THE COMPLETE

CROSSWORD
SOLVER

THE ULTIMATE CROSSWORD COMPANION

THE COMPLETE
CROSSWORD
SOLVER

THE ULTIMATE CROSSWORD COMPANION

ABBEYDALE PRESS

THE COMPLETE CROSSWORD SOLVER

This edition published in 2001
by Abbeydale Press
An imprint of Bookmart Limited
Desford Road, Enderby
Leicester LE19 4AD
England

ISBN 1-86147-022-3
Reprinted 2002 (twice)

Production by Omnipress, Eastbourne
Printed in Great Britain

CONTENTS

NATURAL HISTORY

ANIMALS

3
APE
ASS
BAT
CAT
DOG
ELK
FOX
GNU
KOB
PIG
RAT
YAK
4
ANOA
BEAR
CAVY
CONY
DEER
GAUR
GOAT
HARE
IBEX
KUDU
LION
LYNX
MINK
MOLE
MULE
ORYX
PACA
PIKA
PUMA
SAKI
SEAL
SIKA
TAHR
TITI
VOLE
WOLF
ZEBU
5
ADDAX
BISON
BONGO
CAMEL
CHIRU
CIVET

COATI
COYPU
DHOLE
DINGO
DRILL
ELAND
FOSSA
GAYAL
GENET
GORAL
HINNY
HORSE
HUTIA
HYENA
HYRAX
INDRI
KIANG
KOALA
LEMUR
LIGER
LLAMA
LORIS
MOOSE
MOUSE
NYALA
OKAPI
ORIBI
OTTER
OUNCE
PANDA
POTTO
RATEL
SABLE
SAIGA
SEROW
SHEEP
SHREW
SKUNK
SLOTH
STOAT
TAPIR
TIGER
TIGON
WHALE
ZEBRA

6
AGOUTI
ALPACA
AOUDAD
ARGALI
AUROCH
AYE-AYE
BABOON
BADGER
BEAVER
BOBCAT
CATTLE
CHITAL
COLUGO
COUGAR
COYOTE
CUSCUS
DESMAN
DIK-DIK
DONKEY
DUGONG
DUIKER
ERMINE
FENNEC
FERRET
FISHER
GALAGO
GELADA
GERBIL
GIBBON
GOPHER
GRISON
GUENON
HYAENA
IMPALA
JACKAL
JAGUAR
JERBOA
LANGUR
MAMMAL
MARGAY
MARMOT
MARTEN
MONKEY
MUSK OX
NILGAI
NUMBAT
NUTRIA

OCELOT
OLINGO
ONAGER
POSSUM
RABBIT
RED FOX
RODENT
SEA COW
SERVAL
SIFAKA
TENREC
VERVET
VICUNA
WALRUS
WAPITI
WEASEL
WISENT
WOMBAT
7
ACOUCHI
ANT BEAR
BANTENG
BIGHORN
BLESBOK
BLUE FOX
BUFFALO
CANE RAT
CARIBOU
CHAMOIS
CHEETAH
COLOBUS
DOLPHIN
ECHIDNA
FELIDAE
GAZELLE
GEMSBOK
GERENUK
GIRAFFE
GLUTTON
GORILLA
GRAMPUS
GUANACO
GYMNURE
HAMSTER
LEMMING
LEOPARD
LINSANG
MACAQUE

ANIMALS

7 continued
MAMMOTH
MANATEE
MARKHOR
MEERKAT
MOLE RAT
MOON RAT
MOUFLON
MUSKRAT
NARWHAL
NOCTULE
OPOSSUM
PACK RAT
PANTHER
PECCARY
POLECAT
PRIMATE
RACCOON
RED DEER
ROE DEER
RORQUAL
SEALION
SIAMANG
SOUSLIK
SUN BEAR
TAMARIN
TAMAROU
TARSIER
WALLABY
WARTHOG
WILDCAT
ZORILLA

8
AARDVARK
AARDWOLF
ANTEATER
ANTELOPE
AXIS DEER
BABIRUSA
BONTEBOK
BUSHBABY
BUSHBUCK
CACHALOT
CAPYBARA
CHIPMUNK
DORMOUSE
ELEPHANT
ENTELLUS
FRUIT BAT
HEDGEHOG
IRISH ELK

KANGAROO
KINKAJOU
MANDRILL
MANGABEY
MARMOSET
MONGOOSE
MUSK DEER
MUSQUASH
PANGOLIN
PLATYPUS
PORPOISE
REEDBUCK
REINDEER
RUMINANT
SEA OTTER
SEI WHALE
SQUIRREL
STEINBOK
TALAPOIN
TAMANDUA
VISCACHA
WALLAROO
WATER RAT
WILD BOAR

9
ARCTIC FOX
ARMADILLO
BANDICOOT
BINTURONG
BLACK BEAR
BLACKBUCK
BLUE WHALE
BROWN BEAR
DEER MOUSE
DESERT RAT
DROMEDARY
FLYING FOX
GOLDEN CAT
GROUNDHOG
GUINEA PIG
HAMADRYAS
MARSUPIAL
MONOTREME
MOUSE DEER
ORANG-UTAN
PACHYDERM
PALM CIVET
PAMPAS CAT
PHALANGER
POLAR BEAR
PORCUPINE

PRONGHORN
PROSIMIAN
SILVER FOX
SITATUNGA
SLOTH BEAR
SOLENODON
SPRINGBOK
THYLACINE
TREE SHREW
WATERBUCK
WATER VOLE
WOLVERINE
WOODCHUCK

10
ANGWANTIBO
BARBARY APE
BOTTLENOSE
CACOMISTLE
CHEVROTAIN
CHIMPANZEE
CHINCHILLA
CHIROPTERA
FALLOW DEER
FIELD MOUSE
GOLDEN MOLE
HARTEBEEST
HONEY MOUSE
HOODED SEAL
JAGUARUNDI
KODIAK BEAR
MONA MONKEY
OTTER SHREW
PALLAS'S CAT
PILOT WHALE
PINE MARTEN
POUCHED RAT
PRAIRIE DOG
RACCOON DOG
RHINOCEROS
RIGHT WHALE
SPERM WHALE
SPRINGHAAS
TIMBER WOLF
VAMPIRE BAT
WATER SHREW
WHITE WHALE
WILDEBEEST

11
BARBASTELLE
BARKING DEER
DOUROUCOULI

FLYING LEMUR
GRASS MONKEY
GRIZZLY BEAR
HARBOUR SEAL
HONEY BADGER
KANGAROO RAT
KILLER WHALE
LEOPARD SEAL
PATAS MONKEY
PIPISTRELLE
PRAIRIE WOLF
RAT KANGAROO
RED SQUIRREL
SEROTINE BAT
SNOW LEOPARD

12
ELEPHANT SEAL
HARVEST MOUSE
HIPPOPOTAMUS
HORSESHOE BAT
HOWLER MONKEY
JUMPING MOIJSE
KLIPSPRINGER
MOUNTAIN LION
POCKET GOPHER
RHESUS MONKEY
ROAN ANTELOPE
SNOWSHOE HARE
SPIDER MONKEY
TREE KANGAROO
WATER BUFFALO
WOOLLY MONKEY

13
ANTHROPOID APE
CRABEATER SEAL
DORCAS GAZELLE
HUMPBACK WHALE
MARSUPIAL MOLE
ROYAL ANTELOPE
SABLE ANTELOPE
TASMANIAN WOLF

14
CAPUCHIN MONKEY
CLOUDED LEOPARD
FLYING SQUIRREL
GROUND SQUIRREL
MOUNTAIN BEAVER
NEW WORLD
  MONKEY
OLD WORLD
  MONKEY

14 continued

PERE DAVID'S DEER
SPECTACLED BEAR
SQUIRREL MONKEY
TASMANIAN DEVIL
15+
CHINESE WATER DEER
DUCK-BILLED PLATYPUS
FLYING PHALANGER

PROBOSCIS MONKEY
PYGMY HIPPOPOTAMUS
SCALY-TAILED SQUIRREL
WHITE RHINOCEROS
WOOLLY RHINOCEROS
WOOLLY SPIDER MONKEY

MALE AND FEMALE ANIMALS

ANIMAL	MALE	FEMALE
ANTELOPE	BUCK	DOE
ASS	JACKASS	JENNYASS
BADGER	BOAR	SOW
BEAR	BOAR	SOW
BOBCAT	TOM	LIONESS
BUFFALO	BULL	COW
CAMEL	BULL	COW
CARIBOU	STAG	DOE
CAT	TOM	QUEEN
CATTLE	BULL	COW
CHICKEN	COCK	HEN
COUGAR	TOM	LIONESS
COYOTE	DOG	BITCH
DEER	STAG	DOE
DOG	DOG	BITCH
DONKEY	JACKASS	JENNYASS
DUCK	DRAKE	DUCK
ELAND	BULL	COW
ELEPHANT	BULL	COW
FERRET	JACK	JILL
FISH	COCK	HEN
FOX	FOX	VIXEN
GIRAFFE	BULL	COW
GOAT	BILLYGOAT	NANNYGOAT
GOOSE	GANDER	GOOSE
HARE	BUCK	DOE
HARTEBEAST	BULL	COW
HORSE	STALLION	MARE
IMPALA	RAM	EWE
JACK RABBIT	BUCK	DOE
KANGAROO	BUCK	DOE
LEOPARD	LEOPARD	LEOPARDESS
LION	LION	LIONESS
MOOSE	BULL	COW
OX	BULLOCK	COW
PEACOCK	PEACOCK	PEAHEN
PHEASANT	COCK	HEN

ANIMALS – MALE & FEMALE / YOUNG / COLLECTIVE NAMES

ANIMAL	MALE	FEMALE
PIG	BOAR	SOW
RHINOCEROS	BULL	COW
ROEDEER	ROEBUCK	DOEDEER
SEAL	BULL	COW
SHEEP	RAM	EWE
SWAN	COB	PEN
TIGER	TIGER	TIGRESS
WALRUS	BULL	COW
WEASEL	BOAR	COW
WHALE	BULL	COW
WOLF	DOG	BITCH
ZEBRA	STALLION	MARE

YOUNG ANIMALS

ANIMAL	YOUNG	ANIMAL	YOUNG
ANTELOPE	KID	HARE	LEVERET
BADGER	CUB	HARTEBEAST	CALF
BEAR	CUB	HAWK	CHICK
BEAVER	KITTEN	HORSE	FOAL
BOBCAT	KITTEN	JACKRABBIT	KITTEN
BUFFALO	CALF	KANGAROO	JOEY
CAMEL	CALF	LEOPARD	CUB
CARIBOU	FAWN	LION	CUB
CAT	KITTEN	MONKEY	INFANT
CATTLE	CALF	OX	STOT
CHICKEN	CHICK	PHEASANT	CHICK
COUGAR	KITTEN	PIG	PIIGLET
COYOTE	PUPPY	RHINOCEROS	CALF
DEER	FAWN	ROEDEER	KID
DOG	PUPPY	SEAL	CALF
DUCK	DUCKLING	SHEEP	LAMB
ELAND	CALF	SKUNK	KITTEN
ELEPHANT	CALF	SWAN	CYGNET
ELK	CALF	TIGER	CUB
FISH	FRY	TOAD	TADPOLE
FROG	TADPOLE	WALRUS	CUB
FOX	CUB	WEASEL	KIT
GIRAFFE	CALF	WHALE	CALF
GOAT	KID	WOLF	CUB
GOOSE	GOSLING	ZEBRA	FOAL

COLLECTIVE NAMES

ANIMAL	COLLECTIVE NAME	ANIMAL	COLLECTIVE NAME
ANTELOPE	HERD	BEAR	SLEUTH
APE	SHREWDNESS	BEAVER	COLONY
ASS	DROVE	BLOODHOUND	SUTE
BADGER	CETE	BOAR	SOUNDER

ANIMAL	COLLECTIVE NAME	ANIMAL	COLLECTIVE NAME
BUFFALO	HERD	HORSE	HERD
CAMEL	TRAIN	IMPALA	COUPLE
CARIBOU	HERD	JACKRABBIT	HUSK
CAT	CLUSTER	KANGAROO	TROOP
CATTLE	HERD	KINE	DROVE
CHAMOIS	HERD	LEOPARD	LEAP
CHICKEN	FLOCK	LION	PRIDE
CHOUGH	CHATTERING	MOLE	LABOUR
COLT	RAG	MONKEY	TROOP
COOT	FLEET	MOOSE	HERD
COYOTE	PACK	MOUSE	NEST
DEER	HERD	OX	TEAM
DOG	PACK	PEACOCK	PRIDE
DONKEY	DROVE	PHEASANT	BROOD
DUCK	PADDLING	PIG	TRIP
ELAND	HERD	RHINOCEROS	CRASH
ELEPHANT	HERD	ROEDEER	BEVY
ELK	GANG	ROOK	BUILDING
FERRET	BUSINESS	SEAL	POD
FISH	SCHOOL	SHEEP	FLOCK
FOX	TROOP	SNAKE	KNOT
GELDING	BRACE	TOAD	NEST
GIRAFFE	HERD	WALRUS	POD
GOAT	FLOCK	WEASEL	PACK
GOOSE	GAGGLE	WHALE	SCHOOL
HARE	HUSKE	WOLF	PACK
HARTEBEAST	HERD	ZEBRA	HERD
HAWK	CAST		

CATS

3	8	13	19
REX	DEVON REY	CHESTNUT BROWN	LILAC-POINTED
4	RED TABBY	RED ABYSSINIAN	SIAMESE
MANX	9	TORTOISESHELL	TABBY-POINTED
5	BLUE CREAM	14	SIAMESE
CREAM	10	LONG HAIRED	20+
SMOKE	ABYSSINIAN	BLUE	CHOCOLATE-
TABBY	BROWN TABBY	TORTIE AND	POINTED
6	CHINCHILLA	WHITE	SIAMESE
BIRMAN	CORNISH REY	15	
HAVANA	11	RED-POINT	
SPHYNX	BLUE BURMESE	SIAMESE	
7	BRITISH BLUE	BLUE-POINTED	
BURMESE	COLOURPOINT	SIAMESE	
PERSIAN	RUSSIAN BLUE	SEAL-POINTED	
RED SELF	SILVER TABBY	SIAMESE	
SIAMESE	12	TORTIE-POINT	
SPOTTED	BROWN BURMESE	SIAMESE	
TURKISH			

DOGS

DOGS

3
PUG
4
PULI
5
BOXER
CORGI
HUSKY
SPITZ
6
BEAGLE
BORZOI
BRIARD
COLLIE
KELPIE
POODLE
SALUKI
SETTER
7
BASENJI
BULLDOG
GRIFFON
HARRIER
LOWCHEN
MALTESE
MASTIFF
POINTER
SAMOYED
SHELTIE
SHIH TZU
SPANIEL
TERRIER
WHIPPET
8
ALSATIAN
CHOW CHOW
ELKHOUND
FOXHOUND
KEESHOND
PAPILLON
SHEEPDOG

9
CHIHUAHUA
DACHSHUND
DALMATIAN
DEERHOUND
GREAT DANE
GREYHOUND
LHASA APSO
PEKINGESE
RETRIEVER
SCHNAUZER
STAGHOUND
ST BERNARD
10
BLOODHOUND
FOX TERRIER
OTTERHOUND
POMERANIAN
ROTTWEILER
SCHIPPERKE
WEIMARANER
WELSH CORGI
11
AFGHAN HOUND
BASSET HOUND
BULL MASTIFF
BULL TERRIER
IBIZAN HOUND
IRISH SETTER
SKYE TERRIER
12
CAIRN TERRIER
FINNISH SPITZ
IRISH TERRIER
JAPANESE CHIN
NEWFOUNDLAND
PHARAOH HOUND
SILKY TERRIER
WELSH TERRIER
13
AFFENPINSCHER
BORDER TERRIER

BOSTON TERRIER
COCKER SPANIEL
ENGLISH SETTER
HUNGARIAN PULI
14
GERMAN SHEPHERD
IRISH WOLFHOUND
15
AIREDALE TERRIER
ALASKAN MALAMUTE
BERNESE MOUNTAIN
GOLDEN RETRIEVER
HUNGARIAN VIZSLA
LAKELAND TERRIER
SCOTTISH TERRIER
SEALYHAM TERRIER
SPRINGER SPANIEL
16
KERRY BLUE TERRIER
PYRENEAN MOUNTAIN
SHETLAND SHEEPDOG
YORKSHIRE TERRIER
17
BEDLINGTON TERRIER
DOBERMANN PINSCHER
LABRADOR RETRIEVER
18
JACK RUSSELL TERRIER
KING CHARLES SPANIEL
LARGE MUNSTERLANDER
OLD ENGLISH SHEEPDOG
RHODESIAN RIDGEBACK
20
DANDIE DINMONT
 TERRIER
STAFFORDSHIRE BULL
 TERRIER
WEST HIGHLAND WHITE
 TERRIER
WIREHAIRED POINTING
 GRIFFON

HORSES AND PONIES

3
COB
DON

4
ARAB
BARB

FELL
POLO
RUSS

5
DALES
FJORD

8

5 continued
HUCUL
KONIK
LOKAI
ORLOV
PINTO
SHIRE
TERSK
TIMOR
WELSH
6
ALBINO
BASUTO
EXMOOR
MERENS
MORGAN
TARPAN
VIATKA

7
CASPIAN
COMTOIS
CRIOLLO
FURIOSA
HACKNEY
JUTLAND
LLANERO
MUSTANG
NORIKER
QUARTER
SORRAIA
8
BUDEONNY
CAMARGUE
8
DARTMOOR
GALICENO
HIGHLAND

HOLSTEIN
KABARDIN
KARABAIR
KARABAKH
LUSITANO
PALOMINO
SHETLAND
9
AKHAL-TEKE
ALTER-REAL
APPALOOSA
CONNEMARA
FALABELLA
HAFLINGER
KNABSTRUP
NEW FOREST
OLDENBURG
PERCHERON
SCHLESWIG

10
ANDALUSIAN
AVELIGNESE
CLYDESDALE
GELDERLAND
HANOVERIAN
IRISH DRAFT
LIPIZZANER
11
NOVOKIRGHIZ
12
CLEVELAND BAY
SUFFOLK PUNCH
THOROUGHBRED
13
WELSH MOUNTAIN
16
TENNESSEE
WALKING

CATTLE

5 AND UNDER
DEVON
GIR
KERRY
LUING
6
DEXTER
JERSEY
SUSSEX
7
BEEFALO
BRANGUS

8
AYRSHIRE
FRIESIAN
GALLOWAY
GUERNSEY
HEREFORD
HIGHLAND
LIMOUSIN
9
CHAROLAIS
SHORTHORN
SIMMENTAL

10
BROWN SWISS
LINCOLN RED
MURRAY GREY
WELSH BLACK
11
JAMAICA HOPE
MARCHIGIANA
13
ABERDEEN ANGUS
DROUGHTMASTER
TEXAS LONGHORN

SHEEP

4
LONK
MULE
SOAY
5
CARDY
CHIOS
JACOB
LLEYN
6
MASHAM
MERINO
ROMNEY

7
CHEVIOT
GOTLAND
KARAKUL
LACAUNE
SUFFOLK
8
HERDWICK
LONGMYND
POLWARTH
PORTLAND
SHETLAND

9
HEBRIDEAN
LONGWOOLS
ROUGH FELL
SWALEDALE
TEESWATER
10
CORRIEDALE
DORSET HORN
EXMOOR HORN
POLL DORSET
11
MANX LOGHTAN
WENSLEYDALE

13
WELSH MOUNTAIN
WILTSHIRE HORN
15
FRIES
  MELKSCHAPP
17
SCOTTISH
  BLACKFACE
18
WHITEFACED
  WOODLAND

PIGS

5
DUROC
WELSH
8
PIETRAIN
TAMWORTH

9
BERKSHIRE
HAMPSHIRE
10
LARGE WHITE

15
SWEDISH LANDRACE
17
BRITISH SADDLEBACK
GLOUCESTER OLD SPOT

POULTRY

4
BUFF (goose)
5
MARAN (chicken)
PEARL (guinea fowl)
PEKIN (duck)
ROMAN (goose)
ROUEN (duck)
WHITE (guinea fowl)
6
ANCONA (chicken)
CAYUGA (duck)
EMBDEN (goose)
SILKIE (chicken)
7
AFRICAN (goose)
CHINESE (goose)
CRESTED (duck)
DORKING (chicken)
LEGHORN (chicken)

MUSCOVY (duck)
PILGRIM (goose)
8
LAVENDER (guinea fowl)
TOULOUSE (goose)
9
AYLESBURY (duck)
WELSUMMER (chicken)
10
BARNVELDER (chicken)
BELTSVILLE (turkey)
BOURBON RED (turkey)
INDIAN GAME (chicken)
ROSS RANGER (chicken)
SEBASTOPOL (goose)
CUCKOO MARAN (chicken)
LIGHT SUSSEX (chicken)
12
BLACK NORFOLK (turkey)
INDIAN RUNNER (duck)

NARRAGANSETT (turkey)
PLYMOUTH ROCK (chicken)
WHITE HOLLAND (turkey)
13
BUFF ORPINGTON (duck)
KHAKI CAMPBELL (duck)
MAMMOTH BRONZE
(turkey)
WHITE AUSTRIAN (turkey)
14
BLACK EAST INDIE (duck)
RHODE ISLAND RED
(chicken)
WELSH HARLEQUIN (duck)
WHITE WYANDOTTE
(chicken)
15
CAMBRIDGE BRONZE
(turkey)

BIRDS

3
AUK
EMU
JAY
MOA
OWL
TIT
TUI
4
CHAT
COLY
COOT
CROW
DODO
DOVE
DUCK

GULL
HAWK
HUIA
IBIS
KAGU
KITE
KIWI
KNOT
LARK
LORY
RAIL
RHEA
ROOK
RUFF
SHAG
SKUA

SMEW
SWAN
TEAL
TERN
WREN
5
BOOBY
CRAKE
CRANE
DIVER
EAGLE
EGRET
EIDER
FINCH
GOOSE
GREBE

HERON
HOBBY
MACAW
MYNAH
NODDY
OUZEL
PIPIT
PRION
QUAIL
RAVEN
ROBIN
SCAUP
SERIN
SNIPE
STILT
STORK

6
AVOCET
BARBET
BULBUL
CANARY
CHOUGH
CONDOR
CUCKOO
CURLEW
DARTER
DIPPER
DRONGO
DUNLIN
FALCON
FULMAR
GANNET
GODWIT
HOOPOE
JABIRU
JACANA
KAKAPO
LINNET
MAGPIE
MARTIN
MERLIN
MOTMOT
ORIOLE
OSPREY
PARROT
PEEWIT
PETREL
PIGEON
PLOVER
PUFFIN
QUELEA
RATITE
ROLLER
SHRIKE
SISKIN
TAKAHE
THRUSH
TOUCAN
TROGON
TURACO
TURKEY
WHIDAH
WHYDAH
WIGEON
7
ANTBIRD
BABBLER

BARN OWL
BITTERN
BLUETIT
BUNTING
BUSTARD
BUZZARD
COAL TIT
COURSER
DUNNOCK
EMU WREN
FANTAIL
FINFOOT
FISH OWL
GADWALL
GOSHAWK
GRACKLE
HARRIER
HAWK OWL
HOATZIN
JACAMAR
JACKDAW
KESTREL
LAPWING
MALLARD
MANAKIN
MARABOU
MINIVET
MOORHEN
OILBIRD
ORTOLAN
OSTRICH
PEACOCK
PEAFOWL
PELICAN
PENGUIN
PINTAIL
POCHARD
QUETZAL
REDPOLL
REDWING
ROSELLA
SEAGULL
SERIEMA
SKIMMER
SKYLARK
SPARROW
SUNBIRD
SWALLOW
TANAGER
TINAMOU
TOURACO

VULTURE
WAGTAIL
WARBLER
WAXBILL
WAXWING
WRYBILL
WRYNECK
8
ACCENTOR
AVADAVAT
BATELEUR
BEE-EATER
BLACKCAP
BLUEBIRD
BOATBILL
BOBOLINK
CARACARA
CARDINAL
COCKATOO
CURASSOW
DABCHICK
DOTTEREL
EAGLE OWL
FISH HAWK
FLAMINGO
GAMEBIRD
GARGANEY
GREAT TIT
GROSBEAK
HAWFINCH
HORNBILL
LOVEBIRD
LYREBIRD
MANNIKIN
MEGAPODE
MUTE SWAN
NIGHTJAR
NUTHATCH
OVENBIRD
OXPECKER
PARAKEET
PHEASANT
PYGMY OWL
REDSHANK
REDSTART
REEDLING
RIFLEMAN
ROCKDOVE
SCOPS OWL
SCREAMER
SEA EAGLE

SHELDUCK
SHOEBILL
SNOWY OWL
SONGBIRD
STARLING
SWIFTLET
TAWNY OWL
TITMOUSE
TRAGOPAN
WHEATEAR
WHIMBREL
WHINCHAT
WHIPBIRD
WHITE-EYE
WILDFOWL
WOODCHAT
WOODCOCK
9
ALBATROSS
BALD EAGLE
BLACKBIRD
BLACK SWAN
BOWERBIRD
BRAMBLING
BROADBILL
BULLFINCH
CASSOWARY
CHAFFINCH
COCKATIEL
CORMORANT
CORNCRAKE
CROSSBILL.
CURRAWONG
FIELDFARE
FIRECREST
FRANCOLIN
FRIARBIRD
FROGMOUTH
GALLINULE
GOLDCREST
GOLDENEYE
GOLDFINCH
GUILLEMOT
GYRFALCON
HILL MYNAH
KITTIWAKE
LITTLE OWL
MERGANSER
MOUSEBIRD
PARTRIDGE
PHALAROPE

9 continued
PTARMIGAN
RAZORBILL
RED GROUSE
RIFLEBIRD
RING OUZEL
SANDPIPER
SCRUB BIRD
SNAKEBIRD
SNOW GOOSE
SPOONBILL
STONECHAT
THICKHEAD
THORNBILL
TRUMPETER
TURNSTONE
10
ARCTIC TERN
BEARDED TIT
BRENT GOOSE
BUDGERIGAR
CHIFFCHAFF
CRESTED TIT
DEMOISELLE
DIVING DUCK
FLYCATCHER
GRASSFINCH
GREENFINCH
GREENSHANK
GUINEA FOWL
HAMMERHEAD
HARPY EAGLE
HONEYEATER
HONEY GUIDE
HOODED CROW
JUNGLE FOWL
KINGFISHER
KOOKABURRA
MALLEE FOWL
MUTTONBARD
NIGHT HERON

NUTCRACKER
PRATINCOLE
SACRED ISIS
SADDLEBACK
SAGE GROUSE
SANDERLING
SANDGROUSE
SCREECH OWL
SHEARWATER
SHEATHBILL
SONG THRUSH
SUN BITTERN
TAILORBIRD
TROPIC BIRD
TURTLE DOVE
WEAVERBIRD
WOODPECKER
WOOD PIGEON
ZEBRA FINCH
11
BLACK GROUSE
BRUSH TURKEY
BUTCHERBIRD
BUTTON QUAIL
CANADA GOOSE
CARRION CROW
DIAMONDBIRD
FRIGATEBIRD
GNATCATCHER
GOLDEN EAGLE
HERRING GULL
HUMMINGBIRD
LAMMERGEIER
LAUGHING OWL
MOCKINGBIRD
MUSCOVY DUCK
NIGHTINGALE
REED WARBLER
SNOW BUNTING
SPARROWHAWK
STONE CURLEW

STORM PETREL
TREECREEPER
WALLCREEPER
WEAVERFINCH
WHITETHROAT
WOODCREEPER
WREN BABBLER
12
BURROWING OWL
CAPERCAILLIE
CUCKOO-SHRIKE
DABBLING DUCK
FAIRY PENGUIN
FLOWERPECKER
GREYLAG GOOSE
HEDGE SPARROW
HONEYCREEPER
HOUSE SPARROW
LANNER FALCON
MANDARIN DUCK
MARSH HARRIER
MISTLE THRUSH
MOURNING DOVE
PERCHING DUCK
SHOVELER DUCK
STANDARDWING
UMBRELLA BIRD
WHIPPOORWILL
YELLOWHAMMER
13
ADJUTANT STORK
AMERICAN EAGLE
BARNACLE GOOSE
CROCODILE BIRD
ELEPHANT BIRDS
FAIRY BLUEBIRD
HARLEQUIN DUCK
HAWAIIAN GOOSE
LONG-TAILED TIT
OYSTERCATCHER
PASSERINE BIRD

SECRETARY BIRD
WHISTLING DUCK
WHOOPING CRANE
14
BEARDED VULTURE
BIRD OF PARADISE
DARWIN'S FINCHES
EMPEROR PENGUIN
GOLDEN PHEASANT
GRIFFON VULTURE
OWLET FROG-
  MOUTH
PLAINS-WANDERER
15+
BALTIMORE ORIOLE
GREAT CRESTED
  GREBE
IVORY-BILLED
  WOODPECKER
LAUGHING
  JACKASS
PASSENGER
  PIGEON
PEREGRINE
  FALCON
PHILIPPINE EAGLE
TYRANT
  FLYCATCHER

FISH

3	4		
COD	BASS	GOBY	RUDD
DAB	CARP	HAKE	SHAD
EEL	CHAR	LING	SOLE
GAR	CHUB	OPAH	TOPE
IDE	DACE	ORFE	TUNA
RAY	DORY	PIKE	

5
BLEAK
BREAM
BRILL
DANIO
GRUNT
GUPPY
LOACH
MOLLY
PERCH
PORGY
ROACH
SAURY
SHARK
SKATE
SMELT
SPRAT
TENCH
TETRA
TROUT
TUNNY
6
BARBEL
BELUGA
BLENNY
BONITO
BOWFIN
BURBOT
GUNNEL
KIPPER
MARLIN
MINNOW
MULLET
PLAICE
PUFFER
REMORA
SAITHE
SALMON
TARPON
TURBOT
WEEVER
WRASSE
7
ALEWIFE
ANCHOVY
BATFISH
CATFISH
CICHLID
CROAKER
DOGFISH
EELPOUT

GARFISH
GARPIKE
GOURAMI
GROUPER
GUDGEON
GURNARD
HADDOCK
HAGFISH
HALIBUT
HERRING
HOGFISH
ICEFISH
LAMPREY
MUDFISH
OARFISH
PIRANHA
POLLACK
POMPANO
RATFISH
SARDINE
SAWFISH
SCULPIN
SEA BASS
SNAPPER
SUNFISH
TELEOST
TORPEDO
WHITING
8
ALBACORE
BLUEFISH
BRISLING
BROTULID
BULLHEAD
CAVE FISH
CHARACIN
CHIMAERA
DEVIL RAY
DRAGONET
DRUMFISH
FILEFISH
FLATFISH
FLATHEAD
FLOUNDER
FROGFISH
GOLDFISH
GRAYLING
JOHN DORY
LUNGFISH
MACKEREL
MANTA RAY

MONKFISH
MOONFISH
MORAY EEL
PILCHARD
PIPEFISH
SAILFISH
SEA BREAM
SEA HORSE
SEA PERCH
SEA ROBIN
SKIPJACK
STINGRAY
STURGEON
SWAMP EEL
TOADFISH
WOLF FISH
9
ANGELFISH
BARRACUDA
BLUE SHARK
CLINGFISH
CONGER EEL
GLASSFISH
GLOBEFISH
GOOSEFISH
GRENADIER
KILLIFISH
LATIMERIA
LEMON SOLE
MURRAY COD
PEARLFISH
PIKEPERCH
PILOT FISH
PLACODERM
PORBEAGLE
RED MULLET
RED SALMON
STARGAZER
STONE BASS
STONEFISH
SWORDFISH
SWORDTAIL
THREADFIN
TIGERFISH
TOP MINNOW
TRUNKFISH
WHITEBAIT
WHITEFISH
WRECKFISH
ZEBRA FISH

10
ANGLERFISH
ARCHER FISH
BOMBAY DUCK
COELACANTH
DAMSELFISH
DRAGONFISH
FLYING FISH
GHOST SHARK
GUITAR FISH
LUMPSUCKER
MIDSHIPMAN
MUDSKIPPER
NEEDLEFISH
NURSESHARK
PADDLEFISH
PARROT FISH
PINK SALMON
PLACODERMI
RIBBONFISH
SILVERSIDE
TIGER SHARK
WHALE SHARK
WHITE SHARK
11
ELECTRIC EEL
ELECTRIC RAY
GOBLIN SHARK
HATCHETFISH
LANTERN FISH
MOORISH IDOL
STICKLEBACK
SURGEONFISH
TRIGGERFISH
12+
BASKING SHARK
CLIMBING PERCH
FIGHTING FISH
FOUR-EYED FISH
GREENLAND
  SHARK
HAMMERHEAD
  SHARK
LABYRINTH FISH
MACKEREL SHARK
PORCUPINE FISH
REQUIEM SHARK
SCORPION FISH
SOCKEYE SALMON
THRESHER SHARK
YELLOWFIN TUNA

SEASHELLS

SEASHELLS

3
SUN
4
HARP
5
TULIP
6
NUTMEG
7
JUNONIA
SUNDIAL
8
DYE MUREX
LION'S PAW
NOBLE PEN
PHEASANT
TURK'S CUP
9
ANGEL WING
BAT VOLUTE
BURSA FROG
GIANT CLAM
PINK CONCH
ROTA MUREX
SPINY VASE
TELESCOPE
TENT OLIVE
WEDGE CLAM
10
BLUE MUSSEL
COAT-OF-MAIL
CROWN CONCH
DELPHINULA
DRUPE SNAIL
EYED COWRIE
PAPERY RAPA
QUAHOG CLAM
SCALED WORM
WINGED FROG
11
BEAR PAW CLAM
CAMEO HELMET
CLIONE SNAIL
FRONS OYSTER
GREEN TURBAN
HEART COCKLE
MUSIC VOLUTE
ONYX SLIPPER
OSTRICH FOOT

PAPER BUBBLE
PEARL OYSTER
SACRED CHANK
TEXTILE CONE
TIGER COWRIE
12
AMORIA VOLUTE
ATLANTIC CONE
FLORIDA MITER
GAUDY ASAPHIS
GOLDEN COWRIE
GOLDEN TELLIN
LIMA FILE CLAM
MONEY COWRIES
PACIFIC AUGER
PARTRIDGE TUN
PELICAN'S FOOT
SCOTCH BOBINET
SPIKED LIMPET
SPINDLE TIBIA
13
ANGULAR VOLUTE
BABLYON TURRID
BLEEDING TOOTH
CARDINAL MITER
COMMERCIAL TOP
COSTATE COCKLE
FIGHTING CONCH
GEOGRAPHY CONE
JACKKNIFE CLAM
JAPANESE CONES
PAPER NAUTILUS
RIDGED ABALONE
SPIRAL BABYLON
SUNRISE TELLIN
TURKEY WING ARK
VENUS COMB CLAM
14
CHANNELED WHELK
DISTAFF SPINDLE
ELEGANT FIMBRIA
EPISCOPAL MITER
IMPERIAL VOLUTE
INDONESIAN CLAM
LEUCODON
   COWRIE
LEWIS' MOON
   SNAIL
LIGHTNING WHELK

PANAMANIAN
   CONE
PHILIPPINE CONE
POLYNESIAN
   CONE
TAPESTRY
   TURBAN
TRITON'S
   TRUMPET
VENUS COMB
   MUREX
15
BITTERSWEET
   CLAM
BULL-MOUTH
   HELMET
JAPANESE
   CARRIER
NEW ENGLAND
   WHELK
PANAMANIAN
   AUGER
PILGRIM'S SCALLOP
SUNBURST
   CARRIER
TURRITELLA SNAIL
WATERING POT
   CLAM
WEST INDIAN
   CHANK
WEST AFRICAN
   CONE
16
ASIAN MOON
   SCALLOP
ATLANTIC SURF
   CLAM
DONKEY EAR
   ABALONE
EDIBLE BAY
   SCALLOP
FRILLED
   DOGWINKLE
GLORY-OF-INDIA
   CONE
ORANGE-MOUTH
   OLIVE
PAGODA
   PERIWINKLE

PERPLICATE
   VOLUTE
PINK-MOUTHED
   MUREX
ROOSTERTAIL
   CONCH
WEDDING CAKE
   VENUS
17
AUSTRALIAN
   TRUMPET
CHAMBERED
   NAUTILUS
FLORIDA HORSE
   CONCH
PACIFIC WING
   OYSTER
SANTA CRUZ
   LATIAXIS
VIOLET SPIDER
   CONCH
18
ATLANTIC DEER
   COWRIE
GIANT KNOBBED
   CERITH
GLORY-OF-THE
   SEAS CONE
GREAT KEYHOLE
   LIMPET
PACIFIC GRINNING
   TUN
PRECIOUS
   WENTLETRAP
WHITE-SPOTTED
   MARGIN
19
TANKERVILLE'S
   ANCILLA
20+
ARTHRITIC SPIDER
   CONCH
ATLANTIC THORNY
   OYSTER

REPTILES AND AMPHIBIANS / INSECTS

REPTILES AND AMPHIBIANS

3
ASP
BOA
OLM
4
FROG
NEWT
TOAD
5
ADDER
AGAMA
COBRA
GECKO
KRAIT
MAMBA
SIREN
SKINK
SNAKE
TOKAY
VIPER
6
CAYMAN
GAVIAL
IGUANA
LIZARD
MOLOCH
MUGGER
PYTHON
TAIPAN
TURTLE
ZALTYS

7
AXOLOTL
GHARIAL
REPTILE
TUATARA
8
ANACONDA
BASILISK
BULLFROG
CONGO EEL
MATAMATA
MOCCASIN
MUD PUPPY
PIT VIPER
RINGHALS
SEA SNAKE
SLOWWORM
TERRAPIN
TORTOISE
TREE FROG
9
ALLIGATOR
BLINDWORM
BOOMSLANG
BOX TURTLE
CAECILIAN
CHAMELEON
CROCODILE
HAIRY FROG
PUFF ADDER
TREE SNAKE
VINESNAKE
WART SNAKE
WHIP SNAKE

10
BLACK SNAKE
BUSHMASTER
CHUCKWALLA
CLAWED FROG
COPPERHEAD
CORAL SNAKE
FER-DE-LANCE
GLASS SNAKE.
GRASS SNAKE
HELLBENDER
HORNED TOAD
NATTERJACK
POND TURTLE
SALAMANDER
SAND LIZARD
SIDEWINDER
WATER SNAKE
WORM LIZARD
11
AMPHISBAENA
CONSTRICTOR
COTTONMOUTH
DIAMONDBACK
FLYING SNAKE
GABOON VIPER
GILA MONSTER
GOLIATH FROG
GREEN TURTLE
HORNED VIPER
MIDWIFE TOAD
RATTLESNAKE
SMOOTH SNAKE

12
FLYING LIZARD
HORNED LIZARD
KOMODO
 DRAGON
13
BEARDED LIZARD
FRILLED LIZARD
GIANT TORTOISE
MANGROVE
 SNAKE
MONITOR LIZARD
RUSSELL'S VIPER
SPADEFOOT
 TOAD
WATER
 MOCCASIN
14+
FIRE
 SALAMANDER
HAWKSBILL
 TURTLE
LEATHERBACK
 TURTLE
SNAKE-NECKED
 TURTLE
SOFT-SHELLED
 TURTLE

INSECTS

3
ANT
BEE
BUG
FLY
4
FLEA
GNAT
WASP

5
APHID
DRONE
LOUSE
MIDGE
6
BEDBUG
BEETLE
BOT FLY
CAPSID

CHAFER
CHIGOE
CICADA
EARWIG
GAD FLY
HORNET
IO MOTH
LOCUST
LOOPER
MAGGOT

MANTIS
MAYFLY
SAWFLY
THRIPS
WEEVIL
7
ANTLION
ARMY ANT
BLOWFLY
CRICKET

15

INSECTS

7 continued
CUTWORM
DIPTERA
FIRE ANT
FIREFLY
KATYDID
MONARCH
(butterfly)
PEACOCK
(butterfly)
PROTURA
RINGLET
SANDFLY
SATYRID
(butterfly)
SKIPPER
(butterfly)
STYLOPS
TERMITE
WAX MOTH

8
ALDERFLY
ARMY WORM
BLACKFLY
BOOKWORM
CINNABAR
CRANEFLY
FIREBRAT
FRUIT FLY
GALL WASP
GLOWWORM
GOAT MOTH
GREENFLY
HAWK MOTH
HONEY ANT
HONEYBEE
HORNTAIL
HORSE FLY
HOUSEFLY
HOVERFLY
LACEWING
LADYBIRD
LUNA MOTH
MASON BEE
MEALWORM
MEALYBUG
MILKWEED
(butterfly)
MOSQUITO
PHASMIDA
PLANT BUG

PUSS MOTH
SHEEP KED
SILKWORM
SNAKEFLY
STINK BUG
STONEFLY
WATER BUG
WHITE FLY
WIREWORM
WOODWASP
WOODWORM

9
AMAZON ANT
BLOODWORM
BOOKLOUSE
BRIMSTONE
BUMBLEBEE
CADDIS FLY
COCKROACH
CORN BORER
DAMSELFLY
DOBSONFLY
DOR BEETLE
DRAGONFLY
DRIVER ANT
GALL MIDGE
GROUNDBUG
GYPSY MOTH
NYMPHALID
(butterfly)
OIL BEETLE
OWLET MOTH
ROBBER FLY
SCREWWORM
SHIELD BUG
SWIFT MOTH
TIGER MOTH
TSETSE FLY
WARBLE FLY
WHIRLIGIG

10
BARK BEETLE
BLUEBOTTLE
BOLL WEEVIL
CACTUS MOTH
COCKCHAFER
DROSOPHILA
DUNG BEETLE
FROGHOPPER
HAIRSTREAK
JUNE BEETLE

LEAF BEETLE
LEAF HOPPER
LEAF INSECT
PAPILIONID
(butterfly)
POND SKATER
POTTER WASP
RED ADMIRAL
(butterfly)
SILVERFISH
SPANISH FLY
SPIDER WASP
SPITTLEBUG
SPRINGTAIL
STAG BEETLE
TREEHOPPER
WEBSPINNER

11
ASSASSIN BUG
BACKSWIMMER
BLACK BEETLE
BRISTLETAIL
BUFFALO GNAT
BUSH CRICKET
CANTHARIDIN
CATERPILLAR
CLICK BEETLE
CLOTHES MOTH
CODLING MOTH
EMPEROR MOTH
GRASSHOPPER
MOLE CRICKET
PAINTED LADY
(butterfly)
PLANT HOPPER
SCORPION FLY
STICK INSECT
SWALLOWTAIL
(butterfly)
TIGER BEETLE
TUSSOCK MOTH
WATER BEETLE

12
CABBAGE WHITE
(butterfly)
CACTOBLASTIS
CARPENTER BEE
CARPET BEETLE
DIVING BEETLE
GROUND BEETLE
HERCULES MOTH

PEPPERED MOTH
SCARAB BEETLE
SEXTON BEETLE
WATER BOATMAN
WATER STRIDER

13
BLISTER BEETLE
BURYING BEETLE
CLEARWING MOTH
COTTON STAINER
DADDY LONGLEGS
ELM BARK BEETLE
GEOMETRID MOTH
GIANT WATER BUG
GOLIATH BEETLE
LEAF-CUTTER ANT
LEAFCUTTER BEE
SATURNIID MOTH
SOLDIER BEETLE
TORTOISESHELL
(butterfly)
UNDERWING
MOTH
WATER SCORPION

14+
AMBROSIA BEETLE
BOMBARDIER
BEETLE
CABBAGE ROOT
FLY
CAMBERWELL
BEAUTY (butterfly)
COLORADO
BEETLE
CUCKOO-SPIT
INSECT
DARKLING BEETLE
DEATH'S-HEAD
MOTH
DEATHWATCH
BEETLE
DEVIL'S COACH
HORSE
HERCULES
BEETLE
SLAVE-MAKING
ANT
TORTOISE BEETLE

16

PLANTS AND FLOWERS

3
ABE
HOP
IVY
RYE
4
DOCK
FERN
FLAG (*Iris*)
FLAX
HEMP
IRIS (flag, sweet
  flag, gladdon)
JUTE
LILY
PINK (carnation)
RAPE
REED
RICE
ROSE
RUSH
TARE
UPAS
WOAD
5
AGAVE
ASTER (Michaelmas
  daisy)
AVENS
BRIAR
CANNA
CYCAD
DAISY
HENNA
JALAP
KUDZU
LOTUS
LUPIN
OXLIP (*Primula*)
PANSY (*Viola*)
PEONY
PHLOX
POPPY
SEDGE
SENNA
SISAL
TULIP
VIOLA (pansy, violet)

6
ALLIUM
ALSIKE (clover)
BALSAM
BLUETS
BRYONY
CACTUS
CLOVER (trefoil)
COLEUS
COTTON
COWPEA
CROCUS
DAHLIA
DARNEL
FESCUE
HYSSOP
MADDER
MEDICK
MILLET
NETTLE (*Urtica*)
ORCHID
PETREA.
PEYOTE (cactus)
RATTAN
SALVIA
SPURGE
SQUILL (*Scilla*)
SUNDEW
TEASEL
THRIFT
TWITCH (couch
  grass)
VIOLET (*Viola*)
YARROW
ZINNIA
7
ACONITE
  (monkshood)
ALFALFA
ALKANET
ANEMONE
ASTILBE
BEGONIA
BISTORT
  (snakeroot)
BRACKEN (fern)
BUGLOSS
BULRUSH (reed
  mace)

BURDOCK
CAMPION
CATMINT
CLARKIA
COWSLIP (*Primula*)
DAY LILY
DOGBANE
DOG ROSE
FIGWORT
FREESIA
FROG-BIT
GENTIAN
GLADDON (*Iris*)
GUARANA
HEMLOCK
HENBANE
HONESTY (*Lunaria*)
JONQUIL
  (*Narcissus*)
KINGCUP (marsh
  marigold)
LOBELIA
MILFOIL (yarrow)
MULLEIN (Aaron's
  rod)
OPUNTIA (prickly
  pear)
PAPYRUS
PETUNIA
PIGWEED
PRIMULA. (cowslip,
  primrose)
RAGWORT
ROSELLE
SAGUARO
SANICLE
SPURREY
THISTLE
TIMOTHY
TOBACCO
TREFOIL (clover)
VERBENA (vervain)
VERVAIN (*Verbena*)
8
ACANTHUS
AGRIMONY
ARUM LILY
  (cuckoopint, lords
  and-ladies)

ASPHODEL
AURICULA
BEDSTRAW
BERGENIA
BINDWEED
  (*Convolvulus*)
BLUEBELL
CATBRIER
CAT'S TAIL
  (reedmace)
CHARLOCK
CLEAVERS
  (goosegrass)
CLEMATIS (old
  man's beard,
  traveller's joy)
CROWFOOT
CYCLAMEN
DAFFODIL
DIANTHUS
EELGRASS
EUCHARIS (amazon
  lily)
FLEABANE
FLEAWORT
FOXGLOVE
  (*Digitalis*)
FUMITORY
GERANIUM
  (*Pelargonium*)
GLOXINIA
GOUTWEED
  (ground elder)
HAREBELL
HAWKWEED
HENEQUEN
HIBISCUS (rose of
  China, rose of
  Sharon)
HORNWORT
HYACINTH
ICE PLANT
KNAPWEED
LADY FERN
LARKSPUR
LUNGWORT
MARIGOLD
MILKWEED
MILKWORT

PLANTS AND FLOWERS

8 continued
MOSS PINK (*Phlox*)
PLANTAIN
PLUMBAGO
POLYPODY
PRIMROSE
  (*Primula*)
REEDMACE
  (bulrush, cat's-tail)
ROCK ROSE
SAINFOIN
SALTWORT
SAMPHIRE
SCABIOUS
SEED FERN
SELF HEAL
SHAMROCK (clover,
  merrick, wood
  sorrel)
SNOWDROP
SOAPWORT
SWEET PEA
TOAD LILY (fritillary)
TUBEROSE
VALERIAN
VERONICA
  (speedwell)
WAXPLANT
WOODBINE
  (virginia creeper)
WOODRUSH
WORMWOOD
9
AARON'S ROD
  (mullein)
AMARYLLIS
  (belladonna lily)
ANTHURIUM
AQUILEGIA
  (columbine)
ARROWROOT
BLUEGRASS
BROOMRAPE
BRYOPHYTE
BUCKWHEAT
BUTTERCUP
CAMPANULA
  (Canterbury bell)
CANDYTUFT
CARNATION (pink)
CELANDINE

CHICKWEED
CINERARIA
COCKLEBUR
COCKSFOOT
  (orchard grass)
COLTSFOOT
COLUMBINE
  (Aquilegia)
CORDGRASS
CORN POPPY
CORYDALIS
CYMBIDIUM
  (orchid)
DANDELION
DEVIL'S FIG (prickly
  poppy)
DOG VIOLET
EDELWEISS
EGLANTINE (sweet
  briar)
EYEBRIGHT
GERMANDER
GLADIOLUS
GLASSWORT
GOLDENROD
  (Solidago)
GOOSEFOOT
  (pigweed)
GRASS TREE
GROUND IVY
GROUNDSEL
HELLEBORE
  (christmas rose)
HERB PARIS
HOLLYHOCK
HORSETAIL
HOUSELEEK
IMPATIENS (touch
  me-not, busy Lizzie)
JABORANDI
MARE'S TAIL
MONEYWORT
  (creeping jenny)
MONKSHOOD
  (aconite)
MOSCHATEL
  (townhall clock)
NARCISSUS
  (jonquil)
PATCHOULI
PIMPERNEL

PYRETHRUM
QUILLWORT
ROYALFERN
SAFFLOWER
SAXIFRAGE
  (London pride)
SNAKEROOT
  (bistort)
SPEEDWELL
  (*Veronica*)
SPIKENARD
STONECROP
SUNFLOWER
SWEET FLAG (*Iris*)
TORMENTIL
WATER LILY
WITCHWEED
WOUNDWORT
10
AGAPANTHUS
AMARANTHUS
  (love-lies-bleeding)
AMAZON LILY
ASPIDISTRA
BELLADONNA
  (deadly
  nightshade)
BUSY LIZZIE
BUTTERWORT
CHARMOMILE
CINQUEFOIL
CITRONELLA
CLIFFBREAK (fern)
CORNCOCKLE
CORNFLOWER
COUCH GRASS
  (twitch, quack
  grass)
COW PARSLEY
CRANESBILL
CUCKOOPINT
  (arum lily)
DAMASK ROSE
DRAGONROOT
DYER'S BROOM
FRITILLARY
  (snake's head,
  leopard lily, toad
  lily)
GAILLARDIA
  (blanket flowers)

GOATSBEARD
GOOSEGRASS
  (cleavers)
GRANADILLA
  (passionflower)
GREENBRIER
  (catbrier)
HELIOTROPE
HERB ROBERT
JIMSONWEED
  (thorn apple)
LADY'S SMOCK
MARGUERITE
  (oxeye daisy)
MIGNONETTE
MONTBRETIA
MOONFLOWER
  (morning glory)
NASTURTIUM
OPIUM POPPY
OXEYE DAISY
  (marguerite)
PENNYROYAL
PERIWINKLE
POLYANTHUS
  (*Primula*)
QUACK GRASS
  (couch grass)
SHIELD FERN
SNAKE'S HEAD
SNAPDRAGON
  (*Antirrhinum*)
SOW THISTLE
SPIDERWORT
SPLEENWORT
STITCHWORT
SWEET BRIAR
  (eglantine)
THORN APPLE
  (jimsonweed)
TOUCH-ME-NOT
WALLFLOWER
WATERCRESS
WELSH POPPY
WILLOWHERB
WOOD SORREL
11
ANTIRRHINUM
  (snapdragon)
BISHOP'S WEED
  (ground elder)

11 continued
BITTERSWEET
(woody
nightshade)
BLADDERWORT
CALCEOLARIA
CANARY GRASS
CONVOLVULUS
(bindweed)
FIG MARIGOLD
FORGET-ME-NOT
GILLYFLOWER
(gilliflower, pink,
carnation)
GLOBE FLOWER
GROUND ELDER
(goutweed,
bishop's weed)
HELLEBORINE
(orchid)
HONEYSUCKLE
IPECACUANHA
KANGAROO PAW
LADY'S SLIPPER
LEOPARD LILY
(fritillary, blackberry
lily)
LONDON PRIDE
(saxifrage)
LOVE-IN-A-MIST
MARRAM GRASS
MARSH MALLOW
MEADOWSWEET
PAMPAS GRASS
PONTENTILLA
(cinquefoil)
PRICKLY PEAR
(cactus)
RAGGED ROBIN
RED-HOT POKER
ROSE OF CHINA
(Hibiscus)

RUBBER PLANT
SEA LAVENDER
SHRIMP PLANT
SPIDER PLANT
ST JOHN'S WORT
(Hibiscus)
STRAWFLOWER
WELWITSCHIA
WINTERGREEN

12
AUTUMN CROCUS
(meadow saffron)
CENTURY PLANT
COMPASS PLANT
(turpentine plant)
GLOBE THISTLE
MONKEYFLOWER
MORNING GLORY
(moonflower)
OLD MAN CACTUS
OLD MAN'S BEARD
(Clematis)
ORCHARD GRASS
(cockstoot)
PITCHER PLANT
PRICKLY POPPY
(devil's fig)
QUAKING GRASS
ROSE OF SHARON
(Hibiscus)
SOLOMON'S SEAL
SWEET WILLIAM
VENUS FLYTRAP
13
AFRICAN VIOLET
BIRD'S NEST FERN
BLEEDING HEART
CALYPSO ORCHID
CARRION FLOWER
CHRISTMAS ROSE
(hellebore)

CHRYSANTHEMUM
CREEPING JENNY
(moneywort)
ELEPHANT GRASS
GARLIC MUSTARD
(jack-by-the-
hedge)
GRAPE HYACINTH
MARSH MARIGOLD
(kingcup)
MEADOW SAFFRON
(autumn crocus)
PASSIONFLOWER
(granadilla)
RANUNCULACEAE
ROSE OF JERICHO
SLIPPER ORCHID
TOWNHALL CLOCK
(rnoschatel)
TRAVELLER'S JOY
(Clematis)
WINTER ACONITE
14
BELLADONNA LILY
(Amaryllis)
BLACKBERRY LILY
(leopard lily)
BLANKET FLOWERS
CANTERBURY
BELL (Campanula)
CASTOR-OIL PLANT
HEDGEHOG
CACTUS
JACK-BY-THE-
HEDGE (garlic
mustard)
LORDS-AND-
LADIES (arum lily)
MAIDENHAIR FERN
TRUMPET
CREEPER
15+

BIRD-OF-
PARADISE
FLOWER
BIRD'S NEST
ORCHID
BLACK NIGHT-
SHADE
DEADLY
NIGHTSHADE
(belladonna)
DOG'S TOOTH
VIOLET
ENCHANTER'S
NIGHTSHADE
GRASS OF
PARNASSUS
LILY-OF-THE-
VALLEY
LOVE-LIES-
BLEEDING
(Amaranthus)
MICHAELMAS
DAISY
(Aster)
ORGAN-PIPE
CACTUS
SNOW-ON-THE-
MOUNTAIN
SQUIRTING
CUCUMBER
STAR OF
BETHLEHEM
15
TURPENTINE
PLANT
(compass plant)
WOODY
NIGHTSHADE
(bittersweet)

19

TREES AND SHRUBS

3
ASH
BOX
ELM
FIG
FIR
MAY (hawthorn)
OAK
TEA
YEW
4
ANIL
COCA
DATE
KAVA
KOLA (cola)
NIPA (palm)
PALM
PINE
TEAK
5
ALDER
ASPEN
BALSA
BEECH (*Fagus*)
BIRCH
BROOM
CACAO
CAPER
CEDAR
EBONY
ELDER
ERICA (heath, heather)
FURZE (gorse)
GORSE (furze)
HAZEL
HEATH (*Erica*)
HOLLY
KARRI
LARCH
LILAC
MAPLE
OSIER (willow)
PECAN (hickory)
ROWAN (mountain ash)
SAVIN (juniper)

YUCCA
6
ACACIA
AZALEA
BAMBOO
BANYAN
BAOBAB
BONSAI
BO TREE
CASSIA
DAPHNE
DATURA
DEODAR (cedar)
DERRIS
DURIAN
GINKGO (maidenhair tree)
GOMUTI (sugar palm)
JARRAH
JINBUL (coolabar)
JUJUBE
LAUREL
LOCUST (carob tree, St John's bread)
MIMOSA
MOOLAR (coolabar)
MYRTLE
NUTMEG
ORACHE
POPLAR
PRIVET
PROTEA
REDBUD (judas tree)
RED GUM (Eucalyptus)
SALLOW (willow)
SALVIA
SAPPAN
SPRUCE
WILLOW
7
AMBOYNA
ARBUTUS
BEREERU (greenheart)

BLUE GUM (Eucalyptus)
CAMELIA
CORK OAK
CYPRESS
DOGWOOD
DURMAST (oak)
FUCHSIA
GUM TREE (Eucalyptus)
HEATHER (*Erica*, ling)
HEMLOCK
HICKORY (pecan)
HOLM OAK (holly oak)
JASMINE
JUNIPER
MUGWORT (wormwood)
OIL PALM
PALMYRA
REDWOOD
ROSEBAY (oleander)
SEQUOIA (redwood, wellingtonia, big tree)
SOURSOP
SPIRAEA
SYRINGA (lilac, mock orange)
8
BARBERRY (Berberis)
BASSWOOD
BAYBERRY
BERBERIS (barberry)
BERGAMOT
BLACKBOX (coolabar)
BOX ELDER (maple)
CALABASH
CINCHONA
COOLABAR (jinbul,

moolar, blackbox, dwarf box)
CORKWOOD (balsa)
DWARF BOX (coolabar)
EUONYMUS (spindle tree)
GARDENIA
GUAIACUM
HAWTHORN (may)
HORNSEAM
IRONWOOD
JAPONICA
LABURNUM (golden chain, golden rain)
LAVENDER
MAGNOLIA (umbrella tree)
OLEANDER (rosebay)
QUANDONG
RAMBUTAN
ROSEWOOD
SAGO PALM
SALTBUSH
SILKY OAK
SWEET GUM
SWEETSOP
SYCAMORE (maple)
TAMARISK
TOLU TREE
VIBURNUM (snowball tree)
WISTERIA
WOODBINE (virginia creeper)
WORMWOOD (mugwort)
9
ARAUCARIA (monkey puzzle tree)
BEARBERRY
BUCKTHORN
CAROB TREE (locust)

CORAL TREE
EUPHORBIA (crown
  of thorns,
  poinsettia, snow-
  onthe-mountain)
FIRETHORN
  (pyracantha)
FLAME TREE
  (flamboyant)
FORSYTHIA (golden
  bell)
JACARANDA
JUDAS TREE
  (redbud)
KALANCHOE
KAURI PINE
MANGROVES
MISTLETOE
PLANE TREE
POINCIANA
POISON IVY
SASSAFRAS
SATINWOOD
SCREW PINE
STINKWOOD
STONE PINE
SWEETWOOD
  (greenheart)
TULIP TREE
WHITEBEAM
10
ARBOR VITAE
BIRD CHERRY
BRAZILWOOD

COFFEE TREE
COTTONWOOD
DOUGLAS FIR
DRAGON TREE
EUCALYPTUS (blue
  gum, red gum)
FRANGIPANI
  (pagoda tree,
  temple flower)
GOLDEN BELL
  (forsythia)
GOLDEN RAIN
  (laburnum)
GREENHEART
  (sweetwood,
  bebeeru)
JOSHUA TREE
MANGOSTEEN
MOCK ORANGE
PAGODA TREE
  (frangipani)
POINSETTIA
PYRACANTHA
RAFFIA PALM
RUBBER TREE
WITCH HAZEL
YELLOWWOOD
11
BOTTLEBRUSH
CABBAGE PALM
CAMPHOR TREE
CHAULMOOGRA
COTONEASTER
CYPRESS PINE

DAWN REDWOOD
GOLDEN CHAIN
  (laburnum)
GUELDER ROSE
HONEY LOCUST
JUMPING BEAN
MOUNTAIN ASH
  (rowan)
PENCIL CEDAR
  (juniper)
PHYLLANTHUS
SERVICE TREE
SLIPPERY ELM
SPINDLE TREE
STEPHIANOTIS
TALIPOT PALM
12
CHERRY LAUREL
CREOSOTE BUSH
CUCUMBER TREE
CUSTARD APPLE
  (soursop, sweet
  sop)
INCENSE CEDAR
MONKEY PUZZLE
SNOWBALL TREE
ST JOHN'S BREAD
  (locust)
SWAMP CYPRESS
TEMPLE FLOWER
  (frangipani)
TREE OF HEAVEN
UMBRELLA TREE
(Magnolia)

13
BOUGAINVILLEA
BUTCHER'S
  BROOM
CROWN OF
  THORNS
HORSE CHESTNUT
JAPANESE CEDAR
JAPANESE MAPLE
PAPER MULBERRY
PEACOCK
  FLOWER
  (flamboyant)
WAYFARING TREE
14+
FLAMBOYANT
TREE (flame tree,
  Peacock flower)
FLOWERING
  CURRANT
JERUSALEM
  CHERRY
MAIDENHAIR TREE
  (ginkgo)
STRAWBERRY
  TREE
TRAVELLER'S
  TREE
TURPENTINE TREE
VIRGINIA
  CREEPER
  (Woodbine)

FRUIT AND VEGETABLES

3
FIG
PEA
YAM
4
BEET
EDDO (taro)
KALE
KIWI
LEEK
LIME (linden)
OKRA (lady's
  fingers, gumbo)

PEAR
PLUM
SLOE
TARO (eddo,
  dasheen,
  elephant's ear)
5
APPLE
CAROB
CHARD (swiss
  chard)
CRESS
GRAPE

GUAVA
GUMBO (okra)
LEMON
MANGO
MELON (musk,
  honeydew,
  canteloupe, water)
OLIVE
ONION
(spring onion,
  scallion)
PEACH
SWEDE

6
ALMOND
BANANA
CARROT
CASHEW
CELERY
CHERRY
CITRON
COB NUT
DAMSON
ENDIVE
LENTIL
LICHEE

FRUIT AND VEGETABLES / FUNGI

6 continued
LINDEN (lime)
LITCHI
LOQUAT
LYCHEE (litchi, lichee)
MANIOC (cassava)
MARROW
MEDLAR
ORANGE
PAWPAW
PEANUT (groundnut)
POTATO
PRUNUS (plum, almond, apricot, cherry)
QUINCE
RADISH
SQUASH
TOMATO
TURNIP
WALNUT
7
APRICOT
AVOCADO
BRAMBLE (blackberry)
BULLACE (plum)
CABBAGE
CASSAVA (manioc)
CHICORY
CURRANT
DASHEEN (tard)
FILBERT
GENIPAP

GHERKIN
KUMQUAT
LETTUCE
PARSNIP
PUMPKIN
RHUBARB
SALSIFY
SATSUMA (tangerine)
SHALLOT
SPINACH
8
BEETROOT
BILBERRY (blaeberry, huckleberry, whortleberry)
BRASSICA (broccoli, cabbage)
BROCCOLI
CAPSICUM (pepper, chilli, paprika)
CELERIAC
CHESTNUT
CHICK PEA
CUCUMBER
DEWBERRY
EARTHNUT (groundnut)
EGGPLANT (aubergine)
KOHLRABI (cabbage)
MANDARIN (tangerine)
MULBERRY
MUNG BEAN

MUSHROOM
OLEASTER (russian olive, trebizond date)
SCALLION
SOYA BEAN
TAMARIND
ZUCCHINI (courgette)
9
ARTICHOKE
ASPARAGUS
AUBERGINE (eggplant)
BLAEBERRY (bilberry)
BROAD BEAN
COCODEMER
COURGETTE (marrow, zucchini)
CRAB APPLE
CRANBERRY
GREENGAGE
GROUNDNUT (peanut, earthnut)
MANGETOUT
NECTARINE
PERSIMMON
PINEAPPLE
PISTACHIO
RASPBERRY
STAR APPLE
SWEETCORN
TANGERINE
10
BLACKBERRY (bramble)

CLEMENTINE
ELDERBERRY
FRENCH BEAN (kidney bean)
GOOSEBERRY
GRAPEFRUIT
KIDNEY BEAN
LOGANBERRY
REDCURRANT
RUNNERBEAN
SNAKE GOURD
STRAWBERRY
11
CAULIFLOWER
COCONUT PALM
HORSE-RADISH
HUCKLEBERRY (bilberry)
POMEGRANATE
SWEET POTATO
12+
BLACKCURRANT
BRUSSELS SPROUT
ELEPHANT'S EAR (taro)
JERUSALEM ARTICHOKE
LADY'S FINGERS (okra)
MANGEL-WURZEL (beet)
WATER CHESTNUT
WHORTLEBERRY (bilberry)

FUNGI

4
CEPE
5
MOREL
YEAST
6
AGARIC
INK CAP
7
AMANITA
BOLETUS

CANDIDA
TRUFFLE
8
DEATH CAP
MUSHROOM
PUFFBALL
9
CUP FUNGUS
EARTHSTAR
FLY AGARIC
RUST FUNGI

STINKHORN
TOADSTOOL
10
BREAD MOULD
CHAMPIGNON
11
ASCOMYCETES
ASPERGILLUS
CHANTERELLE
HONEY FUNGUS
PENICILLIUM

SLIME MOULDS
13
BRACKET FUNGUS
14
BASIDIOMYCETES
15
PARASOL MUSHROOM

FAMOUS PEOPLE

ARTISTS AND ARCHITECTS

3

ARP, Jean (1887–1966; French sculptor/poet)
DOU, Gerrit (1613–75; Dutch painter)
FRY, Roger (1866–1934; British painter and art critic)
RAY, Man (1890–1976; US photographer and painter)

4

ADAM, Robert (1728–92; British architect and interior designer)
CAPP, Al (Alfred Caplin, 1909–79; US cartoonist)
CUYP, Aelbert Jacobsz (1620–91; Dutch landscape painter)
DADD, Richard (1817–86; British painter)
DALI, Salvador (1904–89; Spanish surrealist painter)
DIOR, Christian (1905–57; French fashion designer).
DORE, Gustave (1832–83; French illustrator, painter, and sculptor)
DUFY, Raoul (1877–1953; French painter)
ERTE (Romain de Tirtoff, 1892–90; French fashion illustrator and designer, born in Russia)
ETTY, William (1787–1849; British painter)
GILL, Eric (1882–1940; British sculptor, illustrator and typographer
GOES, Hugo van der (c. 1440–82; Flemish painter)
GOYA, Francesco de (1746–1828; Spanish painter)
GRIS, Juan (José Victoriano González, 1887–1927; Spanish-born cubist painter)
GROS, Antoine Jean, Baron (1771–1835; French painter)
HALS, Frans (c. 1581–1666; Dutch painter)
HILL, David Octavius (1802–70; Scottish painter and photographer)
HUNT, William Holman (1827–1910; British painter)
JOHN, Augustus (1878–1961; British painter)
KAHN, Louis Isadore (1901–74; US architect)
KENT, William (1685–1748; English architect, landscape gardener, and interior designer)

KLEE, Paul (1879–1940; Swiss painter and etcher)
LAMB, Henry (1885–1960; Australian-born British painter).
LELY, Sir Peter (Pieter van der Faes, 1618–80; English portrait painter of Dutch descent)
LOOS, Adolph (1870–1933; Austrian architect)
MAES, Nicolas (or N. Maas, 1634–93; Dutch painter)
MARC, Franz (1880–1916; German expressionist painter)
MIRO, Joan (1893–1983; Spanish painter)
NASH, John (1752–1835; British architect)
NASH, Paul (1889–1946; British painter)
NEER, Aert van der (c. 1603–77; Dutch landscape painter)
OPIE, John (1761–1807; British portrait and history painter)
RENI, Guido (1575–1642; Italian painter)
ROSA, Salvator (1615–73; Italian painter and etcher)
SHAW, Norman (1831–1912; British architect)
WARD, Sir Leslie (1851–1922; British caricaturist)
WEST, Benjamin (1738–1820; British painter of American birth)
WOOD, Christopher (1901–30; English painter)
WOOD, Grant (1892–1942; US painter)
WOOD, John, of Bath (1704–54; English architect)
WREN, Sir Christopher (1632–1723; English architect and scientist)
ZORN, Anders (1860–1920; Swedish artist)

5

AALTO, Alvar (1898–1976; Finnish architect)
ATGET, Eugène (1856–1927; French photographer)
BACON, Francis (1909–92; British painter, born in Dublin)
BAKST, Léon (Lev Samoilovich Rosenberg, 1866–1924; Russian artist)
BALLA, Giacomo (1871–1958; Italian futurist painter)

ARTISTS AND ARCHITECTS

5 continued

BARRY, Sir Charles (1795–1860; British architect)

BLAKE, Peter (1932– ; British painter)

BOSCH, Hieronymus (Jerome van Aeken, c. 1450– c. 1516; Dutch painter)

BOUTS, Dierick (c. 1400–75; Dutch painter)

BROWN Capability (Lancelot B, 1716–83; British landscape gardener)

BROWN, Ford Madox (1821–93; British painter, born in Calais)

BURRA, Edward (1905–76; British painter)

CAMPI, Giulio (1502–72; Italian Renaissance architect)

COROT, Jean Baptiste Camille (1796–1875; French landscape painter)

CRANE, Walter (1845–1915; British illustrator, painter, and designer of textiles and wallpaper)

PROME, John (1768–1821; British landscape painter and etcher)

DAGLY, Gerhard (c. 1653–?1714; Belgian artist)

DANBY, Francis (1793–1861; Irish painter)

DANCE, George (c. 1700–68; British architect)

DAVID, Gerard (c. 1460–1523; Dutch painter)

DAVID, Jacques Louis (1748–1825; French neoclassical painter)

DEGAS, Edgar (1834–1917; French painter and sculptor)

DENIS, Maurice (1870–1943; French painter, designer, and art theorist)

DURER, Albrecht (1471–1528; German painter)

ENSOR, James Sydney, Baron (1860–1949; Belgian painter)

ERNST, Max (1891–1976; German artist)

FOLEY, John Henry (1818–74; British sculptor)

GADDI, Taddeo (c. 1300–?1366; Florentine painter)

GIBBS, James (1682–1754; British architect)

GILES, Carl Ronald (1916– ; British cartoonist)

GORKY, Arshile (Vosdanig Adoian, 1905–48; US painter, born in Armenia).

GOYEN, Jan Josephszoon van (1596–1656; Dutch landscape painter and etcher)

GRANT, Duncan James Corrower (1885–1978; British painter and designer)

GROSZ George (1893–1959; German painter)

HOMER, Winslow (1836–1910; US painter)

HOOCH, Pieter de (1629 – c. 1684; Dutch painter)

HORTA, Victor (1861–1947; Belgian architect)

JOHNS, Jasper (1930– ; US artist)

JONES, Inigo (1573–1652; English classical architect)

KEENE, Charles Samuel (1823–91; British artist and illustrator)

KLIMT, Gustav (1862–1918; Viennese Art Nouveau artist)

KLINT, Kaare (1888–1954; Danish furniture designer)

LEACH, Bernard (1887–1979; British potter, born in Hong Kong)

LEECH, John (1817–64; British caricaturist)

LEGER, Fernand (1881–1955; French painter)

LE VAU, Louis (1612–70; French baroque architect)

LIPPI, Fra.Filippo (c. 1406–69; Florentine painter)

LOTTO, Lorenzo (c. 1480–1556; Venetian painter)

LOWRY, L.S. (1887–1976; British painter)

MACKE, August (1887–1914; German painter)

MANET, Edouard (1832–83; French painter)

MENGS, Anton Raphael (1728–79; German painter)

METSU, Gabriel (1629–67; Dutch painter)

MONET, Claude (1840–1926; French impressionist painter)

MOORE, Henry (1898–1986; British sculptor)

MOSES, Grandma (Anna Mary Robertson M, 1860–1961; US primitive painter)

MUNCH, Edvard (1863–1944; Norwegian painter and printmaker)

MYRON (5th century BC; Athenian sculptor)

NADAW (Gaspard Felix Tournachon, 1820 – 1910; French photographer and caricaturist)

NERVI, Pier Luigi (1891–1979; Italian architect)

NOLAN, Sir Sidney (1917–92; Australian painter)

NOLDE, Emil (E. Hansen, 1867–1956; German expressionist painter and printmaker)

OUDRY, Jean-Baptiste (1686–1755; French rococo painter and tapestry designer)

5 continued

PHYFE, Duncan (or Fife, 1768–1854; US furniture designer, born in Scotland)

PIPER, John (1903–92; British painter and writer)

PUGIN, Augustus Welby Northmore (1812–52; British architect and theorist)

QUANT, Mary (1934– ; British fashion designer)

REDON, Odilon (1840–1916; French symbolist, painter and lithographer)

RICCI, Sebastiano (1659–1734; Venetian painter)

RILEY, Bridget Louise (1931– ; British painter)

RODIN, Auguste (1840–1917; French sculptor)

SCOTT, Sir George Gilbert (1811–78; British architect)

SHAHN, Ben (1898–1969; Lithuanian-born US artist)

SOANE, Sir John (1753–1837; British architect)

STEEN, Jan (c. 1626–79; Dutch painter)

STOSS, Veit (c. 1445–1533; German gothic sculptor and woodcarver)

TOBEY, Mark (1890–1976; US painter)

VICKY (Victor Weisz, 1913–66; British cartoonist, born in Berlin)

WATTS, George Frederick (1817–1904; British artist)

WYATT, James (1747–1813; British architect)

6

ALBERS, Josef (1888–1976; German abstract painter)

ARCHER, Thomas (1668–1743; English baroque architect)

BEATON, Sir Cecil (1904–80; British photographer)

BEHZAD (c. 1455– c. 1536; Persian painter)

BENTON, Thomas Hart (1889–1975; US painter)

BEWICK, Thomas (1753–1828; British wood engraver)

BOUDIN, Eugène (1824–98; French painter)

BOULLE, Andre Charles (or Buhl, 1642–1732; French cabinetmaker)

BRANDT, Bill (1905–83; British photographer)

BRAQUE, Georges (1882–1963; French painter)

BRATBY, John (1928– ; British painter and writer)

BREUER, Marcel Lajos (1902–81; US architect. born in Hungary)

BUFFET, Bernard (1928– ; French painter)

BUTLER, Reg Cotterell (1913–81; British sculptor)

CALDER, Alexander (1898–76; US sculptor)

CALLOT, Jacques (c. 1592–1635; French graphic artist)

CANOVA, Antonio (1757–1822; Italian sculptor)

CARDIN, Pierre (1922– ; French fashion designer)

CASSON, Sir Hugh (1910– British architect)

CHANEL, Coco (Gabrielle C, 1883–1971; French fashion designer)

CLOUET, Jean (c. 1485–1540; French portrait, painter)

COOPER, Samuel (1609–72; British miniaturist)

COSWAY, Richard (1742–1821; British portrait miniaturist)

COTMAN, John Sell (1782–1842; British landscape watercolourist and etcher)

DERAIN, André (1880–1954; French postimpressionist painter)

DE WINT, Peter (1784–1849; British landscape painter)

EAKINS, Thomas (1844–1916; US painter)

FLORIS, Cornelis (1514–75; Flemish artist)

FLORIS, Frans (c. 1516–70; Flemish artist)

FULLER, Richard Buckminster (1895–1983; US inventor and architect)

FUSELI, Henry (Johann Heinrich Füssli, 1741–1825: British painter of Swiss birth)

GÉRARD, François, Baron (1770–1837; French painter)

GIOTTO (Giotto di Bondone, c. 1266–1337; Italian painter and architect)

GIRTIN, Thomas (1775–1802; British painter)

GOUJON, Jean (c. 1510–68; French Renaissance sculptor)

GREUZE, Jean-Baptiste (1725–1805; French painter)

GUARDI, Francesco (1712–93; Venetian painter)

HOLLAR, Wenceslaus (1607–77; Bohemian etcher)

HOUDON, Jean Antoine (1741–1828; French sculptor)

ARTISTS AND ARCHITECTS

6 continued

INGRES, Jean-Auguste-Dominique (1780–1867; French painter)

ISABEY, Jean Baptiste (1767–1855; French portrait painter and miniaturist)

JOCHHO (d.1057; Japanese sculptor)

KNIGHT, Dame Laura (1877–1970; British painter)

LASDUN, Sir Denys (1914– ; British architect)

LA TOUR, Georges de (1593–1652; French painter)

LA TOUR, Maurice-Quentin de (1704–88; French portrait pastellist)

LE BRUN, Charles (1619–90; French history and portrait painter and designer)

LE NAIN, Antoine (c. 1588–1648; French painter)

LE NAIN, Louis (c. 1593–1648; French painter)

LE NAIN, Mathieu (c. 1607–77; French painter)

LESCOT, Pierre (c. 1510–78; French architect)

LONGHI, Pietro (Pietro Falca, 1702–85; Venetian painter)

LURCAT, Jean (1892–1966; French painter)

MARINI, Marino (1901–80; Italian sculptor and painter)

MARTIN, John (1789–1854; British painter)

MASSYS, Quentin (or Matsys, Messys, Metsys, c. 1466–1530; Flemish painter)

MILLET, Jean François (1814–75; French painter)

MOREAU, Gustave (1826–98; French symbolist painter)

MORONI, Giovanni Battista (c. 1525–78; Italian painter)

MORRIS, William (1834–96; British designer and artist)

OLIVER, Isaac (?1556–1617; English portrait miniaturist, born in France)

OROZCO, José (1883–1949; Mexican mural painter)

OSTADE, Adrian van (1610–85; Dutch painter)

PALMER, Samuel (1805–81; British landscape painter and etcher)

PAXTON, Sir Joseph (1801–65; British architect)

PISANO, Andrea (Andrea de Pontedera c. 1290–1348; Italian sculptor)

PISANO, Nicola (c. 1220– c. 1278; Italian sculptor)

RENOIR, Pierre Auguste (1841–1919; French impressionist painter)

RIBERA, José de (or Jusepe R, 1591–1652; Spanish-born painter and etcher)

RIVERA, Diego (1886–1957; Mexican mural painter)

ROMNEY, George (1734–1802; British portrait painter)

ROTHKO, Mark (Marcus Rothkovitch. 1903–70; Russian-born US painter)

RUBENS, Peter Paul (1577–1640 Flemish painter)

SCARFE, Gerald (1936– ; British cartoonist)

SEARLE, Ronald William Fordharn (1920– ; British cartoonist)

SESSHU (Sesshu Toyo, 1420–1506; Japanese landscape painter)

SEURAT, Georges (1859–91; French painter)

SIGNAC, Paul (1863–1935; French painter and art theorist)

SISLEY, Alfred (1839–99; Impressionist painter)

SLUTER, Claus, (c. 1345–1406; Dutch sculptor)

SPENCE, Sir Basil (1907–76; British architect)

STUBBS, George (1724–1806; British animal painter)

TANGUY, Yves (1900–55; French surrealist painter)

TISSOT, James Joseph Jacques (1836–1902; French painter and etcher)

TITIAN (Tiziano Vecellio, c. 1488–1576; Venetian painter)

TURNER, Joseph Mallord William (1775–1851; British landscape and marine painter)

VASARI, Giorgio (1511–74; Italian painter, architect, and writer)

VOYSEY, Charles Francis Annesley (1857–1941; British architect and designer)

WARHOL, Andy (Andrew Warhola, 1926–87; US pop artist)

WEYDEN, Rogier van der (c. 1400–64; Flemish painter)

WILKIE, Sir David (1785–1841; Scottish painter)

WILSON, Richard (1714–82; British painter)

WRIGHT, Frank Lloyd (1869–1959; US architect).

XIA GUI (or Hsia: Knei, c. 1180–c. 1230, Chinese landscape painter)

ZEUXIS (late 5th century BC; Greek painter)

ARTISTS AND ARCHITECTS

7

ALBERTI, Leon Battista (1404–72; Italian Renaissance architect)

ALLSTON, Washington (1779–1843; US Romantic painter)

ANTENOR (late 6th century BC; Athenian sculptor)

APELLES (4th century BC; Greek painter)

ASTBURY, John (1688–1743; English potter)

BARLACH, Ernst (1870–1938; German expressionist sculptor and playwright)

BASSANO, Jacopo (Jacopo *or* Giacomo da Ponte, *c.* 1517–92; Italian painter)

BEHRENS, Peter (1868–1940; German architect)

BELLINI, Jacopo (*c.* 1400– *c.* 1470; Venetian painter)

BERNINI, Gian Lorenzo (1598–1680; Italian sculptor and architect)

BONNARD, Pierre (1867–1947; French painter)

BORGLUM, Gutzon (1867–1941; US sculptor)

BOUCHER, François (1703–70; French rococo painter)

BROUWER, Adriaen (*c.* 1605–38; Flemish painter)

CAMERON, Julia Margaret (1815–79; British photographer, born in Calcutta)

CASSATT, Mary (1844–1926; US painter)

CELLINI, Benvenuto (1500–71; Florentine goldsmith and sculptor)

CENNINI, Cennino (*c.* 1370– *c.* 1440; Florentine painter)

CEZANNE, Paul (1839–1906; French postimpressionist painter)

CHAGALL, Marc (1887–1985; Russian-born painter and printmaker) .

CHARDIN, Jean-Baptiste-Siméon (1699–1779; French painter)

CHIRICO, Giorgio de (1888–1978; Italian painter, born in Greece).

CIMABUE, Giovanni (Cenni de Peppi, *c.* 1240– *c.* 1302; Florentine painter)

CLODION (Claude Michel, 1738–1814; French rococo sculptor)

COURBET, Gustave (1819–77; French painter)

DAUMIER, Honoré (1808–79; French caricaturist, painter, and sculptor)

DELORME, Philibert (?1510–70; French Renaissance architect)

DELVAUX, Paul (1897–94; Belgian painter)

DUCHAMP, Marcel (1887–1968; French artist)

EL GRECO (Dornenikos Theotokopoulos, 1541–1614; Painter of Greek parentage born in Crete)

EPSTEIN, Sir Jacob (1880–1959; British sculptor of US birth)

EXEIKIAS (6th century BC; Athenian potter and vase painter)

FABERGÉ, Peter Carl (1846–1920; Russian goldsmith and jeweller)

FLAXMAN, John Henry (1755–1826; British sculptor and book illustrator)

FONTANA, Domenico (1543–1607; Italian architect)

FOUQUET, Jean (*c.* 1420–81; French painter and manuscript illuminator)

GAUGUIN, Paul (1848–1903; French postimpressionist painter)

GIBBONS, Grinling (1648–1721; English wood carver and sculptor)

GILLRAY, James (1756–1815; British caricaturist)

GOZZOLI, Benozzo (Benozzo di Lese, 1420–97; Florentine painter)

GROPIUS, Walter (1883–1969; German architect)

GUARINI, Guarino (1624–83; Italian baroque architect)

HASSALL, John (1868–1948; British artist)

HERRERA, Juan de (1530–97; Spanish, architect)

HOBBEMA, Meindert (1638–1709; Dutch landscape painter

HOCKNEY, David (1937– ; British painter, draughtsman, and printmaker)

HOGARTH, William (1697–1764; British painter and engraver)

HOKUSAI, (Katsushika H, 1760–1849; Japanese painter and book illustrator)

HOLLAND, Henry (1745–1806; British architect)

HOPPNER, John (1758–1810; British painter)

ICTINUS (5th century BC; Greek architect)

JOHNSON, Cornelius (Janssen van Ceulen, 1593–1661; English portrait painter)

KNELLER, Sir Godfrey (1646–1723; English portrait painter of German birth)

LALIQUE, René (1860–1945; French Art Nouveau jeweller and glassmaker)

LAMERIE, Paul de (1688–1751; English silversmith)

29

ARTISTS AND ARCHITECTS

7 continued

L'ENFANT, Pierre-Charles (1754–1825; US architect and town planner of French birth)

LE NÔTRE, André (1613–1700; French, land scape gardener)

LIMBURG, Pol, de (active *c.* 1400– *c.* 1416; French manuscript illuminator)

LIMOSIN, Léonard (or Limousin, *c.* 1505– *c.* 1577; French artist)

LOCHNER, Stefan (*c.* 1400–51; German painter)

LUTYENS, Sir Edwini Landseer (1869–1944; British architect)

MACLISE, Daniel (1806–70; Irish portrait and history painter)

MADERNA, Carlo (1556–1629; Roman architect)

MAILLOL, Aristide (1861–1944; French sculptor)

MANSART, François (or Mansard, 1596–1666; French classical architect)

MARTINI, Simone (*c.* 1294–1344; Italian painter)

MATISSE, Henri (1869–1954; French painter)

MEMLING, Hans, (or Memlinc *c.* 1430–1494; German painter)

MILLAIS, Sir John Everett (1829–96; British painter)

MORANDI, Giorgio (1890–1964; Italian still-life painter, and etcher)

MORISOT, Berthe (1841–95; French painter)

MORLAND, George (1763–1804; British painter)

MURILLO, Bartolomé Esteban (1617–82; Spanish painter)

NEUMANN, Balthasar (1687–1753; German architect)

O'KEEFFE, Georgia (1887–1986; US painter)

ORCAGNA, Andrea (Andrea di Cione, *c.* 1308– *c.* 1368; Florentine artist)

PALISSY, Bernard (1510–89; French potter)

PASMORE, Victor (1908–98; British artist)

PATINIR; Joachim (or Patenier, *c.* 1485–1524; Flemish painter),

PEVSNER, Antoine (1886–1962; Russian sculptor and painter)

PHIDIAS (*c.* 490– *c.* 417 BC; Athenian sculptor)

PICABIA, Francis (1879–1953; French painter and writer)

PICASSO, Pablo (1881–1973; Spanish artist)

POLLOCK, Jackson (1912–56; US painter)

POUSSIN,Nicolas (1594–1665; French painter)

PRUD'HON, Pierre Paul (1758–1823; French painter and draughtsman)

RACKHAM, Arthur (1867–1939; British water colourist and book illustrator)

RAEBURN, Sir Henry (1756–1823; Scottish portrait painter)

RAPHAEL, (Raffaello Sanzio, 1483–1520; Italian Renaissance painter and architect)

REDOUTÉ, Pierre Joseph (1759–1841; French flower painter)

ROBERTS, Tom (1856–1931; Australian painter, born in Britain)

ROUAULT, Georges (1871–1958; French artist)

RUBLYOV, Andrey (or A Rublev, *c.* 1370–1430; Russian icon painter)

SARGENT, John Singer (1856–1925; US portrait painter, born in Florence)

SCHIELE, Egon (1890–1918; Austrian expressionist painter)

SEGHERS, Hercules Pieterzoon (*c.* 1589– *c.* 1638; Dutch landscape painter and etcher)

SHEPARD, Ernest Howard (1879–1976; British artist)

SICKERT, Walter Richard (1860–1942; British impressionist painter/etcher, born Munich)

SNOWDON, Antony Armstrong-Jones, Earl of (1930– ; British photographer)

SNYDERS, Frans (1579–1657; Flemish animal painter)

SOUTINE, Chaim (1893–1943; Lithuanian born painter, who emigrated to Paris)

SPENCER, Sir Stanley (1891–1959: British painter)

TENNIEL, Sir John (1820–1914; British cartoonist and book illustrator)

TIBALDI, Pellegrino (1527–96; Italian architect and painter)

TIEPOLO, Giovanni Battista (1696–1770; Venetian rococo painter)

UCCELLO, Paolo (P. di Dono, 1397–1475; Florentine painter and craftsman)

UTRILLO, Maurice (1883–1955; French painter)

VAN DYCK, Sir Anthony (or Vandyke, 1599–1641; Flemish baroque painter)

VAN EYCK, Jan (*c.* 1390–1441; Flemish painter)

7 continued
VAN GOGH, Vincent (1853–90; Dutch post impressionist painter)
VERMEER, Jan (1632–75; Dutch painter)
VIGNOLA, Giacomo da (1507–73; Roman mannerist architect)
WATTEAU, Antoine (1684–1721; French rococo painter)
ZADKINE, Ossip (1890–1967; French sculptor of Russian birth)
ZOFFANY, Johann (c. 1733–1810; German born English painter)
ZUCCARO, Federico (1543–1609; Italian painter)
ZUCCARO, Taddeo (1529–66; Italian painter)

8
AALTONEN, Wäino (1894–1966; Finnish sculptor)
AMMANATI, Bartolommeo (1511–92; Florentine mannerist architect and sculptor)
ANGELICO, Fra (Guido di Pietro, c. 1400–55; Italian painter)
ANNIGONI, Pietro (1910– ; Italian painter)
ANTELAMI, Benedetto (active 1177–1233; Italian sculptor)
BECKMANN, Max (1884–1950; German expressionist painter)
BOCCIONI Umberto (1882–1916; Italian futurist painter and sculptor)
BRAMANTE, Donato (1444–1514; Italian Renaissance architect)
BRANCUSI, Constantin (1876–1957; Romanian sculptor)
BRONZINO, Il (Agnolo di Cosimo, 1503–72; Florentine mannerist painter)
CARRACCI, Annibale (1560–1609; Italian painter)
CASTAGNO, Andrea del (Andrea di Bartolo de Simone, c. 1421–57; Italian painter)
CHAMBERS, Sir William (1723–96; British architect and interior designer)
CRESSENT, Charles (1685–1768; French cabinetmaker)
CRIVELLI, Carlo (c. 1430–95; Venetian painter)
DAUBIGNY, Charles-François (1817–78; French landscape painter)
DELAUNAY, Robert (1885–1941; French painter)
DRYSDALE, Sir Russell (1912–81; Australian painter, born in England)

DUBUFFET, Jean (1901–85; French painter and sculptor)
FILARETE (Antonio Averlino, c. 1400– c. 1469; Italian Renaissance architect)
FRAMPTON, Sir George James (1860–1928; British sculptor)
GHIBERTI, Lorenzo (c. 1378–1455; Florentine Renaissance sculptor)
GIORDANO, Luca (1632–1705; Neapolitan painter, nicknamed LUCA FA PRESTO)
GOSSAERT, Jan (c. 1478– c. 1532; Flemish painter)
GUERCINO (Giovanni Francesco Barbieri, 1591–1666; Italian painter)
HEPWORTH, Dame Barbara (1903–75; British sculptor)
HILLIARD, Nicholas (1547–1619; English portrait miniaturist)
JACOBSEN, Arne (1902–71; Danish architect and designer of furniture and wallpaper)
JONGKIND, Johan Barthold (1819–91; Dutch landscape painter and etcher)
JORDAENS, Jakob (1593–1678; Flemish painter)
KIRCHNER, Ernst Ludwig (1880–1938; German expressionist painter and printmaker)
LANDSEER, Sir Edwin Henry (1802–73; British artist)
LAWRENCE, Sir Thomas (1769–1830; British painter)
LIPCHITZ, Jacques (1891–1973; Lithuanian cubist sculptor)
LOMBARDO, Pietro (c. 1438–1515; Italian sculptor and architect)
LYSIPPUS (4th century BC; Court sculptor of Alexander the Great)
MAGRITTE, René (1898–1967; Belgian surrealist painter)
MALEVICH, Kazimir (1878–1935; Russian painter and art theorist)
MANTEGNA, Andrea (c. 1431–1506; Italian Renaissance painter and engraver)
MASACCIO (Tommaso di Giovanni di Simone Guidi, 1401–28; Florentine painter)
MASOLINO, (Tommaso di Cristoforo Fini, 1383–?1447; Italian painter)
MEEGEREN, Hans van (1889–1947; Dutch painter)
MONDRIAN Piet (Pieter Cornelis Mondrian, 1872–1944; Dutch painter)

ARTISTS AND ARCHITECTS

8 continued

MULREADY, William (1786–1863; British painter)

MUNNINGS, Sir Alfred (1878–1959; British painter)

NIEMEYER, Oscar (1907– ; Brazilian architect)

PALLADIO, Andrea (1508–80; Italian architect)

PIRANESI, Giambattista (1720–78; Italian etcher)

PISSARRO, Camille (1830–1903; French impressionist painter, born West Indies)

PONTORMO, Jacopo da (J. Carrucci, 1494–1557; Italian mannerist painter)

REYNOLDS, Sir Joshua (1723–92; British portrait painter)

ROBINSON, William Heath (1872–1944; British cartoonist and book illustrator)

ROUSSEAU, Henri (1844–1910; French painter)

ROUSSEAU, Théodore (1812–67; French Romantic painter)

RUISDAEL, Jacob van (?1628–82; Dutch landscape painter)

SAARINEN, Eero (1910–61; US architect. born in Finland)

SASSETTA (Stefano di Giovanni, c. 1392–c. 1450; Italian painter)

SEVERINI, Gino (1883–1966; Italian painter)

SHERATON, Thomas (1751–1806; British furniture designer)

SOUFFLOT, Jacques Germain (1713–80; French architect)

SULLIVAN, Louis Henry (1856–1924; US architect)

TERBORCH, Gerard (1617–81; Dutch painter)

VANBRUGH, Sir John (1664–1726; English architect)

VASARELY, Victor (1908–97; Hungarian-born painter)

VERONESE, Paolo (P.Caliari, 1528–88; Italian painter)

VLAMINCK, Maurice de (1876–1958; French painter)

VUILLARD, Edouard (1868–1940; French artist)

WEDGWOOD, Josiah (1730– 95; British potter, industrialist, and writer)

WHISTLER, James McNeill (1834–1903; US painter)

WHISTLER, Rex (1905–44; British artist)

WOOLLETT, William (1735–85; British engraver)

ZURBARAN, Francisco de (1598–1664; Spanish painter)

9

ALTDORFER, Albrecht (c. 1480–1538; German artist)

BARTHOLDI, Frédéric August (1834–1904; French sculptor)

BEARDSLEY, Aubrey Vincent (1872–98; British illustrator)

BONINGTON, Richard Parkes (1801–28; British painter)

BORROMINI, Francesco (1599–1667; Italian baroque architect)

BOURDELLE, Émile (1861–1929; French sculptor)

CANALETTO (Antonio Canal, 1697–1768; Venetian painter)

CARPACCIO, Vittore (c. 1460– c. 1525; Venetian painter)

CAVALLINI, Pietro (c. 1250–c. 1330; Italian painter)

COCKERELL, Charles Robert (1788–1863; British architect)

CONSTABLE, John (1776–1837; British landscape painter)

CORNELIUS, Peter, von (1783–1867; German painter)

CORREGGIO (Antonio Allegri, c. 1494–1534; Italian Renaissance painter)

COURRÉGES, André (1923– ; French fashion designer)

DE KOONING, Willem (1904– ; US painter of Dutch birth)

DELACROIX, Eugène (1798–1863; French Romantic painter)

DELAROCHE, Paul (1797–1859; French history and portrait painter)

DONATELLO (Donato de Nicolo di Betti Bardi, c. 1386–1466; Florentine sculptor)

FABRITIUS, Carel (1622–54; Dutch painter)

FEININGER, Lyonel (1871–1956; US painter)

FRAGONARD, Jean Honoré (1732–1806; French rococo painter)

FRIEDIRICH, Caspar David (1774–1840; German Romantic landscape painter)

GERICAULT, Théodore (1791–1824; French, painter)

9 continued

GIORGIONE (*c.* 1477–1510; Italian painter)

GREENAWAY, Kate (1846–1901; British artist and book illustrator)

GREENOUGH, Horatio (1805–52; US neoclassical sculptor)

GRUNEWALD, Matthias (Mathis Gothardt, *d.*1528; German painter)

HAWKSMOOR, Nicholas (1661–1736; English baroque architect)

HIROSHIGE, (Ando Tokitaro, 1797–1858; Japanese colour-print artist)

HONTHORST, Gerrit von (1590–1656; Dutch painter)

JAWLENSKY, Alexey von (1864–1941; Russian expressionist painter)

KANDINSKY, Wassily (1866–1944; Russian expressionist painter and art theorist)

KAUFFMANN, Angelica (1741–1807; Swiss painter)

KOKOSCHKA, Oskar (1886–1980; Austrian expressionist painter and writer)

LISSITZKY, El (Eliezer L, 1890–1941; Russian painter and architect)

MESTROVIC, Ivan (1883–1962; US sculptor, born in Yugoslavia)

MUYBRIDGE, Eadweard (Edward James Muggeridge, 1830–1904; US photographer, born in Britain)

NICHOLSON, Ben (1894–1982; British artist)

NOLLEKENS, Joseph (1737–1823; British neoclassical sculptor)

OLDENBURG, Claes; (1929– ; US sculptor, born in Sweden)

PISANELLO (Antonio Pisano, *c.* 1395– *c.* 1455; Italian international gothic painter, draughtsman, and medallist)

ROUBILLAC, Louis Franiçois (or L.F. Roubiliac, 1695–1762; French sculptor)

SIQUEIROS, David Alfaro (1896–1974; Mexican painter)

STIEGLITZ, Alfred (1864–1946; US photographer

THORNHILL, Sir Jarnes (1675–1734; English baroque decorative painter)

VELAZQUEZ, Diego Rodriguez de Silva (1599–1660; Spanish painter)

VITRUVIUS (Marcus Vitruvius Pollio, 1st century BC; Roman architect)

WOUWERMAN, Philips (1619–68; Dutch painter)

10

ALMA-TADEMA, Sir Lawrence (1836–1912; Dutch painter)

ALTICHIER0 (*c.* 1330– *c.* 1390; Italian painter)

ARCHIPENKO, Alexander (1887–1964; Russian-born sculptor and painter)

ARCIMBOLDO, Giuseppe (1527–93; Mannerist painter)

BERRUGUETE, Alfonso (*c.* 1488–1561; Castillian painter)

BERRUGUETE, Pedro (*c.* 1450 – *c.* 1504; Castillian painter)

BOTTICELLI, Sandro (Alessandro di Mariano Filipepi, *c.* 1445–1510; Florentine Renaissance painter)

BURLINGTON, Richard Boyle, 3rd Earl of (1694–1753; English architect)

BURNE-JONES, Sir Edward Coley (1833–98; Pre-Raphaelite painter)

CARAVAGGIO (Michelangelo Merisi, 1573–1610; Italian painter)

CHAMPAIGNE, Philippe de (1602–74; French portrait painter)

CRUIKSHANK, George (1792–1872; British caricaturist, painter and illustrator)

EUPHRONIOS (late 6th–early 5th centuries BC: Athenian potter and vase painter)

GIACOMETTI, Aberto (1901–66; Swiss sculptor and painter)

LORENZETTI, Ambrogio (*c.* 1290–?1348; Italian painter)

MACKINTOSH, Charles Rennie (1868–1928; Scottish architect and designer)

MEISSONIER, Jean-Louis-Ernest (1815–91; French painter)

MODIGLIANI, Amedeo (1884–1920; Italian painter and sculptor)

MOHOLY-NAGY, Làszió (1895–1946; Hungarian artist)

MOTHERWELL, Robert (1915– ; US abstract painter)

POLLAIUOLO, Antonio (*c.* 1432–98; Florentine Renaissance artist)

POLYCLITUS (5th century BC; Greek sculptor)

PRAXITELES (mid-4th century BC; Athenian sculptor)

RICHARDSON, Henry Hobson (1838–86; US architect)

ARTISTS AND ARCHITECTS

10 continued

ROWLANDSON, Thomas (1756–1827; British caricaturist)

SCHWITTERS, Kurt (1887–1958; German artist and poet)

SENEFELDER, Aloys (1771–1834; German playwright and engraver)

SIGNORELLI, Luca (c. 1441–1523; Italian Renaissance painter)

SUTHERLAND, Graham Vivian (1903–80; British artist)

TANGE KENZO (1913– ; Japanese architect)

TINTORETTO (Jacopo Robusti, 1518–94; Venetian painter)

VAN DE VELDE, Henry (1863–1957; Belgian Art Nouveau architect, interior designer, and painter)

VERROCCH Andrea del (Andrea del Cione, c. 1435–88; Italian sculptor, painter, and goldsmith

WATERHOUSE, Alfred (1830–1905; British architect)

ZUCCARELLI, Francesco (1702–88; Italian painter)

11

ABERCROMBIE, Sir Patrick (1879–1957; British architect)

BARTOLOMMEO, Fra (Baccio della Porta, c. 1472–1517; Florentine Renaissance painter)

BUTTERFIELD, William (1814–1900; British architect)

CALLICRATES (5th century BC; Athenian architect)

CALLIMACHUS (late 5th century BC; Greek sculptor)

CHIPPENDALE, Thomas (1718–79; British cabinetmaker)

CHODOWIECKI, Daniel Nikolaus (1726–1801; German painter and engraver)

DELLA ROBBIA Luca (1400–82; Florentine renaissance sculptor)

DOMENICHINO, (Domenico Zampieri, 1581–1641; Italian painter)

GHIRLANDAIO, Domenico (Domenico di Tommaso Bigordi, 1449–94; Florentine painter)

GIAMBOLOGNA (Giovanni da Bologna or Jean de Boulogne, 1529–1608; Italian mannerist sculptor)

GISLEBERTUS (early 12th century; French romanesque sculptor)

HEPPLEWHITE, George (d. 1786; British furniture designer and cabinetmaker)

LE CORBUSIER (Charles-Édouard Jeanneret, 1887–1965; French architect, born in Switzerland)

TERBRUGGHEN, Hendrik (1588–1629; Dutch painter)

THORVALDSEN, Bertel (or B.Thorwaldsen, 1768–1844; Danish sculptor)

12

BRUNELLESCHI, Filippo (1377–1446; Italian architect)

FANTIN-LATOUR, Henri (1836–1904; French painter)

GAINSBOROUGH, Thomas (1727–88; British portrait and landscape painter)

GAUDI Y CORNET, Antonio (1852–1926; Spanish architect)

GIULIO ROMANO (Giulio Pippi, c. 1499–1546; Italian mannerist painter and architect)

LICHTENSTEIN, Roy (1923–97; US painter)

LUCA FA PRESTO (Nickname of Luca Giordano)

PALMA VECCHIO, Jacopo (J Negretti, c. 1480–1528; Italian painter)

PARMIGIANINO (Girolamo Francesco Maria Mazzola, 1503–40; Italian painter)

PINTURICCHIO (Bernardino di Betto, c. 1454–1513; Italian Renaissance painter)

RAUSCHENBERG, Robert (1925– ; US artist)

SAINT-LAURENT, Yves (1936– ; French fashion designer)

SCHIAPARELLI, Elsa (1896–1973; Italian-born fashion designer)

VIOLLET-LE-DUC, Eugéne Emmanuel (1814–79; French architect and author)

WINTERHALTER, Franz Xavier (1806–73; German painter and lithographer)

13

LORENZO MONACO (Piero di Giovanni, c. 1370–1425; Italian painter)

PIERO DI COSIMO (P di Lorenzo, 1462–1521; Florentine Renaissance painter)

WILLIAMS-ELLIS, Sir Clough (1883–1978; Welsh architect

14

ANDREA DEL SARTO (Andrea d'Agnolo, 1486–1530; Italian painter)

BÉRAIN THE ELDER, Jean (1637–1711; French designer, engraver, and painter)

CARTIER-BRESSON, Henri (1908– ; French photographer)

CLAUDE LORRAINE (Claude Gellbe, 1600–82; French landscape painter).

COUSIN THE ELDER, Jean (1490–1560; French artist and craftsman)

GAUDIER-BRZESKA, Henri (1891–1915; French sculptor)

LUCAS VAN LEYDEN (Lucas Hugensz or Jacobsz, c. 1494–1533; Dutch artist)

MIES VAN DER ROHE, Ludwig (1886–1969; German architect)

15

CRANACH THE ELDER, Lucas (Lucas Müller, 1472–1553; German artist)

HARDOUIN-MANSART, Jules (1646–1708; French baroque architect)

KITAGAWA UTAMARO (1753–1806; Japanese artist)

LEONARDO DA VINCI (1452–1519; Italian artistic and scientific genius of the Renaissance)

TOULOUSE-LAUTREC, Henri de (1864–1901; French artist)

16

BRUEGHEL THE ELDER, Pieter (*or* Bruegel, 1525–69; Flemish painter)

FISCHER VON ERLACH, Johann Bernhard (1656–1723; Austrian architect)

PUVIS DE CHAVANNES, Pierre (1824–98; French painter)

REMBRANDT VAN RIJN (1606–69; Dutch painter and etcher)

UTAGAWA KUNIYOSHI (Igusa Magosaburo, 1797–1861; Japanese painter and printmaker)

17

DOMENICO VENEZIANO (active c. 1438–1461; Italian painter)

GENTILE DA FABRIANO (Niccolo di Giovanni di Massio, c. 1370–1427; Florentine painter)

HERRERA THE YOUNGER, Francisco de (1622–85; Spanish baroque painter and architect)

HOLBEIN THE YOUNGER, Hans (c. 1497–1543; German painter)

TENIERS THE YOUNGER, David (1610–90; Flemish painter)

18

ANTONELLO DA MESSINA (c. 1430–c.1479; Italian painter)

JACOPO DELLA QUERCIA (c. 1374–1438; Italian Renaissance sculptor)

LEIGHTON OF STRETTON, Frederic, Baron (1830–96; British painter and sculptor)

19

DUCCIO DI BUONINSEGNA (c. 1255–c. 1318; Italian painter)

PIERO DELLA FRANCESCA (c. 1420–92; Italian Renaissance painter)

20+

DESIDERIO DA SETTIGNANO (c. 1430–64; Italian Renaissance sculptor)

MICHELANGELO BUONARROTI (1475–1564; Italian sculptor, painter, and architect)

MICHELOZZO DI BARTOLOMMEO (1396–1472; Florentine Renaissance sculptor and architect)

WRITERS

3

FRY, Christopher (C. Harris, 1907– ; British dramatist)

GAY, John (1685–1732; British poet and dramatist)

KYD, Thomas (1558–94; English dramatist)

PAZ, Octavio (1914–98; Mexican poet)

SUE, Eugéne (Joseph Marie S, 1804–57; French novelist)

4

AGEE, James (1909–55; US poet arid novelist)

AMIS, Sir Kingsley (1922–95; British novelist and poet)

AMIS, Martin (1949–; British novelist)

BANA (7th century AD; Sanskrit writer)

BAUM, L.Frank (1856–1919; US novelist)

BENN, Gottfried (1886–1956; German Poet)

BLOK, Aleksandr Aleksandrovich (1880–1921; Russian symbolist poet)

BÖLL, Heinrich (1917–85; German novelist)

BOLT, Robert Oxton (1924–95; British dramatist)

BUCK, Pearl S. (1892–1973; US novelist)

CARY, Joyce (1888–1957; British novelist)

CRUZ Sor Juana Inéz de la (1651–95; Mexican poet)

DAHL, Roald (1916–90; British author)

DEUS, João de (1830–96; Portuguese poet)

DU FU (or Tu Fu; 712–70 AD; Chinese poet)

FORD, Ford Madox (Ford Hermann Hueffer, 1873–1939; British novelist)

FORD, John (1586– c. 1640; English dramatist)

FOXE, John (1516–87; English religious writer)

GALT, John (1779–1839; Scottish novelist)

GIDE, André (1869–1951; French novelist and critic)

GRAY, Thomas (1716–71; British poet)

GUNN, Thomson W (1929– ; British poet)

HART, Moss (1904–61; US dramatist)

HOGG, James (1770–1835; Scottish poet and writer)

HOOD, Thomas (1799–1845; British poet)

HOPE, Anthony (Sir Anthony Hope Hawkins; 1863–1933; British novelist)

HUGO, Victor (1802–85; French poet, dramatist, and novelist)

HUNT, Leigh (1784–1859; British poet and journalist)

KIVI, Alexis (A Stenvall, 1834–72; Finnish poet, dramatist, and novelist)

LAMB, Charles (1775–1834; British essayist and critic)

LEAR, Edward (1812–88; British artist/poet)

LIVY (Titus Livius, 59 BC–17 AD; Roman writer)

LOTI, Pierre (Julien Viaud; 1850–1923; French novelist)

LYLY, John (c. 1554–1606; English dramatist and writer)

MANN, Thomas (1875–1955; German novelist)

MUIR, Edwin (1887–1959; Scottish poet),

NASH, Ogden (1902–71; US humorous writer)

NEXO, Martin Andersen (1869–1954; Danish novelist) .

OVID (Publius Ovidius Naso 43 BC– 17 AD; Roman poet)

OWEN, Wilfred (1893–1918; British poet

POPE, Alexander (1688–1744; British poet)

READ, Sir Herbert (1893–1968; British poet)

RHYS, Jean (1894–1979; British novelist)

ROTH, Philip, (1933– ; US novelist)

ROWE, Nicholas (1674–1718; British dramatist)

RUIZ, Juan (c. 1283–1350; Spanish poet)

SADE, Donatien Alphonse François, Marquis de (1740–1814; French novelist)

SA'DI (Mosieh al-Din S. c. 1215–92; Persian poet

SAKI (H.H. Munro; 1870–1916; British humorous short-story writer)

SAND, George (Aurore Dupin, Baronne Dudevani, 1804–76; French novelist)

SHAW, George Bernard (1856–1950; Irish dramatist)

SNOW, C.P. Baron (1905–80; British novelist)

TATE, Allen (1899–79; US poet and critic)

TATE, Nahum (1652–1715; British poet)

URFÉ, Honoré d' (1568–1625; French novelist)

VEGA, Lope Félix de (1562–1635; Spanish poet and dramatist)

WAIN, John (1925–94; British novelist and poet)

4 continued

WARD, Artemus (Charles Farrar Browne, 1834–67; US humorous writer)

WARD, Mrs Humphry (1851–1920; British novelist)

WEBB, Mary (1881–1927; British novelist)

WEST, Dame Rebecca (Cicely Isabel Fairfield, 1892–1983; British novelist and journalist)

WEST, Nathanael (Nathan Weinstein, 1903–40; US novelist)

WOOD, Mrs Henry (1814–87; British novelist)

WREN, P.C. (1885–1941; British novelist)

WYSS, Johann Rudolph (1782–1830; Swiss writer)

ZOLA, Emile (1840–1902; French novelist)

5

ADAMS, Henry (1838–1918; US historian)

ADAMS, Richard (1920– ; British novelist)

AGNON, Shmuel Yosef (Samuel Josef Czaczkes, 1888–1970; Jewish novelist)

ALBEE, Edward (1928– ; US dramatist)

ARANY, János (1817–82; Hungarian poet)

AUDEN, W.H. (1907–73; British poet)

BABEL, Isaac Emmanuilovich (1894–1941; Russian short-story writer)

BARTH, John (1930– ; US novelist)

BATES, H.E. (1905–74; British writer)

BEHAN, Brendan (1923–64; Irish playwright)

BELLO, Andrés (1781–1865; Venezuelan scholar and poet)

BELYI, Andrei (Boris Nikolaevich Bugaev, 1880–1934; Russian symbolist poet/critic)

BEMBO, Pietro (1470–1547; Italian scholar)

BENDA, Julien (1867–1956; French novelist)

BENET, Stephen Vincent (1898–1943; US poet and novelist)

BETTI, Ugo (1892–1953; Italian dramatist)

BOWEN, Elizabeth (1899–1973; British novelist, born in Dublin)

BRANT, Sebastian (?1458–1521; German poet)

BROCH, Hermann (1886–1951; Austrian novelist).

BUNIN, Ivan Alekseevich (1879–1953; Russian poet and novelist)

BURNS, Robert (1759–96; Scottish poet)

BUTOR, Michel (1926– ; French experimental novelist and critic)

BYRON, George Gordon, Lord (1788–1824; British poet)

CAMUS, Albert (1913–60; French novelist)

CAREW, Thomas (c. 1595–1640; British poet)

CLARE, John (1793–1864; British poet)

COLUM, Padraic (Patrick Colm; 1881–1972; Irish poet)

CRAIK, Dinah Maria Mulock (1826–87; British novelist)

CRANE, Hart (1899–1932; US poet)

CRANE, Stephen (1871–1900; US novelist)

DARIO, Rubén (Félix Garcia Sarmiento; 1867–1916; Nicaraguan poet).

DEFOE, Daniel (1660– 1731; British novelist)

DONNE, John (1572–1631; English poet)

DOYLE, Sir Arthur Conan (1859–1930; British author)

DUMAS, Alexandre (1802–70; French novelist and dramatist)

DURAS, Marguerite (1914–96; French novelist)

ELIOT, George (Mary Ann Evans, 1819–80; British novelist)

ELIOT, T.S. (1888–1965; Anglo-American poet, critic, and dramatist)

ELYOT Sir Thomas (c. 1490–1546; English Scholar)

EWALD, Johannes (1743–81; Danish poet and playwright)

FROST, Robert Lee (1874–1963; US poet)

GENET, Jean (1910–86; French novelist and dramatist)

GOGOL, Nikolai Vasilievich (1804–52; Russian novelist and dramatist)

GORKI, Maksim (Aleksei Maksimovich Peshkov; 1868–1936; Russian novelist)

GOSSE, Sir Edmund (1849–1928; British critic)

GOWER, John (c. 1330–1408; English poet)

GRASS, Günter (1927– ; German novelist)

GREEN; Henry (Henry Vincent Yorke; 1905–73; British novelist)

HAFIZ, Shams al-Din Muhammad (?1326–90 Persian lyric poet)

HALLE, Adam de la (c. 1240–90; French poet and musician)

HARDY, Thomas (1840–1928; British novelist and poet)

HARTE, Brett (1836–1902; US short-story writer)

HASEK,Jaroslav (1883–1923; Czech novelist)

HEINE, Heinrich (1797–1856; German Jewish poet and writer)

HENRY, O. (William-Sidney Porter, 1862–1910; US short-story writer)

WRITERS

5 continued

HESSE, Hermann (1877–1962; German novelist and poet)HOMER (8th century BC; Greek epic poet)

HOOFT, Pieter Corneliszoon (1581–1647; Dutch poet)

IBSEN, Henrik (1828–1906; Norwegian playwright and poet)

JAMES, Henry (1843–1916; US novelist and critic)

JARRY, Alfred (1873–1907; French dramatist)

JONES, David (1895–1974: Anglo-Welsh writer)

JONES, LeRoi (1934– ; US dramatist and poet; also called Amiri Baraka)

JOYCE, James (1882–1941; Irish novelist and poet)

KAFKA, Franz (1883–1924; Czech writer)

KEATS, John (1795–1821; British poet)

KEMAL, Namik (1840–88; Turkish poet, novelist, and dramatist)

KESEY, Ken (1935– ; US novelist)

LEWIS, C.S. (1898– 1963; British writer)

LEWIS, Matthew Gregory (1775–1818; British novelist)

LEWIS, Sinclair (1885–1951; US novelist)

LEWIS, Wyndham (1882–1457; British novelist)

LODGE, Thomas (1558–1625; English poet, dramatist, and writer)

LOWRY, Malcolm (1909–57; British novelist)

LUCAN (Marcus Annaeus Lucanus, 39–65 AD; Roman poet)

MAROT, Clement (1496–1544; French poet)

MARSH, Dame Ngaio (1899–1981; New Zealand detective-story writer)

MARTI, José Julián (1853–95; Cuban, poet)

MASON, A.E.W. (1865–1948, British novelist)

MILNE, A.A. (1882–1956; British novelist and dramatist)

MOORE, Marianne (1887–1972; US poet)

MOORE, Thomas (1779–1852; Irish poet)

MURRY, John Middleton (1889–1957; British literary critic)

MUSIL, Robert (1880–1942; Austrian novelist)

MYERS, F.W.H, (1843–1901 British essayist and poet)

NASHE, Thomas (1567– c. 1601; British dramatist).

NOYES, Alfred (1880–1958; British poet)

ODETS, Clifford (1906–63; US dramatist)

O'HARA, John (1905–70; US novelist)

OPITZ, Martin (1597–1639; German poet)

ORCZY, Baroness Emmusca (1865–1947; British novelist)

OTWAY, Thomas (1652–85; British dramatist)

OUIDA (Marie Louise de la Ramée, (1839–1908; British novelist).

PAN GU (or P'an Ku; 32–92 AD; Chinese historian)

PATON, Alan (1903–88; S.African novelist)

PEAKE, Mervyn (1911–68; British novelist)

PEELE, George (1556–96; English dramatist)

PÉGUY, Charles (1873–1914; French poet and essayist)

PERSE, Saint-John (Alexis Saint-Léger, 1887–1975; French poet)

PLATH, Sylvia (1932–63; US poet and writer)

POUND, Ezra (1885–1972; US poet and critic)

POWYS, John Cowper (1812–1963; British novelist)

PRIOR, Matthew (1664–1721; British poet)

PULCI, Luigi (1432–84; Italian poet)

RAINE, Kathleen (1908– ; British poet)

READE, Charles (1814–84; British novelist)

RILKE, Rainer Maria (1875–1926; Austrian poet)

ROLFE, Frederick William (1860–1913; British novelist)

SACHS, Hans (1494–1576; German poet and folk dramatist)

SACHS, Nelly (1891–1970; German Jewish poet and dramatist)

SAGAN, Françoise (Françoise Quoirez, 1935– ; French writer)

SCOTT, Sir Walter (1771–1832; Scot novelist)

SETON, Ernest Thompson (1860–1946; US writer)

SHUTE, Nevil (Nevil Shute Norway 1899–1960; British novelist)

SIMMS, William Gilmore (1806–70; US novelist)

SMART, Christopher (1722–71; British poet)

SMITH, Stevie (Florence Margaret S, 1902–71; British poet)

SPARK, Muriel (1918– ; British novelist)

STAEL, Anne Louise Germaine Necker, Madame de (1766–1817; French writer)

STEIN, Gertrude (1874–1946; US writer)

STORM, Theodor Woldsen (1817–1888; German writer)

5 continued

STOWE, Harriet Beecher (1811–96; US novelist)

SVEVO, Italo (Ettore Schmitz, 1861–1928; Italian novelist)

SWIFT, Jonathan (1667–1745; Anglo-Irish poet and satirist)

SYNGE, John Millington (1871–1909; Anglo-Irish dramatist)

TASSO, Torquato (1544–95; Italian poet)

TIECK, Ludwig (1773–1853; German writer)

TWAIN, Mark (Samuel Langhorne Clernens, 1835–1910; US.novelist)

UDALL, Nicholas (1505–56; English dramatist)

VARRO, Marcus Terentius (116–27 BC; Roman scholar and poet)

VERNE, Jules (1828–1905; French writer)

VIDAL, Gore (1925– ; US novelist and essayist)

VIGNY, Alfred de (1797–1863; French poet, novelist, and dramatist)

WALEY, Arthur (1889–1966; British translator and poet)

WAUGH, Evelyn (1903–66; British novelist)

WEISS, Peter (1916–82; German dramatist and novelist)

WELLS, H.G. (1866–1946; British novelist)

WHITE, Patrick (1912–90;Australian novelist)

WHITE, T.H. (1906–64; British novelist)

WILDE, Oscar (O. Fingal O'Flahertie Wills W, 1854–1900; British dramatist and poet)

WOLFE, Charles (1791–1823; Irish poet)

WOLFE, Thomas (1900–38; US novelist)

WOOLF, Virginia (1882–1941; British novelist)

WYATT, Sir Thomas (1503–42; English poet)

YEATS, William Butler (1865–1939; Irish poet and dramatist)

YONGE, Charlotte (1823–1901; British novelist)

ZWEIG, Arnold (1887–1968; East German Jewish novelist)

ZWEIG, Stefan (1881–1942: Austrian Jewish writer)

6

ACCIUS, Lucius (170– c. 85 BC; Roman tragic dramatist)

ADAMOV, Arthur (1908–70; French dramatist)

ALCOTT, Louisa May (1832–88; US novelist)

ALDISS, Brian W (1925– ; British novelist)

ALEMAN, Mateo (1547–?1614; Spanish writer)

ALGREN, Nelson (1909–81; US novelist)

AMBLER, Eric (1909–98; British novelist)

ANDRIC, Ivo (1892–1975; Serbian writer)

ARAGON, Louis (1897–1982; French poet, novelist, and journalist)

ASCHAM, Roger (1515–68; English scholar and writer)

ASIMOV, Isaac (1920–92; US science fiction writer, born in Russia)

AUBREY, John (1626–97; English antiquary)

AUSTEN, Jane (1775–1817; British novelist)

AZORIN (José Martinéz Ruiz, 1874–1967; Spanish novelist, essayist, and critic)

AZUELA, Mariano (1873–1952; Mexican novelist)

BALZAC, Honoré de (1799–1850; French novelist)

BARHAM, Richard Harris (1788–1845; British humorous writer).

BARKER, George (1913–91; British poet)

BARNES, William (1801–86; British poet)

BAROJA, Pio (1872–1956; Spanish novel

BARRÉS, MAURICE (1862–1923; French writer)

BARRIE, Sir James (1860–1937; British dramatist and novelist)

BELLAY, Joachim de (1522–60; French poet

BELLOC, Hilaire (1870–1953; British poet and essayist)

BELLOW, Saul (1915– ; Canadian-born US novelist)

BESANT, Sir Waiter (1836–1901; British novelist)

BIALIK, Chaim Nachman (1873–1934; Jewish poet and translator)

BIERCE, Ambrose Gwinnett (1842–1914; US writer)

BINYON, Laurence (1869–1943; British poet)

BLYTON, Enid (1897–1968; British writer of children's books)

BORGES, Jorge Luis (1899–1986; Argentinian writer)

BORROW, George Henry (1803–81; British writer)

BRECHT, Bertolt (1898–1956; German dramatist and poet)

BRETON, André (1896–1966; French poet)

BRIDIE, James (Osborne Henry Mavor; 1888–1951; British dramatist)

BRONTE, Anne (1820–49; British novelist)

BRONTE, Charlotte (1816–55; British novelist)

6 continued

BRONTE, Emily (1818–48; British novelist)

BROOKE, Rupert (1887–1915; British poet)

BROWNE, Sir Thornas (1605–82; English writer)

BRYANT, William Cullen (1794–1878; US poet, journalist, and critic)

BUCHAN, John, 1st Baron Tweedsmuir (1875–1940; British novelist)

BUNYAN, John (1628–88; English writer)

BURGER, Gottfried (1747–94; German poet)

BURNEY, Fanny (Mrs Frances Burney D'Arblay; 1752–1840; British novelist)

BUTLER, Samuel (1612–80; British poet)

BUTLER, Samuel (1835–1902; British novelist)

CAMOES, Luis de (c. 1524–80; Portuguese poet)

CAPOTE, Truman (1924–84; US novelist)

CARSON, Rachel Louise (1907–64; US science writer)

CAVAFY, Constantine (C. Kavafis, 1863–1933; Greek poet)

CELINE, Louis Ferdinand. (L.F. Destouches, 1884–1961; French novelist)

CIBBER, Colley (1671–1757; British dramatist)

CLARKE, Marcus (1846–81; Australian novelist, born in London)

COLMAN, George (1732–94; British dramatist)

CONRAD, Joseph (Teodor Josef Konrad Watecz Korzeniowski; 1857–1924; Polish born British novelist)

COOPER, James Fenimore (1789–1851; US novelist)

COWLEY, Abraham (1618–67; English poet)

COWPER, William (1731–1800; British poet)

CRABBE, George (1754–1832; British poet)

CRONIN, A.J. (1896–1981; British novelist)

DANIEL, Samuel (?1562–1619; English poet, dramatist, and critic)

DAUDET, Alphonse (1840–97; French novelist)

DAVIES, W.H. (1871–1940; British poet)

DEKKER, Thomas (c. 1572–1632; British dramatist and pamphleteer)

DOWSON, Ernest (1867–1900; British poet)

DRYDEN, John (1631–1700; British poet)

DUNBAR, William (c. 1460– c. 1530; Scots poet)

ELUARD, Paul (Eugene Grindel, 1895–1952; French poet)

EMPSON, Sir William (1906–84; British poet)

ENNIUS, Quintus (238–169 BC; Roman poet)

EVELYN, John (1620–1706; English diarist)

FOUQUE, Friedrich Heinrich Karl, Baron de la Motte (1777–1843; German novelist and dramatist)

FOWLES, John (1926– ; British novelist).

FRANCE, Anatole (Jacques Anatole François Thibault, 1844–1924; French novelist)

FRISCH, Max (1911–91; Swiss dramatist and novelist)

FUGARD, Athol (1932– ; South African dramatist)

FULLER, Roy (1912–91; British poet / novelist)

FULLER, Thomas (1608–61; British historian)

GEORGE, Stefan (1868–1933; German poet)

GIBBON, Edward (1737–94; British historian)

GIBRAN, Khalil (1883–1931; Lebanese mystic and poet)

GOETHE, Johann Wolfgang von (1749–1832; German poet)

GRAVES, Robert (1895–1985; British poet, critic, and novelist)

GREENE, Graham (1904–91; British novelist)

GREENE, Robert (c. 1558–92; English dramatist)

HAMSUN, Knut (1859–1952; Norwegian novelist)

HARRIS, Joel Chandler (1848–1908; US novelist and short-story writer)

HEBBEL, Friedrich (1813–63; German dramatist)

HELLER, Joseph (1923– ; US novelist)

HESIOD (8th century BC; Greek poet)

HILTON, James (1900–54; British novelist)

HOLMES, Olive Wendell (1809–94; US essayist and poet)

HORACE (Quintus Horatius Flaccus; 65–8 BC; Roman poet)

HUDSON, W.H. (1841–1922; British naturalist and.writer)

HUGHES, Richard (1900–76; British novelist)

HUGHES, Ted (1930–98; British poet)

HUGHES, Thomas (1822–96; British writer)

IRVING, Washington (1783–1859; US short story writer)

ISAACS, Jorge (1837–95; Colombian novelist)

JENSEN, Johannes (1873–1950; Danish novelist and poet)

JONSON, Ben (1572–1637; English dramatist and poet)

6 continued

KAISER, Georg (1878–1945; German dramatist)

KELLER, Gottfried (1819–90; German Swiss poet and novelist)

KLEIST, Heinrich von (1777–1811; German dramatist)

LACLOS, Pierre Choderlos de (1741–1803; French novelist)

LANDOR, Walter Savage (1775–1864; British poet and prose writer)

LANIER, Sidney (1842–81; US poet)

LARKIN, Philip (1922–85; British poet)

LAWLER, Ray (1921– ; Australian dramatist)

LE FANU, Sheridan (1814–73; Irish novelist)

LEONOV, Leonid (1899–94; Russian novelist)

LESAGE, Alain-René (1668–1747; French novelist)

LONDON, Jack (1876–1916; US novelist)

LOWELL, Amy (1874–1925; US poet)

LOWELL, James Russell (1819–91; US poet)

LOWELL, Robert (1917–77; US poet)

LU HSUN (or Chou Shu-jen; 1881–1936; Chinese writer)

MACHEN,Arthur (1863–1947; Welsh novelist)

MAILER, Norman (1923– ; US. writer)

MALORY, Sir Thomas (?1400– 71; English writer)

MERCER, David (1928–80; British dramatist)

MILLAY, Edna St Vincent (1892–1950; US poet)

MILLER, Arthur (1915– ; US dramatist)

MILLER, Henry (1891–1980; US novelist)

MILTON, John (1608–74; English poet)

MOLNAR, Ferenc (1878–1952; Hungarian dramatist)

MORGAN, Charles (1894–1958; British novelist and dramatist)

MORIKE, Eduard Friedrich (1804–75; German poet and novelist)

MUNTHE, Axel (1857–1949; Swedish author)

MUSSET, Alfred de (1810–57; French poet and dramatist)

NERUDA, Pablo (Neftali Ricardo Reyes; 1904–73; Chilean poet)

NERVAL, Gérard de (Gérard Labrunie; 1808–55; French poet)

NESBIT, Edith (1858–1924; British children's writer)

O'BRIEN, Flann (Brian O'Nolan; 1911–66; Irish novelist and journalist)

O'CASEY, Sean (1880–1964; Irish dramatist)

O'NEILL, Eugene (1888–1953; US dramatist)

ORWELL, George (Eric Blair, 1903–60; British novelist, born in India)

PARKER, Dorothy Rothschild (1893–1967; US humorous writer)

PAVESE, Cesare (1908–50; Italian novelist)

PETOFI, Sandor (1823–49; Hungarian poet)

PINDAR (518–438 BC; Greek poet)

PINERO, Sir Arthur Wing (1855–1934; British dramatist)

PINTER, Harold (1930– ; British dramatist)

PIOZZI, Hester Lynch (1741–1821; British writer)

PLOMER, William (1903–73; South African poet and novelist)

PORTER, Katherine Anne (1890–1980; US short-story writer and novelist)

PORTER, Peter (1929– ; British poet)

POTTER, Beatrix (1866–1943; British children's writer / illustrator)

POTTER, Stephen (1900–70; British writer)

POWELL, Anthony (1905– ; British novelist)

PROUST, Marcel (1871–1922; French novelist)

RACINE, Jean (1639–99; French dramatist)

RAMSAY, Allan (?1685–1758; Scottish poet)

RANSOM, John Crowe (1888–1974; US poet)

RUNYON, Damon (1884–1946; US humorous writer)

SAPPER (H.C. McNeile; 1888–1937; British novelist)

SAPPHO (c. 612– c. 580 BC; Greek poet)

SARDOU, Victorien (1831–1908; French dramatist)

SARTRE, Jean-Paul (1905–80; French philosopher, novelist, dramatist, and critic)

SAVAGE, Richard (c. 1696–1743; British poet)

SAYERS, Dorothy L. (1893–1957; British writer)

SIDNEY, Sir Philip (1554–86; English poet)

SILONE, Ignazio (Secondo Tranquilli, 1900–78; Italian novelist)

SINGER, Isaac Bashevis (1904–91; US novelist and short-story writer)

SMILES, Samuel (1812–1904; British writer)

STEELE, Sir Richard (1672–1729; British essayist and dramatist)

STERNE, Laurence (1713–68; British novelist)

STOKER, Bram (Abraham S, 1847–1912; Irish novelist)

41

WRITERS

6 continued

STOREY, David (1933– ; British novelist and dramatist)

SURREY, Henry Howard, Earl of (1517–47; English poet)

SYMONS, Arthur (1865–1945; British poet)

TAGORE, Rabindranath (1861–1941; Indian poet)

THOMAS, Dylan (1914–53; Welsh poet)

THOMAS, Edward (1878–1917; British poet)

TOLLER, Ernst (1893–1939; German playwright and poet

TRAVEN, B. (Berick Traven Torsvan, 1890–1969; US novelist)

UHLAND, Ludwig (1787–1862; German poet)

UNDSET, Sigrid (1882–1949; Norwegian novelist)

UPDIKE, John (1932– ; US novelist and short-story writer)

VALERY, Paul (1871–1945; French poet, essayist, and critic)

VILLON, Franiçois (1431– ?1463; French poet)

VIRGIL (Publius Vergilius Maro, 70–19 BC; Roman poet)

VONDEL, Joost van den (1587–1679; Dutch dramatist and poet)

WALLER, Edmund (1606–87; British poet)

WALTON, Izaak (1593–1683; English writer)

WARTON, Joseph (1722–1800; British poet and critic)

WERFEL, Franz (1890–1945; Austrian Jewish poet, dramatist, and novelist)

WESKER, Arnold (1932– ; British dramatist)

WILDER, Thornton (1897–1975; US novelist and dramatist)

WILSON, Colin (1931– ; British critic and novelist)

WILSON, Edmund (1895–1972; US critic and essayist)

WILSON, Sir Angus (1913–91; British novelist)

WOTTON, Sir Henry (1568–1639; English poet)

WRIGHT, Judith (1915– ; Australian poet)

WRIGHT, Richard (1908–60; US novelist and critic)

7

ADDISON, Joseph (1672–1719; British essayist and poet)

AELFRIC, (c. 955– c. 1020; Anglo-Saxon prose writer)

ALARCON, Pedro Antonio de (1833–91; Spanish novelist)

ALBERTI, Raphael (1902– ; Spanish poet)

ALCAEUS (6th century BC; Greek lyric poet)

ALDANOV, Mark (M Ateksandrovich Landau, 1886–1957; Russian novelist)

ALDRICH, Thornas Bailey (1836–1907; US. short-story writer and poet)

ALEGRiA, Ciro (1909–61; Peruvian novelist)

ALFIERI, Vittorio, Count (1749–1803; Italian poet and dramatist)

ANEIRIN (6th century AD; Welsh poet)

ARETINO, Pietro (1492–1556; Italian satirist)

ARIOSTO, Ludovico (1474–1533; Italian poet)

ARRABAL, Fernando (1932– ; Spanish playwright and novelist)

BALCHIN, Nigel (1908–70; British novelist)

BALDWIN, James Arthur (1924–87; US novelist, essayist, and dramatist)

BARBOUR, John (1316–95; Scottish poet)

BECKETT, Samuel (1906–89; Irish novelist, dramatist, and poet)

BENNETT, Alan (1934–; British writer, actor, director

BENNETT, Arnold (1837–1931; British writer)

BENTLEY, Edmund Clerihew (1875–1956; British writer)

BERGMAN, Hjalmar (1883–1931; Swedish novelist and dramatist)

BLUNDEN, Edmund Charles (1896–1974; British poet and critic)

BOIARDO, Matteo Maria, Conte di Scandiano (1441–94; !talian poet)

BOILEAU (Despreaux), Nicolas (1636–1711; French poet and critic)

BOSWELL, James (1740–95; Scottish writer)

BO ZHU YI (or Po Chü-i; 772–846; Chinese poet)

BRADLEY, Andrew Cecil (1851–1935; British literary critic)

BRIDGES, Robert Seymour (1844–1930; British poet)

BUCHNER, Georg (1813–37; German dramatist)

BURGESS, Anthony (John Burgess Wilson; 1917–93; British novelist and critic)

BURNETT, Frances Eliza Hodgson (1849–1924; British novelist)

7 continued

CAEDMON (*d. c.* 680 AD; English poet)

CAO CHAN (*or* Zao Zhan; ? 1715–63; Chinese novelist)

CAROSSA, Hans (1878–1956; German novelist)

CARROLL, Lewis (Charles Lutwidge Dodgson; 1832–98; British writer)

CHAPMAN, George (*c.* 1560–1634; British poet and dramatist)

CHAUCER, Geoffrey (*c.* 1342–1400; English poet)

CHEKHOV, Anton Pavlovich (1860–1904; Russian dramatist and short-story writer)

CHENIER, André de (1762–94; French poet, born in Istanbul)

CHU WAN (*c.* 343BC– *c.* 289BC; Chinese poet)

CLAUDEL, Paul (1868–1955; French dramatist and poet)

CLELAND, John (1709–89; English novelist)

COCTEAU, Jean (1889–1963; French poet and artist)

COLETTE (Sidonie-Gabrielle *c.* 1873–1954; French novelist)

COLLINS, William (1721–59, British poet)

COLLINS, William Wilkie (1824–89; British novelist)

CORELLI, Marie (1854–1924; British novelist)

CRASHAW, Richard, (*c.* 1613–49; British poet)

CREELEY, Robert (1926– ; US poet)

DA PONTE, Lorenzo 1749–1838; Italian author)

DELEDDA, Grazia (1871–1936; Italian novelist)

DICKENS, Charles (1812–70; British novelist)

DINESEN, Isak (Karen Blixen, Baroness Blixen-Finecke, 1885–1962; Danish author)

DOUGLAS, Gavin (?1474–1522; Scot poet)

DOUGLAS, Norman (1868–1952; British novelist)

DRABBLE, Margaret (1939– ; British writer)

DRAYTON, Michael (1563–1631; English poet)

DREISER; Theodore (1871–1945; US novelist)

DUHAMEL, Georges (1884–1966; French novelist)

DUNSANY, Edward John Moreton Drax Plunkett, 18th Baron (1878–1957; Irish author)

DURRELL, Lawrence George (1912–90; British novelist and poet, born in India)

EMERSON, Ralph Waldo (1803–82; US essayist and poet)

ERCILLA, Alonso de (1533–94; Spanish poet)

EUPOLIS (late 5th century BC; Greek dramatist)

FERRIER, Susan Edmonstone (1782–1854; Scottish novelist)

FEYDEAU, Georges (1862–1921; French playwright)

FIRBANK, Ronald (1886–1926; British novelist)

FLECKER, James Efroy (1884–1915; British poet)

FLEMING, Ian (1908–64; British author)

FLEMING, Paul (1609–40; German poet)

FONTANE, Theodor (1819–98; German novelist)

FORSTER, E. M. (1879–1970; British novelist)

FOSCOLO, Ugo (1778–1827; Italian poet)

FRENEAU, Philip (1752–1832; US poet)

FRODING, Gustaf (1860–1911; Swedish lyric poet)

GASKELL, Elizabeth Cleghorn (1810–65; British novelist)

GAUTIER, Théophile (1811–72; French poet)

GILBERT, Sir William Schwenk (1836–1911; British comic dramatist)

GISSING, George Robert (1857–1903; British novelist)

GOLDING, William (1911–93; British novelist)

GOLDONI, Carlo (1707–93; Italian comic playwright)

GRAHAME, Kenneth (1859–1932; British children's writer)

GUARINI, Giovanni Battista (1538–1612; Italian poet)

HAGGARD, Sir H. Rider (1856–1925; British novelist)

HAMMETT, Dashiell (1894–1961; US novelist)

HARTLEY, L.P. (1895–1972; British novelist)

HELLMAN. Lillian (1905–84; US dramatist)

HERBERT, George (1593–1633; English poet)

HERRICK, Robert (1591–1674; English poet)

HEYWOOD, Thomas (*c.* 1574–1641; English dramatist)

HOLBERG, Ludvig, Baron (1684–1754; Danish playwright and poet)

HOPKINS, Gerard Manley (1844–89; British poet)

WRITERS

7 continued

HOUSMAN, A.E. (1859–1936; British poet and scholar)

IBN EZRA, Abraham Ben Meir (1093–1167; Hebrew poet and scholar)

IONESCO, Eugène (1912–94; French dramatist)

JEFFERS, Robinson (1887–1962; US poet)

JIMENEZ, Juan Ramon (1881–1958; Spanish poet)

JUVENAL (Decimus Junius Juvenalis, c. 60– c. 130 AD; Roman satirist)

KASTNER, Erich (1899–1974; German novelist and poet)

KAUFMAN, George S. (1889–1961; US dramatist)

KENDALL, Henry (1841–82; Australian poet)

KEROUAC, Jack (1922–69; US novelist)

KIPLING, Rudyard (1865–1936; British writer)

KLINGER, Friedrich Maximilian von (1752–1831; German dramatist)

LABICHE, Eugène (1815–88; French dramatist)

LARDNER, Ring (1885–1933; US short-story writer)

LAXNESS, Halldor (1902–98 Icelandic novelist and essayist)

LAYAMON (early 13th century; English poet)

LEACOCK, Stephen (1869–1944; English-born Canadian humorist)

LE CARRÉ, John (David Cornwell, 1931– British novelist)

LESSING, Doris (1919– ;British novelist)

LESSING, Gotthold Ephraim (1729–81; German dramatist and writer)

LINDSAY, Vachel (1879–1931; US poet)

LYDGATE, John (c. 1370–c. 1450; English poet)

MACHAUT, Guillaume de (c. 1300–77; French poet)

MALAMUD, Bernard (1914–86; US novelist)

MALRAUX, André (1901–76; French novelist and.essayist)

MANZONI Alessandro (1785–1873; Italian poet and novelist)

MARLOWE, Christopher (1564–93; English dramatist and poet)

MARRYAT, Captain Frederick (1792–1848; British novelist)

MARSTON, John (1576–1634; English dramatist)

MARTIAL (Marcus Valerius Martialis, c. 40– c. 104 AD; Roman poet)

MARVELL, Andrew (1621–78; English poet)

MASTERS. Edgar Lee (1868–1950; US poet)

MAUGHAM, W. Somerset (1874–1965; British novelist and dramatist)

MAURIAC, François (1885–1970; French novelist)

MAUROIS, André (Emile Herzog; 1885–1967; French biographer, novelist, and critic)

MERIMEE, Prosper (1803–70; French novelist)

MISHIMA, Yukio (Kimitake Hiraoka; 1925–70; Japanese novelist and playwright)

MISTRAL, Frédéric, (1830–1914; French poet)

MISTRAL, Gabriela (Lucila Godoy Alcayaga, 1889–1957; Chilean poet)

MOLIERE (Jean-Baptiste Poquelin, 1622–73; French dramatist)

MONTAGU, Lady Mary Wortley (1689–1762; English writer)

MONTALE, Eugenio (1896–1981; Italian poet)

MORAVIA, Alberto (Alberto Pincherle, 1907–90; Italian novelist)

MURDOCH, Dame Iris (1919–98; British novelist)

NABOKOV, Vladimir (1899–1977; US novelist)

NAEVIUS, Gnaeus (c. 270– c. 200 BC; Roman poet)

NAIPAUL, Sir V.S. (1932– ; West Indian novelist)

NOVALIS (Friedrich Leopold, Freiherr von Hardenberg; 1772–1801; German poet and writer)

O'CONNOR, Frank (Michael O'Donovan; 1903–66; Irish short-story writer)

OSBORNE, John (1929–94; British dramatist)

PATMORE, Coventry (1823–96; British poet)

PEACOCK, Thomas Love (1785–1866; British satirical novelist)

PLAUTUS, Titus Maccius (c. 254-184 BC; Roman dramatist)

PREVERT, Jacques (1900–77; French poet)

PUSHKIN, Aleksandr (1799–1837; Russian poet, novelist, and dramatist)

PYNCHON, Thomas (1937– ; US novelist)

QUENEAU, Raymond (1903–79; French novelist and poet)

RANSOME, Arthur Mitchell (1884–1967; British journalist and children's writer)

7 continued

REGNIER, Henri François Joseph de (1864–1936; French poet)

RICHLER, Mordecai (1931– ; Canadian novelist)

RIMBAUD, Arthur (1854–91; French poet)

ROLLAND, Romain (1866–1944; French novelist, dramatist, and essayist)

ROMAINS, Jules (Louis Farigoule; 1885–1972; French poet, novelist, and dramatist)

RONSARD, Pierre de (1524–85; French poet)

ROUSSEL, Raymond (1877–1933; French writer and dramatist)

ROWLING, J.K. (Joanne, 1965– ; British children's writer)

SAROYAN, William (1908–81; US dramatist and fiction writer)

SASSOON, Siegfried (1886–1967; British poet and writer)

SCARRON, Paul (1610–60; French poet, dramatist, and satirist)

SEFERIS, George (Georgios Seferiadis, 1900–71; Greek poet)

SHAFFER, Peter (1926– ; British dramatist)

SHELLEY, Percy Bysshe (1792–1822; British poet)

SIMENON, Georges (1903–89; Belgian novelist)

SIMONOV, Konstantin (1915–79; Soviet novelist, playwright, poet, and journalist)

SITWELL, Edith (1887–1964; British poet and writer)

SKELTON, John (c. 1460–1529; English poet)

SOUTHEY, Robert (1774–1843; British poet and writer)

SOYINKA, Wole (1934– ; Nigerian dramatist)

SPENDER, Stephen (1909–95; British poet and critic)

SPENSER, Edmund (c. 1552–99; English poet)

STEVENS, Wallace (1879–1955; US poet)

SURTEES, Robert Smith (1803–64; British novelist)

TERENCE (Publius Terentius Afer; c. 185–159 BC; Roman dramatist)

THESPIS (6th century BC; Greek poet)

THOMSON, James (1700–48; British poet).

THURBER, James (1894–1961; US humorous writer and cartoonist)

TOLKIEN, J.R.R. (1892–1973; British scholar and writer)

TOLSTOY, Leo, Count (1828–1910; Russian writer)

TRAVERS, Ben (1886–1980; British dramatist)

TUTUOLA, Amos (1920–97; Nigerian writer)

VAUGHAN, Henry (c. 1622–95; English poet)

VICENTE, Gil (c. 1465–1536; Portuguese dramatist)

WALLACE, Edgar (1875–1932; British novelist)

WALPOLE, Sir Hugh (1884–1941; British novelist)

WEBSTER, John (c. 1580– c. 1625; English dramatist)

WHARTON, Edith (1862–1937; US novelist)

WHITMAN, Walt (1819–92; US Poet)

WIELAND, Christoph Martin (1733–1813; German novelist and poet)

YESENIN, Sergei Aleksandrovich (1895–1925; Russian poet)

8

ABU NUWAS (c. 762– c. 813 AD; Arab poet)

ANACREON (6th century BC; Greek lyric poet)

ANCHIETA, José de (1534–97; Portuguese poet)

ANDERSEN, Hans Christian (1805–75; Danish author)

ANDERSON, Sherwood (1876–1941; US author)

APULEIUS, Lucius (2nd century AD; Roman writer and rhetorician)

ASTURIAS, Miguel Angel (1899–1974; Guatemalan novelist and poet)

BANDEIRA, Manuel Carneiro de Sousa (1886–1968; Brazilian poet)

BANVILLE, Theodore Faullain de (1823–89; French poet)

BARBUSSE, Henri (1873–1935; French novelist)

BEAUMONT, Francis (1584–1616; British dramatist)

BEAUVOIR, Simone de (1908–86; French novelist and essayist)

BECKFORD, William (?1760–1844; British writer)

BEERBOHM, Sir Max (1872–1956; British caricaturist and writer)

BELINSKY, Vissarion (1811–48; Russian literary critic)

8 continued

BENCHLEY. Robert Charles (1889–1945; US humorist)

BERANGER, Pierre Jean de (1780–1857; French poet and songwriter)

BERNANOS, Georges (1888–1948; French novelist)

BETJEMAN, Sir John (1906–84; British poet)

BJORNSON, Bjornstjerne (1832–1910; Norwegian novelist, poet and playwright)

BRADBURY, Ray (1920– ; US science-fiction writer)

BRENTANO, Clemens (1778–1842; German writer)

BROWNING, Robert 1812–89; British poet)

CAMPBELL, Roy (1901–57; South African poet)

CAMPBELL, Thomas (1777–1844; British poet)

CARDUCCI, Giosuè (1835–1907; Italian poet and critic)

CASTILHO, Antonio Feliciano de (1800–75; Portuguese poet)

CATULLUS, Valerius (c. 84– c. 54 BC; Roman poet)

CHANDLER, Raymond (1888–1959; US novelist)

CHARTIER, Alain (c. 1385– c. 1440; French poet and prose writer)

CHRISTIE, Dame Agatha (1891–1976; British author of detective fiction and playwright).

CLAUDIAN (c. 370–404 AD; Roman poet)

CONGREVE, William (1670–1729; British dramatist)

CONSTANT, Benjamin (1767–1830; French novelist)

CROMPTON, Richmal (Richmal Crompton Lamburn, 1890–1969; British children's author)

CUMMINGS, e.e. (1894–1962; US poet)

CYNEWULF (early 9th Century AD; Anglo-Saxon religious poet)

DAVENANT, Sir William (1606–68; English dramatist and poet)

DAY LEWIS, C. (1904–72; British poet)

DE LA MARE, Walter (1873–1956; British poet, novelist, and anthologist)

DONLEAVY, J.P. (1926– ; Irish-American novelist)

ETHEREGE, Sir George (c. 1635– c. 1692; English dramatist)

FARQUHAR, George (1678–1707; Irish dramatist)

FAULKNER, William (1897–1962: US novelist)

FIELDING, Henry (1707–54, British novelist and dramatist)

FIRDAUSI (Abul Qasim Mansur; c. 935– c. 1020; Persian poet)

FLAUBERT, Gustave (1821–80; French novelist)

FLETCHER, John (1579–1625; English dramatist)

FORESTER, C.S. (1899–1966; British novelist)

GINSBERG., Allen (1926– ; US poet)

GONCOURT, Edmond de (1822–96; French writer)

HENRYSON, Robert (15th century; Scottish poet)

HOCHHUTH, Rolf (1933– ; Swiss dramatist)

HUYSMANS, Joris Karl, (1848–1907; French novelist)

JEAN PAUL (Johann Paul Friedrich Richter, 1763–1825; German novelist)

KALIDASA (5th century AD; Indian poet)

KINGSLEY, Charles (1819–79; British writer)

KOESTLER, Arthur (1905–83; British writer)

KOTZEBUE, August von (1761–1819; German dramatist and novelist)

LAFORGUE, Jules (1860–87; French poet)

LAGERLOF, Selma Ottiliana Lovisa 1858–1940; Swedish novelist)

LANGLAND, William (c. 1330– c. 1400; English poet)

LAS CASES, Emmanuel, Comte de 1776–1842; French writer)

LAWRENCE, D.H. (1885–1930; British novelist, poet, and painter)

LOCKHART, John Gibson (1794–1854; Scottish biographer and journalist)

LONGINUS, (1st century; Greek rhetorician)

LOVELACE, Richard (1618–57; English Cavalier poet)

MACAULAY, Dame Rose (1881–1958; British novelist)

MACLEISH, Archibald (1892–1982; US poet)

MACNEICE, Louis (1907–63; Irish-born British poet)

MALHERBE, François de (1555–1628; French poet and critic)

MALLARME, Stéphane (1842–98; French poet)

MARIVAUX, Pierre Carlet de Chamblain de (1688–1763; French dramatist).

8 continued
MARQUAND, J.P. (1893–1960; US novelist)
MCCARTHY, Mary (1912–89 ; US novelist)
MELVILLE, Herman (1819–91; US novelist)
MENANDER (*c.* 341– *c.* 290 BC; Greek dramatist)
MEREDITH, George (1828–1909; British poet and novelist)
MICHELET, Jules (1798–1874; French historian)
MITCHELL, Margaret (1909–49; US novelist)
NEKRASOV, Nikolai Alekseevich (1821–78; Russian poet)
NICOLSON, Sir Harold (1886–1968; British literary critic)
PALGRAVE, Francis Turner, (1824–97; British poet and anthologist)
PERELMAN, S.J. (1904–79; US writer)
PERRAULT, Charles (1628–1703; French poet and fairytale writer)
PETRARCH (Frafficesco Petrarca, 1304–74; Italian poet)
PHAEDRUS, (1st century AD; Roman writer)
PHILEMON (*c.* 368– *c.* 264 BC; Greek dramatist)
PLUTARCH (*c.* 46– *c.* 120 AD; Greek biographer and essayist)
RABELAIS, François (1483–1553; French satirist)
RADIGUET, Raymond (1903–23; French. novelist)
RATTIGAN, Sir Terence (1911–77; British dramatist)
REMARQUE, Erich Maria (1898–1970; German novelist)
RICHARDS, Frank (Charles Hamilton, (1876–1961; British children's writer)
RUNEBERG, Johan Ludvig (1804–77; Finnish poet)
SALINGER, J.D. (1919– ; US novelist)
SANDBURG, Carl (1878–1967; US poet)
SARRAUTE, Nathalie (1902– ; French novelist born in Russia)
SCALIGER, Julius Caesar (1484–1558; Italian humanist scholar)
SCHILLER, Friedrich (1759–1805; German dramatist, poet and writer)
SHADWELL, Thomas (*c.* 1642–92; British dramatist)
SHERIDAN, Richard Brinsley (1751–1816; Anglo-Irish dramatist)

SILLITOE, Alan (1928– ; British novelist)
SINCLAIR, Upton (1878–1968; US novelist)
SMOLLETT, Tobias (1721–71; British novelist)
SPILLANE, Mickey (Frank Morrison 1918– ; US detective-story writer)
STENDHAL (Henri Beyle, 1783–1842; French novelist)
STOPPARD, Tom (1937– ; British dramatist)
SUCKLING, Sir John (1609–42; English poet and dramatist)
SU DONG PO (*or* Su Tung-p'o, 1036–1101; Chinese poet)
TALIESIN (6th century AD; Welsh poet)
TENNYSON, Alfred, Lord (1809–92; British poet)
THOMPSON, Francis (1859–1907; British poet and critic)
TIBULLUS, Albius (*c.* 55– *c.* 19 BC; Roman poet)
TOURNEUR, Cyril (*c.* 1575–1626; English dramatist)
TRAHERNE, Thomas (*c.* 1637–74; English poet)
TRILLING, Lionel (1905–75; US literary critic)
TROLLOPE, Anthony (1815–82; British writer)
TULSIDAS (*c.* 1532–1623; Indian poet)
TURGENEV, Ivan (1818–83; Russian novelist)
VERLAINE, Paul (1844–96; French poet)
VOLTAIRE (François-Marie Arouet, 1694–1778; French writer)
VONNEGUT, Kurt (1922– ; US novelist)
WEDEKIND, Frank (1864–1918; German dramatist)
WHITTIER, John Greenleaf (1807–92; US poet)
WILLIAMS, Tennessee (1911–83; US dramatist)
WILLIAMS, William Carlos (1883–1963; US poet)
ZAMYATIN, Yevgenii Ivanovich (1884–1937; Russian novelist)

9
AESCHYLUS (*c.* 525– 456 BC; Greek tragic dramatist)
AINSWORTH, W. Harrison (1805–82; British historical novelist)
AKHMATOVA, Anna (Anna Andreevna Gorenko, 1889–1966; Russian poet)
ALDINGTON, Richard (1892–1962; British poet, novelist, and biographer)

WRITERS

9 continued

ALLINGHAM, Margery (1904–66; British detective-story writer)

ARBUTHNOT, John (1667–1735; Scot writer)

AYCKBOURN, Alan (1939–; British dramatist)

BLACKMORE, R.D. (1825–1900; British historical novelist)

BLACKWOOD, Algernon Henry (1869–1951; British novelist and short-story writer)

BOCCACCIO, Giovanni (1313–75; Italian writer and poet)

BURROUGHS, Edgar Rice (1875–1950; US novelist)

BURROUGHS, William (1914–97; US novelist)

CERVANTES, Miquel de (1547–1616; Spanish novelist)

CHARTERIS, Leslie (L Charles Bowyer Yin, 1907–93 ; British novelist)

CHURCHILL, Charles (1731–64; British poet)

COLERIDGE, Samuel Taylor (1772–1834; British poet)

CORNEILLE, Pierre (1606–84; French dramatist)

D'ANNUNZIO, Gabriele (1863–1938; Italian poet, novelist, and dramatist)

DE LA ROCHE, Mazo (1885–1961; Canadian novelist)

DE QUINCEY, Thomas (1785–1859; British essayist and critic)

DICKINSON, Ernily (1830–86; US poet)

DOOLITTLE, Hilda (1886–1961; US poet)

DOS PASSOS, John (1896–1970; US writer)

DU MAURIER, George (1834–96; British caricaturist and novelist)

ECKERMANN, Johann Peter (1792–1854; German writer)

EDGEWORTH, Maria (1767–1849; Anglo-Irish writer)

EHRENBERG, Iliya Grigorievich (1891–1967; Soviet author)

EURIPIDES, (c. 480– 406 BC; Greek dramatist)

FROISSART, Jean (1337– c. 1400; French chronicler and poet)

GIRAUDOUX, Jean (1882–1944; French dramatist and novelist)

GOLDSMITH, Oliver (1730–74; Anglo-Irish writer)

GONCHAROV, Ivan Aleksandrovich (1812–91; Russian novelist)

GOTTSCHED, Johann Christoph (1700–66; German critic)

GREENWOOD, Walter (1903– ; British novelist)

HAUPTMANN, Gerhart (1862–1946; German dramatist)

HAWTHORNE, Nathaniel (1804–64; US novelist and short-story writer)

HEMINGWAY, Ernest (1899–1961; US novelist)

HIGHSMITH, Patricia (1921–95; US author of crime fiction)

HOLDERLIN, Friedrich (1770–1843; German poet)

ISHERWOOD, Christopher (1904–86; British novelist)

JEFFERIES, Richard (1848–87; British novelist and naturalist)

KLOPSTOCK. Friedrich Gottlieb (1724–1803; German poet)

LA BRUYER, Jean de (1645–96; French satirist)

LA FAYETTE, Mme de (Marie Madeleine, Comtesse de L F, 1634–93; French novelist)

LAMARTINE, Alphonse de (1790–1869; French poet)

LAMPEDUSA, Giuseppe Tornasi di (1896–1957; Italian novelist)

LERMONTOV, Mikhail (1814–41; Russian Poet and novelist)

LINKLATER, Eric (1889–1974; Scottish novelist)

LLEWELLYN, Richard (R.D.V.L. Lloyd, 1907–83; Welsh novelist)

LOMONOSOV, Mikhaii Vasilievich (1711–65; Russian poet)

LOVECRAFT, H.P. (1890–1937; US novelist and short-story writer)

LUCRETIUS (Titus Lucretius Carus. c. 95– c. 55 BC; Roman philosopher and poet)

MACKENZIE, Sir Compton (1883–1972; British novelist)

MALAPARTE, Curzio (Kurt Erich Suckert;. 1898–1957; Italian novelist and dramatist)

MANSFIELD, Katherine (Kathleen Mansfield Beauchamp, 1888–1923; New Zealand short-story writer)

MARINETTI, Filippo Tommaso (1876–1944; Italian poet and novelist)

MARTINEAU, Harriet (1802–76; British writer)

MASEFIELD, John (1878–1967; British poet)

MASSINGER, Philip (1583 –1640; English dramatist)

9 continued

McCULLERS, Carson (1917–67; US novelist and playwright)

MIDDLETON, Thomas (1580–1627 English dramatist)

MONSARRAT, Nicholas (John Turney, 1910–79; British novelist)

MONTAIGNE, Michel de (1533–92; French essayist)

MUTANABBI, Abu At-Tayyib Ahmad Ibn Husayn al- (915–65 AD; Arab poet)

O'FLAHERTY, Liam (1897–1984; Irish novelist)

PARKINSON, Northcote (1909–93; British author)

PASTERNAK, Boris (1890–1960, Russian poet and novelist)

POLIZIANO (or Politian; 1454–94; Italian poet and scholar)

PRITCHETT, V.S. (1900–97 ; British short-story writer and critic)

RADCLIFFE-Ann (1764–1823; British novelist)

ROCHESTER, John Wilmot, 2nd Earl of (1647–80; British poet)

SACKVILLE, Thomas, 1st Earl of Dorset (1536–1608; British poet and dramatist)

SCHREINER, Olive (1855–1920; South African novelist)

SHENSTONE, William (1714–63; British poet)

SHOLOKHOV, Mikhail (1905–84; Russian novelist)

SOPHOCLES (c. 496– 406 BC; Greek dramatist)

STEINBECK, John (1902–68; US novelist)

STEVENSON, Robert Louis (1850–94; British novelist)

SWINBURNE, Algernon Charles (1837–1909; British poet)

THACKERAY, William Makepeace (1811–63; British novelist)

TSVETAEVA, Marina (1892–1941; Russian poet)

UNGARETTI, Giuseppe (1888–1970; Italian poet)

VERHAEREN, Emile (1844–96; Belgian poet)

VITTORINI, Elio (1908–66; Italian novelist)

WERGELAND, Henrik Arnold (1808–45; Norwegian poet)

WODEHOUSE, Sir P.G. (1881–1975; US humorous writer)

WYCHERLEY, William (1640–1716; English dramatist)

10

BAUDELAIRE, Charles (1821–67; French poet)

BILDERDIJK, Willem (1756–1831; Dutch poet and dramatist)

CAVALCANTI, Guido (c. 1255–1300; Italian poet)

CHATTERJEE, Bankim Chandra (1838–94; Indian novelist)

CHATTERTON, Thomas (1752–70; British poet)

CHESTERTON, G.K. (1874–1936; British essayist, novelist and poet)

CONSCIENCE, Hendrik (1812–83; Flemish novelist)

DAZAI OSAMU (Tsushima Shuji; 1909–48; Japanese novelist)

DIO CASSIUS (c. 150–235 AD; Roman historian)

DRINKWATER, John (1882–1937; British poet and dramatist)

DURRENMATT, Friedrich (1921–90; Swiss dramatist and novelist)

FITZGERALD, Edward (1809–83; British poet)

FITZGERALD, F. Scott (1896–1940; US novelist)

GALSWORTHY, John (1867–1933; British novelist and dramatist)

JEAN DE MEUN (c. 1240–c. 1305; French poet)

KHLEBNIKOV, Velimir (Victor K, 1885–1922; Russian poet)

LA FONTAINE, Jean de (1621–95; French poet)

LAGERKVIST, Pär (1891–1974; Swedish novelist, poet and dramatist)

LONGFELLOW, Henry Wadsworth (1807–82; US poet)

MACDIARMID, Hugh (Christopher Murray Grieve, 1892–1978; Scottish poet)

MANDELSTAM, Osip (1891–?1938, Russian poet)

MAUPASSANT, Guy de (1850–93; French short-story writer and novelist)

McGONAGALL, William (1830–1902; Scottish poet)

MICKIEWICZ, Adam (1798–1855; Polish poet)

OSTROVSKII, Aleksandr Nikolaevich (1823–86; Russian dramatist)

10 continued

PIRANDELLO, Luigi (1867–1936; Italian dramatist and novelist)

PROPERTIUS, Sextus (*c.* 50– *c.* 16 BC Roman poet)

RICHARDSON, Henry Handel (Ethel Florence R, 1870–1946; Australian novelist)

RICHARDSON, Sarnuel (1689–1761; British novelist)

RUTHERFORD, Mark (William Hale White, 1831–1913; British novelist)

SCHNITZLER, Arthur (1862–1931; Austrian Jewish dramatist and novelist)

STRINBERG, August (1849–1912; Swedish dramatist and writer)

TANNHAUSER (*c.* 1200– *c.* 1270; German poet)

THEOCRITUS (*c.* 310–250 BC; Greek poet)

VAN DER POST, Sir Laurens (1906–96; South African novelist)

WILLIAMSON, Henry (1895–1977; British novelist)

WORDSWORTH, William (1770–1850; British poet)

XENOPHANES (6th century BC: Greek poet)

11

ANZENGRUBER, Ludwig (1839–89; Austrian dramatist and novelist)

APOLLINAIRE, Guillaume (Wlihelm de Kostrowitzky, 1880–1918; French poet)

ARCHILOCHUS (*c.* 680 BC; Greek poet)

BACCHYLIDES (*c.* 516– *c.* 450 BC; Greek lyric poet)

BLESSINGTON, Marguerite, Countess of (1789–1849; Irish author)

CALLIMACHUS (*c.* 305–*c.* 240 BC; Greek poet)

CASTIGLIONE, Baldassare (1478–1529; Italian writer)

DOSTOIEVSKI, Fedor Mikhailovich 1821–81; Russian novelist)

EICHENDORFF, Josef, Freiherr von (1788–1857; German writer)

GARCIA LORCA, Federico (1898–1936; Spanish poet and dramatist)

GRILLPARZER, Franz (1791–1892; Austrian dramatist)

KAZANTZAKIS, Nikos (1885–1957; Greek novelist and poet)

LAUTREAMONT, Comte de (Isidore, Ducasse, 1846–70; French writer)

MAETERLINCK, Maurice (1862–1949; Belgian poet and dramatist)

MATSUO BASHO (Matsuo Munefusa, 1644–94; Japanese poet

MAYAKOVSKII, Vladimir (1893–1930; Russian poet)

MONTHERLANT, Henry de (1896–1972; French novelist and dramatist)

OMAR KHAYYAM (?1048–?1122; Persian poet)

PEREZ GALDOS, Benito (1843–1920; Spanish novelist)

SHAKESPEARE, William (1564–1616; English dramatist).

SIENKIEWICZ, Henryk (1846–1916; Polish novelist)

STIERNHIELM, Georg Olofson (1598–1672; Swedish poet)

YEVTUSHENKO, Yevgenii (1933– ;Russian poet)

12

ARISTOPHANES (*c.* 450– *c.* 385 BC: Greek comic dramatist)

BEAUMARCHAIS, Pierre-Augustin Caron de 1732–99; French dramatist)

BLASCO IBANEZ Vicente (1867–1928; Spanish novelist)

FERLINGHETTI, Lawrence (1919– ; US poet)

FEUCHTWANGER, Lion (1884–1958; German novelist and dramatist)

HOFMANNSTHAL, Hugo von (1874–1929; Austrian poet and dramatist)

LOPEZ DE AYALA, Pero (*c.* 1332– *c.* 1407; Spanish poet and chronicler)

MARTIN DU GARD, Roger (1881–1958; French novelist)

MATTHEW PARIS (*c.* 1200–59; English writer)

ROBBE-GRILLET, Alain (1922– ; French novelist)

SAINT-EXUPERY, Antoine de (1900–44; French novelist)

SOLZHENITSYN, Aleksandr (1918– ; Russian novelist)

VOZNESENSKII Andrei (1933– ; Russian poet)

13

BERTRAN DE BORN (?1140 –?1215;
French troubadour poet)

CASTELO BRANCO, Camilo (1825–95;
Portuguese novelist).

CHATEAUBRIAND, Vicomte de (1768–1848;
French writer)

CSOKONAI VITEZ, Mihaly (1773–1805;
Hungarian poet)

HARISHCHANDRA (1850–85; Hindi poet,
dramatist, and essayist, also known as
Bharatendu)

MARIE DE FRANCE (12th century AD;
French poet)

TIRSO DE MOLINA (Gabriel Tellezz,
c. 1584–1648; Spanish dramatist).

ZEAMI MOTOKIYO (1363– c. 1443;
Japanese playwright)

14

BRILLAT-SAVARIN, Anthelme (1755–1826;
French writer)

COMPTON-BURNETT, Dame Ivy
(1892–1969; British novelist)

DAFYDD AP GWILYM (c. 1320– c. 1380;
Welsh poet)

DANTE ALIGHIERI (1265–1321; Italian poet)

DROSTE-HULSHOFF, Annette von
(1797–1848; German poet and novelist)

GONGORA Y ARGOTE, Luis de (1561–1627;
Spanish poet)

GRIMMELSHAUSEN, Hans Jacob-Christoph
von (c. 1625–76; German novelist)

JACOPONE DA TODI (c. 1236–1306; Italian
religious poet)

LECONTE DE LISLE, Charles Marie Rene
(1818–94; French poet)

OEHLENSCHLAGER, Adam (1779–1850;
Danish poet and playwright)

PREVOST D'EXILES, Antoine François,
Abbé (1697–1763; French novelist)

SULLY-PRUDHOMME., René, François
Armand (1839–1907; French poet)

WOLLSTONECRAFT, Mary (1759–97; British
writer)

ZORRILLA Y MORAL, José (1817–93;
Spanish poet and dramatist)

15

ALARCON Y MENDOZA, Juan Ruiz de
(1581–1639; Spanish dramatist)

DIODORUS SICULUS (1st century BC; Greek
historian)

PLINY THE YOUNGER (Gaius Plinius
Caecitius Secundus, c. 61– c. 113 AD.;
Rornan writer)

16

CHRETIEN DE TROYES (12th century AD,
French poet)

CYRANO DE BERGERAC, Savinien
(1619–55; French writer and dramatist)

KAWABATA YASUNARI (1899–1972;
Japanese novelist).

PETRONIUS ARBITER (1st century AD;
Roman satirist)

17

CALDERON DE LA BARCA, Pedro
1600–81; Spanish dramatist)

GUILLAUME DE LORRIS (13th century;
French poet and author)

TANIZAKI JUN-ICHIRO (1886–1965;
Japanese novelist)

18

APOLLONIUS OF RHODES (3rd century BC;
Greek epic poet)

KAKINOMOTO, HITOMARO (c. 680–710;
Japanese poet)

THOMAS OF ERCELDOUNE (13th century;
English poet and prophet)

19

BENOIT DE SAINTE-MAURE (12th century
AD; French poet)

CHIKAMATSU MONZAEMON (Sugimori
Nobumori; 1653–1724; Japanese dramatist)

VILLIERS DE LISLE-ADAM, Philippe
Auguste, Comte de (1838–89; French poet,
novelist, and dramatist)

20+

BERNARDIN DE SAINT-PIERRE, Jacques
Henri (1737–1814; French naturalist and
writer)

DIONYSIUS OF HALICARNASSUS, (1st
century BC; Greek historian)

DRUMMOND OF HAWTHORNDEN, William
(1585–1649; Scots poet)

ECHEGARAY Y EIZAGUIRRE, José
(1832–1916; Spanish dramatist)

CLASSICAL MUSICIANS AND COMPOSERS

CLASSICAL MUSICIANS AND COMPOSERS

3

BAX, Sir. Arnold Edward Trevor (1883–1953; British composer)

4

ADAM, Adolphe-Charles (1803–56; French composer)
ARNE, Thomas Augustine (1710–78; British composer)
BACH, Johann Sebastian (1685–1750; German composer and keyboard player)
BERG, Alban (1885–1935; Austrian composer)
BING, Sir Rudolf (1902– ; British opera administrator)
BLOW, John (1649–1708; English composer)
BOHM, Karl (1894–1981; Austrian conductor)
BULL, John (c. 1562–1628; English composer and organist)
BUSH, Alan Dudley (1900– ; British composer)
BUTT, Dame Clara (1873–1936; British contralto singer)
BYRD, William (?1543–1623; English composer)
CAGE, John (1912–92; US composer)
HESS, Dame Myra (1890–1965; British pianist)
IVES, Charles (1874–1954; US composer)
LALO, Edouard (1823–92; French cornposer)
LILL, John (1944– ; British pianist)
LIND, Jenny (1820–87; Swedish soprano)
NONO, Luigi (1924–90; Italian composer)
ORFF, Cart (1895–1982; German composer and conductor)
WOLF, Hugo (1860–1903; Austrian composer)
WOOD, Sir Henry (1869–1944; British conductor)

5

ALKAN, Charles Henri Valentin (C.H.V. Morhange, 1813–88; French pianist and composer)
ARRAU, Claudio (1903–91; Chilean pianist)
AUBER, Daniel François Esprit (1782–1871; French composer)
AURIC, Georges (1899–83; French composer)
BAKER, Dame Janet (1933– ; British mezzo-soprano)
BERIO, Luciano (1925– ; Italian composer)

BIZET, Georges (Alexandre César Léopold B, 1838–75; French composer)
BLISS, Sir Arthur Edward Drummond (1891–1975; British composer)
BLOCH, Ernest (1880–1959; Swiss-born composer)
BOEHM, Theobald (1794–1881; German flautist)
BOULT, Sir Adrian (1889–1983; British conductor)
BOYCE, William (c. 1710–79; British composer)
BREAM, Julian Alexander (1933– ; British guitanst and lutenist)
BRIAN, Havergal (1876–1972; British composer)
BRUCH, Max (1838–1920; German composer)
BULOW, Hans Guido, Freherrr von (1830–94: German pianist and conductor)
DAVIS, Sir Colin (1927– ; British conductor)
D'INDY, Vincent (1851–1931; French composer)
DUFAY, Guillaume (c. 1400–74; Burgundian composer)
DUKAS, Paul (1865–1935; French composer)
DUPRE, Marcel (1886–1971; French organist and composer)
ELGAR, Sir Edward (1857–1934; British composer)
EVANS, Sir Geraint (1922– ; Welsh baritone)
FALLA, Manuel de (1876–1946; Spanish composer)
FAURE, Gabriel (1845–1924; French composer and organist)
FIELD, John (1782–1837; Irish pianist and composer)
FRIML, Rudolph (1879–1972; Czech-born composer and pianist)
GIGI, Beniamino (1890–1957; Italian tenor)
GLUCK, Christoph Willibald (1714–87; German composer)
GOBBI, Tito (1915–84; Italian baritone)
GRIEG, Edvard Hagerup (1843–1907; Norwegian composer)
GROVE, Sir George (1820–1900; British musicologist)
HALLÉ, Sir Charles (Karl Hallé, 1819–1895; German conductor and pianist)

5 continued

HAYDN, Franz Joseph (1732–1809; Austrian composer)

HENZE, Hans Werner (1926– ; German composer)

HOLST, Gustav (1874–1934; British composer and teacher)

IBERT, Jacques (1890–1962; French composer)

LEHAR, Franz (Ferencz L, 1870–1948; Hungarian composer)

LISZT, Franz (Ferencz L, 1811–86; Hungarian pianist and composer)

LOCKE, Matthew (c. 1622–77; English composer)

LULLY, Jean Baptiste (Giovanni Battista Lulli, 1632–87; French composer)

MELBA, Dame Nellie (Helen Porter Armstrong, 1861–1931; Australian soprano)

MOOR E, Gerald (1899–1987; British pianist).

MUNCH, Charles (1892–1968; French conductor)

OGDON, John (1937– ; British pianist)

PARRY, Sir Hubert (1848–1918; British composer)

PATTI, Adelina (Adela Juana Maria, 1843–1919; Italian-born operatic soprano)

PEARS, Sir Peter (1910–86; British tenor)

RAVEL, Maurice (1875–1937; French composer)

REGER; Max (1873–1916; German composer, organist, and teacher)

SATIE, Erik (1866–1925; French composer)

SHARP, Cecil (1859–1924; British musician)

SOLTI, Sir Georg (1912–97; Hungarian-born British conductor)

SOUSA, John Philip (1854–1933; US composer and bandmaster)

SPOHR, Louis (Ludwig S, 1784–1859; German violinist and composer)

STERN, Isaac (1920– ; Russian-born US violinist)

SZELL, George (1897–1970; Hungarian conductor)

TEYTE, Dame Maggie (1888–1976; British soprano)

VERDI, Giuseppe (1813–1901; Itallan composer)

WEBER, Carl Maria von (1786–1826, German composer)

WEILL, Kurt (1900–50; German composer)

WIDOR, Charles Marie (1844–1937; French organist and composer)

6

ARNOLD, Malcolm (1921– ; British composer).

BARBER, Samuel (1910–81; US composer)

BARTOK, Béla (1881–1945; Hungarian composer)

BISHOP, Sir Henry Rowley (1786–1855; British composer and conductor)

BOULEZ, Pierre (1925– ; French composer and conductor)

BRAHMS, Johannes (1833–97; German composer)

BRIDGE, Frank (1879–1941; British composer)

BURNEY, Charles (1726–1814; British musicologist, organist, and composer)

BUSONI, Ferruccio (1866–1924; Italian virtuoso pianist and composer)

CALLAS, Maria (Maria Anna Kalageropoulos, 1923–77; US soprano)

CARTER, Elliott (1908– ; U.S. composer)

CARUSO, Enrico (1873–1921; Italian tenor)

CASALS, Pablo (Pau C.,1876–1973; Spanish cellist, conductor, and composer)

CHOPIN, Frédéric (François, 1810–49; Polish composer)

CLARKE, Jeremiah (?1673–1707; English composer and organist)

CORTOT, Alfred (1877-1962; French pianist)

COWELL, Henry (1891–1965; US composer)

CURWEN John (1816–80; British teacher who perfected the Tonic Sol-fa system)

CURZON, Sir Clifford (1907–82; British pianist)

DAVIES, Sir Peter Maxwell (1934– ; British composer)

DELIUS, Frederick (1862–1934; British composer)

DIBDIN, Charles (1745–1814; British composer, actor, and singer)

DUPARC, Henri (Marie Eugène Henri Foucques D, 1848–1933; French composer)

DVORAK, Antonin (1841–1904; Czech composer)

ENESCO, Georges (G. Enescu, 1881–1955; Romanian violinist and composer)

FLOTOW, Friedrich von (1812–83; German composer)

6 continued

FRANCK, César Auguste (1822–90; Belgian composer; organist, and teacher)

GALWAY, James (1939– ; Irish flautist)

GOUNOD, Charles François (1818–93; French composer)

GROVES, Sir Charles (1915– ; British conductor)

HALEVY, Jacques François (Fromental Elias Levy, 1799–1862; French composer)

HANDEL, George Frederick (1685–1759; German composer)

HARRIS, Roy (1898–1979; US composer)

HOTTER, Hans (1909– ; German baritone)

HUMMEL, Johann Nepomuk (1778–1837; Hungarian pianist and composer)

JOCHUM, Eugen (1902– ; German conductor)

KODALY, Zoltan (1882–1967; Hungarian composer)

KRENEK, Ernst (1900– ; Austrian composer)

LASSUS, Roland de (c. 1532–94; Flemish composer)

LIGETI, Gyorgy (1923– ; Hungarian composer)

MAAZEL, Lorin (1930– ; US conductor)

MAHLER, Gustav (1860–1911; Austrian, composer and conductor)

MORLEY, Thomas (1557–1603; English composer, music printer, and organist)

MOZART, Wolfgang Amadeus (1756–91; Austrian composer)

PREVIN, André (Andreas L. Priwin, 1929– ; German-born conductor, pianist, composer)

RATTLE, Sir Simon (1955–; British conductor and musical director)

RUBBRA, Edmund (1901–86; British composer)

SCHUTZ, Heinrich (1585–1672; German composer)

TALLIS, Thomas (c. 1505–85; English composer)

VARESE, Edgard (1883–1965; French composer)

WAGNER, Richard (1813–83; German composer)

WALTER, Bruno (B.W. Schlesinger, 1876–1962; German conductor)

WALTON, Sir William (1902–83; British composer)

WEBERN, Anton von (1883–1945; Austrian composer)

7

ALBENIZ, Isaac Manuel Francisco (1860–1909; Spanish composer and pianist)

ALLEGRI, Gregorio (1582–1652; Italian composer)

ANTHEIL, George (1900–59; US composer)

BABBITT, Milton (1916– ; US composer)

BEECHAM, Sir Thomas (1879–1961; British conductor)

BELLINI, Vincenzo (1801–35; Italian composer)

BENNETT, Richard Rodney (1936– ; British composer)

BENN, Sir William Sterndale (1816–75; British pianist)

BERLIOZ, Hector (1803–69; French composer and conductor)

BORODIN, Aleksandr Porfirevich (1833–87; Russian composer)

BRENDEL, Alfred (1931– ; Austrian pianist)

BRITTEN, Benjamin, Baron (1913–76; British composer and pianist)

CABALLE, Montserrat (1933– ; Spanish soprano)

CACCINI, Giulio (c. 1545– c. 1618; Italian singer and composer)

CAMPION, Thomas (or Campian,1567–1620; English composer)

CAVALLI, Francesco (1602–76; Italian composer)

COPLAND, Aaron (1900– ; US composer)

CORELLI, Ardangelo (1653–1713; Italian violinist and composer)

DEBUSSY, Claude (1862–1918; French composer)

DELIBES, Leo, (1836–1918; French composer)

DOMINGO, Placido (1941– ; Spanish tenor)

DOWLAND, John (1563–1626; English composer and lutenist)

FARNABY, Giles (c. 1565–1640; English composer)

FERRIER, Kathleen (1912–53; British contralto)

GALUPPI, Baldassare (1706–85; Venetian composer)

GIBBONS, Orlando (1583–1625; English composer, organist, and virginalist)

GIULINI,Carlo Maria(1914– ; Italian conductor)

HAMMOND, Dame Joan (1912–96; New Zealand soprano)

HOFMANN, Joseph Casimir (1876–1957; Polish-born pianist)

7 continued

IRELAND, John Nicholson (1879–1962; British composer)

JANACEK, Leos (1854–1928; Czech composer)

JOACHIM, Joseph (1831–1907; Hungarian violinist and composer)

KARAJAN, Herbert von (1908–89; Austrian conductor)

KUBELIK, Rafael (1914–96; Czech conductor)

LAMBERT, Constant (1905–51; British composer and conductor)

LEHMANN, Lilli (1848–1929; German soprano)

LEHMANN, Lotte (1885–1976; German soprano)

MALCOLM, George John (1917– ; British harpsichordist)

MARTINO, Bohuslav (1890–1959; Czech composer)

MENOTTI, Gian Carlo (1911– ; Italian-born US composer)

MENUHIN, Sir Yehudi (1916– ; British violinist)

MILHAUD, Darius (1892–1974; French composer)

MONTEUX, Pierre (1875–1964; French conductor)

NICOLAI, Otto Ehrenfried (1810–49; German conductor and composer)

NIELSEN, Carl (1865–1931; Danish composer and conductor)

NIKISCH, Arthur (1855–1922; Hungarian conductor)

NILSSON, Birgit Marta (1918– ; Swedish soprano)

OKEGHEM, Jean d' (*c*. 142– *c*. 1495; Flemish composer)

ORMANDY, Eugene (E. Blau, 1899–1985; Hungarian-born US conductor)

PEROTIN (Latin name: Perotinus Magnus, *c*. 1155– *c*. 1202; French composer)

POULENC, Francis (1899–1963; French composer)

PUCCINI, Giacomo (1858–1924; Italian opera composer)

PURCELL, Henry (1659–95; English composer and organist)

RICHTER, Hans (1843–1916; Hungarian conductor)

RICHTER, Sviatoslav (1914– ; Russian pianist)

RODRIGO, Joaquin (1901– ; Spanish guitar composer)

ROSSINI, Gioacchino Antonio (1792–1868; Italian composer)

ROUSSEL, Albert (1869–1937; French composer)

RUGGLES, Carl (1876–1971; US composer)

SALIERI, Antonio (1750–1825; Italian composer and conductor)

SARGENT, Sir Malcolm (1895–1967; British conductor)

SCHUMAN, William (1910– ; US composer)

SMETANA, Bedrich (1824–84; Bohemian composer)

SOLOMON (S. Cutner, 1902– ; British pianist)

STAINER, Sir John (1840–1901; British composer and organist)

STAMITZ, Johann (Jan Stamic, 1717–57; Bohemian composer)

STRAUSS, Richard (1864–1949; German composer and conductor)

THIBAUD, Jacques (1880–1953; French violinist)

THOMSON, Virgil (1896–89; US composer and conductor)

TIPPETT, Sir Michael (1905– ; British composer)

VIVALDI, Antonio (1678–1741; Italian composer and violinist)

WARLOCK, Peter (Philip Heseltine, 1894–1930; British composer)

WEELKES, Thomas (*c*. 1575–1623; English composer and organist)

WELLESZ, Egon (1885–1974; Austrian composer)

XÉNAKIS, Yannis (1922– ; Greek composer)

8

ALBINONI, Tomaso (1671–1750; Italian composer)

ANSERMET, Ernest (1883–1969; Swiss conductor)

BERKELEY, Sir Lennox Randal Francis (1903–89; British composer)

BRUCKNER, Anton (1824–96; Austrian composer and organist)

CARRERAS, Jose (1946–; Spanish tenor)

CHAUSSON, Ernest (1855–99; French composer)

CIMAROSA, Domenico (1749–1801; Italian composer)

CLEMENTI, Muzio (1752–1832; Italian pianist)

CLASSICAL MUSICIANS AND COMPOSERS

8 continued

DOHNANYI, Erno (Ernst von D, 1877–1960; Hungarian composer and pianist)

FLAGSTAD, Kirsten Malfrid (1895–1962; Norwegian soprano)

GERSHWIN, George (Jacob Gershvin, 1898–1937; US composer)

GESUALDO, Carlo, Prince of Venosa (c. 1560–1631; Italian composer)

GLAZUNOV, Aleksandr Konstantinovich (1865–1936; Russian composer)

GOOSSENS, Sir Eugene (1893–1962; British conductor and composer)

GRAINGER, Percy Aldridge (1882–1961; Australian composer and pianist)

GRANADOS, Enrique (1867–1916; Spanish composer and pianist)

HONEGGER, Arthur (1892–1955; French composer)

HOROWITZ, Vladimir (1904–89; Russian pianist)

KREISLER, Fritz (1875–1962; Austrian violinist)

MACONCHY, Elizabeth (1907– ; British composer)

MASCAGNI, Pietro (1863–1945; Italian composer)

MESSAGER, Andre (1853–1929; French composer and conductor)

MESSIAEN, Olivier (1908–92; French composer, organist, and teacher)

MILSTEIN, Nathan (1904– ; US violinist)

MUSGRAVE, Thea (1928– ; Scot composer)

OISTRAKH, David (1908–75; Russian violinist)

PAGANINI, Niccolo (1782–1840; Italian violinist)

RESPIGHI, Ottorino (1879–1936; Italian composer)

SCHNABEL, Artur (1882–1951; Austrian pianist)

SCHUBERT, Franz (1797–1828; Austrian composer)

SCHUMANN, Elisabeth (1885–1952; German born soprano)

SCHUMANN, Robert (1810–56; German composer)

SCRIABIN, Alexander (1872–1915; Russian composer and pianist)

SIBELIUS, Jean (Johan Julius Christian S, 1865–1957; Finnish composer)

SONDHEIM, Stephen (1930– ; US composer and lyricist)

STANFORD, Sir Charles (1852–1924; Irish composer)

SULLIVAN, Sir Arthur (1842–1900; British composer)

TAVERNER, John (c. 1495–1545; English composer)

TE KANAWA, Dame Kiri (1944– ; New Zealand soprano)

TELEMANN, Georg Philipp (1681–1767; German composer)

VICTORIA, Tomás Luis de (c. 1548–1611; Spanish composer)

WILLIAMS, John (1941– ; Australian guitarist)

ZABALETA, Nicanor (1907– ; Spanish harpist)

9

ADDINSELL, Richard (1904–77; British composer)

ASHKENAZY, Vladimir (1937– ; Russian pianist and conductor)

BARENBOIM, Daniel (1942– ; Israeli pianist and composer)

BEETHOVEN, Ludwig van (1770–1827; German composer)

BERNSTEIN, Leonard (1918–90; US conductor) composer, and pianist)

CHERUBINI, Maria Luigi (1760–1842; Italian composer)

DOLMETSCH, Arnold (1858–1940; British musician and instrument maker)

DONIZETTI, Gaetano (1797–1848; Italian composer)

HINDEMITH, Paul (1895–1963; German composer and viola player)

KLEMPERER, Otto (1885–1973; German conductor)

MACKERRAS, Sir Charles (1925– ; US-born Australian conductor)

OFFENBACH, Jacques (J. Eberst, 1819–80; French composer)

PAVAROTTI, Luciano (1935– ; Italian tenor)

SCARLATTI, Domenico (1685–1757; Italian composer, harpsichordist, and organist)

STOKOWSKI, Leopold (1882–1977; British born conductor)

TORTELIER, Paul (1914–90; French cellist)

TOSCANINI, Arturo (1867–1957; Italian conductor)

10

BARBIROLLI, Sir John (1899–1970; British conductor)

BIRTWISTLE, Sir Harrison (1934– ; British composer)

BOCCHERINI, Luigi (1743–1805; Italian violoncellist and composer)

GALLI-CURCI, Amelita (1882–1963; Italian soprano)

LOS ANGELES, Victoria de (1923– ; Spanish soprano)

MENGELBERG, William (1871–1951; Dutch conductor)

MONTEVERDI, Claudio (1567–1643; Italian composer)

MUSSORGSKI, Modest Petrovich (1839–81; Russian composer)

PADEREWSKI, Ignacy (1860–1941; Polish pianist and composer)

PALESTRINA, Giovanni Pierluigi da (?1525–94; Italian composer)

PRAETORIUS, Michael (M Schultheiss, 1571–1621; German composer)

RUBINSTEIN, Anton (1829–94; Russian pianist and composer)

RUBINSTEIN, Artur (1888–1982; Polish-born pianist)

SAINT-SAENS, Camille (1835–1921; French composer, conductor, pianist, and organist)

SCHOENBERG, Arnold (1874–1951; Austrian born composer)

STRADIVARI, Antonio (?1644–1737; Italian violin maker)

STRAVINSKY, Igor (1882–1971; Russian-born composer)

SUTHERLAND, Dame Joan (1926– ; Australian soprano)

VILLA-LOBOS, Heitor (1887–1959; Brazilian composer)

11

CHARPENTIER, Gustave (1860–1956; French composer)

FURTWANGLER, Wilhelm (1886–1954; German conductor)

HUMPERDINCK, Engelbert (1854–1921; German composer)

LEONCAVALLO, Ruggiero (1858–1919; Italian composer)

LESCHETIZKY, Theodor (1830–1915; Polish pianist and piano teacher)

MENDELSSOHN, Felix (Jacob Ludwig Felix Mendelssohn-Bartholdy, 1809–47; German composer)

RACHMANINOV, Sergei (1873–1943; Russian composer, pianist, and conductor)

SCHWARZKOPF, Elisabeth (1915– ; German soprano)

STOCKHAUSEN, Karlheinz (1928– ; German composer)

SZYMANOWSKI, Karol (1882–1937; Polish composer)

TCHAIKOVSKY, Peter Ilich (1840–93; Russian composer)

WOLF-FERRARI, Ermanno (1876–1948; Italian composer)

12

DALLAPICCOLA, Luigi (1904–1975; Italian composer and pianist)

GUIDO D'AREZZO (c. 990– c. 1050; Italian monk and musical theorist)

KHACHATURIAN, Aram Ilich (1903–78; Russian composer)

KOUSSEVITSKY, Sergei (1874–1951; Russian composer)

13

ROUGET DE L'ISLE, Claude Joseph (1760–1836; French composer)

14

FISCHER-DIESKAU, Dietrich (1925– ; German baritone)

JAQUES-DALCROZE, Émile (1865–1950; Swiss composer)

JOSQUIN DES PREZ (c. 1450–1521; Flemish composer)

RIMSKY-KORSAKOV, Nikolai (1844–1908; Russian composer)

15

COLERIDGE-TAYLOR, Samuel (1875–1912; British composer)

VAUGHAN WILLIAMS, Ralph (1872–1958; British composer)

17

STRAUSS THE YOUNGER, Johann (1825–99; Austrian violinist, conductor, and composer)

POP AND ROCK MUSICIANS

2
U2

3
ABC
ANT, Adam
DAY, Doris
ENO, Brian
JAM, The
LEE, Brenda
MUD
O.M.D. (Orchestral Manoeuvres in the Dark)
ONO, Yoko
RAY, Johnny
REA, Chris
R.E.M.
UFO
VEE, Bobby
WAR
WHO, The
YES

4
10cc
ABBA
AC/DC
ANKA, Paul
BAEZ, Joan
BAND, The
BART, Lionel
BECK, Jeff
BLUE, Barry
BLUR
BROS
BUSH, Kate
BYRD, Charlie
CALE, J.J.
CARS, The
CASH, Johnny
CHER
COLE, Nat 'King'
COMO, Perry
CURE, The
DIDO
DION
DURY, Ian

EDDY, Duane
FAME, Georgie
FORD, Tennessee Ernie
FREE
FURY, Billy
GAYE, Marvin
GETZ, Stan
IDOL, Billy
INXS
JOEL, Billy
JOHN, Elton
KALE, J J
KIDD, Johnny
KING, B B
KING, Carole
KING, Jonathon
KISS
KITT, Eartha
LOWE, Nick
LULU
LYNN, Vera
MANN, Barry
MAZE
MOBY
MONK, Thelonius
MOST, Mickie
MOVE, The
NICE, The
PAUL, Billy
PIAF, Edith
REED, Lou
RICH, Charlie
ROSS, Diana
RUSH
SADE
SHAW, Artie
SHAW, Sandie
STYX
T REX
UB40
WHAM!
WOLF, Howlin'
WOOD, Roy
WRAY, Link

5
ADAMS, Bryan
ADLER, Larry
ADLER, Lou
ASWAD
BAKER, 'Ginger'
BASIE, Count
BERRY, Chuck
BLACK, Cilla
BOLAN, Marc
BONDS, Gary US
BOONE, Pat
BOWIE, David
BREAD
BROWN, James
BYRDS, The
CHINN, Nicky
CLARK, Dave
CLARK, Petula
CLASH, The
CLIFF, Jimmy
COHEN, Leonard
COOKE, Sam
CORRS, The
CREAM
CROCE, Jim
DARIN, Bobby
DAVIS, Miles
DAVIS, Sammy, Jnr
DAVIS, Spencer, Group
DELLS, The
DOORS, The
DYLAN, Bob
ESSEX, David
FACES, The
FERRY, Bryan
FLACK, Roberta
FREED, Alan
GREEN, Al
HALEY, Bill
HANDY, William Christopher
HAYES, Isaac
HEART
HINES, Earl
HOLLY, Buddy
ISAAK, Chris

JAMES, Bob
JAMES, Tommy, & The Shondells
JARRE, Jean-Michel
JONES, Quincy
JONES, Tom
KINKS, The
KLEIN, Allen
LAINE, Frankie
LEWIS, Huey, & The News
LEWIS, Jerry Lee
LYMON, Frankie, & The Teenagers
McCOY, Van
MOORE, Gary
MOYET, Alison
NASH, Graham
NUMAN, Gary
OASIS
O'JAYS, The
PERRY, Richard
PETTY, Tom
PRICE, Alan
PROBY, P J
QUEEN
REDDY, Helen
SAXON
SAYER, Leo
SCOTT, Ronnie
SEGER, Bob
SIMON, Carly
SLADE
SMITH, Bessie
STARR, Ringo
STING
SWEET
TATUM, Art
WHITE, Barry
WYMAN, Bill
YAZOO
YOUNG, Neil
YOUNG, Paul
ZAPPA, Frank
ZZ TOP

6

ALPERT, Herb
ARGENT
ATKINS, Chet
ATWELL, Winifred
AVALON, Frankie
BALDRY, Long John
BASSEY, Shirley
BECHET, Sidney
BENSON, George
BERLIN, Irving
BOLDEN, Buddy
BONEY M
BOSTON
BROWNE, Jackson
BURDON, Eric
CHAPIN, Harry
COCKER, Joe
COODER, Ry
COOPER, Alice
CREOLE, Kid, & The
  Coconuts
CROSBY, Bing
CROSBY, David
DAMNED, The
DEKKER, Desmond
DENVER, John
DOMINO, Fats
DR HOOK
EAGLES, The
EASTON, Sheena
EQUALS, The
FABIAN
FAMILY
FISHER, Eddie
GELDOF, Bob
HARRIS, Emmylou
HOOKER, John Lee
HUNTER, Ian
JAGGER, Mick
JOLSON, Al
JOPLIN, Janis
KNIGHT, Gladys, &
  The Pips
KOOPER, Al
KORNER, Alexis
KRAMER, Billy J
LAUPER, Cyndi
LEIBER, Jerry,
LENNON, John
LENNOX, Annie

LERNER, Alan Jay
MARLEY, Bob, &
  The Wailers
MARTIN, George
MARTYN, John
MATHIS, Johnny
MAYALL, John
McLEAN, Don
MERCURY, Freddie
MIDLER, Bette
MILLER, Glenn
MILLER, Steve
MINGUS, Charlie
MONTEZ, Chris
MORTON, Jelly Roll
NELSON, Ricky
NELSON, Willie
NEWMAN, Randy
NUGENT, Ted
OSMOND, Donny
PALMER, Robert
PARKER, Charlie
PARKER, Colonel
  Tom
PARTON, Dolly
PAXTON, Tom
PITNEY, Gene
POLICE, The
PORTER, Cole
PRINCE
REEVES, Jim
REVERE, Paul, &
  The Raiders
RICHIE, Lionel
ROGERS, Kenny
SCAGGS, Boz
SEDAKA, Neil
SEEGER, Pete
SIMONE, Nina
SLEDGE, Percy
STILLS, Stephen
SUMMER, Donna
TAUPIN, Bernie
TAYLOR, James
THOMAS, B J
TROGGS, The
TURNER, Tina
TWITTY, Conway
VALENS, Ritchie
WALLER, Fats
WATERS, Muddy

WEBBER, Andrew
  Lloyd
WELLER, Paul
WILSON, Jackie
WINTER, Edgar
WINTER, Johnny
WOMACK, Bobby
WONDER, Stevie

7

AMERICA
ANIMALS, The
BALLARD, Hank
BEATLES, The
BEE GEES, The
BENNETT, Tony
BLONDIE
BON JOVI
BOYZONE
BRUBECK, Dave
CALVERT, Eddie
CASSIDY, David
CHAPMAN, Mike
CHARLES, Ray
CHECKER, Chubby
CLANNAD
CLAPTON, Eric
CLOONEY,
  Rosemary
COCHRAN, Eddie
COLLINS, Judy
COLLINS, Phil
DE BURGH, Chris
DIAMOND, Neil
DIDDLEY, Bo
DONEGAN, Lonnie
DONOVAN
EDMUNDS, Dave
EPSTEIN, Brian
FRANCIS, Connie
GABRIEL, Peter
GENESIS
GLITTER, Gary
GOODMAN, Benny
GUTHRIE, Woody
HAMPTON, Lionel
HANCOCK, Herbie
HENDRIX, Jimi
HOLIDAY, Billie
HOLLIES, The
HOUSTON, Whitney

IGGY POP
JACKSON, Janet
JACKSON, Michael
JACKSON, Millie
JARREAU, Al
KEATING, Ronan
LOFGREN, Nils
MADNESS
MADONNA
MANILOW, Barry
MICHAEL, George
MINOGUE, Kylie
MONKEES, The
M PEOPLE
NILSSON, Harry
NIRVANA
ORBISON, Roy
OSMONDS, The
PERKINS, Carl
PICKETT, Wilson
PRESLEY, Elvis
PRESTON, Billy
RAINBOW
REDDING, Otis
RICHARD, Cliff
RICHARD, Keith
RODGERS, Richard
  Charles
RUSSELL, Leon
SANTANA
SEEKERS, The
SHADOWS, The
SHANKAR, Ravi
SHANNON, Del
SINATRA, Frank
SPECTOR, Phil
SQUEEZE
STEVENS, Cat
STEWART, Rod
TRAFFIC
TURTLES, The
VAUGHAN, Sarah
VINCENT, Gene
WAKEMAN, Rick
WARWICK, Dionne
WINWOOD, Steve
WIZZARD
WYNETTE, Tammy
ZOMBIES, The

8

ANDERSON, Ian
AZNAVOUR,
Charles
BOY GEORGE
CAMPBELL, Glen
CHI-LITES, The
COASTERS, The
COLD PLAY
COLTRANE, John
CRYSTALS, The
DRIFTERS, The
FOUR ACES, The
FOUR TOPS, The
FRAMPTON, Peter
FRANKLIN, Aretha
HAMLISCH, Marvin
HAWKWIND
HEATWAVE
INK SPOTS
JENNINGS, Waylon
MARSALIS, Wynton
MAYFIELD, Curtis
MEAT LOAF
MINNELLI, Liza
MIRACLES, The
MITCHELL, Joni
MORRISON, Van
OLDFIELD, Mike
OSBOURNE, Ozzy
PETERSON, Oscar
Emmanuel
PLATTERS, The
RAFFERTY, Gerry
ROBINSON,
Smokey
RONETTES, The
RONSTADT, Linda
SONDHEIM,
Stephen
SPECIALS, The
STIGWOOD, Robert
STROLLER, Mike
SUPREMES, The
ULTRAVOX
VANDROSS, Luther
VAN HALEN

9

AEROSMITH
ARMSTRONG, Louis
BACHARACH, Burt
BADFINGER
BEACH BOYS, The
BEEFHEART,
Captain
BELAFONTE, Harry
BUCKS FIZZ
CHIPMUNKS, The
CRUSADERS, The
ECHOBELLY
ELLINGTON, Duke
FAITHFULL,
Marianne
FOGELBERG, Dan
FOREIGNER
GALLAGHER, Rory
GILLESPIE, Dizzy
GOLDSBORO,
Bobby
GRAPPELLI,
Stephane
LEADBELLY
LITTLE EVA
LYTTELTON,
Humphrey
MARMALADE
MARILLION
McCARTNEY, Paul
MEN AT WORK
MOTORHEAD
O'SULLIVAN, Gilbert
PINK FLOYD
REINHARDT,
Django
ROSE ROYCE
ROXY MUSIC
SCORPIONS
SEARCHERS, The
SHIRELLES, The
SIMPLY RED
STATUS QUO
STEELY DAN
STREISAND, Barbra
THIN LIZZY
TOWNSHEND, Pete
URIAH HEEP
WET WET WET
YARDBIRDS, The

10

AMEN CORNER
BAD COMPANY
BANANARAMA
BLACK CROWS-
CANNED HEAT
CARMICHAEL,
Hoagy
CARPENTERS, The
COMMODORES,
The
DEEP PURPLE
DR FEELGOOD
DURAN DURAN
EURYTHMICS, The
FITZGERALD, Ella
FUNKADELIC
GUNS 'N' ROSES
IRON MAIDEN
JETHRO TULL
LITTLE FEAT
LONG RYDERS
MOODY BLUES
MUNGO JERRY
NEWTON-JOHN,
Olivia
PRETENDERS, The
SCOTT-HERON, Gil
SEX PISTOLS, The
SMALL FACES, The
SPICE GIRLS
STONE ROSES
STRANGLERS, The
STYLISTICS, The
WASHINGTON,
Dinah
WHITESNAKE
ZAGER & EVANS

11

ARMATRADING,
Joan
BEIDERBECKE, Bix
CULTURE CLUB
DIRE STRAITS
FOUNDATIONS
FOUR SEASONS,
The
HUMAN LEAGUE
IMPRESSIONS, The
JACKSON FIVE

JOY DIVISION
KING CRIMSON
LED ZEPPELIN
LINDISFARNE
MANFRED MANN
MARVELETTES, The
PET SHOP BOYS
PROCUL HARUM
SIMPLE MINDS
SPRINGFIELD, Dusty
SPRINGFIELD, Rick
SPRINGSTEEN,
Bruce
TEMPTATIONS, The
WISHBONE ASH

12

BLACK SABBATH
BOOMTOWN RATS
COCKNEY REBEL
CROWDED HOUSE
FLEETWOOD MAC
GRATEFUL DEAD
HALL AND OATES
HOT CHOCOLATE
HOUSEMARTINS,
The
SONNY AND CHER
STYLE COUNCIL
TALKING HEADS
YOUNG RASCALS

13

GEORGE MICHAEL
HAMMERSTEIN II,
Oscar
ISLEY BROTHERS
KRISTOFFERSON,
Kris
LITTLE RICHARD
LOVIN' SPOONFUL
LYNYRD SKYNYRD
MAMAS AND PAPAS
MOTT THE
HOOPLE
REO SPEEDWAGON
ROLLING STONES
SPANDAU BALLET
STAPLE SINGERS
TEARS FOR FEARS
THREE DOG NIGHT

14
ALLMAN BROTHERS
BAY CITY ROLLERS
BLUE OYSTER CULT
DOOBIE BROTHERS
FIFTH DIMENSION
HERMAN'S HERMITS
JON AND VANGELIS
KOOL AND THE GANG

15
DETROIT SPINNERS
EVERLEY BROTHERS

16
AVERAGE WHITE BAND
BOOKER T AND THE MG'S
EARTH WIND AND FIRE
PETER, PAUL AND MARY

17
GRAND FUNK RAILROAD
JEFFERSON AIRPLANE
RIGHTEOUS BROTHERS
SIMON AND GARFUNKEL
SWINGING BLUE JEANS
THUNDERCLAP NEWMAN

18
BLOOD SWEAT AND TEARS
BUFFALO SPRINGFIELD
FAIRPORT CONVENTION
FINE YOUNG CANNIBALS
PUBLIC IMAGE LIMITED
RED HOT CHILI PEPPERS

19
BARCLAY JAMES HARVEST
DEREK AND THE
  DOMINOES
MIKE AND THE MECHANICS

20+
BACHMAN TURNER
  OVERDRIVE
CREEDENCE CLEARWATER
  REVIVAL
CROSBY, STILLS, NASH
  AND YOUNG
DEXYS MIDNIGHT
  RUNNERS
ELECTRIC LIGHT
  ORCHESTRA
EMERSON, LAKE AND
  PALMER

FREDDIE AND THE
  DREAMERS
GERRY AND THE
  PACEMAKERS
HOOTIE AND THE
  BLOWFISH
K.C. AND THE SUNSHINE
  BAND
LADYSMITH BLACK
  MAMBAZO
MANIC STREET PREACHERS
SIOUXSIE AND THE
  BANSHES
SLY AND THE FAMILY
  STONE

STAGE AND SCREEN STARS

STAGE AND SCREEN STARS

3

BOW, Clara (US film actress)
COX, Robert (English comic actor)
FOY, Eddie (US actor)
HAY, Will (British comedian)
LAW, Jude (British actor)
LEE, Bruce (US actor)
LEE, Gypsy Rose (US entertainer)
RAY, Satyajit (Indian film director)
RIX, Sir Brian (British actor)
SIM, Alastair (Scottish actor)

4

ARNE, Susanna Maria (British actress)
BIRD, Theophilus (English actor)
BOND, Edward (British dramatist)
CAGE, Nicolas (US actor)
CANE, Andrew (English actor)
CHAN, Jackie (Hong Kong actor)
CHER (US actress)
COBB, Lee J. (US actor)
COOK, Peter (British comedy actor)
DALY, Augustin (US theatre manager)
DEAN, James (US film actor)
DEPP, Johnny (US actor)
DERN, Bruce (US actor)
DERN, Laura (US actress)
DIAZ, Cameron (US actress)
DUFF, Mrs (US actress)
DUSE, Eleonora (Italian actress)
FORD, John (US film director)
FORD, Harrison (US actor)
GISH, Lillian (US actress)
GOLD, Jimmy (British comedian)
GRAY, 'Monsewer' Eddie (British comedian)
HALL, Sir Peter (British theatre director)
HAWN, Goldie (US actress)
HOPE, Bob (US comedian, born in Britain)
HUNT, Helen (US actress)
HURT, William (US actor)
KEAN, Edmund (British actor)
KNOX, Teddy (British comedian)
JUDD, Ashley (US actress)
LAHR, Bert (US actor)
LANG, Fritz (German film director)
LEAN, Sir David (British film director)
MARX, Groucho (US comedian)
OWEN, Alun Davies (British dramatist)
PAGE, Geraldine (US actress)

PIAF, Edith (French cabaret singer)
PITT, Brad (US actor)
RANK, J.Arthur (British industrialist and film executive)
REED, Sir Carol (British film director)
REID, Beryl (British actress)
RIGG, Diana (British actress)
RYAN, Meg (US actress)
SHER, Anthony (British actor)
TREE, Sir Herbert Beerbohm (British actor and theatre manager)
WEST, Mae (US actress)
WISE, Ernie (British comedian)

5

ALLEN, Chesney (British comedian)
ALLEN, Woody (US film actor and director)
ARMIN, Robert (British actor)
ASKEY, Arthur (British comedian)
BADEL, Alan (British actor)
BARON, André (French actor)
BARON, Michel (French actor)
BARRY, Elizabeth (English actress)
BARRY, Spranger (Irish actor)
BATES, Alan (British actor)
BATES, Kathy (British actress)
BETTY, William Henry West (British boy actor)
BLAIR, Linda (US actress)
BLETHYN, Brenda (British actress)
BLOOM, Claire (British actress)
BOOTH, Barton (British actor)
BOOTH, Edwin Thomas (US actor)
BOOTH, Junius Brutus (US actor)
BOYER, Charles (French film actor)
BRICE, Fanny (US actress)
BROOK, Peter (British theatre director)
BROWN, Pamela (British actor)
BRYAN, Dora (British actress)
CAINE, Sir Michael (British actor)
CANDY, John (US actor)
CAPRA, Frank (US film director, born in Italy)
CAREY, Joyce (British actress)
CARNÉ, Marcel (French film director)
CLAIR, René (French film director)
CLIVE, Kitty (British actress)
CLOSE, Glenn (US actress)
CONTI, Italia (British actress)
CROWE, Russell (NZ actor)
DAFOE, Willem (US actor)

62

5 continued
DAMON, Matt (US actor)
DAVIS, Bette (US film actress)
DENCH, Dame Judi (British actress)
DUNST, Kirsten (US actress)
EDWIN, John (British actor)
EKHOF, Konrad (German actor and director)
EVANS, Dame Edith (British actress)
FLYNN, Errol (Australian actor, born in Tasmania
FONDA, Henry (US film actor and director)
FONDA, Jane (US film actress)
GABIN, Jean (French film actor)
GABLE, Clark (US film actor)
GARBO, Greta (Swedish actress)
GOZZI, Carlo (Italian dramatist)
GRANT, Cary (US film actor, born in England)
GRANT, Hugh (British actor)
GWYNN, Nell (English actress)
HAIGH, Kenneth (British actor)
HANDL, Dame Irene (British actress)
HANKS, Tom (US actor)
HAWKS, Howard (US film director)
HICKS, Sir Seymour (British actor-manager)
HOGAN, Paul (Australian actor)
IRONS, Jeremy (British actor)
JAMES, Sid (British actor)
KAZAN, Elia (US stage and film director and novelist)
KELLY, Grace (US film actress)
KORDA, Sir Alexander (British film producer and director)
LANGE, Jessica (US actress)
LA RUE, Danny (British female impersonator)
LEIGH, Vivien (British actress)
LENYA, Lotte (German actress and singer)
LEWIS, Juliette (US actress)
LIFAR, Serge (Russian ballet dancer and choreographer)
LLOYD, Harold (US film comedian)
LLOYD, Marie (British music-hall entertainer)
LOCKE, Sondra (US actress)
LOPEZ, Jennifer (US actress)
LOREN, Sophia (Italian film actress)
LOSEY, Joseph (US film director)
LUCAS, George (US film director, writer)
MAYER, Louis B (US film producer, born in Russia)
MILES, Bernard (British theatre director)
MILLS, Sir John (British actor)
MOORE, Demi (US actress)
MOORE, Dudley (British actor and song writer)
NERVO, Jimmy (British comedian)
NIVEN, David (British film actor)
O'NEAL, Ryan (US actor)
PAIGE, Elaine (British actress and singer)
PASCO, Richard (British actor)
PETIT, Roland (French ballet dancer and choreographer)
POLUS (Greek tragic actor)
POPOV, Alexei Dmitrevich (Russian director)
POPOV, Oleg Konstantinovich (Russian clown)
POWER, Tyrone (US actor)
PRYCE, Jonathan (British actor)
QUAID, Dennis (US actor)
RYDER, Winona (US actress)
ROBEY, Sir George Edward (British music-hall comedian)
RUSSO, Rene (US actress)
SCOTT, Ridley (British film director)
SEGAL, Steven (US actor)
SMITH, Maggie Natalie (British actress)
SMITH, Will (US actor)
STONE, Sharon (US actress)
TANDY, Jessica (US actress)
TERRY, Dame Ellen Alice (British actress)
TOPOL, Chaim (Israeli actor)
TRACY, Spencer (US film actor)
TUTIN, Dorothy (British actress)
TYLER, Liv, (US actress)
WAJDA, Andrzej (Polish film director)
WAYNE, John (US film actor)

6
ADRIAN, Max (British actor)
AINLEY, Henry (British actor)
AITKEN, Maria (British actress)
ALIZON (French actor)
ALLEYN, Edward (English actor)
ALTMAN, Robert (US film director)
ARNAUD, Yvonne Germaine (French actress)
ARTAUD, Antonin (French actor, poet, producer, and theoretician of the theatre)
ASHTON, Sir Frederick (British ballet dancer and choreographer, born in Ecuador)
ATKINS, Eileen (British actress)
BACALL, Lauren (US actress)
BARDOT, Brigitte (French film actress)
BARNUM, Phineas Taylor (US showman)

STAGE AND SCREEN STARS

6 continued

BAYLIS, Lilian (British theatre manager)
BEATTY, Warren (US actor)
BEJART, Joseph (French actor)
BEJART, Maurice (French ballet dancer and choreographer)
BENING, Annette (US actress)
BENSON, Sir Frank (British actor-manager)
BLASIS, Carlo (Italian dance teacher)
BOCAGE (French actor)
BOGART, Humphrey (US film actor)
BRANDO, Marlon (US actor)
BRIERS, Richard (British actor)
BROOKE, Gustavus Vaughan (British actor)
BROUGH, Lionel (British actor)
BROWNE, Robert (English actor)
BRYANT, Michael (British actor)
BUNUEL, Luis (Spanish film director)
BURTON, Richard Walter (British actor, born in Wales)
CAGNEY, James (US actor)
CALLOW, Simon (British actor)
CANTOR, Eddie (US singer and actor)
CARREY, Jim (US actor)
CASSON, Sir Lewis (British actor and director)
CIBBER, Colley (British actor-manager)
COLMAN, Ronald (British actor)
CONWAY, William Augustus (British actor)
COOPER, Dame Gladys (British actress)
COOPER, Gary (US film actor)
COWARD, Sir Noel (British dramatist, composer, and actor)
COWELL, Joe Leathley (British actor)
CRANKO, John (British choreographer, born in South Africa)
CROSBY, Bing (US popular singer and film actor)
CRUISE, Tom (US actor)
CURTIS, Tony (US film actor)
DE NIRO, Robert (US actor)
DE SICA, Vittorio (Italian film director)
DEVINE, George Alexander Cassady (British theatre manager, director, and actor)
DEVITO, Danny (US actor)
DIGGES, Dudley (British actor)
DISNEY, Walt (US film producer and animator)
DRAPER, Ruth (US actress)
DREYER, Carl Theodor (Danish film director)
DRIVER, Minnie (British actress)

DUNCAN, Isadora (US dancer)
DUVALL, Robert (US actor)
FIELDS, Gracie (British popular entertainer)
FIELDS, W.C. (US actor)
FINLAY, Frank (British actor)
FINNEY, Albert (British actor)
FISHER, Carrie (US actress)
FLEURY (French actor)
FOKINE, Michel (Russian ballet dancer and choreographer)
FORMAN, Milos (Czech film director)
FORMBY, George (British music hall, singer)
FOSTER, Jodie (US actress)
GIBSON, Mel (US actor/director)
GODARD, Jean-Luc (French film director)
GORING, Marius (British actor)
GRAHAM, Martha (US ballet dancer and choreographer)
GUITRY, Sacha (French actor and dramatist)
HARLOW, Jean (US film actress)
HERZOG, Werner (German film director)
HILLER, Dame Wendy (British actress)
HOWARD, Leslie (British actor of Hungarian descent)
HUNTER, Holly (US actress)
IRVING, Sir Henry (British actor and manager)
JACOBI, Derek (British actor)
JOLSON, Al (US actor and singer)
JONES, Vinny (British actor)
JORDAN, Dorothy (British actress)
JOUVET, Louis (French actor and theatre
KEATON, Buster (US silent film comedian)
KEITEL, Harvey (US actor)
KEMBLE, John Philip (British actor and manager)
KENDAL, Felicity (British actress)
KIDMAN, Nicole (Australian actress)
KILMER, Val (US actor)
KOONEN, Alisa Georgievna (Russian actress)
LANDEN, Dinsdale (British actor)
LAUDER, Sir Harry (Scottish singer and music-hall comedian)
LEMMON, Jack (US actor)
LESSER, Anton (British actor)
LILLIE, Beatrice Gladys (British actress, born in Canada)
LIPMAN, Maureen (British actress)
MARTIN, Mary (US actress)
MARTIN, Steve (US Actor)
MASSEY, Daniel (British actor)

64

6 continued

McEWAN, Geraldine (British actress)
McKERN, Leo (British actor)
MERMAN, Ethel (US actress)
MONROE, Marilyn (US film actress)
MORLEY, Robert (British actor)
MURPHY, Eddie (US actor)
NEESON, Liam (Irish actor)
NEWMAN, Paul (US actor)
O'TOOLE, Peter (British actor)
PACINO, Al (US actor)
PORTER, Eric (British actor)
QUAYLE, Sir Anthony (British actor)
REEVES , Keanu (US actor)
ROBSON, Dame Flora (British actress)
ROGERS, Ginger (US actress and singer)
ROWLEY, Thomas (English dramatist and actor)
SHARIF, Omar (Egyptian born US film actor)
SHUTER, Ned (British actor)
SINDEN, Donald (British actor)
SLATER, Christian (US actor)
SNIPES, Wesley (US actor)
SPACEK, Sissy (US actress)
STEELE, Tommy (British singer and actor)
STREEP, Meryl (US actress)
SUZMAN, Janet (British actress)
TAYLOR, Elizabeth (US film actress, born in England)
TEARLE, Godfrey Seymour (British actor)
TEMPLE, Shirley (US film actress)
TILLEY, Vesta (British music-hall entertainer)
WALKEN, Christopher (US actor)
WARREN, William (US actor, born in Britain)
WEAVER, Signourney (US actress)
WELCHE, Rachel (French actress)
WELLES, Orson (US film actor and director)
WILDER, Billy (US film director, born in Austria)
WILLIS, Bruce (US actor)
WOLFIT, Sir Donald (British actor)

7

ACHURCH, Janet (British actress)
ACKLAND, Joss (British actor)
AESOPUS, Claudius (Roman tragic actor)
AFFLECK, Ben (US actor)
ALLGOOD, Sara (Irish actress)
ANISTON, Jennifer (US actress)
ANTOINE, André (French actor, director, and theatre manager)

ASTAIRE, Fred (US actor and dancer)
BALDWIN, Alec (US actor)
BEAUVAL (French actor)
BELLAMY, George Anne (British actress)
BENNETT, Hywel (British actor)
BENNETT, Jill (British actress)
BERGMAN, Ingmar (Swedish film and stage director)
BERGMAN, Ingrid (Swedish actress)
BERGNER, Elisabeth (Austrian actress)
BINOCHE, Juliette (US actress)
BLAKELY, Colin (British actor)
BOGARDE, Dirk (British film actor)
BRANAGH, Kenneth (British actor)
BRESSON, Robert (French film director)
BROSNAN, Pierce (Irish actor)
BULLOCK, Sandra (US actress)
BURBAGE, Richard (English actor)
BURSTYN, Ellen (US actress)
CALVERT, Louis (British actor)
CAMERON, James (Canadian born US film director)
CARLYLE, Robert (British actor)
CASARÉS, Maria (French actress)
CELESTE, Céline (French actress)
CHABROL, Claude (French film director)
CHAPLIN, Charlie (US film actor, born in Britain)
CLOONEY, George (US actor)
COLBERT, Claudette (US film actress, born in France)
COLLIER, Constance (British actress)
COLLINS, Joan (British actress)
COMPTON, Fay (British actress)
CONNERY, Sean (Scottish actor)
CORALLI, Jean (Italian ballet dancer and choreographer
COSTNER, Kevin (US actor/director)
DEBURAU, Jean-Gaspard (French
DEJAZET, Pauline-Virginie (French actress)
DELYSIA, Alice (French actress and singer)
DE MILLE, Cecil B (US film producer and director)
DENEUVE, Catherine (French actress)
DOGGETT, Thomas (British actor)
DOTRICE, Roy (British actor)
DOTRICE Michel (British actress)
DOUGLAS, Kirk (US film actor)
DOUGLAS, Michael (US film actor)
DUNAWAY, Faye (US actress)
DURANTE, Jimmy (US actor and singer)

7 continued

EDWARDS, Blake (US film director)
ELLIOTT, Denholm (British actor)
FELLINI, Federico (Italian film director)
FIENNES, Ralph (British actor)
FONTEYN, Dame Margot (British ballet dancer)
GARLAND, Judy (US singer and film actress)
GARRICK, David (English actor)
GIELGUD, Sir John (British actor)
GINGOLD, Hermione (British actress)
GOLDWYN, Samuel (US film producer)
GOODING Jnr, Cuba (US film director)
GREGORY, Lady Augusta (Irish theatre patron and dramatist
GUTHRIE, Tyrone (British theatre director)
HANCOCK, Sheila (British actress)
HANCOCK, Tony (British comedian)
HAWTREY, Sir Charles (British actor-manager
HEPBURN, Audrey (British actress)
HEPBURN, Katherine (US actress)
HOFFMAN, Dustin (US film actor)
HOPKINS, Sir Anthony (British actor)
HORDERN, Sir Michael (British actor)
HOSKINS, Bob (British actor)
HOUDINI, Harry (US magician)
IFFLAND, August Wilheim (German actor)
JACKSON, Glenda (British actress)
JOHNSON, Dame Celia (British actress)
KARLOFF, Boris (British character actor)
KUBRICK, Stanley (US film writer, director, and producer)
LACKAYE, Wilton (US actor)
LANGTRY, Lillie (British actress, known as the 'Jersey Lily')
LAROQUE (French actor)
LEDOYER, Virginnie (French actress)
LEOTARD, Jules (French acrobat and music-hall performer)
MADONNA (US actress and singer)
MARCEAU, Marcel (French mime)
MARKOVA, Dame Alicia (British ballet dancer)
MASSINE, Leonide (Russian ballet dancer choreographer)
McKENNA, Siobhan (Irish actress)
McQUEEN, Steve (US film actor)
MICHELL, Keith (Australian actor)
NUREYEV, Rudolf (Russian ballet dancer)
OLIVIER, Laurence Kerr, Lord (British actor)
OXBERRY, William (British actor)

PALTROW, Gwyneth (British actress)
PAVLOVA, Anna (Russian ballet dancer)
PAXINOU, Katina (Greek actress)
PLUMMER, Christopher (Canadian actor)
PORTMAN, Eric (British actor)
QUILLEY, Denis (British actor)
RAMBERT, Dame Marie (British ballet dancer and choreographer
REDFORD, Robert (US film actor-director)
RISTORI, Adelaide (Italian actress)
RITCHIE, Guy (British film director)
ROBARDS, Jason (US actor)
ROBBINS, Jerome (US ballet dancer and choreographer)
ROBERTS, Julia (US actress)
ROBESON, Paul Bustil (US singer/actor)
RUSSELL, Ken (British film director)
RUSSELL, Kurt (US actor)
SALVINI, Tommaso (Italian actor)
SELLERS, Peter (British comic actor)
SIDDONS, Sarah (English actress)
STEWART, James (US film actor)
STRITCH, Elaine (US actress)
SWAYZEE, Patrick (US actor)
TEMPEST, Dame Marie (British actress)
ULANOVA, Galina (Russian ballet dancer)
USTINOV, Peter Alexander (British actor, director, and dramatist)
VESTRIS, Madame (British actress)
WINDSOR, Barbra (British actress)
WINSLET, Kate (British actress)
WITHERS, Googie (British actress)

8

ABINGTON, Frances (British actress)
ALDRIDGE, Ira Frederick (US actor)
ANDERSON, Dame Judith (Australian actress)
ANDREINI, Francesco (Italian actor-manager and playwright)
ANDREINI, Giovann Battista (Italian actor)
ANDREINI, Isabella (Italian actress)
ASHCROFT, Dame Peggy (British actress)
BADDELEY, Hermione (British actress)
BANCROFT, Anne (US actress)
BANDERAS, Antonio (US actor)
BANKHEAD, Tallulah (US actress)
BARRAULT, Jean-Louis (French director)
BASINGER, Kim (US actress)
BERENGER, Tom (US actor)
BERKELEY, Busby (US dance director)

8 continued

BORISOVA, Yulia Konstantinovna (Russian actress)
BRASSEUR, Pierre (French actor)
BUCHANAN, Jack (Scottish actor-manager)
CALDWELL, Zoë (Australian actress)
CAMPBELL, Mrs Patrick (British actress)
CHANNING, Carol (US actress and singer)
CLEMENTS, Sir John (British actor-manager)
CONNOLLY, Billy (British actor)
CRAWFORD, Joan (US film actress)
CRAWFORD, Michael (British actor)
DANCOURT, Florent (French actor and play wright)
DE LA TOUR, Frances (British actress)
DE VALOIS, Dame Ninette (British ballet dancer and choreographer, born in Ireland)
DEVRIENT, Ludwig (German actor)
DICAPRIO, Leonardo (US actor)
DIETRICH, Marlene (German film actress and singer)
DUFRESNE (French actor)
EASTWOOD, Clint (US film actor-director)
ESTCOURT, Richard (English actor)
FLAHERTY, Robert (US film director)
FLANAGAN, Bud (British comedian)
FLETCHER, Louise (US actress)
FLORENCE, William Jermyn (US actor)
GOLDBERG, Whoopi (US actress)
GOLDBLUM, Jeff (US actor)
GRENFELL, Joyce (British actress)
GRIERSON, John (British film director)
GRIFFITHS, Melanie (US actress)
GRIMALDI, Joseph (British clown)
GUINNESS, Sir Alec (British actor)
HARRISON, Rex (British actor)
HELPMANN, Sir Robert Murray (Australian ballet dancer, choreographer, and actor)
KINGSLEY, Ben (British actor)
KUROSAWA, Akira (Japanese film director)
KYNASTON, Ned (English actor)
LANSBURY, Angela (US actress)
LAUGHTON, Charles (British actor)
LAWRENCE, Gertrude (British actress)
LEIGHTON, Margaret (British actress)
LUHRMANN, Baz (US film director0
MacREADY, William Charles (British actor and theatre manager)
MATTHEWS, Jessie (British actress)
McGREGOR, Ewan (British actor)
McKELLEN, Ian (British actor)

MERCOURI, Melina (Greek actress and
NAUGHTON, Charlie (British comedian)
NAZIMOVA, Alla (Russian actress)
NIJINSKY, Vaslav (Russian ballet dancer)
PFEIFFER, Michelle ((US actress)
PICKFORD, Mary (Canadian-born US film actress)
POLANSKI, Roman (Polish film director, born in Paris)
REDGRAVE, Amanda (British actress)
REDGRAVE, Corin (British actor)
REDGRAVE, Lynn (British actress)
REDGRAVE, Sir Michael (British actor)
REDGRAVE, Vanessa (British actress)
ROBINSON, Edward G (US film actor, born in Romania
SARANDON, Susan (US actress)
SCOFIELD, Paul (British actor)
SELZNICK, David O. (US film producer)
STALLONE, Sylvester (US actor)
STROHEIM, Erich von (US film director and actor
THOMPSON, Emma (British actress)
TRAVOLTA, John (US actor)
VISCONTI, Luchino (Italian film director)
WHITELAW, Billie (British actress)
WILLIAMS, Kenneth (British comic actor)
WILLIAMS, Michael (British actor)
WILLIAMS, Robin (US actor)
ZIEGFELD, Florenz (US theatrical producer)

9

ANTONIONI, Michelangelo (Italian film maker)
BARKWORTH, Peter (British actor)
BARRYMORE, Drew (US actress)
BARRYMORE, Ethel (US actress)
BARRYMORE, John (US actor)
BARRYMORE, Lionel (US actor)
BARRYMORE, Maurice (British actor)
BELLECOUR (French actor)
BELLEROSE (French actor-manager)
BERIOSOVA, Svetlana (Russian ballet dancer)
BERNHARDT, Sarah (French
BETTERTON, Thomas (English actor)
CHEVALIER, Maurice (French singer/actor)
COURTENAY, Tom (British actor)
DEPARDIEU, Gerard (french actor)
DIAGHILEV, Sergei (Russian ballet impresario)
DU MAURIER, Sir Gerald (British actor)

STAGE AND SCREEN STARS

9 continued
FAIRBANKS Jr, Douglas (US film actor)
FAVERSHAM, William (US actor)
FERNANDEL, (French comedian)
FEUILLERE, Edwige (French actress)
GRAMATICA, Irma (Italian actress)
GROSSMITH, George (British actor)
GRUNDGENS, Glustav (German actor)
LAPOTAIRE Jane (British actress)
MacMILLAN, Sir Kenneth (British ballet
  dancer and choreographer)
MALKOVICH, John (US actor)
MONCREIFF, Gladys (Australian actress)
MORECOMBE, Eric (British comedian)
NICHOLSON, Jack (US film actor)
PECKINPAH, Sam (US film director)
PLEASENCE, Donald (British actor)
PLOWRIGHT, Joan Anne (British actress)
PREMINGER, Otto (US film director, born in
  Austria)
REINHARDT, Max (Austrian theatre director)
SPIELBERG, Steven (US film director)
STERNBERG, Josef von (US film director,
  born in Austria)
STREISAND, Barbra (US singer and actress)
TARANTINO, Quentin (US film director)
THORNDIKE, Dame Sybil (British actress)
VALENTINO, Rudolf (US film actor, born in
  Italy)
ZELLURGER, Renee (US actress)
ZETA JONES, Catherine (British actress)

10
BALANCHINE, George (US ballet dancer and
  choreographer, born in Russia)
BASSERMANN, Albert (German actor)
BELLEROCHE (French actor)
BERTOLUCCI, Bernardo (Italian film director)
BOUCICAULT, 'Dot' (British actor-manager)
BOUCICAULT, Nina (British actress)
CARTWRIGHT, William (English actor)
CUNNINGHAM, Merce (US dancer and
  choreographer)
D' OYLY CARTE, Richard (British theatre
  impresario and manager)
EISENSTEIN, Sergei (Russian film director)
FASSBINDER, Rainer Werner (German film
  director)
GUTTENBURG, Steve (US actor)
LITTLEWOOD, Joan (British theatre director)
MONTFLEURY (French actor)

RICHARDSON, Ian (British actor)
RICHARDSON, Joely (British actress)
RICHARDSON, Sir Ralph (British actor)
ROSSELLINI, Roberto (Italian film director)
RUTHERFORD, Dame Margaret (British
  actress)
WASHINGTON, Denzel (US actor)
WOFFINGTON, Peg (Irish actress)
ZEFFIRELLI, G. Franco (Italian director and
  stage designer)

11
BEAUCHÂTEAU (French actor)
BIANCOLELLI, Giuseppe Domenico (French
  actor)
BONHAM CARTER, Helena (British actress)
BRACEGIRDLE, Anne (English actress)
BRAITHWAITE, Dame Lilian (British actress)
COURTNEIDGE, Dame Cicely (British
  actress)
DAUVILLIERS (French actor)
MACLIAMMÓIR, Micheál (Irish actor and
  dramatist)
MASTROIANNI, Marcello (Itallan actor)
MISTINGUETT (French singer and
  comedienne)
SCHLESINGER, John (British film director)
SCOTT THOMAS, Kristin (US actress)
SILVERSTONE, Alicia (US actress)

12
ATTENBOROUGH, Sir Richard (British film
  actor/ director)
MARX BROTHERS (US family of comic film
  actors)
STANISLAVSKY, Konstantin (Russian actor
  and theatre director)

13
ROSCIUS GALLUS, Quintus (Roman actor

14
MIZOGUCHI KENJI (Japanese film director)
SCHWARZENEGGER, Arnold (US actor)

15
FORBES-ROBERTSON, Sir Johnston (British
  actor-manager)
GRANVILLE-BARKER, Harley (British theatre
  director)

SCIENTISTS AND INVENTORS

3

DAM, Carl Peter Henrik 1895–1976; Danish biochemist)

· KAY, John (1704– *c.* 1764; British inventor)

LEE, Tsung-Dao (1926– ; US physicist)

OHM, Georg Simon (1787–1854; German physicist)

RAY, John (1627–1705; English naturalist)

4

ABEL, Niels Henrik (1802–29; Norwegian

ABEL, Sir Frederick Augustus (1827–1902; British chemist)

ADER, Clément (1841–1926; French engineer and inventor)

AIRY, Sir George Biddell (1801–92; British astronomer

BAER, Kart Ernest von (1792–1876; Russian embryologist)

BELL, Alexander Graham (1847–1922; Scottish scientist and inventor)

BENZ, Karl (1844–1929; German engineer)

BIRO, Laszio (1900–85; Hungarian inventor)

BOHR, Niels Henrik David (1885–1962; Danish physicist)

BORN, Max (1882–1970; British physicist)

BOSE, Sir Jagadis Chandra (1858–1937; Indian plant physiologist and physicist)

COHN, Ferdinand Julius (1839–1884; German botanist)

COKE, Thomas William, of Holkham, Earl of Leicester (1752–1842; British agriculturalist)

CORT, Henry (1740–1800; British inventor)

DAVY, Sir Humphry (1778–1829; British chemist and inventor)

EADS, John Buchanan (1820–87; US civil engineer)

FUST, Johann (1400–66; German printer)

GOLD, Thomas (1920– ; Austrian-born astronomer)

GRAY, Asa (1810–88; US botanist)

HAHN, Otto (1879–1968; German chemist and physicist)

HESS, Victor Francis (1883–1964; US physicist)

HOWE, Elias (1819–67; US inventor)

KOCH, Robert (1843–1910; German bacteriologist)

LAND, Edwin Herbert (1909–91; US inventor)

LAUE, Max Theodor Felix Von (1879–1960; German physicist)

LOEB, Jacques (1859–1924; US zoologist)

MACH, Ernest (1838–1916; Austrian physicist)

MAYO (family of US medical researchers)

OTIS, Elisha Graves (1811–61; US inventor)

OTTO, Nikolaus August (1832–91; German engineer)

RABI, Isidor Isaac (1898–88 ; US physicist)

RYLE, Sir Martin (1918–84; British astronomer)

SWAN, Sir Joseph Wilson (1828–1914; British physicist)

TODD, Alexander Robertus, Baron (1907–97; British biochemist)

TULL, Jethro (1674–1741; English agriculturalist and inventor of the seed drill)

UREY, Harold Clayton (1893–1981; US physicist)

WATT, James (1736–1819; British engineer)

YANG, Chen Ning (1922– ; US physicist)

5

ADAMS, John Couch (1819–92; English astronomer)

AIKEN, Howard Hathaway (1900–73; US mathematician)

AMICI, Giovanni Battista (1786–1863; Italian astronomer, microscopist, and optical instrument maker)

ASTON, Francis William (1877–1945; British chemist)

AVERY, Oswald Theodore (1877–1955; Canadian bacteriologist)

BACON, Roger (*c.* 1214– *c.* 1292; English scientist)

BAILY, Francis (1774–1844; British amateur astronomer)

BAIRD, John Logie (1888–1946; British electrical engineer)

BAKER, Sir Benjamin (1840–1907; British civil engineer)

BANKS, Sir Joseph (1743–1820; British botanist and explorer)

BATES, Henry Walter (1825–92; British naturalist and explorer)

BEEBE, Charles William (1877–1962; US explorer and mathematican)

BETHE, Hans Albrecht (1906– ; US physicist)

5 continued

BLACK, Joseph (1728–99; Scottish physician)

BLOCH, Felix (1905–83 ; US physicist)

BOOLE, George (1815–64; British cosmologist and mathematician)

BOSCH, Carl (1874–1940; German chemist)

BOTHE, Walther Wilhelm Georg Franz (1891–57; German experimental physicist)

BOVET, Daniel (1907–92; Swiss pharmacologist)

BOWEN, Norman Levi (1887–1956; Canadian experimental petrologist)

BOWER, Frederick Orpen (1855–1948; British botanist)

BOYLE, Robert (1627–91; British physicist and chemist)

BRAGG, Sir Williarn Henry (1862–1942; British physicist)

BRAHE, Tycho (1546–1601; Danish astronomer)

BROWN, Robert (1773–1858; Scottish botanist)

BURGE, Joost (1552–1632; Swiss mathematician

CHAIN, Sir Ernst Boris (1906–79; British biochemist)

CREED, Frederick (1871–1957; Canadian inventor)

CRICK, Francis Harry Compton (1916– ; British biophysicist)

CURIE, Marie (1867–1934; Polish chemist)

CURIE, Pierre (1859–1906; French physicist biochemist)

DEBYE, Peter Joseph Wilhelm (1884–1966; Dutch physicist and chemist)

DIELS, Otto Paul Hermann (1876–1954; German chemist)

DIRAC, Paul Adrien Maurice (1902–84; British physicist)

ELTON, Charles (1900–91; British zoologist)

EULER, Leonhard (1707–83; Swiss mathematician)

EVANS, Oliver (1755–1819; US engineer)

FABRE, Jean Henri (1823–1915; French entomologist)

FABRY, Charles (1867–1945; French physicist)

FERMI, Enrico (1901–54; US physicist)

FREGE, Gottlob (1848–1925; German mathematician and logician)

GABOR, Dennis (1900–79; British electrical engineer)

GALLE, Johann Gottfried (1812–1910; German astronomer)

GAUSS, Karl Friedrich (1777–1855; German mathematician)

GEBER, (14th century; Spanish alchemist)

GIBBA, Josiah Willard (1839–1903; US physicist)

GODEL, Kurt (1906–78; US mathematician)

HABER, Fritz (1868–1934; German chemist and inventor)

HARDY, Godfrey Harold (1877–1947; British mathematician)

HENRY, Joseph (1797–1878; US physicist)

HOOKE, Robert (1635–1703; British physicist)

HOYLE, Sir Fred (1915– ; British astronomer)

JEANS, Sir James Hopwood (1877–1946; British mathematician and astronomer)

JOULE, James Prescott (1818–89; British physicist)

KOLBE, Hermann (1818–84; German chemist)

KREBS, Sir Hans Adolf (1900–81; British biochemist)

LAWES, Sir John Bennet (1814–1900; British agriculturalist)

LIBBY, Willard Frank (1908–80; US chemist)

LODGE, Sir Oliver Joseph (1851–1940; British physicist)

LYELL, Sir Charles (1797–1875; British geologist)

MAXIM, Sir Hiram Stevens (1840–1916; British inventor)

MAYER, Julius Robert Von (1814–78; German physicist)

MONGE, Gaspard (1746–1818; French mathematician)

MONOD, Jacques-Lucien (1910–76; French biochemist)

MORSE, Samuel Finley Breese (1791–1872; US inventor)

NOBEL, Alfred Bernhard (1833–96; Swedish chemist)

NOBLE, Sir Andrew (1831–1915; British physicist)

PAULI, Wolfgang (1900–58; US physicist)

POPOV, Aleksandr Stepanovich (1859–1905; Russian physicist)

PROUT, William (1785–1850; British chemist)

RAMAN, Sir Chandrasekhara Venkata (1888–1970; Indian physicist)

5 continued

RHINE, Joseph Banks (1895–1980; US psychologist)

ROSSE, William Parsons, 3rd Earl Of (1800–67; Irish astronomer)

SEGRÈ, Emilio (1905–89; US physicist)

SMITH, Sir Keith Macpherson (1890–1955; Australian aviator)

SODDY, Frederick (1877–1956; British chemist)

STAHL, Georg Ernst (1660–1734; German physician and chemist)

TATUM, Edward Lawrie (1909–75; US geneticist)

TESLA, Nikola (1856–1943; US electrical engineer)

VOLTA, Alessandro Giuseppe Antonio, Anastasio, Count (1745–1827; Italian physicist)

WEBER, Ernst Heinrich (1795–1878; German physiologist)

WHITE, Gilbert (1720–93; English naturalist)

YOUNG, Thomas (1773–1829; British physician and physicist)

6

ACHARD, Franz Karl (1753–1821; German chemist)

ADRIAN, Edgar Douglas, 1st Baron (1889–1977; British physiologist)

AGNESI, Maria Gaetana (1718–99; Italian mathematician and philosopher)

ALFVEN, Hannes Olof Gösta (1908–95; Swedish astrophysicist)

AMPÈRE, André Marie (1775–1836; French physicist)

APPERT, Nicolas (1750–1841; French inventor)

ARCHER, Frederick Scott (1813–57; British inventor and sculptor)

BAEYER, Adolf Von (1835–1917); German chemist)

BEADLE, George Wells (1903–89; US geneticist)

BODONI, Giambattista (1740–1813; Italian printer)

BOLAYI, János (1802–60; Hungarian mathematician)

BONNET, Charles (1720–93); Swiss naturalist)

BORDET, Jules Jean Baptiste Vincent (1870–1961; Belgian bacteriologist)

BRAMAH, Joseph (1748–1814; British inventor)

BRIGGS, Henry (1561–1630; English mathematician)

BRUNEL, Isambard Kingdom (1806–59; British engineer)

BUFFON, Georges Louis Leclerc, Comte de (1707–88; French naturalist)

BUNSEN, Robert Wilhelm (1811–99; German chemist)

CALVIN, Melvin (1911–97; US biochemist)

CANTOR, Georg (1845–1918; Russian mathematician

CARNOT, Sadi (1796–1832; French scientist and soldier)

CARREL, Alexis (1843–1944; French surgeon)

CARVER, George Washington (1864–1943; US agriculturalist)

CAUCHY, Augustin Louis, Baron (1789–1857; French mathematician)

CAXTON, William (*c.* 1422–91; first English printer)

CAYLEY, Arthur (1821–95; British mathematician)

CAYLEY, Sir George (1773–1857; British engineer and pioneer of flying machines)

CUVIER, Georges, Baron (1769–1832; French zoologist)

DALTON, John (1766–1844; British chemist)

DARWIN, Charles Robert (1809–1882; British naturalist)

DE BARY, Heinrich Anton (1831–88; German botanist)

DE DUVE, Christian (1917– ; Belgian biochemist)

DREYER, Johan Ludvig Emil (1852–1926; Danish astronomer)

DU MONT, Alien Balcom (1901–65; US engineer)

DUNLOP, John Boyd (1840–1921; Scottish inventor)

ECKERT, John Presper (1919–95; US electronics engineer)

EDISON, Thomas Alva (1847–1931; US inventor)

ENDERS, John Franklin (1897–1985; US microbiologist)

ENGLER, Gustav Heinrich Adolf (1844–1930; German botanist)

EUCLID (*c.* 300 BC; Greek mathematician)

FERMAT, Pierre de (1601–65; French printer)

SCIENTISTS AND INVENTORS

6 continued

FINSEN, Niels Ryberg (1860–1904; Danish physician)

FOKKER, Anthony Hermann Gerard (1890–1939; Dutch aircraft manufacturer)

FRISCH, Karl Von (1886–1982; Austrian zoologist)

FRISCH, Otto Robert (1904–79; Austrian-born physicist)

FULTON, Robert (1765–1815; American inventor) '

GALOIS, Evariste (1811–32; French mathematician)

GALTON, Sir Francis (1822–1911; British scientist)

GEIGER, Hans (1882–1945; German physicist)

GESNER, Conrad (1516–65; Swiss physician)

GRAHAM, Thomas (1805–69; British physicist)

HALLEY, Edmund (1656–1742; British astronomer)

HEVESY, George Charles Von (1885–1966; Hungarian-born chemist)

HOOKER, Sir William Jackson (1785–1865; British botanist)

HUBBLE, Edwin Powell (1889–1953; US astronomer)

HUTTON, James (1726–97; Scottish physician)

HUXLEY, Thomas Henry (1825–95; British biologist)

JANSKY, Karl Guthe (1905–50; US radio engineer)

JENSON, Nicolas (c. 1420–80; French printer

JOLIOT, Frédéric (1900–59; French physicist)

KELVIN, William Thomson, 1st Baron (1824–1907, Scottish physicist)

KEPLER, Johannes (1571–1630; German astronomer)

KINSEY, Alfred (1894–1956: US zoologist and sociologist)

LANDAU, Lev Davidovich (1908–68; Russian physicist)

LARTET, Édouard Armand Isidore Hippolyte (1801–71; French archaeologist)

LIEBIG, Justus, Baron Von (1803–73; German chemist)

LORENZ, Konrad (1903–89; Austrian zoologist)

LOVELL, Sir Bernard (1913– ; British astronomer)

MARKOV, Andrei Andreevich (1856–1922; Russian mathematician)

MARTIN, Archer John Porter (1910– ; British biochemist)

MARTIN, Pierre-Émile (1824–1915; French engineer)

MCADAM, John Loudon (1756–1836; British inventor)

MENDEL, Gregor Johann (1822–84; Austrian botanist)

MORGAN, Thomas Hunt (1866–1945; US geneticist)

MORLEY, Edward Williams (1838–1923; US chemist)

MORRIS, Desmond John (1928– ; British zoologist)

MULLER, Hermann Joseph (1890–1967; US geneticist)

MULLER, Paul Hermann (1899–1965; Swiss chemist)

NAPIER, John (1550–1617; Scottish mathematician)

NERNST, Walther Hermann (1864–1941; German physical chemist)

NEWTON, Sir Isaac (1642–1727; British physicist and mathematician)

OLBERS, Heinrich Wilhelm Matthäus (1758–1840; German astronomer)

PASCAL, Blaise (1623–62; French mathematician and physicist)

PENNEY, William George Baron (1909–91; British mathematician)

PERKIN, Sir William Henry (1838–1907; British chemist)

PERRIN, Jean-Baptiste (1870–1942; French physicist)

PLANCK, Max Karl Ernst Ludwig (1858–1947; German physicist)

POWELL, Cecil Frank (1903–69; British physicist)

PROUST, Joseph-Louis (1754–1826; French chemist)

RAMSAY, Sir William (1852–1916; Scottish chemist)

RENNIE, John (1761–1821; British civil engineer)

SANGER, Frederick (1918– ; British chemist)

SAVERY, Thomas (c. 1650–1715; English engineer)

SHOLES, Christopher Latham (1811–90; US inventor)

6 continued

SINGER, Isaac Merrit (1811–75; US inventor)
SLOANE, Sir Hans (1660–1753; British physician and naturalist)
STOKES, Sir George Gabriel (1819–1903;
STRUVE, Otto (1897–1963; US astronomer)
SUTTON, Walter Stanborough (1877–1916; US geneticist)
TALBOT, William Henry Fox (1800–77; British botanist and physicist)
TAYLOR, Brook (1685–1737; English mathematician)
TAYLOR, Frederick Winslow (1856–1915; US engineer)
TELLER, Edward (1908– ; US physicist)
TOWNES, Charles Hard (1915– ; US physicist)
VAUBAN, Sébastian Le Prestre de (1633–1707; French military engineer)
WALLIS, Sir Barnes (1887–1979; British aeronautical engineer)
WALTON, Ernest Thomas Sinton (1903–95; Irish physicist)
WATSON, James Dewey (1928– ; US geneticist)
WIENER, Norbert (1894–1964; US mathematician)
WILSON, Eugene Paul (1902–95; US physicist)
WILSON, Charles Thomson Rees (1869–1959; British physicist)
WILSON, Edmund Beecher (1856–1939; US biologist)
WÖHLER, Friedrich (1800–82; German chemist)
WRIGHT, Orville (1871–1948; US aviator)
YUKAWA, Hideki (1907–81; Japanese physicist)
ZEEMAN, Pieter (1865–1943; Dutch physicist)

7

AGASSIZ, Jean Louis Rodolphe (1807–73; Swiss natural historian)
ALVAREZ, Luis Walter (1911–85; US physicist)
AUDUBON, John James, (1785–1851; US naturalist)
BABBAGE, Charles (1792–1871; British mathematician and inventor)
BARDEEN, John (1908–91; US physicist)
BARNARD, Edward Emerson (1857–1923; US astronomer)
BATESON, William (1861–1926; British biologist)

BATTANI, Al- (c. 858–929; Islamic astronomer)
BERGIUS, Friedrich (1884–1949; German chemist)
BORLAUG, Norman Ernest (1914– ; US plant breeder)
BRAILLE, Louis (1809–52; French inventor of system of writing and printing for the blind)
BROUWER, Luitzen Egbertus Jan (1881–1966; Dutch mathematician)
BURBANK, Luther (1849–1926; US plant breeder)
CANDELA, Felix (1910–97; Mexican engineer)
CARDANO, Girolamo (1501–76; Italian mathematician)
COMPTON, Arthur Holly (1892–1962; US physicist)
CORRENS, Carl Erich (1864–1933; German botanist and geneticist)
COULOMB, Charles, Augustin de (1736–1806; French physicist)
CROOKES, Sir William (1832–1919; British physicist)
CURTISS, Glenn (1878–1930; US aviator and aeronautical engineer)
DAIMLER, Gottlieb (1834–1900; German inventor)
DANIELL, John Frederic (1790–1845; British chemist)
DE LA RUE, Warren (1815–89; British astronomer)
DE VRIES, Hugo Marie (1848–1935; Dutch botanist)
DOPPLER, Christian Johann (1803–53; Austrian physicist)
DRIESCH, Hans Adolf Eduard (1867–1941; German zoologist)
EICHLER, August Wilhelm (1839–87; German botanist)
FARADAY, Michael (1791–1867; British chemist and physicist)
FEYNMAN, Richard Phillips (1918–88; US physicist)
FISCHER, Emil Hermann (1852–1919; German chemist)
FLEMING, Sir John Ambrose (1849–1945; British electrical engineer)
FOURIER, Jean Baptiste Joseph, Baron (1768–1830; French mathematician and physicist)

SCIENTISTS AND INVENTORS

7 continued

FRESNEL, Augustin Jean (1788–1827; French physicist)

GAGARIN, Yuri Alekseevich (1934–68; Russian cosmonaut)

GALVANI, Luigi (1737–98; Italian physician)

GILBERT, William (1544–1603; English physicist)

GODDARD, Robert Hutchings (1882–1945; US physicist)

GREGORY, James (1638–75; Scottish mathematician and astronomer)

HAECKEL, Ernst Heinrich (1834–1919; German zoologist)

HAWORTH, Sir Walter Norman (1883–1950; British biochemist)

HELMONT, Jan Baptist van (1580–1644; Belgian alchemist and physician)

HERMITE, Charles (1822–1901; French mathematician)

HILBERT, David (1862–1943; German mathematician)

HODGKIN, Dorothy Mary Crowfoot (1910–94 British biochemist)

HOPKINS, Sir Frederick Gowland (1861–1947; British biochemist)

HUGGINS, Sir William (1824–1910; British astronomer)

HUYGENS, Christiaan (1629–95; Dutch astronomer and physicist)

KAPITZA, Peter Leonidovich (1894–1984; Russian physicist

KENDALL, Edward Calvin (1886–1972; US biochemist)

KENDREW, Sir John Cowdery (1917–97 British biochemist)

KHORANA, Har Gobind (1922– ; US biochemist)

KIDINNU (4th century BC; Babylonian mathematician and astronomer)

KOZYREV, Nikolai Aleksandrovich (1908– Russian astronomer)

LALANDE, Joseph-Jérôme le Français de (1732–1807; French astronomer)

LAMARCK, Jean-Baptiste de Monet, Chevalier de (1744–1829; French naturalist)

LAMBERT, Johann Heinrich (1728–77; German mathematician and astronomer)

LANGLEY, Samuel Pierpont (1834–1906; US astronomer)

LAPLACE, Pierre Simon, Marquis de (1749–1827; French mathematician and astronomer)

LESSEPS, Ferdinand de (1805–94; French diplomat)

LOCKYER, Sir Joseph Norman (1836–1920; British astronomer)

LORENTZ, Hendrick Antoon (1853–1928; Dutch physicist)

LUMIÉRE, Auguste (1862–1954; French photographer and inventor)

LYSENKO, Trofim Denisovich (1898–1976; Russian biologist

MARCONI, Guglielmo (1874–1937; Italian electrical engineer

MAXWELL, James Clerk (1831–79; Scottish physicist)

MEITNER, Lise (1878–1968; Austrian physicist)

MESSIER, Charles (1730–1817; French astronomer)

MOSELEY, Henry Gwyn Jeffries (1887–1915, British physicist)

NEUMANN, John Von (1903–57; US mathematician)

OERSTED, Hans Christian (1777–1851; Danish physicist)

ONSAGER, Lars (1903–76; US chemist)

OSTWALD, Wilhelm (1853–1932; German chemist)

PARSONS, Sir Charles Algernon (1854–1931; British engineer)

PASTEUR, Louis (1822–95; French chemist and microbiologist)

PAULING, Linus Carl (1901–94; US chemist)

PICCARD, (family of Swiss scientists)

POISSON, Siméon Dénis (1781–1840; French mathematician)

PRANDTL, Ludwig (1875–1953; German physicist)

PTOLEMY (Claudius Ptolemaeus, 2nd century AD; Egyptian mathematician, astronomer and geographer)

PURCELL, Edward Mills (1912–97; US physicist)

RÉAMUR, René-Antoine Ferchault de (1683–1757; French physicist)

RIEMANN, Georg Friedrich Bernhard (1826–66; German mathematician

RUMFORD, Benjamin Thompson, Count (1753–1814; American-born scientist)

7 continued

SANDAGE, Allan Rex (1926– ; US astronomer)

SCHEELE, Carl Wilhelm (1742–86; Swedish chemist)

SCHWANN, Theodor (1810–82; German physiologist)

SEABORG, Glenn Theodore (1912–99; US physicist)

SHEPARD Jr, Alan Bartlett (1923–98; US astronaut)

SIEMENS, Ernst Werner von (1816–92; German electrical engineer)

SIMPSON, George Gaylord (1902–84; US palaeontologist)

SZILARD, Leo (1898–1964; US physicist)

TELFORD, Thomas (1757–1834; British civil engineer)

THENARD, Louis-Jacques (1777–1857; French chemist)

THOMSON, Sir Joseph John (1856–1940; British physicist)

TUPOLEV, Andrei Niklaievich (1888–1972; Russian designer

TYNDALL, John (1820–93; Irish physicist)

VAVILOV, Nikolai Ivanovich (1887–1943; Russian plant geneticist)

WAKSMAN, Selman Abraham (1888–1973; US microbiologist)

WALLACE, Alfred Russel (1823–1913; British naturalist)

WEGENER, Alfred Lothar (1880–1930; German geologist)

WHITNEY, Eli (1765–1825; American inventor)

WHITTLE, Sir Frank (1907–96; British aeronautical engineer)

WILKINS, Maurice Hugh Frederick (1916– New Zealand physicist)

ONSAGER, Lars (1903–76; US chemist)

OSTWALD, Wilhelm (1853–1932; German chemist)

PARSONS, Sir Charles Algernon (1854–1931; British engineer)

ZIEGLER, Karl (1898–1973, German chemist)

8

AGRICOLA, Georgius (1494–1555; German physician and mineralogist)

ANDERSON, Carl David (1905–91; US physicist)

ANGSTRÖM, Anders Jonas (1814–74; Swedish physicist and astronomer)

AVOGADRO, Amedeo, Conte di Quaregna e Ceretto (1776–1856; Italian physicist)

BAKEWELL, Robert (1725–95; British agriculturalist)

BESSEMER, Sir Henry (1813–98; British engineer and inventor)

BIRKHOFF, George David (1864–1944; US mathematician)

BJERKNES, Vilhelm Friman Koren (1862–1951; Norwegian meteorologist and physicist)

BLACKETT, Patrick Maynard Stuart, Baron (1897–1974; British physicist)

BRATTAIN, Walter Houser (1902–87; US physicist)

BREWSTER, Sir David (1781–1868; Scottish physicist)

BRIDGMAN, Percy Williams (1882–1961; US physicist)

BRINDLEY, James (1716–72; British canal builder)

BUSHNELL, David (1742–1824; US inventor; built the first submarine)

CALMETTE, Albert Léon Charles (1863–1933; French bacteriologist)

CHADWICK, Sir James (1891–1974; British physicist)

CLAUSIUS, Rudolf Julius Emanuel (1822–88, German physicist)

CROMPTON, Samuel (1753–1827; British inventor)

CULPEPER, Nicholas (1616–54; English physician)

DAGUERRE, Louis-Jacques-Mandé (1789–1851; French inventor)

DEDEKIND, Richard (1831–1916; German mathematician)

DE FOREST, Lee (1873–1961; US electrical engineer)

DE MORGAN, Augustus (1806–71; British mathematician and logician)

EINSTEIN, Albert (1879–1955; German physicist)

ERICSSON, John (1803–89; US naval engineer and inventor)

FOUCAULT, Jean Bernard Léon (1819–68, French physicist)

GASSENDI, Pierre (1592–1655; French physicist)

GUERICKE, Otto Von (1602–86; German physicist)

8 continued

HAMILTON, Sir William Rowan (1805–65; Irish mathematician)

HERSCHEL, Sir William (1738–1822; British astronomer)

ILYUSHIN, Sergei Vladimirovich (1894–1977; Russian aircraft designer)

IPATIEFF, Vladimir Nikolaievich (1867–1952; US physicist)

JACQUARD, Joseph-Marie (1752–1834; French inventor)

KENNELLY, Arthur Edwin (1861–1939; US electrical engineer)

KLAPROTH, Martin Heinrich (1743–1817; German chemist)

KOROLIOV, Sergei Pavlovich (1906–66; Russian aeronautical engineer)

LAGRANGE, Joseph Louis, Comte de (1736–1813; French mathematician and astronomer)

LAWRENCE, Ernest Orlando (1901–58; US physicist)

LEGENDRE, Adrien Marie (1752–1833; French mathematician)

LEMAÎTRE, Georges Édouard, Abbé (1894–1966; Belgian priest and astronomer)

LEUCKART, Karl Georg Friedrich Rudolph

LINNAEUS, Carolus (Carl Linné; 1707–78;

LIPSCOMB, William Nunn (1919– ; US chemist)

LONSDALE, Dame Kathleen (1903–71; Irish

MAUDSLAY, Henry (1771–1831; British engineer)

MCMILLAN, Edwin Mattison (1907–91; US physict

MERCATOR, Gerardus (1512–94; Flemish geographer)

MEYERHOF, Otto Fritz (1884–1951; US biochemist)

MILLIKAN, Robert Andrews (1868–1953; physicist)

MITCHELL, Reginald Joseph (1895–1937 British aeronautical engineer)

MULLIKEN, Robert Sanderson (1896–1986; US chemist and physicist)

NEWCOMEN, Thomas (1663–1729; English blacksmith and inventor of steam engine)

OLIPHANT, Sir Mark Laurence Elwin (1901–2000; Australian physicist)

POINCARÉ, Jules Henri (1854–1912; French mathematician)

RAYLEIGH, John William Strutt, 3rd Baron (1842–1919; British physicist)

RHETICUS (1514–76; German mathematician)

ROBINSON, Sir Robert (1886–1975; British chemist)

ROEBLING, John Augustus (1806–69; US engineer

ROENTGEN, Wilhelm Konrad (1845–1923; German physicist)

SABATIER, Paul (1854–1941; French chemist)

SAKHAROV, Andrei Dimitrievich (1921–89 Russian physicist)

SHOCKLEY, William Bradfield (1910–89, US physicist

SHRAPNEL, Henry (1761–1842; British army officer, who invented the shrapnel shell)

SIKORSKY, Igor Ivan (1889–1972; aeronautical engineer)

STIRLING, James (1692–1770; Scottish mathematician)

VAN ALLEN, James Alfred (1914– ; US physicist)

VAN'T HOFF, Jacobus Henricus (1852–1911; Dutch chemist)

WEISMANN, August Friedrich Leopold (1834–1914; German biologist)

WOODWARD, Robert Burns (1917–79; US chemist)

ZERNICKE, Frits (1888–1966; Dutch physicist)

ZWORYKIN, Vladimir Kosma (1889–1982; US physicist)

9

ABU-AL-WAFA (940–98 AD; Persian mathematician and astronomer)

ARKWRIGHT, Sir Richard (1732–92; British inventor)

ARMSTRONG, Edwin Howard (1890–1954 US electrical engineer)

ARMSTRONG, William George, Baron (1810–1900; British engineer)

ARRHENIUS, Svante August (1859–1927; Swedish physicist and chemist)

BECQUEREL, Henri (1852–1908; French physicist)

BERNOULLI (family of Swiss scientists)

BERTHELOT, Marcelin (1827–1907; French

BERZELIUS, Jöns Jakob, Baron (1779–1848;

BOLTZMANN, Ludwig Eduard (1844–1906; Austrian physicist)

9 continued

BRONOWSKI, Jacob (1908–74; British mathematician

CAVENDISH, Henry (1731–1810; British physicist

CHEBISHEV, Pafnuti Lvovich (1821–94; Russian mathematician

CHERENKOV, Pavel Alekseievich (1904–90 Russian physicist)

COCKCROFT Sir John Douglas (1897–1967; British physicist)

CORNFORTH, Sir John Warcup (1917– ; Australian chemist)

D'ALEMBERT, Jean Le Rond (1717–83; French mathematician)

DAUBENTON, Louis Jean Marie (1716–1800; French naturalist)

DAVENPORT, Charles Benedict (1866–1944; US zoologist)

EDDINGTON, Sir Arthur Stanley (1882–1944; British theoretical astronomer)

ENDLICHER, Stephan Ladislaus (1804–49; Hungarian botanist)

FIBONACCI, Leonardo (c. 1170– c. 1230; Italian mathematician)

FLAMSTEED, John (1646–1719; English astronomer)

GAY-LUSSAC, Joseph Louis (1778–1850; French chemist and physicist)

GUTENBERG, Johann (c. 1400– c. 1468; German printer)

HEAVISIDE, Oliver (1850–1925; British physicist)

HELMHOLTZ, Hermann Ludwig Ferdinand von (1821–94; German physicist and physiologist)\

HOPKINSON, John (1849–98; British physicist and electrical engineer)

JOHANNSEN, Wilhelm Ludvig (1857–1927; Danish geneticist)

JOSEPHSON, Brian David (1940– ; British physicist)

KIRCHHOFF, Gustav Robert (1824–87; German physicist)

KURCHATOV, Igor Vasilievich (1903–60; Russian physicist)

LANKESTER, Sir Edwin Ray (1847–1929;

LAVOISIER, Antoine Laurent (1743–94; French chemist)

LEVERRIER, Urbain Jean Joseph (1811–77; French astronomer)

LIOUVILLE, Joseph (1809–82; French mathematician)

MACINTOSH, Charles (1766–1843; Scottish chemist)

MACMILLAN, Kirkpatrick (d. 1878; Scottish inventor)

MICHELSON, Albert Abraham (1852–1931; US physicist

NICHOLSON, William (1753–1815; British chemist)

NIRENBERG, Marshall Warren (1927– ; US biochemist)

PELLETIER, Pierre Joseph (1788–1842; French chemist)

PRIESTLEY, Joseph (1733–1804; British chemist)

REMINGTON, Eliphalet (1793–1863; US inventor)

SCHLEIDEN, Matthias Jakob (1804–81; German botanist)

STEINMETZ, Charles Proteus (1865–1923; US electrical engineer)

TINBERGEN, Nikolaas (1907–88; Dutch zoologist and pioneer ethologist)

ZSIGMONDY, Richard Adolph (1865–1929; Austrian chemist)

ZUCKERMAN, Solly, Baron (1904–84; British anatomist)

10

ARCHIMEDES (c. 287– c. 212 BC; Greek mathematician and inventor)

ARROWSMITH, Aaron (1750–1823; British cartographer)

BARKHAUSEN, Heinrich (1881–1956; German physicist)

BERTHOLLET, Claude Louis, Comte (1748–1822; French chemist and physician)

BLENKINSOP, John (1783–1831; British engineer)

CANNIZZARO, Stanislao (1826–1910; Italian chemist)

CARTWRIGHT, Edmund (1743–1823; British inventor)

COPERNICUS, Nicolaus (1473–1543; Polish astronomer)

DOBZHANSKY, Theo (1900–75;geneticist)

FITZGERALD, George Francis (1851–1901; Irish physicist)

FOURNEYRON, Benolit (1802–67; French engineer

SCIENTISTS AND INVENTORS

10 continued

FRAUNHOFER, Joseph Von (1787–1826; German physicist)

HARGREAVES, James (d. 1778; English inventor

HEISENBERG, Werner Karl (1901–76; German physicist)

HIPPARCHUS (c. 190– c. 120 BC; Greek astonomer

HOFMEISTER, Wilhelm Friedrich Benedict (1824–77; German botanist)

INGENHOUSZ, Jan (1730–99; Dutch physician and plant physiologist)

KOLMOGROV, Andrei Nikoloaevich (1903– ; Russian mathematician)

LILIENTHAL, Otto (1848–96; German aeronautical engineer)

LIPPERSHEY, Hans (d. c. 1689; Dutch lens grinder)

MAUPERTUS, Pierre Louis Morceau de (1698–1759; French mathematician)

MENDELEYEV, Dimitri Ivanovich (1834–1907; Russian chemist)

METCHNIKOV, Ilya Ilich (1845–1916; Russian zoologist)

RUTHERFORD, Ernest, 1st Baron (1871–1837; English physicist)

SOMMERFELD, Arnold Johannes Wilheim (1868–1951; German physicist)

STAUDINGER, Hermann (1881–1965; German chemist)

STEPHENSON, George (1781–1848; British engineer)

SWAMMERDAM, Jan (1637–80; Dutch naturalist and microscopist)

TORRICELLI, Evangelista (1608–47; Italian physicist)

TOURNEFORT, Joseph Pitton de (1656–1708; French botanist)

TREVITHICK, Richard (1771–1833; British engineer)

WATSON-WATT, Sir Robert Alexander (1892–1973; Scottish physicist)

WHEATSTONE, Sir Charles (1802–75; British physicist)

11

AL-KHWARIZMI, Muhammed Ibn Musa (c. 780– c. 850 AD; Arabic mathematician)

BASKERVILLE, John (1706–75; British printer)

BHOSKHARA II (1114– c. 1185; Indian mathematician)

CHAMBERLAIN, Owen (1920– ; US physicist)

GOLDSCHMIDT, Richard Benedict (1878–1958; US geneticist)

HINSHELWOOD, Sir Cyril Norman (1897–1967; British chemist)

JOLIOT-CURIE, Irène (1896–1956; French chemist)

LE CHATELIER, Henri-Louis (1850–1936;

LEEUWENHOEK, Antonie van (1632–1723; Dutch scientist)

LOBACHEVSKI, Nikolai Ivanovich (1793–1856; Russian mathematician)

MONTGOLFIER, Jacques-Éttienne (1745–99; French balloonist and inventor)

NOSTRADAMUS (1503–66; French physician and astrologer)

OPPENHEIMER, J Robert (1904–67; US physicist)

SCHRODINGER, Erwin (1887–1961; Austrian physicist)

SHERRINGTON, Sir Charles Scott (1857–1952; British physiologist)

SPALLANZANI, Lazzaro (1729–99; Italian physiologist)

TSIOLKOVSKI, Konstantin Eduardovich (1857–1935; Russian aeronautical engineer)

VAN DER WAALS, Johannes Diderik (1837–1923; Dutch physicist)

12

AMBARTSUMIAN, Viktor Amazaspovich (1908–96; Russian astrophysicist)

SZENT-GYORGYI, Albert (1893–1986; US biochemist)

13

ARAGO FRANCOIS (1786–1853; French astronomer and physicist)

CHANDRASEKHAR, Subrahmanyan (1910–95; US astronomer)

REGIOMONTANUS (1436–76; astronomer and mathematician)

14

GALILEO GALILEI (1564–1642; Italian mathematician, physicist, and astronomer) Greek astronomer and mathematician)

EXPLORERS AND ADVENTURERS

4

BYRD, Richard E (1888–1957; US explorer)

CANO, Juan Sebastian del (c. 1460–1526; Spanish navigator)

COOK, Captain James (1728–79; British navigator)

DIAS, Bartolomeu (c. 1450– c. 1500; Portugese navigator)

EYRE, Edward John (1815–1901; British explorer)

GAMA, Vasco da (c. 1469–1524; Portugese navigator)

HUME, Hamilton (1797–1873; Australian explorer)

HUNT, John, Baron (1910–98; British mountaineer)

KIDD, William (c. 1645–1701; Scottish sailor)

PARK, Mungo (1771– c. 1806; Scottish explorer)

POLO, Marco (c. 1254–1324; Venetian traveller)

ROSS, Sir James Clark (1800–62; British explorer)

SOTO, Hernando de (?1496–1542; Spanish explorer)

5

BAKER, Sir Samuel White (1821–93; British explorer)

BARTH, Heinrich (1821–65; German explorer and geographer)

BOONE, Daniel (1734–1820; American pioneer)

BRUCE, James (1730–94; British explorer)

BURKE, Robert O'Hara (1820-61; Irish explorer)

CABOT, John (Giovanni Caboto, c. 1450– c. 1499; Italian explorer)

DAVIS, John (or J Davys, c. 1550-1605; English navigator)

FUCHS, Sir Vivian (1908–99; British explorer)

LAIRD, Macgregor (1808–61;.Scottish explorer)

OATES, Lawrence Edward Grace (1880–1912; British explorer)

ONATE, Juan de (d. 1630; Spanish conquistador)

PARRY, Sir William Edward (1790–1855; British navigator)

PEARY, Robert Edwin (1856–1920; US explorer)

SCOTT, Robert Falcon (1868–1912; British explorer)

SPEKE, John Hanning (1827–64; British explorer)

STURT, Charles (1795–1869; British explorer)

TEACH, Edward (d. 1718; British pirate)

6

ALCOCK, Sir John (1892–1919; British aviator)

BAFFIN, William (c. 1584–1622; English navigator)

BALBOA, Vasco Nunez de (c. 1475–1517; Spanish explorer)

BERING, Vitus Jonassen (1681–1741; Danish navigator)

BRAZZA, Pierre Paul Francois Camille. Savorgnan de (1852–1905; French explorer)

BROOKE, Sir James (1803–68; British explorer)

BURTON, Sir Richard (1821–90; British explorer)

CABRAL, Pedro Alvares (?1467–1520; Portuguese navigator)

CARSON, Kit (Christopher c, 1809–68; US frontiersman)

CORTES, Hernan (1485–1547; Spanish conquistador)

HUDSON, Henry (d. 1611; English navigator)

MORGAN, Sir Henry (c. 1635–88; Welsh buccaneer)

NANSEN, Fridtjof (1861–1930; Norwegian explorer)

NOBILE, Umberto (1885–1978; Italian aviator)

STUART, John McDouall (1815–66; Scottish explorer)

TASMAN, Abel Janszoon (c. 1603– c. 1659; Dutch navigator)

7

BARENTS, Willem (c. 1550–97; Dutch navigator)

BLERIOT, Louis (1872–1936; French aviator)

CARPINI, Giovanni da Pian del (c. 1180– c. 1252; Italian traveller)

CÓRDOBA, Francisco Fernandez do (d. 1518; Spanish explorer)

EXPLORERS AND ADVENTURERS

7 continued

COVILHÃ, Pêro da (c. 1460– c. 1526; Portuguese explorer)

EARHART, Amelia (1898–1937; US aviator)

FIENNES, Sir Ranulph (1944– ; British, "The World's Greatest Living Explorer")

GILBERT, Sir Humphrey (c. 1539–83; English navigator)

HAWKINS, Sir John (1532–95; English navigator)

HILLARY, Sir Edmund (1919– New Zealand mountaineer and explorer)

HINKLER, Herbert John Lewis (1892–1933; Australian aviator)

LA SALLE, Robert Cavelier, Sieur de (1643–87; French explorer)

MCCLURE, Sir Robert John Le Mesurier (1807–73; Irish explorer)

PIZARRO, Francisco (c. 1475–1541; Spanish conquistador)

PYTHEAS (4th century BC; Greek navigator)

RALEIGH, Sir Walter (1554–1618; British explorer)

SELKIRK, Alexander (1676–1721; Scottish sailor)

STANLEY, Sir Henry Morton (1841–1904; British explorer)

WILKINS, Sir George Hubert (1888–1958; British explorer)

WRANGEL, Ferdinand Petrovich, Baron von (1794–1870; Russian explorer)

8

AMUNDSEN, Roald (1872-1928; Norwegian explorer)

COLUMBUS, Christopher (1451–1506; Italian navigator)

FLINDERS, Matthew (1774–1814; British navigator and hydrographer)

FRANKLIN, Sir John (1786–1847; British explorer)

MAGELLAN, Ferdinand (c. 1480–1521; Portuguese explorer)

MARCHAND, Jean Baptiste (1863–1934; French explorer)

VESPUCCI, Amerigo (1454–1512; Italian navigator)

9

BLANCHARD, Jean Pierre François (1753–1809; French balloonist)

FROBISHER, Sir Martin (c. 1535–94; English navigator)

HEYERDAHL,Thor (1914– ;Norwegian ethnologist)

IBERVILLE, Pierre Le Moyne, Sieur d' (1661–1706; French-Canadian explorer)

LEICHARDT, Ludwig (1813–48; German explorer)

LINDBERGH, Charles A. (1902–74; US aviator)

MARQUETTE, Jacques (1637–75; French explorer)

RASMUSSEN, Knud Johan Victor (1879–1933; Danish explorer)

VANCOUVER, George, (c. 1758–98; British navigator)

VELASQUEZ, Diego (?1465–1522; Spanish explorer)

10

BARBAROSSA (Khayr ad-Din, d. 1546; Turkish pirate)

ERIC THE RED (late 10th century; Norwegian explorer)

SHACKLETON, Sir Ernest Henry (1874–1922; British explorer)

11

IBN BATTUTAH (1304–?1368; Arab traveller)

LA CONDAMINE, Charles Marie de (1701–74; French geographer)

LIVINGSTONE, David (1813–73; Scottish missionary and explorer)

PONCE DE LEON, Juan (1460–1521; Spanish explorer)

12

BOUGAINVILLE, Louis Antoine do (1729–1811; French navigator)

LEIF ERIKSSON (11th century; Icelandic explorer)

14

BELLINGSHAUSEN, Fabian Gottlieb, Baron von (1778–1852; Russian explorer)

DUMONT D'URVILLE, Jules Sébastien César (1790–1842; French navigator)

17

HENRY THE NAVIGATOR (1394–1460; Portuguese navigator and patron of explorers)

WORLD LEADERS

3

FOX, Charles James (1749–1806; British Whig politician)

LIE, Trygve (Halvdan) (1896–1968; Norwegian Labour politician)

4

BENN, Anthony Neil Wedgwood (1925– ; British Labour politician)

BLUM, Léon (1872–1950; French socialist)

BOSE, Subhas Chandra (*c.* 1897– *c.* 1945; Indian nationalist leader)

BUSH, George Herbert Walker (1900–; US statesman and president)

BUSH, George W. (1946–;US statesman and president).

COOK, Sir Joseph (1860–1947; Australian statesman)

DIAZ, Porfirio (1830–1915; Mexican soldier)

FOOT, Michael (Mackintosh) (1913– ;British Labour politician)

HILL, Sir Rowland (1795–1879; British-postal expert)

HOLT, Harold Edward (1908–67; Australian statesman)

HOWE, Sir Richard Edward Geoffrey (1926– ; British Conservative politician)

HULL, Cordell (1871–1955; US Democratic politician)

KING, Jr, Martin Luther (1929–68; US Black civil-rights leader)

KING, William Lyon Mackenzie (1874–1950; Canadian statesman)

KIRK, Norman Eric (1923–74; New Zealand statesman)

MEIR, Golda (1898–1978; Israeli stateswoman)

NAGY, Imre (1896–1958; Hungarian statesman)

OWEN, Dr David (1938– ; British politician)

RHEE, Syngman (1875–1965; Korean statesman)

TOJO (Hideki) (1884–1948, Japanese general)

TONE, Theobald Wolfe (1763–98; Irish nationalist)

TUTU, Desmond (1931– ; SouthAfrican clergyman)

WARD, Sir Joseph George (1856–1930; New Zealand statesman)

5

ADAMS, Gerry (1946– ; Northern Ireland Republican leader)

AGNEW, Spiro Theodore(1918– ;US Republican politician)

ASTOR, Nancy Witcher, Viscountess (1879–1964; British politician)

BANDA, Hastings Karnuzu (1905–97; Malawi statesman)

BEGIN, Menachem (1913–92; Israeli statesman)

BEVAN, Aneurin (1897–1960; British Labour politician)

BEVIN, Ernest (1881–1951; British politician)

BOTHA, Louis (1862–1919; South African statesman)

CLARK, Charles Joseph (1939– ; Canadian statesman)

DAYAN, Moshe (1915–81; Israeli general)

DEBRÉ, Michel (1912–96; French statesman)

DESAI, Shri Morarji Ranchhodji (1896–1995; Indian statesman)

DE WET, Christian Rudolf (1854–1922; Afrikaner politician and soldier)

EBERT, Friedrich (1871–1925; German statesman)

EMMET, Robert (1778–1803; Irish nationalist)

LAVAL, Pierre (1883–1945; French statesman)

LENIN, Vladimir Ilich (V I Ulyanov, 1870–1924; Russian revolutionary)

LODGE, Henry Cabot (1850–1924; US Republican politician)

LYNCH, Jack (1917–99; Irish statesman)

LYONS, Joseph Aloysius (1879–1939; Australian statesman)

MANIN, Daniele (1804–57; Italian patriot)

MENON, Krishna (Vengalil Krishnan Krishna Menon, 1896–1974; Indian diplomat)

NEHRU, Jawaharlal (1889–1964; Indian statesman)

NIXON, Richard Milhous (1913–99; US statesman and president)

NKOMO, Joshua (1917–99; Zimbabwean politician)

OBOTE, Apollo Milton (1924– ; Ugandan statesman)

PERÓN, Juan Domingo (1895–1974: Argentine statesman)

5 continued

SADAT, Anwar (1918–81; Egyptian leader)

SMITH, Ian Douglas (1919– ; Rhodesian prime minister)

SMUTS, Jan Christiaari (1870–1950; South African statesman and general)

SPAAK, Paul Henri (1899–1972; Belgian statesman)

STEEL, David Martin Scott (1938– ; British politician)

VANCE, Cyrus (1917– ;US statesman)

VILLA, Pancho (Francesco V, 1878–1923; Mexican revolutionary)

6

ARAFAT, Yassir (1929– ; Palestinian leader)

BARTON, Sir Edmund (1849–1920; Australian statesman)

BHUTTO, Benazir (1953– ; Pakistani politician)

BORDEN, Sir Robert Laird (1854–1937; Canadian statesman)

BRANDT, Willy (1913–92; West German statesman)

BRIGHT, John (1811–89; British radical politician)

BUTLER, Richard Austen, Baron (1902–82; British Conservative politician)

CHIRAC, Jacques (1932– ; French statesman)

COATES, Joseph Gordon (1878–1943; New Zealand statesman)

COBDEN, Richard (1804–65; British politician

CRIPPS, Sir Richard Stafford (1889–1952; British Labour politician)

CURTIN, John Joseph (1885–1945; Australian statesman)

CURZON, George Nathaniel, 1st Marquess (1859–1925; British politician)

DAVITT, Michael (1846–1906; Irish nationalist)

DEAKIN, Alfred (1856–1919; Australian statesman)

DJILAS, Milovan (1911–95;Yugoslav politician)

DUBCEK, Alexander (1921– ; Czechoslovak statesman)

DULLES, John Foster (1888–1959; US Republican politician and diplomat)

ERHARD, Ludwig (1897–1977; German statesman)

FADDEN, Sir Arthur William (1895–1973; Australian statesman)

FISHER, Andrew (1862–1928; Australian statesman)

FLEURY, André Hercule de, Cardinal (1653–1743; French statesman)

FORBES, George William (1869–1947; New Zealand statesman)

FRANCO, Francisco (1892–1975; Spanish general and statesman)

FRASER, John Malcolm (1930– ; Australian statesman)

FRASER, Peter (1884–1950; New Zealand statesman)

GANDHI, Indira (1917–84; Indian stateswoman)

GANDHI, Mohandas Karamchand (1869–1948; Indian nationalist leader)

GORING, Hermann Wilhelm (1893–1946, German Nazi politician)

GORTON, Sir John Grey (1911– ; Australian statesman)

GRIVAS, Georgios (1898–1974; Greek general)

HEALEY, Denis Winston (1917– ; British Labour politician)

HUGHES, William Morris (1864–1952; Australian statesman)

JUÁREZ, Benito Pablo (1806–72; Mexican statesman)

KAUNDA, Kenneth David (1924– ; Zambian statesman)

KRUGER, Stephanus Johannes Paulus (1825–1904; Afrikaner statesman)

MARCOS, Ferdinand Edralin (1917–89; Philippine statesman)

MASSEY, William Ferguson (1856–1925; New Zealand statesman)

MOBUTU, Sese Seko (Joseph Désiré M, 1930– ; Zairese statesmen)

MOSLEY, Sir Oswald Ernald (1896–1980; British fascist)

NASSER, Gamal Abdel (1918–70; Egyptian statesman)

O'BRIEN, Conor Cruise (1917– ; Irish diplomat)

O'NEILL, Terence, Baron (1914– ; Northern Irish statesman)

PÉTAIN, Henri Philippe (1856–1951; French general and statesman)

POWELL, John Enoch (1912–98; British politician)

REAGAN, Ronald Wilson (1912– ; US statesman and president)

WORLD LEADERS

6 continued
REVERE, Paul (1735–1818; American revolutionary
RHODES, Cecil John (1853–1902; South African financier and statesman)
SAVAGE, Michael Joseph (1872–1940; New Zealand statesman)
SEDDON, Richard John (1845–1906; New Zealand statesman)
STALIN, Joseph (1879–1953; Russian leader)
SUÁREZ, Adolfo, Duke of (1932– ;Spanish statesman)
THORPE, John Jeremy (1929– ; British Liberal politician)
WATSON, John Christian (1867–1941; Australian statesman)
WILKES, John (1725–97; British journalist and politician)
ZAPATA, Emiliano (?1877–1919: Mexican revolutionary)

7
ACHESON, Dean Gooderham (1893–1971; US lawyer and statesman)
ASHDOWN, Paddy (1941– ; Social and Liberal Democrat politician)
ATATURK, Kemal (Mustafa Kemal, (1881–1938; Turkish statesman
BATISTA (y Zaldivar), Fulgencio (1901–73; Cuban statesman)
BENNETT, Richard Bedford, Viscount (1870–1947; Canadian statesman)
BOLIVAR, Simon (1783–1830; South American statesman)
BORMANN, Martin (1900–45; German Nazi leader
CLINTON, de Witt (1769–1828; US statesman)
CLINTON, William Jefferson (1946– ; US statesman and president)
COLLINS, Michael (1890–1922; Irish nationalist)
GADDAFI, Moammar Al- (*or* Qaddafi, 1942– ; Libyan colonel and statesman)
GRATTAN, Henry (1746–1820, Irish politician)
GRIMOND, Joseph (1913–93; British politician)
GROMYKO, Andrey (1909–89; Russian statesman)
HIMMLER, Heinrich (1900–45, German Nazi politician)
HOLLAND, Sir Sidney George (1893–1961; New Zealand statesman)

HUSSEIN (ibn.Talal) (1935–99 ;King of Jordan)
JENKINS, Roy Harris (1920– ; British politician and historian)
KINNOCK, Neil (1942– ; Labour politician)
KOSYGIN, Aleksei Nikolaevich (1904–80; Russian statesman)
LUMUMBA, Patrice Hemery (1925–61; Congolese statesman)
MACLEOD, Iain Norman (1913–70; British Conservative politician)
MANDELA, Nelson (Rolihlahla) (1918– ; South African lawyer and politician)
MAZZINI, Giuseppe (1805–72; Italian patriot)
MCMAHON, William (1908– ; Australian statesman)
MENZIES, Sir Robert Gordon (1894–1978; Australian statesman)
MINTOFF, Dominic (1916– ; Maltese statesman)
MOLOTOV, Vyacheslav Mikhailovich (1890–1986; Russian statesman)
NYERERE, Julius Kambarage (1922–99; Tanzanian statesman)
PAISLEY, Ian (1926– ; Northern Ireland politician)
PARNELL, Charles Stewart (1846–91; Irish politician)
PEARSON, Lester Bowles (1897–1972; Canadian statesman)
RAFFLES, Sir Thomas Stamford (1781–1826; British colonial administrator)
SALAZAR, Antonio de Oliveira (1889–1970; Portuguese dictator)
SCHMIDT, Helmut (1918– ; West German statesman)
SCULLIN, James Henry (1876–1953; Australian statesman)
SHASTRI, Shri Lal Bahadur (1904–66; Indian statesman)
SUHARTO (1921– ; Indonesian statesman and general)
TROTSKY, Leon (1879–1940; Russian revolutionary)
TRUDEAU, Pierre Elliott (1919–2000; Canadian statesman)
VORSTER, Balthazar Johannes (1915–83; South African statesman)
WHITLAM, Edward Gough (1916– ; Australian statesman)

83

WORLD LEADERS

8

ADENAUER, Konrad (1876–1967; German statesman)

AMIN DADA, Idi (*c.* 1925– ; Ugandan politician and president)

AYUB KHAN, Mohammad (1907–74; Pakistani statesman)

BEN BELLA, Ahmed (1916– ; Algerian statesman)

BISMARCK, Otto Eduard Leopold, Prince Von (1815–98; Prussian statesman)

BREZHNEV, Leonid Ilich (1906–82; Russian statesman)

BUKHARIN, Nikolai Ivanovich (1888–1938; Russian politician)

BULGANIN, Nikolai Aleksandrovich (1895–1975; Russian statesman)

COSGRAVE, William Thomas (1880–1965; Irish statesman)

CROSSMAN, Richard Howard Stafford (1907–74; British Labour politician)

DALADIER, Édouard (1884–1970; French statesman)

DE GAULLE, Charles André Joseph Marie (1890–1970; French general and statesman)

DE VALERA, Eamon (1882–1975; Irish statesman)

DOLLFUSS, Engelbert (1892–1934; Austrian statesman)

DUVALIER, Frangois (1907–71; Haitian politician)

EICHMANN, Adolf (1906–62; German Nazi politician)

FRANKLIN, Benjamin (1706–90; US diplomat)

GOEBBELS, Paul Joseph (1897–1945; German Nazi politician)

GRIFFITH, Arthur (1872–1922; Irish journalist and nationalist)

HARRIMAN, William Averell (1891–1986; US diplomat)

HASTINGS, Warren (1732–1818; British colonial administrator)

HIROHITO (1901–89; Emperor of Japan)

HOLYOAKE, Sir Keith Jacka (1904–83; New Zealand statesman)

HONECKER, Erich (1912-94; East German statesman)

HUMPHREY, Hubert Horatio (1911–1978; US Democratic politician)

IBARRURI, Dolores (1895–1989; Spanish politician)

KENYATTA, Jomo (*c.* 1891–1978; Kenyan statesman)

KHOMEINI, Ayatollah Ruhollah (1900–89; Iranian Shiite Muslim leader)

MALENKOV, Georgi Maksimilianovich (1902–88; Russian statesman)

MCCARTHY, Joseph Raymond (1908–57; US Republican senator)

MORRISON, Herbert Stanley, Baron (1888–1965; British Labour politician)

MUZOREWA, Bishop Abel Tendekayi (1925– ; Zimbabwean statesman)

O'CONNELL, Daniel (1775–1847; Irish politician)

O'HIGGINS, Bernardo (?1778–1842; Chilean national hero)

PINOCHET, Augusto (1915– ; Chilean general)

PODGORNY, Nikolay (1903–83; Russian statesman)

POINCARÉ, Raymond (1860–1934; French statesman)

POMPIDOU, Georges Jean Raymond (1911–74; French statesman)

QUISLING, Vidkun Abraharn Lauritz Jonsson (1887-1945; Norwegian army officer and Nazi collaborator)

RASPUTIN, Grigori Yefimovich (*c.* 1872–1916; Russian mystic)

SIHANOUK, Norodim, Prince (1922– ; King of Cambodia)

SIKORSKI, Wladyslaw (1881–1943; Polish general and statesman)

ULBRICHT, Walter (1893–1973; East German statesman)

VERWOERD, Hendrik Frensch (1901–66; South African statesman)

WALDHEIM, Kurt (1918– ; Austrian diplomat and statesman)

WEIZMANN, Chaim Azriel (1874–1952; Israeli statesman)

WELENSKY, Sir Roy (1907–91; Rhodesian statesman)

WILLIAMS, Shirley Vivien Teresa Brittain (1930– ; British politician)

9

AGA KHAN IV (1937– ; Imamate of the Ismailite sect of Muslims)

BEN-GURION, David (1886–1973; Israeli statesman)

CASTRO RUZ, Fidel (1926– ; Cuban leader)

9 continued

CHOU EN-LAI (*or* Zhou En Lai, 1898–1976; Chinese communist statesman)

CHURCHILL, Lord Randolph Henry Spencer (1849–95; British Conservative politician)

CHURCHILL, Sir Winston Leonard Spencer (1874–1965; British statesman and prime minister during Worl War II)

GAITSKELL, Hugh (1906–63; British politician)

GARIBALDI, Giuseppe (1807–82; Italian soldier)

GORBACHOV, Mikhail Sergeevich (1931– ; Russian statesman)

HENDERSON, Arthur (1863–1935; British Labour politician)

HO CHI MINH (Nguyen That Thanh, 1890–1969; Vietnamese statesman)

KISSINGER, Henry Alfred (1923– ; US diplomat and political scientist)

LA GUARDIA, Fiorello Henry (1882–1947; US politician

LUXEMBURG, Rosa (1871–1919; German revolutionary)

MACDONALD, James Ramsay (1866–1937; British statesman)

MACDONALD, Sir John Alexander (1815–91; Canadian statesman)

MUSSOLINI, Benito Amilcare Andrea (1883–45; Italian fascist dictator)

PANKHURST, Emmeline (1858–1928; British suffragette)

STEVENSON, Adlai Ewing (1900–65; US Democratic politician)

10

BERNADOTTE, Jean Baptiste Jules (*c.* 1763–1844; French marshal)

CARRINGTON, Peter Alexander Rupert, 6th Baron (1919– ; British Conservative politician)

CLEMENCEAU, Georges (1841–1929; French statesman)

KHRUSHCHEV, Nikita Sergeevich (1894–1971; Russian statesman)

LEE KUAN YEW (1923– ; Singaporean statesman)

MAO TSE-TUNG (*or* Mao Ze Dong, 1893–1976; Chinese communist statesman)

MITTERRAND, Francois Maurice (1916–96; French socialist politician)

RIBBENTROP, Joachim von (1893–1946; German Nazi politician)

VOROSHILOV, Kliment Yefremovich (1881–1969; Russian marshal and statesman)

11

ABDUL RAHMAN, Tunku (1903–73; Malaysian statesman)

CASTLEREAGH, Robert Stewart, Viscount (1769–1822; British statesman)

DIEFENBAKER, John George (1895–1979; Canadian statesman)

HORE-BELISHA, Isaac Leslie, 1st Baron (1893–1957; British politician)

MAKARIOS III, Mikhail Khristodolou Mouskos (1913-77; Cypriot churchman/statesman)

MOUNTBATTEN (of Burma), Louis, 1st Earl (1900–79; British admiral and colonial administrator)

SELWYN LLOYD, John, Baron (1904–78; British Conservative politician)

WILBERFORCE, William (1759–1833; British philanthropist)

12

BANDARANAIKE, Solomon (1899–1959; Sri Lankan statesman)

FREI MONTALVA, Eduardo (1911–82; Chilean statesman)

MENDÈS-FRANCE, Pierre (1907–82; French statesman)

PAPADOPOULOS, George(1919– ;Greek colonel)

13

CHIANG KAI-SHEK (*or* Jiang Jie Shi, 1887–75; Nationalist Chinese statesman)

14

ALLENDE GOSSENS, Salvador (1908–73; Chilean statesman)

CLIVE OF PLASSEY, Robert Baron (1725–74; British soldier and colonial administrator)

15

GISCARD D'ESTAING, Valéry (1926– ; French statesman)

MILITARY LEADERS

3

LEE, Robert E. (1807–70; US Confederate commander)

NEY, Michel, Prince of Moscow (1769–1815; French marshal)

4

ALBA, Fernando Alvarez de Toledo, Duke of (1507–83; Spanish general)

BART, Jean (1650–1702; French admiral)

BYNG, George. Viscount Torrington (1663–1733; English admiral)

DIAZ, Porfirio (1830–1915; Mexican soldier)

FOCH, Ferdinand (1851–1929; French marshal)

HAIG, Douglas, 1st Earl (1861–1928; British field marshal)

HOOD, Samuel, 1st Viscount (1724–1816; British admiral)

HOWE, Richard, Earl (1726–99; British admiral)

JODL, Alfred (1890-1946; German general)

RAIS, Gilles de (or G de Retz, 1404–40; French marshal)

RÖHM, Ernst (1887–1934; German soldier)

ROON, Albrecht, Graf von (1803–79; Prussian general)

SAXE, Maurice, Comte de (1696–1750; Marshal of France)

SLIM, William Joseph, 1st Viscount (1891–1970; British field marshal)

TOGO (Heihachiro) (1847–1934; Japanese admiral)

5

ANDRÉ, John (1751–80; British soldier)

ANSON, George Anson, Baron (1697–1762; British admiral)

BLAKE, Robert (1599–1657; English admiral)

BLIGH, William (1754–1817; British admiral)

CIMON (d. c. 450 BC Athenian general and politician)

DEWEY, George (1837–1917; US admiral)

DRAKE, Sir Francis (1540–96; English navigator and admiral)

EL CID (Rodrigo Diaz de Vivar, c. 1040–99; Spanish warrior)

GATES, Horatio (?1728–1806; American general)

HAWKE, Edward, 1st Baron (1705–81; British admiral)

JONES, John Paul (1747–92; American naval commander)

LALLY, Thomas, Corrite de (1702–66; French general)

LEVEN, Alexander Leslie, 1st Earl of (1580–1661; Scottish general)

MOORE, Sir John (1761–1809; British general)

MURAT, Joachim (1767–1815; French marshal)

PERRY, Matthew C. (1794–1858; US naval officer)

PRIDE, Thomas (d. 1658; English parliamentary soldier)

SULLA, Lucius Cornelius (c. 138–78 BC; Roman dictator)

TILLY, Johan Tserclaes, Graf von (1559–1632; Bavarian general)

TROMP, Maarten (1598–1653; Dutch admiral)

WOLFE, James (1727–59; British soldier)

6

AETIUS, Flavius (d. 454 AD; Roman general)

ARNOLD, Benedict (1741–1801; American general)

BAYARD, Pierre Terrail, Seigneur de (c. 1473–1524; French soldier)

BEATTY, David, 1st Earl (1871–1936; British admiral)

BENBOW, John (1653–1702; English naval officer)

CRONJE, Piet Arnoldus (c. 1840–1911; South African general)

CUSTER, George Armstrong (1839–76; US cavalry general)

DARLAN, Jean (Louis Xavier) François (1881–1942; French admiral)

DÖNITZ, Karl (1891–1981; German admiral)

DUNDEE, John Graham of Claverhouse, 1st Viscount (c. 1649–89; Scottish soldier)

DUNOIS, Jean d'Orleans, Comte, de (1403–68, French general)

FISHER, John Arbuthnot, 1st Baron (1841–1920; British admiral)

FRENCH, John, 1st Earl of Ypres (1852–1925; British field marshal)

6 continued

GINKEL, Godert de, 1st Earl of Athlone (1644–1703; Dutch general)

GORDON, Charles George (1833–85; British general)

GRANBY, John Manners, Marquess of (1721–70; British soldier)

GREENE, Nathaneal (1742–86; American general)

HALSEY, William F. (1882–1959; US admiral)

JOFFRE, Joseph Jacques Césaire (1852–931; French marshal)

KEITEL, Wilhelm (1882–1946; German field marshal)

KLÉBER, Jean Baptiste (1753–1800; French general)

KONIEV, Ivan Stepanovich (1897–1973; Russian marshal)

MARIUS, Gaius (c. 157–86 BC; Roman general)

MOLTKE, Helmuth, Graf von (1800–91; Prussian field marshal)

MOREAU, Jean Victor (1763–1813; French general)

NAPIER (of Magdala), Robert Cornelis, 1st Baron (1810–90; British field marshal)

NAPIER, Sir Charles James (1782–1853; British general)

NARSES (c. 480– 574 AD; Byzantine general)

NELSON, Horatio, Viscount (1758–1805; British admiral)

NIMITZ, Chester W. (1885–1966; US admiral)

OUTRAM, Sir James (1803–63; British soldier)

PATTON, George S. (1885–1945; US general)

PAULUS, Friedrich (1890–1957; German field marshal)

PÉTAIN, (Henri) Philippe (1856–1951; French general and statesman)

RAEDER, Erich (1876–1960; German admiral)

RAGLAN, Fitzroy James Henry Somerset, 1st Baron (1788–1855; British field marshal)

RODNEY, George Brydges, 1st Baron (1719–92; British admiral)

ROMMEL, Erwin (1891–1944; German general)

RUPERT, Prince (1619–82; Cavalry officer)

RUYTER, Michiel Adriaanszoon de (1607–76; Dutch admiral)

TEDDER, Arthur William, 1st Baron (1890–1967; British air marshal)

VERNON, Edward (1684–1757; British admiral)

WAVELL, Archibald Percival, 1st Earl (1883–1950; British field marshal)

WILSON, Henry Maitland, 1st Baron (1881–1964; British field marshal)

WILSON, Sir Henry Hughes (1864–1922; British field marshal)

ZHUKOV, Georgi Konstantinovich (1896–1974; Russian marshal)

7

AGRIPPA, Marcus Vipsanius (?63–12 BC; Roman general)

ALLENBY, Edmund Henry Hynman, 1st Viscount (1861–1936; British field marshal)

ARTIGAS, José Gervasio (1764–1850; national hero of Uruguay)

ATHLONE, Alexander Cambridge. 1st Earl of (1874-1957; British soldier)

BAZAINE, Achille Frangois (1811–88; French marshal)

BERWICK, James Fitzjames, Duke of (1670–1734; Marshal of France)

BLUCHER, Gebhard Leberecht von, Prince of Wahlstatt (1742–1819; Prussian general)

BRADLEY, Omar Nelson (1893–1981; US general)

DECATUR, Stephen (1779-1820; US naval officer)

DENIKIN, Anton Ivanovich (1872–1947; Russian general)

DOWDING, Hugh Caswall Tremenheere, 1st Baron (1882–1970; British air chief marshal)

FAIRFAX, Thomas, 3rd Baron (1612–71; English general)

JACKSON, Andrew (1767–1845; US statesman and general)

JACKSON, Stonewall (Thomas Jonathan J, 1824–63; US Confederate general)

KOLCHAK, Alexander Vasilievich (1874–1920; Russian admiral)

LAMBERT, John (1619–83; English parliamentary general)

LYAUTEY, Louis Hubert Gonzalve (1854–1934; French marshal)

MASSÉNA, André (?1756–1817; French marshal)

METAXAS, Ioannis (1871–1941; Greek general)

MORTIER, Édouard Adolphe Casimir Joseph, Duc de Trévise (1768–1835; French marshal)

PHILLIP, Arthur (1738–1814; British admiral)

REGULUS, Marcus Attilus (d. c. 251 BC; Roman general)

7 continued

ROBERTS, Frederick Sleigh, 1st Earl
(1832–1914; British field marshal)

SHERMAN, William Tecumseh (1820–91; US
Federal general)

SHOVELL, Sir Cloudesley (1650–1707;
English admiral)

SUVOROV, Aleksandr Vasilievich, Count
(1729–1800; Russian field marshal)

TANCRED (c. 1078–1112; Norman
Crusader)

TIRPITZ, Alfred von (1849–1930; German
admiral)

TURENNE, Henri de la Tour d'Auvergne,
Vicomte de (1611–75; French marshal)

VENDÔME, Louis Joseph, Duc de
(1654–1712; French marshal)

VILLARS, Claude Louis Hector, Duc de
(1653–1734; French marshal)

WINGATE, Orde Charles (1903–44; British
soldier)

WRANGEL, Peter Nikolaievich, Baron
(1878–1928; Russian general)

8

AGRICOLA, Gnaeus Julius (40–93 AD Roman
govenor)

ANGLESEY, Henry William Paget, 1st
Marquess of (1768–1854; British field
marshal)

AUGEREAU, Pierre François Charles, Duc
de Castiglione (1757–1816; French
marshal)

BADOGLIO, Pietro (1871–1956; Italian
general)

BERTRAND, Henri Gratien, Comte
(1773–1844; French marshal)

BOURMONT, Louis Auguste Victor de
Ghaisnes, Comte de (1773–1846; French
marshall)

BURGOYNE, John (1722–92; British general)

CAMPBELL, Colin, Baron Clyde (1792–1863;
British field marshal)

CARDIGAN, James Thomas Brudenell, 7th
Earl of (1797–1868; British cavalry officer)

CARRANZA, Venustiano (1859–1920;
Mexican statesman and soldier)

CROMWELL, Oliver (1599–1658; English
soldier and statesman)

GUESCLIN, Bertrand du (c. 1320–80; French
commander)

HANNIBAL (247– c. 183 BC; Carthaginian
general)

IRONSIDE, William Edmund, 1st Baron
(1880–1959; British field marshall)

JELLICOE, John Rushworth, 1st Earl
(1859–1935; British admiral)

KORNILOV, Lavrentia Georgievich
(1870–1918; Russian general)

LUCULLUS, Lucius Licinius (d. c. 57 BC;
Roman general)

LYSANDER (d. 395 BC; Spartan general)

MARSHALL, George C (1880–1959; US
general)

MONTCALM, Louis Joseph do Montcalm-
Grozon, Marquis de (1712–59; French
general)

O'HIGGINS, Bernardo (?1778–1842; Chilean
national hero)

PERSHING, John J (1860–1948; US general)

SANDWICH, John Montagu, 4th Earl of
(1718–92; First lord of the admiralty)

SHERIDAN, Philip H (1831–88; US Federal
general)

WOLSELEY, Garnet Joseph, 1st Viscount
(1833–1913; British field marshal)

9

ANGOULÊME, Charles de Valois, Duc d'
(1573–1650; French soldier)

ANTIPATER (397–319 BC; Macedonian
general)

BONAPARTE, Napoleon (1769–1821; French
emperor)

DUMOURIEZ, Charles François Du Périer
(1739–1823; French general)

GNEISENAU, August, Graf Neithardt von
(1760–1831; Prussian field marshal)

GRENVILLE, Sir Richard (?1541–91; British
sailor)

KITCHENER (of Khartoum), Horatio Herbert,
1st Earl (1850–1916; British field marshal)

LAFAYETTE, Marie Joseph Gilbert Motier,
Marquis de (1757–1834; French general
and politican)

MACARTHUR, Douglas (1880–1964; US
general)

MARCELLUS, Marcus Claudius (d. 208 BC;
Roman general)

MCCLELLAN, George B (1826–85;. Federal
general)

MILTIADES (c. 550– 489 BC; Athenian general)

MILITARY LEADERS

9 continued

NEWCASTLE, William Cavendish, Duke,of (1592–1676; English soldier)

OLDCASTLE, Sir John (*c.* 1378–1417; English soldier)

PRETORIUS, Andries (1799–1853; Afrikaner leader)

RUNDSTEDT, Gerd von (1875–1953; German field marshal)

SANTA ANNA, Antonio López de (1794–1876; Mexican soldier)

TRENCHARD, Hugh Montague, 1st Viscount (1873–1956; The first British air marshal)

10

ABERCROMBY, Sir Ralph (1734–1801; British general)

ALANBROOKE, Alan Francis Brooke, 1st Viscount (1883–1963; British field marshal)

ALCIBIADES (*c.* 450– 404 BC; Athenian general and politician)

AUCHINLECK, Sir Claude (1884–1981; British field marshal)

BERNADOTTE, Jean Baptiste Jules (1763–1844)

CORNWALLIS, Charles, 1st Marquess (1738–1805; British general)

CUMBERLAND, William Augustus, Duke of (1721–65; British general)

FLAMININUS, Titus Quinctius (*c.* 230– *c.* 174 BC; Roman general)

HINDENBURG, Paul von Beneckendorff und von (1847–1934; German general)

KESSELRING, Albert (1885–1960; German general)

KUBLAI KHAN (1215–94; Mongol conqueror of China)

MANNERHEIM, Carl Gustaf Emil, Baron von (1867–1951; Finnish general)

MONTGOMERY (of Alamein), Bernard Law, 1st Viscount (1887–1976; British field marshal)

RICHTHOFEN, Manfred, Freiherr von (1892–1918; German air ace)

SCHLIEFFEN, Alfred, Graf von (1833–1913; German general)

TIMOSHENKO, Semyon Konstantinovich (1895–1970; Russian marshal)

VILLENEUVE, Pierre (1763–1806; French admiral)

WELLINGTON, Arthur Wellesley, Duke of (1769–1852; British general)

11

ALBUQUERQUE, Alfonso de (1453–1515; Portuguese governor in India)

BADEN-POWELL, Robert Stephenson Smyth, 1st Baron (1857–1941; British general)

BEAUHARNAIS. Alexandre, Vicomte de (1760-94; French general)

COLLINGWOOD, Cuthbert, 1st Baron (1750–1810; British admiral)

LIDDELL HART, Sir Basil Henry (1895–1970; British soldier)

MARLBOROUGH, John Churchill, 1st Duke of (1650–1722; British general)

MÜNCHHAUSEN, Karl Friedrich, Freiherr von (1720–97; German soldier)

12

IBRAHIM PASHA (1789–1848; Ottoman general)

SCHWARZKOPF, H. Norman (1934– ; US military commander – Gulf War 1991)

13

EUGENE OF SAVOY, Prince (1663–1736; Austrian general)

FABIUS MAXIMUS, Quintus (d. 203 BC; Roman general)

14

BARCLAY DE TOLLY, Mikhail Bogdanovich, Prince (1761–1818; Russian field marshal)

CLIVE OF PLASSEY, Robert, Baron (1725–74; British soldier and colonial administrator)

15

CASSIUS LONGINUS, Gaius (*d.* 42 BC Roman general)

SCIPIO AFRICANUS (236–183 BC; Roman general)

16

ALEXANDER OF TUNIS, Harold, 1st Earl (1891–1969; British field marshal)

17

HOWARD OF EFFINGHAM, Charles, 2nd Baron (1536–1624; English Lord High Admiral)

20+

BERNHARD OF SAXE-WEIMAR, Duke (1604–39; German general)

SCIPIO AEMILIANUS AFRICANUS (*c.* 185–29 BC; Roman general)

BRITISH PRIME MINISTERS (from 1721)

ROBERT WALPOLE (1721–42)
SPENCER COMPTON, Earl of
Wilmington (1742–43)
HENRY PELHAM (1743–54)
THOMAS PELHAM-HOLLES, Duke of
Newcastle (1754–56)
WILLIAM CAVENDISH, Duke of
Devonshire (1756–57)
THOMAS PELHAM-HOLLES, Duke of
Newcastle (1757–62)
JOHN STUART, Earl of Bute (1762–63)
GEORGE GRENVILLE (1763–65)
CHARLES WATSON-WENTWORTH,
Marquis of Rockingham (1765–66)
WILLIAM PITT, Earl of Chatham (1766–68)
AUGUSTUS HENRY FITZROY, Duke of
Grafton (1768–70)
FREDERICK NORTH (1770–82)
CHARLES WATSON-WENTWORTH,
Marquis of Rockingham (1782)
WILLIAM PETTY, Earl of Shelburne
(1782-83)
WILLIAM HENRY CAVENDISH BENTINCK,
Duke of Portland (1783)
WILLIAM PITT (Son of Earl of Chatham)
(1783–1801)
HENRY ADDINGTON (1801–04)
WILLIAM PITT (1804–06)
WILLIAM WYNDHAM GRENVILLE, Baron
Grenville (1806–07)
WILLIAM BENTINCK, Duke of Portland
(1807–09)
SPENCER PERCEVAL (1809–12)
ROBERT BANKS JENKINSON, Earl of
Liverpool (1812–27)
GEORGE CANNING (1827)
FREDERICK JOHN ROBINSON, Viscount
Goderich (1827–28)
ARTHUR WELLESLEY, Duke of
Wellington (1828–30)
CHARLES GREY, Earl Grey (1830–34)
WILLIAM LAMB, Viscount Melbourne
(1835–41)
ROBERT PEEL (1841–46)
JOHN RUSSELL (1846–52)
EDWARD GEORGE GEOFFREY SMITH
STANLEY, Earl of Derby (1852)

GEORGE HAMILTON GORDON, Earl of
Aberdeen (1852–55)
HENRY JOHN TEMPLE, Viscount
Palmerston (1855–58)
EDWARD STANLEY, Earl of Derby
(1858–59)
HENRY TEMPLE, Viscount Palmerstone
(1859–65)
JOHN RUSSELL, Earl Russell (1865–66)
EDWARD STANLEY, Earl of Derby
(1866–68)
BENJAMIN DISRAELI (1868)
WILLIAM EWART GLADSTONE (1868–74)
BENJAMIN DISRAELI, Earl of
Beaconsfield (1874–80)
WILLIAM EWART GLADSTONE (1880–85)
ROBERT GASCOYNE-CECIL, Marquis of
Salisbury (1895–1902)
ARTHUR JAMES BALFOUR (1902–05)
HENRY CAMPBELL-BANNERMAN (1905–08)
HERBERT HENRY ASQUITH (1908–16)
DAVID LLOYD GEORGE (1916–22)
ANDREW BONAR LAW (1922–23)
STANLEY BALDWIN (1923–24)
NEVILLE CHAMBERLAIN (1937–40)
WINSTON CHURCHILL (1940–45)
CLEMENT RICHARD ATTLEE (1945–51)
WINSTON CHURCHILL (1951–55)
ANTHONY EDEN (1955–57)
HAROLD MACMILLAN (1957–63)
ALEC DOUGLAS-HOME (1963–64)
HAROLD WILSON (1964–70)
EDWARD HEATH (1970–74)
HAROLD WILSON (1974–76)
JAMES CALLAGHAN (1976–79)
MARGARET THATCHER (1979–90)
JOHN MAJOR (1990–97)
TONY BLAIR (1997–)

US PRESIDENTS

GEORGE WASHINGTON (1789–97)
JOHN ADAMS (1797–1801)
THOMAS JEFFERSON (1801–09)
JAMES MADSON (1809–17)
JAMES MONROE (1817–25)
JOHN QUINCY ADAMS (1825–29)
ANDREW JACKSON (1829–37)
MARTIN VAN BUREN (1837–41)
WILLIAM HENRY HARRISON (1841)
JOHN TYLER (1841–45)
JAMES KNOX POLK (1845–49)
ZACHARY TAYLOR (1849–50)
MILLARD FILLMORE (1850–53)
FRANKLIN PIERCE (1853–57)
JAMES BUCHANAN (1857–61)
ABRAHAM LINCOLN (1861–65)
ANDREW JOHNSON (1865–69)
ULYSSES SIMPSON GRANT (1869–77)
RUTHERFORD BIRCHARD HAYES (1877–81)
JAMES ABRAM GARFIELD (1881)
CHESTER ALAN ARTHUR (1881–85)
GROVER CLEVELAND (1885–89)
BENJAMIN HARRISON (1889–93)

GROVER CLEVELAND (1893–97)
WILLIAM MCKINLEY (1897–1901)
THEODORE ROOSEVELT(1901–09)
WILLIAM HOWARD TAFT (1909–13)
WOODROW WILSON (1913–21)
WARREN GAMALIEL HARDING (1921–23)
CALVIN COOLIDGE (1923–29)
HERBERT CLARK HOOVER (1929–33)
FRANKLIN DELANO ROOSEVELT
  (1933–45)
HARRY S TRUMAN (1945–53)
DWIGHT DAVID EISENHOWER (1953–61)
JOHN FITZGERALD KENNEDY (1961–63)
LYNDON BAINES JOHNSON (1963–69)
RICHARD MILHOUS NIXON (1969–74)
GERALD RUDOLPH FORD (1974–77)
JAMES EARL CARTER (1977–81)
RONALD WILSON REAGAN (1981–89)
GEORGE HERBERT WALKER BUSH
  (1989–93)
WILLIAM JEFFERSON CLINTON (1993–2001)
GEORGE WALKER BUSH (2001–

RULERS OF ENGLAND

KINGS OF KENT

HENGEST (c. 455–488)
GERIC surnamed OISC (488–?512)
OCTA (?512–?)
EORMENRIC (?–560)
ETHELBERT II (560–616)
EADBALD (616–640)
EARCONBERT (640–664)
EGBERT I (664–673)
HLOTHERE* (673–685)
EADRIC* (685–686)
SUAEBHARD* (676–692)
OSWINI* (?688–?690)
WIHTRED* (690–725)
ETHELBERT II* (725–762)
EADBERT* (?725–?762)
ALRIC* (c. 750s)
EARDWULF* (747–762)
SIGERED* (?762)
EANMUND* (c. 759–765)
HEABERHT* (764–765)

EGBERT II (c. 765–780)
EALHMUND (784–786)
EADBERT (PRAEN) (796–798)
EADWALD (?798 or 807)
CUTHRED (798–807)
BALDRED (?–825)

KINGS OF DEIRA
AELLI (c. 560–590)
EDWIN (?590–592)
ETHELFRITH (592–616)
EDWIN (616–632)
OSRIC (632–633)
OSWALD (ST.) (633–641)
OSWINE (644–651)
ETHELWALD (651–654)

KINGS OF NORTHUMBRIA
ETHELFRITH (592–616)
EDWIN (616–632)
OSWALD (St.) (633–641)
0SWIU (654–670)

RULERS OF ENGLAND

Kings of Northumbria continued
EWRITH (670–685)
ALDFRITH (685–704)
OSRED I (704–716)
COENRED (716–718)
OSRIC (718–729)
CEOLWULF (729–737)
EADBERT (737–758)
OSWULF (c. 758)
ETHELWALD MOLL (758–765)
ALCHRED (765–774)
ETHELRED I (774–778)
ELFWALD I (778–788)
OSRED II (788–790)
ETHELRED I (790–796)
ELFWALD I (778–788)
OSRED II (788–790)
ETHELRED I (790–796)
OSBALD (796)
EARDWULF (796–806)
ELFWALD II (806–808)
EARDWULF (?808)
EANRED (808–840)
ETHELRED II (840–844)
REDWULF (844)
ETHELRED II (844–849)
OSBERT (849–862)
AELLE (862–867)
EGBERT I (867–873)
RICSIG (873–876)
EGBERT II (876–?878)

KINGS OF MERCIA
CEARL (c. 600)
PENDA (632–654)
WULFHERE (657–674)
ETHELRED (674–704)
COENRED (704–709)
CEOLRED (709–716)
ETHELBALD (716–?757)
BEORNRED (757)
OFFA (757–796)
EGFRITH (796)
COENWULF (796–?821)
CEOLWULF I (821–823)
BEORNWULF (823–825)
LUDECAN (825–827)
WIGLAF (827–840)
BEORHTWULF (840–852)
CEOLWULF II (874–?883)

KINGS OF THE WEST SAXONS
CERDIC (519–534)
CYNRIC (534–560)
CEAWLIN (560–591)
CEOL (591–597)
CEOLWULF (597–611)
CYNEGILS (611–643)
CENWALH (643–672)
SEAXBURH (Queen) (?672–?674)
AESCWINE (674–676)
CENTWINE (676–685)
CAEDWALLA (685–688)
INI (688–726)
AETHELHEARD (726–?740)
CUTHRED (740–756)
SIGEBERHT (756–757)
CYNEWULF (757–786)
BEORHTRIC (786–802)
EGBERT (802–839)
ETHELWULF (839–855)
ETHELBALD (855–860)
ETHELBERT (860–866)
ETHELRED (866–871)
ALFRED (871–899)
EDWARD THE ELDER (899–925)
ATHELSTAN (925–939)
EDMUND (939–946)
EDRED (946–955)

RULERS OF ENGLAND
EDWY (955–959)
EDGAR (959–975)
EDWARD THE MARTYR (975–979)
ETHELDRED (979–1013)
SWEGN FORKBEARD (1013–14)
ETHELRED (1014–16)
EDMUND IRONSIDE (1016)
CANUTE (1016–35)
HAROLD HAREFOOT (1035–40)
HARTACNUTM (1040–42)
EDWARD THE CONFESSOR (1042–66)
HAROLD GODWINSON (1066)
EDGAR ETHELING (1066)(
WILLIAM I (THE CONQUEROR) (1066–87)
WILLIAM II (RUFUS) (1087–1100)
HENRY I (1100–35)
STEPHEN (1135–54)
HENRY II (1154–89)
RICHARD I (1189–99)
JOHN (1199–1216)
HENRY III (1216–72)

EDWARD I (1272–1307)
EDWARD II (1307–27)
EDWARD III (1327–77)
RICHARD II (1377–99)
HENRY IV (1399–1413)
HENRY V (1413–22)
HENRY VI (1422–61)
EDWARD IV (1461–70)
HENRY VI (1470–71)
EDWARD IV (1471–83)
RICHARD III (1483–85)
HENRY VII (1485–1509)
HENRY VIII (1509–47)
EDWARD VI (1547–53)
JANE (LADY JANE GREY) (1553)
MARY (1553–58)
PHILIP (1554–58)
ELIZABETH I (1558–1603)
JAMES I (1603–25)
CHARLES I (1625–49)
THE COMMONWEALTH (1649–60);
OLIVER CROMWELL (Lord Protector,
  1653–58); RICHARD CROMWELL (Lord
  Protector, 1658–59)

CHARLES II (1660–85)
JAMES II (1685–88)
WILLIAM AND MARY (1689–94)
WILLIAM III (1694–1702)
ANNE (1702–14)
GEORGE I (1714–27)
GEORGE II (1727–60)
GEORGE III (1760–1820)
GEORGE IV (1820–30)
WILLIAM IV (1830–37)
VICTORIA (1837–1901)
EDWARD VII (1901–10)
GEORGE V (1910–36)
EDWARD VIII (Duke of Windsor) (1936)
GEORGE VI (1936–52)
ELIZABETH II (1952–)

NOBEL PRIZE WINNERS

PHYSICS

1901	W. RÖNTGEN	1944	I.RABI
1902	H. ANTOON LORNEZ	1945	W.PAULI
	P. ZEEMAN	1946	P. BRIDGMAN
1903	A. BECQUEREL	1947	Sir E. APPLETON
	P .CURIE	1948	P. BLACKETT
	M. CURIE	1949	H. YUKAWA
1904	LORD RAYLEIGH	1950	C. POWELL
1905	P .LENARD	1951	Sir J. COCKCROFT
1906	Sir J.J. THOMSON		E. WALTON
1907	A.A .MICHELSON	1952	F. BLOCH
1908	G LIPPMANN		F. PURCELL
1909	G. MARCONI	1953	F. ZERNIKE
	K. BRAUN	1954	M. BORN
1910	J. VAN DER WAALS		W. BOTHE
1912	N.G. DALEN	1955	W. LAMB, Jr.
1913	H. KAMERLINGH ONNES		P. KUSCH
1914	M.VON LAUE	1956	W. SHOCKLEY
1915	Sir W. BRAGG		J. BARDEEN
	Sir L. BRAGG		W. BRATTAIN
1916	(NO AWARD)	1957	TSUNG-DAO-LEE
1917	C. BARKLA		C.N. YANG
	M. PLANCK	1958	P.A. CHERENKOV
1919	J. STARK		I.M. FRANK
1920	C. GUILLAME		I.Y. TAMM
1921	A. EINSTEIN	1959	E. SEGRÈ
1922	N. BOHR		O. CHAMBERLAIN
1923	R. MILLIKAN	1960	D. GLASER
1925	J. FRANCK	1961	R. HOFSTADTER
	G. HERTZ		R. MÖSSBAUER
1926	J. PERRIN	1962	L.D. LANDAU
1927	A.H. COMPTON	1963	J.H.D. JENSEN
1927	C. WILSON		M.G. MAYER
1928	Sir O. RICHARDSON		E.P. WIGNER
1929	PRINCE L.DE BROGLIE	1964	C.H. TOWNES
1930	Sir C. RAMAN		N.G. BASOV
1931	NO AWARD		A.M. PROKHOROV
1932	W. HEISENBERG	1965	J.S. SCHWINGER
1933	P.A.M. DIRAC		R.P. FEYNMAN
	E. SCHRÖDINGER		S. TOMONAGA
1934	(NO AWARD)	1966	A. KASTLER
1935	Sir J.CHADWICK	1967	H.A.BETHE
1936	V.HESS	1968	L. W.ALVAREZ
	C.ANDERSON	1969	M. GELL-MANN
1937	C.DAVISSON	1970	H. ALVEN
	Sir G.P.THOMSON		N. NEEL
1938	E.FERMI	1971	D. GABOR
1939	E.LAWRENCE	1972	J. BARDEEN
1943	O.STERN		L.N. COOPER
			J.R. SCRIEFFER

1973	L. EASAKI		1997	S. CHU
	I. GIAEVER			C. COHEN-TANNOUDJI
	B. JOSEPHSON			W.D. PHILLIPS
1974	Sir M. RYLE		1998	D.M. LEE
	A. HEWISH			D.D. OSHEROFF
1975	J. RAINWATER			R.C. RICHARDSON
	A. BOHR			H. STÖRMER
	B. MOTTLESON			D.C. TSUI
1976	B. RICHTER		1999	G. HOOFT
	S. TING			J.G. VELTMAN
1977	P.W. ANDERSON		2000	Z.I. ALFEROV
	Sir N.F. MOTT			H. KROEMER
	J.H. VAN VLECK			J. ST CLAIR KILBY
1978	P.L. KAPITSA			
	A.A. PENZIAS		**CHEMISTRY**	
	R.W. WILSON		1901	J.V. HOFF
1979	S.L. GLASHOW		1902	E. FISCHER
	A. SALAM		1903	S. ARRHENIUS
	S. WEINBERG		1904	Sir W. RAMSAY
1980	J. CRONIN		1905	A. VON BAEYER
	V. FITCH		1906	H. MOISSAN
1981	K. SIEGBAHN		1907	E. BUCHNER
	N. BLOEMBERGEN		1908	LORD RUTHERFORD
	A. SCHAWLON		1909	W. OSTWALD
1982	K.G. WILSON		1910	O. WALLACH
1983	S. CHANDRASEKHAR		1911	M. CURIE
	W. FOWLER		1912	V. GRIGNARD
1984	C. RUBBIA			P. SABATIER
	S. VAN DER MEER		1913	A. WERNER
1985	K. VON KLITZING		1914	T. RICHARDS
1986	E. RUSKA		1915	R. WILLSTÄTTER
	G. BINNIG		1916	(NO AWARD)
	H. ROHRER		1917	(NO AWARD)
1987	A. MULLER		1918	F. HABER
	G. BEDNORZ		1919	(NO AWARD)
1988	L.M. LEDERMAN		1920	W. NERNST
	M. SCHWARTZ		1921	F. SODDY
	J. STEINBERGER		1922	F. ASTON
1989	W. PAUL		1923	F. PREGL
	N.F. RAMSEY		1924	(NO AWARD)
1990	J.I. FRIEDMAN		1925	R. ZSIGMONDY
	H.W. KENDALL		1926	T. SVEDBERG
	R.E. TAYLOR		1927	H. WIELAND
1991	P.G.DE GENNES		1928	A. WINDAUS
1992	G. CHARPAK		1929	Sir A. HARDEN
1993	R.A. HULSE			H. VON EULER-CHELPIN
	J.H. TAYLOR,JR		1930	H. FISCHER
1994	B.N. BROCKHOUSE		1931	K. BOSCH
	C.G. SHULL			F. BERGIUS
1995	F. REINES		1932	I. LANGMUIR
	M.L. PERL		1933	(NO AWARD)

Chemistry continued

Year	Winner	Year	Winner
			W.H. STEIN
1934	H. UREY	1973	E. FISCHER / G. WILKINSON
1935	F. JOLIOT-CURIE / I. JOLIOT-CURIE	1974	P.J. FLORY
1936	P. DEBYE	1975	J.W. CORNFORT
1937	Sir W. HAWORTH		V. PRELOG
	P. KARRER	1976	W.M. LIPSCOMB
1938	R. KUHN	1977	I. PRIGOGINE
1939	A. BUTENANDT	1978	P. MITCHELL
	L. RUZICKA	1979	H.C. BROWN
1943	G. DE HEVESY		G. WITTIG
1944	O. HAHN	1980	P. BERG
1945	A. VIRTANEN		W. GILBERT
1946	J. SUMNER		F. SANGER
	J. NORTHROP	1981	K. FUKUI
	W. STANLEY		R. HOFFMAN
1947	Sir R. ROBINSON	1982	A. KLUG
1948	A. TISELIUS	1983	H. TAUBE
1949	W. GIAUQUE	1984	R.B. MERRIFIELD
1950	O. DIELS	1985	H. HAUPTMAN
	K. ALDER		J. KARLE
1951	E. MCMILLAN	1986	D. HERSCHBACH
	G. SEABORG		Y. TSEH LEE
1952	A. MARTIN		J. POLANYI
	R. SYNGE	1987	D. CRAM
1953	H. STAUDINGER		J. LEHN
1954	L.C. PAULING		C. PEDERSEN
1955	V. DU VIGNEAUD	1988	R. HUBER
1956	N. SEMYONOV		H. MICHEL
	Sir C. HINSHELQWOOD	1989	S. ALTMAN
1957	Sir A. TODD	1990	E.J. COREY
1958	F. SANGER	1991	R.R. ERNST
1959	J. HEYROVSKY	1992	R.A. MARCUS
1960	W. LIBBY	1993	K.B. MULLIS
1961	M. CALVIN	1994	G.A. OLAH
1962	J.C. KENDREW	1995	P. CRUTZEN
	M.F. PERUTZ		M. MOLINA
1963	G. NATTA		F.S. ROWLAND
	K. ZIELGER	1996	R.F. CURL JR
1964	D.M.C. HODGKIN		R.E. SMALLEY
1965	R.B. WOODWARD	1997	P.D. BOYER
1966	R.S. MULLIKEN		J.C. SKOU
1967	M. EIGEN		J.E. WALKER
	R.G. W. NORRISH	1998	J.A. POPLE
	G. PORTER		W. KOHN
1968	L. ONSAGER	1999	A. ZEWAIL
1969	D.H.R. BARTON	2000	A.J. HEEGER
	O. HASSEL		A.G. MACDIARMID
1970	L.F. LELOIR		HIDEKA SHIRAKAWA
1971	G. HERZBERG		
1972	C.B. ANFINSEN		
	S. MOORE		

PHYSIOLOGY AND MEDICINE

1901	E. VON BEHRING
1902	Sir R. ROSS
1903	N.R. FINSEN
1904	I. PAVLOV
1905	R. KOCH
1906	C. GOLGI / S. RAMON Y CAJAL
1907	A. LAVERAN
1908	P. ERLICH
	I. MECHNIKOV
1909	E. KOCHER
1910	A. KOSSEL
1911	A. GULLSTRAND
1912	A. CARREL
1913	C. RICHET
1914	R. BARANY
1915	(NO AWARD)
1916	(NO AWARD)
1917	(NO AWARD)
1918	(NO AWARD)
1919	J. BORDET
1920	A. KROGH
1921	(NO AWARD)
1922	A.V. HILL
	O. MEYERHOF
1923	Sir F.G. BANTING
	J.J.R. MACLEOD
1924	W. EINTHOVEN
1925	(NO AWARD)
1926	J. FIBIGER
1927	J. WAGNER VON JAUREGG
1928	C. NICOLLE
1929	C. EIJKMAN
	Sir F. HOPKINS
1930	K. LANSTEINER
1931	O. WARBURG
1932	E.D. ADRIAN
	Sir C. SHERRINGTON
1933	T.H. MORGAN
1934	G.R. MONIT
	W.P. MURPHY
	G.H. WHIPPLE
1935	H. SPEMANN
1936	Sir H.H. DALE
	O. LOEWI
1937	A. SZENT-GYÖRGYI
1938	C. HEYMANS
1939	G. DOMAGK
1940	(NO AWARD)
1941	(NO AWARD)
1942	(NO AWARD)

1943	H. DAM (DEN)
	E.A. DOISY)
1944	J. EARLANGER
	H.S. GASSER
1945	Sir A. FLEMING
	E.B. CHAIN / LORD FLOREY
1946	H.J. MULLER
1947	C.F. CORI
	G.T. CORI
	B. HOUSSAY
1948	P. MÜLLER
1949	W.R. HESS
	A.E. MONIZ
1950	P.S. HENCH
	E.C. KENDALL
	T. REICHSTEIN
1951	M. THEILER
1952	F.A. LIPMANN
	Sir H.A. KREBS
1954	J.F. ENDERS
	T.H. WELLER
	F. ROBBINS
1955	A.H. THEORELL
1956	W. FORSSMANN
	D. RICHARDS
	A.F. COURNAND
1957	D. BOVET
1958	G.W. BEADLE
	E.L. TATUM
	J. LEDERBERG
1959	S. OCHOA
	A .KORNBERG
1960	Sir F. MACFARLANE BURNET
	P.B. MEDWAR
1961	G. VON BÉKÉSY
1962	F.H.C. CRICK
	J.D. WATSON
	M. WILKINS
1963	Sir J.C. ECLES
	A.L. HODGKIN
	A.F. HUXLEY
1964	K. BLOCH
	F. LYNEN
1965	F. JACOB
	A. LWOFF
	J. MONOD
1966	C.B. HUGGINS
	F.P. ROUS
1967	H.K. HARTLINE
	G. WALD
	R.A. GRANIT

Physiology and Medicine continued

1968	R.W. HOLLEY
	H.G. KHORANA
	M.W. NIRENBERG
1969	M. DELBRÜCK
	A.D. HERSHEY
	S.E. LURIA
1970	J. AXELROD
	Sir B. KATZ
	U. VON EULER
1971	E.W. SUTHERLAND, Jr.
1972	G.M. EDELMAN
	R.R. PORTER
1973	K. VON FRISCH
	K. LORENZ
	N. TINBERGEN
1974	A. CLAUDE
	C. DE DUVE
	G.E. PALADE
1975	D. BALTIMORE
	R.D. ULBECCO
	H.M. TEMIN
1976	B.S. BLUMBERG
	D.G. GAJDUSEK
1977	R.S. YALOW
	R. GUILLEMIN
	A.V. SCHALLY
1978	W. ARBER
	D. NATHANS
	H. SMITH
1979	A.M. HOUNSFIELD
1980	G. SNELL
	J. DAUSSET
	B. BENACERRAF
1981	R. SPERRY
	D. HUBEL
	T. WIESEL
1982	S.K. BERGSTROM
	B.I. SAMUELSON
	J.R. VANE
1983	B. MCCLINTOCK
1984	N.K. JERNE
	G.J.F. KÖHLER
	C. MILSTEIN
1985	J. GOLDSTEIN
	M. BROWN
1986	S. COHEN
	R. LEVI-MONTALCINI
1987	S. TONEGAWA
1988	G.B. ELION
	G.H. HITCHINGS
1989	H.E. VARMUS
1990	J.E .MURRAY
	E.D. THOMAS
1991	B. SAKMANN
	E. NEHER
1992	E.H. FISCHER / E.G. KREBS
1993	R.J. ROBERTS
	P.A. SHARP
1994	A.G. GILMAN
	M. RODBELL
1995	E.B. LEWIS
	C. NUSSLEIN-VOLHARD
	E.F. WIESCHAUS
1996	P.C. DOHERTY
	R.M. ZINKERNAGEL
1997	S.B. PRUSINER
1998	R.F. FURCHGOTT
	L.J. IGNARRO
	F. MURAD
1999	G. BLOBEL
2000	A. CARLSSON
	P. GREENGARD
	E. KANDEL

LITERATURE

1901	S. PRUDHOMME
1902	T. MOMMSEN
1903	B. BJØRNSON
1904	F. MISTRAL
	J. ECHEGARAY Y EIZAGUIRRE
1905	H. SIENKIEWICZ
1906	G. CARDUCI
1907	R. KIPLING
1908	R. EUCKEN
1909	S. LAGERLÖF
1910	P. VON HEYSE
1911	M. MAETERLINCK
1912	G. HAUPTMANN
1913	Sir R. TAGORE
1914	(NO AWARD)
1915	R. ROLLAND
1916	V. VON HEIDENSTAM
1917	K. GJELLERUP
	H. PONTOPPIDAN
1919	C. SPITTELER
1920	K. HAMSUN
1921	A. FRANCE
1922	J. BENAVENTE Y MARTINEZ
1923	W.B. YEATS
1924	W.S. REYMONT
1925	G.B. SHAW

1926	G. DELEDDA	1977	S. ALEIXANDRE
1927	H. BERGSON	1978	I.B. SINGER
1928	S. UNDSET	1979	O. ALEPOUDELLIS
1929	T. MANN	1980	C. MILOSZ
1930	S. LEWIS	1981	E. CANETTI
1931	E.A. KARLFELDT	1982	G. GARCIA MARQUEZ
1932	J. GALSWORTHY	1983	W. GOULDING
1933	I. BUNIN	1984	J. SEIFERT
1934	L. PIRANDELLO	1985	C. SIMON
1935	(NO AWARDS)	1986	W. SOYINKA
1936	E. O'NEILL	1987	J. BRODSKY
1937	R.M.DU GARD	1988	N. MAHFOUZ
1938	P. BUCK	1989	C.J. CELA
1939	F.E. SILLANPÄÄ	1990	O. PAZ
1943	(NO AWARD)	1991	N. GORDIMER
1944	J.V. JENSEN	1992	D. WALCOTT
1945	G. MISTRAL	1993	T. MORRISON
1946	H. HESSE	1994	K. OE
1947	A. GIDE	1995	S. HEANEY
1948	T.S. ELIOT	1996	W. SYMBORSKA
1949	W. FAULKNER	1997	D. FO
1950	B. RUSSELL	1998	J. SARAMAGO
1951	P.F. LAGERKVIST	1999	G. GRASS
1952	F. MAURIAC	2000	GAO XINGJIAN
1953	Sir WINSTON CHURCHILL		
1954	E. HEMINGWAY	**PEACE**	
1955	H.K. LAXNESS	1901	J.H. DUNANT / F. PASSY
1956	J.R. JIMÉNEZ	1902	E. DUCOMMUN /C.A. GOBAT
1957	A. CAMUS	1903	Sir W. CREMER
1958	B.L. PASTERNAK (DECLINED AWARD)	1904	INSTITUTE OF INTERNATIONAL LAW (FOUNDED, 1873)
1959	S. QUASIMODO	1905	BARONESS VON SUTTNER
1960	S.J. PERSE	1906	T. ROOSEVELT
1961	I. ANDRIC	1907	E. TEODORO MONETA
1962	J. STEINBECK		L. RENAULT
1963	G. SEFERIS (	1908	K.P. ARNOLDSON
1964	J.P. SARTRE (DECLINED AWARD)	1909	BARON D'ESTOURNELLES DE CONSTANT
1965	M. SHOLOKHOV		
1966	S.Y. AGNON		A. BEERNAERT
	N. SACHS	1910	INSTITUTE PEACE BUREAU (FOUNDED, 1891)
1967	M.A. ASTURIAS		
1968	K. YASUNARI	1911	T. ASSER
1969	S. BECKETT		A. FRIED
1970	A.I. SOLZHENITSYN	1912	E. ROOT
1971	P. NERUDA	1913	H. LAFONTAINE
1972	H. BÖLL	1914	(NO AWARD)
1973	P. WHITE	1915	(NO AWARD)
1974	E. JOHNSON	1916	(NO AWARD)
	H. MARTINSON	1917	INTERNATIONAL RED CROSS COMMITTEE (FOUNDED, 1863)
1975	E. MONTALE		
1976	S. BELLOW	1918	(NO AWARD)

NOBEL PRIZE WINNERS

Peace continued

1919	W. WILSON
1920	L. BOURGEOIS
1921	K. BRANTING
	C.L. LANGE
1922	F. NANSEN
1923	(NO AWARD)
1924	(NO AWARD)
1925	Sir A. CHAMBERLAIN
	C.G. DAWES
1926	A. BRIAND
	G. STRESEMAN
1927	F. BUISSON
	L. QUIDDE
1928	(NO AWARD)
1929	F.B. KELLOGG
1930	N. SÖNDERBLOM
1931	J. ADDAMS
	N.M. BUTLER
1932	(NO AWARD)
1933	Sir N. ANGEL
1934	A. HENDERSON
1935	C. VON OSSIETZKY
1936	C.S. LAMAS
1937	VISCOUNT CECIL OF CHELWOOD
1938	NANSEN INTERNATIONAL OFFICE FOR REFUGEES (FOUNDED, 1931)
1939	(NO AWARD)
1940	(NO AWARD)
1941	(NO AWARD)
1942	(NO AWARD)
1943	(NO AWARD)
1944	INTERNATIONAL RED CROSS COMMITTEE (FOUNDED, 1863)
1945	C. HULL
1946	E.G. BALCH
	J.R. MOTT
1947	AMERICAN FRIEND'S SERVICE COMMITTEE
	FRIENDS' SERVICE COUNCIL
1948	(NO AWARD)
1949	LORD BOYD-ORR
1950	R. BUNCHE
1951	L. JOUHAUX
1952	A. SCHWEITZER
1953	G.C. MARSHALL
1954	OFFICE OF THE UNITED NATIONS HIGH COMMISSION FOR REFUGEES FOUNDED, 1951)
1955	(NO AWARD)
1956	(NO AWARD)
1957	L.B. PEARSON
1958	D.G. PIRE
1959	P.J. NOEL-BAKER
1960	A.J. LUTHULI
1961	D. HAMMARSKJÖLD
1962	L.C. PAULING
1963	INTERNATIONAL RED CROSS COMMITTEE (FOUNDED, 1863) LEAGUE OF RED CROSS SOCIETIES
1964	M. LUTHER KING, Jr.
1965	UNITED NATIONS CHILDREN'S FUND (FOUNDED, 1946)
1966	(NO AWARD)
1967	(NO AWARD)
1968	R. CASSIN
1969	INTERNATIONAL LABOUR ORGANISATION (FOUNDED, 1919)
1970	N.E. BORLAUG
1971	W. BRANDT
1972	(NO AWARD)
1973	H. KISSINGER LE DUC THO (DECLINED AWARD)
1974	S. MACBRIDE /E. SATO
1975	A.S. SAKHAROV
1976	MRS B. WILLIAMS MISS M. CORRIGAN
1977	AMNESTY INTERNATIONAL (FOUNDED IN UK, 1961)
1978	A. SADAT M. BEGIN
1979	MOTHER TERESA
1980	A.P. ESQUIVEL
1981	OFFICE OF THE U.N. HIGH COMMISSION FOR REFUGEES (FOUNDED, 1951)
1982	A. GARCIA ROBLES MRS A. MYRDAL
1983	L. WALESA
1984	BISHOP D. TUTU
1985	INTERNATIONAL PHYSICIANS FOR THE PREVENTION OF NUCLEAR WAR (FOUNDED, 1980)
1986	E. WIESEL
1987	OSCAR ARIAS SANCHEZ
1988	THE UNITES NATIONS PEACE KEEPING FORCES

1989	DALAI LAMA	1979	Sir A. LEWIS / T.W. SCHULTZ
1990	M.S. GORBACHEV	1980	L.R. KLEIN
1991	A.S.S. KYI	1981	J. TOBIN
1992	R.M. TUM	1982	G.J. STIGLER
1993	F.W. DE KLERK / N. MANDELA	1983	G. DEBREU
1994	Y. ARAFAT / S. PEREZ / Y. RABIN	1984	Sir R. STONE
1995	J. ROTBLAT	1985	F. MODIGLIANI
	PUGWASH CONFERENCES ON	1986	J.M. BUCHANAN Jr.
	SCIENCE AND WORLD AFFAIRS	1987	R.M. SOLOW
1996	C.F.X. BELO / J. RAMOS-HORTA	1988	M. ALLAIS
1997	INTERNATIONAL CAMPAIGN TO	1989	T. HAAVELMO
	BAN LANDMINES	1990	H.M. MARKOWITZ
	JODY WILLIAMS		M.M. MILLER / W.F. SHARPE
1998	J. HUME	1991	R.H. COASE
	D. TRIMBLE	1992	G.S. BECKER
1999	DOCTORS WITHOUT BORDERS	1993	R.W. FOGEL / D.C. NORTH
	(MÉDECINS SANS FRONTIÈRS	1994	J.C. HARSANYI
2000	KIM DAE JUNG		J.F. NASH / R. SELTEN
		1995	R. LUCAS

ECONOMICS

1969	R. FRISCH/J. TINBERGEN	1996	J.A. MIRRLEES / W. VICKREY
1970	P.A. SAMUELSON	1997	R.C. MERTON / M.S. SCHOLES
1971	S. KUZNETS	1998	A. SEN
1972	K.J. ARROW/Sir J.R. HICKS	1999	R.A. MUNDELL
1973	W. LEONTIEF	2000	J.J. HECKMAN
1974	F.A.VON HAYEK / G. MYRDAL		D.L.MCFADDEN
1975	L.V. KANTOROVICH		
	T.C. KOOPMANS		
1976	M. FRIEDMAN		
1977	J.E. MEADE / B. OHLIN		
1978	H.A. SIMON		

SPORTS PERSONALITIES

3
ALI, Muhammad (Cassius Marcellus Clay) – boxing
COE, Lord Sebastian – Athletics
COX, Mark – Tennis
ELS, Ernie – Golf
LAW, Denis – Football
LEE, Bruce – Kung fu

4
AMIS, Dennis – Cricket
ASHE, Arthur – Tennis
BEST, George – Football
BIRD, Dickie – Cricket umpire
BORG, Bjorn – Tennis
CLAY, Cassius. *See* Ali, Muhammad.

CRAM, Steve – Middle-distance running
DUKE, Geoffrey E. – Motor cycling
FIGO, Louis – Football
GRAF, Steffi – Tennis
HALL, Wes – Cricket
HILL, Damen – Motor racing
HILL, Graham – Motor-racing
HOAD, Lewis – Tennis
HUNT, James – Motor-racing
HUNT, Lord – Mountaineering
JOHN, Barry – Rugby Union
KHAN, Imran – Cricket
KING, Billie Jean *born* Moffitt, – Tennis
KITE, Tom – Golf
LAMB, Allan – Cricket
LARA, Brian – Cricket

SPORTS PERSONALITIES

4 continued

MANS, Perrie – Snooker
MILO – Wrestling
MOSS, Stirling – Motor-racing
OWEN, Michael – Football
PELÉ – Footballer
RUSH, Ian – Football
WADE, Virginia – Tennis

5

ADAMS, Tony – Football
BANKS, Gordon – Goal keeper
BATES, Jeremy – Tennis
BRUNO, Frank – Heavyweight boxing
BUDGE, Don – Tennis
BUENO, Maria – Tennis
BUSBY, Sir Matt – Football
CLARK, Jim – Motor-racing
COURT, Margaret *born* Smith, – Tennis
CURRY, John Anthony – Ice skating
DAVIS, Joe – Billiards
DAVIS, Steve – Snooker
DURIE, Jo – Tennis
EVERT, Christine – Tennis
FALDO, Nick – Golfer
GIGGS, Ryan – Football
GOOCH, Graham – Cricket
GOUGH, Darren – Cricket
GOWER, David – Cricket
GRACE, Dr. William Gilbert – Cricket
GREIG, Tony – Cricket
HAGEN, Walter Charles – Golf
HOBBS, Sir Jack – Cricket
HOGAN, Ben – Golf
HURST, Geoff, Sir – Football
JAMES, Steve – Snooker
JEEPS, Dickie – Rugby Union
JONES, Ann – Tennis
JONES, Bobby – Golf, amateur
JONES, Steve – Athletics
KEANE, Roy – Football
KNOTT, Alan – Cricket
LAUDA, Niki – Motor-racing
LAVER, Rod – Tennis
LEWIS, Carl – Athletics
LEWIS, Lennox – Boxing
LLOYD, Clive – Cricket
LOCKE, Bobby – Golf
LOUIS, Joe – Boxing
MEADE, Richard – Three-day-eventing
MEADS, Colin – Rugby Union

MOORE, Bobby – Football
OVETT, Steve – Middle-distance running
OWENS, Jesse – Sprinter, long jumper, and hurdler
PERRY, Fred – Tennis and table tennis
PROST, Alain – Motor-racing
REVIE, Don – Football
ROCHE, Tony – Tennis
SENNA, Ayrton – Motor-racing
SHORT, Nigel – Chess
SMITH, Harvey – Showjumping and equestrian
SMITH, Stan – Tennis
SNEAD, Sam – Golf
SPITZ, Mark – Swimmer
TYSON, Mike – Boxing
VIREN, Lasse – Athletics
VIRGO, John – Snooker
WALSH, Courtney – Cricket
WARNE, Shane – Cricket
WAUGH, Mark – Cricket
WAUGH, Steve – Cricket
WHITE, Jimmy – Snooker
WILLS, Helen – Tennis
WOODS, Tiger – Golf

6

AGASSI, Andre – Tennis
ALCOTT, Amy – Golf
ANDREW, Rob – Rugby
BARKER, Sue – Tennis
BAXTER, Jim – Football
BECKER, Boris – Tennis
BORDER, Allan – Cricket
BOTHAM, Ian – Cricket
BROOME, David – Showjumping
BROUGH, Louise – Tennis
BUGNER, Joe – Boxing
BUTTON, Jenson – Motor-racing
CARLOS, Roberto – Football
CARSEN, Willie – Jockey
CASALS, Rosemary – Tennis
CAWLEY, Evonne *born* Goolagong, Tennis
COOPER, Henry – Boxing
COTTON, Henry – Golf
CRUYFF, Johann – Football
DAVIES, Jonathan – Rugby
DAVIES, Laura – Golf
DEXTER, Ted – Cricket
D'INZEO, Colonel Piero – Showjumping
EDBERG, Stefan – Tennis

6 continued

EDRICH, John – Cricket
FANGIO, Juan Manuel – Motor-racing
FOSTER, Brendan – Athletics
GINOLA, David – Football
GULLIT, Ruud – Football
HENDRY, Stephen – Snooker
HENMAN, Tim – Tennis
HINGIS, Martina – Tennis
HUGHES, Mark – Football
HUTTON, Sir Len – Cricket
IRVINE, Eddie – Motor-racing
KARPOV, Anatoly – Chess
KEEGAN, Kevin – Football
KORBUT, Olga – Gymnastics
LANGER, Bernhard – Golf
LASKER, Emanuel – Chess
LAWRIE, Paul – Golf
LILLEE, Dennis – Cricket
LISTON, Sonny – Boxing
MERCKX, Eddy – Cycling
MONTGOMERIE, Colin – Golfer
MORPHY, Paul – Chess
NORMAN, Greg – Golf
PALMER, Arnold – Golf
PARROT, John – Snooker
PETERS, Mary – Athletics
PIQUET, Nelson – Motor-racing
PLAYER, Gary – Golf
RAMSAY, Sir Alf – Football
RHODES, Wilfred – Cricket
ROBSON, Bobby – Football
ROBSON, Brian – Football
SHEENE, Barry – Motor cycling
SMYTHE, Pat – Showjumping and
  equestrian
SOBERS, Sir Garfield – Cricket
STOLLE, Fred – Tennis
TAYLOR, Dennis – Snooker
TAYLOR, Roger – Tennis
THORNE, Willy – Snooker
TITMUS, Fred – Cricket
TURPIN, Randolph – Boxing
WATSON, Tom – Golf
VIALLA, Gianluca – Football
WALKER, Murray – Motor racing commentator
WENGER, Arsene – Football
WILKIE, David – Swimming
WILLIS, Bob – Cricket
ZIDANE, Zinedine – Football

7

AMBROSE, Curtly – Cricket
BECKHAM, David – Football
BOYCOTT, Geoff – Cricket
BRABHAM, Sir Jack – Motor-racing
BRADMAN, Sir Donald – Cricket
CARLING, Will – Rugby
CARNERA, Primo – Boxing
CAUTHEN, Steve – Jockey
COMPTON, Denis – Cricket
CONNORS, Jimmy – Tennis
COWDREY, Colin – Cricket
DEMPSEY, Jack – Boxing
DETTORI, Frankie – Jockey
EDWARDS, Gareth – Rugby
FERRARI, Enzo – Motor-racing
FISCHER, Bobby – Chess
FOGARTY, Carl – Motor cycling
FOREMAN, George – Boxing
FRAZIER, Joe – Boxing
FRENZEN, Heinz Harald – Motor racing
GREAVES, Jimmy – Footballer/commentator
HAMMOND, Wally – Cricket
HIGGINS, Alex – Snooker
HILLARY, Sir Edmund – Mountaineering
HUSSAIN, Nasser – Cricket
JACKLIN, Tony – Golf
JOHNSON, Amy – Aviation
JOHNSON, Joe – Snooker
KLINSMAN, Jurgen – Football
LENGLEN, Suzanne – Tennis
LINEKER, Gary – Football
MCCOIST, Ally – Football
MCENROE, John – Tennis
MCLAREN, Bruce, – Motor-racing
MANSELL, Nigel – Motor-racing
MOTTRAM, Buster – Tennis
NASTASE, Ilie – Tennis
NIELSEN, Gunnar – Athletics
PIGGOTT, Lester – Jockey
PINSENT, Mathew – Rowing
REARDON, Ray – Snooker
REDGRAVE, Sir Steve – Rowing
RIVALDO – Football
ROBERTS, Andy – Cricket
RONALDO – Football
SHEARER, Alan – Football
SPASSKY, Boris – Chess
SPENCER, John – Snooker
STEVENS, Kirk – Snooker
STEWART, Alec – Cricket

SPORTS PERSONALITIES

7 continued
STEWART, Jackie, – Motor-racing
STEWART, Payne – Golf
SURTEES, John – Motor sports
THOMSON, Jeff – Cricket
THOMSON, Peter – Cricket
TREVINO, Lee – Golf
TRUEMAN, Fred – Cricket
WINKLER, Hans Günther – Showjumping
ZATOPEK, Emil – Long-distance running

8
AGOSTINI, Giacomo – Motor cycling
ALEKHINE, Alexander – Chess
ATHERTON, Michael – Cricket
BERGKAMP, Denis – Football
BROOKING, Trevor – Football
CAMPBELL, Sir Malcolm – Land-and
water-speed racing
CHAPPELL, Greg – Cricket
CHAPPELL, Ian – Cricket
CHARLTON, Sir Bobby – Football
CHARLTON, Jackie – Football
CHATAWAY, Sir Christopher – Athletics
CHRISTIE, Linford – Athletics
COMANECI, Nadia – Gymnastics
DOCHERTY, Tommy – Football
FERGUSON, Sir Alex – Football
FRANCOME, John – Jockey
GRAVENEY, Tom – Cricket
HAILWOOD, Mike – Motor cycling
HASTINGS, Gavin – Rugby
HAWTHORN, Mike – Motor-racing
JOSELITO – Matador
KASPAROV, Gary – Chess
KORCHNOI, Victor – Chess
LINDWALL, Raymond – Cricket
MARADONA, Diego – Football
MARCIANO, Rocky – Boxing
MATTHEWS, Sir Stanley – Football
MOUNTJOY, Doug – Snooker
NEWCOMBE, John – Tennis
NICKLAUS, Jack – Golf
OLAZABAL, José Maria – Golf
PHILLIPS, Capt. Mark – Show jumping
RICHARDS, Sir Gordon – Jockey
RICHARDS, Sir Vivian – Cricket
ROBINSON, Sugar Ray – Boxing
RUSEDSKI, Greg – Tennis
THOMPSON, Daley – Decathlon
THORBURN, Cliff – Snooker

WILLIAMS, J.P.R. – Rugby Union
WILLIAMS, Venus – Tennis
ZAHARIOS, Mildred – Golf, athletics

9
BANNISTER, Sir Roger – Athletics
BEARDSLEY, Peter – Football
BONINGTON, Chris – Mountaineering
COULTHARD, David – Motor racing
DALGLISH, Kenny – Football
D'OLIVIERA, Basil – Cricket
GASCOIGNE, Paul – Football
GOOLAGONG, Evonne. *See* Cawley, Evonne.
GRIFFITHS, Terry – Snooker
HOLYFIELD, Evander – Boxing
IMRAN KHAN – Cricket
LINDBERGH, Charles – Aviation
LLEWELLYN, Harry – Showjumping
MACARTHUR, Ellen – Yachting
PATTERSON, Floyd – Boxing
PATTISSON, Rodney – Yachting
SUTCLIFFE, Herbert – Cricket
SZEWINSKA, Irena – Athletics
UNDERWOOD, Derek – Cricket

10
BARRINGTON, Jonah – Squash
CARPENTIER, Georges – Boxing
CHICHESTER, Sir Francis – Yachting
CULBERTSON, Ely – Bridge authority
FITTIPALDI, Emerson – Motor racing
JUANTORENA, Alberto – Athletics
KOURNIKOVA, Anna – Tennis
LONSBOROUGH, Anita – Swimming
SCHUMACHER, Michael – Motor racing
SCHUMACHER, Willie – Jockey
SHERINGHAM, Teddy – Football
WILLS MOODY, Helen – Tennis

11
BALLESTEROS, Severiano – Golfer
BECKENBAUER, Franz – Football
CONSTANTINE, Learie Nicholas Baron – Cricket
ILLINGWORTH, Ray – Cricket
NAVRATILOVA, Martina – Tennis
WEISSMULLER, Johnny – Swimming

13
TENZING NORGAY – Mountaineering

14
SANCHEZ-VICARIO, Arantxa – Tennis

GIRLS' NAMES

2	NAT	CORA	IVAH
DI	ONA	DAFF	JADE
EM	PAM	DALE	JAEL
JO	PAT	DANA	JANE
VI	PEG	DAPH	JEAN
3	PEN	DAWN	JESS
ADA	PIA	DOLL	JILL
AMY	PRU	DORA	JOAN
ANN	RAE	EDEN	JODI
AUD	RIA	EDIE	JODY
AVA	ROS	EDNA	JOSS
ABA	SAL	EILY	JUDI
BEA	SAM	EIRA	JUDY
BEE	SIB	ELLA	JUNE
BEL	SUE	ELMA	KARA
CIS	UNA	ELSA	KATE
DEB	VAL	EMMA	KATH
DEE	VIV	ENID	KATY
DOT	WIN	ERIN	KERI
EDA	ZOË	ERYL	KYLE
ENA	**4**	ESME	LANA
ETH	ABBY	ETTA	LELA
EVA	ADAH	ETTY	LANA
EVE	ADDY	EVIE	LETA
FAN	AINE	FAYE	LILA
FAY	ALDA	FERN	LILI
FLO	ALEX	FIFI	LILY
GAY	ALIX	FLOY	LINA
GUS	ALLY	FRAN	LISA
IDA	ALMA	GABI	LISE
INA	ALVA	GABY	LITA
ISA	ALYS	GAIL	LIZA
ITA	ANIS	GALE	LOIS
IVY	ANNA	GAYE	LOLA
JAN	ANNE	GERT	LORA
JEN	ANYA	GILL	LORI
JOY	AVIS	GINA	LORN
KAY	BABS	GLAD	LUCE
KIM	BEAT	GWEN	LUCY
KIT	BELL	GWYN	LULU
LEE	BESS	HEBE	LYNN
LES	BETA	HEDY	LYRA
LIL	BETH	HOPE	MAIR
LIZ	BINA	ILMA	MARA
LOU	CARA	ILSE	MARY
LYN	CARY	IMMY	MAUD
MAE	CASS	INEZ	META
MAY	CATH	IOLA	MIMA
MEG	CERI	IONA	MIMI
MEL	CISS	IRIS	MINA
MIA	CLEM	IRMA	MIRA
NAN	CLEO	ISLA	MOLL

105

GIRLS' NAMES

4 continued	WYNN	BONNY	EMMIE
MONA	ZANA	BRIDE	EPPIE
MYRA	ZARA	BRITA	ERICA
NADA	ZENA	BRITT	ERIKA
NELL	ZITA	CANDY	ESMEE
NEST	ZOLA	CAREY	ESSIE
NEVA	ZORA	CARLA	ETHEL
NINA	5	CARLY	ETHNE
NITA	ABBEY	CAROL	ETTIE
NOLA	ABBIE	CARYL	EVITA
NONA	ADDIE	CARYS	FAITH
NORA	ADELE	CASEY	FANNY
NOVA	ADLAI	CATHY	FARON
OLGA	AGGIE	CELIA	FIONA
OONA	AGNES	CERYS	FLEUR
OPAL	AILIE	CHLOE	FLORA
OZZY	AILSA	CHRIS	FLOSS
PETA	AIMEE	CILLA	FREDA
PHIL	ALANA	CINDY	FREYDA
POLL	ALEXA	CISSY	GABBY
PRUE	ALICE	CLARA	GAYLE
RENA	ALINA	CLARE	GEMMA
RENE	ALINE	CORAL	GERDA
RHEA	ALVIE	DAISY	GERRY
RICA	AMATA	DARCY	GILDA
RIKA	AMBER	DEBRA	GINNY
RINA	AMICE	DELIA	GRACE
RITA	ANGEL	DELLA	GRETA
ROMA	ANGIE	DELMA	GUSTA
RONA	ANITA	DERYN	HAGAR
ROSA	ANNIE	DIANA	HATTY
ROSE	ANNIS	DIANE	HAZEL
ROXY	ANONA	DILYS	HEDDA
RUBY	ANWEN	DINAH	HEIDI
RUTH	APHRA	DIONE	HELEN
SARA	APRIL	DODIE	HELGA
SIAN	ASTRA	DOLLY	HENNY
SÍLE	AUDRA	DONNA	HEPSY
SÌNE	AUREA	DORIA	HETTY
SUZY	AVICE	DORIS	HILDA
TACY	AVRIL	DREDA	HOLLY
TARA	BEATA	DULCE	HORRY
TESS	BECKY	EDITH	HULDA
THEA	BELLA	EFFIE	HYLDA
TINA	BELLE	ELAIN	ILONA
TONI	BERNY	ELENA	IRENE
TRIS	BERRY	ELISE	ISMAY
TRIX	BERTA	ELIZA	JACKY
TYRA	BERYL	ELLEN	JANET
VERA	BESSY	ELLIE	JANEY
VIDA	BETSY	ELROY	JANIE
VINA	BETTE	ELSIE	JANIS
VITA	BETTY	ELVIE	JAYNE
VIVA	BIDDY	EMILY	JEMMA

5 continued

JENNA	MAGDA	NUALA	SISSY
JENNY	MAIRE	NYREE	SONIA
JEWEL	MAMIE	ODILE	SONJA
JINNY	MANDY	OLIFF	SOPHY
JODIE	MARAH	OLIVE	SACY
JOSIE	MARCY	OLLIE	SUKEY
JOYCE	MARGE	OLWEN	SUSAN
JUDOC	MARGO	OLWYN	SUSIE
JULIA	MARIA	ORIEL	SYBIL
JULIE	MARIE	OWENA	TACEY
KAREN	MARLA	PANSY	TAMAR
KARIN	MARNI	PATSY	TAMMY
KATHY	MARTA	PATTI	TANIA
KATIE	MARTI	PATTY	TANSY
KELDA	MARTY	PAULA	TANYA
KELLY	MATTY	PEACE	TEGAN
KEREN	MAUDE	PEARL	TERRI
KERRI	MAURA	PEGGY	TERRY
KERRY	MAVIS	PENNY	TESSA
KEZIA	MEAVE	PETRA	TETTY
KIRBY	MEGAN	PHEBE	THORA
KITTY	MEGGY	PIPPA	THYRA
KYLIE	MELBA	POLLY	TIBBY
LAURA	MELVA	POPPY	TILDA
LAURI	MERCY	RAINA	TILLY
LEIGH	MERLE	RAINE	TISHA
LEILA	MERRY	REINE	TONIA
LENNY	MERYL	RENÉE	TONYA
LEONA	MILLY	RENIE	TOPAZ
LETTY	MINNA	RHIAN	TOPSY
LIANA	MINTY	RHODA	TOTTY
LIBBY	MITZI	RHONA	TRACY
LIDDY	MOIRA	ROBYN	TRINA
LILAC	MOLLY	RONNA	TRUDI
LILLA	MORAG	ROSIE	TRUDY
LINDA	MORNA	ROWAN	UNITY
LINDY	MOYNA	SADIE	VALDA
LIZZY	MOYRA	SALLY	VANDA
LOLLY	MYSIE	SAMMY	VELDA
LOREN	NADIA	SANDY	VENUS
LORNA	NAHUM	SARAH	VICKI
LORNE	NANCE	SARAI	VICKY
LOTTY	NANNY	SARRA	VIKKI
LUCIA	NAOMI	SELMA	VIOLA
LUCIE	NELLY	SENGA	VIVIA
LUCKY	NERYS	SHANI	WANDA
LYDIA	NESSA	SHARI	WENDA
LYNDA	NESTA	SHEBA	WENDY
LYNNE	NETTA	SHENA	WILLA
MABEL	NICKY	SHELA	WILMA
MADDY	NIKKI	SHIRL	WYNNE
MADGE	NOELE	SHONA	XENIA
MAEVE	NORAH	SIBBY	ZELDA
	NORMA	SIBYL	ZELMA

GIRLS' NAMES

6

AGACIA	BEULAH	DENNIE	GLENIS
AGATHA	BIANCA	DIONNE	GLENNA
AGNETA	BILLIE	DORCAS	GLENYS
AILEEN	BIRDIE	DOREEN	GLINYS
AILITH	BIRGIT	DORICE	GLORIA
AITHNE	BLANCH	DORITA	GLYNIS
ALANNA	BLODYN	DORRIE	GOLDIE
ALBINA	BLYTHE	DOTTIE	GRACIE
ALDITH	BOBBIE	DULCIE	GRANIA
ALEXIA	BONITA	DYMPNA	GRETEL
ALEXIS	BONNIE	EARTHA	GRIZEL
ALICIA	BRENDA	EASTER	GUSSIE
ALISON	BRIDIE	EDWINA	GWENDA
ALTHEA	BRIGID	EILEEN	HAIDEE
ALVINA	BRIGIT	EILWEN	HANNAH
AMABEL	BRIONY	EIRIAN	HATTIE
AMALIA	BRYONY	EITHNE	HAYLEY
AMICIA	CANICE	ELAINE	HEDWIG
AMINTA	CARINA	ELINOR	HELENA
ANDREA	CARITA	ELISHA	HELENE
ANDRÉE	CARMEL	ELISSA	HENNIE
ANEIRA	CARMEN	ELOISA	HEPSEY
ANGELA	CAROLA	ELOISE	HERMIA
ANNICE	CAROLE	ELSPIE	HESTER
ANNIKA	CARRIE	ELUNED	HILARY
ANNORA	CASSIE	ELVINA	HONORA
ANSTEY	CATRIN	ELVIRA	HOWARD
ANTHEA	CECILE	EMELYN	HULDAH
ARIANE	CECILY	EMILIA	IANTHE
ARLEEN	CELINA	ESTHER	IDONEA
ARLENE	CELINE	EUNICE	IMOGEN
ARLINE	CHARIS	EVADNE	INGRID
ARMINA	CHERIE	EVELYN	ISABEL
ARMINE	CHERRY	EVONNE	ISEULT
ASHLEY	CHERYL	FARRAN	ISHBEL
ASTRID	CICELY	FARREN	ISOLDA
ATHENE	CISSIE	FEDORA	ISOLDE
AUDREY	CLAIRE	FELICE	JACKIE
AURIEL	COLINA	FINOLA	JACOBA
AURIOL	CONNIE	FLAVIA	JACQUI
AURORA	DAGMAR	FLOWER	JANICE
AURORE	DANITA	FOSTER	JANINE
AVERIL	DANUTA	FRANCA	JANSIS
BARBIE	DAPHNE	FRANNY	JEANIE
BARBRA	DAVIDA	FRIEDA	JEANNE
BAUBIE	DAVINA	GABBIE	JEHANE
BEATTY	DEANNA	GAENOR	JEMIMA
BENITA	DEANNE	GARNET	JENNIE
BERNIE	DEBBIE	GAYNOR	JENNIE
BERTHA	DECIMA	GERTIE	JESSIE
BESSIE	DELWEN	GINGER	JOANNA
BETHAN	DELWYN	GISELA	JOANNE
BETHIA	DELYTH	GLADYS	JOLEEN
	DENISE	GLENDA	JOLENE

6 continued

JUDITH	MARINA	REGINA	THECLA
JULIET	MARION	RENATA	THEKLA
KARINA	MARISA	RHONDA	THELMA
KEELEY	MARITA	ROBINA	THIRSA
KELLIE	MARLIN	ROISIN	THIRZA
KENDRA	MARLYN	ROSINA	TIRZAH
KERRIE	MARNIE	ROSITA	TRACEY
KEZIAH	MARSHA	ROSLYN	TRICIA
KIRSTY	MARTHA	ROWENA	TRISHA
LALAGE	MARTIE	ROXANA	TRIXIE
LAUREL	MATTIE	ROXANE	TRUDIE
LAUREN	MAUDIE	RUBINA	ULRICA
LAURIE	MAXINE	RUTHIE	URSULA
LAVENA	MEGGIE	SABINA	VASHTI
LAVINA	MAGHAN	SALENA	VERENA
LEANNE	MEHALA	SALINA	VERITY
LEILAH	MELODY	SALOME	VERONA
LENNIE	MERCIA	SANDIE	VICKIE
LENORE	MERIEL	SANDRA	VINNIE
LEONIE	MIGNON	SARINA	VIOLET
LESLEY	MILLIE	SARITA	VIVIAN
LESLIE	MINNIE	SELENA	VIVIEN
LETTIE	MIRIAM	SELINA	VYVYAN
LIANNE	MONICA	SERENA	WALLIS
LIESEL	MURIEL	SHARON	WINNIE
LILIAN	MYRTLE	SHAUNA	XANTHE
LILIAS	NADINE	SHEENA	YASMIN
LILITH	NELLIE	SHEILA	YVONNE
LILLAH	NERINA	SHELLY	ZANDRA
LILLIE	NESSIE	SHERRI	ZILLAH
LINNET	NETTIE	SHERRY	ZINNIA
LIZZIE	NICOLA	SHERYL	**7**
LLINOS	NICOLE	SIBBIE	ABIGAIL
LOLITA	NOELLE	SIDONY	ADAMINA
LOREEN	NOREEN	SILVIA	ADELINA
LOTTIE	ODETTE	SIMONA	ADELINE
LOUISA	ODILA	SIMONE	ADRIANA
LOUISE	OLIVET	SINEAD	INSLEY
LUCINA	OLIVIA	SISELY	AINSLIE
LUELLA	OONAGH	SISSIE	AISLING
MADDIE	ORIANA	SOPHIA	AISLINN
MAGGIE	PAMELA	SOPHIE	ALBERTA
MAHALA	PATTIE	SORCHA	ALBINIA
MAIDIE	PEPITA	STACEY	ALBREDA
MAIRIN	PETULA	STELLA	ALDREDA
MAISIE	PHEMIE	STEVIE	ALEDWEN
MARCIA	PHOEBE	SYLVIA	ALETHEA
MARCIE	PORTIA	SYLVIE	ALFREDA
MARGIE	PRISCA	TAMARA	ALLEGRA
MARGOT	PRISSY	TAMSIN	ALLISON
MARIAM	QUEENA	TANITH	ALOISA
MARIAN	QUEENY	TEGWEN	ALOYSIAA
MARIEL	RACHEL	TERESA	ANNABEL
	RAMONA	TESSIE	ANNAPLE

GIRLS' NAMES

7 continued

ANNETTE	CHARLEY	FLOSSIE	LARISSA
ANOUSKA	CHARLIE	FORTUNE	LAUREEN
ANSELMA	CHATTIE	FRANCES	LAURINA
ANSTICE	CHRISSY	FRANCIE	LAVERNE
ANTOINE	CHRISTY	FRANKIE	LAVINIA
ANTONIA	CLARICE	FRANNIE	LEONORA
ARIADNE	CLARRIE	GENEVRA	LETITIA
ARIANNA	CLAUDIA	GEORGIA	LETTICE
ARLETTA	CLODAGH	GEORGIE	LILLIAN
ARLETTE	COLETTE	GILLIAN	LILLIAS
ASPASIA	COLLEEN	GINETTE	LINDSAY
AUGUSTA	CORALIE	GINEVRA	LINDSEY
AURELIA	CORINNA	GISELLE	LINETTE
AUREOLA	CORINNE	GRAINNE	LISBETH
AUREOLE	CRYSTAL	GWLADYS	LISETTE
AVELINE	CYNTHIA	GWYNEDD	LIZBETH
BABETTE	DAMARIS	GWYNETH	LORAINE
BARBARA	DANETTE	HALCYON	LORETTA
BARBARY	DARLENE	HARRIET	LORETTE
BASILIA	DAVINIA	HEATHER	LORINDA
BASILIE	DEBORAH	HÉLOÏSE	LOUELLA
BASILLA	DEIRDRE	HEULWEN	LOURDES
BEATRIX	DELILAH	HILLARY	LOVEDAY
BEATTIE	DEMELZA	HONORIA	LUCASTA
BEDELIA	DESIREE	HORATIA	LUCETTA
BELINDA	DIAMOND	HYPATIA	LUCETTE
BERNICE	DOLORES	ISADORA	LUCIANA
BETHANY	DONALDA	ISIDORA	LUCILLA
BETTINA	DORETTE	JACINTHA	LUCILLE
BETTRYS	DORINDA	JACINTH	LUCINDA
BEVERLY	DOROTHY	JANETTA	LUCRECE
BLANCHE	DYMPHNA	JANETTE	LYNETTE
BLODWEN	EILUNED	JASMINE	MABELLA
BLOSSOM	ELDREDA	JEANNIE	MABELLE
BRANWEN	ELEANOR	JENIFER	MAHALAH
BRIDGET	ELFREDA	JESSICA	MAHALIA
BRONWEN	ELFRIDA	JILLIAN	MALVINA
BRONWYN	ELSPETH	JOCASTA	MANUELA
CAITLIN	EMELINE	JOCELYN	MARILYN
CAMILLA	EMERALD	JOHANNA	MARISSA
CAMILLE	ESTELLA	JONQUIL	MARLENE
CANDACE	ESTELLE	JOSEPHA	MARTINA
CANDICE	EUGENIA	JOSETTE	MARTINE
CARLEEN	EUGENIE	JUANITA	MATILDA
CARLENE	EULALIA	JULIANA	MAUREEN
CARMELA	EULALIE	JULITTA	MEHALAH
CARMINA	EVELEEN	JUSTINA	MEHALIA
CAROLYN	EVELINA	JUSTINE	MEIRION
CECILIA	FABIANA	KATHRYN	MELANIA
CECILE	FELICIA	KATRINA	MELIORA
CEINWEN	FENELLA	KATRINE	MELISSA
CELESTE	FEODORA	KIRSTIN	MELODIE
CHARITY	FIDELIA	KRISTEN	MELVINA
	FLORRRIE	LARAINE	MERILYN

110

7 continued

MERRION	ROXANNE	ANTONINA	FLORENCE
MICHELE	RUPERTA	ANTONNIA	FLORETTA
MILDRED	SABRINA	APPOLINA	FLORETTE
MINERVA	SAFFRON	APPOLINE	FLORINDA
MIRABEL	SANCHIA	ARABELLA	FRANCINE
MIRANDA	SARANNA	ARAMINTA	FREDRICA
MODESTY	SCARLET	BEATRICE	FREDRIKA
MONIQUE	SEPTIMA	BERENICE	GEORGINA
NANETTE	SHANNON	BEVERLEY	GERMAINE
NATALIA	SHARRON	BIRGITTA	GERTRUDE
NATLIE	SHEILAH	BRIGITTA	GILBERTA
NATASHA	SHELAGH	BRIGITTE	GRETCHEN
NERISSA	SHELLY	BRUNETTA	GRISELDA
NICHOLA	SHIRLEY	CARLOTTA	GULIELMA
NINETTE	SIBELLA	CAROLINA	GWYNNETH
NOELINE	SIBILLA	CAROLINE	HADASSAH
OCTAVIA	SIBYLLA	CATHLEEN	HELEWISE
OLYMPIA	SIDONIA	CATRIONA	HEPZIBAH
OPHELIA	SIDONIE	CERIDWEN	HERMIONE
OTTILIA	SILVANA	CHARISSA	HORTENSE
OTTILIE	SIOBHAN	CHARLENE	HYACINTH
PAMELA	SUSANNA	CHARMAIN	INGEBORG
PANDORA	SUSANNE	CHRISSIE	IOLANTHE
PASCALE	SUZANNA	CHRISTIE	IASBELLA
PAULINE	SUZANNE	CLARIBEL	ISABELLE
PEARLIE	SUZETTE	CLARINDA	JACOBINA
PERDITA	SYBELLA	CLARISSA	JAMESINA
PERONEL	SYBILLA	CLAUDINE	JEANETTE
PETRINA	TABITHA	CLEMENCE	JEANNINE
PHILLIS	TALITHA	CLEMENCY	JENNIFER
PHYLLIS	TATIANA	CLOTILDA	JESSAMYN
QUEENIE	THERESA	CONCEPTA	JOSCELIN
RACHAEL	THÉRÈSE	CONCETTA	JULIANNE
RAELENE	TIFFANY	CORDELIA	JULIENNE
RAFAELLA	TRISSIE	CORNELIA	KATHLEEN
REBECCA	VALERIA	COURTNEY	KIMBERLY
REBEKAH	VALERIE	CRESSIDA	KRISTINA
RHONWEN	VANESSA	CYTHEREA	KRISTINE
RICARDA	VENETIA	DANIELLA	LAETITIA
RICHMAL	VIVIANA	DANIELLE	LARRAINE
ROBERTA	YOLANDA	DELPHINE	LAURAINE
ROMAINE	YOLANDE	DIONYSIA	LAURETTA
RONALDA	ZENOBIA	DOMINICA	LAURETTE
ROSABEL	ZULEKIA	DOROTHEA	LAURINDA
ROSALIA	**8**	DOWSABEL	LORRAINE
ROSALIE	ADELAIDE	DRUSILLA	LUCIENNE
ROSALYN	ADELHEID	ELEANORA	LUCRETIA
ROSANNA	ADRIANNE	ELEONORA	LUCREZIA
ROSANNE	ADRIENNE	EMANUELA	LYNNETTE
ROSEANN	ANGELICA	EMMELINE	MADELINA
ROSETTA	ANGELINA	EUPHEMIA	MADELINE
ROSSLYN	ANGELINE	EUSTACIA	MAGDALEN
ROXANNA	ANGHARAD	FAUSTINA	MAGNOLIA
	ANNALISA	FELICITY	MARCELLA

GIRLS' NAMES

8 continued

MARCELLE
MARGARET
MARIAMNE
MARIANNE
MARIETTA
MARIETTE
MARIGOLD
MARJORIE
MELICENT
MELISENT
MELLONEY
MERCEDES
MEREDITH
MERRILYN
MICHAELA
MICHELLE
MORWENNA
MYRTILLA
PATIENCE
PATRICIA
PAULETTE
PENELOPE
PERPETUA
PHILIPPA
PHILLIDA
PHILLIPA
PHYLLIDA
PRIMROSE
PRUDENCE
PRUNELLA
RAPHAELA
RAYMONDE
RHIANNON
RICHENDA
ROCHELLE
RONNETTE
ROSALEEN
ROSALIND
ROSALINE
ROSAMOND
ROSAMUND
ROSEANNA
ROSEANNE
ROSELINE
ROSEMARY
SAMANTHA
SAPPHIRA
SAPPHIRE
SCARLETT
SHEELAGH
STEFANIE
SUSANNAH
TALLULAH

TAMASINE
THEODORA
THERESIA
THOMASIN
TIMOTHEA
VERONICA
VICTORIA
VIOLETTA
VIOLETTE
VIRGINIA
VIVIENNE
WILFREDA
WILFRIDA
WINEFRED
WINIFRED
9
ALBERTINA
ALBERTINE
ALEXANDRA
ANASTASIA
ANGELIQUE
ANNABELLA
ANNABELLE
ANNELIESE
ARTHURINA
ARTHURINE
AUGUSTINA
BATHSHEBA
BENEDICTA
BERNADINA
BERNADINE
CARMELITA
CASSANDRA
CATHARINE
CATHERINE
CELESTINA
CELESTINE
CHARLOTTE
CHARMAINE
CHRISTIAN
CHRISTINA
CHRISTINE
CHRISTMAS
CLAUDETTE
CLEMENTIA
CLEOPATRA
COLUMBINA
COLUMBINE
CONSTANCE
CONSTANCY
COURTENAY
DESDEMONA
DOMINIQUE
DONALDINA

ELISABETH
ELIZABETH
EMMANUELA
ESMERELDA
ETHELINDA
FIONNUALLA
FRANCESCA
FRANCISCA
FREDERICA
FREDERIKA
GABRIELLA
GABRIELLE
GENEVIEVE
GEORGETTE
GEORGIANA
GERALDINE
GHISLAINE
GUENDOLAN
GUINEVERE
GWENDOLAN
GWENDOLYN
GWENLLIAN
HARRIETTE
HENRIETTA
HENRIETTE
HILDEGARD
HIPPOLYTA
HORTENSIA
HYACINTHA
JAQUELYN
JACQUETTA
JEANNETTE
JESSAMINE
JOSEPHINE
KATHARINE
KATHERINE
KIMBERLEY
LAURENCIA
LAURENTIA
MADELEINE
MAGDALENA
MAGDALENE
MARGARETA
MARGARITA
MEHETABEL
MEHITABEL
MILLICENT
MIRABELLA
MIRABELLE
NICOLETTE
PHILLIPPA
PHILOMENA
PLEASANCE
POLLYANNA

PRISCILLA
ROSABELLA
ROSABELLE
ROSALINDA
ROSEMARIE
STEPHANIE
THEODOSIA
THEOPHILA
THOMASINA
THOMASINE
VALENTINA
VALENTINE
VÉRONIQUE
VICTORINE
VINCENTIA
WINNIFRED
10
ALEXANDRIA
ALPHONSINE
ANTOINETTE
ARTHURETTA
BERNADETTE
BERNARDINA
BERNARDINE
CHRISTABEL
CHRISTIANA
CINDERELLA
CLEMENTINA
CLEMENTINE
CONSTANTIA
DULCIBELLA
ERMINTRUDE
ERMYNTRUDE
ETHELDREDA
EVANGELINA
EVANGELINE
GILBERTINE
GWENDOLINE
HILDEGARDE
JACQUELINE
KINBOROUGH
PETRONELLA
PETRONILLA
TEMPERANCE
THEOPHANIA
WILHELMINA
WILLIAMINA
11
ALEXANDRINA
AHRISTIANIA
FIONNGHUALA
12
PHILADELPHIA

112

BOYS' NAMES

BOYS' NAMES

2	LEO	ALVA	EWAN
AL	LES	AMOS	EWEN
ED	LEW	ANDY	EZRA
3	LEX	ARTY	FRED
ABE	LOU	AXEL	GARY
ALF	LYN	BART	GENE
ART	MAT	BEAU	GLEN
ASA	MAX	BILL	GLYN
BAS	MEL	BING	GREG
BAT	NAT	BOAZ	GWYN
BAZ	NED	BOYD	HAMO
BEN	NYE	BRAD	HANK
BOB	ODO	BRAM	HANS
BUD	PAT	BRET	HERB
CAI	PIP	BRYN	HUEY
DAI	RAB	BURT	HUGH
DAN	RAY	CARL	HUGO
DEE	REG	CARY	IAGO
DEL	REX	CERI	IAIN
DES	ROB	CHAD	IFOR
DON	ROD	CHAS	IGOR
DUD	RON	CHAY	IOLO
ELI	ROY	CLEM	IVAN
ERN	SAM	COLM	IVES
GIB	SEB	CONN	IVOR
GIL	SID	CURT	JACK
GUS	SIM	DALE	JAGO
GUY	STU	DANA	JAKE
HAL	SYD	DAVE	JEFF
HAM	TAM	DAVY	JOCK
HEW	TED	DEAN	JOEL
HOB	TEL	DEWI	JOEY
HUW	TEX	DICK	JOHN
IAN	TIM	DION	JOSÉ
IKE	TOM	DIRK	JOSH
IRA	VIC	DOUG	JUAN
IVO	VIN	DREW	JUDD
JAN	WAL	DUKE	JUDE
JAY	WAT	EARL	KANE
JED	WIN	EBEN	KARL
JEM	ZAK	EDDY	KEIR
JIM	**4**	EDEN	KENT
JOB	ABEL	EDOM	KING
JOE	ADAM	EMIL	KIRK
JON	ALAN	ENOS	KRIS
KAY	ALDO	ERIC	KURT
KEN	ALEC	ERIK	KYLE
KIM	ALED	ERLE	LARS
KIT	ALEX	ESAU	LEON
LEE	ALGY	ESME	LEVI
LEN	ALUN	EVAN	LIAM

BOYS' NAMES

4 continued	THOM	ARMIN	COLUM
LORI	TINO	ARTIE	CONAN
LORN	TOBY	ASHER	CONOR
LUDO	TODD	ATHOL	COSMO
LUKE	TONY	AULAY	CRAIG
LYLE	TREV	AVERY	CUDDY
MARC	TROY	BARON	CYRIL
MARK	VERE	BARRY	CYRUS
MATT	VICK	BASIE	DAMON
MERV	WADE	BASIL	DANNY
MICK	WALT	BENET	DANTE
MIKE	WARD	BENJY	DARBY
MILO	WILF	BENNY	DARCY
MORT	WILL	BERNY	DARYL
MOSS	WYNN	BERRY	DAVID
MUIR	YVES	BEVIS	DENIS
NEAL	ZACK	BILLY	DENNY
NEIL	ZANE	BJORN	DENYS
NICK	ZEKE	BLAIR	DERBY
NOAH	5	BLAKE	DEREK
NOEL	AARON	BLANE	DERRY
NORM	ABNER	BLASE	DERYK
OLAF	ABRAM	BOBBY	DERRY
OLAV	ADAIR	BONAR	DERYK
OMAR	ADOLF	BORIA	DICKY
OSSY	AIDAN	BOYCE	DIGBY
OTHO	ALAIN	BRENT	DONAL
OTIS	ALBAN	BRETT	DONNY
OTTO	ALBIN	BRIAN	DORAN
OWEN	ALDEN	BRICE	DRODO
PAUL	ALDIS	BROCK	DUANE
PETE	ALDUS	BRUCE	DYLAN
PHIL	ALFIE	BRUNO	EAMON
RAFE	ALGAR	BRYAN	EDDIE
RENÉ	ALGER	BRYCE	EDGAR
RHYS	ALGIE	BYRON	EDWIN
RICH	ALICK	CADEL	EDWYN
RICK	ALLAN	CAIUS	ELDON
ROLF	ALLEN	CALEB	ELIAS
ROLY	ALVAH	CALUM	ELIHU
RORY	ALVAR	CAREY	ELIOT
ROSS	ALVIE	CARLO	ELLIS
RUDO	ALVIN	CAROL	ELMER
RUDY	ALVIS	CASEY	ELTON
RUSS	ALWYN	CECIL	ELVIN
RYAN	AMIAS	CHRIS	ELVIS
SAUL	AMYAS	CHUCK	ELWYN
SEAN	ANCEL	CLARK	EMERY
SETH	ANDRÉ	CLAUD	EMILE
SHAW	ANGEL	CLIFF	EMLYN
SHEM	ANGUS	CLINT	EMRYS
STAN	ANSEL	CLIVE	ENOCH
STEW	ANTON	CLYDE	EPPIE
THEO	ARCHY	COLIN	ERNIE

114

5 continued	JESSE	NIGEL	SOLLY
ERROL	JESUS	NIKKI	STEVE
ETHAN	JIMMY	NOLAN	TAFFY
FARON	JONAH	OGDEN	TEDDY
FELIX	JONAS	OLAVE	TERRI
FIDEL	JUDAH	OLLIE	TERRY
FLOYD	JUDAS	ORSON	TIMMY
FRANK	JULES	ORVAL	TITUS
GAIUS	KAROL	OSCAR	TOLLY
GARRY	KEITH	OSSIE	TOMMY
GARTH	KENNY	OSWIN	TUDOR
GAVIN	KEVIN	OWAIN	ULRIC
GEOFF	KIRBY	OZZIE	UPTON
GERRY	LABAN	PABLO	URBAN
GILES	LANCE	PADDY	URIAH
GLENN	LANTY	PAOLO	VINCE
GRANT	LARRY	PARRY	VITUS
GREGG	LAURI	PEDRO	WALDO
GUIDO	LEIGH	PERCE	WALLY
GYLES	LEROY	PERCY	WAYNE
HAMON	LEWIS	PERRY	WILLY
HARDY	LLOYD	PETER	WYATT
HARRY	LOREN	PIERS	WYNNE
HAYDN	LORIN	PIRAN	6
HEATH	LORNE	QUINN	ALDWYN
HEBER	LOUIE	RALPH	ALEXIS
HENRI	LOUIS	RAMON	ALFRED
HENRY	LUCAS	RANDY	ALONSO
HERVÉ	LYULF	RAOUL	ALONZO
HIRAM	MADOC	RICKI	ALURED
HOMER	MANNY	RICKY	ANDREW
HONOR	MANUS	RIKKI	ANGELO
HORRY	MARCO	ROALD	ANSELL
HOWEL	MARIO	ROBIN	ANSELM
HUMPH	MARTY	RODDY	ANTONY
HYMAN	MICAH	RODGE	ARCHER
HYMIE	MICKY	ROGER	ARCHIE
HYWEL	MILES	ROLLO	ARMAND
IDRIS	MITCH	ROLLY	ARNAUD
INIGO	MONTE	ROLPH	ARNOLD
IRVIN	MONTY	ROWAN	ARTHUR
IRWIN	MORAY	ROYAL	ASHLEY
ISAAC	MORTY	RUFUS	AUBERT
ITHEL	MOSES	SACHA	AUBREY
IZAAK	MOSHE	SAMMY	AUGUST
JABEZ	MUNGO	SAXON	AUSTEN
JACKY	MYLES	SCOTT	AUSTIN
JACOB	MYRON	SELBY	AYLMER
JAMES	NEDDY	SERGE	AYLWIN
JAMIE	NEILL	SHANE	AYRTON
JARED	NEVIL	SHAUN	BARNET
JASON	NIALL	SHAWN	BARNEY
JEMMY	NICKY	SILAS	BARRIE
JERRY	NICOL	SIMON	BARRON

BOYS' NAMES

6 continued

BARTLE	DUGALD	HAMLET	LAURIE
BENITO	DUGGIE	HARLEY	LAWRIE
BENNET	DUNCAN	HAROLD	LAYTON
BERNIE	DURAND	HARVEY	LEMUEL
BERTIE	DUSTIN	HAYDEN	LENNOX
BETHEL	DWAYNE	HAYDON	LESLIE
BILLIE	DWIGHT	HECTOR	LESTER
BLAINE	EAMOND	HEDLEY	LIONEL
BLAISE	EDMUND	HERBIE	LONNIE
BOBBIE	EDWARD	HERMAN	LOVELL
BONAMY	EGBERT	HERVEY	LOWELL
BUTOLF	ELDRED	HILARY	LUCIAN
BOTULF	ELIJAH	HOBART	LUCIEN
BUSTER	ELLERY	HOLDEN	LUCIUS
CADELL	ELLIOT	HONOUR	LUTHER
CAESAR	EOGHAN	HORACE	LYNDON
CALLUM	ERNEST	HOWARD	LYULPH
CALVIN	ESMOND	HOWELL	MAGNUS
CARLOS	EUGENE	HUBERT	MALISE
CAROLE	EVELYN	HUGHIE	MALORY
CARTER	FABIAN	ONGRAM	MALVIN
CASPAR	FARREN	IRVINE	MANLEY
CEDRIC	FERGIE	IRVING	MANSEL
CERDIC	FERGUS	ISAIAH	MANUEL
CLAUDE	FINLAY	ISRAEL	MARCEL
COLLEY	FLURRY	JACKIE	MARCUS
CONNOR	FRANCO	JACQUI	MARIUS
CONRAD	FRASER	JARRED	MARTIN
CORMAC	FRAZER	JARROD	MARTYN
CORNEY	FREDDY	JARVIS	MARVIN
COSIMO	GARETH	JASPER	MARVYN
CUDDIE	GARNET	JEREMY	MERLIN
CURTIS	GARRET	JEROME	MERTON
DAFYDD	GASPAR	JETHRO	MERVIN
DAMIAN	GAWAIN	JOHNNY	MERVYN
DAMIEN	GEORGE	JOLYON	MICKEY
DANIEL	GERALD	JORDAN	MILTON
DARREL	GERARD	JOSEPH	MORGAN
DARREN	GERWYN	JOSHUA	MORRIS
DARRYL	GETHIN	JOSIAH	MURRAY
DECLAN	GIDEON	JOSIAS	NATHAN
DENNIS	GILROY	JOTHAM	NEDDIE
DENZIL	GODWIN	JULIAN	NELSON
DERMOT	GORDON	JULIUS	NEWTON
DERYCK	GRAEME	JUNIOR	NINIAN
DEXTER	GRAHAM	JUSTIN	NORMAN
DICKIE	GREGOR	KELVIN	NORRIS
DICKON	GROVER	KENDAL	NORTON
DONALD	GUNTER	KENELM	NOWELL
DORIAN	GUSSIE	KENTON	OBERON
DOUGAL	GUSTAF	KESTER	OLIVER
DOUGIE	GUSTAV	KIERAN	ORRELL
DUDLEY	GWILYM	LAUNCE	OSBERT
	HAMISH	LAUREN	OSBORN

6 continued

OSMOND	STUART	BARNARD	EVERARD
OSMUND	SYDNEY	BARRETT	EZEKIEL
OSWALD	TALBOT	BARTLET	FEARGUS
PALMER	TAYLOR	BASTIAN	FITZROY
PARKER	TEDDIE	BEDFORD	FLORIAN
PASCAL	THOMAS	BENNETT	FRANCIS
PASCOE	TOBIAS	BENTLEY	FRANKIE
PELHAM	TRAVIS	BERNARD	FREDDIE
PHILIP	TREFOR	BERTRAM	FREDRIC
PIERRE	TREVOR	BETHELL	FULBERT
POLDIE	TYBALT	BOTOLPH	GABRIEL
PRINCE	TYRONE	BRADLEY	GARRETT
QUINCY	VAUGHN	BRANDAN	GARRICK
RABBIE	VICTOR	BRANDON	GAYLORD
RAFAEL	VIRGIL	BRENDAN	GEORDIE
RAINER	WALLIS	CANERON	GEORGIE
RAMSAY	WALTER	CARADOC	GERAINT
RAMSEY	WARNER	CARADOG	GERRARD
RANALD	WARREN	CARLTON	GERSHOM
RANDAL	WESLEY	CAROLUS	GERVAIS
RAYNER	WILBUR	CEDRYCH	GERVASE
RAYNOR	WILLIE	CHARLES	GILBERT
REGGIE	WILLIS	CHARLEY	GILLEAN
REUBEN	WILMER	CHARLIE	GILLIAN
RICHIE	WILMOT	CHAUNCY	GODFREY
ROBBIE	WINNIE	CHESTER	GOLDWIN
ROBERT	WYBERT	CHRISTY	GOLDWYN
RODGER	WYSTAN	CLAYTON	GRAHAME
RODNEY	XAVIER	CLEDWYN	GREGORY
ROLAND	YEHUDI	CLEMENT	GUNTHER
RONALD	**7**	CLIFTON	GUSTAVE
RONNIE	ABRAHAM	CLINTON	GWYNFOR
RUDOLF	ABSALOM	COLUMBA	HADRIAN
RUPERT	ABSOLON	CRISPIN	HAMMOND
RUSSEL	ADAMNAN	CRYSTAL	HARTLEY
SAMSON	ADOLPHE	CYPRIAN	HERBERT
SAMUEL	AINSLEY	DARRELL	HERMANN
SEAMUS	AINSLIE	DECIMUS	HILLARY
SEFTON	ALBERIC	DENHOLM	HORATIO
SELWYN	ALDHELM	DERRICK	HUMBERT
SERGEI	ALFONSO	DESMOND	ICHABOD
SERGIO	AMBROSE	DIGGORY	ISIDORE
SEUMAS	ANDREAS	DOMINIC	JACQUES
SEWARD	ANEIRIN	DONOVAN	JAPHETH
SEXTUS	ANEURIN	DOUGLAS	JEFFERY
SHAMUS	ANTHONY	DUNSTAN	JEFFREY
SHELLY	ANTONIO	EARNEST	JILLIAN
SHOLTO	ARTEMAS	ELEAZAR	JOACHIM
SIDNEY	ARTEMUS	ELKANAH	JOCELYN
SIMEON	AUBERON	ELLIOTT	JOHNNIE
STEVEN	AZARIAH	EMANUEL	KENDALL
STEVIE	BALDWIN	EPHRIAM	KENNETH
ST JOHN	BARCLAY	ERASMUS	KENRICK
	BARNABY	EUSTACE	KIMBALL

117

BOYS' NAMES

7 continued

LACHLAN	RODOLPH	BARDOLPH	HUMPHREY
LAMBERT	RODRIGO	BARNABAS	IGNATIUS
LAZARUS	ROWLAND	BARTLETT	IORWERTH
LEANDER	ROYSTON	BENEDICK	JEDIDAH
LEOFRIC	RUDOLPH	BENEDICT	JEPHTHAH
LEOLINE	RUSSELL	BENJAMIN	JEREMIAH
LEONARD	SALAMON	BERENGER	JEREMIAS
LEOPOLD	SAMPSON	BERKELEY	JERMAINE
LINCOLN	SERGIUS	BERNHARD	JOHANNES
LINDSAY	SEYMOUR	BERTHOLD	JONATHAN
LORENZO	SHANNON	BERTRAND	JOSCELIN
LUDOVIC	SHELDON	BEVERLEY	KIMBERLY
MALACHI	SHELLEY	BONIFACE	KINGSLEY
MALACHY	SIGMUND	CAMILLUS	LANCELOT
MALCOLM	SOLOMON	CAMPBELL	LAURENCE
MALLORY	SPENCER	CARLETON	LAWRENCE
MANFRED	STANLEY	CARTHACH	LEIGHTON
MANSELL	STEPHEN	CHARLTON	LLEWELYN
MATTHEW	STEWART	CHAUNCEY	MANASSEH
MAURICE	SWITHIN	CHRISTIE	MANASSES
MAXWELL	TANCRED	CHRYSTAL	MARSHALL
MAYNARD	TERENCE	CLARENCE	MATTHIAS
MEIRION	TERTIUS	CLAUDIUS	MELVILLE
MERRION	THORLEY	CLIFFORD	MEREDITH
MICHAEL	TIMOTHY	CONSTANT	MITCHELL
MILBURN	TORQUIL	COURTNEY	MONTAGUE
MONTAGU	TRAVERS	CRISPIAN	MORDECAI
MURDOCH	TRISTAN	CUTHBERT	MORTIMER
MURTAGH	ULYSSES	DIARMAIT	NAPOLEON
NEVILLE	VAUGHAN	DIARMUID	NEHEMIAH
NICOLAS	VINCENT	DOMINICK	NICHOLAS
NORBERT	WALLACE	EBENEZER	OCTAVIAN
OBADIAH	WARWICK	EMMANUEL	OCTAVIUS
OLIVER	WENDELL	ETHELRED	PERCEVAL
ORLANDO	WILBERT	FARQUHAR	PERCIVAL
ORVILLE	WILFRED	FERNANDO	PHILEMON
OSBORNE	WILFRID	FLETCHER	PHINEHAS
PADRAIG	WINSTON	FLORENCE	RADCLIFF
PATRICK	WOODROW	FLUELLEN	RANDOLPH
PHILLIP	WYNDHAM	FRANKLIN	REGINALD
PHINEAS	WYNFORD	FREDERIC	RODERICK
PRESTON	ZACHARY	FREDRICK	SALVADOR
QUENTIN	**8**	GAMALIEL	SEPTIMUS
QUINTIN	ADOLPHUS	GARFIELD	SHERIDAN
RANDALL	ALASDAIR	GEOFFREY	SILVANUS
RAPHAEL	ALASTAIR	GRAYBURN	SINCLAIR
RAYMOND	ALGERNON	GRIFFITH	STAFFORD
RAYMUND	ALISTAIR	GUSTAVUS	STANFORD
REDVERS	ALOYSIUS	HAMILTON	STIRLING
REYNARD	ALPHONSE	HANNIBAL	SYLVANUS
REYNOLD	ALPHONSO	HARRISON	TALIESIN
RICARDO	AUGUSTIN	HERCULES	TERRENCE
RICHARD	AUGUSTUS	HEREWARD	THADDEUS
	AURELIAN	HEZEKIAH	THEOBALD

8 continued
THEODORE
THORNTON
THUSTAN
THURSTON
TRISTRAM
TURLOUGH
WINTHROP
ZEDEKIAH
9
ALEXANDER
ALPHONSUS
AMBROSIUS
ARCHELAUS
ARCHIBALD
ATHELSTAN
AUGUSTINE
BALTHAZAR
BRODERICK
CADWALADR
CHRISTIAN

CHRISTMAS
CORNELIUS
COURTENAY
DIONYSIUS
ETHELBERT
FERDINAND
FRANCESCO
FRANCISCO
FREDERICK
GERONTIUS
GRANVILLE
GRENVILLE
JEFFERSON
KENTIGERN
KIMBERLEY
LAUNCELOT
LLEWELLYN
MARCELLUS
MARMADUKE
NATHANAEL
NATHANIEL

NICODEMUS
ONUPHRIUS
PEREGRINE
PHILIBERT
RADCLIFFE
SALVATORE
SEBASTIAN
SIEGFRIED
SIGISMUND
SILVESTER
SPARTACUS
STANISLAS
SYLVESTER
THEODORIC
VALENTINE
ZACCHAEUS
ZACHARIAS
ZECHARIAH
ZEPHANIAH

10
BARRINGTON
CARACTACUS
FORTUNATUS
HIERONYMUS
HILDEBRAND
HIPPOLYTUS
MAXIMILIAN
MONTGOMERY
STANISLAUS
THEOPHILUS
WASHINGTON
WILLOUGHBY
11
BARTHOLOMEW
CADWALLADER
CHRISTOPHER
CONSTANTINE
SACHEVERELL

ART AND CULTURE

ART

2	MAESTA	TEMPERA	COLOURIST
OP	MEDIUM	VANITAS	DISTEMPER
3	MOBILE	VARNISH	ENGRAVING
FEC	MOSAIC	WOODCUT	GRISAILLE
INC	PASTEL	**8**	GROTESQUE
INK	PATINA	ABSTRACT	INTIMISME
OIL	PENCIL	AIR-BRUSH	LANDSCAPE
POP	PURISM	ALLEGORY	MAHL-STICK
4	RELIEF	ANCIENTS	MAULSTICK
BODY	ROCOCO	AQUATINT	MEZZOTINT
BUST	SCHOOL	ARMATURE	MINIATURE
CAST	SKETCH	ARRICCIO	POLYPTYCH
DADA	STUCCO	BARBIZON	PRIMITIVE
HERM	STYLUS	BOZZETTO	SCULPTURE
KORE	TUSCAN	CARYATID	STILL LIFE
SIZE	VEDUTA	CHARCOAL	STIPPLING
SWAG	VERISM	DROLERIE	SYMBOLISM
TERM	**7**	DRYPOINT	TENEBRISM
WASH	ACADEMY	EMULSION	VORTICISM
5	ARCHAIC	FIXATIVE	**10**
BRUSH	ATELIER	FROTTAGE	ARRICCIATO
BURIN	BAROQUE	FUTURISM	ART NOUVEAU
CHALK	BAUHAUS	GRAFFITI	ASSEMBLAGE
EASEL	BITUMEN	HATCHING	AUTOMATISM
FECIT	BODEGON	INTAGLIO	AVANTGARDE
GESSO	CABINET	INTONACO	BIOMORPHIC
GLAZE	CAMAIEU	MANDORLA	CARICATURE
MODEL	CARTOON	MAQUETTE	CIRE-PERDUE
NAIVE	COLLAGE	PASTICHE	CRAQUELURE
PUTTO	COSMATI	PLEURANT	FLORENTINE
SALON	DIPTYCH	POUNCING	METALPOINT
SCULP	DRAWING	PREDELLA	MONOCHROME
SECCO	ECORCHE	REPOUSSÉ	MORBIDEZZA
SEPIA	ETCHING	SCULPSIT	NATURALISM
STYLE	GOUACHE	STAFFAGE	PENTIMENTO
TONDO	IMPASTO	TACHISME	PROVENANCE
6	INCIDIT	TESSERAE	QUADRATURA
ASHCAN	LINOCUT	TRECENTO	REPOUSSOIR
BSTRE	LOST WAX	TRIPTYCH	ROMANESQUE
CANVAS	MODELLO	VENETIAN	SURREALISM
CUBISM	MONTAGE	**9**	SYNTHETISM
FRESCO	PALETTE	ALLA PRIMA	TURPENTINE
GOTHIC	PIGMENT	ANTI-CERNE	XYLOGRAPHY
GROUND	POCHADE	AOUARELLE	**11**
KIT-CAT	REALISM	AUTOGRAPH	BAMBOCCANTI
KITSCH	SCUMBLE	BRUSHWORK	BIEDERMEIER
KOUROS	SFUMATO	BYZANTINE	CAROLINGIAN
LIMNER	SINOPIA	CAPRICCIO	CHIAROSCURO

11 continued
CONTÉ CRAYON
DIVISIONISM
ECLECTICISM
ILLUSIONISM
IMPRIMATURA
LITHOGRAPHY
MASTERPIECE
PERSPECTIVE
PICTURESQUE

POINTILLISM
PORTRAITURE
RENAISSANCE
RETROUSSAGE
STYLIZATION
SUPREMATISM
TROMPE L'OEIL
WATERCOLOUR

12
ACRYLIC PAINT
ANAMORPHOSIS
CLOISONNISME
CONTRAPPOSTO
COUNTERPROOF
ILLUMINATION
PRECISIONISM
QUATTROCENTO
SUPERREALISM

13
ARCHITECTONIC
EXPRESSIONISM
FETE CHAMPETRE
IMPRESSIONISM
PAPIERS COLLES
14
CONSTRUCTIVISM

ARCHITECTURE

3
BAY
CAP
DIE
EVE
KEY
4
AMBO
ANTA
APSE
ARCH
BAND
BEAD
BELL
BOSS
DADO
DAIS
DOME
FRET
FROG
FUST
NAVE
PELE
STOA
5
AISLE
AMBRY
ARRIS
ATTIC
CONGE
CROWN
CRYPT
DORIC
FOILS
GABLE
GLYPH
HELIX
INLAY

IONIC
LOBBY
NEWEL
ROMAN
SCAPE
SHAFT
SHANK
TALON
TENIA
TUDOR
VERGE
6
ABACUS
ACCESS
ALCOVE
ARCADE
ATRIUM
ATTICK
AUMBRY
BELFRY
BONNET
BROACH
CANOPY
CHEVET
COLUMN
CORONA
CRENEL
CUPOLA
DAGGER
DENTIL
DIAPER
FACADE
FILLET
FINIAL
FLECHE
FRESCO
FRIEZE
GABLET

GAZEBO
GOTHIC
GUTTAE
HEROIC
LESENE
LINTEL
LINTOL
LOGGIA
LOUVRE
MANTEL
MERLON
METOPE
MUTULE
NORMAN
OCULUS
PAGODA
PATERA
PLINTH
PULPIT
QUADRA
REGULA
ROCOCO
SCAPUS
SCROLL
SEDILE
SOFFIT
TROPHY
URELLA
VESTRY
VOLUTE
WREATH
XYSTUS
ZIG-ZAG
7
ANNULET
ARCH RIB
ASTYLAR
BALCONY

BAROQUE
BASTION
BOULTIN
BUTMENT
CAPITAL
CAVETTO
CHANCEL
CHEVRON
CORNICE
CROCHET
CROCKET
DISTYLE
ECHINUS
ENCARPA
ENTASIS
EUSTYLE
FESTOON
FLEURON
FLUTING
GADROON
GALILEE
GALLERY
LACUNAR
LANTERN
LATTICE
LEQUEAR
LUNETTE
NARTHEX
NULLING
OBELISK
ORATORY
PARVISE
PORTAIL
PORTICO
POSTERN
PTEROMA
REEDING
REGENCY

7 continued
REREDOS
ROSETTE
ROTUNDA
ROUNDEL
SCALLOP
SPANISH
SYSTYLE
TESSARA
TONDINO
TRACERY
TRUMEAU
8
ABUTMENT
ACANTHUS
AEDICUL A
APOPHYGE
ASTRAGAL
ATLANTES
BALUSTER
BARTIZAN
BASILICA
BEAK HEAD
CARYATID
CIMBORIO
CINCTURE
CRENELLE
CRESTING
CYMATIUM
DIASTYLE
DIPTERAL
DOG-TOOTH
EDGE ROLL
EXTRADOS
FORMERET
GARGOYLE
INTRADOS
KEEL ARCH
KEYSTONE

LICH GATE
LYCH GATE
MISERERE
PAVILION
PEDESTAL
PEDIMENT
PILASTER
PREDELLA
PULPITUM
ROCAILLE
SPANDREL
SPANDRIL
TORCHING
TRANSEPT
TRIGLYPH
TYMPANUM
VERANDAH
VIGNETTE
WAINSCOT
9
ACROPOLIS
ANTEFIXAE
ANTHEMION
APEX STONE
ARABESQUE
ARCH BRICK
ARCHIVOLT
ATTIC BASE
BIRD'S BEAK
BYZANTINE
CAMPANILE
CANEPHORA
CARTOUCHE
CAULICOLI
CLOISTERS
COLONNADE
COMPOSITE
DRIPSTONE
FOLIATION

GROTESQUE
HEXASTYLE
HYPOCAUST
HYPOSTYLE
INGLE NOOK
LABEL STOP
LACUNARIA
LINENFOLD
MEZZANINE
MOULDINGS
OCTASTYLE
PALLADIAN
REFECTORY
SGRAFFITO
STRAPWORK
STYLOBATE
TRABEATED
TRIFORIUM
TRILITHON
VESTIBULE
ZOOPHORUS
10
ACROTERION
AMBULATORY
ARAEOSTYLE
ARCHITRAVE
BALDACHINO
BALL FLOWER
BALUSTRADE
BATTLEMENT
CINQUEFOIL
COLONNETTE
CORINTHIAN
EGG AND DART
ENRICHMENT
HAGIOSCOPE
LADY CHAPEL
LANCET ARCH
MISERICORD

MODILLIONS
PIETRA DURA
PRESBYTERY
PYCNOSTYLE
QUATREFOIL
ROMANESQUE
ROOD SCREEN
ROSE WINDOW
SEXPARTITE
TETRASTYLE
TRACHELION
11
CASTELLATED
ENTABLATURE
FAN VAULTING
HARELIP ARCH
LEADED LIGHT
MANTELPIECE
MANTELSHELF
ORIEL WINDOW
RENAISSANCE
RETICULATED
12
AMPHITHEATRE
BLIND TRACERY
COCKLE STAIRS
EGG AND TONGUE
LANCET WINDOW
PORTE-COCHERE
13
AMPHI-PROSTYLE
14
ANGULAR CAPITAL
FLYING BUTTRESS
HYPOTRACHELION

LITERATURE

3
ODE
WIT
4
EPIC
FOOT
IAMB
MYTH

5
ELEGY
FABLE
GENRE
ICTUS
IRONY
LYRIC
METRE
NOVEL

OCTET
PROSE
RHYME
STYLE
THEME
VERSE
6
BALLAD
BATHOS

CESURA
CLICHE
DACTYL
HUBRIS
LAMENT
MONODY
OCTAVE
PARODY
PATHOS

125

LITERATURE / MUSIC

6 continued

6 continued	8	10	14
SATIRE	ALLEGORY	BLANK VERSE	EXISTENTIALISM
SCHOOL	ANAPAEST	CARICATURE	FEMININE ENDING
SEPTET	AUGUSTAN	DENOUEMENT	MILTONIC SONNET
SESTET	DIDACTIC	EPIC SIMILE	ROMANTIC
SIMILE	ELEMENTS	HEPTAMETER	POETRY
SONNET	EXEMPLUM	MOCK HEROIC	SENTIMENTALITY
STANZA	EYE RHYME	NATURALISM	**15**
STRESS	METAPHOR	PENTAMETER	MASCULINE
SYMBOL	OXYMORON	PICARESQUE	ENDING
7	PASTORAL	SPOONERISM	PATHETIC
CAESURA	QUATRAIN	SUBJECTIVE	FALLACY
CONCEIT	RHETORIC	TETRAMETER	PERSONIFICATION
COUPLET	SCANSION	**11**	**16**
DICTION	SYLLABLE	ANACHRONISM	PETRARCHAN
ELISION	TRIMETER	COURTLY LOVE	SONNET
EPIGRAM	**9**	END STOPPING	**18**
EPISTLE	AMBIGUITY	GOTHIC NOVEL	METAPHYSICAL
EPITAPH	ASSONANCE	HORATIAN ODE	POETRY
EUPHONY	BURLESQUE	MALAPROPISM	NEGATIVE
HUMOURS	CATHARSIS	NOBLE SAVAGE	CAPABILITY
IMAGERY	CLASSICAL	OBJECTIVITY	OMNISCIENT
NEMESIS	EUPHEMISM	TRAGICOMEDY	NARRATOR
PARADOX	FREE VERSE	**12**	**20+**
PROSODY	HALF RHYME	ALLITERATION	STREAM OF
PYRRHIC	HEXAMETER	ONOMATOPOEIA	CONSCIOUSNESS
REALISM	HYPERBOLE	**13**	
SPONDEE	MONOMETER	ANTHROPOMORPH	
SUBPLOT	OCTAMETER	HEROIC COUPLET	
TRAGEDY	PARARHYME	INTERNAL RHYME	

MUSIC

1 & 2
F - loud
FF - very loud
MF - half loud
P - soft
PP - very soft
SF - strongly accented

3
BIS - repeat
DIM - becoming softer
PED - abbr. for pedal
PIU - more
PIZ - plucked
RFZ - accentuated RIT - slowing down,
  holding back
SFZ - strongly accented
TEN - held
VIF - lively (Fr.)

4
CODA - final part of a movement
MOTO - motion
RALL - slowing down
SINO - up to; until
TIEF - deep; low (Ger.)

5
AD LIB - at will
ASSAI - very
SUFFO - comic
DOLCE - sweet
FORTE - loud
LARGO - very slow
LENTO - slowly .
MESTO - sad, mournful
MEZZO - half
MOLTO - very much
MOSSO - moving, fast

5 continued

PIANO - soft
QUASI - almost, as if
SEGNO - sign
SENZA - without
SOAVE - sweet; gentle
STARK - strong, loud (Ger.)
TACET - instrument is silent
TANTO - so much
TEMPO - the speed of a composition
TUTTI - all
ZOPPA - in syncopated rhythm

6

ADAGIO - slow
AL FINE - to the end
CHIUSO - stopped (of a note); closed
DA CAPO - from the beginning
DEHORS - outside; prominent
DIVISI - divided
DOPPIO - double
FACILE - easy, fluent
LEGATO - bound, tied (of notes), smoothly
MARCIA - march
NIENTE - nothing
NOBILE - noble
RETENU - held back
SEMPRE - always, still
SUBITO - immediately
TENUTO - held

7

AGITATO - agitated; rapid tempo
ALLEGRO - lively, brisk
AL SEGNO - as far as the sign
AMOROSO - loving, emotional
ANIMATO - spirited
ATTACCA - attack; continue without a pause
CALANDO - ebbing., lessening of tempo
CODETTA - small coda; to conclude a
   passage
CON BRIO - with vigour
DOLENTE - sorrowful
ESTINTO - very softly, almost without tone
GIOCOSO - merry; playful
MARCATO - accented
MORBIDO - soft, delicate
PESANTE - heavily, firmly
SCHNELL - fast (Ger.)
SFOGATO -effortless; in a tree manner
SORDINO - mute
STRETTO - accelerating or intensifying;
   overlapping of entries of fugue

8

A BATTUTA - return to strict time
A PIACERE - as you please
BRILLANT - brilliant
COL CANTO - accompaniment to follow solo
   line
COL LEGNO - to strike strings with stick of
   the bow
CON FIJOCO - fiery; vigorous
DAL SEGNO - from the sign
IN MODO DI - in the manner of
MAESTOSO - majestic
MODERATO - moderately
PORTANDO - carrying one note into the next
RITENUTO - slowing down, holding back
SOURDINE - mute (Fr.)
STACCATO - detached
VIVEMENT - lively (Fr.)

9

ADAGIETTO - quite.slow
CANTABILE - in a singing fashion
CANTILENA - lyrical, flowing
FIORITURA - decoration of a melody
GLISSANDO - sliding scale played on
   instrument
MENO MOSSO - slower pace
MEZZA VOCE - at half power
OBBLIGATO - not to be omitted
PIUTTOSTO - somewhat
PIZZICATO - plucked
SCHNELLER - faster (Ger.)
SFORZANDO - strongly accented
SIN'AL FINE - up to the end
SLENTANDO - slowing down
SOSTENUTO - sustained
SOTTO VOCE - quiet subdued tone

10

AFFETTUOSO - tender
ALLA CACCIA - in hunting style
ALLARGANDO - broadening; more dignified
ALLEGRETTO - quite lively, brisk
DIMINUENDO - becoming softer
FORTISSIMO - very loud
MEZZOFORTE - half loud
NOBILMENTE - nobly
PERDENDOSI - dying away gradually
PIANISSIMO - very soft
PORTAMENTO - carrying one note into next
RAVIVANDO - quickening
RITARDANDO - slowing down, holding back
SCHERZANDO - joking; playing

127

MUSIC / SOL- FA / INSTRUMENTS

10 continued
SCHLEPPEND - dragging; deviating from
  correct speed (Ger.)
SCORREVOLE - gliding; fluent
STRINGENDO - tightening; intensification
11
ACCELERANDO - accelerating
AFFRETTANDO - hurrying
MINACCIANDO - menacing

RALLENTANDO - slowing down
RINFORZANDO - accentuated
12
ALLA CAPPELLA - in church style
LEGGERAMENTE - lightly
13
LEGGIERAMENTE - lightly

SOL-FA SCALE

DOH	ME	SOH	TE
RAY	FAH	LAH	

MUSICAL INSTRUMENTS

2
UD (lute)
YU (scraper)
3
BIN (vina)
KIT (fiddle)
LUR (horn)
OUD (ud)
SAZ (lute)
SHO (mouth organ)
TAR (drum; lute)
UTI (lute)
4
BATA (drum)
BIWA (lute)
CH'IN (zither)
DRUM
FIFE
FUYE (flute)
GONG
HARP
HORN
KENA (quena)
KHEN (mouth organ)
KOTO (zither)
LIRA (fiddle)
LUTE
LYRA (lyre)
LYRE
MU YU (drum)
MVET (zither)
OBOE
OUTI (lute)
P'I P'A (lute)

PIPE
ROTE (lyre)
RUAN (lute)
SONA (shawm)
TRO-U (fiddle)
URUA (clarinet)
VINA (stringed instrument
  related to sitar)
VIOL
WHIP (percussion)
ZOBO (mirliton)
5
AULOI (shawm)
BANJO
BELLS
BHAYA (kettledrum)
BUGLE
BUMPA (clarinet)
CELLO
CHANG (dulcimer)
CHIME
CLAVE
COBZA (lute)
CORNU (trumpet)
CRWTH (tyre)
DAULI (drum)
DHOLA (drum)
DOBRO (guitar)
ERH-HU (fiddle)
FIDEL (fiddle)
FIDLA (zither)
FLUTE
GAITA (bagpipe)
GAJDY (bagpipe)

GUSLE (fiddle)
HURUK (drum)
KAKKO (drum)
KANUN (qanun)
KAZOO (mirliton)
KERAR (lyre)
MBILA (xylophone)
NGOMA (drum)
NGURU (flute)
OKEDO (drum)
ORGAN
PIANO
QANUN (zither)
QUENA (flute)
RASPA (scraper)
REBAB (fiddle)
REBEC (fiddle)
SARON
  (metallophone)
SHAWM
SHENG (mouth organ)
SITAR (lute)
TABLA (drum)
TABOR (drum)
TAIKO (drum)
TIBIA (shawm)
TIPLE (shawm)
TUDUM (drum)
TUMYR (drum)
TUPAN (drum)
VIOLA
YUN LO (gong)
ZURLA (shawm)
ZURNA (shawm)

6

ALBOKA (hornpipe)
ARGHUL (clarinet)
BAGANA (lyre)
BINIOU (bagpipe)
CARNYX (trumpet)
CHAKAY (zither)
CHA PEI (lute)
CORNET
CURTAL (double reed)
DARBUK (drum)
FANDUR (fiddle)
FIDDLE
FUJARA (flute)
GEKKIN (lute)
GENDER (metallophone)
GONGUE (percussion)
GUITAR
HU CH'IN (fiddle)
HUMMEL (zither)
KENONG (gong)
KISSAR (lyre)
KOBORO (drum)
LIRICA (fiddle)
LIRONE (fiddle)
LITUUS (trumpet)
LONTAR (clappers)
MAYURI (lute)
MOROPI (drum)
NAKERS (drums)
NAQARA (drums)
NTENGA (drum)
O-DAIKO (drum)
OMBGWE (flute)
P'AI PAN (clappers)
POMMER (shawm)
RACKET (double reed)
RAMKIE (lute)
RATTLE
SANTIR (dulcimer)
SHAING (horn)
SHAKER
SHANAI (shawm)
SHIELD (percussion)
SHOFAR (horn)
SOPILE (shawm)
SPINET
SPOONS (clappers)
SRALAY (shawm)
SURNAJ (shawm)
SWITCH (percussion)

SYRINX (panpipe)
TAM-TAM (gong)
TOM-TOM (drum)
TXISTU (flute)
VALIHA (zither)
VIELLE (fiddle)
VIOLIN
YANGUM (dulcimer)
ZITHER

7

ADENKUM (stamping tube)
ALPHORN (trumpet)
ANKLUNG (rattle)
ATUMPAN (kettledrum)
BAGPIPE
BARYTON (viol)
BASSOON
BODHRAN (drum)
BONNANG (gong)
BOW HARP
BOXLYRE
BUCCINA (trumpet)
BUISINE (trumpet)
BUMBASS
CELESTE
CHANGKO (drum)
CITTERN
CORNETT
COWBELL
CROTALS (percussion)
CYMBALS
DA-DAIKO (drum)
DIPLICE (clarinet)
DUGDUGI (drum)
ENZENZE (zither)
FITHELE (fiddle)
GADULKA (fiddle)
GITTERN
GLING-BU (flute)
HULA IPU
  (percussion)
INGUNGU (drum)
ISIGUBU (drum)
KACHAPI (zither)
KALUNGU (talking drum)
KAMANJE (fiddle)
KANTELE (zither)
KEMANAK (clappers)
KITHARA (lyre)
KOMUNGO (zither)
MACHETE (lute)

MANDOLA (lute)
MARACAS (percussion)
MASENQO (fiddle)
MIGYAUN (zither)
MOKUGYO (drum)
MURUMBU (drum)
MUSETTE (bagpipe)
MUSETTE (shawm)
OBUKANO (lyre)
OCARINA (flute)
OCTAVIN (wind)
ORPHICA (piano)
PANDORA (cittern)
PANPIPE
PIANINO
PIBCORN (hornpipe)
PICCOLO
PIFFARO (shawm)
QUINTON (viol)
RESHOTO (drum)
RINCHIK (cymbals)
SACKBUT (trombone)
SALPINX (trumpet)
SAMISEN (lute)
SANTOOR (dulcimer)
SARANGI (fiddle)
SARINDA (fiddle)
SAW-THAI (fiddle)
SAXHORN
SAXTUBA
SERPENT
SHIWAYA (flute)
SISTRUM (rattle)
SORDINE (kit)
SORDONE (double reed)
SPAGANE (clappers)
TAM AM LA (gong)
TAMBURA (lute)
TERBANG (drum)
THEORBO (lute)
TIKTIRI (clarinet)
TYMPANY
TRUMPET
TSUZUMI (drum)
UJUSINI (flute)
UKULELE
VIHUELA (guitar)
VIOLONE (viol)
WHISTLE
YUN NGAO (gong)
ZUMMARA (clarinet)

MUSICAL INSTRUMENTS

8

ALGHAITA (shawm)
ALTOHORN
AUTOHARP
BANDOURA (lute)
BASS DRUM
BASS HORN
BOMBARDE (shawm)
BOUZOUKI (lute)
BOWL LYRE
BUZZ DISK
CALLIOPE (mechanical
  organ)
CARILLON
CHIME BAR
CIMBALOM (dulcimer)
CIPACTLI (flute)
CLAPPERS
CLARINET
CLAVICOR (brass family)
CLAW BELL
COURTAUT (double reed)
CRECELLE (cog rattle)
CRUMHORN (double reed)
DULCIMER
DVOYNICE (flute)
GONG DRUM
HANDBELL
HAND HORN
HAWKBELL
JEW'S HARP
KAYAKEUM (zither)
KHUMBGWE (flute)
LANGLEIK (zither)
LANGSPIL (zither)
LAP ORGAN (melodeon)
MANDOLIN (lute)
MELODEON
MELODICA
MIRLITON (kazoo)
MRIDANGA (drum)
OLIPHANT (horn)
O-TSUZUMI (drum)
OTTAVINO (virginal)
P'AI HSIAO (panpipe)
PENORCON (cittern)
POCHETTE (kit)
PSALTERY (zither)
PUTORINO (trumpet)
RECORDER
RKAN-DUNG (trumpet)

RKAN-LING (horn)
RONEAT-EK (xylophone)
SAN HSIEN (lute)
SIDE DRUM
SLIT DRUM
SONAJERO (rattle)
SRINGARA (fiddle)
SURBAHAR (lute)
TALAMBAS (drum)
TARABUKA (drum)
TAROGATO (clarinet;
  shawm)
TIMBALES (drum)
TRIANGLE
TRO-KHMER (fiddle)
TROMBONE
VIOLETTA (viol)
VIRGINAL
YANGCHIN (dulcimer)
YUEH CH'IN (lute)
ZAMPOGNA (bagpipe)

9

ACCORDION
ANGLE HARP
ARPANETTA (zither)
BALALAIKA (lute)
BANDURRIA (lute)
BANJOLELE
BASSONORE (bassoon)
BOMBARDON (tuba)
CASTANETS
CHALUMEAU (clarinet)
COG RATTLE
COMPONIUM (mechanical
  organ)
CORNEMUSE (bagpipe)
CORNOPEAN (brass family)
CROOK HORN
DAIBYOSHI (drum)
DARABUKKE (drum)
DJUNADJAN (zither)
DUDELSACK (bagpipes)
DVOJACHKA (flute)
EUPHONIUM (brass family)
FLAGEOLET (flute)
FLEXATONE (percussion)
GONG AGENG
HACKBRETT (dulcimer)
HARMONICA
HARMONIUM
HYDRAULIS (organ)

KELONTONG (drum)
KONIGHORN (brass family)
LAUNEDDAS (clarinet)
MANDOBASS (lute)
MANDOLONE (lute)
MORIN-CHUR (fiddle)
ORPHARION (citlern)
PICCO PIPE (flute)
PIEN CH'ING
  (lithophone)
ROMMELPOT (drum)
SAXOPHONE
TALLHARPA (lyre)
TOTOMBITO (zither)
TUBA-DUPRE
WOOD BLOCK
WURLITZER
XYLOPHONE
XYLORIMBA
  (xylophone)

10

BANANA DRUM
BARREL DRUM
BASSANELLO (double reed)
BASSET HORN
BIBLE REGAL (organ)
BICITRABIN (vina)
BIRD SCARER
BONGO DRUMS
BULL-ROARER
CHENGCHENG (cymbals)
CHITARRONE (lute)
CLAVICHORD
CLAVIORGAN
COLASCIONE (lute)
CONTRABASS (double
  bass)
COR ANGLAIS
DIDGERIDOO (trumpet)
DOUBLE BASS
FLUGELHORN
FRENCH HORN
GEIGENWERK (mechanical
  harpsichord)
GONG CHIMES
GRAND PIANO
HANDLE DRUM
HURDY GURDY
KETTLEDRUM
LITHOPHONE
  (percussion)

MUSICAL INSTRUMENTS / THEATRE

10 continued

MANDOCELLO (lute)
MELLOPHONE (horn)
MOSHUPIANE (drum)
MOUTH ORGAN
OPHICLEIDE (brass
family)
RANASRINGA (horn)
SAXOTROMBA
SHAKUHACHI (flute)
SOUSAPHONE
SPITZHARFE (zither)
SYMPHONIUM (mouthorgan)
TAMBOURINE (drum)
TEPONAZTLI (drum)
THUMB PIANO (Jew's harp)
TIN WHISTLE
TLAPIZTALI (flute)
TSURI DAIKO (drum)

11

AEOLIAN HARP
ANGEL CHIMES
BARREL ORGAN
BELL CITTERN
BIVALVE BELL
BLADDER PIPE
BOARD ZITHER
CLAPPER BELL
FIPPLE FLUTE
GAMBANG KAYA
(xylophone)
GUITAR-BANJO
HAND TRUMPET
HARPSICHORD
HECKELPHONE (oboe)
NYCKELHARPA,
PAIMENSARVI (horn)
PANHUEHUETL
(drum)

SARON DEMONG
(metallophone)
SLEIGH BELLS
SPIKE FIDDLE
THEORBO -LUTE
UCHIWA DAIKO
(drum)
VIOLA D'AMORE
(viol)
VIOLONCELLO

12

DIPLO-KITHARA (zither)
GANSA GAMBANG
(metallophone)
GANSAJONGKOK
(metallophone)
GLOCKENSPIEL
(metallophone)
GUITAR-VIOLIN
HI-HAT CYMBALS
KANTELEHARPE (tyre)
MANDOLINETTO (ukulele)
PEACOCK SITAR (lute)
RAUSCHPFEIFE (double
reed)
SARRUSOPHONE (brass)
SHOULDER HARP
STOCK-AND-HORN
(hornpipe)
TIPPOO'S TIGER
(organ)
TUBULAR BELLS
VIOLA DA GAMBA (viol)
WHISTLE FLUTE

13

COCKTAIL DRUMS
CONTRABASSOON
DOUBLE BASSOON

(contrabassoon)
HARDANGERFELE (fiddle)
HECKELCLARINA (clarinet)
SAVERNAKE HORN
SCHRILLPFIEFE (flute)
SLIDE TROMBONE
VIOLA BASTARDA (viol)

14

CLARINET D'AMORE
CLAVICYTHERIUM
(harpsichord)
CYTHARA ANGLICA (harp)
JINGLING JOHNNY
TLAPANHUEHUETL (drum)
TRICCABALLACCA
(clappers)

15

CLASSICAL GUITAR
MOOG SYNTHESIZER
TURKISH CRESCENT
(jingling johnny)

16

CHINESE WOOD BLOCK
CHITARRA BATTENTE
(guitar)
CYLINDRICAL DRUMS
DEUTSCHE SCHALMEI
(double reed)
STRUMENTO DI PORCO
(zither)

THEATRE

2	LEG	EXIT	OLIO
OP	PIT	FLAT	PIPE
SM	RUN	GAFF	PROP
3	SET	GOBO	RAIL
ACT	4	GODS	RAKE
ARC	BLUE	GRID	SOCK
ASM	BOOK	IRIS	TABS
GEL	BOOM	LEKO	TAIL
HAM	DROP	MASK	WING

131

5
ABOVE
ACTOR
AD LIB
AGENT
APRON
ARENA
ASIDE
BELOW
BRACE
CLOTH
CLOUD
FLIES
FLOAT
FOYER
GAUZE
GLORY
HALLS
HEAVY
HOIST
INSET
LYRIC
MANET
ODEUM
PERCH
SCENE
SCRIM
SKENE
SLIPS
SLOTE
SOUND
STAGE
STALL
STILE
TRAPS
TRUCK
VISOR
6
BARREL
BATTEN
BOARDS
BORDER
BOX SET
BRIDGE
BUSKER
CELLAR
CENTRE
CIRCLE
CRITIC
GEGGIE
GROOVE

MAKE-UP
NEUMES
OLD MAN
POSTER
PUPPET
RETURN
RUNWAY
SCRUTO
SEA ROW
TEASER
TELARI
TOGGLE
WALK-ON
7
ACT DROP
ACTRESS
AULAEUM
BALCONY
BENEFIT
CALL BOY
CATWALK
CIRCUIT
CURTAIN
DIORAMA
FLIPPER
GALLERY
JORNADA
MANAGER
MATINEE
ON STAGE
PINSPOT
RAIN BOX
ROLL-OUT
ROSTRUM
ROYALTY
SCENERY
SKY DOME
SPOT BAR
TABLEAU
TOP DROP
TRILOGY
TUMBLER
TWO-FOLD
UPSTAGE
VALANCE
8
AUDITION
BLACKOUT
BOOK FLAT
BOOK WING
CALL DOOR

CHAIRMAN
CUT-CLOTH
DESIGNER
DIRECTOR
DUMBSHOW
ELEVATOR
EPILOGUE
FAUTEUIL
FOX WEDGE
JUVENILE
LASHLINE
LIBRETTO
LIGHTING
OFF STAGE
OLD WOMAN
PANORAMA
PARADISO
PARALLEL
PASS DOOR
PLATFORM
PLAYBILL
PRODUCER
PROLOGUE
PROMPTER
SCENARIO
SET PIECE
SILL IRON
SIPARIUM
SKY CLOTH
STAR TRAP
VAMP TRAP
WARDROBE
9
ACOUSTICS
BACKCLOTH
BACKSTAGE
BOAT TRUCK
BOX OFFICE
CALL BOARD
CARPET CUT
CYCLORAMA
DOWNSTAGE
FAN EFFECT
FOOTLIGHT
GRAVE TRAP
GREEN ROOM
GROUNDROW
HAND-PROPS
HEMP HOUSE
LIGHT PIPE
LIMELIGHT

LOFT BLOCK
NOISES OFF
OPEN STAGE
ORCHESTRA
PENNY GAFF
PERIAKTOI
PROJECTOR
PROMENADE
PROVINCES
REFLECTOR
REHEARSAL
REPERTORY
ROD-PUPPET
ROPE HOUSE
SAND-CLOTH
SCENE DOCK
SET WATERS
SIGHT LINE
SKY BORDER
SLAPSTICK
SLIP STAGE
SOUBRETTE
SPOTLIGHT
STAGE CREW
STAGE DOOR
STAGE PROP
STAGE RAKE
THREE-FOLD
THROWLINE
THYRISTOR
TORMENTOR
TRAVELLER
TRICKWORK
WATER ROWS
10
ANTI-MASQUE
AUDITORIUM
AVANT-GARDE
BUILT STUFF
CORNER TRAP
CURTAIN SET
DRAG ARTIST
FLOODLIGHT
FOLLOW SPOT
GHOST GLIDE
HALL KEEPER
HOUSE LIGHT
IMPRESARIO
INNER STAGE
LYCOPODIUM
MARIONETTE

10 continued
PIPE BATTEN
PROMPT SIDE
SADDLE-IRON
SCIOPTICON
SHOW PORTAL
SPECTATORY
STAGE CLOTH
STRIP LIGHT
THUNDER RUN
TREE BORDER
UNDERSTUDY
11
BACKING FLAT
BOOK CEILING
BORDER LIGHT
BRISTLE TRAP
CURTAIN CALL
DRESS CIRCLE
FALLING FLAP
FORMAL STAGE
FRESNEL SPOT
LIGHT BATTEN
LOW COMEDIAN
OFF-BROADWAY
PROFILE SPOT
RISE-AND-SINK
ROLL CEILING
SCENE RELIEF
SPIELTREPPE
STAGE-KEEPER
STROBE LIGHT
SWITCHBOARD
TRITAGONIST
UPPER CIRCLE
WAGGON STAGE
WIND MACHINE
12
ACTOR-MANAGER
AMPHITHEATRE
AUTHOR'S NIGHT
CAULDRON TRAP
CEILING-CLOTH
CHOREOGRAPHY
CONCERT PARTY
CORSICAN TRAP
COSTUME DRAMA
CURTAIN-MUSIC
FLYING EFFECT
FRONT OF HOUSE
LIGHT CONSOLE

LOBSTERSCOPE
MASKING PIECE
PEPPER'S GHOST
PROFILE BOARD
REVERBERATOR
RUNDHORIZONT
SCISSOR CROSS
SOUND EFFECTS
STAGE MANAGER
STAGE SETTING
STOCK COMPANY
THUNDERSHEET
TRANSPARENCY
TWOPENNY GAFF
13
DETAIL SCENERY
DEUS EX MACHINA
IMPROVISATION
LATERNA MAGICA
MAZARINE FLOOR
PLATFORM STAGE
PORTAL OPENING
SAFETY CURTAIN
STAGE LIGHTING
SUPERNUMERARY
WORD
  REHEARSAL
14
CONTOUR
  CURTAIN
COURTROOM
  DRAMA
DRAPERY
  SETTING
DRESS
  REHEARSAL
FOOTLIGHTS TRAP
GENERAL UTILITY
JACKKNIFE STAGE
KUPPELHORIZONT
MEZZANINE
  FLOOR
OFF-OFF-
  BROADWAY
PAGEANT
  LANTERN
PRIVATE THEATRE
PROSCENIUM
  ARCH
REVOLVING STAGE
STAGE DIRECTION

15
BARN DOOR
  SHUTTER
FLEXIBLE STAGING
HAND WORKED
  HOUSE
INCIDENTAL MUSIC
MULTIPLE
  SETTING
PROSCENIUM
  DOORS
QUICK-CHANGE
  ROOM
STAGE-DOOR
  KEEPER
TRAVERSE
  CURTAIN
16
ALIENATION
  EFFECT
ASPHALEIAN
  SYSTEM
COMPOSITE
  SETTING
DRAMATIS
  PERSONAE
DRAWING-ROOM
  DRAMA
PROSCENIUM
  BORDER
TOURING
  COMPANIES
17
CUP-AND-SAUCER
  DRAMA
18
BESPEAK
  PERFORMANCE
CARBON ARC
  SPOTLIGHT
DRUM-AND-SHAFT
  SYSTEM
FEMALE
  IMPERSONATOR
GRAND MASTER
  CONTROL
LINSEN-
  SCHEINWERFER
TECHNICAL
  REHEARSAL

19
COUNTERWEIGHT
  SYSTEM
SIMULTANEOUS
  SETTING
TRANSFORMATION
  SCENE
20
ADVERTISEMENT
  CURTAIN
ASSISTANT STAGE
  MANAGER
CARRIAGE-AND
  FRAME SYSTEM
CHARIOT-AND-
  POLE SYSTEM
PROMENADE
  PRODUCTIONS
SILICON
  CONTROLLED
  RECTIFIER
SYNCHRONOUS
  WINCH SYSTEM

BALLET / NOVELS

BALLET

4	CHAINE	MARQUER	EQUILIBRE
BRAS	CHANGE	POISSON	HORTENSIA
DEMI	CHASSE	RAMASSE	JUPONNAGE
JETE	CROISE	RETOMBE	LIMBERING
PLIE	DEGAGE	SISSONE	MARCHEUSE
POSE	DETIRE	SOUTENU	PAS DE DEUX
SAUT	DEVANT	TAQUETE	PIROUETTE
TUTU	ECARTE	**8**	RACCOURCI
VOLE	EFFACE	ASSEMBLE	REVERENCE
5	ELANCE	ATTITUDE	REVOLTADE
ARQUE	ENTREE	BACK BEND	**10**
BARRE	EPAULE	BALLONNE	BATTEMENTS
BATTU	ETENDU	BALLOTTE	ENLEVEMENT
BEATS	ETOILE	BATTERIE	EPAULEMENT
BRISE	FAILLI	CABRIOLE	SOUBRESAUT
COLLE	JARRET	CAGNEAUX	TAQUETERIE
COUPE	MONTER	CORYPHEE	**11**
DECOR	PENCHE	DANSEUSE	CONTRETEMPS
ELEVE	POINTE	DEBOULES	PAS DE BASQUE
FONDU	RELEVE	DERRIERE	**12**
LIGNE	RETIRE	DETOURNE	CHOREOGRAPHY
PASSE	VOYAGE	GLISSADE	ENCHAINEMENT
PIQUE	**7**	PISTOLET	GARGOUILLADE
PIVOT	ALLONGE	RENVERSE	**13**
PORTE	ARRONDI	SERPETTE	CHOREOGRAPHER
ROSIN	ATTAQUE	SPOTTING	CORPS DE BALLET
SAUTE	BALANCE	STULCHIK	**14**
SERRE	DANSEUR	TONNELET	CLOSED POSITION
TOMBE	DEBOITE	**9**	DIVERTISSEMENT
6	ECHAPPE	ARABESQUE	PRIMA BALLERINA
APLOMB	EMBOITE	BALLABILE	**15**
A TERRE	ETENDRE	COU DE PIED	AUTOUR DE LA
ATTACK	FOUETTE	DEVELOPPE	SALLE
BAISSE	JARRETE	ELEVATION	**17**
BALLON	LEOTARD	ENTRECHAT	REGISSEUR-
CAMBRE	MAILLOT	ENVELOPPE	GENERALE

NOVELS

3
SHE (H. Rider Haggard)
KIM (Rudyard Kipling)
4
DR NO (Ian Fleming)
EMMA (Jane Austen)
GIGI (Colette)
NANA (Emile Zola)

5
CHERI (Colette)
KIPPS (H.G. Wells)
SCOOP (Evelyn Waugh)
SYBIL (Benjamin Disraeli)
ZADIG (Voltaire)
6
AMELIA (Henry Fielding)
BEN HUR (Lew Wallace)

134

6 continued
CHOCKY (John Wyndham)
LOLITA (Vladimir Nabokov)
PAMELA (Henry Fielding)
ROB ROY (Walter Scott)
7
CAMILLA (Fanny Burney)
CANDIDE (Voltaire)
CECILIA (Fanny Burney)
DRACULA (Bram Stoker)
EREWHON (Samuel Butler)
EVELINA (Fanny Burney)
IVANHOE (Walter Scott)
REBECCA (Daphne Du Maurier)
SHIRLEY (Charlotte Bronte)
THE FALL (Albert Camus)
ULYSSES (James Joyce)
8
ADAM BEDE (George Eliot)
CRANFORD (Mrs Gaskell)
JANE EYRE (Charlotte Bronte)
LUCKY JIM (Kingsley Amis)
SWAN SONG (John Galsworthy)
THE IDIOT (Fyodor Mikhailovich Dostoevsky)
THE MAGUS (John Fowles)
THE REBEL (Albert Camus)
TOM JONES (Henry Fielding)
VILLETTE (Charlotte Bronte)
WAVERLEY (Walter Scott)
9
AGNES GREY (Anne Bronte)
BILLY LIAR (Keith Waterhouse)
CONINGSBY (Benjamin Disraeli)
DUBLINERS (James Joyce)
GLENARVON (Lady Caroline Lamb)
HARD TIMES (Charles Dickens)
I CLAUDIUS (Robert Graves)
KIDNAPPED (R.L. Stevenson)
LOVE STORY (Erich Segal)
ROGUE MALE (Geoffrey Household)
THE CHIMES (Charles Dickens)
THE DEVILS (Fyodor Dostoevsky)
THE HEROES (Charles Kingsley)
THE HOBBIT (J.R.R. Tolkien)
THE PLAGUE (Albert Camus)
VICE VERSA (F. Anstey)
10
ANIMAL FARM (George Orwell)
BLEAK HOUSE (Charles Dickens)
CANCER WARD (Alexander Solzhenitsyn)
CLAYHANGER (Arnold Bennett)

DON QUIXOTE (Cervantes)
GOLDFINGER (Ian Fleming)
IN CHANCERY (John Galsworthy)
KENILWORTH (Walter Scott)
LORNA DOONE (R.D. Blackmore)
PERSUASION (Jane Austen)
THE RAINBOW (D.H. Lawrence)
TITUS ALONE (Mervyn Peake)
TITUS GROAN (Mervyn Peake)
VANITY FAIR (William Makepeace Thackeray)
11
BLACK BEAUTY (Anna Sewell)
BURMESE DAYS (George Orwell)
CAKES AND ALE (W. Somerset Maugham)
COUSIN BETTE (Honore de Balzac)
DAISY MILLER (Henry James)
GORMENGHAST (Mervyn Peake)
LITTLE WOMEN (Louisa M. Alcott)
LOST HORIZON (James Hillon)
MIDDLEMARCH (George Eliot)
MRS DALLOWAY (Virginia Woolf)
OLIVER TWIST (Charles Dickens)
SILAS MARNER (George Eliot)
THE BIG SLEEP (Raymond Chandler)
THE OUTSIDER (Albert Camus)
WAR AND PEACE (Leo Tolstoy)
WOMEN IN LOVE (D.H. Lawrence)
12
ANNA KARENINA (Leo Tolstoy)
A SEVERED HEAD (Iris Murdoch)
BARNABY RUDGE (Charles Dickens)
BRIGHTON ROCK (Graham Greene)
CASINO ROYALE (Ian Fleming)
DOMBEY AND SON (Charles Dickens)
FRANKENSTEIN (Mary Shelley)
GUY MANNERING (Walter Scott)
HEADLONG HALL (Thomas Love Peacock)
LITTLE DORRIT (Charles Dickens)
MADAME BOVARY (Gustave Flaubert)
MOLL FLANDERS (Daniel Defoe)
OF MICE AND MEN (John Steinbeck)
ROGUE JUSTICE (Geoffrey Household)
ROOM AT THE TOP (John Braine)
THE DECAMERON (Boccaccio)
THE GO-BETWEEN (L.P. Hartley)
THE LOST WORLD (Arthur Conan Doyle)
THE MOONSTONE (Wilkie Collins)
THE PROFESSOR (Charlotte Bronte)

NOVELS

13
A KIND OF LOVING (Stan Barstow)
A MODERN COMEDY (John Galsworthy)
BRAVE NEW WORLD (Aldous Huxley)
DANIEL DERONDA (George Eliot)
DOCTOR ZHIVAGO (Boris Pasternak)
FANNY AND ZOOEY (J.D. Salinger)
JACOB FAITHFUL (Captain Marryat)
JUST-SO STORIES (Rudyard Kipling)
LES MISERABLES (Victor Hugo)
LIVE AND LET DIE (Ian Fleming)
LIZA OF LAMBETH (W. Somerset Maugham)
MANSFIELD PARK (Jane Austen)
NORTH AND SOUTH (Mrs Gaskell)
PINCHER MARTIN (William Golding)
SKETCHES BY BOZ (Charles Dickens)
SMILEY'S PEOPLE (John Le Carre)
SONS AND LOVERS (D.H. Lawrence)
TARKA THE OTTER (Henry Williamson)
THE BLUE LAGOON (H. de Vere Stacpoole)
THE CHRYSALIDS (John Wyndham)
THE GOLDEN BOWL (Henry James)
THE HISTORY MAN (Malcolm Bradbury)
THE LAST TYCOON (F. Scott Fitzgerald)
THERESE RAQUIN (Emile Zola)
ZULEIKA DOBSON (Max Beerbohm)
14
A MAN OF PROPERTY (John Galsworthy)
A ROOM OF ONE'S OWN (Virginia Woolf)
A ROOM WITH A VIEW (E.M. Forster)
A TOWN LIKE ALICE (Neville Shute)
CHANGING PLACES (David Lodge)
CIDER WITH ROSIE (Laurie Lee)
CROTCHET CASTLE
   (Thomas Love Peacock)
DEATH ON THE NILE (Agatha Christie)
DECLINE AND FALL (Evelyn Waugh)
GOODBYE, MR CHIPS (Jarnes Hilton)
JUDE THE OBSCURE (Thomas Hardy)
LORD OF THE FLIES (William Golding)
NIGHTMARE ABBEY
   (Thomas Love Peacock)
OUR MAN IN HAVANA (Graham Greene)
PICKWICK PAPERS (Charles Dickens)
RITES OF PASSAGE (William Golding)
ROBINSON CRUSOE (Daniel Defoe)
THE AMBASSADORS (Henry James)
THE CORAL ISLAND (R.M. Ballantyne)
THE FIRST CIRCLE
   (Alexander Solzhenitsyn)
THE FORSYTE SAGA (John Galsworthy)

THE GREAT GATSBY (F. Scott Fitzgerald)
THE KRAKEN WAKES (John Wyndham)
THE LONG GOODBYE (Raymond Chandler)
THE SECRET AGENT (Joseph Conrad)
THE SILVER SPOON (John Galsworthy)
THE TIME MACHINE (H.G. Wells)
THE WATER-BABIES (Charles Kingsley)
THE WHITE MONKEY (John Galsworthy)
THE WOODLANDERS (Thomas Hardy)
TREASURE ISLAND (R.L. Stevenson)
TRISTRAM SHANDY (Laurence Sterne)
WHAT MAISIE KNEW (Henry James)
15
A CHRISTMAS CAROL (Charles Dickens)
A FAREWELL TO ARMS (Ernest Hemingway)
A PASSAGE TO INDIA (E.M. Forster)
COLD COMFORT FARM (Stella Gibbons)
EUSTACE AND HILDA (L.P. Hartley)
GONE WITH THE WIND (Margaret Mitchell)
GOODBYE TO BERLIN
   (Christopher Isherwood)
NORTHANGER ABBEY (Jane Austen)
OUR MUTUAL FRIEND (Charles Dickens)
PORTRAIT OF A LADY (Henry James)
PORTRAIT OF CLARE (Francis Brett Young)
STRAIT IS THE GATE (André Gide)
THE COUNTRY GIRLS (Edna O'Brien)
THE INVISIBLE MAN (H.G. Wells)
THE SECRET GARDEN
   (Frances Hodgson Burnett)
THE SILMARILLION (J.R.R. Tolkien)
THE TRUMPET MAJOR (Thomas Hardy)
THE WHITE COMPANY
   (Arthur Conan Doyle)
THE WOMAN IN WHITE (Wilkie Collins)
THREE MEN IN A BOAT (Jerome K. Jerome)
16
A CLOCKWORK ORANGE
   (Anthony Burgess)
A TALE OF TWO CITIES (Charles Dickens)
DAVID COPPERFIELD (Charles Dickens)
GULLIVER'S TRAVELS (Jonathan Swift)
MARTIN CHUZZLEWIT (Charles Dickens)
MR MIDSHIPMAN EASY (Captain Marryat)
NICHOLAS NICKLEBY (Charles Dickens)
TENDER IS THE NIGHT (F. Scott Fitzgerald)
THE GRAPES OF WRATH (John Steinbeck)
THE PLUMED SERPENT (D.H. Lawrence)
THE SCARLET LETTER
   (Nathaniel Hawthorne)
WUTHERING HEIGHTS (Emily Bronte)

17

ALICE IN WONDERLAND (Lewis Carroll)
DR JEKYLL AND MR HYDE
  (R.L. Stevenson)
GREAT EXPECTATIONS (Charles Dickens)
KING SOLOMON'S MINES
  (H. Rider Haggard)
MY BROTHER JONATHAN
  (Francis Brett Young)
POINT COUNTER POINT (Aldous Huxley)
PRIDE AND PREJUDICE (Jane Austen)
THE DEVILS OF LOUDUN (Aldous Huxley)
THE DIARY OF A NOBODY
  (G. and W.Grossmith)
THE LORD OF THE RINGS (J.R.R. Tolkien)
THE MIDWICH CUCKOOS (John Wyndham)
THE MILL ON THE FLOSS (George Eliot)
THE WAR OF THE WORLDS (H.G. Wells)
THE WINGS OF THE DOVE (Henry James)
WIVES AND DAUGHTERS (Mrs Gaskell)

18

A HIGH WIND IN JAMAICA
  (Richard Hughes)
ANNA OF THE FIVE TOWNS
  (Arnold Bennett)
CRIME AND PUNISHMENT
  (Fyodor Dostoevsky)
NINETEEN EIGHTY-FOUR (George Orwell)
SWALLOWS AND AMAZONS
  (Arthur Ransome)
THE CATCHER IN THE RYE (J.D. Salinger)
THE MOON AND SIXPENCE
  (W. Somerset Maugham)
THE OLD MAN AND THE SEA
  (Ernest Hemingway)
THE PRISONER OF ZENDA (Anthony Hope)
THE THIRTY-NINE STEPS (John Buchan)
THE THREE MUSKETEERS
  (Alexandre Dumas)

19

BRIDESHEAD REVISITED (Evelyn Waugh)
FOR WHOM THE BELL TOLLS
  (Ernest Hemingway)
SENSE AND SENSIBILITY (Jane Austen)
THE DAY OF THE TRIFFIDS
  (John Wyndham)
THE GULAG ARCHIPELAGO
  (Alexander Solzhenitsyn)
THE HISTORY OF MR POLLY (H.G. Wells)
THE MAN IN THE IRON MASK
  (Alexandre Dumas)

THE OLD CURIOSITY SHOP
  (Charles Dickens)
THE PILGRIM'S PROGRESS (John Bunyan)
THE RIDDLE OF THE SANDS
  (Erskine Childers)
THE SCARLET PIMPERNEL
  (Baroness Orczy)
THE SCREWTAPE LETTERS (C.S. Lewis)
THE VICAR OF WAKEFIELD
  (Oliver Goldsmith)
THE WIND IN THE WILLOWS
  (Kenneth Grahame)
TOM BROWN'S SCHOOLDAYS
  (Thomas Hughes)

20+

A CONNECTICUT YANKEE IN KING
  ARTHUR'S COURT (Mark Twain)
A DANCE TO THE MUSIC OF TIME
  (Anthony Powell)
AS I WALKED OUT ONE MIDSUMMER
  MORNING (Laurie Lee)
CHILDREN OF THE NEW FOREST
  (Captain Marryat)
FAR FROM THE MADDING CROWD
  (Thomas Hardy)
JOHN HALIFAX, GENTLEMAN (Mrs Craik)
KEEP THE ASPIDISTRA FLYING
  (George Orwell)
LADY CHATTERLEY'S LOVER
  (D.H. Lawrence)
LARK RISE TO CANDLEFORD
  (Flora Thompson)
LITTLE LORD FAUNTLEROY
  (Frances Hodgson Burnett)
MURDER ON THE ORIENT EXPRESS
  (Agatha Christie)
OUT OF THE SILENT PLANET (C.S. Lewis)
AROUND THE WORLD IN EIGHTY DAYS
  (Jules Verne)
TESS OF THE D'URBERVILLES
  (Thomas Hardy)
THE ADVENTURES OF HUCKLEBERRY
  FINN (Mark Twain)
THE ADVENTURES OF TOM SAWYER
  (Mark Twain)
THE BEAUTIFUL AND DAMNED
  (F. Scott Fitzgeraid)
THE BRIDE OF LAMMERMOOR
  (Walter Scott)
THE BROTHERS KARAMAZOV
  (Fyodor Dostoevsky)

NOVELS / PLAYS

20+ continued
THE CRICKET ON THE HEARTH
  (Charles Dickens)
THE FRENCH LIEUTENANT'S WOMAN
  (John Fowles)
THE HEART OF MIDLOTHIAN (Walter Scott)
THE HISTORY OF HENRY ESMOND
  (William Makepeace Thackeray)
THE HONOURABLE SCHOOLBOY
  (John Le Carré)
THE INNOCENCE OF FATHER BROWN
  (G.K. Chesterton)
THE ISLAND OF DOCTOR MOREAU
  (H.G. Wells)
THE LAST OF THE MOHICANS
  (James Fenimore Cooper)
THE MEMOIRS OF SHERLOCK HOLMES
  (Arthur Conan Doyle)
THE MYSTERIES OF UDOLPHO
  (Mrs Radcliffe)
THE MYSTERIOUS AFFAIR AT STYLES
  (Agatha Christie)

THE MYSTERY OF EDWIN DROOD
  (Charles Dickens)
THE PICTURE OF DORIAN GRAY
  (Oscar Wilde)
THE PRIME OF MISS JEAN BRODIE
  (Muriel Spark)
THE RED BADGE OF COURAGE
  (Stephen Crane)
THE RETURN OF THE NATIVE
  (Thomas Hardy)
THE TENANT OF WILDFELL HALL
  (Anne Bronte)
TINKER, TAILOR, SOLDIER, SPY
  (John Le Carre)
TWENTY THOUSAND LEAGUES UNDER
  THE SEA (Jules Verne)
TWO YEARS BEFORE THE MAST
  (Richard Henry Dana)
UNDER THE GREENWOOD TREE
  (Thomas Hardy)

PLAYS

4
LOOT (Joe Orton)
ROSS (Terence Rattigan)
5
CASTE (T.W. Robertson)
FAUST (Goethe)
MEDEA (Euripides)
ROOTS (Arnold Wesker)
6
HOSTS (Henrik Ibsen)
HAMLET (William Shakespeare)
HENRY V (William Shakespeare)
PHEDRE (Jean Racine)
PLENTY (David Hare)
STRIFE (John Galsworthy)
7
AMADEUS (Peter Shaffer)
ATHALIE (Jean Racine)
CANDIDA (G.B. Shaw)
ELECTRA (Sophocies)
GALILEO (Bertolt Brecht)
HENRY IV (William Shakespeare)
HENRY VI (William Shakespeare)
JUMPERS (Tom Stoppard)
MACBETH (William Shakespeare)
OTHELLO (William Shakespeare)

THE LARK (Jean Anouilh)
THE ROOM (Harold Pinter)
VOLPONE (Ben Jonson)
8
ANTIGONE (Sophocies)
HAY FEVER (Noel Coward)
KING JOHN (William Shakespeare)
KING LEAR (William Shakespeare)
PERICLES (William Shakespeare)
PETER PAN (J.M. Barrie)
TARTUFFE (Moliere)
THE BIRDS (Aristophanes)
THE FROGS (Aristophanes)
THE MISER (Moliere)
9
ALL MY SONS (Arthur Miller)
BILLY LIAR (Willis Hall and Keith
  Waterhouse)
CAVALCADE (Noel Coward)
CYMBELINE (William Shakespeare)
DR FAUSTUS (Christopher Marlowe)
FLARE PATH (Terence Rattigan)
GOLDEN BOY (Clifford Odets)
HAPPY DAYS (Samuel Beckett)
HENRY VIII (William Shakespeare)
PYGMALION (G.B. Shaw)

9 continued

RICHARD II (William Shakespeare)
SAINT JOAN (G.B. Shaw)
THE CIRCLE (W. Somerset Maugham)
THE CRITIC (Sheridan)
THE DEVILS (John Whiting)
THE RIVALS (Sheridan)

10

ALL FOR LOVE (John Dryden)
ANDROMAQUE (Jean Racine)
AURENG-ZEBE (John Dryden)
CORIOLANUS (William Shakespeare)
I AM A CAMERA (John Van Druten)
OEDIPUS REX (Sophocles)
RICHARD III (William Shakespeare)
THE BACCHAE (Euripides)
THE BALCONY (Jean Genet)
THE HOSTAGE (Crendan Behan)
THE SEAGULL (Anton Chekhov)
THE TEMPEST (William Shakespeare)
UNCLE VANYA (Anton Chekhov)

11

A DOLL'S HOUSE (Henrik Ibsen)
AS YOU LIKE IT (William Shakespeare)
JOURNEY'S END (R.C. Sherriff)
LOVE FOR LOVE (William Congreve)
PANDORA'S BOX (Frank Wedekind)
ROOKERY NOOK (Ben Travers)
THE BANKRUPT (Alexander Ostrovsky)
THE CONTRAST (Royall Tyler)
THE CRUCIBLE (Arthur Miller)
THE WILD DUCK (Henrik Ibsen)

12

AFTER THE FALL (Arthur Miller)
ANNA CHRISTIE (Eugene O'Neill)
BEDROOM FARCE (Alan Ayckbourn)
BLITHE SPIRIT (Noel Coward)
CHARLEY'S AUNT (Brandon Thomas)
DUEL OF ANGELS (Jean Giraudoux)
JULIUS CAESAR (William Shakespeare)
MAJOR BARBARA (G.B. Shaw)
PRIVATE LIVES (Noel Coward)
THE ALCHEMIST (Ben Jonson)
THE ANATOMIST (James Bridie)
THE APPLE CART (G.B. Shaw)
THE BROKEN JUG (Heinrich von Kleist)
THE CARETAKER (Harold Pinter)
THE MOUSETRAP (Agatha Christie)
THREE SISTERS (Anton Chekhov)
TWELFTH NIGHT (William Shakespeare)

13

ARMS AND THE MAN (G.B. Shaw)
A TASTE OF HONEY (Shelagh Delaney)
HOBSON'S CHOICE (Harold Brighouse)
LE MISANTHROPE (Moliere)
QUALITY STREET (J.M. Barrie)
THE ACHARNIANS (Aristophanes)
THE DUMB WAITER (Harold Pinter)
THE JEW OF MALTA (Christopher Marlowe)
THE LINDEN TREE (J.B. Priestley)
THE MAGISTRATE (Pinero)
THE MATCHMAKER (Thornton Wilder)
THE WHITE DEVIL (John Webster)
THE WINSLOW BOY (Terence Rattigan)
TIMON OF ATHENS (William Shakespeare)
UNDER MILK WOOD (Dylan Thomas)

14

AN IDEAL HUSBAND (Oscar Wilde)
MAN AND SUPERMAN (G.B. Shaw)
ROMEO AND JULIET (William Shakespeare)
SEPARATE TABLES (Terence Rattigan)
THE CORN IS GREEN (Emlyn Williams)
THE COUNTRY GIRL (Clifford Odets)
THE DEEP BLUE SEA (Terence Rattigan)
THE FIRE-RAISERS (Max Frisch)
THE GHOST SONATA (August Strindberg)
THE OLD BACHELOR (William Congreve)
THE PHILANDERER (G.B. Shaw)
THE TROJAN WOMEN (Euripides)
THE WINTER'S TALE (William Shakespeare)
THIS HAPPY BREED (Noel Coward)

15

DANGEROUS CORNER (J.B. Priestley)
DESIGN FOR LIVING (Noel Coward)
HEARTBREAK HOUSE (G.B. Shaw)
LOOK BACK IN ANGER (John Osborne)
MARRIAGE A LA MODE (John Dryden)
PRESENT LAUGHTER (Noel Coward)
THE CONSTANT WIFE
    (W. Somerset Maugham)
THE ICEMAN COMETH (Eugene O'Neill)
TITUS ANDRONICUS (William Shakespeare)
TWO NOBLE KINSMEN
    (William Shakespeare)
VENICE PRESERVED (Thomas Otway)
WAITING FOR GODOT (Samuel Beckett)

16

A CUCKOO IN THE NEST (Ben Travers)
AN INSPECTOR CALLS (J.B. Priestley)
CAT ON A HOT TIN ROOF
    (Tennessee Williams)

PLALYS

CHARACTERS IN FICTION

3

FOX, Brer (*Uncle Remus*, J.C. Harris)

GOG (*The Tower of London*, W.H. Ainsworth)

HUR, Judah (*Ben Hur*, L. Wallace)

JIM, 'Lord' (*Lord Jim*, J. Conrad)

KIM (*Kim*, Rudyard Kipling)

LEE, Lorelei (*Gentlemen Prefer Blondes*, Anita Loos)

OWL (*Winnie the Pooh*, A.A. Milne)

ROO (*Winnie the Pooh*, A.A. Milne)

TOM (The Water Babies, C. Kingsley)

TOM, 'Uncle' (*Uncle Tom's Cabin*, Harriet B. Stowe)

4

ABEL (*Middlemarch*, George Eliot)

CASS, Eppie (*Silas Marner*, George Eliot)

CASY, Rev. Jim (*The Grapes of Wrath*, J.Steinbeck)

CUFF, Sergeant (*The Moonstone*, W Collins)

DEAN, Ellen (*Wuthering Heights*, Emily Bronte)

EAST (*Tom Brown's Schooldays*, T. Hughes)

EASY, John (*Mr Midshipman Easy*, Captain Marryat)

EYRE, Jane (*Jane Eyre*, Charlotte Bronte)

FAWN, Lord Frederic (*Phineas Finn*, A. Trollope)

FELL, Dr Gideon (*The Black Spectacles*, J.Dickson Carr)

FINN, Huckleberry (*Huckleberry Finn, Tom Sawyer*, M. Twain)

FINN, Phineas (*Phineas Finn*, A. Trollope)

GRAY, Dorian,(*The Picture of Dorian Gray*, Oscar Wilde)

GRAY, Nelly (*Faithless Nelly Gray*, T. Hood)

GUNN, Ben (*Treasure Island*, R.L.Stevenson)

HOOK, Captain James (*Peter Pan*, J.M.Barrie)

HYDE, Edward (*Dr Jekyll and Mr Hyde*, R.L.Stevenson)

LAMB, Leonard (*Middlemarch*, George Eliot)

MOLE, Mr (*The Wind in the Willows*, Kenneth Grahame)

NANA (*Peter Pan*, J.M. Barrie)

NASH, Richard (Beau) (*Monsieur Beaucaire*, Booth Tarkington)

PUCK (Robin Goodfellow) (*Puck of Pook's Hill*, R. Kipling)

RAMA (Tiger Tiger) (*The Jungle Book*, R. Kipling)

REED, Mrs (*Jane Eyre*, Charlotte Bronte)

RIDD, John (*Lorna Doone*, R.D. Blackmore)

SEAL, Basil (*Put Out More Flags*, E. Waugh)

SMEE (*Peter Pan*, J.M. Barrie)

TOAD, Mr (*The Wind in the Willows*, K.Grahame)

TROY, Sergeant Francis (*Far from the Madding Crowd*, T. Hardy)

VANE, Harriet (*Strong Poison*, Dorothy L. Sayers)

VANE, Lady Isabel (*East Lynne*, Mrs Henry Wood)

WOLF, 'Brer' (*Uncle Remus*, J.C. Harris)

5

ADLER, Irene (*The Adventures of Sherlock Holmes*, A. Conan Doyle)

AKELA (*The Jungle Book*, R. Kipling)

ALIBI, Tom (*Waverley*, W. Scott)

ATHOS (*The Three Musketeers*, Alexandre Dumas),

BALOO (*The Jungle Book*, R.. Kipling)

BLAKE, Franklin (*The Moonstone*, W. Collins)

BONES, Captain Billy (*Treasure Island*, R.L. Stevenson)

BOOBY, Sir Thomas (*Joseph Andrews*, H.Fielding)

BRUFF (*The Moonstone*, W. Collins)

BULBO, Prince (*The Rose and the Ring*, W. M.Thackeray)

CHANT, Mercy (*Tess of the D'Urbervilles*, , Thomas Hardy)

CLACK, Drusilla (*The Moonstone*, W. Collins)

CLARE, Angel (*Tess of the D'Urbervilles*, Thomas Hardy)

DARCY, Fitzwilliam (*Pride and Prejudice*, Jane Austen)

DEANS, Effie/Jeanie (*The Heart of Midlothian*, W. Scott)

DIXON, Jarnes (*Lucky Jim*, K. Amis)

DOONE, Lorna (*Lorna Doone*, R.D.Blackmore)

EAGER, Rev. Cuthbert (*Room with a View*, E.M. Forster)

FANNY (*Fanny's First Play*, G.B. Shaw)

FLYNN, Father James (*The Dubliners*, James Joyce)

CHARACTERS IN FICTION

5 continued

GESTE, Beau (*Beau Geste*, P.C. Wren)

HANDS, Israel (*Treasure Island*, R.L.Stevenson)

HATCH, Bennet (*The Black Arrow*, R.L.Stevenson)

JONES, Tom (*Tom Jones*, H. Fielding)

KANGA (Winnie the Pooh, A.A. Milne)

KIPPS, Arthur (*Kipps*, H.G. Wells)

LEIGH, Captain Sir Amyas (*Westward Ho!*, C. Kingsley)

MAGOG (*The Tower of London*, W.H. Ainsworth)

MARCH, Amy/Beth/Josephine (Jo)/Meg (*Little Women* etc., Louisa M. Alcott)

MERCY (*Pilgrim's Progress*, J. Bunyan)

MITTY, Walter (The Secret Life of Walter Mitty, J. Thurber)

MOORE, Mrs (*A Passage to India*, E.M. Forster)

O'HARA, Kimball (*Kim*, Rudyard Kipling)

O'HARA, Scarlett (*Gone with the Wind*, Margaret Mitchell)

OTTER, Mr (*The Wind in the Willows*, K. Grahame)

PAGET, Jean (*A Town like Alice*, N. Shute)

POLLY , Alfred (*The History of Mr Polly*, H.G. Wells)

POOLE, Grace (*Jane Eyre*, Charlotte Bronte)

PORGY (*Porgy*, Du Bose Heywood)

PRISM, Miss Laetitia (*The Importance of Being Earnest*, Oscar Wilde)

PUNCH (*Wee Willie Winkie*, R. Kipling)

READY, Masterman (*Masterman Ready*, F. Marryat)

REMUS, Uncle (*Uncle Remus* series, J.C. Harris)

RYDER, Charles (*Brideshead Revisited*, E. Waugh)

SALLY (*Sally in Our Alley*, H. Carey)

SAMBO (*Just So Stories*, R. Kipling)

SHARP, Rebecca (Becky) (*Vanity Fair*, W.M. Thackeray)

SLOPE, Rev. Obadiah (*Barchester Towers*, A. Trollope)

SLOTH (*Pilgrim's Progress*, J. Bunyan)

SMITH, Winston (*1984*, G. Orwell)

SNOWE, Lucy (Villette, Charlotte Bronte)

TARKA (Tarka the Otter, H. Williamson)

THUMB, Tom (*The Tale of Two Bed Mice*, Beatrix Potter)

TOPSY (*Uncle Tom's Cabin*, Harriet B. Stowe)

UNCAS (*The Last of the Mohicans*, J. Fennimore Cooper)

6

ARAMIS (The Three Musketeers, Alexandre Dumas)

AYESHA (*She*, H. Rider Haggard)

BENNET, Catherine/Elizabeth/Jane/Lydia/ Mary (*Pride and Prejudice*, Jane Austen)

BESSIE (Jane Eyre, Charlotte Bronte)

BINKIE, Lady.Grizzel (*Vanity Fair*, W.M. Thackeray)

BOVARY, Emma (*Madame Bovary*, G. Flaubert)

BUTLER, Rhett (*Gone with the Wind*, Margaret Mitchell)

CACKLE (*Vanity Fair*, W.M. Thackeray)

CARDEW, Cecily (*The Importance of Being Earnest*, Oscar Wilde)

CRUSOE, Robinson (*Robinson Crusoe*, D. Defoe)

DANGLE (*The Critic*, R.B. Sheridan)

EEYORE (*Winnie the Pooh*, A.A. Milne)

ELAINE (*Idylls of the King*, Lord Tennyson)

'FRIDAY' (*Robinson Crusoe* D. Defoe)

FRITHA (*The Snow Goose*, P. Gallico)

GARTER, Polly (*Under Milk Wood*, D. Thomas)

GATSBY, Major Jay (*The Great Gatsby*, F. Scott Fitzgerald)

GEORGE (*Three Men in a Boat*, J.K. Jerome)

GERARD, Etienne (*The Exploits of Brigadier Gerard*, A. Conan Doyle)

GILPIN, John (*John Gilpin*, W. Cowper)

GLOVER, Catherine (*The Fair Maid of Perth*, W. Scott)

GORDON, Squire (*Black Beauty*, A. Sewell)

GRIMES (*The Water Babies*, C. Kingsley)

HANNAY, Richard (*The Thirty-Nine Steps*, J. Buchan)

HARKER, Jonathan/Minna (*Dracula*, Brarn Stoker)

HARMAN, Joe (*A Town like Alice*, N. Shute)

HAROLD, Childe (*Childe Harold's Pilgrimage*, Lord Byron)

HEARTS, King of/Knave of/Queen of (*Alice in Wonderland*, L. Garroll)

HOLMES, Mycroft (*The Return of Sherlock Holmes*, A. Conan Doyle).

6 continued

HOLMES, Sherlock (*A Study in Scarlet, The Sign of Four, The Hound of the Baskervilles*, etc., A. Conan Doyle)

HOOPER, Fanny (*Fanny by Gaslight*, M. Sadleir)

JEEVES (*Thank you, Jeeves*, P.G. Wodehouse)

JEKYLL, Henry (*Dr Jekyll and Mr Hyde*, R.L. Stevenson)

LAURIE (*Little Women*, Louisa M. Alcott)

LAURIE, Annie (*Annie Laurie*, Douglass)

LEGREE, Sirnon (*Uncle Tom's Cabin*, Harriet B. Stowe)

LINTON, Edgar (*Wuthering Heights*, Emily Bronte)

MANGAN, Boss (*Heartbreak House*, G.B. Shaw)

MANSON, Dr Andrew (*The Citadel*, A.J. Cronin)

MARPLE, Jane (*A Pocket Full of Rye*, Agatha Christie)

MERLIN (*Idylls of the King*, Lord Tennyson)

MODRED, Sir (*Idylls of the King*, Lord Tennyson)

MOREAU, Andre-Louis (*Scaramouche*, R. Sabatini)

MOREAU, Dr (*The Island of Dr Moreau*, H.G. Wells)

MORGAN, Angharad/Huw (*How Green Was My Valley*, R. Llewellyn)

MORGAN, Organ (*Under Milk Wood*, D. Thomas)

MOWGLI (*The Jungle Book*, R. Kipling)

NUTKIN, Squirrel, (*The Tale of Squirrel Nutkin*, Beatrix Potter)

OMNIUM, Duke of (Family name Palliser) (*The Barsetshire series*, Angela Thirkell)

PICKLE, Peregrine (*Peregrine Pickle*, T. Smollett)

PIGLET, Henry Pootel (*Winnie the Pooh*, A.A. Milne)

POIROT, Hercule (*The Mysterious Affair at Styles*, Agatha Christie)

RABBIT (*Winnie the Pooh*, A.A. Milne)

RABBIT, 'Brer', (*Uncle Remus*, J. C. Harris)

RABBIT, The White (*Alice in Wonderland*, L. Carroll)

RIVERS, St John (*Jane Eyre*, Charlotte Bronte)

SAWYER, Tom (*The Adventures of Tom Sawyer*, M. Twain)

SHANDY, Tristram (*Tristram Shandy*, L. Sterne)

SILVER, Long John (*Treasure Island*, R.L. Stevenson)

SIMNEL, Lambert (*Perkin Warbeck*, John Ford)

TEMPLE, Miss (*Jane Eyre*, Charlotte Bronte)

THORNE, Dr Thomas (*Doctor Thorne*, A. Trollope)

THORPE, Isabella (*Northanger Abbey*, Jane Austen)

TILNEY, Henry (*Northanger Abbey*, Jane Austen)

TURNER, Jim (Captain Flint) (*Swallows and Amazons*, A. Ransome)

UMPOPA (*King Solomon's Mines*, H. Rider Haggard)

WALKER, John/ Roger/ Susan /Tifty/Vicky (*Swallows and Amazons*, A. Ransome)

WESTON, Mrs (*Emma*, Jane Austen)

WILKES, Ashley/India (*Gone with the Wind*, Margaret Mitchell)

WIMSEY, Lord Peter Death Bredon (*Whose Body?*, Dorothy L. Sayers)

7

AISGILL, Alice (*Room at the Top*, J. Braine)

BAGSTER (*Middlemarch*, George Eliot)

BEESLEY (*Lucky Jim*, Kingstey Amis)

BINGLEY, Charles (*Pride and Prejudice*, Jane Austen)

BRANDON, Colonel (*Sense and Sensibility*, Jane Austen)

CANDOUR, Mrs (*The School for Scandal*, R.B. Sheridan)

CHESNEY, Jack (*Charley's Aunt*, Brandon Thomas)

COLLINS, Rev. William (*Pride and Prejudice*, Jane Austen)

CYPRESS, Mr (*Nightmare Abbey*, T.L. Peacock)

DANVERS, Mrs (*Rebecca* Daphne du Maurier)

DESPAIR, Giant (*Pilgrim's Progress*, J. Bunyan)

DRACULA, Count (*Dracula*, Bram Stoker)

EPICENE (*Epicene*, B. Jonson)

FAIRFAX, Gwendolen (*The Importance of Being Earnest*, Oscar Wilde)

FAIRFAX, Jane (*Emma*, J. Austen)

FAIRFAX, Mrs (*Jane Eyre*, Charlotte Bronte)

FAIRLIE, Frederick (Woman in White, W. Collins)

CHARACTERS IN FICTION

7 continued

FAUSTUS (*The History of Dr Faustus*, C. Marlowe)

FORSYTE, Fleur/Irene/Jolyon/don/Soames (*The Forsyte Saga*, J. Galsworthy)

GALAHAD (*Idylls of the King*, Lord Tennyson)

GERAINT (Idylls of the King, Lord Tennyson)

GRANTLY, Bishop of Barchester (The Warden, Barchester Towers, A. Trollope)

HAWKINS, Jim (Treasure Island, R.L. Stevenson)

HENTZAU, Rupert of (*The Prisoner of Zenda*, A. Hope)

HERRIES, Francis (*Rogue Herries*, H. Walpole)

HIGGINS, Henry (*Pygmalion*, G.B. Shaw)

IVANHOE, Wilfred, Knight of (*Ivanhoe*, W. Scott)

JENKINS, Rev. Eli (*Under Milk Wood*, D. Thomas)

KEELDAR, Shirley (*Shirley*, Charlotte Bronte)

LAMPTON, Joe (Room at the Top, J. Braine)

LATIMER, Darsie (Redgauntlet, W. Scott)

LAWLESS (*The Slack Arrow*, R.L. Stevenson)

LINCOLN, Abraham (*Abraham Lincoln*, J. Drinkwater)

LUCIFER (*Faustus*, C. Marlowe)

MESSALA (*Ben Hur*, L. Wallace)

MICHAEL, Duke of Strelsau (*The Prisoner of Zenda*, A. Hope)

MINIVER, Mrs Caroline (*Mrs Miniver*, Jan Struther)

MORLAND, Catherine (*Northanger Abbey*, Jane Austen)

NOKOMIS (Song of Hiawatha, H.W. Longfellow)

PORTHOS (*The Three Musketeers*, Alexandre Dumas)

PROUDIE, Dr/Mrs (*Framley Parsonage*, A. Trollope)

RAFFLES, A.J. (*Raffles* series, E.W. Hornung)

RANDALL, Rebecca (*Rebecca of Sunnybrook Farm*, Kate D. Wiggin)

RATTLER, Martin (*Martin Rattler*, R.M. Ballantyne)

REBECCA (*Rebecca*, Daphne du Maurier)

REBECCA (*Rebecca of Sunnybrook Farm*, Kate D. Wiggin)

RED KING (*Alice Through the Looking Glass*, L. Carroll)

ROBSART, Amy (*Kenilworth*, W. Scott)

SANDERS (Sandi) (*Sanders of the River*, E. Wallace)

SHELTON, Richard (*The Black Arrow*, R.L. Stevenson)

SHIPTON, Mother (*The Luck of Roaring Camp*, Bret Harte)

SMOLLET, Captain (*Treasure Island*, R.L. Stevenson)

SORRELL, Christopher (Kit) (*Sorrell and Son*, W. Deeping)

ST CLARE, Evangeline (Little Eva) (*Uncle Tom's Cabin*, Harriet B. Stowe)

TIDDLER, Tom (*Adam's Opera,* Clemence Dane)

WARBECK, Perkin (*Perkin Warbeck*, John Ford)

WESTERN, Mrs/Sophia/Squire, (*Tom Jones*, H. Fielding)

WILLIAM (*Just William*, Richmal Crompton)

WINSLOW, Ronnie (*The Winslow Boy*, T. Rattigan)

WOOSTER, Bertie (*Thank You, Jeeves*, P.G. Wodehouse)

8

ABSOLUTE, Sir Anthony (The Rivals, R.B. Sheridan)

ANGELICA (The Rose and the Ring, W.M. Thackeray)

APOLLYON (*Pilgrim's Progress*, J. Bunyan)

ARMITAGE, Jacob (*The Children of the New Forest*, Captain Marryat)

BACKBITE, Sir Benjamin (*The School for Scandal*, R.B. Sheridan)

BAGHEERA (*The Jungle Book*, R. Kipling)

BLACK DOG (*Treasure Island*, R.L. Stevenson)

CARRAWAY, Nick (*The Great Gatsby*, F. Scott Fitzgerald)

CASAUBON, Rev. Edward, (*Middlemarch*, George Eliot)

CRAWFURD, David (*Prester John*, J. Buchan)

CRICHTON, Bill (*The Admirable Crichton*, J.M. Barrie)

DASHWOOD, Henry (*Sense and Sensibility*, Jane Austen)

DE BOURGH, Lady Catherine (*Pride and Prejudice*, Jane Austen)

DE WINTER, Maximilian (*Rebecca*, Daphne du Maurier)

EARNSHAW, Catherine (*Wuthering Heights*, Emily Bronte)

8 continued

EVERDENE, Bathsheba (*Far from the Madding Crowd*, T. Hardy)

FFOULKES, Sir Andrew (*The Scarlet Pimpernel*, Baroness Orczy)

FLANDERS, Moll (*Moll Flanders*, D. Defoe)

FLASHMAN (*Tom Brown's Schooldays*, T. Hughes)

GLORIANA (*The Faerie Queen*, E. Spenser)

GOLLANTZ, Emmanuel (*Young Emmanuel*, N. Jacob)

GULLIVER, Lemuel (*Gulliver's Travels*, J. Swift)

GUNGA DIN (*Barrack-room Ballads*, R. Kipling)

HIAWATHA (*The Song of Hiowatha*, H.W. Longfellow)

KNIGHTLY, George (*Emma*, J. Austen)

LANCELOT, Sir (*Idylls of the King*, Lord Tennyson)

LANGUISH, Lydia (*The Rivals*, R.B. Sheridan)

LAURENCE, Theodore (*Little Women*, Louisa M. Alcott)

LESSWAYS, Hilda (*The Clayhanger Trilogy*, Arnold Bennett)

LESTRADE, of Scotland Yard (*A Study in Scarlet*, A. Conan Doyle)

LOCKWOOD (*Wuthering Heights*, Emily Bronte)

MACAVITY (*Old Possum's Book of Practical Cats*, T.S. Eliot)

MALAPROP, Mrs (*The Rivals*, R.B. Sheridan)

MARY JANE (*When We Were Very Young*, A.A. Milne)

MORIARTY, Professor James (*Memoirs of Sherlock Holmes*, A. Conan Doyle)

O'FERRALL, Trilby (*Trilby*, George du Maurier)

OLIFAUNT, Nigel (*The Fortunes of Nigel*, W. Scott)

O'TRIGGER, Sir Lucius (*The Rivals*, R.B. Sheridan)

PALLISER, Lady Glencora/Plantagenet (*Phineas Finn*, A. Trollope)

PRIMROSE, Dr Charles (*The Vicar of Wakefield*, 0. Goldsmith)

QUANTOCK, Mrs Daisy (*Queen Lucia*, E.F. Benson)

RED QUEEN (*Alice Through the Looking Glass*, L. Carroll)

SHOTOVER, Captain (*Heartbreak House*, G.B. Shaw)

ST BUNGAY, Duke of (*Phineas Finn*, A. Trollope)

SVENGALI (*Trilby*, George du Maurier)

THATCHER, Becky (*The Adventures of Tom Sawyer*, M. Twain)

TRISTRAM (*Idylls of the King*, Lord Tennyson)

TULLIVER, Maggie/Torn (*The Mill on the Floss*, George Eliot)

VERINDER, Lady Julia (*The Moonstone*, W. Collins)

WATER RAT (Ratty) (*The Wind in the Willows*, K. Grahame)

WAVERLEY, Edward (*Waverley*, W. Scott)

WHITEOAK (family) (*The Whiteoak Chronicles*, Mazo de la Roche)

WHITE-TIP (*Tarka the Otter*, Henry Williamson)

WHITTIER, Pollyanna (*Pollyanna*, Eleanor H. Porter)

WILLIAMS, Percival William (*Wee Willie Winkie*, R. Kipling)

WORTHING, John (*The Importance of Being Earnest*, Oscar Wilde)

9

ABBEVILLE, Horace (*Cannery Row*, J. Steinbeck)

ABLEWHITE, Godfrey (*The Moonstone*, W. Collins)

ALLWORTHY, Squire (*Tom Jones*, H. Fielding)

BABBERLEY, Lord Fancourt (*Charley's Aunt*, Brandon Thomas)

BARRYMORE (*The Hound of the Baskervilles*, A. Conan Doyle)

BRACKNELL, Lady (*The Importance of Being Earnest*, Oscar Wilde)

BULSTRODE, Nicholas (*Middlemarch*, George Eliot)

CHAINMAIL (*Crotchet Castle*, T.L. Peacock)

CHRISTIAN (*Pilgrim's Progress*, J. Bunyan)

CHURCHILL, Frank (*Emma*, Jane Austen)

D'ARTAGNAN (*The Three Musketeers*, Alexandre Dumas)

DOOLITTLE, Eliza (*Pygmalion*, G.B. Shaw)

GREYSTOKE, Lord (*Tarzan* series, Edgar R. Burroughs)

GUINEVERE (*Idylls of the King*, Lord Tennyson)

INDIAN JOE (*The Adventures of Tom Sawyer*, M. Twain)

CHARACTERS IN FICTION

9 continued

LEICESTER, Earl of (*Kenilworth*, W. Scott)

MACGREGOR, Robin (*Rob Roy*, W. Scott)

MARCH HARE, The (*Alice in Wonderland*, L. Carroll)

MARCHMAIN, Lady Cordelia/Lady Julia/Lord Sebastian/Marquis ofTeresa/The Earl of Brideshead (*Brideshead Revisited*, E. Waugh)

MEHITABEL, the cat (*Archy and Mehitabel*, D. Marquis)

MERRILES, Meg (*Guy Mannering*, W. Scott)

MINNEHAHA (*The Song of Hiawatha*, H.W. Longfellow)

MONCRIEFF, Algernon (*The Importance of Being Earnest, Oscar Wilde*)

PENDENNIS, Arthur (Pen) (*Pendennis*, W.M. Thackeray)

PERCIVALE (*Idylls of the King*, Lord Tennyson)

RED KNIGHT (*Alice Through the Looking Glass*, L. Carroll)

ROCHESTER, Bertha/Edward Fairfax (*Jane Eyre*, Charlotte Bronte)

SHERE KHAN (Lungri) (*The Jungle Book*, R. Kipling)

SOUTHDOWN, Earl of (*Vanity Fair*, W.M. Thackeray)

TAMERLANE (Tamerlane, N. Rowe)

TANQUERAY, Aubrey (*The Second Mrs Tanqueray*, A.W. Pinero)

TIGER LILY (*Peter Pan*, J.M. Barrie)

TRELAWNEY, Rose (*Trelawney of the Wells*, A.W. Pinero)

TRELAWNEY, Squire (Treasure Island, R.L. Stevenson)

TWITCHETT, Mrs Tabitha (*The Tale of Tom Kitten*, Beatrix Potter)

VIRGINIAN, The (*The Virginian*, O. Wister)

WAYNFLETE, Lady Cicely (*Captain Brassbound's Conversion*, G.B. Shaw)

WOODHOUSE, Emma/Isabella (*Emma*, Jane Austen)

10

ABRAMS MOSS (*Pendennis*, W.M. Thackeray)

ALLAN-A-DALE (*Ivanhoe*, W. Scott)

ARROWPOINT (*Daniel Deronda*, George Eliot)

BELLADONNA (*Vanity Fair*, W.M. Thackeray)

CHALLENGER, Professor (*The Lost World*, A. Conan Doyle)

CRIMSWORTH, William (*The Professor*, Charlotte Bronte)

EVANGELINE (*Evangeline*, H.W. Longfellow)

FAUNTLEROY, Lord Cedric Errol (*Little Lord Fauntleroy*, F.H. Burnett)

GOODFELLOW, Robin (*St Ronan's Well*, W. Scott)

HEATHCLIFF (*Wuthering Heights*, Emily Bronte)

HORNBLOWER, Horatio (*The Hornblower* series, C. S. Forester.)

HUNCA MUNCA (*The Tale of Two Bad Mice*, Beatrix Potter)

HUNTER-DUNN, Joan (*A Subaltern's Love Song*, J. Betjeman)

JACKANAPES (*Jackanapes*, Juliana H. Ewing)

LETHBRIDGE, Daphne (*The Dark Tide*, Vera Brittain)

MAN IN BLACK (*A Citizen of the World*, 0.Goldsmith)

MAULEVERER, Lord (*Cranford*, Mrs Gaskell)

MOCK TURTLE, THE (*Alice in Wonderland*, L. Carroll)

PUDDLEDUCK, Jemima (*The Tale of Jemima Puddleduck*, Beatrix Potter)

QUATERMAIN, Allan (*King Solomon 's Mines*, H. Rider Haggard)

RASSENDYLL, Rudolf (*The Prisoner of Zenda*, A. Hope)

STARKADDER, Judith/Old Mrs (*Cold Comfort Farm*, Stella Gibbons)

TINKER BELL (Peter Pan, J.M. Barrie)

TWEEDLEDEE (*Alice Through the Looking Glass*, L. Carroll)

TWEEDLEDUM (*Alice Through the Looking Glass*, L. Carroll)

UNDERSHAFT, Barbara (*Major Barbara*, G.B. Shaw)

WILLOUGHBY, John (*Sense and Sensibility*, Jane Austen)

WINDERMERE, Lord Arthur/Margaret (*Lady Windermere's Fan*, Oscar Wilde)

11
ADDENBROOKE, Bennett (*Raffles*, E.W. Hornung)
DURBEYFIELD, Tess (*Tess of the D'Urbervilles*, T. Hardy)
JABBERWOCKY (*Alice Through the Looking Glass*, L. Carroll)
11 continuedMACCROTCHET (*Crotchet Castle*, T.L. Peacock)
MONTMORENCY, the dog (*Three Men in a Boat*, J.K. Jerome)
REDGAUNTLET, Sir Arthur Darsie (*Redgauntlet*, W. Scott)
TAMBURLAINE (Tamburlaine, C. Marlowe)
TAM O'SHANTER (*Tam O'Shanter*, R. Burns)
TIGGY-WINKLE, Mrs (*The Tale of Mrs TiggyWinkle*, Beatrix Potter)
TITTLEMOUSE, Mrs Thomasina (*The Tale of Mrs Tittlemouse*, Beatrix Potter)
TRUMPINGTON, Lady (*The Virginians*, W.M. Thackeray)
12
BROCKLEHURST (*Jane Eyre*, Charlotte Bronte)
CAPTAIN FLINT (*Swallows and Amazons*, A. Ransome)
FRANKENSTEIN, Victor (*Frankenstein* M.W. Shelley)

HUMPTY-DUMPTY (*Alice Through the Looking-Glass*, L. Carrofi)
PENNYFEATHER, Paul (*Decline and Fall*, E. Waugh)
13
WINNIE-THE-POOH (Edward Bear) (Winnie-the-Pooh, A.A. Milne)
14
MARKHAM, Gilbert (*The Tenant of Wildfell Hall*, Anne Bronte)
MEPHISTOPHELES (*Doctor Faustus*, C.Marlowe)
RIKKI-TIKKI-TAVI (*The Jungle Book*, R. Kipling)
SAMUEL WHISKERS (*The Tale of Samuel Whiskers*, Beatrix Potter)
WORDLY-WISEMAN (*Pilgrim's Progress*, J.Bunyan)
15
OGMORE-PRITCHARD, Mrs (*Under Milk Wood*, D. Thomas)
VALIANT-FOR-TRUTH (*Pilgrim's Progress*, J. Bunyan)
VIOLET ELIZABETH (*Just William*, Richmal Crompton)

CHARACTERS IN DICKENS

2
J0 (Bleak House)
3
AMY (Oliver Twist)
BET, Betsy (Oliver Twist)
BUD, Rosa (Edwin Drood)
CLY (A Tale of Two Cities)
GAY, Walter (Dombey and Son)
JOE (Pickwick Papers)
TOX (Miss (Dombey and Son)
4
ANNE (Dombey and Son)
BAPS (Dombey and Son)
BEGS, Mrs Ridger (David Copperfield)
BRAY, Madeline (Nicholas Nickleby)
BRAY, Waiter (Nicholas Nickleby)
DICK, Mr (Oliver Twist)
DUFF (Oliver Twist)

FIPS, Mr (Martin Chuzzlewit)
FOGG (Pickwick Papers)
GAMP, Mrs Sarah (Martin Chuzzlewit)
GRIP (Barnaby Rudge)
HAWK, Sir Mulberry (Nicholas Nickleby)
HEEP, Uriah (David Copperfield)
HUGH (Barnaby Rudge)
JOWL, Mat (The Old Curiosity Shop)
JUPE, Cecilia (Hard Times)
KAGS (Oliver Twist)
KNAG, Miss (Nicholas Nickelby)
LIST, Isaac (The Old Curiosity Shop)
MANN, Mrs (Oliver Twist)
MARY (Pickwick Papers)
MELL, Charles (David Copperfield)
MIFF, Mrs (Dombey and Son)
OMER (David Copperfield)
PEAK (Barnaby Rudge)

CHARACTERS IN DICKENS

4 continued

PELL, Solomon (Pickwick Papers)
PEPS, Dr Parker (Dombey and Son)
POTT, Minverva (Pickwick Papers)
RIAH (Our Mutual Friend)
RUGG, Anastasia (Little Dorrit)
TIGG, Montague (Martin Chuzzlewit)
WADE, Miss (Little Dorrit)
WEGG, Silas (Our Mutual Friend)

5

ADAMS, Jack (Dombey and Son)
ALLEN, Arabella/Benjamin (Pickwick Papers)
BATES, Charley (Oliver Twist)
BETSY (Pickwick Papers)
BRASS, Sally/Sampson (The Old Curiosity Shop)
BRICK, Jefferson (Martin Chuzzlewit)
BROWN, Alice/Mrs (Dombey and Son)
BUZUZ, Sergeant (Pickwick Papers)
CASBY, Christopher (Little Dorrit)
CHICK, John/ Louisa (Dom bey and Son)
CLARE, Ada (Bleak House)
CLARK (Dombey and Son)
CLIVE (Little Dorrit)
CROWL (Nicholas Nickleby)
CRUPP, Mrs (David Copperfield)
DAISY, Solomon (Barnaby Rudge)
DAVID (Nicholas Nickleby)
DAWES, Mary (Dombey and Son)
DINGO, Professor (Bleak House)
DIVER, Colonel (Martin Chuzzlewit)
DONNY, Mrs (Bleak House)
DOYCE, Daniel (Little Dorrit)
DROOD, Edwin (Edwin Drood)
DUMPS, Nicodemus (Pickwick Papers)
FAGIN (Oliver Twist)
FLITE, Miss (Bleak House)
GILES (Oliver Twist)
GILLS, Solomon (Dombey and Son)
GOWAN, Harry (Little Dorrit)
GREEN, Tom (Barnaby Rudge)
GRIDE, Arthur (Nicholas Nickleby)
GUPPY, William (Bleak House)
HEXAM, Charlie/Jesse/Lizzie (Our Mutual Friend)
JANET (David Copperfield)
JONES, Mary (Barnaby Rudge)
KROOK (Bleak House)
LOBBS, Maria/'Old'(Pickwick Papers)
LORRY, Jarvis (A Tale of Two Cities)
LUCAS, Solomon (Pickwick Papers)

LUPIN, Mrs (Martin Chuzzlewit)
MEALY (David Copperfield)
MELIA (Dombey and Son)
MIGGS, Miss (Barnaby Rudge)
MILLS, Julia (David Copperfield)
MOLLY (Great Expectations)
MOULD (Martin Chuzzlewit)
NANCY (Oliver Twist)
NANDY, John Edward (Little Dorrit)
NOGGS, Newman (Nicholas Nickleby)
PERCH (Dombey and Son)
PINCH, Ruth/Tom (Martin Chuzzlewit)
PRICE, 'Tilda (Nicholas Nickleby)
PROSS, Miss/Solomon (A Tale of Two Cities)
QUALE (Bleak House)
QUILP, Daniel (The Old Curiosity Shop)
RUDGE, Barnaby/Mary (Barnaby Rudge)
SALLY, Old (Oliver Twist)
SCOTT, Tom (The Old Curiosity Shop)
SHARP (David Copperfield)
SIKES, Bill (Oliver Twist)
SLURK (Pickwick Papers)
SLYME, Chevy (Martin Chuzzlewit)
SMIKE (Nicholas Nickleby)
SNOBB, The Hon (Nicholas Nickleby)
SQUOD, Phil (Bleak House)
STAGG (Barnaby Rudge)
TOOTS, Mr P (Dombey and Son)
TRABB (Great Expectations)
TRENT, Frederick/Nellie (The Old Curiosity Shop)
TWIST, Oliver (Oliver Twist)
VENUS, Mr (Our Mutual Friend)
WATTY (Pickwick Papers)

6

BADGER, Dr Bayharn/Laura/Malta/Matthew/ Quebec/Woolwich (Bleak House)
BAILEY, Benjamin (Martin Chuzzlewit)
BAILEY, Captain (David Copperfield)
BAMBER, Jack (Pickwick Papers)
BANTAM, Angelo Cyrus (Pickwick Papers)
BARKER, Phil (Oliver Twist)
BARKIS (David Copperfield)
BARLEY, Clara (Great Expectations)
BARNEY (Oliver Twist)
BEDWIN, Mrs (Oliver Twist)
BETSEY, Jane (Dombey and Son)
BITZER (Hard Times)
BOFFIN, Henrietta/Nicodemus (Our Mutual Friend)
BONNEY (Nicholas Nickleby)

BRIGGS (Dombey and Son)
BUMBLE (Oliver Twist)
BUNSBY, Captain (Dombey and Son)
CARKER, Harriet/ James /John (Dombey and Son)
CARTON, Sydney (A Tale of Two Cities)
CHEGGS, Alick (The Old Curiosity Shop)
CLARKE (Pickwick Papers)
CODGER, Mrs (Martin Chuzzlewit)
CODLIN, Thomas (The Old Curiosity Shop)
CONWAY, General (Barnaby Rudge)
CORNEY, Mrs (Oliver Twist)
CURDLE (Nicholas Nickleby)
CUTLER, Mr/Mrs (Nicholas Nickleby)
CUTTLE, Captain Ned (Dombey and Son)
DARNAY, Charles (A Tale of Two Cities)
DARTLE, Rosa (David Copperfield)
DENNIS, Ned (Barnaby Rudge)
DIBABS, Mrs (Nicholas Nickleby)
DODSON (Pickwick Papers)
DOMBEY, Fanny/Florence/Louisa /Paul (Dombey and Son)
DORKER (Nicholas Nickleby)
DORRIT, Amy/Edward /Fanny/ Frederick/ William (Little Dorrit)
DOWLER, Captain (Pickwick Papers)
FEEDER (Dombey and Son)
FEENIX (Dombey and Son)
FIZKIN, Horatio (Pickwick Papers)
FOLIAR (Nicholas Nickleby)
GEORGE (The Old Curiosity Shop)
GEORGE (Pickwick Papers)
GEORGE, Mr (Bleak House)
GORDON, Lord George (Barnaby Rudge)
GRAHAM, Mary (Martin Chuzzlewit)
GROVES, 'Honest'James (The Old Curiosity Shop)
GUNTER (Pickwick Papers)
HARMON, John (Our Mutual Friend)
HARRIS, Mrs (Martin Chuzzlewit)
HAWDON, Captain (Bleak House)
HIGDEN, Betty (Our Mutual Friend)
HOMINY, Major (Martin Chuzzlewit)
HOWLER, Rev M (Dombey and Son)
JARLEY, Mrs (The Old Curiosity Shop)
JASPER, Jack (Edwin Drood)
JINGLE, Alfred (Pickwick Papers)
KETTLE, La Fayette (Martin Chuzzlewit)
LAMMLE, Alfred (Our Mutual Friend)
LOBLEY (Edwin Drood)
LUMLEY, Dr (Nicholas Nickleby)

MAGNUS, Peter (Pickwick Papers)
MALDEN, Jack (David Copperfield)
MARLEY, Jacob (A Christmas Carol)
MARTON (The Old Curiosity Shop)
MAYLIE, Harrie/Mrs/Rose (Oliver Twist)
MERDLE, Mr (Little Dorrit)
MILVEY, Rev Frank (Our Mutual Friend)
MIVINS (Pickwick Papers)
MODDLE, Augustus (Martin Chuzzlewit)
MORFIN (Dornbey and Son)
MULLET, Professor (Martin Chuzzlewit)
NIPPER, Susan (Dombey and Son)
PANCKS (Little Dorrit)
PERKER (Pickwick Papers)
PHUNKY (Pickwick Papers)
PIPKIN, Nathaniel (Pickwick Papers)
PIRRIP, Philip (Great Expectations)
POCKET, Herbert/Matthew/Sarah (Great Expectations)
POGRAM, Elijah (Martin Chuzzlewit)
RADDLE, Mr and Mrs (Pickwick Papers)
RIGAUD, Monsieur (Little Dorrit)
SAPSEA, Thomas (Edwin Drood)
SAWYER. Bob (Pickwick Papers)
SCALEY (Nicholas Nickleby)
SLEARY, Josephine (Hard Times)
'SLOPPY'(Our Mutual Friend)
SOWNDS (Dombey and Son)
STRONG, Dr (David Copperfield)
TACKER (Martin Chuzzlewit)
TAPLEY, Mark (Martin Chuzzlewit)
TARTAR (Edwin Drood)
TIPPIN, Lady (Our Mutual Friend)
TISHER, Mrs (Edwin Drood)
TOODLE (Dombey and Son)
TUPMAN, Tracy (Pickwick Papers)
VARDEN, Dolly/Gabriel (Barnaby Rudge)
VHOLES (Bleak House)
VUFFIN (The Old Curiosity Shop)
WALKER, Mick (David Copperfield)
WARDLE, Emily/Isabella/Mr/Rachel (Pickwick Papers)
WELLER, Sam/Tony (Pickwick Papers)
WILFER, Belia/Lavinia/Reginald (Our Mutual Friend)
WILLET, Joe/John (Barnaby Rudge)
WINKLE, Nathaffiel (Pickwick Papers)
WOPSLE (Great Expectations)

7

BAILLIE, Gabriel (Pickwick Papers)
BANGHAM, Mrs (Little Dorrit)
BARBARA (The Old Curiosity Shop)
BARBARY, Miss (Bleak House)
BARDELL, Mrs Martha/Tommy (Pickwick Papers)
BAZZARD (Edwin Drood)
BELLING, Master (Nicholas Nickleby)
BLIMBER, Dr (Dombey and Son)
BLOTTON (Pickwick Papers)
BOBSTER, Cecilia/Mr (Nicholas Nickleby)
BOLDWIG, Captain (Pickwick Papers)
BROGLEY (Dombey and Son)
BROOKER (Nicholas Nickleby)
BROWDIE, John (Nicholas Nickleby)
BULLAMY (Martin Chuzzlewit)
CHARLEY (David Copperfield)
CHESTER, Edward/Sir John (Barnaby Rudge)
CHILLIP, Dr (David Copperfield)
CHIVERY, John (Little Dorrit)
CHOLLOP, Hannibal (Martin Chuzzlewit)
CHUFFEY (Martin Chuzzlewit)
CLEAVER, Fanny (Our Mutual Friend)
CLENNAM, Arthur (Little Dorrit)
CLUBBER, Sir Thomas.(Pickwick Papers)
CRACKIT, Toby (Oliver Twist)
CRAWLEY, Young Mr (Pickwick Papers)
CREAKLE (David Copperfield)
CREWLER, Mrs/Rev Horace/Sophy (David Copperfield)
CRIMPLE, David (Martin Chuzzlewit)
CROOKEY (Rickwick Papers)
DAWKINS, Jack (Oliver Twist)
DEDLOCK, Sir Leicester/Volumnia (Bleak House)
DEFARGE, Madame (A Tale of Two Cities)
DOLLOBY (David Copperfield)
DRUMMLE, Bentley (Great Expectations)
DUBBLEY (Pickwick Papers)
DURDLES (Edwin Drood)
EDMUNDS, John (Pickwick Papers)
ESTELLA (Great Expectations)
FLEMING, Agnes (Oliver Twist)
GABELLE, Theophile (A Tale of Two Cities)
GARGERY, Biddy/Joe/Pip (Great Expectations)
GARLAND, Abel/Mrs/Mr (The Old Curiosity Shop)
GASPARD (A Tale of Two Cities)

GAZINGI, Miss (Nicholas Nickleby)
GENERAL, Mrs (Little Dorrit)
GILBER, Mark (Barnaby Rudge)
GRANGER, Edith (Dombey and Son)
GRIDLEY (Bleak House)
GRIMWIG (Oliver Twist)
GRUDDEN, Mrs (Nicholas Nickleby)
HAGGAGE, Dr (Little Dorrit)
HEYLING, George (Pickwick Papers)
JAGGERS (Great Expectations) .
JELLYBY, Caddy/Mrs/Peepy (Bleak House)
JINKINS (Martin Chuzzlewit)
JOBLING, Dr John (Martin Chuzzlewit)
JOBLING, Tony (Bleak House)
JOHNSON, Mr (Nicholas Nickleby)
JORKINS (David Copperfield)
KEDGICK, Captain (Martin Chuzzlewit)
KENWIGS, Morleena (Nicholas Nickleby)
LARKINS, Mr (David Copperfield)
LEEFORD, Edward (Oliver Twist)
LEWSOME (Martin Chuzzlewit)
MALLARD (Pickwick Papers)
MANETTE, Dr/Lucie (A Tale of Two Cities)
MEAGLES (Little Dorrit)
MINERVA (Pickwick Papers)
MOWCHER, Miss (David Copperfield)
NADGETT (Martin Chuzzlewit)
NECKETT, Charlotte/ Ernma/Torn (Bleak House)
NUBBLES, Christopher (The Old Curiosity Shop)
NUPKINS, George (Pickwick Papers)
PAWKINS, Major (Martin Chuzzlewit)
PILKINS, Dr (Dombey and Son)
PIPCHIN, Mrs (Dombey and Son)
PODSNAP, Georgiana/Mr (Our Mutual Friend)
QUINION (David Copperfield)
SAMPSON, George (Our Mutual Friend)
SCADDER, Zephaniah (Martin Chuzzlewit)
SCROOGE, Ebenezer (A Christmas Carol)
SIMMONS, William (Martin Chuzzlewit)
SKEWTON, Hon Mrs (Dombey and Son)
SKYLARK, Mr (David Copperfield)
SLAMMER, Dr (Pickwick Papers)
SLUMKEY, Hon Samuel (Pickwick Papers)
SNAGSBY (Bleak House)
SNAWLEY (Nicholas Nickleby)
SNUBBIN, Sergeant (Pickwick Papers)
SPARSIT, Mrs (Hard Times)
SPENLOW, Dora (David Copperfield)

7 continued

SQUEERS, Fanny/Wackford (Nicholas Nickleby)
STARTOP (Great Expectations)
STRYVER, C.J. (A Tale of Two Cities)
TAMAROO, Miss (Martin Chuzzlewit)
TODGERS, Mrs (Martin Chuzzlewit)
TROTTER, Job (Pickwick Papers)
TRUNDLE (Pickwick Papers)
WACKLES, Jane/Melissa/Sophie (The Old Curiosity Shop)
WATKINS (Nicholas Nickleby)
WEMMICK (Great Expectations)
WICKHAM, Mrs (Dombey and Son)
WITHERS (Dombey and Son)

8

AKERSHEM, Sophronia (Our Mutual Friend)
BAGSTOCK, Major (Dombey and Son)
BARNWELL, B.B. (Martin Chuzzlewit)
BILLIKIN, Mrs (Edwin Drood)
BLATHERS (Oliver Twist)
BOYTHORN, Lawrence (Bleak House)
BRAVASSA, Miss (Nicholas Nickleby)
BROWNLOW, Mr (Oliver Twist)
CLAYPOLE, Noah (Mver Twist)
CLUPPINS (Pickwick Papers)
CRADDOCK, Mrs (Pickwick Papers)
CRATCHIT, Belinda/Bob/Tiny Tim (A Christmas Carol)
CRIPPLES, Mr (Little Dorrit)
CRUMMLES, Ninetta/Vincent (Nicholas Nickleby)
CRUNCHER, Jeremiah/Jerry (A Tale of Two Cities)
CRUSHTON, Hon Mr (Pickwick Papers)
DATCHERY, Dick (Edwin Drood)
D'AULNAIS (A Tale of Two Cities)
FINCHING, Mrs Flora (Little Dorrit)
FLEDGEBY, Old/Young (Our Mutual Friend)
GASHFORD (Barnaby Rudge)
HAREDALE, Emma/Geoffrey/Reuben (Barnaby Rudge)
HAVISHAM, Miss (Great Expectations)
HORTENSE (Bleak House)
JARNDYCE, John (Bleak House)
LA CREEVY, Miss (Nicholas Nickleby)
LANDLESS, Helena/Neville (Edwin Drood)
LANGDALE (Barnaby Rudge)
LENVILLE (Nicholas Nickleby)
LITTIMER (David Copperfield)
LOSBERNE (Oliver Twist)

MAGWITCH, Abel (Great Expectations)
MARY ANNE (David Copperfield)
MATTHEWS (Nicholas Nickleby)
MICAWBER, Wilkins (David Coppertield)
MUTANHED, Lord (Pickwick Papers)
NICKLEBY, Godfrey/Kate/Nicholas/Ralph (Nicholas Nickleby)
PEGGOTTY, Clara/Daniel /Ham/ Little Emily (David Copperfield)
PICKWICK, Samuel (Pickwick Papers)
PLORNISH, Thomas (Little Dorrit)
POTATOES (David Copperfield)
SCADGERS, lady (Hard Times)
SKIFFINS, Miss (Great Expectations)
SKIMPOLE, Arethusa/Harold /Kitty/ Laura (Bleak House)
SKITTLES, Sir Barnet (Dombey and Son)
SMIGGERS, Joseph (Pickwick Papers)
SPARKLER, Edmund (Little Dorrit)
STIGGINS (Pickwick Papers)
TRADDLES, Tom (David Copperfield)
TROTWOOD, Betsey (David Copperfield)
WESTLOCK, John (Martin Chuzzlewit)
WRAYBURN, Eugene (Our Mutual Friend)

9

BELVAWNEY, Miss (Nicholas Nickleby)
BERINTHIA (Dombey and Son)
BLACKPOOL, Stephen (Hard Times)
BOUNDERBY, Josiah (Hard Times)
CHARLOTTE (Oliver Twist)
CHEERYBLE, Charles/ Frank/Ned (Nicholas Nickleby)
CHICKWEED, Conkey (Oliver Twist)
CHUCKSTER (The Old Curiosity Shop)
COMPEYSON (Great Expectations)
FIBBITSON, Mrs (David Copperfield)
GRADGRIND, Louisa/Thomas (Hard Times)
GREGSBURY (Nicholas Nickelby)
GREWGIOUS (Edwin Drood)
HARTHOUSE, James (Hard Times)
HEADSTONE, Bradley (Our Mutual Friend)
LIGHTWOOD, Mortimer (Our Mutual Friend)
LILLYVICK (Nidholas Nickleby)
MANTALINI, Mr (Nicholas Nickleby)
MURDSTONE, Edward/Jane (David Copperfield)
OLD BARLEY (Great Expectations)
PARDIGGLE, Francis/O.A. (Bleak House)
PECKSNIFF, Charity/ Mercy/ Seth (Martin Chuzzlewit)
PRISCILLA (Bleak House)

CHARACTERS IN DICKENS / SHAKESPEARE

9 continued

RIDERHOOD, Pleasant/Roger (Our Mutual Friend)
SMALLWEED, Bartholemew/Joshua/Judy (Bleak House)
SMORLTORK, Count (Pickwick Papers)
SNODGRASS, Augustus (Pickwick Papers)
SUMMERSON, Esther (Bleak House)
SWIVELLER, Richard (The Old Curiosity Shop)
TAPPERTIT, Simon (Barnaby Rudge)
VENEERING, Anastasia /Hamilton (Our Mutual Friend)
VERISOPHT, Lord Frederick (Nicholas Nickleby)
WICKFIELD, Agnes/Mr (David Copperfield)
WITHERDEN, Mr (The Old Curiosity Shop)
WOODCOURT, Allan (Bleak House)

10

AYRESLEIGH, Mr (Pickwick Papers)
CHUZZLEWIT, Anthony/Diggory/George/ Jonas/ Martin/Mrs Ned/Toby (Martin Chuzzlewit)
CRISPARKLE, Rev Septimus (Edwin Drood)
FLINTWINCH, Affery/Ephraim/Jeremiah (Little Dorrit)
MACSTINGER, Mrs (Dombey and Son)
ROUNCEWELL, Mrs (Bleak House)
SNEVELLICI, Miss (Nicholas Nickleby)

SOWERBERRY (Oliver Twist)
STARELEIGH, Justice (Pickwick Papers)
STEERFORTH, James, (David Copperfield)
TATTYCORAM (Little Dorrit)
TURVEYDROP, Prince (Bleak House)
TWINKLETON, Miss (Edwin Drood)
WATERBROOK (David Copperfield)
WITITTERLY, Julia (Nicholas Nickleby)

11

COPPERFIELD, Clara/David (David Copperfield)
'DISMAL JIMMY' (Pickwick Papers)
'GAME CHICKEN', The (Dombey and Son)
MARCHIONESS, The (The Old Curiosity Shop)
PUMBLECHOOK (Great Expectations)
SPOTTLETOES, Mrs (Martin Chuzzle.it)
ST EVREMONDE, Marquis de/Marquise de (A Tale of Two Cities)
SWEEDLEPIPE, Paul (Martin Chuzzlewit)
TULKINGHORN (Bleak House)

12

HONEYTHUNDER, Luke (Edwin Drood)
'SHINY WILLIAM' (Pickwick Papers)
SWEET WILLIAM (The Old Curiosity Shop)
TITE-BARNACLE, Clarence/Ferdinand/ Junior/Lord Decimus/Mr (Little Dorrit)

15

VON KOELDWETHOUT (Nicholas Nickleby)

CHARACTERS IN SHAKESPEARE

3

HAL (Henry IV, part 1)
NYM (Henry V, The Merry Wives of Windsor)

4

ADAM (As You Like It)
AJAX (Troilus and Cressida)
EROS (Antony and Cleopatra)
FORD, Mistress (The Merry Wives of Windsor)
HERO (Much Ado About Nothing)
IAGO (Othello)
IRAS (Antony and Cleopatra)
LEAR (King Lear)
PAGE, Mistress (The Merry Wives of Windsor)
PETO (Henry IV, part 2)
PUCK (A Midsummer Night's Dream)
SNUG (A Midsummer Night's Dream)

5

AARON (Titus Andronicus)
ARIEL (The Tempest)
BELCH, Sir Toby (Twelfth Night)
BLUNT (2 Henry IV)
CAIUS, Doctor (The Merry Wives of Windsor)
CELIA (As You Like It)
CLEON (Pericles)
CORIN (As You Like It)
DIANA (All's Well that Ends Well)
EDGAR (King Lear)
ELBOW (Measure for Measure)
FESTE (Twelfth Night)
FLUTE (A Midsummer Night's Dream)
FROTH (Measure tor Measure)
GOBBO, Launcelot (The Merchant of Venice)
JULIA (The Two Gentlemen of Verona)
LAFEW (All's Well That Ends Well)

5 continued

MARIA (Love's Labour's Lost, Twelfth Night)
PARIS (Troilus and Cressida)
PERCY (Henry IV part 1)
PHEBE (As You Like It)
PINCH (The Comedy of Errors)
POINS (Henry IV part 1,Henry IV part 2)
PRIAM (Troilus and Cressida)
REGAN (King Lear)
ROMEO (Romeo and Juliet)
SNOUT (A Midsummer Night's Dream)
TIMON (Timon of Athens)
TITUS (Titus Andronicus)
VIOLA (Twelfth Night)

6

AEGEON (The Comedy of Errors)
ALONSO (The Tempest)
ANGELO (Measure for Measure)
ANTONY (Antony and Cleopatra)
ARCITE (The Two Noble Kinsmen)
ARMADO (Love's Labour's Lost)
AUDREY (As You Like It)
BANQUO (Macbeth)
BIANCA (The Taming of the Shrew, Othello)
BOTTOM (A Midsummer Night's Dream)
BRUTUS (Coriolanus, Julius Caesar)
CASSIO (Othello)
CHIRON (Titus Andronicus)
CLOTEN (Cymbeline)
DENNIS (As You Like It)
DROMIO (The Comedy of Errors)
DUMAIN (Love's Labour's Lost)
DUNCAN (Macbeth)
EDMUND (King Lear)
EMILIA (Othello, The Two Noble Kinsmen)
FABIAN (Twelfth Night)
FENTON (The Merry Wives of Windsor)
FULVIA (Antony and Cleopatra)
HAMLET (Hamlet)
HECATE (Macbeth)
HECTOR (Troilus and Cressida)
HELENA (A Midsummer Night's Dream, All's Well That Ends Well)
HERMIA (A Midsummer Night's Dream)
IMOGEN (Cymbeline)
JULIET (Romeo and Juliet, Measure for Measure)
LUCIUS (Titus Andronicus)
OBERON (A Midsummer Night's Dream)
OLIVER (As You Like, It)
OLIVIA (Twelfth Night)

ORSINO (Twelfth Night)
OSWALD (King Lear)
PISTOL (Henry IV, part 2, Henry V, The Merry Wives of Windsor)
POMPEY (Measure for Measure, Antony and Cleopatra)
PORTIA (The Merchant of Venice)
QUINCE (A Midsummer Night's Dream)
RUMOUR (Henry IV part 2)
SCROOP (Henry IV part 1, Henry IV part 2)
SILVIA (The Two Gentlemen of Verona)
TAMORA (Titus Andronicus)
THURIO (The Two Gentlemen of Verona)
TYBALT (Romeo and Juliet)
VERGES (Much Ado About Nothing)

7

ADRIANA (The Comedy of Errors)
AEMILIA (The Comedy of Errors)
AGRIPPA (Antony and Cleopatra)
ALARBUS (Titus Andronicus)
ANTONIO (The Merchant of Venice, The Tempest)
BEROWNE (Love's Labour's Lost)
BERTRAM (All's Well That Ends Well)
CALCHAS (Troilus and Cressida)
CALIBAN (The Tempest)
CAPULET (Romeo and Juliet)
CESARIO (Twelfth Night)
CLAUDIO (Much Ado About Nothing, Measure for Measure)
COSTARD (Love's Labour's Lost)
DOUGLAS (Henry IV, part 1)
ESCALUS (Measure for Measure)
FLEANCE (Macbeth)
GONZALO (The Tempest)
HORATIO (Hamlet)
HOTSPUR (Henry IV, part 1)
JACQUES (As You Like It)
JESSICA (The Merchant of Venice)
LAERTES (Hamlet)
LAVINIA (Titus Andronicus)
LEONTES (The Winter's Tale)
LORENZO (The Merchant of Venice)
LUCIANA (The Comedy of Errors)
MACBETH (Macbeth)
MACDUFF (Macbeth)
MALCOLM (Macbeth)
MARIANA (Measure for Measure, All's Well That Ends Well)
MARTIUS (Titus Andronicus)
MIRANDA (The Tempest)

CHARACTERS IN SHAKESPEARE

7 continued

OCTAVIA (Antony and Cleopatra)
OPHELIA (Hamlet)
ORLANDO (As You Like It)
OTHELLO (Othello)
PAULINA (The Winter's Tale)
PERDITA (The Winter's Tale)
PROTEUS (The Two Gentlemen of Verona)
QUICKLY, Mistress (Henry IV part 1, Henry IV part 2, The Merry Wives of Windsor)
SHALLOW, Justice (Henry IV part 2, The Merry Wives of Windsor)
SHYLOCK (The Merchant of Venice)
SILENCE (Henry IV part 2)
SILVIUS (As You Like It)
SLENDER (The Merry Wives of Windsor)
SOLINUS (The Comedy of Errors)
THESEUS (A Midsummer Night's Dream, The Two Noble Kinsmen)
TITANIA (A Midsummer Night's Dream)
TROILUS (Troilus and Cressida)
ULYSSES (Troilus and Cressida)

8

ACHILLES (Troilus and Cressida)
BAPTISTA (The Taming of the Shrew)
BARDOLPH (Henry IV, Henry V, The Merry Wives of Windsor)
BASSANIO (The Merchant of Venice)
BEATRICE (Much Ado About Nothing)
BENEDICK (Much Ado About Nothing)
BENVOLIO (Romeo and Juliet)
CHARMIAN (Antony and. Cleopatra)
CLAUDIUS (Hamlet)
CORDELIA (King Lear)
CRESSIDA (Troilus and Cressida)
DIOMEDES (Antony and Cleopatra, Troilus and Cressida)
DOGBERRY (Much Ado About Nothing)
DON PEDRO (Much Ado About Nothing)
FALSTAFF (The Merry Wives of Windsor, Henry IV)
GERTRUDE (Hamlet)
GRATIANO (The Merchant of Venice)
HERMIONE (The Winter's Tale)
ISABELLA (Measure for Measure)
LUCENTIO (The Taming of the Shrew)
LYSANDER (A Midsummer Night's Dream)
MALVOLIO (Twelfth Night)
MERCUTIO (Romeo and Juliet)
MONTAGUE (Romeo and Juliet)
MORTIMER (Henry IV part 1)

OCTAVIUS (Antony and Cleopatra)
PAROLLES (All's Well That Ends Well)
PERICLES (Pericles)
POLONIUS (Hamlet)
PROSPERO (The Tempest)
RODERIGO (Othello)
ROSALIND (As You Like It)
ROSALINE (Love's Labour's Lost)
STEPHANO (The Tempest)
TRINCULO (The Tempest)
VIOLENTA (All's Well That Ends Well)
VOLUMNIA (Corialanus)

9

ANTIOCHUS (Pericles)
ARVIRAGUS (Cymbeline)
AUGECHEEK, Sir Andrew (Twelfth Night)
BASSIANUS (Titus Andronicus)
CAMBRIDGE (Henry V)
CLEOPATRA (Antony and Cleopatra)
CYMBELINE (Cymbeline)
DEMETRIUS (A Midsummer Night's Dream, Antony and Cleopatra, Titus Andronicus)
DESDEMONA (Othello)
ENOBARBUS (Antony and Cleopatra)
FERDINAND (Love's Labour's Lost, The Tempest)
FREDERICK (As You Like It)
HIPPOLYTA (A Midsummer Night's Dream, The Two Noble Kinsmen)
HORTENSIO (The Taming of the Shrew)
KATHERINA (The Taming of the Shrew)
KATHERINE (Henry V, Love's Labour's Lost)
SEBASTIAN (The Tempest, Twelfth Night)
TEARSHEET, Doll (Henry IV part2)
VALENTINE (The Two Gentlemen of Verona)
VINCENTIO (Measure for Measure, The Taming of the Shrew)

10

ALCIBIADES, (Timon of Athens)
ANTIPHOLUS (The Comedy of Errors)
CORIOLANUS (Coriolanus)
FORTINBRAS (Hamlet)
JAQUENETTA (Love's Labour's Lost)
LONGAVILLE (Love's Labour's Lost)
SATURNINUS (Titus Andronicus)
TOUCHSTONE (As You Like It)

11

ROSENCRANTZ (Hamlet)

12

GUILDENSTERN (Hamlet)

154

FILMS

2
E.T.

3
Hud

4
Dr. No
Gigi
Jaws
MASH

5
Alien
Annie
Bambi
Ghost
Giant
Klute
Marty
Rocky
Seven
Shane
Twins
Wings

6
Bat Man
Ben Hur
Frenzy
Gandhi
Grease
Hamlet
Henry V
Oliver
Psycho
Scream
Top Gun
Top Hat

7
Airport
Amadeus
Bus Stop
Cabaret
Charade
Platoon
Rain Man
Rebecca
The Firm

The Mask
The Robe
Titanic
Tootsie
Vertigo

8
Cocktail
Fantasia
Duck Soup
Gas Light
High Noon
King Kong
Mon Oncle
Music Man
Oklahoma!
Peter Pan
Rashomon
Rio Brave
Scar Face
Star Wars
Superman
The Birds
The Sting
Tom Jones

9
China Town
Annie Hall
Cavalcade
Cimmarron
Cleopatra
Dr. Zhivago
Easy Rider
Funny Face
Funny Girl
Gladiator
House Boat
Local Hero
Moonraker
Octopussy
Pinocchio
Suspicion
Viridiana

10
Blue Velvet
Casablanca
Cinderella
City Lights

Family Plot
Forest Gump
42nd Street
Going My Way
Goldfinger
Goodfellas
L'Avventura
Mrs Miniver
My Fair Lady
Nine To Five
Now Voyager
Raging Bull
Rear Window
Spell Bound
Stage Coach
Taxi Driver
The General
The Misfits
The 39 Steps
Way Out West
Woman In Red

11
A Chorus Line
All About Eve
A Star is Born
A View to Kill
Blade Runner
Call Me Madam
Citizen Kane
Dead of Night
High Society
Intolerance
Mary Poppins
Mickey Mouse
Modern Times
Out of Africa
Pretty Woman
Pulp Fiction
The Big Sleep
The Cruel Sea
The Exorcist
The Graduate
The Lion King
The Magic Bow
The Naked Gun
The Third Man
Thunderball
Torn Curtain

12
African Queen
A Patch of Blue
Casino Royale
Cool Hand Luke
Dirty Dancing
Duel in the Sun
49th Parallel
Frankenstein
Ghostbusters
Jerry Maguire
Jurassic Park
La Règle du Jeu
Rome - Open City
Room at the Top
Seven Samurai
South Pacific
The Apartment
The Godfather
The Producers
The Searchers
The Wild Bunch

13
Apocalypse Now
Dr. Strangelove
Licence to Kill
101 Dalmations
Some Like it Hot
The Blue Lagoon
The Deer Humter
The Dirty Dozen
The Jungle Book
The Terminator
The Wizard of Oz
This is the Army
To Be or Not To Be
Trainspotting
West Side Story

14
Above and Beyond
Above Suspicion
Adam and Evelyne
A Day at the Races
All the King's Men
Bicycle Thieves
Bonnie and Clyde
Brief Encounter
Broadway Melody

155

FILMS

14 continued
Chariots of Fire
Kramer vs Kramer
Midnight Cowboy
Ordinary People
Sleeping Beauty
Song of the South
The Lst Emporer
The Long Weekend
The Lost Weekend

15
Back to the Future
Beverly Hills Cop
Crocodile Dundee
Double Indemnity
Fatal Attraction
For Your Eyes Only
Gone With The Wind
Lady and the Tramp
Life of Emile Zola
On the Waterfront
Return of the Jedi
River of no Return
Singin' in the Rain
Sunset Boulevard
The Sound of Music
The Invisable Man
The Tamarind Seed

16
A Clockwork Orange
American Graffiti
A Night at the Opera
Dances with Wolves
David Copperfield
Dead Poets Society
In the Heat of the Night
La Grande Illusion
Lawrence of Arabia
Night of the Hunter
North by Northwest
Samson and Delilah
Shirley Valentine
The Grapes of Wrath
The Great Ziegfeld
The Maltese Falcon
The Seven Year Itch
The Spy Who Loved Me
Three Men and a Baby

17
A Man for All Seasons
An American in Paris
Arsenic and Old Lace
It's a Wonderful LIfe
Mutiny on the Bounty
Saving Private Ryan
Terms of Endearment
The Bells of Saint Mary's
The English Patient
2001:A Space Odyssey
Victor and Victoria

18
Battleship Potemkin
Diamonds are Forever
From Here to Eternity
Good Morning Vietnam
Never say Never Again
Saturday Night Fever
The Lavender Hill Mob
The Living Daylights
The Prisoner of Zenda
The Ten Commandments
The Towering Inferno

19
Breakfast at Tiffany's
Greatest Show on Earth
How Green Was My Valley
Les Enfants du Paradis
Miracle on 34th Street
Raiders of the Lost Ark
The French Connection

20
Nigthmare on Elm Street
Sleeping with the Enemy
The Empire Strikes Back
The Man Who Knew Too Much
The Poseidon Adventure
Who Framed Roger Rabbit?
You Can't Take It With You

21
Kind Hearts and Coronets

22
Far From the Madding Crowd
Gentlemen Prefer Blonds
How to Marry a Millionaire
Once Upon a Time in the West
The Madness of King George
The Manchurian Candidate

23
Four Weddings and a Funeral
Mr. Smith Goes to Washington
The Bridge on the River Kwai
The Prince and the Showgirl

24
The Adventures of Robin Hood

25
All Quiet on the Western Front
One Flew Over the Cuckoo's Nest

26
Around the World in Eighty Days
Invasion of the Body Snatchers
Snow White and the Seven Dwarfs

29
Butch Cassidy and the
  Sundance Kid
Close Encounters of the
  Third Kind
Indiana Jones and the Last
  Crusade

30
Indiana Jones and the
  Temple of Doom

31
There's No Business Like
  Show Business

156

LANGUAGE

LANGUAGES OF THE WORLD

2	BIHARI	FRISIAN	MANDARIN
WU	BRETON	ITALIAN	ROMANSCH
3	DANISH	LATVIAN	RUMANIAN
MIN	FRENCH	MARATHI	ROMANIAN
4	GAELIC	PUNJABI	UKRANIAN
URDU	GERMAN	RUSSIAN	9
5	KOREAN	SLOVENE	AFRIKAANS
DUTCH	PAHARI	SORBIAN	BULGARIAN
GREEK	POLISH	SPANISH	CANTONESE
HINDI	ROMANY	SWEDISH	ICELANDIC
IRISH	SINDHI	TURKISH	NORWEGIAN
MALAY	SLOVAK	8	SINHALESE
ORIYA	TELUGU	ASSAMESE	10
TAMIL	7	GUJARATI	LITHUANIAN
WELSH	BANGALI	JAPANESE	PORTUGUESE
6	CATALAN	JAVANESE	RAJASTHANI
ARABIC	ENGLISH	KASHMIRI	SERBO-CROAT

THE GREEK ALPHABET

ALPHA	XI
BETA	OMICRON
GAMMA	PI
DELTA	RHO
EPSILON	SIGMA
ZETA	TAU
ETA	UPSILON
THETA	TAU
IOTA	UPSILON
KAPPA	PHI
LAMBDA	CHI
MU	PSI
NU	OMEGA

THE HEBREW ALPHABET

ALEPH	MEM
BETH	NUN
GIMEL	SAMEKH
DALETH	AYIN
HE	PE
VAV	SADI
ZAYIN	KOPH
CHETH	RESH
TETH	SHIN
YOD	SIN
KAPH	TAV
LAMED	

159

FOREIGN WORDS

ENGLISH	FRENCH	GERMAN	ITALIAN	SPANISH	LATIN
AND	ET	UND	E, ED	E	ET
BUT	MAIS	ABER	MA	PERO	SED
FOR	POUR	FÜR	PER	PARA, POR	PER
TO	À	AUF, NACH	A	A	AD
WITH	AVEC	MIT	CON	CON	CUM
MISTER	MONSIEUR	HERR	SIGNOR	SEÑOR	DOMINUS
MADAM	MADAME	FRAU, FR.	SIGNORA	SEÑORA	DOMINA
MRS.	MME.		SIG.A., SIG.RA.	SRA.	
MISS.	MADEMOI-SELLE,	FRÄULEIN, FRL	SIGNORINA SIG.NA.	SEÑORITA SRTA.	
FROM	DE	AUS, VON	DA	DE	AB
OF	DE	VON	DI	DE	DE
GIRL	FILLE	MÄDCHEN	RAGAZZA	CHICA, NIÑA	PUELLA
BOY	GARCON	JUNGE	RAGAZZO	CHICO, NIÑO	PUER
BIG	GRAND	GROSS	GRANDE	GRANDE	MAGNUS
LITTLE	PETIT	KLEIN	PICCOLO	PEQUENO CHICO POCO	PAUCUS
VERY	TRÉS	SEHR	MOLTO	MUCHO	
FASHION-ABLE	À LA MODE	MODISCH	DI MODA	DE MODA	
GENTLEMAN	MONSIEUR	HERR	SIGNORE	CABALLERO	DOMINUS
LADY	DAME	DAME	SIGNORA	SEÑORA	DOMINA
MAN	HOMME	MANN	UOMO	HOMBRE	HOMO
WOMAN	FEMME	FRAU	DONNA	DOÑA	MULIER
WHO	QUI	WER	CHI	QUIÉN, QUE	QUIS
I	JE	ICH	IO	YO	EGO
YOU	TU, VOUS	DU, SIE, IHR	TU, VOI, LEI	TU, VOSOTROS/AS	TU, VOS
WHAT	QUOI, QUEL	WAS	CHE COSA	QUE	QUOD
HE	IL	ER	EGLI	EL	IS
SHE	ELLE	SIE	ELLA	ELLA	EA
WE	NOUS	WIR	NOI	NOSOTROS/AS	NOS
THEY	ILS, ELLES	SIE	ESSI	ELLOS,ELLAS	EI,EAE
AT HOME	CHEZ MOI/NOUS or À LA MAISON	ZU HAUSE	A CASA	EN CASA	DOMO
HOUSE	MAISON	HAUS	CASA	CASA	VILLA, DOMUS
STREET	RUE	STRASSE	STRADA	CALLE	VIA
ROAD	ROUTE	WEG	VIA	CAMINO	VIA
BY	PAR	BEI	PER	POR	PER
BEFORE	AVANT	VOR	PRIMA	(DEL) ANTE	ANTE
AFTER	APRÈS	NACH	DOPO	DESPUTES	POST
UNDER	SOUS	UNTER	SOTTO	(DE)BAJO	SUB
OVER	SUR	OBER	SOPRA, SU	SOBRE	SUPER

FOREIGN WORDS / NUMBERS

ENGLISH	FRENCH	GERMAN	ITALIAN	SPANISH	LATIN
NEAR	PRÈS DE	NAHE, BEI	VICINO	CERCA	PROPE
OUT	DEHORS	AUS	VIA, FUORI	FUERA	EX
IN	DANS	IN	IN	EN	IN
HOW	COMMENT	WIE	COME	COMO	QUO MODO
HY	POURQUOI	WARUM	PERCHE	POR QUE	CUR
THE	LE, LA, LES	DER,DIE,DAS	IL, LO, LA,I GLI, LE	EL, LA, LO, LOS, LAS	
A	UN, UNE	EIN, EINE	UN,UNO,UNA	UN, UNA	
RED	ROUGE	ROT	ROSSA	ROJO	RUBER
BLUE	BLEU	BLAU	AZZURRO	AZUL	CAERULEUS
YELLOW	JAUNE	GELB	GIALLO	AMARILLO	FULVUS
GREEN	VERT	GRUN	VERDE	VERDE	VIRIDIS
BLACK	NOIR	SCHWARZ	NERO	NEGRA	NIGER
WHIE	BLANC OR BLANCHE	WEISS	BANCO	BLANCO	ALBUS
SHORT	COURT	KURZ	CORTO, BREVE	CORTO	BREVIS
LONG	LONG	LANG	LUNGO	LARGO	LONGUS

NUMBERS

ENGLISH	ROMAN NUMERALS	FRENCH	GERMAN	ITALIAN	SPANISH
ONE	I	UN	EIN	UNO	UNO
TWO	II	DEUX	ZWEI	DUE	DOS
THREE	III	TROIS	DREI	TRE	TRES
FOUR	IV	QUATRE	VIER	QUATTRO	CUATRO
FIVE	V	CINQ	FÜNF	CINQUE	CINCO
SIX	VI	SIX	SECHS	SEI	SEIS
SEVEN	VII	SEPT	SIEBEN	SETTE	SUETE
EIGHT	VIII	HUIT	ACHT	OTTO	OCHO
NINE	IX	NEUF	NEUN	NOVE	NUEVE
TEN	X	DIX	ZEHN	DIECI	DIEZ
TWENTY	XX	VINGT	ZWANZIG	VENTI	VEINTE
TWENTY-FIVE	XV	VINGT-CINQ	FÜNF UND ZWANZIG	VENTICI-NQUE	VEINTICI-NCO
THIRTY	XXX	TRENTE	DREISSIG	TRENTA	TREINTA
FOURTY	XL	QUARANTE	VIERZIG	QUARANTA	CUARENTA
FIFTY	L	CINQUANTE	FÜNFZIG	CINQUANTA	CINCUENTA
SIXTY	LX	SOIXANTE	SECHZIG	SESSANTA	SESENTA
SEVENTY	LXX	SOIXANTE-DIX	SIEBZIG	SETTANTA	SETENTA
EIGHTY	LXXX	QUATRE-VINGT	ACHTZI	OTTANTA	OCHENTA
NINETY	XC	QUATRE-VINGT-DIX	NEUNZIG	NOVANTA	NOVENTA

161

NUMBERS / FRENCH PHRASES

ENGLISH	ROMAN NUMERALS	FRENCH	GERMAN	ITALIAN	SPANISH
ONE HUNDRED	C	CENT	HUNDERT	CENTO	CIEN (CIENTO)
FIVE HUNDRED	D	CINQ CENTS	FÜNFHUN-DERT	CINQUE-CENTO	QUINIENTOS
ONE THOUSAND	M	MILLE	TAUSEND	MILLE	MIL

FRENCH PHRASES

5
MÊLÉE - brawl
ON DIT - piece of gossip, rumour
6
DE TROP - unwelcome
7
À LA MODE - fashionable
À PROPOS - to the point
CAP-À-PIE - from head to foot
DE RÈGLE - customary
EN MASSE - all together
EN ROUTE - on the way
8
BÊTE NOIR - person or thing particularly
  disliked
IDÉE FIXE - obsession
MAL DE MER - seasickness
MOT JUSTE - the appropriate word
9
DE RIGUEUR - required by custom
EN PASSANT - by the way
EN RAPPORT - in harmony
ENTRE NOUS - between you and me
10
À BON MARCHÉ - cheap
BILLET DOUX - love letter
DERNIER CRI - latest fashion, the last word
NOM DE PLUME - writer's assumed name
PENSE À BIEN - think for the best
11
AMOUR PROPRE - self-esteem

GARDEZ LA FOI - keep the faith
LÈSE MAJESTÉ - treason
NOM DE GUERRE - assumed name
RAISON D'ÊTRE - justification for existence
SAVOIR FAIRE - address, tact
TOUR DE FORCE - feat or accomplishment
  of great strength
12
FORCE MAJEURE - irresistable force or
  compulsion
HORS DE COMBAT - out of the fight,
  disabled
SANS DIEU RIEN - nothing without God
VENTRE À TERRE - at great speed
14
DOUBLE ENTENDRE - double meaning
ENFANT TERRIBLE - child who causes
  embarrassment
NOBLESSE OBLIGE - privilege entails
  responsibility
PREUX CHEVALIER - gallant knight
VÉRTÉ SANS PEUR - truth without fear
15
AMENDE HONORABLE - reperation
CHERCHEZ LA FEMME - look for the woman
17
PIÈCE DE RESISTANCE - the most
  outstanding item, main dish at a meal
20+
AUTRE TEMPS, AUTRES MOEURS - other
  times, other manners

LATIN PHRASES

4
FIAT - let it be done or made
IN RE - concerning
STET - let it stand
5
AD HOC - for this special purpose
AD LIB - to speak off the cuff, without notes

AD REM - to the point
CIRCA - about
FECIT - he did it
6
AD USUM - as customary
IN SITU - in its original situation
IN TOTO - entirely

LATIN PHRASES

IN VIVO - in life, describing biological
occurances with living bodies
PRO TEM - temporary, for the time being

7

AD FINEM - to the end
A PRIORI - by deduction
CUI BONO? - whom does it benefit?
DE FACTO - in fact
FIAT LUX - let there be light
IN VITRO - in glass, describing
biological experiments outside the body
PECCAVI - a confession of guilt (I have
sinned)
PER DIEM - by the day
SINE DIE - without a day being appointed
SUB ROSA - confidential
UNA VOCE - with one voice, unanimously

8

ALTER EGO - another self
BONA FIDE - in good faith
EMERITUS - one retired from active official
duties
MEA CULPA - an acknowledgement of guilt
(I am to blame)
NOTA BENE - observe or note wel
PRO FORMA - for the sake of form
UT PROSIM - that I may be of use

9

AD INTERIM - meanwhile
AD LITERAM - to the letter
AD NAUSEAM - to a disgusting, sickening
degree
CARPE DIEM - seize the day
DEI GRATIA - by the grace of God
ET TU, BRUTE - and you, Brutus
EXCELSIOR - still higher
EX OFFICIO - by the right position or price
HIC ET NUNC - here and now
INTER ALIA - among other things
PRO PATRIA - for our country
STATUS QUO - the existing situation or state
of affairs
SUB JUDICE - under consideration
VICE VERSA - the terms being exchanged,
the other way round
VOX POPULI - popular opinion

10

ANNO DOMINI - in the year of our Lord
DEO GRATIAS - thanks be to God
EX CATHEDRA - with authority
IN EXTREMIS - in dire straits, at the
point of death
IN MEMORIAM - to the memory of
LOCO CITATO - in the place quoted

POST MORTEM - after death
PRIMA FACIE - at first sight
SINE QUA NON - something indispensable
TERRA FIRMA - solid ground

11

AD INFINITUM - endlessly, to infinity
ANIMO ET FIDE - by courage and faith
DE DIE EN DIEM - from day to day
DE PROFUNDIS - from the depths of misery
EX POST FACTO - after the event
GLORIA PATRI - glory to the Father
LOCUS STANDI - the right to be heard (Law)
NON SEQITUR - an unwarranted conclusion
PAX VOBISCUM -peace be with you
TEMPUS FUGIT - time flies

12

ANTE MERIDIEM - before noon
CAVEAT EMPTOR - let the buyer beware
COMPOS MENTIS - of sane mind
FESTINA LENTE - hasten slowly, be quick
without impetuosity
PERSEVERANDO - by perseverance
POST MERIDIEM - after noon
SERVABO FIDEM - I will keep faith
VENI, VIDI, VICI - I came, I saw, I conquered
VOLO NON VALEO - I am willing but unable

13

CORPUS DELICTI - body of facts that
constitute an offence
DUM SPIRO, SPERO - while I breathe, I hope
IN VINO VERITAS - there is truth in wine,
that is, the truth comes out
MODUS OPERANDI - a method of operating
NE FRONTI CREDE - trust not to
appearances
VINCIT VERITAS - truth conquers
VIRTUTIS AMORE - by love of virtue

14

CETERIS PARRIBUS   - other things being
equal
EDITO PRINCEPS - the original edition
IN LOCO PARENTIS - in place of a parent
NIL DESPERANDUM - never despair
PRO BONO PUBLICO - for the public good

15

ANIMO NON ASTUTIA - by courage not craft
FORTITER ET RECTE - courageously and
honourably
FORTUNA SEQUATUR - let fortune follow
INFRA DIGITATEM - beneath one's dignity
NON COMPOS MENTIS - mentally unsound
OMNIA VINCIT AMOR - love conquers all
PERSONA NON GRATA - an unacceptable
person

LATIN PHRASES / AMERICANISATION

16
GLORIA IN EXCELSIS - glory to God in the highest
17
LABOR IPSE VOLUMPTAS - labour itself is pleasure
NUNQUAM NON PARATUS - always ready
PROBUM NON PAENITET - honesty repents not
VER NON SEMPER VIRET - Spring does not always flourish
18
NEC TEMERE NEC TIMIDE - neither rashly nor timidly
PRO REGE, LEGE, ET GREGE - for the King, the law, and the people
REDUCTIO AD ABSURDAM - reducing to absurdity
19
CANDIDE ET CONSTANTER - fairly and firmly
SOLA NOBILITAS VIRTUS - virtue alone is true nobility
VIRTUTI NON ARMIS FIDO - I trust to virtue and not to arms

20+
DE MORTUIS NIL NISI BONIUM - speak only good of the dead
DULCE ET DECORUM EST PRO PATRIA MORI - it is sweet and seemingly to die for one's country
FORTUNA FAVET FORTIBUS - fortune favours the brave
PATRIA CARA CARIOR LIBERTAS - my country is dear, but liberty is dearer
QUOD ERAT DEMONSTRANDUM - which was to be demonstrated
SIC TRANSIT GLORIA MUNDI - thus passes the glory from the world
TIMEO DANAOS ET DONA FERENTES - I fear the Greeks, even when bearing gifts
VIVIT POST FUNERA VIRTUS - virtue survives the grave

AMERICANISATION

BRITISH	AMERICAN	BRITISH	AMERICAN
ACTION REPLAY	INSTANT REPLAY	BREATHALYZER	DRUNKOMETER
ADRENALINE	EPINEPHRINE	BREEZE BLOCK	CINDER BLOCK
AERODROME	AIRDROME	CAMBERWELL BEAUTY	MOURNING CLOAK
AEROFOIL	AIRFOIL		
AEROPLANE	AIRPLANE	CANDYFLOSS	COTTON CANDY
ANAESTHETIST	ANESTHESIOLOGIST	CARAVAN	TRAILER
ANAESTHETICS	ANESTHESIOLOGY	CATAPULT	SLINGSHOT
ARMISTICE DAY	VETERANS DAY	CATCH PIT	CATCH BASIN
AUBERGINE	EGGPLANT	CENTRAL RESERVE	MEDIAN STRIP
AUTOCUE	TELEPROMPTER	CORN FLOUR	CORNSTARCH
BACK BOILER	WATER BACK	COS	ROMAINE
BARYTES	BARITE	COURGETTE	ZUCCHINI
BEETROOT	RED BEET	CREEPING THISTLE	CANADA THISTLE
BILL	CHECK	CROTCHET	QUARTER NOTE
BISCUIT	COOKIE	CURRENT ACCOUNT	CHECKING ACCOUNT
BLACK PUDDING	BLOOD SAUSAGE	CUTTHROAT	STRAIGHT RAZOR
BLOWLAMP	BLOWTORCH	DELIVERY VAN	PANEL TRUCK
BLUE-EYED BOY	FAIR-HAIRED BOY	DEMISEMIQUAVER	THIRTY-SECOND NOTE
BONNET	HOOD		
BOOT	TRUNK	DICKY	RUMBLE SEAT
BOWLER	DERBY	DINNER JACKET	TUXEDO
BRACES	SUSPENDER	DOSSHOUSE	FLOPHOUSE

BRITISH	AMERICAN	BRITISH	AMERICAN
DOWNPIPE	DOWNSPOUT	MUSIC HALL	VAUDEVILLE
DRAUGHTS	CHECKERS	NAPPY	DIAPER
DRAWING PIN	THUMBTACK	NORADRENALINE	NOREPINEPHRINE
DUAL CARRIAGEWAY	DIVIDED HIGHWAY	NOSEBAG	FEEDBAG
DUMBWAITER	LAZY SUSAN	NOTICE BOARD	BULLETIN
DUSTBIN	GARBAGE CAN; TRASH CAN	OPEN DAY	OPEN HOUSE
		ORDINARY SHARES	COMMON STOCK
DUSTCART	GARBAGE TRUCK	OVERHEAD-VALVE ENGINE	VALVE-IN-HEAD ENGINE
DUSTER	DUST CLOTH		
ÉTRIER	STIRRUP	PATIENCE	SOLITAIRE
FANLIGHT	TRANSOM	PAVEMENT	SIDEWALK
FLAT	APARTMENT	PEDESTRIAN CROSSING	CROSSWALK
FLEX	CORD		
FLY-PAST	FLYOVER	PENNY-FARTHING	ORDINARY
FOUR-STROKE	FOUR-CYCLE	PEPPERWORT	PEPPERGRASS
FRENCH WINDOWS	FRENCH DOORS	PETROL	GASOLINE
FRIESIAN	HOLSTEIN	PLOUGH	BIGDIPPER
FUNERAL PARLOUR	FUNERAL HOME	PRAM	BABY CARRIAGE
FUNNY BONE	CRAZY BONE	PREFERENCE SHARES	PREFERED STOCK
GRAMOPHONE	PHONOGRAPH		
GREY MULLET	MULLET	PROTEOSE	ALBUMOSE
GUDGEON PIN	WRIST PIN	QUAVER	EIGHTH NOTE
HAIRSLIDE	BARRETTE	RAGWORM	CLAMWORM
HEMIDEMISEMI-QUAVER	SIXTY-FORTH NOTE	REAR LIGHT	TAILLIGHT; TAIL LAMP
HEMLOCK	POISON HEMLOCK	RED MULLET	GOAT FISH
HEN HARRIER	MARSH HAWK; MARSH HARRIER	REPERTORY COMPANY	STCK COMPANY
HOLDALL	CARRYALL	REVERSING LIGHT	BACK-UP LIGHT
INSULATING TAPE	FRICTION TAPE	RIGHT-ANGLED TRIANGLE	RIGHT TRIANGLE
JAM	JELLY		
JELLY	JELLO	RING ROAD	BELTWAY
JUMP LEADS	JUMPER CABLES	ROOF RACK	CARRIER
KENNEL	DOGHOUSE	ROUNDABOUT	TRAFFIC CIRCLE
LADYBIRD	LADYBUG	RUBBER	ERASER
LEFT-LUGGAGE OFFICE	CHECKROOM	RUCKSACK	BACKPACK
		SEASON TICKET	COMMUTATION TICKET
LEVEL CROSSING	GRADE CROSSING		
LIFT	ELEVATOR	SEMIBREVE	WHOLE OTE
LIGNOCAINE	LIDOCAINE	SEMIQUAVER	SIXTEENTH NOTE
LOOSE COVER	SLIP COVER	SHOPWALKER	FLOORWALKER
LORRY	TRUCK	SHORTHAND TYPIST	STENOGRAPHER
LOUD-HAILER	BULL HORN	SILENCER	MUFFLER
LOUD-SPEAKER VAN	SOUND TRUCK	SKIRTING BOARD	BASEBOARD; MOPBOARD
LUGGAGE VAN	BAGGAGE CAR		
MAIZE	CORN	SLEEVE	JACKET
MERRY-GO-ROUND	CAROUSEL	SOCKET	OUTLET
MILEOMETER	NAPOLEON	STEAM ORGAN	CALLIOPE
MILLEFEUILLE	HALF-NOTE	STOCKBROKER BELT	EXURBIA
MINIM	FENDER	SUSPENDER BELT	GARTER BELT
MUDGAURD	VAUDEVILLE	SWALLOW DIVE	SWAN DIVE
SWEDE	RUTABAGA	TURN UP	CUFF

AMERICANISATION

BRITISH	AMERICAN	BRITISH	AMERICAN
TAP	FAUCET	UNDERGROUND	SUBWAY
TEA TOWEL	DISHTOWEL	UNDERSEAL	UNDERCOAT
TERYLENE	DACRON	URSA MINOR	LITTLE DIPPER
THORN APPLE	JIMSONWEED	VALVE	VACUUM TUBE
TIE	NECKTIE	VIRGINIA CREEPER	BOSTON IVY
TIE PIN	STICK PIN	WAISTCOAT	VEST
TORSK	CUSK	WINDMILL	PINWHEEL
TRAM	STREETCAR; TROLLEY CAR	WINDSCREEN	WINDSHIELD
		WIPER	WIPER
TRAPEZIUM	TRAPEZOID	WING	FENDER
TREACLE	MOLASSES	WINTERGREEN	SHINLEAF
TROUSERS	PANTS		
TRUNCHEON	NIGHTSTICK		

166

PROVERBS

A bad penny always turns up.
A bad workman always blames his tools.
A bird in the hand is worth two in the bush.
Absence makes the heart grow fonder.
A cat has nine lives.
A cat may look at a king.
Accidents will happen in the best regulated families.
A chain is no stronger than its weakest link.
Actions speak louder than words.
A drowning man will clutch at a straw.
A fool and his money are soon parted.
A fool at forty is a fool indeed.
A friend in need is a friend indeed.
All cats are grey in the dark.
All good things must come to an end.
All is fair in love and war.
All roads lead to Rome.·
All's grist that comes to the mill.
All's well that ends well.
All that glitters is not gold.
All the world loves a lover.
All work and no play makes Jack a dull boy.
A miss is as good as a smile.
An apple a day keeps the doctor away.
An Englishman's home is his castle.
An Englishman's word is his bond.
A nod is as good as a wink to a blind horse.
Any port in a storm.
Any publicity is good publicity.
A trouble shared is a trouble halved.
Attack is the best form of defence.
A watched pot never boils.
A woman's work is never done.
A young physician fattens the churchyard.
Bad news travels fast.
Beauty is in the eye of the beholder.
Beauty is only skin-deep.
Beggars can't be choosers.
Better to be an old man's darling than a young man's slave.
Better to be safe than sorry.
Better late than never.
Birds of a feather flock together.
Blood is thicker than water.
Books and friends should be few but good.
Caesar's wife must be above suspicion.
Charity begins at home.
Christmas comes but once a year.
Civility costs nothing.
Cold hands, warm heart.

Constant dripping wears away the stone.
Curiosity killed the cat.
Cut your coat according to your cloth.
Dead men tell no tales.
Death is the great leveller.
Divide and rule.
Do as I say, not as I do.
Do as you would be done by.
Dog does not eat dog.
Don't count your chickens before they've hatched.
Don't cross the bridge until you come to it.
Don't cut your nose off to spite your face.
Don't meet troubles half way.
Don't put all your eggs in one basket.
Don't spoil the ship for a ha'porth of tar.
Don't teach your grandmother to suck eggs.
Don't throw the baby out with the bathwater.
Don't wash your dirty linen in public.
Early to bed and early to rise makes a man healthy, wealthy and wise.
Easier said than done.
East, West, home's best.
Easy come, easy go.
Empty vessels make the greatest sound.
Even a worm will turn.
Every cloud has a silver lining.
Every dog has his day.
Every dog is allowed one bite.
Every man for himself and the devil take the hindmost.
Everything comes to he who waits.
Experience is the best teacher.
Faith will move mountains.
Familiarity breeds contempt.
Fight fire with fire.
Fine feathers make fine birds.
Fine words butter no parsnips.
Fish and guests smell in three days.
Forewarned and forearmed.
Forgive and forget.
For want of a nail the shoe was lost, for want of a shoe the horse was lost, for want of a horse the rider was lost.
From logs to clogs in just three generations.
Give a dog a bad name and hang him.
Give him an inch and he'll take a yard.
Great minds think alike.
Great oaks from little acorns grow.

Handsome is as handsome does.

He that fights and runs away may live to fight another day.

He travels fastest who travels alone.

He who hesitates is lost.

He who lives by the sword dies by the sword.

He who pays the piper calls the tune.

He who sups the Devil should have a long spoon.

History repeats itself.

Honesty is the best policy.

If a job's worth doing, it's worth doing well.l

If at first you don't succeed, try, try again.

If the mountain won't come to Mohamet, Mohamet must go to the mountain.

If you can't stand the heat, get out of the kitchen.

Imitation is the sincerest form of flattery.

In for a penny, in for a pound.

In the county of the blind, the one-eyed man is king.

It is no use crying over spilt milk.

It never rains but it pours.

It's an ill wind that blows nobody any good.

It's too late to shut the stable door after the horse has bolted.

It will all come out in the wash.

It will all be the same in a hundred years.

Jack of all trades, master of none.

Keep something for a rainy day.

Kill not the goose that lays the golden egg.

Least said soonest mended.

Let bygones be bygones.

Let sleeping dogs lie.

Let the cobbler stick to his last.

Life begins at forty.

Life is a bowl of cherries.

Life is not all beer and skittles.

Look before you leap.

Love is blind.

Love laughs at locksmiths.

Lucky in cards, unlucky in love.

Many a true word is spoken in jest.

Many hands make light work.

March comes in like a lion and goes out like a lamb.

March winds and April showers bring forth May flowers.

Marry in haste, and repent at leisure.

More haste, less speed.

Necessity is the mother of invention.

Needs must when the devil drives.

Ne'er cast a clout till May be out.

Never look a gift horse in the mouth.

No time like the present.

Old habits die hard.

Old sins cast long shadows.

One for sorrow, two for joy, three for a girl, four for a boy, five for silver, six for gold, seven for a secret, never to be told, eight for heaven, nine for hell, ten for the devil's own self.

One good turn deserves another.

One man's meat is another man's poison.

One swallow does not make a summer.

Out of sight, out of mind.

Patience is a virtue.

Penny wise, pound foolish.

Prevention is better than a cure.

Red sky at night, shepherd's delight; red sky in the morning, shepherd's warning.

Revenge is a dish that tastes better cold.

Revenge is sweet.

See a penny and pick it up and all that day you'll have good luck.

See a pin and pick it up and all that day you'll have good luck; see a pin and let it lie, you'll want a pin before you die.

Seeing is believing.

See Naples and die.

Silence is golden.

Spare the rod and spoil the child.

Sticks and stones may break my bones but names will never hurt me.

Still waters run deep.

St. Swithin's Day, if thou dost rain for forty days it will remain; St. Swithin's Day, if thou be fair, for forty days 'twill rain no more.

Take a hair of the dog that bit you.

The darkest hour is just before dawn.

The devil finds work for idle hands to do.

The devil looks after his own.

The early bird catches the worm.

The end justifies the means.

The exception proves the rule.

The hand that rocks the cradle rules the world.

Time is a great healer.

There is honour among thieves.

There is more than one way to skin a cat.

There is no accounting for taste.

There is safety in numbers.

There's many a good tune played on an old fiddle.

There's many a slip' twixt the cup and the lip.

There's no place like home.

There's no place like home

There's no smoke without fire.

The road to hell is paved with good intentions.
Time and tide wait for no man.
Time is a great healer.
Too many cooks spoil the broth.
Truth is stranger than fiction.
Two heads are better than one.
Two wrongs do not make a right.
United we stand, divided we fall.
Waste not, want not.
We must learn to walk before we can run.
What you lose on the swings you gain on the roundabouts.
When poverty comes in at the door, love flies out the window.

When the cat's away, the mice will play.
When the wine is in, the wit is out.
Where there's a will there's a way.
Why keep a dog and bark at yourself?
You can lead a horse to water, but you can't make him drink.
You cannot run with the hare and hunt with the hounds.
You can't make an omelette without breaking eggs.
You can't judge a book by its cover.
You can't teach an old dog new tricks.

SIMILES

as bald as a coot
as black as a pitch
as black as the ace of spades
as blind as a bat
as blind as a mole
as bold as brass
as bright as a button
as busy as a bee
as calm as a millpond
as cheap as dirt
as chirpy as a cricket
as clean as a whistle
as clear as a bell
as clear as crystal
as clear as mud
as cold as charity
as common as muck
as cool as a cucumber
as cross as two sticks
as daft as a brush
as dead as a dodo
as dead as a doornail
as dead as mutton
as deaf as a post
as different as chalk and cheese
as drunk as a lord
as dry as a bone
as dry as dust
as dull as dishwater
as easy as falling off a log
as easy as pie
as fit as a flea
as flat as panake
as free as a bird
as free as air

as free as the wind
as fresh as a daisy
as good as gold
as green as grass
as happy as a lark
as happy as a sandboy
as happy as Larry
as happy as the day is long
as hard as nails
as keen as mustard
as large as life
as light as a feather
as like as two peas in a pod
as lively as a cricket
as mad as a hatter
as mad as a March hare
as meek as a lamb
as merry as a cricket
as neat as a new pin
as nutty as a fruitcake
as obstinate as a mule
as old as the hills
as pale as death
as plain as a pikestaff
as plain as the nose on your face
as pleased as Punch
as poor as the church mouse
as poor as Lazarus
as pretty as a picture
as proud as a peacock
as pure as driven snow
as quick as a flash
as quick as lightening
as quick as thought
as quiet as a mouse

as safe as houses
as sharp as a needle
as sick as a dog
as simple as falling off a log
as slippery as an eel
as snug as a bug in a rug
as sound as a bell
as steady as a rock
as stiff as a board
as stiff as a poker
as stiff as a ramrod
as straight as a die
as straight as an arrow
as stubborn as a mule
as sure as eggs is eggs

as sure as hell
as thick as thieves
as thick as two short planks
as thin as a lath
as thin as a rake
as thin as a stick
as tough as nails
as tough as old boots
as ugly as sin
as warm as toast
as weak as a kitten
as weak as dishwater
as welcome as the flowers in May
as white as a sheet

NURSERY RHYMES

A frog he would a-wooing go,
Heigh ho! says Rowley,
A frog he would a-wooing go,
Whether his mother would let him or no.
With a rowley, powley, gammon and spinach
Heigh ho! says Anthony Rowley.

As I was going to St Ives,
I met a man with seven wives.
Each wife had seven sacks,
Each sack had seven cats,
Each cat had seven kits,
How many were going to St. Ives?

Baa, baa, black sheep
Have you any wool?
Yes, sir, yes, sir,
Three bags full;
One for the master,
And one for the dame,
And one for the little boy
Who lives down the lane.

Bobby Shafto's gone to sea,
Silver buckles on his knee;
He'll come back and marry me,
Bonny Bobby Shafto!

Come, let's to bed
Says Sleepy-head;
Tarry a while, says Slow;
Put on the pan,
Says Greedy Nan,
Let's sup before we go.

Ding dong, bell,
Pussy's in the well.
Who put her in?
Little Johnny Green.
Who pulled her out?
Little Tommy Stout.

Doctor Foster went to Gloucester
In a shower of rain:
He stepped in a puddle,
Right up to his middle,
And never went there again.

Georgie Porgie, pudding and pie,
Kissed the girls and made them cry;
When the boys came out to play
Georgie Porgie ran away.

Goosey, goosey gander,
Whither shall I wander?
Upstairs and downstairs
And in my lady's chamber.

Hey diddle diddle,
The cat and the fiddle,
The cow jumped over the moon;
The little dog laughed
To see such sport,
And the dish ran away with the spoon.

Humpty Dumpty sat on a wall,
Humpty Dumpty had a great fall.
All the king's horses and
All the king's men,
Couldn't put Humpty together again.

How many miles to Babylon?
Three score miles and ten.
Can I get there by candle-light?
Yes and back again.
If your heels are nimble and light,
You may get there by candle light.

Jack and Jill went up the hill
To fetch a pail of water;
Jack fell down and broke his crown,
And Jill came tumbling after.

Jack Sprat could eat no fat,
And his wife could eat no lean,
And so between them both you see,
They licked the platter clean.

Little Bo-peep has lost her sheep,
And can't tell where to find them;
Leave them alone, and they'll come home,
Bringing their tails behind them.

Little Boy Blue,
Come blow your horn,
The sheep's in the meadow,
The cows in the corn.

Little Jack Horner
Sat in the corner,
Eating a Christmas pie;
He put in his thumb,
And pulled out a plum,
And said, What a good boy am I!

Little Miss Muffet,
Sat on her tuffet,
Eating her curds and whey;
There came a big spider,
Who sat down beside her
And frightened Miss Muffet away.

Little Tommy Tucker,
Sings for his supper:
What shall we give him?
White bread and butter.
How shall we cut it
Without a knife?
How will he be married
Without a wife?

Mary, Mary, quite contrary,
How does your garden grow?
With silver bells and cockle shells,
And pretty maids all in row.

Monday's child is fair of face,
Tuesday's child is full of grace,
Wednesday's child is full of woe,
Thursday's child has far to go,
Friday's child is loving and giving,
Saturday's child works hard for a living,
And the child that is born on the Sabbath day,
Is bonny and blithe, and good and gay.

Oh! the grand old Duke of York,
He had ten thousand men;
He marched them up to the top of the hill,
And he marched them down again.
And when they were up they were up,
And when they were down they were down,
And when they were only halfway up,
they were neither up nor down.

Old King Cole
Was a merry old soul,
And a merry old soul was he;
He called for his pipe,
And he called for his bowl,
And he called for his fiddlers three.

Old Mother Hubbard
Went to the cupboard,
To fetch her poor dog a bone;
But when she got there,
The cupboard was bare,
And so the poor dog had none.

One, two,
Buckle my shoe;
Three, four,
Knock at the door.
Five, six,
Pick up sticks;
Seven, eight,
Close the gate.
Nine, ten,
Big fat hen;
Eleven, twelve,
Dig and delve.
Thirteen, fourteen,
Maids a'courting;
Fifteen, sixteen,
Maids in the kitchen;
Seventeen, eighteen,
Maids a'waiting;
Nineteen, twenty,
My plate's empty.

Oranges and lemons,
Say the bells of St Clement's.
You owe me five farthings,
Say the bells of St Martin's.
When will you pay me?
Say the bells of Old Bailey.
When I grow rich,
Say the bells of Shoreditch.
When will that be?
Say the bells of Stepney.
I'm sure I don't know,
Says the great bell at Bow.

Here comes a candle to light you to bed,
Here comes a chopper to chop off your head.

Peter Piper picked a peck of pickled pepper;
A peck of pickled pepper Peter Piper picked;
If Peter Piper picked a peck of pickled pepper,
Where's the peck of pickled pepper Peter
 Piper picked?

Polly put the kettle on,
Polly put the kettle on,
Polly put the kettle on,
We'll all have tea.
Sukey take it off again,
Sukey take it off again,
Sukey take it off again,
They've all gone home.

Pussy cat, pussy cat, where have you been?
I've been to London to look at the queen.
Pussy cat, pussy cat, what did you there?
I frightened a little mouse under her chair.

Ride a cock-horse to Banbury Cross,
To see a fine lady upon a white horse;
Rings on her fingers and bells on her toes,
And she shall have music wherever she goes.

Ring-a-ring o' roses,
A pocket full of posies,
A-tishoo! A tishoo!
We all fall down.

Rub-a-dub-dub,
Three men in a tub,
And who do you think they be?
The butcher, the baker,
The candlestick-maker,
And they all sailed out to sea.

See-saw, Margery Daw,
Jacky shall have a new master;
Jacky shall have but a penny a day,
Because he can't work any faster.

Simple Simon met a pieman,
Going to the fair;
Says Simple Simon to the pieman,
Let me taste your ware.
Says the pieman to Simple Simon,
Show me first your penny;
Says Simple Simon to the pieman,
Indeed I have not any.

Sing a song of sixpence,
A pocket full of rye;
Four and twenty blackbirds,
Baked in a pie.
When the pie was opened,
The birds began to sing;
Was not that a dainty dish,
To set before the king?
The king was in his counting-house,
Counting out his money;
The queen was in the parlour,
Eating bread and honey.
The maid was in the garden,
Hanging out the clothes,
When down came a blackbird,
And pecked off her nose.

Solomon Grundy,
Born on a Monday,
Christened on Tuesday,
Married on Wednesday,
Took ill on Thursday,
Worse on Friday,
Died on Saturday,
Buried on Sunday.
This is the end
Of Solomon Grundy.

The lion and the unicorn
Were fighting for the crown;
The lion beat the unicorn
All round about the town.

There was a crooked man, and he walked a
 crooked mile,
He found a crooked sixpence against a
 crooked stile:
He bought a crooked cat, which caught a
 crooked mouse,
And they all lived together in a little crooked
 house.

There was an old woman who lived in a shoe,
She had so many children she didn't know
   what to do;
She gave them some broth without any bread;
She whipped them all soundly and put them to
   bed.

The twelfth day of Christmas,
My true love sent to me:
Twelve lords a-leaping,
Eleven ladies dancing,
Ten pipers piping,
Nine drummers drumming,
Eight maids a-milking,
Seven swans a-swimming,
Six geese a-laying,
Five gold rings,
Four calling birds,
Three french hens,
Two turtle doves, and
A partridge in a pear tree.

Thirty days hath September,
April, June and November,
All the rest have thirty-one,
Excepting February alone
And that has twenty-eight days clear
And twenty-nine in each leap year.

This little piggy went to market,
This little piggy stayed at home,
This little piggy had roast beef,
This little piggy had none,
And this little piggy cried,
   Wee-wee-wee-wee-wee,
I can't find my way home.

Three blind mice, see how they run!
They all run after the farmer's wife,
Who cut off their tails with a carving knife,
Did you ever see such a thing in your life,
As three blind mice?

Tinker,
Tailor,
Soldier,
Sailer,
Rich man,
Poor man,
Beggarman,
Thief.

Tom, Tom, the piper's son,
Stole a pig and away he run;
The pig was eat
And Tom was beat,
And Tom went howling down the street.

Two little dicky birds,
Sitting on a wall;
One named Peter,
The other named Paul,
Fly away Peter!
Fly away Paul!
Come back Peter!
Come back Paul!

Wee Willie Winkie runs through he town
Upstairs and downstairs and in his nightgown,
Rapping at the window, crying through the lock,
Are the children all in bed? It's past eight o'clock.

What are little boys made of?
Frogs and snails
And puppy-dogs' tails,
That's what little boys are made of.
What are little girls made of?
Sugar and spice
And all that's nice,
That's what little girls are made of.

MOTTOES

A DEA ET REGE - By God and the King (Earl of Chesterfield)

AD MAJOREM DEI GLORIAM - to the greater glory of God (The Jesuits)

A MARI USQUE AD MARE - from sea to sea (Canada)

APRES NOUS LE DELUGE - after us the deluge (617 Squadron, 'The Dam Busters')

ARS LONGA, VITA BREVIS - art is long, life is short (Millais)

AUDI, VIDE, TACE - hear, see, keep silence (United Grand Lodge of Freemasons)

AUSPICIUM MELIORIS AEVI - the sign of a better age (Duke of St Albans, Order of St Michael and St George)

BE PREPARED - (Scout Association, 1908)

CAVENDO TUTUS - safe by being cautious (Duke of Devonshire)

CHE SERA SERA - what will be will be (Duke of Bedford)

DARE QUAM ACCIPERE - to give rather than to receive (Guy's Hospital)

DE PRAESCIENTIA DEI - from the foreknowledge of God (Barber's Company,1461)

DICTUM MEUN PACTUM - my word is my bond (Stock Exchange)

DIEU ET MON DROIT - God and my right (British Sovereigns)

DILIGENT AND SECRET - (College of Arms, 1484)

DOMINE DIRIGE NOS - Lord, guide us (City of London)

DOMINUS ILLUMINATIO MEA - the Lord is my light (Oxford University)

DONORUM DEI DISPENSATIO FIDELIS - faithful dispensation of the gifts of God (Harrow Schooll)

ENALENTÉ À PARLER D'ARMES - equipped to speak of arms (The Heraldry Society, 1957)

ESPÉRANCE EN DIEU - hope in God (Duke of Northumberland)

FIDES ATQUE INTEGRITAS - faith and integrity (Society of Incorporated Accoutants and Auditors)

FLOREAT ETONA - may Eton flourish (Eton College)

FOR COUNTRY NOT FOR SELF (226 Squadron, RAF)

GARDEZ BIEN - watch well (Montgomery)

HEAVEN'S LIGHT OUR GUIDE (Order of the Star of India)

HELP (Foundling Hospital, London)

HINC LUCEM ET POCULA SACRA - hence light and sacred cups (Cambridge University)

HONI SOIT QUI MAL Y PENSE - evil be to him who thinks evil (Order of the Garter)

HONNEUR ET PATRIE - honour and country (Order of the legion of Honour)

ICH DIEN - I serve (Prince of Wales)

IMPERATRICUS AUSPICIIS - imperial in its auspices (Order of the Indian Empire)

IN ACTION FAITHFUL AND IN HONOUR CLEAR (Order of the Companions of Honour, 1917)

IN FIDE SALUS - safety in faith (Star of Rumania)

IN SOMNO SECURITAS - security in sleep (Association of Anaesthetists of Great Britain and Ireland)

JUSTITA VIRTUTUM REGINA - justice in the queen of virtues (Goldmiths' Company)

LABORARE EST ORARE - to labour is to pray (Benedictine Order)

LABOR VIRUS CONVENIT - labour becomes men (Richard I)

LIFE IN OUR HANDS (Institute of Hospital Engineers)

MIHI ET MEA - to me and mine (Anne Boleyn)

NATION SHALL SPEAK PEACE UNTO NATION (British Broadcasting Corporation)

NEC ASPERA TERRENT - difficulties do not daunt (3rd Foot, 'The Buffs', East Kent Regiment)

NEC CUPIAS NEC METUAS - neither desire nor fear (Earl of Hardwicke)

NEMO ME IMPUNE LACESSIT - no one injures me with impunity (Order of the Thistle)

NOLI ME TANGERE - touch me not (Graeme of Garvock, 103 Squadron, RAF)

NON EST VIVERE SED VALERE VITA - life is not living, but health is life (Royal Society of Medicine)

NON SIBI, SED PATRIAE - not for himself, but for his country (Earl of Romney)

NULLIUS IN VERBA - in no man's words (Royal Society)

PAX IN BELLO - peace in war (Godolphin, Duke of Leeds)

PEACE THROUGH UNDERSTANDING (President Eisenhower)

PER ARDUA AD ASTRA - through endeavour to the stars (RAF motto)

PER CAELUM VIA NOSTRA - our way through heaven (Guild of Air Pilots and Navigators)

PISCATORES HOMINUM - fishers of men (National Society)

POWER IN TRUST (Central Electricity Generating Board)

QUIS SEPARABIT? - who shall separate? (Order of St Patrick)

QUOD PETIS HIC EST - here is what you seek (Institute of British Engineers)

RATIONE ET CONCILIO - by reason and counsel (Magistrates Association)

RERUM COGNOSCERE CAUSAS - to know the causes of things (Institute of Brewing)

SEMPER FIDELIS - always faithful (Devonshire regiment, East Devon Militia)

SEMPER PARATUS - always prepared (207 Squadron, RAF)

SOLA VIRTUS INVICTA - virtue alone is invincible (The Duke of Norfolk)

TOUCH NOT THE CAT BUT A GLOVE (Macpherson Clan)

TRIA JUNCTA IN UNO - three joined in one (Order of the Bath)

UNITATE FORTIOR - stronger by union (Building Societies Association; Army and Navy Club)

VER NON SEMPER VIRET - the spring does not always flourish

VERNON SEMPER VIRET - Vernon always flourishes (Lord Lyveden)

WHO DARES WINS (Special Air Force)

AROUND THE WORLD

GAZETTEER OF COUNTRIES

AFGHANISTAN
Capital: Kabul
Currency: afghani (pul)
Language: Pushtoo, Dari Persian

ALBANIA
Capital: Tirana
Currency: lek (qindar)
Language: Albanian

ALGERIA
Capital: Algiers
Currency: dinar (centime)
Language: Arabic, French

ANGOLA
Capital: Luanda
Currency: kwanza (lweis)
Language: Portuguese

ANTIGUA AND BARBUDA
Capital: St Johns
Currency: dollar (cent)
Language: English

ARGENTINA
Capital: Buenos Aires
Currency: peso (centavo)
Language: Spanish

ARMENIA
Capital: Erevan
Currency: dram (luma)
Language: Armenian

AUSTRALIA
Capital: Canberra
Currency. dollar (cent)
Language: English

AUSTRIA
Capital: Vienna
Currency: euro (cent)
Language: German

AZERBAIJAN
Capital: Baku
Currency: manat (kepik)
Language: Turkish

BAHAMAS
Capital: Nassau
Currency: dollar (cent)
Language: English

BAHRAIN
Capital: Manama
Currency: dinar (fils)
Language: Arabic

BANGLADESH
Capital: Dhaka
Currency: taka (poisha)
Language: Bengali, English

BARBADOS
Capital: Bridgetown
Currency: dollar (cent)
Language: English

BELARUS
Capital: Minsk
Currency: rouble (kopek)
Language: Russian

BELGIUM
Capital: Brussels
Currency: euro (cent)
Language: English

BELIZE
Capital: Belmopan
Currency: dollar (cent)
Language: French, Flemish, German

BOLIVIA
Capital: La Paz
Currency: boliviano (centavo)
Language: Spanish

BOSNIA-HERZEGOVINA
Capital: Sarajevo
Currency: mark (fening)
Language: French, Flemish, German

BOTSWANA
Capital: Gaborone
Currency: pula (thebe)
Language: English

179

BRAZIL
Capital: Brasilia
Currency: real (centavo)
Language: Portuguese

BRUNEI
Capital: Bandar Seri Begawan
Currency: dollar (sen)
Language: Malay

BULGARIA
Capital: Sofia
Currency: lev (stotinka)
Language: Bulgarian

CAMBODIA
Capital: Phnom Penh
Currency: riel (sen)
Language: Khmer

CAMEROON
Capital: Yaounde
Currency: franc CFA (centime)
Language: French, English

CANADA
Capital: Ottowa
Currency: dollar (cent)
Language: English, French

CENTRAL AFRICAN REBUBLIC
Capital: Bangui
Currency: franc CFA (centime)
Language: French, Sango

CHAD
Capital: Ndjamena
Currency: franc CFA (centime)
Language: French

CHILE
Capital Santiago
Currency: peso (centavo)
Language: Spanish

CHINA
Capital: Peking
Currency: yuan (fen)
Language: Mandarin Chinese

COLOMBIA
Capital: Bogota
Currency: peso (centavo)
Language: Spanish

CONGO
Capital: Brazzaville
Currency: franc CFA (centime)
Language: French

COSTA RICA
Capital: San Jose
Currency: colon (céntimo)
Language: Spanish

COTE D'IVOIRE
Capital: Abidjan
Currency: franc CFA (centime)
Language: French

CROATIA
Capital: Zagreb
Currency: kuna (lipa)
Language: Serbo-Croat

CUBA
Capital: Havana
Currency: peso (centavo)
Language: Spanish

CYPRUS
Capital: Nicosia
Currency: pound (cent)
Language: Greek, Turkish

CZECH REPUBLIC
Capital: Prague
Currency: koruna (hailér)
Language: Czech

DENMARK
Capital: Copenhagen
Currency: krone (øre)
Language: Danish

DOMINICA
Capital: Roseau
Currency: dollar (cent)
Language: English

DOMINICAN REPUBLIC
Capital: Santo Domingo
Currency: peso (centavo)
Language: Spanish

ECUADOR
Capital: Quito
Currency: US dollar (cent)
Language: Spanish

EGYPT
Capital: Cairo
Currency: pound (piastre)
Language: Arabic

EL SALVADOR
Capital: San Salvador
Currency: colon (centavo)
Language: Spanish

ESTONIA
Capital: Tallinn
Currency: kroon (sent)
Language: Estonian, Russian

ETHIOPIA
Capital: Addis Ababa
Currency: birr (cent)
Legislature: Shengo (National Assembly)

FIJI
Capital: Suva
Currency: dollar (cent)
Language: English

FINLAND
Capital: Helsinki
Currency: euro (cent)
Language: Finnish, Swedish

FRANCE
Capital: Paris
Currency: euro (cent)
Language: French

THE GABON
Capital: Libreville
Currency: franc CFA (centime)
Language: French

GAMBIA
Capital: Banjul
Currency: dalasi (butut)
Language: English

GERMANY
Capital: Bonn
Currency: euro (cent)
Language: German

GHANA
Capital: Accra
Currency: cedi (pesewa)
Language: English

GREECE
Capital: Athens
Currency:euro (cent)
Language: Greek

GUATEMALA
Capital: Guatemala City
Currency: euro (cent)
Language: Spanish

HAITI
Capital: Port-au-Prince
Currency: gourde (centime)
Language: French, Creole

HONDURAS
Capital: Tegucigalpa
Currency: lempira (centavo)
Language: Spanish

HONG KONG
Capital: Victoria
Currency: dollar (cent)
Language: Mandarin Chinese

HUNGARY
Capital: Budapest
Currency: (forint filler)
Language: Hungarian

ICELAND
Capital: Reykjavik
Currency: króna (eyrir)
Language: Icelandic

INDIA
Capital: New Delhi
Currency: rupee (paisa)
Language: Hindi, English

INDONESIA
Capital: Jakarta
Currency: rupiah (sen)
Language: Bahasa Indonesian

IRAN
Capital: Tehran
Currency: rial (dinar)
Language: Farsi (Persian)

IRAQ
Capital: Baghdad
Currency: dinar (fils)
Language: Arabic

IRELAND, REPUBLIC OF
Capital: Dublin
Currency: pound (pence)
Language: Irish Gaelic, English

ISRAEL
Capital: Jerusalem
Currency: shekel (agora)
Language: Hebrew, Arabic

ITALY
Capital: Rome
Currency: euro (cent)
Language: Italian

JAMAICA
Capital: Kingston
Currency: dollar (cent)
Language: English

JAPAN
Capital: Tokyo
Currency: yen (sen)
Language: Japanese

JORDAN
Capital: Amman
Currency: dinar (fils)
Language: Arabic

KAZAKHSTAN
Capital: Alma-Ata
Currency: tenge (tign)
Language: Russian, Kazakh

KENYA
Capital: Nairobi
Currency: shilling (cent)
Language: English, Swahili

KOREA, DEMOCRATIC PEOPLE'S REPUBLIC OF (North Korea)
Capital: P'yongyang
Currency: won (chon)
Language: Korean

KOREA, REPUBLIC OF (South Korea)
Capital: Seoul
Currency: won (jeon)
Language: Korean

KUWAIT:
Capital: Kuwait
Currency: dinar (fils)
Language: Arabic

LAOS
Capital: Vientiane
Currency: kip (at)
Language: Lao

LATVIA
Capital: Riga
Currency: lats (santims)
Language: Latvian, Russia

LEBANON
Capital: Beirut
Currency: pound (piastre)
Language: Arabic

LIBERIA
Capital: Monrovia
Currency: dollar (cent)
Language: English

LIBYA
Capital: Tripoli
Currency: dinar (dirham)
Language: Arabic

LITHUANIA
Capital: Vilnius
Currency: litas (centas)
Language: Lithuanian

LUXEMBOURG
Capital: Luxembourg
Currency: euro (cent)
Language: Letzeburgesch

MACEDONIA
Capital: Skopje
Currency: dinar (para)
Language: Macedonian

MADAGASCAR
Capital: Antananaivo
Currency: franc (centime)
Language: French

MALAWI
Capital: Lilongwe
Currency: kwacha (tambala)
Language: English

MALAYSIA
Capital: Kuala Lumpur
Currency: riggit (sen)
Language: Malay

MALTA
Capital: Valletta
Currency: lira (cent)
Language: Maltese

MEXICO
Capital: Mexico City
Currency: peso (centavo)
Language: Spanish

MONGOLIA
Capital: Ulan Bator
Currency: tugrik (mongo)
Language: Khalkha Mongolian

MONTENEGRO
Capital: Podgorica
Currency: dinar (paras)
Language: Serbo-Croat

MOROCCO
Capital: Rabat
Currency: dirham (centime)
Language: Arabic

MOZAMBIQUE
Capital: Maputo
Currency: metical (centavo)
Language: Portuguese

MYANMAR (FORMERLY BURMA)
Capital: Yangon (Rangoon)
Currency: kyat (pya)
Language: Burmese

NAMIBIA
Capital: Windhoek
Currency: dollar (cent)
Language: English

NEPAL
Capital: Kathmandu
Currency: rupee (paisa)
Language: Nepali

NETHERLANDS
Capital: Amsterdam
Currency: euro (cent)
Language: Dutch

NEW ZEALAND
Capital: Wellington
Currency: dollar (cent)
Language: English

NICARAGUA
Capital: Managua
Currency: cordoba (centavo)
Language: Spanish

NIGERIA
Capital: Abuja
Currency: naira (kobo)
Language: English

NORWAY
Capital: Oslo
Currency: krone (øre)
Language: Norwegian

PAKISTAN
Capital: Islamabad
Currency: rupee (paisa)
Language: English

PANAMA
Capital:Panama City
Currency: balboa (centésimo)
Language: Spanish

PAPUA NEW GUINEA
Capital: Port Moresby
Currency: kina (toea)
Language: English, French

PARAGUAY
Capital: Asuncion
Currency: guarani (céntimo)
Language: Spanish

PERU
Catpital: Lima
Currency: new sol (centimo)
Language: Spanish

PHILIPPINES
Capital: Manila
Currency: peso (centavo)
Language: Filipino, English

POLAND
Capital: Warsaw
Currency: zolty (grosz)
Language: Polish

PORTUGAL
Capital: Lisbon
Currency: euro (cent)
Language: Portuguese

ROMANIA
Capital: Bucharest
Currency: leu (ban)
Language: Romanian

RUSSIA
Capital: Moscow
Currency: rouble (kopek)
Language: Russian

RWANDA
Capital: Kigali
Currency: franc (centime)
Language: Kinyarwanda, English

SAUDI ARABIA
Capital: Riyadh
Currency: riyal (halala)
Language: Arabic

SERBIA
Capital: Belgrade
Currency: dinar (paras)
Language: Serbo-Croat

SIERRA LEONE
Capital: Freetown
Currency: leone (cent)
Language: English

SINGAPORE
Capital: Singapore City
Currency: dollar (cent)
Language: Malay, English, Tamil, Chinese

SLOVAKIA
Capital: Bratislava
Currency: koruna (halier)
Language: Slovak

SOUTH AFRICA
Capital: Pretoria
Currency: rand (cent)
Language: Afrikaans

SPAIN
Capital: Madrid
Currency: euro (cent)
Language: Cortes: Spanish

SRI LANKA
Capital: Colombo
Currency: rupee (cent)
Language: Sinhalese, Tamil, English

SUDAN
Capital: Khartoum
Currency: pound (piastre)
Language: Arabic

SWEDEN
Capital: Stockholm
Currency: krona (øre)
Language: Swedish

SWITZERLAND
Capital: Bern
Currency: franc (centime)
Language: French, German, Italian

SYRIA
Capital: Damascus
Currency: pound (piastre)
Language: Arabic

TAIWAN
Capital: Taipei
Currency: dollar (fen)
Language: Mandarin Chinese

TANZANIA
Capital: Dodoma
Currency: shilling (cent)
Language: Swahili, English

THAILAND
Capital: Bangkok
Currency: baht (satang)
Language: Thai

TUNISIA
Capital: Tunis
Currency: dinar (millime)
Language: Arabic

TURKEY
Capital: Ankara
Currency: lira (kurus)
Language: Turkish

UGANDA
Capital: Kampala
Currency: shilling (cent)
Language: Swahili, English

UKRAINE
Capital: Kiev
Currency: hryvnia (kopiyka)
Language: Ukrainian

UNITED KINGDOM
Capital: London
Currency: pound (pence)
Language: English

UNITED STATES OF AMERICA
Capital: Washington,DC
Currency: dollar (cent)
Language: English

URUGUAY
Capital: Montevideo
Currency: peso (centésimo)
Language: Spanish

UZBEKISTAN
Capital: Tashkent
Currency: sum (tiyin)
Language: Uzbek

VENEZUELA
Capital: Caracas
Currency: bolivar (centavo)
Language: Spanish

VIETNAM
Capital: Hanoi
Currency: dong
Language: Vietnamese

YEMEN
Capital: Sana'a
Currency: dinar (fils/riyal)
Language: Arabic

ZAIRE
Capital: Kinshasa
Currency: zaire (makuta/senghi)
Language: French

ZAMBIA
Capital: Lusaka
Currency: kwacha (ngwee)
Language: English

ZIMBABWE
Capital: Harare
Currency: dollar (cent)
Language: English, Shona, Ndebele

ENGLISH COUNTIES

COUNTY (Administrative Centre)

4
AVON (Bristol)
KENT (Maidstone)

5
DEVON (Exeter)
ESSEX(Chelmstord)
SALOP (name for
Shropshire between
1974 and 1980)
WIGHT, ISLE OF
(Newport, IOW)

6
DORSET
(Dorchester)
DURHAM (Durham)
SURREY (Kingston
Upon Thames)
SUSSEX, EAST
(Lewes)
SUSSEX, WEST
(Chichester)

7
CUMBRIA (Carlisle)
NORFOLK
(Norwich)
RUTLAND*
(Oakham)
SUFFOLK (Ipswich)
8
CHESHIRE
(Chester)

CORNWALL (Truro)
SOMERSET
(Taunton)

9
BERKSHIRE
(Reading)
CLEVELAND
(Middlesborough)
HAMPSHIRE
(Winchester)
WILTSHIRE
(Trowbridge)
W. MIDLANDS
(Birmingham)

10
CUMBERLAND*
(Carlisle)
DERBYSHIRE
(Matlock)
E. YORKSHIRE
(Beverley)
LANCASHIRE
(Preston)
MERSEYSIDE
(Liverpool)
N. YORKSHIRE
(Northallerton)
SHROPSHIRE
(Shrewsbury)
S. YORKSHIRE
(Barnsley)

W. YORKSHIRE
(Wakefield)

11
OXFORDSHIRE
(Oxford)
TYNE AND WEAR
(Newcastle-Upon-
Tyne)
WESTMORLAND
(Kendal)

12
BEDFORDSHIRE
(Bedford)
LINCOLNSHIRE
(Lincoln)
WARWICKSHIRE
(Warwick)

13
HEREFORDSHIRE*
(Hereford)
HERTFORDSHIRE
(Hertford)
STAFFORDSHIRE
(Stafford)

14
CAMBRIDGESHIRE
(Cambridge)
LEICESTERSHIRE
(Leicester)

NORTHUMBER-
LAND
(Morpeth)

15
BUCKING-
HAMSHIRE
(Aylesbury)
GLOUCESTER-
SHIRE (Gloucester)
HUNTINGDON-
SHIRE*
(Huntingdon)
NOTTINGHAM-
SHIRE (Nottingham)

16
NORTHAMPTON-
SHIRE
(Northampton)

17
GREATER MAN-
CHESTER
(Manchester)
20
HEREFORD AND
WORCESTER
(Worcester)

* indicates a former
county

WELSH COUNTIES

COUNTY (Administrative Centre)

5
CLWYD (Mold)
DYFED
(Carmarthen)
GWENT (Cwmbran)
POWYS
(Llandrindod Wells)

7
GWYNEDD
(Caernarton)

8
ANGLESEY*
(Llangefni)

9
GLAMORGAN*
(Cardiff)
MERIONETH
(Dolgellan)

10
FLINTSHIRE* (Mold)
S. GLAMORGAN
(Cardiff)
W. GLAMORGAN
(Swansea)

11
BRECONSHIRE*
(Brecon)

RADNORSHIRE*
(Llandrindod Wells)

12
DENBIGHSHIRE*
(Ruthin)
MID GLAMORGAN
(Cardiff)

13
CARDIGANSHIRE*
(Aberystwyth)
MONMOUTH-
SHIRE* (Newport)
PEMBROKESHIRE*
(Haverfordwest)

15
CAERNARFON-
SHIRE*
(Caernarfon)
CARMARTHEN-
SHIRE*
(Carmarthen)
MONTGOMERY-
SHIRE (Welshpool)

* a former county

SCOTTISH REGIONS AND COUNTIES

REGION OR COUNTY (Administrative Centre)

3
AYR* (Agr)

4
BUTE* (Rothesay)
FIFE* (Cupar)

5
ANGUS* (Forfar)
BANFF* (Banff)
MORAY* (Elgin)
NAIRN* (Nairn)
PERTH* (Perth)
ARGYLL*
(Lochgilphead)
LANARK* (Hamilton)
ORKNEY* (Kirkwall)

7
BERWICK* (Duns)
BORDERS (Newton
St. Boswells)
CENTRAL (Stirling)
KINROSS* (Kinross)
LOTHIAN
(Edinburgh)

PEEBLES*
(Peebles)
RENFREW*
(Paisley)
SELKIRK* (Selkirk)
TAYSIDE (Dundee)
WIGTOWN*
(Stranraer)
ZETLAND* (Lerwick)

8
ABERDEEN*
(Aberdeen)
DUMFRIES*
(Dumfries)
GRAMPIAN
(Aberdeen)
HIGHLAND
(Inverness)
ROXBURGH*
(Newtown St.
Boswells)
SHETLAND
(Lerwick)
STIRLING* (Stirling)

9
CAITHNESS* (Wick)
DUMBARTON*
(Dumbarton)
INVERNESS*
(Inverness)

10
KINCARDINE*
(Stonehaven)
MIDLOTHIAN*
(Edinburgh)
SUTHERLAND*
(Golspie)

11
CLACKMANNAN*
(Alloa)
EAST LOTHIAN*
(Haddington)
STRATHCLYDE
(Glasgow)
WEST LOTHIAN*
(Linlithgow)

12
WESTERN ISLES
(Lewis)

13
KIRKCUDBRIGHT*
(Kirkcudbright)
15
ROSS AND
CROMARTY*
(Dingwall)
19
DUMFRIES AND
GALLOWAY
(Dumfries)

* a former county

IRISH COUNTIES & PROVINCES / AMERICAN STATES

COUNTIES OF NORTHERN IRELAND

COUNTY (County Town)

4	6	9	11
DOWN	ANTRIM (Belfast)	FERMANAGH	LONDONDERRY
(Downpatrick)	ARMAGH (Armagh)	(Enniskillen)	
	TYRONE (Armagh)		

REPUBLIC OF IRELAND PROVINCES

CONNACHT	LEINSTER	MUNSTER	ULSTER

REPUBLIC OF IRELAND COUNTIES

4		KILDARE	LONGFORD
CORK	SLIGO	LEITRIM	MONAGHAN
MAYO	6	WEXFORD	
	CARLOW	WICKLOW	
5	DUBLIN		9
CAVAN	GALWAY		ROSCOMMON
CLARE	OFFALY	8	TIPPERARY
KERRY		KILKENNY	WATERFORD
LOUTH	7	LAOIGHIS	WESTMEATH
MEATH	DONEGAL	LIMERICK	

AMERICAN STATES

STATE	ABBREVIATION	NICKNAME	CAPITAL
ALABAMA	AL	CAMELLIA	MONTGOMERY
ALASKA	AK		JUNEAU
ARIZONA	AZ	OCOTILLO	PHOENIX
ARKANSAS	AR		LITTLE ROCK
CALIFORNIA	CA	GOLDEN	SACRAMENTO
COLORADO	CO	CENTENNIAL	DENVER
CONNECTICUT	CT	NUTMEG	HARTFORD
DELAWARE	DE	DIAMOND	DOVER
FLORIDA	FL	SUNSHINE	TALLAHASSEE
GEORGIA	GA	PEACH	ATLANTA
HAWAII	HI	ALOHA	HONOLULU
IDAHO	ID	GEM	BOISE
ILLINOIS	IL	PRAIRIE	SPRINGFIELD
INDIANA	IN	HOOSIER	INDIANAPOLIS
IOWA	IA	HAWKEYE	DES MOINES
KANSAS	KS	SUNFLOWER	TOPEKA
KENTUCKY	KY	BLUEGRASS	FRANKFORT
LOUISIANA	LA	PELICAN	BATON ROUGE

STATE	ABBREVIATION	NICKNAME	CAPITAL
MAINE	ME	PINETREE	AUGUSTA
MARYLAND	MD	OLDLINE	ANNAPOLIS
MASSACHUSETTS	MA	BAY	BOSTON
MICHIGAN	MI	WOLVERINE	LANSING
MINNESOTA	MN	NORTHSTAR	ST PAUL
MISSISSIPPI	MS	MAGNOLIA	JACKSON
MISSOURI	MO	SHOWME	JEFFERSON CITY
MONTANA	MT	TREASURE	HELENA
NEBRASKA	NE	CORNHUSKER	LINCOLN
NEVADA	NV	SILVER	CARSON CITY
NEW HAMPSHIRE	NH	GRANITE	CONCORD
NEW JERSEY	NJ	GARDEN	TRENTON
NEW MEXICO	NM	LAND OF ENCHANTMENT	SANTA FE
NEW YORK	NY	EMPIRE	ALBANY
NORTH CAROLINA	NC	TARHEEL	RALEIGH
NORTH DAKOTA	ND	SIOUX	BISMARCK
OHIO	OH	BUCKEYE	COLUMBUS
OKLAHOMA	OK	SOONER	OKLAHOMA CITY
OREGON	OR	BEAVER	SALEM
PENNSYLVANIA	PA	KEYSTONE	HARRISBURG
RHODE ISLAND	RI	OCEAN	PROVIDENCE
SOUTH CAROLINA	SC	PALMETTO	COLUMBIA
SOUTH DAKOTA	SD	COYOTE	PIERRE
TENNESSEE	TN	VOLUNTEER	NASHVILLE
TEXAS	TX	LONESTAR	AUSTIN
UTAH	UT	MORMAN	SALT LAKE CITY
VERMONT	VT	GREEN MOUNTAIN	MONTPELIER
VIRGINIA	VA	OLD DOMINION	RICHMOND
WASHINGTON	WA	EVERGREEN	OLYMPIA
WEST VIRGINIA	WV	MOUNTAIN	CHARLESTON
WISCONSIN	WI	BADGER	MADISON
WYOMING	WY	EQUALITY	CHEYENNE

AUSTRALIAN STATES AND TERRITORIES

AUSTRALIAN CAPITAL TERRITORY	NORTHERN TERRITORY	TASMANIA
NEW SOUTH WALES	QUEENSLAND	VICTORIA
	SOUTH AUSTRALIA	WESTERN AUSTRALIA

TOWNS AND CITIES

AFGHANISTAN	ALGERIA	ANGOLA	ARGENTINA
5	4	6	7
HERAT	ORAN	LOBITO	CORDOBA
KABUL	7	LUANDA	LA PLATA
6	ALGIERS		ROSARIO
KANDAHAR			11
			BUENOS AIRES

TOWNS AND CITIES

ARMENIA
7
YEREVAN

AUSTRALIA
5
PERTH
6
DARWIN
HOBART
SYDNEY
8
ADELAIDE
BRISBANE
CANBERRA
9
MELBOURNE
NEWCASTLE
12
ALICE SPRINGS

AUSTRIA
6
VIENNA
8
SALZBURG
9
INNSBRUCK

AZERBAIJAN
4
BAKU

BANGLADESH
5
DHAKA
10
CHITTAGONG

BELARUS
5
BREST
MINSK

BELGIUM
5
GHENT
LIEGE
NAMUR
YPRES

6
BRUGES
DINANT
OSTEND
7
ANTWERP
MALINES
8
BRUSSELS

BRAZIL
5
BELEM

6
RECIFE
8
BRASILIA
SAO PAULO
11
PORTO ALEGRE
12
R10 DE JANEIRO
13
BELO HORIZONTE

BULGARIA
5
SOF1A
VARNA

CANADA
6
OTTAWA
QUEBEC
REGINA
7
CALGARY
HALIFAX
ST JOHN'S
TORONTO
8
EDMONTON
HAMILTON
KINGSTON
MONTREAL
VICTORIA
WINNIPEG
9
VANCOUVER
SASKATOON

10
THUNDER BAY
11
FREDERICTON
12
NIAGARA FALLS
13
CHARLOTTETOWN

CHILE
8
SANTIAGO
10
VALPARAISO

CHINA
4
LUTA
SIAN
5
WUHAN
ANSHAN
CANTON
DAIREN
HARBIN
MUKDEN
PEKING
7
BEIJING
KUNMING
LANCHOW
NANKING
TAIYUAN
8
SHANGHAI
SHENYANG
TIENTSIN 9
CHANGCHUN
CHUNGKING
10
PORT ARTHUR

COLOMBIA
4
CALI
6
BOGOTA
9
CARTAGENA
12
BARRANQUILLA

CZECH REPUBLIC
4
BRNO
6
PRAGUE

EGYPT
4
GIZA
SUEZ
5
ASWAN
CAIRO
LUXOR
TANTA
6
THEBES
7
MANSURA
MEMPHIS
ZAGAZIG
8
ISMAILIA
PORT SAID
10
ALEXANDRIA

ENGLAND
3
ELY
EYE
RYE
WEM
4
BATH
BRAY
BUDE
BURY
CLUN
DEAL
DISS
ETON
HOLT
HOVE
HULL
HYDE
INCE
LEEK
LOOE
LYDD
ROSS

190

England continued	TRING	LYNTON	YEOVIL
4 continued	TRURO	LYTHAM	**7**
RYDE	WELLS	MALDON	ALNWICK
SHAP	WIGAN	MALTON	ANDOVER
WARE	**6**	MARLOW	APPLEBY
WARK	ALSFORD	MASHAM	ARUNDEL
YARM	ALSTON	MORLEY	ASHFORD
YORK	ASHTON	NASEBY	AYLSHAM
5	BARNET	NELSON	BAMPTON
ACTON	BARROW	NEWARK	BANBURY
ALTON	BARTON	NEWLYN	BARKING
BACUP	BATLEY	NEWTON	BECCLES
BLYTH	BATTLE	NORHAM	BEDFORD
BOURN	BAWTRY	OAKHAM	BELFORD
CALNE	BEDALE	OLDHAM	BERWICK
CHARD	BELPER	ORMSBY	BEWDLEY
CHEAM	BODMIN	OUNDLE	BEXHILL
COLNE	BOGNOR	OXFORD	BICKLEY
COWES	BOLTON	PENRYN	BILSTON
CREWE	BOOTLE	PEWSEY	BOURTON
DERBY	B0STON	PINNER	BOWFELL
DOVER	BRUTON	PUDSEY	BRANDON
EGHAM	BUNGAY	PUTNEY	BRISTOL
EPSOM	BURTON	RAMSEY	BRIXHAM
FILEY	BUXTON	REDCAR	BROMLEY
FOWEY	CASTOR	RIPLEY	BURNHAM
FROME	COBHAM	ROMNEY	BURNLEY
GOOLE	CROMER	ROMSEY	BURSLEM
HAWES	DARWEN	RUGELY	CAISTOR
HEDON	DUDLEY	SEAHAM	CATFORD
HURST	DURHAM	SEATON	CAWSTON
HYTHE	EALING	SELSEY	CHARING
LEEDS	ECCLES	SETTLE	CHATHAM
LEIGH	EPPING	SNAITH	CHEADLE
LEWES	EXETER	ST IVES	CHEDDAR
LOUTH	GORING	STROOD	CHESHAM
LUTON	HANLEY	STROUD	CHESTER
MARCH	HARLOW	SUTTON	CHORLEY
OLNEY	HARROW	THIRSK	CLACTON
OTLEY	HAVANT	THORNE	CLIFTON
POOLE	HENLEY	TOTNES	CRAWLEY
REETH	HEXHAM	WALTON	CROYDON
RIPON	HOWDEN	WATTON	DARSLEY
RISCA	ILFORD	WESTON	DATCHET
RUGBY	ILKLEY	WHITBY	DAWLISH
SARUM	ILSLEY	WIDNES	DEVIZES
SELBY	JARROW	WIGTON	DORKING
STOKE	KENDAL	WILTON	DOUGLAS
STONE	LEYTON	WITHAM	DUNSTER
TEBAY	LONDON	WITNEY	ELSTREE
THAME	LUDLOW	WOOLER	ENFIELD

TOWNS AND CITIES

EVERTON	REDRUTH	AYCLIFFE	LECHLADE
EVESHAM	REIGATE	BAKEWELL	LISKEARD
EXMOUTH	RETFORD	BARNSLEY	LONGTOWN
FAREHAM	ROMFORD	BERKELEY	LYNMOUTH
FARNHAM	ROSSALL	BEVERLEY	MARYPORT
FELTHAM	ROYSTON	BICESTER	MIDHURST
GLOSSOP	RUNCORN	BIDEFORD	MINEHEAD
GOSPORT	SALFORD	BOLSOVER	NANTWICH
GRIMSBY	SALTASH	BRACKLEY	NEWHAVEN
HALIFAX	SANDOWN	BRADFORD	NUNEATON
HAMPTON	SAXELBY	BRAMPTON	ORMSKIRK
HARWICH	SEAFORD	BRIDPORT	OSWESTRY
HAWORTH	SHIFNAL	BRIGHTON	PENZANCE
HELSTON	SHIPLEY	BROMYARD	PERSHORE
HEYWOOD	SHIPTON	BROSELEY	PETERLEE
HITCHIN	ST NEOTS	CAMBORNE	PETWORTH
HONITON	SUDBURY	CARLISLE	PEVENSEY
HORNSEA	SUNBURY	CATERHAM	PLAISTOW
HORNSEY	SWANAGE	CHERTSEY	PLYMOUTH
HORSHAM	SWINDON	CLEVEDON	RAMSGATE
IPSWICH	SWINTON	CLOVELLY	REDDITCH
IXWORTH	TAUNTON	COVENTRY	RICHMOND
KESWICK	TELFORD	CREDITON	RINGWOOD
KINGTON	TENBURY	DAVENTRY	ROCHDALE
LANCING	TETBURY	DEBENHAM	ROTHBURY
LANGTON	THAXTED	DEDWORTH	SANDGATE
LEDBURY	TILBURY	DEPTFORD	SANDWICH
LEYBURN	TORQUAY	DEWSBURY	SEDBERGH
LINCOLN	TWYFORD	EGREMONT	SHANKLIN
MALVERN	VENTNOR	EVERSLEY	SHELFORD
MARGATE	WALSALL	FAKENHAM	SHIPSTON
MATLOCK	WALTHAM	FALMOUTH	SIDMOUTH
MOLESEY	WANTAGE	FOULNESS	SKEGNESS
MORETON	WAREHAM	GRANTHAM	SLEAFORD
MORPETH	WARWICK	GRANTOWN	SOUTHEND
MOSSLEY	WATCHET	HADLEIGH	SPALDING
NEWBURY	WATFORD	HAILSHAM	STAFFORD
NEWPORT	WEOBLEY	HALSTEAD	ST ALBANS
NORWICH	WICKWAR	HASTINGS	STAMFORD
OLDBURY	WINDSOR	HATFIELD	STANHOPE
OVERTON	WINSLOW	HELMSLEY	STANWELL
PADSTOW	WINSTER	HEREFORD	ST HELENS
PENRITH	WISBECK	HERNE BAY	STOCKTON
POULTON	WORKSOP	HERTFORD	STRATTON
PRESCOT	**8**	HINCKLEY	SURBITON
PRESTON	ABINGDON	HOLBEACH	SWAFFHAM
RAINHAM	ALFRETON	HUNMANBY	TAMWORTH
READING	ALNMOUTH	ILKESTON	THETFORD
REDHILL	AMESBURY	KEIGHLEY	THORNABY
	AMPTHILL	KINGSTON	TIVERTON
	AXBRIDGE	LAVENHAM	TUNSTALL

England continued
8 continued
UCKFIELD
UXBRIDGE
WALLASEY
WALLSEND
WANSTEAD
WESTBURY
WETHERAL
WETHERBY
WEYMOUTH
WOODFORD
WOOLWICH
WORTHING
YARMOUTH
9
ALDEBURGH
ALDERSHOT
ALLENDALE
ALRESFORD
AMBLESIDE
ASHBOURNE
ASHBURTON
AVONMOUTH
AYLESBURY
BLACKBURN
BLACKPOOL
BLANDFORD
BLISWORTH
BRACKNELL
BRAINTREE
BRENTFORD
BRENTWOOD
BRIGHOUSE
BROUGHTON
CAMBRIDGE
CARNFORTH
CASTLETON
CHESILTON
CHINGFORD
CLITHEROE
CONGLETON
CRANBORNE
CRANBROOK
CREWKERNE
CRICKLADE
CUCKFIELD
DARTMOUTH
DEVONPORT
DONCASTER
DONINGTON

DROITWICH
DRONFIELD
DUNGENESS
DUNSTABLE
ELLESMERE
FAVERSHAM
FLEETWOOD
GATESHEAD
GODALMING
GRAVESEND
GREENWICH
GRINSTEAD
GUILDFORD
HARROGATE
HASLEMERE
HAVERHILL
HAWKHURST
HOLMFIRTH
ILCHESTER
IMMINGHAM
KETTERING
KING'S LYNN
KINGSWEAR
LAMBOURNE
LANCASTER
LEICESTER
LICHFIELD
LIVERPOOL
LONGRIDGE
LOWESTOFT
LYME REGIS
LYMINGTON
MAIDSTONE
MANSFIELD
MIDDLETON
NEWCASTLE
NEWMARKET
NEW ROMNEY
NORTHWICH
OTTERBURN
PEMBRIDGE
PENISTONE
PENKRIDGE
PENYGHENT
PICKERING
ROCHESTER
ROTHERHAM
SALISBURY
SALTFLEET
SEVENOAKS
SHEERNESS

SHEFFIELD
SHERBORNE
SMETHWICK
SOUTHGATE
SOUTHPORT
SOUTHWELL
SOUTHWOLD
STARCROSS
ST AUSTELL
STEVENAGE
STOCKPORT
STOKESLEY
STOURPORT
STRATFORD
TARPORLEY
TAVISTOCK
TENTERDEN
TODMORDEN
TONBRIDGE
TOWCESTER
TYNEMOUTH
ULVERSTON
UPMINSTER
UPPINGHAM
UTTOXETER
WAINFLEET
WAKEFIELD
WARKWORTH
WEYBRIDGE
WHERNSIDE
WHITHAVEN
WIMBLEDON
WINCANTON
WOKINGHAM
WOODSTOCK
WORCESTER
WYMONDHAM
10
ACCRINGTON
ALDBOROUGH
ALTRINCHAM
BARNSTAPLE
BEDLINGTON
BELLINGHAM
BILLERICAY
BIRKENHEAD
BIRMINGHAM
BRIDGNORTH
BRIDGWATER
BROMSGROVE
BROXBOURNE

BUCKINGHAM
CANTERBURY
CARSHALTO N
CHELMSFORD
CHELTENHAM
CHICHESTER
CHIPPENHAM
CHULMLEIGH
COGGESHALL
COLCHESTER
CULLOMPTON
DARLINGTON
DORCHESTER
DUKINFIELD
EASTBOURNE
ECCLESHALL
FARNINGHAM
FOLKESTONE
FRESHWATER
GILLINGHAM
GLOUCESTER
HALESWORTH
HARTLEPOOL
HASLINGDON
HEATHFIELD
HORNCASTLE
HORNCHURCH
HUNGERFORD
HUNSTANTON
HUNTINGDON
ILFRACOMBE
KENILWORTH
KIRKOSWALD
LAUNCESTON
LEAMINGTON
LEOMINSTER
LITTLEPORT
MAIDENHEAD
MALMESBURY
MANCHESTER
MEXBOROUGH
MICHELDEAN
MIDDLEWICH
MILDENHALL
NAILSWORTH
NOTTINGHAM
OKEHAMPTON
ORFORDNESS
PANGBOURNE
PATRINGTON
PEACEHAVEN

TOWNS AND CITIES

England continued
10 continued
PONTEFRACT
PORTISHEAD
PORTSMOUTH
POTTERS BAR
RAVENGLASS
ROCKINGHAM
SAXMUNDHAM
SHEPPERTON
SHERINGHAM
SHREWSBURY
ST ALBRIDGE
ST LEONARDS
STOWMARKET
SUNDERLAND
TEDDINGTON
TEIGNMOUTH
TEWKESBURY
THAMESMEAD
TORRINGTON
TROWBRIDGE
TWICKENHAM
WALSINGHAM
WARMINSTER
WARRINGTON
WASHINGTON
WEDNESBURY
WELLINGTON
WESTWARD HO
WHITCHURCH
WHITSTABLE
WHITTLESEY
WILLENHALL
WINCHELSEA
WINCHESTER
WINDERMERE
WINDLESHAM
WIRKSWORTH
WITHERNSEA
WOODBRIDGE
WORKINGTON
11
BASINGSTOKE
BEARMINSTER
BOGNOR REGIS
BOURNEMOUTH
BRIDLINGTON
BUNTINGFORD
CLEETHORPES
COCKERMOUTH

EAST RETFORD
GLASTONBURY
GREAT MARLOW
GUISBOROUGH
HALTWHISTLE
HAMPTON WICK
HATHERLEIGH
HIGH WYCOMBE
INGATESTONE
LEYTONSTONE
LITTLESTONE
LUDGERSHALL
LUTTERWORTH
MABLETHORPE
MANNINGTREE
MARKET RASEN
MARLBOROUGH
MUCH WENLOCK
NEW BRIGHTON
NEWTON ABBOT
NORTHAMPTON
PETERSFIELD
POCKLINGTON
RAWTENSTALL
SCARBOROUGH
SHAFTESBURY
SOUTHAMPTON
SOUTH MOLTON
STALYBRIDGE
ST MARGARETS
STOURBRIDGE
TATTERSHALL
WALLINGFORD
WALTHAMSTOW
WESTMINSTER
WHITECHURCH
WOODHALL SPA
12
ATTLEBOROUGH
BEXHILL-ON-SEA
CASTLE RISING
CHESTERFIELD
CHRISTCHURCH
GAINSBOROUGH
GREAT GRIMSBY
GREAT MALVERN
HUDDERSFIELD
INGLEBOROUGH
LONG STRATTON
LOUGHBOROUGH
MACLESFIELD

MILTON KEYNES
MORCAMBE BAY
NORTH BERWICK
NORTH SHIELDS
NORTH WALSHAM
PETERBOROUGH
SHOEBURYNESS
SHOTTESBROOK
SOUTH SHIELDS
STOKE-ON-TRENT
13
BARNARD CASTLE
BERKHAMPSTEAD
BISHOPS CASTLE
BOROUGHBRIDGE
BRIGHTLINGSEA
BURTON-ON-TRENT
BURY ST EDMONDS
CHIPPING ONGAR
GREAT YARMOUTH
HIGHAM FERRERS
KIDDERMINSTER
KIRKBY STEPHEN
KNARESBOROUGH
LITTLEHAMPTON
LYTHAM ST ANNES
MARKET DEEPING
MARKET DRAYTON
MELCOMBE REGIS
MELTON MOWBRAY
MIDDLESBROUGH
NORTHALLERTON
SAFFRON WALDEN
SHEPTON MALLET
WOLVERHAMPTON
WOOTTON BASSET
14
BERWICK ON TWEED
BISHOP AUCKLAND
BISHOPS WALTHAM
CHIPPING BARNET
CHIPPING NORTON
HEMEL HEMPSTEAD
KIRKBY LONSDALE
MARKET BOSWORTH
MORTIMER'S CROSS
STOCKTON-ON-TEES
STONY STRATFORD
SUTTON COURTNEY
TUNBRIDGE WELLS
WELLINGBOROUGH

WEST HARTLEPOOL
15+
ASHTON-UNDER-
  LYNE
BARROW-IN-
  FURNESS
BISHOP'S
  STORTFORD
BURNHAM-ON-
  CROUCH
CASTLE DONINGTON
LEIGHTON BUZZARD
NEWCASTLE-UPON-
  TYNE
ST LEONARDS-ON-
  SEA
STRATFORD-ON-
  AVON
SUTTON COLDFIELD
WELWYN GARDEN
  CITY
WESTON-SUPER-
  MARE

ESTONIA
7
TALLINN

FRANCE
3
AIX
PAU
4
ALBI
CAEN
LYON
METZ
NICE
5
ARLES
ARRAS
BREST
DIJON
EVIAN
LILLE
LYONS
MACON
NANCY
NIMES
PARIS
REIMS

TOWNS AND CITIES

France continued
5 continued
ROUEN
TOURS
6
AMIENS
BAYEUX
CALAIS
CANNES
DIEPPE
LE MANS
NANTES
RHEIMS
ST MALO
TOULON
VERDUN
7
AVIGNON
BAYONNE
DUNKIRK
LE HAVRE
LIMOGES
LOURDES
ORLEANS
8
BESANCON
BIARRITZ
BORDEAUX
BOULOGNE
CHARTRES
GRENOBLE
SOISSONS
ST TROPEZ
TOULOUSE
9
ABBEVILLE
CHERBOURG
DUNKERQUE
MARSEILLE
MONTAUBAN
PERPIGNAN
ST ETIENNE
10
MARSEILLES
MONTELIMAR
STRASBOURG
VERSAILLES
11
ARMENTIERES
MONTPELLIER

GEORGIA
7
TBILISI

GERMANY
4
BONN
GERA
KIEL
KOLN
SUHL
5
ESSEN
HALLE
MAINZ
TRIER
WORMS
6
AACHEN
BERLIN
BOCHUM
BREMEN
CASSEL
ERFURT
KASSEL
LUBECK
MUNICH
TREVES
7
COBLENZ
COLOGNE
COTTBUS
DRESDEN
HAMBURG
HANOVER
HOMBURG
KOBLENZ
LEIPZIG
MUNCHEN
POTSDAM
ROSTOCK
SPANDAU
8
AUGSBURG
DORTMUND
HANNOVER
MANNHEIM
NURNBERG
SCHWERIN
9
BRUNSWICK

DARMSTADT
FRANKFURT
MAGDEBURG
NUREMBERG
STUTTGART
WIESBADEN
10
BADEN BADEN
BAD HOMBURG
DUSSELDORF
HEIDELBERG
11
BRANDENBURG
SAARBRUCKEN
13
AIX-LA-CHAPELLE

GREECE
6
ATHENS
SPARTA
THEBES
7
CORINTH
MYCENAE
PIRAEUS
8
SALONIKA

HUNGARY
4
PECS
8
BUDAPEST

INDIA
4
AGRA
5
AJMER
ALWAR
DELHI
KOTAH
PATNA
POONA
SIML A
6
BARODA
BHOPAL
BOMBAY
H0WRAH

IMPHAL
JAIPUR
JHANSI
KANPUR
KOHIMA
MADRAS
MYSORE
NAGPUR
RAMPUR
7
BENARES
GWALIOR
JODHPUR
LUCKNOW
8
AGARTALA
AMRITSAR
CALCUTTA
CAWNPORE
JAMALPUR
SHILLONG
SRINAGAR
VARANASI
9
AHMEDABAD
ALLAHABAD
BANGALORE
HYDERABAD
10
CHANDIGARH
DARJEELING
JAMSHEDPUR
TRIVANDRUM
11
BHUBANESWAR

INDONESIA
7
BANDUNG
JAKARTA
8
SURABAJA
9
PALEMBANG

IRAN
6
ABADAN
SHIRAZ
TABRIZ
TEHRAN

TOWNS AND CITIES

Iran continued

7
ISFAHAN
MASHHAD

IRAQ
5
BASRA
MOSUL
7
BAGHDAD
KARBALA

IRELAND
4
BRAY
COBH
CORK
5
BALLA
BOYLE
CLARE
KELLS
SLIGO
6
ARKLOW
BANTRY
CARLOW
CASHEL
DUBLIN
GALWAY
TRALEE
7
ATHLONE
BLARNEY
CLONMEL
DUNDALK
KILDARE
SHANNON
WEXFORD
WICKLOW
YOUGHAL
8
CLONTARF
DROGHEDA
KILKENNY
LIMERICK
LISTOWEL
MAYNOUTH
RATHDRUM

9
CONNEMARA
KILLARNEY
ROSCOMMON
TIPPERARY
WATERFORD
10
SHILLELAGH
11
BALLYMURPHY

ISRAEL
4
GAZA
5
HAIFA
JAFFA
7
TEL AVIV
9
BEERSHEBA
JERUSALEM

ITALY
4
BARI
PISA
ROME
5
GENOA
MILAN
OSTIA
PADUA
PARMA
SIENA
TRENT
TURIN
6
NAPLES
REGGIO
VENICE
VERONA
7
BOLOGNA
MESSINA
PALERMO
POMPEII
RAVENNA
SALERNO
SAN REMO
TRIESTE

VATICAN
8
FLORENCE
SYRACUSE
9
AGRIGENTO

JAPAN
4
KO8E
5
KYOTO
OSAKA
TOKYO
6
NAGOYA
7
FUKUOKA
SAPPORO
8
NAGASAKI
YOKOHAMA
9
HIROSHIMA
10
KITAKYUSHU

KENYA
4
LAMU
7
MOMBASA
NAIROBI

KOREA
5
SEOUL
8
PANMUNJON

LATVIA
4
RIGA

LEBANON
4
TYRE
5
SIDON
6
BEIRUT

7
TRIPOLI

LIBYA
4
HOMS

6
TOBRUK

LITHUANIA
6
KAUNAS
7
VILNIUS

MALI
6
BAMAKO
8
TIMBUKTU

MEXICO
6
JUAREZ
PUEBLA
8
ACAPULCO
VERACRUZ
9
MONTERREY
11
GUADALAJARA

MOROCCO
3
FEZ
5
RABAT
6
AGADIR
MEKNES
7
TANGIER
8
TANGIERS
9
MARRAKECH
MARRAKESH
10
CASABLANCA

196

MYANMAR (Burma)
3
AVA
7
RANGOON
8
MANDALAY

NETHERLANDS
5
HAGUE
6
ARNHEM
LEIDEN
LEYDEN
7
UTRECHT
8
THE HAGUE
9
AMSTERDAM
EINDHOVEN
ROTTERDAM

NEW ZEALAND
6
NAPIER
NELSON
7
DUNEDIN
8
AUCKLAND
10
WELLINGTON
12
CHRISTCHURCH

NIGERIA
4
KANO
5
ABUJA
ENUGU
LAGOS
6
IBADAN

**NORTHERN
IRELAND**
4
MUFF

5
DOAGH
GLYNN
KEADY
LARNE
LOUTH
NEWRY
OMAGH
TOOME
6
ANTRIM
AUGHER
BERCOO
BERAGH
CALLAN
CARNEY
COMBER
LURGAN
RAPHOE
SHRULE
7
BELFAST
BELLEEK
CALEDON
CARRICK
CLOGHER
DERVOCK
DUNDRUM
DUNMORE
FINTONA
GILFORD
GLENARM
LIFFORD
LISBURN
8
AHOGHILL
BALLYBAY
DUNGIVEN
HILLTOWN
PORTRUSH
STRABANE
TRILLICK
9
BALLINTRA
BALLYMENA
BALLYMORE
BANBRIDGE
BELTURBET
BUSHMILLS
COLERAINE
COOKSTOWN

DUNGANNON
GLASLOUGH
KILLYBEGS
KIRCUBBIN
MONEYMORE
NEWCASTLE
PORTADOWN
RASHARKIN
ROSTREVOR
TOVERMORE
10
BALLYBOFIR
BALLYCLARE
BALLYHAISE
BALLYMONEY
BALLYRONEY
CASTLEDERG
CASTLEFINN
CUSHENHALL
DONAGHADEL
GLENGARIFF
KILCONNELL
MARKETHILL
PORTAFERRY
SAINTFIELD
STRANGFORD
STRANORLAR
TANDERAGEE
11
BALLYCASTLE
BALLYGAWLEY
CARRICKMORE
CROSSMAGLEN
DOWNPATRICK
DRAPERSTOWN
ENNISKILLEN
LETTERKENNY
LONDONDERRY
MAGHERAFELT
PORTGLENONE
RANDALSTOWN
RATHFRYLAND
12
CASTLEBLANEY
CASTLE DAWSON
CASTLEWELLAN
FIVE MILE TOWN
HILLSBOROUGH
INISHTRAHULL
SLIEVE DONARD
STEWARTSTOWN

13
BROOKEBOROUGH
CARRICKFERGUS
DERRYGONNELLY
14
NEWTOWN
  STEWART

NORWAY
4
OSLO
6
BERGEN
9
TRONDHEIM

PAKISTAN
6
LAHORE
OUETTA
7
KARACHI
8
PESHAWAR
9
HYDERABAD
10
RAWALPINDI

PERU
4
LIMA
5
CUZCO

POLAND
4
LODZ
5
POSEN
6
DANZIG
GDANSK
KRAKOW
LUBLIN
WARSAW
7
BRESLAU
8
PRZEMYSL

TOWNS AND CITIES

PORTUGAL
6
LISBON
OPORTO

RUSSIA
5
GORKY
KAZAN
6
MOSCOW
8
SMOLENSK
9
ASTRAKHAN
VOLGOGRAD
LENINGRAD

SAUDI ARABIA
5
MECCA
JEDDAH
MEDINA
RIYADH

SCOTLAND
3
AYR
UIG
4
ALVA
BARR
DUNS
ELIE
KIRN
LUSS
NIGG
OBAN
REAY
RONA
STOW
WICK
5
ALLOA
ANNAN
APPIN
AVOCH
AYTON
BANFF
BEITH
BRORA

BUNAW
BUSBY
CERES
CLOVA
CLUNE
CRAIL
CUPAR
DENNY
DOWNE
ELGIN
ELLON
ERROL
FYVIE
GOVAN
INSCH
ISLAY
KEISS
KEITH
KELSO
LAIRG
LARGO
LEITH
NAIRN
PERTH
SALEN
TROON

6
ABOYNE
ALFORD
BARVAS
BEAULY
BERVIE
BIGGAR
BO'NESS
BUCKIE
CARRON
CAWDOR
COMRIE
CRIEFF
CULLEN
CULTER
DOLLAR
DRYMEN
DUNBAR
DUNDEE
DUNLOP
DUNNET
DUNOON
DYSART
EDZELL
FINDON

FORFAR
FORRES
GIRVAN
GLAMIS
HAWICK
HUNTLY
IRVINE
KILLIN
KILMUN
LANARK
LAUDER
LESLIE
LINTON
LOCHEE
MEIGLE
MOFFAT
PLADDA
RESTON
RHYNIE
ROSYTH
ROTHES
SHOTTS
THURSO
TONGUE
WISHAW
YARROW

7
AIRDRIE
BALFRON
BALLOCH
BANAVIE
BOWMORE
BRAEMAR
BRECHIN
BRODICK
CANOBIE
CANTYRE
CARBOST
CARGILL
CARLUKE
CRATHIE
CULROSS
CUMNOCK
DENHOLM
DOUGLAS
DUNKELD
DUNNING
EVANTON
FAIRLIE
FALKIRK
GALSTON

GIFFORD
GLASGOW
GLENCOE
GOLSPIE
GOUROCK
GRANTON
GUTHRIE
HALKIRK
KENMORE
KESSOCK
KILMORY
KILSYTH
KINROSS
KINTORE
LAMLASH
LARBERT
LYBSTER
MACDUFF
MAYBOLE
MELDRUM
MELROSE
MELVICH
METHVEN
MILMUIR
MONIKIE
MUTHILL
NEWRORT
PAISLEY
PEEBLES
POLMONT
POOLEWE
PORTREE
PORTSOY
RENFREW
SADDELL
SARCLET
SCOURIE
SELKIRK
STANLEY
STRATHY
TARBERT
TARLAND
TAYPORT
TRANENT
TUNDRUM
TURRIFF
ULLSTER
YETHOLM
8
ABERDEEN
ABERLADY

198

Scotland continued
8 continued
ABINGTON
ARBROATH
ARMADALE
ARROCHAR
AULDEARN
BALLATER
BANCHORY
BARRHILL
BEATTOCK
BLANTYRE
BURGHEAD
CANISBAY
CARNWATH
CREETOWN
CROMARTY
DALKEITH
DALMALLY
DINGWALL
DIRLETON
DUFFTOWN
DUMFRIES
DUNBEATH
DUNBLANE
DUNSCORE
EARLSTON
EYEMOUTH
FINDHORN
FORTROSE
GLENLUCE
GREENLAW
GREENOCK
HAMILTON
INVERARY
INVEBURY
JEANTOWN
JEDBURGH
KILBRIDE
KILNIVER
KILRENNY
KINGHORN
KIRKWALL
LANGHOLM
LATHERON
LEUCHARS
LOANHEAD
MARKINCH
MARYKIRK
MONIAIVE
MONTROSE

MONYMUSK
MUIRKIRK
NEILSTON
NEWBURGH
NEWMILNS
PENICUIK
PITSLIGO
POOLTIEL
QUIRAING
ROTHESAY
ST FERGUS
STIRLING
STRICHEN
TALISKER
TARANSAY
TRAQUAIR
ULLAPOOL
WHITHORN
WOODSIDE
9
ABERFELDY
ABERFOYL E
ARDROSSAN
BERRIDALE
BETTYHILL
BLACKLARG
BRACADALE
BRAERIACH
BROADFORD
BROUGHTON
BUCKHAVEN
CAIRNTOUL
CALLANDER
CARSTAIRS
DUMBARTON
EDINBURGH
FERINTOSH
FOCHABERS
INCHKEITH
INVERARAY
INVERNESS
JOHNSTONE
KILDRUMMY
KINGUSSIE
KIRKCALDY
LEADHILLS
LOCHGELLY
LOCHINVAR
LOCHNAGAR
LOCKERBIE
LOGIERAIT

MAUCHLINE
MILNGAVIE
PETERHEAD
PITLOCHRY
PORT ELLEN
PRESTWICK
RICCARTON
RONALDSAY
ROTHIEMAY
SALTCOATS
SHIELDAIG
SLAMANNAN
ST ANDREWS
STEWARTON
ST FILLANS
STRANRAER
STRATHDON
STRONTIAN
THORNHILL
TOBERMORY
TOMINTOUL
10
ABBOTSFORD
ACHNASHEEN
ANSTRUTHER
ARDRISHAIG
AUCHINLECK
BALLANTRAE
CARNOUSTIE
CARSPHAIRN
CASTLETOWN
COATBRIDGE
COLDINGHAM
COLDSTREAM
DALBEATTIE
DRUMLITHIE
EAST LINTON
GALASHIELS
GLENROTHES
JOHNSAVEN
KILCREGGAN
KILLENAULE
KILMAINHAM
KILMALCOLM
KILMARNOCK
KILWINNING
KINCARDINE
KINGSBARNS
KIRKMAIDEN
KIRKOSWALD
KIRRIEMUIR

LENNOXTOWN
LESMAHAGOW
LINLITHGOW
LIVINGSTON
MILNATHORT
MOTHERWELL
PITTENWEEM
PORTOBELLO
RUTHERGLEN
STONEHAVEN
STONEHOUSE
STONEYKIRK
STRATHAVEN
STRATHEARN
STRATHMORE
TWEEDMOUTH
WEST CALDER
WILSONTOWN
11
ABERCHIRDER
BANNOCKBURN
BLAIRGOWRIE
CAMPBELTOWN
CHARLESTOWN
CUMBERNAULD
DRUMMELZIER
DUNFERMLINE
ECCLEFECHAN
FETTERCAIRN
FORT WILLIAM
FRASERBURGH
HELENSBURGH
INVERGORDON
KIRKMICHAEL
LOSSIEMOUTH
LOSTWITHIEL
MAXWELLTOWN
MUSSELBURGH
PORT GLASGOW
PORT PATRICK
PRESTONPANS
PULTNEYTOWN
STRATHBLANE
12
AUCHTERARDER
BALLACHULISH
EAST KILBRIDE
FORT AUGUSTUS
GARELOCHHEAD
INNERLEITHEN
LAWRENCEKIRK

TOWNS AND CITIES

Scotland continued
12 continued
PORTMAHOMACK
STRATHPEFFER
TILLICOULTRY
13
AUCHTERMUCHTY
CASTLE DOUGLAS
INVERKEITHING
INVERKEITHNIE
KIRKCUDBRIGHT
KIRKINTILLOCH
NEWTON STEWART

SLOVAKIA
6
KOSICE
10
BRATISLAVA

SOUTH AFRICA
6
DURBAN
SOWETO
8
CAPE TOWN
MAFEKING
PRETORIA
9
KIMBERLEY
LADYSMITH
10
SIMONSTOWN
11
GRAHAMSTOWN
SHARPEVILLE
12
BLOEMFONTEIN
JOHANNESBURG
13
PORT ELIZABETH

SPAIN
4
VIGO
5
CADIZ
6
BILBAO
MADRID
MALAGA

7
BADAJOZ
CORDOBA
GRANADA
SEVILLE
ALICANTE
PAMPLONA
VALENCIA
ZARAGOZA
9
BARCELONA
CARTAGENA
LAS PALMAS
SANTANDER
SARAGOSSA
12
SAN SEBASTIAN:

SRI LANKA
5
GALLE
KANDY
7
COLOMBO
11
TRINCOMALEE

SUDAN
6
BERBER
7
DONGOLA
8
KHARTOUM
OMDURMAN

SWEDEN
5
MALMO
7
UPPSALA
GOTEBORG
9
STOCKHOLM
10
GOTHENBURG
11
HELSINGBORG

SWITZERLAND
4
BALE
BERN
5
BASEL
6
GENEVA
ZURICH
LUCERNE
8
LAUSANNE

SYRIA
4
HOMS
6
ALEPPO
7
PALMYRA
8
DAMASCUS

TANZANIA
6
DODOMA
8
ZANZIBAR

TURKEY
5
IZMIR
6
ANKARA
SMYRNA
7
ERZERUM
8
ISTANBUL
9
BYZANTIUM
14
CONSTANTINOPLE

UKRAINE
4
KIEV
LVOV
6
ODESSA

7
DONETSK
SEVASTOPOL

USA
4
GARY
LIMA
RENO
TROY
WACO
YORK
5
AKRON
BOISE
BRONX
BUTTE
FLINT
MIAMI
OMAHA
OZARK
SALEM
SELMA
TULSA
UTICA
6
ALBANY
AUSTIN
BANGOR
BILOXI
BOSTON
CAMDEN
CANTON
DALLAS
DAYTON
DENVER
DULUTH
EL PASO
EUGENE
FRESNO
LOWELL
MOBILE
NASSAU
NEWARK
OXNARD
PEORIA
ST PAUL
TACOMA
TOLEDO
TOPEKA
TUCSON

USA continued
6 continued
URBANA
7
ABILENE
ANAHEIM
ATLANTA
BOULDER
BUFFALO
CHICAGO
CONCORD
DETROIT
HAMPTON
HOBOKEN
HOUSTON
JACKSON
KEY WEST
LINCOLN
MADISON
MEMPHIS
MODESTO
NEW YORK
NORFOLK
OAKLAND
ORLANDO
PHOENIX
RALEIGH
READING
ROANOKE
SAGINAW
SAN JOSE
SEATTLE
SPOKANE
ST LOUIS
WICHITA
YONKERS
8
BERKELEY
BROOKLYN
COLUMBUS
DEARBORN
GREENBAY
HANNIBAL
HARTFORD
HONOLULU
LAS VEGAS
NEW HAVEN
PALO ALTO
PASADENA
PORTLAND
RICHMOND

SAN DIEGO
SANTA ANA
SAVANNAH
STAMFORD
STOCKTON
SYRACUSE
9
ANCHORAGE
ANNAPOLIS
ARLINGTON
BALTIMORE
BETHLEHEM
CAMBRIDGE
CHAMPAIGN
CHARLOTTE
CLEVELAND
DES MOINES
FAIRBANKS
FORT WAYNE
FORT WORTH
GALVESTON
HOLLYWOOD
JOHNSTOWN
KALAMAZOO
LANCASTER
LEXINGTO N
LONG BEACH
MANHATTA N
MILWAUKEE
NASHVILLE
NEW LONDON
NORTHEAST
PRINCETON
RIVERSIDE
ROCHESTER
WATERBURY
WORCESTER
YPSILANTI
10
ATOMIC CITY
BATON ROUGE
BIRMINGHAM
CHARLESTON
CINCINATTI
EVANSVILLE
GREENSBORO
GREENVILLE
HARRISBURG
HUNTSVILLE
JERSEY CITY
KANSAS CITY

LITTLE ROCK
LONG BRANCH
LOS ANGELES
LOUISVILLE
MIAMI BEACH
MONTGOMERY
NEW BEDFORD
NEW ORLEANS
PITTSBURGH
PROVIDENCE
SACRAMENTO
SAINT LOUIS
SAN ANTONIO
WASHINGTON
YOUNGSTOWN
11
ALBUQUERQUE
CEDAR RAPIDS
CHATTANOOGA
GRAND RAPIDS
MINNEAPOLIS
NEWPORT NEWS
PALM SPRINGS
SCHENECTADY
SPRINGFIELD
12
ATLANTIC CITY
BEVERLY HILLS
FAYETTEVILLE
INDEPENDENCE
INDIANAPOLIS
JACKSONVLLE
NEW BRUNSWICK
NIAGARA FAL LS
OKLAHOMA CITY
PHILADELPHIA
POUGHKEEPSIE
SALT LAKE CITY
SAN FRANCISCO
SANTA BARBAR A
13
CORPUS CHRISTI
ST PETERSBURGH
14
FORT-
  LAUDERDALE
COLORADO
  SPRINGS

VENEZUELA
7
CARACAS
9
MARACAIBO

WALES
3
USK
4
BALA
HOLT
MOLD
PYLE
RHYL
5
CHIRK
FLINT
NEATH
NEVIN
TENBY
TOWYN
6
AMLWCH
BANGOR
BRECON
BUILTH
CONWAY
MARGAM
RUABON
RUTHIN
7
CARBURY
CARDIFF
CWMBRAN
DENBIGH
MAESTEG
NEWPORT
NEWTOWN
ST ASAPH
SWANSEA
WREXHAM
8
ABERAVON
ABERDARE
ABERGELE
BARMOUTH
BRIDGEND
CAERLEON
CARDIGAN
CHEPSTOW

TOWNS AND CITIES

Wales continued
8 continued
DOLGELLY
EBBW VALE
HAWARDEN
HOLYHEAD
HOLYWELL
KIDWELLY
KNIGHTON
LAMPETER
LLANELLY
LLANRWST
MONMOUTH
PEMBROKE
RHAYADER
SKERRIES
SKIFNESS
TALGARTH
TREDEGAR
TREGARON
9
ABERAERON

ABERDOVEY
ABERFFRAW
BEAUMARIS
CARNARVON
CRICCIETH
FESTINIOG
FISHGUARD
LLANBERIS
LLANDUDNO
NEW RADNOR
PONTYPOOL
PORTHCAWL
PORTMADOC
PWHLLHELI
WELSHPOOL
10
CADER IDRIS
CAERNAR FON
CAERNARVON
CARMARTHEN
CRICKHOWEL
FFESTINIOG

LLANDOVERY
LLANFYLLIN
LLANGADOCK
LLANGOLLEN
LLANIDLOES
MONTGOMERY
PLINLIMMON
PONTYPRIDD
PORTH NIGEL
PORT TALBOT
PRESTEIGNE
11
ABERGAVENNY
ABERYSTWYTH
MACHYNLLETH
OYSTERMOUTH
12
LLANDILOFAWR
LLANTRISSANT
13
HAVERFORDWEST
MERTHYR TYDFIL

ZAIRE
8
KINSHASA
IO
LUBUMBASHI

PORTS OF THE WORLD

ALGERIA
4
ORAN
6
SKIKDA
7
ALGIERS
9
PORT ARZEW

ANGOLA
6
LOBITO
LUANDA

ARGENTINA
7
LA PLATA
11
BUENOS AIRES

AUSTRALIA
6
SYDNEY
7
DAMPIER
GEELONG
8
ADELAIDE
BRISBANE
9
MELBOURNE
NEWCASTLE
10
FREEMANTLE
11
PORT JACKSON
12
PORT ADELAIDE

AZERBAIJAN
4
BAKU

BELGIUM
6
OSTEND
7
ANTWERP
9
ZEEBRUGGE

BENIN
7
COTONOU
9
PORTO NOVO

BRAZIL
4
PARA
5
SELEM
6
RECIFE
SANTOS

7
TOBARAO

10
PERNAMBUCO
RIO DE JANEIRO

BULGARIA
5
VARNA

BURMA
5
AKYAB
6
SITTWE
7
RANGOON
8
MOULMEIN

202

CAMEROON
6
DOUALA

CANADA
7
HALIFAX
KITIMAT
8
MONTREAL
9
CHURCHILL
ESQUIMALT
OWEN SOUND
VANCOUVER
11
THREE RIVERS

**CHANNEL
ISLANDS**
8
ST HELIER
11
SAINT HELIER
ST PETER PORT

CHILE
5
ARICA
8
COQUIMBO
10
VALPARAISO

CHINA
4
AMOY
6
CHEFOO
HANKOW
SWATOW
WEIHAI
7
FOOCHOW
YINGKOW
8
SHANGHAI
TIENTSIN
10
PORT ARTHUR

COLUMBIA
9
CARTAGENA
12
BARRANQUILLA
BUENAVENTURA

CORSICA
6
BASTIA
AJACCIO

CROATIA
6
RIJEKA

CUBA
6
HAVANA
14
SANTIAGO DE
CUBA

CYPRUS
7
LARNACA
8
LIMASSOL

DENMARK
6
ODENSE
7
AALBORG
HORSENS
8
ELSINORE
HELSINGOR
10
COPENHAGEN
13
FREDERIKSHAVN

ECUADOR
9
GUAYAQUIL

EGYPT
4
SUEZ

8
DAMIETTA
PORT SAID
10
ALEXANDRIA

ENGLAND
4
HULL
5
DOVER
6
LONDON
7
CHATHAM
GRIMSBY
HARWICH
TILBURY
8
FALMOUTH
NEWHAVEN
PENZANCE
PLYMOUTH
PORTLAND
SANDWICH
WEYMOUTH
9
AVONMOUTH
DEVONPORT
GRAVESEND
KING'S LYNN
LIVERPOOL
NEWCASTLE
SHEERNESS
10
BARNSTABLE
COLCHESTER
FELIXSTOWE
FOLKESTONE
HARTLEPOOL
PORTSMOUTH
SUNDERLAND
TEIGNMOUTH
WHITSTABLE
11
CINQUE PORTS
SOUTHAMPTON
12
NORTH SHIELDS
PORT SUNLIGHT

13
MIDDLESBROUGH

ESTONIA
7
TALLINN

FINLAND
8
HELSINKI

FRANCE
5
BREST
6
CALAIS
CANNES
DIEPPE
TOULON
7
DUNKIRK
LE HAVRE
8
BORDEAUX
BOUEOGNE
HONFLEUR
9
CHERBOURG
FOS-SUR-MER
MARSEILLE
10
LA ROCHELLE
MARSEILLES

FRENCH GUIANA
7
CAYENNE

GERMANY
4
KIEL
5
EMDEN
6
BREMEN
WISMAR
7
HAMBURG
ROSTOCK

PORTS OF THE WORLD

Germany
continued
8
CUXHAVEN
9
FLENSBURG
10
TRAVEMUNDE
11
BREMERHAVEN
13
WILHELMSHAVEN

GHANA
4
TEMA
8
TAKORADI

GREECE
5
CANEA
CORFU
6
PATRAS
RHODES
7
PIRAEUS
NAVARINO
10
HERMOPOLIS
11
HERMOUPOLIS

HAWAII
8
HONOLULU
11
PEARL HARBOUR

HUNGARY
8
BUDAPEST

INDIA
6
BOMBAY
COCHIN
HALDIA
KANDLA
MADRAS

8
CALCUTTA
COCANADA
KAKINADA
11
MASULIPATAM
PONDICHERRY
12
MASULIPATNAM

INDONESIA
6
PADANG
7
JAKARTA
8
MACASSAR
MAKASSAR
PARADEEP

IRAN
6
ABADAN
7
BUSHIRE

IRAQ
5
BASRA

IRELAND
4
COBH
CORK
7
DONEGAL
DUNDALK
YOUGHAL
8
DUNLEARY
12
DUN LAOGHAIRE

ISRAEL
4
ACRE
AKKO
ELAT
5
EILAT
HAIFA

6
ASHDOD

ITALY
4
BARI
5
GAETA
GENOA
OSTIA
TRANI
6
ANCONA
NAPLES
VENICE
7
LEGHORN
MARSALA
MESSINA
PALERMO
SALERNO
TRAPANI
TRIESTE
8
BRINDISI

IVORY COAST
7
ABIDJAN

JAMAICA
8
KINGSTON
9
PORT ROYAL
10
MONTEGO BAY

JAPAN
4
KOBE
5
KOCHI
OSAKA
8
HAKODATE
NAGASAKI
YOKOHAMA
9
HIROSHIMA
KAGOSHIMA

11
SHIMONOSEKI

KENYA
7
MOMBASA

KUWAIT
12
MINA AL-AHMADI

LATVIA
4
RIGA

LEBANON
6
BEIRUT

LIBYA
7
TRIPOLI
8
BENGHAZI

MADAGASCAR
8
TAMATAVE

MALAYSIA
6
PENANG
9
PORT KLANG
10
GEORGE TOWN
12
KOTAKINABALU

MAURITIUS
9
PORT LOUIS

MEXICO
7
GUAYMAS
8
VERA CRUZ

PORTS OF THE WORLD

MOROCCO
4
SAFI
5
CEUTA
RABAT
6
AGADIR
TETUAN
7
MELILLA
MOGADOR
TANGIER
9
ESSAOUIRA
10
CASABLANCA

MOZAMBIQUE
5
BEIRA
6
MAPUTO

NETHERLANDS
5
DELFT
8
FLUSHING
9
AMSTERD AM
EUROPOORT
ROTTERDAM
10
VLISSINGEN

NEW ZEALAND
6
NELSON
8
AUCKLAND
GISBORNE
9
LYTTELTON

NIGERIA
5
LAGOS
PORT HARCOURT

NORTHERN IRELAND
7
BELFAST

NORWAY
4
OSLO
6
BERGEN
LARVIK
NARVIK
TROMSO
9
STAVANGER
TRONDHEIM
10
CHRISTIANA
HAMMERFEST
13
CHRISTIANSUND

PAKISTAN
6
CHALNA
7
KARACHI

PANAMA
5
COLON
6
BALBOA
9
CRISTOBAL

PAPUA NEW GUINEA
11
PORT MORESBY

PEOPLE'S DEMOCRATIC REPUBLIC OF YEMEN
4
ADEN

PERU
3
ILO

6
CALLAO
MATARINI
10
SAN JUAN BAY

PHILIPPINES
4
CEBU
6
MANILA

POLAND
6
DANZIG
GDANSK
GDYNIA
7
STETTIN
8
SZCZECIN
9
KOLOBRZEG

PORTUGAL
6
LISBON
OPORTO

PUERTO RICO
7
SAN JUAN

ROMANIA
10
CONSTANTSA

RUSSIA
9
ARCHANGEL
LENINGRAD
11
VLADIVOSTOK
13
PETROPAVLOVSK

SAUDI ARABIA
6
JEDDAH

SCOTLAND
4
TAIN
WICK
5
LEITH
SCAPA
6
DUNBAR
DUNDEE
8
GREENOCK
ARDROSSAN
SCAPA FLOW
STORNAWAY
11
GRANGEMOUTH
PORT GLASGOW

SENEGAL
5
DAKAR

SIERRA LEONE
8
FREETOWN

SOUTH AFRICA
6
DURBAN
8
CAPE TOWN
9
MOSSEL BAY
PORT NATAL
10
EAST LONDON
SIMONSTOWN
RICHARD'S BAY
13
PORT ELIZABETH

SOUTH KOREA
5
PUSAN

SPAIN
5
PALMA
PALOS

PORTS OF THE WORLD

Spain continued
6
BILBAO
FERROL
MALAGA
7
CORUNNA
FUNCHAL
8
ALICAME
ARRECIFE
LA CORUNA
9
ALGECIRAS
BARCELONA
CARTAGENA
LAS PALMAS

SRI LANKA
5
GALLE
7
COLOMBO

SUDAN
6
SUAKIN
9
PORT SUDAN

SWEDEN
5
LULEA
MALMO
WISBY
YSTAD
6
KALMAR
8
GOTEBORG
HALMSTAD

NYKOPING
9
STOCKHOLM
10
GOTHENBURG
11
HELSINGSORG

TAIWAN
6
TAINAN
7
KEELUNG
KAOHSIUNG

TANZANIA
6
MTWARA
11
DAR ES SALAAM

**TRINIDAD AND
TOBAGO**
11
PORT-OF-SPAIN

TURKEY
5
IZMIR
6
SMYRNA
8
ISTANBUL
14
CONSTANTINOPLE

UKRAINE
6
ODESSA

URUGUAY
10
MONTEVIDEO

USA
4
ERIE
7
DETROIT
HOUSTON
NEW YORK
NORFOLK
SEATTLE
8
NEW HAVEN
9
BALTIMORE
GALVESTON
NANTUCKET
PENSACOLA
10
BRIDGEPORT
CHARLESTON
JERSEY CITY
LOS ANGELES
NEW BEDFORD
NEW ORLEANS
PERTH AMBOY
PORTSMOUTH

11
ROCK HARBOUR
SAN FRANCISCO

VENEZUELA
8
LA GUIARA
12
PUERTO HIERRO
13
PUERTO CABELLO

WALES
7
CARDIFF
SWANSEA
HOLYHEAD
LLANELLI
PEMBROKE
9
PORTMADOC
12
MILFORD HAVEN

**YEMEN ARAB
REPUBLIC**
5
MOCHA
6
AHMEDI

YUGOSLAVIA
3
BAR
5
KOTOR
7
CATTARO
9
DUBROVNIK

ZAIRE
6
MATADI
9
MBUJI-MAYI

ISLANDS

4	PENANG	MINDANAO	NEW ZEALAND
BALI	RHODES	SAKHALIN	PUERTO RICO
CEBU	SICILY	SARDINIA	**11**
CUBA	TAFIITI	SOMERSET	AXEL HEIBERG
EDGE	TAIWAN	SRI LANKA	GUADALCANAL
GUAM	**7**	SULAWESI	ISLE OF PINES
JAVA	BAHRAIN	TASMANIA	ISLE OF WIGHT
OAHU	BARENTS	TENERIFE	SOUTHAMPTON
SARK	BERMUDA	TRINIDAD	**12**
5	CELEBES	UNALASKA	BOUGAINVILLE
BANKS	CORSICA	VICTORIA	GREAT BRITAIN
CERAM	CURACAO	VITI LEVU	NEW CALEDONIA
CORFU	GOTLAND	ZANZIBAR	NEWFOUNDLAND
CRETE	GRENADA	ANTICOSTI	NOVAYA ZEMLYA
DEVON	ICELAND	AUSTRALIA	**13**
HAITI	IRELAND	ELLESMERE	NORTH EAST LAND
LEYTE	JAMAICA	GREENLAND	PRINCE OF WALES
LUZON	MADEIRA	HALMAHERA	PRINCE PATRICK
MALTA	MAJORCA	ISLE OF MAN	SANTA CATALINA
PANAY	MINDORO	MANHATTAN	**14**
SAMAR	OKINAWA	MAURITIUS	TIERRA DEL FUEGO
TIMOR	PALAWAN	NANTUCKET	**15**
6	SHIKOKU	NEW GUINEA	MARTHA'S
BAFFIN	ST LUCIA	SINGAPORE	VINEYARD
BORNEO	SUMATRA	ST VINCENT	WEST
CYPRUS	WRANGEL	V ANCOUVER	SPITSBERGEN
FLORES	**8**	**10**	**18**
HAINAN	ALDERNE Y	CAPE BRETON	PRINCE EDWARD
HAWAII	BARBADOS	GUADELOUPE	ISLAND
HONSHU	DOMINICA	HISPANIOLA	
JERSEY	GUERNSEY	LONG ISLAND	
KODIAK	HOKKAIDO	MADAGASCAR	
KYUSHU	HONG KONG	MARTINIQUE	
MADURA	MALAGASY	NEW BRITAIN	
NEGROS	MELVILLE	NEW IRELAND	

OCEANS AND SEAS

3 & 4	**5**	WHITE (SEA)	IONIAN (SEA)
ARAL (SEA)	BANDA (SEA)	**6**	LAPTEV (SEA)
AZOV (SEA OF)	BLACK (SEA)	AEGEAN (SEA)	NANHAI (SEA)
DEAD (SEA)	CHINA (SEA)	ARCTIC (OCEAN)	TASMAN (SEA)
JAYA (SEA)	CORAL (SEA)	BALTIC (SEA)	YELLOW (SEA)
KARA (SEA)	IRISH (SEA)	BERING (SEA)	**7**
RED (SEA)	JAPAN (SEA OF)	CELTIC (SEA)	ANDAMAN (SEA)
ROSS (SEA)	NORTH (SEA)	INDIAN (OCEAN)	ARABIAN (SEA)
SAVA (SEA)	TIMOR (SEA)	INLAND (SEA)	ARAFURA (SEA)

SEAS / LAKES AND LOCHS

7 continued
BARENTS (SEA)
BEHRING (SEA)
CASPIAN (SEA)
DONG HAI (SEA)
GALILEE (SEA)
OKHOTSK (SEA OF)
PACIFIC (OCEAN)

WEDDELL (SEA)

8
ADRIATIC (SEA)
AMUNDSEN (SEA)
ATLANTIC (OCEAN)
BEAUFORT (SEA)
HUANG HAI (SEA)
LIGURIAN (SEA)

SARGASSO (SEA)
TIBERIAS (SEA OF)

9
ANTARCTIC (OCEAN)
CARIBBEAN (SEA)
EAST CHINA (SEA)
GREENLAND (SEA)

10+
BELLINGSHAUSEN (SEA)
MEDITERRANEAN (SEA)
PHILIPPINE (SEA)
SETO-NAIKAI (SEA)
SOUTH CHINA (SEA)

LAKES AND LOCHS

3
AWE (Scotland)
VAN (Turkey)
4
BALA (Wales)
CHAD (Africa)
COMO (Italy)
ERIE (Canada, USA)
EYRE (Australia)
KIVU (Zaire, Rwanda)
NEMI (Italy)
NESS (Scotland)
TANA (Ethiopia)
5
FOYLE (Ireland)
GARDA (Italy)
GREAT (Australia)
GREAT (USA, Canada)
HURON (USA, Canada)
KIOGA (Uganda)
KYOGA (Uganda)
LEMAN (Switzerland, France)
LEVEN (Scotland)
LOCHY (Scotland)
MAREE (Scotland)
NEAGH (Northern Ireland)
NYASA (Malawi, Tanzania, Mozambique)
ONEGA (Russia)
TAUPO (New Zealand)
URMIA (Iran)
6
ALBERT (Uganda, Zaire)
BAIKAL (Russia)
EDWARD (Uganda, Zaire)
GENEVA (Switzerland, France)

KARIBA (Zambia, Zimbabwe)
LADOGA (Russia)
LOMOND (Scotland)
LOP NOR (China)
MALAWI (Malawi, Tanzania, Mozambique)
MOBUTU (Uganda, Zaire)
NASSER (Egypt)
NATRON (Tanzania)
PEIPUS (Russia)
POYANG (China)
RUDOLF (Kenya, Ethiopia)
SAIMAA (Finland)
VANERN (Sweden)
7
BALATON (Hungary)
DERWENT (England)
KATRINE (Scotland)
KOKO NOR (China)
LUCERNE (Switzerland)
NU JIANG (China Burma)
ONTARIO (Canada, USA)
QINGHAI (China)
ST CLAIR (USA , Canada)
TORRENS (Australia)
TURKANA (Kenya, Ethiopia)
8
BALKHASHI (Russia)
CHIEMSEE (Germany)
CONISTON (England)
DONGTING (China)
GRASMERE (England)
ISSYK KUL (Russia)
MAGGIORE (Italy, Switzerland)
MAZURIAN (Poland)
MENINDEE (Australia)

MICHIGAN (USA)
NEUSIEDL (Austria, Hungary)
SUPERIOR (USA, Canada)
TITICACA (Peru, Bolivia)
TONLE SAP (Kampuchea
TUNG-T'ING (China)
VICTORIA (Uganda, Tanzania, Kenya)
WINNIPEG (Canada)
9
ATHABASCA (Canada)
BANGWEULU (Zambia)
CHAMPLAIN (USA)
CONSTANCE (Germany)
ENNERDALE (England)
GREAT BEAR (Canada)
GREAT SALT (USA)
MARACAIBO (Venezuela)
THIRLMERE (England)
TRASIMENO (Italy)
ULLSWATER (England)
WAST WATER (England)
10+
BUTTERMERE (England)
GREAT SLAVE (Canada)
IJSSELMEER (Netherlands)
KARA-BOGAZ-GOL (Russia)
OKEECHOBEE (USA)
TANGANYIKA (Zaire, Burundi, Tanzania, Zambia)
VIERWALDSTATTERSEE (Switzerland)
WINDERMERE (England)

RIVERS

2 & 3
AIN (France)
ALN (England)
BUG (Russia, Poland, Germany)
CAM (England)
DEE (Scotland,Wales, England)
DON (Russia, Scotland, England, France, Australia)
EMS (Germany, Netherlands)
ESK (Australia)
EXE (England)
FAL (England)
FLY (New Guinea)
HAN (China)
KWA (Zaire)
LEA (England)
LEE (Ireland)
LOT (France)
OB (Russia)
PO (Italy)
RED (USA)
RUR (Germany)
RYE (England)
TAY (Scotland)
URE (England)
USA (Russia)
USK (Wales, England)
WEY (England)
WYE (Wales, England)
YEO (England)

4
ADDA (Italy)
ADUR (England)
AIRE (England, France)
ALMA (Russia)
AMUR (Mongolia, Russia, China)
ARNO (Italy)
ARUN (Nepal)
AUBE (France)
AVON (England)
BEAS (India)
BURE (England)
CHER (France)
COLN (England)
DART (England)

DOON (Scotland)
DOVE (England)
EBRO (Spain)
EDEN (England, Scotland)
ELBE (Germany, Czech Rep, Slovakia)
EMBA (Russia)
ISIS (England)
JUBA (E. Africa)
KAMA (Russia)
KURA (Turkey, Russia)
LAHN (Germany)
LECH (Germany, Austria)
LENA (Russia)
LUNE (England)
LUNE (Germany)
MAAS (Netherlands)
MAIN (Germany, Northern Ireland)
MINO (Spain)
MOLE (England)
NILE (Sudan, Egypt)
ODER (Germany, Czech Rep, Slovakia, Poland)
OHIO (USA)
OISE (France)
OUSE (England)
OXUS (Russia)
PEEL (Australia, USA)
RAVI (India, Pakistan)
REDE (England)
RUHR (Germany)
SAAR (Germany, France)
SIDA (Russia)
SPEY (Scotland)
TAFF (Wales)
TAJO (Spain)
TARN (France)
TAWE (Wales)
TAWI (India)
TEES (England)
TEJO (Brazil)
TEST (England)
TYNE (Scotland, England)
URAL (Russia)
VAAL (South Africa)
WEAR (England)
YARE (England)

5
ADIGE (Italy)
AISNE (France)
ALLAN (Scotland, Syria)
ALLER (Spain, Germany)
ANNAN (Scotland)
BENUE (Nigeria)
BRENT (England)
CAMEL (England)
CHARI (Cameroon, Chad)
CLYDE (Scotland, Canada)
COLNE (England)
CONGO (Zaire)
DNEPR (Russia)
DOUBS (France, Switzerland)
DOURO (Spain, Portugal)
DOVEY (Wales)
DRAVA (Italy, Austria, Serbia, Hungary)
DUERO (Spain)
DVINA (Russia)
FORTH (Scotland)
FROME (Australia)
INDUS (India, Pakistan, China)
JAMES (USA, Australia)
JUMNA (India)
JURUA (Brazil)
KAFUE (Zambia)
KASAI (Angola Zaire)
KUBAN (Russia)
LIPPE (Germany)
LOIRE (France)
MARNE (France)
MAROS (Indonesia)
MEUSE (France, Belgium)
MINHO (Spain, Portugal)
MURES (Romania, Hungary)
NEGRO (Spain, Brazil, Argentina, Bolivia, Paraguay, Uruguay, Venezuela)
NEMAN (Russia)
NIGER (Nigeria, Mali, Guinea)
OTTER (England)
PEACE (Canada, USA)
PEARL (USA, China)

RIVERS

5 continued
PECOS (USA)
PIAVE (Italy)
PURUS (Brazil)
RANCE (France)
RHINE (Switzerland,
  Germany, Netherlands)
SAALE (Germany)
SEINE (France)
SLAVE (Canada)
SNAKE (USA)
SOMME (France)
STOUR (England)
SWALE (England)
TAGUS (Portugal, Spain)
TAMAR (England)
TIBER (Italy)
TRENT (England)
TWEED (England, Scotland)
VOLGA (Russia, USA)
VOLTA (Ghana)
WESER (Germany)
XINGU (Brazil)
ZAIRE (Zaire)

6
ALLIER (Prance)
AMAZON (Peru, Brazil)
ANGARA (Russia)
BIO BIO (China)
CHENAB (Pakistan)
CLUTHA (New Zealand)
COOPER (Australia)
COQUET (England)
CROUCH (England)
DANUBE (Germany, Austria,
  Romania, Hungary,
  Czech, Slovakia, Bulgaria)
DNESTR (Russia)
ESCAUT (Belgium, France)
FRASER (Canada)
GAMBIA (The Gambia,
  Senegal)
GANGES (India)
GLOMMA (Norway)
HUDSON (USA)
HUNTER (Australia)
IRTYSH (Russia)
ITCHEN (England)
JAPURA (Brazi)l
JORDAN (Israel, J ordan)
KOLYMA (Russia)

LIFFEY (Eire)
LODDON (Australia,
  England)
MAMORE (Brazil, Bolivia)
MEDINA (USA)
MEDWAY (England)
MEKONG (Laos, China)
MERSEY (England)
MONNOW (England, Wales)
MURRAY (Australia,
  Canada)
NECKAR (Germany)
NEISSE (Poland, Germany)
OGOOUE (Gabon)
ORANGE (South Africa)
ORWELL (England)
PARANA (Brazil)
PLATTE (USA)
RIBBLE (England)
ST JOHN (Liberia, USA)
SALADO (Argentina, Cuba,
  Mexico)
SEVERN (England)
SUTLEJ (Pakistan, India,
  China)
THAMES (England)
TICJNO (Italy, Switzerland)
TIGRIS (Iraq, T urkey)
TUGELA (South Africa)
USSURI (China, Russia)
VIENNE (France)
VLTAVA (Czech / Slovakia)
WABASH (USA)
WEAVER (England)
YELLOW (China, USA,
  Papua New Guinea)

7
BERMEJO (Argentina)
CAUVERY (India)
DAMODAR (India)
DARLING (Australia)
DERWENT (England)
DURANCE (France)
GARONNE (France)
GIRONDE (France)
HELMAND (Afghanistan)
HOOGHLY (India)
HUANG HO (China)
LACHLAN (Australia)
LIMPOPO (South Africa,
  Zimbabwe, Mozambique)

LUALABA (Zaire)
MADEIRA (Brazil)
MARANON (Brazil, Peru)
MARITSA (Bulgaria)
MOSELLE (Germany)
ORONTES (Syria)
PECHORA (Russia)
POTOMAC (USA)
SALWEEN (Burma, China)
SCHELDT (Belgium)
SENEGAL (Senegal)
SHANNON (Eire)
SONGHUA (Vietnam, China)
SUNGARI (China)
SUWANNEE (USA)
URUGUAY (Uruguay, Brazil)
VISTULA (Poland)
WAIKATO (New Zealand)
XI JIANG (China)
YANGTZE (China)
YENISEI (Russia)
ZAMBEZI (Zambia, Angola,
  Zimbabwe, Mozambique)

8
AMU DARYA (Russia)
ARAGUAIA (Brazil)
ARKANSAS (USA)
CANADIAN (USA)
CHARENTE (France)
COLORADO (USA)
COLUMBIA (USA)
DEMERARA (Guyana)
DORDOGNE (France)
GODAVARI (India)
MANAWATU (New Zealand)
MENDERES (Turkey)
MISSOURI (USA)
PARAGUAY (Paraguay)
PUTUMAYO (Ecuador)
RIO BRAVO (Mexico)
SAGUENAY (Canada)
SYR DARYA (Russia)
TORRIDGE (England)
TUNGUSKA (Russia))
VOLTURNO (Italy)
WANSBECK (England)
WINDRUSH (England)

9
ATHABASCA (Canada)
CHURCHILL (Canada)
ESSEQUIBO (Guyana)

210

9 continued
EUPHRATES (Iraq)
GREAT OUSE (England)
HSI CHIANG (China)
IRRAWADDY (Burma)
MACKENZIE (Australia)
MAGDALENA (Colombia)
RIO GRANDE (Jamaica)
TENNESSEE (USA)
10
CHANG JIANG (China)
CHAO PHRAYA (Thailand)

COPPERMINE (Canada)
HAWKESBURY (Australia)
SHENANDOAH (USA)
ST LAWRENCE (USA)
11
ASSINIBOINE (Canada)
BRAHMAPUTRA (Tibet,
   India)
MISSISSIPPI (USA)
SHATT AL ARAB (Iran, Iraq)
SUSQUEHANNA (USA)
YELLOWSTONE (USA)

12
GUADALQUIVIR (Spain)
MURRUMBIDGEE
   (Australia)
RIO DE LA PLATA
   (Argentina, Uruguay)
SASKATCHEWAN (Canada)

MOUNTAINS AND HILLS

3
ASO (MT) (Japan)
IDA (MT) (Turkey)
4
ALPS (France, Switzerland,
   Italy, Austria)
BLUE (MTS) (Australia)
COOK (MT) (New Zealand)
ETNA (MT) (Sicily)
HARZ (MTS) (Germany)
JAYA (MT) (Indonesia) JURA
(MTS) (France,
Switzerland)
OSSA (MT)(Australia)
RIGI (Switzerland)
URAL (MTS) (Russia)
5
ALTAI (MTS) (Russia, China,
Mongolia)
ANDES (South America)
ATHOS (MT) (Greece)
ATLAS (MTS) (Morocco,
Algeria
BLACK (MTS) Wales
COAST (MTS) (Canada)
EIGER (Switzerland)
ELGON (MT) (Uganda,
   Kenya)
GHATS (India)
KAMET (MT) (India)
KENYA (MT) (Kenya)
LENIN (PEAK) (Russia)
LOGAN (MT) (Canada)
PELEE (MT) (Martinique)

ROCKY (MTS) (USA,
   Canada)
SAYAN (MTS) (Russia)
SNOWY (MTS) (Australia)
TATRA (MTS) (Poland,
   Czech, Slovakia)
WEALD (THE) (England)
6
ARARAT (MT) (Turkey)
BALKAN (MTS) (Bulgaria)
CARMEL (MT) (Israel)
EGMONT (MT) (New
   Zealand)
ELBERT (MT) (USA)
ELBRUS (MT) (Russia)
ELBURZ (MTS) (Russia)
EREBUS (MT) (Ross Island)
HERMON (MT) (Syria,
   Lebanon)
HOGGAR (MTS) (Algeria)
KUNLUN (MTS) (China)
LADAKH (RANGE) (India)
MATOPO (HILLS)
   (ZImbabwe)
MENDIP (HILLS) (Enghnd)
MOURNE (MTS)
   (Northem Ireland)
OLIVES (MT OF) (Israel)
PAMIRS (Russia, China,
   Afghanistan)
PINDUS (MTS) (Greece,
   Albania)
TAURUS (MTS) (Turkey)
VOSGES (France)

ZAGROS (MTS) (Iran)
7
AHAGGAR (MTS) (Algeria)
BERNINA (Switzerland)
BROCKEN (Germany)
CHEVIOT (HILLS) (United
   Kingdom)
CHIANTI (Italy)
EVEREST (MT) (Nepal,
   Tibet)
OLYMPUS (MT) (Greece)
PALOMAR (MT) (USA)
RAINIER (MT) (USA)
RORAIMA (MT) (Brazil,
   Guyana, Venezuela)
RUAPEHU) (MT) (NZealand)
SKIDDAW (England)
SNOWDON (Wales)
ST ELIAS (MTS) (Alaska,
   Yukon)
TIBESTI (MTS) (Chad,
   Libya)
8
ARDENNES (Luxembourg,
   Belgium, France)
BEN NEVIS (Scotland)
CAMBRIAN (MTS) (Wales)
CAUCASUS (MTS) (Russia)
CEVENNES (France)
CHILTERN (HILLS)
   (England)
COTOPAXI (Ecuador)
COTSWOLD (HILLS)
   (England)

211

MOUNTAINS

8 continued
FLINDERS (RANGE)
  Australia)
FUJIYAMA (Japan)
HYMETTUS (MT) (Greece)
JUNGFRAU (Switzerland)
KAIKOURA (RANGES) (New
  Zealand)
MUSGRAVE (RANGES)
  (Australia)
PENNINES (England)
PYRENEES (France, Spain)
STANOVOI (RANGE)
  (Russia)
TIAN SHAN (Russia, China,
Mongolia)
VESUVIUS (Italy)
9
ACONCAGUA (MT)
  (Argentina)
ALLEGHENY (MTS) (USA)
ANNAPURNA (MT) (Nepal)
APENNINES (Italy)
CAIRNGORM (MTS)
  (Scotland)
DOLOMITES (Italy)
DUNSINANE (Scotland)
GRAMPIANS (Scotland)
HAMERSLEY (RANGE)
  (Australia)
HELVELLYN (England)
HIMALAYAS (S. Asia)
HINDU KUSH (Central Asia)
HUASCARAN (Peru)
KARAKORAM (RANGE)
  (China, Pakistan, India)
KOSCIUSKO (MT)
  (Australia)
MONT BLANC
  (France, Italy)
NANDA DEVI (MT) (India)
PACARAIMA (MTS) (Brazil,
  Venezuela, Guyana)
PARNASSUS (MT) (Greece)

RUWENZORI (MTS)
  (Uganda, Zaire)
TIRICH MIR (MT) (Pakistan)
ZUGSPITZE (Germany)
10
ADIRONDACK (MTS) (USA)
CADER IDRIS (Wales)
CANTABRIAN (MTS) (Spain)
CARPATHIAN (MTS)
  (Czech, Slovakia, Poland,
Romania, Russia)
CHIMBORAZO (MT) (India)
DHAULAGIRI (MT) (Nepal)
ERZGEBIRGE
  (Czech, Slovakia,
  Germany)
KEBNEKAISE (Sweden)
LAMMERMUIR (HILLS)
  (Scotland)
MACDONNELL (RANGES)
  (Australia)
MAJUBA HILL (South Africa)
MATTERHORN (Switzerland,
  Italy)
MIDDLEBACK (RANGE)
  (Australia)
MONTSERRAT (Spain)
MOUNT LOFTY (RANGES)
  (Australia)
11
ANTI-LEBANON MTS
  (Lebanon, Syria)
APPALACHIAN (MTS) (USA)
DRAKENSBERG (MTS)
  (South Africa)
JOTUNHEIMEN (Norway)
KILIMANJARO (MT)
  (Tanzania)
MONADHLIATH (MTS)
  (Scotland)
NANGA PARBAT (MT)
  (Pakistan)
SCAFELL PIKE) (England)
SIERRA MADRE (Mexico)

12
CITLALTEPETL (Mexico)
GODWIN AUSTEN (MT)
  (Pakistan)
GOLAN HEIGHTS (Syria)
GRAN PARADISO (Italy)
INGLEBOROUGH (England)
KANCHENJUNGA (MT)
  (Nepal)
PEAK DISTRICT (England)
POPOCATEPETL (MT)
  (Mexico)
SIDING SPRING (MT)
  (Australia)
SIERRA MORENA (Spain)
SIERRA NEVADA (Spain,
USA)
WARRUMBUNGLE
  (RANGE) (Australia)
13
CARRANTUOHILL (Ireland)
COMMUNISM PEAK
  (Russia)
GROSSGLOCKNER
  (Austria)
KANGCHENJUNGA (MT)
  (Nepal)
KOMMUNIZMA PIK (Russia)
OJOS DEI SALADO
  (Argentina, Chile)
SIERRA MAESTRA (Cuba)
14
BERNESE OBERLAND
  (Switzerland)
FICHTELGEBIRGE
  (Germany)
FINSTERAARHORN
  (Switzerland)
MACGILLICUDDY'S REEKS
  (Ireland)
SHIRE HIGHLANDS
  (Malawi)

VOLCANOES

3
ASO (Japan)
AWU (Indonesia)
4
ETNA (Sicily)
FOGO (Cape Verde Islands)
GEDE (Indonesia)
KABA (Indonesia)
LAKI (Iceland)
NILA (Indonesia)
POAS (Costa Rica)
SIAU (Indonesia)
TAAL (Philippines)
5
AGUNG (Indonesia)
ASAMA (Japan)
ASKJA (Iceland)
DEMPO (Indonesia)
FUEGO (Guatemala)
HEKLA (Iceland)
KATLA (Iceland)
MANAM (Bismarck
  Archipelago)
MAYON (Philippines)
NOYOE (Iceland)
OKMOK (USA)
PALOE (Indonesia)
PELEE (W. Indies)
SPURR (USA)
6
ALCEDO (Galapagos
  Islands)
AMBRIM (Vanuatu Republic)
BIG BEN (Heard Island)
BULENG (Indonesia)
COLIMA (Mexico)
DUKONO (Indonesia)
IZALCO (El Salvador)
KATMAI (USA)
LASCAR (Chile)
LASSEN (USA)
LLAIMA (Chile)
LOPEVI (Vanuatu Republic)
MARAPI (Indonesia)
MARTIN (USA)
MEAKAN) (Japan)
MERAPI (Indonesia)
MIHARA (Japan)
O'SHIMA (Japan)

OSORNO (Chile)
PACAYA (Guatemala)
PAVLOF (USA)
PURACE (Colombia)
SANGAY(Ecuador)
SEMERU (Indonesia)
SLAMAT (Indonesia)
TACANA (Guatemala
UNAUNA (Indonesia)
7
ATITLAN (Guatemala)
BARCENA (Mexico)
BULUSAN (Philippines)
DIDICAS (Philippines)
EL MSTI (Peru)
GALERAS (Colombia)
JORULLO (Mexico)
KILAUEA (USA)
OMETEPE (Nicaragua)
PUYEHUE (Chile)
RUAPEHU (New Zealand)
SABRINA (Azores)
SOPUTAN (Indonesia)
SURTSEY (Iceland)
TERNATE (Indonesia)
TJAREME (Indonesia)
TOKACHI (Japan)
TORBERT(USA)
TRIDENT (USA)
VULCANO (Italy)
8
BOGOSLOF (USA)
CAMEROON (Cameroon)
COTOPAXI (Ecuador)
DEMAVEND (Iran)
FONUALEI (Tonga Islands)
FUJIYAMA (Japan)
HUALALAI (USA)
KERINTJI (Indonesia)
KRAKATAU (Indonesia)
KRAKATAU (Indonesia)
MAUNA LOA (USA)
NIUAFO'OU (Tonga Islands)
RINDJANI (Indonesla)
SANGEANG (Indonesla)
TARAWERA (New Zealand)
VESUVIUS (Italy)
YAKEDAKE (Japan)

9
AMBUROMBU (Indonesia)
BANDAI-SAN (Japan)
CLEVELAND (USA)
COSEGUINA (Nicuagua)
COTACACHI (Ecuador)
GAMKONORA (Indonesia)
GRIMSVOTN (Iceland)
KORYAKSKY (Russia)
MOMOTOMBO (Nicaragua)
MYOZIN-SYO (Japan)
NGAURUHOE (New
  Zealand)
PARICUTIN (Mexico)
RININAHUE (Chile)
SANTORINI (Greece)
STROMBOLI (Italy)
TONGARIRO (New Zealand)
10
ACATENANGO (Guatemala)
CAPELINHOS (Azores)
CERRO NEGRO
  (Nicaragua)
GUALLATIRI (Chile)
HIBOK HIBOK (Philippines)
ICHINSKAYA (Russia)
LONG ISLAND (Bismarck
  Archipelago)
MIYAKEJIMA (Japan)
NYAMIAGIRA (Zaire)
NYIRAGONGO (Zaire)
SANTA MARIA (Guatemala)
SHISHALDIN (USA)
TUNGURAHUA (Ecuador)
VILLARRICA (Chile)
11
GREAT SITKIN (USA)
KILIMANJARO (Tanzania)
LA SOUFRIERE (W. Indies)
TUPUNGATITO (Chile)
WHITE ISLAND (NZealand)
12
HUAINAPUTINA (Peru)
POPOCATAPETL (Mexico)
SARYCHEV PEAK (Russia)
13
KLYUCHEVSKAYA (Russia)

DESERTS

DESERTS

4
GILA
GOBI
THAR
5
NAMIB
NEFUD
NEGEV
OLMOS
ORDOS
SINAI
STURT
6
ARUNTA
GIBSON
MOJAVE
NUBIAN
SAHARA
SYRIAN
UST-URT

7
ALASHAN
ARABIAN
ATACAMA
KARA KUM
MORROPE
PAINTED
SECHURA
SIMPSON
8
COLORADO
KALAHARI
KYZYL KUM
MUYUNKUM
VIZCAINO
9
BLACK ROCK
DASHT-I-LUT
DZUNGARIA

10
AUSTRALIAN
BET-PAK-DALA
GREAT SANDY
PATAGONIAN
RUB'AL KHALI
11
DASHT-I-KAVIR
DASHT-I-MARGO
DEATH VALLEY
13
GREAT SALT LAKE
GREAT VICTORIA
14
BOLSON DE MAPIMI
16
TURFAN DEPRESSION

SCIENCE AND MEASUREMENT

WEIGHTS AND MEASURES

2	GRAM	MINIM	DECIBEL
CC	HAND	NEPER	DIOPTER
CM	HIDE	OUNCE	FARADAY
FT	HOUR	PERCH	FURLONG
GR	INCH	POINT	GILBERT
HL	KILO	POISE	HECTARE
IN	KNOT	POUND	KILOBAR
KG	LINE	QUART	KILOTON
KM	LINK	QUIRE	LAMBERT
LB	MILE	STADE	MAXWELL
MG	MOLE	STERE	MEGATON
ML	NAIL	STILB	OERSTED
MM	PECK	STOKE	POUNDAL
0Z	PHON	STONE	QUARTER
YD	PHOT	TESLA	QUINTAL
3	PICA	THERM	RONTGEN
AMP	PINT	TOISE	SCRUPLE
ARE	PIPE	TONNE	SIEMENS
BAR	POLE	WEBER	8
BEL	REAM	6	ANGSTROM
BIT	ROOD	AMPERE	CHALDRON
CWT	SLUG	BARREL	HOGSHEAD
DWT	SPAN	BUSHEL	KILOGRAM
ELL	TORR	CANDLE	KILOWATT
ERG	TROY	CENTAL	QUADRANT
LUX	VOLT	DEGREE	MEGAWATT
MHO	WATT	DENIER	MICROOHM
MIL	YARD	DRACHM	WATT-HOUR
MIM	5	FATHOM	9
NIT	CABLE	FIRKIN	BOARD-FOOT
OHM	CARAT	GALLON	CENTIGRAM
RAD	CHAIN	GRAMME	CUBIC FOOT
REM	CRITH	KELVIN	CUBIC INCH
ROD	CUBIT	LEAGUE	CUBIC YARD
TON	CURIE	MEGOHM	DECALITRE
TUN	CUSEC	MICRON	DECAMETRE
4	CYCLE	MINUTE	DECILITRE
ACRE	DEBYE	NEWTON	DECIMETRE
BALE	FARAD	PARSEC	FOOT-POUND
BARN	FERMI	PASCAL	HECTOGRAM
BOLT	GAUGE	RADIAN	KILOCYCLE
BYTE	GAUSS	REAMUR	KILOHERTZ
CASK	GRAIN	SECOND	KILOLITRE
CORD	HENRY	STOKES	KILOMETRE
CRAN	HERTZ	7	LIGHT-YEAR
DRAM	JOULE	CALORIE	MEGACYCLE
DYNE	LITRE	CANDELA	MEGAFARAD
FOOT	LUMEN	CENTNER	MEGAHERTZ
GILL	METRE	COULOMB	METRIC TON

WEIGHTS AND MEASURES

9 continued	10+		RUTHERFORD
MICROGRAM	BARLEYCORN	HORSEPOWER	SQUARE
MICROWATT	CENTILITRE	HUNDREDWEIGHT	CENTIMETRE
MILLIGRAM	CENTIMETRE	KILOGRAMME	SQUARE INCH
NANOMETRE	CUBIC METRE	MICROFARAD	SQUARE
SCANTLING	DECAGRAMME	MILLILITRE	KILOMETRE
STERADIAN	DECIGRAMME	MILLIMETRE	SQUARE MILE
	FLUID OUNCE	MILLISTERES	SQUARE YARD
	HECTOLITRE	NANOSECOND	
		PENNYWEIGHT	

PAPER MEASURES

4	QUIRE	FOOLSCAP	SUPER ROYAL
BALE	ROYAL	HAVEN CAP	11
COPY	6	IMPERIAL	ANTIQUARIAN
DEMY	BAG CAP	9	IMPERIAL CAP
POST	BUNDLE	CARTRIDGE	PINCHED POST
POTT	CASING	COLOMBIER	14
REAM	MEDIUM	LARGE POST	DOUBLE
5	7	MUSIC DEMY	ELEPHANT
ATLAS	EMPEROR	10	15
BRIEF	KENT CAP	DOUBLE DEMY	DOUBLE LARGE
CROWN	8	DOUBLE POST	POST
DRAFT	ELEPHANT	GRAND EAGLE	

ELEMENTARY PARTICLES

2	GLUON	7	12
XI	MESON	FERMION	ANTIPARTICLE
3	OMEGA	HYPERON	BETA PARTICLE
ETA	QUARK	NEUTRON	13
PHI	SIGMA	TACHYON	ALPHA PARTICLE
PSI	6	DEUTERON	
4	BARYON	ELECTRON	
KAON	HADRON	GRAVITON	
MUON	LAMBDA	NEUTRINO	
PION	LEPTON	POSITRON	
5	PHOTON	9	
BOSON	PROTON	NEUTRETTO	

THE CHEMICAL ELEMENTS

ACTINIUM (AC)	BISMUTH (BI)	CHROMIUM (CR)	FLUORINE (F)
ALUMINIUM (AL)	BORON (B)	COBALT(CO)	FRANCIUM (FR)
AMERICIUM (AM)	BROMINE (BR)	COLUMBIUM (CB)	GADOLINIUM (GD)
ANTIMONY (SB)	CADMIUM (CD)	COPPER (CU)	GALLIUM (GA)
ARGON (AR)	CAESIUM (CS)	CURMIUM (CM)	GERMANIUM (GE)
ARSENIC (AS)	CALCIUM (CA)	DYSPROSIUM (DY)	GOLD(AU)
ASTATINE (AT)	CALIFORNIUM (CF)	EINSTEINIUM (ES)	HAFNIUM (HF)
BARIUM (BA)	CARBON(C)	ERBIUM (ER)	HELIUM (HE)
BERKELIUM (BK)	CERIUM (CE)	EUROPIUM (EU)	HOLMIUM (HO)
BERYLLIUM (BE)	CHLORINE (CL)	FERMIUM (FM)	HYDROGEN (H)

INDIUM (IN)
IODINE (I)
IRIDIUM (IR)
IRON (FE)
KRYPTON(KR)
LANTHANUM (LA)
LAWRENCIUM (LR)
LEAD (PB)
LITHIUM (LI)
LUTETIUM (LU)
MAGNESIUM (MG)
MANGANESE (MN)
MENDELEVIUM
 (MD)
MERCURY (HG)
MOLYBDENUM
 (MO)
NEODYMIUM (ND)
NEON (NE)

NEPTUNIUM (NP)
NICKEL (NI)
NIOBIUM (NB)
NITROGEN (N)
NOBELIUM (NO)
OSMIUM (OS)
OXYGEN(O)
PALLADIUM (PD)
PHOSPHORUS(P)
PLATINUM (PT)
PLUTONIUM (PU)
POLONIUM (PO)
POTASSIUM (K)
PRASEODYMIUM
 (PR)
PROMETHIUM (PM)
PROTACTINIUM
 (PA)
RADIUM (RA)

RADON(RN)
RHENIUM (RE)
RHODIUM (RH)
RUBIDIUM (RB)
RUTHENIUM (RU)
SAMARIUM (SM)
SCANDIUM (SC)
SELENIUM (SE)
SILICON (SI)
SILVER (AG)
SODIUM (NA)
STRONTIUM (SR)
SULPHUR (S)
TANTALUM(TA)
TECHNETIUM (TC)
TELLURIUM (TE)
TERBIUM (TB)
THALLIUM (TL)
THORIUM (TH).

THULIUM (TM)
TIN (SN)
TITANIUM (TI)
TUNGSTEN (W)
URANIUM (U)
VANADIUM (V)
WOLFRAM (W)
XENON (XE)
YTTERBIUM (YB)
YTTRIUM (Y)
ZINC (ZN)
ZIRCONIUM (ZR)

ALLOYS

4
ALNI - iron, nickel, aluminium, copper
BETA -titanium, aluminium, vanadium, chromium
5
ALPHA - titanium, aluminium, tin, copper, zirconium, niobium, molybdenum
BRASS - copper, zinc
INVAR - iron, nickel
MAZAC - zinc, aluminium, magnesium, copper
MONEL - nickel, cobalt, iron
STEEL - iron, carbon
6
ALNICO - aluminium, nickel, cobalt
BABBIT - tin, lead, antimony, copper
BRONZE - copper, tin
CUNICO - iron, cobalt, copper, nickel
CUNIFE - iron, cobalt, nickel
FEROBA - iron, barium oxide, ironoxide
PEWTER - tin, lead
SOLDER - lead, tin (soft), copper, zinc (brazing)
7
ALCOMAX - aluminium, cobalt, nickel, copper, lead, niobium
ALUMNEL - aluminium, chromium
AMALGAM - mercury, various
CHROMEL - nickel, chromium

COLUMAN - iron, chromium, nickel, aluminium, nobium, copper
ELINVAR - iron, nickel, chromium, tungsten
INCONEL - nickel, chromium, iron
KANTHAL - chromium, aluminium, iron
MUMETAL - iron, nickel, copper, chromium
NIMONIC - nickel, chromium, iron, titanium, aluminium, manganese, silicon
8
CAST IRON - carbon, iron
DOWMETAL - magnesium, aluminium, zinc, manganese
GUNMETAL - copper, tin, zinc
HIPERNIK - nickel, iron
KIRKSITE - zinc, aluminium, copper
MANGANIN - copper, manganese, nickel
NICHROME - nickel, iron, chromium
VICALLOY - iron, cobalt, vanadium
ZIRCALOY - zirconium, tin, iron, nickel, chromium
9
DURALUMIN - alurninium, copper, silicon, magnesium, manganese, zinc
HASTELLOY - nickel, molybdenum, iron, chromium, cobalt, tungsten
PERMALLOY - nickel, iron
PERMINVAR - nickel, iron, cobalt
TYPE METAL - lead, tin, antimony

ALLOYS / GEOMETRIC FIGURES & CURVES

10
CONSTANTAN - copper, nickel
MISCH METAL - cerium, various
MUNTZ METAL - copper, zinc
ROSE'S METAL - bismuth, lead, tin
SUPERALLOY - type of stainless steel
WOOD'S METAL - lead, tin, bismuth,
 cadmium
11
CUPRONICKEL - copper, nickel
ELECTROTYPE - lead, tin, antimony
SUPERMALLOY - iron, nickel
SUPERMENDUR - iron, cobalt
12
FERROSILICON - iron, silicon

GERMAN SILVER - copper, nickel, zinc, lead,
 tin
SILVER SOLDER - copper, silver, zinc
13
FERROCHROMIUM - iron, chromium
FERROTUNGSTEN - iron, tungsten
FERROVANADIUM - iron, vanadium
14
ADMIRALTY METAL - copper, zinc
BRITANNIA METAL - tin, antimony, copper
FERROMANGANESE - iron, manganese
PHOSPHOR BRONZE - copper, tin,
 phosphorus
STAINLESS STEEL - iron, chromium,
 vanadium

GEOMETRIC FIGURES AND CURVES

3	NORMAL	CONCHOID	PENTAGRAM
ARC	OCTANT	CONICOID	PENTANGLE
4	PENCIL	CYLINDER	RHUMB LINE
CONE	RADIUS	ENVELOPE	SINE CURVE
CUBE	SECTOR	EPICYCLE	STROPHOID
KITE	SPHERE	EXCIRCLE	TRAPEZIUM
LINE	SPIRAL	FRUSTRUM	TRAPEZOID
LOOP	SPLINE	GEODESIC	**10**
LUNE	SQUARE	HEPTAGON	ACUTE ANGLE
OVAL	**7**	INCIRCLE	ANCHOR RING
ROSE	ANNULUS	INVOLUTE	CYLINDROID
ZONE	CISSOID	PARABOLA	EPICYCLOID
5	CYCLOID	PENTAGON	HEMISPHERE
CHORD	DECAGON	PRISMOID	HEXAHEDRON
CONIC	ELLIPSE	QUADRANT	KAPPA CURVE
HELIX	EVOLUTE	RHOMBOID	LEMNISCATE
LOCUS	FRACTAL	ROULETTE	OCTAHEDRON
NAPPE	HEXAGON	SPHEROID	PARABOLOID
OGIVE	LIMACON	TRACTRIX	PEANO CURVE
PLANE	OCTAGON	TRIANGLE	POLYHEDRON
PRISM	PERIGON	TROCHOID	PRISMATOID
RHOMB	POLYGON	**9**	QUADRANGLE
SHEET	PYRAMID	ANTIPRISM	QUADREFOIL
SOLID	RHOMBUS	CRUCIFORM	RIGHT ANGLE
TORUS	SEGMENT	DIRECTRIX	SEMICIRCLE
WEDGE	SURFACE	DODECAGON	SERPENTINE
WITCH	TANGENT	ELLIPSOID	TRISECTRIX
6	TREFOIL	HYPERBOLA	**11**
CIRCLE	TRIDENT	ISOCHRONE	CORNU SPIRAL
CONOID	**8**	KOCH CURVE	EPITROCHOID
FOLIUM	CATENARY	LOXODROME	HEPTAHEDRON
LAMINA	CATENOID	MULTIFOIL	HYPERBOLOID

220

GEOMETRIC FIGURES / PLANET / COMETS

11 continued
HYPOCYCLOID
ICOSAHEDRON
KLEIN BOTTLE
LATUS RECTUM
MOBIUS STRIP
OBTUSE ANGLE
PENTAHEDRON
REFLEX ANGLE
TAUTOCHRONE

TETRAHEDRON
12
HYPOTROCHOID
PSEUDOSPHERE
RHOMBOHEDRON
SIGMOID CURVE
13
CIRCUMFERENCE
CUBOCTAHEDRON
PARALLELOGRAM

PARALLELOTOPE
PEDAL TRIANGLE
PERPENDICULAR
QUADRILATERAL
14
SNOWFLAKE
 CURVE
15
BRACHIS-
 TOCHRONE

SCALENE
 TRIANGLE
17
ICOSIDODECA
 HEDRON
ISOSCELES
 TRIANGLE
19
EQUILATERAL
 TRIANGLE

PLANETS AND SATELLITES

MAIN PLANETS (NAMED SATELLITES)
MERCURY
VENUS
EARTH (MOON)
MARS (PHOBOS, DEIMOS)
JUPITER (METIS, ADRASTEA, AMALTHEA,
 THEBE, IO, EUROPA, GANYMEDE,
 CALLISTO, LEDA, MILALIA, LYSITHEA,
 ELARA, ANANKE, CARME, PASIPHAE,
 SINOPE)
SATURN (MIMAS, ENCELADUS, TETHYS,
 DIONE, RHEA, TITAN, HYPERION,
 IAPETUS, PHOEBE, JANUS)
URANUS (MIRANDA, ARIEL, UMBRIEL,
TITANIA, OBERON)
NEPTUNE (TRITON, NEREID)
PLUTO (CHARON)

MINOR PLANETS
ACHILLES
ADONIS
AMOR
APOLLO
ASTRAEA
ATEN
CERES
CHIRON
EROS
EUNOMIA
EUPHROSYNE
HEBE
HERMES
HIDALGO
HYGIEA
ICARUS
IRIS
JUNO
PALLAS
VESTA

COMETS

4
FAYE
5
BIELA
ENCKE
KOPFF
6
HALLEY
OLBERS
TUTTLE
7
BENNETT
D'ARREST
VAISALA

WHIPPLE
8
BORRELLY
DAYLIGHT KOHOUTEK
WESTIPHAL
9
COMAS SOLA
CROMMELIN
10
PONS-BROOKS
SCHAUMASSE
11
AREND-ROLAND

12
PONS-WINNECKE
13
STEPHAN-OTERMA
14
BRONSEN-METCALF
15
GIACOBINI-ZINNER
GRIGG-SKIELLERUP

NEAREST AND BRIGHTEST STARS

4	ALTAIR	LALANDE	BELLATRIX
ROSS	CASTOR	PROCYON	FOMALHAUT
VEGA	CRUCIS	REGULUS	**10+**
WOLF	KRUGER	TAU CETI	BETELGEUSE
5	LUYTEN	**8**	EPSILON INDI
CYGNI	POLLUX	ACHERNAR	ALPHA CENTAURI
DENEB	SHAULA	ARCTURUS	EPSILON ERIDANI
RIGEL	SIRIUS	BARNARD'S	PROXIMA
SIRUS	**7**	CENTAURI	CENTAURI
SPICA	ANTARES	KAPTEYN'S	
6	CANOPUS	**9**	
ADHARA	CAPELLA	ALDEBARAN	

THE CONSTELLATIONS

3	CARINA	SCORPIUS
ARA	CORVUS	SCULPTOR
LEO	CRATER	**9**
4	CYGNUS	ANDROMEDA
APUS	DORADO	CENTAURUS
CRUX	FORNAX	CHAMELEON
GRUS	GEMINI	DELPHINUS
LYNX	HYDRUS	MONOCEROS
LYRA	OCTANS	OPHIUCHUS
PAVO	PICTOR	RETICULUM
VELA	PISCES	URSA MAJOR
5	PUPPIS	URSA MINOR
ARIES	SCUTUM	VULPECULA
CETUS	TAURUS	**10**
DRACO	TUCANA	CANIS MAJOR
HYDRA	VOLANS	CANIS MINOR
INDUS	**7**	CASSIOPEIA
LEPUS	CEPHEUS	HOROLOGIUM
LIBRA	COLUMBA	TRIANGULUM
LUPUS	LACERTA	**11**
MENSA	PEGASUS	CAPRICORNUS
MUSCA	PERSEUS	SAGITTARIUS
NORMA	PHOENIX	TELESCOPIUM
ORION	SAGITTA	**12+**
PYXIS	SERPENS	CAMELOPARDALIS
VIRGO	SEXTANS	CANES VENATICI
6	**8**	COMA BERENICES
ANTLIA	AQUARIUS	CORONA AUSTRALIS
AQUILA	CIRCINUS	CORONA BOREALIS
AURIGA	EQUULEUS	MICROSCOPIUM
BOOTES	ERIDANUS	PISCIS AUSTRINUS
CAELUM	HERCULES	TRIANGULUM
CANCER	LEO MINOR	AUSTRALE

222

METEOR SHOWERS

6	8	OPHIUCHIDS
LYRIDS	CEPHEIDS	PHOENICIDS
URSIDS	GEMINIDS	11
7	ORIONIDS	QUADRANTIDS
CYGNIDS	PERSEIDS	12
LEONIDS	10	CAPRICORNIDS
TAURIDS	AUSTRALIDS	

ASTRONOMERS ROYAL

JOHN FLAMSTEED (1675–1719)
EDMUND HALLEY (1720–42)
JAMES BRADLEY (1742–62)
NATHANIEL BLISS (1762–64)
NEVIL MASKELYNE (1765–1811)
JOHN POND (1811–35)
SIR GEORGE SIDDELL AIRY (1835–81)

SIR WILLIAM H.M. CHRISTIE (1881–1910)
SIR FRANK WATSON DYSON (1910–33)
SIR HAROLD SPENCER JONES (1933–55)
SIR RICHARD WOOLLEY (1955–71)
SIR MARTIN RYLE (1972–82)
PROF. E. GRAHAM SMITH (1982–

GEOLOGICAL TIME SCALE

CENOZOIC		HOLOCENE
	QUATERNARY	PLEISTOCENE
		PLIOCENE
	TERTIARY	MIOCENE
		OLIGOCENE
		EOCENE
		PALAEOCENE
MESOZOIC	CRETACEOUS	
	JURASSIC	
	TRIASSIC	
PALAEOZOIC	PERMIAN	
	CARBONIFEROUS	
	DEVONIAN	
	SILURIAN	
	ORDOVICIAN	
	CAMBRIAN	
PRECAMBRIAN	PRECAMBRIAN	

CLOUDS

ALTOCUMULUS	CUMULONIMBUS
ALTOSTRATUS	CUMULUS
CIRROCUMULUS	NIMBOSTRATUS
CIRROSTRATUS	STRATOCUMULUS
CIRRUS	STRATUS

PREHISTORIC ANIMALS

8
EOHIPPUS
RUTIODON
SMILODON
9
IGUANODON
TRACHODON
10
ALLOSAURUS
ALTISPINAX
BAROSAURUS
DIPLODOCUS
DRYOSAURUS
EUPARKERIA
MESOHIPPUS
ORTHOMERUS
PLIOHIPPUS
PTERANODON
STEGOCERAS
11
ANATOSAURUS
ANCHISAURUS
APATOSAURUS
APHANERAMMA
CETIOSAURUS
COELOPHYSIS
DEINONYCHUS
KRITOSAURUS
MANDASUCHUS
MERYCHIPPUS
MONOCLONIUS

POLACANTHUS
PTERODACTYL
RIOJASAURUS
SAUROLOPHUS
SCOLOSAURUS
SPINOSAURUS
STEGOSAURUS
TARBOSAURUS
TRICERATOPS
12
ANKYLOSAURUS
BRONTOSAURUS
CAMPTOSAURUS
CERATOSAURUS
CHASMOSAURUS
DEINOCHEIRUS
HYLAEOSAURUS
KENTROSAURUS
LAMBEOSAURUS
MEGALOSAURUS
ORNITHOMIMUS
OURANOSAURUS
PLATEOSAURUS
TICINOSUCHUS
13
BRACHIOSAURUS
COMPSOGNATHUS
CORYTHOSAURUS
DESMATOSUCHUS
DILOPHOSAURUS
EDMONTOSAURUS

ERYTHROSUCHUS
HYPSELOSAURUS
HYPSILOPHODON
LESOTHOSAURUS
PANOPLOSAURUS
PENTACERATOPS
PROTOCERATOPS
PTERODACTYLUS
SCELIDOSAURUS
SCLEROMOCHLUS
STYRACOSAURUS
TENONTOSAURUS
TYRANNOSAURUS
14
BALUCHITHERIUM
CETIOSAURISCUS
CHASMATOSAURUS
EUOPLOCEPHALUS
MASSOSPONDYLUS
PSITTACOSAURUS
THESCELOSAURUS
15
PARASAUROLOPHUS
PROCHENEOSAURUS
16
PACHYRHINOSAURUS
PROCOMPSOGNATHUS
17
HETERODONTOSAURUS
18
PACHYCEPHALOSAURUS

ROCKS AND MINERALS

4
GOLD
MICA
OPAL
RUBY
TALC
5
AGATE
BERYL
BORAX
EMERY
FLINT
SHALE
SHARD

SKARN
TOPAZ
TRONA
6
ACMITE
ALBITE
ARKOSE
AUGITE
BARITE
BASALT
COPPER
DACITE
DUNITE
GABBRO

GALENA
GARNET
GNEISS
GYPSUM
HALITE
HAUYNE
HUMITE
ILLITE
LEVYNE
MINIUM
NORITE
NOSEAN
PELITE
PYRITE

PYROPE
QUARTZ
RUTILE
SALITE
SCHIST
SCHORL
SILICA
SILVER
SPHENE
SPINEL
URTITE
ZIRCON

7
ALNOITE
ALTAITE
ALUNITE
ANATASE
APATITE
ARSENIC
AXINITE
AZURITE
BARYTES
BAUXITE
BIOTITE
BISMUTH
BORNITE
BRECCIA
BRUCITE
CALCITE
CALOMEL
CELSIAN
CITRINE
COESITE
CUPRITE
DIAMOND
DIORITE
EMERALD
EPIDOTE
FELSITE
GAHNITE
GEDRITE
GRANITE
GUMMITE
HELVITE
HESSITE
HOPEITE
HUNTITE
IJOLITE
JADEITE
KAINITE
KERNITE
LEUCITE
LIGNITE
MELLITE
MULLITE
OLIVINE
ORTHITE
RASPITE
REALGAR
SPARITE
SYENITE
SYLVITE
THORITE

THULITE
ZEOLITE
ZINCITE
ZOISITE
8
AEGIRINE
ALLANITE
ALUNOGEN
ANALCIME
ANALCITE
ANDESINE
ANDORITE
ANKERITE
ANTIMONY
ARCANITE
AUGELITE
AUTUNITE
BASANITE
BIXBYITE
BLOEDITE
BLUE JOHN
BOEHMITE
BORACITE
BRAGGITE
BRAUNITE
BRAVOITE
BRONZITE
BROOKITE
CALAMINE
CHIOLITE
CHLORITE
CHROMITE
CINNABAR
CORUNDUM
CROCOITE
CRYOLITE
CUBANITE
DATOLITE
DIALLAGE
DIASPORE
DIGENITE
DIOPSIDE
DIOPTASE
DOLERITE
DOLOMITE
ECLOGITE
ENARGITE
EPSOMITE
ESSEXITE
EULYTITE
EUXENITE

FAYALITE
FELDSPAR
FLUORITE
GIBBSITE
GOETHITE
GRAPHITE
HANKSITE
HAWAIITE
HEMATITE
HYACINTH
IDOCRASE
ILMENITE
IODYRITE
JAROSITE
LAZURITE
LIMONITE
LITHARGE
MARSHITE
MEIONITE
MELANITE
MELILITE
MESOLITE
MIERSITE
MIMETITE
MONAZITE
MONETITE
MYLONITE
NEPHRITE
ORPIMENT
PARISITE
PERIDOTE
PERTHITE
PETALITE
PLATINUM
PORPHYRY
PREHNITE
PSAMMITE
PYRIBOLE
PYROXENE
RHYOLITE
ROCKSALT
SANIDINE
SAPPHIRE
SELLAITE
SIDERITE
SMECTITE
SODALITE
STANNITE
STEATITE
STIBNITE
STILBITE

STOLSITE
STRUVITE
TITANITE
TONALITE
TRACHYTE
VARISITE
VATERITE
WEHRLITE
WURTZITE
XENOTIME
9
ACANTHITE
ALMANDINE
ALUMINITE
AMPHIBOLE
ANDRADITE
ANGLESITE
ANHYDRITE
ANORTHITE
ARAGONITE
ARGENTITE
ATACAMITE
BENITOITE
BRIMSTONE
BROMYRITE
BUNSENITE
BYTOWNITE
CARNALITE
CARNOTITE
CELESTITE
CERUSSITE
CHABAZITE
CHINACLAY
COBALTITE
COLUMBITE
COPIAPITE
COTUNNITE
COVELLITE
DANBURITE
DERBYLITE
DIATOMITE
ENSTATITE
ERYTHRITE
EUCAIRITE
EUCLASITE
EUDIALITE
FERBERITE
FIBROLITE
FLUORSPAR
GEHIENITE
GMELINITE

ROCKS AND MINERALS

9 continued
GOSLARITE
GRANULITE
GREYWACKE
GROSSULAR
GRUNERITE
HARMOTOME
HERCYNITE
HERDERITE
HORNSTONE
KAOLINITE
KIESERITE
LANARKITE
LAWSONITE
LEUCITITE
LIMESTONE
LODESTONE
MAGNESITE
MAGNETITE
MALACHITE
MALIGNITE
MANGANITE
MARCASITE
MARGARITE
MARIALITE
MENDIPITE
MICROLITE
MIGMATITE
MILLERITE
MISPICKEL
MONZONITE
MORDENITE
MUGEARITE
MUSCOVITE
NANTOKITE
NATROLITE
NEPHELINE
NICCOLITE
OLDHAMITE
OLIVENITE
PECTOLITE
PENNINITE
PERCYLITE
PERICLASE
PHENAKITE
PHONOLITE
PIGEONITE
PISTACITE
POLLUCITE
POWELLITE
PROUSTITE

PULASKITE
QUARTZITE
RHODONITE
SANDSTONE
SCAPOLITE
SCHEELITE
SCOLECITE
SCORODITE
SMALLTITE
SOAPSTONE
SPODUMENE
STRENGITE
SYLVANITE
TACHYLITE
TANTALITE
TAPIOLITE
THERALITE
THOLEIITE
TREMOLITE
TRIDYMITE
TURQUOISE
URANINITE
VIVIANITE
WAGNERITE
WAVELLITE
WILLEMITE
WITHERITE
WULFENITE
ZEUNERITE
10
ACTINOLITE
AKERMANITE
ALABANDITE
ANDALUSITE
ANKARAMITE
ARSENOLITE
BOROLONITE
BOURNONITE
BRONZITITE
CACOXENITE
CALEDONITE
CANCRINITE
CERVANTITE
CHALCEDONY
CHALCOCITE
CHLORITOID
CHRYSOLITE
CLAUDETITE
CLINTONITE
COLEMANITE
CONNELLITE

COQUIMBITE
CORDIERITE
DOUGLASITE
DYSCRASITE
EMPLECTITE
EMPRESSITE
EPIDIORITE
FORSTERITE
GANOMALITE
GARNIERITE
GAYLUSSITE
GEIKIELITE
GLAUBERITE
GLAUCONITE
GREENSTONE
HAMBERGITE
HEULANDITE
HORNBLENDE
HUEBNERITE
IGNIMBRITE
JAMESONITE
KIMBERLITE
LANTHANITE
LAUMONTITE
LAURIONITE
LEPIDOLITE
LHERZOLITE
LIMBURGITE
MASCAGNITE
MATLOCKITE
MEERSCHAUM
MELILITITE
MELTEIGITE
MICROCLINE
MIRABILITE
MOISSANITE
NEWBERYITE
OLIGOCLASE
ORTHOCLASE
PARAGONITE
PEKOVSKITE
PERIDOTITE
PERTHOSITE
PHLOGOPITE
PHOSGENITE
PIEMONTITE
POLYBASITE
PYRALSPITE
PYROCHLORE
PYROLUSITE
PYRRHOTITE

RHYODACITE
RICHTERITE
RIEBECKITE
SAFFLORITE
SAMARSKITE
SAPPHIRINE
SERPENTINE
SHONKINITE
SPERRYLITE
SPHALERITE
STAUROLITE
STERCORITE
STISHOVITE
TESCHENITE
THENARDITE
THOMSONITE
THORIANITE
TORBERNITE
TOURMALINE
TRAVERTINE
TROEGERITE
ULLMANNITE
ULVOSPINEL
VANADINITE
VITROPHYRE
WEBSTERITE
WHEWELLITE
WOLFRAMITE
ZINCBLENDE
11
ALLEMONTITE
AMBLYGONITE
ANORTHOSITE
APOPHYLLITE
BADDELEYITE
BERTRANDITE
BERYLLONITE
BROCHANTITE
CALCARENITE
CALCILUTITE
CALCIRUDITE
CARBONATITE
CARBORUNDUM
CASSITERITE
CERARGYRITE
CHARNOCKITE
CHIASTOLITE
CHLOANTHITE
CHONDRODITE
CHRYSOBERYL
CHRYSOCOLLA

11 continued
CLINOCHLORE
COBALTBLOOM
DAUBREELITE
EGLESTONITE
FERROAUGITE
FRANKLINITE
GLAUBER SALT
GLAUCOPHANE
GREENOCKITE
HARZBURGITE
HASTINGSITE
HAUSMANNITE
HYPERSTHENE
ICELAND SPAR
KATOPHORITE
LAPIS LAZULI
LEADHILLITE
LOELLINGITE
MANGANOSITE
MELANTERITE
MOLYBDENITE
MONTROYDITE
NEPHELINITE
NORDMARKITE
PENFIELDITE
PENTLANDITE
PHILLIPSITE
PITCHBLENDE
PLAGIOCLASE
PSILOMELANE
PUMPELLYITE
PYRARGYRITE

PYROCHROITE
RADIOLARITE
ROCK CRYSTAL
SILLIMANITE
SMITHSONITE
SPESSARTITE
TITANAUGITE
TRIPHYLUTE
VALENTINITE
VERMICULITE
VESUVIANITE
VILLIAUMITE
ZINNWALDITE
12
ANORTHOCLASE
ARSENOPYRITE
BISMUTHINITE
BOULANGERITE
CALCISILTITE
CHALCANTHITE
CHALCOPYRITE
CLAY MINERALS
CLINOPTOLITE
CLINOZOISITE
CRISTOBALITE
EDDINGTONITE
FELDSPATHOID
FERGUSSONITE
FLUORAPATITE
GROSSULARITE
HEDENBERGITE
HEMIMORPHITE
LUXULLIANITE

METACINNABAR
MONTICELLITE
PYROMORPHITE
PYROPHYLLITE
RHODOCROSITE
SENARMONTITE
SKUTTERUDITE
STRONTIANITE
SYENOMORITE
TERLINGUAITE
TETRAHEDRITE
THOMSENOLITE
TRACHYBASALT
WOLLASTONITE
13
ANTHOPHYLLITE
BREITHAUPTITE
CLINOPYROXENE
CUMMINGTONITE
JACUPIRANGITE
KALIOPHYLLITE
LEPIDOCROCITE
LITCHFIELDITE
ORTHOPYROXENE
QUARTZARENITE
RHODOCHROSITE
STILPNOMELANE
THERMONATRITE
UNCOMPAHGRITE
14
CRYOLITHIONITE
HYDROMAGNE-
  SITE

LECHATELIERITE
LITHIOPHYLLITE
ORTHOQUARTZITE
PSEUDOBROOKITE
RAMMELSBERGITE
TRACHYANDESITE
XANTHOPHYLL ITE
15
MONTMORIL-
  LONITE
PSEUDO-
  TACHYLITE
STIBIOTANTALITE
16
GALENABISMUTH-
  ITE
ORTHOFER-
  ROSILITE
PHARMA-
  COSIDERITE
17
HYDROGROSSU-
  LARITE
TELLUROBIS-
  MUTHITE

ORES

3
TIN - cassiterite
4
IRON - haematite, magnetite
LEAD - galena
ZINC - sphalerite, smithsonite, calamine
5
BORON - kernite
6
BARIUM - barite, witherite
CERIUM - monazite, bastnaesite
COBALT - cobaltite, smaltite, erythrite
COPPER - malachite, azurite, chalcopyrite
  bornite, cuprite
ERBIUM - monazite, bastnaesite

INDIUM - sphalerite, smithsonite, calamine
NICKEL - pentlandite, pyrrhotite
OSMIUM - iridosime
RADIUM - pitchblende, carnotite
SILVER - argentite, horn silver
SODIUM - salt
7
ARSENIC - realgar, orpiment, arsenopyrite
CADMIUM - greenockite
CAESIUM - lepidolite, pollucite
CALCIUM - limestone, gypsum, fluorite
GALLIUM
HAFNIUM - zircon
HOLMIUM - monazite
IRIDIUM

ORES

7 continued
LITHIUM - lepidolite, spodumene
MERCURY - cinnabar
NIOBIUM - columbite-tantalite, pyrochlore,
 euxenite
RHENIUM - molybdenite
RHODIUM
SILICON - silica
THORIUM - monazite
THULIUM - monazite
URANIUM - pitchblende, uraninite, carnotite
YTTRIUM - monazite
8
ANTIMONY - stibnite
CHROMIUM - chromite
LUTETIUM - monazite
PLATINUM - sperrylite
RUBIDIUM - lepidolite
SAMARIUM - monazite, bastnaesite
SCANDIUM - thortveitite, davidite
SELENIUM - pyrites
TANTALUM - columbite-tantalite
THALLIUM - pyrites
TITANIUM - rutile, ilmenite, sphere

TUNGSTEN - wolframite, scheelite
VANADIUM - carnotite, roscoelite, vanadinite
9
ALUMINIUM - bauxite
BERYLLIUM - beryl
GERMANIUM - germanite, argyrodite
LANTHANUM - monazite, bastnaesite
MAGNESIUM - magnesite, dolomite
MANGANESE -pyrolusite, rhodochrosite
NEODYMIUM - monazite, bastnaesite
PALLADIUM
POTASSIUM - sylvite, carnallite, polyhalite
RUTHENIUM - pentlandite, pyroxinite
STRONTIUM - celestite, strontianite
TELLURIUM
YTTERBIUM - monazite
10
DYSPROSIUM - monazite, bastnaesite
GADOLINIUM - monazite, bastnaesite
MOLYBDENUM - molybdenite, wulfenite
PHOSPHORUS - apatite
12
PRASEODYMIUM - inonazite, bastnaesite
PROTACTINIUM - pitchblende

GEMSTONES

4
JADE (green, mauve, brown)
ONYX (various colours. banded)
OPAL (white, milky blue, or black with
 rainbow coloured reflections)
RUBY (red)
5
AGATE (brown, red, blue, green, yellow)
BERYL (green, blue, pink)
TOPAZ (usually yellow or colourless)
6
GARNET (red)
ZIRCON (all colours)
7
CITRINE (yellow)
DIAMOND (colourless)
EMERALD (green)
8

AMETHYST (purple)
SAPPHIRE (blue and other colours except
 red)
SUNSTONE (whitish-red-brown flecked with
gold)
9
MALACHITE (dark green banded)
MOONSTONE (white with bluish tinge)
SOAPSTONE (white or greenish)
TURQUOISE (greenish-blue)
10
AQUAMARINE (turquoise, greenish-blue)
BLOODSTONE (green with red spots)
CHALCEDONY (red, brown, grey, or black)
SERPENTINE (usually green or white)
TOURMALINE (all colours)
11
LAPIS LAZULI (deep blue)

MEDICINE

3		4	
GUT	JAW	ANUS	CUSP
HIP	RIB	BILE	GALL
			HEEL

4 continued
IRIS
LENS
NOSE
ULNA
VEIN
5
ANKLE
AORTA
BOLUS
BOWEL
CHYLE
CHYME
COLON
FEMUR
FOVEA
HEART
HYOID
ILEUM
ILIUM
INCUS
JOINT
LIVER
MALAR
MEDIA
NARES
NASAL
NERVE
OPTIC
PUBIS
PULSE
PUPIL
SENSE
SINEW
SINUS
SKULL
SPINE
TALUS
TIBIA
UVULA
VALVE
VOMER
WRIST
6
ARTERY
ATRIUM
BICEPS
CAECUM
CARDIA
CARPAL
CARPUS

COCCYX
CORNEA
CUBOID
DERMIS
FIBULA
GULLET
KIDNEY
LUNATE
MUSCLE
MYELIN
PELVIS
PEPSIN
RADIUS
RECTUM
REFLEX
RENNET
RETINA
SACRUM
SALIVA
SCLERA
SQUAMA
STAPES
TARSUS
TENDON
TONGUE
TUNICA
URETER
VASTUS
VENULE
VESSEL
7
AURICLE
BLADDER
CAROTID
CHOROID
COCHLEA
CRANIUM
CUTICLE
DELTOID
ECCRINE
ETHMOID
FRONTAL
GEMMULE
GLOTTIS
HUMERUS
INGESTA
JEJUNUM
JUGULAR
LACTEAL
MALLEUS
MAMMARY

MEDULLA
NEPHRON
NEURONE
NOSTRIL
PATELLA
PHALANX
PHARYNX
PTYALIN
PYLORUS
SAPHENA
SCAPULA
SENSORY
STERNUM
STOMACH
SYNAPSE
SYSTOLE
THYROID
TRICEPS
URETHRA
8
ADDUCTOR
APOCRINE
APPENDIX
BACKBONE
BILE DUCT
CEREBRUM
CLAVICLE
CORMARY
DIASTOLE
DUODENUM
EXOCRINE
GANGLION
LIGAMENT
MANDIBLE
MENINGES
PALATINE
PANCREAS
PARIETAL
PERINEUM
PISIFORM
RECEPTOR
SACCULUS
SALIVARY
SCAPHOID
SPHENOID
TEMPORAL
TUBINATE
TYMPANUM
UNCIFORM
VENA CAVA
VERTEBRA

9
ARTERIOLE
BILIRUBIN
BRAINSTEM
CAPILLARY
CUNEIFORM
DIAPHRAGM
DIGESTION
ENDOCRINE
ENDORPHIN
EPICARDIA
EPIDERMIS
GOLGI BODY
HAMSTRING
INGESTION
INTESTINE
LACHRYMAL
LYMPHATIC
LYMPH NODE
MAXILLARY
NAVICULAR
OCCIPITAL
PACEMAKER
SPHINCTER
TASTE BUDS
TRAPEZIUM
TRAPEZIUS
TRAPEZOID
UTRICULUS
VENTRICLE
10
ADAM'S APPLE
ADRENALINE
ASTRAGALUS
BILIVERDIN
BREASTBONE
CEREBELLUM
COLLAR BONE
EPICARDIUM
EPIGLOTTIS
GREY MATTER
HEMISPHERE
HENLE'S LOOP
INNOMINATE
METACARPAL
METACARPUS
METATARSAL
METATARSUS
MYOCARDIUM
QUADRICEPS
SUPRARENAL

MEDICINE

11
CONJUNCTIVA
ENDOCARDIUM
GALLBLADDER
PERICARDIUM
PERISTALSIS
VASA VASORUM
12
ADRENAL GLAND
HAIR FOLLICLE
MOTOR NEURONE
PELVIC GIRDLE
RECEPTACULUM
SCHWANN CELLS
SCIATIC NERVE

SPINAL COLUMN
SUBMAXILLARY
13
AQUEOUS
 HUMOUR
BICUSPID VALVE
BLOOD PRESSURE
KUPFFER'S CELLS
NERVOUS SYSTEM
NODE OF RANVIER
NORADRENALINE
PEYER'S PATCHES
PURKINJE CELLS
SUBMANDIBULAR

14
ACHILLES TENDON
BOWMAN'S
 CAPSULE
BRUNNER'S
 GLANDS
EUSTACHIAN TUBE
PURKINJE FIBRES
VITREOUS
 HUMOUR
15
ALIMENTARY
 CANAL
MALPIGHIAN
 LAYER

OBTURATOR
 MUSCLE
ORGAN OF
 JACOBSON
PECTORAL
 MUSCLES
16
MEDULLA
 OBLONGATA
18
ISLETS OF
 LANGERHANS
SEMICIRCULAR
 CANALS

FOOD AND CLOTHES

COOKERY

4
BARD
BEAT
BLEU (AU)
BOIL
BONE
CHOP
COAT
HANG
HASH
LARD
PIPE
RARE
TOSS
5
BASTE
BERNY
BLANC (À)
BLANC (AU)
BROIL
BROWN
BRULÉ
CARVE
CHILL
CROWN
DAUBE
DRAIN
DRESS
GLAZE
GRILL
KNEAD
MELBA
PLUCK
POACH
POINT(À)
PROVE

PURÉE
REINE (À LA)
ROAST
RUB IN
SAUTÉ
SCALD
STEAM
SWEAT
TRUSS
6
AURORE
BRAISE
CONFIT
CREOLE (À LA)
DECANT
DESALT
DIABLE (À LA)
FILLET
FONDUE
GRATIN
GREASE
MAISON
MIGNON
NATURE
REDUCE
SIMMER
ZEPHYR
7
AL DENTE
ARRÊTER
BLANCHE
BLONDIR
CHEMISE (EN)
COLBERT
CROUTON
DEGLAZE

EMINCER
FLAMBER
GRECQUE (À LA)
MARENGO
MÉDICIS
NICOISE (À LA)
REFRESH
SUPRÊME
TARTARE (À LA)
8
ALLONGER
ANGLAISE (À L')
APPAREIL
ASSATION
BARBECUE
BELLEVUE (EN)
BRETONNE (À LA)
CATABORD
CHASSEUR
CRUDITÉS
DAUPHINE (À LA)
DEVILLED
DUCHESSE (À LA)
EMULSION
ESCALOPE
FERMIÈRE (À LA)
FLAMANDE (À LA)
INFUSION
JULIENNE
MACERATE
MARINATE
MEUNIÈRE (À LA)
PISTACHE
POT-ROAST
SURPRISE (EN)

9
ACIDULATE
BAKE BLIND
CANELLING
DETAILLER
DIEPPOISE (À LA)
ESPAGNOLE (À L')
FRICASSÉE
KNOCK BACK
LIÉGEOISE (À LA)
LYONNAISE (À LA)
MARINIÈRE (À LA)
MEDALLION
MILANAISE
10
ANTILLAISE (À L')
BALLOTTINE
BLANQUETTE
BONNE FEMME
BORDELAISE (À LA)
BOULANGÈRE (À LA)
CHAUD FROID
DIJONNAISE (À LA)
FLORENTINE (À LA)
PROVENCALE (À LA)
11
BELLE HÉLÈNE
BOURGUIGNON
CHARCUTERIE
DAUPHINOISE (À LA)
HOLLANDAISE (À LA)
13
BOURGUIGNONNE
 (À LA)
CLARIFICATION
DEEP-FAT FRYING

KITCHEN UTENSILS AND TABLEWARE

3
CUP
HOB
JAR
JUG
LID
MUG
PAN
POT
TIN
WOK

4
BOWL
DISH
EWER
FORK
MILL
RACK
SPIT
TIAN
TRAY

5
BAHUT
BASIN
BOARD
CHOPE
CHURN
FLUTE
GRILL
KNIFE
LADLE
MIXER

MOULD
PELLE
PLATE
PRESS
RUSSE
SIEVE
SPOON
STEEL
STRAW
TONGS
WHISK

6
BASKET
BUCKET
CARAFE
CLOCHE
COOLER
CRIBLE
DIABLE
EGG CUP
FUNNEL
GOBLET
GRADIN
GRATER
KETTLE
MINCER
MORTAR
MUSLIN
PESTLE
PICHET
PITTER
POÊLON
SAUCER
SHAKER
SHEARS
SIPHON
SKEWER
STRING
TAJINE
TOUPIN
TUREEN
7
ALEMBIC
ATTELET
BLENDER
BROILER
CAISSES
CHINOIS
CHIP PAN
CHOPPER
COCOTTE
DRAINER

ÉCUELLE
GRINDER
MARMITE
PITCHER
RAMEKIN
RONDEAU
SALT BOX
SAMOVAR
SKILLET
SKIMMER
SPATULA
SYRINGE
TÂTE-VIN
TOASTER
8
CAQUELON
CAULDRON
COLANDER
CRÊPE PAN
CROCKER
DAUBIÈRE
EGG TIMER
FLAN RING
HOTPLATE
MAZAGRAN
MOUVETTE
SAUCEPAN
SAUTÉ PAN
SCISSORS
STOCKPOT
STRAINER
TART RING
TASTE-VIN
TRENCHER
9
ALCARRAZA
AUTOCLAVE
BAIN-MARIE
BAKING TIN
CAFETIÈRE
CASSEROLE

COMPOTIER
CORKSCREW
CRUMB TRAY
DÉCOUPOIR
FISH SLICE
FRYING-PAN
KILNER JAR
MANDOLINE
MIJOTEUSE
PASTRY BAG
PIPING BAG
RING MOULD
SALAD BOWL
SAUCEBOAT
SHARPENER
STEAK BATT
TISANIÈRE
TOURTIÈRE
10
APPLE-CORER
CAISSETTES
CASSOLETTE
CHOPSTICKS
CRUET STAND
DIPPING PAN
FISH KETTLE
LIQUIDISER
MUSTARD POT
PERCOLATOR
ROLLING PIN
ROTISSERIE
SALAMANDER
SALT CELLAR
SALTING TUB
SLOW COOKER
STERILIZER
WAFFLE IRON
11
BAKING SHEET
BRAISING PAN
CANDISSOIRE

CHAFING DISH
CHEEESECLOTH
COFFEE MAKER
DOUGH TROUGH
DRIPPING PAN
FRUIT STONER
GARGOULETTE
JAMBONNIÈRE
NUTCRACKERS
PASTRY BRUSH
PASTRY WHEEL
SERVING DISH
THERMOMETER
YOGURT-MAKER
12
CARVING KNIFE
DEEP-FAT FRYER
MEASURING JUG
PALETTE KNIFE
PASTRY CUTTER
TURBOT KNIFE
13
BUTCHER'S BLOCK
FOOD PROCESSOR
ICE-CREAM MAKER
KITCHEN SCALES
LARDING NEEDLE
PRESERVING JAR
SACCHAROMETER
VEGETABLE DISH
14
JUICE EXTRACTOR
KNEADING TROUGH
KNIFE SHARPENER
PRESSURE COOKER
TRUSSING NEEDLE
16
MEAT-CARVING
   TONGS

BAKING

3
BAP
BUN
COB
FAR
PIE
4
BABA
CHOU

FLAN
PAVÉ
RUSK
TART
5
BAGEL
BÂTON
BREAD
CRÊPE

FLUTE
ICING
PLAIT
SABLÉ
SCONE
STICK
TOAST
6
COOKIE

CORNET
ECLAIR
FINGER
LEAVEN
MUFFIN
OUBLIE
ROCHER
TOURTE
WAFFLE

7
BAKLAVA
BANNOCK
BISCUIT
BLOOMER
BRIOCHE
CHAPATI
COTTAGE
CRACKER
CRUMPET
FICELLE
FRITTER
GALETTE
PALMIER
PANCAKE
PRALINE
PRETZEL
STOLLEN

STRUDEL
TARTINE
TARTLET
8
AMANDINE
BAGUETTE
BARM CAKE
BÂTONNET
BISCOTTE
DOUGHNUT
DUCHESSE
DUMPLING
FROSTING
GRISSINI
SANDWICH
SPLIT TIN
TORTILLA
TURNOVER

9
ALLUMETTE
BARQUETTE
CROISSANT
FEUILLETÉ
FRIANDISE
KUGELHOPF
PETIT FOUR
VOL-AU-VENT
10
CRISPBREAD
FRANGIPANE
PÂTISSERIE
PUFF PASTRY
RELIGIEUSE
SHORTBREAD
SPONGE CAKE

11
CHOUX PASTRY
PETIT-BEURRE
PROFITEROLE
12
LANGUE-DE-CHAT
PUMPERNICKEL
SPONGE FINGER
13
GENOESE
  SPONGE
14
PAIN AU CHOCOLAT
15
SAVOY SPONGE
  CAKE

CEREALS

3
RYE
4
BRAN
CORN
OATS
RICE

5
MAIZE
SPELT
WHEAT
6
BARLEY
BULGUR

MÉTEIL
MILLET
7
BURGHUL
FROMENT
SORGHUM

9
BUCKWHEAT
12
CRACKED WHEAT

CHEESES

4
BRIE (France)
CURD (cheese)
EDAM (Netherlands)
FETA (Greece)
TOME (France)
5
BANON (France)
BRICK (US)
CABOC (Scotland)
COMTÉ (France)
DANBO (Denmark)
DERBY (England)
FETTA (Greece)
GOUDA (Netherlands)
HERVE (Belgium)
LEIGH (England)
MOLBO (Denmark)
MUROL (France)
NIOLO (Corsica)
TAMIÉ (France)

6
ASIAGO (Italy)
BAGNES (Switzerland)
BRESSE (France)
CACHAT (France)
CANTAL (France)
CENDRE (France)
DUNLOP (Scotland)
FOURME (France)
GAPRON (France)
GÉROMÉ (France)
HALUMI (Greece)
HRAMSA (Scotland)
LEIDEN (Netherlands)
MORVEN (Scotland)
OLIVET (France)
POURLY (France)
ROLLOT (France)
SALERS (France)
SAMSOË (Denmark)
SBRINZ (Switzerland)

SURATI (India)
TILSIT (Switzerland;
Germany; Austria)
VENACO (Corsica)
7
BONDARD (France)
BRINZEN (Hungary)
BROCCIO Corsica)
BROCCIU (Corsica)
BROUSSE (France)
BRUCCIU (Corsica)
CABÉCOU (France)
CHEDDAR (England)
CROWDIE (Scotland)
DAUPHIN (France)
DEMI-SEL (France)
FONTINA (Italy)
GAPERON (France)
GJETÖST (Norway)
GRUYÈRE (France;
Switzerland)

CHEESES

7 continued
JONCHÉE (France)
LANGRES (France)
LEVROUX (France)
LIMBURG (Belgium)
LIVAROT (France)
MAQUÉE (France)
MONT-D'OR (France)
MORBIER (France)
MÜNSTER (France)
NANTAIS (France)
PICODON (France)
QUARGEL (Austria)
RICOTTA (Italy)
SAPSAGO (Switzerland)
STILTON (England)
VENDÔME (France)
8
AUVERGNE (France)
AYRSHIRE (Scotland)
BEAUFORT (France)
BOULETTE (France)
CHAOURCE (France)
CHESHIRE (England)
EDELPILZ (Germany)
EMMENTAL (Switzerland)
EPOISSES (France)
MANCHEGO (Spain)
PARMESAN (Italy)
PECORINO (Italy)
PÉLARDON (France)
REMOUDOU (Belgium)
SCAMORZE (Italy)
TALEGGIO (Italy)
VALENCAY (France)
9
APPENZELL (Switzerland)
BROODKAAS (Netherlands)
CAITHNESS (Scotland)
CAMBOZOLA (Italy; Germany)
CAMEMBERT (France)
CHABICHOU (France)
CHEVRETON (France)
EMMENTHAL (Switzerland)
EXCELSIOR (France)
LA BOUILLE (France)
LEICESTER (England)
LIMBURGER (Belgium)
MAROILLES (France)
MIMOLETTE (France)
PAVÉ D'AUGE (France)
PORT-SALUT (France)
PROVOLONE (Italy)
REBLOCHON (France)

ROQUEFORT (France)
10
CAERPHILLY (Wales)
DANISH BLUE (Denmark)
DOLCELATTE (Italy)
GLOUCESTER (England)
GORGONZOLA (Italy)
LANCASHIRE (England)
MOZZARELLA (Italy)
NEUFCHÂTEL (Switzerland)
PITHIVIERS (France)
RED WINDSOR (England)
SAINGORLON (France)
STRACCHINO (Italy)
11
CARRÉ DE L'EST (France)
COEUR BE BRAY (France)
COULOMMIERS (France)
KATSHKAWALJ (Bulgaria)
PETIT-SUISSE (France)
PONT-L'ÉVÊQUE (France)
SAINTE- MAURE (France)
SAINT-PAULIN (France)
SCHABZIEGER (Switzerland)
SCHLOSSKÄSE (Austria)
TÊTE-DE-MOINE (Switzerland)
WEISSLACKER (Germany)
WENSLEYDALE (England)
12
CACIOCAVALLO (Italy)
RED LEICESTER (England)
SOUMAINTRAIN (France)
13
SAINT NECTAIRE (France)
SELLES-SUR-CHER (France)
14
BRILLAT-SAVARIN (Fance)
FEUILLE DE DREUX (France)
LAGUIOLE-AUBRAC (France)
SAINT-FLORENTIN (France)
SAINT-MARCELLIN (France)
TRAPPISTENKÄSE (Germany)
15
BOUTON-DE-CULOTTE (France)
16
DOUBLE GLOUCESTER (England)
17
RIGOTTE DE PELUSSIN (France)
18
CHEVROTIN DES ARAVIS (France)
CROTTIN DE CHAVIGNOL (France)
19
POULIGNY-SAINT PIERRE (France)

HERBS AND SPICES

3	BORAGE	OREGANO	ROSEMARY
BAY	BURNET	PAPRIKA	TARRAGON
RUE	CICELY	PARSLEY	TURMERIC
4	FENNEL	PERILLA	**9**
BALM	GARLIC	PIMENTO	CHAMOMILE
DILL	GINGER	SAFFRON	CORIANDER
MINT	LOVAGE	SALSIFY	FENUGREEK
SAGE	PEPPER	TABASCO	SPEARMINT
5	SAVORY	VANILLA	**10+**
ANISE	SESAME	**8**	ASAFOETIDA
BASIL	SORREL	ALLSPICE	BLACK-EYED SUSAN
CHIVE	**7**	ANGELICA	HERB OF GRACE
CLOVE	BONESET	CAMOMILE	HORSERADISH
CUMIN	CARAWAY	CARDAMOM	HOTTENTOT FIG
TANSY	CHERVIL	CARDAMON	OYSTER PLANT
THYME	COMFREY	DROPWORT	PEPPERMINT
6	DITTANY	FEVERFEW	POT MARIGOLD
BETONY	MUSTARD	MARJORAM	VEGETABLE OYSTER

DRINKS

WINES AND APERITIFS

4	MÁLAGA	GIGONDAS	BULL'S BLOOD
FINO	SAUMUR	MERCUREY	MANZANILLA
HOCK	SHERRY	MONTAGNY	MONTRACHET
PORT	VOLNAY	MONTILLA	RICHEBOURG
5	**7**	MUSCADET	RIVESALTES
BYRRH	ALIGOTÉ	PAUILLAC	VINHO VERDE
CRÉPY	CAMPARI	RIESLING	**11**
FITOU	CHABLIS	ROSÉ WINE	ALOXE-CORTO
MÉDOC	CHIANTI	SANCERRE	AMONTILLADO
MOSEL	CLAIRET	SANTENAY	MONBAZILLAC
RIOJA	CRÉMANT	VALENCAY	POUILLY-FUMÉ
SOAVE	FALERNO	VERMOUTH	SAINT JULIEN
TAVEL	GAILLAC	VIN JAUNE	VIN DE PAILLE
TAKAY	MADEIRA	**9**	**12**
6	MARGAUX	BOURGUEIL	CÔTES-DU-RHÔNE
ALSACE	MARSALA	CHAMPAGNE	ROMANÉE-CONTI
BANDOL	MARTINI	CLAIRETTE	SAINT-EMILION
BAROLO	MOSELLE	CÔTE-RÔTIE	SAINT ESTEPHE
BARSAC	ORVIETO	HERMITAGE	VALPOLICELLA
BEAUNE	POMMARD	LAMBRUSCO	VOSNE-ROMANÉE
CAHORS	RETSINA	MEURSAULT	**13**
CASSIS	VOUVRAY	MONTLOUIS	CHÂTEAU D'YQUEM
CHINON	**8**	SAUTERNES	CHÂTEAU LAFITE
CLARET	BORDEAUX	**10**	CHÂTEAU LATOUR
FRANGY	BROUILLY	BARBARESCO	ENTRE-DEUX-MERS
GRAVES	DUBONNET	BEAUJOLAIS	POUILLY-FUISSÉ

237

DRINKS

Wines and Aperitifs continued

14
CHÂTEAU MARGAUX
CÔTES-DU-VENTOUX
GEWÜRZTRAMINER
LACRIMA CHRISTI
15
CÔTES-DE-
 PROVENCE
CÔTES-DU-VIVARAIS
CROZES-HERMITAGE
HAUT POITOU WINES
MOREY-SAINT-DENIS

16
CHAMBOLLE-MUSIGNY
CHÂTEAU HAUT-BRION
GEVREY-CHAMBERTIN
SAVIGNY-LES-BEAUNE
17
CORTON-CHARLEMAGNE
CÔTES-DU-ROUSSILLON
NUITS-SAINT-GEORGES
18
BLANQUETTE DE LIMOUX
19
CHASSAGNE-
 MONTRACHET

20
CHÂTEAU MOUTON
 ROTHSCHILD

COCKTAILS AND MIXED DRINKS

3
FIX
KIR
NOG
4
FIZZ
FLIP
GROG
RAKI
SOUR
5
JELEP
NEGUS
PUNCH
SHOTZ
TODDY
6
BEADLE
BISHOP
GIMLET
POSSET

7
BACARDI
MARTINI
SAGRIA
SIDECAR
WALDORF
8
APPLE CAR
DAIQUIRI
GIN AND IT
GIN SLING
HIGH BALL
NIGHT CAP
PINK LADY
WHIZ BANG
9
ALEXANDER
APPLEJACK
BEE'S KNEES
BUCK JONES
BUCKS FIZZ

COMMODORE
MANHATTEN
MINT JULEP
MOONLIGHT
MOONSHINE
MULLED ALE
WHITE LADY
10
ANGEL'S KISS
ARCHBISHOP
BLACK MARIA
BLOODY MARY
HORSE'S NECK
MERRY WIDOW
MULLED WINE
PINA COLADA
RUM COLLINS
TOM COLLINS
11
BEACHCOMBE
BLACK VELVET

FALLEN ANGEL
WASSAIL BOWL
12
CHURCHWARDEN
ELEPHANT'S EAR
FINE AND DANDY
OLD-FASHIONED
WHITE GIN SOUR
WHITE RUSSIAN
13
CHAMPAGNE BUCK
CORPSE REVIVER
KNICKERBOCKER
MAIDEN'S PRAYER
PLANTER'S PUNCH
PRAIRIE OYSTER
16
BETWEEN THE
 SHEETS
HARVEY
 WALLBANGER

BEERS AND BEVERAGES

3
ALE
4
MEAD
MILD
5
CIDER
KVASS
LAGER
PERRY
STOUT

6
BITTER
LAMBIC
SHANDY
8
GUINNESS
HYDROMEL

10
BARLEY BEER
BARLEY WINE

238

DRINKS

SPIRITS

3	6	7	8
GIN	BOUKHA	AQUAVIT	ARMAGNAC
RUM	BRANDY	AQUAVIT	CALVADOS
4	CHICHA	BACARDI	FALERNUM
ARAK	COGNAC	BOUKHRA	SCHNAPPS
MARC	GRAPPA	BOURBON	9
OUZO	MESCAL	SCHNAPS	FRAMBOISE
5	METAXA	TEQUILA	SLIVOVITZ
CHOUM	PASTIS	WHISKEY	10
VODKA	PERNOD		RYE WHISKEY
	PULQUE		11
	WHISKY		AGUARDIENTE

LIQUEURS

4	7	9	12
SAKÉ	ALCAMAS	ARQUEBUSE	CHERRY BRANDY
SAKI	ALLASCH	COINTREAU	CRÈME DE CACAO
5	BAILEYS	FRAMBOISE	GRAND MARNIER
ANISE	CURACAO	GUIGNOLET	13
ANRAM	ESCUBAC	MIRABELLE	CRÈME DE MENTHE
6	RATAFIA	TRIPLE SEC	15
CASSIS	SAMBUCA	10	SOUTHERN
KÜMMEL	8	BROU DE NOIX	COMFORT
MÊLISS	ABSINTHE	CHARTREUSE	17
QETSCH	ADVOCAAT	MARASCHINO	AMARETTO DI
SCUBAC	ANISETTE	11	SARANNO
STREGA	DRAMBUIE	BENEDICTINE	
	PERSICOT	TRAPPISTINE	

NON-ALCOHOLIC DRINKS

3	5	7	9
CHA (TEA)	LASSI	BEEF TEA	GRENADINE
TEA	WATER	DIABOLO	MILKSHAKE
4	6	SELTZER	ORANGEADE
CHAR (TEA)	COFFEE	8	10
COLA	ORGEAT	LEMONADE	GINGER BEER
SODA	TISANE		TONIC WATER

239

CLOTHES

3
ABA
ALB
BAL
BAS
BAT
BIB
BRA
CAP
FEZ
HAT
LEI
OBI
TAM
4
ABBA
AGAL
ALBA
BAJU
BARB
BECK
BELT
BENN
BOTA
BUSK
CACK
CAPE
CLOG
COAT
COPE
COTE
COWL
DAPS
DIDO
DISK
GARB
GETA
GOWN
HAIK
HOOD
HOSE
IZAR
JAMA
KEPI
KILT
MASK
MAXI
MIDI

MINI
MITT
MUFF
MULE
PUMP
ROBE
RUFF
SARI
SASH
SAYA
SHOE
SLIP
SLOP
SOCK
SPAT
SUIT
TABI
TOGA
TOGS
TOPI
TUTU
VAMP
VEIL
VEST
WRAP
5
ABNET
ACTON
AEGIS
AMICE
AMPYX
APRON
ARCAN
ARMET
ASCOT
BARBE
BARRY
BENJY
BERET
BLAKE
BLUEY
BOINA
BOOTS
BURKA
BUSBY
CABAS
CADET
CAPPA

CHALE
CHAPS
CHOGA
CHOLI
CLOAK
CORDY
COTTA
COTTE
CREST
CROWN
CURCH
CYLAS
CYMAR
DERBY
DHOTI
EPHOD
FICHU
FROCK
GANSY
GILET
GIPPO
GLOVE
HABIT
HULLS
IHRAM
JABOT
JAMAH
JEANS
JELAB
JUPON
LAMMY
LODEN
LUNGI
MIDDY
MUFTI
MULES
NUBIA
PAGNE
PAGRI
PALLA
PANTS
PARKA
PILCH
PIRNY
PUMPS
SABOT
SAREE
SCARF

SHAKO
SHAWL
SHIFT
SHIRT
SKIRT
SMOCK
SNOOD
STOCK
STOLA
STOLE
TAILS
TEDDY
TIARA
TONGS
TOPEE
TOQUE
TREWS
TUNIC
VISOR
VIZOR
WEEDS
6
ABOLLA
ALMUCE
ANADEM
ANALAV
ANKLET
ANORAK
ARCTIC
ARMOUR
ARTOIS
BALKAN
BANYAN
BARRET
BARVEL
BASQUE
BAUTTA
BEANIE
BEAVER
BÉQUIN
BERTHA
BICORN
BIETLE
BIGGIN
BIKINI
BIRRUS
BISHOP
BLAZER

6 continued

BLIAUD	COTHUM	RUFFLE	BERDASH
BLOUSE	COVERT	SANDAL	BERETTA
BOATER	CRAVAT	SARONG	BETSIES
BODICE	DIADEM	SERAPE	BIRETTA
BOLERO	DICKEY	SHIMMY	BOTTINE
BONNET	DIRNDL	SHORTS	BOX CAPE
BOOTEE	DOLMAN	SHROUD	BOX COAT
BOWLER	DOMINO	SLACKS	BRIMMER
BOXERS	DUSTER	SONTAG	BROIGNE
BRACAE	EARCAP	STEP-IN	BURNOUS
BRACES	FEDORA	SUN HAT	BUSSKIN
BRAGAS	FILLET	TABARD	CALECON
BRAIES	GAITER	TAMISE	CALOTTE
BRETON	GANSEY	TIGHTS	CAMOURO
BRIEFS	GARTER	TIPPET	CANEZOU
BROGAN	GAUCHO	TOP HAT	CAPE HAT
BROGUE	GILLIE	TOPPER	CAPUCHE
BUSKIN	GUIMPE	TRILBY	CAPULET
BYRNIE	HALTER	TRUNKS	CASAQUE
BYRRUS	HENNIN	T-SHIRT	CASSOCK
CABAAN	HUIPIL	TUCKER	CATSKIN
CADDIE	JACKET	TURBAN	CAUBEEN
CAFTAN	JERKIN	TUXEDO	CEREVIS
CALASH	JERSEY	TWEEDS	CHAINSE
CALCEI	JUBBAH	ULSTER	CHALWAR
CALIGA	JUMPER	UNDIES	CHAPLET
CALPAC	KABAYA	UPLIFT	CHEMISE
CAMAIL	KIMONO	VAMPAY	CHEVRON
CAMISA	KIRTLE	VESTEE	CHIMERE
CAMISE	LAMMIE	WEDGES	CHIP HAT
CAPOTE	LOAFER	WIMPLE	CHLAMYS
CAPUCE	LUNGEE	WOOLLY	CHOPINE
CAPUTI	MAGYAR	ZOUAVE	CHOU HAT
CARACO	MANTEE	**7**	CHRISOM
CASQUE	MANTLE	AMICTUS	CHUDDAR
CASTOR	MANTUA	APPAREL	CHUDDER
CAUSIA	MITTEN	ARISARD	COMMODE
CESTUS	MOBCAP	ARM BAND	CORONEL
CHADAR	MOGGAN	BABOOSH	CORONET
CHITON	OUTFIT	BALDRIC	COSSACK
CHOKER	PEG-TOP	BALTEUS	COXCOMB
CILICE	PEPLOS	BANDEAU	CRISPIN
CIMIER	PEPLUM	BANDORE	CROP TOP
CLAQUE	PILEUS	BARBUTE	CUCULLA
CLOCHE	PINNER	BAROQUE	CUIRASS
COBCAB	PIRNIE	BASHLYK	CULOTTE
COCKET	PONCHO	BASINET	CURCHEF
CORNET	PUGREE	BAVETTE	CUTAWAY
CORONA	PUTTEE	BAVOLET	DOPATTA
CORSET	RAGLAN	BEDIZEN	DOUBLET
	REEFER	BELCHER	DRAWERS

7 continued

DULBAND
DUL HOSE
EARMUFF
ETON CAP
EVERETT
FANCHON
FASHION
FILIBEG
GARMENT
GHILLIE
G STRING
GUM BOOT
GUM SHOE
GYM SHOE
HANDBAG
HIGH-LOW
HOMBURG
HOSIERY
JODHPUR
KLOMPEN
LAYETTE
LEOTARD
MAILLOT
MANTEAU
MONTERA
MONTERO
MUFFLER
OLIVERS
OVERALL
OXFORDS
PANTIES
PARASOL
PATTERN
PELISSE
PETASOS
PIERROT
PILLBOX
PLUVIAL
PUGGREE
PYJAMAS
RAIMENT
REGALIA
ROMPERS
RUBBERS
SANDALS
SARAFAN
SHALWAR
SILK HAT
SINGLET
SKI BOOT

SLIPPER
SLYDERS
SMICKET
SNEAKER
SOUTANE
SPENCER
SPORRAN
SULTANE
SUN SUIT
SURCOAT
SURTOUT
SWEATER
TANK TOP
TEA GOWN
TOPBOOT
TOP COAT
TRAHEEN
TRICORN
TUNICLE
TWIN SET
UNIFORM
VEILING
WATTEAU
WEDGIES
WING TIE
WOOLLEN
WRAPPER
YASHMAK
Y-FRONTS
ZIMARRA
8
ABBE CAPE
ALL-IN-ONE
ANALABOS
ANTELOPE
BABUSHKA
BALADRAN
BALMORAL
BANDANNA
BARBETTE
BASQUINE
BATH ROSE
BEARSKIN
BED SOCKS
BENJAMIN
BIGGONET
BINNOGUE
BLOOMERS
BODY COAT
BOMBARDS
BOOBTUBE

BOOT-HOSE
BOTTEKIN
BREECHES
BURGONET
BURNOOSE
BYCOCKET
CABASSET
CAMISOLE
CANOTIER
CAPE COAT
CAPELINE
CAPRIOLE
CAPUCINE
CAPUTIUM
CARCANET
CARDIGAN
CARDINAL
CAROLINE
CASAQUIN
CATERCAP
CHANDAIL
CHAPERON
CHAQUETA
CHASUBLE
CHAUSSES
CHONGSAM
CODPIECE
COLOBIUM
COPATAIN
CORSELET
COUCH HAT
COVERALL
CRUSH HAT
CUCULLUS
DANCE SET
DANDY HAT
DJELLABA
DOM PEDRO
DORMEUSE
DUCK-BILL
DUNCE CAP
DUST COAT
DUTCH CAP
FALDETTA
FLANNELS
FLIMSIES
FOOTWEAR
GAMASHES
GAUNTLET
GUERNSEY
HALF-HOSE

HALF SLIP
HEADGEAR
JACK BOOT
JUDO COAT
JUMP SUIT
KERCHIEF
KNICKERS
KNITWEAR
LARRIGAN
LEGGINGS
LINGERIE
LIRIPIPE
MANTELET
MANTILLA
MOCCASIN
NECKLACE
NIGHTCAP
OPERA HAT
OVERALLS
OVERCOAT
OVERSHOE
PARAMENT
PEASECOD
PEIGNOIR
PHILIBEG
PILEOLUS
PINAFORE
PLASTRON
PLATINUM
PLIMSOLL
PULLOVER
SABOTINE
SKULL-CAP
SLIP-OVER
SNOWSHOE
SOMBRERO
STOCKING
SURPLICE
SWIM SUIT
TAIL COAT
TAILLEUR
TARBOOSH
TOQUETTE
TRAINERS
TRENCHER
TRICORNE
TROUSERS
TWO-PIECE
WOOLLENS
WOOLLIES
ZOOT SUIT

CLOTHES

9
ALPARGATA
ALPINE HAT
ANKLE BOOT
APON DRESS
ARMILAUSA
BABY SKIRT
BALAYEUSE
BALL DRESS
BALMACAAN
BAMBIN HAT
BANDOLEER
BARCELONA
BED JACKET
BEEGUM HAT
BELL SKIRT
BILLICOCK
BILLYCOCK
BLOUSETTE
BODY LINEN
BOURRELET
BRASSIERE
BROADBRIM
BRODEQUIN
BRUNSWICK
BYZANTINE
CABRIOLET
CAPE DRESS
CAPE STOLE
CARTWHEEL
CASENTINO
CASQUETTE
CASSIMERE
CHEMILOON
CHIN-CLOTH
CHIVARRAS
CHOLO COAT
COAT DRESS
COAT SHIRT
COCKED HAT
COOLIE HAT
COPINTANK
CORNERCAP
COVERSLUT
COWBOY HAT
CREEDMORE
CRINOLINE
DOG COLLAR
DOMINICAL
DRESS COAT
DRESS SHOE

DRESS SUIT
DUNGAREES
DUNSTABLE
ESCOFFIAN
FLIP FLOPS
FORAGE CAP
FROCK COAT
FULL DRESS
GABARDINE
GABERDINE
GARIBALDI
GLENGARRY
GREATCOAT
HEADDRESS
HEADPIECE
HELMET CAP
HOURI-COAT
HOUSE-COAT
HULA SKIRT
INVERNESS
JOCKEY CAP
JULIET CAP
LOINCLOTH
MILLINERY
NECKCLOTH
NIGHTGOWN
OUTERWEAR
OVERDRESS
OVERSHIRT
OVERSKIRT
PANAMA HAT
PANTALETS
PANTOFFLE
PANTY HOSE
PEAJACKET
PETTICOAT
PILOT COAT
PLUS FOURS
POLONAISE
QUAKER HAT
SANDSHOES
SANSENITO
SHAKSHEER
SHINTIYAN
SHOVEL HAT
SLOPPY JOE
SLOUCH HAT
SNEAKERS
SOU'WESTER
STOMACHER
STRING TIE

SUNBONNET
SURCINGLE
TENT DRESS
THIGH BOOT
TROUSSEAU
TRUNK-HOSE
UNDERCOAT
UNDERGOWN
UNDERVEST
UNDERWEAR
VESTMENTS
VICTORINE
WAISTCOAT
WATCH COAT
WIDE-AWAKE
WITCH'S HAT
WYLIECOAT
10
ANGELUS CAP
APRON TUNIC
BABY BONNET
BASIC DRESS
BATHING CAP
BEER JACKET
BELLBOY CAP
BERRETTINO
BIBI BONNET
BICYCLE BAL
BLOUSE COAT
BOBBY SOCKS
BOSOM SHIRT
BOUDOIR CAP
BRIGANDINE
BRUNCH COAT
BUCKET TOPS
BUMPER BRIM
BUSH JACKET
BUSKJACKET
CALZONERAS
CANVAS SHOE
CAPE COLLAR
CAPPA MAGNA
CARMAGNOLE
CERVELIERE
CHARTREUSE
CHATELAINE
CHEMISETTE
CHIGNON CAP
CHOUQUETTE
CLOCK-MUTCH
COOLIE COAT

COQUELUCHE
CORPS PIQUE
COSSACK CAP
COTE-HARDIE
COUVRE-CHEF
COVERCHIEF
COVERT COAT
CROSSCLOTH
CUMMERBUND
DANCE DRESS
DESHABILLE
DINNER SUIT
DIPLOIDIAN
DOUILLETTE
DRESS PLAID
DRESS SHIRT
DUFFEL COAT
ECLIPSE TIE
ESPADRILLE
ETON JACKET
EUGENIE HAT
FANCY DRESS
FASCINATOR
FLYING SUIT
FORE-AND-AFT
FUSTANELLA
GARMENTURE
GRASS SKIRT
HAREM SKIRT
HUG-ME-TIGHT
JIGGER COAT
LIRIPIPIUM
LOUNGE SUIT
LUMBERJACK
MESSJACKET
NIGHTDRESS
NIGHTSHIRT
OPERA CLOAK
OVERBLOUSE
OVERGAITER
OXFORD BAGS
OXFORD GOWN
PANTALOONS
PICTURE HAT
PITH HELMET
POKE BONNET
PORK PIE HAT
RIDING-HOOD
SERVICE CAP
SHIRTWAIST
SPORTS COAT

10 continued
SPORT SHIRT
SPORTSWEAR
STICHARION
STRING VEST
SUNDAY BEST
SUSPENDERS
SWEAT SHIRT
THREE-PIECE
TRENCH COAT
UNDERDRESS
UNDERLINEN
UNDERPANTS
UNDERSHIRT
UNDERSKIRT
VELDSCHOEN
WINDSOR TIE
WING COLLAR
11
ALSATIAN BOW
BALLET SHOES
BATHING SUIT
BIB-AND-BRACE
BIKER JACKET
BOILED SHIRT
BOXER SHORTS
BREECHCLOTH
BRITISH WARM
CANCAN DRESS
CAVALIER HAT
CORSET COVER
COWBOY BOOTS
DANCING CLOG
DEERSTALKER
DINNER DRESS
EMPIRE SKIRT
ESPADRILLES
EVENING GOWN
EVENING SLIP
FORMAL DRESS
FORTUNY GOWN
HOBBLE SKIRT
HOSTESS GOWN
HUNTING BOOT
MIDDY BLOUSE
NECKERCHIEF
OVERGARMENT
PANTY GIRDLE
RIDING HABIT
RUBBER APRON
RUNNING SHOE

RUSSIAN BOOT
SEWING APRON
SNAP-BRIM HAT
SOUP-AND-FISH
SOUTHWESTER
SPATTERDASH
STOCKING CAP
STRING GLOVE
SWAGGER COAT
TAM-O'SHANTER
TYROLEAN HAT
UNDERGIRDLE
UNDERTHINGS
WALKING SHOE
WEDDING GOWN
WEDDING VEIL
WELLINGTONS
WINDBREAKER
WINDCHEATER
12
AMISH COSTUME
BALKAN BLOUSE
BALLOON SKIRT
BASEBALL BOOT
BATTLE JACKET
BELLY DOUBLET
BLOOMER DRESS
BUSINESS SUIT
CAVALIER BOOT
CHEMISE DRESS
CHEMISE FROCK
CHESTERFIELD
CHUKKER SKIRT
CORSET BODICE
COTTAGE CLOAK
DINNER JACKET
DIVIDED SKIRT
DRESS CLOTHES
DRESSING GOWN
EASTER BONNET
ENGLISH DRAPE
EVENING DRESS
EVENING SHOES
EVENING SKIRT
HANDKERCHIEF
HEADKERCHIEF
HELMET BONNET
KNEE BREECHES
LOUNGING ROBE
MANDARIN COAT
MONKEY JACKET

MORNING DRESS
MOTORING VEIL
PEDAL PUSHERS
QUAKER BONNET
ROLL-ON GIRDLE
SCOTCH BONNET
SLEEPING COAT
SLEEPING SUIT
SMALLCLOTHES
STOVEPIPE HAT
SUGAR-LOAF HAT
TAILORED SUIT
TEN-GALLON HAT
TROUSERETTES
UNDERCLOTHES
UNDERGARMENT
ZOUAVE JACKET
13
ACROBATIC SHOE
AFTER-SKI SOCKS
BACK-STRAP SHOE
BEEFEATER'S HAT
BELLBOY JACKET
BUNGALOW APRON
COACHMAN'S COAT
COMBING JACKET
COTTAGE BONNET
DRESSING SAQUE
ELEVATOR SHOES
HAWAIIAN SKIRT
KNEE-HIGH BOOTS
MOTHER HUBBARD
MOURNING DRESS
NORFOLK JACKET
PEEK-A-BOO WAIST
PRINCESS DRESS
SAM BROWNE BELT
SMOKING JACKET
SPORTS CLOTHES
SUSPENDER BELT
TEDDYBEAR COAT
UNDERCLOTHING
14
AFTERNOON DRESS
BAREFOOT SANDAL
BATHING COSTUME
CAMOUFLAGE SUIT
CARDIGAN BODICE
CONGRESS GAITOR
CONTINENTAL HAT
DRESSING JACKET

DRESSMAKER SUIT
EGYPTIAN SANDAL
EVENING SWEATER
KNICKERBOCKERS
SHOOTING JACKET
THIGH-HIGH BOOTS
15
BOUDOIR SLIPPERS
CARDIGAN SWEATER
CHAPEAU FRANCAIS
CHEMISE À LA REINE
CHEVALIER BONNET
DOUBLE-DUTY
 DRESS
ENVELOPE CHEMISE
FAIR ISLE SWEATER
MONTGOMERY
 BERET
16
BALLERINA
 COSTUME
CALMEL'S HAIR
 SHAWL
CHICKEN SKIN
 GLOVE
EISENHOWER
 JACKET
ELBERT HUBBARD
 TIE
GOING AWAY
 COSTUME
SWADDLING
 CLOTHES
17
CHEMISE À
 L'ANGLAISE
COAL SCUTTLE
 BONNET
CONFIRMATION
 DRESS
FOUNDATION
 GARMENT
SWALLOW-TAILED
 COAT
18
BETHLEHEM
 HEADDRESS
CHARLOTTE
 CORDAY CAP
19
SALVATION ARMY
 BONNET

MATERIALS

3	DORIA	ANGORA	FRIEZE
ABB	FITCH	ARALAC	GRENAI
BAN	GAUZE	ARIDEX	GURRAH
FUR	GENET	ARMURE	KERSEY
NET	GUNNY	BALINE	LAMPAS
REP	HONAN	BARÉGE	LASTEX
4	JUPON	BEAVER	LINENE
ACCA	KAPOK	BENGAL	LIZARD
ALMA	LAINE	BERBER	MADRAS
BAKU	LAPIN	BIRETZ	MARMOT
BRIN	LINEN	BLATTA	MARTEN
BURE	LINON	BUREAU	MELTON
CALF	LISLE	BURLAP	MERINO
CORD	LLAMA	BURNET	MILIUM
CREA	LUREX	BURRAH	MOHAIR
FELT	MOIRE	BYSSUS	MOUTON
FUJI	NINON	CAFFOY	MULMUL
GROS	NYLON	CALICO	MUSLIN
HEMP	ORLON	CAMACA	OCELOT
HIDE	OTTER	CAMLET	OSPERY
JEAN	PEKIN	CANGAN	OXFORD
LACE	PIQUÉ	CANVAS	PAILLE
LAMÉ	PLUSH	CASTOR	PONGEE
LAWN	PRINT	CATGUT	POPLIN
LYNX	RAYON	CHILLO	PYTHON
MULL	SATIN	CHINTZ	RABBIT
PELT	SCRIM	CHROME	RED FOX
ROAN	SERGE	CHUNAN	RIBBON
SILK	SISAL	COBURG	RUBBER
SKIN	SISOL	CONTRO	SAMITE
VAIR	SKUNK	COSSAS	SATEEN
WOOL	STRAW	CÔTELÉ	SAXONY
5	STUFF	CREPON	SENNIT
ABACA	SUEDE	CROISE	SHODDY
ACELE	SURAH	CUBICA	SISSOL
ACETA	TAMMY	DAMASK	SKIVER
ARDIL	TISSUE	DIAPER	SOUPLE
BAIZE	TOILE	DIMITY	TARTAN
BASCO	TULLE	DJERSA	TINSEL
BASIN	TWEED	DOMETT	TISSUE
CADIS	TWILL	DOWLAS	TRICOT
CAFFA	UNION	DUCAPE	TUSSAH
CASHA	VOILE	ÉPONGE	TUSSEH
CLOTH	**6**	ERMINE	VELURE
CRAPE	ALACHA	FABRIC	VELVET
CRISP	ALASKA	FAILLE	VICUNA
CROWN	ALPACA	FISHER	WINCEY
DENIM	AMAZON	FORFAR	WITNEY

7
ACRILON
ACRYLIC
ALAMODE
ART SILK
BAGGING
BATISTE
BATTING
BEMBERG
BLUE FOX
BRABANT
BRUNETE
BUNTING
BUSTIAN
CAMBAYE
CAMBRIC
CANTOON
CAPENET
CARACAL
CARACUL
CATALIN
CHALLIS
CHAMOIS
CHARVET
CHEKMAK
CHEVIOT
CHEYNEY
CHIFFON
COOTHAY
COWHIDE
DAMMASÉ
DELAINE
DOESKIN
DORNICK
DRABBET
DRUGGET
DUCHESS
DURANCE
DUVETYN
EARL GLO
ÉPINGLÉ
ESPARTO
ETAMINE
FAKE FUR
FISHNET
FITCHEW
FLANNEL
FOULARD
FUR FELT
FUSTIAN
GALATEA

GINGHAM
GOBELIN
GROGRAM
GUANACO
GUIPURE
HESSIAN
HOLLAND
JACONET
JAP SILK
KASHMIR
KIDSKIN
LEATHER
LEGHORN
LEOPARD
LIBERTY
MINIVER
MOROCCO
NANKEEN
NETTING
OILSKIN
ORGANDY
ORGANZA
OTTOMAN
PAISLEY
PARAGON
PECCARY
PERCALE
PIGSKIN
RACCOON
RAWHIDE
RAW SILK
ROMANE
SACKING
SAFFIAN
SATINET
SUITING
TAFFETA
TEXTILE
TICKING
TIE SILK
TIFFANY
TUSSORE
VALENCE
VELOURS
VISCOSE
VIYELLA
WEBING
WOOLLEN
WORSTED
8
AGA BANEE

ALOE LACE
ANTELOPE
ARMOZEEN
ARMOZINE
ART LINEN
ASBESTOS
BAGHEERA
BARATHEA
BARRACAN
BATSWING
BAUDEKIN
BEUTANOL
BLANCARD
BOBBINET
BOMBAZET
BOX CLOTH
BUCKSKIN
BUFFSKIN
CALFSKIN
CAPESKIN
CASHMERE
CELANESE
CELENESE
CHAMBRAY
CHARMEEN
CHENILLE
CHIRMEN
CHIVERET
CIVET CAT
CORDUROY
COTELINE
CRETONNE
CROSS FOX
DIAPHANE
DRAP D'ÉTÉ
DUCHESSE
ECRU SILK
EOLIENNE
ESTAMENE
EVERFAST
FARADINE
FLORENCE
GOATSKIN
GOSSAMER
HOMESPUN
INDIENNE
KOLINSKY
LAMBSKIN
LUSTRINE
LUSTRING
MARABOUT

MARCELLA
MAROCAIN
MATERIAL
MILANESE
MOGADORE
MOLESKIN
MOQUETTE
MUSLINET
MUSQUASH
NAINSOOK
OILCLOTH
ORGANDIE
PURE SILK
SARCENET
SARSENET
SEALSKIN
SHAGREEN
SHANTUNG
SHIRTING
SHOT SILK
SQUIRREL
TAPESTRY
TARLATAN
TARLETAN
TOILINET
VALENCIA
WAX CLOTH
WHIPCORD
WHITE FOX
WILD MINK
WILD SILK
ZIBELINE
9
ADA CANVAS
AGRA GAUZE
ALBATROSS
ALLIGATOR
ASBESTALL
ASTRAKHAN
BARK CLOTH
BARK CREPE
BENGALINE
BOMBAZINE
BOMBYCINE
BOOKCLOTH
BOOK LINEN
BROCATELL
BYRD CLOTH
CALAMANCO
CANNEQUIN
CATALOWNE

MATERIALS

9 continued
CHARMEUSE
CHINA SILK
COTTONADE
COTTON REP
CREPELINE
CUT VELVET
DACCA SILK
ECRU CLOTH
ELASTIQUE
FLANNELET
FUR FABRIC
GABARDINE
GEORGETTE
GRENADINE
GROSGRAIN
HAIRCLOTH
HORSEHAIR
HUCKABACK
LONGCLOTH
MARCELINE
MESSALINE
MOSS CREPE
ORGANZINE
PATCHWORK
RANCH MINK
SACKCLOTH
SAIL CLOTH
SATINETTE
SHARKSKIN
SHEEPSKIN
SILVER FOX
SNAKESKIN
STOCKINET
SWANSDOWN
TARPAULIN
TOWELLING
TRICOTINE
VELVETEEN
WOLVERINE
WORCESTER
10
ABBOT CLOTH
AIDA CANVAS
ANGOLA YARN
AUSTINIZED
BALBRIGGAN
BARLEYCORN
BAUM MARTEN
BEAVERETTE
BEAVERTEEN

BOOK MUSLIN
BOUCLÉ YARN
BROADCLOTH
BROAD GOODS
CADET CLOTH
CAMBRESINE
CHINCHILLA
CHINO CLOTH
CIRCASSIAN
CONGO CLOTH
CREPE LISSE
DRESS LINEN
GRASS CLOTH
HOP SACKING
HORSECLOTH
INDIAN LAMB
IRISH LINEN
MARSEILLES
MOUSSELINE
PEAU DE SOIE
PILOT CLOTH
SEERSUCKER
SUEDE CLOTH
TERRY CLOTH
TOILINETTE
WINCEYETTE
11
ABRADED YARN
AERATED YARN
ALBERT CREPE
ARABIAN LACE
ARMURE-LAINE
BABY FLANNEL
BAG SHEETING
BANDLE LINEN
BASKET CLOTH
BATH COATING
BEDFORD CORD
BOMBER CLOTH
BRUSHED WOOL
CANTON CREPE
CANTON LINEN
CHAMOISETTE
CHEESECLOTH
CHESS CANVAS
CHINA COTTON
CLAY WORSTED
COTTON CREPE
DACCA MUSLIN
DIAPER CLOTH
DREADNOUGHT

DRUID'S CLOTH
ESKIMO CLOTH
EVERLASTING
FLANNELETTE
HARRIS TWEED
IRISH POPLIN
LEATHERETTE
OVERCOATING
PERSIAN LAMB
SCOTCH PLAID
SPONGE CLOTH
STONE MARTEN
TOILE DE JOUY
WAFFLE CLOTH
12
ACETATE RAYON
BALLOON CLOTH
BERLIN CANVAS
BOLIVIA CLOTH
BOLTING CLOTH
BRILLIANTINE
BROWN HOLLAND
BRUSHED RAYON
BUTCHER LINEN
CARACUL CLOTH
CAVALRY TWILL
CONVENT CLOTH
COTTON VELVET
CRINKLE CLOTH
CROISÉ VELVET
DENMARK SATIN
DOUBLE DAMASK
DRESS FLANNEL
ELEMENT CLOTH
EMPRESS CLOTH
GLAZED CHINTZ
MUTATION MINK
SHETLAND WOOL
SLIPPER SATIN
VISCOSE RAYON
WELSH FLANNEL
13
AIRPLANE CLOTH
AMERICAN CLOTH
BRITTANY CLOTH
CANTON FLANNEL
CARDINAL CLOTH
CASEMENT CLOTH
CLOISTER CLOTH
COSTUME VELVET
COTTON FLANNEL

COTTON SUITING
COTTON WORSTED
CRUSHED VELVET
DIAGONAL CLOTH
DIAPER FLANNEL
EGYPTIAN CLOTH
END-TO-END CLOTH
LINSEY-WOOLSEY
PATENT LEATHER
RUSSIA LEATHER
14
ALGERIAN STRIPE
AMERICAN COTTON
ARGENTINE CLOTH
BANDOLIER CLOTH
BARONETTE SATIN
BROADTAIL CLOTH
CORKSCREW TWILL
EGYPTIAN COTTON
ELECTORAL CLOTH
FRUIT OF THE LOOM
HONEYCOMB CLOTH
JACQUARD FABRIC
SHEPHERD'S PLAID
15
ABSORBENT
   COTTON
ADMIRALITY CLOTH
CACHEMIRE DE
   SOIE
CAMEL'S HAIR
   CLOTH
EMBROIDERY
   LINEN
OSTRICH FEATHERS
PARACHUTE FABRIC
SEA-ISLAND COTTON
SHIRTING FLANNEL
TATTERSALL CHECK
TATTTERSALL PLAID
TROPICAL SUITING
16
CANDLEWICK FABRIC
CONSTITUTION
   CORD
TURKISH TOWELLING
17
CROSS-STITCH
   CAVAS

248

SPORT AND GAMES

SPORTS

4
GOLF
JUDO
PATO
POLO
5
BOWLS
FIVES
KENDO
RALLY
RODEO
6
AIKIDO
BOULES
BOXING
HOCKEY
KARATE
KUNG FU
PELOTA
ROWING
SHINTY
SKIING
SQUASH
TENNIS
7
ANGLING
ARCHERY
BOWLING
CRICKET
CROQUET
CURLING
FENCING
HURLING
JUJITSU

KABBADI
KARTING
NETBALL
RACKETS
SHOT PUT
SURFING
8
BASEBALL
BIATHLON
CANOEING
COURSING
DRESSAGE
FALCONRY
GYMKHANA
HANDBALL
HURDLING
LACROSSE
LONG JUMP
MARATHON
PETANQUE
PING-PONG
ROUNDERS
SHOOTING
SPEEDWAY
SWIMMING
TUG OF WAR
9
ATHLETICS
BADMINTON
DECATHLON
ICE HOCKEY
MOTO-CROSS
POLE VAULT
SKYDIVING

TAE KWON-DO
WATER POLO
WRESTLING
10
BASKETBALL
DRAG RACING
FLAT RACING
FOXHUNTING
GYMNASTICS
HEPTATHLON
ICE SKATING
PENTATHLON
REAL TENNIS
RUGBY UNION
TRIPLE JUMP
VOLLEYBALL
11
BLOOD SPORTS
BOBSLEDDING
DISCUS THROW
HAMMER THROW
HAND-GLIDING
HORSE RACING
HORSE TRAILS
MARTIAL ARTS
MOTOR RACING
PARACHUTING
RUGBY LEAGUE
TABLE TENNIS
TOBOGGANING
WATER SKIING
WIND SURFING
12
BULLFIGHTING

CABER TOSSING
ETON WALL GAME
JAVELIN THROW
ORIENTEERING
PIGEON RACING
POINT-TO-POINT
STEEPLECHASE
13
EQUESTRIANISM
HARNESS RACING
SKATEBOARDING
WEIGHT LIFTING
14
FOOTBALL LEAGUE
MOUNTAINEERING
STOCK-CAR RACING
15
GREYHOUND
 RACING
16
AMERICAN
 FOOTBALL
MOTORCYCLE
 RACING
18
CLAY-PIGEON
 SHOOTING
FREESTYLE
 WRESTLING
19
ASSOCIATION
FOOTBALL

GAMES

2
GO
4
I-SPY
LUDO
POOL
SNAP
5
BINGO
CARDS
CHESS
CRAPS
DARTS

FIVES
POKER
RUMMY
SHOGI
SPOOF
WHIST
6
CLUEDO
HOOPLA
PAC-MAN
TIPCAT

7
BOWLING
HANGMAN
LOTTERY
MAHJONG
MARBLES
MATADOR
OLD MAID
PACHISI
PONTOON
SNOOKER
YAHTZEE

8
BACCARAT
BIRD CAGE
CRIBBAGE
DADDLUMS
DOMINOES
DRAUGHTS
LEAPFROG
MONOPOLY
PATIENCE
ROULETTE
SCRABBLE
SKITTLES

GAMES / DANCES

9
AUNT SALLY
BILLIARDS
BLACK-JACK
KISS CHASE
POKER DICE
RED LETTER
SNAKE-EYES
VINGT-ET-UN

10
BACKGAMMON
BAT AND TRAP
CASABLANCA
RUNNING OUT
11
CHEMIN DE FER
PLAYSTATION
TIDDLYWINKS

12
BAR BILLIARDS
KNUR AND SPELL
SHOVE HA'PENNY
13
HAPPY FAMILIES
SPACE INVADERS
14
CONTRACT BRIDE

TRIVIAL PURSUIT
SNIP-SNAP-
  SNORUM
16
SNAKES AND
  LADDERS
20
DEVIL AMONG THE
  TAILORS

DANCES

3
DOG
GIG
JIG
OLE
4
AHIR
BUMP
CANA
HAKA
HORA
JIVE
JOTA
POGO
SHAG
VIRA
5
BARIS
BULBA
CAROL
CONGA
CUECA
DANSA
DEBKA
GAVOT
GIGUE
GOPAK
HALOA
HOPAK
KUMMI
L'AG-YA
LIMBO
LOURE
MAMBO
NAZUN
NUMBA
OKINA
POLKA
RUEDA
RUMBA
SALSA

SAMBA
SARBA
SHAKE
SIBEL
SIBYL
STOMP
TANGO
TRATA
TWIST
VELAL
WALTZ
6
ABUANG
AMENER
ATINGA
BATUTA
BOLERO
BOOGIE
CALATA
CANARY
CAN-CAN
CAROLE
CEBELL
CHA CHA
DJOGED
EIXIDA
GANGAR
GIENYS
HUSTLE
JACARA
JARABE
JARANA
KAGURA
KALELA
MINUET
PAVANE
PESSAH
POLSKA
SHIMMY
TIRANA
VALETA

VELETA
YUMARI
7
ABRASAX
ABRAXAS
AHIDOUS
APARIMA
ARNAOUT
BABORÁK
BALL PLA
BAMBUCO
BANJARA
BATUQUE
BHARANG
BOURRÉE
CANARIE
CANARIO
CINQ PAS
CSARDAS
FORLANA
FOX-TROT
FURIANT
FURLANA
GAVOTTE
GERANOS
GLOCSEN
GOMBEYS
GONDHAL
GOSHIKI
HIMINAU
JABADAO
JON-NUKE
LAMBADA
LAMENTO
LANCERS
LANDLER
LLORONA
MADISON
MAYPOLE
MAZURKA
MEASURE

MILONGA
MUNEIRA
PASILLO
PERICON
PLANXTY
PURPURI
SARDANA
SATACEK
SIKINIK
TANDAVA
TANTARA
TRAIPSE
WAKAMBA
8
ALEGRIAS
Ã MOLESON
AURRESKU
BALZTANZ
BULL-FOOT
CACHUCHA
CAKEWALK
CANACUAS
CANDIOTE
CHARRADA
COURANTE
FANDANGO
GALLIARD
GYMNASKA
HABANERA
HAND JIVE
HORN PIPE
HUAPANGO
MAILEHEN
MOHOBELO
MOONWALK
MUTCHICO
OXDANSEN
PERICOTE
RIGAUDON
RUTUBURI
TSAMIKOS

9
BAGUETTES
BAILECITO
BARN DANCE
BOULANGER
CARDADORS
CLOG DANCE
COTILLION
ECOSSAISE
FARANDOLE
GALLEGANDA
HAJDUTÂNC
HORN DANCE
JITTER BUG
KOLOMEJKA
LINE DANCE
MISTLETOE
MOKOROTLO
PASSEPIED
POLONAISE
QUADRILLE
QUICKSTEP
RENNINGEN
ROCK 'N' ROLL

SARABANDE
SATECKOVA
TAMBORITO
TROYANATS
10
ATNUMOKITA
BANDLTANTZ
BATON DANCE
BERGERETTA
CHANIOTIKO
CHARLESTON
ESPRINGALE
FACKELTANZ
FARANDOULO
FURRY DANCE
GAY GORDONS
HOKEY-COKEY
KYNDELDANS
LAUTERBACH
LOCOMOTION
RUNNING SET
STRATHSPEY
STRIP TEASE
SURUVAKARY

TARANTELLA
TRENCHMORE
TURKEY TROT
11
BABORASCHKA
BLACKBOTTOM
DANSURINGUR
DITHYRAMBOS
FLORAL DANCE
GHARBA DANCE
LAMBETH WALK
MORRIS DANCE
PALAIS GLIDE
PAMPERRUQUE
ROCK AND ROLL
SCHOTTISCHE
SQUARE DANCE
12
BREAKDANCING
CREUX DE VERVI
DANSE MACABRE
FUNKY CHICKEN
GREEN GARTERS
REEL O'TULLOCH

13
EIGHTSOME REEL
GHILLIE CALLUM
HIGHLAND FLING
14
BABBITY BOWSTER
MILKMAIDS' DANCE
STRIP THE WILLOW
15
COUNTRY BUMPKIN
MILITARY TWO-STEP
SELLINGER'S ROUND
17
HASTE TO THE
    WEDDING
18
SIR ROGER DE
    COVERLEY

HOBBIES AND CRAFTS

3
DIY
5
BATIK
BINGO
6
BONSAI
SEWING
7
COLLAGE
COKERY
CROCHET
DANCING
KEEP FIT
MACRAMÉ
MOSAICS
ORIGAMI
POTTERY
READING
TATTING
TOPARY
WEAVING
8
AEROBICS
APPLIQUÉ
BASKETRY

CANEWORK
FRETWORK
KNITTING
LAPIDARY
PAINTNG
QUILTING
SPINNING
TAPESTRY
WOODWORK
9
ASTROLOGY
ASTRONOMY
DÉCOUPAGE
GARDENING
GENEALOGY
MARQUETRY
PALMISTRY
PATCHWORK
PHILATELY
RUG MAKING
10
BEE-KEEPING
BEER-MAKING
CROSSWORDS
EMBROIDERY
ENAMELLING

KITE FLYING
LACE MAKING
UPHOLSTERY
WINE MAKING
11
ARCHEOLOGY
BARK RUBBING
BOOK BINDING
CALLIGRAPHY
DRESS MAKING
HANG GLIDING
LEPIDOPTERY
MODEL MAKING
PHOTOGRAPHY
STENCILLING
VINTAGE CARS
12
BEACH COMBING
BIRD WATCHING
BRASS RUBBING
CANDLE-MAKING
FLOWER DRYING
TROPICAL FISH
13
FOSSIL HUNTING
JIG-SAW PUZZLES

MODEL RAILWAYS
TRAIN SPOTTING
14
BADGER WATCHING
CAKE DECORATING
COIN COLLECTING
FLOWER PRESSING
GLASS ENGRAVING
PIGEON FANCYING
15
FLOWER ARRANGING
LAMPSHADE MAKING
SHELL COLLECTING
STAMP COLLECTING
16
AMATEUR
    DRAMATICS
AUTOGRAPH
    HUNTING
19
BUTTERFLY
    COLLECTING

STADIUMS AND VENUES

AINTREE (horse racing)
ANAHEIM (baseball)
ASCOT (horse racing)
AZTECA STADIUM, MEXICO CITY
(olympics, football)
BELFRY, THE (golf)
BELMONT PARK, LONG ISLAND
(horse racing)
BERNABAU STADIUM, MADRID (football)
BIG FOUR CURLING RINK (curling)
BRANDS HATCH (motor racing)
BROOKLANDS (motor racing)
CAESAR'S PALACE, LAS VEGAS (boxing)
CENTRAL STADIUM, KIEV (football)
CLEVELAND MUNICIPAL STADIUM
(baseball)
CORPORATION STADIUM, CALICUR
(cricket)
CROKE PARK, DUBLIN (Gaelic football,
hurling)
CRUCIBLE, SHEFFIELD (snooker)
CRYSTAL PALACE (athletics)
DAYTONA INTERNATIONAL SPEEDWAY
(motor racing, motor cycling)
EDEN GARDENS, CALCUTTA (cricket)
EDGBASTON (cricket)
EPSOM DOWNS (horse racing)
FLUSHING MEADOW, USA (tennis)
FRANCORCHAMPS,BELGIUM (motor
racing)
HAMPDEN PARK, GLASGOW (football)
HEADINGLEY (cricket)
HEYSEL STADIUM, BRUSSELS (football)
IBROX PARK GLASGOW, (football)

LANDSDOWNE ROAD, DUBLIN (rugby)
LORDS CRICKET GROUND (cricket)
LOUISIANA SUPERDOME (most sports)
MADISON SQUARE GARDENS,
NEW YORK (boxing)
MARACANA STADIUM, BRAZIL (football)
MEADOWBANK (athletics)
MILLENNIUM STADIUM,CARDIFF (rugby)
MOOR PARK, RICKMANSWORTH (golf)
MUNICH OLYMPIC STADIUM (athletics,
football)
MURRAYFIELD (rugby)
NEWMARKET (horse racing)
NEU CAMP, BARCELONA (football)
ODSAL STADIUM, BRADFORD (rugby
league)
OLD TRAFFORD (Man.U. football ground)
OLD TRAFFORD (cricket ground)
OVAL, THE (cricket)
ROYAL AND ANCIENT GOLF CLUB OF
ST.ANDREWS (golf)
SHANGHAI STADIUM (gymnastics)
SILVERSTONE (motor racing)
STAHAV STADIUM, PRAGUE (gymnastics)
ST JAMES' PARK NEWCASTLE (football)
SYDNEY CRICKET GROUND
TWICKENHAM (rugby union)
WEMBLEY CONFERENCE CENTRE (darts)
WHITE CITY (greyhound racing)
WIMBLEDON (tennis)
WINDSOR PARK, BELFAST (football)

TROPHIES, EVENTS AND AWARDS

ADMIRAL'S CUP (sailing)
SILVER BROOM (curling)
ALL-IRELAND CHAMPIONSHIP (Gaelic
football)
ALL-IRELAND CHAMPIONSHIPS (hurling)
ALPINE CHAMPIONSHIPS (skiing)
AMERICA'S CUP (sailing)
ASHES (cricket)
BADMINTON THREE DAY EVENT (equestrian)
BBC SPORTS PERSONALITY OF THE YEAR
(all-round)
BENSON & HEDGES MASTERS (snooker)

BOAT RACE (rowing)
BRITISH OPEN CHAMPIONSHIP (golf)
BRONZE MEDAL (most sports)
CHELTENHAM GOLD CUP (horse racing)
CLASSICS (horse racing)
COMMONWEALTH GAMES (athletics)
CORNHILL TESTS (cricket)
DAVIS CUP (tennis)
DAYTONA 500 (motor racing)
DERBY (horse racing)
EMBASSY WORLD PROFESSIONAL
SNOOKER CHAMPIONSHIP (snooker)

ENGLISH GREYHOUND DERBY (greyhound racing)
EUROPEAN CHAMPIONS CUP (basketball)
EUROPEAN CHAMPIONS LEAGUE(football)
EUROPEAN FOOTBALLER OF THE YEAR (football)
EUROPEAN ORDER OF MERIT (golf)
FEDERATION CUP (tennis)
FA CARLING PREMIERSHIP (football)
FA AXA CHALLENGE CUP (football)
FA CHARITY SHIELD (football)
FOOTBALL LEAGUE CHAMPIONSHIP (football)
FULL CAP (football, rugby)
FA FOOTBALLER OF THE YEAR (football)
GOLDEN BOOT AWARD (football)
GOLD MEDAL (most sports)
GORDEN INTERNATIONAL MEDAL (curling)
GRAND NATIONAL (greyhound racing)
GRAND NATIONAL STEEPLECHASE (horse racing)
GRAND PRIX (motor racing)
GRAND SLAM (rugby)
HARMSWORTH TROPHY (power boat racing)
HENLEY REGATTA (rowing)
HIGHLAND GAMES
ICY SMITH CUP (ice hockey)
INDIANAPOLIS 500 (motor racing)
INTERNATIONAL CHAMPIONSHP (bowls)
INTERNATIONAL CROSS-COUNTRY CHAMPIONSHIP (athletics)
IROQUOIS CUP (lacrosse)
ISLE OF MANN TT (motorcycle racing)
JULES RIMET TROPHY (world cup football)
KING GEORGE V GOLD CUP (equestrian)
LE MANS 24 HOUR (motor racing)
LITTLEWOODS CHALLENGE CUP (football)
LOMBARD RALLY (motor racing)
LONSDALE BELT (boxing)
MAN OF THE MATCH (any team gamel)
MARATHON (athletics)
MIDDLESEX SEVENS (rugby union)
MILK RACE (cycling)
MONTE CARLO RALLY (motor racing)
MOST VALUABLE PLAYER (American football)
NATIONAL ANGLING CHAMPIONSHIP (angling)
NATIONAL HUNT JOCKEY CHAMPIONHIP (horse racing)
NATIONAL WESTMINSTER BANK TROPHY (cricket)

NATIONWIDE LEAGUE (football)
NORDIC CHAMPIONSHIPS (skiing)
OAKS (horse racing)
OLYMPIC GAMES (most sports)
ONE THOUSAND GUINEAS (horse racing)
OPEN CROQUET CHAMPIONSHIP (croquet)
OXFORD BLUE (most sports)
PFA FOOTBALLER OF THE YEAR (football)
PREMIER LEAGUE (football)
QUEEN ELIZABETH II CUP (equestrian)
RAC TOURIST TROPHY (motor racing)
ROSE BOWL (American football)
ROYAL HUNT CUP (horse racing)
RUGBY LEAGUE CHALLENGE CUP (rugby league)
RUNNERS-UP MEDAL (most sports)
RYDER CUP (golf)
SCOTTISH FOOTBALL ASSOCIATION CUP (football)
SILVER MEDAL (most sports)
SIX NATIONS CHAMPIONSHIP (rugby)
SOUTH AMERICAN CHAMPIONSHIP (football)
STANLEY CUP (ice hockey)
ST LEGER (horse racing)
STRATHCONA CUP (curling)
SUPER BOWL (American football)
SUPER CUP (handball)
SWAYTHLING CUP (table tennis)
TENANTS SCOTTISH LEAGUE (football)
THOMAS CUP (badminton)
TOUR DE FRANCE (cycling)
TRIPLE CROWN (rugby union)
TWO THOUSAND GUINEAS (horse racing)
UEFA CUP (football)
WALKER CUP (amateur golf)
WEIGHTMAN CUP (sailing)
WIMBLEDON CHAMPIONSHIP (tennis)
WINGFIELD SKULLS (rowing)
WINNER'S MEDAL (most sports)
WOODEN SPOON! (most sports)
WORLD CLUB CHAMPIONSHIP (football)
WORLD CUP (football/rugby/cricket)
WORLD MASTERS CHAMPIONSHIPS (darts)
WORLD SERIES (baseball)
WORTHINGTON CUP (football)
YELLOW JERSEY (cycling)

FOOTBALL TEAMS

TEAM	GROUND	NICKNAME
ABERDEEN	PITTODRIE STADIUM	DONS
AIRDRIEONIANS	BROOMFIELD PARK	DIAMONDS; WAYSIDERS
ALBION ROVERS	CLIFTON HALL	WEE ROVERS
ALLOA	RECREATION PARK	WASPS
ARBROATH	GAYFIELD PARK	RED LICHTIES
ARSENAL	HIGHBURY	GUNNERS
ASTON VILLA	VILLA PARK	VILLANS
AYR UNITED	SOMERSET PARK	HONEST MEN
BARNET	UNDERHILL STADIUM	BEES
BARNSLEY	OAKWELL GROUND	TYKES; REDS;COLLIERS
BERWICK RANGERS	SHIELFIELD PARK	BORDERERS
BIRMINGHAM CITY	ST ANDREWS	BLUES
BLACKBURN ROVERS	EWOOD PARK	BLUE WHITES; ROVERS
BLACKPOOL	BLOOMFIELD ROAD	SEASIDERS
BOLTON WANDERERS	REEBOK STADIUM	TROTTERS
BOURNEMOUTH	DEAN COURT	CHERRIES
BRADFORD CITY	VALLEY PARADE	BANTAMS
BRECHIN CITY	GLEBE PARK	CITY
BRENTFORD	GRIFFIN PARK	BEES
BRIGHTON HOVE ALBION	WITHDEAN STADIUM	SEAGULLS
BRISTOL CITY	ASHTON GATE	ROBINS
BRISTOL ROVERS	MEMORIAL STADIUM	PIRATES
BURNLEY	TURF MOOR	CLARETS
BURY	GIGG LANE	SHAKERS
CAMBRIDGE UNITED	ABBEY STADIUM	UNITED
CARDIFF CITY	NINIAN PARK	BLUEBIRDS
CARLISLE UNITED	BRUNTON PARK	CUMBRIANS; BLUES
CELTIC	CELTIC PARK	BHOYS
CHARLTON ATHLETIC	THE VALLEY	HADDICKS; ROBINS;
CHELSEA	STAMFORD BRIDGE	BLUES
CHELTENHAM TOWN	WHADDON ROAD	ROBINS
CHESTERFIELD	RECREATION GROUND	BLUES; SPIREITES
CLYDEBANK	KILBOWIE PARK	BANKIES
CLYDE	FIRHILL PARK	BULLY WEE
COLCHESTER CITY	LAYER ROAD	U'S
COVENTRY CITY	HIGHFIELD ROAD	SKY BLUES
COWDENBEATH	CENTRAL PARK	COWDEN
CREWE ALEXANDRA	GRESTY ROAD	RAILWAYMEN
CRYSTAL PALACE	SELHURST PARK	EAGLES
DARLINGTON	FEETHAMS GROUND	QUAKERS
DERBY COUNTY	PRIDE PARK	RAMS
DUMBARTON	BOGHEAD PARK	SONS
DUNDEE	DENS PARK	DARK BLUES; DEE
DUNDEE UNITED	TANNADICE PARK	TERRORS; TANGERINES
DUNFERMLINE ATHLETIC	EAST END PARK	PARS
EAST FIFE	BAYVIEW PARK	FIFERS
EAST STIRLINGSHIRE	FIRS PARK	SHIRE
ELGIN CITY	BOROUGH BRIGGS	CITY
EVERTON	GOODISON PARK	TOFFEES

TEAM	GROUND	NICKNAME
EXETER CITY	ST JAMES PARK	GRECIANS
FALKIRK	BROCKVILLE PARK	BAIRNS
FORFAR ATHELETIC	STATION PARK	LOONS
FULHAM	CRAVEN COTTAGE	COTTAGERS
GILLINGHAM	PRIESTFIELD STADIUM	GILLS
GRIIMSBY TOWN	BLUNDELL PARK	MARINERS
HALIFAX TOWN	SHAY GROUND	SHAY MEN
HAMILTON ACADEMICALS	DOUGLAS PARK	ACCIES
HARTLEPOOL UNITED	VICTORIA GROUND	POOL
HEART OF MIDLOTHIAN	TYNECASTLE PARK	HEARTS
HEREFORD UNITED	EDGAR STREET	UNITED
HIBERNIAN	EASTER ROAD	HIBEES
HUDDERSFIELD TOWN	MACALPINE STADIUM	TERRIERS
HULL CITY	BOOTHFERRY PARK	TIGERS
INVERNESS CALEDONIAN THISTLE	CALEDONIAN STADIUM	THISTLE; CALEY
IPSWICH TOWN	PORTMAN ROAD	BLUES; TOWN
KIDDERMINSTER HARRIERS	AGGBOROUGH STADIUM	HARRIERS
KILMARNOCK	RUGBY PARK	KILLIE
LEEDS UNITED	ELLAND ROAD	UNITED
LEICESTER CITY	FILBERT STREET	FILBERTS; FOXES
LEYTON ORIENT	BRISBANE ROAD	O'S
LINCOLN CITY	SINCIL BANK	RED IMPS
LIVERPOOL	ANFIELD	REDS; POOL
LIVINGSTON	COURIER STADIUM	TONS
LUTON TOW	KENILWORTH ROAD	HATTERS
MACCLESFIELD TOWN	MOSS ROSE	SILK MEN
MANCHESTER CITY	MAINE ROAD	BLUES; CITY
MANCHESTER UNITED	OLD TRAFFORD	RED DEVILS
MANSFIELD TOWN	FIELD MILL GROUND	STAGS
MIDDLESBROUGH	RIVERSIDE STADIUM	BORO
MILLWALL	THE NEW DEN	LIONS
MONTROSE	LINKS PARK	GABLE ENDRS
MORTON	CAPPIELOW PARK	TON
MOTHERWELL	FIR PARK	WELL
NEWCASTLE UNITED	ST JAMES PARK	MAGPIES
NORTHAMPTON TOWN	COUNTY GROUND	COBBLERS
NORWICH CITY	CARROW ROAD	CANARIES
NOTTINGHAM FOREST	CITY GROUND	REDS; FOREST
NOTTS COUNTY	MEADOW LANE	MAGPIES
OLDHAM ATHLETIC	BOUNDARY PARK	LATICS
OXFORD UNITED	MANOR GROUND	U'S
PATRICK THISTLE	FIRHILL PARK	JAGS
PETERBOROUGH UNITED	LONDON ROAD	POSH
PETERHEAD	BALMOOR STADIUM	BLUE TOONS
PLYMOUTH ARGYLE	HOME PARK	PILGRIMS
PORTSMOUTH	FRATTON PARK	POMPEY
PORT VALE	VALE PARK	VALIANTS
PRESTON NORTH END	DEEPDALE	LILYWHITES; NORTH END
QUEEN OF THE SOUTH	PALMERSTON PARK	DOONHAMERS
QUEEN'S PARK	HAMPDEN PARK	SPIDERS
QUEEN'S PARK RANGERS	LOFTUS ROAD	RANGERS; R's

FOOTBALL TEAMS

TEAM	GROUND	NICKNAME
RAITH ROVERS	STARK'S PARK	ROVERS
RANGERS	IBROX STADIUM	GERS
READING	MAJEWSKI STADIUM	ROYALS
ROCHDALE	SPOTLAND	DALE
ROSS COUNTY	VICTORIA PARK	COUNTY
ROTHERHAM UNITED	MILLMOOR GROUND	MERRY MILLERS
SCUNTHORPE UNITED	GLANFORD PARK	IRONS
SHEFFIELD UNITED	BRAMHALL LANE	BLADES
SHEFFIELD WEDNESDAY	HILLSBOROUGH	OWLS
SHREWSBURY TOWN	GAY MEADOW	SHREWS; TOWN
SOUTHAMPTON	THE DELL	SAINTS
SOUTHEND UNITED	ROOTS HALL	SHRIMPERS
STENHOUSEMUIR	OCHILVIEW PARK	WARRIORS
STIRLING ALBION	ANNFIELD PARK	ALBION
ST JOHNSTONE	McDIARMIDPARK	SAINTS
ST MIRREN	LOVE STREET	BUDDIES; SAINTS
STOCKPORT COUNTY	EDGELEY PARK	COUNTY; HATTERS
STOKE CITY	VICTORIA GROUND	POTTERS
STRANRAER	STAIR PARK	BLUES
SUNDERLAND	THE STADIUM OF LIGHT	WEARSIDERS
SWANSEA CITY	VETCH FIELD	SWANS
SWINDON TOWN	COUNTY GROUND	ROBINS
TORQUAY UNITED	PLAINMOOR GROUND	GULLS
TOTTENHAM HOTSPUR	WHITE HART LANE	SPURS
TRANMERE ROVERS	PRENTON PARK	ROVERS
WALSALL	FELLOWS PARK	SADDLERS
WATFORD	VICARAGE ROAD	HORNETS
WEST BROMWICH ALBION	HAWTHORNS	BAGGIES; ALBION
WEST HAM UNITED	UPTON PARK	HAMMERS
WIGAN ATHLETIC	JJB STADIUM	LATICS
WIMBLEDON	SELHURST PARK	DONS
WOLVERHAMPTON WANDERERS	MOLINEUX	WOLVES
WREXHAM	RACECOURSE GROUND	ROBINS
WYCOMBE WANDERERS	ADAMS PARK	CHAIRBOYS; BLUES
YORK CITY	BOOTHAM CRESCENT	MINSTERMEN

OCCUPATIONS

PROFESSIONS, TRADES AND OCCUPATIONS

2	AGENT	QUACK	BURSAR
GP	BAKER	QUILL	BUSKER
MD	BONZE	RABBI	BUTLER
MO	BOOTS	RATER	CABBIE
PA	BOSUN	REEVE	CABMAN
PM	CADDY	RUNER	CALKER
3	CHOIR	SCOUT	CANNER
DOC	CLERK	SEWER	CARTER
DON	CLOWN	SHOER	CARVER
GYP	COACH	SLAVE	CASUAL
PRO	COMIC	SMITH	CENSOR
REP	CRIER	SOWER	CLERGY
SPY	CRIMP	STAFF	CLERIC
VET	CURER	SWEEP	CODIST
4	DAILY	TAMER	COINER
AMAH	ENVOY	TAWER	COMBER
AYAH	EXTRA	TAXER	CONDER
BABU	FAKIR	TILER	COOLIE
BARD	FENCE	TUNER	COOPER
BOSS	FIFER	TUTOR	COPPER
CHAR	FILER	TYLER	CO-STAR
CHEF	FINER	USHER	COSTER
COOK	FLIER	VALET	COWBOY
CREW	GIPSY	VINER	COWMAN
DIVA	GLUER	**6**	CRITIC
DYER	GROOM	AIRMAN	CUTLER
GANG	GUARD	ARCHER	CUTTER
GRIP	GUIDE	ARTIST	DANCER
HACK	GUILD	AURIST	DEALER
HAND	HAKIM	AUTHOR	DIGGER
HEAD	HARPY	BAGMAN	DOCKER
HERD	HELOT	BAILER	DOCTOR
HIND	HIRER	BAILOR	DOWSER
MAGI	HIVER	BALKER	DRAPER
MAID	HOPPO	BANKER	DRAWER
MATE	LAMIA	BARBER	DRIVER
MIME	LEECH	BARGEE	DROVER
PAGE	LUTER	BARKER	EDITOR
PEON	MASON	BARMAN	FABLER
POET	MEDIC	BATMAN	FACTOR
SEER	MINER	BEARER	FARMER
SERF	NAVVY	BINDER	FELLER
SYCE	NURSE	BOFFIN	FICTOR
TOUT	OILER	BOOKIE	FISHER
WARD	OWLER	BOWMAN	FITTER
WHIP	PILOT	BREWER	FLAYER
5	PIPER	BROKER	FORGER
ACTOR	PLYER	BUGLER	FOWLER
AD-MAN	PUPIL	BURLER	FRAMER

PROFESSIONS, TRADES AND OCCUPATIONS

6 continued

FULLER	MEDICO	RENTER	TINKER
GAFFER	MENDER	RIGGER	TINMAN
GANGER	MENIAL	RINGER	TINNER
GAOLER	MENTOR	ROBBER	TOLLER
GAUCHO	MERCER	ROOFER	TOUTER
GAUGER	MILKER	ROOTER	TRACER
GIGOLO	MILLER	SACKER	TRADER
GILDER	MINTER	SAILOR	TUBMAN
GILLIE	MONGER	SALTER	TURNER
GLAZER	MORISK	SALVOR	TYCOON
GLOVER	MUMMER	SAPPER	TYPIST
GRAVER	MUMPER	SARTOR	USURER
GROCER	MYSTIC	SAWYER	VACHER
GUIDER	NAILER	SCRIBE	VALUER
GUIDON	NOTARY	SEA-DOG	VAMPER
GUNMAN	NURSER	SEALER	VANMAN
GUNNER	OBOIST	SEAMAN	VASSAL
HARPER	OILMAN	SEINER	VENDER
HATTER	ORATOR	SEIZOR	VENDOR
HAWKER	OSTLER	SELLER	VERGER
HEALER	PACKER	SERVER	VERSER
HEAVER	PARSON	SETTER	VIEWER
HODMAN	PASTOR	SEXTON	WAITER
HOOPER	PAVIER	SHROFF	WALLER
HORNER	PAVIOR	SINGER	WARDEN
HOSIER'	PEDANT	SIRCAR	WARDER
HUNTER	PEDLAR	SKIVVY	WARPER
INTERN	PENMAN	SLATER	WASHER
ISSUER	PICKER	SLAVER	WEAVER
JAILER	PIEMAN	SLAVEY	WEEDER
JAILOR	PIRATE	SLEUTH	WELDER
JOBBER	PITMAN	SNARER	WHALER
JOCKEY	PLATER	SOCMAN	WORKER
JOINER	PLAYER	SORTER	WRIGHT
JOWTER	PORTER	SOUTER	WRITER
JURIST	POTBOY	SPICER	**7**
KEELER	POTTER	SQUIRE	ABACIST
KEEPER	PRIEST	STAGER	ABIGAIL
KILLER	PRUNER	STOKER	ACOLYTE
LACKEY	PURSER	STORER	AGOLYTH
LANDER	QUERRY	SUTLER	ACROBAT
LASCAR	RABBIN	TABLER	ACTRESS
LAWYER	RAGMAN	TAILOR	ACTUARY
LECTOR	RANGER	TAMPER	ALEWIFE
LENDER	RATTER	TANNER	ALMONER
LOADER	READER	TASKER	ANALYST
LOGMAN	REAPER	TASTER	APPOSER
LUMPER	REAVER	TELLER	ARABIST
MARKER	RECTOR	TERMER	ARBITER
MATRON	REGENT	TESTER	ARTISAN
	RELIEF	TILLER	ARTISTE

7 continued

ASSAYER	COWHERD	GRANTOR	ORDERLY
ASSIZER	COWPOKE	GRAZIER	PACKMAN
ASSURED	CROFTER	GRINDER	PAGEBOY
ASSURER	CROPPER	GYMNAST	PAINTER
AUDITOR	CURATOR	HACKLER	PALMIST
AVIATOR	CURRIER	HARPIST	PANTLER
AWARDER	CUSTODE	HAULIER	PEDDLER
BAILIFF	DANSEUR	HELOTRY	PIANIST
BANDMAN	DENTIST	HERBIST	PICADOR
BARMAID	DIALIST	HERDMAN	PLANNER
BELLBOY	DIETIST	HERITOR	PLANTER
BELLHOP	DITCHER	HIGGLER	PLEADER
BEST BOY	DOMINIE	HOGHERD	PLUMBER
BIRDMAN	DOORMAN	HOSTLER	POACHER
BLASTER	DRAGMAN	INDEXER	POSTBOY
BLENDER	DRAPIER	INLAYER	POSTMAN
BOATMAN	DRAWBOY	IRONIST	PRESSER
BONDMAN	DRAYMAN	JANITOR	PRESTOR
BOOKMAN	DREDGER	JUGGLER	PRINTER
BOTTLER	DRESSER	JUNKMAN	PUDDLER
BRIGAND	DROGMAN	JURYMAN	RANCHER
BUILDER	DRUMMER	KEELMAN	REALTOR
BURGLAR	DUSTMAN	KNACKER	REFINER
BUTCHER	FARRIER	KNITTER	RIVETER
BUTTONS	FASCIST	LACEMAN	ROADMAN
CALLBOY	FIDDLER	LINKBOY	ROASTER
CAMBIST	FIREMAN	LINKMAN	RUSTLER
CARRIER	FLESHER	LOCKMAN	SACRIST
CASEMAN	FLORIST	LOMBARD	SADDLER
CASHIER	FLUNKEY	MALTMAN	SAMPLER
CATERER	FLUTIST	MANAGER	SAMURAI
CAULKER	FOOTBOY	MANGLER	SCOURER
CELLIST	FOOTMAN	MARBLER	SCRAPER
CHANTER	FOOTPAD	MARCHER	SERVANT
CHAPMAN	FOREMAN	MARINER	SETTLER
CHEMIST	FOUNDER	MARSHAL	SHARPER
CHORIST	FRISEUR	MATADOR	SHEARER
CLEANER	FROGMAN	MATELOT	SHIPPER
CLICKER	FUELLER	MEALMAN	SHOPBOY
CLIPPIE	FURRIER	MEATMAN	SHOWMAN
COALMAN	GATEMAN	MIDWIFE	SHUNTER
COBBLER	GIRDLER	MILKMAN	SILKMAN
COCKLER	GLAZIER	MODISTE	SIMPLER
COLLIER	GLEANER	MONEYER	SKINNER
CO-PILOT	GLEEMAN	MONITOR	SKIPPER
COPYIST	GLOSSER	MOOTMAN	SLIPPER
CORONER	GRAFFER	MOULDER	SMELTER
CORSAIR	GRAFTER	NEWSBOY	SNIPPER
COUNSEL	GRAINER	OCULIST	SOCAGER
COURIER	GRANGER	OFFICER	SOLDIER
	GRANTEE	ORDERER	SOLOIST

PROFESSIONS, TRADES AND OCCUPATIONS

7 continued

SPENCER
SPINNER
SPOTTER
STAINER
STAMPER
STAPLER
STATIST
STEERER
STEWARD
SURGEON
SWABBER
SWEEPER
TABORER
TALLIER
TAPSTER
TAXI-MAN
TEACHER
TIPSTER
TRACKER
TRAINER
TRAPPER
TRAWLER
TRIMMER
TRUCKER
TRUSTEE
TUMBLER
TURNKEY
VINTNER
VIOLIST
WAGONER
WARRIOR
WEBSTER
WEIGHER
WHEELER
WHETTER
WIREMAN
WOODMAN
WOOLMAN
WORKMAN
WRAPPER
8
ADSCRIPT
AERONAUT
ALGERINE
ANALYSER
APHORIST
APIARIST
ARBORIST
ARMORIST
ARMOURER

ARRESTOR
ASSESSOR
ATTORNEY
BAGMAKER
BANDSMAN
BARGEMAN
BEARHERD
BEDESMAN
BEDMAKER
BIT-MAKER
BLEACHER
BOATSMAN
BONDMAID
BONDSMAN
BOTANIST
BOWMAKER
BOXMAKER
BREWSTER
BROACHER
CABIN BOY
CELLARER
CERAMIST
CHANDLER
CHOIRBOY
CIDERIST
CLAQUEUR
CLOTHIER
COACHMAN
CO-AUTHOR
CODIFIER
COISTRIL
COLLATOR
COMEDIAN
COMPILER
COMPOSER
CONCLAVE
CONJURER
CONVEYOR
COURTIER
COW-LEECH
COXSWAIN
CROUPIER
CUTPURSE
DAIRYMAN
DANSEUSE
DECKHAND
DEFENDER
DESIGNER
DIRECTOR
DOG-LEECH

DOMESTIC
DOUGHBOY
DRAGOMAN
DRUGGIST
EDUCATOR
EMBALMER
EMISSARY
ENGINEER
ENGRAVER
ENROLLER
EPIC POET
ESSAYIST
ESSOINER
EXORCIST
EXPLORER
EXPORTER
FABULIST
FACTOTUM
FALCONER
FAMULIST
FARMHAND
FERRYMAN
FIGURANT
FILMSTAR
FINISHER
FISHWIFE
FLATFOOT
FLAUTIST
FLETCHER
FODDERER
FORESTER
FORGEMAN
FUGLEMAN
GANGSTER
GARDENER
GAVELMAN
GENDARME
GLASSMAN
GOATHERD
GODSMITH
GOSSIPER
GOVERNOR
GUARDIAN
GUNSMITH
HAMMERER
HANDMAID
HANDYMAN
HATMAKER
HAYMAKER
HEAD COOK
HEADSMAN

HELMSMAN
HENCHMAN
HERDSMAN
HIRELING
HISTRION
HOME HELP
HOTELIER
HOUSEBOY
HUCKSTER
HUNTSMAN
IMPORTER
IMPROVER
INKMAKER
INVENTOR
JAPANNER
JET PILOT
JEWELLER
KIPPERER
LABOURER
LANDGIRL
LANDLADY
LANDLORD
LAPIDARY
LARCENER
LARDERER
LEADSMAN
LECTURER
LINESMAN
LUMBERER
MAGICIAN
MAGISTER
MALTSTER
MASSEUSE
MEASURER
MECHANIC
MEDALIST
MELODIST
MERCATOR
MERCHANT
METAL-MAN
MILKMAID
MILLHAND
MILLINER
MINISTER
MINSTREL
MODELLER
MULETEER
MURALIST
MUSICIAN
NEWSHAWK
NOVELIST

8 continued

ONION-MAN	ROMANCER	TRUCKMAN	BONDSLAVE
OPTICIAN	RUGMAKER	TURNCOCK	BONDWOMAN
ORDAINER	RUMOURER	TURNSPIT	BOOKMAKER
ORDINAND	SALESMAN	TUTORESS	BOOTBLACK
ORGANIST	SATIRIST	UNIONIST	BOOTMAKER
OUTRIDER	SAWBONES	VALUATOR	BUCCANEER
OVERSEER	SCULLION	VINTAGER	BURNISHER
PARGETER	SCULPTOR	VIRTUOSO	BUS DRIVER
PARODIST	SEAMSTER	VOCALIST	CAB DRIVER
PENMAKER	SEA-ROVER	VOLUMIST	CAFE OWNER
PERFUMER	SEASONER	WAITRESS	CAMERAMAN
PETERMAN	SEEDSMAN	WALKER-ON	CAR DRIVER
PEWTERER	SEMPSTER	WARDRESS	CARETAKER
PICAROON	SERVITOR	WARRENER	CARPENTER
PLOUGHER	SHEARMAN	WATCHMAN	CARVANEER
POLISHER	SHEPHERD	WATERMAN	CASEMAKER
PORTRESS	SHIPMATE	WET NURSE	CATECHIST
POSTILER	SHIP'S BOY	WHALEMAN	CELLARMAN
POTMAKER	SHOPGIRL	WHITENER	CHARWOMAN
PREACHER	SHOWGIRL	WHITSTER	CHAUFFEUR
PREFACER	SIDESMAN	WIGMAKER	CHEAPJACK
PRELUDER	SIMPLIST	WINNOWER	CHORISTER
PRESSMAN	SKETCHER	WOOL-DYER	CLARIFIER
PROBATOR	SMUGGLER	WRESTLER	CLERGYMAN
PROCURER	SOLDIERY	**9**	CLINICIAN
PROMOTER	SPACEMAN	ALCHEMIST	CLOGMAKER
PROMPTER	SPEARMAN	ALLUMINOR	COALMINER
PROSAIST	SPEEDCOP	ANATOMIST	COALOWNER
PROVIDER	SPURRER	ANNOTATOR	COLLECTOR
PSALMIST	STARCHER	ANNOUNCER	COLOURIST
PUBLICAN	STITCHER	ARBORATOR	COLUMNIST
PUGILIST	STOCKMAN	ARCHERESS	COMPRADOR
PURVEYOR	STOREMAN	ARCHITECT	CONCIERGE
QUARRIER	STRIPPER	ARCHIVIST	CONDUCTOR
RAFTSMAN	STRUMMER	ART CRITIC	CONSERVER
RANCHERO	STUNTMAN	ART DEALER	COSMONAUT
RAPPEREE	SUPPLIER	ARTIFICER	COST CLERK
RECEIVER	SURVEYOR	ASTRONAUT	COSTUMIER
REGRATER	SWINDLER	ATTENDANT	COURTESAN
RELESSEE	TABOURER	AUTHORESS	COUTURIER
RELESSOR	TALLYMAN	BALLADIST	COWFEEDER
REPAIRER	TAVERNER	BALLERINA	COWKEEPER
REPORTER	TEAMSTER	BANK AGENT	CRACKSMAN
RESETTER	THATCHER	BARRISTER	CRAFTSMAN
RESTORER	THESPIAN	BARROW BOY	CRAYONIST
RETAILER	THRESHER	BEEFEATER	CYMBALIST
RETAINER	TIN MINER	BEEKEEPER	DAILY HELP
REVIEWER	TINSMITH	BIOLOGIST	DAIRYMAID
REWRITER	TORTURER	BOATSWAIN	DECORATOR
RIVETTER	TOYMAKER	BODYGUARD	DECRETIST
	TRIPEMAN	BOILERMAN	DESK CLERK

PROFESSIONS, TRADES AND OCCUPATIONS

9 continued

DETECTIVE
DICE-MAKER
DIE-SINKER
DIETETIST
DIETITIAN
DIRECTRIX
DISPENSER
DISSECTOR
DISTILLER
DRAFTSMAN
DRAMATIST
DRAWLATCH
DRUM-MAKER
DRYSALTER
ECOLOGIST
EMBEZZLER
ENAMELLER
ENGROSSER
EPITOMIST
ERRAND BOY
ESTIMATOR
EXAMINANT
EXCAVATOR
EXCERPTOR
EXCHANGER
EXCISEMAN
EXECUTIVE
EXERCITOR
EXORCISER
FABRICANT
FASHIONER
FELT-MAKER
FIGURANTE
FILM ACTOR
FILM EXTRA
FILM-MAKER
FINANCIER
FIRE-EATER
FISH-CURER
FISHERMAN
FISH-WOMAN
FLAG-MAKER
FLAX-WENCH
FLYFISHER
FREELANCE
FREIGHTER
FRIPPERER
FRUITERER
FURBISHER
FURNISHER

GALVANIST
GASFITTER
GAZETTEER
GEM-CUTTER
GEOLOGIST
GLADIATOR
GLUEMAKER
GOLDSMITH
GONDOLIER
GOSPELLER
GOVERNESS
GROUNDMAN
GUARDSMAN
GUERRILLA
GUITARIST
GUN-RUNNER
HARLEQUIN
HARMONIST
HARPOONER
HARVESTER
HELLENIST
HERBALIST
HERBARIAN
HERBORIST
HERB-WOMAN
HIRED HAND
HIRED HELP
HISTORIAN
HOG-RINGER
HOMEOPATH
HOP-PICKER
HOSTELLER
HOUSEMAID
HOUSEWI FE
HYGIENIST
HYPNOTIST
INCUMBENT
INGRAFTER
INNHOLDER
INNKEEPER
INSCRIBER
INSPECTOR
INTENDANT
IRONSMITH
ITINERANT
JACK-SMITH
JOB-MASTER
KENNEL-MAN
LACEMAKER
LACQUERER
LADY'S MAID

LAND AGENT
LANDREEVE
LARCENIST
LAUNDERER
LAUNDRESS
LEGIONARY
LIBRARIAN
LINOTYPER
LIONTAMER
LIVERYMAN
LOAN AGENT
LOCKMAKER
LOCKSMITH
LOG-ROLLER
LUMBERMAN
MACHINIST
MAGNETIST
MAJORDOMO
MALE MODEL
MALE NURSE
MAN-AT-ARMS
MANNEQUIN
MECHANIST
MEDALLIST
MEMOIRIST
MERCENARY
MESMERIST
MESSENGER
METALLIST
METRICIAN
MILL-OWNER
MODELGIRL
MORTICIAN
MUFFIN-MAN
MUSKETEER
MUSKETOON
MYOLOGIST
NAVIGATOR
NEGOTIANT
NEOLOGIAN
NEOLOGIST
NEWSAGENT
NURSEMAID
ODD JOB MAN
OFFICE BOY
OPERATIVE
ORDINATOR
OSTEOPATH
OTOLOGIST
OUTFITTER
PASQUILER

PAYMASTER
PEDAGOGUE
PERFORMER
PHYSICIAN
PHYSICIST
PINKMAKER
PITSAWYER
PLANISHER
PLASTERER
PLOUGHBOY
PLOUGHMAN
PLURALIST
POETASTER
POINTSMAN
POLICEMAN
POP ARTIST
PORTERESS
PORTRAYER
PORTREEVE
POSTILION
POSTWOMAN
POULTERER
PRACTISER
PRECENTOR
PRECEPTOR
PREDICANT
PRELECTOR
PRIESTESS
PRIVATEER
PROFESSOR
PROFILIST
PROVEDORE
PUBLICIST
PUBLISHER
PULPITEER
PUPPETEER
PYTHONESS
QUALIFIER
QUARRYMAN
RACKETEER
RAILMAKER
RECRUITER
REFORMIST
REHEARSER
RIBBONMAN
ROADMAKER
ROPEMAKER
ROUNDSMAN
RUM-RUNNER
SACRISTAN
SAFEMAKER

9 continued

SAILMAKER
SCARIFIER
SCAVENGER
SCENARIST
SCHOLIAST
SCHOOLMAN
SCIENTIST
SCRIVENER
SCYTHEMAN
SEA-ROBBER
SECRETARY
SHIPOWNER
SHIP'S MATE
SHOEBLACK
SHOEMAKER
SIGHTSMAN
SIGNALMAN
SINOLOGUE
SOAPMAKER
SOLICITOR
SONNETEER
SORCERESS
STABLEBOY
STABLEMAN
STAGEHAND
STATIONER
STAY-MAKER
STEERSMAN
STEVEDORE
SUBEDITOR
SUCCENTOR
SUR-MASTER
SWAN-UPPER
SWINEHERD
SWITCHMAN
SWORDSMAN
SYNDICATE
SYNOPTIST
TABLEMAID
TACTICIAN
TAILORESS
TEATASTER
TENTMAKER
TEST PILOT
THERAPIST
THEURGIST
THROWSTER
TIMBERMAN
TIRE-WOMAN
TOOLSMITH

TOWN CLERK
TOWNCRIER
TRADESMAN
TRAGEDIAN
TRAVELLER
TREASURER
TRE PANNER
TRIBUTARY
TRUMPETER'
TYMPANIST
USHERETTE
VARNISHER
VERSIFIER
VETTURINO
VEXILLARY
VIOLINIST
VOLCANIST
VOLTIGEUR
WARRANTEE
WARRANTER
WASHERMAN
WAXWORKER
WEB MASTER
WHITESTER
WINEMAKER
WOOD-REEVE
WORKWOMAN
ZOOKEEPER
ZOOLOGIST
ZOOTOMIST

10

ABLE SEAMAN
ACCOMPTANT
ACCOUCHEUR
ACCOUNTANT
ACOLOTHIST
ADVERTISER
AEROLOGIST
AGROLOGIST
AGRONOMIST
AIR HOSTESS
AIR STEWARD
ALGEBRAIST
AMANUENSIS
APOTHECARY
APPRENTICE
ARBALISTER
ARBITRATOR
ASTROLOGER
ASTRONOMER
ATMOLOGIST

AUCTIONEER
AUDIT CLERK
BALLOONIST
BALLPLAYER
BANDMASTER
BASEBALLER
BASSOONIST
BEADSWOMAN
BEAUTICIAN
BELL-HANGER
BELL-RINGER
BIOCHEMIST
BIOGRAPHER
BLACKSMITH
BLADESMITH
BLOCKMAKER
BLUEJACKET
BOMBARDIER
BONDSWOMAN
BONESETTER
BOOKBINDER
BOOKHOLDER
BOOKKEEPER
BOOKSELLER
BOOTLEGGER
BRICKLAYER
BRICKMAKER
BRUSHMAKER
BUREAUCRAT
BUTTERWIFE
CAREER GIRL
CARTOONIST
CARTWRIGHT
CASH-KEEPER
CAT BREEDER
CAT BURGLAR
CERAMICIST
CHAIR-MAKER
CHARGEHAND
CHARIOTEER
CHIRURGEON
CHORUS GIRL
CHRONICLER
CIRCUITEER
CLAIM AGENT
CLAPPER BOY
CLOCKMAKER
CLOG DANCER
CLOTH MAKER
COACHMAKER
COAL-BACKER

COAL-FITTER
COALHEAVER
COAL-MASTER
CO-ASSESSOR
COASTGUARD
COLLOCUTOR
COLLOQUIST
COLPORTEUR
COMEDIENNE
COMPOSITOR
COMPOUNDER
CONCORDIST
CONTRACTOR
CONTROLLER
COPYHOLDER
COPYWRITER
CORDWAINER
COUNSELLOR
CULTIVATOR
CUSTOMS MAN
CYTOLOGIST
DELINEATOR
DIRECTRESS
DISC JOCKEY
DISCOUNTER
DISCOVERER
DISHWASHER
DISPATCHER
DISTRAINER
DISTRAINOR
DOCKMASTER
DOG BREEDER
DOG-FANCIER
DOORKEEPER
DRAMATURGE
DRESSMAKER
DRUMMER-BOY
DRY CLEANER
EMBLAZONER
EMBOWELLER
ENAMELLIST
EPHEMERIST
EPITAPHIST
EPITOMIZER
EVANGELIST
EXAMINATOR
EXPLORATOR
EYE-SERVANT
FELL-MONGER
FILE-CUTTER
FILIBUSTER

PROFESSIONS, TRADES AND OCCUPATIONS

10 continued
FILM EDITOR
FIREMASTER
FIRE-WORKER
FISHMONGER
FLIGHT CREW
FLOWERGIRL
FLUVIALIST
FOLK-DANCER
FOLK-SINGER
FORECASTER
FRAME-MAKER
FREEBOOTER
FUND RAISER
GAMEKEEPER
GAME WARDEN
GEAR-CUTTER
GEISHA GIRL
GENETICIST
GEOGRAPHER
GLEE-SINGER
GLOSSARIST
GLUE-BOILER
GOLD-BEATER
GOLD-DIGGER
GOLD-WASHER
GOVERNANTE
GRAMMARIAN
GUNSLINGER
HACKNEY-MAN
HALL PORTER
HANDMAIDEN
HARVESTMAN
HATCHELLER
HEAD PORTER
HEAD WAITER
HIEROPHANT
HIGHWAYMAN
HORN PLAYER
HOROLOGIST
HORSECOPER
HOR SE-LEECH
HOUSE AGENT
HUCKSTRESS
HUSBANDMAN
INOCULATOR
INSTITUTOR
INSTRUCTOR
INTERAGENT
IRONMONGER
IRONWORKER

JOURNALIST
JOURNEYMAN
KENNELMAID
KEYBOARDER
LAUNDRYMAN
LAW OFFICER
LEGISLATOR
LIBRETTIST
LIGHTERMAN
LIME-BURNER
LINOTYPIST
LIQUIDATOR
LOBSTERMAN
LOCK-KEEPER
LUMBERJACK
MAGISTRATE
MANAGERESS
MANICURIST
MANSERVANT
MATCHMAKER
MEAT-HAWKER
MEDICAL MAN
MILITIAMAN
MILLWRIGHT
MINERALIST
MINISTRESS
MINTMASTER
MISSIONARY
MOONSHINER
NATURALIST
NAUTCH GIRL
NEGOTIATOR
NEWSCASTER
NEWS EDITOR
NEWSVENDOR
NEWSWRITER
NIGHT NURSE
NOSOLOGIST
NURSERYMAN
OBITUARIST
OIL PAINTER
ORCHARDIST
OSTEOLOGER
OVERLOOKER
PANEGYRIST
PANTRYMAID
PARK-KEEPER
PARK-RANGER
PASQUILANT
PASTRY-COOK
PATHFINDER

PAWNBROKER
PEARL-DIVER
PEDIATRIST
PEDICURIST
PELTMONGER
PENOLOGIST
PERRUQUIER
PHARMACIST
PHILOLOGER
PIANO TUNER
PICKPOCKET
PLATELAYER
PLAYWRIGHT
POLITICIAN
PORTIONIST
POSTILLION
POSTMASTER
PRESCRIBER
PRIMA DONNA
PRIVATE EYE
PROCURATOR
PROGRAMMER
PRONOUNCER
PROPRIETOR
PROSPECTOR
PROTRACTOR
PROVEDITOR
PUNCTURIST
PYROLOGIST
QUIZ-MASTER
RAILWAYMAN
RAT-CATCHER
RECITALIST
RESEARCHER
RINGMASTER
ROADMENDER
ROPEDANCER
ROUGHRIDER
SAFEBLOWER
SALES FORCE
SALESWOMAN
SCHOOLMARM
SCRUTINEER
SCULPTRESS
SEA-CAPTAIN
SEAMSTRESS
SECOND MATE
SEMINARIST
SERVING-MAN
SEXOLOGIST
SHIP-BROKER

SHIP-HOLDER
SHIPMASTER
SHIPWRIGHT
SHOPFITTER
SHOPKEEPER
SHOPWALKER
SIGNWRITER
SILENTIARY
SILK-MERCER
SILK-WEAVER
SINOLOGIST
SKIRMISHER
SNEAK THIEF
SOAP-BOILER
SPECIALIST
STAFF NURSE
STEERSMATE
STEWARDESS
STIPULATOR
STOCKTAKER
STONE-BORER
STONEMASON
STRATEGIST
STREET-WARD
SUPERCARGO
SUPERVISER
SURCHARGER
SURFACE-MAN
SWAN-KEEPER
SYMPHONIST
TALLY CLERK
TASKMASTER
TAXI-DRIVER
TEA-BLENDER
TEA PLANTER
TECHNICIAN
TECHNOCRAT
THEOGONIST
THEOLOGIAN
THEOLOGIST
THRENODIST
TIMEKEEPER
TRACTARIAN
TRADE UNION
TRAFFIC COP
TRAFFICKER
TRAM-DRIVER
TRANSACTOR
TRANSLATOR
TRAWLERMAN
TROUBADOUR

PROFESSIONS, TRADES AND OCCUPATIONS

10 continued

TYPESETTER	BATTI-WALLAH	DEMOGRAPHER	HOUSEMASTER
UNDERTAKER	BATTOLOGIST	DISPENSATOR	HOUSEMOTHER
ETERINARY	BEACHCOMBER	DRAUGHTSMAN	HYMNOLOGIST
VICTUALLER	BELL-FOUNDER	DUTY OFFICER	ILLUMINATOR
VIVANDIERE	BILL-STICKER	ELECTRICIAN	ILLUSIONIST
VOCABULIST	BIRD-CATCHER	EMBLEMATIST	ILLUSTRATOR
WAINWRIGHT	BIRD-FANCIER	EMBROIDERER	INFANTRYMAN
WARRIORESS	BIRD-WATCHER	ENTERTAINER	INSTITUTIST
WATCHMAKER	BOATBUILDER	ESTATE AGENT	INTERPRETER
WATERGUARD	BODY SERVANT	ETHNOLOGIST	INTERVIEWER
WHARFINGER	BOILERSMITH	ETYMOLOGIST	IRON-FOUNDER
WHITESMITH	BONDSERVANT	EXECUTIONER	IVORY-CARVER
WHOLESALER	BOOT-CATCHER	EXTORTIONER	IVORY-TURNER
WINEGROWER	BROADCASTER	FACE-PAINTER	IVORY-WORKER
WINE-WAITER	BULLFIGHTER	FACTORY HAND	KITCHENMAID
WIREWORKER	CANDLEMAKER	FAITH HEALER	LAMPLIGHTER
WOODCARVER	CAR SALESMAN	FANCY-MONGER	LAND STEWARD
WOODCUTTER	CAT'S-MEAT-MAN	FIELD WORKER	LAUNDRYMAID
WOOD-MONGER	CHAIR-MENDER	FIGURE-MAKER	LEADING LADY
WOODWORKER	CHALK-CUTTER	FILING CLERK	LEDGER CLERK
WOOL-CARDER	CHAMBERMAID	FINESTILLER	LIFEBOATMAN
WOOL-COMBER	CHIFFONNIER	FIRE BRIGADE	LIGHTKEEPER
WOOL-DRIVER	CHIROLOGIST	FIRE INSURER	LINEN DRAPER
WOOL-GROWER	CHIROMANCER	FLAX-DRESSER	LITHOLOGIST
WOOL-SORTER	CHIROPODIST	FLESH-MONGER	LITHOTOMIST
WOOL-TRADER	CHOIRMASTER	FOURBISSEUR	LORRY DRIVER
WOOL-WINDER	CHRONOLOGER	FRINGE-MAKER	MADRIGALIST
YARDMASTER	CINDER-WENCH	FRUIT PICKER	MAIDSERVANT
ZINC-WORKER	CLOCK-SETTER	FUNAMBULIST	MAMMALOGIST
ZOOGRAPHER	CLOTH-WORKER	GALLEY-SLAVE	MASTER BAKER
ZYMOLOGIST	COAL-WHIPPER	GENEALOGIST	MECHANICIAN
11	COFFIN-MAKER	GHOSTWRITER	MEDICINE MAN
ACCOMPANIST	COGNOSCENTE	GLASS-BENDER	MEMORIALIST
ACCOUCHEUSE	COLLAR-MAKER	GLASS-BLOWER	MERCHANTMAN
ACOUSTICIAN	CONDISCIPLE	GLASS-CUTTER	METAL WORKER
ADJUDICATOR	CONDOTTIERE	GLASS-WORKER	MINIATURIST
ALLOPATHIST	CONDUCTRESS	GRAVE-DIGGER	MONEY-BROKER
ANNUNCIATOR	CONFEDERATE	GREENGROCER	MONEY-LENDER
ANTIQUARIAN	CONGRESSMAN	HABERDASHER	MONOGRAPHER
APPLE-GROWER	CONSECRATOR	HAGIOLOGIST	MULE-SPINNER
ARBITRATRIX	CONSERVATOR	HAIRDRESSER	MUSIC CRITIC
ARMY OFFICER	CONSTITUENT	HAIR STYLIST	MUSIC MASTER
ARQUEBUSIER	CONVEYANCER	HARDWAREMAN	MYOGRAPHIST
ARTILLERIST	COPPERSMITH	HEDGE-PRIEST	MYSTERIARCH
AUDIO TYPIST	COSMOGONIST	HEDGE-WRITER	MYTHOLOGIST
AUSCULTATOR	COSMOLOGIST	HIEROLOGIST	NECROLOGIST
BANK CASHIER	CRANE DRIVER	HISTOLOGIST	NECROMANCER
BANK MANAGER	CRIMEWRITER	HORSE DOCTOR	NEEDLEWOMAN
BARGEMASTER	CUB REPORTER	HORSE TRADER	NEUROLOGIST
BASKETMAKER	CYPHER CLERK	HOSPITALLER	NEUROTOMIST
	DELIVERY MAN.	HOTEL-KEEPER	NIGHT PORTER

PROFESSIONS, TRADES AND OCCUPATIONS

11 continued

NIGHTWORKER
NOMENCLATOR
NUMISMATIST
OFFICE STAFF
ONION-SELLER
OPERA SINGER
OPHIOLOGIST
ORIENTALIST
ORTHOPEDIST
OSTEOLOGIST
PAMPHLETEER
PANEL-BEATER
PANTOMIMIST
PAPERHANGER
PARLOURMAID
PATHOLOGIST
PATTENMAKER
PEARLFISHER
PETROLOGIST
PETTIFOGGER
PHILATELIST
PHILOLOGIST
PHONOLOGIST
PHYTOLOGIST
POLYPHONIST
PORK BUTCHER
PORTRAITIST
PRECEPTRESS
PRINT-SELLER
PROBATIONER
PROMULGATOR
PROOFREADER
PROPERTY MAN
PROPRIETRIX
QUESTIONARY
RADIOLOGIST
RAG MERCHANT
REPRESENTER
REPUBLISHER
RHETORICIAN
ROADSWEEPER
SAFEBREAKER
SANDWICH MAN
SANSCRITIST
SAXOPHONIST
SCOUTMASTER
SCRAPDEALER
SCRIP-HOLDER
SECRET AGENT
SEDITIONARY

SERVANT GIRL
SERVING-MAID
SHARE-BROKER
SHEEPFARMER
SHEPHERDESS
SHIPBREAKER
SHIPBUILDER
SHIP'S MASTER
SHOPSTEWARD
SILK-THROWER
SILVERSMITH
SLAUGHTERER
SLAVE-DRIVER
SLAVE-HOLDER
SMALLHOLDER
SOCIOLOGIST
STAGE-DRIVER
STEEPLEJACK
STOCKBROKER
STOCKJOBBER
STONECUTTER
STOREKEEPER
SUNDRIESMAN
SYSTEM-MAKER
TAXIDERMIST
TELEGRAPHER
TELEPHONIST
TICKET AGENT
TOASTMASTER
TOBACCONIST
TOOTH-DRAWER
TOPOGRAPHER
TORCH-BEARER
TOWN PLANNER
TOXOPHILITE
TRAIN-BEARER
TRANSCRIBER
TRANSPORTER
TRAVEL AGENT
TYPE-FOUNDER
TYPOGRAPHER
UNDERBEARER
UNDERLETTER
UNDERWRITER
UPHOLSTERER
VERSEMONGER
VINE-DRESSER
WASHERWOMAN
WATCHKEEPER
WAX-CHANDLER
WHEEL-CUTTER

WHEELWRIGHT
WHITEWASHER
WITCH-DOCTOR
WOOL-STAPLER
XYLOPHONIST
ZOOGRAPHIST

12

ACCORDIONIST
ACTOR MANAGER
AMBULANCE MAN
ANAESTHETIST
ANIMALCULIST
ARCHEOLOGIST
ARTILLERYMAN
BALLET DANCER
BALLET MASTER
BANTAMWEIGHT
BELLOWS-MAKER
BIBLIOLOGIST
BIBLIOLOGIST
BIBLIOPEGIST
BOOKING CLERK
BUS CONDUCTOR
CABINET-MAKER
CALLIGRAPHER
CARICATURIST
CARPET-FITTER
CARTOGRAPHER
CATACLYSMIST
CEROGRAPHIST
CHEESEMONGER
CHIEF CASHIER
CHIMNEY-SWEEP
CHIROPRACTOR
CHRONOLOGIST
CHURCHWARDEN
CIRCUIT RIDER
CIVIL SERVANT
CLARINETTIST
CLERK OF WORKS
CLOTH-SHEARER
COACH-BUILDER
COLEOPTERIST
COMMISSIONER
CONCHOLOGIST
CONFECTIONER
CORN CHANDLER
COSMOGRAPHER
COSTERMONGER
CRAFTS-MASTER
CRANIOLOGIST

CRYPTOGAMIST
DANCE HOSTESS
DEEP-SEA DIVER
DEMONOLOGIST
DEMONSTRATOR
DENDROLOGIST
DRAMATURGIST
ECCLESIASTIC
EGYPTOLOGIST
ELECUTIONIST
ENGASTRIMUTH
ENGINE-DRIVER
ENTOMOLOGIST
ENTOMOTOMIST
ENTREPRENEUR
ESCAPOLOGIST
ETHNOGRAPHER
EXPERIMENTER
FAMILY DOCTOR
FARM LABOURER
FILM DIRECTOR
FILM PRODUCER
FIRST OFFICER
FLYING DOCTOR
FOOTPLATEMAN
GEOMETRICIAN
GERIATRICIAN
GLASS-GRINDER
GLOSSOLOGIST
GREASEMONKEY
GUILD BROTHER
GYMNOSOPHIST
GYNECOLOGIST
HAGIOGRAPHER
HALIOGRAPHER
HARNESS-MAKER
HEAD GARDENER
HOMEOPATHIST
HORSE-BREAKER
HORSE-COURSER
HORSE-KNACKER
HOTEL MANAGER
HOUSEBREAKER
HOUSEPAINTER
HOUSESTEWARD
HOUSESURGEON
HYDROGRAPHER
HYDROPATHIST
HYPOTHECATOR
IMMUNOLOGIST
IMPROPRIATOR

12 continued
INSTRUCTRESS
INVOICE CLERK
JERRY-BUILDER
JOINT-TRUSTEE
JURISCONSULT
JUVENILE LEAD
KING'S COUNSEL
KNIFE-GRINDER
KNIFE-THROWER
LABOURING MAN
LAND SURVEYOR
LATH-SPLITTER
LEADER-WRITER
LEXICOLOGIST
LITHOGRAPHER
LONGSHOREMAN
LOSS ADJUSTER
LUMBER-DEALER
MAITRE D'HOTEL
MAKE-UP ARTIST
MALACOLOGIST
MANUAL WORKER
MANUFACTURER
MASSPRODUCER
MEAT-SALESMAN
METALLURGIST
MEZZO SOPRANO
MICROSCOPIST
MINERALOGIST
MISCELLANIST
MONEY-CHANGER
MONOGRAPHIST
MORRIS-DANCER
MOSAIC-ARTIST
MOSAIC-WORKER
MYTHOGRAPHER
NEWSPAPERMAN
NUTRITIONIST
OBSTETRICIAN
OFFICE JUNIOR
ONEIROCRITIC
ORCHESTRATOR
ORGAN-BUILDER
ORGAN-GRINDER
ORTHODONTIST
ORTHOGRAPHER
OVARIOTOMIST
PAPER-STAINER
PATTERN-MAKER
PEDIATRICIAN

PHONOGRAPHER
PHOTOGRAPHER
PHRENOLOGIST'
PHYSIOLOGIST
PLANT MANAGER
PLOUGHWRIGHT
PLUMBER'S MATE
PLYER-FOR-HIRE
POSTMISTRESS
PRACTITIONER
PRESS OFFICER
PRESTIGIATOR
PRISON WARDER
PRIZE-FIGHTER
PROFESSIONAL
PROPAGANDIST
PROPRIETRESS
PSYCHIATRIST
PSYCHOLOGIST
PUBLICITY MAN
PUPIL-TEACHER
PUPPET-PLAYER
QUARRY MASTER
RACING DRIVER
RADIOGRAPHER
RECEPTIONIST
REMEMBRANCER
RESTAURATEUR
RIDING-MASTER
RIGHT-HAND MAN
RUBBER-GRADER
SALES MANAGER
SCENE-PAINTER
SCENE-SHIFTER
SCHOOLMASTER
SCREENWRITER
SCRIPTWRITER
SCULLERY-MAID
SEED-MERCHANT
SEISMOLOGIST
SHARECROPPER
SHARPSHOOTER
SHIP CHANDLER
SHIP'S HUSBAND
SHOE-REPAIRER
SILVER-BEATER
SLAUGHTERMAN
SNAKE-CHARMER
SOCIAL WORKER
SOIL MECHANIC
SPECIAL AGENT

SPEECHWRITER
SPICE-BLENDER
SPORTSCASTER
SPORTSWRITER
STAGE MANAGER
STATISTICIAN
STENOGRAPHER
STONEBREAKER
STONEDRESSER
STONESQUARER
STREET-TRADER
STREET-WALKER
SUGAR-REFINER
TAX-COLLECTOR
TECHNOLOGIST
TELEGRAPH BOY
TELEGRAPHIST
TEST ENGINEER
THERAPEUTIST
THIEF-CATCHER
TICKET-PORTER
TIMBER TRADER
TOLL-GATHERER
TOURIST AGENT
TOXICOLOGIST
TRADESPEOPLE
TRANSPLANTER
TRICHOLOGIST
UNDERMANAGER
UNDERSERVANT
VETERINARIAN
WAITING-WOMAN
WAREHOUSEMAN
WATER DIVINER
WINE MERCHANT
WOOD-ENGRAVER
WORKS MANAGER
ZINCOGRAPHER
13
ADMINISTRATOR
AGRICULTURIST
ANTIQUE DEALER
ARACHNOLOGIST
ARCHAEOLOGIST
ARITHMETICIAN
ARTICLED CLERK
ASSYRIOLOGIST
BARBER-SURGEON
BIBLIOGRAPHER
CALICO-PRINTER
CAMPANOLOGIST

CARTOGRAPHIST
CHARTOGRAPHER
CHICKEN-FARMER
CHIROGRAPHIST
CHOREOGRAPHER
CHRONOGRAPHER
CIVIL ENGINEER
CLEARING AGENT
COFFEE-PLANTER
COMETOGRAPHER
CONTORTIONIST
CONTRABANDIST
COTTON-SPINNER
COUNTER-CASTER
COUNTERFEITER
CRANIOSCOPIST
CRYPTOGRAPHER
DANCING MASTER
DEIPNOSOPHIST
DERMATOLOGIST
DIAGNOSTICIAN
DIAMOND-CUTTER
DRAWING-MASTER
DRESS DESIGNER
DRILL SERGEANT
ELECTROPLATER
ELECTROTYPIST
EMIGRATIONIST
ENCYCLOPEDIST
ENTOZOOLOGIST
EPIGRAMMATIST
ESTATE MANAGER
EXHIBITIONIST
FENCING-MASTER
FORTUNE-TELLER
FRIEGHT-BROKER
GALVANOLOGIST
GASTRILOQUIST
GATOR WRESTLER
GLOSSOGRAPHER
GLYPHOGRAPHER
GROUND-BAILIFF
GYNAECOLOGIST
HARBOUR MASTER
HIEROGLYPHIST
HORSE-MILLINER
HOSPITAL NURSE
ICHTHYOLOGIST
INDUSTRIALIST
INTELLIGENCER
JOINT-EXECUTOR

PROFESSIONS, TRADES AND OCCUPATIONS

13 continued
LETTER-CARRIER
LETTER-FOUNDER
LEXICOGRAPHER
LIGHTHOUSE-MAN
MAID-OF-ALL-WORK
MASTER-BUILDER
MASTER MARINER
MATHEMATICIAN
MELODRAMATIST
METAPHYSICIAN
METEOROLOGIST
METOPOSCOPIST
NIGHT-WATCHMAN
OLD-CLOTHES-MAN
ORNITHOLOGIST
ORTHOGRAPHIST
PARK ATTENDANT
PERIODICALIST
PHARMACEUTIST
PHYSIOGNOMIST
PHYSIOGRAPHER
POSTURE-MASTER
POULTRY FARMER
PRIVATEERSMAN
PROCESS-SERVER
PSALMOGRAPHER
PSYCHOANALYST
PTERIDOLOGIST
PUBLIC SPEAKER
QUEEN'S COUNSEL
RACING-TIPSTER
REVOLUTIONARY
REVOLUTIONIST
RUBBER-PLANTER
SAILING MASTER
SCHOOLTEACHER
SCIENCE MASTER
SHOP ASSISTANT
SILK-THROWSTER
SINGING-MASTER
STATION-MASTER
STENOGRAPHIST
STEREOSCOPIST
STETHOSCOPIST
STREET-SWEEPER
SUB-CONTRACTOR
SUPERINTENDER
SUPERNUMERARY
THAUMATURGIST
THIMBLE-RIGGER

TOLL COLLECTOR
TRADE UNIONIST
TRAMCAR-DRIVER
TRAM CONDUCTOR
VENTRILOQUIST
VIOLONCELLIST
WINDOW-CLEANER
WINDOW-DRESSER
WOOLLEN-DRAPER
WRITING-MASTER
14
ANTHROPOLOGIST
AUTOBIOGRAPHER
BACTERIOLOGIST
BILLIARD-MARKER
BILLIARD-PLAYER
CHAMBER COUNSEL
CHIMNEY-SWEEPER
CITIZEN-SOLDIER
CLASSICS MASTER
COLOUR SERGEANT
COMMISSIONAIRE
DANCING PARTNER
DISCOUNT-BROKER
ECCLESIOLOGIST
EDUCATIONALIST
ENCYCLOPAEDIST
EXCHANGE-BROKER
GRAMMATICASTER
HANDICRAFTSMAN
HERESIO-GRAPHER
HORSE WHISPERER
HORTICULTURIST
HOUSE DECORATOR
HOUSE FURNISHER
LANGUAGE MASTER
LEATHER-DRESSER
MANUAL LABOURER
MARKET-GARDENER
MEDICAL OFFICER
MERCHANT-TAILOR
MISCELLANARIAN
MONEY-SCRIVENER
MOTHER SUPERIOR
MUSIC PUBLISHER
NAVAL PENSIONER
OPHTHALMOLOGIST
PAINTER STAINER
PHARMACOLOGIST
PNEUMATOLOGIST
PSALMOGRAPHIST

RECEPTION CLERK
REPRESENTATIVE
SHIP'S-CARPENTER
SIDEROGRAPHIST
SPECTACLE MAKER
SPECTROSCOPIST
SUPERINTENDENT
SYSTEMS ANALYST
TALLOW CHANDLER
WATER COLOURIST
WEATHER-PROPHET
15
ARBORICULTURIST
BOW STREET RUNNER
CROSSING-SWEEPER
CRUSTACEOLOGIST
DIAMOND MERCHANT
DOMESTIC SERVANT
FORWARDING AGENT
GENTLEMAN-FARMER
HEART SPECIALIST
HELMINTHOLOGIST
HIEROGRAMMATIST
HISTORIO-GRAPHER
INSTRUMENTALIST
INSURANCE BROKER
MUSICAL DIRECTOR
NUMISMATOLOGIST
PALAEONTOLOGIST
PLATFORM-SPEAKER
PORTRAIT-PAINTER
PROGRAMME SELLER
PROVISION DEALER
RAILWAY ENGINEER
RESURRECTIONIST
SCRIPTURE-READER
SLEEPING PARTNER
STRETCHER-BEARER
TICKET COLLECTOR
TIGHTROPE WALKER

16
FREIGHT FORWARDER
CLEARING AGENT

TOOLS

3	AUGER	RAZOR	MULLER
AWL	BEELE	SARSE	OLIVER
AXE	BENCH	SCREW	PALLET
BIT	BESOM	SPADE	PENCIL
DIE	BETTY	SPIKE	PESTLE
FAN	BEVEL	SPILE	PITSAW
GAD	BLADE	SPILL	PLANER
GIN	BORER	SWAGE	PLIERS
HOD	BRACE	TEMSE	PLOUGH
HOE	BURIN	TOMMY	PONTEE
JIG	CHUCK	TONGS	POOLER
LOY	CHURN	TROMP	RAMMER
SAW	CLAMP	TRONE	RASPER
ZAX	CLAMS	WEDGE	REAPER
4	CLASP	WINCH	RIDDLE
ADZE	CLEAT	6	RIPSAW
BI LL	CRAMP	BENDER	RUBBER
BORE	CRANE	BLOWER	SANDER
BROG	CROOM	BODKIN	SAW-SET
BURR	CROZE	BORCER	SCREEN
CART	CUPEL	BOW-SAW	SCYTHE
CRAB	DOLLY	BRAYER	SEGGER
FILE	DRILL	BROACH	SHEARS
FORK	FLAIL	BURTON	SHOVEL
FROW	FLANG	CHASER	SICKLE
GAGE	FORGE	CHISEL	SIFTER
HINK	GAUGE	COLTER	SKEWER
HOOK	GAVEL	CREVET	SLEDGE
JACK	GOUGE	CRUSET	SLICER
LAST	HOIST	DIBBER	SQUARE
LOOM	INCUS	DIBBLE	STIDDY
MALL	JACKS	DOFFER	STITHY
MAUL	JEMMY	DREDGE	STRIKE
MULE	JIMMY	DRIVER	TACKLE
NAIL	KNIFE	FANNER	TENTER
PICK	LATHE	FAUCET	TREPAN
PIKE	LEVEL	FERRET	TROWEL
PLOW	LEVER	FOLDER	TUBBER
RAKE	MOWER	GIMLET	TURREL
RASP	PARER	GRAVER	WIMBLE
RULE	PLANE	HACKLE	WRENCH
SOCK	PLUMB	HAMMER	7
SPUD	PREEN	HARROW	BOASTER
TOOL	PRISE	JAGGER	BRADAWL
TRUG	PRONG	JIGGER	CAPSTAN
VICE	PUNCH	JIG SAW	CATLING
WHIM	QUERN	LADDER	CAUTERY
5	QUOIN	MALLET	CHAMFER
ANVIL	RATCH	MORTAR	CHIP-AXE

TOOLS

7 continued
CHOPPER
CLEAVER
COULOIR
COULTER
CRAMPON
CRISPER
CROWBAR
CUVETTE
DERRICK
DIAMOND
DOG-BELT
DRUDGER
FISTUCA
FORCEPS
FRETSAW
FRUGGIN
GRADINE
GRAINER
GRAPNEL
GRUB AXE
HACKSAW
HANDSAW
HATCHET
HAY FORK
JOINTER
MANDREL
MATTOCK
NIPPERS
NUT HOOK
PICKAXE
PIERCER
PINCERS
PLUMMET
POLE AXE
POUNDER
PRICKER
SALT-PAN
SCALPEL
SCAUPER
SCRAPER
SCREWER
SCRIBER
SEED LOP
SPADDLE
SPANNER
SPITTLE
SPRAYER
STROCAL
TENONER
THIMBLE

TRESTLE
TRIBLET
T-SQUARE
TWIBILL
TWISTER
WHIP-SAW
WHITTLE
WOOLDER
8
BARK MILL
BAR SHEAR
BEAKIRON
BENCH PEG
BILL HOOK
BISTOURY
BLOOMARY
BLOWLAMP
BLOWPIPE
BOATHOOK
BOWDRILL
BULL NOSE
BUTTERIS
CALIPERS
CANTHOOK
CHOPNESS
CROW MILL
CRUCIBLE
DIE STOCK
DOWEL BIT
DRILL BOW
EDGE TOOL
FILATORY
FIRE KILN
FLAME GUN
FLAX COMB
GAVELOCK
GEE CRAMP
HANDLOOM
HANDMILL
HAND VICE
HAY KNIFE
HORSE HOE
LAPSTONE
LEAD MILL
MITRE BOX
MOLEGRIP
MUCK RAKE
NUTSCREW
OILSTONE
PAINT PAD
PANEL SAW

PICKLOCK
PINCHERS
PLUMB BOB
POLISHER
POWERSAW
PRONG-HOE
PUNCHEON
REAP HOOK
SAW WREST
SCISSORS
SCUFFLER
SLATE AXE
STILETTO
STRICKLE
TENON SAW
THROSTLE
TOOTH KEY
TWEEZERS
TWIST BIT
WATERCAN
WATER RAM
WEED HOOK
WINDLASS
WINDMILL
9
BELT PUNCH
BENCH HOOK
BOLTAUGER
BOOT CRIMP
CANKER SIT
CANNIPERS
CAN OPENER
CENTRE BIT
COMPASSES
CORKSCREW
COTTON GIN
CRAMP IRON
CURRY COMB
CUTTER BAR
DOG CLUTCH
DRAW KNIFE
DRAW-PLATE
EXCAVATOR
EYELETEER
FILLISTER
FINING POT
FORK CHUCK
GAS PLIERS
HAMMER AXE
HANDBRACE
HANDSCREW

HANDSPIKE
HOLING AXE
HUMMELLER
IMPLEMENT
JACKKNIFE
JACKPLANE
JACKSCREW
LACE FRAME
LAWNMOWER
NAIL PUNCH
NUT WRENCH
PITCH FORK
PLANE IRON
PLANISHER
PLUMBLINE
PLUMBRULE
SCREWJACK
SCRIBE AWL
SHEARLEGS
SHEEP HOOK
STEELYARD
SUGAR MILL
TIN OPENER
TRY SQUARE
TURF SPADE
TURN BENCH
TURNSCREW
WATERMILL
10
BUSH HARROW
CLASPKNIFE
CLAWHAMMER
COLD CHISEL
CRANE'S BILL
CULTIVATOR
DRAY PLOUGH
DRIFT BOLTS
DRILLPRESS
DRILLSTOCK
EMERY WHEEL
FIRE ENGINE
FIRING IRON
GRINDSTONE
INSTRUMENT
MASONRY BIT
MASTICATOR
MITRE BLOCK
MOTOR MOWER
MOULD BOARD
NAIL DRAWER
PAINTBRUSH

274

10 continued
PERFORATOR
PIPE WRENCH
POINTED AWL
SAFETY LAMP
SCREW PRESS
SLEEK STONE
SNOWPLOUGH
SPOKESHAVE
STEAM PRESS
STEPLADDER
TENTERHOOK
THUMBSCREW
THUMBSTALL
TILT HAMMER
TRIP HAMMER
TURF CUTTER
TURNBUCKLE
WATERCRANE
WATERGAUGE
WATERLEVEL
WHEEL BRACE
11
BRACE-AND-BIT
BREAST DRILL
CHAFF CUTTER
CHAIN BLOCKS
CHAIN WRENCH
CHEESE PRESS
COUNTERSINK
CRAZING MILL
CRISPING PIN
CROSSCUT SAW
DRILL BARROW
DRILL HARROW
DRILL PLOUGH
FANNING MILL
GRUBBING HOE
HELVEHAMMER
JAGGING IRON
MACHINE TOOL
MONKEY BLOCK
PAINT ROLLER
PLOUGHSHARE
PRUNING HOOK
RABBET PLANE
REAPING-HOOK
SAWING STOOL
SCREWDRIVER
SINGLE-EDGED
SKIM COULTER

SNATCH BLOCK
SPIRIT LEVEL
SQUARING ROD
STEAM HAMMER
STONE HAMMER
STRAW CUTTER
STRIKE BLOCK
STUBBLE RAKE
SWARD CUTTER
SWINGPLOUGH
TAPE MEASURE
TURFING IRON
TWO-FOOT RULE
WARPING HOOK
WARPING POST
WEEDING FORK
WEEDING HOOK
WEEDING RHIM
WHEELBARROW
12
BARKING IRONS
BELT ADJUSTER
BRANDING IRON
BREASTPLOUGH
CAULKING TOOL
COUNTER GAUGE
CRADEL SCYTHE
CRAMPING IRON
CRIMPING IRON
CRISPING IRON
CURLING TONGS
DRILL GRUBBER
DRIVING SHAFT
DRIVING WHEEL
EMERY GRINDER
FLOUR DRESSER
GLASS FURNACE
HYDRAULIC RAM
MANDREL LATHE
MARLINE SPIKE
MONKEY WRENCH
PRUNING KNIFE
PULLEY BLOCKS
RUNNING BLOCK
SCRIBING IRON
SLEDGE HAMMER
SLIDING BEVEL
SOCKET CHISEL
STONE BREAKER
STRAIGHTEDGE
SWINGLE KNIFE

TOUCH NEEDLES
TRENCH PLOUGH
TURFING SPADE
TURNING LATHE
WATER BELLOWS
WEEDING TONGS
13
BUTCHER'S BROOM
CHOPPING BLOCK
CHOPPING KNIFE
CYLINDER PRESS
ELECTRIC DRILL
GRAPPLING-IRON
HYDRAULIC JACK
PACKING NEEDLE
SCRIBING BLOCK
SEWING MACHINE
SOLDERING BOLT
SOLDERING IRON
SOWING MACHINE
SPINNING JENNY
SPINNING WHEEL
STOCKING FRAME
SUBSOIL PLOUGH
TWO-HOLE PLIERS
WEEDING CHISEL
14
BLOWING MACHINE
CARDING MACHINE
DRAINING ENGINE
DRAINING PLOUGH
PENUMATIC DRILL
REAPING MACHINE
SMOOTHING PLANE
SWINGLING KNIFE
THRUSTING SCREW
WEEDING FORCEPS
15
CARPENTER'S BENCH
CRIMPING MACHINE
DREDGING MACHINE
DRILLING MACHINE
ENTRENCHING TOOL
PESTLE AND MORTAR
PUMP SCREWDRIVER
WEIGHING MACHINE

TRANSPORT

VEHICLES

3
BMX
BUS
CAB
CAR
FLY
GIG
VAN
4
AUTO
BIKE
CART
DRAG
DRAY
EKKA
HACK
JEEP
LUGE
SHAY
SLED
TAXI
TRAM
TRAP
TUBE
WAIN
5
ARABA
BRAKE
BUGGY
COACH
COUPE
CRATE
CYCLE
DANDY
DOOLY
LORRY
METRO
MOPED
MOTOR
PALKI
SEDAN
SULKY
TONGA
TRAIN
TRUCK
WAGON
6
BERLIN
CALASH

CHAISE
DIESEL
FIACRE
GO-CART
HANSOM
HEARSE
HOTROD
HURDLE
JALOPY
JITNEY
LANDAU
LIMBER
LITTER
MAGLEV
MODEL-T
ROCKET
SALOON
SLEDGE
SLEIGH
SNOCAT
SURREY
TANDEM
TANKER
TOURER
TRICAR
WEASEL
7
AUTOBUS
AUTOCAR
BICYCLE
BOB-SLED
BRITZKA
BROWSER
CALCHE
CARAVAN
CAROCHE
CHARIOT
COASTER
DOG-CART
DROSHKY
FLIVVER
GROWLER
HACKERY
HARD-TOP
OMNIBUS
OPEN-CAR
PHAETON
PULLMAN
SCOOTER

SHUNTER
SIDE-CAR
TALLY-HO
TAXI-CAB
TILBURY
TRACTOR
TRAILER
TROLLEY
TUMBRIL
TWO-DOOR
UNICORN
VIS-A-VIS
WHISKEY
8
BAROUCHE
BRANCARD
BROUGHAM
CABLE-CAR
CAPE-CART
CARRIAGE
CARRIOLE
CLARENCE
CURRICLE
DEAD-CART
DORMEUSE
FOUR-DOOR
HORSE-BUS
HORSE-CAB
HORSE-VAN
ICE-YACHT
KIBITZKA
MONORAIL
MOTOR-CAR
MOTOR-VAN
OLD CROCK
PONY-CART
PUSH-BIKE
QUADRIGA
RICKSHAW
ROADSTER
RUNABOUT
SOCIABLE
STAFF CAR
STEAM-CAR
TOBOGGAN
TRICYCLE
UNICYCLE
VICTORIA

9
AMBULANCE
BOAT-TRAIN
BOB-SLEIGH
BUBBLECAR
BUCKBOARD
CABRIOLET
CHAR-A-BANC
DILIGENCE
ESTATE-CAR
FUNICULAR
HORSE-CART
LIMOUSINE
MAIL-COACH
MILKFLOAT
MILK TRAIN
MONOCYCLE
MOTOR-BIKE
PALANKEEN
PALANQUIN
RACING CAR
SPORTS CAR
STREET-CAR
STRETCHER
TARANTASS
TIN LIZZIE
TWO-SEATER
WAGONETTE
10
AUTOMOBILE
BAIL GHARRY
BEACHWAGON
BLACK MARIA
FIRE-ENGINE
FOUR-IN-HAND
GOODS TRAIN
JINRICKSHA
LOCAL TRAIN
LOCOMOTIVE
MOTOR-COACH
MOTOR-CYCLE
NIGHT-TRAIN
OUTSIDE CAR
PADDYWAGON
PEDAL-CYCLE
PONY-ENGINE
POST-CHAISE
RATTLETRAP
SEDAN-CHAIR

10 continued
SHANDRYDAN
SINCLAIR C5
SNOWPLOUGH
STAGE-COACH
STAGE-WAGON
STATE COACH
TROLLEY-BUS
TROLLEY-CAR
TWO-WHEELER
VELOCIPEDE

11
BONE-BREAKER
BULLOCK-CART
CONVERTIBLE
DIESEL TRAIN
FOUR-WHEELER
GUN-CARRIAGE
JAUNTING-CAR

JINRICKSHAW
LANDAULETTE
MAIL-PHAETON
QUADRICYCLE
SIT-UP AND-BEG
SOUPED-UP CAR
STEAM-ENGINE
STEAM-ROLLEFR
THIKA-GHARRY
WHITECHAPEL

12
COACH AND FOUR
DESOBLIGEANT
DOUBLE-DECKER
EXPRESS TRAIN
FREIGHT TRAIN
HORSE-AND-CART
LUGGAGE TRAIN
PANTECHNICON

PUFFING BILLY
RAILWAY TRAIN
SINGLE-DECKER
STATION-WAGON
STEAM-OMNIBUS
THROUGH TRAIN

13
CYCLE-RICKSHAW
ELECTRIC TRAIN
GOVERNESS-CART
HORSE-CARRIAGE
PENNYFARTHING
RACING CHARIOT
SHOOTING-BRAKE

14
PASSENGER
  TRAIN
RIDING-CARRIAGE
TRACTION ENGINE

15
HACKNEY-
  CARRIAGE
PRAIRIE-
  SCHOONER

16
MOTORIZED
  BICYCLE
UNDERGROUND
  TRAIN

17
HORSELESS
  CARRIAGE

18
TRAVELLING
  CARRIAGE

SHIPS AND BOATS

3
ARK
COG
HOY
TUG

4
ARGO
BARK
BOAT
BRIG
BUSS
DHOW
DORY
GRAB
JUNK
PROA
PUNT
RAFT
SAIC
SNOW
TROW
YAWL

5
BARGE
CANOE
COBLE
DANDY
FERRY
FUNNY

KAYAK
KETCH
LINER
NOBBY
PRAHU
SHELL
SKIFF
SLOOP
SMACK
TRAMP
U-BOAT
UMIAK
XEBEC
YACHT

6
BARQUE
BAWLEY
BIREME
CAIQUE
CARVEL
CUTTER
DINGHY
DOGGER
DUG-OUT
GALLEY
HOOKER
HOPPER
LAUNCH
LORCHA

LUGGER
PACKET
RANDAN
SAMPAN
SEALER
SLAVER
TANKER
TENDER
WHALER

7
BUMBOAT
CARAVEL
CARRACK
CLIPPER
COASTER
COLLIER
CORACLE
CORSAIR
CURRACH
DREDGER
DRIFTER
DROMOND
FELUCCA
FLY-BOAT
FRIGATE
GABBARD
GALLEON
GONDOLA
JANGADA

PINNACE
PIRAGUA
POLACCA
POLACRE
ROWBOAT
SCULLER
STEAMER
TARTANE
TOWBOAT
TRAWLER
TRIREME
WAR SHIP

8
BILANDER
BUDGEROW
COCKBOAT
CORVETTE
CRUMSTER
DAHABIYA
FIRESHIP
FOLDBOAT
LIFEBOAT
LONG-BOAT
MAIL-SHIP
NOAH'S ARK
OUTBOARD
SAILBOAT
SCHOONER
SHOWBOAT

SHIPS AND BOATS / AIRCRAFT / MOTORING

9	STEAMSHIP	COCKLE-SHELL	13
BUCENTAUR	STORESHIP	DOUBLE-CANOE	HERRING-FISHER
CARGO-BOAT	SUBMARINE	FISHING-BOAT	PASSENGER SHIP
CATAMARAN	**10**	HOPPER-BARGE	TRANSPORT SHIP
CRIS-CRAFT	BANANA-BOAT	MAIL-STEAMER	**14**
FREIGHTER	BRIGANTINE	PENTECONTER	CHANNEL
HOUSEBOAT	PADDLE-BOAT	PILOT VESSEL	STEAMER
JOLLY-BOAT	PICKET BOAT	QUINQUEREME	COASTING
LIGHTSHIP	PIRATE-SHIP	SAILING-SHIP	VESSEL
MOTORBOAT	PRISON-SHIP	THREE-MASTER	FLOATING PALACE
MOTORSHIP	QUADRIREME	**12**	OCEAN
MUD-HOPPER	ROWING BOAT	CABIN-CRUISER	GREYHOUND
OUTRIGGER	TEA-CLIPPER	ESCORT VESSEL	
RIVER-BOAT	TRAIN-FERRY	FISHING SMACK	
ROTOR SHIP	VIKING-SHIP	HOSPITAL SHIP	
SHIP'S BOAT	WIND-JAMMER	MERCHANT SHIP	
SLAVE-SHIP	**11**	PLEASURE BOAT	
SPEEDBOAT	BARQUENTINE	SAILING BARGE	
STEAMBOAT	CHASSE-MAREE	STERN-WHEELER	

AIRCRAFT

3	FIGHTER	9	12
JET	JUMP-JET	AEROPLANE	FREIGHT-PLANE
4	SHUTTLE	DIRIGIBLE	**13**
KITE	**8**	MAIL-PLANE	STRATOCRUISER
5	AEROSTAT	MONOPLANE	**14**
PLANE	AIRPLANE	SAILPLANE	FLYING BEDSTEAD
6	AUTOGIRO	TURBO-PROP	PASSENGER
AIR CAR	CONCORDE	**10**	PLANE
BOMBER	JUMBO-JET	FLYING-BOAT	**18**
GLIDER	ROTODYNE	GAS-BALLOON	MONTGOLFIER
7	SEA-PLANE	HELICOPTER	BALLOON
AIRSHIP	TRIPLANE	HOVERCRAFT	
BALLOON	TURBO-JET	HYDROPLANE	
BIPLANE	WARPLANE	**11**	
CLIPPER	ZEPPELIN	FIRE-BALLOON	

MOTORING

2	AXLE	CHOKE	DECOKE
C.C.	BOOT	SERVO	ENGINE
3	BUSH	SHAFT	FILTER
BHP	COIL	VALVE	GASKET
CAM	GEAR	WHEEL	HEATER
FAN	HORN	**6**	HUB CAP
HUB	LOCK	BIG END	IDLING
JET	SUMP	BONNET	PISTON
REV	TYRE	CAMBER	REBORE
ROD	**5**	CLUTCH	STROKE
4	BRAKE	DAMPER	TAPPET

281

MOTORING / NAUTICAL

6 continued
TORQUE
TUNING
7
BATTERY
BEARING
BRACKET
CHASSIS
DYNAMIC
EXHAUST
FAN BELT
GEARBOX
OIL SEAL
8
ADHESION
BRAKE PAD
BULKHEAD
CALLIPER
CAMSHAFT
CROSS-PLY
CYLINDER
DIPSTICK
FLYWHEEL
FUEL PUMP
IGNITION
KICK-DOWN
KNOCKING
LIVE AXLE
MANIFOLD
MOUNTING
RADIATOR
ROTOR ARM
SELECTOR

SILENCER
SMALL END
STEERING
THROTTLE
TRACK ROD
9
BRAKESHOE
CONDENSER
DISC BRAKE
DRUM BRAKE
GEAR STICK
GENERATOR
HALF-SHAFT
HANDBRAKE
INDUCTION
MISFIRING
OVERDRIVE
OVERSTEER
PROP SHAFT
RADIAL-PLY
SIDE VALVE
SPARK PLUG
TWO-STROKE
UNDERSEAL
WHEELBASE
10
AIR CLEANER
ALTERNATOR
BRAKE FLUID
CRANKSHAFT
DETONATION
DRIVE SHAFT
FOUR-STROKE

GUDGEON PIN
HORSEPOWER
PISTON RING
REV COUNTER
SUSPENSION
TACHOMETER
THERMOSTAT
UNDERSTEER
WINDSCREEN
11
ANTI-ROLL BAR
CARBURETTER
CARBURETTOR
COMPRESSION
CROSSMEMBER
DISTRIBUTOR
SERVO SYSTEM
SYNCHROMESH
12
ACCELERATION
CYLINDER HEAD
DIESEL ENGINE
DIFFERENTIAL
SPARKING PLUG
SUPERCHARGER
TRANSMISSION
TURBOCHARGER
VISCOUS DRIVE
13
COOLING SYSTEM
DECARBONIZING
FUEL INJECTION
OVERHEAD VALVE

POWER STEERING
RACK-AND-PINION
SHOCK ABSORBER
SLAVE CYLINDER
SPARK IGNITION
14
FOUR-WHEEL
 DRIVE
PROPELLER
 SHAFT
UNIVERSAL JOINT
15
FRONT-WHEEL
 DRIVE
HYDRAULIC
 SYSTEM
PETROL
 INJECTION
17
INDUCTION
 MANIFOLD
REVOLUTION
 COUNTER
19
CROWN WHEEL
 AND PINION
20+
AUTOMATIC
 TRANSMISSION
INDEPENDENT
 SUSPENSION
POWER ASSISTED
 STEERING

NAUTICAL

3
AFT
BOW
FID
LEE
4
ALEE
BEAM
BITT
BOOM
FORE
HOLD
HULL
KEEL
KNOT

LIST
MATE
POOP
PORT
PROW
STAY
STEM
WAKE
WARP
5
ABAFT
ABEAM
ABOUT
ALOFT
AVAST

BELAY
BELLS
BILGE
BOSUN
CABLE
CAULK
CLEAT
DAVIT
HATCH
HAWSE
STERN
TRICK
TRUCK
WAIST
WEIGH

WINCH
6
BRIDGE
BUNKER
FATHOM
FENDER
FLUKES
FO'C'SLE
GALLEY
HAWSER
JETSAM
LEAGUE
LEEWAY
OFFING
PURSER

282

6 continued
SHROUD
YAWING
7
ADMIRAL
BALLAST
BOLLARD
BULWARK
CAPSTAN
CATWALK
COAMING
DRAUGHT
FLOTSAM
GANGWAY
GRAPNEL
GUNWALE
INBOARD
LANYARD
MOORING
QUARTER

RIGGING
SEA MILE
TONNAGE
TOPSIDE
WATCHES
8
BINNACLE
BOWSPRIT
BULKHEAD
COXSWAIN
DOG WATCH
HALYARDS
HATCHWAY
LARBOARD
PITCHING
SCUPPERS
SPLICING
TAFFRAIL
WINDLASS
WINDWARD

9
AMIDSHIPS
COMPANION
CROW'S NEST
FREEBOARD
SHIP'S BELL
STARBOARD
WATER-LINE
10
BATTEN DOWN
DEADLIGHTS
DEADWEIGHT
FIRST WATCH
FORE-AND-AFT
FORECASTLE
NIGHT WATCH
11
MIDDLE WATCH
QUARTER-DECK
WEATHER SIDE

12
DISPLACEMENT
JACOB'S LADDER
MARLINE SPIKE
NAUTICAL MILE
PLIMSOLL L.INE
13
QUARTERMASTER
14
SUPER-
  STRUCTURE
15
COMPANION-
  LADDER
DAVY JONES
  LOCKER

ARMS & MILTARIA

TITLES

ARMY RANKS
FIELD MARSHAL
GENERAL
LIEUTENANT-GENERAL
MAJOR-GENERAL
BRIGADIER
COLONEL
LIEUTENANT-COLONEL
MAJOR
CAPTAIN
LIEUTENANT
SECOND-LIEUTENANT
SERGEANT-MAJOR
QUARTERMASTER-
  SERGEANT
SERGEANT
CORPORAL
LANCE-CORPORAL
BOMBARDIER
PRIVATE

ROYAL NAVY RANKS
ADMIRAL OF THE
  FLEET

ADMIRAL
VICE-ADMIRAL
REAR-ADMIRAL
COMMODORE
CAPTAIN
COMMANDER
LIEUTENANT-
  COMMANDER
LIEUTENANT
SUB-LIEUTENANT
CHIEF PETTY OFFICER
PETTY OFFICER
LEADING SEAMAN
ABLE SEAMAN
ORDINARY SEAMAN
JUNIOR SEAMAN

ROYAL AIR FORCE RANKS
MARSHAL OF THE ROYAL
  AIR FORCE
AIR CHIEF MARSHAL
AIR MARSHAL
AIR VICE-MARSHAL
AIR COMMODORE

GROUP CAPTAIN
WING COMMANDER
SQUADRON LEADER
FLIGHT LIEUTENANT
FLYING OFFICER
PILOT OFFICER
MASTER AIR
  LOADMASTER
MASTER AIR
  ELECTRONIC OPERATOR
MASTER ENGINEER
MASTER NAVIGATOR
MASTER SIGNALLER
MASTER PILOT
WARRANT OFFICER
CHIEF TECHNICIAN
FLIGHT SERGEANT
SERGEANT CORPORAL
JUNIOR TECHNICIAN
SENIOR AIRCRAFTMAN
LEADING AIRCRAFTMAN
AIRGRAFTMAN 1ST CLASS
AIRCRAFTMAN 2ND
  CLASS

DECORATIONS AND MEDALS

AIR FORCE CROSS (AFC)
AIR FORCE MEDAL (AFM)
ALBERT MEDAL (AM)
CONSPICUOUS GALLANTRY MEDAL
  (CGM)
DISTINGUISHED FLYING CROSS (DFC)
DISTINGUISHED FLYING MEDAL (DFM)
DISTINGUISHED SERVICE CROSS (DSC)
DISTINGUISHED SERVICE MEDAL (DSM)

GEORGE CROSS (GC)
GEORGE MEDAL (GM)
MEDAL FOR DISTINGUISHED CONDUCT
  IN THE FIELD (DCM)
MILITARY CROSS (MC)
MILITARY MEDAL (MM)
THE DISTINGUISHED SERVICE ORDER
  (DSO)
VICTORIA CROSS (VC)

BATTLES

2
RE, ILE DE (1627, Anglo-French Wars)
3
ACS (1849, Hungarian Rising)
AIX, ILE D' (1758, Seven Years' War)
DEE, BRIG OF (1639, Bishops' War)
DIU (1537,1545, Portuguese in India)
GOA (1511, 1570, Portuguese Conquest)
HUE (1968, Vietnam War)

UJI (1180, Taira War)
ULM (1805, Napoleonic Wars)
4
ACRE (1189-1191,Third Crusade; 1291,
  Crusader-Turkish Wars; 1799, French
  Revolutionary Wars; 1840, Egyptian Revolt)
AGRA (1713, Farrukhsiyar's Rebellion; 1803,
  Second British-Maratha War, 1857, Indian
  Mutiny)

BATTLES

4 continued

ALMA (1854, Crimean War)

AONG (1857, Indian Mutiny)

ARAS (1775, First British-Maratha War)

AVUS (198 B.C., Second Macedonian War)

BAZA (1489, Spanish-Muslim Wars)

BEDR (623, Islamic Wars)

BEGA (1696, Ottoman Wars)

CUBA (1953, Castro Revolt)

CYME (474 B.C., Etruscan-Greek Wars)

DEEG (1780, First British-Maratha War; 1804, Second British-Maratha War)

DYLE (896, German States' Wars)

GAZA (332 B.C., Alexander's Asiatic Campaigns; 312 B.C., Wars of Alexander's Successors; 1917, World War I)

GELT, THE (1570, Anglo-Scottish Wars)

GUAM (1944, World War II)

IRUN (1837, First Carlist War)

ISLY (1844, Abd-el-Kader's Rebellion)

IVRY (1590, French Religious Wars)

JENA (1806, Napoleonic Wars)

KARS (1855, Crimean War; 1877, Russo-Turkish War)

KIEV (1941, World War 11)

KISO (1180, Taira War)

KULM (1813, Napoleonic Wars)

LADE (494 B.C., Ionian War; 201 B.C., Macedonian Wars)

LAON (1814, Napoleonic Wars)

LECK, THE (1632, Thirty Years' War)

LENS (1648, Thirty Years' War)

LODZ (1914, World War I)

LOJA (1482, Spanish-Muslim Wars)

MAIN, THE (9 B.C., Germanic War)

MAYA, COLDE, (1813, Peninsular War)

METZ (1870, Franco-Prussian War)

MUTA (636, Muslim Invasion of Syria)

NEON (354 B.C., Sacred War)

NILE (1798, French Revolutionary Wars)

NIVE (1813, Peninsular War)

NOVI (1799, French Revolutionary Wars)

OFEN (1849, Hungarian Rising)

OHUD (623, Mohammed's War with the Koreish)

ONAO (1857, Indian Mutiny)

CRAN (1509, Spanish invasion of Morocco; 1940, World War II)

OREL (1943, World War I

ORUO (1862, Bolivian Civil War)

POLA (1380, War of Chioggia)

RAAB (1809, Napoleonic Wars)

RIGA (1621, Swedish-Polish Wars)

ROME (387 B.C.,First Invasion of the Gauls, 408, Wars of the Western Roman Empire, 472, Ricimer's Rebellion; 537, 546, Wars of the Byzantine Empire; 1082, Norman Seizure; 1527, Wars of Charles V; 1849, Italian Wars of Independence)

SCIO (1769, Ottoman Wars)

SETA (1183, Yoshinaka's Rebellion)

SOHR (1745, War of the Austrian Succession)

ST LO (1944, World War II)

TOBA (1868, Japanese Revolution)

TORO (1476, War of the Castilian Succession)

TROY (1100 B.C.)

TRUK (1944, World War II)

TYRE (332 B.C., Alexander's Asiatic Campaigns)

VEII (405 B.C., Rise of Rome)

ZAMA (202 B.C., Second Punic War)

ZEIM (1877, Russo-Turkish War)

ZELA (67 B.C., Third Mithridatic War; 47 B.C., Wars of the First Triumvirate)

5

ACCRA (1824,1825, First British-Ashanti War)

ADUWA (1896, Italian Invasion of Ethiopia)

ALAMO, STORMING OF THE (1836, Texan Rising)

ALAND (1714, Great Northern War)

ALLIA, THE (390 B.C., The First Invasion of the Gauls)

ALSEN (1864, Schleswig-Holstein War)

AMBUR (1749, Carnatic War; 1767, First British-Mysore War)

AMIDA (359, Roman-Persian Wars)

ANZIO (1944, World War II)

ARCOT (1751, Carnatic War)

ARGOS (195 B.C., Roman Invasion of Greece)

ARIUS (214 B.C., The Wars of the Hellenistic Monarchies)

ARNEE (1751, Carnatic War; 1782, First British-Mysore War)

ARRAH (1857, Indian Mutiny)

ARRAS (1654, Wars of Louis XIV; 1917, World War I)

A SHAU (1966, Vietnam War)

AURAY (1364, Hundred Years' War)

5 continued

BAHUR (1752, Seven Years' War)
BANDA (1858, Indian Mutiny)
BANDS, THE (961, Danish Invasion of Scotland)
BASRA (665, Islamic Wars)
BAVAY (57 B.C., Gallic Wars)
BEREA (1852, Kaffir Wars)
BETWA, THE (1858, Indian Mutiny)
BOSRA (632, Muslim Invasion of Syria)
BOYNE, THE (1690, War Grand Alliance)
BREST (1512,War of the Holy League)
BRILL (1572, Netherlands War of Independence)
BURMA (1942, 1943, World War II)
BUXAR (1764, British Conquest of Bengal)
CADIZ (1587, Anglo-Spanish War)
CAIRO (1517, Ottoman Wars)
CANEA (1644, Candian War)
CAPUA (212 B.C., Second Punic War)
CARPI (1701, War of the Spanish Succession)
CESME (1770, Ottoman Wars)
CHIOS (357 B.C., Social War; 201 B.C., Wars of the Hellenistic Monarchies)
CRECY (1346, Hundred Years' War)
CRETE (1941, World War II)
CUZCO (1536, Conquest of Peru)
DAK TO (1967, Vietnam War)
DAMME (1213, Wars of Philip Augustus)
DELHI (1297, First Tatar Invasion of India; 1398, Second Tatar Invasion; 1803, Second British-Maratha War; 1804, Second British-Maratha War; 1857, Indian Mutiny)
DOUAI (1710, War of the Spanish Succession)
DOURO (1809, Peninsular War)
DOVER (1652, Anglo-Dutch Wars)
DOWNS, THE (1666, Anglo-Dutch Wars)
DREUX (1562, French Religious Wars)
DUBBA (1843, Sind Campaign)
DUNES (1658, Wars of Louis XIV)
DWINA, THE (1701, Swedish-Polish War)
ELENA (1877, Russo-Turkish War)
EL TEB (1884, British-Sudan Campaigns)
EMESA (272, Wars of the Roman Empire)
ENGEN (1800, French Revolutionary Wars)
EYLAU (1807, Napoleonic Wars)
GENOA (1746, Patriotic Rising; 1795, 1800, French Revolutionary Wars)
GIHON, THE (1362, Wars of Tamerlane)

GINGI (1689, Mughal Invasion of the Deccan)
GOITS (1848, Italian Wars of Independence)
GUBAT (1885, British Sudan Campaigns)
HANAU (1813, Napoleonic Wars)
HERAT (1220, Tatar Invasion of Afghanistan; 1837, Persian-Afghan Wars)
HIPPO (430, Wars of the Western Roman Empire)
IMMAC (218, Revolt of Elagabalus)
IMOLA (1797, French Revolutionary Wars)
INDUS, THE (1221,Tatar Invasion of Central Asia)
IPSUS (306 B.C., Wars of Alexander's Successors)
ISSUS (333 B.C., Alexander's Asiatic Campaigns; 1488, Ottoman Wars)
JASSY (1620, Ottoman Wars)
JIRON (1829, Peruvian-Colombian War)
JUNIN (1824, Peruvian War of Independence)
KAGUL (1770, Ottoman Wars)
KALPI (1858, Indian Mutiny)
KAREE (1900, Second Boer War)
KAZAN (1774, Cossack Rising)
KIOGE (1677, Northern War)
KOLIN (1757, Seven Years' War)
KOTAH (1858, Indian Mutiny)
KUMAI (1355, Moronoshi's Rebellion)
LAGOS (1693, War of the Grand Alliance)
LA PAZ (1865, Bolivian Civil War)
LARGS (1263, Norse Invasion of Scotland)
LESNO (1708, Russo-Swedish War)
LEWES (1264, Barons' Wars)
LEYTE (1944, World War II)
LIEGE (1914, World War I)
LIGNY (1815, Napoleonic Wars)
LILLE (1708, War of the Spanish Succession)
LIPPE (11 B.C., Germanic Wars)
LISSA (1866, Seven Weeks' War)
LUZON (1945, World War II)
LYONS (197, Civil Wars of the Roman Empire)
MAIDA (1806, Napoleonic Wars)
MALTA (1565, Ottoman Wars; 1798, French Revolutionary Wars; 1942, World War II)
MARNE (1914, 1918, World War I)
MAXEN (1759, Seven Years' War)
MAYPO (1818, Chile War of Independence)
MERTA (1561, Mughal Invasion of the Deccan)

289

BATTLES

5 continued

MORAT (1476, Burgundian Wars)

MOTYA (398 B.C., Carthaginian Invasion of Sicily)

MUDIKI (1845, First British-Sikh War)

MUNDA (45 B.C., Civil War of Caesar and Pompey)

MURET (1213, Albigensian Crusade)

MURSA (351, Civil Wars of the Roman Empire)

MYLAE (260 B.C., First Punic War)

MYLEX (36 B.C., Wars of the Second Triumvirate)

NAMUR (1914, World War I)

NARVA (1700, Great Northern War)

NAXOS (376 B.C., Wars of the Greek City States)

NIKKO (1868, Japanese Revolution)

NISSA (1064, Scandinavian Wars)

NIZIB (1839, Mehmet Ali's Second Rebellion)

OLPAE (426 B.C., Great Peloponnesian War)

OSTIA (1500, Italian Wars)

OTRAR (1219, Tatar Invasion of Khorezm)

PARIS (1814, Napoleonic Wars; 1870, Franco-Prussian War)

PAR MA (1734, War of the Polish Succession)

PATAY (1429, Hundred Years' War)

PAVIA (271, Invasion of the Alemanni; 568, Lombard Conquest of Italy; 1431, Italian Wars; 1525, Wars of Charles V)

PERED (1849, Hungarian Rising)

PETRA (549, Persian Wars)

PIROT (1885, Serbo-Bulgarian War)

PODOL (1866, Seven Weeks' War)

POONA (1802, Maratha Wars)

PRUTH, THE (1770, Ottoman Wars)

PYDNA (168 B.C., Third Macedonian War)

RAMLA (1177, Crusader-Turkish Wars)

REBEC (1524, Wars of Charles V)

REDAN, THE GREAT (1855, Crimean War)

REIMS (1814, Napoleonic Wars)

REVAL (1790, Russo-Swedish Wars)

RIETI (1821, Italian Wars of Independence)

ROUEN (1418, Hundred Years' War)

SEDAN (1870, Franco-Prussian War)

SELBY (1644, English Civil War)

SEOUL (1950, Korean War)

SLUYS (1340, Hundred Years' War)

SOMME (1916,1918, World War 1)

SPIRA (1703, War of Spanish Succession)

SPURS (1302, Flemish War; 1513, Anglo-French Wars)

STOKE (1487, Lambert Simnel's Rebellion)

SUERO, THE (75 B.C., Civil War of Sertorius)

TACNA (1880, Peruvian-Chilean War)

TAMAI (1884, British Sudan Campaigns)

TEGEA (473 B.C., Ways of Sparta)

TEXEL (1653, Anglo-Dutch Wars)

THALA (22, Numidian Revolt)

THORN (1702, Great Northern War)

TOURS (732, Muslim Invasion of France)

TUNIS (255 B.C., First Punic War; 1270, Eighth Crusade)

TURIN (312, Civil Wars of the Roman Empire; 1706, War of the Spanish Succession)

UCLES (1109, Spanish-Muslim Wars)

UTICA (49 B.C., Civil War of Caesar and Pompey; 694, Muslim Conquest of Africa)

VALMY (1792, French Revolutionary Wars)

VARNA (1444, Anti-Turkish Crusade; 1828, Ottoman Wars)

VARUS, DEFEAT OF (A.D. 9, Wars of the Roman Empire)

VASAQ (1442, Ottoman Wars)

WAVRE (1815, Napoleonic Wars)

WISBY (1613, Danish-Swedish Wars)

WORTH (1870, Franco-Prussian War)

XERES (711, Spanish-Muslim Wars)

YPRES (1914, 1915, 1917, World War I)

ZENTA (1679, Ottoman Wars)

ZNAIM (1809, Napoleonic Wars)

6

AACHEN (1944, World War II)

ABUKIR (1799,1801, French Revolutionary Wars)

ABU KRU (1885, British Sudan Campaigns)

ACTIUM (31 B.C., Wars of the Second Triumvirate)

AEGINA (458 B.C., Third Messenian War)

AEGUSA (241 B.C., First Punic War)

ALEPPO (638, Muslim Invasion of Syria; 1400, Tatar Invasion of Syria; 1516, Ottoman Wars)

ALESIA (52 B.C., Gallic Wars)

ALFORD (1645, English Civil War)

ALHAMA (1482, Spanish-Muslim Wars)

ALIWAL (1846, First British-Sikh War)

AMBATE (1532, Conquest of Peru)

AMIENS (1870, Franco-Prussian War)

6 continued

ANCONA (1860, Italian Wars of Independence)
ANGORA (1402, Tatar Invasion of Asia Minor)
ANTIUM (1378, War of Chioggia)
ARBELA (331 B.C., Alexander's Asiatic Campaigns)
ARCOLA (1796, French Revolutionary Wars)
ARGAON (1803, Second British-Maratha War)
ARKLOW (1798, Irish Rebellion)
ARNHEM (1944, World War II)
ARQUES (1589, French Religious Wars)
ARSOUF (1191, Third Crusade)
ARTOIS (1915, World War I)
ASHTEE (1818, Third British-Maratha War)
ASIAGO (1916, World War I)
ASPERN (1809, Napoleonic Wars)
ASSAYE (1803, Second British-Maratha War)
ATBARA (1898, British Sudan Campaigns)
AUSSIG (1426, Hussite War)
AZORES (1591, Anglo-Spanish War)
BAMIAN (1221, Tatar Invasion of Kharismia)
BARDIA (1941, World War II)
BARNET (1471, Wars of the Roses)
BASING (871, Danish Invasion of Britain)
BAYLEN (1808, Peninsular War)
BEAUGE (1421, Hundred Years' War)
BENDER (1768, Ottoman Wars)
BERGEN (1759, Seven Years' War)
BEYLAN (1831, Egyptian Revolt)
BILBAO (1836, First Carlist War; 1937, Spanish Civil War)
BINGEN (70, Gallic Revolt)
BIRUAN (1221, Tatar Invasion of Kharismia)
BOYACA (1819, Colombian War of Independence)
BUSACO (1810, Peninsular War)
CABALA (379 B.C., Second Carthaginian Invasion of Sicily)
CABRIA (72 B.C., Third Mithridatic War)
CALAIS (1346, Hundred Years' War; 1558, Anglo-French Wars)
CALLAO (1866, Peruvian War of Independence)
CALVEN, THE (1499, Swiss-Swabian War)
CAMDEN (1780, American RevolutionWar)
CAMPEN (1759, Seven Years' War)
CANDIA (1648, Candian War)
CANNAE (216 B.C., Second Punic War)

CEPEDA (1859, Argentine Civil War)
CHANDA (1818, Third British-Maratha War)
CHIARI (1701, War of Spanish Succession)
CHILOE (1826, Chilean War of Independence)
CHIZAI (1372, Hundred Years' War)
CHUNAR (1538, Hindu-Mughal Wars)
CNIDUS (394 B.C., Wars of Greek City States)
CONCON (1891, Chilean Civil War)
CUNAXA (401 B.C., Expedition of Cyrus the Younger)
CYSSUS (191 B.C., Wars of the Hellenistic Monarchies)
DANZIG (1627, Thirty Years' War; 1807, 1813, Napoleonic Wars)
DARGAI (1897, British Northwest Frontier Campaign)
DELIUM (424 B.C., Peloponnesian War)
DELPHI (355 B.C., Sacred War)
DENAIN (1712, War of the Spanish Succession)
DESSAU (1626, Thirty Years' War)
DIEPPE (1942, World War II)
DIPAEA (471 B.C., Arcadian War)
DJERBA (1560, Ottoman Wars)
DOLLAR (875, Danish Invasions of Scotland)
DUNBAR (1296, 1339, Wars of Scottish Independence; 1650, Cromwell's Scottish Campaign)
DUNDEE (1899, Second Boer War)
DUPPEL (1864, Schleswig-Holstein War)
EDESSA (259, Persian Wars)
ELINGA (206 B.C., Second Punic War)
EMBATA (356 B.C., Social War)
ERBACH (1800, French Revolutionary Wars)
FAENZA (541, Wars of the Byzantine Empire)
FERKEH (1896, British Sudan Campaigns)
GAZALA (1942, World War II)
GEBORA (1811, Peninsular War)
GERONA (1809, Peninsular War)
GHAZNI (1839, First British-Afghan War)
GISORS (1197, Anglo-French Wars)
GROZKA (1739, Ottoman Wars)
HALLUE (1870, Franco-Prussian War)
HARLAW (1411, Scottish Civil Wars)
HASHIN (1885, British Sudan Campaigns)
HATVAN (1849, Hungarian Rising)
HAVANA (1748, War of the Austrian Succession; 1762, Seven Years' War)
HEXHAM (1464 , Wars of the Roses)

BATTLES

6 continued

HIMERA (480 B.C., First Carthaginian Invasion of Sicily; 409 B.C., Second Carthaginian Invasion of Sicily)
HOCHST (1622, Thirty Years' War)
HONAIN (629, Muslim Conquest of Arabia)
HUESCA (1105, Spanish-Muslim Wars; 1837, First Carlist War)
HYSIAE (668 B.C., Sparta against Argos)
INCHON (1950, Korean War)
INGAVI (1841, Bolivian-Peruvian War)
INGOGO (1881, First Boer War)
ISMAIL (1790, Ottoman Wars)
ISONZO (1915, World War I)
JALULA (637, Muslim Invasion of Persia)
JARNAC (1569, Third French Religious War)
JERSEY (1550 Anglo-French Wars)
JHANSI (1857, Indian Mutiny)
KAPPEL (1531, Swiss Religious Wars)
KARAKU (1218, Tatar Invasion of Khwarizm)
KHELAT (1839, First British-Afghan War)
KIRKEE (1817, Third British-Maratha War)
KOKEIN (1824, First Burma War)
KOMORN (1849, Hungarian Rising)
KONIAH (1831, Mehemet Ali's First Rebellion)
KOTZIN (1622,1673, Ottoman Wars)
KRONIA (1738, Ottoman Wars)
LAHORE (1296, First Tatar Invasion of India)
LANDAU (1702, War of the Spanish Succession)
LANDEN (1693, War of the Grand Alliance)
LANNOY (1567, Netherlands War of Independence)
LARCAY (1829, Chilean Revolution)
LAUPEN (1339, Burgundian Wars)
LAWARI (1803, Second British-Maratha War)
LE MANS (1871, Franco-Prussian War)
LERIDA (1642,1647, Thirty Years' War)
LEYDEN (1574, Netherlands War of Independence)
LONATO (1796, French Revolutionary Wars)
LUCENA (1483, Spanish-Muslim Wars)
LUNDEN (1676, Danish-Swedish Wars)
LUTTER (1626, Thirty Years' War)
LUTZEN (1632, Thirty Years' War; 1813, Napoleonic Wars)
MACALO (1427, Italian Wars)
MADRAS (1746, War of the Austrian Succession; 1758, Seven Years' War)
MADRID (1936, Spanish Civil War)

MAIDAN (1842, First British-Afghan War)
MAJUBA (1881, First Boer War)
MALAGA (1487, Spartish-Muslim Wars; 1704, War of the Spanish Succession)
MALAYA (1941, World War II)
MALDON (991, Danish Invasions of Britain)
MANILA (1898, Spanish-American War)
MANTUA (1797, French Revolutionary Wars)
MARDIS (315, War of the Two Empires)
MARGUS (285, Civil Wars of the Roman Empire)
MEDINA (625, Muslim Conquest of Arabia)
MEDOLA (1796, French Revolutionary Wars)
MEERUT (1398, Second Tatar Invasion of India)
MERIDA (712, Spanish-Muslim Wars)
MERTON (871, Danish Invasions of Britain)
MEXICO (1520, Conquest of Mexico)
MINDEN (1759, Seven Years' War)
MIYAKO (1353, Moronoshi's Rebellion; 1391, Mitsuyakis' Revolt)
MOHACZ (1526,1687, Ottoman Wars)
MORAWA (1443, Ottoman Wars)
MOSCOW (1941, World War II)
MUKDEN (1905, Russo-Japanese War; 1948,Chinese Civil War)
MULTAN (1848, Second British-Sikh War)
MUTHUL, THE (108 B.C., Jugurthine War)
MUTINA (43 B.C., Roman Civil Wars)
MYCALE (479 B.C., Persian-Greek Wars)
MYTTON (1319, Wars of Scottish Independence)
NACHOD (1866, Seven Weeks' War)
NAJARA (1367, Hundred Years' War)
NANHAN (1904, Russo-Japanese War)
NASEBY (1645, English Civil War)
NICAEA (1097, First Crusade)
NORWAY (1940, World War II)
NOTIUM (407 B.C,, Peloponnesian War)
NOVARA (1513, Italian Wars; 1849, Italian Wars of Independence)
OCKLEY (851, Danish Invasions of Britain)
OLMEDO (1467, War of the Castilian Succession)
OLMOTZ (1758, Seven Years' War)
OPORTO (1809, Peninsular War)
ORTHEZ (1814, Peninsular War)
OSTEND (1601, Netherlands War of Independence)
OTUMBA (1520, Spanish Conquest of Mexico)

6 continued

PANION (198 B.C., Wars of the Hellenistic Monarchies)

PARANA (1866, Paraguayan War)

PATILA (1394, Tatar Invasion of Persia)

PEKING (1214, Tatar Invasion of China)

PLEI ME (1965, Vietnam War)

PLEVNA (1877, Russo-Turkish War)

POLAND (1939, World War II)

PONANI (1780, First British-Mysore War)

POTOSI (1825, Bolivian War of Independence)

PRAGUE (1620, Thirty Years' War; 1757, Seven Years' War)

PUENTE (1816, Colombian War of Independence)

QUEBEC (1759,1760, Seven Years' War)

RABAUL (1943, World War II)

RAGATZ (1446, Armagnac War)

RAPHIA (217 B.C., Wars of the Hellenistic Monarchies)

RASZYN (1809, Napoleonic Wars)

RHODES (1480, Ottornan Wars)

RIVOLI (1797, French Revolutionary Wars)

ROCROI (1643, Thirty Years' War)

ROLICA (1808, Peninsular War)

RUMANI (1915, World War I)

SACILE (1809, Napoleonic Wars)

SADOWA (1866, Seven Weeks' War)

SAIGON (1968, Vietnam War)

SAINTS, THE (1782, American Revolutionary War)

SALADO (1340, Spanish-Muslim Wars)

SANGRO (1943, World War II)

SARDIS (280 B.C., Wars of Alexander's Successors)

SEPEIA (494 B.C., Argive War)

SESKAR (1790, Russo-Swedish Wars)

SHILOH (1862, American Civil War)

SICILY (1943, World War II)

SIFFIN (657, Muslim Civil Wars)

SILPIA (206 B.C., Second Punic War)

SINOPE (1853, Crimean War)

SON-TAI (1883, Tongking War)

SORATA (1780, Inca Rising)

STE FOY (1760, Seven Years' War)

ST KITS (1667, Anglo-Dutch Wars)

SYBOTA (433 B.C., Peloponnesian Wars)

TAURIS (47 B.C., Civil War of Caesar and Pompey)

TEGYRA (373 B.C., Boeotian War)

TERTRY (687, Rise of the Franks)

TETUAN (1860, Spanish-Moroccan War)

THEBES (335 B.C., Macedonian Conquest)

THURII (282 B.C., Roman Civil Wars)

TIFLIS (1386, Tatar Invasion of the Caucasus)

TIGRIS (363, Persian Wars)

TOBRUK (1941, 1942, World War II)

TOFREK (1885, British-Sudan Campaigns)

TORGAU (1760, Seven Years' War)

TOULON (1707, War of the Spanish Succession; 1744, War of the Austrian Succession; 1793, French Revolutionary Wars)

TOWTON (1461, Wars of the Roses)

TSINAN (1948, Chinese Civil War)

TUDELA (1808, Peninsular War)

ULUNDI (1879, Zulu-British War)

UROSAN (1595, Japanese Invasion of Korea)

USHANT (1794, French Revolutionary Wars)

VARESE (1859, Italian Wars of Independence)

VARMAS (1813, Colombian War of Independence)

VENICE (1848, Italian Wars of Independence)

VERDUN (1916, World War I)

VERONA (312, Civil Wars of the Roman Empire)

VIENNA (1529,1683, Ottoman Wars)

VYBORG (1918, Russo-Finnish War)

WAGRAM (1809, Napoleonic Wars)

WAIZAN (1849, Hungarian Rising)

WARSAW (1831, Second Polish Rising; 1914,World War I; 1918, Russo-Polish War; 1939, 1944, World War II)

WERBEN (1631, Thirty Years' War)

WIAZMA (1812, Napoleonic Wars)

YARMUK (636, Muslim Invasion of Syria)

YAWATA (1353, War of the Northern and Southern Empires)

ZALAKA (1086, Moorish against Castile)

ZAMORA (901, Spanish-Muslim Wars)

ZURICH (1799, French Revolutionary Wars)

7

ABRAHAM, PLAINS OF (1759, Seven Years' War)

ABU KLEA (1885, British Sudan Campaigns)

ACRAGAS (406 B.C., Second Carthaginian Invasion of Sicily)

BATTLES

7 continued

AGORDAT (1893, Italian Sudan Campaigns)

ALARCOS (1195, Spanish-Muslim Wars)

ALCOLEA (1868, Isabel II of Spain Deposed)

ALGHERO (1353, Aragonese Conquest of Sardinia)

ALGIERS (1775, Spanish-Algerian War; 1816, Bombardment of)

ALIGARH (1803, First British-Maratha War)

ALKMAAR (1573, Netherlands War of Independence; 1799, French Revolutionary Wars)

ALMANSA (1707, War of the Spanish Succession)

ALMORAH (1815, British-Gurkha War)

ALNWICK (1093, Anglo-Scottish Wars)

AMAKUSA (1638, Revolt of the Christians in Japan)

AMOAFUL (1874, Second British-Ashanti War)

AMORIUM (838, Muslim Invasion of Asia Minor)

ANCYRAE (242 B.C., Hierax's Rebellion)

ANTIOCH (244 B.C., Syrian Wars; 1097, First Crusade)

ANTWERP (1576, Netherlands War of Independence; 1832, Liberation of Belgium; 1914, World War I)

ARAUSIO (105 B.C., Fourth Gallic Invasion)

ARIKERA (1791, Second British-Mysore War)

ASCALON (1099, First Crusade)

ASCULUM (279 B.C., Pyrrhus' Invasion of Italy; 89 B.c., Social War)

ASHDOWN (871, Danish Invasion of Britain)

ATHENRY (1316, Conquest of Ireland)

AUGHRIM (1691, War of English Succession)

BAGHDAD (1401, Mongul Invasion of Mesopotamia)

BALKANS (1940,1944, World War II)

BAPAUME (1871, Franco-Prussian War)

BAROSSA (1811, Peninsular War)

BASSANO (1796, French Revolutionary Wars)

BASSEIN (1780, First British-Maratha War)

BATAVIA (1811, Napoleonic Wars)

BATOCHE (1885, Riet's Second Rebellion)

BAUTZEN (1813, Napoleonic Wars)

BELMONT (1899, Second Boer War)

BENBURB (1646, Great Irish Rebellion)

BETHUNE (1707, War of the Spanish Succession)

BETIOCA (1813, Colombian War of Independence)

BEZETHA (66, Jewish Wars of Roman Empire)

BIBERAC (1796, French Revolutionary Wars)

BITONTO (1734, War of the Polish Succession)

BOKHARA (1220, Tatar Invasion of Kharismia)

BOURBON (1810, Napleonic Wars)

BRESCIA (1849, Italian Rising)

BRESLAU (1757, Seven Years' War)

BRIENNE (1814, Napoleonic Wars)

BULL RUN (1861, 1862, American Civil War)

CADESIA (636, Muslim Invasion of Persia)

CADSAND (1357, Hundred Years' War)

CALAFAT (1854, Crimean War)

CARACHA (1813, Colombian War of Independence)

CARIGAT (1791, Second British-Mysore War)

CARNOUL (1739, Persian Invasion of India)

CARRHAE (53 B.C., Parthian War)

CASSANO (1705, War of Spanish Succession)

CASSINO (1944, World War II)

CHALONS (271, Revolt of the Legions of Aquitaine; 366, Invasion of the Alemanni; 451, Wars of the Western Roman Empire)

CHETATE (1854, Crimean War)

CHOCZIM (1769, Ottoman Wars)

CHONG-JU (1904, Russo-Japanese War)

CIBALIS (315, War of the Two Empires)

CLISSAU (1702, Swedish-Polish Wars)

CLUSIUM (225 B.C., Conquest of Cisalpine Gaul)

COLENSO (1899, Second Boer War)

COLOMBO (1796, French Revolution Wars)

CORDOVA (1010, Spanish-Muslim Wars)

CORINTH (429 B.C., Peloponnesian War; 394 B.C., Corinthian War; 1862, American Civil War)

CORONEA (447 B.C., First Peloponnesian War; 394 B.C., Corinthian War)

CORONEL (1914, World War I)

CORUMBA (1877, Paraguayan War)

CORUNNA (1809, Peninsular War)

CRAONNE (1814, Napoleonic Wars)

CRAVANT (1423, Hundred Years' War)

CREFELD (1758, Seven Years' War)

CREMONA (198 B.C., Second Gallic Invasion; 69, Civil Wars of the Roman Empire; 1702, War of Spanish Succession)

7 continued

CRONION (379 B.C., Second Carthaginian Invasion of Sicily)

CROTONE (982, German Invasion of Italy)

CROTOYE (1347, Hundred Years' War)

CUASPAD (1862, Ecuador-Colombia War)

CURICTA (49 B.C., Civil War of Caesar and Pompey)

CUSTOZA (1866, Italian Wars of Independence)

CYZICUS (410 B.C., Peloponnesian War; 88 B.C., First Mithridatic War)

WASLAU (1742, War of the Austrian Succession)

DAZAIFU (1281, Chinese Invasion of Japan)

DEORHAM (577, Wessex against the Welsh)

DODOWAH (1826, First British-Ashanti War)

DONABEW (1825, First Burma War)

DRESDEN (1813, Napleonic Wars)

DRISTEN (973, Wars of the Byzantine Empire)

DUNDALK (1318, Scottish Invasion of Ireland)

DUNKELD (1689, Jacobite Rising)

DUNKIRK (1940, World War II)

DUPPLIN (1332, Baliol's Rising)

DURAZZO (1081, Norman Invasion of Italy)

ECKMOHL (1809, Napoleonic Wars)

ECNOMUS (256 B.C., First Punic War)

EL CANEY (1898, Spanish-American War)

ELK HORN (1862, American Civil War)

ENTHOLM (1676, Northern Wars)

EPHESUS (499 B.C., Ionian War; 262 B.c., Gallic Invasion of Asia)

ESSLING (1809, Napoleonic Wars)

ETAMPES (604, Burgundians against Neustrians)

EVESHAM (1265, Barons' War)

FALKIRK (1298, Wars of Scottish independence; 1746, The Forty-five Rebellion)

FERRARA (1815, Napoleon's Hundred Days)

FLEURUS (1622, Thirty Years' War; 1690. War of the Grand Alliance; 1794, French Revolutionary Wars)

FLOODEN (1513, Anglo-Scottish Wars)

FOCSANI (1789, Ottoman Wars)

FORNOVO (1495,Italian Wars)

FRANLIN (1864, American Civil War)

FULFORD (1066, Norse Invasion of England)

FUSHIMI (1868, Japanese Revolution)

GALICIA (1914, World War I)

GATE PAH (1864, Maori-British War)

GHERAIN (1763, British Conquest of Bengal)

GHOAINE (1842, First British-Afghan War)

GORARIA (1857, Indian Mutiny)

GORLICE (1915, World War I)

GRANADA (1319,1491, Spanish-Muslim Wars)

GRANGAM (1721, Great Northern War)

GRANSON (1476, Burgundian Wars)

GRASPAN (1899, Second Boer War)

GRENADA (1779, American Revolutionary War; 1983, American Invasion)

GROCHOW (1831, Second Polish Rising)

GUJERAT (1849, Second British-Sikh War)

GWALIOR (1780, First British-Maratha War; 1858, Indian Mutiny)

HAARLEM (1572, Netherlands War of Independence)

HASLACH (1805, Napoleonic Wars)

HELORUS (492 B.C., Wars of Sicily)

HERNANI (1836, 1837, First Carlist War)

HERRERA (1837, First Carlist War)

HILL 875 (1967, Vietnam War)

HILL 881 (1967, Vietnam War)

HOGLAND (1789, Russo-Swedish Wars)

HOOGHLY, THE (1759, Anglo-Dutch Wars in India)

HUMAITA (1866,1868, Paraguayan War)

HWAI-HAI (1948, Chinese Civil War)

ISASZCQ (1849, Hungarian Rising)

IWO-JIMA (1945, World War II)

JAMAICA (1655, Anglo-Spanish Wars)

JAVA SEA (1942, World War II)

JITGURH (1815, British Gurkha War)

JUTLAND (1916, World War I)

KAIPING (1895, Sino-Japanese War)

KALISCH (1706, Great Northern War)

KALUNGA (1814, British-Gurkha War)

KAMARUT (1824, First Burma War)

KAMBULA (1879, Zulu War)

KAPOLNA (1849, Hungarian Rising)

KASHGAL (1883, British Sudan Campaigns)

KHARKOV (1942,1943, World War II)

KHE SANH (1968, Vietnam War)

KILSYTH (1645, English Civil War)

KINEYRI (1848, Second British-Sikh War)

KINLOSS (1009, Danish Invasion of Scotland)

KINSALE (1601, O'Neill's Rebellion)

KIUCHAU (1904, Russo-Japanese War)

BATTLES

7 continued
KOJENDE (1219, Tatar Invasion of Central Asia)

KOMATSU (1062, Japanese Nine Years' War)

KOSSOVA (1398, 1448, Ottoman Wars)

KRASNOI (1812, Napoleonic Wars)

KROTZKA (1739, Ottoman Wars)

KURDLAH (1795, Maratha Wars)

LA HOGUE (1692, War of the Grand Alliance)

LARISSA (171 B.C., Third Macedonian War)

L'ECLUSE (1340, Hundred Years' War)

LEGHORN (1653, Anglo-Dutch Wars)

LEGNANO (1176, Wars of the Lombard League)

LEIPZIG (1631, Thirty Years' War; 1813, Napoleonic Wars)

LEPANTO (1571, Cyprus War)

LEUCTRA (371 B.C., Wars of the Greek City States)

LEUTHEN (1757, Seven Years' War)

LINCOLN, FAIR OF (1217, First Barons' War)

LINDLEY (1900, Second Boer War)

LOCNINH (1967, Vietnam War)

LOFTCHA (1877, Russo-Turkish War)

LUCKNOW (1857, Indian Mutiny)

LUZZARA (1702, War of the Spanish Succession)

MAGENTA (1859, Italian Wars of Independence)

MAIWAND (1880, Second British-Afghan War)

MALACCA (1513, Portuguese Conquests)

MALAKOV (1855, Crimean War)

MALNATE (1859, Italian Wars of Independence)

MANSURA (1250, Seventh Crusade)

MARENGO (1800, French Revolution Wars)

MARGATE (1387, Hundred Years' War)

MAROSCH, THE (101, Roman Empire Wars)

MATAPAN, CAPE (1941, World War II)

MATCHIN (1791, Ottoman Wars)

MEEANEE (1843, Sind Campaign)

MEMPHIS (459 B.C., Athenian Expedition to Egypt, 638, Muslim Conquest of Egypt; 1862, American Civil War)

MENTANA (1867, Italian Wars of Independence)

MESSINA (1284, Aragonese Conquest of Sicily; 1718, War of the Quadruple Alliance)

METHVEN (1306, Wars of Scottish (Independence)

MILAZZO (1860, Italian Wars of Independence)

MINORCA (1756, Seven-Years' War; 1762, American Revolutionary War)

MOGILEV (1812, Napoleonic Wars)

MONARDA (1501, Moorish Insurrection)

MONTIEL (1369, Castilian Civil War)

MORELLA (1840, First Carlist War)

MORTARA (1849, Italian Wars of Independence)

MOSKOWA (1812, Napoleonic Wars)

NAEFELS (1388, Swiss-Austrian Wars)

NAISSUS (269, Gothic Invasion of the Roman Empire)

NAM DONG (1964, Vietnam War)

NANKING (1949, Chinese Civil War)

NEUWIED (1797, French Revolutionary Wars)

NEWBURN (1640, Anglo-Scottish Wars)

NEWBURY (1643, 1644, English Civil War)

NEW ROSS (1798, Irish Rebellion)

NIAGARA (1759, Seven Years' War)

NINEVEH (627, Persian Wars)

NISIBIS (338, 346. 350, Persian Wars of the Roman Empire)

NIVELLE (1813, Peninsular War)

OCZAKOV (1737, Ottoman Wars)

ODAWARA (1590, Hojo Rebellion)

OKINAWA (1945, World War II)

OOSCATA (1768, First British-Mysore War)

OPEQUAN (1864, American Civil War)

ORLEANS (1428, Hundred Years' War)

PAGAHAR (1825, First Burma War)

PALERMO (1848, Italian Wars of Independence)

PALMYRA (272, Roman Empire Wars)

PANIPAT (1526, Third Mughal Invasion of India; 1556, Hindu Revolt; 1759, Afghan-Maratha Wars)

PARKANY (1663, Ottoman Wars)

PLASSEY (1757, Seven Years' War)

PLATAEA (479 B.C., Third Persian Invasion; 429 B.C., Great Peloponnesian War)

PLESCOW (1615, Russo-Swedish Wars)

PLOVDIV (1878, Russo-Turkish War)

POLOTSK (1812, Napoleonic Wars)

PRESTON (1648, English Civil War; 1715, The Fifteen Rebellion)

PULTAVA (1709, Great Northern War)

PULTUSK (1703, Great Northern War; 1806, Napoleonic Wars)

7 continued

PUNNIAR (1843, Gwalior Campaign)
RASTADT (1796, French Revolution Wars)
RAVENNA (729, Byzantine Empire Wars;
1512, War of the Holy League)
READING (871, Danish Invasions of Britain)
REVOLAX (1808, Russo-Swedish Wars)
RIMNITZ (1789, Ottoman Wars)
RIO SECO (1808, Peninsular War)
ROSTOCK (1677, Danish-Swedish Wars)
ROUCOUX (1746, War of the Austrian
Succession)
RUMANIA (1916, World War I)
RUSPINA (46 B.C., Civil War of Caesar and
Pompey)
SABUGAL (1811, Peninsular War)
SAGUNTO (1811, Peninsular War)
SALAMIS (480 B.C., Third Persian Invasion;
307 B.C., Wars of Alexander's Successors)
SALERNO (1943, World War II)
SAN JUAN (1898, Spanish-American War)
SARKANY (1848, Hungarian Rising)
SCUTARI (1474, Ottoman Wars)
SEALION, OPERATION (1940, World War II)
SECCHIA, THE (1734, War of the Polish
Succession)
SEGEWAR (1849, Hungarian Rising)
SELINUS (409 B.C., Second Carthaginian
Invasion of Sicily)
SEMPACH (1386, Swiss War of
Independence)
SENEFFE (1674, Wars of Louis XIV)
SENEKAL (1900, Second Boer War)
SHARQAT (1918, World War I)
SIMGARA (348, 360, Persian Wars of the
Roman Empire)
SINNACA (53 B.C., Parthian War)
SINUIJU (1951, Korean War)
SKALITZ (1866, Seven Weeks' War)
SOBRAON (1846, First British-Sikh War)
SOCZAWA (1676, Ottoman Wars)
SOMNATH (1024, Mahmud's Twelfth
Invasion of India)
ST DENIS (1567, French Religious Wars;
1837, French-Canadian Rising)
ST LUCIA (1794, French Revolutionary Wars)
SURINAM (1804, Napoleonic Wars)
SURSUTI, THE (1191, 1192, Mohammed
Ghori's Invasion)
SVISTOV (1877, Russo-Turkish War)
SZIGETH (1566, Ottoman Wars)

TAGINAE (552, Byzantine Empire Wars)
TALKHAN (1221, Talar Invasion of
Khorassan)
TALNEER (1818, Third British-Maratha War)
TANAGRA (457 B.C., Peloponnesian Wars)
TANJORE (1758, Seven Years' War; 1773,
First British-Mysore War)
TARANTO (1501, Italian Wars; 1940, World
War II)
TELAMON (225 B.C., Conquest of Cisalpine
Gaul)
TE-LI-SSU (1904, Russo-Japanese War)
TERGOES (1572, Netherlands War of
Independence)
THAPSUS (46 B.C., Civil War of Caesar and
Pompey)
TICINUS (218 B.C., Second Punic War)
TOLBIAC (496, Rise of the Franks)
TOLENUS (90 B.C., Social War)
TOURNAI (1581, Netherlands War of
Independence; 1709, War of the Spanish
Succession)
TREBBIA (218 B.C. Second Punic War;
1799, French Revolutionary Wars)
TREVERI (55 B.c., Gallic Wars)
TRIPOLI (643, Muslim Conquest of Africa)
TUNISIA (1942, World War II)
TURBIGO (1859, Italian Wars of
Independence)
UKRAINE (1943, World War II)
UPPSALA (1520,1521, Danish-Swedish
Wars)
VESERIS (339 B.C., Latin War)
VIGO BAY (1702, War of the Spanish
Succession)
VILLACH (1492, Ottoman Wars)
VILLETA (1868, Paraguayan War)
VIMEIRO (1808, Peninsular War)
VINAROZ (1938, Spanish Civil War)
VITORIA (1813, Peninsular War)
VOUILLE (507, Rise of the Franks)
WARBURG (1760, Seven Years' War)
WARGAOM (1779, First British-Maratha War)
WEPENER (1900, Second Boer War)
WIMPFEN (1622, Thirty Years' War)
WINKOVO (1812, Napoleonic Wars)
YASHIMA (1184, Taira War)
ZLOTSOW (1676, Ottoman Wars)
ZURAKOW (1676, Ottoman Wars)
ZUTPHEN (1586, Netherlands War of
Independence)

BATTLES

8

ABERDEEN (1644, English Civil War)
ABU HAMED (1897, British Sudan
  Campaigns)
ACAPULCO (1855, Mexican Liberal Rising)
ADUATUCA (52 B.C., Gallic Wars)
AIZNADIN (634, Muslim Invasion of Syria)
ALICANTE (1706, War of the Spanish
  Succession)
ALMENARA (1710, War of the Spanish
  Succession)
AMALINDE (1818, Kaffir Wars)
ANAQU ITO (1546, Conquest of Peru)
ANTIETAM (1862, American Civil War)
AQUILEIA (394, Roman Civil Wars)
ARRETILIM (283 B.C., Etruscan War)
ASIRGHAR (1819, Third British-Maratha
  War)
ASPENDUS (191 B.C., Wars of the
Hellenistic
  Monarchies)
ASSUNDUN (1016, Danish Invasions of
  Britain)
ATLANTIC (1917, World War I)
AUGSBURG (900, Germans versus
  Hungarians)
AULDEARN (1645, English Civil War)
AVARICUM (53 B.C. Gallic Wars)
AXARQUIA (1483, Spanish-Muslim Wars)
AYACUCHO (1824, Peruvian War of
  Independence)
AZIMGHUR (1858, Indian Mutiny)
BAGRADAS (49 B.C., Wars of the First
  Triumvirate)
BASTOGNE (1944, World War II)
BEAUMONT (1870, Franco-Prussian War)
BEDA FOMM (1941, World War II)
BELGRADE (1456, 1717, 1789, Ottoman
  Wars)
BELLEVUE (1870, Franco-Prussian War)
BEREZINA (1812, Napoleonic War)
BEYMAROO (1841, First British-Afghan War)
BIBRACTE (58 B.C., Gallic Wars)
BISMARCK (1941, World War II)
BLENHEIM (1704, War of the Spanish
  Succession)
BLUEBERG (1806, Napoleonic Wars)
BORNHOLM (1676, Northern War)
BORODINO (1812, Napoleonic Wars)
BOULOGNE (1544, Anglo-French Wars)
BOUVINES (1214, Anglo-French Wars)

BOVIANUM (305 B.C., Second Samnite War)
BR IHUEGA (1710, War of Spanish Succession)
BROOKLYN (1776, American Revolutionary
  War)
BUZENVAL (1871, Franco-Prussian War)
CALCUTTA (1756, Seven Years' War)
CALDIERO (1796, French Revolutionary
  Wars; 1805, Napoleonic Wars)
CAPE BONA (468, Wars of the Western
  Roman Empire)
CARABOBO (1821, Venezuelan War of
  Independence)
CARLISLE (1745, The Forty-five Rebellion)
CARRICAL (1758, Seven Years' War)
CARTHAGE (152 B.C., Third Punic War; 533,
  Byzantine Empire Wars)
CASTELLA (1813, Peninsular War)
CAWNPORE (1857, Indian Mutiny)
CHERITON (1644, English Civil War)
CHEVILLY (1870, Franco-Prussian War)
CHIOGGIA (1380, War of Chioggia)
CHIPPEWA (1814, War of 1812)
CLONTARF (1014, Norse Invasion of Ireland)
COCHEREL (1364, Hundred Years' War)
COLOMBEY (1870, Franco-Prussian War)
COPRATUS, THE (316 B.C., Wars of
  Alexander's Successors)
CORAL SEA (1942, World War II)
COURTRAI (1302, Flemish War)
CRAYFORD (456, Jutish Invasion)
CRIMISUS (341 B.C., Third Carthaginian
  Invasion of Sicily)
CULLODEN (1746, The Forty-five Rebellion)
CZARNOVO (1806, Napoleonic Wars)
DAMASCUS (635, Muslim Invasion of Syria;
  1401, Tatar Invasion of Syria; 1918, WWI)
DAN-NO-URA (1185, Taira War)
DNIESTER (1769, Ottoman Wars)
DOMINICA (1782, American Revolutionary
  War)
DREPANUM (249 B.C. First Punic Wars)
DROGHEDA (1641, Great Irish Rebellion;
  1649, Cromell's Campaign in Ireland)
DRUMCLOG (1679, Covenanters' Rising)
EDGEHILL (1642, English Civil War)
ESPINOSA (1808, Peninsular War)
ETHANDUN (878, Danish Invasions of
  Britain)
FAIR OAKS (1862, American Civil War)
FAVENTIA (82 B.C., Civil War of Marius and
  Sulla)

8 continued

FLANDERS (1940, World War II)

FLORENCE (406, Wars of the Western Roman Empire)

FLUSHING (1809, Napoleonic Wars)

FONTENOY (1745, War of the Austrian Succession)

FORMIGNY (1450, Hundred Years' War)

FRASTENZ (1499, Swiss-Swabian War)

FREIBURG (1644, Thirty Years' War)

FRETEVAL (1194, Anglo-French Wars)

GADEBESK (1712, Great Northern War)

GAULAULI (1858, Indian Mutiny)

GEMBLOUX (1578, Netherlands War of Independence)

GEOK TEPE (1878, Russian Conquest of Central Asia)

GERBEROI (1080, Norman Revolt)

GERGOVIA (52 B.C., Gallic Wars)

GISLIKON (1847, War of the Sonderbund)

GITSCHIN (1866, Seven Weeks' War)

GOODWINS, THE (1666, Anglo-Dutch Wars)

GRAF SPEE (1939, World War II)

GRANICUS, THE (334 B.C., Alexander's Asiatic Campaigns)

GUNZBURG (1805, Napoleonic Wars)

HADRANUM (344 B.C., Sicilian Wars)

HAHOZAKI (1274, Tatar Invasion of Japan)

HASTINGS (1066, Norman Conquest)

HERACLEA (280 B.C., Pyrrhus' Invasion of Italy; 313, Roman Civil Wars)

HERDONEA (210 B.C., Second Punic War)

HERRINGS, THE (1429, Hundred Years' War)

HONG KONG (1941, World War II)

HYDASPES, THE (326 B.C., Alexander's Asiatic Campaigns)

INKERMAN (1854, Crimean War)

ITABITSU (740, Hirotsuke's Rebellion)

JEMAPPES (1792, French Revolution Wars)

JIDBALLI (1904, Somali Expedition)

JOTAPATA (67 A.D. Jewish Wars of Roman Empire)

KANDAHAR (1221, Tatar Invasion of Afghanistan; 1545, Mughal Invasion of Afghanistan; 1648, Perso-Afghan Wars., 1834, Afghan Tribal Wars; 1880, Second British-Afghan War)

KATZBACH (1813, Napoleonic Wars)

KHARTOUM (1884, British-Sudan Campaigns)

KIRBEKAN (1885, British Sudan Campaigns)

KLUSHINO (1610, Russo-Polish Wars)

KORYGAOM (1818, Third British-Maratha War)

KULEVCHA (1829, Ottoman Wars)

KUMAMOTO (1876, Satsuma Rebellion)

KUMANOVO (1912, 1st Balkan War)

LANGPORT (1645, English Civil War)

LANGSIDE (1568, Scottish Civil Wars)

LA PUEBLA (1862, 1863, Franco-Mexican war)

LARISSUS, THE (209 B.C., Wars of the Achaean League)

LAUFFELD (1747, War of the Austrian Succession)

LAUTULAE (316 B.C., Second Samnite War)

LE CATEAU (1914, World War I)

LEITSKAU (1813, Napoleonic Wars)

LEONTINI (211 B.C., Second Punic War)

LIAOYANG (1904, Russo-Japanese War)

LIEGNITZ (1760, Seven Years' War)

LOBOSITZ (1756, Seven Years' War)

LUNCARTY (980, Danish Invasions of Scotland)

LYS RIVER (1918, World War I)

MAFEKING (1899, Second Boer War)

MAGNESIA (190 B.C., Wars of the Hellenistic Monarchies)

MAHIDPUR (1817, Third British-Maratha War)

MANDONIA (338 B.C., Macedonian Wars)

MANTINEA (418 B.C., Peloponnesian War; 362 B.C., Wars of the Greek City States; 208 B.C., Wars of the Achaean League)

MARATHON (490 B.C., Persian-Greek Wars)

MEDELLIN (1809, Peninsular War)

MEDENINE (1943, World War II)

MELITENE (578, Persian-Byzantine Wars)

MESSINES (1917, World War I)

METAURUS (207 B.C., Second Punic War)

MOLLWITZ (1741, War of the Austrian Succession)

MONTREAL (1760, Seven Years War)

MORTLACK (1010, Danish Invasions of Scotland)

MOSKIRCH (1800, French Revolutionary Wars)

MOUSCRON (1794, French Revolutionary Wars)

MUHLBERG (1547, German Reformation Wars)

BATTLES

8 continued

MOHLDORF (1322, Civil War of the Holy Roman Empire)

MUSA BAGH (1858, Indian Mutiny)

MYTILENE (428 B.C., 406 B.C., Great Peloponnesian War)

NAVARINO (1827, Greek War of Independence)

NEHAVEND (A.D. 641, Muslim Invasion of Persia)

NIQUITAS (1813, Colombian War of Independence)

NUMANTIA (142 B.C., Lusitanian War)

OBLIGADO (1845, Uruguayan Civil War)

OMDURMAN (1898, British-Sudan Campaigns)

ONESSANT (1778, American Revolutionary War)

OSTROWNO (1812, Napoleonic Wars)

OVERLORD, OPERATION (1944, World War II)

PALESTRO (1859, Italian Wars of Independence)

PALO ALTO (1846, American-Mexican War)

PANDOSIA (331 B.C., Macedonian Wars)

PANORMUS (251 B.C., First Punic War)

PEA RIDGE (1862, American Civil War)

PELUSIUM (525 B.C., Persian Conquest of Egypt; 321 B.C., War of Alexander's Successors)

PESHAWAR (1001, Afghan Invasion of India)

PHIL IPPI (42 B.c., Roman Civil Wars)

PODHAJCE (1667, Polish-Turkish Wars)

POITIERS (507, Gothic Invasion of France; 1356, Hundred Years' War)

PORTLAND (1653, Anglo-Dutch Wars)

PYRAMIDS (1798, French Revolutionary Wars)

PYRENEES (1813, Peninsular War)

RATHENOW (1675, Swedish Invasion of Brandenburg)

RICHMOND (1862, American Civil War)

ROSSBACH (1757, Seven Years' War)

ROVEREDO (1796, French Revolution Wars)

SAALFELD (1806, Napoleonic Wars)

SAMAGHAR (1658, Rebellion of Aurungzebe)

SANTAREM (1834, Portuguese Civil War)

SAPIENZA (1490, Ottoman Wars)

SARATOGA (1777, American Revolutionary War)

SAUCOURT (861, Norse Invasion of France)

SEMINARA (1495, French Wars in Italy)

SENTINUM (298 B.C., Third Samnite War)

SHANGHAI (1937, Sino-Japanese War)

SHOLAPUR (1818, Third British-Maratha War)

SIDASSIR (1799, Third Britishr-Mysore War)

SIKAJOKI (1808, Russo-Swedish Wars)

SILISTRA (1854, Crimean War)

SINSHEIM (1674, Wars of Louis XIV)

SLIVNICA (1885, Serbo-Bulgarian War)

SMOLENSK (1708, Great Northern War; 1812, Napoleonic Wars; 1941, World War II)

SOISSONS (486, Rise of the Franks)

SORAUREN (1813, Peninsular War)

SPION KOP (1900, Second Boer War)

SPLITTER (1679, Swedish Invasion of Brandenburg)

ST ALBANS (1455,1461, Wars of the Roses)

STANDARD, THE (1138, Anglo-Scottish Wars)

STE CROIX (1807, Napoleonic Wars)

ST GEORGE (1500, Ottoman Wars)

ST MIKEL (1918, World War I)

STOCKACH (1799, French Revolutionary Wars)

ST PRIVAT (1870, Franco-Prussian War)

STRATTON (1643, English Civil War)

ST THOMAS (1807, Napoleonic Wars)

SYRACUSE (415 B.C., Peloponnesian Wars; 387 B.C., Second Carthaginian Invasion of Sicily; 213 B.C., Second Punic War)

TACUBAYA (1859. Mexican Liberal Rising)

TALAVERA (1809, Peninsular War)

TARAPACA (1879, Peruvian-Chilean War)

TAYEIZAN (1868, Japanese Revolution)

TEMESVAR (1849, Hungarian Rising)

THETFORD (870, Danish Invasions of England)

TIBERIAS (1187, Crusader-Saracen Wars)

TOULOUSE (1814, Napoleonic Wars)

TRINIDAD (1797; French Revolutionary Wars)

TSINGTAO (1914, World War I)

TSUSHIMA (1419, Mongol Invasion of Japan)

TURNHOUT (1597, Netherlands War of Independence)

VALLETTA (1798, French Revolutionary Wars)

VALUTINO (1812, Napoleonic Wars)

8 continued

VELENEZE (1848, Hungarian Rising)
VELLETRI (1849, Italian Wars of Independence)
VERNEUIL (1424, Hundred Years' War)
VILLIERS (1870, Franco-Prussian War)
VOLTURNO (1860, Italian Wars of Independence)
WATERLOO (1815, Napoleonic Wars)
WATIGAON (1825, First Burma War)
YAMAZAKI (1582, Mitsuhide Rebellion)
YENIKALE, GULF OF (1790, Ottoman Wars)
YORKTOWN (1781, American Revolutionary War; 1862, American Civil War)
ZENDECAN (1039, Turkish Invasion of Afghanistan)
ZORNDORF (1758, Seven Years' War)

9

ABENSBERG (1809, Napoleonic Wars)
AGENDICUM (52 B.C., Gallic Wars)
AGINCOURT (1415, Hundred Years' War)
AGNADELLO (1509, War of the League of Cambrai)
AHMADABAD (1780, First British-Maratha War)
AHMED KHEL (1880, Second British-Afghan War)
AIGUILLON (1347, Hundred Years' War)
ALCANTARA (1580, Spanish Conquest of Portugal; 1706, War of the Spanish Succession)
ALHANDEGA (939, Spanish-Muslim Wars)
ALRESFORD, (1644, English Civil War)
ALTENDORF (1632, Thirty Years' War)
AMSTETTEN (1805, Napoleonic Wars)
ANGOSTURA (1847, American-Mexican War; 1868, Paraguayan War)
AQUIDABAN (1870, Paraguayan War)
ARGINUSAE (406 B.C., Great Peloponnesian War)
ARKENHOLM (1455, Douglas Rebellion)
ASKULTSIK (1828, Ottoman Wars)
ASTRAKHAN (1569,Turkish Invasion of Russia)
ATAHUALPA (1531, Conquest of Peru)
AUERSTADT (1806, Napoleonic Wars)
AYLESFORD (456, Jutish Invasion of Britain)
BALACLAVA (1854, Crimean War).
BALLYMORE (1798, Irish Rebellion)
BANGALORE (1791, Second British-Mysore War)

BARCELONA (1705, War of the Spanish Succession; 1938, Spanish Civil War)
BEDRIACUM (69, Civil Wars of the Roman Empire)
BENEVENTO (1266, Franco-Italian Wars)
BERGFRIED (1807, Napleonic Wars)
BHURTPORE (1805, Second British-Maratha War; 1827, Second Siege of)
BLACK ROCK (1812, War of 1812)
BLUFF COVE (1982, Falkland Isles)
BOIS-LE-DUC (1794, French Revolutionary Wars)
BORGHETTO (1796, French Revolutionary Wars)
BORNHOVED (1227, War of Scandinavia)
BRENTFORD (1642, English Civil War)
BRIG OF DEE (1639, Bishops' Wars)
BUCHAREST (1771, Ottoman Wars)
BURNS HILL (1847, Kaffir Wars)
BYZANTIUM (318 B.C., Wars of Alexander's Successors; 323, Civil Wars of the Roman Empire)
CAMERINUM (298 B.C., Third Samnite War)
CAPE HENRY (1781, American Revolutionary War)
CAPORETTO (1917, World War I)
CAPRYSEMA (743 B.C., First Messenian War)
CASILINUM (554, Byzantine Empire Wars)
CASTILLON (1453, Hundred Years' War)
CERIGNOLA (1503, Italian Wars)
CHACABUCO (1817, Chilean War of Independence)
CHAERONEA (338 B.C., Amphictyonic War; 86 B.C., First Mithridatic War)
CHALCEDON (74 B.C., Third Mithridatic War)
CHAMPAGNE (1915, World War I)
CHARASIAS (1879, Second British-Afghan War)
CHARENTON (1649, War of the Fronde)
CHE-MUL-PHO (1904, Russo-Japanese War)
CHORILLOS (1861, Peruvian-Chilean War)
CHOTUSITZ (1742, War of the Austrian Succession)
CIVITELLA (1033 Norman Invasion of Italy)
CORRICHIE (1562, Huntly's Rebellion)
COULMIERS (1870, Franco-Prussian War)
CROSSKEYS (1862, American Civil War)
CUDDALORE (1783, American Revolutionary War)

301

BATTLES

9 continued

CYNOSSEMA (411 B.C., Peloponnesian War)

DENNEWITZ (1813, Napoleonic Wars)

DETTINGEN (1743, War of the Austrian Succession)

DEVICOTTA (1749, Carnatic War)

DORYLAEUM (1097, First Crusade)

DUNSINANE (1054, Anglo-Scottish Wars)

EBRO RIVER (1938, Spanish Civil War)

EDERSBERG (1809, Napoleonic Wars)

EDGEWORTH (1469, Wars of the Roses)

EL ALAMEIN (1942, World War II)

ELCHINGEN (1805, Napoleonic Wars)

ELLANDUNE (825, Wessex versus Mercia)

ELLEPORUS (389 B.C., Italiot Invasion of Sicily)

EMPINGHAM (1470, Wars of the Roses)

EURYMEDON, THE (466 B.C., Third Persian Invasion)

FAMAGUSTA (1570, Cyprus War)

FISH CREEK (1855, Riel's Second Rebellion)

FIVE FORKS (1865, American Civil War)

FRIEDLAND (1807, Napoleonic Wars)

FRONTIERS, BATTLE OF THE (1914, World War I)

GALLIPOLI (1915, World War I)

GERMAGHAH (1193, Tatar Conquest of Central Asia)

GIBRALTAR (1704, War of the Spanish Succession; 1779, American Revolutionary War)

GLADSMUIR (1745, The Forty-five Rebellion)

GLEN FRUIN (1604, Scottish Civil Wars)

GLENLIVET (1594, Huntly's Rebellion)

GRAMPIANS, THE (Roman Invasion Of Scotland)

GRANDELLA (1266, Italian Wars)

GUAL-EL-RAS (1860, Spanish-Moroccan War)

GUINEGATE (1513, Anglo-French Wars)

GUMBINNEN (1914, World War I)

HALIARTUS (395 B.C. Wars of Greek City States)

HEILSBERG (1807, Napoleonic Wars)

HEMUSHAGU (1595, Japanese Invasion of Korea)

HERICOURT (1474, Burgundian Wars)

HOCHKIRCH (1758, Seven Years' War)

HOCHSTADT (1800, French Revolutionary Wars)

HYDERABAD (1843, Conquest of Sind)

JERUSALEM (70 A.D., Jewish Wars of Roman Empire; 637, Muslim Invasion of Syria; 1099, First Crusade; 1187, Crusader-Turkish Wars; 1917, World War 1; 1948, Israeli-Arab Wars)

JUGDULLUK (1842, First British-Afghan War)

KAGOSHIMA (1877, Satsuma Rebellion)

KARA BURUR (1791, Ottoman Wars)

KARAGAULA (1774, Cossack Rising)

KARAMURAN (1225, Tatar Conquest of Central Asia)

KASSASSIN (1882, Egyptian Revolt)

KEMENDINE (1824, First Burma War)

KERESZTES (1596, Ottoman Wars)

KHARISMIA (1220, Tatar Invasion of Central Asia)

KIMBERLEY (1899, Second Boer War)

KISSINGEN (1866, Seven Weeks' War)

KIZIL-TEPE (1877, Russo-Turkish War)

KRAKOVICZ (1475, Ottoman Wars)

KUNOBITZA (1443, Ottoman Wars)

LADYSMITH (1899, Second Boer War)

LANG'S NECK (1881, First Boer War)

LANSDOWNE (1643, English Civil Wars)

LE BOURGET (1870, Franco-Prussian War)

LENINGRAD (1944, World War II)

LEXINGTON (1775, American Revolutionary War; 1861, American Civil War)

LEYTE GULF (1944, World War II)

LILYBAEUM (250 B.C., First Punic War)

LINKOPING (1598, Swedish-Polish Wars)

LOWENBERG (1813, Napoleonic Wars)

MAGOEBURG (1631, Thirty Years' War)

MALAVILLY (1799, Third British-Mysore War)

MALEGNANO (1859, Italian Wars of Independence)

MANGALORE (1783, First British-Mysore War)

MANSFIELD (1864, American Civil War)

MARIA ZELL (1805, Napoleonic Wars)

MARIGNANO (1515, Italian Wars)

MARSAGLIA (1693, War of the Grand Alliance)

MERSEBURG (934, Germans versus Hungarians)

MILLESIMO (1796, French Revolution Wars)

MIOHOSAKI (764, Oshikatsa's Rebellion)

MITA CABAN (1362, Tatar Wars)

MOHRUNGEN (1807, Napoleonic Wars).

MONTEREAU (1814, Napoleonic Wars)

9 continued

MONTERREY (1846, Amercian-Mexican War)
MONTLHERY (1465, Franco-Burgundian War)
MORAZZONE (1848, Italian Wars of Independence)
MUKWANPUR (1816, British-Gurkha War)
MYONNESUS (190 B.C., Wars of the Hellenistic Monarchies)
NAGY-SARLO (1849, Hungarian Rising)
NASHVILLE (1863, American Civil War)
NAULOCHUS (36 B.C, Wars of the Second Triumvirate)
NAUPACTUS (429 B.C., Great Peloponnesian War)
NAVARRETE (1367, Hundred Years' War)
NEGAPATAM (1746, War of the Austrian Succession; 1781, Second British Mysore War 1782, American Revolutionary War)
NEW GUINEA (1942, World War II)
NEW MARKET (1864, American Civil War)
NICOPOLIS (66 B.C., 47 B.C., Third Mithridatic War; 1396, Ottoman Wars; 1877, Russo-Turkish War)
NUJUFGHUR (1857, Indian Mutiny)
OCEAN POND (1864, American Civil War)
OENOPHYTA (457 B.C., First Peloponnesian War)
OLTENITZA (1853, Crimean War)
OTTERBURN (1388, Wars of Scottish Independence)
OUDENARDE (1708, War of the Spanish Succession)
PELEKANON (1329, Ottoman Wars)
PELISCHAT (1877, Russo-Turkish War)
PERISABOR (363, Persian Wars)
PERPIGNAN (1474, Franco-Spanish War)
PHARSALUS (48 B.C., Civil War of Caesar and Pompey; 1897, Greco-Turkish,Wars)
PLACENTIA (271, Invasion of the Alemanni)
POLLENTIA (402, Wars of the Western Roman Empire)
POLLICORE (1781, First British-Mysore War)
PONTEVERT (57 B.C., Gallic Wars)
PORTO NOVO (1781, First British-Mysore War)
PRIMOLANO (1796, French Revolution Wars)
PRINCETON (1777, American Revolutionary War)

PYONGYANG (1894, Sino-Japanese War)
QUISTELLO (1734, War of the Polish Succession)
RAMILLIES (1706, War of the Spanish Succession)
RAMNUGGUR (1849, Second British-Sikh War)
RATHMINES (1649, Cromwell's Campaign in Ireland)
RHINELAND, THE (1945, World War II)
RIACHUELA (1865, Paraguayan War)
ROSBECQUE (1382, Flemish-French Wars)
ROSEBURGH (1460, Anglo-Scottish Wars)
RYNEMANTS (1578, Netherlands War of Independence)
SADULAPUR (1848, Second British-Sikh War)
SALAMANCA (1812, Peninsular War; 1858, Mexican Liberal Rising)
SAMARKAND (1220, Tatar Invasion of Khorezm)
SAN LAZARO (1746, War of the Austrian Succession)
SANTANDER (1937, Spanish Civil War)
SARAGOSSA (1700, War of the Spanish Succession; 1808, Peninsular War)
SAXA RUBRA (312, Revolt of Maxentius)
SCARPHEIA (146 B.C., War of the Achaean League)
SCHWECHAT (1848, Hungarian Rising)
SEDGEMOOR (1685, Monmouth's Rebellion)
SERINGHAM (1753, Carnatic War)
SEVENOAKS (1450, Cade's Rebellion)
SHAHJEHAN (1221, Tatar Invasion of Khorezm)
SHEERNESS (1667, Anglo-Dutch Wars)
SHERSTONE (1016, Danish Invasion of England)
SHINOWARA (1183, Yoshinaka's Rebellion)
SHIROGAWA (1876, Satsuma Rebellion)
SHOLINGUR (1781, First British-Mysore War)
SINGAPORE (1942, World War II)
SITABALDI (1817, Third British-Maratha War)
SOLFERINO (1859, Italian Wars of Independence)
SOUTHWARK (1450, Cade's Rebellion)
SPICHEREN (1870, Franco-Prussian War)
STADTLOHN (1623, Thirty Years' War)
STAFFARDA (1690, War of the Grand Alliance)

BATTLES

10 continued

COPENHAGEN (1801, French Revolutionary Wars; 1807, Napoleonic Wars)

CORTE NUOVA (1237 Guelfs and Ghibellines)

CORUPEDION (281 B.C., Wars of the Hellenistic Monarchies)

DALMANUTHA (1900, Second Boer War)

DOGGER BANK (1781, American Revolutionary War, 1915, World War I)

DONAUWORTH (1704, War of the Spanish Succession)

DUFFINDALE (1549, Kett's Rebellion)

DUNGANHILL (1647, Great Irish Rebellion)

DYRRACHIUM (48 B.C., Civil War of Caesar and Pompey)

ENGLEFIELD (871, Danish Invasion of Britain)

FEHRBELLIN (1675, Swedish Invasion of Brandenburg)

FEROZESHAH (1845, First British-Sikh War)

FETHANLEAG (584, Saxon Conquests)

FUTTEYPORE (1857, Indian Mutiny)

GAINES MILL (1862, American Civil War)

GARIGLIANO (1503, Italian Wars; 1850, Italian Wars of Independence)

GERMANTOWN (1777, American Revolutionary War)

GETTYSBURG (1863, American Civil War)

GLEN MALONE (1580, Colonization of Ireland)

GOLDEN ROCK (1753, Carnatic War)

GORODECZNO (1812, Napoleonic Wars)

GOTHIC LINE (1944, World War II)

GRANT'S HILL (1758, Seven Years' War)

GRAVELINES (1558, Franco-Spanish Wars)

GRAVELOTTE (1870, Franco-Prussian War)

GUADELOUPE (1794, French Revolutionary Wars)

HABBANIYAH (1941, World War II)

HARDENBERG (1580, Netherlands War of Independence)

HASTENBECK (1757 Seven Years' War)

HEATHFIELD (633, Mercia against Northumbria)

HEKITAI-KAN (1595, Japanese Invasion of Korea)

HELIGOLAND (1807, Napoleonic Wars)

HELIOPOLIS (1800, French Revolutionary Wars)

HELLESPONT (323, War of the Two Empires)

HOLLABRUNN (1805, Napleonic Wars)

HUMBLEBECK (1700, Great Northern War)

ICHINOTANI (1189, Taira War)

INVERLOCHY (1645, English Civil War)

JELLALABAD (1842, First British-Afghan War)

KHOJAH PASS (1842, First British-Afghan War)

KONIGGRATZ (1866, Seven Weeks' War)

KORNSPRUIT (1900, Second Boer War)

KRINGELLEN (1612, Danish-Swedish Wars)

KUNERSDORF (1759, Seven Years' War)

KLIT-EL-AMARA (1915, World War I)

LA FAVORITA (1797, French Revolutionary Wars)

LAKE GEORGE (1755, Seven Years' War)

LANDSKRONE (1676, Danish-Swedish Wars)

LA PLACILLA (1891, Chilean Civil War)

LA ROCHELLE (1372, Hundred Years' War; 1627, French Religious Wars)

LA ROTHIERE (1814, Napoleonic Wars)

LAS SALINAS (1538, Conquest of Peru)

LEUCOPETRA (146 B.C., Wars of the Achacan League)

LOUDON HILL (1307, Wars of Scottish Independence)

LOUISBOURG (1745, War of the Austrian Succession; 1758, Seven Years' War)

LULEBURGAZ (1912, Balkan Wars)

LUNDY'S LANE (1814, War of 1812)

MAASTRICHT (1579, Netherlands War of Independence)

MAHARAJPUR (1843, Gwalior Campaign; 1857, Indian Mutiny)

MALPLAQUET (1709, War of the Spanish Succession)

MARETH LINE (1943, World War II)

MARIENDAHL (1645, Thirty Years' War)

MARS-LA-TOUR (1870, Franco-Prussian War)

MARTINIQUE (1794, French Revolutionary Wars; 1809, Napoleonic Wars)

MASERFIELD (642, Northumbria against Mercia)

MELANTHIAS (559, Wars of the Byzantine Empire)

MICHELBERG (1805, Napoleonic Wars)

MIDDELBURG (1593, Netherlands War of Independence)

MIRAFLORES (1881, Peruvian-Chilean War)

BATTLES

10 continued

MONTEBELLO (1800, French Revolutionary Wars; 1859, Italian Wars of Independence)

MONTENOTTE (1796, French Revolutionary Wars)

MONTEVIDEO (1807, Napoleonic Wars; 1843, 1851, 1863, Uruguayan Civil War)

MONTFAUCON (886, Norman Invasion of France)

MONTMIRAIL (1814, Napoleonic Wars)

MORTGARTEN (1315, First Swiss-Austrian War)

MOUNT TABOR (1799, French Revolutionary Wars)

MOHLHAUSEN (58 B.C., Gallic War)

NAROCH LAKE (1916, World War I)

NEERWINDEN (1693, War of the Grand Alliance; 1793, French Revolutionary Wars)

NEW ORLEANS (1814, War of 1812; 1862, American Civil War)

NIEUWPOORT (1600, Netherlands War of Independence)

NORDLINGEN (1634,1645, Thirty Year's War)

ORCHOMENUS (85 B.C., First Mithridatic War)

OSTROLENKA (1853, Crimean War)

PAARDEBERG (1 9OG, Second Boer War)

PALESTRINA (1849, Italian Wars of Independence)

PANDU NADDI (1857, Indian Mutiny)

PEN SELWOOD (1016, Danish Invasions of Britain)

PEREMBACUM (1780, First British-Mysore War)

PERRYVILLE (1862, American Civil War)

PERSEPOLIS (316 B.C., Wars of Alexander's Successors)

PETERSBURG (1864, American Civil War)

PIAVE RIVER (1918, World War I)

PONT VALAIN (1370, Hundred Years' War)

PORT ARTHUR (1894, Sino-Japanese War; 1904, Russo-Japanese, War)

PORT HUDSON (1863, American Civil War)

PORTO BELLO (1740, War of the Austrian Succession)

QUATRE BRAS (1815, Napoleonic Wars)

QUIPUAYPAN (1532, Conquest of Peru)

RAKERSBERG (1416, Ottoman Wars)

ROMERSWAEL (1574, Netherlands War of Independence)

RUHR POCKET (1945, World War II)

RUMERSHEIM (1709, War of the Spanish Successsion)

SALANKEMEN (1691, Ottoman Wars)

SAN ISODORO (1870, Paraguayan War)

SAN JACINTO (1836, Texan Rising; 1867, Franco-Mexican War)

SANNA'S POST (1900, Second Boer War)

SANTA LUCIA (1842, Rio Grande Rising)

SAVANDROOG (1791, Second British-Mysore War)

SEINE MOUTH (1416, Hundred Years' War)

SEXIGAHARA (1600, Rebellion of Hideyori)

SEVASTOPOL (1854, Crimean War)

SEVEN PINES (1862, American Civil War)

SHREWSBURY (1403, Percy's Rebellion)

SHROPSHIRE (A.D. 50, Roman Conquest of Britain)

SIDI REZEGH (1941, World War II)

SOLWAY MOSS (1542, Anglo-Scottish Wars)

SPHACTERIA (425 B.c., Great Peloponnesian War)

STALINGRAD (1942, World War II)

STEENKERKE (1692, War of the Grand Alliance)

ST EUSTACHE (1837, French-Canadian Rising)

STILLWATER (1777, American Revolutionary War)

STOLHOFFEN (1707, War of the Spanish Succession)

STONE RIVER (1862, American Civil War)

TAIKEN GATE (1157, Hogen Insurrection)

TALANA HILL (1899, Second Boer War)

TANNENBERG (1410, German-Polish Wars; 1914, World War I)

TASHKESSEN (1877, Russo-Turkish War)

TEL-EL-KEBIR (1882, Egyptian Revolt)

TETTENHALL (910, Danish Invasions of England)

TEWKESBURY (1471, Wars of the Roses)

TINCHEBRAI (1106, Norman Civil War)

TIPPERMUIR (1644, English Civil War)

TRAVANCORE (1789, Second British-Mysore War)

TRICAMERON (533, Invasion of the Vandals)

UTSONOMIYA (1868, Japanese Revolution)

VAL-ES-DUNES (1047, Rise of Normandy)

WARTEMBERG (1813, Napoleonic Wars)

WATTIGNIES (1793, French Revolutionary Wars)

306

10 continued

WILDERNESS, THE (1864, American Civil War)

WINCHESTER (1863, American Civil War)

ZIEZICKSEE (1302, Flemish War)

11

AEGOSPOTAMI (405 B.C., Peloponnesian War)

ALAM EL HALFA (1942, World War II)

ALESSANDRIA (1799, French Revolutionary Wars)

ALJUBAROTTA (1385, Spanish-Portuguese Wars)

AN LAO VALLEY (1966, Vietnam War)

AQUAE SEXTIA (102 B.C., Cimbric War)

BANNOCKBURN (1314, Wars of Scottish Independence)

BELLEAU WOOD (1918, World War I)

BISMARCK SEA (1943, World War II)

BLADENSBURG (1814, War of 1812)

BLANQUEFORT (1450, Hundred Years' War)

BORYSTHENES, THE (1512, Russo-Polish Wars)

BRAMHAM MOOR (1408, Northumberland's Rebellion)

BREITENFELD (1642, Thirty Years' War)

BRENNEVILLE (1119, Anglo-French Wars)

BUENOS AIRES (1806,1807, Napoleonic Wars; 1874, Mitre's Rebellion)

BUNKER'S HILL (1775, American Revolutionary War)

CALPULALPAM (1860, Mexican Liberal Rising)

CAMELODUNUM (43, Roman Invasion of Britain)

CAPE PASSERO (1718, War of the Quadruple Alliance)

CARBIESDALE (1650, English Civil War)

CARENAGE BAY (1778, American Revolutionary War)

CASTIGLIONE (1706, War of the Spanish Succession; 1796, French Revolutionary Wars)

CASTILLEJOS (1860, Spanish-Moroccan War)

CECRYPHALEA (458 B.C., Third Messenian War)

CHAMPAUBERT (1814, Napoleonic Wars)

CHAPULTEPEC (1847, American-Mexican War)

CHATTANOOGA (1863, American Civil War)

CHICKAMAUGA (1863, American Civil War)

CHUANWALA (1849, Second British-Sikh War)

CHRYSOPOLIS (324, War of the Two Empires)

COLDHARBOUR (1864, American Civil War)

COLLINE GATE (82 B.C., Civil War of Marius and Sulla)

CONSTANTINE (1836, Conquest of Algeria)

DESERT STORM (1991, Gulf War)

DIAMOND HILL (1900, Second Boer War)

DINGAAWS DAY (1838, Afrikaner-Zulu War)

DOLNI-DUBNIK (1877, Russo-Turkish War)

DRIEFONTEIN (1900, Second Boer War)

DORRENSTEIN (1805, Napoleonic Wars)

ELANDS RIVER (1900, Second Boer War)

FARRUKHABAD (1804, Second British-Maratha War)

FERRYBR IDGE (1461, Wars of the Roses)

FISHER'S HILL (1864, American Civil War)

FORT ST DAVID (1758, Seven Years' War)

FRAUBRUNNEN (1376, Invasion of the 'Guglers')

FRAUENSTADT (1706, Great Northern War)

GIBBEL RUTTS (1798, Irish Rebellion)

GOOSE GREEN (1985, Falklands War)

GROSS-BEEREN (1813, Napoleonic Wars)

GUADALAJARA (1937, Spanish Civil War)

GUADALCANAL (1942, World War II)

HADRIANOPLE (323, War of the Two Empires; 378, Second Gothic Invasion of the East)

HALIDON HILL (1333, Wars of Scottish Independence)

HEAVENFIELD (634, Northumbria against the British)

HEILIGERLEE (1568, Netherlands War of Independence)

HEISINGBORG (1710, Great Northern War)

HENNERSDORF (1745, War of the Austrian Succession)

HERMANSTADT (1442, Ottoman Wars)

HOHENLINDEN (1800, French Revolutionary Wars)

HONDSCHOOTE (1793, French Revolutionary Wars)

ILE DE FRANCE (1810, Napoleonic Wars)

ISANDHWANA(1879,Zulu-British War)

KLAUSENBURG (1660, Ottoman Wars)

LAKE KERGUEL (1391, Tatar Invasion of Russia)

BATTLES

12 continued

ARCIS-SUR-AUBE (1814, Napoleonic Wars)

ARGENTORATUM (357, Invasion of the Alemanni)

ARROYO GRANDE (1842, Uruguayan Civil War)

ATHERTON MOOR (1643, English Civil War)

BANDA ISLANDS (1796, French Revolutionary Wars)

BARQUISIMETO (1813, Colombian War of Independence)

BERGEN-OP-ZOOM (1747, War of the Austrian Succession; 1799, French Revolutionary Wars)

BLOEMFONTEIN (1900, Second Boer War)

BRADDOCK DOWN (1643, English Civil War)

CAUDINE FORKS (321 B.C., Second Samnite War)

CHICKAHOMINY (1864, American Civil War)

CONCHA RAYADA (1818, Chilean War of Independence)

ELANDSLAAGTE (1899, Second Boer War)

EUTAW SPRINGS (1781, American Revolutionary War)

FORT DON ELSON (1862, American Civil War)

FREDRIKSHALD (1718, Great Northern War)

HAMPTON ROADS (1862, American Civil War)

HARPER'S FERRY (1862, American Civil War)

HEDGELEY MOOR (1464, Wars of the Roses)

HENGESTESDUN (837, Danish Invasions of Britain)

HOMILDON HILL (1402, Anglo-Scots Wars)

ICLSTAVISUS (16 A.D., Germanic Wars)

KIRCH-DENKERN (1761, Seven Years' War)

KIU-LIEN-CHENG (1904, Russo-Japanese War)

KONIGSWARTHA (1813, Napoleonic Wars)

KURSK SALIENT (1943, World War II)

LAKE REGILLUS (497 B.C., Roman Civil Wars)

LYNN HAVEN BAY (1781, American Revolutionary War)

MALAKAND PASS (1895, Chitral Campaign)

MIDWAY ISLAND (1942, World War II)

MONS-EN-PEVELE (1304, Flemish War)

MONTE CASEROS (1852, Argentine Civil War)

MONT VALERIEN (1871, Franco-Prussian War)

MONCHENGRATZ (1866, Seven Weeks' War)

MURFREESBORO (1862, American Civil War)

NECHTAN'S MERE (685, Northumbrian Invasion of Scotland)

NOVA CARTHAGO (209 B,C, Second Punic War)

OONDWA NULLAH (1763, British Conquest of Bengal)

PENOBSCOT BAY (1779, American Revolutionary War)

PETERWARDEIN (1716, Ottoman Wars)

PHILIPPSBURG (1734, War of the Polish Succession)

PINKIE CLEUGH (1547, Anglo-Scottish Wars)

PORT REPUBLIC (1862, American Civil War)

PRAIRIE GROVE (1862, American Civil War)

RADCOT BRIDGE (1387, Appellants' Rebellion)

RICH MOUNTAIN (1861, American Civil War)

RONCESVALLES (778, Charlemagne's Conquests; 1813, Peninsular War)

ROUNDWAY DOWN (1643, English Civil War)

RULLION GREEN (1666, Covenanters' Rising)

SAN SEBASTIAN (18,13, Peninsular War; 1836, First Carlist War)

SECUNDERBAGH (1857, Indian Mutiny)

SERINGAPATAM (1792, Second British-Mysore War, 1799, Third British-Mysore War)

SOUTHWOLD, BAY (1672, Anglo-Dutch Wars)

SPOTSYLVANIA (1864, American Civil War)

ST MARY'S CLYST (1549, Arundel's Rebellion)

SUNGARI RIVER (1947, Chinese Civil War)

TET OFFENSIVE, THE (1968, Vietnam War)

TIGRANOCERTA (69 B.C., Third Mithridatic War)

VALENCIENNES (1566, Netherlands War of Independence; 1656, Franco-Spanish Wars)

VILLA VICIOSA (1710, War of the Spanish Succession)

WILLIAMSBURG (1862. American Civil War)

BATTLES

12 continued

WILSON'S CREEK (1861, American Civil
War)

WROTHAM HEATH (1554, Wyatt's
Insurrection)

13

ADMAGETOBRIGA (61 B.C., Gallic Tribal
Wars)

AIX-LA-CHAPELLE (1795, French
Revolutionary Wars)

AMSAAOAN GULF (435 B.C., Corcyrean
Corinthian War)

BADULI-KI-SERAI (1857, Indian Mutiny)

BELLE-ILE-EN-MER (1759, 1761, Seven
Years' War; 1795, French Revolutionary
Wars)

BOROUGHBRIDGE (1322, Rebellion of the
Marches)

BOSWORTH FIELD (1485, Wars of the
Roses)

CAPE ST VINCENT (1797, French
Revolutionary Wars)

CASTELFIDARDO (1860, Italian Wars of
Independence)

CASTELNAUDARY (1632, French Civil
Wars)

CEDAR MOUNTAIN (1862, American Civil
War)

CHANDERNAGORE (1757, Seven Years'
War)

CHRISTIANOPLE (1611, Danish-Swedish
Wars)

CHRYSLER'S FARM (1813, War of 1812)

CIUDAD RODRIGO (1812, Peninsular War)

CYNOSCEPHALAE (364 B.C., Wars of
Greek City States; 197 B.C., Second
Macedonian War)

FALKLAND ISLES (1914, World War I; 1982,
Falklands War)

FAROUHAR'S FARM (1899, Second Boer
War)

FORT FRONTENAC (1758, Seven
Years' War)

FRANKENHAUSEN (1525, Peasants' War)

GLENMARRESTON (683, Angles' Invasion of
Britain)

HORNS OF HATTIN (1187, Crusader-
Saracen Wars)

INVERKEITHING (1317, Anglo-Scottish
Wars)

KASSERINE PASS (1943, World War II)

KILLIECRANKIE (1689, Jacobite Rising)

LITTLE BIG HORN (1876, Sioux Rising)

LOIGNY-POUPREY (1870, Franco-Prussian
War)

MAGERSFONTEIN (1899, Second Boer War)

MARCIANOPOLIS (376, Gothic Invasion of
Thrace)

MASURIAN LAKES (1914, 1915, WWI)

MEGALETAPHRUS (740 B.C., First
Messenian War)

MOLINOS DEL REY (1808, Peninsula War)

MOUNT SELEUCUS (353, Civil Wars of the
Roman Empire)

NEVILLE'S CROSS (1346, Anglo-Scottish
Wars)

NEWTOWN BUTLER (1689, War of the
Grand Alliance)

NORTHALLERTON (1138, Anglo-Scottish
Wars)

NORTH FORELAND (1666, Anglo-Dutch
Wars)

PAGASAEAN GULF (352 B.C., Sacred War)

PALAIS GALLIEN (1649, War of the Fronde)

PASSCHENDAELE (1917, World War I)

PELELIU-ANGAUR (1944, World War II)

PHILIPPINE SEA (1944, World War II)

PHILIPPOPOLIS (251, First Gothic Invasion
of the Roman Empire; 1878, Russo-Turkish
War)

PORTO PRAIA BAY (1781, American
Revolutionary War)

ROANOKE ISLAND (1862, American Civil
War)

SANTA VITTOR IA (1702, War of the Spanish
Succession)

SIEVERSHAUSEN (1553, German
Reformation
Wars)

SOUTH MOUNTAIN (1862, American Civil
War)

SPANISH ARMADA (1588, Anglo-Spanish
War)

SUDLEY SPRINGS (1862, American Civil
War)

SUGAR-LOAF ROCK (1753, Carnatic War)

WHITE OAK SWAMP (1862, American Civil
War)

YOUGHIOGHENNY (1754, Seven Years'
War)

ZUSMARSHAUSEN (1647, Thirty Years' War)

14

BERWICK-ON-TWEED (1296, Wars of Scottish Independence)

BOTHWELL BRIDGE (1679, Covenanters' Rising)

BRISTOE STATION (1863, American Civil War)

CAMPUS CASTORUM (69, Revolt of Vitellius)

CAPE FINISTERRE (1747, War of the Austrian Succession; 1805, Napoleonic Wars)

CHALGROVE FIELD (1643, English Civil War)

CHATEAU-THIERRY (1814, Napoleonic Wars)

CONSTANTINOPLE (668, Muslim Invasion of Europe; 1203-04, Fourth Crusade, 1261, Reconquest by Byzantines: 1422, Ottoman Invasion of Europe; 1453, Turkish Conquest)

CROPREDY BRIDGE (1644, English Civil War)

DRUMMOSSIE MOOR (1746, The Forty-five Rebellion)

FREDERICKSBURG (1862, American Civil War)

FUENTES DE ONORO (1811, Peninsular War)

HOHENFRIEDIBERG (1745, War of the Austrian Succession)

KOVEL-STANISLAV (1916, World War I)

LA BELLE FAMILLE (1759, Seven Years' War)

LOOSECOAT FIELD (1470, Wars of the Roses)

MARIANA ISLANDS (1944, World War II)

MORTIMER'S CROSS (1461, Wars of the Roses)

MOUNT LACTARIUS (553, Wars of the Byzantine Empire)

NICHOLSON'S NECK (1899, Boer War)

PASO DE LA PATRIA (1866, Paraguayan War)

PEACH TREE CREEK (1864, American Civil War)

PORTE ST ANTOINE (1652, War of the Fronde)

PUSAN PERIMETER (1950, Korean War)

ROUVRAY-ST-DENIS (1429, Hundred Years' War)

SANTIAGO DE CUBA (1898, Spanish-American War)

SAVAGE'S STATION (1862, American Civil War)

SECESSIONVILLE (1862, American Civil War)

SINAI PENINSULA (1956, Israeli-Arab War)

SOLOMON ISLANDS (1942, World War II)

STAMFORD BRIDGE (1066, Norse invasion of Britain; 1453, Wars of the Roses)

STIRLING BRIDGE (1297, Wars of Scottish Independence)

TEARLESS BATTLE (368 B.C., Wars of Sparta)

TONDEMAN'S WOODS (1754, Carnatic War)

TSUSHIMA STRAIT (1905, Russo-Japanese War)

VITTORIO VENETO (1918, World War I)

15

ALEUTIAN ISLANDS (1943, World War II)

AMATOLA MOUNTAIN (1846, Kaffir Wars)

APPOMATTOX RIVER (1865, American Civil War)

BATTLE OF BRITAIN (1940, World War II)

BEAUNE-LA-ROLANDE (1870, Franco-Prussian War)

BEAVER'S DAM CREEK (1862, American Civil War)

FORUM TEREBRONII (251, First Gothic Invasion of the Roman Empire)

FRANKFURT-ON-ODER (1631, Thirty Years' War)

GROSS-AGERSDORF (1757, Seven Years' War)

HELIGOLAND BIGHT (1914, World War I)

KHOORD KABUL PASS (1842, First British-Afghan War)

MALOYAROSLAVETS (1812, Napoleonic Wars)

MISSIONARY RIDGE (1863, American Civil War)

PLAINS OF ABRAHAM (1759, Seven Years' War)

PUENTE DE LA REYNA (1872, Second Carlist War)

SEVEN DAYS' BATTLE (1862, American Civil War)

SPANISH GALLEONS (1702, War of the Spanish Succession)

BATTLES

16

BATAAN-CORREGIDOR (1941, World War II)
BRONKHORST SPRUIT (1880, First Boer War)
CAMBRAI-ST QUENTIN (1918, World War I)
CHANCELLORSVILLE (1863, American Civil War)
FARRINGTON BRIDGE (1549 Arundel's Rebellion)
FORT WILLIAM HENRY (1757, Seven Years' War)
KINNESAW MOUNTAIN (1864, American Civil War)
LAS NAVAS DE TOLOSA (1212, Spanish Muslim Wars)
LIPARAEAN ISLANDS (257 B.C., First Punic War)
MADONNA DELL'OLENO (1744, War of the Austrian Succession)
MONONGAHELA RIVER (1755, Seven Years' War)
QUEENSTON HEIGHTS (1812, War of 1812)
SALUM-HALFAYA PASS (1941, World War II)
SAMPFORD COURTNEY (1549, Arundel's Rebellion)
ST JAKOB AN DER BIRS (1444, Armagnac War)

17

BURLINGTON HEIGHTS (1813, War of 1812)
DODECANESE ISLANDS (1943, World War II)
GUSTAV-CASSINO LINE (1943, World War II)
INHLOBANE MOUNTAIN (1879, Zulu War)
KWAJALEIN-ENIWETOK (1944, World War II)

LA FERE CHAMPENOISE (1814, Napoleonic Wars)
PITTSBURGH LANDING (1862, American Civil War)
POLAND-EAST PRUSSIA (1944, World War II)
VAN TUONG PENINSULA (1965, Vietnam War)

18

FORNHAM ST GENEVIEVE (1173, Rebellion of the Princes)
GUILFORD COURTHOUSE (1781, American Revolutionary War)
MEUSE-ARGONNE FOREST (1918, World War I)
PYLOS AND SPHACTERIA (425 B.C., Great Peloponnesian War)

19

CHU PONG-IA DRANG RIVER (1965, Vietnam War)
'GLORIOUS FIRST OF JUNE' 1794, French Revolutionary Wars)

20+

BARBOSTHENIAN MOUNTAINS (192 B.C., Wars of the Achaean League)
PARAETAKENE MOUNTAINS (316 B.C., Wars of Alexander's Successors)
RHINE AND THE RUHR POCKET, THE (1945, World War II)
SHANNON AND CHESAPEAKE (1813, War of 1812)
THIRTY-EIGHTH PARALLEL (1951, Korean War)

ARMOUR

4	LAMES	CASSIS	MORION
JACK	SALET	CELATE	SALADE
MAIL	VISOR	CHEEKS	SHIELD
5	6	CRENEL	TABARD
ARMET	ALETES	CRINET	OMBRIL
BACYN	BASNET	CUELLO	7
BUFFE	BHANJU	GORGET	AILETES
CREST	BRACER	GUSSET	BACINET
CULET	BRIDLE	HEAUME	BALDRIC
GIPON	BRUGNE	HELMET	BARBUTE
IMBER	CALOTE	MASCLE	BASINET
JUPEL	CAMAIL	MESAIL	BUCKLER
JUPON	CASQUE	MORIAN	CHAUCES

7 continued
CORSLET
CRUPPER
CUIRASS
CUISSES
CULESET
FENDACE
FRONTAL
GAUCHET
GOUCHET
GREAVES
HAUBERK
HOGUINE
LANIERS
MURSAIL
PANACHE
PLACARD
POITRAL
SURCOAT
VISIERE
8
ALLECRET

BARDINGS
BASCINET
BAUDRICK
BRASSARD
BRAYETTE
BUFF COAT
BURGINOT
BURGONET
CABASSET
CHAMPONS
CHANFRON
CHAUCHES
CHAUSSES
COD PIECE
COLLERET
COLLETIN
CORSELET
CRINIERE
GAUNTLET
HALECRET
JAMBEAUX
JAZERANT

PAULDRON
PECTORAL
PLASTRON
SABATONS
SOLERETS
TESTIERE
9
BAINBERGS
BEINBERGS
CHAIN MAIL
CHAMPFRON
CHAUSSONS
EPAULETTE
HAUSSE-COL
JACK BOOTS
POURPOINT
REREBRACE
SABATYNES
10
AVENTAILLE
BANDED MAIL
BARREL HELM

BRICHETTES
BRIGANDINE
CROISSANTS
ECREVISSES
EMBOITMENT
FLANCHARDS
LAMBREQUIN
11
BREASTPLATE
BREASTSTRAP
BRIGANDYRON
BRIGANTAYLE
CHAPEL DE FER
ESPALLIERES
PLATE ARMOUR
13
ARMING DOUBLET
15
IMBRICATE
ARMOUR

WEAPONS

2
NU
V1
V2
3
AXE
BOW
DAG
GUN
GYN
TNT
4
ADZE
BARB
BILL
BOLO
BOLT
BOMB
CLUB
DIRK
FANG
FOIL
KORA
KRIS
MACE
MINE

PIKE
SCUD
SHOT
TANK
TUCK
5
A-BOMB
ANCUS
ANKUS
ANLAS
ARROW
ASWAR
BATON
BIDAG
BILSO
BOLAS
BOSON
BRAND
ESTOC
FLAIL
FUSEE
FUSIL
GUPTI
H-BOMB
KERIS
KHORA

KILIG
KILIJ
KNIFE
KUKRI
KYLIE
LANCE
LATCH
PILUM
PRODD
RIFLE
SABRE
SHELL
SLING
SPEAR
STAKE
STAVE
SWORD
TACHI
WADDY
6
AMUKTA
ARMLET
BARKAL
BARONG
BASTON
BODKIN

BULLET
CANNON
CARCAS
CEMTEX
CUDGEL
DAGGER
DAISHO
DRAGON
DUM-DUM
DUSACK
EXOCET
KATANA
KERRIE
KHANDA
KIKUKI
KODOGU
MASSUE
MAZULE
MORTAR
MUSKET
NAPALM
PARANG
PETARD
PISTOL
POP GUN
QILLIJ

313

WEAPONS

6 continued
QUIVER
RAMROD
RAPIER
ROCKET
SCYTHE
SEMTEX
SUMPIT
TALWAR
VGO GUN

7
ASSEGAI
AWL-PIKE
BALASAN
BALISTA
BAYONET
BELFREY
BILJONG
BOMBARD
BOURDON
BREN GUN
CALIVER
CALTRAP
CARABEN
CARBINE
CARREAU
CHAKRAM
CHALCOS
CHOPPER
CURRIER
CUTLASS
DUDGEON
DUSSACK
FAUCHON
FIRE-POT
GRENADE
HALBARD
HALBART
HALBERD
HAND GUN
HARPOON
KASTANE
KINDJAL
LONG BOW
MISSILE
MUSQUET
PONIARD
PUNT GUN

QUARREL
SHASHQA
SHINKEN
STEN GUN
TORPEDO
TRIDENT

8
AMUSETTE
ARBALEST
ARBALETE
ARQUEBUS
ATOM BOMB
AXE-KNIFE
BASELARD
BASILARD
BLOWPIPE
CALTHORP
CANISTER
CARABINE
CATAPULT
CHACHEKA
CLADIBAS
CLAYMORE
CROSSBOW
DERINGER
DESTRIER
FALCHION
FALCONET
FAUCHARD
FIRELOCK
HACKBUTT
HAIL SHOT
HAQUEBUT
HASSEGAI
HOWITZER
PETRONEL
POIGNARD
REPEATER
REVOLVER
SCIMITAR
SHAMSHIR
SHRAPNEL
SPONTOON
SUMPITAN
TOMAHAWK
TOMMYGUN

9
ACK-ACK GUN
ARTILLERY
BADELAIRE
BANDELEER
BANDOLIER
BANNEROLE
BATTLE-AXE
BIG BERTHA
BOOMERANG
CARRONADE
CARTOUCHE
CARTRIDGE
CHAIN SHOT
DETONATOR
DOODLE-BUG
FALCASTRA
FLAGELLUM
FLAMBERGE
FLINTLOCK
GELIGNITE
GRAPESHOT
GUNPOWDER
HARQUEBUS
KNOBSTICK
MATCHLOCK
MAZZUELLE
MILLS BOMB
MUSKETOON
POISON GAS
SLUNG SHOT
SMART BOMB
TRUNCHEON

10
ARTILLATOR
BANDEROLLE
BRANDESTOC
BROAD ARROW
BROADSWORD
CANNON BALL
FIRE-STICKS
FLICK KNIFE
GATLING GUN
KNOBKERRIE
LETTER BOMB
LIMPET MINE
MACHINE GUN
PEA-SHOOTER

POWDERHORN
SIDEWINDER
SMALL SWORD
SWORD STICK

11
ANTI-TANK GUN
ARMOURED CAR
BLUNDERBUSS
HAND GRENADE
KHYBER KNIFE
MISERICORDE
NEUTRON BOMB

12
BATTERING RAM
BREECH LOADER
BRIDLE CUTTER
FIRE CARRIAGE
FLAME-THROWER
HYDROGEN BOMB

13
BRASS KNUCKLES
DUELLING SWORD
GUIDED MISSILE
KNUCKLE DUSTER
THROWING KNIFE

14
DUELLING PISTOL
INCENDIARY BOMB
NUCLEAR
  WEAPONS
PATRIOT MISSILE
ROCKET
  LAUNCHER
SAWN-OFF
  SHOTGUN
TWO-HANDED
  SWORD

15
ANTI-AIRCRAFT
  GUN

16
BALLISTIC MISSILE
HEAT-SEEKING
  MISSILE

20+
DOUBLE-
  BARRELLED
  SHOTGUN

RELIGION AND MYTHOLOGY

BOOKS OF THE BIBLE

OLD TESTAMENT
GENESIS
EXODUS
LEVITICUS
NUMBERS
DEUTERONOMY
JOSHUA
JUDGES
RUTH
1 SAMUEL
2 SAMUEL
1 KINGS
2 KINGS
1 CHRONICLES
2 CHRONICLES
EZRA
NEHEMIAH
ESTHER
JOB
PSALMS
PROVERBS
ECCLESIASTES
SONG OF SOLOMON
ISAIAH
JEREMIAH
LAMENTATIONS
EZEKIEL
DANIEL
HOSEA
JOEL

AMOS
OBADIAH
JONAH
MICAH
NAHUM
HABAKKUK
ZEPHANIAH
HAGGAI
ZECHARIAH
MALACHI

APOCRYPHA
I ESDRAS
II ESDRAS
TOBIT
JUDITH
THE REST OF
  ESTHER
WISDOM
ECCLESIASTICUS
BARUCH, WITH EPISTLE
  OF JEREMIAH
SONG OF THE THREE
  CHILDREN
SUSANNA
BEL AND THE DRAGON
PRAYER OF MANASSES
I MACCABEES
II MACCABEES

NEW TESTAMENT
MATTHEW
MARK
LUKE
JOHN
THE ACTS
ROMANS
1 CORINTHIANS
2 CORINTHIANS
GALATIANS
EPHESIANS
PHILIPPIANS
COLOSSIANS
1 THESSALONIANS
2 THESSALONIANS
1 TIMOTHY
2 TIMOTHY
TITUS
PHILEMON
HEBREWS
JAMES
1 PETER
2 PETER
1 JOHN
2 JOHN
3 JOHN
JUDE
REVELATION

BIBLICAL CHARACTERS

AARON - elder brother of Moses; 1st high priest of Hebrews

ABEL - second son of Adam and Eve; murdered by brother Cain

ABRAHAM - father of Hebrew nation

ABSALOM - David's spoilt third son; killed after plotting against his father

ADAM - the first man created; husband of Eve

BAAL - fertility god of Canaanites and Phoenicians

BATHSHEBA - mother of Solomon

BELSHAZZAR - last king of Babylon, son of Nebuchadnezzar; Daniel interpreted his vision of writing on the wall as foretelling the downfall of his kingdom

BENJAMIN - youngest son of Jacob and Rachel. His descendants formed one of the 12 tribes of Israel

CAIN - first son of Adam and Eve; murdered his brother Abel

DANIEL - prophet, court of Nebuchadnezzar with a gift for interpreting dreams

DAVID - slayed the giant Goliath

DELILAH - a Philistine seducer and betrayer of Samson

ELIJAH - Hebrew prophet, taken into heaven in a fiery chariot

ELISHA - prophet and disciple of Elijah

ENOCH - father of Methuselah

EPHRAIM - son of Joseph; founded one of the 12 tribes of Israel

BIBLICAL CHARACTERS

ESAU - elder of Isaac's twin sons; tricked out of his birthright by his brother

ESTHER - beautiful Israelite woman; heroically protected her people

EVE - first woman; created as companion for Adam in Garden of Eden

EZEKIEL - prophet of Israel captured by Babylonians

GIDEON - Israelite hero and judge

GOLIATH - Philistine giant killed by David

HEZEIKIAH - king of Judah (c. 715–686 AD)

ISAAC - son of Abraham and Sarah, conceived in their old age; father of Jacob and Esau

ISAIAH - the greatest old testament prophet

ISHMAEL - Abraham's son by Hagar, hand maiden to his wife, Sarah; rival of Isaac

ISRAEL - new name given to Jacob after his reconciliation with Esau

JACOB - second son of Isaac, and Rebekah, younger twin of Esau, whom he tricked out of his inheritance. The 12 tribes of Israel ware named after his 12 descendants

JEREMIAH - one of the great prophets; foretold destruction of Jerusalem

JEZEBEL - cruel and lustful wife of Ahab, king of Israel

JOB - long-suffering inhabitant of UZ

JONAH - after ignoring God's commands he was swallowed by a whale

JONATHAN - eldest son of Saul and close friend of David

JOSEPH - favourite son of Jacob and Rachel with his 'coat of many colours'

JOSHUA - succeeded Moses and led Israelites against Canaan. He defeated Jericho where the walls fell down

JUDAH - son of Jacob and Leah; founded tribe of Judah

LOT - nephew of Abraham; he escaped the destruction of Sodom, but his wife was turned into a pillar of salt for looking back

METHUSELAH - son of Enoch, the oldest person ever (969 years)

MIRIAM - sister of Aaron and Moses; prophetess and leader of Israelites

MOSES - Israel's great leader and lawgiver, he led the Israelites out of captivity in Egypt to the promised land of Canaan. Received ten commandments from Jehovah on Mt Sinai

NEBUCHADNEZZAR - king of Babylon

NOAH - grandson of Methuselah, father of Shem, Ham, and Japheth; built ark to save his family and all animal species from the great flood

REBEKAH - wife of Isaac, mother of Jacob and Esau

RUTH - Moabite who accompanied her mother-in-law Naomi to Bethlehem.

SAMSON - Israelite judge of great physical strength; seduced and betrayed by Delilah

SAMUEL - prophet and judge of Israel

SARAH - wife of Abraham, mother of Isaac

SAUL - first king of Israel

SOLOMON - son of David and Bathsheba; remembered for his wisdom and wealth

NEW TESTAMENT

ANDREW - fisherman and brother of Peter; one of 12 Apostles

BARABBAS - robber and murderer; in prison with Jesus and released instead of him

BARNABAS - Cypriot missionary, introduced Paul to the Church

BARTHOLOMEW - possibly same person as Nathaniel, one of the 12 Apostles

CAIAPHAS - high priest of the Jews; Jesus brought to him after arrest

GABRIEL - angel who announced birth of Jesus to Mary

HEROD - 1. the Great, ruled when Jesus was born 2. Antipas, son of Herod the Great, ruled when John the Baptist was murdered 3. Agrippa, killed James (brother of John) 4. Agrippa 11, before whom Paul was tried

JAMES - 1. the Greater, one of 12 Apostles, brother of John 2. the Less, one of 12 Apostles 3. leader of the Church in Jerusalem and author of the New Testament epistle

JESUS - founder of Christianity

JOHN - youngest of 12 Apostles

JOHN THE BAPTIST - announced coming of Jesus, and baptized him

JOSEPH -1. husband of Mary the mother of Jesus 2. of Arimathea, a secret disciple of Jesus

JUDAS ISCARIOT - the disciple who betrayed Jesus

LAZARUS - brother of Mary and Martha, raised from the dead by Jesus

BIBLICAL CHARACTERS / PATRON SAINTS

LUKE - companion of Paul, author of Luke and Acts

MARK - author of the gospel; companion of Paul, Barnabas, and Peter

MARTHA - sister of Mary and Lazarus, friend of Jesus

MARY - **1**. mother of Jesus **2**. sister of Martha and Lazarus **3**. Magdalene, cured by Jesus and the first to see him after the resurrection

MATTHEW - one of 12 Apostles, author of the gospel

MATTHIAS - chosen to replace the apostle Judas

MICHAEL - a chief archangel

NATHANIEL - see Bartholomew

NICODEMUS - a Pharisee who had a secret meeting with Jesus

PAUL - formerly Saul of Tarsus, persecutor of Christians; renamed after his conversion. Apostle to Gentiles, author of epistles

PETER - Simon, one of 12 Apostles; denied Jesus before the crucifixion but later became leader of the Church

PHILIP - one of 12 Apostles

PILATE - Roman procurator of Judea; allowed Jesus to be crucified

SALOME - **1**. wife of Zebedee, mother of James and John **2**. daughter of Herodias; danced before Herod for the head of John the Baptist

SAUL - *see* Paul

SIMON - **1**. Simon Peter see Peter **2**. the Canaanite, one of 12 Apostles **3**. one of Jesus' four brothers **4**. the leper, in whose house Jesus was anointed **5**. of Cyrene, carried the cross of Jesus **6**. the tanner, in whose house Peter had his vision

STEPHEN - Christian martyr, stoned to death

THOMAS - one of 12 Apostles, named 'Doubting' because he doubted the resurrection

TIMOTHY - Paul's fellow missionary; two of Paul's epistles are to him

TITUS - convert and companion of Paul, who wrote him one epistle

PATRON SAINTS

AGATHA (bell-founders)
ALBERT THE GREAT (students of natural sciences)
ANDREW (Scotland)
BARBARA (gunners and miners)
BERNARD OF MONTJOUX (mountaineers)
CAMILLUS (nurses)
CASIMIR (Poland)
CECILIA (musicians)
CHRISTOPHER (wayfarers)
CRISPIN (shoemakers)
DAVID (Wales)
DIONYSIUS (DENIS) OF PARIS (France)
DUNSTAN (goldsmiths, jewellers, locksmiths)
DYMPNA (insane)
ELIGIUS or ELOI (metalworkers)
ERASMUS (sailors)
FIACRE (gardeners)
FRANCES CABRINI (emigrants)
FRANCES OF ROME (motorists)
FRANCIS DE SALES (writers)
FRANCIS XAVIER (foreign missions)
FRIDESWIDE (Oxford)

GEORGE (England)
GILES (cripples)
HUBERT (huntsmen)
JEROME EMILIANI (orphans and abandoned children)
JOHN OF GOD (hospitals and booksellers)
JUDE (hopeless causes)
JULIAN (innkeepers, boatmen, travellers)
KATHERINE OF ALEXANDRIA (students, philosophers, and craftsmen)
LUKE (physicians and surgeons)
MARTHA (housewives)
NICHOLAS (children, sailors, unmarried girls, merchants, pawnbrokers, apothecaries, and perfumeries)
PATRICK (Ireland)
PETER NOLASCO (midwives)
SAVA (Serbian people)
VALENTINE (lovers)
VITUS (epilepsy and nervous diseases)
WENCESLAS (Czechoslovakia)
ZITA (domestic servants)

RELIGIOUS MOVEMENTS

3
BON
I AM
ZEN
4
AINU
5
BOSCI
ISLAM
KEGON
THAGS
THUGS
6
BABISM
PARSIS
QUAKER
SHINTO
TAOISM
VOODOO
7
AJIVIKA
BAHAISM
GIDEONS
JAINISM
JUDAISM
JUMPERS
LAMAISM
MORMONS
PARSEES
SHAKERS
SIKHISM
WAHABIS
ZIONISM

8
ABELIANS
ABELITES
ACOEMETI
ADAMITES
ADMADIYA
AHMADIYA
AMARITES
BAPTISTS
BUDDHISM
CATHOLIC
HINDUISM
HUMANISM
MAR THOMA
NICHIREN
NOSAIRIS
PURITANS
STUDITES
9
CALVINISM
CHUNTOKYO
FRANKISTS
HICKSITES
HUGUENOTS
JANSENISM
METHODIST
PANTHEISM
10
ABSTINENTS
ADVENTISTS
AGONIZANTS
AMBROSIANS
BUCHANITES
CALIXTINES

11
ABODE OF LOVE
ABRAHAMITES
ANABAPTISTS
ANGLICANISM
ARNIKANISM
BASILIDEANS
BERNARDINES
COVENANTERS
12
ABECEDARIANS
BENEDICTINES
CHRISTIANITY
PRESBYTERIAN
SPIRITUALISM
UNITARIANISM
13
MOHAMMEDANISM
PROTESTANTISM
REDEMPTORISTS
ROMAN CATHOLIC
SALVATION ARMY
14
CONGREGATIONAL
FUNDAMENTALISM
16
ABYSSINIAN CHURCH
CHRISTIAN SCIENCE
MORAVIAN BRETHREN
PLYMOUTH BRETHREN
17
ANTIPAEDOBAPTISTS
JEHOVAH'S WITNESSES

RELIGIOUS ORDERS

AUGUSTINIAN
BARNABITE
BENEDICTINE
BRIGITTINE
CAMALDOLESE
CAPUCHINS
CARMELITE
CARTHUSIAN
CISTERCIAN
DOMINICAN
FRANCISCAN

HOSPITALLERS
JERONYMITE
MINIMS
POOR CLARES
PREMONSTRATENSIAN
SALESIAN
SERVITE
SYLVESTRINE
TEMPLARS
THEATINE
TRAPPIST

TRINITARIAN
URSULINE
VISITANDINE
VISITATION

CLERGY

ARCHBISHOP	CURATE	POPE
ARCHDEACON	DEACON	PRIEST
BISHOP	DEAN	RECTOR
CANON	ELDER	VICAR
CARDINAL	MINISTER	VICAR-FORANE
CHAPLAIN	PARSON	

POPES

ST PETER (42)
ST LINUS (67)
ST ANACLETUS (Cletus) (76)
ST CLEMENT I (88)
ST EVARISTUS (97)
ST ALEXANDER I (105)
ST SIXTUS 1 (115)
ST TELESPHORUS (125)
ST HYGINUS (136)
ST PIUS I (140)
ST ANICETUS (155)
ST SOTERUS (166)
ST ELEUTHERIUS (175)
ST VICTOR I (189)
ST ZEPHYRINUS (199)
ST CALLISTUS I (217)
ST URBAN I (222)
ST PONTIAN (230)
ST ANTERUS (236)
ST FABIAN (236)
ST CORNELIUS (251)
ST LUCIUS I (253)
ST STEPHEN I (254)
ST SIXTUS II (257)
ST DIONYSIUS (259)
ST FELIX I (269)
ST EUTYCHIAN (275)
ST CAIUS (283)
ST MARCELLINUS

(296)
ST MARCELLUS I (308)
ST EUSEBIUS (309)
ST MELCHIADES (311)
ST SYLVESTER I (314)
ST MARCUS (336)
ST JULIUS I (337)
LIBERIUS (352)
ST DAMASUS I (366)
ST SIRICIUS (384)
ST ANASTASIUS I (399)
ST INNOCENT I (401)
ST ZOSIMUS (417)
ST BONIFACE I (418)
ST CELESTINE I (422)
ST SIXTUS III (432)
ST LEO I (the Great) (440)
ST HILARY (461)
ST SIMPLICIUS (468)
ST FELIX III (483)
ST GELASIUS 1 (492)
ANASTASIUS II (496)
ST SYMMACHUS (4911)
ST HORMISDAS (514)
ST JOHN I (523)

ST FELIX IV (526)
BONIFACE II (530)
JOHN II (533)
ST AGAPETUS I (535)
ST SILVERIUS (536)
VIGILIUS (537)
PELAGIUS I (556)
JOHN III (561)
BENEDICT I (575)
PELAGIUS II (579)
ST GREGORY I (the Great) (590)
SABINIANUS (604)
BONIFACE III (607)
ST BONIFACE IV (608)
ST DEUSDEDIT (Adeodatus I) (615)
BONIFACE V (619)
HONORIUS I (625)
SEVERINUS (640)
JOHN IV (640)
THEODORE I (642)
ST MARTIN I (649)
ST EUGENE I (654)
ST VITALIAN (657)
ADEODATUS II (672)
DONUS (676)
ST AGATHO (678)
ST LEO II (682)
ST BENEDICT II (684)
JOHN V (685)
CONON (686)
ST SERGIUS I (687)
JOHN VI (701)

JOHN VII (705)
SISINNIUS (708)
CONSTANTINE (708)
ST GREGORY II (715)
ST GREGORY III (731)
ST ZACHARY (741)
STEPHEN II (III)* (752)
ST PAUL I (757)
STEPHEN III (IV) (768)
ADRIAN I (772)
ST LEO III (795)
STEPHEN IV (V) (816)
ST PASCHAL I (817)
EUGENE II (824)
VALENTINE (827)
GREGORY IV (827)
SERGIUS II (844)
ST LEO IV (847)
BENEDICT III (855)
ST NICHOLAS I (855)
ADRIAN II (867)
JOHN VIII (872)
MARINUS I (882)
ST ADRIAN III (884)
STEPHEN V (VI) (885)
FORMOSUS (891)
BONIFACE VI (896)
STEPHEN VI (VII) (896)
ROMANUS (897)
THEODORE II (897)

321

POPES

JOHN IX (898)
BENEDICT IV (900)
LEO V (903)
SERGIUS III (904)
ANASTASIUS III
 (911)
LANDUS (913)
JOHN X (914)
LEO VI (928)
STEPHEN VII (VIII)
 (928)
JOHN XI (931)
LEO VII (936)
STEPHEN VIII (IX)
 (939)
MARINUS II (942)
AGAPETUS II (946)
JOHN XII (955)
LEO VIII (963)
BENEDICT V (964)
JOHN XIII (965)
BENEDICT VI (973)
BENEDICT VII (974)
JOHN XIV (983)
JOHN XV (985)
GREGORY V (996)
SYLVESTER II (999)
JOHN XVII (1003)
JOHN XVIII (1004)
SERGIUS IV (1009)
BENEDICT VIII
 (1012)
JOHN XIX (1024)
BENEDICT IX
 (1032)
GREGORY VI
 (1045)
CLEMENT II (1046)
BENEDICT IX
 (1047)
DAMASUS II (1048)
ST LEO IX (1049)
VICTOR II (1055)
STEPHEN IX(X)
 (1057)
NICHOLAS II (1059)
ALEXANDER II
 (1061)
ST GREGORY VII
 (1073)
VICTOR III (1086)

URBAN II (1088)
PASCHAL II (1099)
GELASIUS II (1118)
CALLISTUS II (1119)
HONORIUS II (1124)
INNOCENT II (1130)
CELESTINE II
 (1143)
LUCIUS II (1144)
EUGENE III (1145)
ANASTASIUS IV
 (1153)
ADRIAN IV (1154)
ALEXANDER III
 (1159)
LUCIUS III (1181)
URBAN III (1185)
GREGORY VIII
 (1187)
CLEMENT III
 (1187)
CELESTINE III
 (1191)
INNOCENT III
 (1198)
HONORIUS III
 (1216)
GREGORY IX
 (1227)
CELESTINE IV
 (1241)
INNOCENT IV
 (1243)
ALEXANDER IV
 (1254)
URBAN IV (1261)
CLEMENT IV (1265)
GREGORY X (1271)
INNOCENT V (1276)
ADRIAN V (1276)
JOHN XXI (1276)
NICHOLAS III
 (1277)
MARTIN IV (1281)
HONORIUS IV
 (1285)
NICHOLAS IV
 (1288)
ST CELESTINE V
 (1294)
BONIFACE VIII (1294)

BENEDICT XI
 (1303)
CLEMENT V (1305)
JOHN XXII (1316)
BENEDICT XII
 (1334)
CLEMENT VI (1342)
INNOCENT VI
 (1352)
URBAN V (1362)
GREGORY XI
 (1370)
URBAN VI (1378)
BONIFACE IX
 (1389)
INNOCENT VII
 (1404)
GREGORY XII
 (1406)
MARTIN V (1417)
EUGENE IV (1431)
NICHOLAS V (1447)
CALLISTUS III
 (1455)
PIUS II (1458)
PAUL II (1464)
SIXTUS IV (1471)
INNOCENT VIII
 (1484)
ALEXANDER VI
 (1492)
PIUS III (1503)
JULIUS II (1503)
LEO X (1513)
ADRIAN VI (1522)
CLEMENT VII (1523)
PAUL III (1534)
JULIUS III (1550)
MARCELLUS II
 (1555)
PAUL IV (1555)
PIUS (1559)
ST PIUS V (1566)
GREGORY XIII
 (1572)
SIXTUS V (1585)
URBAN VII (1590)
GREGORY XIV
 (1590)
INNOCENT IX
 (1591)

CLEMENT VIII
 (1592)
LEO XI (1605)
PAUL V (1605)
GREGORY XV
 (1621)
URBAN VIII (1623)
INNOCENT X (1644)
ALEXANDER VII
 (1655)
CLEMENT IX (1667)
CLEMENT X (1670)
INNOCENT XI
 (1676)
ALEXANDER VIII
 (1689)
INNOCENT XII
 (1691)
CLEMENT XI (1700)
INNOCENT XIII
 (1721)
BENEDICT XIII
 (1724)
CLEMENT XII
 (1730)
BENEDICT XIV
 (1740)
CLEMENT XIII
 (1758)
CLEMENT XIV
 (1769)
PIUS VI (1775)
PIUS VII (1800)
LEO XII (1823)
PIUS VIII (1829)
GREGORY XVI
 (1831)
PIUS IX(1846)
LEO XIIII (1878)
ST PIUS X (1903)
BENEDICT XV
 (1914)
PIUS XI (1922)
PIUS XII (1939)
JOHN XXIII (1958)
PAUL VI (1963)
JOHN PAUL I (1978)
JOHN PAUL II
 (1978)

ARCHBISHOPS OF CANTERBURY

AUGUSTINE (597)
LAURENTIUS (604)
MELLITUS (619)
JUSTUS (624)
HONORIUS (627)
DEUSDEDIT (655)
THEODORUS (668)
BEORHTWEALD (693)
TATWINE (731)
NOTHELM (735)
CUTHBEORHT (740)
BREGUWINE (761)
JAENBEORHT (765)
AETHELHEARD (793)
WULFRED (805)
FEOLOGILD (832)
CEOLNOTH (833)
AETHELRED (870)
PLEGMUND (890)
AETHELHELM (914)
WULFHELM (923)
ODA (942)
AELFSIGE (959)
BEORHTHELM (959)
DUNSTAN (960)
AETHELGAR (988)
SIGERIC SERIO (990)
AELFRIC (995)
AELFHEAH (1005)
LYFING (1013)
AETHELNOTH (1020)
EADSIGE (1038)
ROBERT OF JUMIEGES (1051)
STIGAND (1052)
LANFRANC (1070)
ANSELM (1093)
RALPH D'ESCURES (1114)
WILLIAM OF CORBEIL (1123)
THEOBALD OF BEC (1139)
THOMAS BECKET (1162)
RICHARD OF DOVER (1174)
BALDWIN (1184)
REGINALD FITZJOCELIN (1191)
HUBERT WALTER (1193)
REGINALD (1205)

JOHN DE GRAY (1205)
STEPHEN LANGTON (1213)
WALTER OF EVESHAM (1128)
RICHARD GRANT (Wethershed) (1229)
RALPH NEVILL (1231)
JOHN OF SITTINGBOURNE (1232)
JOHN BLUND (1232)
EDMUND RICH (1234)
BONIFACE OF SAVOY (1245)
ADAM OF CHILLENDEN (1270)
ROBERT KILWARDBY (1273)
ROBERT BURNELL (1278)
JOHN PECHAM (1279)
ROBERT WINCHELSEY (1295)
THOMAS COBHAM (1313)
WALTER REYNOLDS (1314)
SIMON MEPHAM (1328)
JOHN STRATFORD (1334)
JOHN OFFORD (1348)
THOMAS BRADWARDINE (1349)
SIMON ISLIP (1349)
SIMON LANGHAM (1366)
WILLIAM WHITTLESEY (1369)
SIMON SUDBURY (1375)
WILLIAM COURTENAY (1381)
THOMAS ARUNDEL (1397)
ROGER WALDEN (1398)
THOMAS ARUNDEL (1399)
HENRY CHICHELE (1414)
JOHN STAFFORD (1443)
JOHN KEMPE (1452)
THOMAS BOURGCHIER (1454)
JOHN MORTON (1486)
HENRY DEANE (1501)
WILLIAM WARHAM (1504)
THOMAS CRANMER (1533)
REGINALD POLE (1556)

MATTHEW PARKER (1559)
EDMUND GRINDAL (1576)
JOHN WHITGIFT (1583)
RICHARD BANCROFT (1604)
GEORGE ABBOT (1611)
WILLIAM LAUD (1633)
WILLIAM JUXON (1660)
GILBERT SHELDON (1663)
WILLIAM SANCROFT (1678)
JOHN TILLOTSON (1691)
THOMAS TENISON (1695)
WILLIAM WAKE (1716)
JOHN POTTER (1737)
THOMAS HERRING (1747)
MATTHEW HUTTON (1757)
THOMAS SECKER (1758)
FREDERICK CORNWALLIS (1768)
JOHN MOCRE (1783)
CHARLES MANNERS SUTTON (1805)
WILLIAM HOWLEY (1828)
JOHN BIRD SUMNER (1848)
CHARLES THOMAS LONGLEY (1862)
ARCHIBALD CAMPBELL TAIT (1868)
EDWARD WHITE BENSON (1883)
FREDERICK TEMPLE (1896)
RANDALL THOMAS DAVIDSON (1903)
COSMO GORDON LANG (1928)
WILLIAM TEMPLE (1942)
GEOFFREY FRANCIS FISHER (1945)
ARTHUR MICHAEL RAMSEY (1961)
FREDERICK DONALD COGGAN (1974)
ROBERT ALEXANDER KENNEDY RUNCIE (1980)
GEORGE LEONARD CAREY(1991)

RELIGIOUS TERMS

2	AISLE	ADVENT	SANGHA
BA	ALLEY	AGUNAH	SERMON
HO	ALTAR	AHIMSA	SERVER
OM	AMBRY	AKASHA	SHARI'A
3	AMICE	AKEDAH	SHRIVE
ALB	ANGEL	AL CHET	SPIRIT
ARA	APRON	ANOINT	SUTRAS
AUM	ARMOR	ANTHEM	TAUHID
HAJ	BANNS	AUMBRY	TIPPET
PEW	BASON	AVODAH	VERGER
PIX	BEADS	BARSOM	VESTRY
PYX	BIBLE	BAT KOL	**7**
YAD	BIMAH	BEADLE	ACCIDIA
4	BODHI	BELFRY	ACCIDIE
AMBO	BRIEF	CANTOR	ACOLYTE
APSE	BUGIA	CHOHAN	AGRAPHA
AZAN	BURSE	CHOVAH	AMPULLA
BEMA	COTTA	CHRISM	ANGELUS
BUJI	CREED	CLERGY	APOSTIL
BULL	CROSS	DHARMA	APOSTLE
COPE	CRUET	DHYANA	APPAREL
COWL	DIKKA	DITTHI	ASHAMNU
FONT	EMETH	DOSSAL	ATHEISM
HADJ	EPHOD	DUCHAN	AUREOLE
HAJJ	FALDA	EASTER	BADCHAN
HALO	GOHEI	FLECHE	BANKERS
HELL	HYLIC	FRATER	BAPTISM
HOOD	IHRAM	GLORIA	BATHING
HOST	KALPA	HEAVEN	BELL COT
HYMN	KARMA	HEKHAL	BERAKAH
JUBE	LAVER	HESPED	BIRETTA
KAMA	LIMBO	KAIROS	CASSOCK
KNOP	MOTZI	KIBLAH	CHALICE
LENT	NICHE	KISMET	CHAMETZ
MACE	PASCH	KITTEL	CHANCEL
MASS	PESAH	LITANY	CHANTRY
NAOS	PESHA	MANTRA	CHAPTER
NAVE	PSALM	MATINS	CHAZZAN
OLAH	ROSHI	MISSAL	CHRISOM
RAMA	SHIVA	NIGGUN	COLLECT
SOMA	STOUP	NIMBUS	COMPLIN
TIEN	SYNOD	ORATIO	CORNICE
VOID	TOTEM	ORISON	CROSIER
WAKE	USHER	PARVIS	CROZIER
YOGA	VEDAS	PESACH	DHARANI
5	WAFER	PRAYER	DIOCESE
ABBOT	**6**	PULPIT	DIPTYCH
ABYSS	ABBACY	ROCHET	EILETON
AGATI	ABODAH	ROSARY	FISTULA

324

7 continued
GAYATRI
GELILAH
GEULLAH
GRADINE
GREMIAL
HASSOCK
HEATHEN
HEKDESH
INTROIT
KHEREBU
LECTERN
LOCULUS
MANIPLE
MINARET
MOZETTA
NARTHEX
NIRVANA
NOCTURN
PALLIUM
PENANCE
PILGRIM
PURUSHA
REQUIEM
REREDOS
SAMSARA
STHIBEL
TALLITH
TONSURE
TRINITY
TZADDIK
VESPERS
WORSHIP
8
ABLUTION
ABSTEMII
A CAPELLA
AFFLATUS
AFFUSION
AFIKOMEN
AGNUS DEI
ANTIPHON
ARMORIUM
AUTO DA FE
AVE MARIA
BEADROLL
BELL COTE
BEMIDSAR
BENEFICE
BREVIARY
BUTSUDEN

CANCELLI
CANTICLE
CIBORIUM
CINCTURE
COMPLINE
CONCLAVE
CORPORAL
CRUCIFIX
DALMATIC
DIKERION
DISCIPLE
DOXOLOGY
EPIPHANY
EVENSONG
FRONTLET
HABDALAH
MANIPULE
NATIVITY
NER TAMID
NIVARANA
OBLATION
PAROKHET
PASSOVER
PREDELLA
RESPONSE
SACRISTY
SURPLICE
TASHLICH
TRIPTYCH
VESTMENT
9
ADIAPHORA
ANAMNESIS
APOCRYPHA
ARBA KOSOT
ARCHANGEL
ASPERSION
CANDLEMAS
CARTOUCHE
CATACOMBS
CATECHISM
CERECLOTH
CHALITZAH
CHRISTMAS
COLLATION
COMMUNION
EPHPHETHA
EUCHARIST
FALDSTOOL
FLABELLUM
FORMULARY

MUNDATORY
OFFERTORY
PACE-AISLE
PURGATORY
SANCTUARY
YOM KIPPUR
10
ABSOLUTION
AGATHOLOGY
ALLOCUTION
AMBULATORY
ANTECHAPEL
APOCALYPSE
BALDACHINO
BAR MITZVAH
SAS MITZVAH
BAT MITZVAH
BENEDICTUS
CATAFALQUE
CLERESTORY
CUTTY STOOL
HAGIOSCOPE
INDULGENCE
INTINCTION
INVOCATION
LADY CHAPEL
PRESBYTERY
SEXAGESIMA
11
ABBREVIATOR
ABOMINATION
AGNOSTICISM
ALITURGICAL
ANTEPENDIUM
ANTIMINSION
ASPERGILLUM
BENEDICTION
CHRISTENING
HUMERAL VEIL
INQUISITION
INVESTITURE
SCRIPTORIUM
12
ANTILEGOMENA
ARON HA-KODESH
ASH WEDNESDAY
CONFIRMATION
CONGREGATION
SEPTUAGESIMA

13
BEATIFICATION
BIRKAT HA-MAZON
EPITRACHELION
14
FOLDED
  CHASUBLE
MAUNDY
  THURSDAY

325

RELIGIOUS BUILDINGS

3	JINGU	DEANERY	SYNAGOGUE
WAT	JINJA	MINSTER	**12**
4	**6**	**8**	BET HA-KNESSET
CELL	CHAPEL	BASILICA	BET HA-MIDRASH
KIRK	CHURCH	CLOISTER	CHAPTER HOUSE
5	MOSQUE	HOUNFORT	MEETINGHOUSE
ABBEY	PAGODA	LAMASERY	**13**
BET AM	PRIORY	**9**	ANGELUS TEMPLE
CELLA	**7**	BADRINATH	
DUOMO	CHANTRY	CATHEDRAL	
HONDO	CONVENT	MONASTERY	

HINDU DEITIES

BRAHMA - the Creator

SHIVA - the Destroyer

VISHNU - the Preserver

INDFIA - king of the gods; god of war and storm

AGNI - god of fire

AHI *or* IHI - the Sistrum Player

AMIRITA - water of life

YAMA - king of the dead

VARUNA - god of water

SURYA - the sun-god

VAW - god of the wind

KUBERA - god of wealth; guardian of the north

KARTTIKEYA - war-god; god of bravery

VISVAKARMA - architect for the gods

KAMA - god of desire

SARASVATI - goddess of speech

LAKSHMI - goddess of fortune

DEVI - a mother goddess

ADITI - goddess of heaven; mother of the gods

SARANYU - goddess of the clouds

PRITHIVI - earth-goddess; goddess of fertility

DITI - mother of the demons

MANASA - sacred mountain and lake

SHITALA - goddess of smallpox

GANESHA - god of literature, wisdom, and prosperity

GARUDA - the devourer, identified with fire and the sun

HANUMAN - a monkey chief

SUGRIVA - monkey king

BALI - demon who became king of heaven and earth

AMARAVATI - city of the gods

GANDHARVAS - celestial musicians

JYESTHA - goddess of misfortune

SOMA - ambrosial offering to the gods

GREEK AND ROMAN MYTHOLOGY

Mythological Characters

ACHILLES - Greek hero; invulnerable except for his heel

ADONIS - renowned for his beauty

AGAMEMNON - king of Mycenae

AJAX - Greek warrior

ATLAS - bore heaven on his shoulders

BELLEROPHON - Corinthian hero who rode winged horse Pegasus

BOREAS - the north wind

CERBERUS - three-headed dog, guarded Hades

CHARON - boatman who rowed dead across river Styx

CHARYBDIS - violent whirlpool

CIRCE - sorceress who had the power to turn men into beasts

CYCLOPS - one of a race of one-eyed giant (cyclopes)

DAEDALUS - craftsman; designed and built the labyrinth in Crete

GORGONS - three sisters (Stheno, Euryale, and Medusa) who had snakes for hair and whose appearance turned people to stone

HADES - the Underworld

HELEN OF TROY - famed for her beauty; cause of Trojan war

HERACLES - famed for his courage and strength; performed the twelve labours

HERCULES - Roman name for HERACLES

HYDRA - many-headed snake

JASON - led the Argonauts in search of the Golden Fleece

LETHE - river in Hades whose water caused forgetfulness

MIDAS - King of Phrygia whose touch turned everything to gold

MINOTAUR - monster with the head of a bull and the body of a man. It was kept in the Cretan labyrinth and fed with human flesh

NARCISSUS - beautiful youth, who fell in love with his own reflection

ODYSSEUS - Greek hero of the Trojan war

OEDIPUS - king of Thebes; married his mother

OLYMPUS - a mountain; the home of the gods

ORPHEUS - skilled musician

PANDORA - the first woman; opened the box that released all varieties of evil

PERSEUS - Greek hero who killed the Gorgon Medusa

POLYPHEMUS - leader of the Cyclopes

ROMULUS - founder of Rome

SATYRS - hoofed spirits of fore sts, fields, and streams

SCYLLA - six-headed sea monster

SIBYL - a prophetess

SIRENS - creatures depicted as half women, half birds, who lured sailors to their deaths

STYX - main river of Hades, across which Charon ferried the souls of the dead

THESEUS - Greek hero who kilied the Cretan Minotaur ULYSSES - Roman name tor ODYSSEUS

Greek Gods (*Roman equivalent*)

APHRODITE - goddess of beauty and love (VENUS)

APOLLO - god of poetry, music, and prophecy (APOLLO)

ARES - god of war (MARS)

ARTEMIS - goddess of the moon (DIANA)

ASCLEPIUS - god of medical art (AESCULAPIUS)

ATHENE - goddess of wisdom (MINERVA)

CHARITES - 3 daughters of Zeus: Euphrosyne, Aglaia, and Thalia; personified grace, beauty, and charm (GRACES)

CRONOS - god of agriculture (SATURN)

DEMETER - goddess of agriculture (CERES)

DIONYSUS - god of wine and fertility (BACCHUS)

EOS - goddess of dawn (AURORA)

EROS - god of love (CUPID)

FATES - 3 goddesses who determine man's destiny: Clotho, Lachesis, and Atropos

HEBE - goddess of youth (JUVENTAS)

HECATE - goddess of witchcraft (HECATE)

HELIOS - god of the sun (SOL)

HEPHAESTUS - god of destructive fire (VULCAN)

HERA - queen of heaven, goddess of women and marriage (JUNO)

HERMES - messenger of gods (MERCURY)

HESTIA - goddess of the hearth (VESTA)

HYPNOS - god of sleep (SOMNUS)

NEMESIS - goddess of retribution

PAN - god of woods and fields (FAUNUS)

PERSEPHONE - goddess of the Underworld (PROSERPINE)

PLUTO - god of the Underworld (PLUTO)

PLUTUS - god of wealth

POSEIDON - god of the sea (NEPTUNE)

RHEA - goddess of nature (CYBELE)

SELENE - goddess of the moon (LUNA)

THANATOS - god of death (MORS)

ZEUS - supreme god; god of sky and weather (JUPITER)

GREEK AND ROMAN MYTHOLOGY / NORSE MYTHOLOGY

Roman Gods (*Greek equivalent*)

AESCULAPIUS (ASCLEPIUS)	FAUNUS (PAN)	(HERMES)	SOL (HELIOS)
APOLLO (APOLLO)	GRACES (CHARITES)	MINERVA (ATHENE)	SOMNUS (HYPNOS)
AURORA (EOS)	HECATE (HECATE)	MORS (THMATOS)	VENUS (APHRODITE)
BACCHUS (DIONYSUS)	JUNO (HERA)	NEPTUNE (POSEIDON)	VESTA (HESTIA)
CERES (DEMETER)	JUPITER (ZEUS)	PLUTO (PLUTO)	VULCAN (HEPHAESTUS)
CUPID (EROS)	JUVENTAS (HEBE)	PROSERPINE (PERSEPHONE)	
CYBELE (RHEA)	LUNA (SELENE)		
DIANA (ARTEMIS)	MARS (ARES)	SATURN (CRONOS)	
	MERCURY		

The Nine Muses

CALLIOPE (EPIC POETRY)
CLIO (HISTORY)
ERATO (LOVE POETRY)
EUTERPE (LYRIC POETRY)
MELPOMENE (TRAGEDY)
POLYHYMNIA (SACRED SONG)
TERPSICHORE (DANCING)
THALIA (COMEDY)
URANIA (ASTRONOMY)

The Twelve Labours of Hercules

THE NEMEAN LION
THE LERNAEAN HYDRA
THE WILD BOAR OF ERYMANTHUS
THE STYMPHALIAN BIRDS
THE CERYNEIAN HIND
THE AUGEAN STABLES
THE CRETAN BULL
THE MARES OF DIOMEDES
THE GIRDLE OF HIPPOLYTE
THE CATTLE OF GERYON
THE GOLDEN APPLES OF THE HESPERIDES
THE CAPTURE OF CERBERUS

NORSE MYTHOLOGY

AEGIR - god of the sea
ALFHEIM - part of Asgard inhabited by the light elves
ASGARD - the home of the gods
ASK - name of the first man created from a fallen tree
BALDER - god of the summer sun
BRAGI - god of poetry
EIR - goddess of healing
EMBLA - name of first woman created from a fallen tree
FORSETI - god of justice
FREY - god of fertility and crops
FREYJA - goddess of love and night
FRIGG - Odin's wife; supreme goddess
GUNGNIR - Odin's magic spear
HEIJADAL - guardian of Asgard
HEL - goddess of the dead
HODUR - god of night
IDUN - wife of Bragi; guardian of the golden apples of youth
LOKI - god of evil
MIDGARD - the world of men
NORNS - three goddesses of destiny: Urd (Fate), Skuld (Being), and Verdandi (Necessity)
ODIN - supreme god; god of battle, inspiration, and death
RAGNAROK - final battle between gods and giants in which virtually all life is destroyed
SIF - Thor's wife; her golden hair was cut off by Loki
SLEIPNIR - Odin's eight-legged horse
THOR - god of thunder
TYR - god of war
VALHALLA - hall in Asgard where Odin welcomed souls of heroes killed in battle
VALKYRIES - nine handmaidens of Odin who chose men doomed to die in battle
YGGDRASILL - the World Tree, an ash linking all the worlds
YMIR - giant from whose body the world was formed

EGYPTIAN MYTHOLOGY

AMON-RA - supreme god

ANUBIS - jackel-headed son of Osiris; god of the dead

BES - god of marriage

GEB - earth-god

HATHOR - co-headed goddess of love

HORUS - hawk-headed god of light

ISIS - goddess of fertility

MAAT - goddess of law, truth, and justice

MONT - god of war

MUT - wife of Amon-Ra

NEHEH - god of eternity

NUN *or* NU - the primordial Ocean

NUT - goddess of the sky

OSIRIS - ruler of the afterlife

PTAH - god of the arts

RA - the sun god

RENPET - goddess of youth

SEKHMET - goddess of war

SET or SETH - god of evil

SHU - god of air

TEFNUT - goddess of dew and rain

THOTH - god of wisdom

UPUAUT - warrior-god; god of the dead

ARTHURIAN LEGEND

ARTHUR - legendary British leader of the Knights of the Round Table

AVALON - paradise

CAMELOT - capital of Arthur's kingdom

EXCALIBUR - Arthur's magic sword

GALAHAD - son of Lancelot., purest of the Knights of the Round Table; succeeded in the quest of the Grail

GAWAIN - nephew of Arthur, son of Morgan Le Fay; searched for the Grail

GRAIL (SANGREAL, THE HOLY GRAIL) - said to be the vessel of the Last Supper; in the custody of the Fisher King

GUINEVERE - wife of Arthur, lover of Lancelot

KAY - foster brother of Arthur

LANCELOT or LAUNCELOT - knight and lover of Queen Guinevere

MERLIN - magician and bard who prepared Arthur for kingship

MODRED or MORDRED - nephew of Arthur, son of Morgan le Fay

MORGAN LE FAY - sorceress and healer; sister of Arthur

PERCIVAL or PERCEVAL - knight who vowed to seek the Grail

UTHER PENDRAGON - father of Arthur

VIVIANE - the Lady of the Lake

MISCELLANEOUS

COLOURS

3	GRÈGE	MATARA	SEA BLUE
AAL	HAZEL	MOTLEY	SKY BLUE
BA	HENNA	ORANGE	TEA ROSE
DUN	IVORY	ORCHID	THISTLE
JET	JASPÉ	OYSTER	TILE RED
RED	JAUNE	PASTEL	TILLEUL
TAN	JEWEL	PEARLY	TUSSORE
4	KHAKI	PIRNED	VIOLINE
BLEU	LODEN	PURPLE	**8**
BLUE	MAIZE	RAISIN	ABSINTHE
BOIS	MAUVE	RESEDA	ALIZARIN
BURE	OCHRE	RUSSET	AMARANTH
CUIR	OLIVE	SALMON	AURULENT
DRAB	OMBRÉ	SHRIMP	BABY BLUE
EBON	PEACH	SILVER	BABY PINK
ÉCRU	PEARL	TITIAN	BORDEAUX
GOLD	PÊCHE	VIOLET	BURGUNDY
GREY	PRUNE	YELLOW	CAPUCINE
GRIS	ROUGE	ZIRCON	CHALDERA
HOPI	SEPIA	**7**	CHÂTAINE
IRIS	SHADE	ANAMITE	CHESTNUT
JADE	TAUPE	APRICOT	CIEL BLUE
LAKE	TOPAZ	ARDOISE	CINNAMON
LARK	UMBER	AUREATE	CREVETTE
NAVY	WHITE	BISCUIT	CYCLAMEN
NOIR	**6**	CALDRON	EAU DE NIL
ONYX	ACAJOU	CARAMEL	ÉCARLATE
OPAL	ALESAN	CARMINE	EGGPLANT
PIED	ARGENT	CHAMOIS	EGGSHELL
PINK	AUBURN	CORBEAU	GRIZZLED
PLUM	BASANÉ	CRIMSON	GUN METAL
PUCE	BISTRE	EMERALD	HAZEL NUT
ROSE	BLONDE	FILBERT	HYACINTH
RUBY	BRONZE	FUCHIA	LARKSPUR
SAND	BURNET	GRIZZLE	LAVENDER
SHOT	CASTOR	HEATHER	MOHOGANY
VERT	CENDRÉ	INGÉNUE	MOLE GREY
5	CERISE	JACINTH	MULBERRY
AMBER	CHERRY	JONQUIL	NAVY BLUE
BEIGE	CHROMA	LACQUER	PEA GREEN
BLACK	CITRON	LAVANDE	PISTACHE
BROWN	CLARET	MAGENTA	POPPY RED
CAMEL	COPPER	MOTTLED	PRIMROSE
CAPRI	DORADO	MUSTARD	SAPPHIRE
CHAIR	LAXEN	NACARAT	SEA GREEN
COCOA	GARNET	NATURAL	SHAGREEN
CORAL	GOLDEN	NEUTRAL	SPECTRUM
CREAM	INDIGO	OLD ROSE	VIRIDIAN
CYMAR	JASPER	PEARLED	
DELFT	MADDER	PLATINA	
FLESH	MARTON	SAFFRON	
GREEN	MAROON	SCARLET	

333

COLOURS / CALENDARS

9
ALICE BLUE
AUBERGINE
AZURE BLUE
BLUE-GREEN
CADET BLUE
CADET GREY
CARNATION
CARNELIAN
CHAMPAGNE
CHOCOLATE
COCHINEAL
DELPH BLUE
DUTCH BLUE
FLESH PINK
GREEN-BLUE
HARLEQUIN
LEAF GREEN
MOONSTONE
MOSS GREEN
NILE GREEN
OLIVE DRAB
PARCHMENT
PEARL GREY
RASPBERRY
ROYAL BLUE
TANGERINE
TOMATO RED
TURKEY RED

TURQUOISE
VERDIGRIS
VERMILION
WALLY BLUE
10
AQUAMARINE
AURICOMOUS
BOIS DE ROSE
CAFÉ AU LAIT
CASTOR GREY
COBALT BLUE
CONGO BROWN
ENSIGN BLUE
LIVER BROWN
MARINA BLUE
MARINE BLUE
OXFORD BLUE
PETROL BLUE
POLYCHROME
POWDER BLUE
TERRACOTTA
ZENITH BLUE
11
BOTTLE GREEN
BURNT ALMOND
CARDINAL RED
CLAIR DE LUNE
FOREST GREEN
GOBELIN BLUE

HORIZON BLUE
HUNTER'S PINK
LAPIS LAZULI
LEMON YELLOW
LIPSTICK RED
PARROT GREEN
PEACOCK BLUE
POMEGRANATE
SMOKED PEARL
SOLID COLOUR
ULTRAMARINE
VERSICOLOUR
WALNUT BROWN
YELLOW OCHRE
12
BALL PARK BLUE
CANARY YELLOW
CARROT COLOUR
CASTILIAN RED
CELADON GREEN
HUNTER'S GREEN
HYACINTH BLUE
LOGWOOD BROWN
MIDNIGHT BLUE
OVERSEAS BLUE
SAPPHIRE BLUE
SOLERINO RED
TYRIAN PURPLE
VERDANT GREEN

13
BISHOP'S PURPLE
BISHOP'S VIOLET
CAMBRIDGE BLUE
MOTHER-OF-PEARL
PARTI-COLOURED
PEPPER-AND-SALT
PRIMARY COLOUR
TORTOISE SHELL
TURQUOISE BLUE
14
HEATHER MIXTURE
PERIWINKLE BLUE
PISTACHIO GREEN
TURQUOISE GREEN
15
CALEDONIAN BROWN
CHARTREUSE
 GREEN
SECONDARY
 COLOUR
16
CHARTREUSE
 YELLOW

CALENDARS

GREGORIAN
JANUARY
FEBRUARY
MARCH
APRIL
MAY
JUNE
JULY
AUGUST
SEPTEMBER
OCTOBER
NOVEMBER
DECEMBER

HEBREW
SHEVAT (Jan/Feb)
ADAR (Feb/Mar)
NISAN (Mar/April)
IYAR (Apr/May)
SIVAN (May/June)
TUMMUZ (June/July)
AV (July Aug)

ELUL (Aug/Sept)
TISHRI (Sept/Oct)
HESHVAN (Oct/Nov)
KISLEV (Nov/Dec)
TEVET (Dec/Jan)

ISLAMIC
MUHARRAN (Jan)
SAFAR (Feb)
RAB I (Mar)
RAB II (Apr)
JUMĀDĀ I (May)
JUMĀDĀ II (June)
RAJAB (July)
SHA'BAN (Aug)
RAMADĀN (Sept)
SHAWWĀL (Oct)
DHUAL-QA'DAH (Nov)
DHUAL-HIJJAH (Dec)

CHINESE
XIAO HAN (Jan)

DA HAN (Jan/Feb)
LI CHUN (Feb)
YU SHUI (Feb/Mar)
JINGSHUI (Mar)
CHUN FEN (Mar/Apr)
QING MING (Apr)
GU YU (Apr/May)
LI XIA (May)
XIAO MAN (May/June)
MANG ZHONG (June)
XIA ZHI (June/July)
XIAO SHU (July)
LI QUI (July/Aug)
CHU SHU (Aug)
BAI LU (Aug/Sept)
QUI FEN Sept)
HAN LU (Sept/Oct)
SHUANG JIANG (Oct)
LI DONG (Oct/Nov)
XIAO XUE (Nov)
DA XUE (Nov/Dec)
DONG ZHI (Dec)

ZODIAC SIGNS / BIRTHSTONES / ANNIVERSARIES

THE SIGNS OF THE ZODIAC

SIGN (Symbol; Dates)

ARIES (Ram; 21 Mar - 19 Apr)
TAURUS (Bull; 20 Apr - 20 May)
GEMINI (Twins; 21 May - 21 June)
CANCER (Crab; 22 June - 22 July)
LEO (Lion; 23 July - 22 Aug)
VIRGO (Virgin; 23 Aug - 22 Sept)

LIBRA (Scales; 23 Sept - 23 Oct)
SCORPIO (Scorpion; 24 Oct - 21 Nov)
SAGITTARIUS (Archer; 22 Nov - 21 Dec)
CAPRICORN (Goat; 22 Dec - 19 Jan)
AQUARIUS (Water-carrier; 20 Jan - 18 Feb)
PISCES (Fish; 19 Feb - 20 Mar)

THE TWELVE SIGNS OF THE CHINESE ZODIAC

RAT	RABBIT	HORSE	ROOSTER
OX	DRAGON	SHEEP	DOG
TIGER	SNAKE	MONKEY	BOAR

BIRTHSTONES

Month - STONE

January - GARNET
February - AMETHYST
March - BLOODSTONE/AQUAMARINE
April - DIAMOND
May - EMERALD
June - PEARL

July - RUBY
August - SARDONYX/PERIDOT
September - SAPPHIRE
October - OPAL
November - TOPAZ
December - TURQUOISE

WEDDING ANNIVERSARIES

1st - PAPER
2nd - COTTON
3rd - LEATHER
4th - FRUIT/FLOWERS
5th - WOOD
6th - IRON
7th - WOOL/COOPER
8th - BRONZE/POTTERY
9th - POTTERY/WILLOW
10th - TIN/ALUMINIMUM
11th - STEEL
12th - SILK/LINEN

13th - LACE
14th - IVORY
15th - CRYSTAL
20th - CHINA
25th - SILVER
30th - PEARL
35th - CORAL
40th - RUBY
45th - SAPPHIRE
50th - GOLD
55th - EMERALD
60th - DIAMOND

PEERAGE / HERALDRY / SINS / WONDERS / VIRTUES

PEERAGE

DUKE	DUCHESS	MARQUIS	MARCHIONESS
EARL	BARONESS	MARQUESS	VISCOUNTESS
BARON	COUNTESS	VISCOUNT	

HERALDRY

TINCTURES
OR (gold)
ARGENT (silver)
ERMINE
VAIR
POTENT
AZURE (blue)
GULES (red)
SABLE (black)
VERT (green)
PURPURE (purple)

DIVISIONS OF FIELDS
PER PALE
PER FESS
PER CROSS
PER BEND
PER SALTIRE
PER CHEVRON

DESCRIPTIONS OF FIELDS
PARTLY
BARRY
BURELY
BENDY
QUARTERLY
ENTY
FRETTY
GIRONNY
BEZANTY

PARTS OF THE ESCUTCHEON
DEXTER (right)
SINISTER (left)
MIDDLE
CHIEF (top)
FLANK (side)
BASE
NOMBRIL
FESS POINT

HONOUR POINT
TRESSURE (border)

LINES
ENGRAILED
EMBATLED
INDENTED
INVECTED
WAVY, UNDY
NEBULY
DANCETTY
RAGULY
POTENTÉ
DOVETAILED
URDY

CROSSES
FORMY
PATY
FLORY
MOLINE
BOTONNY

CROSLETTED
FITCHY
SALTIRE

OTHER OBJECTS AND DECORATIONS
LOZENGES
ROUNDELS (circles)
ANNELETS (rings)
FOUNTAINS (wavey lines on a circle)
BILLETS (upright objects)
MOLET (star)
RAMPANT (rearing up)
COUCHANT (sleeping or sitting)
PASSANT (standing)
BAR

SEVEN DEADLY SINS

PRIDE	LUST	GLUTTONY	SLOTH
COVETOUSNESS	ENVY	ANGER	

SEVEN WONDERS OF THE WORLD

PYRAMIDS OF GIZA, EGYPT	STATUE OF ZEUS AT OLYMPIA
COLOSSUS OF RHODES	TEMPLE OF ARTEMIS AT EPHESUS
HANGING GARDENS OF BABYLON	PHAROS LIGHTHOUSE OF ALEXANDRIA
MAUSOLEUM OF HALICARNASSUS	

SEVEN VIRTUES

FAITH	HOPE	LOVE (CHARITY)	TEMPERANCE
FORTITUDE	JUSTICE	PRUDENCE	

MONEY

3
BIT
BOB
COD
DAM
ECU
FAR
KIP
LAT
MIL
MNA
PIE
REE
REI
SHO
SOL
SOU
4
ANNA
BEKA
BIGA
BUCK
CASH
DAUM
DIME
DOIT
JOEY
KRAN
MAIL
MERK
MITE
OBAL
PEAG
PICE
PONY
QUID
REAL
RYAL
TAEL
UNIK
5
ANGEL
ASPER
BELGA
BETSO
BROA
CONTO
COPEC
CROWN
DARIC
DUCAT

EAGLE
GROAT
LIARD
LIBRA
LITAS
LIVRE
LOCHO
LOUIS
MEDIO
MOHAR
MOHUR
NOBLE
OBANG
PAOLO
PENCE
OENGO
PENNY
PLACK
QURSH
SCEAT
SCUDO
STICA
STYCA
SYCEE
TICAL
TICCY
TOMAN
UNCIA
UNITE
6
AMANIA
AUREUS
BAUBEE
BAWBEE
BEZART
CONDOR
COPANG
COPPER
DÉCIME
DOBLON
FLORIN
FUORTE
GUINEA
GULDEN
KOPECK
MONKEY
NICKEL
PAGODE
SCEATT
SEQUN
STATER

STIVER
TALARI
TALENT
TANNER
TESTER
TESTON
THALER
TOMAUN
ZECHIN
7
ANGELOT
CAROLUS
CENTAVA
DENARII
GUILDER
JACOBUS
MILREIS
MOIDORE
NGUSANG
PISTOLE
QUARTER
SEXTANS
STOOTER
TESTOON
UNICORN
8
AMBROSIN
DENARIUS
DIDRACHM
DOUBLOON
DUCATOON
FARTHNG
FLORENCE
JOHANNES
KREUTZER
LOUIS D'OR
MARAVEDI
NAPOLEON
PICAYUNE
QUETZALE
SESTERCE
SHILLING
SIXPENCE
9
BOLIVIANO
CUARTILLO
DIDRACHMA
DUPONDIUS
GOLD BROAD
GOLD NOBLE
GOLD PENNY

HALF PENNY
PISTAREEN
RIXDOLLAR
ROSE-NOBLE
SESTERTII
SOVEREIGN
SPUR ROYAL
YELLOW BOY
10
EASTERLING
FIRST BRASS
GOLD STATER
QUADRUSSIS
SESTERTIUM
SILVERLING
STOUR-ROYAL
THREEPENCE
TRIPONDIUS
VENEZOLANO
11
HONG KONG
  DOLLAR
MILL SIXPENCE
SILVER PENNY
SPADE GUINEA
12
SILVER-STATER
TETRADRACHMA
TRIBUTE PNNY
13
THREEPENNY BIT

COLLECTIVE NAMES

ACROBATS - troupe	LAPWING - desert
APES - shrewdness	LARKS - exaltation
BABOONS - troop	LEOPARDS - leap,lepe
BAKERS - tabernacle	LIONS - pride,sawt,sowse
BARBERS - babble	LOCUSTS - swarm
BARMEN - promise	MAGPIES - tittering
BAYONETS - grove	MERCHANTS - faith
BEES - erst,swarm	MESSENGERS - diligence
BELLS - change	MOLES - labour
BISHOPS - bench,psalter	MULES - span
BISON - herd	NIGHTINGALES - watch
BREWERS -feast	ORCHIDS - coterie
BUFFALOES - obstinacy	OWLS - parliament, stare
BULLFINCHES - bellowing	PAINTERS - curse,illusion
BULLOCKS - drove	PARROTS - pandemonium
BUTCHERS - goring	PEKINGESE - pomp
BUTLERS -sneer	PENGUINS - parcel
CANONS - chapter, dignity	PIGS - litter
CATERPILLARS - army	PIPERS - skirl
CATTLE - herd	PORPOISES -turmoil
CHOUGHS - chattering	PREACHERS - converting
COBBLERS - cutting	RABBITS - bury
CROCODILES - bask	RHINOCEROS crash-
CROWS - murder	ROBBERS - band
DEANS - decanter,decorum	SHEEP - flock
DONS - obscuration	SHERIFFS - posse
DUCKS - paddling, safe	SHIPS - fleet,armada
ELEPHANTS - herd, parade	SHOEMAKERS - blackening
FERRETS - busyness	STARLINGS - murmuration
FLIES - swarm	SWALLOWS - gulp
GAMBLERS - talent	SWINE - doylt
GEESE - gaggle	TAILORS - disguising
GOLDFINCHES - charm	TAVERNERS - closing
GOVERNESSES - galaxy	TROUT - hover
GRAMMARIANS - conjunction	TURKEY - rafter
HARES - down	TURTLES - turn
HARPIST - melody	UNDERTAKERS - unction
HERONS - serge	WIDOWS - ambush
HIPPOPOTOMI -bloat	WILDCATS - destruction, dout
HUNTERS - blast	WOODPECKERS - descent
JELLYFISH - fluther,smack	WRITERS - worship
JUGGLERS - neverthriving	ZEBRAS - zeal
KITTENS - litter	

TYPEFACES

4	5	FOLIO	6
BELL	ASTER	IONIC	AACHEN
GILL	BEMBO	KABEL	BECKET
	BLOCK	LOTUS	CASLON
	DORIC	TIMES	COOPER

338

6 continued
FUTURA
GLYPHA
GOTHIC
HORLEY
IMPACT
ITALIA
LUCIAN
MELIOR
MINION
MODERN
MONACO
ONDINE
OPTIMA
ROMANA
TECHNO
7
ANTIQUE
BASILIA
BAUHAUS
BERNARD
BOOKMAN
BRAMLEY

CANDIDA
CENTURY
CORONET
COURIER
CUSHING
ELECTRA
FLOREAL
GEORGIA
IMPRINT
MADISON
MEMPHIS
NEW YORK
RALEIGH
SPARTAN
SYMBOLS
TEXTILE
TIFFANY
UNIVERS
WINDSOR
8
BERKELEY
BEROLINA
CLOISTER

CONCORDE
CHARCOAL
EGYPTIAN
EHRHARDT
FRANKLIN
FRUTIGER
GALLIARD
GARAMOND
MONOTYPE
NOVARESE
OLYMPIAN
PALATINO
PERPETUA
ROCKWELL
SOUVENIR
TELETEXT
9
AMERICANA
BARCELONA
BRITANNIC
CALEDONIA
CLARENDON
CLEARFACE

DOMINANTE
EUROSTILE
FAIRFIELD
HELVETICA
WORCESTER
10
AVANT GARDE
CHELTENHAM
CHURCHWARD
EGYPTIENNE
LEAMINGTON
TIMES ROMAN
11
OPTICAL BETA
12
ZAPF DINGBATS
13
TIMES NEW
ROMAN
14
TRUMP
 MEDIAEVAL

AMERICAN INDIANS

3
FOX
OTO
UTE
4
CREE
CROW
HOPI
HUPA
IOWA
SAUK
TUPI
5
AZTEC
CADDO
CREEK
HAIDA
HURON
KASKA
KIOWA
OMAHA
OSAGE
SIOUX
SLAVE
TETON
WAPPO
YUROK

6
ABNAKI
APACHE
ATSINA
CAYUGA
DAKOTA
DOGRIB
MICMAC
MIXTEC
MOHAWK
NAVAJO
NOOTKA
OJIBWA
ONEIDA
OTTAWA
PAIUTE
PAWNEE
QUAPAW
SALISH
SANTEE
SENECA
TANANA
TOLTAC
YAKIMA

7
ARIKARA
BEOTHUK
CATAWBA
CHINOOK
CHOKTAW
HIDATSA
INGALIK
KUTCHIN
SHAWNEE
SHUSWAP
TLINGIT
WICHTA
WYANDOT
8
CHEROKEE
CHEYENNE
COMANCE
DELAWARE
ILLINOIS
IROQUOIS
KICKAPOO
NEZPERCÉ
ONONDAGA
SHOSHONI
TUTCHONE

9
ALGONQUIN
BLACKFOOT
CHICKASAW
CHIPEWYAN
MENOMINEE
PENOBSCOT
TAHAGMIUT
TILLAMOOK
TSIMSHIAN
TUSCARORA
WINNEBAGO
10+
KAVIAGMIUT
POTAWATOMI

WORDS

3 LETTERS
ACE
ACT
ADD
ADO
AFT
AGE
AGO
AHA
AID
AIL
AIM
AIR
ALE
ALL
AMP
AND
ANT
ANY
APE
APT
ARC
ARK
ARM
ART
ASH
ASK
ASP
ASS
ATE
AUK
AWE
AWL
AXE
AYE

4 LETTERS
ABBA
ABED
ABET
ABLE
ABLY
ABUT
ACES
ACHE
ACID
ACME
ACNE
ACRE
ACTS
ADAM
ADEN
ADZE

AEON
AERO
AFAR
AFRO
AGED
AGES
AGOG
AGUE
AHEM
AHOY
AIDE
AIDS
AIMS
AIRS
AIRY
AJAR
AKIN
ALAS
ALIT
ALLY
ALMS
ALOE
ALPS
ALSO
ALTO
ALUM
AMEN
AMID
AMIR
AMOK
AMPS
ANAL
ANEW
ANON
ANTE
ANTI
ANTS
ANUS
APED
APES
APEX
APSE
AQUA
ARAB
ARCH
ARCS
AREA
ARIA
ARID
ARKS
ARMS
ARMY
ARTS
ARTY

ASHY
ASIA
ASPS
ATOM
ATOP
AUKS
AUNT
AURA
AUTO
AVER
AVID
AVOW
AWAY
AWED
AWLS
AWOL
AWRY
AXED
AXES
AXIS
AXLE
AYAH
AYES

5 LETTERS
ABACK
ABASE
ABASH
ABATE
ABBEY
ABBOT
ABEAM
ABHOR
ABIDE
ABODE
ABORT
ABOUT
ABOVE
ABUSE
ABYSS
ACHED
ACHES
ACIDS
ACORN
ACRES
ACRID
ACTED
ACTOR
ACUTE
ADAGE
ADAMS
ADAPT
ADDED

ADDER
ADDLE
ADD-ON
ADEPT
AD HOC
ADIEU
ADIOS
ADLIB
ADMAN
ADMEN
ADMIT
ADMIX
ADOBE
ADOPT
ADORE
ADORN
ADULT
ADZES
AEGIS
AEONS
AFFIX
AFIRE
AFOOT
AFOUL
AFROS
AFTER
AGAIN
AGAMA
AGAPE
AGATE
AGAVE
AGENT
AGGRO
AGILE
AGING
AGISM
AGILT
AGLOW
AGONY
AGORA
AGREE
AGUES
AHEAD
AIDED
AIDES
AILED
AIMED
AISLE
AITCH
ALACK
ALAMO
ALARM
ALATE
ALBUM

ALDER
ALECK
ALERT
ALGAE
ALGAL
ALGID
ALGIN
ALIAS
ALIBI
ALIEN
ALIGN
ALIKE
ALIVE
ALLAY
ALLEY
ALLOT
ALLOW
ALLOY
ALOFT
ALOIN
ALONE
ALONG
ALOOF
ALOUD
ALPHA
ALTAR
ALTER
AMBIT
AMBLE
AMBRY
AMEND
AMIDE
AMINE
AMINO
AMIRS
AMISS
AMITY
AMMAN
AMONG
AMOUR
AMPLE
AMPLY
AMUCK
AMUSE
ANDES
ANGEL
ANGER
ANGLE
ANGST
ANILE
ANIMA
ANION
ANISE
ANJOU

ANKLE
ANNAL
ANNEX
ANNOY
ANNUL
ANODE
ANOLE
ANTES
ANTIC
ANVIL
ANZAC
ANZIO
AORTA
APACE
APART
APEAK
APERY
APHID
APHIS
A PIED
APING
APISH
APORT
APPAL
APPEL
APPLE
APPLY
APRIL
APRON
APSES
APSIS
APTLY
ARABS
ARBOR
AREAL
AREAS
ARENA
ARENT
ARGON
ARGOT
ARGUE
ARIAN
ARIAS
ARIEL
ARIEN
ARIES
ARISE
ARMED
AROID
AROMA
AROSE
ARRAY
ARRIS
ARROW

ARSON	AYLES	ACETIC	AFFIRM	ALECKS	AMOUNT
ARYAN	AYAHS	ACETUM	AFFLUX	ALEGAR	AMOURS
ASCII	AZIDE	ACETYL	AFFORD	ALEPPO	AMPERE
ASCOT	AZINE	ACHAEA	AFFRAY	ALERTS	AMPULE
ASHEN	AZOIC	ACHENE	AFGHAN	A LEVEL	AMRITA
ASHES	AZOLE	ACHING	AFIELD	ALGOID	AMULET
ASIAN	AZTEC	ACIDIC	AFLAME	ALIBIS	AMUSED
ASIDE	AZURE	ACINIC	AFLOAT	ALIENS	AMYLUM
ASKED		ACINUS	AFRAID	ALIGHT	ANALOG
ASKER		ACORNS	AFRESH	ALIPED	ANCHOR
ASKEW	**6 LETTERS**	ACQUIT	AFRICA	ALKALI	ANCONA
ASPEN	ABACUS	ACROSS	AFTERS	ALKANE	ANDEAN
ASPER	ABADAN	ACTING	AGADIR	ALKENE	ANEMIA
ASPIC	ABATED	ACTION	AGAMIC	ALKYNE	ANEMIC
ASSAI	ABATIS	ACTIVE	AGARIC	ALLEGE	ANERGY
ASSAM	ABATOR	ACTORS	AGATES	ALLEYS	ANGARY
ASSAY	ABBACY	ACTUAL	AGEING	ALLIED	ANGELS
ASSES	ABBESS	ACUITY	AGEISM	ALLIER	ANGERS
ASSET	ABBEYS	ACUMEN	AGEIST	ALLIES	ANGINA
ASTER	ABBOTS	ADAGES	AGENCY	ALLIUM	ANGLED
ASTIR	ABDUCT	ADAGIO	AGENDA	ALLOYS	ANGLER
ASTRO	ABIDED	ADDEND	AGENTS	ALLUDE	ANGLES
ASWAN	ABIDER	ADDERS	AGHAST	ALLURE	ANGOLA
ATLAS	ABJECT	ADDICT	AGNATE	ALMADA	ANGORA
ATOLL	ABJURE	ADDING	AGOGIC	ALMOND	ANIMAL
ATOMS	ABLAUT	ADDLED	AGREED	ALMOST	ANIMUS
ATONE	ABLAZE	ADD-ONS	AIDING	ALPACA	ANKARA
ATONY	ABOURD	ADDUCE	AIKIDO	ALPHAS	ANKLES
ATRIA	ABODES	ADDUCT	AILING	ALPINE	ANKLET
ATRIP	ABORAL	ADEPTS	AIMING	ALSACE	ANLAGE
ATTAR	ABOUND	ADHERE	AIRBAG	ALTAIR	ANNABA
ATTIC	ABRADE	ADIEUS	AIRBED	ALTARS	ANNALS
AUDIO	ABROAD	ADIEUX	AIRBUS	ALTONA	ANNEAL
AUDIT	ABRUPT	ADJOIN	AIRGUN	ALUMNI	ANNECY
AUGER	ABSEIL	ADJURE	AIRIER	ALWAYS	ANNEXE
AUNTS	ABSENT	ADJUST	AIRILY	AMATOL	ANNUAL
AURAL	ABSORB	ADMIRE	AIRING	AMAZED	ANODES
AURAS	ABSURD	ADORED	AIRMAN	AMAZON	ANODIC
AURIC	ABUSED	ADRIFT	AIRMEN	AMBALA	ANOINT
AUTOS	ABUSER	ADROIT	AIRWAY	AMBARY	ANOMIC
AUXIN	ABUSES	ADSORB	AISLES	AMBITS	ANOMIE
AVAIL	ACACIA	ADULTS	AKIMBO	AMBLED	ANORAK
AVOID	ACADIA	ADVENT	ALARMS	AMBLER	ANOXIA
AWAIT	ACARID	ADVICE	ALASKA	AMBUSH	ANOXIC
AWAKE	ACARUS	ADVISE	ALBANY	AMEBIC	ANSATE
AWARD	ACCEDE	AEDILE	ALBEDO	AMENDS	ANSHAN
AWARE	ACCENT	AEGEAN	ALBEIT	AMIDIC	ANSWER
AWASH	ACCEPT	AERATE	ALBINO	AMIDOL	ANTEED
AWFUL	ACCESS	AERIAL	ALBION	AMIDST	ANTHEM
AWOKE	ACCORD	AERIFY	ALBITE	AMIENS	ANTHER
AXILE	ACCOST	AEROBE	ALBUMS	AMMINE	ANTICS
AXING	ACCRUE	AFFAIR	ALCOVE	AMNION	ANTLER
AXIOM	ACCUSE	AFFECT	ALDOSE	AMOEBA	ANTRUM
AXLES	ACETAL	AFFINE	ALDRIN	AMORAL	ANTUNG

ANURAN	ARENAS	ASLEEP	AU LAIT	ABLATOR	ACTABLE
ANURIA	AREOLA	ASMARA	AU PAIR	ABOLISH	ACTINIA
ANUSES	ARETES	ASPECT	AUREUS	ABORTED	ACTINIC
ANVILS	ARGALI	ASPIRE	AURORA	ABRADED	ACTINON
ANYANG	ARGENT	ASSAIL	AUROUS	ARADER	ACTIONS
ANYHOW	ARGOSY	ASSAYS	AUSSIE	ABREACT	ACTRESS
ANYONE	ARGOTS	ASSENT	AUSTRO-	ABREAST	ACTUARY
ANYWAY	ARGUED	ASSERT	AUTEUR	ABRIDGE	ACTUATE
AORIST	ARGUER	ASSESS	AUTHOR	ABRUZZI	ACULEUS
AORTAS	ARGYLE	ASSETS	AUTISM	ABSCESS	ACUTELY
AORTIC	ARGYLL	ASSIGN	AUTUMN	ABSCISE	ACYCLIC
AOUDAD	ARIEGE	ASSIST	AVATAR	ABSCOND	ADAGIOS
APACHE	ARIGHT	ASSIZE	AVENGE	ABSENCE	ADAMANT
APATHY	ARIOSO	ASSORT	AVENUE	ABSINTH	ADAPTED
APEMAN	ARISEN	ASSUME	AVERSE	ABSOLVE	ADAPTER
APERCU	ARISTA	ASSURE	AVIARY	ABSTAIN	ADDENDA
APEXES	ARKOSE	ASTERN	AVIATE	ABUSING	ADDICTS
APHIDS	ARMADA	ASTHMA	AVIDIN	ABUSIVE	ADDRESS
APHITH	ARMAGH	ASTRAL	AVIDLY	ABUTTAL	ADDUCED
APIARY	ARMFUL	ASTRAY	AVOCET	ABUTTED	ADENINE
APICAL	ARMIES	ASTUTE	AVOWAL	ABUTTER	ADENOID
APICES	ARMING	ASWARM	AVOWED	ABYSMAL	ADENOMA
APIECE	ARMLET	ASYLUM	AVOWER	ABYSSAL	ADEPTLY
APLITE	ARMOUR	ATAXIA	AWAKED	ABYSSES	ADHERED
APLOMB	ARMPIT	ATHENS	AWAKEN	ACACIAS	ADIPOSE
APNOEA	ARMURE	AT-HOME	AWARDS	ACADEMY	ADJOINT
APODAL	ARNICA	ATOLLS	AWEIGH	ACADIAN	ADJOURN
APOGEE	AROMAS	ATOMIC	AWHILE	ACAROID	ADJUDGE
APOLLO	AROUND	ATONAL	AWNING	ACAUDAL	ADJUNCT
APPEAL	AROUSE	ATONES	AWOKEN	ACCEDED	ADJURED
APPEAR	ARRACK	ATONER	AXENIC	ACCEDER	ADJURER
APPEND	ARRANT	ATONIC	AXILLA	ACCENTS	ADMIRAL
APPLES	ARRAYS	ATRUM	AXIOMS	ACCLAIM	ADMIRED
APPOSE	ARREST	ATTACH	AYMARA	ACCORDS	ADMIRER
APRILS	ARRIVE	ATTACK	AZALEA	ACCOUNT	ADOPTED
APRONS	ARROBA	ATTAIN	AZORES	ACCRUAL	ADORING
APULIA	ARROWS	ATTEND	AZOTIC	ACCRUED	ADORNED
AQUILA	ARSINE	ATTEST		ACCUSED	ADRENAL
ARABIA	ARTERY	ATTICA		ACCUSER	ADULATE
ARABIC	ARTFUL	ATTICS	**7 LETTERS**	ACERBIC	ADVANCE
ARABLE	ARTIER	ATTIRE	ABALONE	ACEROSE	ADVENTS
ARAGON	ARTIST	ATTORN	ABANDON	ACETATE	ADVERBS
ARARAT	ARTOIS	ATTUNE	ABASHED	ACETIFY	ADVERSE
ARBOUR	ASARUM	AUBADE	ABASING	ACETONE	ADVICES
ARCADE	ASCEND	AUBURN	ABATING	ACETOUS	ADVISED
ARCANA	ASCENT	AUDILE	ABAXIAL	ACHIEVE	ADVISER
ARCANE	ASCOTS	AU FAIT	ABDOMEN	ACIDIFY	AEGISES
ARCHED	ASHIER	AU FOND	ABETTED	ACIDITY	AEONIAN
ARCHER	ASHLAR	AUGEND	ABETTOR	ACOLYTE	AERATED
ARCHES	ASHORE	AUGERS	ABIDING	ACQUIRE	AERATOR
ARCHILY	ASIANS	AUGITE	ABILITY	ACREAGE	AERIALS
ARCTIC	ASIDES	AUURY	ABIOSIS	ACROBAT	AEROBIC
ARDENT	ASKING	AUGUST	ABJURED	ACRONYM	AEROGEL
ARDOUR	ASLANT	AUKLET	ABJURER	ACRYLIC	AEROSOL

345

AETOLIA	ALARMED	ALRIGHT	ANKLETS	APOCARP	ARDECHE
AFFABLE	ALASKAN	ALSO-RAN	ANNATES	APOCOPE	ARDENCY
AFFABLY	ALBANIA	ALTERED	ANNEATO	APOGAMY	ARDUOUS
AFFAIRE	ALBERTA	ALTHAEA	ANNELID	APOGEES	AREAWAY
AFFAIRS	ALBINIC	ALTHING	ANNEXED	APOLOGY	ARENITE
AFFIXED	ALBINOS	ALTHORN	ANNEXES	APOLUNE	AREOLAR
AFFIXES	ALBITIC	ALUMNAE	ANNOYED	APOMICIT	ARGONNE
AFFLICT	ALBUMEN	ALUMNUS	ANNUALS	APOSTIL	ARGOTIC
AFFRAYS	ALBUMIN	ALUNDUM	ANNUITY	APOSTLE	ARGUING
AFFRONT	ALCAZAR	ALUNITE	ANNULAR	APOTHEM	ARDIETY
AFGHANS	ALCHEMY	ALYSSUM	ANNULET	APPAREL	ARIETTA
AFRICAN	ALCOHOL	AMALGAM	ANNULUS	APPEASE	ARISING
AGAINST	ALCOVES	AMANTIA	ANODIZE	APPEASE	ARIZONA
AGEISTS	ALERTED	AMASSED	ANODYNE	APPLAUD	ARMADAS
AGELESS	ALERTLY	AMASSER	ANOMALY	APPLIED	ARMAND
AGENDAS	A LEVELS	AMATEUR	ANORAKS	APPLIER	ARMENIA
AGENDUM	ALFALFA	AMATORY	ANOSMIA	APPOINT	ARMFULS
AGGRADE	ALGEBRA	AMAZING	ANOTHER	APPRISE	ARMHOLE
AGGRESS	ALGERIA	ANCHUSA	ANSWERS	APPROVE	ARMIGER
AGILELY	ALGIERS	ANCIENT	ANTACID	APPULSE	ARMLESS
AGILITY	ALAISES	ANCONAL	ANTEFIX	APRAXIA	ARMOIRE
AGITATE	ALIGNED	ANDANTE	ANTEING	APAXIC	ARMOURY
AGONIES	ALIMENT	ANDIRON	ANTENNA	APRICOT	ARMPITS
AGONIST	ALIMONY	ANDORRA	ANTHEMS	A PRIORI	ARMREST
AGONIZE	ALIQUOT	ANDROID	ANTHERS	APROPOS	AROUSAL
AGRAFFE	ALIUNDE	ANEROID	ANTHILL	APSIDAL	AROUSED
AGRAPHA	ALKALIC	ANEURIN	ANTHRAX	APTERAL	AROUSER
AGROUND	ALKALIS	ANGERSK	ANTIBES	APTNESS	ARRAIGN
AILERON	ALKANET	ANGELIC	ANTIGEN	AQUARIA	ARRANGE
AILMENT	ALLAYED	ANGELUS	ANTIGUA	AQUATIC	ARRAYAL
AIMLESS	ALLEGED	ANGERED	ANTIQUE	AQUAVIT	ARRAYED
AIRBASE	ALLEGRO	ANGEVIN	ANTLERS	AQUEOUS	ARREARS
AIRBEDS	ALLELIC	ANGINAL	ANTLION	AQUIFER	ARRESTS
AIRCREW	ALLERGY	ANGIOMA	ANTONYM	ARABIAN	ARRIVAL
AIRDROP	ALLHEAL	ANGLIAN	ANUROUS	ARABIST	ARRIVED
AIRFLOW	ALLONYM	ANGLIFY	ANXIETY	ARACAJU	ARRIVER
AIRGUNS	ALLOWED	ANGLING	ANXIOUS	ARAMAIC	ARROWED
AIRIEST	ALLOYED	ANGOLAN	AYBODY	ARANEID	ARSENAL
AIRINGS	ALLSEED	ANGORAS	ANYWISE	ARAPAHO	ARSENIC
AIRLANE	ALL-STAR	ANGRIER	APOGOGE	ARAROBA	ART DECO
AIRLESS	ALL-TIME	ANGRILY	APATITE	ARBITER	ARTICLE
AIRLIFT	ALLUDED	ANGUINE	APELIKE	ARBOUS	ARTISAN
AIRLINE	ALLURED	ANGUISH	APETALY	ARBUTUS	ARTISTE
AIRLOCK	ALLUVIA	ANGULAR	APHAGIA	ARCADES	ARTISTS
AIRMAIL	ALLYING	ANILINE	APHASIA	ARCADIA	ARTLESS
AIRPORT	ALMANAC	ANILITY	APHESIS	ARCANUM	ARTWORK
AIR RAID	ALMERIA	ANIMALS	APHONIA	ARCHAIC	ASCARID
AIRSHIP	ALMONDS	ANIMATE	APHONIC	ARCHERS	ASCENTS
AIRSICK	ALMONER	ANIMATO	APHOTIC	ARCHERY	ASCETIC
AIRWAYS	ALOETIC	ANIMISM	APHYLLY	ARCHINE	ASCITES
AITCHES	ALOOFLY	ANIMIST	APIEZON	ARCHING	ASCITIC
ALABAMA	ALPACAS	ANIONIC	APLASIA	ARCHIVE	ASCRIBE
A LA	ALPHORN	ANISEED	APLENTY	ARCHWAY	ASEPTIC
MODE	ALREADY	ANISOLE	APLITIC	ARCUATE	ASEXUAL

ASHAMED	AUBERGE	AWESOME	ABSENTED	ACHROMIC
ASHANTI	ACTIONS	AWFULLY	ABSENTEE	ACICULAR
ASHIEST	AUDIBLE	AWKWARD	ABSENTER	ACICULUM
ASHTRAY	AUDIBLY	AWLWORT	ABSENTLY	ACID-FAST
ASIATIC	AUDITED	AWNINGS	ABSINTHE	ACIDNESS
ASITINE	AUDITOR	AXOLOTL	ABSOLUTE	ACIDOSIS
ASKANCE	AUGITIC	AZIMUTH	ABSOLVED	ACIDOTIC
ASOCIAL	AUGMENT	AZURITE	ABSOLVER	ACID-RAIN
ASPECTS	AUGURAL	AZYGOUS	ABSORBED	ACID-TEST
ASPERSE	AUGURED		ABSORBER	ACIERATE
ASPHALT	AU PAIRS		ABSTRACT	ACOLYTES
ASPIRED	AURALLY	**8 LETTERS**	ABSTRUSE	ACONITIC
ASPIRER	AUREATE	AARDVARK	ABSURDLY	ACOUSTIC
ASPIRIN	AUREOLE	ABACUSES	ABUNDANT	ACQUAINT
ASSAULT	AURICLE	ABAMPERE	ABUTILON	ACQUIRED
ASSAYED	AURORAE	ABATTOIR	ABUTMENT	ACQUIRER
ASSAYER	AURORAL	ABBATIAL	ABUTTALS	ACRE-FOOT
ASSEGAI	AURORAS	ABBESSES	ABUTTING	ACRE-INCH
ASSIZES	AUSPICE	ABDICATE	ACADEMIA	ACRIDINE
ASSAUGE	AUSSIES	ABOMENS	ACADEMIC	ACRIDITY
ASSUMED	AUSTERE	ABDUCENT	ACANTHUS	ACRIMONY
ASSUMER	AUSTRAL	ABDUCTED	ACARPOUS	ACROBATS
ASSURED	AUSTRIA	ABELMOSK	ACCEDING	ACRODONT
ASSURER	AUTHORS	ABEOKUTA	ACCENTED	ACROLEIN
ASSYRIA	AUTOCUE	ABERDEEN	ACCENTOR	ACROLITH
ASTATIC	AUTOMAT	ABERRANT	ACCEPTED	ACROMION
ASTOUND	AUTOPSY	ABETTING	ACCEPTOR	ACRONYMS
ASTRIDE	AUTUMNS	ABETTORS	ACCESSED	ACROSTIC
ASTROID	AUXESIS	ABEYANCE	ACCESSES	ACRYLICS
ASTYLAR	AVAILED	ABHORRED	ACCIDENT	ACTINIDE
ASUNDER	AVARICE	ABIDANCE	ACCOLADE	ACTINISM
ASYLEMS	AVATARS	AB INITIO	ACCORDED	ACTINIUM
ATACTIC	AVENGED	ABJECTLY	ACCORDER	ACTINOID
ATAVIAM	AVENGER	ABJURING	ACCOSTED	ACTIVATE
ATAVIST	AVENUES	ABLATION	ACCOUNTS	ACTIVELY
ATELIER	AVERAGE	ABLATIVE	ACCREDIT	ACTIVISM
ATHEISM	AVERRED	ABNEGATE	ACCRUING	ACTIVIST
ATHEIST	AVERTED	ABNORMAL	ACCURACY	ACTIVITY
ATHLETE	AVESTAN	ABORTING	ACCURATE	ACT OF GOD
ATHWART	AVEYRON	ABORTION	ACCURSED	ACTUALLY
ATLANTA	AVIATOR	ABORTIVE	ACCUSERS	ACTUATED
ATLASES	AVIDITY	ABOUNDED	ACCUSING	ACTUATOR
ATOMISM	AVGNON	ABOVE PAR	ACCUSTOM	ACULEATE
ATOMIST	AVIONIC	ABRADANT	ACCUTRON	ACUTANCE
ATOMIZE	AVOCADO	ABRADING	ACENTRIC	ADAMSITE
ATONING	AVOIDED	ABRASION	ACERBATE	ADAPTERS
ATROPHY	AVOIDER	ABRASIVE	ACERBITY	ADAPTING
ATTACHE	AVOWALS	ABRIDGED	ACERVATE	ADAPTIVE
ATTACKS	AVOWING	ABRIDGER	ACESCENT	ADDENDUM
ATTAINT	AWAITED	ABROGATE	ACHENIAL	ADDICTED
ATTEMPT	AWAKING	ABRUPTLY	ACHIEVED	ADDICTION
ATTIRED	AWARDED	ABSCISSA	ACHIEVER	ADDICTIVE
ATTRACT	AWARDEE	ABSEILED	ACHILLES	ADDUCENT
ATTUNED	AWARDER	ABSENCES	ACHROMAT	ADDUCING

ADDUCTOR	AEROGRAM	AIRBUSES	ALIENAGE	ALTERING
ADELAIDE	AEROLITE	AIRCRAFT	ALIENATE	ALTHOUGH
ADENITIS	AEROLOGY	AIRCREWS	ALIENISM	ALTITUDE
ADENOIDS	AERONAUT	AIREDALE	ALIENIST	ALTRUISM
ADEQUACY	AEROSOLS	AIRFIELD	ALIGHTED	ALTRUIST
ADEQUATE	AEROSTAT	AIRFORCE	ALIGNING	ALUMROOT
ADHERENT	AESTHETE	AIRFRAME	ALIQUANT	ALVEOLAR
ADHERING	AFEBRILE	AIRINESS	ALIZARIAN	ALVEOLUS
ADHESION	AFFECTED	AIRLANES	ALKAHEST	AMALGAMS
ADHESIVE	AFFERENT	AIRLIFTS	ALKALIES	AMARANTH
ADJACENT	AFFIANCE	AIRLINER	ALKALIFY	AMARELLE
ADJOINED	AFFINITY	AIRLINES	ALKALINE	AMARILLO
ADJUDGED	AFFIRMED	AIRLOCKS	ALKALIZE	AMASSING
ADJUNCTS	AFFIRMER	AIRPLANE	ALKALOID	AMATEURS
ADJURING	AFFIXING	AIRPORTS	ALLANITE	AMAZONAS
ADJUSTED	AFFLATUS	AIR RAIDS	ALLAYING	AMBEROID
ADJUTANT	AFFLUENT	AIRSCREW	ALL CLEAR	AMBIENCE
ADJUVANT	AFFORDED	AIRSHIPS	ALLEGING	AMBITION
AD-LIBBED	AFFOREST	AIRSPACE	ALLEGORY	AMBIVERT
AD-LIBBER	AFFRONTS	AIRSPEED	ALLELISM	AMBROSIA
ADMIRALS	AFFUSION	AIRSTRIP	ALLELUIA	AMBULANT
ADMIRERS	AFLUTTER	AIRTIGHT	ALLEPPEY	AMBULATE
ADMIRING	AFRICANS	AIR-TO-AIR	ALLERGEN	AMBUSHED
ADMITTED	AGARTALA	AIRWAVES	ALLERGIC	AMBUSHES
ADMONISH	AGE GROUP	AIRWOMAN	ALLEYWAY	AMENABLE
ADOPTING	AGENCIES	AIRWOMEN	ALLIANCE	AMENDING
ADOPTION	AGENESIS	A LA CARTE	ALLOCATE	AMERICAN
ADOPTIVE	AGENETIC	ALACRITY	ALLODIAL	AMETHYST
ADORABLE	AGENTIAL	ALARMING	ALLODIUM	AMICABLE
ADORNING	AGENTIVE	ALARMISM	ALLOGAMY	AMICABLY
ADRIATIC	AGERATUM	ALARMIST	ALLOPATH	AMITOSIS
ADROITLY	AGGRIEVE	ALBACORE	ALLOTTED	AMITOTIC
ADULARIA	AGIOTAGE	ALBANIAN	ALLOTTEE	AMMETERS
ADULATOR	AGITATED	ALBANISM	ALLOWING	AMMONIAC
ADULTERY	AGITATOR	ALCATRAZ	ALL RIGHT	AMMONIFY
ADUMBRAL	AGITPROP	ALCHEMIC	ALL-ROUND	AMMONITE
ADVANCED	AGMINATE	ALCIDINE	ALLSPICE	AMMONIUM
ADVANCER	AGNOSTIC	ALCOHOLS	ALLUDING	AMNESIAC
ADVANCES	AGONIZED	ALDEHYDE	ALLURING	AMNIOTIC
ADVERTED	AGRAPHIA	ALDERMAN	ALLUSION	AMOEBOID
ADVISING	AGRARIAN	ALDERMEN	ALLUSIVE	AMORETTO
ADVISORY	AGRESTAL	ALDERNEY	ALLUVIAL	AMORTIZE
ADVOCAAT	AGROLOGY	ALDOXIME	ALLUVIUM	AMOUNTED
ADVOCACY	AGRONOMY	ALEATORY	ALMANACS	AMPERAGE
ADVOCATE	AGUEWEED	ALEHOUSE	ALMIGHTY	AMPHIPOD
ADYNAMIA	AIGRETTE	ALERTING	ALMONERS	AMPHORAE
ADYNAMIC	AIGUILLE	ALFRESCO	ALOPECIA	AMPHORAS
AEGROTAT	AILMENTS	ALGERIAN	ALPHABET	AMPOULES
AERATING	AIRBASES	ALGERINE	ALPHOSIS	AMPULLAR
AERATION	AIRBORNE	ALGINATE	ALPINISM	AMPUTATE
AERIALLY	AIRBRAKE	ALGOLOGY	ALPINIST	AMPUTEES
AEROBICS	AIRBRICK	ALGORISM	ALSATIAN	AMRAVATI
AERODYNE	AIRBRUSH	ALHAMBRA	ALSO-RANS	AMRITSAR
AEROFOIL	AIRBURST	ALICANTE	ALTER EGO	AMYGDALA

AMYGDALE	ANIMATED	APATETIC	APYRETIC	ARMS RACE
ANABAENA	ANIMATOR	APERIENT	AQUALUNG	AROMATIC
ANABASIS	ANIMISTS	APERITIF	AQUANAUT	AROUSING
ANABATIC	ANISETTE	APERTURE	AQUARIST	ARPEGGIO
ANABLEPS	ANKERITE	APHANITE	AQUARIUM	ARRANGED
ANABOLIC	ANKYLOST	APHELIAN	AQUARIUS	ARRANGER
ANACONDA	ANNALIST	APHELION	AQUATICS	ARRAYING
ANAEROBE	ANNEALED	APHORIAM	AQUATINT	ARRESTED
ANAGLYPH	ANNEALER	APHORIST	AQUEDUCT	ARRESTER
ANAGOGIC	ANNEXING	APHORIZE	AQUILINE	ARRAYING
ANAGRAMS	ANNOTATE	APIARIAN	ARACHNID	ARRESTED
ANALCITE	ANNOUNCE	APIARIES	ARAPAIMA	ARRESTER
ANALECTS	ANNOYING	APIARIST	ARAWAKAN	ARRIVALS
ANALEMMA	ANNUALLY	APIOLOGY	ARBITERS	ARRIVING
ANALOGUE	ANNULATE	APLASTIC	ARBITRAL	ARROGANT
ANALYSED	ANNULOSE	APOCRINE	ARBOREAL	ARROGATE
ANALYSER	ANODYNES	APODOSIS	ARCADIAN	ARROWING
ANALYSES	ANOINTED	APOGAMIC	ARCATURE	ARSENALS
ANALYSIS	ANOINTER	APOLOGIA	ARCHAEAN	ARSENATE
ANALYSTS	ANOREXIA	APOLOGIA	ARCHAISM	ARSENIDE
ANALYTIC	ANSERINE	APOLOGUE	ARCHAIST	ARSENITE
ANAPAEST	ANSWERED	APOMIXIS	ARCHAIZE	ARSONIST
ANAPHASE	ANTABUSE	APOPHYGE	ARCHDUKE	ARTEFACT
ANAPHORA	ANTEATER	APOPLEXY	ARCHIVAL	ARTERIAL
ANARCHIC	ANTECEDE	APOSPORY	ARCHIVES	ARTERIES
ANASARCA	ANTEDATE	APOSTAST	ARCHNESS	ARTESIAN
ANATHEMA	ANTELOPE	APOSTATE	ARCHWAYS	ARTFULLY
ANATOLIA	ANTENNAS	APOSTLES	ARCTURUS	ARTICLED
ANCESTOR	ANTERIOR	APPALLED	ARDENNES	ARTICLES
ANCHORED	ANTEROOM	APPANAGE	ARDENTLY	ARTIFACT
ANCIENTS	ANTEVERT	APPARENT	AREA CODE	ARTIFICE
ANDANTES	ANTHELIX	APPEALED	ARENITIC	ARTINESS
ANDESINE	ANTHESIS	APPEALER	ATEQUIPA	ARTISANS
ANDESISTE	ANTHILLS	APPEARED	ARETHUSA	ARTISTES
ANDIRONS	ANTIBODY	APPEASED	ARGENTIC	ARTISTIC
ANDIZHAN	ANTIDOTE	APPELLEE	ARGININE	ARTISTRY
ANDORRAN	ANTIGENS	APPENDED	ARGUABLE	ARYANIZE
ANDROGEN	ANTIHERO	APPENDIX	ARGUABLY	ASBESTOS
ANDROIDS	ANTI-ICER	APPESTAT	ARGUMENT	ASCENDED
ANECDOTE	ANTILLES	APPETITE	ARIANIAM	ASCENDER
ANECHOIC	ANTIMERE	APPLAUSE	ARILLATE	ASCETICS
ANEMONES	ANTINODE	APPLE PIE	ARILLODE	ASCIDIAN
ANETHOLE	ANTINOMY	APPLIQUE	ARISTATE	ASCIDIUM
ANEURYSM	ANTIPHON	APPLYING	ARKANSAS	ASCOCARP
ANGELENO	ANTIQUES	APPOSITE	ARMAGNAC	ASCORBIC
ANGELICA	ANTITANK	APPRAISE	ARMAMENT	ASCRIBED
ANGERING	ANTONYMS	APPRISED	ARMATURE	ASHTRAYS
ANGINOSE	ANTRORSE	APPROACH	ARMBANDS	ASNIERES
ANGLESEY	ANURESIS	APPROVAL	ARMCHAIR	ASPERSER
ANGLICAN	ANYPLACE	APPROVED	ARMENIAN	ASPHODEL
ANGRIEST	ANYTHING	APRES-SKI	ARMHOLES	ASPHYXIA
ANGSTROM	ANYWHERE	APRICOTS	ARMORIAL	ASPIRANT
ANGULATE	ANORISTIC	APTEROUS	ARMOURED	ASPIRATE
ANHEDRAL	APAGOGIC	APTITUDE	ARMOURER	ASPIRING

349

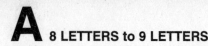

ASPIRINS	ATROPHIC	AVAILING	ABJECTION	ACCORDION
ASSAILED	ATROPINE	AVENGERS	ABLUTIONS	ACCOSTING
ASSAILER	ATTACHED	AVENGING	ABNEGATOR	ACCOUNTED
ASSAMESE	ATTACHER	AVERAGED	ABOLISHED	ACCREATION
ASSASSIN	ATTACHES	AVERAGES	ABOLISHER	ACCRETIVE
ASSAULTS	ATTACKED	AVERMENT	ABOLITION	ACCRUMENT
ASSAYING	ATTACKER	AVERRING	ABOMINATE	ACCUMBENT
ASSEGAIS	ATTAINED	AVERSION	ABORIGINE	ACELLULAR
ASSEMBLE	ATTEMPTS	AVERSIVE	ABORTIONS	ACESCENCE
ASSEMBLY	ATTENDED	AVERTING	ABOUNDING	ACETAMIDE
ASSENTED	ATTESTED	AVIARIES	ABOUT-TURN	ACETIFIER
ASSENTOR	ATTIRING	AVIATION	ABRASIONS	ACETYLATE
ASSERTED	ATTITUDE	AVIATORS	ABRASIVES	ACETYLENE
ASSERTER	ATTORNEY	AVIATRIX	ABRIDGING	ACETYLIDE
ASSESSED	ATTUNING	AVIDNESS	ABROGATED	ACHEULIAN
ASSESSOR	ATYPICAL	AVIEMORE	ABROGATOR	ACHIEVING
ASSIGANT	AUBUSSON	AVIFAUNA	ABSCESSES	ACICULATE
ASSIGNED	AUCKLAND	AVIONICS	ABSCONDED	ACIDIFIED
ASSIGNEE	AUCTIONS	AVOCADOS	ABSCONDER	ACIDIFIER
ASSIGNER	AUDACITY	AVOIDING	ABSEILING	ACIDOPHIL
ASSIGNOR	AUDIENCE	AVOWABLE	ABSENTEES	ACID TESTS
ASSISTED	AUDITING	AVULSION	ABSENTING	ACIDULATE
ASSISTER	AUDITION	AWAITING	ABSOLVING	ACIDULOUS
ASSONANT	AUDITORY	AWAKENED	ABSORBENT	ACINIFORM
ASSORTED	AUGSBURG	AWARDING	ABSTRACTS	ACOUSTICS
ASSORTER	AUDERIES	AWEATHER	ABSURDITY	ACQUIENCE
ASSUAGED	AUGURING	AXILLARY	ABUNDANCE	ACQUIRING
ASSUAGER	AUGUSTLY	AXIOLOGY	ABU SIMBEL	ACQUITTAL
ASSUMING	AUREOLES	AXLETREE	ABUSIVELY	ACQUITTED
ASSURING	AU REVOIR	AYRESHIRE	ABUTMENTS	ACQUITTER
ASSYRIAN	AURICLES	AZIMUTHS	ABYSSINIA	ACROBATIC
ASTATINE	AURICULA	AZOTEMIA	ACADEMICS	ACRODROME
ASTERISK	AUSPICES	AZOTEMIC	ACANTHINE	ACROGENIC
ASTERISM	AUSTRAIN		ACANTHOID	ACRONYMIC
ASTERNAL	AUTACOID		ACANTHOUS	ACROPETAL
ASTEROID	AUTARCHY	**9 LETTERS**	ACARIASIS	ACROPOLIS
ASTHENIA	AUTARKIC	ABACTINAL	ACAROLOGY	ACROSPIRE
ASTHENIC	AUTHORED	ABANDONED	ACCEDENCE	ACROSTICS
ASTONISH	AUTISTIC	ABASEMENT	ACCENTING	ACTINOPOD
ASTRAGAL	AUTOBAHN	ABASHEDLY	ACCENTUAL	ACTIVATED
ASTURIAS	AUTOCRAT	ABATEMENT	ACCEPTANT	ACTIVATOR
ASTUTELY	AUTOCUES	ABATTOIRS	ACCEPTING	ACTIVISTS
ASUNCION	AUTOGAMY	ABCOULOMB	ACCESSING	ACTRESSES
ATARAXIA	AUTOGIRO	ABDICABLE	ACCESSION	ACTS OF GOD
ATHEISTS	AUTOLYSE	ABDICATED	ACCESSORY	ACTUALITY
ATHENIAN	AUTOMATA	ABDICATOR	ACCIDENCE	ACTUALIZE
ATHEROMA	AUTOMATE	ABDOMINAL	ACCIDENTS	ACTURAIAL
ATHLETES	AUTOMATS	ABDUCTING	ACCIPITER	ACTUARIES
ATHLETIC	AUTONOMY	ABDUCTION	ACCLAIMED	ACTUATION
ATLANTIS	AUTOSOME	ABERRANCE	ACCLIVITY	ACUMINATE
ATOMIZER	AUTOTOMY	ABHORRENT	ACCOLADES	ACUMINOUS
ATONABLE	AUTOTYPE	ABHORRING	ACCOMPANY	ACUTENESS
ATONALLY	AUTOTYPY	ABIDINGLY	ACCORDANT	ADAMANTLY
ATROCITY	AUTUMNAL	ABILITIES	ACCORDING	ADAPTABLE

ADDICTION	ADVENTURE	AFTERMATH	ALIENABLE	ALTITUDES
ADDICTIVE	ADVERBIAL	AFTERNOON	ALIENATED	ALTRICIAL
ADDITIONS	ADVERSARY	AFTERWORD	ALIENATOR	ALTRUISTS
ADDITIVES	ADVERSELY	AGE GROUPS	ALIGHTING	ALUMINATE
ADDRESSED	ADVERSITY	AGGRAVATE	ALIGNMENT	ALUMINIUM
ADDRESSEE	ADVERTING	AGGREGATE	ALIPHATIC	ALUMINIZE
ADDRESSER	ADVERTISE	AGGRESSOR	ALKALOSIS	ALUMINOUS
ADDRESSES	ADVISABLE	AGGRIEVED	ALLAHABAD	ALVEOLARS
ADDUCTION	ADVISEDLY	AGITATION	ALLANTOIC	ALVEOLATE
ADEMPTION	ADVOCATED	AGITATORS	ALLANTOID	AMAGASAKI
ADENOIDAL	ADVOCATES	AGNOMICAL	ALLANTOIS	AMARYLLIS
ADENOSINE	AEOLIPILE	AGNOSTICS	ALL-AROUND	AMAUROSIS
ADHERANCE	AEPYORNIS	AGONIZING	ALLEGEDLY	AMAUROTIC
ADHERANTS	AEROBATIC	AGREEABLE	ALLELUIAS	AMAZEMENT
ADHESIONS	AERODROME	AGREEABLY	ALLENTOWN	AMAZINGLY
ADHESIVES	AEROLOGIC	AGREEMENT	ALLERGIES	AMAZONIAN
ADIABATIC	AEROMETER	AGRONOMIC	ALLERGIST	AMAZONITE
AD INTERIM	AEROMETRY	AHMEDABAD	ALLETHRIN	AMBERGRIS
ADIPOCERE	AEROPAUSE	AILANTHUS	ALLEVIATE	AMBERJACK
ADJACENCY	AEROPHONE	AIMLESSLY	ALLEYWAYS	AMBIENCES
ADJECTIVE	AEROPLANE	AIRBRAKES	ALLIANCES	AMBIGUITY
ADJOINING	AEROSPACE	AIRFIELDS	ALLIGATOR	AMBIGUOUS
ADJOURNED	AESTHESIA	AIRFORCES	ALLOCATED	AMBITIONS
ADJUDGING	AESTHETES	AIR-INTAKE	ALLOGRAPH	AMBITIOUS
ADJUSTING	AESTHETIC	AIRLETTER	ALLOMETRY	AMBLYOPIA
ADJUTANCY	AESTIVATE	AIRLIFTED	ALLOMORPH	AMBLYOPIC
ADJUTANTS	AETHEREAL	AIRLINERS	ALLOPATHY	AMBROSIAL
AD-LIBBING	AETIOLOGY	AIRPLANES	ALLOPHANE	AMBROTYPE
ADMEASURE	AFFECTING	AIRPOCKET	ALLOPHONE	AMBULANCE
ADMINICLE	AFFECTION	AIRSTREAM	ALLOPLASM	AMBUSHING
ADMIRABLE	AFFECTIVE	AIRSTRIPS	ALLOTMENT	AMENDIBLE
ADMIRABLY	AFFIANCED	AIRWORTHY	ALLOTROPE	AMENDMENT
ADMIRALTY	AFFIDAVIT	AITCHBONE	ALLOTROPY	AMENITIES
ADMISSION	AFFILIATE	ALABASTER	ALLOTTING	AMERICANA
ADMISSIVE	AFFIRMINY	ALBATROSS	ALLOWABLE	AMERICANS
ADMITTING	AFFIXTURE	ALBERTITE	ALLOWABLY	AMERICIUM
ADMIXTURE	AFFLICTED	ALBESCENT	ALLOWANCE	AMERINDIC
AD NAUSEAM	AFFLUENCE	ALCHEMIST	ALLOWEDLY	AMETHYSTS
ADNOMINAL	AFFORDING	ALCHEMIZE	ALLUSIONS	AMETROPIA
ADOPTIONS	AFFRICATE	ALCOHOLIC	ALMA MATER	AMIANTHUS
ADORATION	AFFRONTED	ALDEBARAN	ALMANDINE	AMIDSHIPS
ADORNMENT	AFLATOXIN	ALEHOUSES	ALMS-HOUSE	AMINO ACID
ADRENALIN	AFORESAID	ALEMANNIC	ALONGSIDE	AMMOCOETE
ADSORBATE	A FORTIORI	ALEPH-NULL	ALOOFNESS	AMMONIATE
ADSORBENT	AFRIKAANS	ALERTNESS	ALPENGLOW	AMMONICAL
ADULATION	AFRIKANER	ALFILARIA	ALPHABETS	AMMONITIC
ADULATORY	AFRO-ASIAN	ALGARROBA	ALSATIANS	AMNESTIES
ADULTERER	AFTERBODY	ALGEBRAIC	ALTERABLE	AMOEBAEAN
ADUMBRATE	AFTERCARE	ALGECIRAS	ALTERCATE	AMORALITY
AD VALOREM	AFTERDAMP	ALGOMETER	ALTER EGOS	AMOROUSLY
ADVANCING	AFTERDECK	ALGOMETRY	ALTERNATE	AMORPHISM
ADVANTAGE	AFTERGLOW	ALGONQUIN	ALTIMETER	AMORPHOUS
ADVECTION	AFTERHEAT	ALGORITHM	ALTIPLANO	AMORTIZED
ADVENTIVE	AFTERLIFE	ALICYCLIC	ALTISSIMO	AMOUNTING

AMPERSAND	ANCHORESS	ANORTHITE	APERTURES	APPROBATE
AMPHIBIAN	ANCHORING	ANOSMATIC	APETALOUS	APPROVING
AMPHIBOLE	ANCHORITE	ANOXAEMIA	APICULATE	APPULSIVE
AMPHIGORY	ANCHOVIES	ANOXAEMIC	APISHNESS	APRIL FOOL
AMPHIOXUS	ANCILLARY	ANSWERING	APIVOROUS	APRIORITY
AMPLIFIED	ANCIPITAL	ANTALKALI	APLANATIC	APTITUDES
AMPLIFIER	ANDALUSIA	ANTARCTIC	APOCOPATE	AQUALUNGS
AMPLITUDE	ANDANTINO	ANTEATERS	APOCRYPHA	AQUAPLANE
AMPUTATED	ANDRADITE	ANTECHOIR	APODICTIC	AQUARELLE
AMSTERDAM	ANDROMEDA	ANTEDATED	APOENZYME	AQUARIUMS
AMUSEMENT	ANECDOTAL	ANTEFIXAL	APOGAMOUS	AQUATINTS
AMUSINGLY	ANECDOTES	ANTELOPES	APOLOGIAS	AQUEDUCTS
AMYGDALIN	ANECDOTIC	ANTENATAL	APOLOGIES	AQUILEGIA
AMYLOPSIN	ANEMOLOGY	ANTENNULE	APOLOGIST	AQUITAINE
ANABANTID	ANGLESITE	ANTEROOMS	APOLOGIZE	ARABESQUE
ANABIOSIS	ANGLEWORM	ANTHELION	APOPHASIS	ARABINOSE
ANABOLISM	ANGLICANS	ANTHEMION	APOPHYSIS	ARACHNOID
ANABOLITE	ANGLECISM	ANTHODIUM	APOSTATES	ARAGONESE
ANACLINAL	ANGLICIZE	ANTHOLOGY	APOSTOLIC	ARAGONITE
ANACLISIS	ANGOSTURA	ANTHOTAXY	APPALLING	ARAUCANIA
ANACLITIC	ANGUISHED	ANTHOZOAN	APPALOOSA	ARAUCARIA
ANACONDAS	ANHYDRIDE	ANTHURIUM	APPARATUS	ARBITRAGE
ANACRUSIS	ANHYDRITE	ANTHOLOGY	APPARITOR	ARBITRAGE
ANAEROBIC	ANHYDROUS	ANTHOTAXY	APPEALING	ARBITRARY
ANALECTIC	ANIMALISM	ANTHOZOAN	APPEARING	ARBITRATE
ANALEPTIC	ANIMALIST	ANTHURIUM	APPEASING	ARBITRESS
ANALGESIC	ANIMALITY	ANTICHLOR	APPELLANT	ARBOREOUS
ANALOGIES	ANIMALIZE	ANTICLINE	APPELLATE	ARBORETUM
ANALOGIST	ANIMATING	ANTIDOTES	APPENDAGE	ARCHAISMS
ANALOGIZE	ANIMATION	ANTIGENIC	APPENDANT	ARCHAIZER
ANALOGOUS	ANIMATISM	ANTIKNOCK	APPENDING	ARCHANGEL
ANALYSAND	ANIMISTIC	ANTIMERIC	APPENZELL	ARCHDUCAL
ANALYSING	ANIMOSITY	ANTIMONIC	APPERTAIN	ARCHDUCHY
ANALYTICS	ANISOGAMY	ANTIPATHY	APPETENCE	ARCHDUKES
ANAMNESIS	ANKLEBONE	ANTIPHONY	APPETITES	ARCHENEMY
ANANDROUS	ANKYLOSIS	ANTIPODAL	APPETIZER	ARCHETYPE
ANANTHOUS	ANNALISTS	ANTIPODES	APPLAUDED	ARCHFIEND
ANAPAESTS	ANNAPURNA	ANTIQUARY	APPLAUDER	ARCHICARP
ANAPESTIC	ANNEALING	ANTIQUATE	APPLE CART	ARCHITECT
ANAPHORAL	ANNELIDAN	ANTIQUITY	APPLEJACK	ARCHIVIST
ANAPLASIA	ANNOTATED	ANTISERUM	APPLE PIES	ARCHIVOLT
ANAPLASTY	ANNOTATOR	ANTITOXIC	APPLIANCE	ARCOGRAPH
ANAPTYXIS	ANNOUNCED	ANTITOXIN	APPLICANT	ARCTOGAEA
ANARCHISM	ANNOUNCER	ANTIVENIN	APPOINTED	ARCTURIAN
ANARCHIST	ANNOYANCE	ANTIWORLD	APPOINTEE	ARCUATION
ANARTHRIA	ANNUITANT	ANXIETIES	APPOINTER	ARDUOUSLY
ANATHEMAS	ANNUITIES	ANXIOUSLY	APPOINTOR	AREA CODES
ANATOLIAN	ANNULLING	APARTHEID	APPORTION	ARGENTINA
ANATOMIES	ANNULMENT	APARTMENT	APPRAISAL	ARGENTINE
ANATOMIST	ANOESTRUS	APATHETIC	APPRAISED	ARGENTITE
ANATOMIZE	ANOINTING	APELDOORN	APPRAISER	ARGENTOUS
ANCESTORS	ANOMALIES	APENNINES	APPREHEND	ARGILLITE
ANCESTRAL	ANOMALOUS	APERIODIC	APPRESSED	ARGUMENTS
ANCHORAGE	ANOPHELES	APERITIFS	APPRISING	ARMADILLO

ARMAMENTS	ASSASSINS	ATOMIZERS	AUTOCLAVE	ABIOGENIST
ARMATURES	ASSAULTED	ATONALISM	AUTOCRACY	ABIRRITANT
ARMCHAIRS	ASSAULTER	ATONALITY	AUTOCRATS	ABIRRITATE
ARMISTICE	ASSAYABLE	ATONEMENT	AUTOCROSS	ABJURATION
ARMOURERS	ASSEMBLED	ATONICITY	AUTOECISM	ABLE-BODIED
ARMOURIES	ASSEMBLER	ATROCIOUS	AUTOGRAFT	ABLE SEAMEN
ARMS RACES	ASSENTING	ATROPHIED	AUTOGRAPH	ABLE SEAMEN
AROMATIZE	ASSERTING	ATTACHING	AUTOICOUS	ABNEGATION
ARPEGGIOS	ASSERTION	ATTACKERS	AUTOLYSIN	ABNORMALLY
ARRAIGNER	ASSERTIVE	ATTACKING	AUTOLYSIS	ABOLISHING
ARRANGING	ASSESSING	ATTAINDER	AUTOLYTIC	ABOMINABLE
ARRESTING	ASSESSORS	ATTAINING	AUTOMATED	ABOMINABLY
ARRIVISTE	ASSIDUITY	ATTEMPTED	AUTOMATIC	ABOMINATED
ARROGANCE	ASSIDUOUS	ATTEMPTER	AUTOMATON	ABORIGINAL
ARROGATED	ASSIGNING	ATTENDANT	AUTONOMIC	ABORIGINES
ARROGATOR	ASSISTANT	ATTENDING	AUTOPHYTE	ABORTICIDE
ARROWHEAD	ASSISTING	ATTENTION	AUTOPSIES	ABORTIONAL
ARROWROOT	ASSOCIATE	ATTENTIVE	AUTOSOMAL	ABORTIVELY
ARROWOOD	ASSONANCE	ATTENUANT	AUTOTIMER	ABOUT-TURNS
ARROWORM	ASSORTING	ATTENUATE	AUTOTOMIC	ABOVEBOARD
ARSENICAL	ASSUAGING	ATTESTANT	AUTOTOXIC	ABRASIVELY
ARSENIOUS	ASSUASIVE	ATTESTING	AUTOTOXIN	ABREACTION
ARSONISTS	ASSUMABLE	ATTITUDES	AUTOTYPIC	ABRIDGABLE
ARTEFACTS	ASSURANCE	ATTORNEYS	AUXILIARY	ABRIDGMENT
ARTIFICER	ASSUREDLY	ATTRACTED	AVAILABLE	ABROGATING
ARTIFICES	ASSURGENT	ATTRACTOR	AVAILABLY	ABROGATION
ARTILLERY	ASTERISKS	ATTRIBUTE	AVALANCHE	ABRUPTNESS
ARTLESSLY	ASTEROIDS	ATTRITION	AVERAGING	ABSCISSION
ARYTENOID	ASTHMATIC	ATTRITIVE	AVERSIONS	ABSCONDING
ASCENDANT	ASTOUNDED	AUBERGINE	AVERTABLE	ABSOLUTELY
ASCENDING	ASTRADDLE	AUBRIETIA	AVIFAUNAL	ABSOLUTION
ASCENSION	ASTRAKHAN	AU COURANT	AVIRULENT	ABSOLUTORY
ASCERTAIN	ASTROCYTE	AUCTIONED	AVOCATION	ABSOLVABLE
ASCOSPORE	ASTRODOME	AUCTORIAL	AVOIDABLE	ABSORBABLE
ASCRIBING	ASTROLAB	AUDACIOUS	AVOIDANCE	ABSORBANCY
ASEPALOUS	ASTROLOGY	AUDIENCES	AVUNCULAR	ABSORBENTS
ASEXUALLY	ASTRONAUT	AUDIOLOGY	AWAKENING	ABSORPTION
ASHAMEDLY	ASTRONOMY	AUDIPHONE	AWARDABLE	ABSORPTIVE
ASHKENAZI	ASTROTURF	AUDITIONS	AWARENESS	ABSTAINERS
ASHKHABAD	ASYLLABIC	AUGMENTED	AWESTRUCK	ABSTAINING
ASININITY	ASYMMETRY	AUGMENTOR	AWFULNESS	ABSTEMIOUS
ASPARAGUS	ASYMPTOTE	AU NATUREL	AWKWARDLY	ABSTENTION
ASPERSION	ASYNDETIC	AURICULAR	AXIOMATIC	ABSTERGENT
ASPERSIVE	ASYNDETON	AUSTENITE	AYATOLLAH	ABSTINENCE
ASPHALTED	ATAVISTIC	AUSTERELY		ABSTRACTED
ASPHALTIC	ATHEISTIC	AUSTERITY		ABUNDANTLY
ASPHALTUM	ATHENAEUM	AUSTRALIA	**10 LETTERS**	ABYSSINIAN
ASPHYXIAL	ATHLETICS	AUTARCHIC	ABANDONING	ACCELERANT
ASPIRANTS	ATLANTEAN	AUTARKIES	ABBREVIATE	ACCELERATE
ASPIRATED	ATMOMETER	AUTHENTIC	ABDICATING	ACCENTUATE
ASPIRATES	ATMOMETRY	AUTHORESS	ABDICATION	ACCEPTABLE
ASPIRATOR	ATOM BOMBS	AUTHORIAL	ABDICATIVE	ACCEPTABLY
ASSAILANT	ATOMICITY	AUTHORITY	ABERRATION	ACCEPTANCE
ASSAILING	ATOMISTIC	AUTHORIZE	ABHORENCE	ACCEPTEDLY

ACCESSIBLE	ACTIVATING	ADVENTURES	AFTERPAINS
ACCESSIONS	ACTIVENESS	ADVERBIALS	AFTERPIECE
ACCESS TIME	ACTIVITIES	ADVERTENCE	AFTERSHAFT
ACCIDENTAL	ACTOMYSIN	ADVERTISED	AFTERSHAVE
ACCIPTIRAL	ADACTYLOUS	ADVERTISER	AFTERSHOCK
ACCLAIMING	ADAMANTINE	ADVOCATING	AFTERTASTE
ACCOMPLICE	ADAM'S APPLE	ADVOCATION	AFTERWARDS
ACCOMPLISH	ADAPTATION	ADVOCATORY	AGAMICALLY
ACCORDABLE	ADDICTIONS	ADZUKI BEAN	AGAPANTHUS
ACCORDANCE	ADDIS ABABA	AECIOSCOPE	AGGLUTININ
ACCORDIONS	ADDITIONAL	AERENCHYMA	AGGRANDIZE
ACCOSTABLE	ADDRESSES	AEROBATICS	AGGRAVATED
ACCOUNTANT	ADDRESSING	AEROBIOSIS	AGGREGATED
ACCOUNTING	ADDUCEABLE	AEROBIOTIC	AGGREGATES
ACCREDITED	ADENECTOMY	AERODROMES	AGGRESSION
ACCRESCENT	ADENOVIRUS	AERO-ENGINE	AGGRESSIVE
ACCRETIONS	ADEQUATELY	AEROGRAMME	AGGRESSORS
ACCUMBENCY	ADIRONDACK	AEROGRAPHY	AGITATIONS
ACCUMULATE	ADJECTIVES	AEROLOGIST	AGREEMENTS
ACCURATELY	ADJOURNING	AEROMETRIC	AGRONOMICS
ACCUSATION	ADJUDICATE	AERONAUTIC	AGRONOMIST
ACCUSATIVE	ADJUNCTION	AEROPHAGIA	AGRYPNOTIC
ACCUSATIVE	ADJURATION	AEROPHOBIC	AHMEDNAGAR
ACCUSINGLY	ADJURATORY	AEROPLANES	AIDE-DE-CAMP
ACCUSTOMED	ADJUSTMENT	AEROSPHERE	AIR-HOSTESS
ACEPHALOUS	ADMINISTER	AEROSTATIC	AIR-LETTERS
ACETABULUM	ADMIRATION	AESTHETICS	AIR LIFTING
ACETIC ACID	ADMIRINGLY	AESTIVATOR	AIR-POCKETS
ACETOMETER	ADMISSIBLE	AFFABILITY	ALACRITOUS
ACETYLENIC	ADMISSIONS	AFFECTEDLY	ALARM CLOCK
ACHIEVABLE	ADMITTANCE	AFFECTIONS	ALARMINGLY
ACHRONDITE	ADMITTEDLY	AFFETTUOSO	ALBESCENCE
ACHROMATIC	ADMIXTURES	AFFIDAVITS	ALBUMENIZE
ACHROMATIN	ADMONISHED	AFFILIATED	ALBUMINATE
ACIDIFYING	ADMONISHER	AFFILIATES	ALBUMINOID
ACIDIMETER	ADMONITION	AFFINITIES	ALBUMINOUS
ACIDOMETER	ADMONITORY	AFFINITIVE	ALCHEMIST
ACIERATION	ADOLESCENT	AFFLICTION	ALCOHOLICS
ACOTYLEDON	ADORNMENTS	AFFLICTING	ALCOHOLISM
ACQUAINTED	ADRENALINE	AFFLICTIVE	ALCOHOLIZE
ACQUIESCED	ADRENERGIC	AFFORDABLE	ALDERMANIAC
ACQUIRABLE	ADROITNESS	AFFORESTED	ALGERBRAIST
ACQUITTALS	ADSORBABLE	AFFRICATES	ALGOLAGNIA
ACQUITTING	ADSORPTION	AFFRONTING	ALGOLAGNIC
ACROBATICS	ADULTERANT	AFICIONADO	ALGONQUIAN
ACROMEGALY	ADULTERATE	AFRIKANDER	ALGORISMIC
ACRONYCHAL	ADULTERERS	AFRIKANERS	ALGORITHMS
ACROPHOBIA	ADULTERESS	AFTERBIRTH	ALIENATING
ACTABILITY	ADULTERINE	AFTERBRAIN	ALIGNMENTS
ACTINIFORM	ADULTEROUS	AFTERGLOWS	ALIMENTARY
ACTINOLITE	ADUMBRATED	AFTERIMAGE	ALKALINITY
ACTINOMERE	ADVANTAGES	AFTERLIVES	ALKYLATION
ACTINOZOAN	ADVENTITIA	AFTERMATHS	ALLARGANDO
ACTIONABLE	ADVENTURER	AFTERNOONS	ALLEGATION

ALLEGIENCE	AMBULATION	ANASTOMOSE	ANOINTMENT
ALLEGORIES	AMBULATORY	ANATOMICAL	ANORTHITIC
ALLEGORIST	AMELIORANT	ANATOMISTS	ANSWERABLE
ALLEGORIZE	AMELIORATE	ANATOMIZER	ANSWERABLY
ALLEGRETTO	AMENDMENTS	ANATROPOUS	ANTAGONISM
ALLERGENIC	AMERINDIAN	ANCESTRESS	ANTAGONIST
ALLEVIATED	AMIABILITY	ANCESTRIES	ANTAGONIZE
ALLEVIATOR	AMINO ACIDS	ANCHORAGES	ANTARCTICA
ALLIACEOUS	AMMONIACAL	ANCHORITES	ANTEBELLUM
ALLIGATORS	AMMUNITION	ANDALUSITE	ANTECEDENT
ALLITERATE	AMOEBIASIS	ANDROECIAL	ANTEDATING
ALLOCATING	AMOEBOCYTE	ANDROECIUM	ANTE-MORTEM
ALLOCATION	AMORTIZING	ANDROGENIC	ANTEPENULT
ALLOCUTION	AMPELOPSIS	ANECDOTAGE	ANTHOPHORE
ALLOGAMOUS	AMPERSANDS	ANECDOTIST	ANTHRACENE
ALLOMERISM	AMPHEATRIC	ANEMICALLY	ANTHRACITE
ALLOMEROUS	AMPHIASTER	ANEMOCHORE	ANTHRAPOID
ALLOMETRIC	AMPHIBIANS	ANEMOGRAPH	ANTIBARYON
ALLOPATHIC	AMPHIBIOUS	ANEMOMETER	ANTIBIOSIS
ALLOPATRIC	AMPHIBOLIC	ANEMOMETRY	ANTIBIOTIC
ALLOPHONIC	AMPHIBRACH	ANEMOPHILY	ANTIBODIES
ALLOTMENTS	AMPHICYTON	ANEMOSCOPE	ANTICHRIST
ALLOTROPIC	AMPHIGORIC	ANESTHESIA	ANTICIPANT
ALLOWANCES	AMPHIMACER	ANESTHETIC	ANTICIPATE
ALL-PURPOSE	AMPHIMIXES	ANEURYSMAL	ANTICLIMAX
ALL-ROUNDER	AMPHOTERIC	ANGELOLOGY	ANTICLINAL
ALLUREMENT	AMPLIFIERS	ANGIOSPERM	ANTIDROMIC
ALLUSIVELY	AMPLIFYING	ANGLICISMS	ANTIFREEZE
ALMA MATERS	AMPUTATING	ANGLICIZED	ANTIHEROES
ALMIGHTIER	AMPUTATION	ANGLOPHILE	ANTILEPTON
ALMIGHTILY	AMUSEMENTS	ANGLOPHOBE	ANTILOGISM
ALMS-HOUSES	AMYGDALATE	ANGLOPHONE	ANTIMATTER
ALONGSHORE	AMYGDALINE	ANGLO-SAXON	ANTIMERISM
ALPENSTOCK	AMYGDALOID	ANGULARITY	ANTIMONIAL
ALPESTRINE	AMYLACEOUS	ANGULATION	ANTIMONOUS
ALTARPIECE	AMYLOLYSIS	ANIMADVERT	ANTIOPHONAL
ALTERATION	ANABOLITIC	ANIMACULE	ANTIPODEAN
ALTERATIVE	ANACHORISM	ANIMATEDLY	ANTIPROTON
ALTERNATIVE	ANACOUSTIC	ANISTROPHY	ANTIPYRINE
ALTERNATED	ANACRUSTIC	ANKYLOSAUR	ANTIQUATED
ALTERNATOR	ANADROMOUS	ANNALISTIC	ANTI-SEMITE
ALTIMETERS	ANAGLYPHIC	ANNEXATION	ANTISEPSIS
ALTOGETHER	ANALGESICS	ANNIHILATE	ANTISEPTIC
ALTRUISTIC	ANALOGICAL	ANNO-DOMINI	ANTISOCIAL
AMALGAMATE	ANALYSABLE	ANNOTATING	ANTISTATIC
AMANUENSIS	ANAMNESTIC	ANNOTATION	ANTITHESIS
AMATUERISH	ANAMORPHIC	ANNOTATIVE	ANTITRADES
AMATUERISM	ANAPAESTIC	ANNOUNCERS	ANTITRAGUS
AMBASSADOR	ANAPLASTIC	ANNOUNCING	APARTMENTS
AMBIVALENT	ANAPTYCTIC	ANNOYANCES	APHORISTIC
AMBOCEPTOR	ANARCHISTS	ANNULATION	APHRODISIA
AMBULACRAL	ANARTHROUS	ANNULLABLE	APICULTURE
AMBULACRUM	ANASARCOUS	ANNULMENTS	APIOLOGIST
AMBULANCES	ANASTIGMAT	ANNUNCIATE	APLACENTAL

355

APOCOLYPSE	APPROXIMAL	ART NOUVEAU	ASTRONAUTS
APOCARPOUS	APRIL FOOLS	ARTY-CRAFTY	ASTRONOMER
APOCHROMAT	AQUAMARINE	ASBESTOSIS	ASTUTENESS
APOCRYPHAL	AQUAPHOBIA	ASCARIASIS	ASYMMETRIC
APOLITICAL	AQUAPLANED	ASCENDANCY	ASYMPTOTIC
APOLOGETIC	AQUAPLANES	ASCENDANTS	ATHERMANCY
APOLOGISTS	ARABESQUES	ASCETICISM	ATMOSPHERE
APOLOGIZED	ARACHNIDAN	ASCRIBABLE	ATOMICALLY
APOLOGIZER	ARAUCANIAN	ASCRIPTION	ATOMIC PILE
APOPHTHEGM	ARBITRABLE	ASEXUALITY	ATROCITIES
APOPHYSATE	ARBITRATED	ASPERSIONS	ATROPHYING
APOPHYSIAL	ARBITRATOR	ASPHALTING	ATTACHABLE
APOPLECTIC	ARCHAISTIC	ASPHALTITE	ATTACHMENT
APOSEMATIC	ARCHANGELS	ASPHYXIANT	ATTAINABLE
APOSTASIES	ARCHBISHOP	ASPHYXIATE	ATTAINMENT
APOSTATIZE	ARCHDEACON	ASPIDISTRA	ATTEMPTING
APOSTOLATE	ARCHERFISH	ASPIRATING	ATTENDANCE
APOSTROPHE	ARCHESPORE	ASPIRATION	ATTENDANTS
APOTHECARY	ARCHETYPAL	ASPIRATORY	ATTENTIONS
APOTHETICAL	ARCHETYPES	ASSAILABLE	ATTENUATED
APOTHETICUM	ARCHIMEDES	ASSAILANTS	ATTENUATOR
APOTHEOSES	ARCHITECTS	ASSAILMENT	ATTESTABLE
APOTROPSIC	ARCHITRAVE	ASSAULTING	ATTORNMENT
APPALACHIA	ARCHIVISTS	ASSEMBLAGE	ATTRACTING
APPARALLED	ARCHOPLASM	ASSEMBLIES	ATTRACTION
APPARENTLY	ARCTOGAEAN	ASSEMBLING	ATTRACTIVE
APPARITION	ARC WELDING	ASSERTIBLE	ATTRIBUTED
APPEALABLE	AREANCEOUS	ASSERTIONS	ATTRIBUTER
APPEARANCE	AREOGRAPHY	ASSESSABLE	ATTRIBUTES
APPEASABLE	AREOLATION	ASSEVERATE	ATYPICALLY
APPENDAGES	ARGILLITIC	ASSIBILATE	AUBERGINES
APPENDICES	ARGUMENTUM	ASSIGNABLE	AUCTIONEER
APPENDICLE	ARTISTOCRAT	ASSIGNMENT	AUCTIONING
APPENDIXES	ARITHMETIC	ASSIMILATE	AUDIBILITY
APPERCEIVE	ARMADILLOS	ASSISTANCE	AUDIOGENIC
APPETIZERS	ARMAGEDDON	ASSISTANTS	AUDIOMETER
APPETIZING	ARMIPOTENT	ASSOCIABLE	AUDIOMETRY
APPLAUDING	ARMISTICES	ASSOCIATED	AUDITIONED
APPLE CARTS	ARRAIGNING	ASSOCIATES	AUGMENTING
APPLIANCES	ARRHYTHMIA	ASSORTMENT	AURICULATE
APPLICABLE	ARROGANTLY	ASSUMPTION	AURIFEROUS
APPLICANTS	ARROGATING	ASSUMPTIVE	AUSCULTATE
APPLICATOR	ARROGATION	ASSURANCES	AUSFORMING
APPOINTEES	ARROGATIVE	ASTERISKED	AUSPICIOUS
APPOINTING	ARROWHEADS	ASTEROIDAL	AUSTRALIAN
APPOSITION	ARTFULNESS	ASTHENOPIA	AUSTRALOID
APPOSITIVE	ARTHRALGIA	ASTHENOPIC	AUSTRALORP
APPRAISALS	ARTHRALGIC	ASTHMATICS	AUTARCHIES
APPRAISING	ARTHRITICS	ASTOMATOUS	AUTECOLOGY
APPRAISIVE	ARTHROMERE	ASTONISHED	AUTHORIZED
APPRECIATE	ARTICHOKES	ASTOUNDED	AUTHORIZER
APPRENTICE	ARTICULATE	ASTRINGENT	AUTHORSHIP
APPROACHED	ARTIFICERS	ASTROLOGER	AUTOCRATIC
APPROACHES	ARTIFICIAL	ASTROMETRY	AUTOECIOUS

AUTOGAMOUS	ABSENTEEISM	ACHROMATISM	ADVANCEMENT
AUTOGENOUS	ABSORBINGLY	ACHROMATIZE	ADVANCINGLY
AUTOGRAPHS	ABSORPTANCE	ACHROMATOUS	ADVENTURERS
AUTOMATICS	ABSTENTIONS	ACID-FORMING	ADVENTURESS
AUTOMATING	ABSTENTIOUS	ACIDIFIABLE	ADVENTURISM
AUTOMATION	ABSTRACTING	ACIDIMETRIC	ADVENTURIST
AUTOMATISM	ABSTRACTION	ACIDOPHILIC	ADVENTUROUS
AUTOMATIST	ABSTRACTIVE	ACIDOPHILUS	ADVERBIALLY
AUTOMATONS	ABSTRICTION	ACIDULATION	ADVERSARIAL
AUTOMATOUS	ABSURDITIES	ACINACIFORM	ADVERSARIES
AUTOMOBILE	ABUSIVENESS	ACKNOWLEDGE	ADVERSATIVE
AUTOMOTIVE	ACADEMICALS	ACLINIC LINE	ADVERSITIES
AUTONOMIST	ACADEMICIAN	ACOUSTICIAN	ADVERTENTLY
AUTONOMOUS	ACADEMICISM	ACQUAINTING	ADVERTISERS
AUTOPHYTIC	ACARPELLOUS	ACQUIESCENT	ADVERTISING
AUTOPLASTY	ACATALECTIC	ACQUIESCING	AERODYNAMIC
AUTOSTRADA	ACAULESCENT	ACQUIREMENT	AEROGRAMMES
AUTOTOMIZE	ACCELERANDO	ACQUISITION	AERONAUTICS
AUTUMNALLY	ACCELERATED	ACQUISITIVE	AEROSTATICS
AUXOCHROME	ACCELERATOR	ACQUITTANCE	AEROSTATION
AVALANCHES	ACCENTUATED	ACROFLAVINE	AESTIVATION
AVANT-GARDE	ACCEPTANCES	ACRIMONIOUS	AETIOLOGIST
AVARICIOUS	ACCEPTATION	ACROCARPOUS	AFFECTATION
AVELLANEDA	ACCESSORIAL	ACROMEGALIC	AFFECTINGLY
AVENTURINE	ACCESSORIES	ACTINICALLY	AFFECTIONAL
AVICULTURE	ACCESSORILY	ACTINOMETER	AFFECTIVITY
AVOCATIONS	ACCIPITRINE	ACTINOMETRY	AFFILIATING
AVENCULATE	ACCLAMATION	ACTINOMYCIN	AFFILIATION
AWAKENINGS	ACCLAMATORY	ACTUALITIES	AFFIRMATION
AXIOLOGIST	ACCLIMATIZE	ACUMINATION	AFFIRMATIVE
	ACCLIVITIES	ACUPUNCTURE	AFFLICTIONS
	ACCLIVITOUS	ADAM'S APPLES	AFFORESTING
11 LETTERS	ACCOMMODATE	ADAPTATIONS	AFFRANCHISE
ABANDONEDLY	ACCOMPANIED	ADIAPHORISM	AFFRICATIVE
ABANDONMENT	ACCOMPANIER	ADIAPHORIST	AFGHANISTAN
ABBEVILLIAN	ACCOMPANIST	ADIAPHOROUS	AFICTIONADOS
ABBREVIATED	ACCOMPLICES	AD INFINITUM	AFRO-ASIATIC
ABBREVIATOR	ACCORDANCES	ADIPOCEROUS	AFTERBIRTHS
ABDICATIONS	ACCORDINGLY	ADJOURNMENT	AFTERBURNER
ABERRATIONS	ACCOUNTABLE	ADJUDICATED	AFTEREFFECT
ABIETIC ACID	ACCOUNTANCY	ADJUDICATOR	AFTERSHAVES
ABIOGENESIS	ACCOUNTANTS	ADJUSTMENTS	AFTERTASTES
ABIOGENERIC	ACCULTURATE	ADMIRATIONS	AGELESSNESS
ABLUTIONARY	ACCUMULABLE	ADMONISHING	AGGLOMERATE
ABNORMALITY	ACCUMULATED	ADMONITIONS	AGGLUTINANT
ABOLISHMENT	ACCUMULATOR	ADOLESCENCE	AGGLUTINATE
ABOMINATING	ACCUSATIONS	ADOLESCENTS	AGGRADATION
ABOMINATION	ACCUSATIVAL	ADOPTIONISM	AGGRANDIZER
ABORIGINALS	ACCUSATIVES	ADOPTIONIST	AGGRAVATING
ABORTIONIST	ACCUSTOMING	ADULTERATED	AGGRAVATION
ABRACADABRA	ACETANILIDE	ADULTERATOR	AGGREGATING
ABRANCHIATE	ACETYLATION	ADUMBRATING	AGGRAGATION
ABRIDGEMENT	ACHIEVEMENT	ADUMBRATION	AGGRIEVEDLY
ABROGATIONS	ACHONDRITIC	ADUMBRATIVE	AGNOSTICISM

AGONIZINGLY	ALTERNATING	ANASTOMOSIS	ANTHOLOGIES
AGONY COLUMN	ALTERNATION	ANASTOMOTIC	ANTHOLOGIST
AGORAPHOBIA	ALTERNATIVE	ANCIENTNESS	ANTHOLOGIZE
AGORAPHOBIC	ALTERNATORS	ANCILLARIES	ANTHERACITIC
AGRARIANISM	ALTITUDINAL	ANDROGENOUS	ANTHRACNOSE
AGRICULTURE	ALTOCUMULUS	ANDROGNOUS	ANTIBIOTICS
AGROBIOLOGY	ALTOGETHERS	ANDROSPHINX	ANTICATHODE
AGROLOGICAL	ALTOSTRATUS	ANEMOGRAPHY	ANTICIPATED
AGROSTOLOGY	ALUMINOSITY	AMEMOMETERS	ANTICIPATOR
AIDE-MEMOIRE	ALVEOLATION	ANEMOMETRIC	ANTICLASTIC
AIDES-DE-CAMP	AMALGAMATED	ANESTHETICS	ANTICYCLONE
AILUROPHILE	ANARANTHINE	ANESTHETIST	ANTIFENRILE
AILUROPHOBE	AMBASSADORS	ANESTHETIZE	ANTIFOULING
AIMLESSNESS	AMBIGUOUSLY	ANFRACTUOUS	ANTIMISSILE
AIRCRAFTMAN	AMBITIOUSLY	ANGLICANISM	ANTINEUTRON
AIRCRAFTMEN	AMBIVALENCE	ANGLICIZING	ANTINUCLEAR
AIRLESSNESS	AMBLYGONITE	ANGLO-INDIAN	ANTINUCLEON
AIRSICKNESS	AMELIORATED	ANGLOPHILES	ANTIOXIDANT
AIR TERMINAL	AMELIORATOR	ANGLOPHILIA	ANTIPATHIES
ALARM CLOCKS	AMENABILITY	ANGLOPHOBES	ANTIPHONARY
ALBATROSSES	AMINOPHENOL	ANGLOPHOBIA	ANTIPHRASIS
ALBUMINURIA	AMINOPYRINE	ANGLO-SAXONS	ANTIPYRESIS
ALBUQUERQUE	AMMONIATION	ANIMOSITIES	ANTIPYRETIC
ALDOSTERONE	AMONTILLADO	ANISODACTYL	ANTIQUARIAN
ALESSANDRIA	AMOROUSNESS	ANISOGAMOUS	ANTIQUITIES
ALGEBRAICAL	AMOR PATRIAE	ANIOSMEROUS	ANTIRRHINUM
ALGINIC ACID	AMORPHOUSLY	ANISOMETRIC	ANTISEMITES
ALGOLAGNIST	AMORTIZABLE	ANISOPTROPIC	ANTISEMITIC
ALGORITHMIC	AMOUR-PROPRE	ANNABERGITE	ANTISEPTICS
ALKALIMETER	AMPHETAMINE	ANNEXATIONS	ANTITUSSIVE
ALKALIMETRY	AMPHIBIOTIC	ANNIHILABLE	ANTOFAGASTA
ALKALIZABLE	AMPHIBOLITE	ANNIHILATED	ANTONOMASIA
ALL-AMERICAN	AMPHIBOLOGY	ANNIHILATOR	ANXIOUSNESS
ALLANTOIDAL	AMPHICHORIC	ANNIVERSARY	APHETICALLY
ALLEGATIONS	AMPHICTYONY	ANNOTATIONS	APHRODISIAC
ALLEGIANCES	AMPHISBAENA	ANNUNCIATOR	APICULTURAL
ALLEGORICAL	AMPHISTYLAR	ANOINTMENTS	APOCALYPSES
ALLEVIATING	AMPHITRICHA	ANOMALISTIC	APOCALYPTIC
ALLEVIATION	AMPLEXICAUL	ANOMALOUSLY	APOCOPATION
ALLEVIATIVE	AMPLIFIABLE	ANONYMOUSLY	APOCYNTHION
ALLOCATIONS	AMPUTATIONS	ANORTHOSITE	APOLOGETICS
ALLOGRAPHIC	AMYLOPECTIN	ANTAGONISMS	APOLOGIZING
ALLOMORPHIC	ANACHRONISM	ANTAGONISTS	APOMORPHINE
ALLOPLASMIC	ANACOLUTHIC	ANTAGONIZED	APONEUROSIS
ALLOPURINOL	ANACOLUTHON	ANTALKALINE	APONEUROTIC
ALL-POWERFUL	ANADIPLOSIS	ANTECEDENCE	APOPHYLLITE
ALL-ROUNDERS	ANAEMICALLY	ANTECEDENTS	APOSIOPESIS
ALLUREMENTS	ANAESTHESIA	ANTECHAMBER	APOSIOPETRIC
ALMIGHTIEST	ANAESTHETIC	ANTEPENDIUM	A POSTERIORI
ALPHABETIZE	ANALEMMATIC	ANTEVERSION	APOSTOPHES
ALTARPIECES	ANALYSATION	ANTHERIDIAL	APOTHEOSIZE
ALTERATIONS	ANAMORPHISM	ANTHERIDIUM	APPALLINGLY
ALTERCATION	ANAPHYLAXIS	ANTHEROZOID	APPARATCHIK
ALTERNATELY	ANARCHISTIC	ANTHOCYANIN	APPARATUSES

APPARELLING	ARCHENTERON	ASSYRIOLOGY	AUSTRALASIA
APPEALINGLY	ARCHIPELAGO	ASTATICALLY	AUSTRALIANS
APPARITIONS	ARDUOUSNESS	ASTERISKING	AUSTRONESIA
APPEALINGLY	ARENICOLOUS	ASTIGMATISM	AUTHORITIES
APPEARANCES	ARGENTINEAN	ASTONISHING	AUTHORIZING
APPEASEMENT	ARISTOCRACY	ASTRAPHOBIA	AUTOCHANGER
APPELLATION	ARISTOCRATS	ASTRAPHOBIC	AUTOCRACIES
APPELLATIVE	ARMED FORCES	ASTRINGENCY	AUTOGENESIS
APPERTAINED	ARMIPOTENCE	ASTRINGENTS	AUTOGENETIC
APPLICATION	ARMOURED CAR	ASTROBOTANY	AUTOGRAPHED
APPLICATIVE	ARMOUR PLATE	ASTROLOGERS	AUTOGRAPHIC
APPLICATORY	AROMATICITY	ASTROMETRIC	AUTOKINETIC
APPOINTMENT	ARONOMASTIC	ASTRONAUTIC	AUTOMOBILES
APPORTIONED	ARRAIGNMENT	ASTRONOMERS	AUTOPLASTIC
APPORTIONER	ARRANGEMENT	ASTROSPHERE	AUTOTROPHIC
APPRECIABLE	ARRESTINGLY	ATELECTASIS	AUXANOMETER
APPRECIABLY	ARTERIALIZE	ATHEISTICAL	AUXILIARIES
APPRECIATED	ARTHROMERIC	ATHERMANOUS	AVOIRDUPOIS
APPREHENDED	ARTHROSPORE	ATHLETICISM	AVUNCULARLY
APPRENTICED	ARTICULATED	ATMOSPHERES	AWESOMENESS
APPRENTICES	ARTICULATOR	ATMOSPHERIC	AWKWARDNESS
APPROACHING	ARTILLERIES	ATOMIC PILES	
APPROBATION	ARTIODACTYL	ATOMIZATION	
APPROBATIVE	ARTLESSNESS	ATROCIOUSLY	**12 LETTERS**
APPROPRIATE	ARYTENODIAL	ATTACHE CASE	ABBREVIATING
APPROVINGLY	ASCENSIONAL	ATTACHMENTS	ABBREVIATION
APPROXIMATE	ASCERTAINED	ATTAINMENTS	ABELIAN GROUP
APPURTENANT	ASCETICALLY	ATTEMPTABLE	ABOLITIONARY
AQUACULTURE	ASKING PRICE	ATTENDANCES	ABOLITIONISM
AQUAMARINES	ASPERGILLUS	ATTENTIVELY	ABOLITIONIST
AQUAPLANNING	ASPHYXIATED	ATTENUATING	ABOMINATIONS
AQUARELLIST	ASPIDISTRAS	ATTENUATION	ABORTIONISTS
AQUATICALLY	ASPIRATIONS	ATTESTATION	ABRACADABRAS
AQUICULTURE	ASSASSIINATE	ATTITUDINAL	ABSENT-MINDED
ARALIACEOUS	ASSEMBLAGES	ATTRACTABLE	ABSOLUTENESS
ARBITRAGEUR	ASSEMBLYMAN	ATTRACTIONS	ABSOLUTE ZERO
ARBITRAMENT	ASSEMBLYMEN	ATTRIBUTING	ABSORPTIVITY
ARBITRARILY	ASSENTATION	ATTRIBUTION	ABSTEMIOUSLY
ARBITRATING	ASSERTIVELY	ATTRIBUTIVE	ABSTRACTEDLY
ARBITRATING	ASSESSMENTS	ATTRITIONAL	ABSTRACTIONS
ARBITRATION	ASSESSORIAL	AUCTIONEERS	ABSTRUSENESS
ARBITRATORS	ASSEVERATED	AUDACIOUSLY	ACADEMICALLY
ARBORESCENT	ASSIDUOUSLY	AUDIOLOGIST	ACADEMICIANS
ARCHAEOLOGY	ASSIGNATION	AUDIOMETRIC	ACANTHACEOUS
ARCHAEOZOIC	ASSIGNMENTS	AUDIOTYPING	ACCELERATING
ARCHAICALLY	ASSIMILABLE	AUDIOTYPIST	ACCELERATION
ARCHANGELLIC	ASSIMILATED	AUDIOVISUAL	ACCELERATIVE
ARCHBISHOPS	ASSOCIATING	AUDITIONING	ACCELERATORS
ARCHDEACONS	ASSOCIATION	AUDITORIUMS	ACCENTUATING
ARCHDIOCESE	ASSOCIATIVE	AUGMENTABLE	ACCENTUATION
ARCHDUCHESS	ASSORTMENTS	AURIGNACIAN	ACCIACCATURA
ARCHEGONIUM	ASSUAGEMENT	AUSCULTATOR	ACCIDENTALLY
ARCHENEMIES	ASSUMPTIONS	AUSTERENESS	ACCLAMATIONS
ARCHENTERIC	ASSUREDNESS	AUSTERITIES	ACCLIMATIZED

ACCLIMATIZER	AFFECTATIONS	AMBASSADRESS	ANNUNCIATIVE
ACCOMMODATED	AFFECTEDNESS	AMBIDEXTROUS	ANTAGONISTIC
ACCOMPANISTS	AFFECTIONATE	AMBITENDENCY	ANTAGONIZING
ACCOMPANYING	AFFILIATIONS	AMBIVALENTLY	ANTECHAMBERS
ACCOMPLISHED	AFFIRMATIVES	AMELIORATING	ANTEDILUVIAN
ACCOMPLISHER	AFORETHOUGHT	AMELIORATIVE	ANTEMERIDIAN
ACCORDIONIST	AFRIKANEROM	AMERICANISMS	ANTHOLOGICAL
ACCOUPLEMENT	AFRO-AMERICAN	AMERICANIZED	ANTEOLOGISTS
ACCOUTREMENT	AFTERBURNING	AMERICANIZER	ANTHROPOIDAL
ACCUMULATING	AFTEREFFECTS	AMITOTICALLY	ANTHROPOLOGY
ACCUMULATION	AFTERTHOUGHT	AMORTIZATION	ANTI-AIRCRAFT
ACCUMULATIVE	AGAMOGENESIS	AMORTIZEMENT	ANTICATALYST
ACCUMULATORS	AGAMOGENETIC	AMPHETAMINES	ANTICIPATING
ACCUSTATORIAL	AGARICACEOUS	AMPHIBRACHIC	ANTICIPATION
ACETALDEHYDE	AGE OF CONSENT	AMPHICOELOUS	ANTICIPATIVE
ACHIEVEMENTS	AGGLOMERATED	AMPHICTYONIC	ANTICIPATORY
ACHILLES' HEEL	AGGLUTINABLE	AMPHIDIPLOID	ANTICLERICAL
ACHLAMYDEOUS	AGGLUTINOGEN	AMPHISBAENIC	ANTICLIMAXES
ACHLORHYDRIA	AGGRAVATIONS	AMPHITHEATRE	ANTICYCLONES
ACKNOWLEDGED	AGGREGATIONS	AMPHITHECIUM	ANTICYCLONIC
ACKNOWLEDGER	AGGRESSIVELY	AMPHITROPOUS	ANTIHALATION
ACOUSTICALLY	AGONY COLUMNS	AMPULLACEOUS	ANTIMACASSAR
ACQUIESCENCE	AGORAPHONICS	AMYGDALOIDAL	ANTIMAGNETIC
ACQUISITIONS	AGRICULTURAL	ANACHRONISMS	ANTINEUTRINO
ACROSTICALLY	AILUROPHILIA	ANAESTHETICS	ANTIPARALLEL
ACTINOMETRIC	AILUROPHOBIA	ANAESTHETIST	ANTIPARTICLE
ACTINOMYCETE	AIR COMMODORE	ANAESTHETIZE	ANTIPATHETIC
ADAPTABILITY	AIR-CONDITION	ANAGOGICALLY	ANTIPERIODIC
ADDITIONALLY	AIRHOSTESSES	ANAGRAMMATIC	ANTIQUARIANS
ADHESIVENESS	AIR TERMINALS	ANALYTICALLY	ANTIRACHITIC
ADJECTIVALLY	ALCOHOLICITY	ANAMORPHOSIS	ANTISEMITISM
ADJOURNMENTS	ALHAMBRESQUE	ANAPHRODISTA	ANTITHETICAL
ADJUDICATING	ALIENABILITY	ANAPHYLACTIC	ANTONOMASTIC
ADJUDICATION	ALIMENTATION	ANARCHICALLY	AORISTICALLY
ADJUDICATORS	ALIMENTATIVE	ANASTIGMATIC	APAGOGICALLY
ADMINISTERED	ALKALIMETRIC	ANATOMICALLY	APERIODICITY
ADMINISTRATE	ALL-IMPORTANT	ANCHORPERSON	APHRODISIACS
ADSCITITIOUS	ALL-INCLUSIVE	ANCIEN REGIME	APICULTURIST
ADULTERATING	ALLITERATION	ANDROSTERONE	APLANOSPERE
ADULTERATION	ALLITERATIVE	ANEMOGRAPHIC	APOCHROMATIC
ADUMBRATIONS	ALLOMORPHISM	ANEMOPHILIOUS	APOCYNACEOUS
ADVANTAGEOUS	ALLUSIVENESS	ANESTHETISTS	APOGEOTROPIC
ADVENTITIOUS	ALMIGHTINESS	ANESTHETIZED	APOSTROPHIZE
ADVISABILITY	ALPHABETICAL	ANGLO-INDIANS	APOTHECARIES
AERIFICATION	ALPHABETIZER	ANGLO-PHILIAC	APPALACHIANS
AERODONETICS	ALPHANUMERIC	ANGUILLIFORM	APPARATCHIKS
AEROEMBOLISM	ALTERABILITY	ANGULARITIES	APPARENTNESS
AEROMECHANIC	ALTERCATIONS	ANIMADVERTED	APPASSIONATO
AERONAUTICAL	ALTERNATIONS	ANNEXATIONAL	APPEASEMENTS
AERONEUROSIS	ALTERNATIVES	ANNIHILATING	APPELLATIONS
AESTHETICIAN	ALTIMETRICAL	ANNIHILATION	APPENDECTOMY
AESTHETICISM	AMALGAMATING	ANNIHILATIVE	APPENDICITIS
AETHEREALITY	AMALGAMATION	ANNOUNCEMENT	APPENDICULAR
AETIOLOGICAL	AMATEURISHLY	ANNUNCIATION	APPERCEPTION

APPERCEPTIVE	ASCENSION DAY	AUTOGRAPHING	AGGLOMERATION
APPERTAINING	ASCERTAINING	AUTOHYPNOSIS	AGGLUTINATION
APPETIZINGLY	ASCOMYCETOUS	AUTOHYPNOTIC	AGGRAVATINGLY
APPLAUDINGLY	ASH WEDNESDAY	AUTOMOBILIST	AGREEABLENESS
APPLICATIONS	ASKING PRICES	AUTONOMOUSLY	AGRICULTURIST
APPOGGIATURA	ASPHYXIATING	AUTOROTATION	AIR COMMODORES
APPOINTMENTS	ASPHYXIATION	AUTOXIDATION	AIRWORTHINESS
APPORTIONING	ASSASSINATED	AVAILABILITY	ALCOHOLICALLY
APPRAISINGLY	ASSEMBLY LINE	AVARICOUSLY	ALGEBRAICALLY
APPRECIATING	ASSEVERATING	AVICULTURIST	ALLEGORICALLY
APPRECIATION	ASSEVERATION	AVITAMINOSIS	ALTERNATIVELY
APPRECIATIVE	ASSIBILATION	AVOGADRO'S LAW	ALUMINIFEROUS
APPREHENDING	ASSIGNATIONS	AWE-INSPIRING	ALUMINOTHERMY
APPREHENSION	ASSIMILATING		AMALGAMATIONS
APPREHENSIVE	ASSIMILATION		AMBASSADORIAL
APPRENTICING	ASSIMILATIVE	**13 LETTERS**	AMBIDEXTERITY
APPROACHABLE	ASSOCIATIONS	ABBREVIATIONS	AMBIGUOUSNESS
APPROPRIABLE	ASTONISHMENT	ABNORMALITIES	AMBITIOUSNESS
APPROPRIATED	ASTOUDINGLY	ABOLITIONISTS	AMERICANIZING
APPROXIMATED	ASTRINGENTLY	ABSORBABILITY	AMNIOCENTESIS
APPURTENANCE	ASTROBIOLOGY	ACCENTUATIONS	AMPITHEATRES
APRON STRINGS	ASTROCOMPASS	ACCEPTABILITY	AMPLIFICATION
AQUICULTURAL	ASTROGEOLOGY	ACCESSIBILITY	AMUSEMENT PARK
ARBITRAGEURS	ASTROLOGICAL	ACCIDENT-PRONE	ANACHRONISTIC
ARBORESCENCE	ASTRONAUTICS	ACCLIMATIZING	ANAESTHETISTS
ARBORIZATION	ASTRONOMICAL	ACCOMMODATING	ANAESTHETIZED
ARCHDEACONRY	ASTROPHYSICS	ACCOMMODATION	ANAGRAMMATISM
ARCHDIOCESAN	ASYMPTOMATIC	ACCOMMODATIVE	ANAGRAMMATIST
ARCHDIOCESES	ASYNCHRONISM	ACCOMPANIMENT	ANAGRAMMATIZE
ARCHESPORIAL	ASYNCHRONOUS	ACCOMPLISHING	ANAPHORICALLY
ARCHETYPICAL	ATHEROMATOUS	ACCOUTREMENTS	ANAPHRODISIAC
ARCHIPELAGIC	ATHLETE'S FOOT	ACCREDITATION	ANATHEMATIZED
ARCHIPELAGOS	ATHLETICALLY	ACCUMULATIONS	ANATOMIZATION
ARCHITECTURE	ATHWARTSHIPS	ACIDIFICATION	ANCHORPERSONS
ARCHOPLASMIC	ATMOSPHERICS	ACKNOWLEDGING	ANESTHETIZING
ARCTIC CIRCLE	ATOMIC ENERGY	ACQUAINTANCES	ANGLICIZATION
ARGILLACEOUS	ATTACHE CASES	ACQUIESCENTLY	ANGLO-AMERICAN
ARISTOCRATIC	ATTESTATIONS	ACQUISITIVELY	ANGLO-CATHOLIC
ARMOURED CARS	ATTESTED MILK	ACRIMONIOUSLY	ANIMADVERSION
ARMOUR-PLATED	ATTITUDINIZE	ACROBATICALLY	ANIMADVERTING
AROMATICALLY	ATTRACTIVELY	ACTUALIZATION	ANIMALIZATION
ARRAIGNMENTS	ATTRIBUTABLE	ADENOIDECTOMY	ANNIVERSARIES
ARRANGEMENTS	AUDIOLOGICAL	ADMINISTERING	ANNOUNCEMENTS
ARSENOPYRITE	AUDIOMETRIST	ADMINISTRATOR	ANSWERABILITY
ARTESIAN WELL	AUGMENTATION	ADMISSIBILITY	ANTAGONIZABLE
ARTHROPODOUS	AUGMENTATIVE	ADMONISHINGLY	ANTICLIMACTIC
ARTHROSPORIC	AULD LANG SYNE	ADVENTURESSES	ANTICLOCKWISE
ARTICULATELY	AUSCULTATION	ADVENTUROUSLY	ANTIHISTAMINE
ARTICULATING	AUSPICIOUSLY	ADVERTISEMENT	ANTIPERSONNEL
ARTICULATION	AUSTRALASIAN	AESTHETICALLY	ANTISPASMODIC
ARTICULATORY	AUSTRONESIAN	AFFIRMATIVELY	ANTISUBMARINE
ARTIFICIALLY	AUTHENTICATE	AFFORESTATION	APATHETICALLY
ARTILLERYMAN	AUTHENTICALLY	AFTERTHOUGHTS	APERIODICALLY
ARTISTICALLY	AUTOANTIBODY	AGGLOMERATING	APOSTROPHIZED

APPLICABILITY
APPORTIONMENT
APPRECIATIONS
APPREHENSIBLE
APPREHENSIONS
APPROPRIATELY
APPROPRIATION
APPROXIMATELY
APPROXIMATION
AQUICULTURIST
ARBITRARINESS
ARBORICULTURE
ARCHAEOLOGIST
ARCHIPELAGOES
ARCHITECTONIC
ARCHITECTURAL
ARGUMENTATION
ARGUMENTATIVE
ARISTOCRACIES
ARITHMETICIAN
AROMATIZATION
ARTESIAN WELLS
ARTICULATIONS

ARTIFICIALITY
ARUNDINACEOUS
ASCERTAINABLE
ASCERTAINMENT
ASSASSINATING
ASSASSINATION
ASSAULT COURSE
ASSEMBLY LINES
ASSERTIVENESS
ASSET-STRIPPER
ASSEVERATIONS
ASSIDUOUSNESS
ASSIGNABILITY
ASTHMATICALLY
ASTONISHINGLY
ASTRODYNAMICS
ASTROPHYSICAL
ATHEISTICALLY
ATROCIOUSNESS
ATTAINABILITY
ATTENTIVENESS
ATTRIBUTIVELY
AUDACIOUSNESS

AUGMENTATIONS
AUSTRALASIANS
AUTHENTICALLY
AUTHENTICATED
AUTHENTICATOR
AUTHORITARIAN
AUTHORITATIVE
AUTHORIZATION
AUTOBIOGRAPHY
AUTOMATICALLY
AXIOMATICALLY

3 LETTERS				5 LETTERS	
3 LETTERS	BALD	BIER	BOTH	**5 LETTERS**	BASES
BAA	BALE	BIFF	BOUT	BABEL	BASIC
BAD	BALE	BIKE	BOWL	BABES	BASIL
BAG	BALK	BILE	BOWS	BABUL	BASIN
BAH	BALL	BILK	BOZO	BABUS	BASIS
BAN	BALM	BILL	BRAE	BACCY	BASRA
BAR	BAND	BIND	BRAG	BACKS	BASSO
BAT	BANE	BINS	BRAN	BACON	BASTE
BAY	BANG	BIRD	BRAS	BADGE	BATCH
BBC	BANK	BIRO	BRAT	BADLY	BATED
BED	BANS	BITE	BRAY	BAGEL	BATHE
BEE	BARB	BITS	BRIM	BAGGY	BATHS
BEG	BARD	BLAB	BRIT	BAHAI	BATIK
BEN	BARE	BLAH	BRNO	BAHOA	BATON
BET	BARK	BLED	BROW	BAILS	BATTY
BIB	BARN	BLEW	BUBO	BAIRN	BATUM
BID	BARS	BLIP	BUBS	BAIZE	BAULK
BIG	BASE	BLOB	BUCK	BAKED	BAWDS
BIN	BASK	BLOC	BUDS	BAKER	BAWDY
BIO-	BASS	BLOT	BUFF	BALAS	BAYED
BIT	BAST	BLOW	BUGS	BALED	BAYOU
BOA	BATH	BLUE	BULB	BALER	BEACH
BOB	BATS	BLUR	BULK	BALES	BEADS
BOD	BAUD	BOAR	BULL	BALKS	BEADY
BOG	BAWD	BOAS	BUMF	BALLS	BEAKS
BOO	BAWL	BOAT	BUMP	BALLY	BEAKY
BOP	BAWL	BOBS	BUMS	BALMS	BEAMS
BOW	BAYS	BODE	BUNA	BALMY	BEANO
BOX	BEAD	BODS	BUNG	BALSO	BEANS
BOY	BEAK	BODY	BUNK	BANAL	BEARD
BRA	BEAM	BOER	BUNS	BANDS	BEARS
BUB	BEAN	BOGS	BUOY	BANDY	BEAST
BUD	BEAR	BOIL	BURK	BANES	BEATS
BUG	BEAT	BOLD	BURN	BANFF	BEAUS
BUM	BEAU	BOLE	BURP	BANGS	BEAUT
BUN	BECK	BOLL	BURR	BANJO	BEAUX
BUR	BEDS	BOLT	BURS	BANKS	BEBOP
BUS	BEEF	BOMB	BURY	BANNS	BECKS
BUT	BEER	BOND	BUSH	BANTU	BEECH
BUY	BEES	BONE	BUSK	BARBS	BEEFY
BYE	BEET	BONN	BUSS	BARDS	BEERS
	BELL	BONY	BUST	BARED	BERRY
	BELT	BOOB	BUSY	BARER	BEETS
4 LETTERS	BEND	BOOK	BUTS	BARGE	BEFIT
BAAS	BERK	BOOM	BUTT	BARIC	BEFOG
BABE	BERN	BOON	BUYS	BARKS	BEGAN
BABU	BEST	BOOR	BUZZ	BARMY	BEGAT
BABY	BETA	BOOS	BYES	BARNS	BEGET
BACK	BETS	BOOT	BYRE	BARON	BEGIN
BADE	BEVY	BOPS	BYTE	BARYE	BEGOT
BAGS	BIAS	BORE		BASAL	BEGUM
BAIL	BIBS	BORT		BASED	BEGUN
BAKE	BIDE	BOSH		BASEL	BEIGE
BAKU	BIDS	BOSS		BASER	BEING

B 5 LETTERS to 6 LETTERS

BEIRA	BITTY	BODGE	BOUTS	BROWS	BUXOM
BELAY	BIYSK	BOERS	BOVID	BRUIN	BUYER
BELCH	BLACK	BOGEY	BOWED	BRUME	BWANA
BELEM	BLADE	BOGGY	BOWEL	BRUNT	BYLAW
BELIE	BLAIN	BOGIE	BOWER	BRUSH	BYRES
BELLE	BLAME	BOGOR	BOWLS	BRUTE	BYTES
BELLS	BLANC	BOGUS	BOXED	BUBAL	BYWAY
BELLY	BLAND	BOHEA	BOXER	BUCKS	
BELOW	BLANK	BOHOL	BOXES	BUDDY	
BELTS	BLARE	BOILS	BOZOS	BUDGE	**6 LETTERS**
BEMBA	BLASE	BOLES	BRACE	BUFFS	BAAING
BENCH	BLAST	BOLLS	BRACT	BUGGY	BABBLE
BENDS	BLAZE	BOLTS	BRAES	BUGLE	BABIED
BENIN	BLEAK	BOLUS	BRAGA	BUILD	BABIES
BENTS	BLEAR	BOMBE	BRAID	BUILT	BABOON
BERKS	BLEAT	BOMBS	BRAIL	BULBS	BACKED
BERRY	BLEED	BONDS	BRAIN	BULGE	BACKER
BERTH	BLEEP	BONED	BRAKE	BULGY	BACKUP
BERYL	BLEND	BONES	BRAND	BULKS	BADGER
BESET	BLESS	BONGO	BRASH	BULKY	BADGES
BESOM	BLEST	BONNY	BRASS	BULLA	BAFFLE
BETAS	BLIMP	BONUS	BRATS	BULLS	BAGELS
BEVEL	BLIND	BOOBS	BRAVE	BULLY	BAGGED
BEZEL	BLINI	BOOBY	BRAVO	BUMPH	BAILED
BHANG	BLINK	BOOED	BRAWL	BUMPS	BAILEE
BIBLE	BLIPS	BOOKS	BRAWN	BUMPY	BAILER
BIDED	BLISS	BOOMS	BRAXY	BUNCH	BAILEY
BIDET	BLITZ	BOONS	BRAYS	BUNGS	BAILOR
BIERS	BLOAT	BOORS	BRAZE	BUNKS	BAIRNS
BIFFS	BLOBS	BOOST	BREAD	BUNNY	BAITED
BIFID	BLOCK	BOOTH	BREAK	BUOYS	BAKERS
BIGHT	BLOCS	BOOTS	BREAM	BURGH	BAKERY
BIGOT	BLOKE	BOOTY	BREDA	BURIN	BAKING
BIHAR	BLOND	BOOZE	BREED	BURKE	BALATA
BIJOU	BLOOD	BOOZY	BRENT	BURKS	BALBOA
BIKED	BLOOM	BORAX	BREVE	BURLY	BALDLY
BIKES	BLOTS	BORED	BRIER	BURMA	BALING
BILGE	BLOWN	BORER	BRILL	BURNS	BALKAN
BILLS	BLOWS	BORES	BRINE	BURNT	BALKED
BILLY	BLOWY	BORIC	BRING	BURPS	BALKER
BINAL	BLUER	BORNE	BRINK	BURRO	BALLAD
BINGE	BLUES	BORNU	BRINY	BURRS	BALLET
BINGO	BLUFF	BORON	BRISK	BURRY	BALLOT
BIOME	BLUNT	BOSKY	BRITS	BURSA	BALSAM
BIOTA	BLURB	BOSOM	BROAD	BURSE	BALSAS
BIPED	BLURT	BOSON	BROIL	BURST	BALTIC
BIPOD	BLUSH	BOSSY	BROKE	BUSBY	BAMAKO
BIRCH	BOARD	BOSUN	BROME	BUSED	BAMBOO
BIRDS	BOARS	BOTCH	BRONX	BUSES	BANANA
BIROS	BOAST	BOUGH	BROOD	BUSHY	BANDED
BIRTH	BOATS	BOULE	BROOK	BUTCH	BANDIT
BISON	BOBBY	BOUND	BROOM	BUTTS	BANGED
BITCH	BOCHE	BOURN	BROTH	BUTTY	BANGER
BITES	BODED	BOUSE	BROWN	BUTYL	BANGLE

BANGUI	BATHER	BEGUMS	BEYOND	BISQUE	BOBBIN
BANISH	BATHOS	BEHALF	BEZOAR	BISSAU	BOBBLE
BANJOS	BATMAN	BEHAVE	BHOPAL	BISTRE	BOBCAT
BANKED	BATMEN	BEHEAD	BHUTAN	BISTRO	BOCHUM
BANKER	BATONS	BEHELD	BIAFRA	BITCHY	BODEGA
BANNED	BATTED	BEHEST	BIASED	BITING	BODICE
BANNER	BATTEN	BEHIND	BIASES	BITTEN	BODIES
BANTAM	BATTER	BEHOLD	BIBLES	BITTER	BODILY
BANTER	BATTLE	BEHOVE	BICEPS	BLACKS	BODING
BANYAN	BATTUE	BEINGS	BICKER	BLADES	BODKIN
BAOBAB	BAUBLE	BEIRUT	BICORN	BLAMED	BOFFIN
BARBED	BAULKS	BELFRY	BIDDEN	BLANCH	BOGEYS
BARBEL	BAWLED	BELIED	BIDETS	BLANKS	BOGOTA
BARBER	BAWLER	BELIEF	BIDING	BLARED	BOILED
BARBET	BAYEUX	BELIER	BIFFED	BLASTS	BOILER
BARDIC	BAYING	BELIZE	BIFFIN	BLAZED	BOLAND
BARELY	BAYOUS	BELLES	BIGAMY	BLAZER	BOLDER
BAREST	BAZAAR	BELLOW	BIG CAT	BLAZES	BOLDLY
BARGED	BEACON	BELONG	BIG END	BLAZON	BOLERO
BARGEE	BEADED	BELSEN	BIGGER	BLEACH	BOLIDE
BARGES	BEADLE	BELTED	BIGGIE	BLENDE	BOLSHY
BARING	BEAGLE	BELUGA	BIGHTS	BLENDS	BOLSON
BARIUM	BEAKER	BEMOAN	BIGOTS	BLENNY	BOLTED
BARKED	BEAMED	BEMUSE	BIG TOP	BLIGHT	BOLTER
BARKER	BEARDS	BENGAL	BIGWIG	BLIMEY	BOMBAY
BARLEY	BEARER	BENIGN	BIHARI	BLIMPS	BOMBED
BARMAN	BEASTS	BENONI	BIKING	BLINDS	BOMBER
BARMEN	BEATEN	BENUMB	BIKINI	BLINKS	BONBON
BARNEY	BEATER	BENZOL	BILGES	BLINTZ	BONDED
BARONA	BEAUNE	BENZYL	BILKED	BLITHE	BONGOS
BARONS	BEAUTS	BERATE	BILKER	BLOCKS	BONIER
BARONY	BEAUTY	BEREFT	BILLED	BLOKES	BONILY
BARQUE	BEAVER	BERETS	BILLET	BLONDE	BONING
BARRED	BECAME	BERGEN	BILLON	BLOODS	BONITO
BARROW	BECKET	BERING	BILLOW	BLOODY	BON MOT
BARTER	BECKON	BERLIN	BINARY	BLOOMS	BONNET
BARYON	BECOME	BERTHS	BINATE	BLOTCH	BONSAI
BASALT	BEDAUB	BESEEM	BINDER	BLOTTO	BONZER
BASELY	BEDBUG	BESOMS	BINGES	BLOUSE	BOOBED
BASEST	BEDDED	BESTED	BINGOS	BLOWER	BOOHOO
BASHED	BEDDER	BESTIR	BINNED	BLOW-UP	BOOING
BASHES	BEDECK	BESTOW	BIOGEN	BLOWZY	BOOKED
BASICS	BEDLAM	BETAKE	BIONIC	BLUEST	BOOKIE
BASIFY	BEDPAN	BETHEL	BIOPIC	BLUFFS	BOOMED
BASING	BEEFED	BETIDE	BIOPSY	BLUISH	BOOSTS
BASINS	BEETLE	BETONY	BIOTIC	BLUNGE	BOOTED
BASION	BEFALL	BETOOK	BIOTIN	BLURBS	BOOTEE
BASKED	BEFELL	BETRAY	BIPEDS	BLURRY	BOOTHS
BASKET	BEFOOL	BETTED	BIRDIE	B-MOVIE	BOOZED
BASQUE	BEFORE	BETTER	BIRTHS	BOARDS	BOOZER
BASSES	BEFOUL	BEVELS	BISCAY	BOASTS	BOPPED
BASSET	BEGGAR	BEVIES	BISECT	BOATED	BORAGE
BASTED	BEGGED	BEWAIL	BISHOP	BOATER	BORANE
BATHED	BEGONE	BEWARE	BISONS	BOBBED	BORATE

BORDER	BRACED	BRONZY	BURBOT	BY-LINE	BALCONY
BOREAL	BRACER	BROOCH	BURDEN	BYPASS	BALDING
BORERS	BRACES	BROODS	BUREAU	BYPLAY	BALEFUL
BORIDE	BRAIDS	BROODY	BURGAS	BYROAD	BALKING
BORING	BRAINS	BROOKS	BURGEE	BYSSUS	BALLADE
BORNEO	BRAINY	BROOMS	BURGER	BYWAYS	BALLADS
BORROW	BRAISE	BROWNS	BURGHS	BYWORD	BALLAST
BORZOI	BRAKED	BROWSE	BURGLE		BALLETS
BOSKET	BRAKES	BRUGES	BURIAL		BALLOON
BOSNIA	BRANCH	BRUISE	BURIED	**7 LETTERS**	BALLOTS
BOSOMS	BRANDS	BRUMAL	BURIER	BABBLED	BALLS-UP
BOSOMY	BRANDY	BRUNCH	BURLAP	BABBLER	BALMIER
BOSSED	BRASHY	BRUNEI	BURLER	BABOONS	BALMILY
BOSSES	BRASOV	BRUTAL	BURLEY	BABYING	BALNEAL
BOSTON	BRASSY	BRUTES	BURNED	BABYISH	BALONEY
BOSUNS	BRAVED	BRYONY	BURNER	BABY-SAT	BALSAMS
BOTANY	BRAVER	BUBBLE	BURNET	BABY-SIT	BALUCHI
BOTCHY	BRAVES	BUBBLE	BURPED	BACCATE	BAMBARA
BOTFLY	BRAVOS	BUCCAL	BURRED	BACILLI	BAMBINO
BOTHER	BRAWLS	BUCKED	BURROS	BACKERS	BAMBOOS
BOTTLE	BRAWNY	BUCKET	BURROW	BACKING	BANANAS
BOTTOM	BRAYED	BUCKLE	BURSAL	BACKLOG	BANDAGE
BOUAKE	BRAYER	BUDDED	BURSAR	BACKSAW	BANDBOX
BOUCLE	BRAZEN	BUDDHA	BURSTS	BACKUPS	BANDEAU
BOUGHS	BRAZER	BUDDLE	BURTON	BACALUM	BANDIED
BOUGHT	BRAZIL	BUDGED	BURYAT	BADAJOZ	BANDIER
BOUGIE	BREACH	BUDGET	BUSBAR	BAD DEBT	BANDING
BOULES	BREAKS	BUFFED	BUS BOY	BAD FORM	BANDITS
BOULLE	BREAST	BUFFET	BUSHED	BADGERS	BANDUNG
BOUNCE	BREECH	BUGGED	BUSHEL	BADNESS	BANEFUL
BOUNCY	BREEZE	BUGGER	BUSHES	BAFFLED	BANGERS
BOUNDS	BREEZY	BUGLER	BUSIED	BAFFLER	BANGING
BOUNTY	BREGMA	BUGLES	BUSIER	BAFFLES	BANKOK
BOURNS	BREMEN	BUILDS	BUSKED	BAGANDA	BANGLES
BOURSE	BRETON	BULBAR	BUSKER	BAGASSE	BANKERS
BOVINE	BREVET	BULBIL	BUSSED	BAGGAGE	BANKSIA
BOVVER	BREWER	BULBUL	BUSTED	BAGGIER	BANNERS
BOWELS	BRIBER	BULGED	BUST-UP	BAGGILY	BANNING
BOWERS	BRIDAL	BULGES	BUTANE	BAGGING	BANNOCK
BOWERY	BRIDLE	BULKED	BUTENE	BAGHDAD	BANQUET
BOWFIN	BRIERY	BULLET	BUTLER	BAG LADY	BANSHEE
BOWING	BRIGHT	BUMBLE	BUTTED	BAGPIPE	BANTAMS
BOWLED	BRITON	BUMMED	BUTTER	BAGWORM	BANTOID
BOWLER	BROACH	BUMPED	BUTTES	BAHAISM	BANYANS
BOWMAN	BROADS	BUMPER	BUTTON	BAHAIST	BAPTISM
BOWMEN	BROCHE	BUNCHY	BUYERS	BAHAMAS	BAPTIST
BOWSAW	BROGUE	BUNDLE	BUYING	BAHRAIN	BAPTIZE
BOW TIE	BROKEN	BUNGE	BUYOUT	BAILEYS	BARBARY
BOW-WOW	BROKER	BUNION	BUZZED	BAILIFF	BATBATE
BOWYER	BROLLY	BUNKED	BUZZER	BAILING	BARBELL
BOXCAR	BROMAL	BUNKER	BUZZES	BAINITE	BARBERS
BOXERS	BROMIC	BUNK-UP	BY-BLOW	BAITING	BARBULE
BOWING	BRONCO	BUOYED	BYGONE	BALANCE	BARCHAN
BOYISH	BRONZE	BURBLE	BYLAWS	BALATON	BAR CODE

BARENTS	BATTLES	BEDLAMS	BENZENE	BIGENER	BITTIER
BARGAIN	BATWING	BEDOUIN	BENZINE	BIG GAME	BITUMEN
BARGEES	BAUBLES	BEDPANS	BENZOIC	BIGGEST	BIVALVE
BARGING	BAUHAUS	BEDPOST	BENZOIN	BIGGIES	BIVOUAC
BARKERS	BAULKED	BEDRAIL	BENZOYL	BIG HEAD	BIZARRE
BARKING	BAUTZEN	BEDROCK	BEQUEST	BIGHORN	BIZERTE
BARMAID	BAUXITE	BEDROOM	BERATED	BIGNAME	BLABBED
BARMIER	BAVARIA	BEDSIDE	BEREAVE	BIGNESS	BLABBER
BARNAUL	BAWDIER	BEDSORE	BERMUDA	BIGOTED	BLACKEN
BARNEYS	BAWDILY	BEDTIME	BERNESE	BIGOTRY	BLACKER
BAROQUE	BAWLING	BEECHES	BERRIES	BIG SHOT	BLACKLY
BAROTSE	BAYAMON	BEEFIER	BERSEEM	BIG TIME	BLADDER
BARQUES	BAYONET	BEEFING	BERSERK	BIG TOPS	BLAMING
BARRACK	BAYWOOD	BEEF TEA	BERTHED	BIGWIGS	BLANDER
BARRAGE	BAZAARS	BEEHIVE	BESEECH	BIJAPER	BLANDLY
BARRELS	BAZOOKA	BEELINE	BESIDES	BAKANER	BLANKET
BARRIER	BEACHED	BEESWAX	BESIEGE	BIKINIS	BLANKLY
BARRING	BEACHES	BEETFLY	BESMEAR	BILBOES	BLARING
BAROWS	BEACONS	BEETLED	BESPEAK	BILIARY	BLARNEY
BARYTES	BEADIER	BEETLES	BESPOKE	BILIOUS	BLASTED
BASCULE	BEADILY	BEGGARS	BESTIAL	BILLOWY	BLATANT
BASENJI	BEADING	BEGGARY	BESTING	BILTONG	BLATHER
BASHFUL	BEADLES	BEGGING	BEST MAN	BILMORPH	BLAUBOK
BASHING	BEAKERS	BEGONIA	BEST-OFF	BINDERS	BLAZERS
BASHKIR	BEAMING	BEGUILE	BESTREW	BINDERY	BLAZING
BASILAR	BEARDED	BEHAVED	BETAINE	BINDING	BLAZONS
BASILIC	BEARERS	BEHINDS	BETAKEN	BINNING	BLEAKER
BASKETS	BEAR HUG	BEJEWEL	BETHELS	BIOCIDE	BLEAKLY
BASKING	BEARING	BELATED	BETHINK	BIODATA	BLEATER
BASOTHO	BEARISH	BELAYED	BETIDED	BIOHERM	BLEEDER
BAS-RHIN	BEASTLY	BELCHED	BETIMES	BIOLOGY	BLEEPED
BASSEIN	BEATERS	BELCHES	BETOKEN	BIOMASS	BLEEPER
BASSETS	BEATIFY	BELFORT	BETROTH	BIONICS	BLEMISH
BASSIST	BEATING	BELGIAN	BETTERS	BIOPICS	BLENDED
BASSOON	BEATNIK	BELGIUM	BETTING	BIOPTIC	BLENDER
BASTARD	BEAVERS	BELIEFS	BETWEEN	BIOTITE	BLESBOK
BASTING	BEATIFY	BELIEVE	BETWIXT	BIOTYPE	BLESSED
BASTION	BEATING	BELLBOY	BEVELED	BIPLANE	BLETHER
BATCHED	BEATNIK	BELLEEK	BEWITCH	BIPOLAR	BLEWITS
BATFISH	BEAVERS	BELLIES	BEYOGLU	BIRCHED	BLIGHTS
BATHERS	BEAR HUG	BELLOWS	BEZIQUE	BIRCHES	BLINDED
BATHING	BEARING	BELOVED	BIASING	BIRD DOG	BLINDLY
BATH-MAT	BEARISH	BELTING	BIASSED	BIRDIES	BLINKED
BATHTUB	BEASTLY	BELTWAY	BIAXIAL	BIRETTA	BLINKER
BATHYAL	BEATERS	BELYING	BIBCOCK	BISCUIT	BLISTER
BATISTE	BEATIFY	BEMUSED	BIBELOT	BISHOPS	BLITZED
BATSMAN	BEATING	BENARES	BICYCLE	BISMUTH	BLITZES
BATSMEN	BEATNIK	BENCHER	BIDDING	BISTORT	BLOATED
BATTENS	BEAVERS	BENCHES	BIFFING	BISTROS	BLOATER
BATTERS	BECAUSE	BENDING	BIFILAR	BITCHED	BLOCKED
BATTERY	BEDBUGS	BENEATH	BIFOCAL	BITCHES	BLONDER
BATTIER	BEDDING	BENEFIT	BIG CATS	BIT PART	BLONDES
BATTING	BEDEVIL	BENGALI	BIG DEAL	BITTENN	BLOODED
BATTLED	BEDEWED	BEETHOS	BIG ENDS	BITTERS	BLOOMED

BLOOMER	BOGGIER	BOROUGH	BRAMBLE	BROILED	BUFFING
BLOOPER	BOGGING	BORSCHT	BRAMLEY	BROILER	BUFFOON
BLOSSOM	BOGGLED	BORSTAL	BRANDED	BROKERS	BUGABOO
BLOTCHY	BOHEMIA	BORZOIS	BRASHER	BROMATE	BUGANDA
BLOTTED	BOILERS	BOSCAGE	BRASHLY	BROMIDE	BUGBANE
BLOTTER	BOILING	BOSNIAN	BRASSES	BROMINE	BUGBEAR
BLOUSES	BOLDEST	BOSSIER	BRASSIE	BROMISM	BUG-EYED
BLOW-DRY	BOLEROS	BOSSILY	BRAVADO	BRONCHI	BUGGERS
BLOWERS	BOLETUS	BOSSING	BRAVAIS	BRONCOS	BUGGERY
BLOWFLY	BOLIVAR	BOTCHED	BRAVELY	BRONZED	BUGGIES
BLOWIER	BOLIVIA	BOTCHER	BRAVERY	BRONZES	BUGGING
BLOWING	BOLLARD	BOTCH-UP	BRAVEST	BROODED	BUGLERS
BLOWOUT	BOLOGNA	BOTTLED	BRAVING	BROODER	BUGLOSS
BLOW-UPS	BOLONEY	BOTTLES	BRAVURA	BROOKED	BUILDER
BLUBBER	BOLSHIE	BOTTOMS	BRAWLED	BROTHEL	BUILDUP
BLUE GUM	BOLSTER	BOTTROP	BRAWLER	BROTHER	BUILT-IN
BLUEING	BOLTING	BOTULIN	BRAYING	BROWNED	BUILT-UP
BLUE JAY	BOLZANO	BOUCHEE	BRAZIER	BROWNER	BULBOUS
BLUE LAW	BANBANS	BOUDOIR	BREADTH	BROWNIE	BULGIER
BLUETIT	BANDAGE	BOULDER	BREAKER	BROWSED	BULKILY
BLUFFED	BONDING	BOUNCES	BREAK-IN	BROWSER	BULKING
BLUFFER	BONE-DRY	BOUNDED	BREATHE	BRUCINE	BULLACE
BLUFFLY	BONESET	BOUNDEN	BREATHY	BRUISED	BULLATE
BLUNDER	BONFIRE	BOUNDER	BRECCIA	BRUISER	BULLDOG
BLUNGER	BONGOES	BOUQUET	BREEDER	BRUISES	BULLETS
BLUNTED	BONIEST	BOURBON	BRENNER	BRUITED	BULLIED
BLUNTLY	BONJOUR	BOURDON	BREVIER	BRUMOUS	BULLIES
BLURRED	BONKERS	BOUYANT	BREVITY	BRUSHED	BULLION
BLURTED	BONNETS	BOWHEAD	BREWAGE	BRUSHER	BULLISH
BLUSHED	BONNIER	BOWKNOT	BREWERY	BRUSHES	BULLOCK
BLUSHER	BONUSES	BOWLERS	BREWING	BRUSH-UP	BULRUSH
BLUSHES	BOOBIES	BOWLINE	BRIBERY	BRUSQUE	BULWART
BLUSTER	BOOBING	BOWLING	BRICOLE	BRUTISH	BUMBLED
B-MOVIES	BOOKEND	BOWSHOT	BRIDOON	BRYANSK	BUMBLER
BOARDED	BOOKING	BOW TIES	BRIGADE	BUBBLED	BUMBOAT
BOARDER	BOORISH	BOWCARS	BRIGAND	BUBBLER	BUMMING
BOARISH	BOOSTED	BOXROOM	BRIMFUL	BUBBLES	BUMPERS
BOASTED	BOOSTER	BOXWOD	BRIMMER	BUBONIC	BUMPIER
BOASTER	BOOTEES	BOYCOTT	BRINDLE	BUCKETS	BUMPILY
BOATERS	BOOTING	BOYHOOD	BRIOCHE	BUCKEYE	BUMPING
BOATING	BOOTLEG	BARBANT	BRISKER	BUCKING	BUMPKIN
BOATMAN	BOOZERS	BRACING	BRISKET	BUCKLED	BUNCHED
BOATMEN	BOOZE-UP	BRACKEN	BRISKLY	BUCKLER	BUNCHES
BOBBERY	BOOZIER	BRACKET	BRISTLE	BUCKLES	BUNDLED
BOBBIES	BOOZILY	BRADAWL	BRISTLY	BUCKRAM	BUNDLER
BOBBING	BOOZING	BRAGGED	BRITISH	BUCKSAW	BUNDLES
BOBBINS	BOPPING	BRAGGER	BRITONS	BUCOLIC	BUNGING
BOBBLES	BORACIC	BRAHMAN	BRITTLE	BUDDIES	BUNGLED
BOBSLED	BORAZON	BRAIDED	BROADEN	BUDDING	BUNGLES
BOBSTAY	BORDERS	BRAIDER	BROADER	BUDGETS	BUNIONS
BOBTAIL	BORDURE	BRAILLE	BROADLY	BUDGING	BUNKERS
BODICES	BOREDOM	BRAINED	BROCADE	BUFFALO	BUNKING
BODKINS	BORNEEL	BRAISED	BROCKET	BUFFERS	BUNK-UPS
BOFFINS	BORNITE	BRAKING	BROGUES	BUFFETS	BUNNIES

BUNTING	BUSTLED	BACKLIST	BALLS-UP	BARONIES
BUOYAGE	BUSTLER	BACKLOGS	BALLYHOO	BAROSTAT
BUOYANT	BUSTLES	BACKPACK	BALMIEST	BAROUCHE
BUOYING	BUST-UPS	BACK SEAT	BALMORAL	BARRACKS
BURBLED	BUSYING	BACKSIDE	BALSAMIC	BARRAGES
BURBLER	BUTANOL	BACKSLID	BALUSTER	BARRATOR
BURDENS	BUTCHER	BACKSPIN	BANALITY	BARRATRY
BURDOCK	BUTLERS	BACKSTAY	BANDAGED	BARRETTE
BUREAUX	BUSTLES	BACKSTOP	BANDAGES	BARRIERS
BURETTE	BUST-UPS	BACK TALK	BANDANNA	BARTERED
BURGEON	BUSYING	BACKWARD	BANDIEST	BARTERER
BURGERS	BUTANOL	BACKWASH	BANDITRY	BARTIZAN
BURGESS	BUTCHER	BACKYARD	BANDSMAN	BASEBALL
BURGHAL	BUTLERS	BACTERIA	BANDSMEN	BASELESS
BURGHER	BUTLERY	BACTERIN	BANDYING	BASELINE
BURGLAR	BUTTERY	BACTRIAN	BANISHED	BASEMENT
BURGLED	BUTTIES	BADALONA	BANISTER	BASENESS
BURIALS	BUTTING	BAD BLOOD	BANKBOOK	BASE RATE
BURLIER	BUTTOCK	BAD DEBTS	BANK NOTE	BASICITY
BURMESE	BUTTONS	BADGERED	BANK RATE	BASIDIAL
BURNERS	BUTYRIC	BADINAGE	BANKROLL	BASIDIUM
BURNING	BUTYRIN	BADLANDS	BANKRUPT	BASILARY
BURNISH	BUYOUTS	BADLY-OFF	BANNOCKS	BASILICA
BURNOUS	BUZZARD	BAD-MOUTH	BANQUETS	BASILISK
BURNOUT	BUZZERS	BAEDEKER	BANSHEES	BASKETRY
BURPING	BUZZING	BAFFLING	BANTERED	BASOPHIL
BURRING	BYE-BYES	BAGGAGES	BANTERER	BASS CLEF
BURRITO	BYGONES	BAGGIEST	BAPTISMS	BASSINET
BURROWS	BYWORDS	BAGPIPES	BAPTISTS	BASSISTS
BURSARS		BAGUETTE	BAPTIZED	BASSOONS
BURSARY		BAHAMIAN	BARATHEA	BASSWOOD
BURSTER	**8 LETTERS**	BAHEAINI	BARBADOS	BASTARDS
BURTHEN	BABBLERS	BAILABLE	BARBARIC	BASTILLE
BURTONS	BABBLING	BAILIFFS	BARBEQUE	BASTIONS
BURUNDI	BABIRUSA	BAILMENT	BARBERRY	BATANGAS
BURWEED	BABYHOOD	BAILSMAN	BARBICAN	BATHETIC
BURYING	BABY TALK	BAKELITE	BARBICEL	BATH MATS
BUSBIES	BACCARAT	BAKERIES	BAR CHART	BATHROBE
BUS BOYS	BACCHIUS	BALANCED	BAR CODES	BATHROOM
BUSHELS	BACHELOR	BALANCER	BAREBACK	BATHTUBS
BUSHIER	BACILLUS	BALANCES	BAREFOOT	BATHURST
BUSHING	BACKACHE	BALDNESS	BARENESS	BATTENED
BUSHIRE	BACKBITE	BALEARIC	BARGAINS	BATTERED
BUSHPIG	BACKBONE	BALINESE	BARGRAPH	BATTERER
BUSHTIT	BACKCHAT	BALLADES	BARITONE	BATTIEST
BUSIEST	BACKCOMB	BALLADRY	BARMAIDS	BATTLING
BUSKERS	BACKDATE	BALLARAT	BARMIESTY	BAUHINIA
BUSKING	BACK DOOR	BALLCOCK	BARNACLE	BAULKING
BUSSING	BACKDROP	BALL GAME	BARNYARD	BAVARIAN
BUS STOP	BACKFILL	BALLONET	BAROGRAM	BAWDIEST
BUSTARD	BACKFIRE	BALLOONS	BARONAGE	BAYBERRY
BUSTERS	BACKHAND	BALLOTED	BARONESS	BAYONETS
BUSTIER	BACKLASH	BALL PARK	BARONETS	BAZOOKAS
BUSTLING	BACKLESS	BALLROOM	BARONIAL	BDELLIUM

BEACHING	BEGGARED	BESTIARY	BILINEAR	BIT PARTS
BEADIEST	BEGGARLY	BESTOWEL	BILLETED	BITSTOCK
BEADINGS	BEGINNER	BESTOWED	BILLFISH	BITTERLY
BEAGLING	BEGOTTEN	BESTOWER	BILLFOLD	BITTERNS
BEAM-ENDS	BEGRUDGE	BESTREWN	BILLHOOK	BITTIEST
BEANPOLE	BEGUILLED	BESTRIDE	BILLIARD	BIVALENT
BEARABLE	BEHAVING	BESTRODE	BILLIONS	BIVALVES
BEARDING	BEHEADED	BETAKING	BILLOWED	BIVOUACS
BEAR HUGS	BEHOLDEN	BETATRON	BILOBATE	BIWEEKLY
BEARINGS	BEHOLDER	BETIDING	BIMANOUS	BIYEARLY
BEARSKIN	BELABOUR	BETRAYAL	BINAURAL	BLABBING
BEATABLE	BELAYING	BETRAYED	BINDINGS	BLACK ART
BEATIFIC	BELCHING	BETRAYER	BINDWEED	BLACK BOX
BEATINGS	BELFRIES	BETTERED	BIN-LINER	BLACKCAP
BEATNIKS	BELGRADE	BEVATRON	BINNACLE	BLACKEST
BEAUTIES	BELIEVED	BEVELING	BINOMIAL	BLACK EYE
BEAUTIFY	BELIEVER	BEVELLED	BIOASSAY	BLACKFLY
BEAUVAIS	BELITTLE	BEVERAGE	BIOCIDAL	BLACK ICE
BEAVERED	BELLBIRD	BEWAILLED	BIOCYCLE	BLACKING
BECALMED	BELLBOYS	BEWAILER	BIODATAS	BLACKISH
BECHAMEL	BELLOWED	BEWARING	BIOLYTIC	BLACKLEG
BECKONED	BELLOWER	BEWIGGED	BIOMETRY	BLACKOUT
BECKONER	BELLPULL	BEWILDER	BIONOMIC	BLACK-TIE
BECOMING	BELLWORT	BHATPARA	BIOPLASM	BLACKTOP
BEDAUBED	BELLYFUL	BIANNUAL	BIOPSIES	BLADDERS
BEDAZZLE	BELMOPAN	BIASSING	BIOSCOPE	BLAMABLE
BEDECKED	BELONGED	BIATHLON	BIOSCOPY	BLAMEFUL
BEDIMMED	BELOVEDS	BIBLICAL	BIOTITIC	BLANCHED
BED LINEN	BELTWAYS	BIBULOUS	BIOTYPIC	BLANDEST
BEDOUINS	BEMOANED	BICKERED	BIPAROUS	BLANDISH
BEDPLATE	BENADRYL	BICKERER	BIPHENYL	BLANKETS
BEDPOSTS	BENEFICE	BICOLOUR	BIPLANES	BLASTEMA
BEDROOMS	BENEFITS	BICONVEX	BIRACIAL	BLASTING
BEDSIDES	BENGHAZI	BICUSPID	BIRADIAL	BLAST-OFF
BEDSORES	BENIGNLY	BICYCLED	BIRAMOUS	BLASTULA
BEDSTEAD	BENTWOOD	BICYCLES	BIRCHING	BLATANCY
BEDSTRAW	BENUMBED	BICYCLIC	BIRDBATH	BLAZONED
BEDTIMES	BENZOATE	BIDDABLE	BIRDCAGE	BLAZONRY
BEEBREAD	BEQUEATH	BIENNIAL	BIRD DOGS	BLEACHED
BEECHNUT	BEQUESTS	BIFACIAL	BIRDLIKE	BLEACHER
BEE-EATER	BERATING	BIFIDITY	BIRDLIME	BLEAKEST
BEEFCAKE	BERCEUSE	BIFOCALS	BIRDSEED	BLEARIER
BEEFIEST	BEREAVED	BIGAMIST	BIRD'S EYE	BLEARILY
BEEFWOOD	BERGAMET	BIGAMOUS	BIRETTAS	BLEATING
BEEHIVES	BERIBERI	BIGHEADS	BIRTHDAY	BLEEPERS
BEELINES	BERTHING	BIGNAMES	BISCUITS	BLEEPING
BEESWING	BERYLINE	BIGNONIA	BISECTED	BLENCHED
BEETLING	BESANCON	BIG SHOTS	BISECTOR	BLENCHER
BEETROOT	BESEIGED	BIG STICK	BISEXUAL	BLENDERS
BEFALLEN	BESEIGER	BIG-TIMER	BISTOURY	BLENDING
BEFITTED	BESMIRCH	BIG WHEEL	BITCHIER	BLENHEIM
BEFOULER	BESOTTED	BIJUGATE	BITCHILY	BLESSING
BEFRIEND	BESOUGHT	BILABIAL	BITCHING	BLIGHTED
BEGETTER	BESPOKEN	BILBERRY	BITINGLY	BLIGHTER

BLIMPISH	BLUNTING	BOOKABLE	BOUNTIES	BREACHED
BLINDAGE	BLURRING	BOOKCASE	BOUQUETS	BREACHES
BLINDERS	BLURTING	BOOK CLUB	BOUTIQUE	BREAD BIN
BLINDING	BLUSHERS	BOOKENDS	BOUZOUKI	BREADNUT
BLINKERS	BLUSHING	BOOKINGS	BOWSHOTS	BREADTHS
BLINKING	BLUSTERY	BOOKLETS	BOWSPRIT	BREAKAGE
BLISSFUL	BOARDERS	BOOKMARK	BOWBERRY	BREAKERS
BLISTERS	BOARDING	BOOKRACK	BOXBOARD	BREAKING
BLITHELY	BOARFISH	BOOKSHOP	BOXROOMS	BREAK -INS
BLITZING	BOASTERS	BOOKWORM	BOYCOTTS	BREATHER
BLIZZARD	BOASTFUL	BOOSTERS	BOYISHLY	BREECHES
BLOATERS	BOASTING	BOOSTING	BOY SCOUT	BREEDING
BLOCKADE	BOAT HOOK	BOOTLACE	BRACELET	BREEZILY
BLOCKAGE	BOAT LOAD	BOOTLESS	BRACHIAL	BRETHREN
BLOCKING	BOBBINET	BOOZE-UPS	BRACHIUM	BREVETCY
BLONDEST	BOBBY PIN	BOOZIEST	BRACKETS	BREVIARY
BLOODFIN	BOBOLINK	BORACITE	BRACKISH	BRIBABLE
BLOODILY	BOBTAILS	BORDEAUX	BRACTEAL	BRICKBAT
BLOODING	BOBWHITE	BORDELLO	BRADAWLS	BRIDGING
BLOOD RED	BOBILESS	BORDERED	BRAGGART	BRIEFING
BLOOMERS	BODLEIAN	BORDERER	BRAGGING	BRIGHTEN
BLOOMERY	BODY BLOW	BOREHOLE	BRAHMANI	BRIGHTON
BLOOMING	BODY WORK	BORINGLY	BRAHMANS	BRIOCHES
BLOOPERS	BOEHMITE	BOROUGHS	BRAIDING	BRISANCE
BLOSSOMS	BOGEYMAN	BORROWED	BRAINIER	BRISKEST
BLOTCHES	BOGGIEST	BORROWER	BRAINING	BRISLING
BLOTTERS	BOGGLING	BORSTALS	BRAINPAN	BRISTLED
BLOTTING	BOHEMIAN	BOSPORUS	BRAISING	BRISTLES
BLOWFISH	BOILABLE	BOSS-EYED	BRAMBLES	BRITCHES
BLOWHARD	BOLDFACE	BOSSIEST	BRANCHED	BRITTANY
BLOWHOLE	BOLDNESS	BOTANIZE	BRANCHIA	BROACHED
BLOWIEST	BOLIVIAN	BOTCHERS	BRANDIES	BROACHER
BLOWLAMP	BOLLARDS	BOTCHIER	BRANDING	BROADEST
BLOWOUTS	BOLLWORM	BOTCHILY	BRANDISH	BROADWAY
BLOWPIPE	BOLSHIER	BOTCHING	BRAND-NEW	BROCADED
BLOW-WAVE	BOLTHOLE	BOTCH-UPS	BRASHEST	BROCCOLI
BLOWZIER	BOLTONIA	BOTHERED	BRASILIA	BROCHURE
BLOWZILY	BOLTROPE	BOTSWANA	BRASSARD	BROILERS
BLUDGEON	BOMBSITE	BOTTLING	BRASS HAT	BROILING
BLUE BABY	BOMBYCID	BOTTOMRY	BRASSICA	BROKENLY
BLUEBELL	BONA FIDE	BOTULISM	BRASSIER	BROLLIES
BLUEBIRD	BONANZAS	BOUDOIRS	BRASSILY	BROMIDES
BLUE BOOK	BONEFISH	BOUFFANT	BRATTICE	BRONCHIA
BLUE CHIP	BONEHEAD	BOUILLON	BRAUNITE	BRONCHOS
BLUE FILM	BONE-IDLE	BOULDERS	BRAWLERS	BRONCHUS
BLUEFISH	BONELESS	BOULLION	BRAWLING	BRONZING
BLUEGILL	BONE MEAL	BOULOGNE	BRAWNIER	BROOCHES
BLUE GUMS	BONFIRES	BOUNCERS	BRAWNILY	BROODERS
BLUE JAYS	BONHOMIE	BOUNCIER	BRAZENED	BROODIER
BLUE LAWS	BONINESS	BOUNCILY	BRAZENLY	BROODILY
BLUE MOON	BONNIEST	BOUNCING	BRAZIARS	BROODING
BLUENESS	BONS MOTS	BOUNDARY	BRAZIERS	BROOKING
BLUFFING	BONTEBOK	BOUNDERS	BRAZILIN	BROOKITE
BLUNDERS	BOOHOOED	BOUNDING	BRAZILEN	BROOKLYN

371

BROTHELS	BULGIEST	BUSYNESS	BAGATELLE	BARBAROUS
BROTHERS	BULKHEAD	BUTANONE	BAGGINESS	BARBECUED
BROUGHAM	BULKIEAT	BUTCHERS	BAG LADIES	BARBECUES
BROUHAHA	BULLDOGS	BUTCHERY	BAILIWICK	BARBICANS
BROWBEAT	BULLDOZE	BUTTERED	BAIN-MARIE	BARBITONE
BROWNEST	BULLETIN	BUTTOCKS	BALACLAVA	BARCAROLE
BROWNIES	BULLFROG	BUTTONED	BALAKLAVA	BARCELONA
BROWNING	BULLHEAD	BUTTRESS	BALALAIKA	BAR CHARTS
BROWNISH	BULHORN	BUTYRATE	BALANCING	BARE BONES
BROWSING	BULLNECK	BUZZARDS	BALCONIES	BAREFACED
BRUISERS	BULLOCKS	BUZZWORD	BALEFULLY	BARGAINED
BRUISING	BULLRING	BY-BIDDER	BALKANIZE	BARGAINER
BRUITING	BULL'S-EYE	BYPASSED	BALLASTED	BARGE POLE
BRUNCHES	BULLYBOY	BY PASSES	BALLCOCKS	BAR GRAPHS
BRUNETTE	BULLYING	BYRONISM	BALLERINA	BARITONES
BRUSHING	BULLY-OFF		BALL GAMES	BARNACLES
BRUSH-OFF	BULWARKS		BALLISTIC	BARN DANCE
BRUSH-UPS	BUMBLING	**9 LETTERS**	BALLOONED	BARNSTORM
BRUSSELS	BUMPIEST	BABY TEETH	BALLOTING	BARNYARDS
BRUTALLY	BUMPKINS	BABY TOOTH	BALLPOINT	BAROGRAPH
BRYOLOGY	BUNCHING	BACCHANAL	BALLROOMS	BAROMETER
BRYOZOAN	BUNDLING	BACCIFORM	BALMINESS	BARONETCY
BUBALINE	BUNGALOW	BACHELORS	BALTHAZAR	BAROSCOPE
BUBBLIER	BUNGHOLE	BACILLARY	BALTIMORE	BARRACKED
BUBBLING	BUNGLERS	BACKACHES	BAMBOOZLE	BARRACUDA
BUHSHEE	BUNGLING	BACKBENCH	BANDAGING	BARRETTES
BUCKAROO	BUOYANCY	BACKBITER	BANDANNAS	BARRICADE
BUCKBEAN	BURBERRY	BACKBOARD	BANDEROLE	BARRISTER
BUCKETED	BURBLING	BACKBONES	BANDICOOT	BARROW BOY
BUCKHORN	BURDENED	BACKCLOTH	BANDOLEER	BARTENDER
BUCKLERS	BURGHERS	BACKCROSS	BANDSTAND	BARTERING
BUCKLING	BURGLARS	BACKDATED	BANDWAGON	BASEBALLS
BUCKSHEE	BURGLARY	BACK DOORS	BANDWIDTH	BASEBOARD
BUCKSHOT	BURGLING	BACK DROPS	BANEBERRY	BASELINES
BUCKSKIN	BURGUNDY	BACKFIRED	BANEFULLY	BASEMENTS
BUDAPEST	BURLIEST	BACKHANDS	BANGALORE	BASE METAL
BUDDHISM	BURNOOSE	BACKPACKS	BANISHING	BASE RATES
BUDDHIST	BURNOUTS	BACKPEDAL	BANISTERS	BASHFULLY
BUDDLEITA	BURRITOS	BACK SEATS	BANKBOOKS	BASICALLY
BUDGETED	BURROWED	BACKSIDES	BANK DRAFT	BASIFIXED
BUFFALOS	BURROWER	BACKSIGHT	BANK NOTES	BASILICAN
BUFFERED	BURSITIS	BACKSLIDE	BANK ROLLS	BASILICAS
BUFFETED	BURSTING	BACKSPACE	BANKRUPTS	BASILISKS
BUFFETER	BURTHENS	BACKSWEPT	BANQUETED	BASIPETAL
BUFFOONS	BUSHBABY	BACKTRACK	BANQUETTE	BAS-RELIEF
BUGABOOS	BUSHBACK	BACKWARDS	BANTERING	BASS CLEFS
BUGBEARS	BUSHBUCK	BACKWATER	BANUSTAN	BASSINETS
BUGGERED	BUSHIEST	BACKWOODS	BAPTISMAL	BASTINADO
BUILDERS	BUSHVELD	BACKYARDS	BAPTIZING	BATH CHAIR
BUILDING	BUSINESS	BACTERIAL	BARBADIAN	BATHOLITH
BUILDUPS	BUS STOPS	BACTERIUM	BARBARIAN	BATHROBES
BUKOVINI	BUSTIEST	BACTEROID	BARBARISM	BATHROOMS
BULAWAYO	BUSTLING	BADGERING	BARBARITY	BATTALION
BULGARIA	BUSYBODY	BADMINTON	BARBARIZE	BATTENING

BATTERIES	BEHOLDERS	BICKERING	BITTERNUT	BLINDFOLD
BATTERING	BEHOLDING	BICONCAVE	BITTINESS	BLINDNESS
BATTINESS	BELATEDLY	BICYCLING	BIVALENCY	BLIND SPOT
BATTLEAXE	BELEAGUER	BICYCLIST	BIZARRELY	BLINKERED
BATTLECRY	BELEMNITE	BIDENTATE	BLABBERED	BLISTERED
BAWDINESS	BELGRAVIA	BIFARIOUS	BLACKBALL	BLIZZARDS
BAYONETED	BELIEVERS	BIFOLIATE	BLACK BELT	BLOCKADED
BAY WINDOW	BELIEVING	BIFURCATE	BLACKBIRD	BLOCKAGES
BEACH BALL	BELITTLED	BAGAMISTS	BLACKBUCK	BLOCKHEAD
BEACHHEAD	BELITTLER	BIG DIPPER	BLACKCOCK	BLOCK VOTE
BEACHWEAR	BELLICOSE	BIGENERIC	BLACKDAMP	BLONDNESS
BEADINESS	BELLOWING	BIG-TIMERS	BLACKENED	BLOOD BANK
BEARBERY	BELLYACHE	BIGUANIDE	BLACK EYES	BLOODBATH
BEARDLESS	BELLY FLOP	BIG WHEELS	BLACK FISH	BLOODFUED
BEARISHLY	BELONGING	BIJECTION	BLACKHEAD	BLOOD HEAT
BEARSKINS	BEMOANING	BIJECTIVE	BLACK HOLE	BLOODLESS
BEASTLIER	BENCHMARK	BILABIALS	BLACKJACK	BLOOD LUST
BEATIFIED	BENEFICES	BILABIATE	BLACK LEAD	BLOOD ROOT
BEATITUDE	BENEFITED	BILATERAL	BLACK LEGS	BLOODSHED
BEAUMONDE	BENGALESE	BILHARZIA	BLACKLIST	BLOODSHOT
BEAUTIFUL	BENGALINE	BILINGUAL	BLACKMAIL	BLOOD TYPE
BEAUX-ARTS	BENIGHTED	BILIRUBIN	BLACK MASS	BLOOD WORM
BEAVERING	BENIGNANT	BILLBOARD	BLACKNESS	BLOSSOMED
BEBEERINE	BENIGNITY	BILLETING	BLACKOUTS	BLOTCHIER
BECCAFICO	BENTONITE	BILLFOLDS	BLACKPOLL	BLOTCHILY
BECKONING	BENZIDINE	BILLHOOKS	BLACK SPOT	BLOW-DRIED
BECQUERAL	BERBERINE	BILLIARDS	BLACKTAIL	BLOW-FLIES
BEDAUBING	BEREAVING	BILLIONTH	BLAMELESS	BLOWHARDS
BEDECKING	BERKELIUM	BILLOWING	BLANCHING	BLOWHOLES
BEDEVILLED	BERYLLIUM	BILLY GOAT	BLANDNESS	BLOWLAMPS
BEDFELLOW	BESEECHED	BILOCULAR	BLANKETED	BLOWPIPES
BEDRAGGLE	BESETTING	BIMONTHLY	BLANKNESS	BLUBBERED
BEDRIDDEN	BESIEGING	BIN-LINERS	BLASPHEME	BLUDGEONS
BED-SITTER	BESMEARED	BINOCULAR	BLASPHEMY	BLUEBEARD
BEDSPREAD	BESPATTER	BINOMIALS	BLASTEMIC	BLUEBELLS
BEDSTEADS	BESTIALLY	BINUCLEAR	BLASTULAR	BLUEBERRY
BEEFEATER	BESTIRRED	BIOGRAPHY	BLATANTLY	BLUEBIRDS
BEEFINESS	BESTOWING	BIOLOGIST	BLATHERED	BLUE-BLACK
BEEFSTEAK	BESTREWED	BIOMETRIC	BLAZONING	BLUE BLOOD
BEEKEEPER	BETE-NOIRE	BIONOMICS	BLEACHERS	BLUE BOOKS
BEELZEBUB	BETHLEHEM	BIONOMIST	BLEACHING	BLUE CHIPS
BEERINESS	BETHOUGHT	BIOSPHERE	BLEAKNESS	BLUE FILMS
BEESTINGS	BETOKENED	BIOSTATIC	BLEARIEST	BLUEGRASS
BEETROOTS	BETRAYALS	BIRTHDAYS	BLEMISHED	BLUE JEANS
BEFALLING	BETRAYERS	BIRTHMARK	BLEMISHER	BLUE PETER
BEFITTING	BETRAYING	BIRTHRATE	BLEMISHES	BLUE PRINT
BEGETTING	BETROTHED	BIRTHROOT	BLENCHING	BLUESTONE
BEGGARING	BETTERING	BIRTHWORT	BLESSEDLY	BLUFFNESS
BEGINNERS	BETTER-OFF	BISECTING	BLESSINGS	BLUNDERED
BEGINNING	BEVELLING	BISECTION	BLETHERED	BLUNTNESS
BEGRUDGED	BEVERAGES	BISECTRIX	BLIGHTERS	BLURREDLY
BEGUILING	BEWAILING	BISSERATE	BLIGHTING	BLUSTERER
BEHAVIOUR	BEWITCHED	BISEXUALS	BLIND DATE	BOARDROOM
BEHEADING	BIBLIOTIC	BITCHIEST	BLINDFISH	BOARDWALK

BOARHOUSE	BOTHERING	BREAKAGES	BUBBLE GUM	BURSIFORM
BOAT HOOKS	BOTTLE-FED	BREAKAWAY	BUBBLIEST	BURTHENED
BOAT HOUSE	BOUILLONS	BREAKDOWN	BUCCANEER	BUSHELLER
BOAT SWAIN	BOULEVARD	BREAKEVEN	BUCHAREST	BUSHINESS
BOAT TRAIN	BOUNCIEST	BREAKFAST	BUCKBOARD	BUTADIENE
BOBSLEIGH	BOUNDLESS	BREAKNECK	BUCKETING	BUTCHERED
BOBTAILED	BOUNTEOUS	BREATHILY	BUCKHOUND	BUTTERBUR
BODY BLOWS	BOUNTIFUL	BREATHING	BUCKTEETH	BUTTERCUP
BODYCHECK	BOURGEOIS	BREECHING	BUCKTHORN	BUTTERFAT
BODYGUARD	BOUTIQUES	BRIC-A-BRAC	BUCKTOOTH	BUTTERFLY
BOGGINESS	BOW-LEGGED	BRICKWORK	BUCKWHEAT	BUTTERINE
BOILINGLY	BOWSPIRITS	BRICKYARD	BUDDHISTS	BUTTERING
BOLDFACED	BOWSTRING	BRIEFCASE	BUDGETARY	BUTTERNUT
BOLSHEVIK	BOW WINDOW	BRIGADIER	BUDGETING	BUTTONING
BOLSHIEST	BOXING DAY	BRILLIANT	BUFFALOES	BUZZWORDS
BOLSTERED	BOX NUMBER	BRIMSTONE	BUFFERING	BYPASSING
BOLSTERER	BOX OFFICE	BRININESS	BUFFETING	BYPRODUCT
BOLTHOLES	BOYCOTTED	BRIOLETTE	BUGLEWEED	BYSTANDER
BOMBARDED	BOYFRIEND	BRIQUETTE	BUILDINGS	
BOMBASTIC	BOY SCOUTS	BRISKNESS	BULGARIAN	
BOMBPROOF	BRACELETS	BRISTLING	BULGINESS	**10 LETTERS**
BOMBSHELL	BRACHIATE	BRITANNIA	BULGINGLY	BABY-MINDER
BOMBSIGHT	BRACINGLY	BRITANNIC	BULKHEADS	BABY-SITTER
BOMBSITES	BRACKETED	BRITISHER	BULKINESS	BACCHANALS
BONA FIDES	BRACTEATE	BROACHING	BULLDOZED	BACITRACIN
BONE CHINA	BRACTEOLE	BROAD BEAN	BULLDOZER	BACKBITERS
BONEHEADS	BRAGGARTS	BROADBILL	BULLETINS	BACKBITING
BON VIVANT	BRAINIEST	BROADCAST	BULLFIGHT	BACKCLOTHS
BOOBY TRAP	BRAINLESS	BROADENED	BULLFINCH	BACKCOMBED
BOOKCASES	BRAINSICK	BROAD JUMP	BULLFROGS	BACKDATING
BOOK CLUBS	BRAINWASH	BROAD LEAF	BULLHORNS	BACKFIRING
BOOK MAKER	BRAINWAVE	BROADLOOM	BULLISHLY	BACKGAMMON
BOOK MARKS	BRAKESHOE	BROADNESS	BULLRINGS	BACKGROUND
BOOK PLATE	BRAKESMAN	BROADSIDE	BULL'S EYES	BACKHANDED
BOOKSHELF	BRAMBLING	BROADTAIL	BULRUSHES	BACKHANDER
BOOKSHOPS	BRANCHIAL	BROCADING	BUMBLEBEE	BACKLASHES
BOOKSTALL	BRANCHING	BROCHETTE	BUMPINESS	BACK NUMBER
BOOKSTAND	BRANDLING	BROCHURES	BUMPTIOUS	BACKPACKER
BOOK TOKEN	BRAND NAME	BROKERAGE	BUNGALOWS	BACKSLIDER
BOOKWORMS	BRASHNESS	BRONCHIAL	BUNGHOLES	BACKSPACES
BOOMERANG	BRASS BAND	BRONZE AGE	BUNKHOUSE	BACKSTAIRS
BOORISHLY	BRASSERIE	BROODIEST	BUOYANTLY	BACKSTITCH
BOOTLACES	BRASS HATS	BROTHERLY	BURDENING	BACK STREET
BOOTSTRAP	BRASSIERE	BROWN RICE	BURGEONED	BACKSTROKE
BOOZINESS	BRASSIEST	BRUNETTES	BURGESSES	BACKWARDLY
BORDELLOS	BRAVENESS	BRUSH-OFFS	BURLESQUE	BACKWATERS
BORDERING	BRAWNIEST	BRUSHWOOD	BURLINESS	BACULIFORM
BOREHOLES	BRAZENING	BRUSHWORK	BURNINGLY	BAFFLEMENT
BORN-AGAIN	BRAZILIAN	BRUSQUELY	BURNSHED	BAGGAGE CAR
BORROWERS	BREACHING	BRUTALITY	BURNISHER	BALACLAVAS
BORROWING	BREAD BINS	BRUTALIZE	BURNOUSES	BALALAIKAS
BOSSINESS	BREADLINE	BRUTISHLY	BURROWING	BALDERDASH
BOTANICAL	BREADROOT	BRYOPHYTE	BURSARIAL	BALDHEADED
BOTANISTS	BREAKABLE	BRYTHONIC	BURSARIES	BALLASTING

BALLERINAS	BARROW BOYS	BEGRUDGING	BIBLIOTIST
BALLFLOWER	BARTENDERS	BEHINDHAND	BICHLORIDE
BALLISTICS	BARYCENTRE	BELABOURED	BICYCLISTS
BALLOONING	BARYSPHERE	BELIEVABLE	BIENNIALLY
BALLOONIST	BASALTWARE	BELIEVABLY	BIFURCATED
BALLPOINTS	BASE METALS	BELITTLING	BIGAMOUSLY
BALNEOLOGY	BASILICATA	BELLADONNA	BIG BROTHER
BALUSTRADE	BASKETBALL	BELLARMINE	BIG DIPPERS
BAMBOOZLED	BASKET-STAR	BELLETRIST	BIJOUTERIE
BAMBOOZLER	BASKETWORK	BELL-RINGER	BILBERRIES
BANALATIES	BAS-RELIEFS	BELLWETHER	BILINGUALS
BANANA SKIN	BASS GUITAR	BELLYACHED	BILIVERDIN
BANDERILLA	BASSOONIST	BELLYACHES	BILLBOARDS
BANDMASTER	BASTARDIZE	BELLY DANCE	BILLET-BOX
BANDOLEERS	BASUTOLAND	BELLY FLOPS	BILLIONTHS
BANDSTANDS	BATH CHAIRS	BELLY LAUGH	BILL OF FARE
BANDWAGONS	BATHOMETER	BELONGINGS	BILL OF SALE
BANGLADESH	BATHOMETRY	BENCH MARKS	BILLY GOATS
BANISHMENT	BATHYMETRY	BENEDICITE	BIMESTRIAL
BANK DRAFTS	BATHYSCAPH	BENEFACTOR	BIMETALLIC
BANKROLLED	BATON ROUGE	BENEFICIENT	BINOCULARS
BANKRUPTCY	BATTALIONS	BENEFICIAL	BINUCLEATE
BANKRUPTED	BATTLEAXES	BENEFITING	BIOCELLATE
BANNERETTE	BATTLEDORE	BENEVOLENT	BIODYNAMIC
BANQUETING	BATTLEMENT	BENIGNANCY	BIOECOLOGY
BAPTISTERY	BATTLESHIP	BENZOCAINE	BIOGENESIS
BARBARIANS	BAYONETING	BENZODRINE	BIOGENETIC
BARBARISMS	BAY WINDOWS	BENZOFURAN	BIOGRAPHER
BARBARIZED	BEACH BALLS	BEQUEATHED	BIOGRAPHIC
BARBEQUING	BEACH BUGGIES	BEQUEATHER	BIOLOGICAL
BARBED WIRE	BEACHCHAIR	BESEECHING	BIOLOGISTS
BARBELLATE	BEACHHEADS	BESMEARING	BIOPHYSICS
BAREHEADED	BEANSPROUT	BESMIRCHED	BIOPLASMIC
BARELEGGED	BEASTLIEST	BESPEAKING	BIOPOIESIS
BARGAINING	BEATIFYING	BESSARABIA	BIORHYTHMS
BARGE POLES	BEATITUDES	BESTIALITY	BIOSTATICS
BARIUM MEAL	BEAUJOLAIS	BESTIALIZE	BIPARIETAL
BARLRYCORN	BEAUTICIAN	BESTIARIES	BIPARTISAN
BARLEY WINE	BEAUTY SPOT	BESTIRRING	BIPETALOUS
BAR MITZVAH	BECOMINGLY	BESTREWING	BIQUADRATE
BARN DANCES	BECQUERELS	BESTRIDDEN	BIRD OF PREY
BAROMETERS	BEDCLOTHES	BESTRIDING	BIRTHMARKS
BAROMETRIC	BEDEVILING	BEST-SELLER	BIRTHPLACE
BARONNESS	BEDEVILLED	BETELGEUSE	BIRTH RATES
BARONETAGE	BED OF ROSES	BETHINKING	BIRTHRIGHT
BARRACKING	BEDRAGGLED	BETOKENING	BIRTHSTONE
BARRACUDAS	BED-SITTERS	BETROTHALS	BISEXUALLY
BARRAMUNDI	BEDSPREADS	BETROTHING	BISHOPBIRD
BARRATROUS	BEEFEATERS	BETTERMENT	BISHOPRICS
BARRENNESS	BEFOREHAND	BEWILDERED	BISMUTHOUS
BARRENWORT	BEFOULMENT	BEWITCHING	BISSEXTILE
BARRICADED	BEFRIENDED	BIANNULATE	BISULPHATE
BARRICADER	BEGGARWEED	BIBLIOPOLE	BISULPHIDE
BARRISTERS	BEGINNINGS	BIBLIOTICS	BISYMMETRY

BITARTRATE	BLINDFOLD	BOBBY SOCKS	BOX NUMBERS
BITCHINESS	BLIND SOPTS	BOBSLEIGHS	BOX OFFICES
BIT OF FLUFF	BLISSFULLY	BODYGUARDS	BOYCOTTING
BITTERLING	BLISTERING	BOILER SUIT	BOYFRIENDS
BITTERNESS	BLITHERING	BOISTEROUS	BOYISHNESS
BITTERWEED	BLITHESOME	BOLLOCKS-UP	BRACHIOPOD
BITTERWOOD	BLOCKADING	BOLL WEEVIL	BRACHYLOGY
BITUMINIZE	BLOCKHEADS	BOLOMETRIC	BRACHYURAN
BITUMUNOUS	BLOCKHOUSE	BOLSHEVIKS	BRACKETING
BIVALVULAR	BLOCK VOTES	BOLSHEVISM	BRADYKININ
BIVOUACKED	BLONDENESS	BOLSTERING	BRAGGINGLY
BLABBERING	BLOOD BANKS	BOMBARDIER	BRAHMANISM
BLACKMOOR	BLOODBATHS	BOMBARDING	BRAINCHILD
BLACK BELTS	BLOOD COUNT	BOMBSHELLS	BRAIN DRAIN
BLACKBERRY	BLOOD FEUD	BONDHOLDER	BRAININESS
BLACK BOXES	BLOOD GROUP	BONEHEADED	BRAINSTORM
BLACK DEATH	BLOODHOUNDS	BONE MARROW	BRAINWAVES
BLACKENING	BLOODINESS	BONESHAKER	BRAKE SHOES
BLACKGUARD	BLOOD LUSTS	BON VIVANTS	BRANCHIATE
BLACKHEADS	BLOOD MONEY	BOOBY PRIZE	BRANDISHED
BLACKHEART	BLOOD SPORT	BOOBY TRAPS	BRANDISHER
BLACK HOLES	BLOODSTAIN	BOOKBINDER	BRAND NAMES
BLACKJACKS	BLOODSTOCK	BOOKKEEPER	BRASHINESS
BLACKLISTS	BLOOD TYPES	BOOKMAKERS	BRASS BANDS
BLACK MAGIC	BLOODY MARY	BOOKMOBILE	BRASSBOUND
BLACK MARIA	BLOSSOMING	BOOKPLATES	BRASSED OFF
BLACK POWER	BLOTCHIEST	BOOKSELLER	BRASSERIES
BLACK SHEEP	BLOW-BY-BLOW	BOOKSTALLS	BRASSIERES
BLACKSHIRT	BLOW-DRYING	BOOK TOKENS	BRASSINESS
BLACKSMITH	BLOWZINESS	BOOMERANGS	BRASS TACKS
BLACKSNAKE	BLUBBERING	BOOTBLACKS	BRATISLAVA
BLACK SPOTS	BLUDGEONED	BOOTLEGGED	BRAVISSIMO
BLACKTHORN	BLUDGEONER	BOOTLEGGER	BRAWNINESS
BLACK WIDOW	BLUE BABIES	BOOTLOADER	BRAZENNESS
BLADDERNUT	BLUEBEARDS	BOOTSTRAPS	BREADBOARD
BLANCMANGE	BLUEBOTTLE	BORDERLAND	BREADCRUMB
BLANKETING	BLUE CHEESE	BORDERLINE	BREADFRUIT
BLANK VERSE	BLUE-COLLAR	BORROWINGS	BREADLINES
BLASPHEMED	BLUE MURDER	BOTANIZING	BREAKAWAYS
BLASPHEMER	BLUE-PENCIL	BOTCHINESS	BREAKDOWNS
BLASTOCOEL	BLUEPRINTS	BOTHERSOME	BREAKFASTS
BLASTOCYST	BLUETHROAT	BOTRYOIDAL	BREAKWATER
BLASTODERM	BLUNDERERS	BOTTLE BANK	BREASTBONE
BLASTOMERE	BLUNDERING	BOTTLE-FEED	BREASTWORK
BLASTOPORE	BLUSHINGLY	BOTTLENECK	BRECCIATED
BLATHERING	BLUSTERERS	BOTTOMLESS	BREEZINESS
BLEACHABLE	BLUSTERING	BOTTOM LINE	BRICKLAYER
BLEARINESS	BOARDROOMS	BOTTOMMOST	BRIDEGROOM
BLEATINGLY	BOARDWALKS	BOULEVARDS	BRIDESMAID
BLEMISHING	BOASTFULLY	BOUNCINESS	BRIDGEABLE
BLETHERING	BOASTINGLY	BOUNDARIES	BRIDGEHEAD
BLIND ALLEY	BOATHOUSES	BOWDLERISM	BRIDGEPORT
BLIND DATES	BOATSWAINS	BOWDLERIZE	BRIDGEWORK
BLIND DRUNK	BOAT TRAINS	BOW WINDOWS	BRIGANTINE

BRIGHTENER
BRIGHTNESS
BRIGHTWORK
BRILLIANCE
BRILLIANCY
BRIQUETTES
BRITISHERS
BROADCASTS
BROADCLOTH
BROADENING
BROAD GUAGE
BROADSHEET
BROADSIDES
BROADSWORD
BROKEN-DOWN
BROKENNESS
BRONCHIOLE
BRONCHITIC
BRONCHITIS
BRONX CHEER
BROODINESS
BROOMSTICK
BROWBEATEN
BROWNED-OFF
BROWNSTONE
BRUTALIZED
BRYOLOGIST
BRYOPHYTIC
BUBONOCELE
BUCCANEERS
BUCCINATOR
BUCHENWALD
BUCKBOARDS
BUCKET SEAT
BUCKET SHOP
BUDGERIGAR
BUFFER ZONE
BUFFLEHEAD
BUFFOONERY
BULLDOZERS
BULLDOZING
BULLFIGHTS
BULLHEADED
BULLNECKED
BUMBLENESS
BUNCHINESS
BUNKHOUSES
BUNYA-BUNYA
BUON GIORNO
BURBERRIES
BURDENSOME
BUREAUCRAT
BURGENLAND
BURGEONING

BURGLARIES
BURGUNDIAN
BURLESQUED
BURLESQUES
BURNISHING
BURTHENING
BUSH BABIES
BUSH HAMMER
BUSH MASTER
BUSH RANGER
BUSINESSES
BUS STATION
BUSYBODIES
BUTCHERING
BUTTER BEAN
BUTTERCUPS
BUTTERFISH
BUTTERMILK
BUTTERWORT
BUTTON-DOWN
BUTTONHOLE
BUTTONHOOK
BUTTONWOOD
BUTTRESSED
BUTTRESSES
BY-ELECTION
BYPRODUCTS
BYSTANDERS

11 LETTERS
BABY-MINDERS
BABY'S-BREATH
BABY-SITTING
BACCHANALIA
BACCIFEROUS
BACCIVOROUS
BACILLIFORM
BACKBENCHER
BACKBENCHES
BACKCOMBING
BACK COUNTRY
BACKGROUNDS
BACKHANDERS
BACK NUMBERS
BACK PACKERS
BACK PASSAGE
BACKPEDALED
BACKROOM BOY
BACKSLAPPER
BACKSLIDERS
BACKSLIDING
BACKSTREETS
BACKSTROKES

BACKTRACKED
BACTERAEMIA
BACTERICIDE
BADDERLOCKS
BAD-MOUTHING
BAGGAGE CARS
BAGGAGE ROOM
BAKER'S DOZEN
BALANCEABLE
BALEFULNESS
BALL BEARING
BALLETOMANE
BALLOONISTS
BALUCHISTAN
BALUSTRADES
BAMBOOZLING
BANANA SKINS
BANDMASTERS
BANGLADESHI
BANK ACCOUNT
BANKER'S CARD
BANK HOLIDAY
BANK ROLLONG
BANKRUPTING
BANTERINGLY
BARBARIIES
BARBARIZING
BARBAROUSLY
BARBITURATE
BAREFACEDLY
BARIUM MEALS
BARLEY SUGAR
BARLEY WATER
BAR MITZVAHS
BARNSTORMED
BARNSTORMER
BAROGRAPHIC
BARONETCIES
BAROTSELAND
BARQUENTINE
BARREL ORGAN
BARRICADING
BASHFULNESS
BASKERVILLE
BASS GUITARS
BASSOONISTS
BASTARDIZED
BASTINADOED
BASTINADOES
BASTNAESITE
BATHING SUITE
BATHOLITHIC
BATHOMETRIC
BATTLE CRIES

BATTLEFIELD
BATTLEMENTS
BATTLE ROYAL
BATTLESHIPS
BEACHCHAIRS
BEACHCOMBER
BEANSPROUTS
BEARISHNESS
BEAR'S-BREECH
BEASTLINESS
BEAUTEOUSLY
BEAUTICIANS
BEAUTIFULLY
BEAUTIFYING
BEAUTY QUEEN
BEAUTY SLEEP
BEAUTY SPOTS
BEAVERBOARD
BEDEVILLING
BEDEVILMENT
BEFITTINGLY
BEFRIENDING
BEGUILEMENT
BEGUILINGLY
BEHAVIOURAL
BELABOURING
BELATEDNESS
BELEAGUERED
BELL-BOTTOMS
BELLICOSITY
BELLIGERENT
BELL-RINGING
BELLY ACHING
BELLY-BUTTON
BELLY DANCER
BELLY DANCES
BELLY LAUGHS
BENEDICTINE
BENEDICTION
BENEDICTORY
BENEFACTION
BENEFACTORS
BENEFICIARY
BENEVOLENCE
BENIGHTEDLY
BEQUEATHING
BEREAVEMENT
BERGSCHRUND
BESMIRCHING
BESPATTERED
BESTSELLERS
BESTSELLING
BETULACEOUS
BEWILDERING

377

BHUBANESWAR	BLACKLEGGED	BODHISATTVA	BREAD BASKET
BIAS BINDING	BLACKLISTED	BODY-CENTRED	BREAD BOARDS
BIBLIOLATRY	BLACKMAILED	BODY POLITIC	BREAD CRUMBS
BIBLIOMANCY	BLACKMAILER	BOILERMAKER	BREAD FRUITS
BIBLIOMANIA	BLACK MARIAS	BOILERPLATE	BREADTHWAYS
BIBLIOPHILE	BLACK MARKET	BOILERSUITS	BREADWINNER
BIBLIOPHISM	BLACK MASSES	BOLL WEEVILS	BREAKFASTED
BIBLIOTHECA	BLACK MUSLIM	BOMBARDIERS	BREASTPLATED
BICARBONATE	BLACK PEPPER	BOMBARDMENT	BREATHALYSE
BICENTENARY	BLACK SHIRTS	BONDHOLDERS	BREATHINESS
BICEPHALOUS	BLACK SMITHS	BONE MARROWS	BREECHBLOCK
BICONCAVITY	BLACK WIDOWS	BONESHAKERS	BREMERHAVEN
BIEDERMEIER	BLADDER WORT	BOOBY PRIZES	BRIDGEBOARD
BIFOLIOLATE	BLAMELESSLY	BOOKBINDERS	BRISTLETAIL
BIFURCATING	BLAMEWORTHY	BOOKBINDERY	BRITTLENESS
BIFURCATION	BLANCMANGES	BOOKBINDING	BRITTLE-STAR
BIG BUSINESS	BLANK CHEQUE	BOOKISHNESS	BROADCASTER
BILATERALLY	BLASPHEMERS	BOOKKEPERS	BROAD GAUGES
BILIOUSNESS	BLASPHEMIES	BOOKKEEPING	BROAD MINDED
BILLETS-DOUX	BLASPHEMING	BOOKMOBILES	BROAD SHEETS
BILLIONAIRE	BLASPHEMOUS	BOOKSELLERS	BROAD SWORDS
BILLOWINESS	BLASTOGENIC	BOOMERANGED	BROMINATION
BILLS OF FARE	BLASTOMERIC	BOORISHNESS	BRONCHIOLAR
BILLS OF SALE	BLASTOPORIC	BOOTLEGGERS	BRONTOSAURI
BIMETALLISM	BLENCHINGLY	BOOTLEGGING	BRONX CHEERS
BIMOLECULAR	BLEPHARITIC	BORDERLANDS	BRONZE MEDAL
BIOCATALYST	BLEPHARITIS	BORDERLINES	BROOMSTICKS
BIOCENOLOGY	BLESSEDNESS	BOTANICALLY	BROTHERHOOD
BIODYNAMICS	BLIND ALLEYS	BOTHERATION	BROWBEATING
BIOENGINEER	BLINDFOLDED	BOTTLE BANKS	BROWNSTONES
BIOFEEDBACK	BLINDSTOREY	BOTTLE GREEN	BRUCELLIOSIS
BIOGRAPHERS	BLOCKBUSTER	BOTTLENECKS	BRUSQUENESS
BIOGRAPHIES	BLOCKHOUSES	BOUNDLESSLY	BRUTALITIES
BIOPHYSICAL	BLOOD COUNTS	BOUNTEOUSLY	BRUTALIZING
BIOPARTITION	BLOOD GROUPS	BOURGEOISIE	BRUTISHNESS
BIOQUADRATIC	BLOODHOUNDS	BOURNEMOUTH	BRYOLOGICAL
BIOQUARTERLY	BLOODLESSLY	BOWDLERIZED	BUCKET SEATS
BIRD-BRAINED	BLOOD PLASMA	BOYSENBERRY	BUCKET SHOPS
BIRDS OF PREY	BLOOD SPORTS	BRACE AND BIT	BUCKLER-FERN
BIRD-WATCHER	BLOOD STAINS	BRACHIATION	BUCOLICALLY
BIROBIDZHAN	BLOOD STREAM	BRADYCARDIA	BUDGERIGARS
BIRTHPLACES	BLOOD SUCKER	BRADYCARDIC	BUENOS AIRES
BIRTHRIGHTS	BLOOD VESSEL	BRAGGADOCIO	BUFFER STATE
BISEXUALISM	BLOTCHINESS	BRAHMAPUTRA	BUFFER STOCK
BISEXUALITY	BLUDGEONING	BRAIN DRAINS	BUFFER ZONES
BISYMMETRIC	BLUEBERRIES	BRAINLESSLY	BULBIFEROUS
BITTERSWEET	BLUE-BLOODED	BRAINSTORMS	BULLDOG CLIP
BIVOUACKING	BLUEBOTTLES	BRAINS TRUST	BULLETPROOF
BLACKMOORS	BLUE CHEESES	BRAINTEASER	BULLFIGHTER
BLACKBALLED	BLUE-EYED BOY	BRAINWASHED	BULLFINCHES
BLACKBOARDS	BLUE MUDERS	BRAINWASHER	BULLISHNESS
BLACK COMEDY	BLUNDERBUSS	BRANCHIOPOD	BULL TERRIER
BLACKGUARDS	BLURREDNESS	BRANDENBURG	BUMPTIOUSLY
BLACK HUMOUR	BOBSLEIGHED	BRANDISHING	BUREAUCRACY

BUREAUCRATS
BURGOMASTER
BURLESQUING
BURNISHAMBLE
BUSHWACKER
BUSINESS END
BUSINESSMAN
BUSINESSMEN
BUS STATIONS
BUTCHERBIRD
BUTTER BEANS
BUTTERFLIES
BUTTONHOLED
BUTTONHOLES
BUTTONMOULD
BUTTRESSING
BY-ELECTIONS

12 LETTERS
BABY CARRIAGE
BACCHANALIAN
BACKBENCHERS
BACKBREAKING
BACKHANDEDLY
BACK OF BEYOND
BACK PASSAGES
BACKPEDALING
BACKPEDALLED
BACKROOM BOYS
BACK SLAPPERS
BACK SLAPPING
BACKTRACKING
BACKWARDNESS
BACKWOODSMAN
BACKWOODSMEN
BACTERICIDAL
BACTERIOLOGY
BAGGAGE ROOMS
BAKING POWDER
BALANCED DIET
BALANCE SHEET
BALL BEARINGS
BALLOTEMENT
BANDJARMASIN
BANK ACCOUNTS
BANKER'S CARDS
BANKER'S ORDER
BANK HOLIDAYS
BANKRUPTCIES
BANTAMWEIGHT
BARBARIANISM
BARBARICALLY
BARBITURATES

BARLEY SUGARS
BARNSTORMERS
BARNSTORMING
BARRELORGANS
BASIDIOSPORE
BASTARDIZING
BATCH PROCESS
BATHING SUITS
BATHYSPHERES
BATTERING RAM
BATTLEFIELDS
BATTLES ROYAL
BEACH BUGGIES
BEACHCOMBERS
BEAUTIFICALLY
BEAUTY QUEENS
BECHUANALAND
BEDAZZLEMENT
BEGGARLINESS
BEGRUDGINGLY
BEHAVIOURISM
BEHAVIOURIST
BELEAGUERING
BELITTLEMENT
BELITTLINGLY
BELLETRISTIC
BELLIGERENCE
BELLIGERENCY
BELLIGERENTS
BELLY BUTTONS
BELLY DANCERS
BENEDICTINES
BENEDICTIONS
BENEFACTIONS
BENEFACTRESS
BENEFICENTLY
BENEFICIALLY
BENEVOLENTLY
BEREAVEMENTS
BESPECTACLED
BEWILDERMENT
BEWITCHINGLY
BIAURICULATE
BIBLIOGRAPHY
BIBLIOMANIAC
BIBLIOPHILES
BICOLLATERAL
BIFLAGELLATE
BIFURCATIONS
BILHARZIASIS
BILINGUALISM
BILL OF HEALTH
BILL OF LADING
BILL OF RIGHTS

BIOCATALYTIC
BIOCHEMISTRY
BIOECOLOGIST
BIOFLAVONOID
BIOGEOGRAPHY
BIOGRAPHICAL
BIOLOGICALLY
BIONOMICALLY
BIOPHYSICIST
BIOSYNTHESIS
BIOSYNTHETIC
BIRD'S EYE VIEW
BIRD WATCHERS
BIRTH CONTROL
BLABBERMOUTH
BLACK AND BLUE
BLACK BALLING
BLACK BERRIES
BLACK COUNTRY
BLACK CURRANT
BLACK ECONOMY
BLACK ENGLISH
BLACKGUARDLY
BLACK-HEARTED
BLACKLEGGING
BLACKLISTING
BLACKMAILERS
BLACKMAILING
BLACK MUSLIMS
BLACK PUDDING
BLADDERWRACK
BLAMEFULNESS
BLANK CHEQUES
BLAST FURNACE
BLASTODERMIC
BLASTOSPHERE
BLINDFOLDING
BLISSFULNESS
BLISTERINGLY
BLOCKBUSTERS
BLOCK LETTERS
BLOEMFONTEIN
BLOOD BROTHER
BLOODLETTING
BLOODSTAINED
BLOODSTREAMS
BLOODSUCKERS
BLOODTHIRSTY
BLOODVESSELS
BLOODY-MINDED
BLUE-EYED BOYS
BLUESTOCKING
BLUNDERINGLY
BLUSTERINGLY

BOARDING CARD
BOASTFULNESS
BOBSLEIGHING
BODY LANGUAGE
BODY SNATCHER
BODY STOCKING
BOILING POINT
BOISTEROUSLY
BOLSTERINGLY
BOMBACACEOUS
BOMBARDMENTS
BOOBY-TRAPPED
BOOK-LEARNING
BOOMERANGING
BOTTOM DRAWER
BOWDLERIZING
BOWLING ALLEY
BOWLING GREEN
BRACHYLOGOUS
BRACKISHNESS
BRAINS TRUSTS
BRAINTEASERS
BRAINWASHING
BREADWINNERS
BREAKFASTING
BREASTSTROKE
BREECHLOADER
BRINKMANSHIP
BROADCASTERS
BROADCASTING
BRONCHOSCOPE
BRONCHOSCOPY
BRONCHOBUSTER
BRONTOSAURUS
BRONZE MEDALS
BROTHERHOODS
BROTHER-IN-LAW
BROWNIE POINT
BUFFER STATES
BUFFER STOCKS
BULLDOG CLIPS
BULLET-HEADED
BULLFIGHTERS
BULLFIGHTING
BULLHEADEDLY
BULL TERRIERS
BUNSEN BURNER
BUREAUCRATIC
BURGLAR ALARM
BUSINESSLIKE
BUSINESS SUIT
BUTTERSCOTCH
BUTTONHOLING
BUYER'S MARKET

BABY CARRIAGES
BACCALAUREATE
BACK FORMATION
BACK PEDALLING
BACKWARDATION
BACTERIOLYSIS
BACTERIOLYTIC
BACTERIOPHAGE
BALANCED DIETS
BALANCE SHEETS
BALKANIZATION
BALLISTICALLY
BALNEOLOGICAL
BALSAMIFEROUS
BAMBOOZLEMENT
BANDSPREADING
BANKER'S ORDERS
BANTAMWEIGHTS
BARBAROUSNESS
BAREFACEDNESS
BASIDOMYCETE
BATTERING RAMS
BATTLE CRUISER
BATTLE-SCARRED
BEAST OF BURDEN
BEATIFICATION
BEAUTY PARLOUR
BEHAVIOURALLY
BEHAVIOURISTS
BELISHA BEACON
BELLES-LETTRES
BELLY-LANDINGS
BENEFICIARIES
BEWILDERINGLY
BIBLIOGRAPHER
BIBLIOGRAPHIC
BICENTENARIES
BIG BANG THEORY
BIG HEADEDNESS
BIGNONIACEOUS
BILLS OF HEALTH

BILLS OF LADING
BIODEGRADABLE
BIOECOLOGICAL
BIOENERGETICS
BIOMETRICALLY
BIOSTATICALLY
BIOTECHNOLOGY
BIRD OF PASSAGE
BIRD'S-EYE VIEWS
BIREFRINGENCE
BLABBERMOUTHS
BLACK AND WHITE
BLACK BERRYING
BLACK COMEDIES
BLACK CURRANTS
BLACKGUARDISM
BLACK PUDDINGS
BLAMELESSNESS
BLANDISHMENTS
BLANTYRE-LIMBE
BLASPHEMOUSLY
BLAST FURNACES
BLASTOGENESIS
BLIND MAN'S BUFF
BLOOD BROTHERS
BLOOD CURDLING
BLOODLESSNESS
BLOOD PRESSURE
BLOOD RELATION
BLOTTING PAPER
BLUE-PENCILLED
BLUESTOCKINGS
BLUNDERBUSSES
BOARDING CARDS
BOARDING HOUSE
BODY SNATCHERS
BODY STOCKINGS
BOILING POINTS
BOMBASTICALLY
BOOBY TRAPPING
BOON COMPANION
BORAGINACEOUS

BOTTLE-FEEDING
BOTTOM DRAWERS
BOUGAINVILLEA
BOUNDLESSNESS
BOUNTIFULNESS
BOUSTROPHEDON
BOWLING ALLEYS
BOWLING GREENS
BRACHYPTEROUS
BRAINLESSNESS
BRAINSTORMING
BRASSICACEOUS
BRASS KNUCKLES
BROADMINDEDLY
BROKEN-HEARTED
BROMELIACEOUS
BRONCHIAL TUBE
BRONCHOSCOPIC
BROTHERLINESS
BROTHERS-IN-LAW
BROWNIE GUIDES
BROWNIE POINTS
BRUTALIZATION
BUBONIC PLAGUE
BUILDING BLOCK
BULLETIN BOARD
BUMPTIOUSNESS
BUNSEN BURNERS
BURDEN OF PROOF
BUREAUCRACIES
BUREAUCRATISM
BURGLAR ALARMS
BURNT OFFERING
BUSH TELEGRAPH
BUSINESS CLASS
BUSINESS SUITS
BUSINESSWOMAN
BUTCHER'S-BROOM
BUTTERFINGERS
BUTYRALDEHYDE

3 LETTERS

CAB
CAD
CAM
CAN
CAP
CAR
CAT
CAW
CIA
CID
COB
COD
COG
COL
CON
COO
COP
COS
COT
COW
COX
COY
CRY
CUB
CUD
CUE
CUM
CUP
CUR
CUT

4 LETTERS

CABS
CADS
CAFE
CAGE
CAKE
CALF
CALK
CALL
CALM
CALX
CAME
CAMP
CAMS
CANE
CANS
CANT
CAPE
CAPS
CARD
CARE

CARP
CARS
CART
CASE
CASH
CASK
CAST
CATS
CAUL
CAVE
CAVY
CAWS
CEDE
CELL
CENT
CERT
CHAP
CHAR
CHAT
CHEF
CHER
CHEW
CHIC
CHID
CHIN
CHIP
CHIT
CHOP
CHOU
CHOW
CHUG
CHUM
CINE-
CITE
CITY
CLAD
CLAM
CLAN
CLAP
CLAW
CLAY
CLEF
CLEW
CLIP
CLOD
CLOG
CLOP
CLOT
CLOY
CLUB
CLUE
COAL
COAT
COAX

COBS
COCK
CODA
CODE
CODS
COED
COGS
COIF
COIL
COIN
COIR
COKE
COLA
COLD
COLS
COLT
COMA
COMB
COME
CONE
CONK
CONS
CONY
COOK
COOL
COON
COOP
COOS
COOT

5 LETTERS

CABAL
CABBY
CABER
CABIN
CABLE
CACAO
CACHE
CACTI
CADDY
CADET
CADGE
CADIZ
CADRE
CAFES
CAGES
CAGEY
CAIRN
CAIRO
CAJUN
CAKED
CAKES
CALIX
CALLA
CALLS
CALOR

CROW
CRUS
CRUX
CUBA
CUBE
CUBS
CUED
CUES
CUFF
CULL
CULM
CULT
CUPS
CURB
CURD
CURE
CURL
CURS
CURT
CUSP
CUSS
CUTE
CUTS
CYAN
CYST
CZAR

CALVE
CALYX
CAMEL
CAMEO
CAMPO
CANAL
CANDY
CANED
CANER
CANES
CANNA
CANNY
CANOE
CANON
CANTO
CANTS
CAPER
CAPES
CAPON
CAPRI
CAP
CARAT
CARDS
CARED
CARES
CARET
CARGO
CARNE
CAROB
CAROL
CARPS
CARRY
CARTS
CARVE
CASED
CASES
CASKS
CASTE
CATCH
CATER
CATTY
CAULK
CASES
CAVED
CAVES
CAVIL
CAWED
CD-ROM
CEARA
CEASE
CEDAR
CEDED
CEDER
CEIBA

CELLA
CELLE
CELLO
CELLS
CENSE
CENTO
CENTS
CERES
CERIC
CERTS
CETUS
CHAFE
CHAFF
CHAIN
CHAIR
CHALK
CHAMP
CHANT
CHAOS
CHAPS
CHARD
CHARM
CHARS
CHART
CHARY
CHASE
CHASM
CHATS
CHEAP
CHEAT
CHECK
CHEEK
CHEEP
CHEER
CHEFS
CHESS
CHEST
CHEWS
CHEWY
CHICK
CHIDE
CHIEF
CHILD
CHILE
CHILL
CHIME
CHINA
CHINE
CHING
CHINK
CHINS
CHIPS
CHIRP
CHIRR

CHAR (partial col) — CORK CORM CORN COSH COST COSY COTS COUP COVE COWL COWS COXA COZY CRAB CRAG CRAM CRAP CREW CRIB CROP

381

CHITS	CLIME	COMIC	COYLY	CROWD	CYNIC
CHIVY	CLINE	COMMA	COYPU	CROWN	CYSTS
CHOCK	CLING	COMPO	COZEN	CROWS	CZARS
CHOIR	CLINK	CONCH	CRABS	CROZE	CZECH
CHOKE	CLIPS	CONES	CRACK	CRUDE	
CHOKY	CLOAK	CONEY	CRAFT	CRUEL	
CHOMP	CLOCK	CONGA	CRAGS	CRUET	**6 LETTERS**
CHOPS	CLODS	CONGE	CRAKE	CRUMB	CABALS
CHORD	CLONE	CONGO	CRAMP	CRUMP	CABANA
CHORE	CLOSE	CONIC	CRANE	CRURA	CABERS
CHOSE	CLOTH	CONKS	CRANK	CRUSE	CABINS
CHOUX	CLOTS	CONTE	CRAPE	CRUSH	CABLED
CHOWS	CLOUD	COOED	CRAPS	CRUST	CABLES
CHRON-	CLOUT	COOKS	CRASH	CRYPT	CABLET
CHUCK	CLOVE	COOLS	CRASS	CUBAN	CABMAN
CHUFF	CLOWN	COONS	CRATE	CUBED	CACHES
CHUMP	CLUBS	COOPS	CRAVE	CUBES	CACHET
CHUMS	CLUCK	CO-OPT	CRAWL	CUBIC	CACHOU
CHUNK	CLUES	COOTS	CRAZE	CUBIT	CACKLE
CHURL	CLUMP	COPED	CRAZY	CUDDY	CACTUS
CHURN	CLUNG	COPES	CREAK	CUFFS	CADCAM
CHUTE	CLUNK	COPSE	CREAM	CUING	CADDIE
CHYME	CLUNY	CORAL	CREDO	CULCH	CADDIS
CIDER	CLWYD	CORDS	CREED	CULET	CADENT
CIGAR	CLYDE	CORED	CREEK	CULEX	CADETS
CINCH	COACH	CORER	CREEL	CULLS	CADGED
CIRCA	COALS	CORES	CREEP	CULPA	CADGER
CISCO	COALY	CORGI	CREME	CULTS	CADRES
CISSY	COAST	CORKS	CREPE	CUMIN	CAECUM
CITED	COATS	CORNS	CREPT	CUPEL	CAELUM
CIVET	COBRA	CORNU	CRESS	CUPIS	CAEOMA
CIVIL	COCKS	CORNY	CREST	CUPPA	CAESAR
CLACK	COCKY	CORPS	CRETE	CURBS	CAFTAN
CLAIM	COCOA	CORSE	CREWS	CURCH	CAGIER
CLAMP	CODAS	COSTA	CRIBS	CURDY	CAGILY
CLAMS	CODED	COSTS	CRICK	CURED	CAGING
CLANG	CODER	COUCH	CRIED	CURES	CAICOS
CLANK	CODES	COUGH	CRIER	CURET	CAIQUE
CLANS	CODEX	COULD	CRIES	CURIA	CAIRNS
CLAPS	COIFS	COUNT	CRIME	CURIE	CAJOLE
CLASH	COIGN	COUPE	CRIMP	CURIO	CAKING
CLASP	COILS	COUPS	CRISP	CURLS	CALAIS
CLASS	COINS	COURT	CROAK	CURLY	CALASH
CLAWS	COKES	COVEN	CROAT	CURRY	CALCAR
CLEAN	COLDS	COVER	CROCK	CURSE	CALCES
CLEAR	COLIC	COVES	CROFT	CURVE	CALCIC
CLEAT	COLON	COVET	CRONE	CUSHY	CALICO
CLEEK	COLTS	COVEY	CRONY	CUSPS	CALIPH
CLEFS	COMAS	COWED	CROOK	CUTER	CALKED
CLEFT	COMBO	COWER	CROON	CUTIS	CALKIN
CLERK	COMBS	COWES	CROPS	CUT UP	CALLAO
CLICK	COMER	COWLS	CRORE	CYCLE	CALLED
CLIFF	COMET	COXED	CROSS	CYDER	CALLER
CLIMB	COMFY	COXES	CROUP	CYMRY	CALL-IN

382

CALLOW	CANYON	CASTER	CERVIX	CHICLY	CHURLS
CALL-UP	CAPERS	CASTES	CETANE	CHIDED	CHUTES
CALLUS	CAPIAS	CASTLE	CEYLON	CHIDER	CICADA
CALMED	CAPONS	CASTOR	CHA-CHA	CHIEFS	CICERO
CALMER	CAPOTE	CASUAL	CHACMA	CHIGOE	CIDERS
CALMLY	CAPPED	CATCHY	CHAETA	CHILES	CIGARS
CALPAC	CAPPER	CATENA	CHAFED	CHILLI	CILICE
CALQUE	CAPSID	CATGUT	CHAFER	CHILLS	CILIUM
CALVED	CAPTOR	CATION	CHAFFY	CHILLY	CINDER
CALVES	CARAFE	CATKIN	CHAINS	CHIMED	CINEMS
CAMASS	CARATS	CATNAP	CHARS	CHIMES	CINEOL
CAMBER	CARBON	CATNIP	CHAISE	CHINES	CINQUE
CAMELS	CARBOY	CATSUP	CHALET	CHINKS	CIPHER
CAMEOS	CARDED	CATTLE	CHALKS	CHINTZ	CIRCLE
CAMERA	CAREEN	CAUCUS	CHALKY	CHIPPY	CIRCUM-
CAMION	CAREER	CAUDAD	CHAMPS	CHIRPS	CIRCUS
CAMISE	CARESS	CAUDAL	CHANCE	CHIRPY	CIRQUE
CAMLET	CARETS	CAUDEX	CHANCY	CHISEL	CIRRUS
CAMPED	CARGOS	CAUDLE	CHANGE	CHITIN	CITIES
CAMPER	CARHOP	CAUGHT	CHANTS	CHITON	CITIFY
CAMPOS	CARIES	CASUAL	CHANTY	CHIVES	CITING
CAMPUS	CARINS	CAUSED	CHAOAN	CHOCKS	CITRAL
CANADA	CARING	CAUSES	CHAPEL	CHOICE	CITRIC
CANLALS	CARMAN	CAVEAT	CHARDS	CHOIRS	CITRIN
CANAPE	CARMEL	CAVE-IN	CHARGE	CHOKED	CITRON
CANARD	CARNES	CAVERN	CHARMS	CHOKER	CITRUS
CANARY	CARNET	CAVIAR	CHARTS	CHOKES	CIVETS
CANCAN	CAROBS	CAVING	CHASED	CHOLER	CIVICS
CANCEL	CAROLS	CAVITY	CHASER	CHOLLA	CIVIES
CANCER	CARPEL	CAVORT	CHASES	CHONJU	CLAIMS
CANDID	CARPET	CAWING	CHASMS	CHOOSE	CLAMMY
CANDLE	CARPUS	CAXTON	CHASSE	CHOOSY	CLAMPS
CANINE	CARREL	CAYMAN	CHASTE	CHOPPY	CLAQUE
CANING	CARROT	CD-ROMS	CHATTY	CHORAL	CLARET
CANKER	CARTED	CEASED	CHEATS	CHORDS	CLASPS
CANNED	CARTEL	CEDARS	CHECKS	CHOREA	CLASSY
CANNEL	CARROT	CEDING	CHECY	CHORES	CLAUSE
CANNES	CARTED	CELAYA	CHEEKS	CHORIC	CLAWED
CANNON	CARTON	CELERY	CHEEKY	CHORUS	CLAWER
CANNOT	CARVED	CELLAR	CHEEPS	CHOSEN	CLAYEY
CANOED	CARVER	CELLOS	CHEERS	CHOUGH	CLEATS
CANOES	CASABA	CELTIC	CHEERY	CHRISM	CLEAVE
CANONS	CASEFY	CEMENT	CHEESE	CHRIST	CLEFTS
CANOPY	CASEIN	CENSER	CHEESY	CHROMA	CLENCH
CANTAL	CASERN	CERCAL	CHEQUE	CHROME	CLEOME
CANTED	CASHED	CERCIS	CHERRY	CHUBBY	CLERGY
CANTER	CASHEW	CERCUS	CHERTY	CHUCKS	CLERIC
CANTIC	CASING	CEREAL	CHERUB	CHUKAR	CLERKS
CANTLE	CASINO	CERES	CHESTS	CHUKKA	CLEVER
CANTON	CASKET	CERISE	CHESTY	CHUMMY	CLEVIS
CANTOR	CASSLON	CERIUM	CHEWED	CHUMPS	CLICHE
CANTOS	CASQUE	CERMET	CHEWER	CHUNKS	CLICKS
CANTUS	CASSIA	CEROUS	CHICKS	CHUNKY	CLIENT
CANVAS	CASSIS	CERVID	CHICLE	CHURCH	CLIFFS

CLIMAX	COCKLE	COMMAS	CORALS	COVERS	CRENEL
CLIMBS	COCK-UP	COMMIS	CORBAN	COVERT	CREOLE
CLIMES	COCOON	COMMIT	CORBEL	COVEYS	CRESOL
CLINAL	CODDLE	COMMON	CORDED	COWAGE	CRESTS
CLINCH	CODGER	COMORO	CORDON	COWARD	CRETAN
CLINES	CODIFY	COMOSE	CORERS	COWBOY	CRETIC
CLINGY	CODING	COMPEL	CORFAM	COWMAN	CRETIN
CLINIC	COELOM	COMPLY	CORGIS	COWMEN	CREUSE
CLOACA	COERCE	CONCHA	CORING	COWPAT	CREWED
CLOAKS	COEVAL	CONCHY	CORIUM	COWPOX	CREWEL
CLODDY	COFFEE	CONCUR	CORKED	COWRIE	CRICKS
CLOGGY	COFFER	CONDOM	CORKER	COXING	CRIERS
CLONAL	COFFIN	CONDOR	CORMEL	COYOTE	CRIKEY
CLONES	COGENT	CONEYS	CORNEA	COYPUS	CRIMEA
CLONIC	COGGED	CONFER	CORNEL	COZIER	CRIMES
CLONUS	COGNAC	CONGAS	CORNE	COZILY	CRINGE
CLOSED	COHEIR	CONGES	CORNET	CRABBY	CRINUM
CLOSER	COHERE	CONGOU	CORONA	CRACKS	CRIPES
CLOSES	COHORT	CONICS	CORPSE	CRACOW	CRISES
CLOSET	COHOSH	CONIES	CORPUS	CRADLE	CRISIS
CLOTHE	COHUNE	CONIUM	CORRAL	CRAFTS	CRISPS
CLOTHS	COILED	CONKED	CORSES	CRAGGY	CRISPY
CLOUDS	COILER	CONKER	CORSET	CRAMBO	CRISTA
CLOUDY	COINED	CONMAN	CORTEX	CRAMPS	CRITIC
CLOUTS	COINER	CANMEN	CORYMB	CRANED	CROAKS
CLOVEN	COITAL	CONNED	CORYZA	CRANES	CROCKS
CLOVER	COITUS	CONOID	COSECH	CRANIA	CROCUS
CLOVES	COLDER	CONSUL	COSHED	CRANKS	CROFTS
CLOWNS	COLDLY	CONTRA-	COSHES	CRANKY	CRONES
CLOYED	COLEUS	CONVEX	COSIER	CRAPPY	CROOKS
CLUBBY	COLEYS	CONVEY	COSIES	CRASIS	CRORES
CLUCKS	COLIMA	CONVOY	COSILY	CRATED	CROSSE
CLUMPS	COLLAR	COOING	COSINE	CRATER	CROTCH
CLUMPY	COLLET	COOKED	COSMIC	CRATES	CROTON
CLUMSY	COLLIE	COOKER	COSMOS	CRAVAT	CROUCH
CLUTCH	COLONS	COOKIE	COSSET	CRAVED	CROUPS
COALED	COLONY	COLLED	COSTAL	CRAVEN	CROWDS
COALER	COLOUR	COOLER	CO-STAR	CRAWLS	CROWED
COARSE	COLUMN	COOLIE	COSTLY	CRAYON	CROWER
COASTS	COLURE	COOLLY	COTTER	CRAZED	CROWNS
COATED	COMATE	COOPED	COTTON	CRAZES	CRUDER
COAXED	COMBAT	COOPER	COUCAL	CREAKS	CRUETS
COAXER	COMBED	COPALM	COUGAR	CREAKY	CRUISE
COBALT	COMBER	COPIED	COUGHS	CREAMS	CRUMBS
COBBER	COMBOS	COPIER	COULEE	CREASE	CRUMBY
COBBLE	COMEDY	COPIES	COUNTS	CREATE	CRUMMY
COBNUT	COMELY	COPING	COUNTY	CRECHE	CRUNCH
COBRAS	COME-ON	COP-OUT	COUPES	CREDIT	CRURAL
COBWEB	COMERS	COPPED	COUPLE	CREDOS	CRUSES
COCCID	COMETS	COPPER	COUPON	CREEDS	CRUSTS
COCCUS	COMFIT	COPSES	COURSE	CREEKS	CRUSTY
COCCYX	COMICS	COPTIC	COURTS	CREELS	CRUTCH
COCHIN	COMING	COPULA	COUSIN	CREEPS	CRUXES
COCKED	COMITY	COQUET	COVENS	CREEPY	CRYING

CRYPTS	CUTEST	CAGIEST	CAMPBED	CAPTIVE	CARTING
CUBANE	CUTLER	CAGOULE	CAMPERS	CAPTORS	CARTONS
CUBBED	CUTLET	CAHOOTS	CAMPHOR	CAPTURE	CARTOON
CUBING	CUTOFF	CAIQUES	CAMPING	CARAFES	CARVERS
CUBISM	CUTOUT	CAISSON	CAMPION	CARAMBA	CARVING
CUBIST	CUTTER	CAJOLED	CAMWOOD	CARAMEL	CASCADE
CUBITS	CUTUPS	CAJUPUT	CANAPES	CARAVAN	CASCARA
CUBOID	CYANIC	CALAMUS	CANARDS	CARAVEL	CASEASE
CUCKOO	CYCLED	CALCIFY	CANASTA	CARAWAY	CASEATE
CUCUTA	CYCLES	CALCINE	CANCANS	CARBENE	CASEOSE
CUFFED	CYCLIC	CALCITE	CANCERS	CARBIDE	CASEOUS
CUIABA	CYDERS	CALCIUM	CANDELA	CARBINE	CASERTA
CULLED	CYGNET	CALCULI	CANDIED	CARBONS	CASHEWS
CULLER	CYGNUS	CALDERA	CANDIES	CARBOYS	CASHIER
CULLET	CYMBAL	CALDRON	CANDLER	CARCASS	CASHING
CULLIS	CYMENE	CALENDS	CANDLES	CARDIAC	CASINGS
CULTIC	CYMOID	CALGARY	CANDOUR	CARDING	CASINOS
CUMANA	CYMOSE	CALIBRE	CANELLA	CARDOON	CASKETS
CUMBER	CYMRIC	CALICHE	CANINES	CAREERS	CASPIAN
CUNEAL	CYNICS	CALICOS	CANKERS	CAREFUL	CASQUED
CUPIDS	CYPHER	CALIPEE	CANNERY	CARFARE	CASQUES
CUPOLA	CYPRUS	CALIPHS	CANNIER	CARGOES	CASSATA
CUPPAS	CYSTIC	CALKING	CANNILY	CARHOPS	CASSAVA
CUPPED		CALLAIS	CANNING	CARIBOU	CASSINO
CUPRIC		CALLANT	CANNONS	CARIOCA	CASSOCK
CUP TIE	**7 LETTERS**	CALL BOX	CANNULA	CARIOLE	CASTERS
CUPULE	CABARET	CALLBOY	CANONRY	CARIOUS	CASTILE
CURACY	CABBAGE	CALLERS	CNOPUS	CARLINE	CASTING
CURARE	CABBALA	CALLING	CANTALA	CARLING	CASTLED
CURATE	CABBIES	CALL-INS	CANTEEN	CARMINE	CASTLES
CURBED	CABEZON	CALLOUS	CANTERS	CARNAGE	CAST-OFF
CURDLE	CABIMAS	CALMEST	CANTHUS	CARNIFY	CASTORS
CURFEW	CABINET	CALMING	CANTING	CAROLED	CASULIST
CURIAE	CABLING	CALOMEL	CANTONS	CAROLUS	CATALAN
CURING	CABOOSE	CALORIC	CANTORS	CAROTID	CATALPA
CURIOS	CAB RANK	CALORIE	CANVASS	CAROUSE	CATANIA
CURIUM	CACHETS	CALOTTE	CANYONS	CARPALE	CATARRH
CURLED	CACKLED	CALTROP	CANZONA	CAR PARK	CATBIRD
CURLER	CACKLER	CALUMNY	CANZONE	CARPETS	CATBOAT
CURLEW	CACKLES	CALVARY	CAPABLE	CARPING	CATCALL
CURSED	CADAVER	CALVING	CAPABLY	CAR POOL	CATCHER
CURSES	CADDIED	CALYCES	CAPELIN	CARPORT	CATCHES
CURSOR	CADDIES	CALYCLE	CAPELLA	CARRICK	CATECHU
CURTLY	CADDISH	CALYPSO	CAPERED	CARRIED	CATERED
CURTSY	CADELLE	CALYXES	CAPITAL	CARRIER	CATERER
CURVED	CADENCE	CAMBERS	CAPITOL	CARRIES	CATFISH
CURVES	CADENCY	CAMBIAL	CAPORAL	CARRION	CATHEAD
CURVET	CADENZA	CAMBIST	CAPPING	CARROTS	CATHODE
CUSCUS	CADGERS	CAMBIUM	CAPRICE	CARROTY	CATKINS
CUSPID	CADGING	CAMBRAI	CAPSIZE	CARRY-ON	CATLING
CUSSED	CADMIUM	CAMBRIC	CAPSTAN	CARSICK	CATMINT
CUSSES	CAESIUM	CAMELOT	CAPSULE	CARTAGE	CATNAPS
CUSTOM	CAESURA	CAMERAL	CAPTAIN	CARTELS	CAT'S-EAR
CUTELY	CAFTANS	CAMERAS	CAPTION	CARTERS	CAR'S EYE

385

CAT'S PAW	CERTAIN	CHARLIE	CHIBOUK	CHORIOD	CLAMANT
CATSUIT	CERTIFY	CHARMED	CHICAGO	CHORTLE	CLAMBER
CATTALO	CERUMEN	CHARMER	CHICANE	CHOWDER	CLAMMED
CATTERY	CERVINE	CHARNEL	CHICANO	CHROMIC	CLAMOUR
CATTIER	CESSION	CHARPOY	CHICKEN	CHROMYL	CLAMPED
CATTILY	CESSPIT	CHARQUI	CHICORY	CHRONIC	CLAMPER
CATTISH	CESTODE	CHARRED	CHIDDEN	CHRONON	CLANGED
CATWALK	CESTOID	CHARTED	CHIDING	CHUCKED	CLANGER
CAUDATE	CHAFFED	CHARTER	CHIEFLY	CHUCKLE	CLANGOR
CAULINE	CHAFFER	CHASERS	CHIFFON	CHUFFED	CLANKED
CAULKED	CHAFING	CHASING	CHIGGER	CHUGGED	CLAPPED
CAULKER	CHAGRIN	CHASMAL	CHIGNON	CHUKKER	CLAPPER
CAUSING	CHAINED	CHASSIS	CHILEAN	CHUMMED	CLAQUES
CAUSTIC	CHAIRED	CHASTEN	CHILIAD	CHURNED	CLARIFY
CAUTERY	CHAISES	CHASTER	CHILIES	CHUTNEY	CLARINO
CAUTION	CHALCID	CHATEAU	CHILLED	CHUVASH	CLARION
CAVALLA	CHALETS	CHATTED	CHILLUM	CHYMOUS	CLARITY
CAVALRY	CHALICE	CHATTEL	CHILUNG	CICADAS	CLARKIA
CAVEATS	CHALKED	CHATTER	CHIMERA	CICHLID	CLASHED
CAVE-INS	CHALLAH	CHAYOTE	CHIMERE	CILIARY	CLASHER
CAVEMAN	CHALLIS	CHEAPEN	CHIMING	CILIATE	CLASHES
CAVEMEN	CHALONE	CHEAPER	CHIMNEY	CIMBRIC	CLASPED
CAVERNS	CHAMBER	CHEAPLY	CHINESE	CINDERS	CLASPER
CAVETTO	CHAMFER	CHEATED	CHINKED	CINDERY	CLASSED
CAVILED	CHAMOIS	CHEATER	CHINOOK	CINEMAS	CLASSES
CAYENNE	CHAMPAC	CHECHEN	CHINTZY	CINERIN	CLASSIC
CEASING	CHAMPED	CHECKED	CHINWAG	CIPHERS	CLASSIS
CEDILLA	CHANCED	CHECK-IN	CHIPPED	CIPOLIN	CLASTIC
CEILING	CHANCEL	CHECK-UP	CHIPPER	CIRCLED	CLATTER
CELADON	CHANCES	CHEDDAR	CHIRPED	CIRCLER	CLAUSAL
CELEBES	CHANCRE	CHEEKED	CHIRPER	CIRCLES	CLAUSES
CELESTA	CHANGER	CHEEPED	CHIRRUP	CIRCLET	CLAVATE
CELLARS	CHANGES	CHEEPER	CHISELS	CIRCUIT	CLAVIER
CELLIST	CHANNEL	CHEERED	CHIVIED	CIRQUES	CLAVIUS
CELLULE	CHANSON	CHEERIO	CHLORAL	CIBRATE	CLAWING
CELSIUS	CHANTED	CHEESES	CHLORIC	CIRSOID	CLAYPAN
CENSORS	CHANTER	CHEETAH	CHOC-ICE	CISSIES	CLEANED
CENSUAL	CHANTRY	CHELATE	CHOCKED	CISSOID	CLEANER
CENSURE	CHAOTIC	CHEMISE	CHOCTAW	CISTERN	CLEANLY
CENTAUR	CHAPEAU	CHEMIST	CHOCIER	CISTRON	CLEANSE
CENTAVO	CHAPELS	CHEQUER	CHOICER	CITABLE	CLEANUP
CENTERS	CHAPLET	CHEQUES	CHOICES	CITABLE	CLEARED
CENTIME	CHAPPAL	CHERISH	CHOKERS	CITADEL	CLEARER
CENTNER	CHAPPED	CHEROOT	CHOKING	CITHARA	CLEARLY
CENTRAL	CHAPTER	CHERUBS	CHOLERA	CITIZEN	CLEAVED
CENTRES	CHARADE	CHERVIL	CHOLINE	CITRATE	CLEAVER
CENTRIC	CHARGED	CHESTED	CHOMPED	CITRINE	CLEMENT
CENTRUM	CHARGER	CHEVIOT	CHOOSER	CITRONS	CLERICS
CENTURY	CHARGES	CHEVRON	CHOPPED	CIVILLY	CLERKED
CEPHEUS	CHARIER	CHEWIER	CHOPPER	CIVVIES	CLICHED
CERAMIC	CHARILY	CHEWING	CHORALE	CLACKED	CLICHES
CERATED	CHARIOT	CHIANTI	CHORDAL	CLADODE	CLICKED
CEREALS	CHARITY	CHIAPAS	CHOREAL	CLAIMED	CLICKER
CEREBRA	CHARKHA	CHIASMA	CHORION	CLAIMER	CLIENTS

CLIMATE	COBBERS	COLLATE	COMPUTE	CONTEMN	CORINTH
CLIMBED	COBBLER	COLLECT	COMRADE	CONTEND	CORKAGE
CLIMBER	COBWEBS	COLLEEN	CONATUS	CONTENT	CORKERS
CLINICS	COCAINE	COLLEGE	CONCAVE	CONTEST	CORKING
CLINKED	COCCOID	COLLIDE	CONCEAL	CONTEXT	CORMOUS
CLINKER	COCCOUS	COLLIER	CONCEDE	CONTORT	CORNCOB
CLIPPED	COCHLEA	COLLIES	CONCEIT	CONTOUR	CORNEAL
CLIPPER	COCKADE	COLLOID	CONCEPT	CONTROL	CORNERS
CLIPPIE	COCKIER	COLLUDE	CONCERN	CONTUSE	CORNETS
CLIQUES	COCKING	COLOBUS	CONCERT	CONVENE	CORNICE
CLIQUEY	COCKLES	COLOGNE	CONCHAL	CONVENT	CORNIER
CLOACAL	COCKNEY	COLOMBO	CONCHES	CONVERT	CORNISH
CLOAKED	COCKPIT	COLONEL	CONCISE	CONVICT	CORNUAL
CLOBBER	COCK-UPS	COLONIC	CONCOCT	CONVOKE	CORNUTE
CLOCHES	COCONUT	COLOSSI	CONCORD	CONVOYS	COROLLA
CLOCKED	COCOONS	COLOURS	CONCUSS	COOKERS	CORONAE
CLOGGED	COCOTTE	COLTISH	CONDEMN	COOKERY	CORONAL
CLOPPED	COCOYAM	COLUMNS	CONDIGN	COOKIES	CORONAS
CLOSELY	CODDLED	COMBATS	CONDOLE	COOKING	CORONER
CLOSEST	CODEINE	COMBERS	CONDOMS	COOKOUT	CORONET
CLOSETS	CODFISH	COMBINE	CONDONE	COOLANT	CORPORA
CLOSE-UP	CODGERS	COMBING	CONDORS	COOLERS	CORPSES
CLOSING	CODICES	COMB-OUT	CONDUCE	COOLEST	CORRADE
CLOSURE	CODICIL	COMBUST	CONDUCT	COOLIES	CORRALS
CLOTHED	CODLING	COMECON	CONDUIT	COOLING	CORRECT
CLOTHES	COELIAC	COMEDIC	CONDYLE	COOLISH	CORREZE
CLOTTED	COEQUAL	COMFIER	CONFECT	COOPERS	CORRIDA
CLOTURE	COERCED	COMFITS	CONFESS	CO-OPTED	CORRODE
CLOUTED	COEVALS	COMFORT	CONFIDE	COPEPOD	CORRUPT
CLOWNED	COEXIST	COMFREY	CONFINE	COPIERS	CORSAGE
CLOYING	COFFERS	COMICAL	CONFIRM	COPILOT	CORSAIR
CLUBBED	COFFINS	COMINGS	CONFORM	COPINGS	CORSETS
CLUCKED	COGENCY	COMMAND	CONFUSE	COPIOUS	CORSICA
CLUMPED	COGGING	COMMEND	CONFUTE	COP-OUTS	CORTEGE
CLUNIAC	COGNACS	COMMENT	CONGEAL	COPPERS	CORVINE
CLUPEID	COGNATE	COMMODE	CONGEST	COPPERY	COSENZA
CLUSTER	COGNIZE	COMMONS	CONGIUS	COPPICE	COSHING
CLUTTER	COHABIT	COMMUNE	CONICAL	COPPING	COSIEST
CLYPEAL	COHERED	COMMUTE	CONIFER	COPULAR	COSINES
CLYPEUS	COHORTS	COMPACT	CONIINE	COPYCAT	COSMINE
COACHED	COILING	COMPANY	CONJOIN	COPYING	COSMOID
COACHES	COIMBRA	COMPARE	CONJURE	COPYIST	COSTARD
COAL GAS	COINAGE	COMPASS	CONQUER	COQUINA	CO-STARS
COALING	COINERS	COMPEER	CONSENT	COQUITO	COSTATE
COAL TAR	COINING	COMPERE	CONSIGN	CORACLE	COSTING
COAMING	COLDET	COMPLETE	CONSIST	CORBEIL	COSTIVE
COARSEN	COLDISH	COMPILE	CONSOLE	CORBELS	COSTUME
COASER	COLD WAR	COMPLEX	CONSOLS	CORDAGE	COTE-D'OR
COASTAL	COLICKY	COMPLIN	CONSORT	CORDATE	COTERIE
COASTED	COLITIC	COMPONY	CONSULS	CORDIAL	COTIDAL
COASTER	COLITIS	COMPORT	CONSULT	CORDING	COTINGA
COATING	COLLAGE	COMPOSE	CONSUME	CORDITE	COTTAGE
COAXIAL	COLLARD	COMPOST	CONTACT	CORDOBA	COTTONY
COAXING	COLLARS	COMPOTE	CONTAIN	CORDONS	COUCHED

C 7 LETTERS to 8 LETTERS

COUCHER	COXCOMB	CRESTED	CRUELLY	CURFEWS	CYPHERS
COUCHES	COYNESS	CRETINS	CRUELTY	CURIOSA	CYPRESS
COUGARS	COYOTES	CREVICE	CRUISED	CURIOUS	CYPRIOT
COUGHES	COZENED	CREWCUT	CRUSIER	CURLERS	CYSTINE
COULDN'T	COZENER	CREWING	CRUISES	CURLEWS	CYSTOID
COULDST	COZIEST	CRIBBED	CRUMBLE	CURLIER	CZARINA
COULOIR	CRABBED	CRICKED	CRUMBLY	CURLING	
COULOMB	CRACKED	CRICKET	CRUMPET	CURRANT	
COULTER	CRACKER	CRICOID	CRUMPLE	CURRENT	**8 LETTERS**
COUNCIL	CRACKLE	CRIMEAN	CRUMPLY	CURRIED	CABBAGES
COUNSEL	CRACKUP	CRIMPED	CRUNCHY	CURRIER	CABINBOY
COUNTED	CRADLED	CRIMPER	CRUSADE	CURRIES	CABINETS
COUNTER	CRADLES	CRIMPLE	CRUSHED	CURRISH	CABLE CAR
COUNTRY	CRAFTED	CRIMSON	CRUSHES	CURSING	CABLEWAY
COUPLED	CRAIOVA	CRINGED	CRYBABY	CURSIVE	CABOCHON
COUPLER	CRAMMED	CRINGLE	CRYOGEN	CURSORS	CABOODLE
COUPLES	CRAMMER	CRINITE	CRYPTAL	CURSORY	CABOOSES
COUPLET	CRAMPED	CRINKLE	CRYPTIC	CURTAIL	CABOTAGE
COUPONS	CRAMPON	CRINKLY	CRYSTAL	CURTAIN	CAB RANKS
COURAGE	CRANIAL	CRINOID	CUBBING	CURTESY	CABRILLA
COURIER	CRANING	CRIPPLE	CUBICAL	CURVING	CABRIOLE
COURSED	CRANIUM	CRISPED	CUBITAL	CUSHIER	CACHALOT
COURSER	CRANKED	CRISPLY	CUCKOLD	CUSHION	CACHEPOT
COURSES	CRAPPED	CRITICS	CUCKOOS	CUSSING	CACHEXIA
COURTED	CRAPPIE	CRITTER	CUDDLED	CUSTARD	CACHUCHA
COURTLY	CRASHED	CROAKED	CUDGELS	CUSTODY	CACKLERS
COUSINS	CRASHES	CROAKER	CUFFING	CUSTOMS	CACKLING
COUTURE	CRASSLY	CROATIA	CUISINE	CUTAWAY	CACTUSES
COUVADE	CRATERS	CROCHET	CULLING	CUTBACK	CADASTER
COVERED	CRATING	CROCKET	CULPRIT	CUTICLE	CADAVERS
COVERER	CRAVATS	CROFTER	CULTISM	CUTLASS	CADDYING
COVERTS	CRAVING	CRONIES	CULTIST	CUTLERS	CADENCES
COVER-UP	CRWLED	CROOKED	CULTURE	CUTLERY	CADENZAS
COVETED	CRAWLER	CROONER	CULVERT	CUTLETS	CADUCEUS
COVETER	CRAYONS	CROPPED	CUMQUAT	CUTOFFS	CADUCITY
COWARDS	CRAZIER	CROPPER	CUMULET	CUTOUTS	CAFFIENE
COWBANE	CRAZILY	CROQUET	CUMULUS	CUTTACK	CAGELING
COWBELL	CREAKED	CROSIER	CUNEATE	CUTTERS	CAGINESS
COWBIND	CREAMED	CROSSED	CUNNING	CUTTING	CAGLIARI
COWBIRD	CREAMER	CROSSER	CUP CAKE	CUTWORK	CAGOULES
COWBOYS	CREASED	CROSSES	CUPOLAS	CUTWORM	CAISSONS
COWERED	CREASES	CROSSLY	CUPPING	CWNBRAN	CAJOLERY
COWFISH	CREATED	CROUTON	CUPRITE	CYANATE	CAJOLING
COWGIRL	CREATOR	CROWBAR	CUPROUS	CYANIDE	CAKEWALK
COWHAND	CRECHES	CROWDED	CUP TIES	CYANINE	CALABASH
COWHERB	CREDENT	CROWING	CURABLE	CYANITE	CALABRIA
COWHERD	CREDITS	CROWNER	CURABLY	CYABLER	CALADIUM
COWHIDE	CREEDAL	CROWDED	CURACAO	CYCLING	CALAMINE
COWLICK	CREEPER	CROZIER	CURATES	CYCLIST	CALAMINT
COWLING	CREMATE	CRUCIAL	CURATOR	CYCLOID	CALAMITE
COWPATS	CRENATE	CRUCIFY	CURBING	CYCLONE	CALAMITY
COWRIES	CREOLES	CRUDELY	CURCUMA	CYCLOPS	CALATHUS
COWSHED	CREOSOL	CRUDEST	CURDLED	CYGNETS	CALCIFIC
COWSLIP	CRESSET	CRUDITY	CURE-ALL	CYMBALS	CALCITIC

388

CALCULUS	CANBERRA	CARAVANS	CASH-BOOK	CAUCUSES
CALCUTTA	CANCELED	CARAWAYS	CASHCARD	CAUDALLY
CALDRONS	CANCROID	CARBINES	CASH CROP	CAULDRON
CALENDAR	CANDIDLY	CARBOLIC	CASH DESK	CAULICLE
CALENDER	CANFIELD	CARBONIC	CASH FLOW	CAULKING
CALF LOVE	CANISTER	CARBONYL	CASHIERS	CAUSABLE
CALFSKIN	CANNABIC	CARBURET	CASHLESS	CAUSALLY
CALIBRED	CANNABIN	CARDAMOM	CASHMERE	CAUSERIE
CALIBRES	CANNABIS	CARDIGAN	CASSETTE	CAUSEWAY
CALIPASH	CANNIBAL	CARDINAL	CASSOCKS	CAUTIONS
CALIPERS	CANNIEST	CARDIOID	CASTAWAY	CAUTIOUS
CALISAYA	CANNIKIN	CARDITIS	CASTINGS	CAVALIER
CALLABLE	CANNONED	CAREENED	CAST-IRON	CAVATINA
CALL GIRL	CANOEING	CAREERED	CASTRATE	CAVEATOR
CALLINGS	CANOEIST	CAREFREE	CASTRATO	CAVEFISH
CALLIOPE	CANONESS	CARELESS	CASUALLY	CAVICORN
CALLIPER	CANONIST	CARESSED	CASUALTY	CAVILING
CALLISTO	CANONIZE	CARESSER	CASUISTS	CAVILLED
CALLUSES	CANOODLE	CARESSES	CATACOMB	CAVILLER
CALMNESS	CANOPIES	CAREWORN	CATALASE	CAVILTIES
CALOR GAS	CANTATAS	CARIBOUS	CATALYST	CAVORTED
CALORIES	CANTEENS	CARILLON	CATAMITE	CEDILLAS
CALUTRON	CANTERED	CARINATE	CATAPULT	CEILINGS
CALVADOS	CANTICLE	CARLISLE	CATARACT	CELERIAC
CALVARIA	CANTONAL	CARNAUBA	CATCALLA	CELERITY
CALYCATE	CANVASES	CARNIVAL	CATCH-ALL	CELIBACY
CALYCINE	CANZONET	CAROLINA	CATCHFLY	CELIBATE
CALYPSOS	CAPACITY	CAROLINE	CATCHIER	CELLARER
CALYPTRA	CAPERING	CAROLING	CATCHILY	CELLARET
CAMAGUEY	CAPESKIN	CAROLLED	CATCHING	CELLISTS
CAMBODIA	CAPITALS	CAROTENE	CATECHIN	CELLULAR
CAMBOGIA	CAPITATE	CAROUSAL	CATECHOL	CELLULOID
CAMBRIAN	CAPONIZE	CAR PARKS	CATEGORY	CEMENTED
CAMELEER	CAPRICES	CARPETED	CATENANE	CEMENTER
CAMELLIA	CAPRIOLE	CARPETED	CATENARY	CEMENTUM
CAMEROON	CAPSICUM	CAR POOLS	CATENATE	CEMETERY
CAMISOLE	CAPSIZED	CARPORTS	CATENOID	CENOTAPH
CAMOMILE	CAPSTANS	CARRIAGE	CATERING	CENOZOIC
CAMPAGNA	CAPSTONE	CARRIERS	CATHEDRA	CENSORED
CAMPAIGN	CAPSULAR	CARRYALL	CATHETER	CENSURED
CAMPANIA	CAPSULES	CARRYCOT	CATHEXIS	CENSURES
CAMP BEDS	CAPTAINS	CARRYING	CATHODES	CENSUSES
CAMPECHE	CAPTIONS	CARRYOUT	CATHODIC	CENTAURS
CAMPFIRE	CAPTIOUS	CARTONS	CATHOLIC	CENTUARY
CAMPHENE	CAPTIVES	CARUNCLE	CATIONIC	CENTAVOS
CAMPINAS	CAPTURED	CARVINGS	CAT'S EYES	CENTERED
CAMPSITE	CAPTURES	CARYATID	CAT'S FOOT	CENTIARE
CAMPUSES	CAPUCHIN	CASANOVA	CAT'S PAWS	CENTIMES
CAMSHAFT	CAPYBARA	CASCADED	CATSUITS	CENTRING
CANADIAN	CARACARA	CASCADES	CATTIEST	CENTRIST
CANAGRE	CARACOLE	CASEMATE	CATTLEYA	CENTROID
CANAILLE	CARAMELS	CASEMENT	CATWALKS	CEPHALAD
CANALIZE	CARANGID	CASEWORK	CAUCASIA	CEPHALIC
CANARIES	CARAPACE	CASHABLE	CAUCASUS	CEPHALIN

CERAMICS	CHAPPING	CHEMISTS	CHLORATE	CINCTURE
CERAMIST	CHAPTERS	CHEMURGY	CHLORIDE	CINEASTE
CERASTES	CHARACIN	CHENILLE	CHLORINE	CINERAMA
CERATOID	CHARADES	CHEQUERS	CHLORITE	CINERARY
CERCARIA	CHARCOAL	CHEROKEE	CHLOROUS	CINNABAR
CEREBRAL	CHARENTE	CHEROOTS	CHOC-ICES	CINNAMON
CEREBRIC	CHARGERS	CHERRIES	CHOCKING	CIPHERED
CEREBRUM	CHARGING	CHERUBIC	CHOICELY	CIRCLETS
CEREMENT	CHARIEST	CHESSMAN	CHOISEST	CIRCLING
CEREMONY	CHARIOTS	CHESTIER	CHOIRBOY	CIRCUITS
CERNUOUS	CHARISMA	CHESTILY	CHOISEUL	CIRCUITY
CEROTYPE	CHARLADY	CHESTNUT	CHOLERIC	CIRCULAR
CERULEAN	CHARLIES	CHEVRONS	CHOMPING	CIRCUSES
CERVELAT	CHARLOCK	CHEWABLE	CHOOSIER	CISTERNA
CERVICAL	CHARMERS	CHEWIEST	CHOP-CHOP	CISTERNS
CERVICES	CHARMING	CHEYENNE	CHOPPERS	CITADELS
CERVIXES	CHARQUID	CHIASMAL	CHOPPIER	CITATION
CESAREAN	CHARRING	CHIASMIC	CHOPPILY	CITIZENS
CESSIONS	CHARTERS	CHIASMUS	CHOPPING	CITREOUS
CESSPITS	CHARTING	CHIASTIC	CHOP SUEY	CITRUSES
CESSPOOL	CHARTISM	CHICANER	CHORALES	CITY HALL
CETACEAN	CHARTIST	CHICANOS	CHORDATE	CIVILIAN
CEVENNES	CHASSEUR	CHICKENS	CHORDING	CIVILITY
CHACONNE	CHASTELY	CHICKPEA	CHORIAMB	CIVILIZE
CHAFFING	CHASTEST	CHICLAYO	CHORTLED	CIVIL LAW
CHAINING	CHASTISE	CHIGETAI	CHORTLES	CIVIL WAR
CHAINMAN	CHASTITY	CHIGGERS	CHORUSED	CLACKING
CHAIN SAW	CHASUBLE	CHIGNONS	CHORUSES	CLAIMANT
CHAIRING	CHAT SHOW	CHILDISH	CHOW-CHOW	CLAIMING
CHAIRMAN	CHATTELS	CHILDREN	CHOW-MEIN	CLAMBAKE
CHAIRMEN	CHATTIER	CHILIASM	CHRISTEN	CLAMMIER
CHALAZAL	CHATTILY	CHILIAST	CHROMATE	CLAMMILY
CHALDRON	CHATTING	CHILLIER	CHROMITE	CLAMMING
CHALICES	CHAUFFER	CHILLIES	CHROMIUM	CLAMOURS
CHALKIER	CHEAPEST	CHILLING	CHROMOUS	CLAMPING
CHAMBERS	CHEATING	CHILOPOD	CHUBBIER	CLANGERS
CHAMBRAY	CHECKERS	CHIMAERA	CHUCKING	CLANGING
CHAMPING	CHEKING	CHIMBOTE	CHUCKLED	CLANKISH
CHAMPION	CHECK-INS	CHIMERAS	CHUCKLER	CLANSMAN
CHANCELS	CHECKOUT	CHIMNEYS	CHUCKLES	CLANSMEN
CHANCERY	CHECKUPS	CHINDWIN	CHUGGING	CLAPPERS
CHANCIER	CHEDDITE	CHINKING	CHUMMIER	CLAPPING
CHANCILY	CHEEKIER	CHINLESS	CHUMMILY	CLAPTRAP
CHANCING	CHEEKILY	CHIPMUNK	CHUMMING	CLARINET
CHANDLER	CHEEKING	CHIPPIES	CHUNKIER	CLARIONS
CHANGING	CHEEPING	CHIPPING	CHURCHES	CLASHING
CHANNELS	CHEERFUL	CHIRPIER	CHURLISH	CLASPING
CHANTIES	CHEERIER	CHIRPILY	CHURNING	CLASSICS
CHANUKAH	CHEERILY	CHIRPING	CHUTZPAH	CLASSIER
CHAPATTI	CHEERING	CHIRRUPY	CICATRIX	CLASSIFY
CHAPBOOK	CHEETAHS	CHISELED	CICERONE	CLASSING
CHAPERON	CHEKIANG	CHITCHAT	CICHLOID	CLASSISM
CHAPLAIN	CHEMICAL	CHIVALRY	CIMBRIAN	CLASSIST
CHAPLETS	CHEMISES	CHIVYING	CINCHONA	CLATTERS

CLATTERY	CLOSE-UPS	COCHLEAE	COLLAGEN	COMMERCE
CLAVICLE	CLOSURES	COCHLEAR	COLLAGES	COMMODES
CLAYLIKE	CLOTHIER	COCKADES	COLLAPSE	COMMONER
CLAYMORE	CLOTHING	COCKATOO	COLLARED	COMMONLY
CLEAN-CUT	CLOTTING	COCKCROW	COLLATED	COMMUNAL
CLEANERS	CLOUDIER	COCKEREL	COLLATOR	COMMUNED
CLEANEST	CLOUDILY	COCKEYED	COLLECTS	COMMUNES
CLEANING	CLOUDING	COCKIEST	COLLEENS	COMMUTED
CLEANSED	CLOUDLET	COCKNEYS	COLLEGES	COMMUTER
CLEANSER	CLOUTING	COCKPITS	COLLIDED	COMPACTS
CLEAR-CUT	CLOWNERY	COCKSPUR	COLLIERS	COMPARED
CLEAREST	CLOWNING	COCKSURE	COLLIERY	COMPARER
CLEARING	CLOWNISH	COCKTAIL	COLLOQUE	COMPARES
CLEAROUT	CLUBBING	COCONUTS	COLLOQUY	COMPEERS
CLEARWAY	CLUBFEET	COCOONED	COLLUDED	COMPERED
CLEAVAGE	CLUBFOOT	CODDLING	COLOMBIA	COMPERES
CLEAVERS	CLUBHAUL	CODICILS	COLONELS	COMPETED
CLEAVING	CLUCKING	CODIFIED	COLONIAL	COMPILED
CLEMATIS	CLUELESS	CODIFIER	COLONIES	COMPILER
CLEMENCY	CLUMPING	CODOMAIN	COLONIST	COMPLAIN
CLENCHED	CLUMPISH	CODPIECE	COLONIZE	COMPLETE
CLENCHES	CLUMSIER	COENURUS	COLOPHON	COMPILED
CLERICAL	CLUMSILY	COENURUS	COLORADO	COMPLIER
CLERIHEW	CLUPEOID	COENZYME	COLORANT	COMPLAIN
CLERKDOM	CLUSTERS	COEQUALS	COLOSSAL	COMPOSED
CLERKING	CLUSTERY	COERCING	COLOSSUS	COMPOSER
CLEVEITE	CLUTCHED	COERCION	COLOTOMY	COMPOTES
CLEVERLY	CLUTCHES	COERCIVE	COLOURED	COMPOUND
CLICKING	COACHING	COEXTEND	COLPITIS	COMPRESS
CLIMATES	COACHMAN	COGENTLY	COLUBRID	COMPRISE
CLIMATIC	COACHMEN	COGITATE	COLUMBIS	COMPUTED
CLIMAXED	COACTOION	COGNATES	COLUMBIC	COMPUTER
CLIMAXES	COACTIVE	COGNOMEN	COLUMBUS	COMRADES
CLIMBERS	COAGULUM	COGWHEEL	COLUMNAR	CONATION
CLIMBING	COAHUILA	COHERENT	COLUMNED	CONATIVE
CLINCHED	COALESCE	COHERING	COMANCHE	CONCEDED
CLINCHER	COALFACE	COHESION	COMATOSE	CONCEITS
CLINCHES	COALFISH	COHESIVE	COMBATED	CONCEIVE
CLINGING	COALHOLE	COHOBATE	COMBATER	CONCEPTS
CLINICAL	COALMINE	COIFFEUR	COMBINED	CONCERNS
CLINKERS	COALPORT	COIFFURE	COMBINER	CONCERTO
CLINKING	COARSELY	COINAGES	COMBINES	CONCERTS
CLIPPERS	COARSEST	COINCIDE	COMEBACK	CONCHOID
CLIPPIES	COASTERS	COINSURE	COMEDIAN	CONCLAVE
CLIPPING	COASTING	COLANDER	COMEDIES	CONCLUDE
CLIQUISH	COATINGS	COLD CUTS	COMEDOWN	CONCRETE
CLOAKING	COAT-TAIL	COLD FEET	COMELIER	CONDENSE
CLOCKING	COAUTHOR	COLD FISH	COMFIEST	CONDOLED
CLODDISH	COBALTIC	COLDNESS	COMFORTS	CONDONED
CLOGGING	COBBLERS	COLD SNAP	COMITIES	CONDONER
CLOISTER	COBBLING	COLD SORE	COMMANDO	CONDUCED
CLOPPING	COBWEBBY	COLD-WELD	COMMANDS	CONDUCER
CLOSE-SET	COCA-COLA	COLESLAW	COMMENCE	CONDUITS
CLOSETED	COCCYGES	COLISEUM	COMMENTS	CONDYLAR

CONFEREE	CONTINUO	CORNEOUS	COURTING	CRANKING
CONFERVA	CONTOURS	CORNERED	COUSCOUS	CRANKPIN
CONFETTI	CONTRACT	CORNETTE	COVALENT	CRANNIED
CONFIDED	CONTRAIL	CORNICES	COVENANT	CRANNIES
CONFIDER	CONTRARY	CORNICHE	COVENTRY	CRASHING
CONFINED	CONTRAST	CORNIEST	COVERAGE	CRAVENLY
CONFINES	CONTRIVE	CORN PONE	COVERING	CRAVINGS
CONFLATE	CONTROS	CORONARY	COVERLET	CRAWFISH
CONFLICT	CONTUSED	CORONERS	COVERTLY	CRAWLERS
CONFOCAL	CONVENED	CORONETS	COVER-UPS	CRAWLING
CONFOUND	CONVENER	CORPORAL	COVETING	CRAYFISH
CONFRERE	CONVENTS	CORRIDOR	COVETOUS	CRAYONED
CONFRONT	CONVERGE	CORRODED	COWARDLY	CRAZIEST
CONFUSED	CONVERSE	CORRODER	COWBELLS	CREAKIER
CONFUTED	CONVERTS	CORSAGES	COWBERRY	CREAKILY
CONFUTER	CONVEXLY	CORSAIRS	COWERING	CREAMERS
CONGENER	CONVEYED	CORSELET	COWHANDS	CREAMERY
CONGRATS	CONVEYOR	CORSETED	COWHERDS	CREAMIER
CONGRESS	CONVICTS	CORSETRY	COWHIDES	CREAMING
CONIDIAL	CONVINCE	CORTEGES	COWLICKS	CREASING
CONIDIUM	CONVOKED	CORTICAL	COWLINGS	CREATINE
CONIFERS	CONVOKER	CORTICES	CO-WORKER	CREATING
CONJOINT	CONVOYED	CORUNDUM	COWSHEDS	CREATION
CONJUGAL	CONVULSE	CORVETTE	COWSLIPS	CREATIVE
CONJUNCT	COOKABLE	CORYPHEE	COXALGIA	CREATORS
CONJURED	COOKBOOK	COSECANT	COXALGIC	CREATURE
CONJURER	COOKOUTS	COSINESS	COXCOMBS	CREDENCE
CONNIVED	COOLABAR	COSMETIC	COXSWAIN	CREDENZA
CONNIVER	COOLANTS	COSTLIER	COZENAGE	CREDIBLE
CONNOTED	COOLNESS	COST-PLUS	COZENING	CREDIBLY
CONODONT	COOPTING	COSTUMES	COZINESS	CREDITED
CONOIDAL	COOPTION	COTDEATH	CRABBIER	CREDITOR
CONQUEST	COPILOTS	COTERIES	CRABBING	CREEPERS
CONSERVE	COPLANAR	COTSWOLD	CRABWISE	CREEPIER
CONSIDER	COPPERAS	COTTAGER	CRACKERS	CREEPILY
CONSOLED	COPULATE	COTTAGES	CRACKLING	CREEPING
CONSOLER	COPYBOOK	COUCHANT	CRACKLED	CREMATED
CONSOLES	COPYCATS	COUCHING	CRACKNEL	CREMATOR
CONSOMME	COPY-EDIT	COUGHING	CRACKPOT	CREODONT
CONSORTS	COPYHOLD	COULISSE	CRACKUPS	CREOSOTE
CONSPIRE	COPYISTS	COUMARIN	CRADLING	CRESCENT
CONSTANT	COQUETRY	COUMARIN	CRAFTIER	CRESTING
CONSTRUE	COQUETTE	COUNCILS	CRAFTILY	CRESYLIC
CONSULAR	COQUILLE	COUNTERS	CRAFTINNG	CRETONNE
CONSUMED	CORACLES	COUNTESS	CRAGGIER	CREVASSE
CONSUMER	CORACOID	COUNTIES	CRAM-FULL	CREVICES
CONTACTS	CORDIALS	COUNTING	CRAMMERS	CERW CUTS
CONTANGO	CORDLESS	COUPLETS	CRAMMING	CREW NECK
CONTEMPT	CORDONED	COUPLING	CRAMPING	CRIBBAGE
CONTENTS	CORDOVAN	COURANTE	CRAMPONS	CRIBBING
CONTESTS	CORDUROY	COURLAND	CRANE FLY	CRICKETS
CONTEXTS	CORDWOOD	COURSING	CRANIATE	CRICKING
CONTINUA	CORKWOOD	COURTESY	CRANIUMS	CRIMINAL
CONTINUE	CORNCOBS	COURTIER	CRANKIER	CRIMPING

CRIMSONS	CRUMBLED	CUP FINAL	CYNOSURE	CALUMNIES
CRINGING	CRUMBLES	CUPIDITY	CYPHERED	CALVARIES
CRINKLED	CRUMHORN	CUPREOUS	CYPRINID	CALVINISM
CRINKLES	CRUMMIER	CUPULATE	CYRILLIC	CALVINIST
CRIPPLED	CRUMPETS	CURATORS	CYSTEINE	CALVITIES
CRIPPLES	CRUMPLED	CURCULIO	CYSTITIS	CAMBISTRY
CRISPATE	CRUNCHED	CURDLING	CYTASTER	CAMELHAIR
CRISPIER	CRUSADED	CURE-ALLS	CYTIDINE	CAMELLIAS
CRISPING	CRUSADER	CURLICUE	CYTOLOGY	CAMEMBERT
CRISTATE	CRUSADES	CURLIEST	CYTOSINE	CAMERAMAN
CRITERIA	CRUSHING	CURRANTS	CZARINAS	CAMERAMEN
CRITICAL	CRUSTIER	CURRENCY		CAMISOLES
CRITIQUE	CRUSTILY	CURRENTS		CAMPAIGNS
CRITTERS	CRUTCHES	CURRICLE	**9 LETTERS**	CAMPANILE
CROAKILY	CRYOLITE	CURRIERY	CABALLERO	CAMPANULA
CROAKING	CRYONICS	CURRYING	CABIN BOYS	CAPFIRES
CROCKERY	CRYOSTAT	CURSEDLY	CABLE CARS	CAMPHORIC
CROCOITE	CRYOTRON	CURTAINS	CABLEGRAM	CAMPSITES
CROCUSES	CRYSTALS	CURTNESS	CABLE-LAID	CAMSHAFTS
CROFTERS	CUBATURE	CURTSIED	CABOODLES	CANAANITE
CROMLECH	CUBE ROOT	CURTSIES	CABRIOLET	CANAL BOAT
CROOKING	CUBICLES	CUSHIEST	CACHECTIC	CANALIZED
CROONERS	CUBIFORM	CUSHIONS	CACODEMON	CANAVERAL
CROONING	CUBISIST	CUSHIONY	CACOETHES	CANCELLING
CROPPERS	CUBISTIC	CUSPIDOR	CACOETHIC	CANCELLED
CROPPING	CUCKOLDS	CUSSEDLY	CACOPHONY	CANCELLER
CROISERS	CUCUMBER	CUSTARDS	CACUMINAL	CANCEROUS
CROSSBAR	CUCURBIT	CUSTOMER	CAECILIAN	CANDIDACY
CROSSBOW	CUDDLIER	CUSTUMAL	CAESAREAN	CANDIDATE
CROSSCUT	CUDDLING	CUTAWAYS	CAFETERIA	CANDLEMAS
CROSSEST	CUDGELED	CUTBACKS	CAINGORM	CANDLENUT
CROSS-EYE	CUFF LINK	CUTENESS	CAITHNESS	CANDYTUFT
CROSSING	CUL-DE-SAC	CUT GLASS	CALABOOSE	CANESCENT
CROSSLET	CULIACAN	CUTICLES	CALAMANCO	CANICULAR
CROSSPLY	CULINARY	CUTICULA	CALCANEAL	CANISTERS
CROTCHES	CULOTTES	CUTINIZE	CALCANEUS	CANKEROUS
CROTCHET	CULOUSLY	CUT-PRICE	CALCICOLE	CANNELURE
CROUCHED	CULPABLE	CUTPURSE	CALCIFIED	CANNERIES
CROUPIER	CULPABLY	CUTTINGS	CALCIFUGE	CANNIBALS
CROUPOUS	CULPRITS	CUTWATER	CALCIMINE	CANNINESS
CROUTONS	CULTIGEN	CYANITIC	CALCULATE	CANNONADE
CROWBARS	CULTIVAR	CYANOGEN	CALCULOUS	CANNONING
CROWBOOT	CULTRATE	CYANOSIS	CALENDARS	CANNULATE
CROWDING	CULTURAL	CYANOTIC	CALENDERS	CANOEISTS
CROWFOOT	CULTURED	CYCLADES	CALENDULA	CANONICAL
CROWNING	CULTURES	CYCLAMEN	CALENTURE	CANONIZED
CROZIERS	CULVERIN	CYCLISTS	CALIBRATE	CANOODLED
CRUCIATE	CULVERTS	CYCLONES	CALIPHATE	CAN OPENER
CRUCIBLE	CUMBERED	CYCLONIC	CALL BOXES	CANTABILE
CRUCIFER	CUMBRIAN	CYCLOSIS	CALL GIRLS	CANTALOUP
CRUCIFIX	CUMQUATS	CYLINDER	CALLOUSITY	CANTERING
CRUDITES	CUMULOUS	CYMATIUM	CALLOUSLY	CANTICLES
CRUISERS	CUPBOARD	CYMOGENE	CALMATIVE	CANTONESE
CRUISING	CUP CAKES	CYNICISM	CALORIFIC	CANVASSED

CANVASSER	CARNATION	CASTRATED	CAUSATIVE	CERUSSITE
CANVASSES	CARNELIAN	CASTRATOR	CAUSEWAYS	CERSAREAN
CAPACIOUS	CARNIVALS	CASUARINA	CAUTERANT	CESSATIONS
CAPACITOR	CARNIVORE	CASUISTIC	CAUTERIZE	CETACEANS
CAPARISON	CARNOTITE	CASUISTRY	CAUTIONED	CHABAZITE
CAPILLARY	CAROLLING	CATABASIS	CAVALCADE	CHA-CHA-CHA
CAPITULAR	CAROTIDAL	CATABATIC	CAVILIERS	CHAETOPOD
CAPITULUM	CAROUSALS	CATABOLIC	CAVENDISH	CHAFFINCH
CAPRICCIO	CAROUSELS	CATACLYSM	CAVERNOUS	CHAGRINED
CAPRICORN	CAROUSING	CATACOMBS	CAVILLERS	CHAIN GANG
CAPSAICIN	CARPENTER	CATALEPSY	CAVILLING	CHAIN MAIL
CAPSICUMS	CARPENTRY	CATALOGUE	CAVORTING	CHAIN SAWS
CAPSIZING	CARPETBAG	CATALONIA	CEASE-FIRE	CHAIR LIFT
CAPSULATE	CARPETING	CATALYSER	CEASELESS	CHALKIEST
CAPTAINCY	CARPOLOGY	CATALYSIS	CELANDINE	CHALLENGE
CAPTAINED	CARRAGEEN	CATALYSTS	CELEBRANT	CHAMELEON
CAPTIVATE	CARREFOUR	CATALYTIC	CELEBRATE	CHAMFERER
CAPTIVITY	CARRIAGES	CATAMARAN	CELEBRITY	CHAMOMILE
CAPTURING	CARRYALLS	CATAMENIA	CELESTIAL	CHAMPAGNE
CARAPACES	CARRYCOTS	CATAMOUNT	CELESTITE	CHAMPAIGN
CARBAMATE	CARRY-OVER	CATAPHYLL	CELIBATES	CHAMPERTY
CARBANION	CARTAGENA	CATAPLASM	CELLARAGE	CHAMPIONS
CARBAZOLE	CARTESIAN	CATAPLEXY	CELLOIDIN	CHAMPLEVE
CARBINEER	CARTHORSE	CATAPULTS	CELLULASE	CHANCIEST
CARBOLIZE	CARTILAGE	CATARACTS	CELLULOID	CHANCROID
CARBONADO	CATOGRAM	CATARRHAL	CELLULOSE	CHANCROUS
CARBONATE	CARTOUCHE	CATATONIA	CELTACIST	CHANDELLE
CARBONIZE	CARTRIDGE	CATATONIC	CEMENTING	CHANDLERS
CARBONOUS	CART TRACK	CATCALLED	CEMENTITE	CHANDLERY
CARBUNCLE	CARTULARY	CATCHCROP	CENOTAPHS	CHANNELED
CARBURIZE	CARTWHEEL	CATCHIEST	CENSORIAL	CHANTEUSE
CARCASSES	CARYATIDS	CATCHMENT	CENSORING	CHAPERONS
CARCINOMA	CARYOPSIS	CATCHWORD	CENSURING	CHAPLAINS
CARDBOARD	CASANOVAS	CATECHISM	CENTAURUS	CHAPLETED
CARDIGANS	CASCADING	CATECHIST	CENTENARY	CHARABANC
CARDINALS	CASEATION	CATECHIZE	CENTERING	CHARACTER
CARD INDEX	CASEBOUND	CATERWAUL	CENTIGRAM	CHARCOALS
CARD PUNCH	CASE STUDY	CATHARSES	CENTIPEDE	CHARINESS
CARD SHARP	CASH CARDS	CATHARSIS	CENTRALLY	CHARITIES
CAREENING	CASH CROPS	CATHARTIC	CENTRIOLE	CHARIVARI
CAREERING	CASH DESKS	CATHEDRAL	CENTRISTS	CHARLATAN
CAREERISM	CASHIERED	CATHEPSIN	CENTURIAL	CHARLOTTE
CAREERIST	CASSATION	CATHETERS	CENTURIES	CHARMEUSE
CAREFULLY	CASSEROLE	CATHOLICS	CENTURION	CHARTABLE
CARESSING	CASSETTES	CATOPTRIC	CERACEOUS	CHARTERED
CARETAKER	CASSIMERE	CATTREIES	CERATODUS	CHARWOMAN
CARIBBEAN	CASSOCKED	CATTINESS	CERCARIAL	CHARWOMEN
CARIBBEES	CASSOULET	CATTLEMAN	CEREBROID	CHASTENED
CARILLONS	CASSOWARY	CAUCASOID	CEREBRUMS	CHASTENER
CARINTHIA	CASTANETS	CAUDATION	CEREBLOTH	CHASTISED
CARIOSITY	CASTAWAYS	CAULDRONS	CERTAINLY	CHASUBLES
CARMELITE	CASTIGATE	CAUSALGIA	CERTAINTY	CHATELAIN
CARNELIST	CASTILIAN	CAUSALITY	CERTIFIED	CHATOYANT
CARNALITY	CASTOR OIL	CAUSATION	CERTITUDE	CHAT SHOWS

CHATTERED	CHIPPINGS	CICATRIZE	CLAVICLES	CLOUDLESS
CHATTERER	CHIROPODY	CICERONES	CLAVICORN	CLOUD NINE
CHATTIEST	CHIROPTER	CIGARETTE	CLAYMORES	CLOYINGLY
CHAUFFEUR	CHIRPIEST	CIGARILLO	CLAYSTONE	CLUYBBABLE
CHEAPENED	CHRRUPER	CILIATION	CLAYTONIA	CLUBHOUSE
CHEAP-JACK	CHISELING	CILIOLATE	CLEANABLE	CLUMSIEST
CHEAPNESS	CHISELLED	CIMMERIAN	CLEANNESS	CLUSTERED
CHECKABLE	CHISELLER	CINCTURES	CLEANSERS	CLUTCH BAG
CHECKERED	CHITINOID	CINEMATIC	CLEANSING	CLUTCHING
CHECKLIST	CHITINOUS	CINERARIA	CLEARANCE	CLUTTERED
CHECKMATE	CHIVALRIC	CINEREOUS	CLEAR-EYED	CNIDARIAN
CHECKOUTS	CHLORDANE	CINGULATE	CLEARINGS	COACHWORK
CHECKROOM	CHLORELLA	CIPHERING	CLEARNESS	COADJUTOR
CHEEKBONE	CHLORIDES	CIRALPINE	CLEARWAYS	COADUNATE
CHEEKIEST	CHLORIDIC	CIRCADIAN	CLEARWING	COAGULANT
CHEERIEST	CHLORITIC	CIRCASSIA	CLEAVAGES	COAGULASE
CHEERLESS	CHLOROSIS	CIRCINATE	CLEMENTLY	COAGULATE
CHELATION	CHLOROTIC	CIRCUITAL	CLENCHING	COALESCED
CHELICERA	CHOCK-FULL	CIRCUITRY	CLERGYMAN	COALFACES
CHELIFORM	CHOCOLATE	CIRCULARS	CLERGYMEN	COALFIELD
CHELONIAN	CHOCOLATY	CIRCULATE	CLERIHEWS	COALHOLES
CHEMICALS	CHOIRBOYS	CIRRHOSED	CLERKSHIP	COALHOUSE
CHEMISORB	CHOKEABLE	CIRRHOSIS	CLIENTELE	COALITION
CHEMISTRY	CHOLEROID	CIRRHOTIC	CLIMACTIC	COALMINES
CHEMOSTAT	CHONDRIFTY	CITATIONS	CLIMAXING	COARCTATE
CHEMURGIC	CHONDRITE	CITIZENERY	CLIMB-DOWN	COARSENED
CHEQUERED	CHONDROMA	CITY HALLS	CLINCHERS	COASTLINE
CHERISHED	CHONDRULE	CITY-STATE	CLINCHING	COAT TAILS
CHERISHER	CHOOSIEST	CIVICALLY	CLINGFILM	COAXINGLY
CHESTIEST	CHOPHOUSE	CIVILIANS	CLINGFISH	COBALTITE
CHESTNUTS	CHOPLOGIC	CIVILIZED	CLINICIAN	COBALTOUS
CHEVALIER	CHOPPIEST	CIVILIZER	CLINOSTAT	COCA-COLAS
CHEVRETTE	CHOPSTICK	CIVIL LIST	LINQUANT	COCAINISM
CHICALOTE	CHORIONIC	CIVIL WARS	CLINTONIA	COCAINIZE
CHICANERY	CHORISTER	CLAIMABLE	CLIPBOAR	COCCOLITH
CHICKADEE	CHOROLOGY	CLAIMANTS	CLIP JOINT	COCCYGEAL
CHICKPEAS	CHORTLING	CLAMBRAKES	CLIPPINGS	COCINEAL
CHICKWEED	CHORUSING	CLAMBERED	CLITELLUM	COCHLEATE
CHIEFTAIN	CHRISTIAN	CLAMMIEST	CLOAKROOM	COCK-A-HOOP
CHIHUAHUA	CHRISTMAS	CLAMOROUS	CLOBBERED	COCKATIEL
CHILBLAIN	CHROMATIC	CLAMOURED	CLOCKWISE	COCKATOOS
CHILDHOOD	CHROMATID	CLAMPDOWN	CLOCKWORK	COCKED HAT
CHILDLESS	CHROMATIN	CLAPBOARD	CLOISONNE	COCKERELS
CHILDLIKE	CHROMOGEN	CLARENDON	CLOISTERS	COCKFIGHT
CHILIADAL	CHRONAXIE	CLARIFIED	CLOISTRAL	COCKHORSE
CHILLIEST	CHRONICLE	CLARIFIER	CLONICITY	COCKINESS
CHINATOWN	CHRYSALIS	CLARINETS	CLOSE CALL	COCKLEBUR
CHINAWARE	CHTHONIAN	CLASSICAL	CLOSEDOWN	COCKNEYFY
CHINKIANG	CHUBBIEST	CLASSIEST	CLOSE-KNIT	COCKROACH
CHINSTRAP	CHUCKLING	CLASSLESS	CLOSENESS	CORKSCOMB
CHINTZIER	CHUMMIEST	CLASSMATE	CLOSETING	COCKSFOOT
CHIPBOARD	CHUNKIEST	CLASSROOM	CLOTHIERS	COCKTAILS
CHIPMUNKS	CHURCHMAN	CLATHRATE	CLOUDBANK	COCOONING
CHIPOLATA	CICATRICE	CLATTERED	CLOUDIEST	CODIFYING

C 9 LETTERS

CODPIECES	COLLIDING	COMMODORE	CONCERNED	CONGENIAL
COELOSTAT	COLLIGATE	COMMONAGE	CONCERTED	CONGER ELL
COENOBITE	COLLIMATE	COMMONERS	CONCERTOS	CONGERIES
COENOCYTE	COLLINEAR	COMMOTION	CONSIERGE	CONGESTED
COENOSARC	COLLINSIA	COMMUNING	CONCILIAR	CONGOLESE
COEQUALLY	COLLISION	COMMUNION	CONCIDELY	CONGRUENT
COERCIBLE	COLLOCATE	COMMUNISM	CONCISION	CONGRUITY
COEVALITY	COLLODION	COMMUNIST	CONCLAVES	CONGROUS
COEXIASTED	COLLOIDAL	COMMUNITY	CONCLUDED	CONHOIDAL
COFFEE BAR	COLLOTYPE	COMMUNIZE	CONCOCTED	CONJOINED
COFFEEPOT	COLLUDING	COMMUTATE	CONCOCTER	CONJOINER
COFFERDAM	COLLUSION	COMMUTERS	CONCORTAT	CONJUGANT
COGITATED	COLLUSIVE	COMMUTING	CONCOURSE	CONJUGATE
COGITATOR	COLLIVIAL	COMPACTED	CONCRETED	CONJURERS
COGNATION	COLLUVIUM	COMPACTER	CONCRUINE	CONJURING
COGNITIVE	COLLYRIUM	COMPACTLY	CONCURRED	CONNECTED
COGNIZANT	COLOCYNTH	COMPANDER	CONCUSSED	CONNECTOR
COGNOMENS	COLOMBIAN	COMPANIES	CONDEMNED	CONNEMARA
COGWHEELS	COLUMBINE	COMPANION	CONDEMNER	CONNIVENT
COHABITED	COLUMBITE	COMPARING	CONDENSED	CONNIVING
COHERENCE	COLUMBIUM	COMPASSES	CONDENSER	CONNOTING
COIFFEURS	COLUMELLA	COMPELLED	CONDIGNLY	CONNUBIAL
COIFFURES	COLUMNIST	COMPELLER	CONDIMENT	CONQUERED
COINCIDED	COMATULID	COMPENDIA	CONDITION	CONQUEROR
COINTREAU	COMBATANT	COMPERING	CONDOLING	CONQUESTS
COKULORIS	COMBATING	COMPETENT	CONDONING	CONSCIOUS
COLANDERS	COMBATIVE	COMPETING	CONDUCING	CONSCRIPT
COLCHICUM	COMBATTED	COMPILERS	CONDUCTIVE	CONSENSUS
COLCOTHAR	COMBINING	COMPILING	CONDUCTED	CONSENTED
COLD CREAM	COMBUSTOR	COMPLAINT	CONDUCTOR	CONSENTER
COLD-DRAWN	COMEBACKS	COMPLETED	CONDYLOID	CONSERVED
COLD FRAME	COMEDIANS	COMPLETER	CONDYLOMA	CONSERVER
COLD FRONT	COMEDOWNS	COMPLEXES	CONFERRED	CONSERVES
COLD SNAPS	COMELIEST	COMPLIANT	CONFERRER	CONSIGNED
COLD SORES	COMFORTED	COMPLYING	CONFERVAL	CONSIGNEE
COLD STEEL	COMFORTER	COMPONENT	CONFESSED	CONSIGNOR
COLD SWEAT	COMICALLY	COMPORTED	CONFESSOR	CONSISTED
COLECTOMY	COMMANDED	COMPOSERS	CONFIDANT	CONSOCIES
COLICROOT	COMMANDER	COMPOSING	CONFIDENT	CONSOLING
COLICWEED	COMMANDOS	COMPOSITE	CONFIDING	CONSOLUTE
COLLAGIST	COMMENCED	COMPOSTED	CONFIRMED	CONSONANT
COLLAPSAR	COMMENDAM	COMPOSURE	CONFITURE	CONSORTED
COLLAPSED	COMMENDED	COMPOUNDS	CONFLATED	CONSORTER
COLLAPSES	COMMENSAL	COMMPRISAL	CONFLICTS	CONSORTIA
COLLARING	COMMENTED	COMPRISED	CONFLUENT	CONSPIRED
COLLATING	COMMENTER	COMPUTERS	CONFORMAL	CONSTABLE
COLLATION	COMMINGLE	COMPUTING	CONFORMED	CONSTANCE
COLLATIVE	COMMINUTE	COMRADELY	CONFORMER	CONSTANCY
COLLEAGUE	COMMISSAR	CONCAVITY	CONFRERES	CONSTANTA
COLLECTED	COMMITTAL	CONCEALED	CONFUCIAN	CONSTANTS
COLLECTOR	COMMITTED	CONCEDING	CONFUSING	CONSTRAIN
COLLEGIAL	COMMITTEE	CONCIETED	CONFUSION	CONSTRICT
COLLEGIAN	COMMITTER	CONCIEVED	CONFUTING	CONSTRUCT
COLLEGIUM	COMMODITY	CONCENTRE	CONGEALED	CONSTRUED

396

CONSTRUER	CONVOLUTE	CORTISONE	COVER NOTE	CREVASSES
CONSULATE	CONVOYING	CORUSCATE	COVERTURE	CREWELIST
CONSULTED	CONVULSED	CORVETTES	COWARDICE	CREW NECKS
CONSULTER	COOKHOUSE	CORYDALIS	CO-WORKERS	CRIBELLUM
CONSUMERS	COOPERAGE	CORYMBOSE	COXCOMBRY	CRICKETER
CONSUMING	COOPERATE	COSEISMAL	COYOTILLO	CRIMINALS
CONTACTED	COORDINAL	COSMETICS	CRAB APPLE	CRIMPLENE
CONTACTOR	COPARTNER	COSMIC RAY	CRABBEDLY	CRIMSONED
CONTAGION	COPESTONE	COSMOGONY	CRABBIEST	CRINKLIER
CONTAGIUM	COPIOUSLY	COSMOLOGY	CRAB STICK	CRINKLING
CONTAINED	COPOLYMER	COSMONAUT	CRACK DOWN	CRINOLINE
CONTAINER	COPROLITE	COSMOTRON	CRACKLING	CRIPPLING
CONTEMNER	COPULATED	COSSETTED	CRACKPOTS	CRISPIEST
CONTENDED	COPYBOOKS	COSTA RICA	CRACKSMAN	CRISPNESS
CONTENDER	COPYRIGHT	CO-STARRED	CRACKSMEN	CRITERION
CONTENTED	COQUETTES	COSTLIEST	CRAGGIEST	CRITICISM
CONTESTED	CORALLINE	COSTOTOMY	CRANBERRY	CRITICIZE
CONTESTER	CORALLOID	COST PRICE	CRANKCASE	CRITIQUES
CONTINENT	CORALROOT	COSTUMIER	CRANKIEST	CROCHETED
CONTINUAL	CORBICULA	COTANGENT	CRAPULOUS	CRICHETER
CONTINUED	COR BLIMEY	COT DEATHS	CRASH-DRIVE	CROCODILE
CONTINUER	CORDIALLY	COTE D'AZUR	CRASH-LAND	CROISSANT
CONTINUOS	CORDIFORM	COTENANCY	CRASSNESS	CROMLECHS
CONTINUUM	CORDONING	COTILLION	CRATEROUS	CROOKEDLY
CONTORTED	COREOPSIS	COTTAGERS	CRAYONING	CROP-EARED
CONTOURED	CORIANDER	COTTONADE	CRAYONIST	CROQUETTE
CONTRACTS	CORKBOARD	COTTON GIN	CRAZINESS	CROSSBARS
CONTRAILS	CORKSCREW	COTTYEDON	CREAMCUPS	CROSSBEAM
CONTRALTO	CORMORANT	COUCHETTE	CREAMIEST	CROSSBILL
CONTRASTS	CORN BREAD	COUNSELED	CREATIONS	CROSSBOWS
CONTRASTY	CORNCRAKE	COUNTABLE	CREATURAL	CROSSBRED
CONTRIVED	CORNELIAN	COUNTDOWN	CREATURES	CROSSEYED
CONTUMACY	CORNERING	COUNTERED	CREDENDUM	CROSSFIRE
CONTUMELY	CORNETIST	COUNTLESS	CREDITING	CROSSHEAD
CONTUSING	CORNFIELD	COUNT NOUN	CREDITORS	CROSSINGS
CONTUSION	CORNFLOUR	COUNTRIES	CREDULITY	CROSS-LINK
CONTUSIVE	CORNSTALK	COUP D'ETAT	CREDULOUS	CROSSNESS
CONUNDRUM	COROLLARY	COUPLINGS	CREEPIEST	CROSSOVER
CONVECTOR	CORPORALE	COURGETTE	CREMATING	CROSSTALK
CONVENERS	CORPORALS	COURTELLE	CREMATION	CROSSTREE
CONVENING	CORPORATE	COURTEOUS	CREMATORY	CROSSWALK
CONVERGED	CORPOREAL	COURTESAN	CRENATION	CROSSWIND
CONVERSED	CORPOSANT	COURTIERS	CRENULATE	CROSSWISE
CONVERSER	CORPULENT	COURTLIER	CREOLIZED	CROSSWORD
CONVERTED	CORPUSCLE	COURTROOM	CREOPHAGY	CROSSWORT
CONVERTER	CORRALLED	COURTSHIP	CREOSOTED	CROTCHETS
CONVEXITY	CORRASION	COURTYARD	CREOSOTIC	CROTCHETY
CONVEYERS	CORROSIVE	COUTURIER	CREPITANT	CROUCHING
CONVEYING	CORRUGATE	COVALENCY	CREPITATE	CROUPIERS
CONVICTED	CORRUPTED	COVENANTS	CRESCENDO	CROWBERRY
CONVINCED	CORRUPTER	COVERALLS	CRESCENTS	CROWNWORK
CONVINCER	CORRUPTLY	COVERINGS	CRETINISM	CROW'S FEET
CONVIVIAL	CORSELETS	COVERLESS	CRETINOID	CROW'S FOOT
CONVOKING	CORTICATE	COVERLETS	CRETINOUS	CROW'S NEST

C 9 LETTERS

CRUCIALLY	CURIOSITY	CYSTOLITH	CAMPAIGNER	CAPTIVATOR
CRUCIBLES	CURIOUSLY	CYSTOTOMY	CAMPANILES	CARAMELIZE
CRUCIFIED	CURLICUES	CYTOPLASM	CAMPESTRAL	CARBOLATED
CRUCIFIER	CURLINESS	CYTOPLAST	CAMPGROUND	CARBONATED
CRUCIFORM	CURLPAPER		CAMPHORATE	CARBON COPY
CRUDITIES	CURRENTLY		CANAL BOATS	CARBONIZED
CRUELTIES	CURRICULA	**10 LETTERS**	CANALIZING	CARBUNCLES
CRUMBLIER	CURRYCOMB	CABANATUAN	CANCELLATE	CARCINOGEN
CRUMBLING	CURSIVELY	CABIN CLASS	CANCELLING	CARDIALGIA
CRUMMIEST	CURSORIAL	CACCIATORE	CANDELABRA	CARDIALGIC
CRUMPLING	CURSORILY	CACHINNATE	CANDIDATES	CARDIOGRAM
CRUNCHIER	CURTAILED	CACK-HANDED	CANDLEFISH	CARDIOLOGY
CRUNCHING	CURTAINED	CACOGENIES	CANDLEPINS	CARDSHIPS
CRUSADERS	CURTILAGE	CACOGRAPHY	CANDLEWICK	CAREERIST
CRUSADING	CURTSYING	CACOMISTLE	CANDLEWOOD	CARELESSLY
CRUSTIEST	CURVATURE	CACOPHONIC	CANDYFLOSS	CARETAKERS
CRYBABIES	CUSHINESS	CACTACEOUS	CANKERWORM	CARICATURE
CRYOMETER	CUSHIONED	CADAVERINE	CANNELLONI	CARNALLITE
CRYOMETRY	CUSPIDATE	CAERPHILLY	CANNONADES	CARNASSIAL
CRYOPHYTE	CUSPIDORS	CAESEREANS	CANNONBALL	CARNATIONS
CRYOSCOPE	CUSTODIAL	CAESPITOSE	CANONICATE	CARNELIANS
CRYOSCOPY	CUSTODIAN	CAFETERIAS	CANONICITY	CARNIVORES
CRYPTOGAM	CUSTOMARY	CALABASHES	CANONIZING	CAROLINIAN
CUTENIDUM	CUSTOMERS	CALABOOSES	CANOODLING	CAROTENOID
CUBBYHOLE	CUSTOMIZE	CALAMANDER	CAN OPENERS	CARPATHIAN
CUBE ROOTS	CUTANEOUS	CALAMITIES	CANTABRIAN	CARPELLARY
CUBISISTS	CUTICULAR	CALAMITOUS	CANTALOUPE	CARPELLATE
CUBSCOUTS	CUTLASSES	CALAMONDIN	CANTALOUPS	CARPENTERS
CUCKOLDED	CUTPURSES	CALAVERITE	CANTATRICE	CARPOPHORE
CUCULLATE	CUTTHROAT	CALCAREOUS	CANTILEVER	CAROSPHORE
CUCUMBERS	CUTTINGLY	CALCEIFORM	CANTILLATE	CARRIER BAG
CUDDLIEST	CYANAMIDE	CALCIFEROL	CANTONMENT	CARRYING-ON
CUDGELING	CYANOTYPE	CALCIFUGAL	CANVASBACK	CARRY-OVERS
CUDGELLED	CYBERNATE	CALCIFYING	CANVASSERS	CARTHORSES
CUDGELLER	CYCLAMATE	CALCITONIN	CANVASSING	CARTHUSIAN
CUFF LINKS	CYCLOIDAL	CALCSINTER	CAPABILITY	CARTILAGES
CUIRASSES	CYCLONITE	CALCULABLE	CAPACITATE	CARTOMANCY
CUL-DE-SACS	CYCLOPSES	CALCULATED	CAPACITIES	CARTOONIST
CULLENDER	CYCLORAMA	CALCULATOR	CAPACITIVE	CARTRIDGES
CULMINANT	CYCLOTRON	CALCULUSES	CAPACITORS	CART TRACKS
CULMINATE	CYLINDERS	CALEDONIAN	CAPARISONS	CARTWHEELS
CULTIVATE	CYMBALIST	CALIBRATED	CAPITALISM	CARUNCULAR
CULTURIST	CYMOGRAPH	CALIBRATOR	CAPITALIST	CARYATIDAL
CUMBERING	CYMOPHANE	CALIFORNIA	CAPITALIZE	CASABLANCA
CUMBRANCE	CYNICALLY	CALIPHATES	CAPITATION	CASCARILLA
CUNEIFORM	CYNOSURES	CALLOWNESS	CAPITATIVE	CASE-HARDEN
CUNNINGLY	CYPHERING	CALORICITY	CAPITULATE	CASEINOGEN
CUPBEARER	CYPRESSES	CALUMINATE	CAPPUCCINO	CASEWORKER
CUPBOARDS	CYPRINOID	CALUMINOUS	CAPREOLATE	CASHIERING
CUP FINALS	CYRENACA	CALVINISTS	CAPRICIOUS	CASSEROLES
CUPOLATED	CYSTEINIC	CALYPTRATE	CAPRICORNS	CASSIOPEIA
CURATIVES	CYSTOCARP	CAMEMBERTS	CAPTAINING	CASTIGATED
CURDINESS	CYSTOCELE	CAMERLENGO	CAPTIOUSLY	CASTIGATOR
CURETTAGE	CYSTOCELE	CAMPAIGNED	CAPTIVATED	CASTRATING

CASTRATION	CELLOBIOSE	CHALKINESS	CHECKMATED
CASUALNESS	CELLOPHANE	CHALLENGED	CHECKMATES
CASUALTIES	CELLULITUS	CHALLENGER	CHECKPOINT
CASUS BELLI	CELLULOSIC	CHALLENGES	CHECKROOMS
CATABOLISM	CEMETERIES	CHALYBEATE	CHEKBONES
CATABOLITE	CENOTAPHIC	CHAMBER POT	CHEEKINESS
CATACLINAL	CENSORABLE	CHAMELEONS	CHEEKPIECE
CATACLYSMS	CENSORIOUS	CHAMOMILES	CHEERFULLY
CATAFALQUE	CENSORSHIP	CHAMPIGNON	CHEERINESS
CATALECTIC	CENSURABLE	CHAMPIONED	CHEESECAKE
CATALEPTIC	CENTENNIAL	CHANCELLOR	CHEESED OFF
CATALOGUED	CENTESIMAL	CHANCERIES	CHEESINESS
CATALOGUER	CENTIGRADE	CHANCINESS	CHELICERAL
CATALOGUES	CENTIGRAMS	CHANDELIER	CHEMICALLY
CATAMARANS	CENTILITRE	CHANDIGRAPH	CHEMISETTE
CATAMENIAL	CENTILLION	CHANGEABLE	CHEMOTAXIS
CATAPLASIA	CENTIMETRE	CHANGEABLY	CHEQUEBOOK
CATAPULTED	CENTIPEDES	CHANGELESS	CHEQUE CARD
CATARRHINE	CENTIPOISE	CHANGELING	CHERISHING
CATASTASIS	CENTRALISM	CHANGEOVER	CHERUBICAL
CAT BURGLAR	CENTRALITY	CHANNELLED	CHESSBOARD
CATCALLING	CENTRALIZE	CHANNELLER	CHESTINESS
CATCH CROPS	CENTRE-FIRE	CHAPERONED	CHEVALIERS
CATCHINESS	CENTRE-FOLD	CHAPFALLEN	CHEVROTAIN
CATCHPENNY	CENTRICITY	CHAPLAINCY	CHEWING GUM
CATCHWORDS	CENTRIFUGE	CHARABANCS	CHICKEN POX
CATECHESIS	CENTROMERE	CHARACTERS	CHIEFTAINS
CATECHISMS	CENTROSOME	CHARGEABLE	CHIFFCHAFF
CATECHISTS	CENTURIONS	CHARGE CARD	CHIFFONIER
CATECHIZED	CEPHALOPOD	CHARGE HAND	CHIHUAHUAS
CATEGORIES	CEREBELLAR	CHARIOTEER	CHILBLIANS
CATEGORIZE	CEREBELLUM	CHARITABLE	CHILDBIRTH
CATENARIAN	CEREBRALLY	CHARITABLY	CHILD'S PLAY
CATENATION	CEREMONIAL	CHARLADIES	CHILIASTIC
CATENULATE	CEREMONIES	CHARLATANS	CHILLINESS
CATHEDRALS	CEROGRAPHY	CHARLESTON	CHIMERICAL
CATHOLICON	CERTIFYING	CHARMINGLY	CHIMNEYPOT
CATOPTRICS	CERUMINOUS	CHARTERING	CHIMPANZEE
CAT'S CRADLE	CERVICITIS	CHARTREUSE	CHINABERRY
CATTLE GRID	CESSATIONS	CHASTENING	CHINATOWNS
CAULESCENT	CESSIONARY	CHASTISING	CHINCHILLA
CAUTERIZED	CETOLOGIST	CHATELAINE	CHINQUAPIN
CAUTIONARY	CHAGRINING	CHATOYANCY	CHINSTRAPS
CAUTIONING	CHAIN GANGS	CHATTERBOX	CHINTZIEST
CAUTIOUSLY	CHAINPLATE	CHATTERERS	CHIPOLATAS
CAVALCADES	CHAIN-REACT	CHATTERING	CHIROMANCY
CAVALRYMAN	CHAIN-SMOKE	CHAUDFROID	CHIRPINESS
CAVALRYMEN	CHAIN STORE	CHAUFFEURS	CHISELLERS
CAVITATION	CHAIR LIFTS	CHAUVINISM	CHISELLING
CAVITY WALL	CHAIR WOMAN	CHAUVINIST	CHITTARONE
CEASE-FIRES	CHAIRWOMEN	CHEAPENING	CHITTAGONG
CEILOMETER	CHALCEDONY	CHEAPSKATE	CHIVALROUS
CELEBRATED	CHALCOCITE	CHEBOKSARY	CHLAMYDATE
CELEBRATOR	CHALKBOARD	CHECKLISTS	CHLORAMINE

CHLORINATE	CISTACEOUS	CLOGGINESS	COELACANTH
CHLOROFORM	CISTERCIAN	CLOISTERED	COENOCYTIC
CHOANOCYTE	CITRIC ACID	CLOSE CALLS	COEQUALITY
CHOCOLATES	CITRONELLA	CLOSED BOOK	COERCIVELY
CHOICENESS	CITRULLINE	CLOSEDOWNS	COERCIVITY
CHOKEBERRY	CITY FATHER	CLOSED SHOP	COEXISTENT
CHRODRITIC	CITY-STATES	CLOSE SHAVE	COEXISTING
CHOPHOUSES	CIVILITIES	CLOSE THING	COFFEE BARS
CHORIAMBIC	CIVILIZING	CLOTHBOUND	COFFEEPOTS
CHORISTERS	CLACTONIAN	CLOTHES PEG	COFFFE SHOP
CHRISTENED	CLADOCERON	CLOUDBANKS	COFFERDAMS
CHRISTENER	CLAMBERING	CLOUDBERRY	COGITATING
CHRISTIANS	CLAMMINESS	CLOUDBURST	COGITATION
CHROMATICS	CLAMOURING	CLOUDINESS	COGITATIVE
CHROMATIST	CLAMPDOWNS	CLOVE HITCH	COGNIZABLE
CHROMOMERE	CLANGOROUS	CLOVERLEAF	COGNIZANCE
CHROMNEMA	CLANSWOMAN	CLOWNISHLY	COHABITANT
CHROMOSOME	CLAPPED-OUT	CLOYEDNESS	COHABITING
CHRONICITY	CLARABELLA	CLUBFOOTED	COHERETNLY
CHRONICLED	CLARIFYING	CLUBHOUSES	COHESIVELY
CHRONICLER	CLASP KNOFE	CLUMSINESS	COIMBATORE
CHRONICLES	CLASSICISM	CLUTCH BAGS	COINCIDENT
CHRONOGRAM	CLASSICIST	CLUTTERING	COINCIDING
CHRONOLOGY	CLASSIFIED	CLYDESDALE	COLATITUDE
CHRYSOLITE	CLASSIFIER	CNIDOBLAST	COLCHICINE
CHUBBINESS	CLASSMATES	COACERVATE	COLD CHISEL
CHUCKER-OUT	CLASSROOMS	COACTIVITY	COLD FISHES
CHUCKWALLA	CLATTERING	COADJUTANT	COLD FRAMES
CHUMMINESS	CLAVICHORD	COADJUTORS	COLD FRONTS
CHUNKINESS	CLAVICULAR	COAGULABLE	COLD TURKEY
CHURCHGOER	CLAY PIGEON	COAGULATED	COLEMANITE
CHURCHYARD	CLEANSABLE	COALBUNKER	COLOEPTILE
CHURLISHLY	CLEAN SWEEP	COALESCENT	COLEORHIZA
CHYLACEOUS	CLEARANCES	COALESCING	COLLAGENIC
CICARTICES	CLEFT STICK	COALFIELDS	COLLAPSING
CICATRICLE	CLEMENTINE	COALHOUSES	COLLARBONE
CICATRIZER	CLERESTORY	COALITIONS	COLLAR STUD
CIGARETTES	CLEVER DICK	COAPTATION	COLLATERAL
CINCHONINE	CLEVERNESS	COARSENES	COLLATIONS
CINCHONISM	CLIENTELES	COASTGUARD	COLLEGUES
CINCHONIZE	CLINGINESS	COASTLINES	COLLECTING
CINCINNATI	CLINGSTONE	COATHANGER	COLLECTIVE
CINDERELLA	CLINICALLY	COAT OF ARMS	COLLECTORS
CINERARIUM	CLINKSTONE	COCHABAMBA	COLLEGIATE
CINNAMONIC	CLINOMETER	COCHINEALS	COLLIERIES
CINQUEFOIL	CLINOMETRY	COCKALORUM	COLLIMATOR
CIRCUITOUS	CLIPBOARDS	COCKCHAFER	COLLISIONS
CIRCULATED	CLIP JOINTS	COCKED HATS	COLLOCATED
CIRCULATOR	CLOAKROOMS	COCKFIGHTS	COLLOQUIAL
CIRCUMCISE	CLOBBERING	COCKHORSES	COLLOQUIES
CIRCUMFLEX	CLOCKMAKER	COCKNEYISM	COLLIQUIAM
CIRCUMFUSE	CLOCK TOWER	COCKSCOMBS	COLLOTYPIC
CIRCUMVENT	CLODDISHLY	COCONUT SHY	COLONIZERS
CISMONTANE	CLODHOPPER	CODSWALLOP	COLONIZING

COLONNADED	COMMUNIONS	CONCEIVING	CONFERRING
COLONNADES	COMMINIQUE	CONCENTRIC	CONFERVOID
COLORATION	COMMUNISTS	CONCEPCION	CONFESSING
COLORATURA	COMMUTABLE	CONCEPTION	CONFESSION
COLOSSALLY	COMMUTATOR	CONCEPTIVE	CONFESSORS
COLOSSUSES	COMPACTING	CONCEPTUAL	CONFIDANTS
COLOURABLE	COMPANIONS	CONCERNING	CONFIDENCE
COLOURFAST	COMPARABLE	CONCERTINA	CONFIRMING
COLOURINGS	COMPARABLY	CONCERTINO	CONFISCATE
COLOURLESS	COMPARATOR	CONCESSION	CONFLATING
COLUMBINES	COMPARISON	CONCESSIVE	CONLFICTED
COLUMELLAR	COMPASSION	CONCHIOLIN	CONFLUENCE
COLUMNISTS	COMPATIBLE	CONCHOLOGY	CONFORMERS
COMANCHEAN	COMPATIBLY	CONCIERGES	CONFORMING
COMBATABLE	COMPATRIOT	CONCILIATE	CONFORMIST
COMBATANTS	COMPELLING	CONCINNITY	CONFORMITY
COMBATTING	COMPENDIUM	CONCINNOUS	CONFOUNDED
COMBINABLE	COMPENSATE	CONCLAVIST	CONFOUNDER
COMBUSTION	COMPETENCE	CONCLUDING	CONFRONTED
COMEDIENNE	COMPETENCY	CONCLUSION	CONFRONTER
COME-HITHER	COMPETITOR	CONCLUSIVE	CONFUSABLE
COMELINESS	COMPLACENT	CONCOCTING	CONFUSEDLY
COMESTIBLE	COMPLAINED	CONCOCTION	CONGEALING
COMFORTERS	COMPLAINER	CONCOCTIVE	CONGENERIC
COMFORTING	COMPLAINTS	CONCORDANT	CONGENITAL
COMIC OPERA	COMPLEMENT	CONCORDATS	CONGER EELS
COMIC STRIP	COMPLETELY	CONCOURSES	CONGESTION
COMMANDANT	COMPLETING	CONCRETELY	CONGESTIVE
COMMANDEER	COMPLETION	CONCRETING	CONGLOBATE
COMMANDERS	COMPLETIVE	CONCRETION	CONGREGATE
COMMEASURE	COMPLEXION	CONCRETIVE	CONGRESSES
COMMENCING	COMPLEXITY	CONCRETIZE	CONGRUECE
COMMENDING	COMPLIANCE	CONCUBINES	CONIFEROUS
COMMENTARY	COMPLICATE	CONCURRENT	CONJECTURE
COMMENTATE	COMPLICITY	CONCUSSING	CONJOINING
COMMENTING	COMPLIMENT	CONCUSSION	CONJOINTLY
COMMERCIALS	COMPONENTS	CONCUSSIVE	CONJUGABLE
COMMISSARS	COMPORTING	CONDEMNING	CONJUGATED
COMMISSARY	COMPOSITES	CONDENSATE	CONJUGATOR
COMMISSION	COMPOSITOR	CONDENSERS	CONNECTING
COMMISSURE	COMPOSTING	CONDENSING	CONNECTION
COMMITTMENT	COMPOUNDED	CONDESCEND	CONNECTIVE
COMMITTALS	COMPOUNDER	CONDIMENTS	CONNIVANCE
COMMITTEES	COMPREHEND	CONDITIONS	CONQUERING
COMMITTING	COMPRESSED	CONDOLENCE	CONQUERORS
COMMODIOUS	COMPRESSOR	CONDUCIBLE	CONSCIENCE
COMMODORES	COMPRISING	CONDUCTING	CONSCRIPTS
COMMONABLE	COMPROMISE	CONDUCTION	CONSECRATE
COMMONALITY	COMPULSION	CONDUCTIVE	CONSENSUAL
COMMONNESS	COMPULSIVE	CONDUCTORS	CONSENTING
COMMON NOON	COMPULSORY	CONEFLOWER	CONSEQUENT
COMMON ROOM	COMPUTABLE	CONFECTION	CONSERVING
COMMONWEAL	CONCEALING	CONFERENCE	CONSIDERED
COMMOTIONS	CONCEDEDLY	CONFERMENT	CONSIDERER

CONSIGNEES	CONTORTION	COOPERATOR	CORRUPTION
CONSIGNING	CONTOURING	COOPTATION	CORRUPTIVE
CONSIGNORS	CONTRABAND	COOPTATIVE	CORSETIERE
CONSISTENT	CONTRABASS	COORDINATE	CORUSCATED
CONSISTING	CONTRACTED	COPARCENER	COS LETTUCE
CONSISTORY	CONTRACTOR	COPENHAGEN	COSMICALLY
CONSOCIATE	CONTRADICT	COPPERHEAD	COSMIC RAYS
CONSOLABLE	CONTRAFLOW	COPROLALIA	COSMODROME
CONSONANCE	CONTRALTOS	COPROLITIC	COSMOGONAL
CONSONANTS	CONTRARIES	COPROPHAGY	COSMOGONIC
CONSORTIAL	CONTRARILY	COPULATING	COSMONAUTS
CONSORTING	CONTRASTED	COPULATION	COSSETTING
CONSORTIUM	CONTRAVENE	COPULATIVE	COSTA RICAN
CONSPECTUS	CONTRIBUTE	COPYHOLDER	CO-STARRING
CONSPIRACY	CONTRITELY	COPYRIGHTS	COSTLINESS
CONSPIRING	CONTRITION	COPYWRITER	COST PRICES
CONSTABLES	CONTRIVING	COQUELICOT	COSTUMIERS
CONSTANTAN	CONTROLLED	COQUETTISH	COTANGENTS
CONSTANTLY	CONTROLLER	COR ANGLAIS	COTILLIONS
CONSTIPATE	CONTROVERT	CORDIALITY	COTTAGE PIE
CONSTITUTE	CONTUSIONS	CORDERITE	COTTON GINS
CONSTRAINT	CONUNDRUMS	CORDILLERA	COTTONSEED
CONSTRUCTS	CONVALESCE	CORDON BLEU	COTTONTAIL
CONSTRUING	CONVECTION	CORIACEOUS	COTTONWOOD
CONSUETUDE	CONVECTIVE	CORINTHIAN	COTTON WOOL
CONSULATES	CONVECTORS	CORKSCREW	COUCHETTES
CONSULSHIP	CONVENABLE	CORMOPHYTE	COUCH GRASS
CONSULTANT	CONVENANCE	CORMORANTS	COULOMETER
CONSULTING	CONVENIENT	CORNACEOUS	COUNCILLOR
CONSUMMATE	CONVENTION	CORNCOCKLE	COUNCILMAN
CONTACTING	CONVENTUAL	CORNCRACKES	COUNCILMEN
CONTACTUAL	CONVERGENT	CORNED BEEF	COUNSELLED
CONTAGIONS	CONVERGING	CORNELIANS	COUNSELLOR
CONTAGIOUS	CONVERSANT	CORNFLAKES	COUNTDOWNS
CONTAINERS	CONVERSELY	CORNFLOWER	COUNTERACT
CONTAINING	CONVERSING	CORNSTARCH	COUNTERING
CONTENDERS	CONVERSION	CORNUCOPIA	COUNTERSPY
CONTENDING	CONVERTING	CORONATION	COUNTESSES
CONTENTING	CONVERTERS	CORPORATOR	COUNT NOUNS
CONTENTION	CONVERTING	CORPOREITY	COUNTRYMAN
CONTESTANT	CONVEYABLE	CORPULENCE	COUNTRYMEN
CONTESTING	CONVEYANCE	CORPUSCLES	COUNTY TOWN
CONTEXTUAL	CONVICTING	CORRALLING	COUP D'ETAT
CONTEXTURE	CONVICTION	CORRECTING	COURAGEOUS
CONTUGUITY	CONVICTIVE	CORRECTION	COURGETTES
CONTINENCE	CONVINCING	CORRECTIVE	COURT CARDS
CONTINENTS	CONVOCATOR	CORRELATED	COURTESANS
CONTINGENT	CONVOLUTED	CORRESPOND	COURTESIES
CONTINUANT	CONVULSING	CORRIENTES	COURTHOUSE
CONTINUING	CONVULSION	CORRIGENDA	COURTLIEST
CONTINUITY	CONVULSIVE	CORRIGIBLE	COURTSHIPS
CONTINUOUS	COOKHOUSES	CORRODIBLE	COURTYARDS
CONTINUUMS	COOL-HEADED	CORRODIBLE	COUTURIERS
CONTORTING	COOPERATED	CORRUGATED	COVARIANCE
		CORRUPTING	

COVENANTAL	CRITICALLLY	CUMULATIVE	CALEFACTORY
COVENANTED	CRITICISMS	CUMULIFORM	CALIBRATING
COVENANTEE	CRITICIZED	CUPBEARERS	CALIBRATION
COVENANTER	CRITICIZER	CURABILITY	CALIFORNIUM
COVENANTOR	CROAKINESS	CURATORIAL	CALLIGRAPHY
COVER NOTES	CROCHETING	CURMUDGEON	CALLIPYGIAN
COVETOUSLY	CROCODILES	CURRENCIES	CALLOUSNESS
COWCATCHER	CROISSANTS	CURRICULAR	CALORIMETER
CRAB APPLES	CROQUETTES	CURRICULUM	CALUMNIATED
CRACKBRAIN	CROSSBONES	CURTAILING	CALVINISTIC
CRACKDOWNS	CROSSBREED	CURTAINING	CALYPTROGEN
CRAFTINESS	CROSSCHECK	CURVACEOUS	CAMARADERIE
CRANE FILES	CROSSHATCH	CURVATURES	CAMERA-READY
CRANESBILL	CROSS-INDEX	CUSHIONING	CAMOULAGED
CRANIOLOGY	CROSSPATCH	CUSSEDNESS	CAMOUFLAGES
CRANIOTOMY	CROSSPIECE	CUSTARD PIE	CAMPAIGNERS
CRANKSHAFT	CROSS-REFER	CUSTODIANS	CAMPAIGNING
CRAPULENCE	CROSSROADS	CUSTOMIZED	CAMPANOLOGY
CRAQUELURE	CROSS-SLIDE	CUSTOM-MADE	CAMPANULATE
CRASH-DIVED	CROSSTREES	CUTTHROATS	CAMPGROUNDS
CRASH-DIVES	CROSSWALKS	CUTTLEBONE	CANALICULAR
CRAVENESS	CROSSWINDS	CUTTLEFISH	CANALICULUS
CRAYFISHES	CROSSWORDS	CYBERNETIC	CANDELABRUM
CREAKINESS	CROWDED OUT	CYCLAMATES	CANDIDACIES
CREAMERIES	CROWN COURT	CYCLICALLY	CANDLEBERRY
CREAMINESS	CROWNPIECE	CYCLOMETER	CANDLELIGHT
CREATININE	CROW'S NESTS	CYCLOMETRY	CANDLEPOWER
CREATIONAL	CRUCIFIXES	CYCLORAMIC	CANDLESTICK
CREATIVELY	CRUCIFYING	CYCLOSTOME	CANDLEWICKS
CREATIVITY	CRUMBLIEST	CYCLOSYTLE	CANINE TEETH
CREDITABLE	CRUNCHIEST	CYLINDTROID	CANINE TOOTH
CREDITIABLY	CRUSTACEAN	CYMIFEROUS	CANNIBALISM
CREDIT CARD	CRUSTINESS	CYSTECTOMY	CANNIBALIZE
CREDIT NOTE	CRYOGENICS	CYSTOSCOPE	CANNONBALLS
CREEPINESS	CRYOPHILIC	CYSTOSCOPY	CANTHARIDES
CREMATIONS	CRYOSCOPIC	CYTOCHROME	CANTILEVERS
CREAMTORIA	CRYPTOZOIC	CYTOLOGIST	CAPACIOUSLY
CRENELLATE	CRYSTAL SET		CAPACITANCE
CREOSOTING	CTENOPHORE		CAPILLARIES
CREPE PAPER	CUBBYHOLES	**11 LETTERS**	CAPILLARITY
CRESCENDOS	CUCKOLDING	CABINET WORK	CAPITALISTS
CRESCENTIC	CUCKOOPINT	CACOGRAPHIC	CAPITALIZED
CRETACEOUS	CUCULIFORM	CACOPHONOUS	CAPITAL LEVY
CREWELWORK	CUDDLESOME	CALCEOLARIA	CAPITATIONS
CRIBRIFORM	CUDGELLING	CALCICOLOUS	CAPITULATED
CRICKETERS	CUERNAVCA	CALCIFEROUS	CAPITULATOR
CRIMINALLY	CULLENDERS	CALCIFEROUS	CAPRICCIOSO
CRIMSONING	CULTIVABLE	CALCIFERGOUS	CAPRICORNUS
CRINKLIEST	CULTIVATED	CALCINATION	CAPSULATION
CRINOLINES	CULTIVATOR	CALCULATING	CAPTIVATING
CRISPATION	CULTURALLY	CALCULATION	CAPTIVATION
CRISPINESS	CUMBERSOME	CALCULATORS	CARABINIERE
CRISSCROSS	CUMMERBUND	CALEFACIENT	CARAVANNING
CRITERIONS	CUMULATION	CALEFACTION	CARBAMIDINE

403

CARBONATION	CAT BURGULARS	CERTAINTIES	CHEF D'OEUVRE
CARBONIZING	CATCH PHRASE	CERTIFIABLE	CHELICERATE
CARBON PAPER	CATCH WEIGHT	CERTIFICATE	CHELIFEROUS
CARBORUNDUM	CATECHISMAL	CETOLOGICAL	CHEMOSMOSIS
CARBOXYLASE	CATECHISTIC	CHAETOGNATH	CHEMOSMOTIC
CARBOXYLATE	CATECHIZING	CHAFFINCHES	CHEMOSPHERE
CARBUNCULAR	CATEGORICAL	CHAFING DISH	CHEMOTACTIC
CARBURETTOR	CATEGORIZED	CHAIN LETTER	CHEMOTROPIC
CARBYLAMINE	CATERPILLAR	CHAIN-SMOKED	CHEQUE CARDS
CARCINOGENS	CATERWAULED	CHAIN-SMOKER	CHERISHABLE
CARDINALATE	CATHETERIZE	CHAIN STITCH	CHESHIRE CAT
CARD INDEXES	CATHOLICISM	CHAIN STORES	CHESS BOARDS
CARDIOGRAPH	CATHOLICITY	CHAIRPERSON	CHEVAL GLASS
CARD PUNCHES	CATHOLICIZE	CHALCANLITE	CHIAROSCURO
CARDUACEOUS	CATTLE GRIDS	CHALCEDONIC	CHIASTOLITE
CAREFULNESS	CAULIFLOWER	CHALKBOARDS	CHICANARIES
CARESSINGLY	CAUSABILITY	CALLENGERS	CHICHIHAERH
CARICATURED	CAUSATIVELY	CHALLENGING	CHICKENFEED
CARICATURES	CAUSTICALLY	CHAMBERLAIN	CHIFFONIERS
CARMINATIVE	CAUSTICNESS	CHAMBERMAID	CHILDMINDER
CARNIVOROUS	CAUTERIZING	CHAMBER POTS	CHIMNEYPOTS
CAROLINGIAN	CAVALIERISM	CHAMELEONIC	CHIMPANZEES
CARPOGONIAL	CAVERNOUSLY	CHAMPERTOUS	CHINCHILLAS
CARPOGONIUM	CAVITY WALLS	CHAMPIONING	CHINOISERIE
CARPOLOGIST	CEASELESSLY	CHANCELLERY	CHIPPENDALE
CARRIAGEWAY	CELEBRATING	CHANCELLOR	CHIROGRAPHY
CARRIER BAGS	CELEBRATION	CHANCROIDAL	CHIROPODIST
CARSICKNESS	CELEBRATIVE	CHANDELIERS	CHIROPTERAN
CARTOGRAPHY	CELEBRITIES	CHANGELINGS	CHITCHATTED
CARTOONISTS	CEMENTATION	CHANGEOVERS	CHLAMYDEOUS
CARTWHEELED	CEMENT MIXER	CHANNELLING	CHLORINATED
CARUNCULATE	CENOSPECIES	CHANTERELLE	CHLORINATOR
CARVEL-BUILT	CENTENARIAN	CHANTICLEER	CHLOROPHYLL
CARVING FORK	CENTENARIES	CHAOTICALLY	CHLOROPLAST
CASE HISTORY	CENTENNIALS	CHAPERONAGE	CHLOROPRENE
CASE STUDIES	CENTIMETRES	CHAPERONING	CHLOROQUINE
CASEWORKERS	CENTRALIZED	CHARGE CARDS	CHOANOCYTAL
CASSITERATE	CENTRE BOARD	CHARGE HANDS	CHOCK-A-BLOCK
CASTELLATED	CENTRE-FOLDS	CHARGE NURSE	CHOIR MASTER
CASTER SUGAR	CENTRE PIECE	CHARGE SHEET	CHOIR SCHOOL
CASTIGATING	CENTRIFUGAL	CHARIOTEERS	CHOKE CHERRY
CASTIGATION	CENTRIFUGES	CHARISMATIC	CHOLESTEROL
CASTING VOTE	CENTRIPETAL	CHASTISABLE	CHOLINERGIC
CASTOR SUGAR	CENTROBARIC	CHATELAINES	CORDOPHONE
CATACAUSTIC	CENTROMERIC	CHATTANOOGA	CHOREODRAMA
CATACHRESIS	CENTROSOMIC	CHAUFFEURED	CHOREOGRAPH
CATACLASTIC	CEPHALALGIA	CHAUVINISTS	CHOROGRAPHY
CATACLYSMIC	CERARGYRITE	CHEAPSKATES	CHRISMATORY
CATADROMOUS	CEREBRATION	CHECKMATING	CHRISTENDOM
CATAFALQUES	CEREBROSIDE	CHECKPOINTS	CHRISTENING
CATALOGUING	CEREMONIALS	CHEERLEADER	CHRISTMASES
CATAPLASTIC	CEREMONIOUS	CHEERLESSLY	CHRISTOLOGY
CATAPULTING	CEROGRAPHIC	CHEESECAKES	CHROMATINIC
CATASTROPHE	CEROPLASTI	CHEESECLOTH	CHROMINANCE

CHROMOGENIC	CLEAR HEADED	COERCIONARY	COMFORTABLY
CHROMONEMAL	CLEFT PALATE	COERCIONIST	COMFORTLESS
CHROMOPHORE	CLEFT STICKS	COESSENTIAL	COMIC OPERAS
CHROMOPLASM	CLEISTOGAMY	COEXISTENCE	COMIC STRIPS
CHROMOPLAST	CLEVER DICKS	COEXTENSION	COMMANDANTS
CHROMOSOMAL	CLIENT STATE	COEXTENSIVE	COMME IL FAUT
CHRMOSOMES	CLIFF HANGER	COFFEE BREAK	COMMEMORATE
CHRONICALLY	CLIMACTERIC	COFFEE HOUSE	COMMENDABLE
CHRONICLERS	CLIMATOLOGY	COFFEE SHOPS	COMMENDABLY
CHRONICLING	CLINANDRIUM	COFFEE TABLE	COMMENTATED
CHRONOGRAPH	CLINOMETRIC	COGITATIONS	COMMENTATOR
CHRONOMETER	CLOCK TOWERS	COGNITIVELY	COMMERCIALS
CHRONOMETRY	CLODHOPPERS	COGNIZANCES	COMMINATION
CHRONOSCOPE	CLOISTERING	COGNOSCENTI	COMMINATORY
CHRYSALISES	CLOSED SHOPS	COINCIDENCE	COMMINUTION
CHRYSAROBIN	CLOSE FISTED	COINSURANCE	COMMISERATE
CHRYSOBERYL	CLOSE-HAULED	COLD-BLOODED	COMMISSIONS
CHRYSOLITIC	CLOSE SEASON	COLD CHISELS	COMMISSURAL
CHRYSOPHASE	CLOSE SHAVES	COLD COMFORT	COMMITMENTS
CHURCHGOERS	CLOSING TIME	COLD-HEARTED	COMMODITIES
CHURCHWOMAN	CLOSTRIDIAL	COLD STORAGE	COMMON NOUNS
CHURCHYARDS	CLOSTRIDIUM	COLEOPTERAN	COMMONPLACE
CICATRICIAL	CLOTHESLINE	COLLABORATE	COMMON ROOMS
CICATRIZANT	CLOTHES PEGS	COLLAPSIBLE	COMMON SENSE
CINDERELLAS	CLOUD BURSTS	COLLARBONES	COMMOTIONAL
CINEMASCOPE	CLOUD-CAPPED	COLLAR STUDS	COMMUNALIST
CIRCULARITY	CLOYINGNESS	COLLECTABLE	COMMUNALITY
CIRCULARIZE	CLUSTERBOMB	COLLECTANEA	COMMUNALIZE
CIRCULAR SAW	COADUNATION	COLLECTEDLY	COMMUNICANT
CIRCULATING	COADUNATIVE	COLLECTIONS	COMMUNICATE
CIRCULATION	COAGULATING	COLLECTIVES	COMMUNIONAL
CIRCULATIVE	COAGULATION	COLLEMBOLAN	COMMUNIQUES
CIRCULATORY	COAGULATIVE	COLLENCHYMA	COMMUNISTIC
CIRCUMCISED	COALBUNKERS	COLLIGATION	COMMUNITIES
CIRCUMLUNAR	COALESCENCE	COLLIMATION	COMMUTATION
CIRCUMPOLAR	COALITIONAL	COLLOCATING	COMMUTATIVE
CIRCUMSPECT	COALSCUTTLE	COLLOCATION	COMMUTATORS
CIRENCESTER	COARCTATION	COLOGARITHM	COMPACT DISC
CITIZENSHIP	COASTGUARDS	COLONIALISM	COMPACTEDLY
CITRONELLAL	COAT HANGERS	COLONIALIST	COMPACTNESS
CITY FATHERS	COATS OF ARMS	COLONIZABLE	COMPARATIVE
CIVIL RIGHTS	COBBLESTONE	COLORATURAS	COMPARISONS
CIVVY STREET	COCCIDIOSIS	COLORIMETER	COMPARTMENT
CLAIRVOYANT	COCCIFEROUS	COLOUR-BLIND	COMPASSABLE
CLAMATORIAL	COCK-A-LEEKIE	COLOURISTIC	COMPATRIOTS
CLANDESTINE	COCKCHAFERS	COLTISHNESS	COMPENDIOUS
CLARINETIST	COCKLESHELL	COLUMBARIUM	COMPENDIUMS
CLASSIFYING	COCKROACHES	COMBATIVELY	COMPENSATED
CLAVICHORDS	CODICILLARY	COMBINATION	COMPENSATOR
CLAY PIGEONS	COD-LIVER OIL	COMBINATIVE	COMPETENTLY
CLEAN LIMBED	COEDUCATION	COMBUSTIBLE	COMPETITIONS
CLEANLINESS	COEFFICIENT	COMESTIBLES	COMPETITIVE
CLEAN-SHAVEN	COELENTERIC	COMEUPPANCE	COMPETITORS
CLEAN SWEEPS	COELENTERON	COMFORTABLE	COMPILATION

COMPLACENCE	CONDUCTANCE	CONNECTIBLE	CONSUMPTIVE
COMPLACENCY	CONDUCTIBLE	CONNECTICUT	CONTACT LENS
COMPLAINANT	CONDUCTRESS	CONNECTIONS	CONTAINMENT
COMPLAINERS	CONFABULATE	CONNOISSEUR	CONTAMINANT
COMPLAINING	CONFECTIONS	CONNOTATION	CONTAMINATE
COMPLAISANT	CONFEDERACY	CONNOTATIVE	CONTEMNIBLE
COMPLEMENTS	CONFEDERATE	CONSCIENCES	CONTEMPLATE
COMPORTMENT	CONFERENCES	CONSCIOUSLY	CONTENTEDLY
COMPOSITION	CONFERMENTS	CONSCRIPTED	CONTENTIONS
COMPOSITORS	CONFESSEDLY	CONSECRATED	CONTENTIOUS
COMPRISABLE	CONFESSIONS	CONSECRATO	CONTENTMENT
COMPROMISED	CONFIDENCES	CONSECUTION	CONTESTANTS
COMPROMISER	CONFIDENTLY	CONSECUTIVE	CONTEXTURAL
COMPROMISES	CONFIDINGLY	CONSENSUSES	CONTINENTAL
COMPTOMETER	CONFINEMENT	CONSENTIENT	CONTINGENCE
COMPTROLLER	CONFISCABLE	CONSEQUENCE	CONTINGENCY
COMPULSIONS	CONFISCATED	CONSERVABLE	CONTINGENTS
COMPUNCTION	CONFISCATOR	CONSERVANCY	CONTINUALLY
COMPUTATION	CONFLATIONS	CONSERVATOR	CONTINUANCE
COMPUTERIZE	CONFLICTING	CONSIDERATE	CONTINUATOR
COMRADESHIP	CONFLICTION	CONSIDERING	CONTORTIONS
COMCATENATE	CONFLICTIVE	CONSIGNABLE	CONTRACTILE
CONCAVITIES	CONFLUENCES	CONSIGNMENT	CONTRACTING
CONCEALMENT	CONFORMABLE	CONSISTENCY	CONTRACTION
CONCEITEDLY	CONFORMABLY	CONSOLATION	CONTRACTIVE
CONCEIVABLE	CONFORMANCE	CONSOLATORY	CONTRACTORS
CONCEIVABLY	CONFORMISTS	CONSOLIDATE	CONTRACTUAL
CONCENTRATE	CONFOUNDING	CONSONANCES	CONTRACTURE
CONCEPTACLE	CONFRONTING	CONSONANTAL	CONTRAFLOWS
CONCEPTIONS	CONFUSINGLY	CONSORTIUMS	CONTRAPTION
CONCERNEDLY	CONFUTATION	CONSPECIFIC	CONTRASTING
CONCERTANTE	CONFUTATIVE	CONSPICUOUS	CONTRASTIVE
CONCERTEDLY	CONGEALMENT	CONSPIRATOR	CONTRAVENED
CONCERT GOER	CONGELATION	CONSTANTINE	CONTRAVENER
CONCERTINAS	CONGENIALLY	CONSTELLATE	CONTRAYERVA
CONCESSIBLE	CONGESTIBLE	CONSTERNATE	CONTRETEMPS
CONCESSIONS	CONGREGATED	CONSTIPATED	CONTRIBUTED
CONCILIATED	CONGREGATOR	CONSTITUENT	CONTRIBUTOR
CONCILIATOR	CONGRESSMAN	CONSTITUTED	CONTRIVANCE
CONCLUSIONS	CONGRESSMEN	CONSTITUTER	CONTROLLERS
CONCOCTIONS	CONGRUENTLY	CONSTRAINED	CONTROLLING
CONCOMITANT	CONGRUITIES	CONSTRAINER	CONTROVERSY
CONCORDANCE	CONJECTURAL	CONSTRAINTS	CONTUMELIES
CONCUBINAGE	CONJECTURED	CONSTRICTED	CONTUSIONED
CONCURRENCE	CONJECTURER	CONSTRICTOR	CONURBATION
CONDEMNABLE	CONJECTURES	CONSTRUCTED	CONVALESCED
CONDENSABLE	CONJOINEDLY	CONSTRUCTOR	CONVENIENCE
CONDITIONAL	CONJUGALITY	CONSULSHIPS	CONVENTICLE
CONDITIONED	CONJUGATING	CONSULTANCY	CONVENTIONS
CONDITIONER	CONJUGATION	CONSULTANTS	CONVERGENCE
CONDOLATORY	CONJUNCTIVA	CONSUMERISM	CONVERGENCY
CONDOLENCES	CONJUNCTIVE	CONSUMMATED	CONVERSABLE
CONDOMINIUM	CONJUNCTURE	CONSUMMATOR	CONVERSANCE
CONDONATION	CONJURATION	CONSUMPTION	CONVERSIONS

CONVERTIBLE	CORS ANGLAIS	CRASH HELMET	CRYSTALLOID
CONVEXITIES	CORTICATION	CRASH-LANDED	CRYSTAL SEATS
CONVEYANCER	CORUSCATING	CRAZY PAVING	CTENOPHORAN
CONVEYANCES	CORUSCATION	CREAM CHEESE	CUCKOO CLOCK
CONVICTABLE	COSIGNATORY	CREDENTIALS	CULMIFEROUS
CONVINCIBLE	COS LETTUCES	CREDIBILITY	CULMINATION
CONVIVIALLY	COSMETICIAN	CREDIT CARDS	CULPABILITY
CONVOCATION	COSMOGONIES	CREDIT NOTES	CULTIVATING
CONVOCATIVE	COSMOGONIST	CREDULOUSLY	CULTIVATION
CONVOLUTION	COSMOLOGIST	CREMATORIUM	CULTIVATORS
CONVOLVULUS	COSMOPOLITE	CRENELLATED	CUMMERBUNDS
CONVULSIONS	COTERMINOUS	CRENULATION	CUNNILINGUS
COOKERY BOOK	COTONEASTER	CREOPHAGOUS	CUPELLATION
COOPERATING	COTTAGE LOAF	CREPITATION	CUPRIFEROUS
COOPERATION	COTTON CANDY	CREPUSCULAR	CUPRONICKEL
COOPERATIVE	COTTONTAILS	CRESTFALLEN	CURATORSHIP
COOPERATORS	COUNCILLORS	CRIMINALITY	CURIOSITIES
COORDINATED	COUNSELLING	CRIMINOLOGY	CURIOUSNESS
COORDINATES	COUNSELLORS	CRINKLEROOT	CURMUDGEONS
COORDINATOR	COUNTENANCE	CRINKLINESS	CURRICULUMS
COPARCENARY	COUNTERFEIT	CRITICIZING	CURRY POWDER
COPLANARITY	COUNTERFOIL	CROCIDOLATE	CURTAILMENT
COPPERPLATE	COUNERMAND	CROCODILIAN	CURTAIN CALL
COPPERSMITH	COUNTERMINE	CROOKEDNESS	CURVILINEAR
COPROPHILIA	COUNTERMOVE	CROP-DUSTING	CUSPIDATION
COPYWRITERS	COUNTERPANE	CROSSBREEDS	CUSTARD PIES
CORNERSTONE	COUNTERPART	CROSS-GARNET	CUSTOMARILY
CORNFLOWERS	COUNTERPLOT	CROSS-LEGGED	CUSTOM-BUILT
CORNICULATE	COUNTERSANK	CROSSPIECES	CUSTOMIZING
CORNUCOPIAS	COUNTERSIGN	CROSS-STITCH	CUT-AND-DRIED
COROLLARIES	COUNTERSUNK	CROWDEDNESS	CUTTING EDGE
CORONOGRAPH	COUNTERTYPE	CROWN COLONY	CYANIDATION
CORONATIONS	COUNTERVAIL	CROWN COURTS	CYANOHYDRIN
CORNERSHOPS	COUNTERWORD	CROWNED HEAD	CYBERNATION
CORPORALITY	COUNTERWORK	CROWN JEWELS	CYBERNETICS
CORPORATELY	COUNTIFIED	CROWN PRINCE	CYCADACEOUS
CORPORATION	COUNTRY CLUB	CRUCIFEROUS	CYCLOALKANE
CORPORATIVE	COUNTRYSIDE	CRUCIFIXION	CYCLOHEXANE
CORPOREALLY	COUNTY COURT	CRUNCHINESS	CYCLOPLEGIA
CORPUSCULAR	COUNTY TOWNS	CRUSTACEANS	CYCLOSTYLED
CORRECTABLE	COUP DE GRACE	CRUSTACEOUS	CYCLOTHYMIA
CORRECTIONS	COURTEOUSLY	CRYOBIOLOGY	CYCLOTHYMIC
CORRECTIVES	COURTHOUSES	CRYOHYDRATE	CYCLINDRICAL
CORRECTNESS	COURTLINESS	CRYOSURGERY	CYSTOSCOPIC
CORRELATING	COVENANTING	CRYOTHERAPY	CYTOKINESIS
CORRELATION	COVER CHARGE	CRYPTICALLY	CYTOLOGICAL
CORROLATIVE	COWCATCHERS	CRYPTOGAMIC	CYTOLOGISTS
CORRIGENDUM	CRABBEDNESS	CRYPTOGENIC	CYTOPLASMIC
CORROBORATE	CRACKERJACK	CRYPTOGRAPH	
CORROSIVELY	CRANBERRIES	CRYPTOZITE	
CORRUGATION	CRANIOMETER	CYRSTAL BALL	
CORRUPTIBLE	CRANIOMETRY	CRYSTALLINE	
CORRUPTIONS	CRANKSHAFTS	CRYSTALLITE	
CORRUPTNESS	CRASH-DRIVING	CRYSTALLIZE	

C 12 LETTERS

12 LETTERS

CABIN CRUISER
CABINET-MAKER
CABLE RAILWAY
CACHINNATION
CAEOGENESIS
CAENOGENETIC
CALAMITOUSLY
CALCULATIONS
CALENDAR YEAR
CALIBRATIONS
CALISTHENICS
CALLIGRAPHER
CALLIGRAPHIC
CALLISTHENIC
CALL OF NATURE
CALORIMETRIC
CALUMNIATING
CALUMINATION
CAMELOPARDUS
CAMI-KNICKERS
CAMOUFLAGING
CAMP-FOLLOWER
CANALIZATION
CANCELLATION
CANDELABRUMS
CANDLESTICKS
CANDY-STRIPED
CANNIBALIZED
CANNON FODDER
CANONIZATION
CANTABRIGIAN
CANTANKEROUS
CAPABILITIES
CAPACITATION
CAPARISONNED
CAPE COLOURED
CAPERCAILLIE
CAPILLACEOUS
CAPITAL GAINS
CAPITALIZING
CAPITULATING
CAPITULATION
CAPRICIOUSLY
CAPTIOUSNESS
CARAVANSERAI
CARVOHYDRATE
CARBONACEOUS
CARBON COPIES
CARBON DATING
CARBON PAPERS
CARBURETTORS
CARCINOGENIC
CARD-CARRYING

CARDIOGRAPHY
CARDIOLOGIST
CARDIOMEGALY
CARELESSNESS
CARICATURING
CARICATURIST
CARILLONNEUR
CARPETBAGGER
CARPOLOGICAL
CARPOPHAGOUS
CARRIAGEWAYS
CARTE BLANCHE
CARTOGRAPHER
CARTOGRAPHIC
CARTWHEELING
CARVING FORKS
CARVING KNIFE
CASH AND CARRY
CASH REGISTER
CASTELLATION
CASTING VOTES
CATACHRESTIC
CATASTROPHES
CATASTROPHIC
CATCHPHRASES
CATECHETICAL
CATEGORIZING
CATERPILLARS
CATERWAULING
CAULIFLOWERS
CAUSE CELEBRE
CAUTIOUSNESS
CAVEAT EMPTOR
CELEBRATIONS
CEMENT MIXERS
CENSORIOUSLY
CENTENARIANS
CENTRALIZING
CENTREPIECES
CENTROCLINAL
CENTROSPHERE
CENTUPLICATE
CEPHALOMETER
CEPHALOMETRY
CEPHALOPODAN
CEPHALOPODIC
CEREMONIALLY
CEROGRAPHIST
CERTIFICATED
CERTIFICATES
CHAIN LETTERS
CHAIN-SMOKERS
CHAIN-SMOKING
CHAIRMANSHIP

CHAIRPERSONS
CHAISE LONGUE
CHALCOGRAPHY
CHALCOPYRITE
CHAMBERLAINS
CHAMBERMAIDS
CHAMBER MUSIC
CHAMPIONSHIP
CHANGELESSLY
CHANGE OF LIFE
CHANGING ROOM
CHAPLAINCIES
CHAPTERHOUSE
CHARACTERFUL
CHARACTERIZE
CHARGE NURSES
CHARGE SHEETS
CHARLATANISM
CHARNEL HOUSE
CHASTISEMENT
CHASTITY BELT
CHATTERBOXES
CHAUFFEURING
CHAUVINISTIC
CHECKERBERRY
CHECKERBLOOM
CHEERFULNESS
CHEERLEADERS
CHEESEBURGER
CHEESEPARING
CHEMOSPHERIC
CHEMOTHERAPY
CHEMOTROPISM
CHEQUERBOARD
CHERUBICALLY
CHESHIRE CATS
CHESTERFIELD
CHIAROSCUROS
CHIEF JUSTICE
CHIEF OF STAFF
CHILDBEARING
CHILDBENEFIT
CHILDISHNESS
CHILDMINDERS
CHILDMINDING
CHILDPRODIGY
CHIMNEYPIECE
CHIMNEYSTACK
CHIMNEYSWEEP
CHIROGRAPHER
CHIROGRAPHIC
CHIROPODISTS
CHIROPRACTIC
CHIROPRACTOR

CHITCHATTING
CHITTERLINGS
CHIVALROUSLY
CHLORAMBUCIL
CHLORENCHYMA
CHLORINATING
CHLORINATION
CHLOROFORMED
CHLOROHYDRIN
CHLOROPICRIN
CHOIRMASTERS
CHOIR SCHOOLS
CHOLERICALLY
CHONDRIOSOME
CHOREOGRAPHS
CHOREOGRAPHY
CHOREOGRAPHER
CHOREOGRAPHIC
CHRISTCHURCH
CHRISTENINGS
CHRISTIAN ERA
CHRISTIANITY
CHRISTIANIZE
CHRISTMAS BOX
CHRISTMAS EVE
CHRIST'S THORN
CHROMATICISM
CHROMATICITY
CHROMATOGRAM
CHROME YELLOW
CHROMOPHORIC
CHROMOSPHERE
CHRONOGRAPHS
CHRONOLOGIES
CHRONOLOGIST
CHRONOMETERS
CHRONOMETRIC
CHRONOSCOPIC
CHURCHWARDEN
CHURLISHNESS
CHYMOTRYPSIN
CINCHONIDINE
CINEMATHEQUE
CIRCUITOUSLY
CIRCULARIZED
CIRCULARIZER
CIRCULAR SAWS
CIRCUMCISING
CIRCUMCISION
CIRCUMFLUOUS
CIRCUMFUSION
CIRCUMNUTATE
CIRCUMSCRIBE
CIRCUMSTANCE

CIRCUMVENTED	COALITIONIST	COMMENTARIES	CONCEPTUALLY
CIRCUMVENTER	COAL SCUTTLES	COMMENTATING	CONCERTGOERS
CIRROCUMULUS	COBBLESTONES	COMMENTATORS	CONCERTINAED
CIRROSTRATUS	COCK FIGHTING	COMMERCIALLY	CONCERT PITCH
CITIZEN'S BAND	COCKLESHELLS	COMMISERATED	CONCILIATING
CITRICULTURE	COCONUT SHIES	COMMISERATOR	CONCILIATION
CIVIL DEFENCE	CODIFICATION	COMMISSARIAL	CONCILIATORS
CIVILIZATION	COEFFICIENTS	COMMISSIONAL	CONCILIATORY
CIVIL LIBERTY	COELENTERATE	COMMISSIONED	CONCLUSIVELY
CIVIL SERVANT	COENESTHESIA	COMMISSIONER	CONCOMITANCE
CIVIL SERVICE	COENESTHESIS	COMMITTEEMAN	CONCOMITANTS
CLAIRVOYANCE	COENESTHETIC	COMMITTEEMEN	CONCORDANCES
CLAIRVOYANTS	COERCIVENESS	COMMODIOUSLY	CONCRESCENCE
CLANGEROUSLY	COFFEE BREAKS	COMMON MARKET	CONCUPISCENT
CLANNISHNESS	COFFEE HOUSES	COMMONPLACES	CONCURRENCES
CLAPERBOARD	COFFEE TABLES	COMMONWEALTH	CONCURRECTLY
CLARINETTIST	COHABITATION	COMMUNICABLE	CONDEMNATION
CLASS ACTIONS	COHESIVENESS	COMMUNICABLY	CONDEMNATORY
CLASSICALITY	COINCIDENCES	COMMUNICANTS	CONDENSATION
CLASSICISTIC	COINCIDENTAL	COMMUNICATED	CONDESCENDED
CLASSIFIABLE	COLD SHOULDER	COMMUNICATOR	CONDITIONERS
CLASSIFIED AD	COLEOPTEROUS	COMMUNIONIST	CONDITIONING
CLAUDICATION	COLLABORATED	COMMUTATIONS	CONDUCTIVITY
CLEAR-SIGHTED	COLLABORATOR	COMPACT DISCS	CONFABULATED
CLEFT PLATES	COLLECTIVELY	COMPANIONATE	CONFABULATOR
CLERESTORIED	COLLECTIVISM	COMPANIONWAY	CONFECTIONER
CLERESTORIES	COLLECTIVIST	COMPARTMENTS	CONFEDERATED
CLERK OF WORKS	COLLECTIVITY	COMPASS POINT	CONFEDERATES
CLIENT STATES	COLLECTIVIZE	COMPATRIOTIC	CONFERENTIAL
CLIFFHANGERS	COLLECTORATE	COMPELLINGLY	CONFESSIONAL
CLIFFHANGING	COLLOCATIONS	COMPENSATING	CONFIDENTIAL
CLIMACTERICS	COLLOIDALITY	COMPENSATION	CONFINEMENTS
CLIMATICALLY	COLLOQUIALLY	COMPENSATIVE	CONFIRMATION
CLIMATOLOGIC	COLLYWOBBLES	COMPENSATORY	CONFIRMATORY
CLIQUISHNESS	COLONIALISTS	COMPETITIONS	CONFISCATING
CLODDISHNESS	COLONIZATION	COMPLACENTLY	CONFISCATORY
CLOSE-CROPPED	COLORIMETRIC	COMPLAISANTS	CONFORMATION
CLOSED SEASON	COLOURLESSLY	COMPLAISANCE	CONFOUNDEDLY
CLOSED-GRAINED	COLOUR SCHEME	COMPLEMENTED	CONFUCIANISM
CLOSE SEASONS	COLUMNIATION	COMPOSITIONS	CONFUCIANIST
CLOSING PRICE	COMBINATIONS	COMPREHENDED	CONGENITALLY
CLOSING TIMES	COMBUSTIBLES	COMPRESSIBLE	CONGLOBATION
CLOTHESHORSE	COME-UPPANCES	COMPROMISING	CONGLOMERATE
CLOTHESLINES	COMFORTINGLY	COMPTROLLERS	CONGLUTINATE
CLOTHES-PRESS	COMMANDEERED	COMPULSIVELY	CONGRATULATE
CLOTTED CREAM	COMMANDMENTS	COMPULSORILY	CONGREGATING
CLOVE HITCHES	COMMEMORATED	COMPUNCTIOUS	CONGREGATION
CLOVER LEAVES	COMMEMORATOR	COMPUTATIONS	CONJECTURING
CLOWNISHNESS	COMMENCEMENT	COMPUTERIZED	CONJUGATIONS
CLUB SANDWICH	COMMENDATION	CONCATENATED	CONJUNCTIONS
CLUSTER BOMBS	COMMENDATORY	CONCENTRATED	CONJUNCTIVAL
COACERVATION	COMMENSALISM	CONCENTRATES	CONJUNCTIVES
COACH BUILDER	COMMENSURATE	CONCENTRATOR	CONJUNCTURAL
COACH STATION	COMMENTARIAL	CONCEPTIONAL	CONJUNCTURES

409

CONNING TOWER
CONNOISSEURS
CONNOTATIONS
CONQUISTADOR
CONSCRIPTING
CONSCRIPTION
CONSECRATING
CONSECRATION
CONTEMPORIZE
CONTEMPTIBLE
CONTEMPTIBLY
CONTEMPTUOUS
CONTENTIONAL
CONTEXTUALLY
CONTIGUOUSLY
CONTINENTALS
CONTINGENTLY
CONTINUALITY
CONTINUATION
CONTINUATIVE
CONTINUINGLY
CONTINUOUSLY
CONTORTIONAL
CONTRACTIBLE
CONTRACTIONS
CONTRADICTED
CONTRADICTER
CONTRAPTIONS
CONTRAPTUNAL
CONTRARINESS
CONTRARIWISE
CONTRAVENING
CONTRIBUTING
CONTRIBUTION
CONTRIBUTIVE
CONTRIBUTORS
CONTRIBUTORY
CONTRIVANCES
CONTROLLABLE
CONTROVERTER
CONURBATIONS
CONVALESCENT
CONVALESCING
CONVECTIONAL
CONVENIENCES
CONVENIENTLY
CONVENTIONAL
CONVERTIBLES
CONVEYANCING
CONVEYER BELT
CONVINCINGLY
CONVIVIALITY
CONVOCATIONS
CONVOLUTEDLY

CONVOLUTIONS
CONVULSIVELY
COOKERY BOOKS
COOKING APPLE
COOPERATIVES
COORDINATELY
COORDINATING
COORDINATION
COPOLYMERIZE
COPROPHAGOUS
COPROPHILOUS
COPTIC CHURCH
COQUETTISHLY
CORNER STONES
CORNISH PASTY
COROLLACEOUS
CORPORALSHIP
CORPORATIONS
CORPOREALITY
CORRECTITUDE
CORRECTIVELY
CORRELATIONS
CORRELATIVES
CORRESPONDED
CORROBORATED
CORROBORATOR
CORRUGATIONS
COSMETICALLY
COSMETICIANS
COSMOLOGICAL
COSMOPOLITAN
COST OF LIVING
COTYLEDONARY
COTYLEDONOUS
COUTENANCED
COUTENANCES
COUNTERACTED
COUNTERBLAST
COUNTERCHECK
COUNTERCLAIM
COUNTERFOILS
COUNTERPANES
COUNTERPARTS
COUNTERPOINT
COUNTERPOSE
COUNTERPROOF
COUNTERSHAFT
COUNTERSIGNS
COUNTERTENOR
COUNTRY CLUBS
COUNTRY DANCE
COUNTRY SEATS
COUNTY COURT
COUPS DE GRACE

COURAGEOUSLY
COURT-MARTIAL
COVER CHARGES
COVERED WAGON
COVETOUSNESS
COWARDLINESS
CRACKBRAINED
CRANIOLOGIST
CRANIOMETRIC
CRASH BARRIER
CRASH HELMETS
CRASH LANDING
CREEPY-CRAWLY
CREMATIONISM
CREMATIONIST
CREMATORIUMS
CRENELLATION
CRISSCROSSED
CRISSCROSSES
CROP-SPRAYER
CROSSBENCHER
CROSSBENCHES
CROSSCHECKED
CROSS-COUNTRY
CROSSCURRENT
CROSS-DRESSER
CROSS-EXAMINE
CROSS GRAINED
CROSSPATCHES
CROSS-SECTION
CROWNED HEADS
CROWN PRINCES
CRUSH BARRIER
CRYPTANALYST
CRYPTOGRAPHY
CRYPTOLOGIST
CRYSTAL BALLS
CRYSTAL CLEAR
CRYSTAL GAZER
CRYSTALLITIC
CRYSTALLIZED
CUCKOO CLOCKS
CUMULATIVELY
CUMULONIMBUS
CUPBOARD LOVE
CURARIZATION
CURATORSHIPS
CURMUDGEONLY
CURTAIN CALLS
CURVACEOUSLY
CUT AND THRUST
CUTTLEFISHES

13 LETTERS

CABIN CRUISERS
CABINET MAKERS
CABLE RAILWAYS
CALCARIFEROUS
CALCIFICATION
CALCULABILITY
CALENDAR MONTH
CALENDAR YEARS
CALLIGRAPHIST
CALLISTHENICS
CALORIFICALLY
CAMPANOLOGIST
CANCELLATIONS
CANNIBALISTIC
CANNIBALIZING
CANONIZATIONS
CAPACIOUSNESS
CAPARISONNING
CAPE COLOURED
CAPITAL LEVIES
CAPITULATIONS
CAPRIFICATION
CARAVANSERAIS
CARBOHYDRATES
CARBON DIOXIDE
CARBONIFEROUS
CARBONIZATION
CARBURIZATION
CARCINOMATOID
CARDINAL POINT
CARDIOGRAPHER
CARDIOGRAPHIC
CARDIOLOGICAL
CARICATURISTS
CARNIFICATION
CARPETBAGGERS
CARPET SWEEPER
CARRIER PIGEON
CARTILAGINOUS
CARTOGRAPHERS
CARVING KNIVES
CASE HISTORIES
CASH DISPENSER
CASH REGISTERS
CASSEGRAINIAN
CASUISTICALLY
CATASTROPHISM
CATASTROPHIST
CATCHMENT AREA
CATECHIZATION
CATECHOLAMINE
CATEGORICALLY
CATHARTICALLY

CAT-O'-NINE-TAILS
CAUTERIZATION
CAYENNE PEPPER
CENTRE FORWARD
CEPHALIZATION
CEPHALOMETRIC
CEPHALOTHORAX
CEREBROSPINAL
CEREMONIALISM
CEREMONIALIST
CEREMONIOUSLY
CERTIFICATION
CERTIFICATORY
CERTIFIED MAIL
CERTIFIED MILK
CHAFING DISHES
CHAIN REACTION
CHAIN STITCHES
CHAIRMANSHIPS
CHAISE LONGUES
CHALCOGRAPHER
CHALCOGRAPHIC
CHALLENGEABLE
CHAMPIONSHIPS
CHANCELLERIES
CHANGEABILITY
CHANGE RINGING
CHANGING ROOMS
CHANTRY CHAPEL
CHARACTERIZED
CHARACTERLESS
CHARGEABILITY
CHARGE ACCOUNT
CHARNEL HOUSES
CHARTER MEMBER
CHASTISEMENTS
CHASTITY BELTS
CHATEAUBRIAND
CHEERLESSNESS
CHEMISORPTION
CHEMORECEPTOR
CHESTERFIELDS
CHEVAL GLASSES
CHIAROSCURISM
CHIAROSCURIST
CHIEF JUSTICES
CHIEFS OF STAFF
CHIEFTAINSHIP
CHILDLESSNESS
CHIMNEYBREAST
CHIMNEY CORNER
CHIMNEYPIECES
CHIMNEYSTACKS
CHIMNEYSWEEPS

CHIROPRACTORS
CHLAMYDOSPORE
CHLOROBENZENE
CHLOROFORMING
CHLOROMYCETIN
CHLOROPLASTIC
CHONDRIOSOMAL
CHONDROMATOUS
CHOREOGRAPHED
CHOREOGRAPHER
CHOREOGRAPHIC
CHRISTIANIZER
CHRISTIAN NAME
CHRISTMAS CAKE
CHRISTMAS CARD
CHRISTMASTIDE
CHRISTMASTIME
CHRISTMAS TREE
CHRISTOLOGIST
CHROMATICALLY
CHROMATICNESS
CHROMATOLYSIS
CHROMATOPHORE
CHROMOPLASMIC
CHROMOPROTEIN
CHROMOSPHERIC
CHRONOBIOLOGY
CHRONOGRAPHER
CHRONOGRAPHIC
CHRONOLOGICAL
CHRYSANTHEMUM
CHURCHWARDENS
CICATRIZATION
CINEMATICALLY
CINEMATOGRAPH
CIRCULARIZING
CIRCUMAMBIENT
CIRCUMCISIONS
CIRCUMFERENCE
CIRCUMFLEXION
CIRCUMSCRIBED
CIRCUMSPECTLY
CIRCUMSTANCES
CIRCUMVALLATE
CIRCUMVENTING
CIRCUMVENTION
CIVIL ENGINEER
CIVILIZATIONS
CIVIL SERVANTS
CLAIRAUDIENCE
CLANDESTINELY
CLAPPERBOARDS
CLARIFICATION
CLARINETTISTS

CLASSIFIED ADS
CLASSLESSNESS
CLASS STRUGGLE
CLAUSTROPHOBE
CLAVICHORDIST
CLEARANCE SALE
CLEAR-HEADEDLY
CLEARINGHOUSE
CLEISTOGAMOUS
CLERKS OF WORKS
CLIMACTERICAL
CLIMATOLOGIST
CLIMBING FRAME
CLIMBING IRONS
CLOSED-CIRCUIT
CLOSED SEASONS
CLOSING PRICES
CLOTHES HANGER
CLOTHESHORSES
CLUSTER-BOMBED
COACHBUILDERS
COACH STATIONS
COBELLIGERENT
COCAINIZATION
COCKER SPANIEL
COCKTAIL STICK
CODECLINATION
CODIFICATIONS
COEDUCATIONAL
COLD-BLOODEDLY
COLD-HEARTEDLY
COLLABORATING
COLLABORATION
COLLABORATIVE
COLLABORATORS
COLLETIVISTIC
COLLOQUIALISM
COLOUR SCHEMES
COMBAT FATIGUE
COMBINING FORM
COMMANDEERING
COMMANDERSHIP
COMMAND MODULE
COMMEMORATING
COMMEMORATION
COMMEMORATIVE
COMMENCEMENTS
COMMENDATIONS
COMMENSURABLE
COMMERCIALISM
COMMERCIALIST
COMMERCIALITY
COMMERCIALIZE
COMMISERATING

COMMISERATION
COMMISERATIVE
COMMISSARIATS
COMMISSIONERS
COMMISSIONING
COMMUNALISTIC
COMMUNICATING
COMMUNICATION
COMMUNICATIVE
COMMUNICATORY
COMMUNITARIAN
COMMUNITY HOME
COMMUNIZATION
COMPANIONABLE
COMPANIONABLY
COMPANIONSHIP
COMPANIONWAYS
COMPARABILITY
COMPARATIVELY
COMPARTMENTAL
COMPASSIONATE
COMPASS POINTS
COMPATIBILITY
COMPATRIOTISM
COMPENDIOUSLY
COMPETITIVELY
COMPLAININGLY
COMPLAISANTLY
COMPLEMENTARY
COMPLEMENTING
COMPLICATEDLY
COMPLICATIONS
COMPLIMENTARY
COMPLIMENTING
COMPOSITIONAL
COMPREHENDING
COMPREHENSION
COMPREHENSIVE
COMPRESSIONAL
COMPUTABILITY
COMPUTATIONAL
COMPUTERIZING
CONCATENATING
CONCATENATION
CONCAVO-CONVEX
CONCENTRATING
CONCENTRATION
CONCENTRATIVE
CONCENTRICITY
CONCEPTUALISM
CONCEPTUALIST
CONCEPTUALIZE
CONCERT GRANDS
CONCERTINAING

CONCESSIONARY
CONCHOLOGICAL
CONCHOLOGISTS
CONCOMITANTLY
CONCRETE MIXER
CONCRETIONARY
CONCUPISCENCE
CONDEMNATIONS
CONDEMNED CELL
CONDENSED MILK
CONDESCENDING
CONDESCENSION
CONDITIONALLY
CONDUCIVENESS
CONDUCTOR RAIL
CONDYLOMATOUS
CONFABULATING
CONFABULATION
CONFABULATORY
CONFECTIONARY
CONFECTIONERS
CONFECTIONERY
CONFEDERACIES
CONFEDERATING
CONFEDERATION
CONFESSIONALS
CONFESSIONARY
CONFIGURATION
CONFIRMATIONS
CONFISCATIONS
CONFLAGRATION
CONFRATERNITY
CONFRONTATION
CONGLOMERATES
CONGLOMERATIC
CONGRATULATED
CONGRATULATOR
CONGREGATIONS
CONGRESSIONAL
CONJUGATIONAL
CONJUNCTIONAL
CONNECTING ROD
CONNING TOWERS
CONNOTATATIVE
CONQUISTADORS
CONSANGUINITY
CONSCIENTIOUS
CONSCIOUSNESS
CONSECUTIVELY
CONSEQUENTIAL
CONSERVANCIES
CONSERVATIVES
CONSERVATOIRE
CONSIDERATELY

CONSIDERATION
CONSISTENCIES
CONSOLIDATING
CONSOLIDATION
CONSPICUOUSLY
CONSPIRATRESS
CONSTELLATION
CONSTELLATORY
CONSTERNATION
CONSTITUTIONS
CONSTRAINEDLY
CONSTRICTIONS
CONSTRUCTIBLE
CONSTRUCTIONS
CONSULTANCIES
CONSULTATIONS
CONSUMMATIONS
CONTACT LENSES
CONTAINERIZED
CONTAMINATING
CONTAMINATION
CONTAMINATORS
CONTEMPLATING
CONTEMPLATION
CONTENTIOUSLY
CONTEXTUALIZE
CONTINGENCIES
CONTINUATIONS
CONTORTIONIST
CONTRABANDIST
CONTRACEPTION
CONTRACEPTIVE
CONTRACTIONAL
CONTRACTUALLY
CONTRADICTING
CONTRADICTION
CONTRADICTIVE
CONTRADICTORY
CONTRAPUNTIST
CONTRAVENTION
CONTRIBUTIONS
CONTROVERSIAL
CONTROVERSIES
CONVALESCENCE
CONVALESCENTS
CONVERSATIONS
CONVERSAZIONE
CONVERTIPLANE
CONVEXO-CONVEX
CONVEYER BELTS
CONVOCATIONAL
CONVOLVULUSES
COOKING APPLES
COOPERATIVELY

CORN EXCHANGES
CORRESPONDENT
CORRESPONDING
CORROBORATING
CORROBORATION
CORROBORATIVE
CORROBORATORS
CORROSIVENESS
CORRUPTIONIST
COSIGNATORIES
COSMOPOLITANS
COST-EFFECTIVE
COTTAGE CHEESE
COTTAGE LOAVES
COTTON-PICKING
COUNTERACTING
COUNTERACTION
COUNTERACTIVE
COUNTERATTACK
COUNTERBLASTS
COUNTERCHARGE
COUNTERCLAIMS
COUNTERFEITED

COUNTERFEITER
COUNTERMANDED
COUNTERPOINTS
COUNTERSIGNED
COUNTRY DANCES
COUNTY COUNCIL
COURTEOUSNESS
COURT MARTIALS
COURTS-MARTIAL
COVERED WAGONS
CRAFTSMANSHIP
CRASH BARRIERS
CRASH LANDINGS
CRASSULACEOUS
CREDIT ACCOUNT
CREDIT SQUEEZE
CRIMINOLOGIST
CRISSCROSSING
CROSSBENCHERS
CROSSBREEDING
CROSSCHECKING
CROSSCURRENTS
CROSS-DRESSERS

CROSS-DRESSING
CROSS-EXAMINED
CROSS-EXAMINER
CROSS-HATCHING
CROSS-PURPOSES
CROSS-QUESTION
CROSS-REFERRED
CROSS-SECTIONS
CROSS-STITCHES
CRUISE MISSILE
CRUSH BARRIERS
CRYPTANALYSIS
CRYPTANALYTIC
CRYTOGRAPHER
CRYPTOGRAPHIC
CRYSTAL GAZERS
CRYSTAL GAZING
CRYSTALLINITY
CRYSTALLIZING
CUMULOSTRATUS
CURTAIN RAISER
CUSTODIANSHIP
CYLINDRICALLY

3 LETTERS

DAB
DAD
DAM
DAY
DDT
DEB
DEM
DEN
DEP
DEW
DID
DIE
DIG
DIM
DIN
DIP
DIY
DJS
DNA
DOC
DOE
DOG
DOH
DON
DOS
DOT
DRY
DTS
DUB
DUD
DUE
DUG
DUN
DUO
DVD
DYE

4 LETTERS

DABS
DADO
DADS
DAFT
DAGO
DAIS
DALE
DAME
DAMN
DAMP
DAMS
DANK
DARE
DARK
DARN
DART
DASH
DATA
DATE
DAUB
DAWE
DAYS
DAZE
D-DAY
DEAD
DEAF
DEAL
DEAN
DEAR
DEBS
DEBT
DECK
DEED
DEEM
DEEP
DEER
DEFT
DEFY
DELE
DELL
DELL
DEMO
DENS
DENT
DENY
DERV
DESK
DEWY
DHOW
DIAL
DICE
DICK
DIED
DIET
DIGS
DIKE
DILL
DIME
DINE
DINS
DINT
DISC
DISH
DISK
DIVE
DOCK
DOCS
DODO
DOES
DOFF
DOGE
DOGS
DOHA
DOLE
DOLL
DOLT
DOME
DONE
DONS
DOOM
DOOR
DOPE
DORY
DISE
DOSS
DOTE
DOTS
DOUR
DOVE
DOWN
DOZE
DOZY
DRAB
DRAG
DRAM
DRAT
DRAW
DRAY
DREW
DRIP
DROP
DRUB
DRUG
DRUM
DUAL
DUCK
DUCT
DUDE
DUDS
DUEL
DUES
DUET
DUFF
DUGS
DUKE
DULL
DULY
DUMB
DUMP
DUNE
DUNG
DUNK
DUNS
DDUOS
DUPE
DUSK
DUST
DUTY
DYAD
DYED
DYES
DYKE
DYNE

5 LETTERS

DACCA
DADDY
DAGGA
DAGOS
DAILY
DAIRY
DAISY
DAKAR
DALES
DALLY
DAMAN
DAMES
DANCE
DANDY
DANIO
DARAF
DARED
DARER
DARES
DARKS
DARNS
DARTS
DATED
DATER
DATES
DATUM
DAUBS
DAUBY
DAUNT
DAVIT
DAWNS
DAZED
DAZES
DEALS
DEALT
DEANS
DEARS
DEARY
DEATH
DEBAR
DEBIT
DEBTS
DEBUG
DUBUT
DECAL
DECAY
DECKS
DECOR
DECOY
DECRY
DEEDS
DEFER
DEGAS
DE-ICE
DEFIY
DEIGN
DEISM
DEIST
DEITY
DEKKO
DELAY
DELFT
DELHI
DELLS
DELOS
DELTA
DELVE
DEMOB
DEMON
DEMOS
DEMUR
DENIM
DENSE
DENTS
DEPOT
DEPTH
DERBY
DERMA
DESKS
DETER
DEUCE
DEVIL
DHOLE
DHOTI
DHOWS
DIALS
DIARY
DIAZO
DICED
DICER
DICEY
DICKS
DICKY
DICTA
DIETS
DIGIT
DIJON
DIKES
DILDO
DIMER
DIMES
DIMLY
DINAR
DINED
DINER
DINGO
DIINGY
DINKA
DIODE
DIRER
DIRGE
DIRKS
DIRTY
DISCO
DISCS
DISHY
DISKS
DITCH
DITTO
DITTY
DIVAN
DIVED
DIVER
DIVES
DIVOT
DIXIE
DIZZY
DIBBY
DOBRO
DOCKS
DODGE
DODGY
DODOS
DOERS
DOGES
DOGGO
DOGGY
DOGIE
DOGMA
DOILY
DOING
DOLBY
DOLCE
DOLED
DOLLS
DOLLY
DOLTS
DOMED

DOMES	DREGS	DUSKY	DAPPLE	DECENT	DEMISE
DONEE	DRESS	DUSTY	DARDIC	DECIDE	DEMIST
DONNA	DRIBS	DUTCH	DARFUR	DECILE	DEMODE
DONOR	DRIED	DUVET	DARING	DECKED	DEMONS
DOOMS	DRIER	DWARF	DARKEN	DECKLE	DEMOTE
DONEE	DRIFT	DWELL	DARKER	DECOCT	DEMURE
DONNA	DRILL	DWELT	DARKLY	DECODE	DEMURS
DONOR	DRILY	DYERS	DARNED	DECOKE	DENARY
DOOMS	DRINK	DYFED	DARNEL	DECORS	DENGUE
DOORS	DRIPS	DYING	DARNER	DECOYS	DENIAL
DOPED	DRIVE	DYKES	DARTED	DECREE	DENIED
DOPES	DROIT		DARTER	DEDUCE	DENIER
DOPEY	DROLL		DASHED	DEDUCT	DENIMS
DORIC	DROME	**6 LETTERS**	DASHER	DEEMED	DENNED
DOSED	DRONE	DABBED	DASHES	DEEPEN	DENOTE
DOSER	DROOL	DABBER	DATARY	DEEPER	DENSER
DOSES	DROOP	DABBLE	DATING	DEEPLY	DENTAL
DOTED	DROPS	DACRON	DATIVE	DEFACE	DENTED
DOTER	DROSS	DACTYL	DATURA	DEFAME	DENTEX
DOTTY	DROVE	DADOES	DAUBED	DEFEAT	DENTIL
DOUBT	DROWN	DAEMON	DAUBER	DEFECT	DENTIN
DOUGH	DRUGS	DAFTER	DAVITS	DEFEND	DENUDE
DOUSE	DRUID	DAFTLY	DAWDLE	DEFIED	DENVER
DOVES	DRUMS	DAGGER	DAWNED	DEFIER	DEODAR
DOWDY	DRUNK	DAHLIA	DAYBOY	DEFILE	DEPART
DOWEL	DRUSE	DAINTY	DAYGLO	DEFINE	DEPEND
DOWER	DRYER	DAISES	DAYTON	DEFORM	DEPICT
DOWNS	DUBAI	DAKOTA	DAZING	DEFRAY	DEPLOY
DOWNY	DUCAL	DALLAS	DAZZLE	DEFTLY	DEPORT
DOWRY	DUCAT	DALTON	DEACON	DEFUSE	DEPOSE
DOWSE	DUCHY	DAMAGE	DEADEN	DEGAGE	DEPOTS
DOYEN	DUCKS	DAMARA	DEADLY	DEGREE	DEPTHS
DOZED	DUCKY	DAMASK	DEAFEN	DEHORN	DEPUTE
DOZER	DUCTS	DANMAR	DEALER	DE-ICED	DEPUTY
DRABS	DUDES	DAMMED	DEARER	DE-ICER	DERAIL
DRAFF	DUELS	DAMNED	DEARLY	DEIFIC	DERIDE
DRAFT	DUETS	DAMPED	DEARTH	DEISTS	DERIVE
DRAGS	DUFFS	DAMPEN	DEATHS	DEIXIS	DERMAL
DRAFF	DUKES	DAMPER	DEBARK	DEJAVU	DERMIC
DRAFT	DULLY	DAMPLY	DEBASE	DEJECT	DERMIS
DRAGS	DULSE	DAMSEL	DEBATE	DE JURE	DERRIS
DRAIL	DUMMY	DAMSON	DEBITS	DELAYS	DESCRY
DRAIN	DUMPS	DANCED	DEBRIS	DELETE	DESERT
DRAKE	DUNCE	DANCER	DEBTOR	DELIAN	DESIGN
DRAMA	DUNES	DANDLE	DEBUNK	DELICT	DESIRE
DRAMS	DUNGY	DANGER	DEBUTS	DELPHI	DESIST
DRANN	DUNKS	DANGLE	DECADE	DELTAS	DESMAN
DRAPE	DUPED	DANISH	DECALS	DELUDE	DESMID
DRAWL	DUPER	DANKER	DECAMP	DELUGE	DESORB
DRAWN	DUPES	DANUBE	DECANE	DE LUXE	DESPOT
DRAWS	DUPLE	DANZIG	DECANT	DELVED	DESSAU
DREAD	DUREX	DAPHNE	DECARE	DELVER	DETACH
DREAM	DURRA	DAPPED	DECCAN	DEMAND	DETAIL
DREAR	DURUM	DAPPER	DECEIT	DEMEAN	DETAIN

DETECT	DINGHY	DODDLE	DOTTER	DRINKS	DUNNER
DETENT	DUNGLE	DODGED	DOTTLE	DRIPPY	DUPERY
DETEST	DINING	DODGEM	DOUALA	DRIVEL	DUPING
DETOUR	DINKUM	DODGER	DOUBLE	DRIVEN	DUPLET
DEUCED	DINNED	DODGES	DOUBLY	DRIVER	DUPLEX
DEVICE	DINNER	DODOES	DOUBTS	DRIVES	DURBAN
DEVILS	DIOXAN	DOFFED	DOUCHE	DROGUE	DURBAR
DEVISE	DIOXIN	DOFFER	DOUGHY	DROLLY	DURESS
DEVOID	DIPLEX	DOF-EAR	DOURLY	DROND	DURIAN
DEVOTE	DIPLOE	DOGGED	DOUSED	DRONES	DURING
DEVOUR	DIPODY	DOGGER	DOUSER	DRONGO	DUSTED
DEWIER	DIPOLE	DOGIES	DOVISH	DROOPY	DUSTED
DEWILY	DIPPED	DOGLEG	DOWNED	DROPSY	DUSTER
DEWLAP	DIPPER	DOGMAS	DOWNER	DROSSY	DUSTUP
DEXTER	DIRECT	DOG TAG	DOWSED	DROVER	DUTIES
DIACID	DIREST	DOINGS	DOWSER	DROVES	DUVETS
DIADEM	DIRGES	DOLINE	DOYENS	DROWSE	DWARFS
DIALED	DIRHAM	DOLING	DOYLEY	DROWSY	DYABLE
DIAPER	DIRNDL	DOLLAR	DOZENS	DRUDGE	DYEING
DIAPIR	DISARM	DOLLED	DOZIER	DRUIDS	DYNAMO
DIARCH	DISBAR	DOLLOP	DOZILY	DRUNKS	DYNAST
DIATOM	DISBUD	DOLMAN	DOZING	DRYADS	DYNODE
DIBBED	DISCOS	DOLMAS	DRABLY	DRYERS	
DIBBER	DISCUS	DOLMEN	DRACHM	DRY ICE	
DIBBLE	DISEUR	DOLOUR	DRAFFY	DRYING	**7 LETTERS**
DICIER	DISHED	DOMAIN	DRAFTS	DRY ROT	DABBLING
DICING	DISHES	DOMINO	DRAFTY	DUBBED	DABBLED
DICKER	DISMAL	DONATE	DRAGEE	DUBBIN	DABBLER
DICTUM	DISMAY	DONJON	DRAGGY	DUBLIN	DAB HAND
DIDDLE	DISOWN	DONKEY	DRAGON	DUCATS	DACTYLS
DIEPPE	DISPEL	DONNED	DRAINS	DUCKED	DADAISM
DIESEL	DISTAL	DONORS	DRAKES	DUCKER	DADAIST
DIESIS	DISTIL	DOODLE	DRAMAS	DUDEEN	DADDIES
DIETED	DISUSE	DOOMED	DRAPED	DUELED	DAEMONS
DIETER	DITHER	DOPANT	DRAPER	DUELLO	DAFTEST
DIFFER	DITTOS	DOPIER	DRAPES	DUFFEL	DAGGERS
DIGAMY	DIVANS	DOPING	DRAWEE	DUFFER	DAGLOCK
DIGEST	DIVERS	DORIAN	DRAWER	DUGOUT	DAHLIAS
DIGGER	DIVERT	DORIES	DRAWLS	DULCET	DAHOMAN
DIGITS	DIVEST	DORMER	DRAWLY	DULLED	DAHOMEY
DIGLOT	DIVIDE	DORMIE	DREADS	DULLER	DAILIES
DIK-DIK	DIVINE	DORSAD	DREAMS	DULUTH	DAIRIES
DIKTAT	DIVING	DORSAL	DREAMT	DUMBER	DAISIES
DILATE	DIJAMBI	DORSUM	DRAEMY	DUMBLY	DAKOTAN
DILDOS	DJINNS	DOSAGE	DREARY	DUMDUM	DALLIED
DILUTE	DOABLE	DOSING	DREDGE	DUMPED	DAMAGED
DIMITY	DOBBIN	DOSSAL	DREGGY	DUMPER	DAMAGER
DIMMED	DOCENT	DOSSED	DRENCH	DUNCES	DAMAGES
DIMMER	DOCILE	DOSSER	DRESSY	DUNDEE	DAMMING
DIMPLE	DOCKED	DOTAGE	DRIERS	DUNITE	DAMNIFY
DIMPLY	DOCKER	DOTARD	DRIEST	DUNKED	DAMNING
DIMWIT	DOCKET	DOT COM	DRIFTS	DUNKER	DAMPERS
DINARS	DOCTOR	DOTING	DRIFTY	DUNLIN	DAMPEST
DINERS	DODDER	DOTTED	DRILLS	DUNNED	DAMPING

DAMPISH	DEAREST	DEFECTS	DENIZEN	DESPONG	DIARCHY
DAMSELS	DEARIES	DEFENCE	DENMARK	DESPOTS	DIARIES
DAMSONS	DEATHLY	DEFIANT	DENNING	DESSERT	DIARIES
DANCERS	DEBACLE	DEFICIT	DENOTED	DESTINE	DIARIST
DANCING	DEBASED	DEFILED	DENSELY	DESTINY	DIASTER
DANDERS	DEBASER	DEFINER	DENSEST	DESTROY	DIAZINE
DANDIER	DEBATED	DEFLATE	DENSITY	DETAILS	DIAZOLE
DANDIES	DEBATER	DEFLECT	DENTATE	DETENTE	DIBASIC
DANDIFY	DEBATES	DEFORCE	DENTINE	DETERGE	DIBBING
DANDLED	DEBAUCH	DEFRAUD	DENTING	DETINUE	DIBBLED
DANDLER	DEBRIEF	DEFROCK	DENTIST	DETOURS	DIBBLER
DANGERS	DEBTORS	DEFRODT	DENTOID	DETRACT	DIBBLES
DANGLED	DECADAL	DEFUNCT	DENTURE	DETRAIN	DICIEST
DANGLER	DECADES	DEFUSED	DENUDED	DETROIT	DICKENS
DANKEST	DECAGON	DEFYING	DENUDER	DETRUDE	DICKIER
DANSEUR	DECANAL	DEGAUSS	DENYING	DEUTZIA	DICKIES
DAPHNIA	DECAPOD	DEGRADE	DEONTIC	DVEALUE	DICLINY
DAPPING	DECAYED	DEGREES	DEPISER	DEVELOP	DICTATE
DAPPLED	DECEASE	DEHISCE	DEPLETE	DEVIANT	DICTION
DARESAY	DECIEVE	DEICIDE	DEPLORE	DEVIATE	DIDTUMS
DARIOLE	DECENCY	DI-ICING	DEPLUME	DEVICES	DIDDLED
DARKEST	DECIARE	DEICTIC	DEPOSAL	DEVILED	DIDICOY
DARLING	DECIBAL	DEIFIED	DEPOSED	DEVILRY	DIEBACK
DARNING	DECIDED	DEIFIER	DEPOSER	DEVIOUS	DIE-CAST
DARTING	DECIDER	DEIFORM	DEPOSIT	DEVISAL	DIEHARD
DASHEEN	DECIDUA	DEIGNED	DEPRAVE	DEVISED	DIESELS
DASHING	DECIMAL	DEISTIC	DEPRESS	DEVISEE	DIETARY
DASHURE	DECKING	DEITIES	DEPRIVE	DEVISER	DIETING
DATABLE	DECLAIM	DEJECTA	DEPSIDE	DEVISOR	DIFFUSE
DAUBERY	DECLARE	DELAINE	DEPUTED	DEVOICE	DIGAMMA
DAUBING	DECLASS	DELAYED	DERANGE	DEVOIRS	DIGESTS
DAUNTED	DECLINE	DELAYER	DERBIES	DEVOLVE	DIGGERS
DAUNTER	DECODED	DELETED	DERIDED	DEVOTED	DIGGING
DAUPHIN	DECORUM	DELIGHT	DERIDER	DEVOTEE	DIGITAL
DAWDLED	DECOYED	DELIMIT	DERIVED	DEWCLAW	DIGNIFY
DAWDLER	DECOYER	DELIVER	DERIVER	DEWDROP	DIGNITY
DAWNING	DECREED	DELOUSE	DERMOID	DEWIEST	DIGRAPH
DAYBOOK	DECREER	DELPHIC	DERRICK	DEWLAPS	DIGRESS
DAYBOYS	DECREES	DELTAIC	DERVISH	DEXTRAL	DILATED
DAY-CARE	DECRIAL	DELTOID	DESCALE	DEXTRAN	DILATOR
DAYLONG	DECRIED	DELUDED	DESCANT	DEXTRIN	DILDOES
DAYROOM	DECRIER	DELUDER	DESCEND	DIABASE	DILEMMA
DAYTIME	DECUPLE	DELUGED	DESCENT	DIABOLO	DILUENT
DAZEDLY	DEDUCED	DELUGES	DESERTS	DIADEMS	DILUTED
DAZZLED	DEEMING	DELVING	DESERVE	DIAGRAM	DILUTEE
DEACONS	DEEPEST	DEMANDS	DESIGNS	DIALECT	DILUTER
DEAD END	DEEP FRY	DEMERIT	DESIRED	DIALING	DIMETER
DEAD EYE	DEFACED	DEMESNE	DESIRER	DIALLED	DIMMERS
DEAD PAN	DEFACER	DEMIGOD	DESKTOP	DIALLER	DIMMEST
DEAF AID	DE FACTO	DEMONIC	DESMOID	DIALYSE	DIMMING
DEALATE	DEFAMED	DEMOUNT	DESPAIR	DIAMINE	DIMNESS
DEALERS	DEFAMER	DEMURER	DESPISE	DIAMOND	DIMORPH
DEALING	DEFAULT	DENIALS	DESPITE	DIANOIA	DIMPLES
DEANERY	DEFEATS	DENIERS	DESPOIL	DIAPERS	DIMWITS

417

DINERIC	DISROBE	DOGGONE	DOUBTER	DRESSES	DUBIETY
DINETTE	DISRUPT	DOGLEGS	DOUCHES	DRIBBLE	DUBIOUS
DINGIER	DIDDECT	DOG TAGS	DOUGHTY	DRIBLET	DUCHESS
DINGILY	DISSENT	DOGTROT	DOUGLAS	DRIFTED	DUCHIES
DINGLES	DISTAFF	DOGVANE	DOURINE	DRIFTER	DUCKIES
DINGOES	DISTANT	DOGWOOD	DOUSING	DRILLED	DUCKING
DINKIER	DISTEND	DOILIES	DOWABLE	DRILLER	DUCKTILE
DINNERS	DISTICH	DOLEFUL	DOWAGER	DRINKER	DUDGEON
DINNING	DISTORT	DOLLARS	DOWDIER	DRIP-DRY	DUELING
DIOCESE	DISTURB	DOLLIES	DOWDILY	DRIPPED	DUELLED
DIOPTRE	DISUSED	DOLLING	DOWNBOW	DRIVE-IN	DUELLER
DIORAMA	DITCHED	DOLLISH	DOWNERS	DRIVERS	DUENNAS
DIORITE	DITCHER	DOLLOPS	DOWNIER	DRIVING	DUFFERS
DIOXIDE	DITCHES	DOLMENS	DOWNING	DRIZZLE	DUGOUTS
DIPHASE	DITTANY	DOLPHIN	DOWRIES	DRIZZLY	DUKEDOM
DIPLOID	DITTIES	DOLTISH	DOWSERS	DROLLER	DULLARD
DIPLOMA	DIURNAL	DOMAINS	DOWSING	DRONING	DULLEST
DIPLONT	DIVERGE	DOMICAL	DOYLEYS	DRONISH	DULLING
DIPNOAN	DIVERSE	DOMINEE	DOZENTH	DROOLED	DULOSIS
DIPOLAR	DIVIDED	DONATED	DOZIEST	DROOPED	DUMBEST
DIPPERS	DIVIDER	DONATOR	DRABBER	DROPLET	DUMMIES
DIPPING	DIVIDES	DONBASS	DRABBLE	DROPOUT	DUMPERS
DIPTYCH	DIVINED	DONEGAL	DRACHMA	DROPPED	DUMPIER
DIREFUL	DIVINER	DONETSK	DRACHMS	DROPPER	DUMPING
DIRNDLS	DIVIDES	DON JUAN	DRAFTED	DROSHKY	DUNGEON
DIRTIED	DIVISOR	DONKEYS	DRAFTEE	DROUGHT	DUNKING
DIRTIER	DIVORCE	DONNING	DRAFTER	DROVERS	DUNKIRK
DIRTILLY	DIVULGE	DONNISH	DRAGGED	DROWNED	DUNNAGE
DISABLE	DIZZIER	DOODLED	DRAGGLE	DROWNER	DUNNEST
DISAVOW	DIZZILY	DOODLER	DRAGNET	DROWSED	DUNNING
DISBAND	DNIEPER	DOODLIES	DRAGONS	DRUBBER	DUNNITE
DISCARD	D-NOTICE	DOOMING	DRAGOON	DRUDGED	DUODENA
DISCERN	DOBRUJA	DO-OR-DIE	DRAINED	DRUDGER	DUOTONE
DISCOID	DOCKAGE	DOORMAN	DRAINER	DRUDGES	DUPABLE
DISCORD	DOCKERS	DOORMAT	DRAPERS	DRUGGED	DURABLE
DISCUSS	DOCKETS	DOORMEN	DRAPERY	DRUGGET	DURABLY
DISDAIN	DOCKING	DOORWAY	DRAPING	DRUIDIC	DURANGO
DISEASE	DOCTORS	DOPIEST	DRASTIC	DRUMMIN	DURMAST
DISEUSE	DODDERY	DORMANT	DRATTED	DRUMMED	DUSKIER
DISGUST	DODDLES	DORMERS	DRAUGHT	DRUMMER	DUSTBIN
DISHFUL	DODGEMS	DORMICE	DRAWBAR	DRUNKEN	DUSTERS
DISHIER	DODGERS	DORNICK	DRAWERS	DRUNKER	DUSTIER
DISHING	DODGIER	DOSAGES	DRAWING	DRYABLE	DUSTING
DISJECT	DODGING	DOSSERS	DRAWLED	DRYADIC	DUSTMAN
DISJOIN	DODOISM	DOSSIER	DRAWLER	DRY DOCK	DUSTMEN
DISLIKE	DOESKIN	DOSSING	DREADED	DRY-EYED	DUSTPAN
DISMAST	DOFFING	DOTAGES	DREAMED	DRY LAND	DUSTUPS
DISMISS	DOGBANE	DOTTIER	DREAMER	DRYNESS	DUTIFUL
DISOBEY	DOGCART	DOTTING	DREDGED	DRY-SALT	DUVETYN
DISPLAY	DOG DAYS	DOUBLED	DREDGER	DRY-SHOD	DUVANDA
DISPORT	DOGFISH	DOUBLER	DRENTHE	DUALISM	DWARFED
DISPOSE	DOGGERY	DOUBLES	DRESDEN	DUALIST	DWARVES
DISPUTE	DOGGIES	DOUBLET	DRESSED	DUALITY	DWELLED
DISRATE	DOGGING	DOUBTED	DRESSER	DUBBING	DWELLER

DWINDLE	DARKENER	DEBUGGED	DEFEATER	DEMANDER
DYARCHY	DARKNESS	DEBUGGER	DEFECATE	DEMARCHE
DYELINE	DARK ROOM	DEBUNKED	DEFECTED	DEMEANED
DYEWOOD	DARLINGS	DEBUNKER	DEFECTOR	DEMENTED
DYNAMIC	DATABASE	DECADENT	DEFENCES	DEMENTIA
DYNAMOS	DATEABLE	DECAMPED	DEFENDED	DEMERARA
DYNASTY	DATELINE	DECANOIC	DEFERENT	DEMERITS
DYSURIA	DATOLITE	DECANTED	DEFERRED	DEMERSAL
DYSURIC	DAUGHTER	DECANTER	DEFERRER	DEMENSES
DZONGKA	DAUNTING	DECAYING	DEFIANCE	DEMIGODS
	DAUPHINE	DECEASED	DEFICITS	DEMIJOHN
	DAUPHINS	DECEIVED	DEFILERS	DEMILUNE
8 LETTERS	DAWDLERS	DECEIVER	DEFILING	DEMISTED
DABBLERS	DAWDLING	DECEMBER	DEFINING	DEMISTER
DABBLING	DAYBREAK	DECENTLY	DEFINITE	DEMIVOLT
DABCHICK	DAYDREAM	DECIBELS	DEFLATED	DEMOBBED
DAB HANDS	DAYLIGHT	DECIDING	DEFLATOR	DEMOCRAT
DACTYLIC	DAYROOMA	DECIDUAL	DEFLEXED	DEMOLISH
DAEMONIC	DAYTIMES	DECIMALS	DEFLOWER	DEMONIAC
DAFFODIL	DAY-TO-DAY	DECIMATE	DEFLOREST	DEMONISM
DAFTNESS	DAZZLING	DECIPHER	DEFORMED	DEMONIST
DAGESTAN	DEACONRY	DECISION	DEFORMER	DEMONIZE
DAINTIER	DEAD BEAT	DECISIVE	DEFRAYAL	DEMOTING
DAINTIES	DEAD DUCK	DECKHAND	DEFRAYED	DEMOTION
DAINTILY	DEAD ENDS	DECLARED	DEFRAYER	DEMOTION
DAIQUIRI	DEADENED	DECLARER	DEFTNESS	DEMOTIST
DAIRYMAN	DEADENER	DECLASSE	DEFUSING	DEMPSTER
DAIRYMEN	DEADFALL	DECLINED	DEGASSER	DEMURELY
DALESMAN	DEAD HEAT	DECLINER	DEGRADED	DEMUREST
DALLYING	DEADLIER	DECLINES	DEGRADER	DEMURRAL
DALMATIA	DEADLINE	DECODING	DEICIDAL	DEMURRED
DALMATIC	DEADLOCK	DECOLOUR	DEIFYING	DEMURRER
DALTONIC	DEADNESS	DECORATE	DEIGNING	DENATURE
DAMAGING	DEAD WOOD	DECOROUS	DEJECTED	DENDRITE
DAMANHUR	DEAF-AIDS	DECOYING	DELAWARE	DENDROID
DAMASCUS	DEAFENED	DECREASE	DELAYING	DENIABLE
DAMNABLE	DEAF-MUTE	DECREPIT	DELEGACY	DENIZENS
DAMNABLY	DEAFNESS	DECRETAL	DELEGATE	DENOTING
DAMOCLES	DEALFISH	DECRYING	DELETING	DENOUNCE
DAMPENED	DEALINGS	DECURVED	DELETION	DENTICLE
DAMPENER	DEANSHIP	DEDICATE	DELICACY	DENTINAL
DAMPNESS	DEARESTS	DEDUCING	DELICATE	DENTURES
DANDIEST	DEARNESS	DEDUCTED	DELIGHTS	DENUDATE
DANDLING	DEATHBED	DEED POLL	DELIRIUM	DENUDING
DANDRUFF	DEATH ROW	DEEMSTER	DELIVERY	DEPARTED
DANDYISH	DEBACLES	DEEPENED	DELOUSED	DEPENDED
DANDYISM	DEBARKED	DEEPENER	DELPHIAN	DEPICTED
DANEWORT	DEBARRED	DEEP-LAID	DELUDING	DEPICTER
DANGLING	DEABASING	DEEPNESS	DELUGING	DEPLIATE
DANKNESS	DEABATERS	DEERSKIN	DELUSION	DEPLETED
DANUBIAN	DEABATING	DEFACING	DELUSIVE	DEPLORED
DARINGLY	DEBILITY	DEFAMING	DELUSORY	DEPLORER
DARK AGES	DEBITING	DEFAULTS	DEMAGOGY	DEPLOYED
DARKENED	DEBONAIR	DEFEATED	DEMANDED	DEPONENT

419

DEPORTED	DETENTES	DIAPAUSE	DILIGENT	DISCLAIM
DEPORTEE	DETERRED	DIAPHONE	DILUTING	DISCLOSE
DEPOSING	DETESTED	DIAPHONY	DILUTION	DISCORDS
DEPOSITS	DETESTER	DIARCHIC	DILUVIAL	DISCOUNT
DEPRAVED	DETHRONE	DIARISTS	DIMERISM	DISCOVER
DEPRAVER	DETONATE	DIASCOPE	DIMEROUS	DISCREET
DEPRIVED	DETRITAL	DIASPORA	DIMETRIC	DISCRETE
DEPRIVER	DETRITUS	DIASPORE	DIMINISH	DISCUSES
DEPURATE	DEUCEDLY	DIASTASE	DINGDONG	DISEASED
DEPUTIES	DEUTERON	DIASTEMA	DINGHIES	DISEASES
DEPUTING	DEVALUED	DIASTOLE	DINGIEST	DISENDOW
DEPUTIZE	DEVIANCE	DIASTRAL	DINKIEST	DISGORGE
DERAILED	DEVIANTS	DIASTYLE	DINOSAUR	DISGRACE
DERANGED	DEVIATED	DIATOMIC	DIOCESAN	DISGUISE
DERELICT	DEVIATOR	DIATRIBE	DIOSESES	DISHEVEL
DERIDING	DEVILING	DIBBLING	DIOPSIDE	DISHFULS
DERISION	DEVILISH	DICENTRA	DIOPTASE	DISHIEST
DERISIVE	DEVILLED	DICHORIC	DIOPTRAL	DISINTER
DERISORY	DEVISING	DICKERED	DIOPTRIC	DISJOINT
DERIVING	DEVOLVED	DICKIEST	DIORMIC	DISJUNCT
DEROGATE	DEVONIAN	DICROTIC	DIORIRIC	DISKETTE
DERRICKS	DEVOTEES	DIDDLING	DIOXIDES	DISLIKED
DESCALED	DEVOTING	DIDYMIUM	DIPHENYL	DISLIKES
DESCANTS	DEVOTION	DIDYMOUS	DIPLEGIA	DISLODGE
DESCENTS	DEVOURED	DIEHARDS	DIPLEXER	DISLOYAL
DESCRIBE	DEVOURER	DIELDRIN	DIPLOMAS	DISMALLY
DESCRIED	DEVOUTER	DIERESES	DIPLOMAT	DISMAYED
DESCRIER	DEWBERRY	DIERESIS	DIPLOPIA	DISMOUNT
DESERTED	DEWDROPS	DIERETIC	DIPLOPIC	DISORDER
DESERTER	DEWINESS	DIESTOCK	DIPLOPOD	DISOWNED
DESERVED	DEWY-EYED	DIETETIC	DIPLOSIS	DISOWNER
DESERVER	DEXTROSE	DIFFERED	DIPSTICK	DISPATCH
DESIGNED	DIABASIC	DIFFRACT	DIPTERAL	DISPENSE
DESIGNER	DIABETES	DIFFUSED	DIPTERAN	DISPERSE
DESINENT	DIABETIC	DIFFUSER	DIRECTED	DISPIRIT
DESIRING	DIABOLIC	DIGAMIST	DIRECTLY	DISPLACE
DESIROUS	DIACIDIC	DIGAMOUS	DIRECTOR	DISPLAYS
DESISTED	DIACONAL	DIGESTED	DIRIMENT	DISPOSAL
DESKWORK	DIAGNOSE	DIGESTER	DIRT BIKE	DISPOSED
DESOLATE	DIAGONAL	DIGESTIF	DIRTIEST	DISPOSER
DESPATCH	DIAGRAMS	DIGGINGS	DIRT ROAD	DISPROOF
DESPISED	DIAGRAPH	DIGITATE	DIRTYING	DISPROVE
DESPOTIC	DIALECTS	DIGITIZE	DISABLED	DISPUTED
DESSERTS	DIALLAGE	DIGITRON	DISABUSE	DISPUTER
DESTINED	DIALLING	DIGRAPHS	DISAGREE	DISPUTES
DESTRUCT	DIALOGUE	DIHEDRAL	DISALLOW	DISQUIET
DETACHED	DIALYSER	DIHEDRON	DISANNUL	DISROBED
DETACHER	DIALYSIS	DIHYBRID	DISARMED	DISROBER
DETAILED	DIALYTIC	DILATANT	DISARMER	DISSEISE
DETAINED	DIAMANTE	DILATING	DISARRAY	DISSENTS
DETAINEE	DIAMETER	DILATION	DISASTER	DISSEVER
DETAINER	DIAMONDS	DILATIVE	DISBURSE	DISSOLVE
DETECTED	DIANTHUS	DILATORY	DISCARDS	DISSUADE
DETECTOR	DIAPASON	DILEMMAS	DISCIPLE	DISTAFFS

DISTANCE	DOCTORED	DOORWAYS	DRAGGLED	DROOLING
DISTASTE	DOCTRINE	DOPINESS	DRAGLINE	DROOPILY
DISTINCT	DOCUMENT	DORDOGNE	DRAGNETS	DROOPING
DISTRACT	DODDERED	DORMANCY	DRAGOMAN	DROPLETS
DISTAINE	DODDERER	DORMOUSE	DRAGONET	DROPOUTS
DISTRAIT	DODGIEST	DORTMUND	DRAGOONS	DROPPERS
DISTRESS	DOGBERRY	DOSSIERS	DRAGROPE	DROPPING
DISTRICT	DOGCARTS	DOTATION	DRAINAGE	DROPSIED
DISTRUST	DOG-EARED	DOTINGLY	DRAINING	DROPWORT
DISUNION	DOGFIGHT	DOTTEREL	DRAMATIC	DROUGHTS
DISUNITE	DOGGEDLY	DOTTIEST	DRAPABLE	DROUGHTY
DISUNITY	DOGGERAL	DOUBLETS	DRATTING	DROWNING
DITCHING	DOGGONED	DOUBLING	DRAUGHTS	DROWSILY
DITHEISM	DOGGY BAG	DOUBLOON	DRAUGHTY	DROWSING
DITHEIST	DOGHOUSE	DOUBLURE	DRAWABLE	DRUBBING
DITHERED	DOGMATIC	DOUBTERS	DRAWBACK	DRUDGERY
DITHERER	DO-GOODER	DOUBTFUL	DRAWBORE	DRUDGING
DIURESIS	DOGSBODY	DOUBTING	DRAWLINGS	DRIGGETS
DIURETIC	DOG'S-TAIL	DOUGHNUT	DRAWLING	DRUGGING
DIVALENT	DOG-TIRED	DOURNESS	DRAWTUBE	DRUGGIST
DIVE-BOMB	DOGTOOTH	DOVECOTE	DREADFUL	DRUIDISM
DIVERGED	DOGTROTS	DOVETAIL	DREADING	DRUMBEAT
DIVERTED	DOGWATCH	DOWAGERS	DREAMERS	DRUMFIRE
DIVERTER	DOGWOODS	DOWDIEST	DREAMILY	DRUMFISH
DIVESTED	DOLDRUMS	DOWNBEAT	DREAMING	DRUMHEAD
DIVIDEND	DOLERITE	DOWNCAST	DREARIER	DRUMMERS
DIVIDERS	DOLOMITE	DOWNFALL	DREARILY	DRUMMING
DIVIDING	DOLOROSO	DOWNHAUL	DREDGERS	DRUNKARD
DIVI-DIVI	DOLOROUS	DOWNHILL	DREDGING	DRUNKEST
DIVINELY	DOLPHINS	DOWNIEST	DRENCHED	DRUPELET
DIVINERS	DOMELIKE	DOWNLOAD	DRENCHER	DRY-CLEAN
DIVINING	DOMESTIC	DOWNPIPE	DRESSAGE	DRY DOCKS
DIVINITY	DOMICILE	DOWNPLAY	DRESSERS	DRY GOODS
DIVINIZE	DOMINANT	DOWNPOUR	DRESSIER	DRY STONE
DIVISION	DOMINATE	DOWNTIME	DRESSILY	DUDDONET
DIVISIVE	DOMINEER	DOWNTOWN	DRESSING	DUCKLING
DIVISORS	DOMINION	DOWNTURN	DRIBBLED	DUCKWEED
DIVORCED	DOMINIUM	DOWNWARD	DRIBBLER	DUCTILES
DIVORCEE	DOMINOES	DOWNWASH	DRIBBLES	DUELLING
DIVORCER	DONATING	DOWNWIND	DRIBLETS	DUELLIST
DIVORCES	DONATION	DOXASTIC	DRIFTAGE	DUETTIST
DIVULGED	DONATIVE	DOXOLOGY	DRIFTERS	DUISBURG
DIVULGER	DONJUANS	DOZINESS	DRIFTING	DUKEDOMS
DIZZIEST	DOODLING	DRABBEST	DRILLING	DULCIANA
DJAKARTA	DOOMSDAY	DRABNESS	DRINKERS	DULCIMER
DJIBOUTI	DOORBELL	DRACAENA	DRINKING	DULLARDS
DNIESTER	DOORJAMB	DRACHMAE	DRIPPING	DULLNESS
D-NOTICES	DOORKNOB	DRACHMAS	DRIVABLE	DUMBBELL
DOCILITY	DOORMATS	DRACONIC	DRIVE-INS	DUMB-CANE
DOCKETED	DOORNAIL	DRAFTEES	DRIVELED	DUMBNESS
DOCKLAND	DOORPOST	DRAFTIER	DRIVEWAY	DUMB SHOW
DOCKSIDE	DOORSILL	DRAFTING	DRIZZLED	DUMMYRUN
DOCKYARD	DOORSTEP	DRAGGIER	DROLLERY	DUMPIEST
DOCTORAL	DOORSTOP	DRAGGING	DROLLEST	DUMPLING

DUNGAREE	DAMNATORY	DEBARMENT	DECOMPOSE	DEFLECTOR
DUNGEONS	DAMNEDEST	DEBARRING	DECONTROL	DEFOLIATE
DUNGHILL	DAMPENING	DEBATABLE	DECORATED	DEFORMING
DUODENAL	DAMP SQUIB	DEBAUCHED	DECORATOR	DEFORMITY
DUODENUM	DAMSELFLY	DEBAUCHEE	DECOUPAGE	DEFRAUDED
DUOLOGUE	DANDELION	DEBAUCHER	DECREASED	DEFRAUDER
DUPLEXES	DANDIFIED	DEBAUCHES	DECREASES	DEFRAYING
DURATION	DANGEROUS	DEBENTURE	DECREEING	DEFROCKED
DURATIVE	DAREDEVIL	DEBOUCHED	DECREMENT	DEFROSTED
DUSHANBE	DARKENING	DEBRIEFED	DECRETIVE	DEFROSTER
DUSKIEST	DARK HOUSE	DEBUGGING	DECRETORY	DEGRADING
DUSTBINS	DARK ROOMS	DEBUNKERS	DECUMBENT	DEGREE-DAY
DUSTBOWL	DARMSTADT	DEBUNKING	DECURRENT	DEHISCENT
DUSTCART	DARTBOARD	DEBUTANTE	DECUSSATE	DEHYDRATE
DUSTIEST	DASHBOARD	DECADENCE	DEDICATED	DEJECTION
DUSTPANS	DASHINGLY	DECAGONAL	DEDICATEE	DELEGABLE
DUTCH CAP	DASTARDLY	DECALCIFY	DEDICATOR	DELEGATED
DUTCHMAN	DATABUSES	DECALOGUE	DEDUCTIBLE	DELEGATES
DUTIABLE	DATEDNESS	DECAMPING	DEDUCTING	DELETIONS
DUTY-FREE	DATELINES	DECANTERS	DEDUCTION	DELICIOUS
DWARFING	DAUNTLESS	DECANTING	DEDUCTIVE	DELIGHTED
DWARFISH	DAVENPORT	DECAPODAL	DEED POLLS	DELIGHTER
DWARFISM	DAYDREAMS	DECASTYLE	DEEDS POLL	DELIMITED
DWELLING	DAYDREAMY	DECATHLON	DEEPENING	DELINEATE
DWINDLED	DAYFLOWER	DECIETFUL	DEEP FRIED	DELIRIANT
DYARCHIC	DAYLIGHTS	DECIEVERS	DEEP SOUTH	DELIRIOUS
DYESTUFF	DAY SCHOOL	DECIEVING	DEERGRASS	DELIRIUMS
DYNAMICS	DEACONESS	DECEMBERS	DEER HOUND	DELIVERED
DYNAMISM	DEADBEATS	DECENCIES	DEFALCATE	DELIVERER
DYNAMIST	DEAD DUCKS	DECENNIAL	DEFAULTED	DELOUSING
DYNAMITE	DEADENING	DECEPTION	DEFAULTER	DELUSIONS
DYNASTIC	DEAD HEATS	DECEPTIVE	DEFEATING	DEMAGOGIC
DYNATRON	DEADLIEST	DECIDABLE	DEFEATISM	DEMAGOGUE
DYSGENIC	DEADLIGHT	DECIDEDLY	DEFEATIST	DEMANDANT
DYSLEXIA	DEADLINES	DECIDUOUS	DEFECATED	DEMANDING
DYSLEXIC	DEADLOCKS	DECILLION	DEFECATOR	DEMANTOID
DYSPNOEA	DEADLY SIN	DECIMALLY	DEFECTING	DEMARCATE
	DEAD MARCH	DECIMATED	DEFECTION	DEMEANING
	DEAFENING	DECIMATOR	DEFECTIVE	DEMEANOUR
9 LETTERS	DEAF-MUTES	DECIMETRE	DEFECTORS	DEMIJOHNS
DACHSHUND	DEALATION	DECISIONS	DEFENDANT	DEMIMONDE
DACTYLICS	DEAMINATE	DECKCHAIR	DEFENDERS	DEMISABLE
DADAISTIC	DEANERIES	DECKHANDS	DEFENDING	DEMISTING
DAFFODILS	DEATHBEDS	DECKHOUSE	DEFENSIVE	DEMITASSE
DAINTIEST	DEATHBLOW	DECLAIMED	DEFERENCE	DEMOBBING
DAIQUIRIS	DEATH DUTY	DECLAIMER	DEFERMENT	DEMOCRACY
DAIRY FARM	DEATHLESS	DECLARANT	DEFERRING	DEMOCRATS
DAIRY MAID	DEATHLIKE	DECLARING	DEFIANTLY	DEMOTIONS
DALAI LAMA	DEATH MASK	DECLINATE	DEFICIENT	DEMULCENT
DALLIANCE	DEATH RATE	DECLINING	DEFINABLE	DEMULSIFY
DALMATION	DEATH TOLL	DECLIVITY	DEFINIENS	DENDRITIC
DALTONISM	DEATH TRAP	DECOCTION	DEFLATING	DENIGRATE
DAMASCENE	DEATH WISH	DECOLLATE	DEFLATION	DENITRATE
DAMNATION	DEBARKING	DECOLLETE	DEFLECTED	DENITRIFY

DENOTABLE	DESCANTER	DETRAINED	DIAPHONIC	DIGITIZER
DENOUNCED	DESCENDED	DETRIMENT	DIAPHRAGM	DIGITOXIN
DENOUNCER	DESCENDER	DETRITION	DIAPHYSIS	DIGLOTTIC
DENSENESS	DESCRIBED	DETRUSION	DIARRHOEA	DIGNIFIED
DENSITIES	DESCRIBER	DEUTERIDE	DIASTASIC	DIGNITARY
DENTALIUM	DESCRYING	DEUTERIUM	DIASTASIS	DIGNITIES
DENTATION	DESCRYING	DEVALUATE	DIASTATIC	DIGRAPHIC
DENTIFORM	DESECRATE	DEVALUING	DIASTOLIC	DIGRESSED
DENTISTRY	DESERTERS	DEVASTATE	DIATHERMY	DIGRESSER
DENTITION	DESERTING	DEVELOPED	DIATHESIS	DILATABLE
DEODORANT	DESERTION	DEVELOPER	DIATHETIC	DILATANCY
DEODORIZE	DESERVING	DEVIATING	DIATOMITE	DILIGENCE
DEOXIDIZE	DESICCANT	DEVIATION	DIATRIBES	DILUTIONS
DEPARTING	DESICCATE	DEVIATORY	DIATROPIC	DIMENSION
DEPARTURE	DESIGNATE	DEVILFISH	DIAZONIUM	DIMIDIATE
DEPASTURE	DESIGNERS	DEVILLING	DIAZOTIZE	DIMISSORY
DEPENDANT	DESIGNING	DEVILMENT	DIBROMIDE	DIM-WITTED
DEPENDENT	DESINENCE	DEVIOUSLY	DICHASIAL	DING DONGS
DEPENDING	DESIRABLE	DEVISABLE	DICHASIUM	DINGINESS
DEPICTING	DESIRABLY	DEVITRIFY	DICHOGAMY	DINING CAR
DEPICTION	DESISTING	DEVOLVING	DICHOTOMY	DINOCERAS
DEPICTIVE	DESMIDIAN	DEVOTEDLY	DICHROISM	DINOSAURS
DEPICTURE	DESOLATED	DEVOTIONS	DICHROITE	DINOTHERE
DEPILATOR	DESOLATER	DEVOURING	DICHROMIC	DIOECIOUS
DEPLETING	DESPAIRED	DEVOUTEST	DICKERING	DIOESTRUS
DEPLETION	DESPERADO	DEXEDRINE	DICKYBIRD	DIPHTHONG
DEPLETIVE	DESPERATE	DEXTERITY	DICLINISM	DIPLOIDIC
DEPLORING	DESPISING	DEXTEROUS	DICLINOUS	DIPLOMACY
DEPLOYING	DESPOILED	DEXTRORSE	DICROTISM	DIPLOMATE
DEPORTEES	DESPOILER	DIABETICS	DICTATING	DIPLOMATS
DEPORTING	DESPOTISM	DIABLERIE	DICTATION	DIPLOTENE
DEPOSABLE	DESPUMATE	DIABOLISM	DICTATORS	DIPSTICKS
DEPOSITED	DESTINIES	DIABOLIST	DIDACTICS	DIPSWITCH
DEPOSITOR	DESTITUTE	DIABOLIZE	DIETETICS	DIPTEROUS
DEPRAVING	DESULTORY	DIACONATE	DIETICIAN	DIRECTING
DEPRAVITY	DETACHING	DIACRITIC	DIETITIAN	DIRECTION
DEPRECATE	DETAILING	DIACTINIC	DIFFERENT	DIRECTIVE
DEPRESSED	DETAINEES	DIAERESES	DIFFERING	DIRECTORS
DEPRESSOR	DETAINING	DIAERESIS	DIFFICULT	DIRECTORY
DEPRIVING	DETECTING	DIAGNOSED	DIFFIDENT	DIRECTRIX
DEPURATOR	DETECTION	DIAGNOSES	DIFFUSELY	DIRECT TAX
DEPUTIZED	DETERGENT	DIAGONALS	DIFFUSING	DIREFULLY
DERAILING	DETERMENT	DIALECTIC	DIFFUSION	DIRIGIBLE
DERELICTS	DETERMINE	DIALOGISM	DIFFUSIVE	DIRT BIKES
DE RIGUEUR	DETERRENT	DIALOGIST	DIGASTRIC	DIRT CHEAP
DERISIBLE	DETERRING	DIALOGIZE	DIGENESIS	DIRTINESS
DERIVABLE	DETERSIVE	DIALOGUER	DIGENETIC	DIRT ROADS
DERMATOID	DETESTING	DIALOGUES	DIGESTANT	DIRT TRACK
DERMATOME	DETHRONED	DIAMAGNET	DIGESTING	DIRTY WORK
DEROGATED	DETHRONER	DIAMETERS	DIGESTION	DISABLING
DERRING-DO	DETONATED	DIAMETRAL	DIGESTIVE	DISABUSAL
DERRINGER	DETONATOR	DIAMETRIC	DIGITALIN	DISABUSED
DERVISHES	DETRACTED	DIANDROUS	DIGITALIS	DISACCORD
DESCALING	DETRACTOR	DIANOETIC	DIGITIZED	DISAFFECT

423

DISAFFIRM	DISHONEST	DISSEMBLE	DIXIELAND	DOSIMETER
DISAGREED	DISHONEST	DISSENTED	DIZZINESS	DOSIMETRY
DISAPPEAR	DISHONOUR	DISSENTER	DOCKETING	DOSSHOUSE
DISARMING	DISH TOWEL	DISSIDENT	DOCKYARDS	DOTTINESS
DISASTERS	DISHWATER	DISSIPATE	DOCTORATE	DOUBLEBED
DISAVOWAL	DISINFECT	DISSOLUTE	DOCTORING	DOUBLETON
DISAVOWED	DISINFEST	DISSOLVED	DOCTRINAL	DOUBLOONS
DISAVOWER	DISK DRIVE	DISSOLVER	DOCTRINES	DOUBTABLE
DISBANDED	DISKETTES	DISSONANT	DOCMENTS	DOUBTLESS
DISBARRED	DISLIKING	DISSUADED	DODDERERS	DOUGHNUTS
DISBELIEF	DISLOCATE	DISSUADER	DODDERING	DOUGHTIER
DISBRANCH	DISLODGED	DISTANCED	DODECAGON	DOVECOTES
DISBURDEN	DISMANTLE	DISTANCED	DOG COLLAR	DOVETAILS
DISBURSED	DISMASTED	DISTANCES	DOG-EAT-DOG	DOWDINESS
DISBURSER	DISMAYING	DISTANTLY	DOGFIGHTS	DOWITCHER
DISCALCED	DISMEMBER	DISTEMPER	DOGFISHES	DOWNCOMER
DISCARDED	DISMISSAL	DISTENDED	DOGGY BAGS	DOWNFALLS
DISCARDER	DISMISSED	DISTENDER	DOGHOUSES	DOWNGRADE
DISCERNED	DISOBEYED	DISTICHAL	DOGLEGGED	DOWNPOURS
DISCERNER	DISOBEYER	DISTILLED	DOGMATICS	DOWNRANGE
DISCHARGE	DISOBLIGE	DISTILLER	DOGMATISM	DOWNRIGHT
DISCIPLES	DISORDERS	DISTINGUE	DOGMATIST	DOWNSPOUT
DISCLIMAX	DISOWNING	DISTORTED	DOGMATIZE	DOWNSTAGE
DISCLOSED	DISPARAGE	DISTORTER	DO-GOODERS	DOWNSWING
DISCLOSER	DISPARATE	DISTRAINT	DOG PADDLE	DOWNTHROW
DISCOIDAL	DISPARITY	DISTRICTS	DOLEFULLY	DOWNTURNS
DISCOLOUR	DISPELLED	DISTURBED	DOLERITIC	DOWNWARDS
DISCOMFIT	DISPELLER	DISTURBER	DOLLYBIRD	DRACONIAN
DISCOMMON	DISPENSED	DISUNITED	DOLOMITES	DRAFTIEST
DISCOUNTS	DISPENSER	DITHERING	DOLOMITIC	DRAFTSMAN
DISCOURSE	DISPERSAL	DITHYRAMB	DOLTISHLY	DRAFTSMEN
DISCOVERT	DISPERSED	DITTANDER	DOMESTICS	DRAGGIEST
DISCOVERY	DISPENSER	DIURETICS	DOMICILED	DRAGHOUND
DISCREDIT	DISPLACED	DIURNALLY	DOMICILES	DRAGOMANS
DISCUSSED	DISPLACER	DIVALENCY	DOMINANCE	DRAGONESS
DISDAINED	DISPLAYED	DIVERGENT	DOMINATED	DRAGONFLY
DISEMBARK	DISPLAYER	DIVERGING	DOMINATOR	DRAGONISH
DISEMBODY	DISPLEASE	DIVERSELY	DOMINICAL	DRAGOONED
DISENABLE	DISPORTED	DIVERSIFY	DOMINICAN	DRAINABLE
DISENGAGE	DISPOSING	DIVERSION	DOMINIONS	DRAINPIPE
DISENTAIL	DISPRAISE	DIVERTING	DONATIONS	DRAMATICS
DISESTEEM	DISPROVAL	DIVERTIVE	DONNISHLY	DRAMATIST
DISFAVOUR	DISPROVED	DIVESTING	DONORSHIP	DRAMATIZE
DISFIGURE	DISPUTANT	DIVIDABLE	DOODLEBUG	DRAPERIED
DISFOREST	DISPUTING	DIVIDENDS	DOORBELLS	DRAPERIES
DISGORGED	DISREGARD	DIVINABLE	DOORFRAME	DRAUGHTER
DISGORGER	DISRELISH	DIVISIBLE	DOORKNOBS	DRAVIDIAN
DISGRACED	DISREPAIR	DIVISIONS	DOORNAILS	DRAWBACKS
DISGRACER	DISREPUTE	DIVORCEES	DOORPLATE	DRAWKNIFE
DISGUISED	DISROBING	DIVORCING	DOORSTEPS	DRAWPLATE
DISGUISER	DISRUPTED	DIVORCIVE	DORDRECHT	DREAMBOAT
DISGUISES	DISRUPTER	DIVULGING	DORMITORY	DREAMLAND
DISGUSTED	DISSECTED	DIVULSION	DORMOBILE	DREAMLESS
DISHCLOTH	DISSECTOR	DIVULSIVE	DORONICUM	DREAMLIKE

DREARIEST	DUPLEXITY	DAMSELFISH	DECISIONAL
DRENCHING	DUPLICATE	DANDELIONS	DECISIVELY
DRESSIEST	DUPLICITY	DAPPLE-GREY	DECKCHAIRS
DRESSINGS	DURALUMIN	DAREDEVILS	DECLAIMING
DRIBBLING	DUSKINESS	DARJEELING	DECLARABLE
DRIFTWOOD	DUSTBOWLS	DARK HORSES	DECLASSIFY
DRILLABLE	DUSTCARTS	DARTBOARDS	DECLENSION
DRINKABLE	DUSTSHEET	DASHBOARDS	DECLINABLE
DRIP-DRIED	DUST STORM	DAUGHTERLY	DECOCTIONS
DRIPSTONE	DUTCH BARN	DAYDREAMED	DECOLLATOR
DRIVELING	DUTCH CAPS	DAYDREAMER	DECOLONIZE
DRIVELLED	DUTCH OVEN	DAY-NEUTRAL	DECOLORANT
DRIVELLER	DUTIFULLY	DAY NURSERY	DECOLORIZE
DRIVEWAYS	DUTY-FREES	DAY SCHOOLS	DECOMPOSED
DRIZZLING	DWELLINGS	DAY-TRIPPER	DECOMPOSER
DROLLNESS	DWINDLING	DEACONSHIP	DECOMPOUND
DROMEDARY	DYER'S WEED	DEACTIVATE	DECOMPRESS
DROPLIGHT	DYNAMETER	DEAD CENTRE	DECORATING
DROPPINGS	DYNAMITED	DEAD LETTER	DECORATION
DROPSICAL	DYNAMITER	DEADLINESS	DECORATIVE
DRUBBINGS	DYNAMITIC	DEADLY SINS	DECORATORS
DRUGGISTS	DYNAMOTOR	DEAD-NETTLE	DECOROUSLY
DRUGSTORE	DYNASTIES	DEAD RINGER	DECOUPLING
DRUMBEATS	DYSENTERY	DEALERSHIP	DECREASING
DRUM MAJOR	DYSGENICS	DEATHBLOWS	DECREEABLE
DRUMSTICK	DYSLECTIC	DEATH MASKS	DECREE NISI
DRUNKARDS	DYSPEPSIA	DEATH RATES	DECRESCENT
DRUNKENLY	DYSPEPTIC	DEATH'S-HEAD	DECUMBENCE
DUALISTIC	DYSPHAGIA	DEATH SQUAD	DEDICATING
DUBIOUSLY	DYSPHAGIC	DEATH TOLLS	DEDICATION
DUBITABLE	DYSPHASIA	DEATH TRAPS	DEDICATORY
DUBROVNIK	DYSPHASIC	DEATHWATCH	DEDUCTIBLE
DUCHESSES	DYSPHONIA	DEBASEMENT	DEDUCTIONS
DUCKBOARD	DYSPHONIC	DEBAUCHEES	DEEP FREEZE
DUCKLINGS	DYSPHORIA	DEBAUCHERY	DEEP FRYING
DUCTILITY	DYSPHORIC	DEBAUCHING	DEEP-ROOTED
DUDE RANCH	DYSPLASIA	DEBENTURES	DEEP-SEATED
DUELLISTS	DYSPNOEAL	DEBILITATE	DE-ESCALATE
DUFFEL BAG	DYSTHYMIC	DEBOUCHING	DEFACEBALE
DULCIMERS	DYSTROPHY	DEBRIEFING	DEFACEMENT
DUMBBELLS		DEBUTANTES	DEFALCATOR
DUMBFOUND		DECADENTLY	DEFAMATION
DUMBSHOWS	**10 LETTERS**	DECAHEDRAL	DEFAMATORY
DUMMYRUNS	DACSHUNDS	DECAMPMENT	DEFAULTERS
DUMPINESS	DAILY BREAD	DECAPITATE	DEFAULTING
DUMPLINGS	DAINTINESS	DECATHLONS	DEFEASANCE
DUNCE'S CAP	DAIRY FARMS	DECEIVABLE	DEFEASIBLE
DUNE BUGGY	DAIRYMAIDS	DECELERATE	DEFEATISTS
DUNGAREES	DAISY WHEEL	DECEPTIONS	DEFECATING
DUNGENESS	DALAI LAMAS	DECIMALIZE	DEFECATION
DUODECIMO	DALMATIONS	DECIMATING	DEFECATIONS
DUODENARY	DAMAGEABLE	DECIMATION	DEFENDABLE
DUODENUMS	DAMP COURSE	DECIPHERED	DEFENDANTS
DUOLOGUES	DAMP SQUIBS	DECIPHERER	DEFENSIBLE

425

DEFENSIBLY	DELIVERING	DEPENDANTS	DESERTIONS
DEFENSIVES	DELOCALIZE	DEPENDENCE	DESERVEDLY
DEFERMENTS	DELPHINIUM	DEPENDENCY	DESHABILLE
DEFERRABLE	DELTIOLOGY	DEPICTIONS	DESICCANTS
DEFICIENCY	DELUSIONAL	DEPILATION	DESICCATED
DEFILEMENT	DELUSIVELY	DEPILATORY	DESICCATOR
DEFINITELY	DEMAGOGUES	DEPLETABLE	DESIDERATA
DEFINITION	DEMANDABLE	DEPLORABLE	DESIDERATE
DEFINITIVE	DEMARCATED	DEPLORABLY	DESIGNABLE
DEFINITUDE	DEMARCATOR	DEPLOYMENT	DESIGNATED
DEFLAGRATE	DEMEANOURS	DEPOLARIZE	DESIGNATOR
DEFLECTING	DEMENTEDLY	DEPOPULATE	DESIGNEDLY
DEFLECTION	DEMICANTON	DEPORTABLE	DESISTANCE
DEFLECTIVE	DEMOBILIZE	DEPORTMENT	DESOLATELY
DEFLOWERED	DEMOCRATIC	DEPOSITARY	DESOLATING
DEFLOWERER	DEMODULATE	DEPOSITING	DESOLATION
DEFOLIANTS	DEMOGRAPHY	DEPOSITION	DESPAIRING
DEFOLIATED	DEMOISELLE	DEPOSITORS	DESPATCHED
DEFOLIATOR	DEMOLISHED	DEPOSITORY	DESPATCHER
DEFORESTED	DEMOLISHER	DEPRECIATED	DESPATCHES
DEFORESTER	DEMOLITION	DEPRECIATOR	DESPERADOS
DEFORMABLE	DEMONETIZE	DEPRECIATE	DESPICABLE
DEFRAUDING	DEMONIACAL	DEPRESSANT	DESPICABLY
DEFRAYABLE	DEMONOLOGY	DEPRESSING	DESPOILING
DEFROCKING	DEMORALIZE	DEPRESSION	DESPONDENT
DEFROSTERS	DEMOTIVATE	DEPRESSIVE	DESQUAMATE
DEFROSTING	DEMURENESS	DEPRIVABLE	DESSIANTINE
DEFUNCTIVE	DEMURRABLE	DEPURATION	DESTROYERS
DEGENERACY	DENATURANT	DEPURATIVE	DESTROYING
DEGENERATE	DENDRIFORM	DEPUTATION	DESTRUCTOR
DEGRADABLE	DENDROLOGY	DEPUTIZING	DETACHABLE
DEGRESSION	DENEGRATION	DERACINATE	DETACHMENT
DEHISCENCE	DENIGRATION	DERAILEUR	DETAINABLE
DEHUMANIZE	DENIGRATED	DERAILMENT	DETAINMENT
DEHUMIDIFY	DENIGRATOR	DEREGULATE	DETECTABLE
DEHYDRATED	DENOMINATE	DERISIVELY	DETECTIVES
DEHYDRATOR	DENOTATION	DERISORILY	DETERGENCY
DEJECTEDLY	DENOTATIVE	DERIVATION	DETERGENTS
DELAMINATE	DENOTEMENT	DERIVATIVE	DETERMINED
DELECTABLE	DENOUEMENT	DERMATITIS	DETERMINER
DELECTABLY	DENOUNCING	DERMATOGEN	DETERRENCE
DELEGATING	DENSIMETER	DERMATOMIC	DETERRENTS
DELEGATION	DENSIMETRY	DERMATOSIS	DETESTABLE
DELIBERATE	DENTIFRICE	DEROGATING	DETESTABLY
DELICACIES	DENUDATION	DEROGATION	DETHRONING
DELICATELY	DEODORANTS	DEROGATIVE	DETONATING
DELIGHTFUL	DEODORIZED	DEROGATORY	DETONATION
DELIGHTING	DEODORIZER	DESALINATE	DETONATIVE
DELIMITING	DEONTOLOGY	DESCENDANT	DETONATORS
DELINEATED	DEOXIDIZER	DESCENDENT	DETOXICANT
DELINEATOR	DEPARTMENT	DESCENDING	DETOXICATE
DELINQUENT	DEPARTURES	DESCRIBING	DETRACTING
DELIQUESCE	DEPENDABLE	DESECRATED	DETRACTION
DELIVERIES	DEPENDABLY	DESECRATOR	DETRACTIVE

DETRACTORS	DIE-CASTING	DIRECTRESS	DISDAINFUL
DETRAINING	DIE-HARDISM	DIRIGIBLES	DISDAINING
DETRIMENTS	DIELECTRIC	DIRT FARMER	DISEMBOWEL
DETRUNCATE	DIETICIANS	DIRT TRACKS	DISEMBROIL
DEUTOPLASM	DIFFERENCE	DIRTY TRICKS	DISENCHANT
DEUX-SEVRES	DIFFICULTY	DISABILITY	DISENDOWER
DEVASTATED	DIFFIDENCE	DISABUSING	DISENGAGED
DEVASTATOR	DIFFRACTED	DISALLOWED	DISENTHRAL
DEVELOPERS	DIFFUSABLE	DISAPPOINT	DISENTITLE
DEVELOPING	DIGESTABLE	DISAPPROVE	DISENTWINE
DEVIATIONS	DIGESTIONS	DISARRANGE	DISEPALOUS
DEVILISHLY	DIGESTIVES	DISASTROUS	DISFEATURE
DEVITALIZE	DIGITALISM	DISAVOWALS	DISFIGURED
DEVOCALIZE	DIGITALIZE	DISAVOWING	DISFIGURER
DEVOLUTION	DIGITATION	DISBANDING	DISGORGING
DEVOTEMENT	DIGITIFORM	DISBANDED	DISGRACING
DEVOTIONAL	DIGITIZING	DISBARMENT	DISGRUNTLE
DEVOUTNESS	DIGITIZERS	DISBARRING	DISGUISING
DEXTRALITY	DIGITIZING	DISBELIEVE	DISGUSTING
DIABOLICAL	DIGNIFYING	DISBURSING	DISHABILLE
DIACAUSTIC	DIGRESSING	DISCARDING	DISHARMONY
DIACHRONIC	DIGRESSION	DISC BRAKES	DISHCLOTHS
DIACRITICS	DIGRESSIVE	DISCERNING	DISHEARTEN
DIACTINISM	DILAPIDATE	DISCHARGED	DISHONESTY
DIADROMOUS	DILATATION	DISCHARGER	DISH TOWELS
DIAGENESIS	DILEMMATIC	DISCHARGES	DISHWASHER
DIAGNOSING	DILETTANTE	DISCIPLINE	DISINCLINE
DIAGNOSTIC	DILETTANTI	DISC JOCKEY	DISINHERIT
DIAGONALLY	DILLIGENTLY	DISCLAIMED	DISJOINTED
DIAKENESIS	DILLYDALLY	DISCLAIMER	DISK DRIVES
DIALECTICS	DIMENSIONS	DISCLOSING	DISLIKABLE
DIALYSABLE	DIMINISHED	DISCLOSURE	DISLOCATED
DIAPASONAL	DIMINUENDO	DISCOMFORT	DISLODGING
DIAPEDESIS	DIMINUITION	DISCOMMODE	DISLOYALLY
DIAPEDETIC	DIMINUITIVE	DISCOMPOSE	DISLOYALTY
DIAPHANOUS	DIMORPHISM	DISCONCERT	DISMALNESS
DIAPHYSIAL	DIMORPHOUS	DISCONNECT	DISMANTLED
DIARRHOEAL	DINING CARS	DISCONTENT	DISMANTLER
DIASTALSIS	DINING ROOM	DISCOPHILE	DISMASTING
DIASTALTIC	DINNER BELL	DISCORDANT	DISMISSALS
DIATHERMIC	DIPETALOUS	DISCOUNTED	DISMISSING
DIATROPISM	DIPHOSGENE	DISCOURAGE	DISMISSIVE
DIABASICITY	DIPHTHERIA	DISCOURSER	DISMOUNTED
DIACHLORIDE	DIPHTHONGS	DISCOURSES	DISOBEYING
DICHROMATE	DIPHYLETIC	DISCOVERED	DISOBLIGED
DICKENSIAN	DIPHYLLOUS	DISCOVERER	DISORDERED
DICKYBIRDS	DIPHYDONT	DISCREETLY	DISORDERLY
DICTAPHONE	DIPLODOCUS	DISCREPANT	DISOWNMENT
DICTATIONS	DIPLOMATIC	DISCRETELY	DISPARAGED
DICTATRESS	DIPSOMANIA	DISCRETION	DISPARAGER
DICTIONARY	DIRECTIONS	DISCURSIVE	DISPASSION
DICTOGRAPH	DIRECTIVES	DISCUSSANT	DISPATCHED
DICYNODONT	DIRECTNESS	DISCUSSING	DISPATCHES
DIDYNAMOUS	DIRECTOIRE	DISCUSSION	DISPELLING

DISPENSARY	DISTINCTLY	DOMINATION	DREAMINGLY
DISPENSERS	DISTORTION	DOMINATIVE	DREAMLANDS
DISPENSING	DISTORTIVE	DOMINEERED	DREAMWORLD
DISPERMOUS	DISTRACTED	DOMINICANS	DREARINESS
DISPERSING	DISTRACTER	DONKEYWORK	DRESSINESS
DISPERSION	DISTRAINED	DONNYBROOK	DRESSMAKER
DISPERSIVE	DISTRAINEE	DOORKEEPER	DRILLSTOCK
DISPERSOID	DISTRAINOR	DOORPLATES	DRIP-DRYING
DISPIRITED	DISTRAUGHT	DORSIGRADE	DRIVELLERS
DISPLACING	DISTRESSED	DOSIMETRIC	DRIVELLING
DISPLAYED	DISTRIBUTE	DOSSHOUSES	DROLLERIES
DISPLEASED	DISTRUSTED	DOTTED LINE	DROOPINESS
DISPORTING	DISTRUSTER	DOUBLE BASS	DROSOPHILA
DISPOSABLE	DISTURBING	DOUBLE BEDS	DROSSINESS
DISPOSSES	DISULFIRAM	DOUBLE BIND	DROWSINESS
DISPRAISER	DISULPHATE	DOUBLE CHIN	DRUGSTORES
DISPROVING	DISULPHIDE	DOUBLE DATE	DRUM MAJORS
DISPUTABLE	DISUNITING	DOUBLE-HUNG	DRUMSTICKS
DISPUTABLY	DISUTILITY	DOUBLE-PARK	DRUPACEOUS
DISQUALIFY	DISYLLABIC	DOUBLE-REED	DRY BATTERY
DISQUIETED	DITHEISTIC	DOUBLE-STOP	DRY-CLEANED
DISRESPECT	DIVARICATE	DOUBLE-TAKE	DRY CLEANER
DISRUPTING	DIVE-BOMBED	DOUBLE-TALK	DUBITATION
DISRUPTION	DIVE-BOMBER	DOUBLE TIME	DUCKBOARDS
DISRUPTIVE	DIVERGENCE	DOUBLETREE	DUFFEL BAGS
DISSATISFY	DIVERGENCY	DOUBTFULLY	DUFFEL COAT
DISSECTING	DIVERSIONS	DOUGHTIEST	DUMBSTRUCK
DISSECTION	DIVERTEDLY	DOVETAILED	DUMBWAITER
DISSEMBLED	DIVERTIBLE	DOWN-AND-OUT	DUNCE'S CAPS
DISSEMBLER	DIVESTIBLE	DOWN-AT-HEEL	DUNDERHEAD
DISSENSION	DIVESTMENT	DOWNGRADED	DUODECIMAL
DISSENTERS	DIVINATION	DOWNLOADED	DUODENITUS
DISSENTING	DIVINATORY	DOWN-MARKET	DUPABILITY
DISSERVICE	DIVING BELL	DOWNPLAYED	DUPLICABLE
DISSIDENCE	DIVINITIES	DOWNSPOUTS	DUPLICATED
DISSIDENTS	DIVISIONAL	DOWNSTAIRS	DUPLICATES
DISSIMILAR	DIVISIVELY	DOWNSTREAM	DUPLICATOR
DISSIPATED	DIVULGENCE	DRAGONHEAD	DURABILITY
DISSIPATER	DOCTORATES	DRAGONROOT	DURATIONAL
DISSOCIATE	DOCTRINISM	DRAGOONAGE	DUSSELDORF
DISSOLUBLE	DOCUMENTED	DRAGOONING	DUST JACKET
DISSOLVING	DODECANESE	DRAINPIPES	DUSTSHEETS
DISSONANCE	DOG BISCUIT	DRAMATISTS	DUST STORMS
DISSUADING	DOGCATCHER	DRAMATIZED	DUTCH BARNS
DISSUASION	DOG COLLARS	DRAMATIZER	DUTCH OVENS
DISSUASIVE	DOGGEDNESS	DRAMATURGE	DUTCH TREAT
DISTANCING	DOGMATISTS	DRAMATURY	DUTCH UNCLE
DISTENDING	DOGMATIZER	DRAWBRIDGE	DYNAMISTIC
DISTENSION	DOGSBODIES	DRAWING PIN	DYNAMITING
DISTICHOUS	DOLLARFISH	DRAWSTRING	DYSENTERIC
DISTILLATE	DOLL'S HOUSE	DREADFULLY	DYSPLASTIC
DISTILLERS	DOLLY BIRDS	DREADLOCKS	DYSPROSIUM
DISTILLERY	DOLOROUSLY	DREAMBOATS	DYSTROPHIC
DISTILLING	DOMINATING	DREAMINESS	

11 LETTERS

DACTYLOLOGY	DECLARATORY	DELINEATIVE	DEPOSITIONS
DAGGERBOARD	DECLENSIONS	DELIQUENCY	DEPRAVATION
DAIRY CATTLE	DECLINATION	DELIQUENTS	DEPRAVITIES
DAIRY FARMER	DECLINATORY	DELIRIOUSLY	DEPRACATING
DAISY WHEEL	DECLIVITIES	DELITESCENT	DEPRACATION
DAMNABILITY	DECLIVITOUS	DELIVERABLE	DEPRACATIVE
DAMP COURSES	DECOLLATION	DELIVERANCE	DEPRACATORY
DANGER MONEY	DECOLLETAGE	DELIVERYMAN	DEPRECIABLE
DANGEROUSLY	DECOLONIZED	DELIVERYMEN	DEPRECIATED
DAPPLE-GREYS	DECOMPOSING	DELPHINIUMS	DEPRECIATOR
DARDANELLES	DECORATIONS	DEMAGNETIZE	DEPREDATION
DAREDEVILRY	DECORTICATE	DEMAGOGERY	DEPRESSIBLE
DATABLENESS	DECREPITATE	DEMARCATING	DEPRESSIONS
DAUNTLESSLY	DECREPITUDE	DEMARCATION	DEPRIVATION
DAYDREAMERS	DECRESCENCE	DEMOCRACIES	DEPUTATIONS
DAYDREAMING	DECRETALIST	DEMOCRATIZE	DERAILMENTS
DEACTIVATOR	DECUSSATION	DEMODULATOR	DERANGEMENT
DEAD LETTERS	DEDICATEDLY	DEMOGRAPHER	DEREGULATED
DEAD MARCHES	DEDICATIONS	DEMOGRAPHIC	DERELICTION
DEAD RINGERS	DEDUCTIVELY	DEMOLISHING	DERIVATIONS
DEAF-AND-DUMB	DEFENCELESS	DEMOLITIONS	DERMATOLOGY
DEALERSHIPS	DEFENSIVELY	DEMONETIZED	DESALINATED
DEAMINATION	DEFERENTIAL	DEMONICALLY	DESCENDABLE
DEATH DUTIES	DEFICIENTLY	DEMONOLATER	DESCENDANTS
DEATHLESSLY	DEFINIENDUM	DEMONOLATRY	DESCENDIBLE
DEATHLINESS	DEFINITIONS	DEMONSTRATE	DESCRIBABLE
DEATH RATTLE	DEFLECTIONS	DEMORALIZER	DESCRIPTION
DEATH'S HEAD	DEFLORATION	DEMOTIVATED	DESCRIPTIVE
DEATHSQUADS	DEFLOWERING	DEMOUNTABLE	DESECRATING
DEBARKATION	DEFOLIATING	DEMULSIFIER	DESECRATION
DEBASEDNESS	DEFOLIATION	DEMYSTIFIED	DESEGREGATE
DEBASEMENTS	DEFORCEMENT	DENIGRATING	DESENSITIZE
DEBILITATED	DEFORESTING	DENIGRATION	DESERVINGLY
DEBOUCHMENT	DEFORMATION	DENITRATION	DESEXUALIZE
DEBRIDEMENT	DEFORMATIES	DENOMINABLE	DESICCATING
DECALCIFIER	DEFRAUDMENT	DENOMINATOR	DESICCATION
DECALESCENT	DEGENERATED	DENOTATIONS	DESICCATIVE
DECAPITATED	DEGENERATES	DENOUEMENTS	DESIDERATUM
DECAPITATOR	DEGLUTINATE	DENSIMETRIC	DESIGNATING
DECARBONIZE	DEGLUTITION	DENTAL FLOSS	DESIGNATION
DECEITFULLY	DEGRADATION	DENTAL PLATE	DESIGNATIVE
DECELERATED	DEHUMANIZED	DENICULATE	DESPATCHING
DECLERATOR	DEHYDRATING	DENTILABIAL	DESPERADOES
DECEPTIVELY	DEHYDRATION	DENUMERABLE	DESPERATELY
DECEREBRATE	DECITICALLY	DENUNCIATOR	DESPERATION
DECILLIONTH	DEIFICATION	DEODORIZING	DESPOILMENT
DECIMALIZED	DELECTATION	DEOXYGENATE	DESPONDANCY
DECIPHERING	DELEGATIONS	DEOXYRIBOSE	DESPUMATION
DECKLE-EDGED	DELETERIOUS	DEPARTMENTS	DESSERT WINE
DECLAMATION	DELIBERATED	DEPLORINGLY	DESTABILIZE
DECLAMATORY	DELIBERATOR	DEPLUMATION	DESTINATION
DECLARATION	DELICIOUSLY	DEPOLARIZER	DESTITUTION
DECLARATIVE	DELINEATING	DEPOPULATED	DESTROYABLE
	DELINEATION	DEPORTATION	DESTRUCTION

DESTRUCTIVE	DICOTYLEDON	DIRTY OLD MAN	DISCREPANCY
DESULTORILY	DICTAPHONES	DIRTY OLD MEN	DISCUSSIBLE
DETACHMENTS	DICTATIONAL	DIRTY TRICKS	DISCUSSIONS
DETERIORATE	DICTATORIAL	DISABLEMENT	DISEMBARKED
DETERMINANT	DIDACTICISM	DISACCREDIT	DISEMBODIED
DETERMINATE	DIE-CASTINGS	DISACCUSTOM	DISENCUMBER
DETERMINERS	DIFFERENCES	DISAFFECTED	DISENGAGING
DETERMINING	DIFFERENTIA	DISAFFOREST	DISENTANGLE
DETERMINISM	DIFFERENTLY	DISAGREEING	DISENTHRALL
DETERMINIST	DIFFIDENTLY	DISALLOWING	DISFIGURING
DETESTATION	DIFFRACTING	DISAPPEARED	DISFORESTED
DETONATIONS	DIFFRACTION	DISAPPROVAL	DISGRACEFUL
DETRAINMENT	DIFFRACTIVE	DISAPPROVED	DISGRUNTLED
DETRIBALIZE	DIFFUSENESS	DISAPPROVER	DISGUISABLE
DETRIMENTAL	DIFFUSIVITY	DISARMAMENT	DISGUSTEDLY
DEUTERANOPE	DIGESTIONAL	DISARRANGED	DISHEVELLED
DEUTEROGAMY	DIGITIGRADE	DISASSEMBLE	DISHONESTLY
DEUTSCHMARK	DIGNITARIES	DISASSEMBLY	DISHONOURED
DEVALUATION	DIGRESSIONS	DISAVOWEDLY	DISHONOURER
DEVASTATING	DIHYBRIDISM	DISBANDMENT	DISHWASHERS
DEVASTATION	DILAPIDATED	DISBELIEVED	DISILLUSION
DEVASTATIVE	DILAPIDATOR	DISBELIEVER	DISILLUSIVE
DEVELOPABLE	DILATOMETER	DISBURSABLE	DISINFECTED
DEVELOPMENT	DILATOMETRY	DISCERNIBLE	DISINFECTOR
DEVIOUSNESS	DILETTANTES	DISCERNIBLY	DISINTEREST
DEVOURINGLY	DIMENSIONAL	DISCERNMENT	DISINTERRED
DEXTEROUSLY	DIMIDIATION	DISCHARGING	DISJOINABLE
DIACRITICAL	DIMINISHING	DISCIPLINAL	DISJUNCTION
DIADELPHOUS	DIMINUENDOS	DISCIPLINED	DISJUNCTIVE
DIAGNOSABLE	DIMINUTIONS	DISCIPLINER	DISJUNCTURE
DIAGNOSTICS	DIMINUTIVES	DISCIPLINES	DISLOCATING
DIALECTICAL	DINING ROOMS	DISC JOCKEYS	DISLOCATION
DIALOGISTIC	DINING TABLE	DISCLAIMERS	DISLODGEMENT
DIALYSATION	DINNER BELLS	DISCLAIMING	DISMANTLING
DIAMAGNETIC	DINNER TABLE	DISCLOSURES	DISMASTMENT
DIAMONDBACK	DINOSAURIN	DISCOGRAPHY	DISMEMBERED
DIAPHORESIS	DIOPTOMETER	DISCOLOURED	DISMEMBERER
DIAPHORETIC	DIOPTOMETRY	DISCOMFITED	DISMISSIBLE
DIAPOPHYSIS	DIPHTHEROID	DISCOMFITER	DISMOUNTING
DIARTHROSIS	DIPHTHONGAL	DISCOMFORTS	DISOBEDIENT
DIASTROPHIC	DIPHYCERCAL	DISCOMMODED	DISOBLIGING
DIATESSARON	DIPLOCOCCAL	DISCOMPOSED	DISORDERING
DIATOMICITY	DIPLOCOCCUS	DISCONTINUE	DISORGANIZE
DIATONICISM	DIPLOMATIST	DISCORDANCE	DISPARAGING
DICEPHALISM	DIPROTODONT	DISCOTHEQUE	DISPARATELY
DICEPHALOUS	DIPSOMANIAC	DISCOUNTING	DISPARITIES
DICHOGAMOUS	DIPSWITCHES	DISCOURAGED	DISPATCH BOX
DICHOTOMIES	DIRECT DEBIT	DISCOURAGER	DISPATCHING
DICHOTOMIES	DIRECTIONAL	DISCOURSING	DISPENSABLE
DICHOTOMIST	DIRECTORATE	DISCOURTESY	DISPIRITING
DICHOTOMIZE	DIRECTORIAL	DISCOVERERS	DISPLEASING
DICHOTOMOUS	DIRECTORIES	DISCOVERIES	DISPLEASURE
DICHROMATIC	DIRECT TAXES	DISCOVERING	DISPOSITION
DICROSCOPE	DIRT FARMERS	DISCREDITED	DISPROVABLE

DISPUTATION	DITTOGRAPHY	DOUBLE-QUICK	**12 LETTERS**
DISQUIETING	DIVARICATOR	DOUBLE-SPACE	DACTYLICALLY
DISQUIETUDE	DIVE-BOMBERS	DOUBLE TAKES	DAEMONICALLY
DISREGARDED	DIVE-BOMBING	DOUBLETHINK	DAIRY FARMERS
DISREGARDER	DIVERGENCIES	DOVETAILING	DANISH PASTRY
DISRELISHED	DIVERGENTLY	DOWN-AND-OUTS	DARBY AND JOAN
DISROBEMENT	DIVERSIFIED	DOWNGRADING	DAY NURSERIES
DISRUPTIPONS	DIVERSIFORM	DOWNHEARTED	DEACTIVATION
DISSECTIBLE	DIVERSIONAL	DOWNLOADING	DEAF-MUTENESS
DISSECTIONS	DIVERTINGLY	DOWN PAYMENT	DEATH RATTLES
DISSEMBLER	DIVESTITURE	DOWNPLAYING	DEATH WARRANT
DISSEMBLING	DIVINATIONS	DOWN-TO-EARTH	DEBARKATIONS
DISSEMINATE	DIVINE RIGHT	DOWNTRODDEN	DEBAUCHERIES
DISSEMINULE	DIVING BELLS	DRAGONFLIES	DEBILITATING
DISSENTIONS	DIVING BOARD	DRAMATIZING	DEBILITATION
DISSENTIENT	DIVISIONISM	DRAMATURICS	DEBILITATIVE
DISSENTIOUS	DIVISIONIST	DRASTICALLY	DELICATESSAN
DISSEPIMENT	DIVORCEABLE	DRAUGHTSMAN	DELIGHTFULLY
DISSIMILATE	DIVORCEMENT	DRAUGHTSMEN	DELIMITATION
DISSIMULATE	DOCTRINAIRE	DRAWBRIDGES	DELIMITATIVE
DISSIPATING	DOCUMENTARY	DRAWING POINS	DELIQUESCENT
DISSIPATION	DOCUMENTING	DRAWING ROOM	DELITESCENCE
DISSIPATIVE	DODDERINGLY	DRAWSTRINGS	DELTIOLOGIST
DISSOCIABLE	DODECAGONAL	DREADNOUGHT	DEMAGNETIZED
DISSOCIATED	DOGBERRYISM	DREAMLESSLY	DEMAGNETIZER
DISSOLUTELY	DOG BISCUITS	DREAM WORLD	DEMENTEDNESS
DISSOLUTION	DOGCATCHERS	DRESS CIRCLE	DEMILITARIZE
DISSOLUTIVE	DOLEFULNESS	DRESSMAKERS	DEMIMONDAINE
DISSOLVABLE	DOLL'S HOUSES	DRESSMAKING	DEMOCRATIZED
DISSONANCES	DOMESTICATE	DRILLMASTER	DEMODULATION
DISSUADABLE	DOMESTICITY	DROMEDARIES	DEMOGRAPHERS
DISSYLLABIC	DOMICILIARY	DRUNKENNESS	DEMOLISHMENT
DISSYLLABLE	DOMICILIATE	DRY CLEANERS	DEMONETIZING
DISSYMMETRY	DOMINEERING	DRY-CLEANING	DEMONIACALLY
DISTASTEFUL	DOORKEEPERS	DSCONTINUER	DEMONOLOGIST
DISTEMPERED	DOORKNOCKER	DUAL-PURPOSE	DEMONSTRABLE
DISTENSIBLE	DOORSTOPPER	DUBIOUSNESS	DEMONSTRABLY
DISTILLABLE	DORMITORIES	DUDE RANCHES	DEMONSTRATED
DISTINCTION	DOTTED LINES	DUFFEL COATS	DEMONSTRATOR
DISTINCTIVE	DOUBLE AGENT	DUMBFOUNDED	DEMOTIVATING
DISTINGUISH	DOUBLE BINDS	DUMBFOUNDER	DEMOTIVATION
DISTORTIONS	DOUBLE-BLIND	DUMBWAITERS	DEMYSTIFYING
DISTRACTING	DOUBLE BLUFF	DUNDERHEADS	DENATURALIZE
DISTRACTION	DOUBLE-CHECK	DUNE BUGGIES	DENATURATION
DISTRACTIVE	DOUBLE CHINS	DUPLICATING	DENDROLOGIST
DISTRAINING	DOUBLE CREAM	DUPLICATION	DENICOTINIZE
DISTRESSFUL	DOUBLE-CROSS	DUPLICATORS	DENOMINATING
DISTRESSING	DOUBLE DATED	DUST JACKETS	DENOMINATION
DISTRIBUTOR	DOUBLE DATES	DUTIABILITY	DENOMINATIVE
DISTRUSTFUL	DOUBLE-DUTCH	DUTIFULNESS	DENOMINATORS
DISTRUSTING	DOUBLE-EDGED	DYNAMICALLY	DENOUNCEMENT
DISTURBANCE	DOUBLE-FACED	DYSFUNCTION	DENSITOMETER
DISULPHURIC	DOUBLE FAULT		DENSITOMETRY
DITHYRAMBIC	DOUBLE-GLAZE		DENTAL PLATES

DENTILINGUAL	DETHRONEMENT	DILATATIONAL	DISCOLOURING
DENUNCIATION	DETOXICATION	DILATABILITY	DISCOMFITING
DENUNCIATORY	DETRUNCATION	DILATATIONAL	DISCOMFITURE
DEONTOLOGIST	DETUMESCENCE	DILATOMETRIC	DISCOMMODING
DEPARTMENTAL	DEUTERANOPIA	DILATORINESS	DISCOMMODITY
DEPENDANCIES	DEUTERANOPIC	DILETTANTISH	DISCOMPOSING
DEPILATORIES	DEUTOPLASMIC	DILETTANTISM	DISCOMPOSURE
DEPOLITICIZE	DEUTSCHE MARK	DILLYDALLIED	DISCONCERTED
DEPOPULATING	DEUTSCHMARKS	DIMINISHABLE	DISCONNECTED
DEPOPULATION	DEVALUATIONS	DIMINISHMENT	DISCONNECTER
DEPORTATIONS	DEVELOPMENTS	DINING TABLES	DISCONSOLATE
DEPOSITORIES	DEVIATIONISM	DINNER JACKET	DISCONTENTED
DEPRAVEDNESS	DEVIATIONIST	DIOPTRICALLY	DISCONTINUED
DEPRECIATING	DEVILISHNESS	DIPHTHERITIC	DISCORDANTLY
DEPRECIATION	DEVIL-MAY-CARE	DIPHTHONGIZE	DISCOTHEQUES
DEPRECIATORY	DEVITALIZING	DIPLOBLASTIC	DISCOUNTABLE
DEPREDATIONS	DEXTROGYRATE	DIPLOCARDIAC	DISCOURAGING
DEPRESSINGLY	DIABOLICALLY	DIPLOMATISTS	DISCOURTEOUS
DEPRIVATIONS	DIAGEOTROPIC	DIPROPELLANT	DISCOVERABLE
DERACINATION	DIAGRAMMATIC	DIPSOMANIACS	DISCOVERTURE
DERANGEMENTS	DIALECTICIAN	DIRECT DEBITS	DISCREDITING
DEREGULATING	DIALECTOLOGY	DIRECT OBJECT	DISCREETNESS
DEREGULATION	DIALLING CODE	DIRECTORIES	DISCRIMINANT
DERELICTIONS	DIALLING TONE	DIRECTORSHIP	DISCRIMINATE
DERESTRICTED	DIALYTICALLY	DIRECT SPEECH	DISCURSIVELY
DERISIVENESS	DIAMAGNETISM	DIRIGIBILITY	DISCUSSIONAL
DERIVATIONAL	DIAPOPHYSIAL	DISABILITIES	DISDAINFULLY
DERIVATIVELY	DIARTHRODIAL	DISABLEMENTS	DISEMBARKING
DERMATOPHYTE	DIASTROPHISM	DISACCHARIDE	DISEMBARRASS
DEROGATORILY	DIATHERMANCY	DISADVANTAGE	DISEMBOWLED
DESALINATING	DIATOMACEOUS	DISAFFECTION	DISENCHANTED
DESALINATION	DIATONICALLY	DISAFFILIATE	DISENCHANTER
DESCRIPTIONS	DIAZOMETHANE	DISAGREEABLE	DISENDOWMENT
DESEGREGATED	DIBRANCHIATE	DISAGREEABLY	DISENTANGLED
DESENSITIZED	DICARBOXYLIC	DISAGREEMENT	DISESTABLISH
DESENSITIZER	DICHROMATISM	DISALLOWABLE	DISFORESTING
DESERVEDNESS	DICHROSCOPIC	DISALLOWANCE	DISFRANCHISE
DESIDERATION	DICTATORSHIP	DISAMBIGUATE	DISGORGMENT
DESIDERATIVE	DICTIONARIES	DISANNULMENT	DISGUSTINGLY
DESIGNATIONS	DIDACTICALLY	DISAPPEARING	DISHEVELMENT
DESIRABILITY	DIENCEPHALIC	DISAPPOINTED	DISHONOURING
DESPAIRINGLY	DIENCEPHALON	DISAPPOINTER	DISINCENTIVE
DESPOLIATION	DIESEL ENGINE	DISAPPROVING	DISINFECTANT
DESPONDENTLY	DIETETICALLY	DISARRANGING	DISINFECTING
DESPOTICALLY	DIENCEPHALIC	DISASSOCIATE	DISINFECTION
DESQUAMATION	DIENCEPHALON	DISASTROUSLY	DISINFLATION
DESSERT SPOON	DIESEL ENGINE	DISBELIEVERS	DISINGENUOUS
DESSERT WINES	DIETETICALLY	DISBELIEVING	DISINHERITED
DESTABILIZED	DIFFERENTIAL	DISBURSEMENT	DISINTEGRATE
DESTINATIONS	DIFFICULTIES	DISCIPLESHIP	DISINTERMENT
DESTRUCTIBLE	DIGITIZATION	DISCIPLINARY	DISINTERRING
DETERIORATED	DIGRESSIONAL	DISCIPLINING	DISJOINTEDLY
DETERMINABLE	DILAPIDATION	DISCLAMATION	DISLOCATIONS
DETERMINANTS	DILATABILITY	DSCOGRAPHER	DISLODGEMENT

DISLOYALTIES
DISMEMBERING
DISMOUNTABLE
DISOBEDIENCE
DISOPERATION
DISORGANIZED
DISORGANIZER
DISORIENTATE
DISPENSARIES
DISPENSATION
DISPENSATORY
DISPIRITEDLY
DISPLACABLE
DISPLACEMENT
DISPOSITIONS
DISPOSSESSED
DISPOSSESSOR
DISPUTATIONS
DISPUTATIOUS
DISQUALIFIED
DISQUALIFIER
DISQUIETEDLY
DISQUISITION
DISREGARDFUL
DISREGARDING
DISRELISHING
DISREPUTABLE
DISREPUTABLE
DISRUPTIVELY
DISSATISFIED
DISSEMBLANCE
DISSEMINATED
DISSEMINATOR
DISSERTATION
DISSEVERANCE
DISSIMILARLY
DISSIMULATED
DISSIMULATOR
DISSOCIATING
DISSOCIATION
DISSOCIATIVE
DISSOLUTIONS
DISSYMMETRIC
DISTEMPERING
DISTILLATION
DISTILLATORY
DISTILLARIES
DISTINCTIONS
DISTINCTNESS
DISTORTIONAL
DISTRACTEDLY
DISTRACTIBLE
DISTRACTIONS
DISTRAINABLE

DISTRAINMENT
DISTRIBUTARY
DISTRIBUTING
DISTRIBUTION
DISTRIBUTIVE
DISTRIBUTORS
DISTURBANCES
DIURETICALLY
DIVARICATION
DIVERSIFYING
DIVERSIONARY
DIVERTICULAR
DIVERTICULUM
DIVERTIMENTO
DIVING BOARDS
DIVINIZATION
DIVISABILITY
DIVISIVENESS
DOCTRINALITY
DOCTRINARIAN
DOGMATICALLY
DO-IT-YOURSELF
DOMESDAY BOOK
DOMESTICABLE
DOMESTICALLY
DOMESTICATED
DOMESTICATOR
DOMINO EFFECT
DOMKEY JACKET
DONKEY'S YEARS
DOORKNOCKERS
DOORSTEPPING
DOORSTOPPERS
DORSIVENTRAL
DORSOVENTRAL
DOUBLE-ACTING
DOUBLE AGENTS
DOUBLE BASSES
DOUBLE-BEDDED
DOUBLE BLUFFS
DOUBLE-DATING
DOUBLE-DEALER
DOUBLE-DECKER
DOUBLE-DOTTED
DOUBLE FAULTS
DOUBLE-GLAZED
DOUBLE-HEADER
DOUBLE-PARKED
DOUBLE-TALKED
DOUBLE-TONGUE
DOWN PAYMENTS
DRACONIANISM
DRACONICALLY
DRAMATICALLY

DRAMATIZABLE
DRAUGHTBOARD
DRAWING BOARD
DRAWING ROOMS
DREADFULNESS
DREADNOUGHTS
DRESS CIRCLES
DRESSING-DOWN
DRESSING GOWN
DRESSING ROOM
DRY BATTERIES
DUCKING STOOL
DUMBFOUNDING
DUTCH AUCTION
DUTCH COURAGE
DWARFISHNESS
DYNAMOMETRIC

13 LETTERS
DADAISTICALLY
DADDY LONGLEGS
DAGUERREOTYPE
DAMAGEABILITY
DARK CONTINENT
DASTARDLINESS
DAUGHTER-IN-LAW
DEAD RECKONING
DEBT OF HONOUR
DECAPITATIONS
DECEITFULNESS
DECENTRALIZED
DECEPTIVENESS
DECEREBRATION
DECLAMATORILY
DECLARATORILY
DECLASSIFYING
DECOMPOSITION
DECOMPRESSING
DECOMPRESSION
DECOMPRESSIVE
DECONGESTANTS
DECONTAMINANT
DECONTAMINATE
DECONTROLLING
DECREPITATION
DEDUCTIBILITY
DEFECTIVENESS
DEFENSIBILITY
DEFENSIVENESS
DEFERENTIALLY
DEFIBRILLATOR
DEFORESTATION
DEGLUTINATION

DELETERIOUSLY
DELIBERATIONS
DELICATESSENS
DELICIOUSNESS
DELINQUENCIES
DELIROUSNESS
DEMAGNETIZING
DEMAGOGICALLY
DEMERARA SUGAR
DEMILITARIZED
DEMOCRATIZING
DEMOLITIONIST
DEMONOLOGICAL
DEMONSTRATING
DEMONSTRATION
DEMONSTRATIVE
DEMONSTRATORS
DENATIONALIZE
DENDRITICALLY
DENDROLOGICAL
DENOMINATIONS
DENSITOMETRIC
DENTAL SURGEON
DENTICULATION
DENUNCIATIONS
DEODORIZATION
DEONTOLOGICAL
DEOXIDIZATION
DEOXYGENATION
DEPENDABILITY
DEPERSONALIZE
DEPRECATINGLY
DEPRECATORILY
DEPRESSOMOTOR
DERMATOLOGIST
DERMATOPHYTIC
DERMATOPLASTY
DESCRIPTIVELY
DESCRIPTIVISM
DESEGREGATION
DESENSITIZING
DESSERTSPOONS
DESTABILIZING
DESTRUCTIVELY
DESULTORINESS
DETACHABILITY
DETERIORATING
DETERIORATION
DETERIORATIVE
DETERMINATION
DETERMINATIVE
DETERMINISTIC
DETESTABILITY
DETRIMENTALLY

DEVASTATINGLY	DISCIPLINABLE	DISINTEGRATOR	DOCUMENTARIES
DEVELOPMENTAL	DISCOLORATION	DISINTERESTED	DOCUMENTARILY
DEVIATIONISTS	DISCOMMODIOUS	DISINTERMENTS	DOCUMENTATION
DEVOLUTIONARY	DISCOMPOSEDLY	DISMANTLEMENT	DOGMATIZATION
DEVOTIONALITY	DISCONCERTING	DISMEMBERMENT	DOG'S BREAKFAST
DEXTEROUSNESS	DISCONCERTION	DISOBEDIENTLY	DOMESTICATING
DEXTROGLUCOSE	DISCONFORMITY	DISOBLIGINGLY	DOMESTICATION
DIAGNOSTICIAN	DISCONNECTING	DISORIENTATED	DOMESTICITIES
DIALECTICIANS	DISCONNECTION	DISPARAGEMENT	DOUBLE-CHECKED
DIALLING CODES	DISCONNECTIVE	DISPARAGINGLY	DOUBLE-CROSSED
DIALLING TONES	DISCONTENTING	DISPASSIONATE	DOUBLE-CROSSER
DIAMETRICALLY	DISCONTINUING	DISPATCH BOXES	DOUBLE-CROSSES
DIAPHRAGMATIC	DISCONTINUITY	DISPENSATIONS	DOUBLE-DEALERS
DICTATORIALLY	DISCONTINUOUS	DISPLACEMENTS	DOUBLE-DEALING
DICTATORSHIPS	DISCOUNT STORE	DISPOSABILITY	DOUBLE-DECKERS
DIESEL ENGINES	DISCOURTESIES	DISPOSITIONAL	DOUBLE FEATURE
DIFFERENTIALS	DISCREDITABLE	DISPOSSESSING	DOUBLE FIGURES
DIFFERENTIATE	DISCREDITABLY	DISPOSSESSION	DOUBLE-GLAZING
DIFFUSIBILITY	DISCREPANCIES	DISPROPORTION	DOUBLE-JOINTED
DIGESTIBILITY	DISCRETIONARY	DISPUTABILITY	DOUBLE-PARKING
DILAPIDATIONS	DISCRIMINATED	DISQUALIFYING	DOUBLE-TALKING
DILLYDALLYING	DISCRIMINATOR	DISRESPECTFUL	DOWNHEARTEDLY
DIMENSIONLESS	DISEMBODIMENT	DISSATISFYING	DOWNING STREET
DIM-WITTEDNESS	DISEMBOWELING	DISSEMINATING	DRAINING BOARD
DINNER JACKETS	DISEMBOWELLED	DISSEMINATION	DRAMATIC IRONY
DINNER SERVICE	DISENABLEMENT	DISSERTATIONS	DRAMATIZATION
DIRECTORSHIPS	DISENGAGEMENT	DISSIMILARITY	DRAWING BOARDS
DISADVANTAGED	DISENTAILMENT	DISSOLUBILITY	DRESSING GOWNS
DISADVANTAGES	DISENTANGLING	DISSOLUTENESS	DRESSING ROOMS
DISAFFECTEDLY	DISFIGUREMENT	DISTASTEFULLY	DRESSING TABLE
DISAFFILIATED	DISFRANCHISED	DISTILLATIONS	DRINKING WATER
DISAFFIRMANCE	DISGRACEFULLY	DISTINCTIVELY	DRUM MAJORETTE
DISAGREEMENTS	DISHARMONIOUS	DISTINGUISHED	DUALISTICALLY
DISAPPEARANCE	DISHONOURABLE	DISTRESSINGLY	DUCKING STOOLS
DISAPPOINTING	DISHONOURABLY	DISTRIBUTABLE	DUPLICABILITY
DISARTICULATE	DISILLUSIONED	DISTRIBUTIONS	DUTCH AUCTIONS
DISASSOCIATED	DISINCENTIVES	DISTRUSTFULLY	DWELLING HOUSE
DISBURDENMENT	DISINFECTANTS	DIVERSIFIABLE	
DISBURSEMENTS	DISINHERITING	DIVISION LOBBY	
DISCHARGEABLE	DISINTEGRATED	DOCTRINAIRISM	

3 LETTERS

EAR
EAT
EBB
ECG
EEC
EEK
EEL
EGG
EGO
ELF
ELK
ELM
EMU
END
EON
ERA
ERE
ERG
ERR
ESP
ESQ
ETC
EVE
EWE
EYE

4 LETTERS

EACH
EARL
EARN
EARS
EASE
ESAT
EASY
EATS
EBBS
ECGS
ECHO
ECRU
EDAM
EDDY
EDEN
EDGE
EDGY
EDIT
EELS
EFIK
EGGS
EGOS
EIRE
ELAN
ELBA

ELBE
ELIA
ELKS
ELMS
ELSE
EMIR
EMIT
EMUS
ENDS
ENVY
EONS
EPEE
EPIC
ERAS
ERGO
ERGS
ERIE
ERSE
ESPY
ET AL
ETCH
EURE
EURO
EVEN
EVER
EVES
EVIL
EWER
EWES
EXAM
EXES
EXIT
EYED
EYES
EYOT

5 LETTERS

EAGER
EAGLE
EAGRE
EARED
EARLS
EARLY
EARTH
EASED
EASEL
EASER
EASTS
EATEN
EATER
EAVES
EBBED
EBONY

ECLAT
EDEMA
EDGED
EDGER
EDGES
EDICT
EDIFY
EDUCE
EDUCT
EERIE
EFFED
EGEST
EGGER
EGRET
EGYPT
EIDER
EIGER
EIGHT
EIKON
EILAT
EJECT
ELAND
ELATE
ELBOW
ELDER
ELECT
ELEGY
ELEMI
ELFIN
ELIDE
ELITE
ELOPE
ELUDE
ELUTE
ELVER
ELVES
E MAIL
EMBED
EMBER
EMBOW
EMCEE
EMEND
EMERY
EMIRN
EMIRS
EMMER
EMOTE
EMPTY
ENACT
ENATE
ENDED
ENDER
ENDOW
ENDUE

ENEMA
ENEMY
ENJOY
ENNUI
ENROL
ENSUE
ENTER
ENTRY
ENUGU
ENURE
ENVOY
EOSIN
EPACT
EPEES
EPICS
EPOCH
EPODE
EPOXY
EQUAL
EQUIP
ERASE
ERBIL
ERECT
ERGOT
ERODE
EROSE
ERRED
ERROR
ERUCT
ERUPT
ESKER
ESSAY
ESSEN
ESTER
ESTOP
ETHER
ETHIC
ETHOS
ETHYL
ETUDE
EVADE
EVENS
EVENT
EVERY
EVICT
EVICS
EVILS
EVOKE
EWERS
EXACT
EXALT
EXAMS
EXCEL
EXERT

EXILE
EXIAT
EXITS
EXPEL
EXTOL
EXTRA
EXUDE
EXULT
EYING
EYOTS
EYRIE

6 LETTERS

EAGLES
EAGLET
EARFUL
EARING
EARNED
EARNER
EARTHS
EARTHY
EARWAX
EARWIG
EASELS
EASIER
EASILY
EASTER
EATERS
EATING
EBBING
ECARTE
ECESIS
ECHARD
ECHOED
ECHOIC
ECLAIR
ECTYPE
ECURIE
ECZEMA
EDDIED
EDDIES
EDGIER
EDGILY
EDGING
EDIBLE
EDICTS
EDITED
EDITOR
EERILY
EFFACE
EFFECT
EFFETE
EFFIGY

EFFING
EFFLUX
EFFORT
EFFUSE
EGESTA
EGGCUP
EGGNOG
EGOISM
EGOIST
EGRESS
EGRETS
EIGHTH
EIGHTS
EIGHTY
EITHER
EJECTA
ELANDS
ELAPID
ELAPSE
ELATED
ELATER
ELBOWS
ELDERS
ELDEST
ELEGIT
ELEVEN
ELEVON
ELFISH
ELICIT
ELIDED
ELIXIR
ELOPED
ELOPER
EL PASO
ELUDED
ELUDER
ELYSEE
EMBALM
EMBANK
EMBARK
EMBERS
EMBLEM
EMBODY
EMBOLY
EMBOSS
EMBRYO
EMERGE
EMESIS
EMETIC
EMIGRE
EMOTER
EMPALE
EMPIRE
EMPLOY

ENABLE	ENWOMB	ETHYNE	EXTORT	ECONOMY	ELEGIES
ENAMEL	ENWRAP	ETYMON	EXTRAS	ECORCHE	ELEGIST
ENATIC	ENZYME	EUBOEA	EXUDED	ECOTONE	ELEGIZE
EN BLOC	EOCENE	EUCHRE	EYEFUL	ECOTYPE	ELEMENT
ENCAGE	EOGENE	EULOGY	EYEING	ECSTASY	ELEUSIS
ENCAMP	EOLITH	EUNUCH	EYELET	ECHYMAL	ELEVATE
ENCASE	EONISM	EUREKA	EYELID	ECTOPIA	ELEVENS
ENCODE	EOZOIC	EUROPE	EYRIES	ECTOPIC	ELIDING
ENCORE	EPARCH	EVADED		ECTYPAL	ELISION
ENCYST	EPIRUS	EVADER		ECUADOR	ELITISM
ENDEAR	EPONYM	EVENLY	**7 LETTERS**	EDACITY	ELITIST
ENDING	EPOPEE	EVENTS	EACH WAY	EDAPHIC	ELIXIRS
ENDIVE	EQUALS	EVILER	EAGERLY	EDDYING	ELLIPSE
ENDUED	EQUATE	EVILLY	EAGLETS	EDGIEST	EL MINYA
ENDURE	EQUINE	EVINCE	EARACHE	EDGINGS	ELOPING
ENEMAS	EQUITY	EVOKED	EARDRUM	EDICTAL	ELUDING
ENERGY	ERASED	EVOKER	EARFLAP	EDIFICE	ELUSION
ENFACE	ERASER	EVOLVE	EARLDOM	EDIFIED	ELUSIVE
ENFOLD	ERBIUM	EVZONE	EARLIER	EDIFIER	ELUVIAL
ENGAGE	ERFUERT	EXAMEN	EARLOBE	EDITING	ELUVIUM
ENGINE	ERLANG	EXARCH	EARMARK	EDITION	ELYSIAN
ENGRAM	ERMINE	EXCEED	EARMUFF	EDITORS	ELYSIUM
ENGULF	ERODED	EXCEPT	EARNERS	EDUCATE	ELYTRON
ENIGMA	EROTIC	EXCESS	EARNEST	EEL-LIKE	EMANATE
ENJOIN	ERRAND	EXCISE	EARNING	EELWORM	EMBARGO
ENLACE	ERRANT	EXCITE	EARPLUG	EFFACED	EMBASSY
ENLIST	ERRATA	EXCUSE	EARRING	EFFACER	EMBLEMS
ENMESH	ERRING	EXEDRA	EARSHOT	EFFECTS	EMBOLIC
ENMITY	ERRORS	EXEMPT	EARTHED	EFFORTS	EMBOLUS
ENNAGE	ERSATZ	EXEUNT	EARTHEN	EGGCUPS	EMBRACE
ENNEAD	ERYNGO	EXHALE	EARTHLY	EGGHEAD	EMBROIL
ENOSIS	ESCAPE	EXHORT	EARWIGS	EGG ROLL	EMBRYOS
ENOUGH	ESCARP	EXHUME	EASEFUL	EGOISTS	EMENDED
ENRAGE	ESCHAR	EXILED	EASIEST	EGOTISM	EMERALD
ENRICH	ESCHEW	EXILES	EAST END	EGOTIST	EMERGED
ENROBE	ESCORT	EXILIC	EASTERN	EGOTRIP	EMERSED
ENROOT	ESCROW	EXITED	EASTERS	EIDETIC	EMETICS
ENSIGN	ESCUDO	EXODUS	EASTING	EIDOLON	EMETINE
ENSILE	ESKIMO	EXONYM	EATABLE	EIGHTHS	EMIGRES
ENSOUL	ESPIAL	EXOTIC	EBB TIDE	EJECTED	EMINENT
ENSUED	ESPIED	EXPAND	EBONITE	EJECTOR	EMIRATE
ENSURE	ESPIER	EXPECT	EBONIZE	ELAMITE	EMITTED
ENTAIL	ESPRIT	EXPEND	ECBOLIC	ELAPSED	EMITTER
ENTICE	ESSAYS	EXPERT	ECCRINE	ELASTIC	EMOTION
ENTIRE	ESTATE	EXPIRE	ECDYSIS	ELASTIN	EMOTIVE
ENTITY	ESTEEM	EXPIRY	ECHELON	ELATION	EMPALER
ENTOMB	ESTRAY	EXPORT	ECHIDNA	ELATIVE	EMPANEL
ENTRAP	ETALON	EXPOSE	ECHINUS	ELBOWED	EMPATHY
ENTREE	ETCHED	EXSERT	ECHOING	ELDERLY	EMPEROR
ENVIED	ETCHER	EXTANT	ECHOISM	ELEATIC	EMPIRES
ENVIER	ETHANE	EXTEND	ECLAIRS	ELECTED	EMPIRIC
ENVIES	ETHENE	EXTENT	ECLIPSE	ELECTOR	EMPLACE
ENVOYS	ETHICS	EXTERN	ECLOGUE	ELEGANT	EMPORTIA
ENWIND	ETHNIC	EXTINE	ECOLOGY	ELEGIAC	EMPOWER

EMPRESS	ENJOYED	EPIDOTE	ESCAPED	EXACTOR	EXPUNGE
EMPTIED	ENJOYER	EPIGEAL	ESCAPEE	EXALTED	EXSCIND
EMPTIER	ENLARGE	EPIGENE	ESCAPER	EXALTER	EXTENTS
EMPTIES	ENLIVEN	EPIGONE	ESCAPES	EXAMINE	EXTINCT
EMPTILY	EN MASSE	EPIGRAM	ESCOLAR	EXAMPLE	EXTRACT
EMPYEMA	ENNOBLE	EPIGYNY	ESCORTS	EXARATE	EXTREME
EMULATE	ENOUNCE	EPIMERE	ESERINE	EXCERPT	EXTRUDE
EMULOUS	ENPLANE	EPISODE	ESKIMOS	EXCISED	EXUDING
ENABLED	ENQUIRE	EPISOME	ESPARTO	EXCITED	EXULTED
ENABLER	ENQUIRY	EPISTLE	ESPOUSE	EXCITER	EXURBIA
ENACTED	ENRAGED	EPITAPH	ESPYING	EXCITON	EXUVIAE
ENACTOR	ENROBER	EPITAXY	ESQUIRE	EXCITOR	EXUVIAL
ENAMOUR	ENROUTE	EPITHET	ESSAYED	EXCLAIM	EX WORKS
ENCASED	ENSIGNS	EPITOME	ESSENCE	EXCLAVE	EYEBALL
ENCHAIN	ENSLAVE	EPIZOIC	ESSONNE	EXCLUDE	EYEBATH
ENCHANT	ENSNARE	EPIZOON	ESTATES	EXCRETA	EYEBOLT
ENCLAVE	ENSUING	EPOCHAL	ESTHETE	EXCRETE	EYEBROW
ENCLOSE	ENSURED	EPOCHES	ESTREAT	EXCUSAL	EYELASH
ENCODED	ENSURER	EPONYMY	ESTUARY	EXCUSED	EYELESS
ENCODER	ENTASIA	EPSILON	ETERNAL	EXCUSES	EYELETS
ENCOMIA	ENTASIS	EQUABLE	ETESIAN	EXECUTE	EYELIDS
ENCORES	ENTEBBE	EQUABLY	ETHANOL	EXEGETE	EYESHOT
ENCRUST	ENTENTE	EQUALID	ETHERIC	EXERGUE	EYESORE
ENDARCH	ENTERED	EQUALLY	ETHICAL	EXERTED	EYEWASH
ENDEMIC	ENTERER	EQUATED	ETHMOID	EXHAULED	
END GAME	ENTERIC	EQUATOR	ETHYLIC	EXHAUST	
ENDINGS	ENTERON	EQUERRY	ETRURIA	EXHIBIT	**8 LETTERS**
ENDIVES	ENTHRAL	EQUINOX	EUCAINE	EXHUMED	EARDROPS
ENDLESS	ENTHUSE	ERASERS	EULOGIA	EXHUMER	EARDRUMS
ENDMOST	ENTICED	ERASING	EUNUCHS	EXIGENT	EARLDOMS
ENDORSE	ENTICER	ERASION	EUPHONY	EXILING	EARLIEST
ENDOWED	ENTITLE	ERASURE	EURASIA	EXISTED	EARLOBES
ENDOWER	ENTOPIC	ERECTED	EVACUEE	EXITING	EARMUFFS
ENDURING	ENTRAIN	ERECTER	EVADING	EXODERM	EARNINGS
ENDURED	ENTRANT	ERECTLY	EVANGEL	EXOGAMY	EARPHONE
END USER	ENTREAT	ERECTOR	EVASION	EXOTICA	EARPIECE
ENDWAYS	ENTREES	EREMITE	EVASIVE	EXPANSE	EARPLUGS
ENEMIES	ENTRIES	EREPSIN	EVENING	EXPENSE	EARRINGS
ENERGID	ENTROPY	ERISTIC	EVEREST	EXPERTS	EARSHOTS
ENFORCE	ENTRUST	ERITREA	EVERTOR	EXPIATE	EARTHIER
ENGAGED	ENTWINE	ERMINES	EVICTED	EXPIRED	EARTHILY
ENGAGER	E NUMBER	ERODENT	EVICTOR	EXPIRER	EARTHING
EN GARDE	ENVELOP	ERODING	EVIDENT	EXPLAIN	EARTHNUT
ENGINES	ENVENOM	EROSION	EVILEST	EXPLANT	EASEMENT
ENGLAND	ENVIOUS	EROSIVE	EVIL EYE	EXPLODE	EASINESS
ENGLISH	ENVIRON	EROTEMA	EVILLER	EXPLOIT	EASTERLY
ENGORGE	ENVYING	EROTICA	EVINCED	EXPLORE	EAST SIDE
ENGRAFT	ENZYMES	ERRANCY	EVOKING	EXPORTS	EBB TIDES
ENGRAIL	EPAULET	ERRANDS	EVOLUTE	EXPOSAL	ECCLESIA
ENGRAIN	EPEEIST	ERRATIC	EVOLVED	EXPOSED	ECHELONS
ENGRAVE	EPERGNE	ERRATUM	EVOLVER	EXPOSER	ECHINATE
ENGROSS	EPICARP	ERUDITE	EWE-NECK	EXPOSES	ECHINOID
ENHANCE	EPICENE	ERUPTED	EXACTED	EXPOUND	ECLECTIC
ENIGMAS	EPICURE	ERZURUM	EXACTLY	EXPRESS	ECLIPSED

ECLIPSER	EJECTING	EMBRACED	ENCROACH	ENQUIRED
ECLIPSES	EJECTION	EMBRACER	ENCUMBER	ENQUIRER
ECLIPSIS	EJECTIVE	EMBRACES	ENCYCLIC	ENRAGING
ECLIPTIC	EKISTICS	EMBRYOID	ENDAMAGE	ENRICHED
ECLOGITE	ELAPSING	EMENDING	ENDANGER	ENRICHER
ECLOSION	ELATERID	EMERALDS	END-BLOWN	ENROLLED
ECONOMIC	ELATERIN	EMERGENT	ENDBRAIN	ENROLLEE
ECOTONAL	ELBOWING	EMERGING	ENDEARED	ENROLLER
ECOTYPIC	EL DORADO	EMERITUS	ENDEMIAL	ENSCHEDE
ECRASEUR	ELDRITCH	EMERSION	ENDEMISM	ENSCONE
ECSTATIC	ELECTING	EMIGRANT	ENDERMIC	ENSEMBLE
ECTODERM	ELECTION	EMIGRATE	END GAMES	ENSHRINE
ECTOMERE	ELECTIVE	EMIRATES	ENDOCARP	ENSHROUD
ECTOSARC	ELECTORS	EMISSARY	ENDOERM	ENSIFORM
ECUMENIC	ELECTRET	EMISSION	ENDOGAMY	ENSILAGE
EDACIOUS	ELECTRIC	EMISSIVE	ENDOGENY	ENSLAVED
EDENTATE	ELECTRON	EMITTING	ENDORSED	ENSLAVER
EDGINESS	ELECTRUM	EMOTIONS	ENDORSEE	ENSNARED
EDIFICES	ELEGANCE	EMPATHIC	ENDORSER	ENSNARER
EDITIONS	ELEMENTS	EMPERORS	ENDOSOME	ENSPHERE
EDUCABLE	ELENCHUS	EMPHASES	ENDOWING	ENSURING
EDUCATED	ELENCTIC	EMPHASIS	ENDPAPER	ENSWATHE
EDUCATOR	ELEPHANT	EMPHATIC	ENDPLATE	ENTAILED
EDUCIBLE	ELEVATED	EMPLOYED	ENDURING	ENTAILER
EDUCTION	ELEVATOR	EMPLOYEE	END USERS	ENTANGLE
EDUCTIVE	ELEVENTH	EMPLOYER	ENERGIZE	ENTELLUS
ELLGRASS	ELICITED	EMPORIUM	ENERVATE	ENTENDRE
EERINESS	ELICITOR	EMPTIEST	ENFEEBLE	ENTENTES
EFFACING	ELIDIBLE	EMPTYING	ENFILADE	ENTERING
EFFECTED	ELIGIBLE	EMPYEMIC	ENFOLDED	ENTHALPY
EFFECTOR	ELISIONS	EMPYREAL	ENFOLDER	ENTHETIC
EFFERENT	ELITISTS	EMPYREAN	ENFORCED	ENTHRONE
EFFICACY	ELKHOUND	EMULATED	ENFORCER	ENTHUSED
EFFIGIAL	ELLIPSES	EMULATOR	ENGADINE	ENTICING
EFFIGIES	ELLIPSIS	EMULSIFY	ENGAGING	ENTIRELY
EFFLUENT	ELONGATE	EMULSION	ENGENDER	ENTIRETY
EFFUSION	ELOQUENT	EMULSIVE	ENGINEER	ENTITLES
EFFUSIVE	ELYTROID	EMULSOID	ENGINERY	ENTITLED
EGESTION	EMACIATE	ENABLING	ENGRAVED	ENTODERM
EGESTIVE	EMANATED	ENACTING	ENGRAVER	ENTOMBED
EGGHEADS	EMANATOR	ENACTIVE	ENGULFED	ENTOZOIC
EGGPLANT	EMBALMED	ENACTORY	ENHANCED	ENTOZOON
EGG ROLLS	EMBALMER	ENAMELED	ENHANCER	ENTRAILS
EGGSHELL	EMBARKED	ENCAENIA	ENJOYING	ENTRANCE
EGG TIMER	EMBATTLE	ENCAMPED	ENKINDLE	ENTRANTS
EGOISTIC	EMBEDDED	ENCASING	ENLARGED	ENTREATY
EGOMANIA	EMBEZZLE	ENCIPHER	ENLARGER	ENTRENCH
EGOTISTS	EMBITTER	ENCIRCLE	ENLISTED	ENTREPOT
EGO TRIPS	EMBLAZON	ENCLAVES	ENLISTER	ENTRESOL
EGYPTIAN	EMBODIED	ENCLITIC	ENMESHED	ENTRYISM
EIGHTEEN	EMBOLDEN	ENCLOSED	ENNOBLED	ENTRYWAY
EIGHTIES	EMBOLISM	ENCLOSER	ENNOBLER	ENTWINED
EISENACH	EMBOSSED	ENCODING	ENORMITY	E NUMBERS
EITHER-OR	EMBOSSER	ENCOMIUM	ENORMOUS	ENURESIS

ENURETIC	ERASABLE	ETHERIFY	EVERYONE	EXHAUSTS
ENVELOPE	ERASURES	ETHERIZE	EVICTING	EXHIBITS
ENVIABLE	ERECTILE	ETHICIST	EVICTION	EXHORTED
ENVIABLY	ERECTING	ETHICIZE	EVIDENCE	EXHORTER
ENVIRONS	EREMITIC	ETHIOPIA	EVILDOER	EXHUMING
ENVISAGE	ERETHISM	ETHIOPIC	EVILLEST	EXIGENCY
ENVISION	ERGOTISM	ETHNARCH	EVILNESS	EXIGIBLE
ENWREATH	ERIGERON	ETHOLOGY	EVINCING	EXIGUITY
ENZOOTIC	ERRANTRY	ETHONONE	EVINCIVE	EXIGUOUS
EOLITHIC	ERUMPENT	ETHOXIDE	EVOCABLE	EXISTENT
EPAULETS	ERUPTING	ETHYLATE	EVOCATOR	EXISTING
EPHEMERA	ERUPTION	ETHYLENE	EVOLVING	EXITANCE
EPIBLAST	ERUPTIVE	ETIOLATE	EXACTING	EX LIBRIS
EPIBOLIC	ERYHEMA	ETIOLOGY	EXACTION	EXOCRINE
EPICALYX	ESCALADE	ETRUSCAN	EXALTING	EXORABLE
EPICOTYL	ESCALATE	EUCHARIS	EXACTION	EXORCISE
EPICURES	ESCALOPE	EUGENICS	EXALTING	EXORCIST
EPICYCLE	ESCAPADE	EULACHON	EXAMINED	EXORSIZE
EPIDEMIC	ESCAPEES	EULOGIES	EXAMINEE	EXORDIAL
EPIDURAL	ESCAPING	EULOGIST	EXAMINER	EXORDIUM
EPIFOCAL	ESCAPISM	EULOGIZE	EXAMPLES	EXOSPORE
EPIGRAMS	ESCAPIST	EUONYMUS	EXCAVATE	EXOTERIC
EPIGRAPH	ESCHEWAL	EUPEPSIA	EXCEEDED	EXOTOXIC
EPILEPSY	ESCHEWED	EUPEPTIC	EXCEEDER	EXOTOXIN
EPILOGUE	ESCHEWER	EUPHONIA	EXCELLED	EXPANDED
EPINASTY	ESCORTED	EUPHORIC	EXCEPTED	EXPANDER
EPIPHANY	ESCULENT	EUPHOTIC	EXCERPTS	EXPECTED
EPIPHYTE	ESKIMOAN	EUPHRASY	EXCESSES	EXPEDITE
EPISCOPE	ESKIMOID	EUPHUISM	EXCHANGE	EXPELLED
EPISODES	ESOTERIC	EUPHUIST	EXCISING	EXPELLEE
EPISODIC	ESPALIER	EUPNOEIC	EXCISION	EXPELLER
EPISTLER	ESPECIAL	EURASIAN	EXCITANT	EXPENDED
EPISTLES	ESPOUSAL	EUROCRAT	EXCITING	EXPENSES
EPISTYLE	ESPOUSED	EUROPEAN	EXCLUDED	EXPERTLY
EPITAPHS	ESPRESSO	EUROPIUM	EXCLUDER	EXPIABLE
EPITASIS	ESSAYING	EUSTATIC	EXCRETAL	EXPIATED
EPITHETS	ESSAYIST	EUTECTIC	EXCRETED	EXPIATOR
EPITOMIC	ESSENCES	EVACUANT	EXCRETER	EXPIRING
EPIZOISM	ESTANCIA	EVACUEES	EXCUSING	EXPLICIT
EPIZOITE	ESTEEMED	EVADABLE	EXECRATE	EXPLOTED
EPONYMIC	ESTERASE	EVALUATE	EXECUTOR	EXPLODER
EQUALING	ESTERIFY	EVANESCE	EXEGESES	EXPLOITS
EQUALITY	ESTHETES	EVASIONS	EXEGESIS	EXPLORED
EQUALIZE	ESTIMATE	EVECTION	EXEGETIC	EXPLORER
EQUALLED	ESTONIAN	EVENINGS	EXEMPLAR	EXPONENT
EQUATING	ESTOPPEL	EVENNESS	EXEMPLUM	EXPORTED
EQUATION	ESTOVERS	EVENSONG	EXEMPTED	EXPORTER
EQUINITY	ESTRAGON	EVENTFUL	EXERCISE	EXPOSING
EQUIPAGE	ESTRANGE	EVENTIDE	EXERTING	EXPOSURE
EQUIPPED	ESURIENT	EVENTUAL	EXERTION	EXPUNGED
EQUIPPER	ETCHINGS	EVERMORE	EXERTIVE	EXPUNGER
EQUITANT	ETERNITY	EVERSION	EX GRATIA	EXTENDED
EQUITIES	ETERNIZE	EVERYDAY	EXHALANT	EXTENDER
ERADIATE	ETHEREAL	EVERYMAN	EXHALING	EXTENSOR

EXTERIOR	EBULLIENT	EIGHTFOLD	EMBOWMENT	ENCHANTER
EXTERNAL	ECCENTRIC	EJACULATE	EMBRACOR	ENCHILADA
EXTOLLED	ECHOLALIA	ELABORATE	EMBRACERY	ENCHORIAL
EXTOLLER	ECHOLALIC	EL ALAMEIN	EMBRACING	ENCIRCLED
EXTORTED	ECLAMPSIA	ELASTOMER	EMBRASURE	ENCLOSING
EXTORTER	ECLAMPTIC	ELATERIUM	EMBROCATE	ENCLOSURE
EXTRACTS	ECLIPSING	ELBOWROOM	EMBROIDER	ENCOMIAST
EXTRADOS	ECOLOGIST	ELDERSHIP	EMBROILED	ENCOMIUMS
EXTREMES	E-COMMERCE	ELECTRONS	EMBROILER	ENCOMPASS
EXTRORSE	ECONOMICS	ELECTUARY	EMBRYONIC	ENCOUNTER
EXTRUDED	ECONOMIES	ELEGANTLY	EMENDABLE	ENCOURAGE
EXULTANT	ECONOMIST	ELEMENTAL	EMENDATOR	ENCRINITE
EXULTING	ECONOMIZE	ELEPHANTS	EMERGENCE	ENCRUSTED
EXUVIATE	ECOSPHERE	ELEVATING	EMERGENCY	ENDAMOEBA
EYEBALLS	ECOSYSTEM	ELEVATION	EMIGRANTS	ENDEARING
EYEBROWS	ECSTATIES	ELEVATORS	EMIGRATED	ENDEAVOUR
EYEGLASS	ECSTATICS	ELEVENSES	EMINENCES	ENDLESSLY
EYELINER	ECTOBLAST	ELEVENTHS	EMINENTLY	ENDOBLAST
EYE PIECE	ECTOMERIC	ELICITING	EMISSIONS	ENDOCRINE
EYESHADE	ECTOMORPH	ELIMINANT	EMMENTHAL	ENDOERGIC
EYESIGHT	ECTOPHYTE	ELIMINATE	EMMOLIENT	ENDOLYMPH
EYESORES	ECTOPLASM	ELLESMERE	EMOLUMENT	ENDOMORPH
EYESTALK	EDDYSTONE	ELLIPSOID	EMOTIONAL	ENDOPHYTE
EYETEETH	EDELWEISS	ELOCUTION	EMOTIVELY	ENDOPLASM
EYETOOTH	EDIBILITY	ELONGATED	EMOTIVISM	ENDORSING
	EDIFICIAL	ELOPEMENT	EMPANELLED	ENDOSCOPE
	EDINBURGH	ELOQUENCE	EMPATHIZE	ENDOSCOPY
9 LETTERS	EDITORIAL	ELSEWHERE	EMPENNAGE	ENDOSPERM
EACH OTHER	EDUCATING	ELUCIDATE	EMPHASIZE	ENDOSPORE
EAGERNESS	EDUCATION	ELUSIVELY	EMPHYSEMA	ENDOSTEAL
EAGLE-EYED	EDUCATIVE	ELUTRIATE	EMPIRICAL	ENDOSTEUM
EAGLEWOOD	EDUCATORS	EMANCIATED	EMPLOYEES	ENDOTOXIN
EARLINESS	EDUCATORY	EMANINTING	EMPLOYERS	ENDOWMENT
EARLY BIRD	EDWARDIAN	EMANATION	EMPLOYING	ENDURABLE
EARMARKED	EFFECTING	EMANATIVE	EMPORIUMS	ENDURANCE
EARNESTLY	EFFECTIVE	EMANATORY	EMPOWERED	ENERGETIC
EARPHONES	EFFECTUAL	EMBALMERS	EMPRESSES	ENERGIZED
EARPIECES	EFFERENCE	EMBALMING	EMPTIABLE	ENERGIZER
EARTHIEST	EFFICIENT	EMBARGOED	EMPTINESS	ENERGUMEN
EARTHLIER	EFFLUENCE	EMBARGOES	EMPYREUMA	ENERVATED
EARTHLING	EFFLUENTS	EMBARKING	EMULATING	ENERVATOR
EARTHRISE	EFFLUVIAL	EMBARRASS	EMULATION	EN FAMILLE
EARTHSTAR	EFFLUVIUM	EMBASSIES	EMULATIVE	ENFEEBLED
EARTHWARD	EFFORTFUL	EMBATTLED	EMULSIONS	ENFEEBLER
EARTHWORK	EFFULGENT	EMBAYMENT	EMUNCTORY	ENFILADED
EARHWORM	EFFUSIONS	EMBEDDING	ENACTMENT	ENFILADES
EASTBOUND	EGGPLANTS	EMBEDMENT	ENAMELING	ENFOLDING
EAST ENDER	EGGSHELLS	EMBELLISH	ENAMELLED	ENFORCING
EASTER EGG	EGG TIMERS	EMBEZZLED	ENAMELLER	ENGINEERS
EASTWARDS	EGOMANIAC	EMBEZZLER	EMAMOURED	ENGLACIAL
EASY CHAIR	EGOTISTIC	EMBODYING	ENCAMPING	ENGRAMMIC
EASYGOING	EGREGIOUS	EMBOLISMS	ENCAUSTIC	ENGRAVERS
EASYTERMS	EGYPTIANS	EMBOSOMED	ENCHAINED	ENGRAVING
EAVESDROP	EIDERDOWN	EMBOSSING	ENCHANTED	ENGROSSED

ENGROSSER	ENTRAPPED	EPITHETIC	ESPLANADE	EUTHERIAN
ENGULFING	ENTRAPPER	EPITOMIST	ESPOUSALS	EUTROPHIC
ENHANCING	ENTREATED	EPITOMIZE	ESPOUSINGS	EVACUATED
ENHANTIVE	ENTRECOTE	EPIZOOTIC	ESPRESSOS	EVACUATOR
ENIGMATIC	ENTREMETS	EPONYMOUS	ESSAYISTS	EVADINGLY
ENJOINING	ENTRE NOUS	EQUAL-AREA	ESSENTIAL	EVAGINATE
ENJOYABLE	ENTRUSTED	EQUALIZED	ESTABLISH	EVALUATED
ENJOYABLY	ENTRYWAYS	EQUALIZER	ESTAMINET	EVALUATOR
ENJOYMENT	ENTWINING	EQUALLING	ESTATE CAR	EVAPORATE
ENKINDLER	ENUCLEATE	EQUATABLE	ESTEEMING	EVAPORITE
ENLARGING	ENUMERATE	EQUATIONS	ESTHETICS	EVASIVELY
ENLIGHTEN	ENUNCIATE	EQUERRIES	ESTIMABLE	EVENTUATE
ENLISTING	ENVELOPED	EQUINOXES	ESTIMATED	EVERGREEN
ENLIVENED	ENVELOPES	EQUIPMENT	ESTIMATES	EVERSLIDE
ENLIVENER	ENVIOUSLY	EQUIPOISE	ESTIMATOR	EVERYBODY
ENMESHING	ENVISAGED	EQUIPPING	ESTOPPAGE	EVICTIONS
ENNOBLING	ENVYINGLY	EQUISETUM	ESTRANGED	EVIDENTLY
EN PASSANT	ENZYMATIC	EQUITABLE	ESTRANGER	EVILDOERS
ENQUIRIES	ENPARCHIAL	EQUITABLY	ESTUARIAL	EVILDOING
ENQUIRING	EPHEDRINE	EQUIVOCAL	ESTUARIES	EVINCIBLE
ENRAGEDLY	EPHEMERAL	EQUIVOQUE	ESTUARINE	EVOCATION
EN RAPPORT	EPHEMERID	ERADICANT	ESURIENCE	EVOLVABLE
ENRAPTURE	EPHEMERIS	ERADICATE	ETCETERAS	EXACTABLE
ENRICHING	EPHEMERON	ERECTABLE	ETERNALLY	EXACTNESS
ENROLLING	EPICENISM	ERECTIONS	ETHIOPIAN	EXALTEDLY
ENROLMENT	EPICENTRE	ERECTNESS	ETHMODIAL	EXAMINERS
ENSCONCED	EPICRISIS	EREMITISM	ETHNARCHY	EXAMINING
ENSEMBLES	EPICRITIC	ERGOGRAPH	ETHNOGENY	EXANIMATE
ENSHRINED	EPICUREAN	ERGOMETER	ETHNOLOGY	EXANTHEMA
ENSLAVING	EPICURISM	ERGONOMIC	ETHNOLOGIC	EXCALIBUR
ENSNARING	EPICYCLIC	ERISTICAL	ETHYLENIC	EXCAUDATE
ENSTATITE	EPIDEMICS	EROGENOUS	ETIOLATED	EXCAVATED
ENSUINGLY	EPIDERMAL	EROSIONAL	ETIQUETTE	EXCAVATOR
ENTAILING	EPIDERMIS	EROTICISM	ETRAMETER	EXCEEDING
ENTAMOEBA	EPIDURALS	ERRONEOUS	ETYMOLOGY	EXCELLENT
ENTANGLED	EPIGENOUS	ERSTWHILE	EUCHARIST	EXCELLING
ENTANGLER	EPIGRAPHY	ERUDITELY	EUCLIDEAN	EXCELSIOR
ENTELECHY	EPIGYNOUS	ERUDITION	EUDEMONIA	EXCEPTING
ENTENDRES	EPILEPTIC	ERUPTIBLE	EUDEMONIC	EXCEPTION
ENTERABLE	EPILOGIST	ERUPTIONS	EULOGISTS	EXCEPTIVE
ETERNALLY	EPILOGUES	ERYTHRISM	EULOGIZED	EXCERPTER
ENTERITIS	EPIMYSIUM	ERYTHRITE	EUPHEMISM	EXCESSIVE
ENTERTAIN	EPINASTIC	ESCALADER	EUPHEMIST	EXCHANGED
ENTHRONED	EPIPHANIC	ESCALATED	EUPHEMIZE	EXCHANGER
ENTHUSING	EPIPHRAGM	ESCALATOR	EUPHONIUM	EXCHANGES
ENTHYMEME	EPIPHYSIS	ESCALOPES	EUPHONIZE	EXCHEQUER
ENTITLING	EPIPHYTIC	ESCAPABLE	EUPHORBIA	EXCIPIENT
ENTOBLAST	EPIROGENY	ESCAPADES	EUPHRATES	EXCISABLE
ENTOMBING	EPISCOPAL	ESCAPISTS	EUPLASTIC	EXCISEMAN
ENTOPHYTE	EPISTASIS	ESCHEWING	EURHYTHMY	EXCISIONS
ENTOURAGE	EPISPAXIS	ESCORTING	EUROCRATS	EXCITABLE
ENTRAINED	EPISTEMIC	ESOPHAGUS	EUROSPORT	EXCITEDLY
ENTRANCED	EPITAPHIC	ESPERANTO	EUTHENICS	EXCLAIMED
ENTRANCES	EPITAXIAL	ESPIONAGE	EUTHENIST	EXCLAIMER

EXCLUDING	EXOSPHERE	EXSTROPHY	EARTHWARDS
EXCLUSIVE	EXOSTOSIS	EXTEMPORE	EARTHWORKS
EXCORIATE	EXOTICISM	EXTENDING	EARTHWORMS
EXCREMENT	EXPANDING	EXTENSION	EAR TRUMPET
EXCRETING	EXPANSILE	EXTENSITY	EAST ANGLIA
EXCRETION	EXPANSION	EXTENSIVE	EAST BERLIN
EXCRETIVE	EXPANSIVE	EXTENUATE	EAST ENDERS
EXCRATORY	EXPATIATE	EXTERIORS	EASTER EGGS
EXCULPATE	EXPECTANT	EXTERNALS	EASTERNERS
EXCURRENT	EXPECTING	EXTIRPATE	EASTERTIDE
EXCURSION	EXPEDIENT	EXTOLLING	EAST INDIAN
EXCURSIVE	EXPEDITED	EXTOLLMENT	EAST INDIES
EXCUSABLE	EXPEDITER	EXTORTING	EASTWARDLY
EXCUSABLY	EXPELLANT	EXTORTION	EASY CHAIRS
EXECRABLE	EXPELLING	EXTORTIVE	EASY STREET
EXECRABLY	EXPENDING	EXTRABOLD	EASY VIRTUE
EXECRATED	EXPENSIVE	EXTRACTED	EBULLIENCE
EXECUTANT	EXPERTISE	EXTRACTOR	EBULLITION
EXECUTING	EXPIATING	EXTRADITE	EBURNATION
EXECUTION	EXPIATION	EXTRAVERT	ECCENTRICS
EXECUTIVE	EXPIATORY	EXTREMELY	ECCHYMOSIS
EXECUTORS	EXPLAINED	EXTREMISM	ECHINODERM
EXECUTORY	EXPLAINER	EXTREMIST	ECHOPRAXIA
EXECUTRIX	EXPLETIVE	EXTREMITY	ECOLOGICAL
EXEGETICS	EXPLICATE	EXTRICATE	ECOLOGISTS
EXEMPLARY	EXPLODNG	EXTRINSIC	ECONOMICAL
EXEMPLIFY	EXPLOITED	EXTROVERT	ECONOMISTS
EXEMPTING	EXPLOITER	EXTRUDING	ECONOMIZED
EXEMPTION	EXPLORERS	EXTRUSION	ECONOMIZER
EXEQUATUR	EXPLORING	EXTRUSIVE	ECOSPECIES
EXERCISED	EXPLOSION	EXUBERANT	ECOSYSTEMS
EXERCISER	EXPLOSIVE	EXUBERATE	ECTODERMAL
EXERCISES	EXPONENTS	EXUDITION	ECTOENZYME
EXERTIONS	EXPONIBLE	EXUDATION	ECTOGENOUS
EXFOLIATE	EXPORTERS	EXUDATIVE	ECTOMORPHY
EXHALABLE	EXPORTING	EYEBALLED	ECUADORIAN
EXHAUSTED	EXPOSABLE	EYEBRIGHT	ECUMENICAL
EXHAUSTER	EXPOSITOR	EYELASHES	ECZEMATOUS
EXHIBITED	EXPOSURES	EYELETEER	EDENTULOUS
EXHIBITOR	EXPOUNDED	EYE-OPENER	EDIFYINGLY
EXHORTING	EXPOUNDER	EYE PIECES	EDITORIALS
EXISTENCE	EXPRESSED	EYE SHADOW	EDITORSHIP
EXODONTIA	EXPRESSER	EYE STRAIN	EDULCORATE
EXOENZYME	EXPRESSES		EDWARDIANS
EX OFFICIO	EXPRESSLY		EFFACEABLE
EXOGAMOUS	EXPULSION	**10 LETTERS**	EFFACEMENT
EXOGENOUS	EXPULSIVE	EARLY BIRDS	EFFECTIBLE
EXONERATE	EXPUNGING	EARMARKING	EFFECTUATE
EXORCISER	EXPURGATE	EARTHBOUND	EFFEMINACY
EXORCISMS	EXQUISITE	EARTHINESS	EFFEMINATE
EXORCISTS	EXSECTION	EARTHLIGHT	EFFERVESCE
EXORSIZED	EXSERTILE	EARTHLINGS	EFFETENESS
EXOSMOSIS	EXSERTION	EARTHQUAKE	EFFECIENCY
EXOSMOTIC	EXSICCATE	EARTHSHINE	EFFLORESCE

EFFORTLESS	ENBARKMENT	ENCASHABLE	ENFLEURAGE
EFFRONTERY	EMBEZZLERS	ENCASHMENT	ENFOLDMENT
EFFULGENCE	EMBEZZLING	ENCEPHALIC	ENFORCEDLY
EFFUSIVELY	EMBITTERED	ENCEPHALON	ENGAGEMENT
EGOCENTRIC	EMBITTERER	ENCHAINING	ENGAGINGLY
EGYPTOLOGY	EMBLAZONED	ENCHANTERS	ENGENDERED
EIDERDOWNS	EMBLAZONRY	ENCHANTING	ENGENDERER
EIGHTEENTH	EMBLEMATIC	ENCHILADAS	ENGINEERED
EIGHTH NOTE	EMBLEMENTS	ENCIPHERER	ENGLISHMAN
EIGHTIETHS	EMBODIMENT	ENCIRCLING	ENGLISHMEN
EISTEDDFOD	EMBOLDMENT	ENCLOSABLE	ENGRAVINGS
EJACULATED	EMBOLISMIC	ENCLOSURES	ENGROSSING
EJACULATOR	EMBONPOINT	ENCODEMENT	ENGULFMENT
ELABORATED	EMBOSSMENT	ENCOUNTERS	ENHARMONIC
ELABORATOR	EMBOUCHURE	ENCOURAGED	ENJAMBMENT
ELAEOPTENE	EMBRASURED	ENCOURAGER	ENJOINMENT
ELASTICITY	EMBRASURES	ENCROACHED	ENJOYMENTS
ELASTICIZE	EMBRECTOMY	ENCROACHER	ENLACEMENT
ELATEDNESS	EMBROIDERY	ENCRUSTANT	ENLISTMENT
ELDERBERRY	EMBROILING	ENCUMBERED	ENLIVENING
ELEATICISM	EMBRYOGENY	ENCYCLICAL	ENORMITIES
ELECAMPANE	EMBRYOLOGY	ENCYSTMENT	ENORMOUSLY
ELECTIVITY	EMENDATION	ENDANGERED	ENPHYTOTIC
ELECTORATE	EMENDATORY	ENDEARMENT	ENRAGEMENT
ELECTRICAL	EMETICALLY	ENDEAVOURS	ENRAPTURED
ELECTRODES	EMIGRATING	ENDOCARPAL	ENRICHMENT
ELECTROJET	EMIGRATION	ENDOCRINAL	ENROLMENTS
ELECTRONIC	EMIGRATIVE	ENDOCRINIC	ENSANGUINE
ELEMENTARY	EMISSARIES	ENDODERMAL	ENSCONCING
ELEVATIONS	EMISSIVITY	ENDODERMIC	ENSHRINING
ELEVEN-PLUS	EMMENTALER	ENDODERMIS	ENSHROUDED
ELICITABLE	EMMETROPIA	ENDODONTIA	ENTAILMENT
ELIMINABLE	EMOLLIENCE	ENDODONTIC	ENTANGLING
ELIMINATED	EMOLLIENTS	ENDOENZYME	ENTEROTOMY
ELIMINATOR	EMOLUMENTS	ENDOGAMOUS	ENTERPRISE
ELLIPTICAL	EMPALEMENT	ENDOGENOUS	ENTHRALLED
ELONGATED	EMPANELING	ENDOMORPHY	ENTHRALLER
ELONGATION	EMPANELLED	ENDOPHYTIC	ENTHRONING
ELONGATIVE	EMPHASIZED	ENDORSABLE	ENTHUSIASM
ELOPEMENTS	EMIPIRICISM	ENDOSCOPIC	ENTHUSIAST
ELOQUENTLY	EMPIRICIST	ENDOSMOSIS	ENTICEMENT
EL SALVADOR	EMPLOYABLE	ENDOSMOTIC	ENTICINGLY
ELUCIDATED	EMPLOYMENT	ENDOSTOSIS	ENTIRENESS
ELUCIDATOR	EMPOWERING	ENDOWMENTS	ENTODERMAL
ELUTRIATOR	EMULSIFIED	END PRODUCT	ENTOMBMENT
ELUVIATION	EMULSIFIER	ENDURINGLY	ENTOMOLOGY
EMACIATION	EMULSIONED	ENERGETICS	ENTOPHYTIC
EMANATIONS	ENACTMENTS	ENERGIZING	ENTOURAGES
EMANCIPATE	EMANELLING	ENERVATING	ENTRAINING
EMARGINATE	ENAMELLIST	ENERVATION	ENTRANCING
EMASCULATE	ENAMELWARE	ENERVATIVE	ENTRAPMENT
EMBALMMENT	ENAMELWORK	ENFACEMENT	ENTRAPPING
EMBANKMENT	ENCAMPMENT	ENFEEBLING	ENTREATIES
EMBARGOING	ENCASEMENT	ENFILADING	ENTREATING

ENTRENCHED	EQUANIMITY	ETERNALITY	EVECTIONAL
ENTRENCHER	EQUANIMOUS	ETERNALIZE	EVEN-HANDED
ENTRUSTING	EQUATIONAL	ETHANEDIOL	EVENTFULLY
ENUCLEATOR	EQUATORIAL	ETHEREALLY	EVENTUALLY
ENUMERATED	EQUESTRIAN	ETHNICALLY	EVERGLADES
ENUMERATOR	EQUIPOTENT	ETHNOGENIC	EVERGREENS
ENUNCIABLE	EQUITATION	ETHNOLOGIC	EVERYTHING
ENUNCIATED	EQUIVALENT	ETHNOLOGIST	EVERYWHERE
ENUNCIATOR	EQUIVOCATE	ETHYLATION	EVIDENTIAL
ENVELOPING	ERADIATION	ETIOLATION	EVIL-MINDED
ENVISAGING	ERADICABLE	EUBACTERIA	EVISCERATE
ENZYMOLOGY	ERADICATED	EUCALYTOL	EVOCATIONS
EOSINOPHIL	ERADICATOR	EUCALYTUS	EVOLVEMENT
EPIBLASTIC	ERECTILITY	EUCHLORINE	EXACERBATE
EPICANTHUS	ERETHISMIC	EUDEMONICS	EXACTINGLY
EPICARDIAC	ERGONOMICS	EUDEMONISM	EXACTITUDE
EPICARDIUM	ERGOSTEROL	EUDIOMETER	EXAGGERATE
EPICENTRAL	ERICACEOUS	EUDOIMETRY	EXALTATION
EPICENTRES	ERINACEOUS	EUGENECIST	EXAMINABLE
EPICUREANS	EROGENIETY	EUHEMERISM	EXASPERATE
EPICYCLOID	EROTEMATIC	EUHEMERIST	EX CATHEDRA
EPIDEICTIC	EROTICALLY	EUHEMERIZE	EXCAVATING
EPIDECIMAL	EROTOGENIC	EULOGISTIC	EXCAVATION
EPIDIDYMIS	EROTOMANIA	EULOGIZING	EXCAVATORS
EPIGASTRIC	ERRATICISM	EUPATORIUM	EXCEEDABLE
EPIGENESIS	ERUBESCENT	EUPHEMISMS	EXCELLENCE
EPIGENETIC	ERUCTATION	EUPHEMIZER	EXCELLENCY
EPIGLOTTAL	ERUCTATIVE	EUPHONIOUS	EXCEPTABLE
EPIGLOTTIS	ERUPTIONAL	EUPHONIUMS	EXCEPTIONS
EPIGRAPHER	ERUPTIVITY	EUPHORIANT	EXCHANGING
EPIGRAPHIC	ERYSIPELAS	EUPHORISTIC	EXCITATION
EPILEPTICS	ERYTHRITOL	EURHYTHMIC	EXCITATIVE
EPILEPTOID	ESCADRILLE	EUROCHEQUE	EXCITEMENT
EPIMORPHIC	ESCALATING	EUROCLYDON	EXCITINGLY
EPINEURIAL	ESCALATION	EURODOLLAR	EXCLAIMING
EPINEURIUM	ESCALATORS	EUROMARKET	EXCLUDABLE
EPIPHONEMA	ESCAPEMENT	EURYPTERID	EXCLUSIVES
EPIPHYSEAL	ESCAPOLOGY	EURYTHMICS	EXCOGITATE
EPIROGENIC	ESCARPMENT	EURYTROPIC	EXCORIATED
EPISCOPACY	ESCHAROTIC	EUSTACHIAN	EXCRESCENT
EPISIOTOMY	ESCRITOIRE	EUTHANASIA	EXCRETIONS
EPISPASTIC	ESCUTCHEON	EVACUATING	EXCRUCIATE
EPISTERNUM	ESPADRILLE	EVACUATION	EXCULPABLE
EPISTOLARY	ESPECIALLY	EVACUATIVE	EXCULPATED
EPITAPHIST	ESPLANADES	EVALUATING	EXCURSIONS
EPITHELIAL	ESSENTIALS	EVALUATION	EXCUSATORY
EPITHELIUM	ESTATE CARS	EVAULATIVE	EXECRATING
EPITOMIZED	ESTHETICAL	EVANESCENT	EXECRATION
EPITOMIZER	ESTIMATING	EVANGELISM	EXECRATIVE
EPOXY RESIN	ESTIMATION	EVANGELIST	EXECUTABLE
EPSOM SALTS	ESITIMATIVE	EVANGELIZE	EXECUTANTS
EQUIBILITY	ESTAMATORS	EVANSVILLE	EXECUTIONS
EQUALIZERS	ESTIPULATE	EVAPORABLE	EXECUTIVES
EQUALIZING	ESTRANGLING	EVAPORATED	EXEMPTIBLE

EXEMPTIONS	EXPLICATOR	**11 LETTERS**	ELASTICALLY
EXENTERATE	EXPLICITLY	EAGER BEAVER	ELASTIC BAND
EXCERCISING	EXPLOITERS	EARNESTNESS	ELASTOMERIC
EXHALATION	EXPLOITING	EARTHENWARE	ELASTOPLAST
EXHAUSTING	EXPLOSIONS	EARTHLINESS	ELBOW GREASE
EXHAUSTION	EXPLOSIVES	EARTHQUAKES	ELECTIONEER
EXHAUSTIVE	EXPORTABLE	EAR TRUMPETS	ELECTORATES
EXHIBITING	EXPOSITION	EASEFULNESS	ELECTORSHIP
EXHIBITION	EXPOSITORY	EAST ANGLICAN	ELECTRIC EYE
EXHIBITIVE	EXPOUNDING	EASTERMOST	ELECTRICIAN
EXHIBITORS	EXPRESSAGE	EATING APPLE	ELECTRICITY
EXHIBITORY	EXPRESSING	EBULLIENTLY	ELECTRIFIED
EXHILIRATE	EXPRESSION	ECCLESIARCH	ELECTRIFIER
EXHILIRATE	EXPRESSWAY	ECCRINOLOGY	ELECTROCUTE
EXHUMATION	EXPULSIONS	ECHCHYMOSED	ELECTROFORM
EXIGENCIES	EXPUNCTION	ECHOPRACTIC	ELECTROLYSE
EXIGUOUSLY	EXPUGATED	ECLECTICISM	ELECTROLYTE
EXISTENCES	EXSANGUINE	ECNOMETRIC	ELECTRONICS
EXOBIOLOGY	EXSICCATOR	ECONOMIZING	ELECTROTYPE
EXOCENTRIC	EXTENDIBLE	ECOSPECIFIC	ELEGIACALLY
EXODONTIST	EXTENSIBLE	ECTOBLASTIC	ELEPHANTINE
EXONERATED	EXTENSIONS	ECTOGENESIS	ELEPHANTOID
EXONERATOR	EXTENUATED	ECTOMORPHIC	ELICITATION
EXORBITANT	EXTENUATOR	ECTOPLASMIC	ELIGIBILITY
EXCORCIZING	EXTERNALLY	ECTOSARCOUS	ELIMINATING
EXOSPOROUS	EXTINCTION	EDAPHICALLY	ELIMINATION
EXOTHERMIC	EXTINCTIVE	EDIFICATION	ELIMINATIVE
EXOTICALLY	EXTINGUISH	EDITORIALLY	ELIZABETHAN
EXOTICNESS	EXTIRPATED	EDUCABILITY	ELLIPSOIDAL
EXPANDBALE	EXTIRPATOR	EDUCATIONAL	ELLIPTICITY
EXPANSIBLE	EXTORTIONS	EFFECTIVELY	ELONGATIONS
EXPANSIONS	EXTRACTING	EFFECTUALLY	ELUCIDATING
EXPATRIATED	EXTRACTION	EFFECTUATED	ELUCIDATION
EXPATRIATOR	EXTRACTIVE	EFFERVESCED	ELUCIDATIVE
EXPATRIATE	EXTRACTORS	EFFICACIOUS	ELUCIDATORY
EXPECTABLE	EXTRADITED	EFFICIENTLY	ELUSIVENESS
EXPECTANCY	EXTRAMURAL	EGALITARIAN	ELUTRIATION
EXPEDIENCE	EXTRANEOUS	EGOCENTRISM	EMANATIONAL
EXPEDIENCY	EXTRAVERTS	EGOMANIACAL	EMANCIPATED
EXPEDIENTS	EXTRICABLE	EGOTISTICAL	EMANCIPATOR
EXPEDITING	EXTRICATED	EGREGIOUSLY	EMASCULATED
EXPEDITION	EXTROVERTS	EIFFEL TOWER	EMASCULATOR
EXPELLABLE	EXTRUSIONS	EIGHTEENTHS	EMBANKMENTS
EXPENDABLE	EXUBERENCE	EINSTEINIAN	EMBARKATION
EXPERIENCE	EXULTANTLY	EINSTEINIUM	EMBARRASSED
EXPERIMENT	EXULTATION	EJACULATING	EMBELLISHED
EXPERTNESS	EXULTINGLY	EJACULATION	EMBELLISHER
EXPIRATION	EYEBALLING	EJACULATIVE	EMBITTERING
EXPIRATORY	EYE-CATCHER	EJACULATORY	EMBLAZONING
EXPLAINING	EYEDROPPER	EJECTOR SEAT	EMBLEMATIZE
EXPLETIVES	EYEGLASSES	ELABORATELY	EMBOLDENING
EXPLICABLE	EYE-OPENERS	ELABORATING	EMBOLECTOMY
EXPLICABLY	EYE SHADOWS	ELABORATION	EMBRACEABLE
EXPLICATED	EYEWITNESS	ELABORATIVE	EMBRACEMENT

EMBRACATION	ENDOCENTRIC	ENTHRALLING	EROTOMANIAC
EMBROIDERED	ENDOCRANIUM	ENTHRALMENT	ERRATICALLY
EMBROIDERER	ENDOCRINOUS	ENTHUSIASMS	ERRONEOUSLY
EMBROILMENT	ENDODONTICS	ENTHUSIASTS	ERUBESCENCE
EMBRYECTOMY	ENDODONTIST	ENTICEMENTS	ERUCTATIONS
EMBRYOGENIC	ENDOMETRIAL	ENTITLEMENT	ERYSIPELOID
EMENDATIONS	ENDOMETRIUM	ENTOBLASTIC	ERYTHEMATIC
EMERGENCIES	ENDOMORPHIC	ENTOMBMENTS	ERYTHRISMAL
EMIGRATIONS	ENDONEURIUM	ENTOMOPHILY	ERYTHROCYTE
EMMENAGOGIC	ENDOPLASMIC	ENTRAINMENT	ESCAPEMENTS
EMMENAGOGUE	ENDORSEMENT	ENTREATMENT	ESCHATOLOGY
EMOTIONALLY	ENDOSCOPIST	ENTRENCHING	ESCUTCHEONS
EMOTIONLESS	ENDOSPERMIC	ENTRUSTMENT	ESEMPLASTIC
EMOTIVENESS	ENDOSPOROUS	ENTWINEMENT	ESOPHAGUSES
EMPANELLING	ENDOTHECIAL	ENUCLEATION	ESOTERICISM
EMPANELMENT	ENDOTHECIUM	ENUMERATING	ESSENTIALLY
EMPERORSHIP	ENDOTHERMIC	ENUMERATION	ESTABLISHED
EMPHASIZING	END PRODUCTS	ENUNCIATIVE	ESTABLISHER
EMPIRICALLY	ENFORCEABLE	ENVELOPMENT	ESTATE AGENT
EMPLACEMENTS	ENFORCEMENT	ENVIOUSNESS	ETHANEDURA
EMPLOYMENTS	ENFRANCHISE	ENVIRONMENT	ETHANEDIOIC
EMPOWERMENT	ENGAGEMENTS	ENZYMOLYSIS	ETHEREALITY
EMPTY-HENDED	ENGENDERING	ENZYMOLYTIC	ETHEREALIZE
EMPTY-HEADED	ENGINEERING	EPHEMERALLY	ETHICALNESS
EMULOUSNESS	ENGLISH HORN	EPIDERMISES	ETHNOBOTONY
EMULSIFYING	ENGORGEMENT	EPIDIASCOPE	ETHNOGENIST
EMULSIONING	ENGRAILMENT	EPIGASTRIUM	ETIOLOGICAL
ENARTHROSIS	ENGROSSEDLY	EPIGENESIST	ETYMOLOGIES
ENCAPSULATE	ENGROSSMENT	EPIGRAPHIST	ETYMOLOGIST
ENCEPHALOMA	ENHANCEMENT	EPIPHYTOTIC	EUCHARISTIC
ENCEPHALOUS	ENLARGEABLE	EPITHALAMIC	EUCHROMATIC
ENCHAINMENT	ENLARGEMENT	EPITHELIOMA	EUCHROMATIN
ENCHANTMENT	ENLIGHTENED	EPITOMIZING	EUDIOMETRIC
ENCHANTRESS	ENLIGHTENER	EPOCH-MAKING	EUGENICALLY
ENCHONDROMA	ENLISTED MAN	EQUIANGULAR	EUPHEMISTIC
ENCOMIASTIC	ENLISTED MEN	EQUIDISTANT	EURHYTHMICS
ENCOMPASSED	ENLISTMENTS	EQUILATERAL	EUROCHEQUES
ENCOUNTERED	ENLIVENMENT	EQUILIBRANT	EURODOLLARS
ENCOUNTERER	ENNEAHEDRAL	EQUILIBRIST	EUROPEANISM
ENCOURAGING	ENNEAHEDRON	EQUILIBRIUM	EUROPEANIZE
ENCROACHING	ENNISKILLEN	EQUINOCTIAL	EURYTHERMAL
ENCUMBERING	ENNOBLEMENT	EQUIPOLLENT	EVACUATIONS
ENCUMBRANCE	ENNOBLINGLY	EQUIVALENCE	EVAGINATION
ENCYCLICALS	ENRAPTURING	EQUIVALENCY	EVALUATIONS
ENDANGERING	ENSHROUDING	EQUIVALENTS	EVANESCENCE
ENDEARINGLY	ENSLAVEMENT	EQUIVOCALLY	EVANGELICAL
ENDEARMENTS	ENTABLATURE	EQUIVOCATED	EVANGELISTS
ENDEAVOURED	ENTABLEMENT	ERADICATING	EVANGELIZED
ENDEAVOURER	ENTEROSTOMY	ERADICATION	EVANGELIZER
ENDEMICALLY	ENTEROVIRUS	ERADICATIVE	EVAPORATING
ENDLESSNESS	ENTERPRISER	ERADICATORS	EVAPORATION
ENDOBLASTIC	ENTERPRISES	ERASTIANISM	EVAPORATIVE
ENDOCARDIAL	ENTERTAINED	ERGATOCRACY	EVASIVENESS
ENDOCARDIUM	ENTERTAINER	EROSIVENESS	EVENING STAR

EVENTUALITY
EVENTUATION
EVERLASTING
EVISCERATED
EVISCERATOR
EXACERBATED
EXAGGERATED
EXAGGERATOR
EXALTEDNESS
EXAMINATION
EXANIMATION
EXASPERATED
EXASPERATER
EXCAVATIONS
EXCEEDINGLY
EXCELLENTLY
EXCEPTIONAL
EXCERPTIBLE
EXCERPTTION
EXCESSIVELY
EXCITEDNESS
EXCITEMENTS
EXCLAMATION
EXCLAMATORY
EXCLUSIVELY
EXCOGITATOR
EXCORIATING
EXCORIATION
EXCULPATORY
EX-DIRECTORY
EXECRATIONS
EXECUTIONER
EXECUTORIAL
EXEMPLARILY
EXEMPLIFIED
EXEMPLIFIER
EXERCISABLE
EXFOLIATION
EXFOLIATIVE
EXHAUSTABLE
EXHIBITIONS
EXHILARATED
EXHILARATOR
EXHORTATION
EXHORTATIVE
EXHUMATIONS
EXISTENSIAL
EXONERATING
EXONERATION
EXONERATIVE
EXORABILITY
EXORBITANCE
EXOSKELETAL
EXOSKELETON

EXOTERICISM
EXPANSIVELY
EXPATIATING
EXPATIATION
EXPATRIATED
EXPATRIATES
EXPECTANTLY
EXPECTATION
EXPECTATIVE
EXPECTORANT
EXPECTORATE
EXPEDIENTLY
EXPEDITIONS
EXPEDITIOUS
EXPENDITURE
EXPENSIVELY
EXPERIENCED
EXPERIENCES
EXPERIMENTS
EXPLAINABLE
EXPLANATION
EXPLANATORY
EXPLOSIVELY
EXPONENTIAL
EXPORTATION
EXPOSEDNESS
EXPOSITIONS
EXPOSTULATE
EXPRESSIBLE
EXPRESSIONS
EXPRESSWAYS
EXPROPRIATE
EXPURGATING
EXPURGATION
EXPURGATORY
EXQUISITELY
EXSICCATION
EXSICCATIVE
EXSTIPULATE
EXPEMPORIZE
EXTENSIONAL
EXTENSIVELY
EXTENUATING
EXTENUATION
EXTENUATORY
EXTERIORIZE
EXTERMINATE
EXTERNALISM
EXTERNALIST
EXTERNALITY
EXTERNALIZE
EXTIRPATING
EXTIRPATION
EXTIRPATICVE

EXTOLLINGLY
EXTRACTABLE
EXTRACTIONS
EXTRADITING
EXTRADITION
EXTRAPOLATE
EXTRAVAGANT
EXTRAVAGATE
EXTRAVASATE
EXTREMENESS
EXTREMITIES
EXTRICATING
EXTRICATION
EXTROVERTED
EXUBERANTLY
EYE-CATCHING

12 LETTERS
EAGER BEAVERS
EARSPLITTING
EARTH SHAKING
EAST BERLINER
EAST GERMANIC
EATING APPLES
EAU DE COLOGNE
EAVESDROPPED
EAVESDROPPER
EBULLIOSCOPY
ECCENTRICITY
ECCLESIASTIC
ECCLESIOLOGY
ECHINOCOCCUS
ECHINODERMAL
ECHOLOCATION
ECLECTICALLY
ECLIPTICALLY
ECOLOGICALLY
ECONOMETRICS
ECONOMICALLY
ECTOPARASITE
ECUMENICALLY
EDACIOUSNESS
EDITORIALIST
EDITORIALIZE
EDULCORATION
EFFECTUALITY
EFFECTUATING
EFFECTUATION
EFFEMINATELY
EFFERVESCENT
EFFERVESCING
EFFLORESCENT
EFFORTLESSLY

EFFUSIVENESS
EGOISTICALLY
EGYPTOLOGIST
EJACULATIONS
EJECTOR SEATS
ELABORATIONS
ELASTICATION
ELASTIC BANDS
ELECTRICALLY
ELECTRIC EYES
ELECTRICIANS
ELECTRIFYING
ELECTROCUTED
ELECTROGRAPH
ELECTROLYSER
ELECTROLYSIS
ELECTROLYTES
ELECTROLYTIC
ELECTROMETER
ELECTROMETRY
ELECTRONVOLT
ELECTROPHONE
ELECTROPLATE
ELECTROSCOPE
ELECTROSHOCK
ELECTROTONIC
ELECTROTONUS
ELEVENTH HOUR
ELIZABETHANS
ELLIPTICALLY
ELOCUTIONARY
ELOCUTIONIST
ELOQUENTNESS
EMANCIPATING
EMANCIPATION
EMANCIPATIVE
EMANCIPATORY
EMARGINATION
EMASCULATING
EMASCULATION
EMASCULATIVE
EMBARKATIONS
EMBARRASSING
EMBELLISHING
EMBEZZLEMENT
EMBITTERMENT
EMBLAZONMENT
EMBRANCHMENT
EMBROCATIONS
EMBROIDERIES
EMBROIDERING
EMBRYOLOGIST
EMIGRATIONAL
EMOTIONALISM

EMOTIONALIST	ENTANGLEMENT	ESCUTCHEONED	EXCRESCENCES
EMOTIONALITY	ENTERKINASE	ESOTERICALLY	EXCRUCIATING
EMOTIONALIZE	ENTERPRISING	ESSENTIALISM	EXCRUCIATION
EMPATHETICALLY	ENTERTAINERS	ESSENTIALIST	EXCURSIONIST
EMPLACEMENTS	ENTERTAINING	ESSENTIALITY	EXECUTIONERS
EMULSIFIABLE	ENTHRONEMENT	ESTABLISHING	EXECUTORSHIP
ENANTIOMORPH	ENTHUSIASTIC	ESTATE AGENCY	EXEGETICALLY
ENARTHRODIAL	ENTHYMEMATIC	ESTATE AGENTS	EXEMPLIFYING
ENCEPHALITIC	ENTICINGNESS	ESTHETICALLY	EXENTERATION
ENCEPHALITIS	ENTOMOLOGIST	ESTRANGEMENT	EXHAUSTIVELY
ENCHANTMENTS	ENTOMOLOGIZE	ETERNIZATION	EXHIBITIONER
ENCIPHERMENT	ENTRANCEMENT	ETHERIZATION	EXHILIRATING
ENCIRCLEMENT	ENTRANCINGLY	ETHNOCENTRIC	EXHILIRATION
ENCLITICALLY	ENTREATINGLY	ETHNOGRAPHER	EXHILIRATIVE
ENCOMPASSING	ENTRENCHMENT	ETHNOGRAPHIC	EXHORTATIONS
ENCOUNTERING	ENTREPRENEUR	ETHNOLOGICAL	EXIGUOUSNESS
ENCROACHMENT	ENUMERATIONS	ETHNOLOGISTS	EXOBIOLOGIST
ENCRUSTATION	ENVIABLENESS	ETHOXYETHANE	EXOPEPTIDASE
ENCUMBRANCER	ENVIRONMENTS	ETHYL ALCOHOL	EXOPHTHALMIC
ENCUMBRANCES	ENVISAGEMENT	ETYMOLOGICAL	EXOPHTHALMOS
ENCYCLOPEDIA	ENZOOTICALLY	ETYMOLOGISTS	EXORBITANTLY
ENCYCLOPEDIC	ENZYMOLOGIST	EUCALYPTUSES	EXOTERICALLY
ENDAMAGEMENT	EOSINOPHILIC	EUHEMERISTIC	EXPANSIONARY
ENDANGERMENT	ENPENCEPHALIC	EUPHONICALLY	EXPANSIONISM
ENDEAVOURING	ENPENCEPHALON	EUPHORICALLY	EXPANSIONIST
ENDOCARDITIC	EPHEMERALITY	EVANGELISTIC	EXPATRIATING
ENDOCARDITIS	EPICUREANISM	EVANGELIZING	EXPATRIATION
ENDOMORPHISM	EPICYCLOIDIAL	EVAPORIMETER	EXPECTATIONS
ENDOPARASITE	EPIDEMIOLOGY	EVENING DRESS	EXPECTORATED
ENDORSEMENTS	EPIGLOTTIDES	EVEN-TEMPERED	EXPECTORATOR
ENDOSKELETAL	EPIGLOTTISES	EVENTFULNESS	EXPEDIENTIAL
ENDOSKELETON	EPIGRAMMATIC	EVISCERATING	EXPERIENCING
ENDOTHELOID	EPIMORPHOSIS	EVISCERATION	EXPERIMENTAL
ENDOTHELIOMA	EPISCOPALISM	EVOLUTIONARY	EXPERIMENTED
ENDOTHERMISM	EPISODICALLY	EVOLUTIONISM	EXPERIMENTER
ENDURABILITY	EPISTEMOLOGY	EVOOLUTIONIST	EXPERT SYSTEM
ENERGETICIST	EPITHALAMIUM	EXACERBATING	EXPLANATIONS
ENFEEBLEMENT	EQUALITARIAN	EXACERBATION	EXPLANTATION
ENFRANCHISED	EQUALIZATION	EXACTINGNESS	EXPLICITNESS
ENFRANCHISER	EQUATABILITY	EXAGGERATING	EXPLOITATION
ENGAGINGNESS	EQUESTRIENNE	EXAGGERATION	EXPLICITNESS
ENGENDERMENT	EQUIDISTANCE	EXAGGERATIVE	EXPLOITATION
ENGINE DRIVER	EQUILIBRADOR	EXAMINATIONS	EXPLOITATIVE
ENGLISH HORNS	EQUIPOLLENCE	EXASPERATING	EXPLORATIONS
ENGLISHWOMAN	EQUVALENTLY	EXASPERATION	EXPOSITIONAL
ENGRAFTATION	EQUIVOCALITY	EXCELLENCIES	EXPOSITOROILY
ENGROSSINGLY	EQUIVOCATING	EXCHANGEABLE	EXPOSTULATED
ENHANCEMENTS	EQUIVOCATION	EXCHANGE RATE	EXPOSTULATOR
ENLARGEMENTS	EQUIVOCATORY	EXCITABILITY	EXPRESSIONAL
ENLIGHTENING	ERGASTOPLASM	EXCLAMATIONS	EXPRESSIVELY
ENLIVENINGLY	ERYTHROBLAST	EXCLUSIONARY	EXPRESSIVITY
ENORMOUSNESS	ERYTHROCYTIC	EXCOGITATION	EXPROPRIABLE
ENSHRINEMENT	ERYTHROMYCIN	EXCOGITATIVE	EXPROPRIATED
ENSILABILITY	ESCAPOLOGIST	EXCORIATIONS	EXPROPRIATOR

EXPURGATIONS
EXSANGUINITY
EX-SERVICEMAN
EX-SERVICEMEN
EXTEMPORIZED
EXTEMPORIZER
EXTENDEDNESS
EXTENSOMETER
EXTERMINABLE
EXTERMINATED
EXTERMINATOR
EXTERNALIZED
EXTEROCEPTER
EXTINGUISHED
EXTINGUISHER
EXTORTIONARY
EXTORTIONATE
EXTORTIONIST
EXTRADITIONS
EXTRAMARITAL
EXTRAMUNDANE
EXTRANEOUSLY
EXTRANUCLEAR
EXTRAPOLATED
EXTRAPOLATOR
EXTRASENSORY
EXTRAUTERINE
EXTRAVAGANCE
EXTRAVAGANZA
EXTROVERSION
EXTROVERSIVE
EYEWITNESSES

13 LETTERS
EAVESDROPPERS
EAVESDROPPING
ECCENTRICALLY
ECCLESIASTICS
ECCLESIOLATER
ECCLESIOLATRY
ECONOMIZATION
ECTOPARASITIC
ECUMENICALISM
EDITORIALIZER
EDUCATED GUESS
EFFECTIVENESS
EFFERVESCENCE
EFFERVESCIBLE
EFFICACIOUSLY
EFFLORESCENCE
EGOCENTRICITY
EGOTISTICALLY
EGREGIOUSNESS

EGYPTOLOGICAL
ELABORATENESS
ELECTIONEERER
ELECTRIC CHAIR
ELECTRIFIABLE
ELECTROCUTING
ELECTROCUTION
ELECTROGRAPHY
ELECTROMAGNET
ELECTROMERISM
ELECTROMETRIC
ELECTROMOTIVE
ELECTROPHILIC
ELECTROPHONIC
ELECTROPHORUS
ELECTROPLATER
ELECTROSCOPIC
ELECTROSTATIC
ELECTROVALENT
ELEPHANTIASIC
ELEPHANTIASIS
EMBARRASSMENT
EMBELLISHMENT
EMBRYOLOGICAL
EMBRYONICALLY
EMINENCE GRISE
EMOTIONLESSLY
EMPHYSEMATOUS
EMPIRICALNESS
EMPLOYABILITY
EMULSION PAINT
ENCAPSULATION
ENCAUSTICALLY
ENCEPHALOGRAM
ENCHANTRESSES
ENCOMPASSMENT
ENCOURAGEMENT
ENCOURAGINGLY
ENCROACHINGLY
ENCROACHMENTS
ENCULTURATION
ENCULTURATIVE
ENCUMBERINGLY
ENCYCLOPEDIAS
ENCYCLOPEDISM
ENCYCLOPEDIST
ENDOCRINOLOGY
ENDODONTOLOGY
ENDOLYMPHATIC
ENDOMETRIOSIS
ENDOPARASITIC
ENDOPEPTIDASE
ENERGETICALLY
ENFRANCHISING

ENGINE DRIVERS
ENIGMATICALLY
ENLIGHTENMENT
ENROLLED NURSE
ENTANGLEMENTS
ENTERTAINMENT
ENTHRALLINGLY
ENTHRONEMENTS
ENTOMOLOGICAL
ENTOMOLOGISTS
ENTOMOPHILOUS
ENTREPRENEURS
ENUNCIABILITY
ENVIRONMENTAL
ENZYMOLOGICAL
EPIGRAMMATISM
EPIGRAMMATIST
EPIGRAMMATIZE
EPILEPTICALLY
EPIPHENOMENAL
EPIPHENOMENON
EPIPHYTICALLY
EPISCOPALIANS
EPITOMIZATION
EPIZOOTICALLY
EQUESTRIANISM
EQUILIBRATION
EQUILIBRISTIC
EQUIMOLECULAR
EQUIPONDERANT
EQUIPONDERATE
EQUIPOTENTIAL
EQUITABLENESS
EQUIVOCATIONS
ERGONOMICALLY
ERRONEOUSNESS
ERYSIPELATOUS
ESCAPOLOGISTS
ESCHATOLOGIST
ESTABLISHMENT
ESTIMABLENESS
ESTRANGEMENTS
ETHNOCENTRISM
ETHNOGRAPHERS
ETHNOLOGICALLY
EVAPORABILITY
EVENTUALITIES
EVERLASTINGLY
EVOCATIVENESS
EXAGGERATEDLY
EXAGGERATIONS
EXAMINATIONAL
EXASPERATEDLY
EXCEPTIONABLE

EXCEPTIONALLY
EXCESSIVENESS
EXCHANGE RATES
EXCLAMATIONAL
EXCLAMATORILY
EXCLUDABILITY
EXCLUSIVENESS
EXCOMMUNICATE
EXCURSIVENESS
EXCUSABLENESS
EXECRABLENESS
EXEMPLARINESS
EXEMPLIFIABLE
EXHIBITIONISM
EXHIBITIONIST
EXPANSIBILITY
EXPANSIONISTS
EXPANSIVESNESS
EXPECTORATING
EXPECTORATION
EXPEDITIONARY
EXPEDITIOUSLY
EXPENDABILITY
EXPENSIVENESS
EXPERIMENTING
EXPERT SYSTEMS

EXPLANATORIES
EXPLANATORILY
EXPLOSIVENESS
EXPONENTIALLY
EXPORTABILITY
EXPOSTULATING
EXPOSTULATION
EXPOSTULATORY
EXPRESSIONISM
EXPRESSIONIST
EXPROPRIATING
EXPROPRIATION
EXPROPRIATORS
EXQUISITNESS
EXTEMPORARILY
EXTEMPORIZING
EXTENDIBILITY
EXTENSIBILITY
EXTENSIVENESS
EXTENUATINGLY
EXTERMINATING
EXTERMINATION
EXTERMINATIVE
EXTERMINATORS
EXTERNALIZING
EXTEROCEPTIVE

EXTERRITORIAL
EXTINGUISHANT
EXTINGUISHERS
EXTINGUISHING
EXTORTIONABLE
EXTORTIONISTS
EXTRACELLULAR
EXTRAGALACTIC
EXTRAJUDICIAL
EXTRAORDINARY
EXTRAPOLATING
EXTRAPOLATION
EXTRAPOLATIVE
EXTRAPOSITION
EXTRAVAGANCES
EXTRAVAGANTLY
EXTRAVAGANZAS
EXTRAVAGATION
EXTRAVASATION
EXTRAVASCULAR
EXTRINSICALLY
EYEBROW PENCIL
EYE-CATCHINGLY

3 LETTERS	FLUE	FACET	FELLS	FIRER	FLOSS
FAB	FLUX	FACIA	FELON	FIRES	FLOUR
FAD	FOAL	FACTS	FEMUR	FIRMS	FLOUT
FAG	FOAM	FADDY	FENCE	FIRRY	FLOWN
FAN	FOBS	FADED	FENNY	FIRST	FLUED
FAR	FOCI	FADER	FERAL	FIRTH	FLUKE
FAT	FOES	FAERY	FERIA	FISHY	FLUKY
FAX	FOGS	FAILS	FERMI	FISTS	FLUME
FAY	FOGY	FAINT	FERNS	FITCH	FLUNG
FBI	FOHN	FAIRS	FERNY	FITLY	FLUNK
FED	FOIL	FAIRY	FERRY	FIVER	FLUOR
FEE	FOLD	FAITH	FESSE	FIVES	FLUSH
FEN	FOND	FAKED	FETAL	FIXED	FLUTE
FEW	FONT	FAKER	FETCH	FIXER	FLUTY
FEY	FOOD	FAKES	FETED	FIXES	FLY-BY
FEZ	FOOL	FAKIR	FETES	FIZZY	FLYER
FIB	FOOT	FALLS	FETID	FLACH	FOALS
FIE	FOPS	FALSE	FETOR	FLAGS	FOAMY
FIG	FORA	FAMED	FETUS	FLAIL	FOCAL
FIN	FORD	FANCY	FEUDS	FLAIR	FOCUS
FIR	FORE	FANGO	FEVER	FLAKE	FOGGY
FIT	FORK	FANGS	FEZES	FLAKY	FOILS
FIX	FORM	FANNY	FIATS	FLAME	FOISM
FLU	FORT	FANON	FIBRE	FLAMY	FOIST
FLY	FOUL	FARAD	FIELD	FLANK	FOLDS
FOB	FOUR	FARCE	FIEND	FLANS	FOLIC
FOE	FOWL	FARED	FIREY	FLAPS	FOLIC
FOG	FOXY	FARER	FIFER	FLARE	FOLKS
FOP	FRAP	FARES	FIFES	FLASH	FOLLY
FOR	FRAU	FARMS	FIFTH	FLASK	FONTS
FOX	FRAY	FASTS	FIFTY	FLATS	FOODS
FRO	FREE	FATAL	FIGHT	FLAWS	FOOLS
FRY	FRET	FATED	FILAR	FLAWY	FOOTS
FUG	FROE	FATES	FILCH	FLEAM	FORAY
FUN	FROG	FATTY	FILED	FLEAS	FORCE
FUR	FROM	FAUGH	FILER	FLECK	FORDS
	FUEL	FAULT	FILES	FLEER	FORGE
	FULL	FAUNA	FILET	FLEET	FORGO
4 LETTERS	FUME	FAUNS	FILLY	FLESH	FORKS
FACE	FUND	FAVUS	FILMS	FLEWS	FORME
FACT	FUNK	FAWNS	FILMY	FLICK	FORMS
FADE	FURL	FAXED	FILTH	FLIER	FORTE
FLAX	FURS	FAZED	FILUM	FLIES	FORTH
FLAY	FURY	FEARS	FINAL	FLING	FORTS
FLEA	FUSE	FEAST	FINCH	FLINT	FORTY
FLED	FUSS	FEATS	FINDS	FLOAT	FORUM
FLEE	FUZZ	FEAZE	FINED	FLOCK	FOSSA
FLEW		FECAL	FINER	FLOES	FOSSE
FLEX		FECES	FINES	FLONG	FOULS
FLIP	**5 LETTERS**	FECIT	FINGO	FLOOD	FOUND
FLIT	FABLE	FED UP	FINIS	FLOOR	FOUNT
FLOE	FACED	FEEDS	FINNY	FLOPS	FOURS
FLOP	FACER	FEIGN	FIORD	FLORA	FOVEA
FLOW	FACES	FEINT	FIRED	FLORY	FOWLS

F

FOXED	FUSED	FANGED	FEMALE	FILIAL	FLABBY
FOXES	FUSEL	FANION	FEMORA	FILING	FLACON
FOYER	FUSES	FANJET	FEMURS	FILLED	FLAGGY
FRAIL	FUSIL	FANNED	FENCED	FILLER	FLAGON
FRAME	FUSSY	FANNER	FENCER	FILLET	FLAILS
FRANC	FUSTY	FARCES	FENCES	FILL-IN	FLAKED
FRANK	FUTON	FARINA	FENDED	FILLIP	FLAKER
FRAUD	FUZZY	FARING	FENDER	FILMED	FLAKES
FREAK	FYLDE	FARMED	FENIAN	FILMIC	FLAMBE
FREED		FARMER	FENNEC	FILOSE	FLAMED
FREER		FAR-OFF	FENNEL	FILTER	FLAMER
FREON	**6 LETTERS**	FAR-OUT	FERBAM	FILTHY	FLAMES
FRESH	FABIAN	FARROW	FERIAL	FIMBLE	FLANKS
FRETS	FABLED	FASCIA	FERMAT	FINALE	FLARED
FRIAR	FABLER	FASTED	FERRET	FINALS	FLARES
FRIED	FABLES	FASTEN	FERRIC	FINDER	FLASHY
FRIER	FABRIC	FASTER	FERULA	FINERY	FLASKS
FRIES	FACADE	FAT CAT	FERULE	FINEST	FLATLY
FRILL	FACETS	FATHER	FERVID	FINGAL	FLATUS
FRISE	FACIAL	FATHOM	FESCUE	FINGER	FLAUNT
FRISK	FACIES	FATTEN	FESTAL	FINIAL	FLAVIN
FRITT	FACILE	FATTER	FESTER	FINING	FLAWED
FRIZZ	FACING	FAUCAL	FETIAL	FINISH	FLAXEN
FROCK	FACTOR	FAUCES	FETING	FINITE	FLAYED
FROGS	FACULA	FAUCET	FETISH	FINNED	FLAYER
FROND	FADE-IN	FAULTS	FETTER	FINNIC	FLECHE
FRONS	FADING	FAULTY	FETTLE	FIORDS	FLECKS
FRONT	FAECAL	FAUNAL	FEUDAL	FIORIN	FLEDGE
FROST	FAECES	FAUNAS	FEUDED	FIPPLE	FLEECE
FROTH	FAENZA	FAVOUR	FEZZAN	FIRING	FLEECY
FROWN	FAERIE	FAWNED	FEZZED	FIRKIN	FLEETS
FROZE	FAG END	FAWNER	FEZZES	FIRMED	FLENSE
FRUIT	FAGGED	FAXING	FIANCE	FIRMER	FLESHY
FRUMP	FAGGOT	FAZING	FIASCO	FIRMLY	FLETCH
FRYER	FAILED	FEALTY	FIBBED	FIRSTS	FLEXED
FRY-UP	FAILLE	FEARED	FIBBER	FIRTHS	FLEXES
FUCUS	FAINTS	FEARER	FIBRED	FISCAL	ELEXOR
FUDGE	FAIRER	FEASTS	FIBRES	FISHED	FLICKS
FUELS	FAIRLY	FECULA	FIBRIL	FISHER	FLIERS
FUGAL	FAITHS	FECUND	FIBRIN	FISHES	FLIGHT
FUGGY	FAKERS	FEDORA	FIBULA	FISTIC	FLIMSY
FUGUE	FAKING	FEEBLE	FICKLE	FITFUL	FLINCH
FULLY	FAKIRS	FEEBLY	FIDDLE	FITTED	FLINTS
FUMED	FALCON	FEEDER	FIDDLY	FITTER	FLINTY
FUMER	FALLAL	FEELER	FIDGET	FIVERS	FLIRTS
FUMES	FALLEN	FEINTS	FIELDS	FIXATE	FLITCH
FUNDS	FALLER	FEISTY	FIENDS	FIXERS	FLOATS
FUNGI	FALLOW	FELINE	FIERCE	FIXING	FLOATY
FUNKS	FALSER	FELLED	FIESTA	FIXITY	FLOCKS
FUNKY	FALTER	FELLER	FIFTHS	FIZGIG	FLOCKY
FUNNY	FAMILY	FELLOE	FIGHTS	FIZZED	FLOODS
FURAN	FAMINE	FELLOW	FIGURE	FIZZER	FLOORS
FURRY	FAMISH	FELONS	FIJIAN	FIZZLE	FLOOZY
FURZE	FAMOUS	FELONY	FILETS	FJORDS	FLOPPY

FLORAL	FORBAD	FRESNO	FUNGAL	FAINTER	FASTING
FLORET	FORBID	FRIARS	FUNGIC	FAINTLY	FATALLY
FLORID	FORCED	FRIARY	FUNGUS	FAIREST	FATBACK
FLOSSY	FORCER	FRIDAY	FUNKED	FAIRIES	FAT CATS
FLOURY	FORFAR	FRIDGE	FUNKER	FAIRING	FATEFUL
FLOWED	FORGES	FRIEND	FUNNEL	FAIRISH	FATHEAD
FLOWER	FORGET	FRIERS	FUN RUN	FAIR SEX	FATHERS
FLUENT	FORGOT	FRIEZE	FURIES	FAIRWAY	FATIGUE
FLUFFY	FORKED	FRIGHT	FURLES	FALANGE	FATLING
FLUIDS	FORMAL	FRIGID	FURLER	FALBALA	FATNESS
FLUKES	FORMAT	FRIJOL	FURORE	FALCATE	FATTEST
FLUKEY	FORMED	FRILLS	FURRED	FALCONS	FATTIER
FLURRY	FORMER	FRILLY	FURROW	FALLACY	FATTIES
FLUTED	FORMIC	FRINGE	FUSILE	FALL GUY	FATTILY
FLUTER	FORMYL	FRINGY	FUSING	FALLING	FATTISH
FLUTES	FORNIX	FRISKS	FUSION	FALLOUT	FATTISM
FLY-BYS	FORTES	FRISKY	FUSSED	FALSELY	FATUITY
FLYERS	FORTIS	FRIULI	FUSSER	FALSEST	FATUOUS
FLYING	FORUMS	FRIVOL	FUSSES	FALSIES	FAUCETS
FLYSCH	FOSSIL	FRIZZY	FUSTIC	FALSIFY	FAULTED
FOALED	FOSTER	FROCKS	FUTILE	FALSITY	FAUVISM
FOAMED	FOUGHT	FROGGY	FUTONS	FAMILLE	FAUX PAS
FOBBED	FOULED	FROLIC	FUTURE	FAMINES	FAVOURS
FODDER	FOULER	FRONDS	FUZZED	FANATIC	FAVRILE
FOETAL	FOULLY	FRONTS		FAN BELT	FAWNING
FOETID	FOUL-UP	FROSTS		FANCIED	FEARFUL
FOETOR	FOUNTS	FROSTY	**7 LETTERS**	FANCIER	FEARING
FOETUS	FOURTH	FROTHS	FABIANS	FANCIES	FEASTED
FOGGED	FOVEAL	FROTHY	FABRICS	FANCILY	FEASTER
FOGGIA	FOWLER	FROWNS	FACADES	FANFARE	FEATHER
FOGIES	FOXIER	FROWSY	FACEBAR	FANNING	FEATURE
FOIBLE	FOXILY	FROZEN	FACE-OFF	FANTAIL	FEBRILE
FOILED	FOXING	FRUGAL	FACIALS	FANTAST	FEDERAL
FOLDED	FOYERS	FRUITS	FACINGS	FANTASY	FEDORAS
FOLDER	FRACAS	FRUITY	FACTFUL	FANZINE	FEEBLER
FOLIAR	FRAMED	FRUMPS	FACTION	FARADAY	FEEDBAG
FOLIOS	FRAMER	FRUNZE	FACTORS	FARADIC	FEEDERS
FOLIUM	FRAMES	FRYING	FACTORY	FARAWAY	FEEDING
FOLKSY	FRANCE	FRY-UPS	FACTUAL	FARCEUR	FEEDLOT
FOLLOW	FRANCS	FUDDLE	FACULAR	FAR EAST	FEEDLER
FOLSOM	FRAPPE	FUELED	FACULTY	FAR-GONE	FEELING
FOMENT	FRATER	FUGATO	FADABLE	FARMERS	FEIGNED
FONDER	FRAUDS	FUGING	FADDISH	FARMING	FEIGNER
FONDLE	FRAUEN	FUGUES	FADDISM	FARNESS	FEINTED
FONDLY	FRAYED	FUHRER	FADDIST	FARRAGO	FELINES
FONDUE	FRAZIL	FULCRA	FADEOUT	FARRIER	FELLERS
FONTAL	FREAKS	FULFIL	FAEROES	FARTHER	FELLING
FOODIE	FREAKY	FULLER	FAG ENDS	FASCIAL	FELLOWS
FOOLED	FREELY	FULMAR	FAGGING	FASCIAS	FELONRY
FOOTER	FREEST	FUMBLE	FAGGOTS	FASCINE	FELSITE
FOOTLE	FREEZE	FUMING	FAIENCE	FASCISM	FELSPAR
FOOZLE	FRENCH	FUNDED	FAILING	FASCIST	FELTING
FORAGE	FRENZY	FUNDIC	FAILURE	FASHION	FELUCCA
FORAYS	FRESCO	FUNDUS	FAINTED	FASTEST	FEMALES

FEMORAL	FIESTAS	FISCALS	FLEECED	FLUENCY	FONDANT
FENCERS	FIFTEEN	FISHERY	FLEECES	FLUFFED	FONDEST
FENDERS	FIFTIES	FISH-EYE	FLEEING	FLUIDAL	FONDLED
FENDING	FIGHTER	FISHGIG	FLEETER	FLUIDIC	FONDLER
FERMATA	FIG LEAF	FISHIER	FLEMING	FLUMMOK	FONDUES
FERMENT	FIGMENT	FISHING	FLEMISH	FLUNKED	FOOCHOW
FERMION	FIGURAL	FISHNET	FLENSER	FLUNKEY	FOODIES
FERNERY	FIGURED	FISSILE	FLESHED	FLUORIC	FOOLERY
FERRATA	FIGURER	FISSION	FLESHER	FLUSHED	FOOLING
FERRATE	FIGURES	FISSURE	FLESHES	FLUSHER	FOOLISH
FERRETS	FIGWORT	FISTULA	FLESHLY	FLUSHES	FOOTAGE
FERRETY	FILARIA	FITMENT	FLEURON	FLUSTER	FOOTBOY
FERRIED	FILBERT	FITNESS	FLEXILE	FLUTING	FOOTING
FERRIES	FILCHED	FITTERS	FLEXING	FLUTIST	FOOTMAN
FERRITE	FILCHER	FITTEST	FLEXION	FLUTTER	FOOTMEN
FERROUS	FILETED	FITTING	FLEXURE	FLUVIAL	FOOTPAD
FERRULE	FILIATE	FIXABLE	FLICKED	FLUXION	FOOTSIE
FERTILE	FILIBEG	FIXATED	FLICKER	FLYABLE	FOOT-TON
FERVENT	FILINGS	FIXEDLY	FLIGHTS	FLYAWAY	FOOTWAY
FERVOUR	FILLETS	FIXTURE	FLIGHTY	FLYBACK	FOOZLER
FESTIVE	FILLIES	FIZZIER	FLINGER	FLYBLOW	FOPPERY
FESTOON	FILLING	FLACCID	FLIPPED	FLYBOAT	FOPPISH
FETCHED	FILL-INS	FLAG DAY	FLIPPER	FLYBOOK	FORAGED
FETCHER	FILLIPS	FLAGGED	FLIRTED	FLY-FISH	FORAGER
FETLOCK	FILMIER	FLAGGER	FLIRTIER	FLY HALF	FORAGES
FETTERS	FILMILY	FLAGMAN	FLITTED	FLYLEAF	FORAMEN
FETUSES	FILMING	FLAGONS	FLITTER	FLYOVER	FORAYED
FEUDING	FILMSET	FLAILED	FLIVVER	FLYPAST	FORAYER
FEVERED	FILTERS	FLAKIER	FLOATER	FLYTRAP	FORBADE
FEWNESS	FIMBRIA	FLAKING	FLOATED	FOALING	FORBEAR
FEYNESS	FINABLE	FLAMING	FLOATER	FOAMIER	FORBORE
FIANCES	FINAGLE	FLANEUR	FLOCCUS	FOAMING	FORCEPS
FIASCOS	FINALLY	FLANKED	FLOCKED	FOBBING	FORCING
FIBBERS	FINANCE	FLANKER	FLOGGED	FOCUSED	FORDING
FIBBING	FINBACK	FLANNEL	FLOGGER	FOCUSER	FOREARM
FIBROID	FINCHES	FLAPPED	FLOODED	FOCUSES	FOREGUT
FIBROIN	FINDING	FLARE-UP	FLOODER	FOGGIER	FOREIGN
FIBROMA	FINEART	FLARING	FLOORED	FOGGILY	FORELEG
FIBROUS	FINE-CUT	FLASHED	FLOPPED	FOGGING	FOREMAN
FIBULAE	FINESSE	FLASHER	FLORIDA	FOGHORN	FOREMEN
FIBULAR	FINFOOT	FLASHES	FLORINS	FOGLAMP	FOREPAW
FIBULAS	FINGERS	FLASKET	FLORIST	FOGYISH	FORERUN
FICTILE	FINICKY	FLAT-BED	FLORUIT	FOIBLES	FORESAW
FICTION	FININGS	FLATLET	FLOSSED	FOILING	FORESEE
FIDDLED	FINLAND	FLATTEN	FLOTAGE	FOISTED	FORESTS
FIDDLER	FINNING	FLATTER	FLOTSAM	FOLACIN	FORETOP
FIDDLES	FINNISH	FLAUNCH	FLOUNCE	FOLDERS	FOREVER
FIDGETS	FIREARM	FLAVONE	FLOURED	FOLDING	FORFEIT
FIDGETY	FIREMEN	FLAVOUR	FLOUTED	FOLDOUT	FORGAVE
FIELDED	FIREPAN	FLAWING	FLOUTER	FOLIAGE	FORGERS
FIELDER	FIRMEST	FLAYING	FLOWAGE	FOLIATE	FORGING
FIERCER	FIRMING	FLEABAG	FLOWERS	FOLIOSE	FORGIVE
FIERIER	FIRSTLY	FLEAPIT	FLOWERY	FOLKISH	FORGOER
FIESOLE	FIRTREE	FLECKED	FLOWING	FOLLIES	FORGONE

FORKFUL	FREAKED	FROWNED	FURTHER	FALDERAL
FORKING	FRECKLE	FROWNER	FURTIVE	FALKLAND
FORLORN	FREEBIE	FROWSTY	FUSCUOS	FALLFISH
FORMANT	FREEDOM	FRUITED	FUSIBLE	FALL GUYS
FORMATE	FREEING	FRUITER	FUSSIER	FALLIBLE
FORMATS	FREEMAN	FRUSTUM	FUSSILY	FALLOUTS
FORMICA	FREEMEN	FUCHSIA	FUSSING	FALSETTO
FORMING	FREESIA	FUCHSIN	FUSSPOT	FALTBOAT
FORMOSA	FREEWAY	FUDDLES	FUSTIAN	FALTERED
FORMULA	FREEZER	FUDGING	FUSTIER	FALTERER
FORSAKE	FREIGHT	FUEGIAN	FUTTOCK	FAMILIAL
FORSOOK	FREMONT	FUELING	FUTURES	FAMILIAR
FORTIES	FRESCOS	FUELLED	FUZZIER	FAMILIES
FORTIFY	FRESHEN	FUELLER	FUZZILY	FAMISHED
FORTUNE	FRESHER	FUGGIER	FUZZING	FAMOUSLY
FORWARD	FRESHET	FUKUOKA		FANAGALO
FORWENT	FRESHLY	FULCRUM		FANATICS
FOSSILS	FRESNEL	FULGENT	**8 LETTERS**	FAN BELTS
FOUETTE	FRETFUL	FULLEST	FABULIST	FANCIERS
FOULARD	FRETSAW	FULMARS	FABULOUS	FANCIEST
FOULEST	FRETTED	FULNESS	FACEABLE	FANCIFUL
FOUL-UPS	FRIABLE	FULSOME	FACE CARD	FANCYING
FOUNDED	FRIBBLE	FULVOUS	FACELESS	FANCY MAN
FOUNDER	FRIDAYS	FUMARIC	FACE-LIFT	FANCY MEN
FOUNDRY	FRIDGES	FUMBLED	FACE PACK	FANDANGO
FOURIER	FRIENDS	FUMBLER	FACIALLY	FANFARES
FOURTHS	FRIEZES	FUMBLES	FACILELY	FANLIGHT
FOUR-WAY	FRIGATE	FUNCHAL	FACILITY	FANTASIA
FOVEATE	FRIGHTS	FUNDING	FACTIONS	FANZINES
FOVEOLA	FRILLED	FUNERAL	FACTIOUS	FARADISM
FOWLING	FRINGED	FUNFAIR	FACTOTUM	FARADIZE
FOXFIRE	FRINGES	FUNGOLD	FADELESS	FARCEUSE
FOXHOLE	FRISBEE	FUNGOUS	FADEOUTS	FARCICAL
FOXHUNT	FRISEUR	FUNICLE	FAEROESE	FAREWELL
FOXIEST	FRISIAN	FUNKIER	FAHLBAND	FAR-FLUNG
FOXLIKE	FRISKED	FUNKING	FAILINGS	FARINOSE
FOXTAIL	FRISKER	FUNNELS	FAIL-SAFE	FARMABLE
FOXTROT	FRISKET	FUNNIER	FAILURES	FARMHAND
FRACTUS	FRISSON	FUNNILY	FAINEANT	FARMLAND
FRAENUM	FRITTER	FUN RUNS	FAINTEST	FARMYARD
FRAGILE	FRIZZED	FURBISH	FAINTING	FARNESOL
FRAILER	FRIZZER	FURCATE	FAINTISH	FAROUCHE
FRAILTY	FRIZZLE	FURCULA	FAIR COPY	FARRIERS
FRAKTUR	FROEBEL	FURIOSO	FAIR GAME	FARRIERY
FRAME-UP	FROG-BIT	FURIOUS	FAIRINGS	FARROWED
FRAMING	FROGMAN	FURLING	FAIRLEAD	FARTHEST
FRANKED	FROGMEN	FURLONG	FAIRNESS	FARTHING
FRANKER	FROLICS	FURNACE	FAIRWAYS	FASCIATE
FRANKLY	FRONDED	FURNESS	FAITHFUL	FASCICLE
FRANTIC	FRONTAL	FURNISH	FAIZABAD	FASCISTS
FRAPPES	FRONTED	FURRIER	FALCHION	FASHIONS
FRAUGHT	FROSTED	FURRING	FALCONER	FASTBACK
FRAYING	FROTHED	FURROWS	FALCONET	FASTENED
FRAZZLE	FROWARD	FURROWY	FALCONRY	FASTENER

455

FAST FOOD	FEMINISM	FIGURATE	FIREDOGS	FLANNELS
FASTNESS	FEMINIST	FIGURINE	FIRE DOOR	FLAPJACK
FATALISM	FEMINIZE	FIGURING	FIRE-PLUG	FLAPPING
FATALIST	FENDERED	FILAGREE	FIRESIDE	FLARE-UPS
FATALITY	FENESTRA	FILAMENT	FIRETRAP	FLASHERS
FATHEADS	FERETORY	FILARIAL	FIREWEED	FLASHEST
FATHERED	FEROCITY	FILATURE	FIREWOOD	FLASHGUN
FATHERLY	FERREOUS	FILCHING	FIREWORK	FLASHIER
FATHOMED	FERRETED	FILECARD	FIRMNESS	FLASHILY
FATHOMER	FERRETER	FILEFISH	FIRMWARE	FLASHING
FATIGUED	FERRIAGE	FILETING	FIRST AID	FLATBOAT
FATIGUES	FERRITIN	FILICIDE	FIRST-DAY	FLAT FEET
FATTENED	FERRULES	FILIFORM	FIR TREES	FLATFISH
FATTENER	FERRYING	FILIGREE	FISCALLY	FLATFOOT
FATTIEST	FERRYMAN	FILIPINO	FISHABLE	FLATHEAD
FAUBOURG	FERRYMEN	FILLETED	FISHBOLT	FLATLETS
FAULTIER	FERVENCY	FILLINGS	FISHBOWL	FLATMATE
FAULTILY	FERVIDLY	FILMIEST	FISHCAKE	FLATNESS
FAULTING	FESTERED	FILM STAR	FISHFACE	FLAT SPIN
FAUSTIAN	FESTIVAL	FILTERED	FISH FARM	FLATTERY
FAUTEUIL	FESTOONS	FILTHIER	FISH HOOK	FLATTEST
FAVONIAN	FETATION	FILTHILY	FISHIEST	FLATTING
FAVOURED	FETCHING	FILTRATE	FISHNETS	FLATTISH
FAVOURER	FETIALES	FIMBRIAL	FISHSKIN	FLATWARE
FAYALITE	FETICIDE	FINAGLER	FISHTAIL	FLATWAYS
FEARLESS	FETISHES	FINALISM	FISHWIFE	FLATWORM
FEARSOME	FETLOCKS	FINALIST	FISSURES	FLAUNTED
FEASIBLE	FETTERED	FINALITY	FITFULLY	FLAUNTER
FEASIBLY	FETTERER	FINALIZE	FITMENTS	FLAUTIST
FEASTING	FETTLING	FINANCED	FITTABLE	FLAVOURS
FEATHERS	FEVERFEW	FINANCES	FITTINGS	FLAWLESS
FEATHERY	FEVERISH	FINDABLE	FIVEFOLD	FLAXSEED
FEATURED	FIASCOES	FINDINGS	FIVEPINS	FLEABAGS
FEATURES	FIBRILAR	FINEABLE	FIVE-STAR	FLEABANE
FEBRIFIC	FIBROSIS	FINE ARTS	FIXATION	FLEABITE
FEBRUARY	FIBROTIC	FINE-DRAW	FIXATIVE	FLEAPITS
FECKLESS	FICTIONS	FINENESS	FIXTURES	FLEAWORT
FECULENT	FIDDLING	FINESPUN	FIZZIEST	FLECKING
FEDERATE	FIDELITY	FINE-TUNE	FLABBIER	FLECTION
FEEBLEST	FIDGETED	FINGERED	FLABBILY	FLEECING
FEEDABLE	FIDUCIAL	FINGERER	FLAG DAYS	FLEETEST
FEEDBACK	FIELD DAY	FINISHED	FLAGGING	FLEETING
FEEDBAGS	FIELDERS	FINISHER	FLAGPOLE	FLESHIER
FEELINGS	FIELDING	FINISHES	FLAGRANT	FLESHING
FEIGNING	FIENDISH	FINITELY	FLAGSHIP	FLESHPOT
FEINTING	FIERCELY	FIREABLE	FLAILING	FLETCHER
FELDSPAR	FIERCEST	FIREARMS	FLAKIEST	FLEXIBLE
FELICITY	FIERIEST	FIREBACK	FLAMBEAU	FLEXIBLY
FELINITY	FIFTIETH	FIREBALL	FLAMENCO	FLEXUOUS
FELLABLE	FIGHTERS	FIREBOAT	FLAMEOUT	FLEXURAL
FELLATIO	FIGHTING	FIREBRAT	FLAMINGO	FLICKERY
FELONIES	FIG LEAFS	FIREBUGS	FLANDERS	FLICKING
FELSITIC	FIGMENTS	FIRE-CURE	FLANERIE	FLIMFLAM
FEMININE	FIGURANT	FIREDAMP	FLANKING	FLIMSIER

FLIMSILY	FLUSHING	FOOTPACE	FORESTAY	FOUR-LEAF
FLINCHED	FLUTISTS	FOOTPADS	FORESTED	FOURSOME
FLINCHER	FLUTTERS	FOOTPATH	FORESTER	FOUR-STAR
FLINGING	FLUTTERY	FOOTRACE	FORESTRY	FOURTEEN
FLINTIER	FLYBLOWN	FOOTREST	FORETELL	FOVEOLAR
FIP-FLOP	FLYOVERS	FOOTROPE	FORETIME	FOWL PEST
FLIPPANT	FLYPAPER	FOOTSIES	FORETOLD	FOXGLOVE
FLIPPERS	FLYPASTS	FOOTSLOG	FOREWARN	FOXHOUND
FLIPPEST	FLYSHEET	FOOTSORE	FOREWENT	FOXHUNTS
FLIPPING	FLYSPECK	FOOTSTEP	FOREWIND	FOXINESS
FLIP SIDE	FLYWHEEL	FOOTWALL	FOREWING	FOXTROTS
FLIRTING	FLYWHISK	FOOTWEAR	FOREWORD	FRACTION
FLITTING	FOAMIEST	FOOTWORK	FOREYARD	FRACTURE
FLOATAGE	FOAMLIKE	FOOTWORN	FORFEITS	FRAGMENT
FLOATERS	FOB WATCH	FORAGING	FORGINGS	FRAGRANT
FLOATING	FOCALIZE	FORAYING	FORGIVEN	FRAILEST
FLOCCOSE	FOCUSING	FORBEARS	FORGIVER	FRAMABLE
FLOCCULE	FOCUSSED	FORBORNE	FORGOING	FRAME-UPS
FLOCKING	FOETUSES	FORCE-FED	FORJUDGE	FRANCIUM
FLOGGING	FOGBOUND	FORCEFUL	FORK-LIFT	FRANKEST
FLOODING	FOGGIEST	FORCIBLE	FORMABLE	FRANKING
FLOODLIT	FOGHORNS	FORCIBLY	FORMALIN	FRANKISH
FLOORAGE	FOG LAMPS	FORDABLE	FORMALLY	FRANKLIN
FLOORING	FOIE GRAS	FOREARMS	FORMERLY	FRAULEIN
FLORALLY	FOILABLE	FOREBEAR	FORMLESS	FRAZZLED
FLORENCE	FOILSMAN	FOREBODE	FORMULAE	FREAKING
FLORIDLY	FOISTING	FORECAST	FORMULAS	FREAKISH
FLORIGEN	FOLDABLE	FOREDECK	FORMWORK	FRECKLED
FLORISTS	FOLDAWAY	FOREDOOM	FORNICAL	FRECKLES
FLOSSING	FOLDBOAT	FOREFEET	FORSAKEN	FREE-BASE
FLOTILLA	FOLIATED	FOREFOOT	FORSAKER	FREEBIES
FLOUNCED	FOLKLORE	FOREGOER	FORSOOTH	FREEBIRD
FLOUNCES	FOLK-ROCK	FOREGONE	FORSWEAR	FREEBOOT
FLOUNDER	FOLKTALE	FOREHAND	FORSWORE	FREEBORN
FLOURING	FOLKWAYS	FOREHEAD	FORSWORN	FREEDMAN
FLOURISH	FOLLICLE	FOREKNOW	FORTIETH	FREE-FALL
FLOUTING	FOLLOWED	FORELAND	FORT KNOX	FREEFONE
FLOWERED	FOLLOWER	FORELEGS	FORTRESS	FREEHAND
FLOWERER	FOLLOW-ON	FORELIMB	FORTUITY	FREEHOLD
FLUE-CURE	FOLLOW-UP	FORELOCK	FORTUNES	FREE KICK
FLUENTLY	FOMENTED	FOREMAST	FORWARDS	FREELOAD
FLUFFIER	FOMENTER	FOREMOST	FOSSETTE	FREE PASS
FLUFFING	FONDANTS	FORENAME	FOSTERED	FREEPORT
FLUIDICS	FONDLING	FORENOON	FOSTERER	FREEPOST
FLUIDITY	FONDNESS	FORENSIC	FOULNESS	FREE REIN
FLUIDIZE	FOOLSCAP	FOREPART	FOUL PLAY	FREESIAS
FLUMMERY	FOOTBALL	FOREPEAK	FOUNDERS	FREEWAYS
FLUNKEYS	FOOTFALL	FOREPLAY	FOUNDING	FREE WILL
FLUNKING	FOOTGEAR	FORESAIL	FOUNTAIN	FREEZERS
FLUORENE	FOOTHILL	FORESEEN	FOUR-BALL	FREEZE-UP
FLOURIDE	FOOTHOLD	FORESEER	FOUR-DEAL	FREEZING
FLOURINE	FOOTLING	FORESIDE	FOUR-EYED	FRENETIC
FLURRIED	FOOTMARK	FORESKIN	FOUR-EYES	FRENULUM
FLURRIES	FOOTNOTE	FORESTAL	FOURFOLD	FRENZIED

FREQUENT	FRUMENTY	FUTURISM	FAMILIARS	FEBRIFUGE
FRESCOES	FRUMPIER	FUTURIST	FAMILY MAN	FEBRILITY
FRESHEST	FRUMPISH	FUTURITY	FAMILY MEN	FECULENCE
FRESHMAN	FRUSTULE	FUZZIEST	FANATICAL	FECUNDATE
FRESHMEN	FUCHSIAS		FANCINESS	FECUNDITY
FRETLESS	FUCOIDAL		FANCY-FREE	FEDERATED
FRETSAWS	FUDDLING	**9 LETTERS**	FANCYWORK	FEELINGLY
FRETTING	FUELLING	FABACEOUS	FANDANGLE	FEE-PAYING
FRETWORK	FUGACITY	FABIANISM	FANDANGOS	FELONIOUS
FREUDIAN	FUGGIEST	FABRICATE	FANLIGHTS	FEMINISTS
FRIARIES	FUGITIVE	FABRIKOID	FAN-TAILED	FENESTRAL
FRIBBLER	FULCRUMS	FACE CARDS	FANTASIES	FENUGREEK
FRICTION	FULLBACK	FACECLOTH	FANTASIZE	FERMANAGH
FRIENDLY	FULL MOON	FACE-LIFTS	FANTASTIC	FERMENTED
FRIESIAN	FULLNESS	FACE PACKS	FARADIZER	FERMENTER
FRIGATES	FULL-PAGE	FACEPLATE	FARANDOLE	FEROCIOUS
FRIGGING	FULL STOP	FACE-SAVER	FAREWELLS	FERRETING
FRIGHTEN	FULL-TIME	FACETIOUS	FARMHANDS	FERROCENE
FRIGIDLY	FUMATORY	FACE VALUE	FARMHOUSE	FERROTYPE
FRILLIER	FUMBLING	FACSIMILE	FARMSTEAD	FERTILITY
FRINGING	FUMELESS	FACTIONAL	FARMYARDS	FERTILIZE
FRIPPERY	FUMIGANT	FACTITIVE	FARRAGOES	FERVENTLY
FRISBEES	FUMIGATE	FACTORAGE	FARROWING	FESTERING
FRISETTE	FUMINGLY	FACTORIAL	FAR-SEEING	FESTIVALS
FRISKIER	FUMITORY	FACTORIES	FARTHINGS	FESTIVITY
FRISKILY	FUNCTION	FACTORING	FASCICLED	FESTOONED
FRISKING	FUNERALS	FACTORIZE	FASCICULE	FETICIDAL
FRISSONS	FUNERARY	FACTUALLY	FASCINATE	FETISHISM
FRITTERS	FUNEREAL	FACULTIES	FASCISTIC	FETISHIST
FRIULAIN	FUNFAIRS	FADDINESS	FASHIONED	FETTERING
FRIZZIER	FUNGIBLE	FADDISHLY	FASHIONER	FETTUCINE
FRONTING	FUNGUSES	FADEDNESS	FASTENERS	FEUDALISM
FRONTLET	FUNKIEST	FAGACEOUS	FASTENING	FEUDALIST
FRONT MAN	FUNNELED	FAGGOTING	FATALISTS	FEUDALITY
FRONT MEN	FUNNIEST	FAINTNESS	FATEFULLY	FEUDALIZE
FROSTIER	FURCATED	FAIRYLAND	FATHEADED	FEUDATORY
FROSTILY	FURLABLE	FAIRY-LIKE	FATHERING	FEVERWORT
FROSTING	FURLONGS	FAIRY-TALE	FATHOMING	FIBRIFORM
FROTHIER	FURLOUGH	FAITHFULS	FATIGABLE	FIBRINOUS
FROTHILY	FURNACES	FAITHLESS	FATIGUING	FICTIONAL
FROSTING	FURRIERS	FALANGISM	FATTENING	FIDGETING
FROTHING	FURRIERY	FALANGIST	FATTINESS	FIDUCIARY
FROWNING	FURRIEST	FALCONERS	FATUITOUS	FIELD DAYS
FROWZIER	FURROWED	FALCONINE	FATUOUSLY	FIELDFARE
FRUCTIFY	FURROWER	FALDSTOOL	FAULTIEST	FIELDSMAN
FRUCTOSE	FURTHEST	FALLACIES	FAULTLESS	FIELDSMEN
FRUGALLY	FURUNCLE	FALLOPIAN	FAVEOLATE	FIELD-TEST
FRUITAGE	FUSELAGE	FALSE DAWN	FAVOURING	FIELD TRIP
FRUIT BAT	FUSIFORM	FALSEHOOD	FAVOURITE	FIELDWORK
FRUIT FLY	FUSILIER	FALSENESS	FAWNINGLY	FIFTEENTH
FRUITFUL	FUSSIEST	FALSIFIED	FEARFULLY	FIFTIETHS
FRUITIER	FUSSPOTS	FALSIFIER	FEATHERED	FIGURINES
FRUITING	FUSTIEST	FALSITIES	FEATURING	FILAMENTS
FRUITION	FUTILITY	FALTERING	FEBRICITY	FILIATION

FILICIDAL	FIRST NAME	FLAUTISTS	FLUTTERED	FORCEMEAT
FILLETING	FIRST-RATE	FLAVOROUS	FLUTTERER	FORCINGLY
FILLISTER	FIRST TIME	FLAVOURED	FLUXIONAL	FOREARMED
FILMINESS	FISHCAKES	FLAVOURER	FLY-FISHER	FOREBEARS
FILM STARS	FISHERIES	FLEABITES	FLY HALVES	FOREBODED
FILM STOCK	FISHERMAN	FLEDGING	FLYING FOX	FOREBODER
FILMSTRIP	FISHERMEN	FLEETNESS	FLYLEAVES	FOREBRAIN
FILOPLUME	FISH FARMS	FLESHIEST	FLYSHEETS	FORECASTS
FILOSELLE	FISHINESS	FLESHINGS	FLYWEIGHT	FORECLOSE
FILTERING	FISH KNIFE	FLESHPOTS	FLYWHEELS	FORECOURT
FILTER TIP	FISHPLATE	FLEURETTE	FLYWHISKS	FOREFRONT
FILTHIEST	FISH SLICE	FLEXIONAL	FOCUSABLE	FOREGOING
FIMBRIATE	FISH STICK	FLEXITIME	FOCUSSING	FOREHANDS
FINALISTS	FISSILITY	FLICKERED	FOETATION	FOREHEADS
FINALIZED	FISTULOUS	FLIMSIEST	FOETICIDE	FOREIGNER
FINANCIAL	FIXATIONS	FLINCHING	FOGGINESS	FOREJUDGE
FINANCIER	FIXATIVES	FLINTIEST	FOLIATION	FORELOCKS
FINANCING	FIXED GAZE	FLINTLOCK	FOLIOLATE	FORENAMED
FINE-GRAIN	FIXED HEAD	FLIP-FLOPS	FOLK DANCE	FORENAMES
FINE PRINT	FIXED-STAR	FLIPPANCY	FOLK TALES	FORENSICS
FINE-TOOTH	FIXED TERM	FLOATABLE	FOLLICLES	FOREREACH
FINGERING	FIZZINESS	FLOAT-FEED	FOLLOWERS	FORESHANK
FINGERTIP	FLABBIEST	FLOGGINGS	FOLLOWING	FORESHEET
FINISHING	FLABELLUM	FLOODABLE	FOLLOW-UPS	FORESHOCK
FINISTERE	FLAGEOLET	FLOODGATE	FOMENTING	FORESIGHT
FIRE ALARM	FLAGPOLES	FLOOD TIDE	FOOD STAMP	FORESKINS
FIREBALLS	FLAGRANCE	FLOOR SHOW	FOODSTUFF	FORESTALL
FIREBOXES	FLAGRANCY	FLOPHOUSE	FOOLERIES	FORESTERS
FIREBRAND	FLAGSHIPS	FLOPPIEST	FOOLHARDY	FORETASTE
FIREBREAK	FLAGSTAFF	FLORIATED	FOOLISHLY	FORETOKEN
FIREBRICK	FLAG-STICK	FLORIDITY	FOOLPROOF	FORETOOTH
FIRECREST	FLAGSTONE	FLORISTIC	FOOTBALLS	FOREWOMAN
FIREDRILL	FLAG-WAVER	FLOTATION	FOOTBOARD	FOREWOMEN
FIRE-EATER	FLAKINESS	FLOTILLAS	FOOTFALLS	FOREWORDS
FIREFLIES	FLAME-LIKE	FLOUNCING	FOOT FAULT	FORFEITED
FIREGUARD	FLAMINGOS	FLOUNDERS	FOOTHILLS	FORFEITER
FIREIRONS	FLAMMABLE	FLOURMILL	FOOTHOLDS	FORGATHER
FIRELIGHT	FLANNELED	FLOWCHART	FOOTLOOSE	FORGEABLE
FIREPLACE	FLAPJACKS	FLOWERAGE	FOOTNOTES	FORGERIES
FIRE-PLUGS	FLARE PATH	FLOWERBED	FOOTPATHS	FORGETFUL
FIREPOWER	FLASHBACK	FLOWERING	FOOTPLATE	FORGETTER
FIREPROOF	FLASHBULB	FLOWERPOT	FOOTPOUND	FORGIVING
FIRESIDES	FLASHCUBE	FLOWINGLY	FOOTPRINT	FORGOTTEN
FIRESTONE	FLASHGUNS	FLUCTUANT	FOOTRACES	FORLORNLY
FIRESTORM	FLASHIEST	FLUCTUATE	FOOTSTALK	FORMALISM
FIRETHORN	FLASHOVER	FLUFFIEST	FOOTSTALL	FORMALIST
FIRETRAPS	FLATMATES	FLUIDIZER	FOOTSTEPS	FORMALITY
FIREWATER	FLAT SPINS	FLUKINESS	FOOTSTOOL	FORMALIZE
FIREWORKS	FLATTENED	FLUMMOXED	FORAMINAL	FORMATION
FIRMAMENT	FLATTENER	FLUORENCE	FORBEARER	FORMATIVE
FIRSTBORN	FLATTERED	FLUOROSIS	FORBIDDEN	FORMATTED
FIRSTHAND	FLATTERER	FLUORSPAR	FORBIDDER	FORMICARY
FIRST LADY	FLATULENT	FLURRYING	FORCEABLE	FORMULAIC
FIRSTLING	FLAUNTING	FLUSTERED	FORCE-FEED	FORMULARY

FORMULATE	FREELANCE	FROSTIEST	FURROWING	FAMILY TREE
FORMULISM	FREE-LIVER	FROSTWORK	FURTHERER	FAMISHMENT
FORMULIST	FREEMASON	FROTHIEST	FURTIVELY	FAMOUSNESS
FORNICATE	FREEPHONE	FROSTWORK	FUSELAGES	FANATICISM
FORSAKING	FREE PORTS	FROTHIEST	FUSILLADE	FANATICIZE
FORSYTHIA	FREE-RANGE	FRUCTUOUS	FUSIONISM	FANCIFULLY
FORTHWITH	FREESHEET	FRUGALITY	FUSIONIST	FANCY DRESS
FORTIETHS	FREESTONE	FRUIT BATS	FUSSINESS	FANCY WOMAN
FORTIFIED	FREESTYLE	FRUITCAKE	FUSTINESS	FANCY WOMEN
FORTIFIER	FREE TRADE	FRUITERER	FUTURISTS	FANTASIZED
FORTITUDE	FREE VERSE	FRUITIEST	FUZZINESS	FARCICALLY
FORTNIGHT	FREEWHEEL	FRUITLESS		FAR EASTERN
FORTUNATE	FREE WORLD	FRUMPIEST		FARFETCHED
FORTY-FIVE	FREEZABLE	FRUSTRATE	**10 LETTERS**	FARMHOUSES
FORWARDED	FREEZE-DRY	FRYING PAN	FABRICATED	FARMSTEADS
FORWARDER	FREIGHTED	FUGACIOUS	FABRICATOR	FARSIGHTED
FORWARDLY	FREIGHTER	FUGITIVES	FABULOUSLY	FASCICULAR
FOSSILIZE	FRENCHIFY	FULFILLED	FACECLOTHS	FASCINATED
FOSSORIAL	FRENCHMAN	FULLBACKS	FACE-HARDEN	FASHIONING
FOSTERAGE	FRENCHMEN	FULL-BLOWN	FACE-SAVERS	FASTENINGS
FOSTERING	FREQUENCE	FULLBOARD	FACE-SAVING	FASTIDIOUS
FOUNDERED	FREQUENCY	FULLDRESS	FACE-TO-FACE	FASTIGIATE
FOUNDLING	FRESHENED	FULL-FACED	FACILENESS	FATALITIES
FOUNDRIES	FRESHENER	FULL-GROWN	FACILITATE	FATHERHOOD
FOUNTAINS	FRESHNESS	FULL HOUSE	FACILITIES	FATHERLAND
FOURSOMES	FRETFULLY	FULL MOONS	FACSIMILIES	FATHERLESS
FOUR-WHEEL	FRETBOARD	FULL-SCALE	FACTITIOUS	FATHER-LIKE
FOVEOLATE	FRETWORKS	FULL STOPS	FACT OF LIFE	FATHOMABLE
FOXGLOVES	FRICASSEE	FULMINANT	FACTORABLE	FATHOMETER
FOXHOUNDS	FRIGHTFUL	FULMINATE	FACTORIZED	FATHOMLESS
FOXHUNTER	FRIGIDITY	FULSOMELY	FACTORSHIP	FAT-SOLUBLE
FRACTIONS	FRILLIEST	FUMIGATED	FACTUALISM	FAULTINESS
FRACTIOUS	FRISKIEST	FUMIGATOR	FACTUALIST	FAVOURABLE
FRACTURAL	FRITTERED	FUNCTIONS	FARHENHEIT	FAVOURABLY
FRACTURED	FRITTERER	FUNDAMENT	FAINTINGLY	FAVOURITES
FRACTURES	FRIVOLITY	FUNGICIDE	FAIR COPIES	FEARLESSLY
FRAGILITY	FRIVOLLER	FUNGIFORM	FAIRGROUND	FEATHER BED
FRAGMENTS	FRIVOLOUS	FUNGISTAT	FAIR-MINDED	FEATHER BOA
FRAGRANCE	FRIZZIEST	FUNICULAR	FAIR-SPOKEN	FEATHERING
FRAILITIES	FRIZZLING	FUNNELING	FAIRYLANDS	FEBRUARIES
FRAMBOISE	FROCK COAT	FUNNELLED	FAIRY LIGHT	FECKLESSLY
FRAMEWORK	FROGMARCH	FUNNINESS	FAIRY TALES	FECUNDATOR
FRANCHISE	FROGMOUTH	FUNNY BONE	FAITHFULLY	FEDERALISM
FRANGIBLE	FROGSPAWN	FUNNY FACE	FALLACIOUS	FEDERALIST
FRANGLAIS	FROLICKED	FUNNY FARM	FALLOW DEAR	FEDERALIZE
FRANKABLE	FROLICKER	FURBISHED	FALLOWNESS	FEDERATING
FRANKNESS	FRONTAGES	FURBISHER	FALSE ALARM	FEDERATION
FRATERNAL	FRONTALLY	FURCATION	FALSE DAWNS	FEDERATIVE
FREEAGENT	FRONTDOOR	FURIOUSLY	FALSEHOODS	FEEBLENESS
FREE-BASED	FRONTIERS	FURLOUGHS	FALSE START	FEET OF CLAY
FREEBOARD	FRONTLINE	FURNISHED	FALSE TEETH	FEIGNINGLY
FREEHOLDS	FRONT-PAGE	FURNISHER	FALSIFYING	FELICITATE
FREE HOUSE	FRONT ROOM	FURNITURE	FAMILIARLY	FELICITIES
FREE KICKS	FROSTBITE	FURRINESS	FAMILY NAME	FELICITOUS

FELLMONGER	FIREBRICKS	FLAVESCENT	FLUORINATE
FELLOWSHIP	FIRE DRILLS	FLAVOURING	FLUSTERING
FEMALENESS	FIRE-EATERS	FLAWLESSLY	FLUTTERING
FEMININITY	FIRE-EATING	FLEA-BITTEN	FLY-BY-NIGHT
FERMENTING	FIRE ENGINE	FLEA MARKET	FLYCATCHER
FEROCITIES	FIRE ESCAPE	FLEDGLINGS	FLY-FISHING
FERTILIZED	FIREGUARDS	FLEECINESS	FLYING BOAT
FERTILIZER	FIREPLACES	FLESHINESS	FLYING FISH
FESTOONERY	FIRE-RAISER	FLESH WOUND	FLYSPECKED
FESTOONING	FIRESTORMS	FLICKERING	FLYSWATTER
FETCHINGLY	FIRING LINE	FLICK KNIFE	FLYWEIGHTS
FETISHISTS	FIRST-CLASS	FLIGHT DECK	FOAMFLOWER
FEVERISHLY	FIRST FLOOR	FLIGHTIEST	FOAM RUBBER
FIBREBOARD	FIRST NAMES	FLIGHTLESS	FOB WATCHES
FIBREGLASS	FIRST NIGHT	FLIGHT PATH	FOCAL POINT
FIBRINOGEN	FISH FINGER	FLIMSINESS	FOLIACEOUS
FIBROBLAST	FISH KNIVES	FLINTINESS	FOLK DANCER
FIBROSITIS	FISHMONGER	FLINTLOCKS	FOLK DANCES
FICKLENESS	FISH SLICES	FLIPPANTLY	FOLKLORIST
FICTIONIST	FISH STICKS	FLIRTATION	FOLKSINESS
FICTICIOUS	FISTICUFFS	FLIRTINGLY	FOLLICULAR
FIDDLEHEAD	FIVE-FINGER	FLOATATION	FOLLICULIN
FIDDLEWOOD	FIXED-POINT	FLOCCULANT	FOLLOWABLE
FIELD EVENT	FIXED STARS	FLOCCULATE	FOLLOWINGS
FIELDMOUSE	FLABBINESS	FLOCCULENT	FONDLINGLY
FIELDSTONE	FLABELLATE	FLOODGATES	FONTANELLE
FIELD-TESTS	FLACCIDITY	FLOODLIGHT	FOOD STAMPS
FIELD TRIPS	FLAGELLANT	FLOODTIDES	FOODSTUFFS
FIENDISHLY	FLAGELLATE	FLOORBOARD	FOOTBALLER
FIERCENESS	FLAGITIOUS	FLOOR CLOTH	FOOTBRIDGE
FIFTEENTHS	FLAGRANTLY	FLOOR SHOWS	FOOT-CANDLE
FIFTY-FIFTY	FLAGSTAFFS	FLOPHOUSES	FOOT FAULTS
FIGURATION	FLAGSTONES	FLOPPINESS	FOOTLIGHTS
FIGURATIVE	FLAG-WAVING	FLOPPY DISK	FOOTPLATES
FIGUREHEAD	FLAMBOYANT	FLORENTINE	FOOTPRINTS
FILARIASIS	FLAMEPROOF	FLORIBUNDA	FOOTSTOOLS
FILIALNESS	FLAMINGOES	FLORISTICS	FORBEARING
FILIBUSTER	FLANNELING	FLOUNDERED	FORBIDDING
FILMSETTER	FLANNELLED	FLOURISHED	FORCEDNESS
FILMSTRIPS	FLARE PATHS	FLOURISHER	FORCEFULLY
FILTERABLE	FLASHBACKS	FLOURISHES	FORE AND AFT
FILTER TIPS	FLASHBOARD	FLOURMILLS	FOREARMING
FILTHINESS	FLASHBULBS	FLOUTINGLY	FOREBODING
FILTRATION	FLASHCUBES	FLOWCHARTS	FORECASTED
FINALIZING	FLASHINESS	FLOWERBEDS	FORECASTER
FINANCIERS	FLASHLIGHT	FLOWER GIRL	FORECASTLE
FINE-TUNING	FLASHPOINT	FLOWERLESS	FORECLOSED
FINGER BOWL	FLATFISHES	FLOWER-LIKE	FORECOURSE
FINGERLING	FLAT-FOOTED	FLOWERPOTS	FORECOURTS
FINGERNAIL	FLAT RACING	FLUCTUATED	FOREDOOMED
FINGERTIPS	FLATTENING	FLUFFINESS	FOREFATHER
FIRE ALARMS	FLATTERIES	FLUGELHORN	FOREFINGER
FIREBRANDS	FLATTERING	FLUMMOXING	FOREGATHER
FIREBREAKS	FLATULENCE	FLUORIDATE	FOREGOINGS

F

10 LETTERS

FOREGROUND	FOURRAGERE	FREQUENTED	FULMINATED
FORIEGN AID	FOURSQUARE	FREQUENTER	FULMINATOR
FOREIGNERS	FOUR-STROKE	FREQUENTLY	FUMATORIUM
FOREIGNISM	FOURTEENTH	FRESHENING	FUMBLINGLY
FOREORDAIN	FOXHUNTERS	FRESHWATER	FUMIGATING
FORERUNNER	FOXHUNTING	FRICASSEES	FUMIGATION
FORESEEING	FOX TERRIER	FRICATIVES	FUNCTIONAL
FORESHADOW	FRACTIONAL	FRICTIONAL	FUNCTIONED
FOREST-LIKE	FRACTURING	FRIENDLESS	FUNEREALLY
FORETELLER	FRAGMENTAL	FRIENDLIER	FUNGICIDAL
FOREWARNED	FRAGMENTED	FRIENDLIES	FUNGICIDES
FOREWARNER	FRAGRANCES	FRIENDLILY	FUNICULARS
FORFEITERS	FRAGRANTLY	FRIENDSHIP	FUNICULATE
FORFEITING	FRAMEWORKS	FRIGHTENED	FUNNELLING
FORFEITURE	FRANCHISED	FRIGHTENER	FUNNY BONES
FORGETTING	FRANCHISES	FRILLINESS	FUNNY FARMS
FORGIVABLE	FRANCISCAN	FRISKINESS	FURBISHING
FORGIVABLY	FRANCONIAN	FRITILLARY	FURNISHING
FORKEDNESS	FRATERNITY	FRITTERING	FURTHERING
FORMALISTS	FRATERNIZE	FRIZZINESS	FURUNCULAR
FORMALIZED	FRATRICIDE	FROCK COATS	FUSIBILITY
FORMALIZER	FRAUDULENT	FROGHOPPER	FUSILLADES
FORMATIONS	FREAKINESS	FROLICKING	FUTURISTIC
FORMATTING	FREAKISHLY	FROLICSOME	FUTUROLOGY
FORMIC ACID	FREE AGENTS	FRONTALITY	
FORMIDABLE	FREE-BASTING	FRONTBENCH	
FORMIDABLY	FREEBOARDS	FRONT DOORS	**11 LETTERS**
FORMLESSLY	FREEBOOTER	FRONT ROOMS	FABRICATING
FORMULATED	FREE CHURCH	FRONTWARDS	FABRICATION
FORMULATOR	FREEDWOMAN	FROSTBOUND	FABRICATIVE
FORNICATED	FREE-FOR-ALL	FROSTINESS	FACE-CENTRED
FORNICATOR	FREE-HANDED	FROTHINESS	FACETIOUSLY
FORSWEARER	FREEHOLDER	FROWNINGLY	FACILITATED
FORTHRIGHT	FREE HOUSES	FROZENNESS	FACILITATOR
FORTIFIERS	FREELANCED	FRUCTIFIED	FACT-FINDING
FORTIFYING	FREELANCER	FRUCTIFIER	FACTORIZING
FORTISSIMO	FREELANCES	FRUITCAKES	FACTORY FARM
FORTNIGHTS	FREE-LIVING	FRUITERERS	FACTS OF LIFE
FORTRESSES	FREELOADED	FRUIT FLIES	FACTUALNESS
FORTUITISM	FREELOADER	FRUITINESS	FACULTATIVE
FORTUITIST	FREEMARTIN	FRUIT SALAD	FAIRGROUNDS
FORTY-NINER	FREEMASONS	FRUSTRATED	FAIR-WEATHER
FORTY WINKS	FREE PARDON	FRUSTRATER	FAIRY LIGHTS
FORWARDING	FREE PASSES	FRYING PANS	FAITH HEALER
FOSSILIZED	FREE-SPOKEN	FUDDY-DUDDY	FAITHLESSLY
FOSTERINGS	FREE-TRADER	FULFILLING	FALCONIFORM
FOUNDATION	FREIGHTAGE	FULFILMENT	FALLIBILITY
FOUNDERING	FREIGHTERS	FULIGINOUS	FALLING STAR
FOUNDLINGS	FREIGHTING	FULL-BODIED	FALSE ALARMS
FOURCHETTE	FRENCH BEAN	FULL HOUSES	FALSE BOTTOM
FOUR-COLOUR	FRENCH HORN	FULL-LENGTH	FALSE STARTS
FOUR-HANDED	FRENCH KISS	FULL-RIGGED	FALSIFIABLE
FOUR-IN-HAND	FRENCH LOAF	FULL-SAILED	FALTERINGLY
FOUR-POSTER	FRENZIEDLY	FULLY-GROWN	FAMILIARITY

FAMILIARIZE	FIBRE OPTICS	FISSIPAROUS	FLYING START
FAMILY NAMES	FIBROMATOUS	FLABBERGAST	FLYSWATTERS
FAMILY TREES	FIBROUSNESS	FLAGELLANTS	FOLK DANCERS
FANATICALLY	FICTIONALLY	FLAGELLATED	FOLLICULATE
FANTASIZING	FIDGETINGLY	FLAMBOYANCE	FOMENTATION
FARCICALITY	FIELD-EFFECT	FLANNELETTE	FOOLISHNESS
FARINACEOUS	FIELD-EVENTS	FLANNELLING	FOOL'S ERRAND
FAR-REACHING	FIELD-HOCKEY	FLASHLIGHTS	FOOTBALLERS
FARTHERMOST	FIELD-TESTED	FLASH POINTS	FOOTBRIDGES
FARTHINGALE	FIELDWORKER	FLAT-CHESTED	FOOTFAULTED
FASCINATING	FIFTH COLUMN	FLATTERABLE	FOOTSLOGGED
FASCINATION	FIFTH-DEGREE	FLAUNTINGLY	FOPPISHNESS
FASCINATIVE	FIGURED BASS	FLAVOURINGS	FORBEARANCE
FASHIONABLE	FIGUREHEADS	FLAVOURSOME	FORBIDDANCE
FAST-BREEDER	FILAMENTARY	FLEA MARKETS	FORBODINGS
FAST-FORWARD	FILIBUSTERS	FLEET STREET	FORECASTERS
FATEFULNESS	FILMOGRAPHY	FLESHINESS	FORECASTING
FATHER-IN-LAW	FILMSETTING	FLESH WOUNDS	FORECLOSING
FATHERLANDS	FILTRATABLE	FLETCHERISM	FORECLOSURE
FATUOUSNESS	FIMBRIATION	FLEURS-DE-LIS	FOREFATHERS
FAULT-FINDER	FINANCIALLY	FLEXIBILITY	FOREFINGERS
FAULTLESSLY	FINE-GRAINED	FLICK KNIVES	FOREGROUNDS
FAVOURINGLY	FINGERBOARD	FLIGHT DECKS	FOREMANSHIP
FAVOURITISM	FINGER BOWLS	FLIGHTINESS	FOREQUARTER
FAWNINGNESS	FINGERNAILS	FLIGHT PATHS	FORERUNNERS
FEARFULNESS	FINGERPLATE	FLINCHINGLY	FORESEEABLE
FEASIBILITY	FINGERPRINT	FLIRTATIONS	FORESHORTEN
FEATHER BEDS	FINGERSTALL	FLIRTATIOUS	FORESIGHTED
FEATHER BOAS	FIRE BRIGADE	FLOATATIONS	FORESTALLED
FEATHEREDGE	FIRECRACKER	FLOCCULENCE	FORESTALLER
FEATURE FILM	FIRE ENGINES	FLOODLIGHTS	FORESTATION
FEATURELESS	FIRE ESCAPES	FLOORBOARDS	FORETELLING
FECUNDATION	FIRE FIGHTER	FLOORCLOTHS	FORETHOUGHT
FECUNDATORY	FIRE HYDRANT	FLOORWALKER	FOREWARNING
FEDERALISTS	FIRE LIGHTER	FLOPPY DISKS	FORFEITABLE
FEDERATIONS	FIRE PROOFED	FLORESCENCE	FORGATHERED
FELICITATED	FIRE-RAISERS	FLOUNDERING	FORGETFULLY
FELICITATOR	FIRE-RAISING	FLOURISHING	FORGET-ME-NOT
FELLOWSHIPS	FIRE STARTER	FLOWCHARTED	FORGETTABLE
FEMME FATALE	FIRE STATION	FLOWER GIRLS	FORGIVENESS
FENESTRATED	FIRING SQUAD	FLOWERINESS	FORGIVINGLY
FERMENTABLE	FIRMAMENTAL	FLUCTUATING	FORLORN HOPE
FEROCIOUSLY	FIRST COUSIN	FLUCTUATION	FORLORNNESS
FERRICYANIC	FIRST-DEGREE	FLUORESCEIN	FORMALISTIC
FERRIFEROUS	FIRST-FOOTER	FLUORESCENT	FORMALITIES
FERRIS WHEEL	FIRST NIGHTS	FLUORIDATED	FORMALIZING
FERROCYANIC	FIRST PERSON	FLUOROMETER	FORMATIONAL
FERTILIZERS	FIRST STRIKE	FLUOROMETRY	FORMATIVELY
FERTILIZING	FIRST-STRING	FLUOROSCOPE	FORMICATION
FERULACEOUS	FISH-EYE LENS	FLUOROSCOPY	FORMULAICLY
FERVENTNESS	FISH FARMING	FLYCATCHERS	FORMATIVELY
FESTINATION	FISH FINGERS	FLYING BOATS	FORMICATION
FETISHISTIC	FISHMONGERS	FLYING FOXES	FORMULAICLY
FEUDALISTIC	FISSIONABLE	FLYING SQUAD	FORMULARIZE

FORMULATING
FORMULATION
FORMULISTIC
FORNICATING
FORNICATION
FORSWEARING
FORTHCOMING
FORTIFIABLE
FORTNIGHTLY
FORTUNATELY
FORWARDNESS
FOSSILIZING
FOUL-MOUTHED
FOUNDATIONS
FOUNTAIN PEN
FOUR-POSTERS
FOURTEENTHS
FOX TERRIERS
FRACTIONARY
FRACTIONATE
FRACTIONIZE
FRACTIOUSLY
FRACTURABLE
FRAGMENTARY
FRAGMENTING
FRAME OF MIND
FRANCHISING
FRANCISCANS
FRANCOPHILE
FRANCOPHOBE
FRANCOPHONE
FRANKFURTER
FRANTICALLY
FRATERNALLY
FRATERNIZED
FRATERNIZER
FRATRICIDAL
FRATRICIDES
FRAUDULENCE
FREEBOOTERS
FREE-FLOATER
FREE-FOR-ALLS
FREE-HEARTED
FREEHOLDERS
FREELANCING
FREELOADERS
FREELOADING
FREEMASONIC
FREEMASONRY
FREE PARDONS
FREE-SWIMMER
FREETHINKER
FREEWHEELED
FREEZE-DRIED

FRENCH BEANS
FRENCH BREAD
FRENCH DOORS
FRENCH FRIES
FRENCH HORNS
FRENCHWOMAN
FREQUENCIES
FREQUENTING
FRETFULNESS
FREUDIANISM
FRIENDLIEST
FRIENDSHIPS
FRIGHTENING
FRIGHTFULLY
FRIVOLITIES
FRIVOLOUSLY
FROGMARCHED
FRONT-RUNNER
FROSTBITTEN
FRUCTIFYING
FRUGIVOROUS
FRUITLESSLY
FRUIT SALADS
FRUSTRATING
FRUSTRATION
FRUTESCENCE
FULGURATING
FULGURATION
FULL-BLOODED
FULL-FLEDGED
FULL-MOUTHED
FULMINATING
FULMINATION
FULMINATORY
FULSOMENESS
FUNAMBULIST
FUNCTIONARY
FUNCTIONING
FUNDAMENTAL
FUNGIBILITY
FUNGISTATIC
FURALDEHYDE
FURIOUSNESS
FURNISHINGS
FURTHERANCE
FURTHERMORE
FURTHERMOST
FURTIVENESS

12 LETTERS
FABRICATIONS
FABULOUSNESS
FACELESSNESS
FACILITATING
FACILITATION
FACILITATIVE
FACTIONALISM
FACTIONALIST
FACTIOUSNESS
FACTORY FARMS
FACTUALISTIC
FAINT-HEARTED
FAIT ACCOMPLI
FAITHFULNESS
FAITH HEALERS
FAITH HEALING
FALLACIOUSLY
FALLING STARS
FALSE BOTTOMS
FAMILIARIZED
FAMILIARIZER
FAMILIARNESS
FAMILY CIRCLE
FAMILY DOCTOR
FANCIFULNESS
FARADIZATION
FARSIGHTEDLY
FASCINATEDLY
FASTIDIOUSLY
FATHER FIGURE
FATHERLINESS
FATHERS-IN-LAW
FATIGABILITY
FAULT-FINDING
FEARLESSNESS
FEARSOMENESS
FEATHERBRAIN
FEATURE FILMS
FECKLESSNESS
FEDERALISTIC
FEEBLEMINDED
FELICITATING
FELICITATION
FELICITOUSLY
FEMINIZATION
FENESTRATION
FENNELFLOWER
FERMENTATION
FERMENTATIVE
FERRICYANIDE
FERRIS WHEELS
FERROCYANIDE
FERTILIZABLE

FEVERISHNESS
FIBRILLATION
FIBRILLIFORM
FIBROBLASTIC
FICTIONALIZE
FICTITIOUSLY
FIDDLESTICKS
FIELD GLASSES
FIELD MARSHAL
FIELD-TESTING
FIELD WORKERS
FIENDISHNESS
FIFTH COLUMNS
FIGURATIVELY
FIGURE GROUND
FIGURE SKATER
FILIBUSTERED
FILIBUSTERER
FILM PREMIERE
FILTER-TIPPED
FINALIZATION
FINGERBOARDS
FINGERPLATES
FINGER PRINTS
FINGERSTALLS
FIRE BRIGADES
FIRECRACKERS
FIRE FIGHTERS
FIRE FIGHTING
FIRE HYDRANTS
FIRELIGHTERS
FIREPROOFING
FIRE STARTERS
FIRE STATIONS
FIRING SQUADS
FIRST COUSINS
FIRST-FOOTING
FIRST-NIGHTER
FIRST REFUSAL
FISSIPALMATE
FLAGELLATING
FLAGELLATION
FLAGELLIFORM
FLAMBOYANTLY
FLAME-THROWER
FLAMMABILITY
FLATTERINGLY
FLEET ADMIRAL
FLOATABILITY
FLOCCULATION
FLOORWALKERS
FLORICULTURE
FLOWCHARTING
FLUCTUATIONS

FLUID EXTRACT
FLUIDIZATION
FLUORESCENCE
FLUORIDATING
FLUORIDATION
FLUORINATION
FLUOROCARBON
FLUOROMETRIC
FLUOROSCOPIC
FLUTTERINGLY
FLUVIOMARINE
FLYING DOCTOR
FLYING SAUCER
FLYING SQUADS
FOCALIZATION
FOOT-AND-MOUTH
FOOT FAULTING
FOOTSLOGGING
FORBEARINGLY
FORBIDDINGLY
FORCE-FEEDING
FORCEFULNESS
FORECLOSABLE
FOREKNOWABLE
FORENSICALLY
FOREORDAINED
FORESHADOWED
FORESHADOWER
FORESTALLING
FORESTALLMENT
FORESTAYSAIL
FORETRIANGLE
FORGATHERING
FORGET-ME-NOTS
FORMALDEHYDE
FORMLESSNESS
FORMULARIZER
FORMULATIONS
FORTUITOUSLY
FOSSILIZABLE
FOUNDATIONAL
FOUNTAINHEAD
FOUNTAIN PENS
FOURTH ESTATE
FOURTH OF JULY
FRACTIONALLY
FRACTIONATOR
FRAMES OF MIND
FRANKINCENSE
FRATERNALISM
FRATERNATIES
FRATERNIZING
FRAUDULENTLY
FREAKISHNESS

FREE CHURCHES
FREE-FLOATING
FREE-STANDING
FREE-SWIMMING
FREE-THINKERS
FREETHINKING
FREEWHEELING
FREEZE-DRYING
FREIGHTLINER
FRENCH KISSES
FRENCH LOAVES
FRENCH POLISH
FRENETICALLY
FREQUENTABLE
FREUDIAN SLIP
FRIENDLINESS
FRIGHTENABLE
FROG MARCHING
FRONDESCENCE
FRONTBENCHER
FRONTBENCHES
FRONTIERSMAN
FRONTIERSMEN
FRONTISPIECE
FRONT-RUNNERS
FRUCTIFEROUS
FRUITFULNESS
FRUIT MACHINE
FRUMPISHNESS
FRUSTRATIONS
FUDDY DUDDIES
FULLY-FLEDGED
FULMINATIONS
FUNCTIONALLY
FUNDAMENTALS
FUTILITARIAN
FUTUROLOGIST

13 LETTERS
FACETIOUSNESS
FACTORABILITY
FACTORIZATION
FAITHLESSNESS
FALLOPIAN TUBE
FALSIFICATION
FAMILIARITIES
FAMILIARIZING
FAMILY DOCTORS
FANTASTICALLY
FASCICULATION
FASCINATINGLY
FASCISTICALLY
FATHEADEDNESS

FATHER FIGURES
FAULTLESSNESS
FEATHERBEDDED
FEATHERSTITCH
FEATHER-VEINED
FEATHERWEIGHT
FEATURE-LENGTH
FEEDING BOTTLE
FELICITATIONS
FELLOW FEELING
FELONIOUSNESS
FEMMES FATALES
FEROCIOUSNESS
FERRIMAGNETIC
FERROCHROMIUM
FERROCONCRETE
FERROELECTRIC
FERROMAGNETIC
FERTILIZATION
FEUDALIZATION
FEUILLETONISM
FEUILLETONIST
FIBROVASCULAR
FICTIONALIZED
FIELD MARSHALS
FIELD OF VISION
FIGHTER-BOMBER
FIGURED BASSES
FIGURE OF EIGHT
FIGURE SKATERS
FIGURE-SKATING
FILIBUSTERING
FILING CABINET
FILM PREMIERES
FILTERABILITY
FINANCIAL YEAR
FINE-TOOTH COMB
FINGERPRINTED
FIRST OFFENDER
FISH-EYE LENSES
FISSION-FUSION
FLABBERGASTED
FLAGELLANTISM
FLAME-THROWERS
FLEET ADMIRALS
FLESH AND BLOOD
FLIRTATIOUSLY
FLOATING-POINT
FLOATING VOTER
FLOODLIGHTING
FLORICULTURAL
FLORISTICALLY
FLOURISHINGLY
FLYING COLOURS

FLYING DOCTORS
FLYING OFFICER
FLYING PICKETS
FLYING SAUCERS
FOLLOW-THROUGH
FONTAINEBLEAU
FOOD POISONING
FOOD PROCESSOR
FOOLHARDINESS
FOOL'S PARADISE
FOOTBALL POOLS
FORAMINIFERAL
FOREIGN OFFICE
FOREJUDGEMENT
FOREKNOWINGLY
FOREKNOWLEDGE
FORENSICALITY
FOREORDAINING
FORESHADOWING
FORESHORTENED
FOREWARNINGLY
FORGETFULNESS

FORGIVINGNESS
FORKLIFT TRUCK
FORMALIZATION
FORMATIVENESS
FORMIDABILITY
FORTIFICATION
FORTITUDINOUS
FORTUNE HUNTER
FORTUNE-TELLER
FOSSILFEROUS
FOSSILIZATION
FOUNDATIONARY
FRACTIONATION
FRACTIOUSNESS
FRACTOCUMULUS
FRACTOSTRATUS
FRAGMENTATION
FRANCHISEMENT
FREEZING POINT
FREIGHTLINERS
FRENCH WINDOWS
FREQUENTATION

FREQUENTATIVE
FREUDIAN SLIPS
FRIDGE-FREEZER
FRIGHTENINGLY
FRIGHTFULNESS
FRINGE BENEFIT
FRIVOLOUSNESS
FRONT BENCHERS
FRONTISPIECES
FRONTOGENESIS
FRUITLESSNESS
FRUIT MACHINES
FRUMENTACEOUS
FULL-FASHIONED
FUNCTIONALISM
FUNCTIONALIST
FUNCTIONARIES
FUNDAMENTALLY
FUNNY BUSINESS
FUTURE PERFECT

3 LETTERS	GAYS	GOOD	GALEA	GEOID	GLUTS
GAB	GAZA	GOOF	GALES	GERMS	GLYPH
GAD	GAZE	GOON	GALLA	GESSO	GNARL
GAG	GCSE	GORE	GALLS	GETUP	GNASH
GAL	G'DAY	GORY	GAMED	GHANA	GNATS
GAS	GEAR	GOSH	GAMES	GHATS	GNOME
GAY	GELD	GOUT	GAMEY	GHENT	GOADS
GEE	GELS	GOWN	GAMIC	GHOST	GOALS
GEL	GEMS	GRAB	GAMIN	GHOUL	GOATS
GEM	GENE	GRAM	GAMMA	GHYLL	GODLY
GEN	GENT	GRAN	GAMMY	GIANT	GOERS
GET	GENU	GRAY	GAMUT	GIBER	GOFER
GIG	GERM	GREW	GANDA	GIBES	GOIAS
GIN	GHAT	GREY	GANGS	GIDDY	GOING
GIS	GHEE	GRID	GANJA	GIFTS	GOLDS
GNU	GIBE	GRIM	GAOLS	GIGOT	GOLEM
GOB	GIFT	GRIN	GAPED	GIGUE	GOLLY
GOD	GIGS	GRIP	GAPER	GIJON	GOMEL
GOO	GILD	GRIT	GAPES	GILET	GONAD
GOP	GILL	GROG	GARDA	GILLS	GONDI
GOT	GILT	GROW	GASES	GILTS	GONER
GUM	GIMP	GRUB	GASPS	GIPSY	GONGS
GUT	GINS	GUFF	GASSY	GIRLS	GOODS
GUV	GIRD	GULF	GATED	GIRON	GOODY
GUY	GIRL	GULL	GATES	GIRTH	GOOEY
GYM	GIRO	GULP	GAUDY	GIVEN	GOOFS
GYP	GIRT	GUMS	GAUGE	GIVER	GOOFY
	GIST	GUNS	GAUNT	GLACE	GOONS
	GIVE	GURU	GAUSS	GLADE	GOOSE
4 LETTERS	GLAD	GUSH	GAUZE	GLAIR	GOOSY
GAFF	GLEE	GUST	GAUZY	GLAND	GORED
GAGA	GLEN	GUTS	GAVEL	GLANS	GORES
GAGE	GLIB	GUVS	GAVLE	GLARE	GORGE
GAGS	GLOW	GUYS	GAWKY	GLARY	GORKI
GAIN	GLUE	GYBE	GAYER	GLASS	GORSE
GAIT	GLUM	GYMS	GAZED	GLAZE	GOUDA
GALA	GLUT	GYRE	GAZER	GLEAM	GOUGE
GALE	GNAT		GCSES	GLEAN	GOURD
GALL	GNAW		GEARS	GLEBE	GOUTY
GALS	GNUS	5 LETTERS	GECKO	GLEES	GOWNS
GAME	GOAD	GABBY	GEESE	GLENS	GRABS
GAMY	GOAL	GABES	GEEST	GLIDE	GRACE
GANG	GOAT	GABLE	GELID	GLINT	GRADE
GOAL	GOBI	GABON	GEMMA	GLITZ	GRAFT
GAPE	GOBO	GADID	GENES	GLOAT	GRAIL
GAPS	GOBS	GAFFE	GENET	GLOBE	GRAIN
GARB	GODS	GAFFS	GENIC	GLOOM	GRAMA
GARD	GOER	GAGED	GENIE	GLORY	GRAMS
GASH	GOES	GAGES	GENII	GLOSS	GRANT
GASP	GO-GO	GAILY	GENOA	GLOVE	GRAPE
GATE	GOLD	GAINS	GENRE	GLUED	GRAPH
GAVE	GOLF	GAITS	GENTS	GLUER	GRASP
GAWK	GONE	GALAH	GENUS	GLUEY	GRASS
GAWP	GONG	GALAS	GEODE	GLUME	GRATE

G
5 LETTERS to 6 LETTERS

GRAVE	GULLY	GALLON	GATHER	GIBBED	GLOSSY
GRAVY	GULPS	GALLOP	GAUCHE	GIBBER	GLOVED
GRAYS	GUMBO	GALORE	GAUCHO	GIBBET	GLOVER
GRAZE	GUMMA	GALOSH	GAUGED	GIBBON	GLOVES
GREAT	GUMMY	GALWAY	GAUGER	GIBE AT	GLOWED
GREBE	GUNGE	GAMBIA	GAUGES	GIFTED	GLOWER
GRECO-	GUPPY	GAMBIT	GAVAGE	GIGGLE	GLUING
GREED	GURUS	GAMBLE	GAVELS	GIGGLY	GLUMLY
GREEK	GUSTO	GAMBOL	GAVIAL	GIGILO	GLUTEN
GREEN	GUSTS	GAMELY	GAWKED	GILDED	GLYCOL
GREET	GUSTY	GAMETE	GAWKER	GILDER	GNAWED
GREYS	GUTSY	GAMIER	GAWPED	GILLED	GNAWER
GRIDS	GUTTA	GAMINE	GAYEST	GILLIE	GNEISS
GRIEF	GUYED	GAMING	GAZEBO	GIMLET	GNOMES
GRILL	GUYOT	GAMMAS	GAZING	GIMMAL	GNOMIC
GRIME	GWENT	GAMMED	GAZUMP	GINGER	GNOMON
GRIMY	GYPSY	GAMMON	GDYNIA	GINKGO	GNOSIS
GRIND	GYRAL	GANDER	GEARED	GIRDED	GOADED
GRINS	GYRES	GANGER	GECKOS	GIRDER	GOATEE
GRIPE		GANGES	GEDACT	GIRDLE	GOBBET
GRIPS	**6 LETTERS**	GANGUE	GEE-GEE	GIRLIE	GOBBLE
GRIST	GABBED	GANNET	GEEZER	GIRTHS	GOBIAN
GRITS	GABBER	GANOID	GEISHA	GIUSTO	GOBLET
GROAN	GABBLE	GANTRY	GELADA	GIVING	GOBLIN
GROAT	GABBRO	GAOLED	GELDED	GLACIS	GODSON
GROIN	GABION	GAOLER	GELLED	GLADES	GODWIT
GROOM	GABLED	GAPING	GEMINI	GLADLY	GOFERS
GROPE	GADDED	GAPPED	GEMMED	GLAIRY	GOFFER
GROSS	GADDER	GARAGE	GENDER	GLANCE	GOGGLE
GROUP	GADFLY	GARBED	GENERA	GLANDS	GOITRE
GROUT	GADGET	GARBLE	GENEVA	GLARED	GO-KART
GROVE	GADOID	GARCON	GENIAL	GLARES	GOLDEN
GROWL	GAELIC	GARDEN	GENIES	GLASSY	GOLFER
GROWN	GAFFER	GARGET	GENOME	GLAZED	GOLLOP
GRUBS	GAFFES	GARGLE	GENRES	GLAZER	GOMUTI
GRUEL	GAGGED	GARISH	GENTLE	GLAZES	GONERS
GRUFF	GAGGER	GARLIC	GENTLY	GLEAMS	GONION
GRUNT	GAGGLE	GARNER	GENTRY	GLEBES	GOODLY
GUANO	GAGING	GARNET	GEONIC	GLEETY	GOOFED
GUARD	GAIETY	GARTER	GERBIL	GLIBLY	GOOGLY
GUAVA	GAINED	GASBAG	GERMAN	GLIDED	GOOGOL
GUESS	GAINER	GASCON	GERMEN	GLIDER	GOOIER
GUEST	GAINLY	GASHED	GERUND	GLIDES	GOPHER
GUIDE	GAITER	GASHES	GETTER	GLINTS	GORGED
GUILD	GALATA	GASIFY	GETUPS	GLIOMA	GORGER
GUILE	GALATI	GASKET	GEYSER	GLITCH	GORGES
GUILT	GALAXY	GASKIN	GEZIRA	GLITZY	GORGON
GUISE	GALENA	GASMAN	GHETTO	GLOATS	GORIER
GULAG	GALERE	GASPED	GHIBLI	GLOBAL	GORILY
GULAR	GALIBI	GASPER	GHOSTS	GLOBES	GORING
GULCH	GALIOT	GASSED	GHOULS	GLOBIN	GO-SLOW
GULES	GALLED	GASSER	GHYLLS	GLOOMY	GOSPEL
GULFS	GALLEY	GASSES	GIANTS	GLORIA	GOSSIP
GULLS	GALLIC	GATEAU	GIAOUR	GLOSSA	GOTHIC

468

GOUGED	GRINDS	GUISES	GAINSAY	GENERIC	GINGERY
GOUGER	GRINGO	GUITAR	GAITERS	GENESIS	GINGHAM
GOUGES	GRIPED	GULDEN	GALATEA	GENETIC	GINGILI
GOURDS	GRIPER	GULLAH	GALEATE	GENEVAN	GINGIVA
GOVERN	GRIPES	GULLED	GALENIC	GENIPAP	GINSENG
GRABEN	GRISLY	GULLET	GALICIA	GENITAL	GIN TRAP
GRACED	GRISON	GULPED	GALILEE	GENITOR	GIPSIES
GRACES	GRISTS	GULPER	GALIPOT	GENOESE	GIAFFE
GRADED	GRITTY	GUMBOS	GALLANT	GENTEEL	GIRASOL
GRADER	GRIVET	GUMMED	GALLEON	GENTIAN	GIRDERS
GRADES	GROANS	GUNDOG	GALLERY	GENTILE	GIRDING
GRADIN	GROATS	GUNG-HO	GALLEYS	GENUINE	GIRDLED
GRADUS	GROCER	GUNMAN	GALLFLY	GEODESY	GIRDLER
GRAECO-	GRODNO	GUNMEN	GALLING	GEOLOGY	GIRDLES
GRAFTS	GROGGY	GUNNED	GALLIUM	GEORDIE	GIRLISH
GRAINS	GROINS	GUNNEL	GALLNUT	GEORGIA	GIONDE
GRAINY	GROOMS	GUNNER	GALLONS	GEORGIC	GIRONNY
GRAMME	GROOVE	GUNSHY	GALLOPS	GERBILS	GISARME
GRANDS	GROOVY	GUNTER	GALLOUS	GERENUK	GITTERN
GRANGE	GROPED	GURGLE	GALLOWS	GERMANE	GIVABLE
GRANNY	GROPER	GURJUN	GALUMPH	GERMANS	GIZZARD
GRANTS	GROPES	GURKHA	GAUCHOS	GERMANY	GLACIAL
GRAPES	GROTTO	GUSHED	GAUDERY	GERUNDS	GLACIER
GRAPHS	GROTTY	GUSHER	GAUDIER	GESTALT	GLADDEN
GRASSY	GROUCH	GUSSET	GAUDILY	GESTAPO	GLADDER
GRATED	GROUND	GUSTED	GAUGING	GESTATE	GLAD EYE
GRATER	GROUPS	GUTTED	GAUHATI	GESTURE	GLAMOUR
GRATES	GROUSE	GUTTER	GAUZIER	GETABLE	GLANCED
GRATIS	GROUTS	GUVNOR	GAVOTTE	GETAWAY	GLANCES
GRAVEL	GROVEL	GUYANA	GAWKERS	GETTING	GLARING
GRAVEN	GROVES	GUYING	GAWKIER	GEYSERS	GLASGOW
GRAVER	GROWER	GUZZLE	GAWKING	GHASTLY	GLASSED
GRAVES	GROWLS	GYPPED	GAWPING	GHERKIN	GLASSES
GRAVID	GROWTH	GYPSUM	GAYNESS	GHETTOS	GLASIER
GRAYER	GROYNE	GYRATE	GAZEBOS	GHILLIE	GLAZING
GRAZED	GROZNY	GYROSE	GAZELLE	GHOSTED	GLEAMED
GRAZER	GRUBBY		GAZETTE	GHOSTLY	GLEANED
GRAZES	GRUDGE		GEARBOX	GIBBETS	GLEANER
GREASE	GRUGRU	**7 LETTERS**	GEARING	GIBBING	GLEEFUL
GREASY	GRUMPY	GABBING	GECKOES	GIBBONS	GLENOID
GREATS	GRUNTS	GABBLED	GEE-GEES	GIBBOUS	GLIADIN
GREBES	GUARDS	GABBLER	GEELONG	GIBLETS	GLIBBER
GREECE	GUAVAS	GADDING	GEEZERS	GIDDIER	GLIDERS
GREEDY	GUENON	GADGETS	GEISHAS	GIDDILY	GLIDING
GREENS	GUESTS	GADGETY	GELATIN	GIGGLED	GLIMMER
GREYED	GUFFAW	GADROON	GELDING	GIGGLER	GLIMPSE
GREYER	GUIANA	GADWALL	GELLING	GIGGLES	GLINTED
GRIEVE	GUIDED	GAFFERS	GEMMATE	GIGOLOS	GLISTEN
GRIFFE	GUIDER	GAGAUZI	GEMMING	GILBERT	GLITTER
GRIGRI	GUIDEN	GAGGING	GEMMULE	GILDING	GLIWACE
GRILLE	GUILDS	GAHNITE	GEMSBOK	GILLIES	GLOATED
GRILLS	GUILTY	GAINERS	GENAPPE	GIMBALS	GLOATER
GRILSE	GUIMPE	GAINFUL	GENDERS	GIMLETS	GLOBATE
GRIMLY	GUINEA	GAINING	GENERAL	GIMMICK	GLOBOID

GLOBOSE	GODLIKE	GRAINER	GREISEN	GROUCHY	GUJARAT
GLOBULE	GODSEND	GRAMMAR	GREMIAL	GROUNDS	GULCHES
GLORIED	GOGGLED	GRAMMES	GREMLIN	GROUPED	GULDENS
GLORIES	GOGGLES	GRAMPUS	GRENADE	GROUPER	GULLETS
GLORIFY	GOIANIA	GRANADA	GREYEST	GROUPIE	GULLIES
GLOSSAL	GO-KARTS	GRANARY	GREYHEN	GROUSED	GULLING
GLOSSED	GOLDEYE	GRANDAD	GREYING	GROUSER	GULPING
GLOSSER	GOLFERS	GRANDEE	GREYISH	GROUSES	GUMBOIL
GLOTTAL	GOLFING	GRANDER	GREYLAG	GROUTER	GUMBOOT
GLOTTIC	GOLIATH	GRANDLY	GRIBBLE	GROWERS	GUMDROP
GLOTTIS	GONADAL	GRANDMA	GRIDDLE	GROWING	GUMMIER
GLOWING	GONDOLA	GRANDPA	GRIEVED	GROWLED	GUMMING
GLUCOSE	GOODBYE	GRANGES	GRIEVER	GROWLER	GUMMITE
GLUEING	GOOD DAY	GRANITE	GRIFFIN	GROWN-UP	GUMSHOE
GLIMMER	GOODIES	GRANOLA	GRIFFON	GROWTHS	GUM TREE
GLUTEAL	GOODISH	GRANTED	GRILLED	GROYNES	GUNBOAT
GLUTEUS	GOFFIER	GRANTEE	GRILLER	GRUBBED	GUNDOGS
GLUTTED	GOOFILY	GRANTER	GRILLES	GRUBBER	GUNFIRE
GLUTTON	GOOFING	GRANTOR	GRIMACE	GRUDGED	GUNLOCK
GLYCINE	GOOIEST	GRANULE	GRIMIER	GRUDGER	GUNNELS
GLYPHIC	GOPHERS	GRAPHIC	GRIMMER	GRUDGES	GUNNERS
GLYPTIC	GORGING	GRAPNEL	GRINDER	GRUFFER	GUNNERY
GNARLED	GORGONS	GRAPPLE	GRINGOS	GRUFFLY	GUNNING
GNASHED	GORIEST	GRASPED	GRINNED	GRUMBLE	GUNSHOT
GNASHES	GORILLA	GRASPER	GRINNER	GRUMOUS	GUNWALE
GNATHIC	GOSHAWK	GRASSED	GRIPERS	GRUNTED	GURGLED
GNAWING	GOSLING	GRASSES	GRIPING	GRUNTER	GURNARD
GNOCCHI	GO-SLOWS	GRATERS	GRIPPED	GRUYERE	GUSHIER
GNOMISH	GOSPELS	GRATIFY	GRIPPER	GRYPHON	GUSHING
GNOSTIC	GOSPLAN	GRATING	GRISTLE	G-STRING	GUSSETS
GOADING	GOSSIPS	GRAUPEL	GRIZZLY	GUANACO	GUSTIER
GO-AHEAD	GOSSIPY	GRAVELY	GRITTED	GUANESE	GUSTILY
GOATEED	GOUACHE	GRAVEST	GRIZZLE	GUANINE	GUSTING
GOATEES	GOUGING	GRAVITY	GROANED	GUARANI	GUTLESS
GOBBETS	GOULASH	GRAVURE	GROANER	GUARDED	GUSTIER
GOBBLED	GORMANI	GRAYEST	GROCERS	GUARDER	GUTTATE
GOBBLER	GOURMET	GRAYING	GROCERY	GUAYULE	GUTTERS
GOBBLES	GRAB BAG	GRAZIER	GROLIER	GUDGEON	GUTTING
GOBELIN	GRABBED	GRAZING	GROMMET	GUESSED	GUVNORS
GOBILIN	GRABBER	GREASED	GROOMED	GUESSER	GUZZLED
GOBIOID	GRABBLE	GREASER	GROOMER	GUESSES	GUZZLER
GOBLETS	GRACILE	GREATER	GROOVED	GUESTED	GWALIOR
GOBLINS	GRACING	GREATLY	GROOVES	GUFFAWS	GWYNIAD
GODDAMN	GRACKLE	GREAVES	GROPING	GUILING	GYMNAST
GODDESS	GRADATE	GRECIAN	GROSSED	GUILDER	GYMSLIP
GODHEAD	GRADING	GREENED	GROSSER	GUINEAN	GYPPING
GODHOOD	GRADUAL	GREENER	GROSSES	GUINEAS	GYPSIES
GODLESS	GRAFTED	GREETED	GROSSLY	GUIPURE	GYRATED
GODLIER	GRAFTER	GREETER	GROTTOS	GUITARS	GYRATOR

8 LETTERS	GARAGING	GENETICS	GIN RUMMY	GLORYING
GABBLING	GARAMOND	GENIALLY	GIN SLING	GLOSSARY
GABBROIC	GARBLESS	GENITALS	GIN TRAPS	GLOSSIER
GABONESE	GARBLING	GENITIVE	GIRAFFES	GLOSSILY
GABORONE	GARBOARD	GENIUSES	GIRDLING	GLOSSING
GADABOUT	GARDENED	GENOCIDE	GIRLHOOD	GLOWERED
GADFLIES	GARDENER	GENOTYPE	GIVEAWAY	GLOW-WORM
GADGETRY	GARDENIA	GENTIANS	GIZZARDS	GLOXINIA
GAFFSAIL	GARGANEY	GENTILES	GLABELLA	GLUCAGON
GAINABLE	GARGLING	GENTRIFY	GLABROUS	GLUCINUM
GAINSAID	GARGOYLE	GEODESIC	GLACIATE	GLUCOSIC
GALACTIC	GARISHLY	GEODETIC	GLACIERS	GLUMMEST
GALANGAL	GARLANDS	GEOGNOSY	GLADDEST	GLUMNESS
GALAXIES	GARLICKY	GEOMANCY	GLAD HAND	GLUTELIN
GALBANUM	GARMENTS	GEOMETER	GLADIATE	GLUTTING
GALENISM	GARNERED	GEOMETRY	GLADIOLI	GLUTTONS
GALENIST	GARRISON	GEOPHAGY	GLADNESS	GLUTTONY
GALICIAN	GARROTTE	GEOPHYTE	GLAD RAGS	GLYCERIC
GALILEAN	GASIFIER	GEOPONIC	GLANCING	GLYCERIN
GALLANTS	GASIFORM	GEORDIES	GLANDERS	GLYCEROL
GALLEASS	GASLIGHT	GEORGIAN	GLANDULE	GLYCERYL
GALLEONS	GAS MASKS	GEOTAXIS	GLASSIER	GLYCOGEN
GALLIARD	GASOLIER	GERANIAL	GLASSINE	GLYCOLIC
GALLIPOT	GASOLINE	GERANIOL	GLASSING	GLYPTICS
GALLOPED	GASSIEST	GERANIUM	GLASSMEN	GNASHING
GALLOPER	GASTIGHT	GERMANIC	GLAUCOMA	GNATHION
GALLOWAY	GASTRULA	GERM CELL	GLAUCOUS	GNATHITE
GALOSHES	GASWORKS	GERMINAL	GLAZIERS	GNAWABLE
GALVANIC	GATEFOLD	GESTALTS	GLAZIERY	GNEISSIC
GAMBLERS	GATEPOST	GESTAPOS	GLEAMING	GNOMONIC
GAMBLING	GATEWAYS	GESTURAL	GLEANING	GOAL LINE
GAMBOLED	GATHERED	GESTURED	GLENDALE	GOAL POST
GAMECOCK	GATHERER	GESTURER	GLIBBEST	GOATHERD
GAMENESS	GAUDIEST	GESTURES	GLIBNESS	GOATSKIN
GAMESTER	GAULLISM	GHANAIAN	GLIMMERS	GOAT'S-RUE
GAMINESS	GAULLIST	GHERKINS	GLIMPSED	GOBBLING
GAMMA RAY	GAUNTLET	GHETTOES	GLIMPSER	GOD-AWFUL
GAMMONER	GAUZIEST	GHOSTING	GLIMPSES	GODCHILD
GANDHIAN	GAZELLES	GHOULISH	GLINTING	GODLIEST
GANG-BANG	GAZETTES	GIANTESS	GLISCADE	GODSENDS
GANGLAND	GAZPACHO	GIBBERED	GLITCHES	GODSPEED
GANGLIAL	GAZUMPED	GIBBSITE	GLITTERS	GOETHITE
GANGLING	GAZUMPER	GIBINGLY	GLITTERY	GO-GETTER
GANGLION	GELATINE	GIDDIEST	GLITZIER	GOGGLING
GANGRENE	GELATION	GIFT-WRAP	GLOAMING	GOIDELIC
GANGSTER	GELDINGS	GIGANTIC	GLOATING	GOINGS-ON
GANGWAYS	GELIDITY	GIGGLING	GLOBALLY	GOITROUS
GANISTER	GEMINATE	GILTHEAD	GLOBULAR	GOLD DUST
GANTLINE	GEMOLOGY	GIMCRACK	GLOBULES	GOLD FISH
GANTRIES	GEMSTONE	GIMMICKS	GLOBULIN	GOLD LEAF
GANYMEDE	GENDARME	GIMMICKY	GLOOMFUL	GOLDMINE
GAOLBIRD	GENERALS	GINGERED	GLOOMIER	GOLD RUSH
GAPEWORM	GENERATE	GINGERLY	GLOOMILY	GOLF BALL
GAPINGLY	GENEROUS	GINGIVAL	GLORIOUS	GOLF CLUB

471

GOLIATHS	GRANDEUR	GRILLAGE	GRUNTING	GYMSLIPS
GOLLIWOG	GRAND MAL	GRILLING	GRYPHONS	GYNANDRY
GOLLOPER	GRANDMAS	GRIMACED	G-STRINGS	GYNARCHY
GOMBROON	GRANDPAS	GRIMACER	GUAIACOL	GYPSEOUS
GONDOLAS	GRANDSON	GRIMACES	GUAIACUM	GYRATING
GONIDIAL	GRANITIC	GRIMIEST	GUARANTY	GYRATION
GONIDIUM	GRANNIES	GRIMMEST	GUARDANT	GYRATORY
GONOCYTE	GRANTING	GRIMNESS	GUARDIAN	
GONOPORE	GRANULAR	GRINDERS	GUARDING	
GOOD BOOK	GRANULES	GRINDERY	GUERNSEY	**9 LETTERS**
GOODBYES	GRAPHEME	GRINDING	GUERRERO	GABARDINE
GOODLIER	GRAPHICS	GRINNING	GUESSING	GABERDINE
GOODNESS	GRAPHITE	GRIPPING	GUESTING	GABIONADE
GOODWILL	GRAPNELS	GRISEOUS	GUFFAWED	GADABOUTS
GOODWORD	GRAPPLED	GRISETTE	GUIANESE	GADOLINIC
GOOFIEST	GRAPPLER	GRISLIER	GUIDABLE	GADROONED
GOOGLIES	GRASPING	GRITTIER	GUIDANCE	GAINFULLY
GORGEDLY	GRASSIER	GRITTILY	GUILDERS	GAINSAYER
GORGEOUS	GRASSING	GRITTING	GUILEFUL	GALACTOSE
GORGERIN	GRATEFUL	GRIZZLED	GUILTIER	GALANTINE
GORILLAS	GRATINGS	GROANING	GUILTILY	GALAPAGOS
GORINESS	GRATUITY	GROGGIER	GUJARATI	GALEIFORM
GORLOVKA	GRAVAMEN	GROGGILY	GULFWEED	GALENICAL
GORMLESS	GRAVELED	GROMWELL	GULLIBLE	GALINGALE
GOSLINGS	GRAVELLY	GROOMING	GULLIBLY	GALLANTLY
GOSPODIN	GRAVITAS	GROOVIER	GUMBOILS	GALLANTRY
GOSSAMER	GRAVITON	GROSCHEN	GUMBOOTS	GALLERIED
GOSSIPED	GRAYLING	GROSSEST	GUMBOTIL	GALLERIES
GOSSIPER	GREASERS	GROSSING	GUMDROPS	GALLISISM
GOTEBORG	GREASIER	GROTTIER	GUMMIEST	GALLISIZE
GOUACHES	GREASILY	GROTTOES	GUMMOSIS	GALLINULE
GOURMAND	GREASING	GROUCHED	GUMPTION	GALLIPOLI
GOURMETS	GREATEST	GROUCHES	GUMSHOES	GALLIVANT
GOUTWEED	GREEDIER	GROUNDED	GUMTREES	GALLONAGE
GOVERNED	GREEDILY	GROUPIES	GUNBOATS	GALLOPING
GOVERNOR	GREENERY	GROUPING	GUNFLINT	GALLSTONE
GRAB BAGS	GREENEST	GROUSING	GUNMETAL	GALUMPHED
GRABBING	GREENFLY	GROVELED	GUNPAPER	GALVANISM
GRABBLER	GREENING	GROWABLE	GUNPOINT	GALVANIZE
GRACEFUL	GREENISH	GROWLERS	GUNSHOTS	GALWEGIAN
GRACIOUS	GREENLET	GROWLING	GUNSMITH	GAMBOLING
GRADABLE	GREEN TEA	GROWN-UPS	GUNSTOCK	GAMECOCKS
GRADIENT	GREETING	GRUBBIER	GUNWALES	GAMMADION
GRADUATE	GREMLINS	GRUBBILY	GURGLING	GAMMA RAYS
GRAECISM	GRENADES	GRUBBING	GURKHALI	GANDHIISM
GRAFFITI	GRENOBLE	GRUDGING	GUSTIEST	GANG-BANGS
GRAFFITO	GREY AREA	GRUESOME	GUTSIEST	GANGLIONS
GRAFTERS	GREYBACK	GRUFFEST	GUTTERED	GANGPLANK
GRAFTING	GREYNESS	GRUFFISH	GUTTURAL	GANGSTERS
GRAINING	GRIDDLES	GRUMBLED	GUYANESE	GAOLBIRDS
GRAMPIAN	GRIDIRON	GRUMBLER	GUZZLERS	GARDENERS
GRANDADS	GRIEVING	GRUMBLES	GUZZLING	GERDENIAS
GRANDEES	GRIEVOUS	GRUMPIER	GYMKHANA	GARDENING
GRANDEST	GRIFFINS	GRUMPILY	GYMNASTS	GARGOYLED

GARGOYLES	GENERALLY	GIBRALTAR	GLOMERATE	GOODLIEST
GARIBALDI	GENERATED	GIDDINESS	GLOMERULE	GOOD LOOKS
GARLANDED	GENERATOR	GIFT HORSE	GLOOMIEST	GOOD NIGHT
GARNERING	GENIALITY	GIGAHERTZ	GLORIFIED	GOOD SIZED
GARNISHED	GENITALIC	GIGANTISM	GLORIFIER	GOOD WORDS
GARNISHER	GENITALLY	GILSONITE	GLORY HOLE	GOOFINESS
GARNISHES	GENITIVAL	GILT-EDGED	GLOSSIEST	GOOSANDER
GARNITURE	GENITIVES	GIMMICKERY	GLOSSITIC	GOOSEFOOT
GARRISONS	GENOCIDAL	GINGER NUT	GLOSSITIS	GOOSENECK
GARROTTED	GENOTYPIC	GIN SLINGS	GLOTTIDES	GOOSESTEP
GARROTTER	GENTEELLY	GIPSYWORT	GLOTTISES	GOOSINESS
GARROTTES	GENTILITY	GIRANDOLE	GLOWERING	GORGEABLE
GARRULITY	GENTLEMAN	GIRL GUIDE	GLOWINGLY	GORGONIAN
GARRULOUS	GENTLEMEN	GIRLISHLY	GLOW-WORMS	GORILLIAN
GAS FITTER	GENTLE SEX	GIRONDISM	GLUCOSIDE	GORILLOID
GASHOLDER	GENUFLECT	GIRONDIST	GLUTAMINE	GOSPELLER
GASLIGHTS	GENUINELY	GIVEAWAYS	GLUTEMOUS	GOSSIPING
GASOLINIC	GEODESIST	GIVEN NAME	GLYCERIDE	GOTHICISM
GASOMETER	GEOGRAPHY	GLABELLAR	GLYCERINE	GOURMANDS
GASOMETRY	GEOLOGIST	GLADDENED	GLYCOSIDE	GOUTINESS
GASPINGLY	GEOLOGIZE	GLADDENER	GOAL LINES	GOVERNESS
GASSINESS	GEOMANCER	GLADIATOR	GOALMOUTH	GOVERNING
GASTRITIC	GEOMANTIC	GLADIOLUS	GOALPOSTS	GOVERNORS
GASTRITIS	GEOMETRIC	GLAIREOUS	GOATHERDS	GRACELESS
GASTROPOD	GEOMETRID	GLAMORIZE	GOATSKINS	GRADATION
GASTRULAR	GEOPHYTIC	GLAMOROUS	GO-BETWEEN	GRADIENTS
GATECRASH	GEOPHONIC	GLANDERED	GODFATHER	GRADUALLY
GATEHOUSE	GEORGETTE	GLANDULAR	GODLESSLY	GRADUATED
GATEPOSTS	GEOTACTIC	GLARINGLY	GODLINESS	GRADUATES
GATHERING	GEOTROPIC	GLASSIEST	GODMOTHER	GRADUATOR
GAUCHERIE	GERANIUMS	GLASSWARE	GODPARENT	GRAMPUSES
GAUDINESS	GERIATRIC	GLASSWORK	GO-GETTERS	GRANARIES
GAUGEABLE	GERMANDER	GLASSWORT	GOGGLE BOX	GRANDADDY
GAUGEABLY	GERMANISM	GLEANABLE	GOING-OVER	GRANDOISE
GAULIETER	GERMANITE	GLEANINGS	GOLD CREST	GRANDIOSO
GAUNTLETS	GERMANIUM	GLEEFULLY	GOLDEN AGE	GRAND JURY
GAUNTNESS	GERMANIZE	GLENGARRY	GOLDEN EYE	GRANDNESS
GAUZINESS	GERMANOUS	GLIDINGLY	GOLDENROD	GRAND PRIX
GAWKINESS	GERM CELLS	GLIMMERED	GOLDFIELD	GRAND SLAM
GAZEHOUND	GERMICIDE	GLIMPSING	GOLDFINCH	GRANDSONS
GAZETTEER	GERMINANT	GLISSADER	GOLD MEDAL	GRANITITE
GAZIANTEP	GERMINATE	GLISSANDO	GOLD-MINER	GRANIVORE
GAZUMPING	GERMISTON	GLISTENED	GOLDMINES	GRANOLITH
GEARBOXES	GERUNDIAL	GLITTERED	GOLD PLATE	GRANTABLE
GEAR LEVER	GERUNDIVE	GLITZIEST	GOLDSMITH	GRANULATE
GEARWHEEL	GESTATION	GLOBALISM	GOLF BALLS	GRANULITE
GEHLENITE	GESTATORY	GLOBALIST	GOLF CLUBS	GRANULOMA
GELIGNITE	GESTURING	GLOBOSITY	GOLF LINKS	GRAPESHOT
GELSEMIUM	GEYSERITE	GLOMERATE	GOLLIWOGS	GRAPEVINE
GEMMATION	GHASTLIER	GLOMERULE	GOMPHOSIS	GRAPHITIC
GEMUTLICH	GHOSTLIER	GLOOMIEST	GONDOLIER	GRAPPLING
GENDARMES	GHOST TOWN	GLABALISM	GONDIATITE	GRASPABLE
GENEALOGY	GIBBERING	GLOBALIST	GONOPHORE	GRASSIEST
GENERABLE	GIBBERISH	GLOBOSITY	GONORRHEA	GRASSLAND

473

GRASSQUIT	GRISLIEST	GUITARIST	GARNISHING
GRATICULE	GRISTLIER	GULPINGLY	GARRISONED
GRATIFIED	GRISTMILL	GUMMATOUS	GARROTTING
GRATIFIER	GRITTIEST	GUMMINESS	GAS FITTERS
GRATINGLY	GRIZZLING	GUMSHIELD	GASHOLDERS
GRATITUDE	GROCERIES	GUN COTTON	GASIFIABLE
GRAVELING	GROGGIEST	GUN POWDER	GASOMETERS
GRAVELISH	GRONINGEN	GUNRUNNER	GASOMETRIC
GRAVELLED	GROOMAMAN	GUNSMITHS	GAS STATION
GRAVENESS	GROOVIEST	GUSHINGLY	GASTRALGIA
GRAVEYARD	GROPINGLY	GUSTATORY	GASTRALGIC
GRAVIDITY	GROUCHING	GUSTINESS	GASTROLITH
GRAVITATE	GROUNDAGE	GUTTERING	GASTRONOME
GRAVY BOAT	GROUNDING	GYMKHANAS	GASTRONOMY
GREASE GUN	GROUNDNUT	GYMNASIUM	GASTROTOMY
GREASIEST	GROUNDSEL	GYMNASTIC	GAS TURBINE
GREAT-AUNT	GROUPINGS	GYNAECOID	GATEHOUSES
GREAT BEAR	GROVELLED	GYNARCHIC	GATEKEEPER
GREAT COAT	GROVELLER	GYNOECIUM	GATHERABLE
GREAT DANE	GRUBBIEST	GYNOPHORE	GATHERINGS
GREATNESS	GRUBSTAKE	GYRATIONS	GAUCHENESS
GREEDIEST	GRUELLING	GYRFALCON	GAULTHERIA
GREENBACK	GRUFFNESS	GYROSCOPE	GAUSSMETER
GREEN BEAN	GRUMBLERS		GAZETTEERS
GREEN BELT	GRUMBLING		GEAR LEVERS
GREENGAGE	GRUMPIEST	**10 LETTERS**	GELATINIZE
GREENHEAD	GUANABARA	GABARDINES	GELATINOID
GREENHORN	GUANIDINE	GADOLINITE	GELATINOUS
GREENLAND	GUANOSINE	GADOLINIUM	GELDERLAND
GREENLING	GUARANTEE	GAFF-RIGGED	GEMINATION
GREENNESS	GUARANTOR	GAILLARDIA	GEMMACEOUS
GREENROOM	GUARDABLE	GAINLINESS	GEMOLOGIST
GREENSAND	GUARDEDLY	GAINSAYING	GENERALIST
GREENWICH	GUARDIANS	GALASHIELS	GENERALITY
GREENWOOD	GUARDRAIL	GALLACIZER	GENERALIZE
GREETINGS	GUARDROOM	GALLOGLASS	GENERATING
GREGARINE	GUARDSMAN	GALLSTONES	GENERATION
GREGORIAN	GUARDSMEN	GALLUP POLL	GENERATIVE
GRENADIER	GUARD'S VAN	GALUMPHING	GENERATORS
GRENADINE	GUATEMALA	GALVANIZED	GENERATRIX
GREY AREAS	GUAYAQUIL	GALVANIZER	GENEROSITY
GREY BEARD	GUERRILLA	GAMEKEEPER	GENEROUSLY
GREYHOUND	GUESSABLE	GAMETOCYTE	GENETICIST
GREY STATE	GUESSWORK	GANG-BANGED	GENICULATE
GRAYWACKE	GUESTROOM	GANGLIONIC	GENIUS LOCI
GRIDIRONS	GUFFAWING	GANGPLANKS	GENTLEFOLK
GRIEVANCE	GUIDELINE	GANGRENOUS	GENTLENESS
GRILLROOM	GUIDEPOST	GARAGE SALE	GENTRIFIED
GRIMACING	GUIDINGLY	GARAGE CAN	GEOCENTRIC
GRIMALKIN	GUILDHALL	GARDEN CITY	GEOCHEMIST
GRIMINESS	GUILDSMAN	GARGANTUAN	GEODYNAMIC
GRINDELIA	GUILELESS	GARISHNESS	GEOGNOSTIC
GRIPINGLY	GUILTLESS	GARLANDING	GEOGRAPHER
GRISAILLE	GUINEA PIG	GARNIERITE	GEOLOGICAL

GEOLOGISTS	GLEAMINGLY	GOLF COURSE	GRAPTOLITE
GEOMETRIZE	GLIMMERING	GONDOLIERS	GRASSFINCH
GEOMORPHIC	GLIOMATOUS	GONIOMETER	GRASSINESS
GEOPHAGIST	GLISTENING	GONIOMETRY	GRASS ROOTS
GEOPHAGOUS	GLITTERATI	GONOCOCCAL	GRASS WIDOW
GEOPHYSICS	GLITTERING	GONOCOCCUS	GRATEFULLY
GEOSCIENCE	GLOATINGLY	GONOPHORIC	GRATIFYING
GEOSTATICS	GLOBALISTS	GONORRHOEA	GRATUITIES
GEOTHERMAL	GLOCHIDERM	GOOD FRIDAY	GRATUITOUS
GEOTROPISM	GLOMERULAR	GOODLINESS	GRAVELLING
GERATOLOGY	GLOMERULUS	GOOD LOOKER	GRAVESTONE
GERIATRICS	GLOOMINESS	GOODY-GOODY	GRAVETTIAN
GERMANIZER	GLORIFYING	GOOSEBERRY	GRAVEYARDS
GERMICIDAL	GLORIOUSLY	GOOSEFLESH	GRAVIMETER
GERMICIDES	GLORY HOLES	GOOSESTEPS	GRAVIMETRY
GERMINATED	GLOSSARIAL	GORGEOUSLY	GRAVITATED
GERUNDIVAL	GLOSSARIES	GORGONZOLA	GRAVITATER
GESTATIONS	GLOSSARIST	GORMANDIZE	GRAVY BOATS
GESUNDHEIT	GLOSSINESS	GORMLESSLY	GRAVY TRAIN
GET-UP-AND-GO	GLOTTIDEAN	GOTHICALLY	GREASE GUNS
GHASTLIEST	GLUCOSIDAL	GOVERNABLE	GREASEWOOD
GHOSTLIEST	GLUMACEOUS	GOVERNANCE	GREASINESS
GHOST TOWNS	GLUTTINGLY	GOVERNMENT	GREATCOATS
GHOSTWRITE	GLUTTONOUS	GRACEFULLY	GREAT DANES
GIANT PANDA	GLYCOGENIC	GRACIOUSLY	GREAT-NIECE
GIFTEDNESS	GLYCOLYSIS	GRADATIONS	GREAT-UNCLE
GIFT HORSES	GLYCOSIDIC	GRADUALISM	GREEDINESS
GINGER ALES	GLYCOSURIA	GRADUALIST	GREEDY-GUTS
GINGER BEER	GLYCOSURIC	GRADUATING	GREENBACKS
GINGER NUTS	GNASHINGLY	GRADUATION	GREEN BEANS
GINGIVITIS	GOALKEEPER	GRAININESS	GREEN BELTS
GIPPY TUMMY	GOALMOUTHS	GRAMICIDIN	GREENBRIER
GIRL FRIDAY	GOATSBEARD	GRAMINEOUS	GREENFINCH
GIRLFRIEND	GO-BETWEENS	GRAMMARIAN	GREENFLIES
GIRL GUIDES	GODFATHERS	GRAMOPHONE	GREENGAGES
GIVEN NAMES	GOD-FEARING	GRANADILLA	GREENHEART
GLACIALIST	GODMOTHERS	GRANDCHILD	GREENHORNS
GLACIATION	GODPARENTS	GRAND OPERA	GREENHOUSE
GLACIOLOGY	GOGGLE-EYED	GRAND PIANO	GREEN LIGHT
GLADDENING	GOINGS-OVER	GRAND SLAMS	GREEN PAPER
GLADIATORS	GOLD-BEATER	GRANDS PRIX	GREENSHANK
GLAGOLITIC	GOLD DIGGER	GRANDSTAND	GREENSTONE
GLAIRINESS	GOLDEN AGES	GRANGERISM	GREEN THUMB
GLAMORIZED	GOLDEN MEAN	GRANGERIZE	GREGARIOUS
GLAMORIZER	GOLDEN RULE	GRANNY KNOT	GRENADIERS
GLANCINGLY	GOLDENSEAL	GRANOPHYRE	GRESSORIAL
GLANDEROUS	GOLDFIELDS	GRANULATED	GREYHOUNDS
GLASS FIBRE	GOLDILOCKS	GRANULATOR	GREY MATTER
GLASSHOUSE	GOLD MEDALS	GRANULITIC	GRIEVANCES
GLASSINESS	GOLD-MINING	GRAPEFRUIT	GRIEVINGLY
GLASS-MAKER	GOLD-PLATED	GRAPEVINES	GRIEVOUSLY
GLASWEGIAN	GOLD RUSHES	GRAPHITIZE	GRIM REAPER
GLAUCONITE	GOLDSMITHS	GRAPHOLOGY	GRINDSTONE
GLAZING-BAR	GOLDTHREAD	GRAPH PAPER	GRIPPINGLY

GRISLINESS
GRISTLIEST
GRITTINESS
GROANINGLY
GROGGINESS
GROTESQUES
GROTTINESS
GROUCHIEST
GROUND BAIT
GROUND CREW
GROUNDLESS
GROUNDLING
GROUNDMASS
GROUNDNUTS
GROUND PLAN
GROUND RENT
GROUND RULE
GROUNDSMAN
GROUNDSMEN
GROUNDWORK
GROVELLERS
GROVELLING
GRUBBINESS
GRUBSTAKES
GRUDGINGLY
GRUESOMELY
GRUMPINESS
GRUNTINGLY
GUADELOUPE
GUARANTEED
GUARANTEES
GUARANTIES
GUARANTORS
GUARDHOUSE
GUARDRAILS
GUARDROOMS
GUARD'S VANS
GUERRILLAS
GUESSINGLY
GUESTHOUSE
GUESTROOMS
GUIDELINES
GUILDHALLS
GUILEFULLY
GUILLEMOTS
GUILLOTINE
GUILTINESS
GUINEA FOWL
GUINEA PIGS
GUITARFISH
GUITARISTS
GULF STREAM
GUNRUNNERS
GUNRUNNING

GURGLINGLY
GYMNASIAST
GYMNASIUMS
GYMNASTICS
GYMNOSPERM
GYNANDROUS
GYNOPHORIC
GYPSOPHILIA
GYROSCOPES
GYROSCOPIC
GYROSTATIC

11 LETTERS
GAFF-TOPSAIL
GAINFULNESS
GALLANTNESS
GALLANTRIES
GALL BLADDER
GALLIVANTED
GALLUP POLLS
GALVANIZING
GAMEKEEPERS
GAMEKEEPING
GAMETANGIAL
GAMETANGIUM
GEMETOGENIC
GAMETOPHORE
GAMETOPHYTE
GAMOGENESIS
GAMOGENETIC
GARAGE SALES
GARBAGE CANS
GARDEN PARTY
GARNISHMENT
GARRISONING
GARRULOULY
GASEOUSNESS
GAS STATIONS
GASTRECTOMY
GASTRONOMES
GASTRONOMIC
GASTROPODAN
GASTROSCOPE
GASTROSCOPY
GASTROSTOMY
GASTROTRICH
GAS TURBINES
GATE CRASHED
GATECRASHER
GATEKEEPERS
GEANTICLINE
GEGENSCHEIN
GELATINIZER

GEMMIPAROUS
GEMMULATION
GEMOLOGICAL
GENDARMERIE
GENEALOGIES
GENEALOGIST
GENERALIZED
GENERALIZER
GENERALNESS
GENERALSHIP
GENERATIONS
GENERICALLY
GENETICALLY
GENETIC CODE
GENETICISTS
GENTEELNESS
GENTIANELLA
GENTLEMANLY
GENTLEWOMAN
GENTRIFYING
GENUFLECTED
GENUFLECTOR
GENUINENESS
GEOCHEMICAL
GEODYNAMICS
GEOGRAPHERS
GEOGRAPHIES
GEOMAGNETIC
GEOPHYSICAL
GEOPOLITICS
GEOSTRATEGY
GEOSTROPHIC
GEOSYNCLINE
GEOTECTONIC
GERATOLOGIC
GERMANENESS
GERMINATING
GERMINATION
GERM WARFARE
GERONTOLOGY
GERRYMANDER
GESTATIONAL
GESTICULATE
GET-TOGETHER
GHASTLINESS
GHOSTLINESS
GHOSTWRITER
GIANT-KILLER
GIANT PANDAS
GIBBOUSNESS
GIFT-WRAPPED
GIGANTESQUE
GILLYFLOWER
GINGER BEERS

GINGERBREAD
GINGER GROUP
GIRL FRIDAYS
GIRLFRIENDS
GIRLISHNESS
GIVE-AND-TAKE
GLADIOLUSES
GLAMORIZING
GLAMOROUSLY
GLARINGNESS
GLASSBLOWER
GLASSCUTTER
GLASSHOUSES
GLASS-MAKING
GLASS-WORKER
GLAUCONITIC
GLEEFUNESS
GLOBEFLOWER
GLOBIGERINA
GLOCHIDIATE
GLOMERATION
GLOMERULATE
GLORIFIABLE
GLOSSECTOMY
GLOSSOLALIA
GLOTTEL STOP
GLOVE PUPPET
GLOWERINGLY
GLUE-SNIFFER
GLYPHOGRAPH
GNATCATCHER
GOALKEEPERS
GOALKEEPING
GODCHILDREN
GODDAUGHTER
GODFORSAKEN
GODLESSNESS
GOLD-BEATING
GOLD DIGGERS
GOLD-DIGGING
GOLDEN EAGLE
GOLDEN SYRUP
GOLDFINCHES
GOLF COURSES
GONIOMETRIC
GONOCOCCOID
GONORRHOEAL
GOOD EVENING
GOOD-LOOKERS
GOOD-LOOKING
GOOD-MORNING
GOOD NATURED
GOOD OFFICES
GORDIAN KNOT

476

GORMANDIZED
GORMANDIZER
GOSSIPINGLY
GOURMANDISE
GOURMANDISM
GOVERNESSES
GOVERNMENTS
GRACELESSLY
GRADABILITY
GRADATIONAL
GRADE SCHOOL
GRADUALNESS
GRADUATIONS
GRAECO-ROMAN
GRAMMARIANS
GRAMMATICAL
GRAMOPHONES
GRANDADDIES
GRANDFATHER
GRANDIOSITY
GRAND JURIES
GRAND MASTER
GRANDMOTHER
GRAND OPERAS
GRANDPARENT
GRAND PIANOS
GRANDSTANDS
GRANGERIZER
GRANITEWARE
GRANIVOROUS
GRANNY KNOTS
GRANOLITHIC
GRANOPHYRIC
GRANULARITY
GRANULATION
GRANULATIVE
GRANULOCYTE
GRAPEFRUITS
GRAPHICALLY
GRAPHOLOGIC
GRAPHOMOTOR
GRASSHOPPER
GRASS WINDOWS
GRAVESTONES
GRAVIMETRIC
GRAVITATING
GRAVITATION
GRAVITATIVE
GREASEPAINT
GREASY SPOON
GREAT-NEPHEW
GREENBOTTLE
GREENGROCER
GREENHOUSES

GREENLANDER
GREENOCKITE
GREEN PAPERS
GREEN PEPPER
GRIDDLECAKE
GRIMACINGLY
GRINDSTONES
GRISTLINESS
GRIZZLY BEAR
GROTESQUELY
GROUCHINESS
GROUND CREWS
GROUND FLOOR
GROUND GLASS
GROUNDLINGS
GROUND PLANS
GROUND RENTS
GROUND RULES
GROUND SHEET
GROUND SPEED
GROUND STAFF
GROUNDSWELL
GRUELLINGLY
GRUMBLINGLY
GUARDEDNESS
GUARDHOUSES
GUESSTIMATE
GUESTHOUSES
GUEST WORKER
GUILELESSLY
GUILLOTINED
GUILLOTINER
GUILLOTINES
GUILTLESSLY
GULLIBILITY
GUN CARRIAGE
GUN SMITHING
GURGITATION
GUTLESSNESS
GUTTA PERCHA
GUTTER PRESS
GUTTER SNIPE
GUTTERALIZE
GYNAECOLOGY
GYPSIFEROUS
GYROCOMPASS
GYROSCOPICS
GYROSTATICS

12 LETTERS
GALACTOGOGUE
GALACTOMETER
GALACTOMETRY
GALL BLADDERS
GALLINACEOUS
GALLIVANTING
GALIVANICALLY
GALVANOMETER
GALVANOMETRY
GALVANOSCOPE
GALVANOSCOPY
GAMESMANSHIP
GAMETOPHORIC
GAMETOPHYTIC
GAMOPETALOUS
GARBAGE TRUCK
GARDEN CITIES
GASIFICATION
GASTIGHTNESS
GASTRONOMIST
GASTROPODOUS
GASTROSCOPIC
GASTRULATION
GATECRASHERS
GATECRASHING
GAVANIZATION
GEANTICLINAL
GENDER-BENDER
GENEALOGICAL
GENEALOGISTS
GENERALITIES
GENERALIZING
GENERAL STAFF
GENEROSITIES
GENEROUSNESS
GENICULATION
GENOTYPICITY
GENUFLECTING
GENUFLECTION
GEOCHEMISTRY
GEOGRAPHICAL
GEOSYNCLINAL
GERANIACEOUS
GERIATRICIAN
GERMANOPHILE
GERMANOPHOBE
GERONTOCRACY
GESTICULATED
GESTICULATOR
GET-TOGETHERS
GHOULISHNESS
GIANT KILLERS
GIBRALTARIAN

GIFT-WRAPPING
GIGANTICALLY
GIGANTICNESS
GINGER GROUPS
GINGERLINESS
GLABROUSNESS
GLACIOLOGIST
GLADIATORIAL
GLASS-BLOWERS
GLASSCUTTERS
GLAUCOMATOUS
GLIMMERINGLY
GLISTENINGLY
GLITTERINGLY
GLOBETROTTER
GLOCKENSPIEL
GLORIOUSNESS
GLOSSOGRAPHY
GLOTTAL STOPS
GLOVE PUPPETS
GLUCOGENESIS
GLUCOGENETIC
GLUE-SNIFFERS
GLUE-SNIFFING
GLUTTONOUSLY
GLYCOGENESIS
GLYCOGENETIC
GLYCOPROTEIN
GLYCOGRAPHY
GNOMONICALLY
GNOTOBIOTICS
GOBBLEDYGOOK
GOLDEN EAGLES
GOLDFISH BOWL
GOLD STANDARD
GONADOTROPIN
GOOD-HUMOURED
GOODY-GOODIES
GOOSEBERRIES
GOOSE PIMPLES
GOOSESTEPPED
GORGEOUSNESS
GORMANDIZING
GOSSIPMONGER
GOVERNMENTAL
GOVERNORSHIP
GRACEFULNESS
GRACIOUSNESS
GRADE SCHOOLS
GRADUALISTIC
GRALLATORIAL
GRAMMATOLOGY
GRAM-NEGATIVE
GRAM-POSITIVE

GRANDFATHERS
GRAND MASTERS
GRANDMOTHERS
GRAND PARENTS
GRANODIORITE
GRANULOCYTIC
GRAPHOLOGIST
GRASSHOPPERS
GRATEFULNESS
GRATIFYINGLY
GRATUITOUSLY
GREASY SPOONS
GREAT CIRCLES
GREEN FINGERS
GREENGROCERS
GREENGROCERY
GREEN PEPPERS
GREGARIOUSLY
GRIEVOUSNESS
GRIZZLY BEARS
GROSSULARITE
GROUND FLOORS
GROUNDLESSLY
GROUNDSHEETS
GROUND STAFFS
GROUNDSWELLS
GROUP CAPTAIN
GROUP THERAPY
GROVELLINGLY
GROWING PAINS
GRUESOMENESS
GUARANTEEING
GUARDIANSHIP
GUERRILLAISM
GUESSTIMATES
GUEST WORKERS
GUILLOTINING
GUN CARRIAGES
GUTTER SNIPES
GYNAECOCRACY
GYROMAGNETIC

13 LETTERS

GALLICIZATION
GALLOWS HUMOUR
GALVANOMETRIC
GALVANOSCOPIC
GALVANOTROPIC
GAMBREL-ROOFED
GAMETOGENESIS
GAMMAGLOBULIN
GARBAGE TRUCKS
GARDEN PARTIES
GARRULOUSNESS
GASTROSCOPIST
GEIGER COUNTER
GENDER-BENDERS
GENERALISSIMO
GENERAL STRIKE
GENERATION GAP
GENTIANACEOUS
GENUFLECTIONS
GEOCHRONOLOGY
GEODYNAMICIST
GEOMETRICALLY
GEOMORPHOLOGY
GEOPOLITICIAN
GEOSTATIONARY
GEOTACTICALLY
GEOTROPICALLY
GERIATRICIANS
GERMANIZATION
GERMAN MEASLES
GERMANOPHILIA
GERMANOPHOBIA
GERONTOCRATIC
GERONTOLOGIST
GERRYMANDERED
GESTICULATING
GESTICULATION
GESTICULATIVE
GHETTO BLASTER
GLACIOLOGICAL
GLAMORIZATION
GLAMOROUSNESS
GLOBETROTTERS
GLOBETROTTING
GLOBULIFEROUS
GLOCKENSPIEL
GLORIFICATION
GLOSSOGRAPHER
GLUTINOUSNESS
GLYPHOGRAPHER

GLYPHOGRAPHIC
GLYPTOGRAPHER
GLYPTOGRAPHIC
GOLDEN JUBILEE
GOLDEN WEDDING
GOLDFISH BOWLS
GOOD AFTERNOON
GOOD-NATUREDLY
GOOD SAMARITAN
GOOSESTEPPING
GOVERNABILITY
GRACELESSNESS
GRADE CROSSING
GRAMINIVOROUS
GRAMMAR SCHOOL
GRAMMATICALLY
GRAM-MOLECULAR
GRANDCHILDREN
GRANDDAUGHTER
GRANDILOQUENT
GRANDULOMATOUS
GRAPHEMICALLY
GRAPHICALNESS
GRAPHIC DESIGN
GRAPHOLOGISTS
GRAPPLING IRON
GRATIFICATION
GRAVITATIONAL
GREEN-FINGERED
GROTESQUENESS
GROUND STROKES
GROUP CAPTAINS
GROUP PRACTICE
GUARDIAN ANGEL
GUBERNATORIAL
GUIDED MISSILE
GUILELESSNESS
GUILTLESSNESS
GYMNOSPERMISM
GYMNOSPERMOUS
GYNAECOCRATIC
GYNAECOLOGIST
GYNANDROMORPH

3 LETTERS	4 LETTERS				
HAD	HAAF	HEAT	HOER	HURT	HAMZA
HAE	HAAR	HEBE	HOES	HUSH	HANCE
HAG	HABU	HECK	HOGG	HUSK	HANDS
HAH	HACK	HEED	HOGS	HUSS	HANDY
HAM	HADE	HEEL	HOKE	HUTS	HANKY
HAN	HADJ	HEFT	HOLD	HUTU	HANOI
HAP	HAEM	HEIR	HOLE	HWAN	HANSA
HAS	HAFT	HELA	HOLM	HWYL	HANSE
HAT	HAGS	HELD	HOLP	HYDE	HANTS
HAW	HA-HA	HELL	HOLS	HYMN	HAPLY
HAY	HAIG	HELM	HOLT	HYPE	HAPPY
HE'D	HAIK	HELP	HOLY	HYPO	HARAR
HEH	HAIL	HEMP	HOMA		HARDS
HEL	HAIR	HEMS	HOME		HARDY
HEM	HAJJ	HENS	HOMO	**5 LETTERS**	HARED
HEN	HAKE	HENT	HOMY	HABER	HAREM
HEP	HALE	HERA	HONE	HABIT	HARES
HER	HALF	HERB	HONG	HACEK	HARPS
HE'S	HALL	HERD	HONK	HACKS	HARPY
HET	HALM	HERE	HOOD	HADAL	HARRY
HEW	HALO	HERL	HOOF	HADES	HARSH
HEX	HALT	HERM	HOOK	HADJI	HARTS
HEY	HAMA	HERN	HOOP	HADN'T	HASN'T
HIC	HAME	HERO	HOOT	HADST	HASPS
HID	HAMS	HERR	HOPE	HAFIZ	HASTE
HIM	HAND	HERS	HOPI	HAFTS	HASTY
HIN	HANG	HESS	HOPS	HAGAR	HATCH
HIP	HANK	HEST	HORA	HAGEN	HASTY
HIS	HARD	HETH	HORN	HAGUE	HATCH
HIT	HARE	HEWN	HOSE	HA-HAS	HATED
HOB	HARK	HICK	HOST	HAUDA	HATES
HOD	HARL	HIDE	HOTS	HAIFA	HAUGH
HOE	HARM	HIED	HOUR	HAIKU	HAULM
HOG	HARP	HI-FI	HOVE	HAILS	HAULS
HOM	HART	HIGH	HOWE	HAIN'T	HAUNT
HOO	HARZ	HIKE	HOYA	HAIRS	HAUSA
HOP	HASA	HILL	HUBS	HAIRY	HAVEN
HOT	HASH	HILT	HUED	HAITI	HAVER
HOW	HASK	HIND	HUES	HAJJI	HAVES
HOY	HASP	HINT	HUFF	HAKEA	HAVOC
HQS	HAST	HIPS	HUGE	HAKES	HAVRE
HUB	HATE	HIRE	HUGO	HAKIM	HAWES
HUE	HATH	HISS	HUGS	HALAL	HAWKS
HUG	HATS	HIST	HULA	HALER	HAWSE
HUH	HAUL	HITS	HULK	HALIC	HAYDN
HUM	HAVE	HIVE	HULL	HALID	HAZED
HUN	HAWK	HOAD	HUME	HALLO	HAZEL
HUT	HAZE	HOAR	HUMP	HALLS	HAZER
	HAZY	HOAX	HUMS	HALMA	HAZES
	HEAD	HOBO	HUNG	HALOS	H-BOMB
	HEAL	HOBS	HUNK	HALTS	HEADS
	HEAP	HOCK	HUNT	HALVE	HEADY
	HEAR	HODS	HUON	HAMAL	HEAPS
		HOED	HURL	HAMMY	HEARD

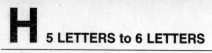

HEARS	HIKER	HONOR	HUMAN	HAIDAN	HARDIE
HEART	HIKES	HOOCH	HUMIC	HAIDUK	HARDLY
HEATH	HILAR	HOODS	HUMID	HAILED	HARD UP
HEAVE	HILLA	HOOEY	HUMPH	HAILER	HAREEM
HEAVY	HILLS	HOO-HA	HUMPS	HAINAN	HAREMS
HEDGE	HILLY	HOOKE	HUMPY	HAIRDO	HARING
HEDGY	HILTS	HOOKS	HUMUS	HAIRIF	HARKED
HEELS	HILUM	HOOKY	HUNAN	HAJJES	HARKEN
HEGEL	HILUS	HOOPS	HUNCH	HAJJIS	HARLEM
HEIRS	HINDI	HOOTS	HUNKS	HAKIMS	HARLEY
HEIST	HINDS	HOPED	HUNTS	HALEST	HARLOT
HEJAZ	HINDU	HOPEH	HUPEH	HALIDE	HARLOW
HEKLA	HINES	HOPER	HURDS	HALITE	HARMED
HELEN	HINGE	HOPES	HURON	HALLAH	HARMER
HELIX	HINNY	HORAE	HURRY	HALLEL	HARNEY
HELLE	HINTS	HORAL	HURST	HALLEY	HAROLD
HELLO	HIPPO	HORDE	HURTS	HALLOO	HARPED
HELLS	HIPPY	HOREB	HUSKS	HALLOS	HARPER
HELMS	HIRAM	HORME	HUSKY	HALLOW	HARRAR
HELOT	HIRED	HORNS	HUSSY	HALLUX	HARRIS
HELPS	HIRER	HORNY	HUTCH	HALOES	HARROW
HELVE	HITCH	HORSA	HYADS	HALOID	HARTAL
HE-MAN	HIVED	HORSE	HYDRA	HALTED	HARVEY
HE-MEN	HIVES	HORST	HYDRO	HALTER	HASHED
HENCE	HOARD	HORSY	HYENA	HALVAH	HASHES
HENGE	HOARY	HORUS	HYING	HALVED	HASLET
HENIE	HOBBS	HOSEA	HYMEN	HALVES	HASSAN
HENNA	HOBBY	HOSED	HYMNS	HAMATE	HASSLE
HENRY	HOBOS	HOSES	HYPED	HAMITE	HASTEN
HERAT	HOCKS	HOSTA	HYPER	HAMLET	HATBOX
HERBS	HOCUS	HOSTS	HYPOS	HAMMED	HATHOR
HERBY	HOFEI	HOTEL		HAMMER	HATING
HERDS	HOFUF	HOTLY	**6 LETTERS**	HAMPER	HATPIN
HERES	HOGAN	HOUGH	HAAKON	HANDED	HATRED
HEROD	HOICK	HOUND	HABANA	HANDEL	HATTER
HERON	HOIST	HOUND	HABILE	HANDLE	HAULED
HERTZ	HOKKU	HOURI	HABITS	HANGAR	HAULER
HESSE	HOKUM	HOURS	HACKED	HANGER	HAUNCH
HET UP	HOLDS	HOUSE	HACKER	HANG-UP	HAUNTS
HEWED	HOLES	HOVEL	HACKLE	HANKER	HAVANA
HEWER	HOLEY	HOVER	HADEAN	HANKIE	HAVANT
HEXAD	HOLLA	HOWDY	HADITH	HANKOW	HAVENS
HEXED	HOLLO	HOWLS	HADJES	HANNAH	HAVEN'T
HEXER	HOLLY	HOYLE	HADJIS	HANSEL	HAVING
HEXES	HOLST	HSIAN	HADRON	HANSOM	HAWAII
HEXYL	HOMER	HUBBY	HAEMAL	HAPPEN	HAWHAW
HICKS	HOMES	HUBLI	HAEMIC	HAPTEN	HAWICK
HIDER	HOMEY	HUFFY	HAEMIN	HAPTIC	HAWKED
HIDES	HONAN	HUFUF	HAERES	HARALD	HAWKER
HI-FIS	HONDO	HUGER	HAFTER	HARASS	HAWSER
HIGHS	HONED	HULKS	HAGBUT	HARBIN	HAYBOX
HIGHT	HONEY	HULLO	HAGGAI	HARD BY	HAYMOW
HIJAZ	HONKS	HULLS	HAGGIS	HARDEN	HAZARD
HIKED	HONKY	HULME	HAGGLE	HARDER	HAZELS

HAZIER	HELIUM	HICCUP	HOEING	HORARY	HULLER
HAZILY	HELLAS	HICKEY	HOGGED	HORDES	HULLOS
HAZING	HELLEN	HICKOK	HOGGER	HORMIC	HUMANE
H-BOMBS	HELLER	HIDDEN	HOGNUT	HORMUZ	HUMANS
HEADED	HELLES	HIDING	HOGTIE	HORNED	HUMBER
HEADER	HELLOS	HIEMAL	HOICKS	HORNET	HUMBLE
HEAD-ON	HELMET	HIGGLE	HOIDEN	HORRID	HUMBLY
HEALED	HELPED	HIGHER	HOISTS	HORROR	HUMBUG
HEALER	HELPER	HIGHLY	HOLDEN	HOSIER	HUMISM
HEALEY	HELVES	HIJACK	HOLDER	HOSING	HUMMED
HEALTH	HEMMED	HIKERS	HOLDUP	HOSTED	HUMMEL
HEAPED	HEMMER	HIKING	HOLIER	HOSTEL	HUMMER
HEAPER	HEMPEN	HILARY	HOLILY	HOSTIE	HUMOUR
HEARER	HENBIT	HILLEL	HOLISM	HOT AIR	HUMPED
HEARSE	HENLEY	HILLER	HOLLER	HOTBED	HUMPTY
HEARST	HEPCAT	HIMEJI	HOLLOW	HOT DOG	HUNGER
HEARTH	HEPTAD	HINDER	HOLMES	HOTELS	HUNGRY
HEARTS	HERALD	HINDOO	HOLMIC	HOTIEN	HUNTED
HEARTY	HERBAL	HINDUS	HOLPEN	HOTPOT	HUNTER
HEATED	HERDED	HINGED	HOMAGE	HOD ROD	HUPPAH
HEATER	HERDER	HINGER	HOMBRE	HOTTER	HURDLE
HEATHS	HERDIC	HINGES	HOMELY	HOTTIE	HURLED
HEATHY	HEREAT	HINTED	HOMIER	HOUDAN	HURLER
HEAVED	HEREBY	HINTER	HOMILY	HOUNDS	HURLEY
HEAVEN	HEREIN	HIPPED	HOMING	HOURIS	HURRAH
HEAVER	HEREOF	HIRRER	HOMINY	HOURLY	HURRAY
HEAVES	HEREON	HIPPIE	HONEST	HOUSED	HURTER
HEBREW	HERERO	HIRING	HONIED	HOUSEL	HURTLE
HEBRON	HERESY	HISPID	HONING	HOUSES	HUSAIN
HECATE	HERETO	HISSED	HONKED	HOVELS	HUSHED
HECKLE	HERIOT	HISSER	HONKER	HOWARD	HUSH-UP
HECTIC	HERMES	HISSES	HONOUR	HOWDAH	HUSKER
HECTOR	HERMIT	HI-TECH	HONSHU	HOWE'ER	HUSSAR
HECUBA	HERMON	HITHER	HOODED	HOWLED	HUSTLE
HEDDLE	HERNIA	HITLER	HOODOO	HOWLER	HUSTON
HEDGED	HEROES	HIT MAN	HOOFED	HOWLET	HUXLEY
HEDGER	HEROIC	HIT MEN	HOOKAH	HOWRAH	HUZZAH
HEDGES	HEROIN	HITTER	HOOKUP	HOYDEN	HYADES
HEDJAZ	HERONS	HIVING	HOOPED	HSIANG	HYAENA
HEEDED	HERPES	HOARDS	HOOPER	HUBBLE	HYALIN
HEEDER	HERREN	HOARSE	HOOP-LA	HUBBUB	HYBRID
HEE-HAW	HESIOD	HOAXED	HOOPOE	HUBCAP	HYBRIS
HEELED	HESTIA	HOAXER	HOORAK	HUBRIS	HYDRAS
HEELER	HETMAN	HOAXES	HOORAY	HUCKLE	HYDRIA
HEENAN	HEWERS	HOBART	HOOTED	HUDDLE	HYDRIC
HEFTER	HEWING	HOBBES	HOOTER	HUDSON	HYENAS
HEGIRA	HEXANE	HOBBLE	HOOVER	HUFFED	HYMENS
HEIDUC	HEXING	HOBNOB	HOOVES	HUGELY	HYMNAL
HEIFER	HEXANE	HOCKED	HOPING	HUGEST	HYMNED
HEIGHT	HEXING	HOCKER	HOPPED	HUGGED	HYPHEN
HEJIRA	HEXONE	HOCKEY	HOPPER	HUGGER	HYPING
HEKATE	HEYDAY	HODDEN	HOPPLE	HUGHES	
HELENA	HIATAL	HODDIN	HOPPUS	HUGHIE	
HELIOS	HIATUS	HODMAN	HORACE	HULLED	

481

H

7 LETTERS	HAMITIC	HARDING	HAULIER	HECKLED	HERALDS
HABITAT	HAMLETS	HARD NUT	HAULING	HECKLER	HERBAGE
HABITED	HAMMERS	HARDPAN	HAUNTED	HECTARE	HERBALS
HABITUE	HAMMING	HARDTOP	HAUNTER	HEDGING	HERBERT
HABITUS	HAMMOCK	HARELIP	HAURAKI	HEDONIC	HERDING
HACHURE	HAMMOND	HARICOT	HAUTBOY	HEEDFUL	HEREDES
HACKBUT	HAMPDEN	HARIJAN	HAUTEUR	HEEDING	HERETIC
HACKERS	HAMPERS	HARKING	HAWKERS	HEELING	HERITOR
HACKING	HAMPTON	HARLOTS	HAWKING	HEELTAP	HERMITS
HACKLER	HAMSTER	HARMFUL	HAWKINS	HEERLEN	HERNIAL
HACKLES	HAMULAR	HARMING	HAWKISH	HEFTIER	HERNIAS
HACKNEY	HAMULUS	HARMONY	HAWORTH	HEFTILY	HEROTIC
HACKSAW	HANAPER	HARNESS	HAWSERS	HEGUMEN	HEROINE
HADAWAY	HANCOCK	HARPIES	HAYCOCK	HEIFERS	HEROISM
HADDOCK	HANDBAG	HARPING	HAYFORK	HEIFETZ	HERONRY
HADRIAN	HANDFUL	HARPINS	HAYRACK	HEIGH-HO	HERRICK
HAEMOID	HANDFUL	HARPIST	HAYSEED	HEIGHTS	HERRING
HAFINUM	HANDGUN	HARPOON	HAYWARD	HEINOUS	HERSELF
HAGFISH	HANDIER	HARRIED	HAYWIRE	HEIRDOM	HERTZOG
HAGGARD	HANDILY	HARRIER	HAZARDS	HEIRESS	HESIONE
HAGGISH	HANDING	HARROWS	HAZIEST	HEISTER	HESSIAN
HAGGLED	HANDLED	HARSHER	HAZLITT	HEITIKI	HESSITE
HAGGLER	HANDLER	HARSHLY	HEADERS	HELICAL	HETAERA
HAGLIKE	HANDLES	HARSLET	HEADIER	HELICES	HETAIRA
HAILING	HANDOUT	HARTLEY	HEADILY	HELICON	HEXADIC
HAIRCUT	HANDSAW	HARVARD	HEADING	HELLBOX	HEXAGON
HAIRDOS	HANDSEL	HARVEST	HEADMAN	HELLCAT	HEXAPLA
HAIRIER	HANDSET	HARWICH	HEADMEN	HELLENE	HEXAPOD
HAIRNET	HANDS-ON	HARYANA	HEADPIN	HELLERY	HEXOSAN
HAIRPIN	HANDS UP	HAS-BEEN	HEADSET	HELLION	HEYDUCK
HAITIAN	HANGARS	HASHING	HEADWAY	HELLISH	HEYSHAM
HAITINK	HANGING	HASHISH	HEALERS	HELLUVA	HEYWOOD
HAKLUYT	HANGMAN	HASIDIC	HEALING	HELMAND	HICCUPS
HALAKAH	HANGMEN	HASIDIM	HEALTHS	HEMETS	HICKORY
HALAKIC	HANGOUT	HASSLED	HEALTHY	HELOISE	HIDABLE
HALAVAH	HANG-UPS	HASSLES	HEAPING	HELOTRY	HIDALGO
HALBERD	HANKIES	HASSOCK	HEARING	HELPFUL	HIDEOUS
HALYCON	HANOVER	HASTATE	HEARKEN	HELPING	HIDINGS
HALDANE	HANSARD	HASTIER	HEARSAY	HEMIOLA	HIELAND
HALFWAY	HANSOMS	HASTILY	HEARSES	HEMIPOD	HIGHBOY
HALF-WIT	HANUMAN	HATBAND	HEARTEN	HEMLINE	HIGHEST
HALIBUT	HANYANG	HATCHED	HEARTHS	HEMLOCK	HIGH TEA
HALIDOM	HA'PENNY	HATCHEL	HEATERS	HEMMING	HIGHWAY
HALIFAX	HAPLESS	HATCHER	HEATHEN	HENBANE	HIJACKS
HALLWAY	HAPLITE	HATCHES	HEATHER	HENCOOP	HILBERT
HALOGEN	HAPLOID	HATCHET	HEATING	HENDRIX	HILLARY
HALTERE	HAPPIER	HATEFUL	HEAVENS	HENGIST	HILLERY
HALTERS	HAPPILY	HATLESS	HEAVIER	HENNERY	HILLIER
HALTING	HAPTENE	HATLIKE	HEAVIES	HENPECK	HILLOCK
HALVING	HARAPPA	HATPINS	HEAVILY	HEPARIN	HIMSELF
HALYARD	HARBOUR	HATTERS	HEAVING	HEPATIC	HINDGUT
HAMADAN	HARDEST	HAUBERK	HEBETIC	HEPBURN	HINGING
HAMBURG	HARDIER	HAUGHTY	HEBRAIC	HEPTANE	HINTING
HAMELIN	HARDILY	HAULAGE	HEBREWS	HAPTOSE	HIONATE

HIPBATH	HOKUSAI	HOSANNA	HUMDRUM	HYDRANT
HIPBONE	HOLDALL	HOSIERS	HUMERAL	HYDRATE
HIPLESS	HOLDERS	HOSIERY	HUMERUS	HYDRIDE
HIPPEST	HOLDING	HOSPICE	HUMIDLY	HYDROID
HIPPIES	HOLDUPS	HOSTAGE	HUMIDOR	HYGIENE
HIPSTER	HOLIDAY	HOSTELS	HUMMING	HYMNALS
HIRABLE	HOLIEST	HOSTILE	HUMMOCK	HYMNING
HIRSUTE	HOLLAND	HOSTING	HUMORAL	HYPED UP
HISSING	HOLLERS	HOSTLER	HUMOURS	HYPHENS
HISTOID	HOLLOWS	HOTBEDS	HUMPING	
HISTONE	HOLMIUM	HOT DOGS	HUNCHED	
HISTORY	HOLSTER	HOTFOOT	HUNCHES	**8 LETTERS**
HITCHED	HOLY SEE	HOTHEAD	HUNDRED	HABITANT
HITCHER	HOMBURG	HOTLINE	HUNGARY	HABITATS
HITCHES	HOMERIC	HOTNESS	HUNGNAM	HABITUAL
HIT LIST	HOME RUN	HOTPOTS	HUNKERS	HABITUDE
HITTING	HOMIEST	HOT RODS	HUNLIKE	HABITUES
HITTITE	HOMOLOG	HOT SEAT	HUNNISH	HABSBURG
HOARDED	HOMONYM	HOT SPOT	HUNTERS	HACIENDA
HOARDER	HONESTY	HOTSPUR	HUNTING	HACKNEYS
HOARIER	HONEYED	HOTTEST	HURDLED	HACKSAWS
HOARILY	HONIARA	HOUDINI	HURDLER	HACKWORK
HOARSEN	HONITON	HOUMOUS	HURDLES	HADRONIC
HOARSER	HONKIES	HOUNDED	HURLING	HAEMATIC
HOATZIN	HONKING	HOUNDER	HURRAYS	HAEMATIN
HOAXERS	HONOURS	HOUSING	HURRIED	HAEREMAI
HOAXING	HOODLUM	HOUSMAN	HURTFUL	HAGGLING
HOBBEMA	HOODOOS	HOUSTON	HURTING	HAILWOOD
HOBBIES	HOOGHLY	HOUTING	HURTLED	HAIPHONG
HOBBIAM	HOOKAHS	HOVERED	HUSBAND	HAIRBALL
HOBBIST	HOOKERS	HOVERER	HUSHABY	HAIRCUTS
HOBBLED	HOOKIES	HOWBEIT	HUSHING	HAIRGRIP
HOBBLER	HOOKING	HOWDAHS	HUSKIER	HAIRIEST
HOBLIKE	HOOKUPS	HOWEVER	HUSKIES	HAIRLESS
HOBNAIL	HOORAYS	HOWLAND	HUSKILY	HAIRLIKE
HOBOISM	HOOTERS	HOWLING	HUSSARS	HAIRLINE
HOBOKEN	HOOTING	HOWDENS	HUSSEIN	HAIRNETS
HOCKING	HOOVERS	HUAI-NAN	HUSSIES	HAIRPINS
HOCKNEY	HOPEFUL	HUBBIES	HUSSISM	HAIRTAIL
HODEIDA	HOPHEAD	HUBCAPS	HUSSITE	HAIRWORM
HODGKIN	HOPKINS	HUDDLED	HUSTLED	HAKODATE
HOEDOWN	HOPLITE	HUDDLER	HUSTLER	HALAFIAN
HOWLIKE	HOPPERS	HUDDLES	HUTCHES	HALATION
HOGARTH	HOPPING	HUFFIER	HUTCHIE	HALBERDS
HOGBACK	HOPPLER	HUFFILY	HUTLIKE	HALCYONE
HOGFISH	HOPSACK	HUFFING	HUTMENT	HALENESS
HOGGING	HORIZON	HUFFISH	HUYGENS	HALFBACK
HOGGISH	HORMONE	HUGGING	HYAENAS	HALFBEAK
HOGLIKE	HORNETS	HULKING	HYAENIC	HALFCOCK
HOGNOSE	HORNER	HULLING	HYALINE	HALF-LIFE
HOGWASH	HORNILY	HUMANLY	HYALITE	HALF MAST
HOGWEED	HORRIFY	HUMBLED	HYALOID	HALF MOON
HOISTED	HORRORS	HUMBLER	HYBRIDS	HALF NOTE
HOISTER	HORSIER	HUMBUGS	HYDATID	HALF TERM

483

HALF TIME	HANKERED	HARRIDAN	HAYMAKER	HECATOMB
HALFTONE	HANKERER	HARRIERS	HAYSTACK	HECKLERS
HALF-WITS	HANNIBAL	HARRIMAN	HAZARDED	HECKLING
HALIBUTS	HANRATTY	HARRISON	HAZELHEN	HECTARES
HALLIARD	HANUKKAH	HARROWED	HAZELNUT	HECTORED
HALLMARK	HAPLICIT	HARROWER	HAZINESS	HEDGEHOG
HALLOWED	HAPLOSIS	HARRUMPH	HEADACHE	HEDGEHOP
HALLOWER	HAPPENED	HARRYING	HEADACHY	HEDGEROW
HALLWAYS	HAPPIEST	HARSHEST	HEADBAND	HEDONICS
HALO-LIKE	HAPSBURG	HARTFORD	HEADFAST	HEDONISM
HALYARDS	HAPTERON	HARTNELL	HEADGEAR	HEDONIST
HAMILTON	HARA-KIRI	HARUSPEX	HEADHUNT	HEEDLESS
HAMMERED	HARAMBEE	HARVESTS	HEADIEST	HEELBALL
HAMMERER	HARANGUE	HAS-BEENS	HEADINGS	HEELLESS
HAMMOCKS	HARAPPAN	HASIDISM	HEADLAND	HEELPOST
HAMPERED	HARASSED	HASSLING	HEADLESS	HEFTIEST
HAMPERER	HARASSER	HASSOCKS	HEADLIKE	HEGELIAN
HAMSTERS	HARBOURS	HASTEFUL	HEADLINE	HEGEMONY
HANDBAGS	HARDBACK	HASTENED	HEADLOCK	HEIGHTEN
HANDBALL	HARDBAKE	HASTENER	HEADLONG	HEIMADALL
HANDBELL	HARDBALL	HASTIEST	HEADMOST	HEIRLESS
HANDBILL	HARD CASH	HASTINGS	HEADRACE	HEORLOOM
HANDBOOK	HARD COPY	HATBANDS	HEADRAIL	HEIRSHIP
HANDCART	HARD-CORE	HATCHERY	HEADREST	HELIACAL
HANDCLAP	HARD DISK	HATCHETS	HEADROOM	HELICOID
HANDCUFF	HARDENED	HATCHING	HEADSAIL	HELIPORT
HANDFAST	HARDENER	HATCHWAY	HEADSETS	HELLADIC
HANDFEED	HARDHACK	HATEABLE	HEADSHIP	HELL-BENT
HANDFULS	HARDIEST	HATFIELD	HEADSMAN	HELLCATS
HANDGRIP	HARD LINE	HATHAWAY	HEADWARD	HELLENES
HANDGUNS	HARD LUCK	HATHORIC	HEADWAYS	HELLENIC
HANDHOLD	HARDNESS	HATTERAS	HEADWIND	HELLFIRE
HANDICAP	HARD NUTS	HAT TRICK	HEADWORK	HELLHOLE
HANDIEST	HARD SELL	HAULIERS	HEALABLE	HELMETED
HANDLERS	HARDSHIP	HAUNCHED	HEARINGS	HELMINTH
HANDLESS	HARD TACK	HAUNCHES	HEARTIER	HELMLESS
HANDLIKE	HARDTOPS	HAUNTING	HEARTILY	HELMSMAN
HANDLING	HARD UPON	HAUSFRAU	HEATEDLY	HELMSMEN
HANDLOOM	HARDWARE	HAUTBOYS	HEATHENS	HELOTISM
HANDMADE	HARDWOOD	HAVELOCK	HEATHERY	HELPABLE
HANDOUTS	HAREBELL	HAVE-NOTS	HEATLESS	HELPINGS
HANDOVER	HARELIKE	HAVERING	HEAT PUMP	HELPLESS
HANDRAIL	HARGEISA	HAVILDAR	HEAT RASH	HELPMANN
HANDS-OFF	HARICOTS	HAVOCKER	HEAT WAVE	HELPMATE
HANDSOME	HARIKARI	HAWAIIAN	HEAVENLY	HELPMEET
HANDYMAN	HARINGEY	HAWFINCH	HEAVIEST	HELINSKI
HANDYMEN	HARKENED	HAWKBILL	HEAVY-SET	HELVETIA
HANGBIRD	HARKENER	HAWK-EYED	HEBDOMAD	HELVETIC
HANGCHOW	HARLOTRY	HAWKLIKE	HEBETATE	HELVETIA
HANGER-ON	HARMLESS	HAWKWEED	HEBETUDE	HEMIOLIC
HANGINGS	HARMONIC	HAWTHORN	HEBRAISM	HEMIPODE
HANGNAIL	HARPINGS	HAYCOCKS	HEBRAIST	HEMLINES
HANGOUTS	HARPISTS	HAY FEVER	HEBRAIZE	HEMLOCKS
HANGOVER	HARPOONS	HAYFORKS	HEBRIDES	HENBANES

HENCHMAN	HIBISCUS	HISPANIC	HOMEMADE	HORNIEST
HENCHMEN	HICCUPED	HISTOGEN	HOMERIAN	HORNLESS
HENEQUEN	HIDDENLY	HISTORIC	HOME RULE	HORNLIKE
HENG-YANG	HIDEAWAY	HITCHING	HOME RUNS	HORNPIPE
HEN HOUSE	HIDELESS	HITHERTO	HOMESICK	HORNTAIL
HEN PARTY	HIDROSIS	HIT LISTS	HOMESPUN	HORNWORK
HENRYSON	HIDROTIC	HIVELIKE	HOMETOWN	HOROLOGE
HENSLOWE	HIERARCH	HOACTZIN	HOMEWARD	HOROLOGY
HEPATICA	HIERATIC	HOARDING	HOMEWORK	HOROWITZ
HEPTAGON	HIGHBALL	HOARIEST	HOMICIDE	HORRIBLE
HEPTARCH	HIGHBORN	HOARSELY	HOMILIES	HORRIBLY
HEPWORTH	HIGHBOYS	HOARSEST	HOMILIST	HORRIDLY
HERACLEA	HIGHBROW	HOBBLING	HOMINESS	HORRIFIC
HERACLES	HIGHER-UP	HOBBYIST	HOMINOID	HORSEBOX
HERALDED	HIGHJACK	HOBNAILS	HOMODONT	HORSEFLY
HERALDIC	HIGH JUMP	HOCKTIDE	HOMOGAMY	HORSEMAN
HERALDRY	HIGHLAND	HOGMANAY	HOMOGEMY	HORSEMEN
HERBLIKE	HIGH LIFE	HOGSHEAD	HOMOGOMY	HORSIEST
HERCULES	HIGH MASS	HOISTING	HOMOLOGY	HOSANNAS
HERDSMAN	HIGHNESS	HOKKAIDO	HOMONYMS	HOSPICES
HERDSMEN	HIGH-RISE	HOLDABLE	HONDURAN	HOSPITAL
HERDWICK	HIGH ROAD	HOLDALLS	HONDURAS	HOSTAGES
HEREDITY	HIGH SEAS	HOLDFAST	HONEGGER	HOSTELRY
HEREFORD	HIGH SPOT	HOLDINGS	HONESTLY	HOSTLERS
HEREINTO	HIGHTAIL	HOLDOVER	HONEWORT	HOTCHPOT
HEREUPON	HIGH TECH	HOLIDAYS	HONEYBEE	HOTELIER
HEREWARD	HIGH TIDE	HOLINESS	HONEYDEW	HOT FLUSH
HEREWITH	HIGH TIME	HOLISTIC	HONG KONG	HOTHEADS
HERITAGE	HIGHVELD	HOLLANDS	HONIEDLY	HOTHOUSE
HERMETIC	HIGHWAYS	HOLLERED	HONOLULU	HOT LINES
HERMITIC	HIJACKED	HOLLIDAY	HONORARY	HOTPLATE
HERODIAS	HIJACKER	HOLLOWED	HONOURED	HOT SPOTS
HERPETIC	HILARITY	HOLLOWER	HONOURER	HOT STUFF
HERRINGS	HILLFORT	HOLLOWLY	HOODLESS	HOT WATER
HERSCHEL	HILLIARD	HOOCENE	HOODLIKE	HOUNDING
HERTFORD	HILLIEST	HOLOGRAM	HOOKLESS	HOUNSLOW
HERTZIAN	HILLOCKS	HOLOTYPE	HOOKLIKE	HOUSEBOY
HESIODIC	HILLSIDE	HOLOZOIC	HOOKNOSE	HOUSEFLY
HESTITANT	HIMATION	HOLSTIEN	HOOKWORM	HOUSEFUL
HESTITATE	HINYANA	HOLSTERS	HOOLIGAN	HOUSEMAN
HESPERIA	HINCKLEY	HOLYHEAD	HOOPLIKE	HOUSEMEN
HESPERUS	HINDERED	HOLYOAKE	HOOSEGOW	HOUSETOP
HESSIANS	HINDERER	HOLYTIDE	HOOVERED	HOUSINGS
HETAERIC	HINDMOST	HOLY WEEK	HOPEFULS	HOVERERS
HEXAGONS	HINDUISM	HOLYWRIT	HOPELESS	HOVERING
HEXAGRAM	HIPBATHS	HOMBURGS	HOPLITIC	HOWITZER
HEXANOIC	HIP FLASK	HOMEBODY	HORATIAN	HRVATSKA
HEXAPLAR	HIPPARCH	HOMEBRED	HORIZONS	HUANG HUA
HEXAPODY	HIPSTERS	HOME BREW	HORMONAL	HUCKSTER
HEZEKIAH	HIRAGANA	HOME HELP	HORMONES	HUDDLING
HIATUSES	HIRELING	HOMELAND	HORNBEAM	HUFFIEST
HIAWATHA	HIRI MOTU	HOMELESS	HORNBILL	HUGENESS
HIBERNAL	HIROHITO	HOMELIER	HORNBOOK	HUGGABLE
HIBERNIA	HISPANIA	HOMELIKE	HORNFELS	HUGUENOT

HULL-LESS	HYDROGEN	HALF-LIVES	HANGERS-ON	HARROVIAN
HUMANELY	HYDROMEL	HALF MOONS	HANGNAILS	HARROWING
HUMANISM	HYGIENIC	HALF NOTES	HANGOVERS	HARSHNESS
HUMANIST	HYMENEAL	HALFPENCE	HANKERING	HARTBEEST
HUMANITY	HYPNOSIS	HALFPENNY	HANSEATIC	HARTSHORN
HUMANIZE	HYPNOTIC	HALFTONES	HAPHAZARD	HARTSPICY
HUMANOID	HYSTERIA	HALF-TRUTH	HAPLESSLY	HARVESTER
HUMBLEIST	HYSTERIC	HALITOSIS	HAPLOLOGY	HASTENING
HUMANITY		HALLELUJA	HAPPENING	HASTINESS
HUMANIZE		HALLIARDS	HAPPINESS	HATCHABLE
HUMANOID	**9 LETTERS**	HALL-JONES	HAPPY HOUR	HATCHBACK
HUMBLEST	HABERGEON	HALLMARKS	HARANGUED	HATCHMENT
HUMBLING	HABITABLE	HALOWE'EN	HARANGUER	HATCHWAYS
HUMBOLDT	HABITABLY	HALLOWING	HARANGUES	HATEFULLY
HUMIDIFY	HABITUATE	HALLOWMAS	HARRASSING	HAT TRICKS
HUMIDITY	HAICIENDAS	HALLSTATT	HARBINGER	HAUGHTIER
HUMILITY	HACKMORE	HALMAHERA	HARBOURED	HAUGHTILY
HUMMOCKS	HACKBERRY	HALOBIONT	HARBOURER	HAVENLESS
HUMMOCKY	HACKNEYED	HALOPHYTE	HARDBACKS	HAVERSACK
HUMORIST	HADROSAUR	HALOTHANE	HARDBOARD	HAVERSIAN
HUMOROUS	HAEMATEIN	HALTINGLY	HARDBOUND	HAVERSINE
HUMOURED	HAEMATITE	HAMADRYAD	HARD CIDER	HAWKSBILL
HUMPBACK	HAEMATOID	HAMADRYAS	HARD CORES	HAWSHOLE
HUMPHREY	HAEMATOMA	HAMAMATSU	HARDCOVER	HAWSEPIPE
HUMPLIKE	HAEMOCOEL	HAMBURGER	HARD DISKS	HAWTHORNE
HUNCHING	HAEMOCYTE	HAMERSLEY	HARD DRINK	HAWTHORNS
HUNDREDS	HAEMOSTAT	HAM-FISTED	HARDENING	HAYMAKING
HUNGERED	HAGBUTEER	HAMMERNG	HARDHEADS	HAYSTACKS
HUNGRIER	HAGGADIST	HAMMERTOE	HARDIHOOD	HAZARDING
HUNGRILY	HAGGARDLY	HAMMURABI	HARDINESS	HAZARDOUS
HUNTEDLY	HAGIARCHY	HAMPERING	HARD-LINER	HEADACHES
HUNTRESS	HAGIOLOGY	HAMPSHIRE	HARD-NOSED	HEADBANDS
HUNTSMAN	HAG-RIDDEN	HAMPSTEAD	HARDSHIPS	HEADBOARD
HUNTSMEN	HAIDAR ALI	HAMSTRING	HARDWOODS	HEADDRESS
HURDLERS	HAILSTONE	HAMSTURNG	HAREBELLS	HEADFIRST
HURDLING	HAILSTORM	HANDBELLS	HARKENING	HEADINESS
HURRYING	HAIRBRUSH	HANDBILLS	HARLEQUIN	HEADLANDS
HURTLING	HAIRCLOTH	HANDBOOKS	HARMATTEN	HEADLIGHT
HUSBANDS	HAIRGRIPS	HANDBRAKE	HARMFULLY	HEADLINED
HUSH-HUSH	HAIRINESS	HANDCARTS	HARMONICA	HEADLINER
HUSKIEST	HAIRLINES	HANDCLAPS	HARMONICS	HEADLINES
HUSKLIKE	HAIRPIECE	HANDLASPS	HARMONIES	HEADPIECE
HUSTINGS	HAIR SHIRT	HANDCRAFT	HARMONIST	HEADREACH
HUSTLERS	HAIR SLIDE	HANDCUFFS	HARMONIUM	HEADREST
HUSTLING	HAIRSTYLE	HANDICAPS	HARMONIZE	HEADSCARF
HWANG HAI	HALEAKALA	HANDINESS	HARMOTOME	HEADSHIPS
HYACINTH	HALESOWEN	HANDIWORK	HARNESSED	HEADSTALL
HYYDER ALI	HALFBACKS	HANDLEBAR	HARNESSER	HEADSTAND
HYDRACID	HALF-BAKED	HANDLOOMS	HARNESSES	HEAD START
HYDRANTH	HALF BOARD	HANDOVERS	HARPOONED	HEADSTOCK
HYDRANTS	HALF-BREED	HANDRAILS	HARPOONER	HEADSTONE
HYDRATED	HALF-CASTLE	HANDSHAKE	HARQUEBUS	HEADWARDS
HYDRATES	HALF CROWN	HANDSPIKE	HARRIDANS	HEADWINDS
HYDRATOR	HALF-LIGHT	HANDSTAND	HARROGATE	HEADWORDS

HEALINGLY	HELLENIZE	HEXAMETER	HINDOOISM	HOLLERING
HEALTHFUL	HELLHOUND	HEXAPODIC	HINDRANCE	HOLLOWEST
HEALTHIER	HELLISHLY	HEXASTICH	HINDSIGHT	HOLLOWING
HEALTHILY	HELPFULLY	HEXASTYLE	HINDU KUSH	HOLLYHOCK
HEARKENED	HELPMATES	HEXATEUCH	HINDUSTAN	HOLLYWOOD
HEARKENER	HELVELLYN	HEY PRESTO	HINGELESS	HOLOCAINE
HEARTACHE	HELVETIAN	HIBERNATE	HINGELIKE	HOLOCAUST
HEARTBEAT	HELVETIUS	HIBERNIAN	HIP FLASKS	HOLOCRINE
HEARTBURN	HEMIALGIA	HICCUPING	HIP POCKET	HOLOGRAMS
HEARTENED	HEMICYCLE	HICKORIES	HIPPOCRAS	HOLOGRAPH
HEARTFELT	HEMINGWAY	HIDDENITE	HIPPOLYTA	HOLOPHYTE
HEARTHRUG	HEMISTITCH	HIDEAWAYS	HIPPOLYTE	HOLOTYPIC
HEARTIEST	HEMITROPE	HIDEABOUND	HIRELINGS	HOLSTEINS
HEARTLAND	HENDIADYS	HIDEOUSLY	HIROSHIGE	HOLSTERED
HEARTLESS	HEN HOUSES	HIERARCHY	HIROSHIMA	HOLY GHOST
HEARTSTICK	HENPECKED	HIERODULE	HIRUNDINE	HOLY GRAIL
HEARTSOME	HEOMANIAC	HIEROGRAM	HISPIDITY	HOLYSTONE
HEARTWOOD	HEPATITIS	HIEROLOGY	HISTAMINE	HOME FRONT
HEARTWORM	HEPTAGONS	HIFALUTIN	HISTADINE	HOMEGROWN
HEATHERED	HEPTARCHY	HIGHBALLS	HISTOGENY	HOME GUARD
HEATHFOWL	HERACLEAN	HIGHBROWS	HISTOGRAM	HOME HELPS
HEATHLIKE	HERALDING	HIGH CHAIR	HISTOLOGY	HOMELANDS
HEAT PUMPS	HERALDIST	HIGH-CLASS	HISTORIAN	HOMELIEST
HEAVINESS	HERBALIST	HIGH COURT	HISTORIES	HOMEMAKER
HEAVISIDE	HERBARIUM	HIGHER-UPS	HIT-AND-RUN	HOME MOVIE
HEAVY-DUTY	HERBICIDE	HIGH-FLIER	HITCHCOCK	HOMEOPATH
HEBRAZIER	HERBIVORE	HIGH-FLOWN	HITCHLIKE	HOMESTEAD
HEBRIDEAN	HERCULEAN	HIGH-GRADE	HITLERISM	HOMETOWNS
HECTOGRAM	HERCYNIAN	HIGH HORSE	HIT-OR-MISS	HOME TRUTH
HECTORING	HEREAFTER	HIGH JINKS	HIT PARADE	HOMEWARDS
HEDGEHOGS	HEREUNDER	HIGH JUMPS	HOARDINGS	HOMEYNESS
HEDGEROWS	HERITABLE	HIGHLANDS	HOARFROST	HOMICIDAL
HEDONISTS	HERTIABLY	HIGH-LEVEL	HOARHOUND	HOMICIDES
HEEDFULLY	HERITRESS	HIGHLIGHT	HOATCHING	HOMILETIC
HEELPIECE	HERMITAGE	HIGH POINT	HOBBESIAN	HOMOGRAFT
HEFTINESS	HERMITIAN	HIGH-RISES	HOBGOBLIN	HOMOGRAPH
HEGEMONIC	HERNIATED	HIGH ROADS	HOBNAILED	HOMOLYSIS
HEGUMENOS	HERODOTUS	HIGH-SPEED	HOBNOBBED	HOMOLYTIC
HEIMDALLR	HESITANCY	HIGH SPOTS	HO CHI MINH	HOMONYMIC
HEINOUSLY	HESITATED	HIGH TABLE	HODOMETER	HOMOPHILE
HEIRESSES	HESITATER	HIGH TIDES	HODOMETRY	HOMOPHONE
HEIRLOOMS	HESPERIAN	HIGH-TONED	HODOSCOPE	HOMOPHONY
HELGOLAND	HESSONITE	HIGH WATER	HOGGISHLY	HOMOPHYLY
HELICALLY	HESYCHAST	HIJACKERS	HOGSHEADS	HOMOPLASY
HELICLINE	HETAERISM	HIJACKING	HOHENLORE	HOMOPOLAR
HELIOSTAT	HETAERIST	HILARIOUS	HOIDENISH	HOMOSPORY
HELIOTYPE	HETAIRISM	HILLBILLY	HOI POLLOI	HOMOTAXIC
HELIOZOAN	HETERODOX	HILLOCKED	HOLARCTIC	HOMOTAXIS
HELIPORTS	HETERONYM	HILLSIDES	HOLDOVERS	HONEYBEES
HELLDIVER	HETEROSIS	HILVERSUM	HOLE IN ONE	HONETCOMB
HELLEBORE	HEURISTIC	HIMALAYAS	HOLIDAYED	HONEYEDLY
HELLENIAN	HEXACHORD	HIMYARITE	HOLINSHED	HONEY-LIKE
HELLENISM	HEXAGONAL	HINDBRAIN	HOLLANDER	HONEYMOON
HELLENIST	HEXAGRAMS	HINDERING	HOLLANDIA	HONKY-TONK

HONORARIA	HOUSEBOATS	HURRICANE	HAEMATURIC
HONORIFIC	HOUSEBOYS	HURRIEDLY	HAEMOLYSIN
HONOR ROLL	HOUSECARL	HURTFULLY	HAEMOLYSIS
HONOURING	HOUSECOAT	HUSBANDED	HAEMOLYTIC
HOODOOISM	HOUSEHOLD	HUBANDER	HAEMOPHILE
HOOFBOUND	HOUSELEEK	HUSBANDRY	HAGIOCRACY
HOOK-NOSED	HOUSELESS	HUSH MONEY	HAGIOLATER
HOOKWORMS	HOUSELINE	HUSKINESS	HAGIOLATRY
HOOLIGANS	HOUSEMAID	HYACINTHS	HAGIOLOGIC
HOOTNANNY	HOUSEROOM	HYBRIDISM	HAGIOSCOPE
HOOVERING	HOUSETOPS	HYBRIDITY	HAILSTONES
HOPE CHEST	HOUSEWIFE	HYBRIDIZE	HAILSTORMS
HOPEFULLY	HOUSEWORK	HYBRISTIC	HAIRPIECES
HOPLOLOGY	HOUSTONIA	HYDANTOIN	HAIR SHIRTS
HOPSCOTCH	HOVERPORT	HYDATHODE	HAIR SLIDES
HOREHOUND	HOWITZERS	HYDERABAD	HAIRSPRING
HORNBILLS	HOWLINGLY	HYDRANGEA	HAIRSTREAK
HORNINESS	HOWSOEVER	HYDRASTIS	HAIRSTYLES
HORNPIPES	HOWOTWDIE	HYDRATION	HALBERDIER
HORNSTONE	HOYDENISH	HYDRAULIC	HALF A CROWN
HOROLOGIC	HSUAN T'UNG	HYDRAZINE	HALF-BREEDS
HOROSCOPE	HUBRISTIC	HYDRAZOIC	HALF-CASTES
HOROSCOPY	HUCKABACK	HYDRIODIC	HALF CROWNS
HORRIFIED	HUCKSTERS	HYDROCELE	HALF-LENGTH
HORSEBACK	HUE AND CRY	HYDROFOIL	HALF-SISTER
HORSEHAIR	HUFFINESS	HYDROLOGY	HALF-TRUTHS
HORSEHIDE	HUGH CAPET	HYDROLYSE	HALF VOLLEY
HORSELESS	HU-HO-HAO T'E	HYDROLYTE	HALF-WITTED
HORSELIKE	HUMANISTS	HYGIENIST	HALLELUJAH
HORSEMINT	HUMANISED	HYPERBOLA	HALLMARKED
HORSEPLAY	HUMANIZER	HYPERBOLE	HALOGENATE
HORSESHIT	HUMAN-LIKE	HYPHENATE	HALOGENOID
HORSESHOE	HUMANNESS	HYPNOTISM	HALOGENOUS
HORSETAIL	HUMANOIDS	HYPNOTIST	HALOPHYTIC
HORSEWEED	HUMAN RACE	HYPNOTIZE	HALTER-LIKE
HORSEWHIP	HUMBLEBEE	HYPOCRISY	HALTERNECK
HORSINESS	HUMBUGGER	HYPOCRITE	HAMBURGERS
HORTATIVE	HUMDINGER	HYSTERICS	HAMMERHEAD
HORTATORY	HUMECTANT		HAMMERLESS
HOSPITALS	HUMERUSES		HAMMER-LIKE
HOSPITIUM	HUMIDNESS	**10 LETTERS**	HAMSHACKLE
HOSTELLER	HUMILIATE	HABILIMENT	HAMSTRINGS
HOSTESSES	HUMORISTS	HABILITATE	HANDBALLER
HOSTILELY	HUMOURFUL	HABITATION	HANDBARROW
HOSTILITY	HUMOURING	HABITUALLY	HANDBRAKES
HOTELIERS	HUMPBACKS	HABITUATED	HANDCUFFED
HOTFOOTED	HUMPINESS	HACKBUSTER	HANDICRAFT
HOTHEADED	HUNCHBACK	HACKNEYISM	HANDLEABLE
HOTHOUSES	HUNDREDTH	HAECKELIAN	HANDLEBARS
HOTPLATES	HUNGARIAN	HAEMAGOGUE	HANDLELESS
HOT POTATO	HUNGERING	HAEMATINIC	HANDMAIDEN
HOTTENTOT	HUNGRIEST	HAEMATITIC	HAND-ME-DOWN
HOT WATERS	HUNKY-DORY	HAEMATOSIS	HANDPICKED
HOURGLASS	HUNNISHLY	HAEMATURIA	HANDSHAKES

HANDSOMELY	HAUSTELLUM	HEEDLESSLY	HEREABOUTS
HANDSPRING	HAUSTORIAL	HEIDELBERG	HEREDITARY
HANDSTANDS	HAUSTORIUM	HEIGHTENED	HEREDETIST
HANDSTROKE	HAVERSACKS	HEISENBERG	HERESIARCH
HANKERINGS	HAZARDABLE	HELIANTHUS	HERETOFORE
HANKY-PANKY	HAZARD-FREE	HELICOPTER	HERMITAGES
HANOVERIAN	HEADBOARDS	HELIGOLAND	HEROICALLY
HAPLOLOGIC	HEADCHEESE	HELIOGRAPH	HESITANTLY
HAPPENINGS	HEADHUNTED	HELIOLATER	HESITATING
HAPPY EVENT	HEADHUNTER	HELIOLATRY	HESITATION
HAPPY HOURS	HEADLIGHTS	HELIOMETER	HESITATIVE
HARANGUING	HEADLINING	HELIOMETRY	HESPERIDES
HARASSMENT	HEADMASTER	HELIOPOLIS	HESPERIDIN
HARBINGERS	HEAD OF HAIR	HELIOTAXIS	HETERODONT
HARBOURAGE	HEADPHONES	HELIOTROPE	HETERODOXY
HARBOURING	HEADPIECES	HELIOTYPIC	HETERODYNE
HARD-BITTEN	HEADSPRING	HELLBENDER	HETEROGAMY
HARD-BOILED	HEADSQUARE	HELLENIZER	HETEROGONY
HARD CIDERS	HEADSTONES	HELLESPONT	HETEROLOGY
HARDHEADED	HEADSTREAM	HELMET-LIKE	HETERONOMY
HARD LABOUR	HEADSTRONG	HELMINTHIC	HETEROTOPY
HARD-LINERS	HEADWATERS	HELPLESSLY	HEULANDITE
HARD LIQUOR	HEADWORKER	HEMELYTRAL	HEURISTICS
HARD PALATE	HEALTH FOD	HEMELYTRON	HEXADECANE
HARELIPPED	HEALTHIEST	HEMICYCLIC	HEXAEMERIC
HARGREAVES	HEARING AID	HEMIHEDRAL	HEXAEMERON
HARLEQUINS	HEARKENING	HEMIPLEGIA	HEXAHEDRAL
HARMLESSLY	HEARTBEATS	HEMIPLEGIC	HEXAHEDRON
HARMONICAS	HEARTBREAK	HEMIPTERAN	HEXAMERISM
HARMONIOUS	HEARTENING	HEMIPTERON	HEXAMEROUS
HARMONIUMS	HEARTHRUGS	HEMISPHERE	HEXAMETERS
HARMONIZED	HEARTINESS	HEMITROPIC	HEXAMETRIC
HARMONIZER	HEARTSEASE	HEMOGLOBIN	HEXANGULAR
HARMSWORTH	HEARTTHROB	HEMOPHILIA	HEXAVALENT
HARNESSING	HEATEDNESS	HEMORRHAGE	HIBERNACLE
HARPOONING	HEATHBERRY	HEMORRHOID	HIBERNATED
HARTEBEEST	HEATHENDOM	HENCEFORTH	HIBERNATOR
HARTLEPOOL	HEATHENISH	HENDECAGON	HIBISCUSES
HARUSPICAL	HEATHENISM	HENOTHEIST	HIDDENESS
HARVESTERS	HEATHENIZE	HEN PARTIES	HIERARCHAL
HARVESTING	HEAT RASHES	HEPARINOID	HIEROCRACY
HARVESTMAN	HEAT SHIELD	HEPHAESTUS	HIERODULIC
HASH BROWNS	HEATSTROKE	HEPHAISTOS	HIEROGLYPH
HASTEFULLY	HEAVEN-SENT	HEPTAGONAL	HIEROLOGIC
HATCHBACKS	HEAVENWARD	HEPTAMETER	HIERONYMIC
HATCHELLER	HEAVY-LADEN	HEPTARCHIC	HIERONYMUS
HATCHERIES	HEAVY WATER	HEPTASTICH	HIEROPHANT
HATCHET JOB	HEBDOMIDAL	HEPTATEUCH	HIGHBINDER
HATCHET MAN	HEBETATION	HERACLIDIN	HIGH CHAIRS
HATCHET MEN	HEBETATIVE	HERACLITUS	HIGH CHURCHES
HATSHEPSUT	HEBRAISTIC	HERBACEOUS	HIGH COURTS
HAUBERGEON	HECTICALLY	HERBALISTS	HIGH-FLIERS
HAUGHTIEST	HECTOGRAPH	HERBICIDAL	HIGH-FLYING
HAUNTINGLY	HEDONISTIC	HERBIVORES	HIGH-HANDED

HIGH HORSES	HOCUS-POCUS	HOMORGANIC	HOT FLUSHES
HIGHJACKER	HODGEPODGE	HOMOSEXUAL	HOTFOOTING
HIGH JUMPER	HOGARTHIAN	HOMOZYGOTE	HOUSEBOATS
HIGHLANDER	HOITY-TOITY	HOMOZYGOUS	HOUSEBOUND
HIGHLIGHTS	HOKEY COKEY	HOMUNCULAR	HOUSECRAFT
HIGH MASSES	HOKEY-POKEY	HOMUNCULUS	HOUSEFLIES
HIGH MINDED	HOLDERSHIP	HONESTNESS	HOUSEHOLDS
HIGHNESSES	HOLES IN ONE	HONEYBUNCH	HOUSEMAIDS
HIGH-OCTANE	HOLIDAYING	HONEYCOMBS	HOUSE OF GOD
HIGH POINTS	HOLINESSES	HONEYDEWED	HOUSE PARTY
HIGH PRIEST	HOLLOWNESS	HONEY-EATER	HOUSEPLANT
HIGH RELIEF	HOLLYHOCKS	HONEYMOONS	HOUSE-PROUD
HIGH SCHOOL	HOLOCAUSTS	HONORARIUM	HOUSEWIVES
HIGH SEASON	HOLOENZYME	HONORIFICS	HOVERCRAFT
HIGH STREET	HOLOFERNES	HONOURABLE	HOVERINGLY
HIGH STRUNG	HOLOGRAPHY	HONOURABLY	HOVERTRAIN
HIGHWAYMAN	HOLOHEDRAL	HONOURLESS	HOW DO YOU DO
HIGHWAYMEN	HOLOPHYTIC	HOODLUMISM	HUA KUO-FENG
HIJACKINGS	HOLUS-BOLUS	HOODWINKED	HUCKLEBONE
HILDEBRAND	HOLY SPIRIT	HOODWINKER	HUDDLESTON
HILLINGDON	HOMEBODIES	HOOKEDNESS	HUGUENOTIC
HIMYARITIC	HOME BREWING	HOOTENANNY	HULLABALOO
HINAYANIST	HOMECOMING	HOPE CHESTS	HUMANENESS
HINDENBURG	HOME GUARDS	HOPELESSLY	HUMANISTIC
HINDERMOST	HOMELINESS	HORIZONTAL	HUMANITIES
HINDRANCES	HOMEMAKERS	HORNBLENDE	HUMANIZING
HINDUSTANI	HOMEMAKEING	HORNEDNESS	HUMBERSIDE
HINTERLAND	HOME MOVIES	HORN-RIMMED	HUMBLENESS
HIPHUGGERS	HOME OFFICE	HOROLOGIST	HUMBLINGLY
HIPPARCHUS	HOMEOPATHS	HOROLOGIUM	HUMBUGGERY
HIP POCKETS	HOMEOPATHY	HOROSCOPES	HUMDINGERS
HIPPOCRENE	HOMEOTYPIC	HOROSCOPIC	HUMIDIFIED
HIPPODROME	HOMESTEADS	HORRENDOUS	HUMIDIFIER
HIPPOGRIFF	HOME TRUTHS	HORRIDNESS	HUMIDISTAT
HIPPOLYTAN	HOMILECTICS	HORRIFYING	HUMILIATED
HIPPOLYTUS	HOMOCERCAL	HORROR FILM	HUMILIATOR
HIPPOMENES	HOMOCYCLIC	HORSEBOXES	HUMORESQUE
HISPANIOLA	HOMOEOPATH	HORSEFLESH	HUMORISTIC
HISTAMINIC	HOMOEROTIC	HORSEFLIES	HUMOROUSLY
HISTIOCYTE	HOMOGAMOUS	HORSELAUGH	HUMOURLESS
HISTIOLTSIS	HOMOGENATE	HORSELEECH	HUMOURSOME
HISTIOLYTIC	HOMOGENIZE	HORSE OPERA	HUMPBACKED
HISTORIANS	HOMOGENOUS	HORSEPOWER	HUNCHBACKS
HISTORICAL	HOMOGONOUS	HORSE SENSE	HUNDREDTHS
HISTRIONIC	HOMOGRAPHS	HORSESHOES	HUNGRINESS
HITCHHIKED	HOMOLOGATE	HORSEWOMAN	HUNTINGDON
HITCHHIKER	HOMOLOGIZE	HORSEWOMEN	HUNTRESSES
HITHERMOST	HOMOLOGOUS	HOSPITABLE	HUNTSVILLE
HIT PARADES	HOMOLOSINE	HOSPITABLY	HURDY-GURDY
HOARSENESS	HOMONIMITY	HOSTELLERS	HURLY-BURLY
HOBBYHORSE	HOMOOUSIAN	HOSTELLING	HURRICANES
HOBGOBLINS	HOMOPHONES	HOSTELRIES	HURRYINGLY
HOBNOBBING	HOMOPHONIC	HOT-BLOODED	HUSBANDING
HOCHHEIMER	HOMOPLASTY	HOTCHPOTCH	HUSBANDMAN

HUSBANDMEN	HAGGISHNESS	HAREBRAINED	HELIOCROME
HYACINTHUS	HAGIOGRAPHIA	HARMFULNESS	HELIOGRAPHS
HYALOPLASM	HAGIOGRAPHY	HARMONISTIC	HELIOGRAPHY
HYALURONIC	HAGIOLOGIST	HARMONIZING	HELIOLITHIC
HYBRIDIZER	HAGIOSCOPIC	HARNESSLESS	HELIOMETRIC
HYDRANGEAS	HAIRBREADTH	HARNESS-LIKE	HELIOSTATIC
HYDRASTINE	HAIRBRUSHES	HARPOON-LIKE	HELIOTACTIC
HYDRAULICS	HAIRDRESSER	HARPSICHORD	HELIOTROPES
HYDROCORAL	HAIRPIN BEND	HARRIS TWEED	HELIOTROPIC
HYDROFOILS	HAIR RAISING	HARROWINGLY	HELIOTROPIN
HYROGRAPH	HAIR SPRINGS	HARTEBEESTS	HELEBORINE
HYDROLOGIC	HAIRSTYLIST	HARUM-SCARUM	HELLENISTIC
HYDROLYSER	HAIR TRIGGER	HARVEST HOME	HELLISHNESS
HYDROLYSIS	HAIRWEAVING	HARVASTLESS	HELMINTHOID
HYDROLYTIC	HALCYON DAYS	HARVEST MOON	HELPFULNESS
HYDROMANCY	HALF-BROTHER	HATCHET JOBS	HELPINGHAND
HYDROPONIC	HALF-HEARTED	HATCHET LIKE	HEMERALOPIA
HYGIENISTS	HALFPENNIES	HATEFULNESS	HEMERALOPIC
HYPERBOLAS	HALF-SISTERS	HAUGHTINESS	HEMIANOPSIA
HYPERBOLIC	HALF-VOLLEYS	HAUSTELLATE	HEMIELYTRAL
HYPHENATED	HALLMARKING	HAWKISHNESS	HEMIELYTRON
HYPNOTISTS	HALLUCINATE	HAZARDOUSLY	HEMIHYDRATE
HYPNOTIZED	HALOPHYTISM	HEADDRESSES	HEMIMORPHIC
HYPOCRITES	HALTEMPRICE	HEADHUNTERS	HEMITERPENE
HYPODERMIC	HALTERNECKS	HEADHUNTING	HEMITROPISM
HYPOTENUSE	HALTINGNESS	HEAD MASTERS	HEMOPHILIAC
HYPOTHESES	HAMILTONIAN	HEALTH FOODS	HEMORRHAGES
HYPOTHESIS	HAMMERSMITH	HEALTHFULLY	HEMHORROIDS
HYSTERICAL	HAMMERSTEIN	HEALTHINESS	HEMSTITCHER
	HAMMOCK-LIKE	HEARING AIDS	HEPPLEWHITE
	HANDBREADTH	HEART ATTACK	HEPTAHEDRON
11 LETTERS	HANDCUFFING	HEART BROKEN	HEPTAMEROUS
HABERDASHER	HANDFASTING	HEARTHSTONE	HEPTANGULAR
HABILITATOR	HANDICAPPED	HEARTLESSLY	HEPTAVALENT
HABITATIONS	HANDICAPPER	HEARTSOMELY	HERBIVOROUS
HABITUATING	HANDICRAFTS	HEARTTHROBS	HERCULANEUM
HABITUATION	HAND LUGGAGE	HEATHENNESS	HEREDITABLE
HABITUDINAL	HAND MAIDENS	HEAT SHIELDS	HEREINAFTER
HADROSAURUS	HAND-ME-DOWNS	HEAVENWARDS	HERETICALLY
HAEMACHROME	HANDWRITTING	HEAVY-HANDED	HERO WORSHIP
HAEMATOCELE	HANDWRITTEN	HEAVY WEIGHT	HERPETOLOGY
HAEMATOCRIT	HANDGLIDING	HEBDOMADARY	HERRING BONE
HAEMATOLOGY	HAPHAZARDLY	HEBEPHRENIA	HERZEGOVINA
HAEMATOZOON	HAPLESSNESS	HEBEPHRENC	HESITATIONS
HAEMOCYANIN	HAPLOGRAPHY	HEBRAICALLY	HESPERIDIUM
HAEMOGLOBIN	HAPPY EVENTS	HECKELPHONE	HESYCHASTIC
HAEMOPHILIA	HAPPY MEDIUM	HECTOGRAPHY	HETAERISTIC
HAEMOPHILIC	HARASSINGLY	HEDGEHOPPER	HETEROCLITE
HAEMOPTYSIS	HARBOURLESS	HEEDFULNESS	HETEROECISM
HAEMORRHAGE	HARD-AND-FAST	HEGELIANISM	HETEROGRAFT
HAEMOSTASIA	HARDECANUTE	HEIGHTENING	HETEROLYSIS
HAEMOSTASIS	HARD PALATES	HEINOUSNESS	HETEROLYTIC
HAEMOSTATIC	HARD-PRESSED	HELICOGRAPH	HETEROPHONY
HAGGARDNESS	HARDWEARING	HELICOPTERS	HETEROPHYTE

HETEROPOLAR	HISTAMINASE	HONEYMOONED	HUMILIATING
HETEROSPORY	HISTIOCYTIC	HONEYMOONER	HUMILIATION
HETEROSTYLY	HISTOLOGIST	HONEYSUCKER	HUMILIATIVE
HETEROTAXIS	HISTORIATED	HONEYSUCKLE	HUMILIATORY
HETEROTOPIA	HISTORICISM	HONORARIUMS	HUMMINGBIRD
HETEROTOPIC	HISTORICIST	HONOURS LIST	HUNCHBACKED
HETEROTYPIC	HISTORICITY	HOODWINKING	HUNGER MARCH
HEXADECIMAL	HISTRIONICS	HOOLIGANISM	HUNNISHNESS
HEXAGONALLY	HITCHHIKERS	HOPEFULNESS	HURRIEDNESS
HEXAHYDRATE	HITCHHIKING	HOPLOLOGIST	HURTFULNESS
HEXASTICHIC	HOBBLEDEHOY	HORIZONLESS	HUSBANDLESS
HEXASTICHON	HOBBYHORSES	HORIZONTALS	HYACINTHINE
HEXATEUCHAL	HOGGISHNESS	HORNBLENDIC	HYDNOCARPIC
HIBERNATING	HOLKARSTATE	HORNET'S NEST	HYDRARGYRIC
HIBERNATION	HOLLANDIASE	HORNSWOGGLE	HYDRARGYRUM
HIBERNICISM	HOLOBLASTIC	HORROR FILMS	HYDROCARBON
HIDE-AND-SEEK	HOLOCAUSTA;L	HORS D'OEUVRE	HYDROCYANIC
HIDEOUSNESS	HOLOGRAPHIC	HORSELAUGHS	HYDROGENATE
HIERARCHIES	HOLOHEDRISM	HORSE OPERAS	HYDROGENIZE
HIERARCHISM	HOLOMORPHIC	HORSE RADISH	HYDROGENOUS
HIEROCRATIC	HOLOTHURIAN	HORTATORILY	HYDROGRAPHY
HIEROGLYPHS	HOMECOMINGS	HOSPITALITY	HYDROLOGIST
HIEROLOGIST	HOMEOPATHIC	HOSPITALIZE	HYDROLYSATE
HIGHFALUTIN	HOMEOSTASIS	HOSPITALLER	HYDROMANCER
HIGH JUMPERS	HOMEOSTATIC	HOSTILITIES	HYDROMANTIC
HIGH LANDERS	HOMERICALLY	HOT-CROSS BUN	HYDROMEDUSA
HIGHLIGHTED	HOMESTEADER	HOTHEADEDLY	HYDROMETEOR
HIGH-PITCHED	HOME STRETCH	HOT POTATOES	HYDROPHOBIA
HIGH-POWERED	HOMICIDALLY	HOT-TEMPERED	HYDROPHONICS
HIGH-PRIESTS	HOMOCENTRIC	HOURGLASSES	HYPERACTIVE
HIGH-PROFILE	HOMEOPATHS	HOUSE ARREST	HYPERMARKET
HIGH-RANKING	HOMEOPATHY	HOUSEBROKEN	HYPHENATING
HIGH-SCHOOLS	HOMOEROTISM	HOUSEFATHER	HYPHENATION
HIGH-SHERIFF	HOMOGENEITY	HOUSEHOLDER	HYPNOTIZING
HIGH-TENSION	HOMOGENEOUS	HOUSEKEEPER	HYPODERMICS
HIGH-TREASON	HOMOGENIZED	HOUSE LIGHTS	HYPOTHERMIA
HIGHWAY CODE	HOMOGENIZER	HOUSEMASTER	
HIGH-WYCOMBE	HOMOGRAPHIC	HOUSEMOTHER	
HILARIOUSLY	HOMOIOUSIAN	HOUSEPARENT	**12 LETTERS**
HILLBILLIES	HOMOLOGICAL	HOUSEPLANTS	HABEAS CORPUS
HINDERINGLY	HOMOLOGIZER	HOUSEWIFELY	HABERDASHERS
HINDQUATER	HOMOMORPHIC	HOUSEWIFERY	HABERDASHERY
HINSHELWOOD	HOMOPHONOUS	HOUSEWORKER	HABILITATION
HIPPEASTRUM	HOMOPHYLLIC	HOVERCRAFTS	HABITABILITY
HIPPOCAMPAL	HOMOPLASTIC	HOW DO YOU DOS	HABITATIONAL
HIPPOAMPUS	HOMOPTEROUS	HUCKLEBERRY	HABITUALNESS
HIPPOCRATES	HOMO SAPIENS	HUCKSTERISM	HACKING COUGH
HIPPOCRATIC	HOMOSEXUALS	HUDIBRASTIC	HAEMATEMESIS
HIPPOPOTAMI	HOMOSPOROUS	HUGUENOTISM	HAEMATOBLAST
HIPPO REGIUS	HOMOTHALLIC	HULLABALOOS	HAEMATOCYRAL
HIRSUTENESS	HOMOTHERMAL	HUMAN RIGHTS	HAEMATOGENIC
HISPANICISM	HOMOZYGOSIS	HUMDRUMNESS	HAEMATOLOGIC
HISPANICIST	HOMOZYGOTIC	HUMIDIFIERS	HAEMATOLYSIS
HISPANICIZE	HONEYCOMBED	HUMIDIFYING	HAEMOPHILIAC

HAEMOPOIESIS
HAEMOPOIETIC
HAEMORRHAGIC
HAEMORRHOIDS
HAGIOGRAPHER
HAGOGRAPHIC
HAGIOLATROUS
HAIRDRESSERS
HAIRDRESSING
HAIRPIN BENDS
HAIR-RESTORER
HAIR'S BREADTH
HAIRSPLITTER
HAIRTRIGGERS
HALF-BROTHERS
HALF-HOLIDAYS
HALF-MEASURES
HALF-TIMBERED
HALFWAY HOUSE
HALF WITTEDLY
HALLOWEDNEDD
HALLSTATTIAN
HALLUCINATED
HALLUCINATOR
HALLUCINOGEN
HALLUSINOSIS
HALOGENATION
HAMBLETONIAN
HAMMARSKJOLD
HAMMER HEADED
HAMPEREDNESS
HAMSTRINGING
HANDICAPPING
HANDKERCHIEF
HANDSOMENESS
HAPPENSTANCE
HAPPY-GO-LUCKY
HAPPY MEDIUMS
HAPTOTROPISM
HARD CURRENCY
HARD FEELINGS
HARD SHOULDER
HARE COURSING
HARLEQUINADE
HARLEY STREET
HARMLESSNESS
HARMONICALLY
HARMONIOUSLY
HARMONIZABLE
HARPSICHORDS
HARQUEBUSIER
HARTHACANUTE
HARVEST MOONS
HATCHET-FACED

HAUTE COUTURE
HAUTE CUISINE
HEADQUARTERS
HEADSHRINKER
HEADSTRONGLY
HAEMOPHILIAC
HEART ATTACKS
HEARTBREAKER
HEART DISEASE
HEARTENINGLY
HEART FAILURE
HEARTRENDING
HEARTSTRINGS
HEAR-TO-HEART
HEARTWARMING
HEATHENISHLY
HEAVENLINESS
HEAVYHEARTED
HEAVYPETTING
HEAVYWEIGHTS
HEBDOMADALLY
HEBETUDINOUS
HEBRAIZATION
HECTOCOTYLUS
HECTOGRAPHIC
HEDGEHOPPING
HEDGE SPARROW
HEEDLESSNESS
HEILUNGKIANG
HEIR APPARENT
HELICOIDALLY
HELIOCENTRIC
HELIOCHROMIC
HELIOGABALUS
HELIOGRAPHER
HELIOGRAPHIC
HELIOGRAVURE
HELIOLATROUS
HELIOTHERAPY
HELIOTROPISM
HELLENICALLY
HELLGRAMMITE
HELPING HANDS
HELPLESSNESS
HEMICHORDATE
HEMIHYDRATED
HEMIMORPHISM
HEMIMORPHITE
HEMIPARASITE
HEMISPHEROID
HENDECAGONAL
HENOTHEISTIC
HERALDICALLY
HERBACOUSLY

HEREDITARILY
HERMETICALLY
HERMITICALLY
HERMOTENSILE
HEROICALNESS
HERPES ZOSTER
HERPETOLOGIC
HERRINGBONES
HERSTMONCEUX
HESITATINGLY
HETEROCERCAL
HETEROCYCLIC
HETERODACTYL
HETEROECIOOUS
HETEROGEMETE
HETEROGAMOUS
HETEROGENOUS
HETEROGONOUS
HETEROGRAPHY
HETEROGYNOUS
HETEROLOGOUS
HETEROMEROUS
HETERONOMOUS
HETERONYMOUS
HETEROOUSIAN
HETEROPHYLLY
HETEROPLASTY
HETEROSEXUAL
HETEROTACTIC
HETEROZYGOTE
HETEROZYGOUS
HEXACOSANOIC
HEXAGRAMMOID
HEXAHYDRATED
HIBERNACULUM
HIBERNIANISM
HIERARCHICAL
HIERATICALLY
HIEROGLYPHIC
HIEROPHANTIC
HIGH FIDELITY
HIGH-HANDEDLY
HIGHLIGHTING
HIGHLY-STRUNG
HIGH-MINDEDLY
HIGH-PRESSURE
HIGH PROFILES
HIGH SHERIFFS
HIGH-SOUNDING
HIGH-SPIRITED
HINAYANISTIC
HINDQUARTERS
HIPPOCRENIAN
HIPPOPOTAMUUS

493

HIRE PURCHASE
HISTOGENESIS
HISTOGENETIC
HISTOLOGICAL
HISTORICALLY
HOBBLEDEHOYS
HOBSON-JOBSON
HOHENZOLLERN
HOLIDAYMAKER
HOLISTICALLY
HOLOPHRASTIC
HOLOPLANKTON
HOLY OF HOLIES
HOME COUNTIES
HOME FROM HOME
HOMELESSNESS
HOMEOMORPHIC
HOMEOPATHIST
HOMESICKNESS
HOMOCHROMOUS
HOMOGENIZING
HOMOGONOUSLY
HOMOLOGATION
HOOMORPHISM
HOMOPOLARITY
HOMOTAXIALLY
HOMOTHALLISM
HOMOZYGOUSLY
HOEYMOONERS
HONEYMOONING
HONEYSUCKLED
HONEYSUCKLES
HOPELESSNESS
HORIZONTALLY
HORNET'S NEST
HORN OF PLENTY
HORRENDOUSLY
HORRIBLENESS
HORRIFICALLY
HORRIFYINGLY
HORS DE COMBAT
HORS D'OEUVRES
HORSEMANSHIP
HORSE-TRADING
HORSEWHIPPED
HORSEWHIPPER
HORTICULTURE
HORTUS SICCUS
HOSPITALIZED
HOT-CROSS BUNS
HOT-GOSPELLER
HOUSE ARRESTS
HOUSEBREAKER
HOUSEFATHERS

HOUSEHOLDERS
HOUSE HUSBAND
HOUSEKEEPERS
HOUSEKEEPING
HOUSEMASTERS
HOUSEMOTHERS
HOUSE OF CARDS
HOUSE OF LORDS
HOUSEPARENTS
HOUSE PARTIES
HOUSE SPARROW
HOUSE-TO-HOUSE
HOUSE-TRAINED
HOUSEWARMING
HOUSEY-HOUSEY
HUBBLE-BUBBLE
HUDDERSFIELD
HUGGER-MUGGER
HUMANITARIAN
HUMANIZATION
HUMILIATIONS
HUMMING BIRDS
HUMOROUSNESS
HUMPTY DUMPTY
HUNGER STRIKE
HURDY-GURDIES
HURSTMONCEUX
HYALOPLASMIC
HYBRIDIZABLE
HYDNOCARPATE
HYDRASTININE
HYDROCARBONS
HYDROCEPHALY
HYDROCHLORIC
HYDRODYNAMIC
HYDROFLUORIC
HYDROGENATOR
HYDROGEN BOMB
HYDROGRAPHER
HYDROGRAPHIC
HYDROKINETIC
HYDROLYSABLE
HYDROMEDUSAN
HYDROTHERAPY
HYGIENICALLY
HYPERMARKETS
HYPNOTICALLY
HYPOCHONDRIA
HYPOCRITICAL
HYPOTHETICAL
HYSTERECTOMY
HYSTERICALLY

13 LETTERS
HAEMATOLOGIST
HAEMODIALYSIS
HAEMOPHILIACS
HAEMORRHOIDAL
HAGIOGRAPHIES
HAIR-RESTORERS
HAIR-SPLITTING
HALF-HEARTEDLY
HALFWAY HOUSES
HALLUCINATING
HALLUCINATION
HALLUCINATORY
HANDKERCHIEFS
HAPHAZARDNESS
HARD-HEARTEDLY
HARD-LUCK STORY
HARD OF HEARING
HARD SHOULDERS
HARMONIZATION
HAZARDOUSNESS
HEADSHRINKERS
HEALTHFULNESS
HEARTBREAKING
HEARTBROKENLY
HEART DISEASES
HEARTLESSNESS
HEARTSICKNESS
HEARTSOMENESS
HEART-TO-HEARTS
HEATH ROBINSON
HEAVY HYDROGEN
HEAVY INDUSTRY
HEDGE SPARROWS
HEEBIE-JEEBIES
HELLENIZATION
HELMINTHIASIS
HELMINTHOLOGY
HELTER-SKELTER
HEMICELLULOSE
HENDECAHEDRON
HEPTADECANOIC
HEPAMETRICAL
HERBIVOROUSLY
HERMAPHRODITE
HERNIORRHAPHY
HEROIC COUPLET
HERPETOLOGIST
HERTFORDSHIRE
HETEROGENEITY
HETEROGENEOUS
HETEROGENESIS
HETEROGENETIC
HETEROGRAPHIC

HETEROMORPHIC
HETEROPLASTIC
HETEROPTEROUS
HETEROSEXUALS
HETEROSPOROUS
HETEROSTYLOUS
HETEROTHALLIC
HETEROTROPHIC
HETEROZYGOSIS
HEURISTICALLY
HIEROGLYPHICS
HIEROGLYPHIST
HIGH-AND-MIGHTY
HIGH CHURCHMAN
HIGH EXPLOSIVE
HIGHLAND FLING
HIGH-PRESSURED
HIGH-WATER MARK
HILARIOUSNESS
HISTOCHEMICAL
HOBSON'S CHOICE
HOLE-AND-CORNER
HOLIDAYMAKERS
HOLIDAYMAKING
HOLY COMMUNION
HOME ECONOMICS

HOMEOMORPHISM
HOMILETICALLY
HOMOCHROMATIC
HOMOEROTICISM
HOMOGENEOUSLY
HOMOIOTHERMIC
HOMOLOGICALLY
HOMOSEXUALITY
HONEYDEW MELON
HONORIFICALLY
HORNS OF PLENTY
HORRIFICATION
HORSE CHESTNUT
HORSEWHIPPING
HORTICULTURAL
HOSPITALIZING
HOT-GOSPELLERS
HOT-GOSPELLING
HOT-HEADEDNESS
HOUSEBREAKERS
HOUSEBREAKING
HOUSEHOLD NAME
HOUSE HUSBANDS
HOUSEMISTRESS
HOUSES OF CARDS
HOUSE SPARROWS

HOUSEWARMINGS
HUCKLEBERRIES
HUMANITARIANS
HUMILIATINGLY
HUNDREDWEIGHT
HUNGER MARCHER
HUNGER MARCHES
HUNGER STRIKER
HUNGER STRIKES
HUNTING GROUND
HURRICANE LAMP
HYALURONIDASE
HYBRIDIZATION
HYDRAULICALLY
HYDROCEPHALIC
HYDOCEPHALUS
HYDROCHLORIDE
HYDRODYNAMICS
HYDROELECTRIC
HYDROGENATION
HYDROGEN BOMBS
HYDROKINETICS
HYDROLYSATION
HYPERCRITICAL
HYPOCHONDRIAC

3 LETTERS	IOTA	INDUS	IBEXES	INCEST	INNUIT
ICE	IOUS	INEPT	IBIBIO	INCHED	INROAD
ICY	IOWA	INERT	IBISES	INCHES	INRUSH
IDS	IPOH	INFER	ICE AGE	INCHON	INSANE
IFS	IRAN	INFIX	ICEBOX	INCISE	INSECT
ILK	IRAQ	INGOT	ICE CAP	INCITE	INSERT
IMF	IRIS	INION	ICEMAN	INCOME	INSETS
INN	IRON	INKED	ICEMEN	INCUBI	INSIDE
ION	ISLE	INKLE	ICHANG	INCUSE	INSIST
IOU	ISMS	IN-LAW	ICICLE	INDEED	IN SITU
IPA	ITCH	INLAY	ICIEST	INDENT	INSOLE
IQS	ITEM	INLET	ICONIC	INDIAN	INSTAR
IRA	IUDS	INNER	ID CARD	INDICT	INSTEP
IRE		INPUT	IDEALS	INDIGO	INSTIL
IRK	**5 LETTERS**	INSET	IDEATE	INDIUM	INSULA
ISM	IAMBS	INTER	IDIOCY	INDOLE	INSULT
ITS	I-BEAM	INTRO	IDIOMS	INDOOR	INSURE
ITV	IBIZA	INUIT	IDIOTS	INDORE	INTACT
IUD	ICIER	INURE	IDLEST	INDRIS	INTAKE
IVF	ICILY	INURN	IDLING	INDUCE	INTEND
IVY	ICING	INVAR	IDYLLS	INDUCT	INTENT
	ICONS	IODIC	IGLOOS	INDULT	INTERN
	ICTIC	IONIC	IGNITE	INFAMY	INTIMA
4 LETTERS	ICTUS	IOTAS	IGNORE	INFANT	INTINE
IAMB	IDAHO	IRAQI	IGUACU	INFECT	INTONE
IBEX	IDEAL	IRATE	ILESHA	INFEST	IN TOTO
IBID	IDEAS	IRBID	ILEXES	INFIRM	INTROS
IBIS	IDIOM	IRISH	ILL-USE	INFLOW	INTUIT
ICBM	IDIOT	IRKED	IMAGES	INFLUX	INUITS
ICED	IDLED	IRONS	IMBIBE	INFORM	INULIN
ICES	IDLER	IRONY	IMBRUE	INFUSE	INURED
ICON	IDOLS	ISERE	IMBUES	INGEST	INVADE
IDEA	IDYLL	ISLAM	IMIDIC	INGOTS	INVENT
IDEM	IGLOO	ISLES	IMMUNE	INHALE	INVERT
IDES	IKONS	ISLET	IMMURE	INHAUL	INVEST
IDLE	ILEAC	ISSUE	IMPACT	INHERE	INVITE
IDLY	ILEUM	ISTLE	IMPAIR	INHUME	INVOKE
IDOL	IMAGE	ITALO-	IMPALA	INJECT	INWARD
IFFY	IMAGO	ITALY	IMPALE	INJURE	IODATE
IKBS	IMAMS	ITCHY	IMPART	INJURY	IODIDE
IKON	IMBED	ITEMS	IMPEDE	INK-CAP	IODINE
ILES	IMBUE	IVIED	IMPEND	INKIER	IODISM
ILEX	IMIDE	IVIES	IMPHAL	INKING	IODIZE
IMAM	IMINE	IVORY	IMPISH	INKPAD	IODOUS
IMPS	IMPEL	IZMIR	IMPORT	INKLAID	IONIAN
INCA	IMPLY	IZMIT	IMPOSE	INLAND	IONIZE
INCH	INANE		IMPOST	IN-LAWS	IONONE
INDO-	INAPT		IMPUGN	INLAYS	IPECAC
INFO	INCUR	**6 LETTERS**	IMPURE	INLETS	IREFUL
INKS	INCUS	IAMBIC	IMPUTE	INLIER	IRENIC
INKY	INDEX	IAMBUS	INARCH	INMATE	IRIDIC
INNS	INDIA	IBADAN	INBORN	INMOST	IRISES
INTO	INDIC	IBAGUE	INBRED	INNATE	IRITIC
IONS	INDRE	IBERIA	INCEPT	INNING	IRITIS

IRKING	IGENOUS	IMPRESS	INFIELD	INSTANT	ISCHIAL
IRONED	IGNITED	IMPREST	INFLAME	INSTATE	ISCHIUM
IRONER	IGNITER	INPRINT	INFLATE	INSTEAD	ISFAHEN
IRONIC	IGNOBLE	IMPROVE	INFLECT	INSTEPS	ISLAMIC
IRRUPT	IGNOBLY	IMPULSE	INFLICT	INSULAR	ISLANDS
IRTYSH	IGNORED	IMPUTED	INFLOWS	INSULIN	ISOBARS
ISATIN	IGNORER	IMPUTER	INFRACT	INSULTS	ISABATH
ISCHIA	IGUANAS	INANELY	INFUSED	INSURED	ISOCHOR
ISLAND	IKEBANA	INANITY	INFUSER	INSURER	ISOGAMY
ISLETS	ILETITIS	INAPTLY	INGENUE	INSWING	ISOGENY
ISOBAR	ILL-BRED	INBOARD	INGESTA	INTAKES	ISOHYET
ISOGEN	ILLEGAL	IMBOUND	INGOING	INTEGER	ISOLATE
ISOHEL	ILLICIT	INBREED	INGRAIN	INTENSE	ISOLINE
ISOLEX	ILLNESS	INCENSE	INGRATE	INTERIM	ISONOMY
ISOMER	ILL WILL	INCHING	INGRESS	INTERNS	ISOTONE
ISOPOD	IMAGERY	INCIPIT	IN-GROUP	INTIMAL	ISOTOPE
ISRAEL	IMAGINE	INCISED	INGROWN	INTONED	ISOTOPY
ISSUED	IMAGISM	INCISOR	INHABIT	INTONER	ISOTRON
ISSUES	IMAGIST	INCITED	INHALED	INTROIT	ISRAELI
ISTRIA	IMAMATE	INCITER	INHALER	INTRUDE	ISSUING
ITALIC	IMBIBED	INCLINE	INHERIT	INTRUST	ISTHMUS
ITCHED	IMBIBER	INCLOSE	INHIBIT	INURING	ISTRIAN
ITCHES	IMBRUTE	INCLUDE	IN-HOUSE	INUTILE	ITALIAN
ITHACA	IMBUING	INCLUDE	INHUMAN	INVADED	ITALICS
ITSELF	IMITATE	INCOMES	INHUMER	INVADER	ITCHIER
	IMMENSE	INCROSS	INITIAL	INVALID	ITCHING
	IMMERSE	INCUBUS	INJURED	INVEIGH	ITEMIZE
7 LETTERS	IMMORAL	INCURVE	INJURER	INVERSE	ITERANT
IAMBICS	IMMURED	INDENTS	INKIEST	INVITED	ITERATE
IAPETUS	IMPACTS	IN-DEPTH	INKLING	INVITER	ITHACAN
IBERIAN	IMPALAS	INDEXED	INKPAADS	IN VITRO	IVANOVO
ICE AGES	IMPALED	INDEXER	INKWELL	INVOOICE	IVORIES
ICEBALL	IMPALER	INDEXES	INLAYER	INVOKED	IZHEVSK
ICEBERG	IMPANEL	INDIANA	INMATES	INVOKER	
ICE CAPS	IMPASSE	INDIANS	INMARDS	INVOLVE	
ICE-COLD	IMPASTE	INDICAN	INNERVE	INWARDS	**8 LETTERS**
ICE FALL	IMPASTO	INDICTIA	INNINGS	INWEAVE	IAMBUSES
ICELAND	IMPEACH	INDDORS	INQUEST	IODIZER	ICEBURGS
ICE PACK	IMPEDED	INDORSE	INQUIET	IONIZED	ICEBLINK
ICE PICK	IMPEDER	INDOXYL	INQUIRE	IONIZER	ICEBOUND
ICE RINK	IMPERIL	INDRAWN	INQUIRY	IPOMOEA	ICEBOXES
ICHNITE	IMPETUS	INDUCED	INROADS	IPSWICH	ICE CREAM
ICICLED	IMPIETY	INDULGE	INSECTS	IRANIAN	ICE LOLLY
ICICLES	IMPINGE	INEPTLY	INSERTS	IRATELY	ICE PACKS
ICINESS	IMPIOUS	INERTIA	INSHORE	IRELAND	ICE PICKS
ICTERIC	IMPLANT	INERTLY	INSIDER	IRENICS	ICE RINKS
ICTERUS	IMPLEAD	INEXACT	INSIDES	IRIDIUM	ICE SHEET
ID CARS	IMPLIED	INFANCY	INSIGHT	IRKSOME	ICE SKATE
IDEALLY	IMPLORE	INFANTA	INSIPID	IRKUKSK	ICE WATER
IDEATUM	IMPORTS	INFANTE	INSOFAR	IRON AGE	ICHTHYIC
IDENTIC	IMPOSED	INFANTS	INSOLES	IRONIES	IDEALISM
IDIOTIC	IMPOSER	INFARCT	INSPECT	IRONING	IDEALIST
IDIOLIZE	IMPOUND	INFERNO	INSPIRE	IRONIST	IDEALITY
IDYLLIC	IMPRESA	INFIDEL	INSTALL	ISAGOGE	IDEALIZE

IDEATION	IMPARTER	INCLUDED	INFESTER	INPUTTED
IDEATIVE	IMPASSES	INCOMING	INFIDELS	INQUESTS
IDEE FIXE	IMPEDING	INCREASE	INFINITE	INQUIRED
IDENTIFY	IMPELLED	INCUBATE	INFINITY	INQUIRER
IDENTITY	IMPELLER	INCUDATE	INFIXION	INSANELY
IDEOGRAM	IMPERIAL	INCURRED	INFLAMED	INSANITY
IDEOLOGY	IMPERIUM	INDAMINE	INFLAMER	INSCRIBE
IDIOCIES	IMPETIGO	INDEBTED	INFLATED	INSECURE
IDIOLECT	IMPINGED	INDECENT	INFLATER	INSERTED
IDLENESS	IMPINGER	INDENTED	INFLEXED	INSERTER
IDOLATER	IMPISHLY	INDENTER	IN-FIGHT	INSETTED
IDOLATRY	IMPLANTS	INDEXERS	INFLUENT	INSETTER
IDOLIZED	IMPLICIT	INDEXING	INFLUXES	INSIDERS
IDOLIZER	IMPLODED	INDICANT	INFORMAL	INSIGHTS
IDYLLIST	IMPLORED	INDICATE	INFORMED	INSIGNIA
IGNITING	IMPLORER	INDICIAL	INFORMER	INSISTED
IGNITION	IMPLYING	INDICTED	INFRA DIG	INSISTER
IGNITRON	IMPOLICY	INDICTEE	INFRARED	INSOLATE
IGNOMINY	IMPOLITE	INDIGENE	INFRINGE	INSOLENT
IGNORANT	IMPORTED	INDIGENT	INFUSING	INSOMNIA
IGNORING	IMPORTER	INDIGID	INFUSION	INSOMUCH
IGUANIAN	IMPOSING	INDIRECT	INFUSIVE	INSPIRED
ILLATIVE	IMPOSTOR	INDOCILE	INGATHER	INSPIRER
ILL-FATED	IMPOTENT	INDOLENT	INGENUES	INSPIRIT
ILLINOIS	IMPRINTS	INDLOGY	INGESTED	INSTANCE
ILLIQUID	IMPRISON	INDORSED	INGRATES	INSTANTS
ILL-TIMED	IMPROPER	INDUSING	IN-GROUPS	INSTINCT
ILL-TREAT	IMRPOVED	INDUCTED	INGROWTH	INSTRUCT
ILLUSION	IMPROVER	INDUCTOR	INGUINAL	INSULANT
ILLUSORY	IMPUDENT	INDULGED	INHALANT	INSULATE
ILMENITE	IMPUGNED	INDULGER	INHALERS	INSULTED
IMAGINAL	IMPUGNER	INDULINE	INHALING	INSULTER
IMAGINED	IMPULSES	INDUSIAL	INHERENT	INSURERS
IMAGINER	IMPUNITY	INDUSIUM	INHUMANE	INSURING
IMBECILE	IMPURITY	INDUSTRY	INIMICAL	INTAGLIO
IMBEDDED	IMPUTING	INEDIBLE	INIQUITY	INTARSIA
IMBIBING	INACTION	INEDIBLY	INITIALS	INTEGERS
IMITABLE	INACTIVE	INEDITED	INITIATE	INTEGRAL
IMITATED	INASMUCH	INEQUITY	INJECTED	INTENDED
IMITATOR	IN CAMERA	INERTIAL	INJECTOR	INTENDER
IMMANENT	INCENSED	INESSIVE	INJURIES	INTENTLY
IMMOBILE	INCEPTOR	INEXPERT	INJURING	INTERACT
IMMODEST	INCHOATE	INFAMIES	INKBERRY	INTERCOM
IMMOLATE	INCIDENT	INFAMOUS	INKINESS	INTEREST
IMMORTAL	INCISING	INFANTAS	INKSTAND	INTERIMS
IMMOTILE	INCISION	INFANTRY	INKWELLS	INTERIOR
IMMUNITY	INCISIVE	INFECTED	INLANDER	INTERLAY
IMMUNIZE	INCISORS	INFECTOR	INNATELY	INTERMIT
IMMURING	INCISURE	INFERIOR	INNERMAN	INTERMIX
IMPACTED	INCITING	INFERNAL	INNOCENT	INTERNAL
IMPAIRED	INCLINED	INFERNOS	INNOVATE	INTERNED
IMPALING	INCLINER	INFERRED	INNUENDO	INTERNEE
IMPARITY	INCLINES	INFERRER	INOCULUM	INTERPOL
IMPARTED	INCLOSED	INFESTED	INOSITOL	INTERRED

INTERRED	IRRIGATE	ICONOLOGY	IMMIGRATE	IMPOTENCE
INTERREX	IRRITANT	IDEALISTS	IMMINENCE	IMPOUNDED
INTERSEX	IRRITATE	IDEALIZED	IMMINGHAM	IMPOUNDER
INTERVAL	ISAGOGIC	IDEALIZER	IMMODESTY	IMPRECATE
INTIMACY	ISATINIC	IDENTICAL	IMMOLATED	IMPRECISE
INTIMATE	ISCHEMIC	IDENTIKIT	IMMOLATOR	IMPRESSED
INTONING	ISLANDER	IDEOGRAMS	IMMORALLY	IMPRESSER
INTRADOS	ISMAILIA	IDEOLOGUE	IMMORTALS	IMPRESSES
INTRENCH	ISOBARIC	IDEOMOTOR	IMMOVABLE	IMPRINTED
INTREPID	ISOCHEIM	IDIOBLAST	IMMOVABLY	IMPRINTER
INTRIGUE	ISOCLINE	IDIOLECTS	IMMUNIZED	IMPROBITY
INTROSE	ISOCRACY	IDIOMATIC	IMMUNIZER	IMPROMPTU
INTRUDED	ISOGLOSS	IDIOPATHY	IMMUTABLE	IMPROVING
INTRUDER	ISOGONIC	IDIOPHONE	IMMUTABLY	IMPROVISE
INTUBATE	ISOLABLE	IDOLATERS	IMPACTING	IMPRUDENT
INTUITED	ISOLATED	IDOLIZING	IMPACTION	IMPUDENCE
INUNDANT	ISOLATER	IGNESCENT	IMPAIRING	IMPUGNING
INUNDATE	ISOLOGUE	IGNITABLE	IMPARTIAL	IMPULSION
INVADERS	ISOMETRIC	IGNORAMUS	IMPARTING	IMPULSIVE
INVADING	ISOMETRY	IGNORANCE	IMPASSION	IMPUTABLE
INVALIDS	ISOMORPH	IGNORATIO	IMMPASIVE	INABILITY
INVASION	ISOPHONE	IGUANODON	IMPATIENS	INAMORATA
INVASIVE	ISOPLETH	ILEOSTOMY	IMPATIENT	INANIMATE
INVEIGLE	ISOPODAN	ILL AT EASE	IMPEACHED	INANITIES
INVENTED	ISOPRENE	ILLEGALLY	IMPEACHER	INANITION
INVENTOR	ISOSTASY	ILLEGIBLE	IMPEDANCE	INAPTNESS
INVERTED	ISOTHERE	ILL-GOTTEN	IMPELLANT	INAUDIBLE
INVESTED	ISOTHERM	ILLICITLY	IMPELLING	INAUDIBLY
INVESTOR	ISOTONIC	ILLNESSES	IMPENDING	INAUGURAL
INVIABLE	ISOTOPES	ILLOGICAL	IMPERFECT	INCAPABLE
INVITING	ISOTOPIC	ILL-OMENED	IMPERILED	INCAPABLY
INVOICED	ISOTROPY	ILLUSIONS	IMPERIOUS	INCARNATE
INVOICES	ISRAELIS	IMAGINARY	IMPETRATE	INCAUTION
INVOKING	ISSUABLE	IMAGINING	IMPETUOUS	INCENSING
INVOLUTE	ISSUANCE	IMAGISTIC	IMPETUSES	INCENTIVE
INVOLVED	ISTANBUL	IMBALANCE	IMPIETIES	INCEPTION
INVOLVER	ISTHMIAN	IMBECILES	IMPINGING	INCEPTIVE
INWARDLY	ISTHMOID	IMBEDDING	IMPIOUSLY	INCESSANT
IODATION	ITALIANS	IMBRICATE	IMPLANTED	INCIDENCE
IODOFORM	ITEMIZED	IMBROGLIO	IMPLANTER	INCIDENTS
IODOPSIN		IMADAZOLE	IMPLEADER	INCIPIENT
IONIZERS		IMITATING	IMPLEMENT	INCISIONS
IONIZING	**9 LETTERS**	IMITAITON	IMPLICATE	INCISURAL
IOTACISM	ICE CREAMS	IMITATIVE	IMPLODING	INCLEMENT
IRAKLION	ICE HOCKEY	IMITATORS	IMPLORING	INCLINING
IRISHMAN	ICELANDER	IMMANENCE	IMPLOSION	INCLOSURE
IRISHMEN	ICELANDIC	IMMANENCY	IMPOLITIC	INCLUDING
IRONBARK	ICE SHEETS	IMMEDIACY	IMPORTANT	INCLUSION
IRONCLAD	ICE-SKATED	IMMEDIATE	IMPORTERS	INCLUSIVE
IRON-REY	ICE-SKATER	IMMENSELY	IMPORTING	INCOGNITO
IRONWARE	ICE SKATES	IMMENSITY	IMPORTUNE	INCOME TAX
IRONWOOD	ICHNEUMON	IMMERSING	IMPOSABLE	INCOMMODE
IRONWORK	ICHNOLOGY	IMMERSION	IMPOSTERS	INCORRECT
IROQUOIS	ICHTHYOID	IMMIGRANT	IMPOSTURE	INCORRUPT

INCREASED	INELASTIC	INHERITOR	INSOMNIAC	INTERLEAF
INCREASER	INELEGANT	INHIBITED	INSPECTED	INTERLINE
INCREASES	INEPTNESS	INHIBITER	INSPECTOR	INTERLINK
INCREMENT	INERTNESS	INHIBITOR	INSPIRING	INTERLOCK
INCRETION	INFANTILE	INITIALED	INSTALLED	INTERLOPE
INCUBATED	INFARCTED	INITIALER	INSTALLER	INTERLUDE
INCUBATOR	INFATUATE	INITIALLY	INSTANCED	INTERMENT
INCUBUSES	INFECTING	INITIATED	INSTANCES	INTERNESS
INCULCATE	INFECTION	INITIATES	INSTANTER	INTERNING
INCULPATE	INFECTIVE	INITIATOR	INSTANTLY	INTERNIST
INCUMBENT	INFERABLE	INJECTING	INSTIGATE	INTERNODE
INCURABLE	INFERENCE	INJECTION	INSTILLED	INTERPLAY
INCURABLY	INFERIORS	INJECTIVE	INSTILLER	INTERPOSE
INCURIOUS	INFERRING	INJURABLE	INSTINCTS	INTERPRET
INCURRENT	INFERTILE	INJURIOUS	INSTITUTE	INTERRING
INCURRING	INFESTING	INJUSTICE	INSULATED	INTERRUPT
INCURSION	INFIELDER	INKSTANDS	INSULATOR	INTERSECT
INCURSIVE	INFIGHTER	INNER CITY	INSULTING	INTERVALS
INCURVATE	INFIRMARY	INNERMOST	INSURABLE	INTERVENE
INDECENCY	INFIRMATY	INNER TUBE	INSURANCE	INTERVIEW
INDECORUM	INFLAMING	INNERVATE	INSURGENT	INTERWOVE
INDELIBLE	INFLATING	INNKEEPPER	INSWINGER	INTESTACY
INDELIBLY	INFLATION	INNOCENCE	INTAGLIOS	INTESTATE
INDEMNIFY	INFLECTED	INNOCUOUS	INTEGRAND	INTESTINE
INDENTING	INFLECTOR	INNOVATED	INTEGRANT	INTIMATED
INDENTION	INFLICTED	INNOVATOR	INTEGRATE	INTIMATES
INDENTURE	INFLICTER	INNSBRUCK	INTEGRITY	INTORSION
INDEXICAL	INFLUENCE	INNUENDOS	INTELLECT	INTRICACY
INDIAN INK	INFLUENZA	INOCULATE	INTENDANT	INTRICATE
INDICATED	INFORMANT	INORGANIC	INTENDEDS	INTRIGUED
INDICATOR	INFORMERS	INOTROPIC	INTENDING	INTRIGUER
INDICTING	INFORMING	IN-PATIENT	INTENSELY	INTRIGUES
INDIGENCE	INFRACTOR	INPUTTING	INTENSIFY	INTRINSIC
INDIGNANT	INFRINGED	INQUILINE	INTENSION	INTRODUCE
INDIGNITY	INFRINGER	INQUIRIES	INTENSITY	INTROITAL
INDIGOTIC	INFURIATE	INQUIRING	INTENSIVE	INTROJECT
INDISPOSE	INFUSCATE	INQUORATE	INTENTION	INTROVERT
INDOCHINA	INFUSIBLE	INSCRIBED	INTER ALIA	INTRUDERS
INDOLENCE	INFUSIONS	INSECTEAN	INTERBRED	INTRUDING
INDONESIA	INGENIOUS	INSELBERG	INTERCEDE	INTRUSION
INDORSING	INGENUITY	INSENSATE	INTERCEPT	INTRUSIVE
INDRAUGHT	INGENUOUS	INSERTION	INTERCITY	INTRUSTED
INDUCIBLE	INGESTING	INSERTING	INTERCOMS	INTUITING
INDUCTILE	INGESTION	IN-SERVICE	INTERCROP	INTUITION
INDUCTING	INGESTIVE	INSETTING	INTERDICT	INTUITIVE
INDUCTION	INGLENOOK	INSIDE JOB	INTERESTS	INTUMESCE
INDUCTIVE	INGRAINED	INSIDIOUS	INTERFACE	INUNCTION
INDULGENT	INGROWING	INSINCERE	INTERFERE	INUNDATED
INDULGING	INHABITED	INSINUATE	INTERFILE	INUNDATOR
INEBRIANT	INHALANTS	INSIPIDLY	INTERFUSE	INUTILITY
INEBRIATE	INHALATOR	INSISTENT	INTERIORS	INVADABLE
INEBRIETY	INHARMONY	INSISTING	INTERJECT	INVALIDED
INEFFABLE	INHERENCE	INSOLENCE	INTERLACE	INVARIANT
INEFFABLY	INHERITED	INSOLVENT	INTERLARD	INVASIONS

INVECTIVE	ISALLOBAR	ICE-SKATING	IMMACULATE	IMPORTANCE
INVEIGHED	ISCHAEMIA	ICHINOMIYA	IMMATERIAL	IMPORTUNED
INVEIGHER	ISINGLASS	ICHTHYOSIS	IMMATURELY	IMPORTUNER
INVEIGLED	ISLAMABAD	ICHTHYOTIC	IMMATURITY	IMPOSINGLY
INVEIGLER	ISLANDERS	ICONOCLASM	IMMEMORIAL	IMPOSITION
INVENTING	ISOBARISM	ICONOCLAST	IMMERSIBLE	IMPOSSIBLE
INVENTION	ISOBATHIC	ICONOLATER	IMMIGRANTS	IMPOSSIBLY
INVENTIVE	ISOCHORIC	ICONOLATRY	IMMIGRATED	IMPOSTROUS
INVENTORS	ISOCLINAL	ICONOMATIC	IMMIGRATOR	IMPOSTURES
INVENTORY	ISOCRATIC	ICONOSCOPE	IMMINENTLY	IMPOTENTLY
INVERNESS	ISOGAMETE	IDEALISTIC	IMMISCIBLE	IMPOUNDAGE
INVERSELY	ISOGAMOUS	IDEALIZING	IMMOBILITY	IMPOUNDING
INVERSION	ISOGENOUS	IDEATIONAL	IMMOBILIZE	IMPOVERISH
INVERSIVE	ISOLATING	IDEMPOTENT	IMMODERACY	IMPREGANTE
INVERTASE	ISOLATION	IDENTIFIED	IMMODERATE	IMPRESARIO
INVERTING	ISOLATIVE	IDENTIFIER	IMMODESTLY	IMPRESSING
INVESTING	ISOLOGOUS	IDENTIKITS	IMMOLATING	IMPRESSION
INVIDIOUS	ISOMERISM	IDENTITIES	IMMOLATION	IMPRESSIVE
INVIOLACY	IOSMERIZE	IDEOGRAPHY	IMMORALIST	IMPRIMATUR
INVIOLATE	ISOMEROUS	IDEOLOGIES	IMMORALITY	IMPRINTING
INVISIBLE	ISOMETRIC	IDEOLOGIST	IMMORTELLE	IMPRISONED
INVISIBLY	ISONIAZID	IDEOLOGUES	IMMOTILITY	IMPRISONER
INVOCABLE	ISOOCTANE	IDIOLECTAL	IMMUNIZING	IMPROBALE
INVOICING	ISOPROPYL	IDIOPATHIC	IMMUNOLOGY	IMPROBABLY
INVOLUCEL	ISOSCELES	IDIOPHONIC	IMPAIRMENT	IMPROPERLY
INVOLUCRE	ISOSMOTIC	IDOLATRIZE	IMPALEMENT	IMPROVABLE
INVOLVING	ISOSTATIC	IDOLATROUS	IMPALPABLE	IMPROVISED
IODOMETRY	ISOSTERIC	IGNOBILITY	IMPANATION	IMPROVISER
IONOPAUSE	ISOTACTIC	IGNOMINIES	IMPANELLED	IMPRUDENCE
IPSO FACTO	ISOTHERAL	IJSSELMEER	IMPARTIBLE	IMPUDENTLY
IRASCIBLE	ISOTHERMS	ILL-ADVISED	IMPASSIBLE	IMPUISSANT
IRASCIBLY	ISOTROPIC	ILLEGALITY	IMPATIENCE	IMPULSIONS
IRIDOTOMY	ISRAELITE	ILLEGALIZE	IMPEACHIING	IMPUNITIES
IRISH STEW	ISTHMUSES	ILLITERACY	IMPECCABLE	IMPURITIES
IRONBOUND	ITALICIZE	ILLITERATE	IMPECCABLY	IMPUTATION
IRONSIDES	ITCHINESS	ILL-NATURED	IMPEDANCES	IMPUTATIVE
IRONSTONE	ITCHY FEET	ILLOCUTION	IMPEDIMENT	IN ABSENTIA
IRONWORKS	ITCHY PALM	ILL-STARRED	IMPEDINGLY	INACCURACY
IROQUOIAN	ITEMIZING	ILL-TREATED	IMPENDENCE	INACCURATE
IRRADIANT	ITERATION	ILLUMINANT	IMPENITENT	INACTIVATE
IRRADIATE	ITERATIVE	ILLUMINATE	IMPERATIVE	INACTIVELY
IRRAWADDY	ITINERANT	ILLUMINATI	IMPERIALLY	INACTIVITY
IRREGULAR	INTINERARY	ILLUMINISM	IMPERILLED	INADEQUACY
IRRIGABLE	ITINERATE	ILLUMINIST	IMPERSONAL	INADEQUATE
IRRIGATED	ITSY-BITSY	ILLUSORILY	IMPERVIOUS	INAMORATAS
IRRIGATOR	IVY LEAGUE	ILLUSTRATE	IMPETRATOR	INAPPOSITE
IRRITABLE		IMAGINABLE	IMPISHNESS	INAPTITUDE
IRRITABLY		IMBALANCES	IMPLACABLE	INARTISTIC
IRRITANTS	**10 LETTERS**	IMBECILITY	IMPLANTING	INAUGURATE
IRRITATED	IAMBICALLY	IMBIBITION	IMPLEMENTS	INBREEDING
IRRITATOR	IATROGENIC	IMBRICATED	IMPLICATED	INCANDESCE
IRRUPTION	ICEBREAKER	IMBROGLIOS	IMPLICITLY	INCAPACITY
IRRUPTIVE	ICE LOLLIES	IMITATIONS	IMPLOSIONS	INCAPARINA
ISAGOGICS	ICE-SKATERS	IMMACULACY	IMPOLITELY	INCARNATED

INCAUTIOUS	INDEXATION	INFERNALLY	INITIATION	INSOMCIACS
INCENDIARY	INDIAN CORN	INFIDELITY	INITIATIVE	INSOMNIOUS
INCENTIVES	INDICATING	INFIELDERS	INITIATORY	INSOUCIANT
INCEPTIONS	INDICATION	INFIGHTING	INJECTIBLE	INSPECTING
INCESSANCY	INDICATIVE	INFILTRATE	INJECTIONS	INSPECTION
INCESTUOUS	INDICATORS	INFINITELY	INJUNCTION	INSPECTIVE
INCHOATION	INDICATORY	INFINITIVE	INJUNCTIVE	INSPECTORS
INCHOATIVE	INDICTMENT	INFINITUDE	INJURY TIME	INSPIRABLE
INCIDENTAL	INDIGENOUS	INFLATABLE	INJUSTICES	INSPIRITER
INCINERATE	INDIRECTLY	INFLATEDLY	INNER TUBES	INSTALLING
INCIPIENCE	INDISCREET	INFLECTING	INNKEEPERS	INSTALMENT
INCIPIENCY	INDISCRETE	INFLECTION	INNOCENTLY	INSTANCING
INCISIVELY	INDISPOSED	INFLECTIVE	INNOMINATE	INSTIGATED
INCITATION	INDISTINCT	INFLEXIBLE	INNOVATING	INSTIGATOR
INCITEMENT	INDIVIDUAL	INFLEXIBLY	INNOVATION	INSTILLING
INCITINGLY	INDOCILITY	INFLICTING	INNOVATIVE	INSTILMENT
INCIVILITY	INDOLENTLY	INFLICTION	INNOVATORS	INSTITUTED
INCLEMENCY	INDOLOGIST	INFLICTIVE	INNUENDOS	INSTITUTES
INCLINABLE	INDONESIAN	INFLUENCED	INNUMERACY	INSTITUTOR
INCLOSURES	INDOPHENOL	INFLUENCER	INNUMERATE	INSTRUCTED
INCLUDABLE	INDUCEMENT	INFLUENCES	INOCULABLE	INSTRUCTOR
INCLUSIONS	INDUCTANCE	INFLUENZAL	INOCULATED	INSTRUMENT
INCOHERENT	INDUCTIONS	INFORMALLY	INOPERABLE	INSUFFLATE
INCOMPLETE	INDULGENCE	INFORMANTS	INORDINACY	INSULARISM
INCONSTANT	INDUSTRIAL	INFORMEDLY	INORDINATE	INSULARITY
INCRASSATE	INDUSTRIES	INFRACTION	INOSCULATE	INSULATING
INCREASING	INEBRIATED	INFRASONIC	IN-PATIENTS	INSULATION
INCREDIBLE	INEBRIATES	INGESTIBLE	INQUIETUDE	INSULATORS
INCREDIBLY	INEDUCABLE	INGLENOOKS	INQUISITOR	INSURANCES
INCREMENTS	INEDUCABLY	INGLORIOUS	INSALIVATE	INSURGENCE
INCRESCENT	INEFFICACY	INGRATIATE	INS AND OUTS	INSURGENCY
INCUBATING	INELEGANCE	INGREDIENT	INSANITARY	INSURGENTS
INCUBATION	INELIGIBLE	INGRESSION	INSATAIBLE	INTANGIBLE
INCUBATIVE	INELOQUENT	INGRESSIVE	INSATIABLY	INTANGIBLY
INCUBATORS	INEPTITUDE	INHABITANT	INSCRIBING	INTEGRABLE
INCULCATED	INEQUALITIY	INHABITING	INSECURELY	INTEGRATED
INCULCATOR	INEQUITIES	INHALATION	INSECURITY	INTEGRATOR
INCULPABLE	INEVTIABLE	INHARMONIC	INSEMINATE	INTEGUMENT
INCULPATED	INEVITABLY	INHERENTLY	INSENSIBLE	INTELLECTS
INCUMBENCY	INEXISTENT	INHERITING	INSENSIBLY	INTENDANCE
INCUMBENTS	INEXORABLE	INHIBITING	INSENTIENT	INTENDANCY
INCUNABULA	INEXORABLY	INHIBITION	INSERTABLE	INTENDMENT
INCURRABLE	INEXPERTLY	INHIBITIVE	INSERTIONS	INTENTIONS
INCURRENCE	INEXPIABLE	INHUMANELY	INSIDE JOB	INTENTNESS
INCURSIONS	INEXPLICIT	INHUMANITY	INSIGHTFUL	INTERACTED
INDECENTLY	IN EXTREMIS	INHUMATION	INSINUATED	INTER ALIOS
INDECISION	INFALLIBLE	INIMITABLE	INSIPIDITY	INTERBRAIN
INDECISIVE	INFALLIBLY	INIMITABLY	INSISTENCE	INTERBREED
INDECOROUS	INFARCTION	INIQUITIES	INSOBRIETY	INTERCEDED
INDEFINITE	INFATUATED	INIQUITOUS	INSOLATION	INTERCEDER
INDELICACY	INFECTIONS	INITIALING	INSOLENTLY	INTERDICTS
INDELICATE	INFECTIOUS	INITIALIZE	INSOLVABLE	INTERESTED
INDENTURED	INFELICITY	INITIALLED	INSOLVENCY	INTERFACED
INDENTURES	INFERENCES	INITIATING	INSOLVENTS	INTERFACES

INTERFERED	INTROVERTS	IRRATIONAL	IDIOMORPHIC
INTERFERER	INTRUSIONS	IRREGULARS	IDIOTICALLY
INTERFERON	INTRUSTING	IRRELATIVE	IDOLITRIZER
INTERFLUVE	INTUBATION	IRRELEVANT	IDOLIZATION
INTERGRADE	INTUITABLE	IRRELIGION	IDYLLICALLY
INTERGROUP	INUNDATING	IRRESOLUTE	IGNIS FATUUS
INTERLACED	INUNDATION	IRREVERENT	IGNOMINIOUS
INTERLAKEN	INUREDNESS	IRRIGATING	IGNORAMUSES
INTERLEAVE	INVAGINATE	IRRIGATION	ILE-DE-FRANCE
INTERLOPER	INVALIDATE	IRRIGATIVE	ILL-ASSORTED
INTERLUDES	INVALIDING	IRRITATING	ILL-FAVOURED
INTERLUNAR	INVALIDISM	IRRITATION	ILLIBERALLY
INTERMARRY	INVALIDITY	IRRITATIVE	ILLIMITABLE
INTERMENTS	INVALUABLE	IRRUPTIONS	ILL-MANNERED
INTERMEZZI	INVARIABLE	ISENTROPIC	ILLOGICALLY
INTERMEZZO	INVARIABLY	ISOANTIGEN	ILL-TEMPERED
INTERNALLY	INVARIENCE	ISOCHEIMAL	ILL-TREATING
INTERNMENT	INVEIGHING	ISOCHRONAL	ILLUMINANCE
INTERNODAL	INVEIGLING	ISOCHROOUS	ILLUMINATED
INTERNSHIP	INVENTIBLE	ISOCYANIDE	ILLUMINATOR
INTERPHASE	INVENTIONS	ISODYNAMIC	ILLUSIONARY
INTERPLEAD	INVERACITY	ISOGAMETIC	ILLUSIONISM
INTERPOSAL	INVERSIONS	ISOGLOSSAL	ILLUSIONIST
INTERPOSED	INVERTIBLE	ISOGLOTTIC	ILLUSTRATED
INTERPOSER	INVESTABLE	ISOLEUCINE	ILLUSTRATOR
INTERREGNA	INVESTMENT	ISOMETRICS	ILLUSIONARY
INTERSPACE	INVETERACY	ISOMORPHIC	ILLUSIONISM
INTERSTATE	INVETERATE	ISOPIESTIC	ILLUSIONIST
INTERSTICE	INVIGILATE	ISOSEISMAL	ILLUSTRATED
INTERTIDAL	INVIGORATE	ISOTHERMAL	ILLSTRATOR
INTERTWINE	INVINCIBLE	ISOTROPOUS	ILLUSTRIOUS
INTERVENED	INVINCIBLY	ISREALITES	ILLUVIATION
INTERVENER	INVIOLABLE	ITALIANATE	IMAGINARILY
INTERVIEWS	INVITATION	ITALICIZED	IMAGINATION
INTERWOVE	INVITATORY	ITCHY PALMS	IMAGINATIVE
INTERWOVEN	INVOCATION	ITINERANCY	IMBRICATION
INTESTINAL	INVOCATORY	IVORY TOWER	IMITABILITY
INTESTINES	INVOLUCRAL		IMITATIONAL
INTIMACIES	INVOLUTION		IMITATIVELY
INTIMATELY	IODIZATION	**11 LETTERS**	IMMEDIATELY
INTIMATION	IODOMETRIC	ICEBREAKERS	IMMEDICABLE
INTIMIDATE	IONIZATION	ICHNOGRAPHY	IMMIGRATING
INTINCTION	IONOSPHERE	ICHTHYOLOGY	IMMIGRATION
INTOLERANT	IRENICALLY	ICONOCLASTS	IMMOBILIZED
INTONATION	IRIDACEOUS	ICONOGRAPHY	IMMOBILIZER
INTOXICANT	IRIDECTOMY	ICONOLOGIST	IMMORTALITY
INTOXICATE	IRIDESCENT	ICOSAHEDRAL	IMMORTALIZE
INTRAMURAL	IRISH STEWS	ICOSAHEDRAL	IMMUNOASSAY
INTRENCHED	IRISHWOMAN	ICOSAHEDRON	IMMUNOGENIC
INTREPIDLY	IRONICALLY	IDENTICALLY	IMMUNOLOGIC
INTRIGUING	IRONMONGER	IDENTIFYING	IMPANELLING
INTRODUCED	IRRADIANCE	IDEOLOGICAL	IMPARTATION
INTRODUCER	IRRADIATED	IDIOBLASTIC	IMPARTIALLY
INTROSPECT	IRRADIATOR	IDIOGRAPHIC	IMPASSIONED

IMPASSIVELY	IMPRESSIBLE	INCREASABLE	INDULGINGLY
IMPASSIVITY	IMPRESSIONS	INCREASEDLY	INDUPLICATE
IMPASTATION	IMPRESSMENT	INCREDULITY	INDUSTRIOUS
IMPATIENTLY	IMPRIMATURS	INCREDULOUS	INEBRITATING
IMPEACHABLE	IMPRISONING	INCREMENTAL	INEBRIATION
IMPEACHMENT	IMPROPRIATE	INCRIMINATE	INEDIBILITY
IMPECUNIOUS	IMPROPRIETY	INCULCATING	INEFFECTIVE
IMPEDIMENTA	IMPROVEMENT	INCULCATION	INEFFECTUAL
IMPEDIMENTS	IMPROVIDENT	INCULPATING	INEFFICIENT
IMPENITENCE	IMPROVINGLY	INCULPATION	INELEGANTLY
IMPERATIVES	IMPROVISING	INCUNABULAR	INELOQUENCE
IMPERFECTLY	IMPRUDENTLY	INCURIOSITY	INELUCTABLE
IMPERFORATE	IMPUGNATION	INCURVATION	INELUCATABLY
IMPERIALISM	IMPUISSANCE	INCURATURE	INEQUITABLE
IMPERIALIST	IMPULSIVELY	INDECIDUOUS	INEQUITABLY
IMPERILLING	IMPUTATIONS	INDEFINABLE	INERTIA REEL
IMPERIOUSLY	INADVERTENT	INDEFINABLY	INESCAPABLE
IMPERMANENT	INADVISABLE	INDEHISCENT	INESCAPABLY
IMPERMEABLE	INALIENABLE	INDEMNIFIER	INESSENTIAL
IMPERSONATE	INALTERABLE	INDEMNITIES	INESTIMABLE
IMPERTINENT	INATTENTION	INDENTATION	INESTIMABLY
IMPETRATION	INATTENTIVE	INDENTURING	INEXACTNESS
IMPETRATIVE	INAUGURATED	INDEPENDENT	INEXCUSABLE
IMPETUOSITY	INAUGURATOR	INDEX FINGER	INEXISTENCE
IMPETUOUSLY	INCALESCENT	INDIA RUBBER	INEXPEDIENT
IMPINGEMENT	INCANTATION	INDICATABLE	INEXPENSIVE
IMPIOUSNESS	INCAPSULATE	INDICATIONS	INFANTICIDE
IMPLAUSIBLE	INCARCERATE	INDICATIVES	INFANTILISM
IMPLAUSIBLY	INCARDINATE	INDICTMENTS	INFANTILITY
IMPLEADABLE	INCARNATING	INDIFFERENT	INFANTRYMAN
IMPLEMENTAL	INCARNATION	INDIGESTION	INFANTRYMEN
IMPLEMENTED	INCERTITUDE	INDIGESTIVE	INFATUATION
IMPLEMENTER	INCESSANTLY	INDIGNANTLY	INFERENTIAL
IMPLICATING	INCIDENTALS	INDIGNATION	INFERIORITY
IMPLICATION	INCINERATED	INDIGNITIES	INFERNALITY
IMPLICATIVE	INCINERATOR	INDIRECTION	INFERTILITY
IMPLORATION	INCIPIENTLY	INDIVIDUALS	INFESTATION
IMPLORATORY	INCLINATION	INDIVIDUATE	INFILTRATED
IMPLORINGLY	INCLUSIVELY	INDIVISIBLE	INFILTRATOR
IMPORTANTLY	INCOERCIBLE	INDIVISIBLY	INFINITIVAL
IMPORTATION	INCOGNIZANT	INDOCHINESE	INFINITIVES
IMPORTUNATE	INCOHERENCE	INDO-HITTITE	INFIRMARIES
IMPORTUNING	INCOME TAXES	INDO-IRANIAN	INFIRMITIES
IMPORTUNITY	INCOMMODING	INDOMITABLE	INFLAMINGLY
IMPOSITIONS	INCOMPETENT	INDOMITABLY	INFLAMMABLE
IMPRACTICAL	INCOMPLIANT	INDO-PACIFIC	INFLECTIONS
IMPRECATION	INCONGRUITY	INDUBITABLE	INFLICTIONS
IMPRECATORY	INCONGRUOUS	INDUBITABLY	INFLUENCING
IMPRECISION	INCONSONANT	INDUCEMENTS	INFLUENTIAL
IMPREGNABLE	INCONSTANCY	INDUCTILITY	INFORMALITY
IMPREGNABLY	INCONTINENT	INDUCTIONAL	INFORMATION
IMPREGNATED	INCORPORATE	INDUCTIVELY	INFORMATIVE
IMPREGNATOR	INCORPOREAL	INDULGENCES	INFORMINGLY
IMPRESARIOS	INCORRECTLY	INDULGENTLY	INFRACOSTAL

504

INFRACTIONS	INSALUBRITY	INTEGRATION	INTERREGNAL
INFRANGIBLE	INSCRIBABLE	INTEGRETIVE	INTERREGNUM
INFREQUENCY	INSCRIPTION	INTEGUMENTS	INTERRELATE
INFURIATING	INSCRIPTIVE	INTELLIGENT	INTERROBANG
INFURIATION	INSCRUTABLE	INTEMPERATE	INTERROGATE
INFUSIONISM	INSCRUTABLY	INTENSIFIED	INTERRUPTED
INFUSIONIST	INSECTARIUM	INTENSIFIER	INTERRUPTER
INGENIOUSLY	INSECTICIDE	INTENTIONAL	INTERSECTED
INGENUOUSLY	INSECTIVORE	INTERACTING	INTERSEXUAL
INGRAINEDLY	INSEMINATED	INTERACTION	INTERSPERSE
INGRATIATED	INSEMINATOR	INTERACTIVE	INTERSTICES
INGRATITUDE	INSENSITIVE	INTERATOMIC	INTERTRIBAL
INGREDIENTS	INSENTIENCE	INTERBEDDED	INTERTWINED
INGURGITATE	INSEPERABLE	INTERCALARY	INTERVENING
INHABITABLE	INSEPERABLY	INTERCALATE	INTERVIEWED
INHABITANCY	INSERTIONAL	INTERCEDING	INTERVIEWEE
INHABITANTS	INSESSORIAL	INTERCEPTING	INTERVIEWER
INHALATIONS	INSIDE TRACK	INTERCEPTOR	INTERWEAVER
INHERITABLE	INSIDIOUSLY	INTERCESSOR	INTIMATIONS
INHERITANCE	INSINCERELY	INTERCHANGE	INTIMIDATED
INHIBITABLE	INSINCERITY	INTERCOSTAL	INTIMIDATOR
INHIBITEDLY	INSINUATING	INTERCOURSE	INTOLERABLE
INHIBITIONS	INSINUATION	INTERDENTAL	INTOLERABLY
INITIALLING	INSINUATIVE	INTERDICTOR	INTOLERANCE
INITIATIONS	INSISTENTLY	INTERESTING	INTONATIONS
INITIATIVES	INSOUCIANCE	INTERFACING	INTOXICABLE
INITIATRESS	INSPECTABLE	INTERFERING	INTOXICANTS
INJUDICIOUS	INSPECTIONS	INTERFUSION	INTOXICATED
INJUNCTIONS	INSPECTORAL	INTERJECTED	INTOXICATOR
INJURIOUSLY	INSPIRATION	INTERLACING	INTRA-ATOMIC
INNER CITIES	INSPIRATIVE	INTERLARDED	INTRACOSTAL
INNERVATION	INSPIRATORY	INTERLINEAR	INTERACTABLE
INOCUOUSLY	INSPIRINGLY	INTERLINGUA	INTERACTABLY
INNOVATIONS	INSTABILITY	INTERLINING	INTRADERMAL
INNS OF COURT	INSTALMENTS	INTERLINKED	INTRAVENOUS
INNUMERABLE	INSTATEMENT	INTERLOCKED	INTRENCHING
INNUTRITION	INSTIGATING	INTERLOCKER	INTREPIDITY
INOBSERVANT	INSTIGATION	INTERLOPERS	INTRICACIES
INOCULATING	INSTIGATIVE	INTERMEZZOS	INTRICATELY
INOCULATION	INSTIGATORS	INTERMINGLE	INTRODUCING
INOCULATIVE	INSTINCTIVE	INTERMOTTOR	INTROVERTED
INOFFENSIVE	INSTITUTING	INTERNALITY	INTRUDINGLY
INOFFICIOUS	INSTITUTION	INTERNALIZE	INTRUSIONAL
INOPERATIVE	INSTITUTIVE	INTERNECINE	INTUITIONAL
INOFFICIOUS	INSTRUCTING	INTERNEURON	INTUITIVELY
INOPERATIVE	INSTRUCTION	INTERNMENTS	INTUITIVISM
INOPORTUNE	INSTRUCTIVE	INTERNSHIPS	INTUITIVIST
INQUILINISM	INSTRUCTORS	INTERNUNCIO	INTUMESCENT
INQUILINOUS	INSTRUMENTS	INTERPOLATE	INUNDATIONS
INQUIRINGLY	INSUFFLATOR	INTERPOSING	INVAGINABLE
INQUISITION	INSUPERABLE	INTERPRETED	INVALIDATED
INQUISITIVE	INSUPERABLY	INTERPRETER	INVALIDATOR
INQUISITORS	INTAGLIATED	INTERRACIAL	INVENTIONAL
IN-RESIDENCE	INTEGRATING	INTERRADIAL	INVENTORIES

INVERTABRAL
INVESTIGATE
INVESTITIVE
INVESTITURE
INVESTMENTS
INVIABILITY
INVIDIOUSLY
INVIGILATED
INVIGILATOR
INVIGORATED
INVIGORATOR
INVITATIONS
INVOCATIONS
INVOLUCRATE
INVOLUNTARY
INVOLVEMENT
IONOSPHERIC
IRIDESCENCE
IRISH COFFEE
IRON CURTAIN
IRONMONGERS
IRONMONGERY
IRON RATIONS
IRRADIATING
IRRADIATION
IRRADIATIVE
IRRECUSABLE
IRREDENTISM
IRREDUCIBLE
IRREDUCIBLY
IRREFUTABLE
IRREFUTABLY
IRREGULARLY
IRRELEVANCE
IRRELIGIOUS
IRREMOVABLE
IRREPAIRABLE
IRREPARABLY
IRRESOLUBLE
IRRETENTIVE
IRREVERENCE
IRREVOCABLE
IRREVOCABLY
IRRITATIONS
ISOCHRONIZE
ISODIAPHERE
ISOELECTRIC
ISOGEOTHERM
ISOLABILITY
ISOLECITHAL
ISOMAGNETIC
ISOMETRICAL
ISOMETROPIA
ISOMORPHISM

ISORHYTHMIC
ISOTONICITY
ITACOLUMITE
ITALICIZING
ITEMIZATION
ITHYPHALLIC
ITINERARIES
ITINERATION
IVORY TOWERS

12 LETTERS
ICE-CREAM SODA
ICHNEUMON FLY
ICHNOGRAPHIC
ICHNOLOGICAL
ICHTHYOLOGIC
ICHTHYOPHAGY
ICONOCLASTIC
ICONOGRAPHER
ICONOGRAPHIC
ICONOLATROUS
ICONOLOGICAL
IDEALIZATION
IDENTIFIABLE
IDENTITY CARD
IDEOLOGICAL
IDIOMORPHISM
IDIOSYNCRASY
IDOLATROUSLY
IGNITABILITY
ILLEGALITIES
ILLEGIBILITY
ILLEGITIMACY
ILLEGITIMATE
ILLIBERALITY
ILLITERATELY
ILLOGICALITY
ILL-TREATMENT
ILLUMINATING
ILLUMINATION
ILLUMINATIVE
ILLUSIONISTS
ILLUSORINESS
ILLUSTRATING
ILLUSTRATION
ILLUSTRATIVE
ILLUSTRATORS
IMAGINATIONS
IMBECILITIES
IMMACULATELY
IMMEASURABLE
IMMEASURABLY
IMMEMORIABLE

IMMERSIONISM
IMMERSIONIST
IMMETHODICAL
IMMOBILIZING
IMMODERATELY
IMMODERATION
IMMORALITIES
IMMORTALIZED
IMMORTALIZER
IMMOVABILITY
IMMUNE SYSTEM
IMMUNIZATION
IMMUNOLOGIST
IMMUTABILITY
IMPARTIALITY
IMPEDIMENTAL
IMPENETRABLE
IMPENITENTLY
IMPERATIVELY
IMPERCEPTION
IMPERCEPTIVE
IMPERFECTION
IMPERFECTIVE
IMPERIALISTS
IMPERISHABLE
IMPERMANENCE
IMPERSONALLY
IMPERSONATED
IMPERSONATOR
IMPERTINENCE
IMPLANTATION
IMPLEMENTING
IMPLICATIONS
IMPLICITNESS
IMPOLITENESS
IMPONDERABLE
IMPORTATIONS
IMPOVERISHED
IMPOVERISHER
IMPRECATIONS
IMPREGNATING
IMPREGNATION
IMPRESSIONAL
IMPERMANENCE
IMPERSONALLY
IMPERSONATED
IMPERSONATOR
IMPERTINENCE
IMPETIGINOUS
IMPLANTATION
IMPLEMENTING
IMPLICATIONS
IMPLICITNESS
IMPOLITENESS

IMPONDERABLE
IMPORTATIONS
IMPOVERISHED
IMPOVERISHER
IMPRECATIONS
IMPREGNATING
IMPREGNATION
IMPRESSIONAL
IMPRESSIVELY
IMPRISONMENT
IMPROVEMENTS
IMPROVIDENCE
IMPUTABILITY
INACCESSIBLE
INACCESSIBLY
INACCURACIES
INACCURATELY
INACTIVATION
INADEQUACIES
INADEQUATELY
INADMISSIBLE
INADMISSIBLY
INADVERTENCE
INAPPLICABLE
INAPPLICABLY
INARTICULATE
INAUDIBILITY
INAUGURATING
INAUGURATION
INAUSPICIOUS
INCALCULABLE
INCALCULABLY
INCALESCENCE
INCANDESCENT
INCANTATIONS
INCAPABILITY
INCAPACITATE
INCARCERATED
INCARCERATOR
INCARNATIONS
INCAUTIOUSLY
INCENDIARISM
INCESTUOUSLY
INCIDENTALLY
INCINERATING
INCINERATION
INCINERATORS
INCISIVENESS
INCIVILITIES
INCLINATIONS
INCLINOMETER
INCOGNIZANCE
INCOHERENTLY
INCOMMODIOUS

INCOMMUTABLE	INDIFFERENCE	INFLECTIONAL	INSURRECTION
INCOMPARABLE	INDIGENOUSLY	INFLORESCENT	INTELLECTION
INCOMPARABLY	INDIGESTIBLE	INFREQUENTLY	INTELLECTIVE
INCOMPATIBLE	INDIGESTIBLY	INFRINGEMENT	INTELLECTUAL
INCOMPATIBLY	INDIRECTNESS	INFUNDIBULAR	INTELLIGENCE
INCOMPETENCE	INDISCIPLINE	INFUNDIBULUM	INTELLIGIBLE
INCOMPETENTS	INDISCREETLY	INFUSIBILITY	INTELLIGIBLY
INCOMPLETELY	INDISCRETION	INGLORIOUSLY	INTEMPERANCE
INCOMPLIANCE	INDISPUTABLY	INGRATIATING	INTENSIFIERS
INCOMPUTABLE	INDISSOLUBLE	INGRATIATION	INTENSIFYING
INCONCLUSIVE	INDISSOLUBLY	INHABITATION	INTERACTIONS
INCONFORMITY	INDISTINCTLY	INHARMONIOUS	INTERCEPTING
INCONSEQUENT	INDIVIDUALITY	INHERITANCES	INTERCEPTION
INCONSISTENT	INDIVIDUATOR	INHOSPITABLE	INTERCEPTIVE
INCONSOLABLE	INDOCTRINATE	INHOSPITABLY	INTERCEPTORS
INCONSOLABLY	INDO-EUROPEAN	INHUMANITIES	INTERCESSION
INCONSONANCE	INDOLEACETIC	INIMICALNESS	INTERCESSORY
INCONSUMABLE	INDOMETHACIN	INIQUITOUSLY	INTERCHANGED
INCONTINENCE	INDUSTRIALLY	INNOVATIONAL	INTERCHANGES
INCONVENIENT	INEFFABILITY	INNUTRITIOUS	INTERCONNECT
INCOORDINATE	INEFFACEABLE	INOBSERVANCE	INTERCURRENT
INCORPORABLE	INEFFICIENCY	INOCULATIONS	INTERDICTION
INCORPORATED	INELASTICITY	INORDINATELY	INTERDICTIVE
INCORPORATOR	INEQUALITIES	INOSCULATION	INTERESTEDLY
INCORPOREITY	INERADICABLE	INQUISITIONS	INTERFERENCE
INCORRIGIBLE	INERADICABLY	INSALIVATION	INTERFERTILE
INCORRIGIBLY	INESSENTIALS	INSALUBRIOUS	INTERFLUVIAL
INCRASSATION	INEXACTITUDE	INSCRIPTIONS	INTERGLACIAL
INCREASINGLY	INEXPEDIENCE	INSECTICIDAL	INTERJECTING
INCRETIONARY	INEXPERIENCE	INSECTICIDES	INTERJECTORY
INCRIMINATED	INEXPERTNESS	INSECTIVORES	INTERLACEDLY
INCRIMINATOR	INEXPLICABLE	INSEMINATING	INTERLAMINAR
INCRUSTATION	INEXPLICABLY	INSEMINATION	INTERLARDING
INCUBATIONAL	INEXPRESSIVE	INSINUATIONS	INTERLINKING
INCUMBENCIES	INEXTENSIBLE	INSOLUBILITY	INTERLOCKING
INCURABILITY	INEXTRICABLE	INSPECTINGLY	INTERLOCUTOR
INDEBTEDNESS	INEXTRICABLY	INSPECTIONAL	INTERMARRIED
INDECISIVELY	INFANTICIDAL	INSPECTORATE	INTERMEDIACY
INDECLINABLE	INFANTICIDES	INSPIRATIONS	INTERMEDIARY
INDECOROUSLY	INFATUATEDLY	INSPIRITMENT	INTERMEDIATE
INDEFEASIBLE	INFATUATIONS	INSTALLATION	INTERMINABLE
INDEFENSIBLE	INFECTIOUSLY	INSTITUTIONS	INTERMINABLY
INDEFENSIBLY	INFELICIOUSLY	INSPIRITMENT	INTERMINGLED
INDEFINITELY	INFELICITOUS	INSTALLATION	INTERMISSION
INDELIBILITY	INFESTATIONS	INSTITUTIONS	INTERMISSIVE
INDELICATELY	INFIDELITIES	INSTRUCTABLE	INTERMITTENT
INDEMNIFYING	INFILTRATING	INSTRUCTIONS	INTERMIXABLE
INDENTATIONS	INFILTRATION	INSTRUMENTAL	INTERMIXTURE
INDEPENDENCE	INFILTRATORS	INSUFFERABLE	INTERNALIZED
INDEPENDENCY	INFLAMMATION	INSUFFERABLY	INTERNUNCIAL
INDEPENDENTS	INFLAMMATORY	INSUFFICIENT	INTEROCEPTOR
INDEX FINGERS	INFLATIONARY	INSUFFLATION	INTERPELLANT
INDIAN SUMMER	INFLATIONISM	INSURABILITY	INTERPELLATE
INDICATIVELY	INFLATIONIST	INSURGENCIES	INTERPLEADER

507

INTERPOLATED
INTERPOSABLE
INTERPRETERS
INTERPRETING
INTERPRETIVE
INTEREGNUMS
INTERROGATED
INTERROGATOR
INTERRUPTING
INTERRUPTION
INTERRUPTIVE
INTERSECTING
INTERSECTION
INTERSPATIAL
INTERTEXTURE
INTERTWINING
INTERVENTION
INTERVIEWEES
INTERVIEWERS
INTERVIEWING
INTERVOCALIC
INTERWEAVING
INTIMIDATING
INTIMIDATION
INTOLERANTLY
INTONATIONAL
INTOXICATING
INTOXICATION
INTOXICATIVE
INTRACARDIAC
INTRACRANIAL
INTRANSIGENT
INTRANSITIVE
INTRANUCLEAR
INTRAUTERINE
INTRIGUINGLY
INTRODUCIBLE
INTRODUCTION
INTRODUCTORY
INTROJECTION
INTROJECTIVE
INTROVERSION
INTROVERSIVE
INTUITIONISM
INTUITIONIST
INTUMESCENCE
INTUSSUSCEPT
INVAGINATION
INVALIDATING
INVALIDATION
INVERTEBRACY
INVERTEBRATE
INVERTED SNOB
INVESTIGABLE

INVESTIGATED
INVESTIGATOR
INVESTITURES
INVIGILATING
INVIGILATION
INVIGILATORS
INVIGORATING
INVIGORATION
INVIGORATIVE
INVISIBILITY
INVOCATIONAL
INVOLUCELATE
INVOLUTIONAL
INVULNERABLE
INVULNERABLY
INVULTUATION
IRASCIBILITY
IRISH COFFEES
IRONING BOARD
IRRADIATIONS
IRRATIONALLY
IRREDEEMABLE
IRREDEEMABLY
IRREFRAGABLE
IRREGULARITY
IRRELEVANCES
IRRELEVANTLY
IRRELIEVABLE
IRREMISSIBLE
IRRESISTIBLY
IRRESOLUTELY
IRRESOLUTION
IRRESOLVABLE
IRRESPECTIVE
IRRESPIRABLE
IRRESPONSIVE
IRREVERENTLY
IRREVERSIBLE
IRREVERSIBLY
IRRIGATIONAL
IRRITABILITY
ISOCHROMATIC
ISODIAMETRIC
ISOLATIONISM
ISOLATIONIST
ISOTOPICALLY
ITALIANESQUE

13 LETTERS
IATROGENICITY
ICE-CREAM SODAS
ICHTHYOLOGIST
ICONOMATICISM
IDEALIZATIONS
IDENTICAL TWIN
IDENTITY CARDS
IDEOLOGICALLY
IDIOMATICALLY
IDIOSYNCRATIC
IGNOMINIOUSLY
ILL-CONSIDERED
ILLOCUTIONARY
ILLUMINATIONS
ILLUSIONISTIC
ILLUSTRATIONS
ILLUSTRIOUSLY
IMAGINATIVELY
IMAGISTICALLY
IMITATIVENESS
IMMATERIALISM
IMMATERIALIST
IMMATERIALITY
IMMATERIALIZE
IMMIGRATIONAL
IMMISCIBILITY
IMMORTALIZING
IMMUNIZATIONS
IMMUNOGENETIC
IMMUNOTHERAPY
IMPALPABILITY
IMPARIPINNATE
IMPARTIBILITY
IMPASSABILITY
IMPASSIONEDLY
IMPASSIVENESS
IMPECCABILITY
IMPECUNIOUSLY
IMPERCEPTIBLE
IMPERCEPTIBLY
IMPERFECTIONS
IMPERFORATION
IMPERIALISTIC
IMPERIOUSNESS
IMPERMISSIBLE
IMPERSONALITY
IMPERSONALIZE
IMPERSONATING
IMPERSONATION
IMPERSONATORS
IMPERTINENTLY
IMPERTURBABLE
IMPERTURBABLY

IMPETUOUSNESS
IMPLACABILITY
IMPONDERABLES
IMPORTUNATELY
IMPOSSIBILITY
IMPOVERISHING
IMPRACTICABLE
IMPRACTICABLY
IMPRACTICALLY
IMPRESSIONISM
IMPRESSIONIST
IMPROBABILITY
IMPROPRIATION
IMPROPRIETIES
IMPROVABILITY
IMPROVIDENTLY
IMPROVISATION
IMPULSIVENESS
INADVERTENTLY
INAPPROPRIATE
INATTENTIVELY
INAUGURATIONS
INCANDESCENCE
INCANTATIONAL
INCAPACITATED
INCAPSULATION
INCARCERATING
INCARCERATION
INCARDINATION
INCLINATIONAL
INCOMBUSTIBLE
INCOMMUNICADO
INCOMPETENTLY
INCONCEIVABLE
INCONCEIVABLY
INCONDENSABLE
INCONGRUITIES
INCONGRUOUSLY
INCONSEQUENCE
INCONSIDERATE
INCONSISTENCY
INCONSPICUOUS
INCONSTANCIES
INCONTESTABLE
INCONTESTABLY
INCONVENIENCE
INCONVERTIBLE
INCONVINCIBLE
INCORPORATING
INCORPORATION
INCORPORATIVE
INCORPOREALLY
INCORRECTNESS
INCORRUPTIBLE

INCORRUPTIBLY
INCREDIBILITY
INCREDULOUSLY
INCREMENTALLY
INCRIMINATING
INCRIMINATION
INCRIMINATORY
INCRUSTATIONS
INCULPABILITY
INDEFATIGABLE
INDEFATIGABLY
INDENTURESHIP
INDEPENDENTLY
INDESCRIBABLE
INDESCRIBABLY
INDETERMINACY
INDETERMINATE
INDETERMINISM
INDETERMINIST
INDIAN SUMMERS
INDIFFERENTLY
INDISCERNIBLE
INDISCRETIONS
INDISPENSABLE
INDISPENSABLY
INDISPOSITION
INDISTINCTIVE
INDIVIDUALISM
INDIVIDUALIST
INDIVIDUALITY
INDIVIDUALIZE
INDIVIDUATION
INDOCTRINATED
INDOCTRINATOR
INDUPLICATION
INDUSTRIALISM
INDUSTRIALIST
INDUSTRIALIZE
INDUSTRIOUSLY
INEDUCABILITY
INEFFECTIVELY
INEFFECTUALLY
INEFFICACIOUS
INEFFICIENTLY
INELIGIBILITY
INEVITABILITY
INEXHAUSTIBLE
INEXHAUSTIBLY
INEXORABILITY
INEXPENSIVELY
INEXPERIENCED
INEXPRESSIBLE
INEXPRESSIBLY
INFALLIBILITY

INFECTIVENESS
INFERENTIALLY
INFILTRATIONS
INFINITESIMAL
INFLAMMATIONS
INFLECTEDNESS
INFLEXIBILITY
INFLORESCENCE
INFLUENCEABLE
INFLUENTIALLY
INFORMATIONAL
INFORMATIVELY
INFRINGEMENTS
INFURIATINGLY
INGENUOUSNESS
INGRAINEDNESS
INHOSPITALITY
INIMITABILITY
INJUDICIOUSLY
INLAND REVENUE
INNOCUOUSNESS
INNOVATIONIST
INOCULABILITY
INOFFENSIVELY
INOPERABILITY
INOPPORTUNELY
INORGANICALLY
INQUISITIONAL
INQUISITIVELY
INQUISITORIAL
INSATIABILITY
INSCRIPTIONAL
INSECTIVOROUS
INSENSIBILITY
INSENSITIVELY
INSENSITIVITY
INSIDIOUSNESS
INSIGNIFICANT
INSPIRATIONAL
INSPIRITINGLY
INSTABILITIES
INSTALLATIONS
INSTANTANEOUS
INSTIGATINGLY
INSTINCTIVELY
INSTITUTIONAL
INSTRUCTIONAL
INSTRUCTIVELY
INSUBORDINATE
INSUBTANTIAL
INSUFFICIENCY
INSUPPORTABLE
INSURRECTIONS
INSUSCEPTIBLE

INTANGIBILITY
INTEGRABILITY
INTEGUMENTARY
INTELLECTUALS
INTELLIGENTLY
INTEMPERATELY
INTENTIONALLY
INTERACTIONAL
INTERACTIVELY
INTERACTIVITY
INTERBREEDING
INTERCALARILY
INTERCELLULAR
INTERCEPTIONS
INTERCESSIONS
INTERCHANGING
INTERCLAVICLE
INTERCOLUMNAR
INTERCURRENCE
INTEREST GROUP
INTERESTINGLY
INTERFACIALLY
INTERFERINGLY
INTERGALACTIC
INTERGRADIENT
INTERJECTIONS
INTERLACEMENT
INTERLAMINATE
INTERLOCUTION
INTERLOCUTORS
INTERLOCUTORY
INTERLUNATION
INTERMARRIAGE
INTERMARRYING
INTERMEDIATOR
INTERMINGLING
INTERMISSIONS
INTERMITTENCE
INTERNALIZING
INTERNATIONAL
INTEROCEPTIVE
INTERPELLATOR
INTERPERSONAL
INTERPOLATING
INTERPOLATION
INTERPOLATIVE
INTERPOSINGLY
INTERPOSITION
INTERPRETABLE
INTERRACIALLY
INTERRELATION
INTERROGATING
INTERROGATION
INTERROGATIVE

INTERROGATORS
INTERROGATORY
INTERRUPTIBLE
INTERRUPTIONS
INTERSECTIONS
INTERSPERSING
INTERSPERSION
INTERSTRATIFY
INTERTROPICAL
INTERVENTIONS
INTRACELLULAR
INTRAMUSCULAR
INTRANSIGENCE
INTRAPERSONAL
INTRAVASATION
INTRAVENOUSLY
INTRINSICALLY
INTRODUCTIONS
INTROGRESSION
INTROSPECTION
INTROSPECTIVE
INTUITIVENESS
INVARIABILITY
INVENTIVENESS
INVENTORIABLE
INVERTEBRATES
INVERTED COMMA
INVERTED SNOBS
INVERTIBILITY
INVESTIGATING
INVESTIGATION
INVESTIGATIVE
INVESTIGATORS
INVIDIOUSNESS
INVINCIBILITY
INVIOLABILITY
INVOLUNTARILY
IRRATIONALITY
IRRECLAIMABLE
IRRECOVERABLE
IRRECOVERABLY
IRRELIGIONIST
IRREPLACEABLE
IRREPRESSIBLE
IRREPRESSIBLY
IRRESPONSIBLE
IRRESPONSIBLY
IRRETRIEVABLE
IRRETRIEVABLY
ISOLATIONISTS
ISOMERIZATION
ITALICIZATION

J 3 LETTERS to 7 LETTERS

3 LETTERS
JAB
JAG
JAM
JAR
JAW
JET
JEW
JIB
JOB
JOG
JOT
JOY
JPS
JUG
JUT

4 LETTERS
JABS
JACK
JADE
JAGS
JAIL
JAMB
JAMS
JAPE
JARS
JAWS
JAYS
JAZZ
JEEP
JEER
JELL
JERK
JEST
JETS
JEWS
JIBE
JIBS
JIGS
JILT
JINN
JINX
JIVE
JOBS
JOCK
JOGS
JOHN
JOIN
JOKE
JOLT
JOSH
JOVE

JOWL
JOYS
JUDO
JUGS
JUJU
JULY
JUMP
JUNE
JUNK
JURA
JURY
JUST
JUTE

5 LETTERS
JABOT
JACKS
JADED
JADES
JAFFA
JAILS
JALAP
JAMBS
JAMMU
JAMMY
JAPAN
JAPER
JAPES
JAUNT
JAWED
JAZZY
JEANS
JEEPS
JEERS
JEHOL
JELLO
JELLY
JEMMY
JENNY
JEREZ
JERKS
JERKY
JESTS
JESUS
JETTY
JEWEL
JEWRY
JIBED
JIBES
JIDDA
JIFFY
JIHAD
JIMMY

JINGO
JINKS
JINNY
JIVED
JOCKS
JOINS
JOINT
JOIST
JOKED
JOKER
JOKES
JOLLY
JOLTS
JONAH
JORUM
JOULE
JOUST
JOVES
JOWEL
JOYED
JUDAS
JUDGE
JUGAL
JUGUM
JUICE
JUICY
JUJUS
JULEP
JUMBO
JUMPS
JUMPY
JUNCO
JUNE
JUNKS
JUNTA
JUNTO
JURAL
JURAT
JUREL
JUROR
JURUA

6 LETTERS
JABBED
JABBER
JABIRU
JACANA
JACKAL
JACKED
JACKET
JAFFNA
JAGGED
JAGUAR

JAILED
JAILER
JAIPUR
JALOPY
JAMMED
JAMMER
JANGLE
JAPERY
JAPURA
JARGON
JARRAH
JARRED
JASPER
JAUNTS
JAUNTY
JAWING
JAZZED
JEERED
JEERER
JEJUNE
JELLED
JENNET
JERBOA
JERKED
JERKER
JERKIN
JERSEY
JESTED
JESTER
JESUIT
JET LAG
JETSAM
JET SET
JETTED
JETTON
JEWELS
JEWESS
JEWISH
JHANSI
JIBBED
JIBBER
JIBING
JIGGED
JIGGER
JIGGLY
JIGSAW
JIHADS
JILTED
JILTER
JINGLE
JINGLY
JINXED
JINXES
JITTER

JIVING
JOBBED
JOBBER
JOB LOT
JOCKEY
JOCOSE
JOCUND
JOGGED
JOGGER
JOGGLE
JOHNNY
JOHORE
JOINED
JOINER
JOINTS
JOISTS
JOKERS
JOKING
JOLTED
JORDAN
JOSHED
JOSHES
JOSTLE
JOTTED
JOTTER
JOULES
JOUNCE
JOURNO
JOVIAL
JOYFUL
JOYING
JOYOUS
JUDAEA
JUDAIC
JUDDER
JUDGED
JUDGED
JUDGER
JUDGES
JUDOGI
JUDOKA
JUGATE
JUGGED
JUGGLE
JUICED
JUICES
JUJUBE
JULEPS
JULIES
JUMBLE
JUMPED
JUMPER
JUNEAU
JUNGLE

JUNGLY
JUNIOR
JUNKED
JUNKET
JUNKIE
JUNTAS
JURIES
JURIST
JURORS
JUSTLY
JUTTED
JUTTER

7 LETTERS
JABBING
JACAMAR
JACKALS
JACKASS
JACKDAW
JACKETS
JACKING
JACKPOT
JACKSON
JACK TAR
JACOBIN
JACONET
JACUZZI
JADEITE
JAGGERY
JAGGING
JAGUARS
JAILERS
JAILING
JALAPIC
JALISCO
JAMACIA
JAMMIER
JAMMING
JANGLED
JANGLER
JANITOR
JANUARY
JARGONS
JARRING
JASMINE
JAUNTED
JAVELIN
JAWBONE
JAYWALK
JAZZIER
JAZZILY
JAZZING
JEALOUS

JEERING	JOG TROT	JUMPING	JAVELINS	JUDDERED
JEHOVAH	JOHN DOE	JUMP-OFF	JAWBONES	JUDGMENT
JEJUNAL	JOINDER	JUNGIAN	JAZZIEST	JUDICIAL
JEJUNUM	JOINERS	JUNGLES	JEALOUSY	JUGGLERS
JELLIED	JOINERY	JUNIORS	JAHOVIAN	JUGGLERY
JELLIED	JOINING	JUNIPER	JEMMYING	JUGGLING
JELLIFY	JOINTED	JUNKETS	JEOPARDY	JUGULARS
JELLING	JOINTER	JUNKIES	JEREMIAH	JUICIEST
JEMMIED	JOINTLY	JUNKING	JERKIEST	JULIENNE
JEMMIES	JOLLIED	JURISTS	JEROBOAM	JUMBLING
JENNIES	JOLLIER	JURY BOX	JESUITIC	JUMBO JET
JERICHO	JOLLIFY	JURYMAN	JET-BLACK	JUMPABLE
JERKIER	JOLLILY	JUSSIVE	JETFOILS	JUMPED-UP
JERKILY	JOLLITY	JUSTIFY	JETLINER	JUMPIEST
JERKING	JOLTING	JUTLAND	JETTISON	JUMPSUIT
JERKINS	JONESES	JUTTING	JEWELLED	JUNCTION
JERSEYS	JONQUIL		JEWELLER	JUNCTURE
JESTERS	JOSHING		JEW'S HARP	JUNGFRAU
JESTING	JOSTLED	**8 LETTERS**	JEZEBELS	JUNIPERS
JESUITS	JOSTLER	JABALPUR	JEGGERED	JUNKETER
JETFOIL	JOTTERS	JABBERED	JIGGLING	JUNK FOOD
JETPORT	JOTTING	JABBERER	JINGLING	JUNK MAIL
JETTIES	JOURNAL	JACKBOOT	JINGOISM	JUNKYARD
JETTING	JOURNEY	JACKDAWS	JINGOIST	JURASSIC
JEWFISH	JOURNOS	JACKFISH	JIPIJAPA	JURATORY
JEW'S-EAR	JOUSTED	JACKPOTS	JIUJITSU	JURISTIC
JEZEBEL	JOUSTER	JACKSTAY	JOCKETED	JUSTICES
JIBBING	JOYLESS	JACK TARS	JOCOSELY	JUSTNESS
JIGGERS	JOYRIDE	JACOBEAN	JOCOSITY	JUVENILE
JIGGING	JUBILEE	JACOBIAN	JODHPURI	
JIGGLED	JUDAEAN	JACOBITE	JODHPURS	
JIGGLES	JUDAICA	JACQUARD	JOGGLING	**9 LETTERS**
JIGSAWS	JUDAISM	JACUZZIS	JOHN BULL	JABBERERS
JILTING	JUDAIST	JAGGEDLY	JOHNNIES	JABBERING
JIMJAMS	JUDAIZE	JAILBIRD	JOINTING	JABORANDI
JIMMMIES	JUDASES	JALOPIES	JOINTURE	JACARANDA
JINGLED	JUDGING	JALOUSIE	JOKINGLY	JACKASSES
JINGLER	JUDOIST	JAMAICAN	JOLLIEST	JACKBOOTS
JINGLES	JUGGING	JAMBOREE	JOLLYING	JACK FROST
JINXING	JUGGLED	JAMMIEST	JOSTLING	JACK KNIFE
JITTERS	JUGGLER	JAMNAGAR	JOTTINGS	JACKSHAFT
JITTERY	JUGULAR	JANGLING	JOURNALS	JACKSMELT
JOBBERS	JUICIER	JANITORS	JOURNEYS	JACKSNIPE
JOBBERY	JUICILY	JAPANESE	JOUSTING	JACOBITES
JOBBING	JUICING	JAPANNED	JOVIALLY	JAILBIRDS
JOBLESS	JUJITSU	JAPINGLY	JOYFULLY	JAILBREAK
JOBLOTS	JUJUBES	JAPONICA	JOYOUSLY	JAMBOREES
JOCKEYS	JUKEBOX	JAROSITE	JOYRIDER	JAM-PACKED
JOCULAR	JUMBLED	JASMINES	JOYRIDES	JANISSARY
JODHPUR	JUMBLER	JAUNDICE	JOYSTICK	JANSENISM
JOGGING	JUMBLES	JAUNTIER	JUBILANT	JANSENIST
JOGGLED	JUMPERS	JAUNTILY	JUBILATE	JANUARIES
JOGGLER	JUMPIER	JAUNTING	JUBILEES	JAPANNING
JOGGLES	JUMPILY	JAVANESE	JUDAIZER	JAPONICAS

511

J

JARGONIZE
JAUNDICED
JAUNTIEST
JAYWALKED
JAYWALKER
JEALOUSLY
JEERINGLY
JELLY BEAN
JELLYFISH
JELLY ROLL
JEREMIADS
JERKINESS
JERKINGLY
JEROBOAMS
JERUSALEM
JESTINGLY
JESUITISM
JET ENGINE
JET-SETTER
JET STREAM
JEWELFISH
JEWELLERS
JEWELLERY
JEWELLING
JEW'S HARPS
JIB-HEADED
JITTERBUG
JOB CENTRE
JOCKEYING
JOCKSTRAP
JOCULARLY
JOCUNDITY
JOE PUBLIC
JOINTRESS
JOINTWORM
JOLLINESS
JORDANIAN
JOSS STICK
JOURNEYED
JOURNEYER
JOVIALITY
JOYLESSLY
JOYRIDERS
JOTRIDING
JOYSTICKS
JUBILANCE
JUDDERING
JUDGEABLE
JUDGEMENT
JUDGESHIP
JUDGINGLY
JUDGMENTS
JUDICABLE
JUDICATOR

JUDICIARY
JUDICIOUS
JUICINESS
JUKEBOXES
JUMBO JETS
JUMPINESS
JUMP-START
JUMPSUITS
JUNCTIONS
JUNCTURES
JUNGLE GYM
JUNKETING
JUNOESQUE
JURIDICAL
JURY BOXES
JUSTICIAR
JUSTIFIED
JUSTIFIER
JUTLANDER
JUVENILES
JUVENILIA
JUXTAPOSE

10 LETTERS
JACKANAPES
JACKHAMMER
JACK-KNIFED
JACK KNIVES
JACKRABBIT
JACK THE LAD
JACOBITISM
JAGUARONDI
JAILBREAKS
JAM SESSION
JANITORIAL
JARDINIERE
JAUNTINESS
JAWBREAKER
JAYWALKERS
JAYWALKING
JEALOUSIES
JELLY BEANS
JELLY ROLLS
JEOPARDIZE
JERRY-BUILD
JERRY-BUILT
JESUITICAL
JET ENGINES
JET-SETTERS
JETTISONED
JIGGERMAST
JINGOISTIC
JITTERBUGS

JOB CENTRES
JOBSHARING
JOCKSTRAPS
JOCULARITY
JOLLY ROGER
JOSS STICKS
JOURNALESE
JOURNALISM
JOURNALIST
JOURNALIZE
JOURNEYING
JOURNEYMAN
JOURNEYMEN
JOYFULNESS
JOYOUSNESS
JUBILANTLY
JUBILATION
JUDGMENTAL
JUDICATIVE
JUDICATORY
JUDICATURE
JUDICIALLY
JUGGERNAUT
JUMBLE SALE
JUMBLINGLY
JUNCACEOUS
JUNCTIONAL
JUNKETINGS
JURY-RIGGED
JUSTICIARY
JUSTIFYING
JUVENILITY
JUXTAPOSED

11 LETTERS
JACKHAMMERS
JACK-KNIFING
JACKRABBITS
JACTITATION
JAM SESSIONS
JANISSARIES\
JAWBREAKERS
JELLYFISHES
JEOPARDIZED
JETTISONING
JOIE DE VIVRE
JOURNALISTS
JOURNALIZER
JOYLESSNESS
JUDAIZATION
JUDGEMENT DAY
JUDICATURES
JUDICOUSLY

JUGGERNAUTS
JUGULAR VEIN
JUMBLE SALES
JUSTICESHIP
JUSTICIABLE
JUSTIFIABLE
JUSTIFIABLY
JUVENESCENT
JUXTAPOSING

12 LETTERS
JACK-IN-THE-BOX
JACK ROBINSON
JACKSONVILLE
JE NE SAIS QUOI
JEOPARDIZING
JET-PROPELLED
JIGSAW PUZZLE
JOHANNESBURG
JOURANALISTIC
JUDICATORIAL
JUGULAR VEINS
JUNIOR SCHOOL
JURISCONSULT
JURISDICTION
JURISDICTIVE
JURISPRUDENT
JUSTIFYINGLY
JUVENESCENCE

13 LETTERS
JARGONIZATION
JELLIFICATION
JET PROPULSION
JIGGERY-POKERY
JIGSAW PUZZLES
JOLLIFICATION
JUDICIOUSNESS
JURISPRUDENCE
JUSTICIARSHIP
JUSTIFICATION
JUSTIFICATORY
JUXTAPOSITION

3 LETTERS	5 LETTERS	KNAVE	KANARA	KILTED	KUMMEL
KEG	KABUL	KNEAD	KANGAS	KILTER	KUNG FU
KEN	KALAT	KNEED	KANPUR	KIMONO	KUNLUN
KEY	KANDY	KNEEL	KANSAS	KINASE	KURGAN
KID	KANGA	KNEES	KAOLIN	KINDER	KUWAIT
KIN	KANSU	KNELL	KARATE	KINDLE	KWACHA
KIP	KAPOK	KNELF	KARATS	KINDLY	KYUSHU
KIT	KAPUT	KNIFE	KARIBA	KINGLY	
	KARAT	KNOBS	KARMIC	KIOSKS	
	KAREN	KNOCK	KASBAH	KIPPED	7 LETTERS
4 LETTERS	KARMA	KNOLL	KASSEL	KIPPER	KAFTANS
KALE	KAROO	KNOTS	KAUNAS	KIRKUK	KAIFENG
KEEL	KARST	KNOWN	KAYAKS	KIRMAN	KAINITE
KEEN	KASAI	KNOWS	KAZAKH	KIRSCH	KAISERS
KEEP	KAYAK	KNURL	KEBABS	KISMET	KALENDS
KEGS	KAZAN	KOALA	KEDIRI	KISSED	KALININ
KELP	KAZOO	KOCHI	KEELED	KISSER	KALMUCK
KENS	KEBAB	KOINE	KEENED	KISSES	KAMPALA
KENT	KEDAH	KONGO	KEENER	KIT BAG	KANNADA
KEPT	KEDGE	KONYA	KEENLY	KITSCH	KANTIAN
KERB	KEELS	KOOKS	KEEPER	KITTED	KARACHI
KERN	KEENS	KOKKY	KELOID	KITTEN	KARAKUL
KEYS	KEEPS	KORAN	KELPIE	KLAXON	KARBALA
KHAN	KENYA	KOREA	KELTIC	KNAVES	KASHGAR
KICK	KERBS	KRAAL	KELVIN	KNAWEL	KASHMIR
KIDS	KERCH	KRAFT	KENED	KNELLS	KASSALA
KIEL	KERRY	KRAIT	KENNEL	KNIFED	KATYDID
KIEV	KETCH	KRILL	KENYAN	KNIFER	KATAKER
KIKE	KEVEL	KRONA	KERALA	KNIGHT	KAYSERI
KILL	KEYED	KRONE	KERMAN	KNIVES	KEELING
KILN	KHAKI	KROON	KERMES	KNOCKS	KEELSON
KILO	KHANS	KUDOS	KERNEL	KNOLLS	KEENEST
KILT	KHMER	KUDZU	KERSEY	KNOTTY	KEENING
KIND	KIANG	KUFIC	KETENE	KNOWER	KEEPERS
KINE	KICKS	KUKRI	KETONE	KOALAS	KEEPING
KING	KIKES	KULAK	KETOSE	KOHIMA	KEEPNET
KINK	KILLS	KURIL	KETTLE	KOKAND	KEITLOA
KIPS	KILNS	KURSK	KEYING	KOLYMA	KELVINS
KIRK	KILOS	KUTCH	KEYWAY	KOPECK	KENNEDY
KISS	KILTS	KWELA	KHALIF	KOREAN	KENNELS
KITE	KINDS	KYOTO	KHULNA	KORUNA	KENNING
KITS	KINGS		KHYBER	KOSHER	KENOSIS
KIWI	KININ		KIBOSH	KOSICE	KENOTIC
KNAP	KINKS	6 LETTERS	KICKED	KOVROW	KENTISH
KNEE	KINKY	KABYLE	KICKER	KOWTOW	KERATIN
KNEW	KIOSK	KADANA	KIDDED	KRAALS	KERBING
KNIT	KIRIN	KAFFIR	KIDDER	KRISES	KERNELS
KNOB	KIRKS	KAFTAN	KIDDIE	KRONER	KERNITE
KNOW	KIROV	KAISER	KIDNAP	KRUGER	KESTREL
KOBE	KITES	KAKAPO	KIDNEY	KRONOR	KESWICK
KOHL	KITTY	KALIMA	KIELCE	KUKRIS	KETCHES
KOOK	KITWE	KALONG	KIKUYU	KUMASI	KETCHUP
KRIS	KIWIS	KALUGA	KILLED	KUMISS	KETONIC
KUDO	KNACK	KAMALA	KILLER		KETOSIS

KETTLES	KITSCHY	KANAZAWA	KIMONOED	KOHLRABI
KEYED UP	KITTENS	KANDAHAR	KINABALU	KOLHAPUR
KEYHOLE	KITTIES	KANGAROO	KINDLIER	KOLINSKY
KEYNOTE	KITTING	KAOLIANG	KINDLING	KOMSOMOL
KEY RING	KITTING	KAOLINIC	KINDNESS	KOOKIEST
KHADDAR	KLAXONS	KARELIAN	KINDREDS	KOOTENAY
KHAKASS	KLEENEX	KASHMIRI	KINETICS	KORDOFAN
KHALIFS	KNAPPER	KATAKANA	KINGBIRD	KOSTROMA
KHALKHA	KNAVERY	KATMANDU	KINGBOLT	KOWTOWED
KHAMSIN	KNAVISH	KATOWICE	KINGDOMS	KOWTOWER
KHANATE	KNEADED	KATTEGAT	KINGFISH	KRAKATOA
KHARKOV	KNEADER	KAEASAKI	KINGLIER	KUMAMOTO
KHERSON	KNEECAP	KAYEKERS	KINGPINS	KUMQUATS
KHINGAN	KNEEING	KEDGEREE	KINGSHIP	KURTOSIS
KHOISAN	KNEELED	KEENNESS	KING-SIZE	KUZNETSK
KIANGSU	KNEEPAD	KEEPSAKE	KINGSTON	KWEICHOW
KIBBUTZ	KNIFING	KEESHOND	KINGWANA	KWEIYANG
KICKING	KNIGHTS	KELANTAN	KINGWOOD	KYPHOSIS
KICKOFF	KNITTED	KELOIDAL	KINKAJOU	KYPHOTIC
KIDDERS	KNITTER	KEMEROVO	KINKIEST	
KIDDIES	KNOBBLY	KENNELED	KINSFOLK	
KIDDING	KNOCKED	KENTUCKY	KINSHASA	**9 LETTERS**
KIDNEYS	KNOCKER	KERATOID	KIRIGAMI	KADIYEVKA
KIDSKIN	KNOCK-ON	KERATOSE	KISHINEV	KAGOSHIMA
KILDARE	KNOCK-UP	KERCHIEF	KISSABLE	KAISERDOM
KILLERS	KNOSSOS	KEROSENE	KITCHENS	KAMCHATKA
KILLICK	KNOTTED	KESTEVEN	KLAIPEDA	KANAMYCIN
KILLING	KNOTTER	KESTRELS	KLONDIKE	KANGAROOS
KILLJOY	KNOW-ALL	KETOXIME	KLYSTRON	KAOSIUNG
KILOTON	KNOW-HOW	KEYBOARD	KNAPSACK	KAOLINITE
KILTERS	KNOWING	KEYHOLES	KNAPWEED	KARABINER
KIMONOS	KNUCKLE	KEY MONEY	KNEADING	KARAGANDA
KINDEST	KNUCKLY	KEYNOTES	KNEECAPS	KARAKORAM
KINDLED	KOOKIER	KEY PUNCH	KNEE-DEEP	KARLSRUHE
KINDLER	KOPECKS	KEY RINGS	KNEE-HIGH	KARYOGAMY
KINDRED	KOWLOON	KEYSTONE	KNEE-JERK	KARYOSOME
KINETIC	KREMLIN	KHARTOUM	KNEELING	KARYOTYPE
KINFOLK	KRISHNA	KHMERIAN	KNICKERS	KATANGESE
KINGCUP	KRYPTON	KHUSKHUS	KNIGHTED	KAWAGUCHI
KINGDOM	KUMQUAT	KIAOCHOW	KNIGHTLY	KEEPSAKES
KINGPIN	KUNZITE	KIBOSHES	KNOCKERS	KELTICISM
KINKIER	KURDISH	KICKABLE	KNOCKING	KELTICIST
KINKILY	KUWAITI	KICKBACK	KNOCKOUT	KENNELING
KINSHIP	KWANGJU	KICKSHAW	KNOCK-UPS	KENNELLED
KINSMAN	KWAZULU	KID-GLOVE	KNOTHOLE	KENTLEDGE
KINGSMEN		KIDNAPED	KNOTTIER	KEPT WOMAN
KIPPERS		KILKENNY	KNOTTILY	KEPT WOMEN
KIPPING	**8 LETTERS**	KILLDEER	KNOTTING	KERATITIS
KIRGHIZ	KAKEMOID	KILLINGS	KNOTWEED	KERATOSIS
KIRUNDI	KALAHARI	KILLJOYS	KNOWABLE	KERBSTONE
KISSERS	KAMACITE	KILOBYTE	KNOW-ALLS	KERCHIEFS
KISSING	KAMACURI	KILOGRAM	KNUCKLED	KERFUFFLE
KITBAGS	KAMAKAZE	KILOVOLT	KNUCKLES	KETONURIA
KITCHEN	KANARESE	KILOWATT	KOHINOOR	KEYBOARDS

KEYSTONES
KEYSTROKE
KIBBUTZES
KIBBUTZIM
KICKBACKS
KID GLOVES
KIDNAPPING
KIDNAPPED
KIDNAPPER
KIESERITE
KILLARNEY
KILLIFISH
KILLINGLY
KILOBYTES
KILOCYCLE
KILOGRAMS
KILOHERTZ
KILOLITRE
KILOMETRE
KILOWATTS
KIMBERLY
KINDLIEST
KINGMAKER
KIING'S EVIL
KINGTOWN
KINKINESS
KINSWOMAN
KIRKCALDY
KIROVABAD
KISANGANI
KITCHENER
KITTENISH
KITTIWAKE
KLEENEXES
KNACKERED
KNAPSACKS
KNAVERIES
KNAVISHLY
KNIFE-EDGE
KNIGHTING
KNITTABLE
KNOBBLER
KNOCKDOWN
KNOCKOUTS
KNOTGRASS
KNOTTIEST
KNOWINGLY
KNOWLEDGE
KNOXVILLE
KNUCKLING
KONIOLOGY
KOOKINESS
KOSCIUSKO
KOWTOWING

KOZHIKODE
KRASNODAR
KRONSTADT
KUIBYSHEV
KURDISTAN
KURRAJONG
KWANGTUNG
KYMOGRAPH

10 LETTERS
KABARAGOYA
KANTIANISM
KARA-KALPAK
KARYOGAMIC
KARYOLYMPH
KARYOPLASM
KARYOTYPIC
KENNELLING
KENTICKIAN
KERATINIZE
KERCHEIFED
KERFUFFLES
KERSEYMERE
KETTLEDRUM
KEYBOARDED
KEYBOARDER
KEYPUNCHED
KEYPUNCHER
KEYPUNCHES
KAHBAROVSK
KIDNAPPERS
KIDNAPPING
KIDNEY BEAN
KILMARNOCK
KILOLITRES
KILOMETRES
KILOMETRIC
KIMBERLITE
KINCARDINE
KINDLINESS
KINDNESSES
KINEMATICS
KINGFISHER
KINGLINESS
KINGMAKERS
KING-OF-ARMS
KING'S BENCH
KISS OF LIFE
KITH AND KIN
KITTIWAKES
KNEECAPPED
KNICK-KNACK
KNIFE-EDGES

KNIGHTHEAD
KNIGHTHOOD
KNOBBLIEST
KNOCKABOUT
KNOCK-KNEED
KOOKABURRA
KRISHNAISM
KRUGERRAND
KU KLUX KLAN

11 LETTERS
KALININGRAD
KANCHIPURAM
KERB CRAWLER
KETTLEDRUMS
KEYBOARDERS
KEYBOARDING
KEYPUNCHERS
KIDNEY BEANS
KILIMANJARO
KILLER WHALE
KIND-HEARTED
KINDREDNESS
KINETICALLY
KINETOPLAST
KINGFISHERS
KISS OF DEATH
KITCHENETTE
KITCHENWARE
KITTENISHLY
KLEPTOMANIA
KNEECAPPING
KNICK-KNACKS
KNIGHTHOODS
KNUCKLEBONE
KOOKABURRAS
KRUGERRANDS
KUALA LUMPUR
KWASHIORKOR
KYANIZATION
KYMOGRAPHIC

12 LETTERS
KALEIDOSCOPE
KARYOKINESIS
KARYOKINETIC
KARYOPLASMIC
KERATOGENOUS
KERATOPLASTY
KERB CRAWLERS
KERB CRAWLING
KEYNESIANISM

KEY SIGNATURE
KILLER WHALES
KILOWATT-HOUR
KINAESTHESIA
KINAESTHETIC
KINDERGARDEN
KING'S COUNSEL
KING'S ENGLISH
KITCHENETTES
KLEPTOMANIAC
KLIPSPRINGER
KNACKER'S YARD
KNEE BREECHES
KNIGHT-ERRANT
KRISTIANSAND

13 LETTERS
KALEIDOSCOPES
KALEIDOSCOPIC
KANGAROO COURT
KERATOPLASTIC
KETTLEDRUMMER
KEY SIGNATURES
KIDDERMINSTER
KIDNEY MACHINE
KINDERGARTENS
KIND-HEARTEDLY
KINEMATICALLY
KINETIC ENERGY
KINETONUCLEUS
KING'S COUNSELS
KING'S EVIDENCE
KIRKCUDBRIGHT
KITCHEN GARDEN
KLEPTOMANIACS
KNIGHTS-ERRANT
KNOWLEDGEABLE
KNOWLEDGEABLY
KNUCKLE-DUSTER

3 LETTERS

LAB	LAND	LILY	LOUD	LARGO	LEVEE

3 LETTERS

3 LETTERS	LAND	LILY	LOUD	LARGO	LEVEE
LAB	LANE	LIMA	LOUR	LARKS	LEVEL
LAD	LANK	LIMB	LOUT	LAROS	LEVER
LAG	LASP	LIME	LOVE	LARVA	LEVIS
LAN	LAPP	LIMN	LOWS	LASER	LEWIS
LAP	LAPS	LIMP	LUCK	LASSO	LEXIS
LAW	LARD	LIMY	LUFF	LASTS	LHASA
LAX	LARK	LINE	LUGS	LATCH	LIANA
LAY	LASH	LING	LULL	LATER	LIARS
LCD	LASS	LINK	LUMP	LATEX	LIBEL
LCM	LAST	LINT	LUNG	LATHE	LIBRA
LEA	LATE	LINZ	LUNY	LATHS	LIBYA
LED	LATH	LION	LURE	LATIN	LICIT
LEE	LAUD	LIPS	LURK	LAUGH	LICKS
LEG	LAVA	LIRA	LUSH	LAVAL	LIDOS
LEI	LAWN	LIRE	LUST	LAVER	LIEGE
LEO	LAWS	LISP	LUTE	LAWNS	LIE-IN
LET	LAYS	LIST	LUVS	LAWNY	LIENS
LIB	LAZE	LIVE	LYNX	LAXLY	LIEUS
LID	LAZY	LOAD	LYON	LAY-BY	LIFER
LIE	LEAD	LOAF	LYRE	LAYER	LIFTS
LIP	LEAF	LOAM		LAZED	LIGER
LIT	LEAK	LOAN		LEACH	LIGHT
LOB	LEAN	LOBE	**5 LETTERS**	LEADS	LIKED
LOG	LEAP	LOBS	LABEL	LEADY	LIKEN
LOO	LEAS	LOCH	LACED	LEAFY	LIKES
LOP	LEEK	LOCI	LACER	LEAKS	LILAC
LOT	LEER	LOCK	LACES	LEAKY	LILLE
LOW	LEES	LOCO	LADEN	LEANT	LILOS
LOX	LEFT	LODE	LADER	LEAPS	LILTS
LPS	LEGS	LODZ	LADLE	LEAPT	LIMBO
LSD	LEIS	LOFT	LAGAN	LEARN	LIMBS
LUG	LEND	LOGO	LAGER	LEASE	LIMED
LUV	LENS	LOGS	LAGOS	LEASH	LIMEN
	LENT	LOGY	LAHTI	LEAST	LIMES
	LETS	LOIN	LAIRD	LEAVE	LIMEY
4 LETTERS	LEVY	LOLL	LAIRS	LEDGE	LIMIT
LABS	LEWD	LONE	LAITY	LEDGY	LINED
LACE	LIAT	LONG	LAKER	LEECH	LINEN
LACK	LIAS	LOOK	LAKES	LEEKS	LINER
LACY	LICE	LOOM	LAMAS	LEERS	LINES
LADE	LICK	LOON	LAMBS	LEERY	LINGO
LADS	LIDO	LOOP	LAMED	LEFTY	LININ
LADY	LIDS	LOOS	LAMER	LEGAL	LINKS
LAGS	LIED	LOOT	LAMPS	LEGER	LINTY
LAID	LIEF	LOPE	LANCE	LEGGY	LIONS
LAIN	LIEN	LORD	LANDS	LEGIT	LIPIS
LAIR	LIES	LORE	LANES	LEMMA	LIRAS
LAKE	LIEU	LORN	LANKY	LEMON	LISLE
LAKH	LIFE	LOSE	LA PAZ	LEMUR	LISTS
LAMA	LIFT	LOSS	LAPEL	LENIS	LITER
LAMB	LIKE	LOST	LAPSE	LENTO	LITHE
LAME	LILO	LOTH	LARCH	LEPER	LITRE
LAMP	LILT	LOTS	LARGE	LETUP	LIVED

516

LIVEN	LOVAT	**6 LETTERS**	LANGUR	LAUDER	LEIDEN
LIVER	LOVED	LAAGER	LANKER	LAUGHS	LE MANS
LIVES	LOVER	LABELS	LANKLY	LAUNCH	LEMONS
LIVID	LOVES	LABIAL	LANNER	LAUREL	LEMONY
LLAMA	LOVEY	LABILE	LANUGO	LAVABO	LEMURS
LLANO	LOWED	LABIUM	LAPDOG	LAVAGE	LENDER
LOACH	LOWER	LABLAB	LAPELS	LAVISH	LENGTH
LOADS	LOWLY	LABOUR	LAPPED	LAWFUL	LENITY
LOAMY	LOYAL	LABRET	LAPPER	LAWYER	LENSES
LOANS	LUCID	LABRUM	LAPPET	LAXITY	LENTEN
LOATH	LOCKY	LACHES	LAPSED	LAY-BYS	LENTIC
LOBAR	LUCRE	LACIER	LAPSER	LAYERS	LENTIL
LOBBY	LUFFA	LACILY	LAPSES	LAYING	LEONID
LOBED	LUGER	LACING	LAPSUS	LAYMAN	LEPERS
LOBES	LUMEN	LACKED	LAP-TOP	LAYMEN	LEPTON
LOCAL	LUMME	LACKEY	LARDED	LAY-OFF	LESION
LOCHS	LUMPS	LACTAM	LARDER	LAYOUT	LESSEE
LOCKS	LUMPY	LACTIC	LARDON	LAZIER	LESSEN
LOCUM	LUNAR	LACUNA	LARGER	LAZILY	LESSER
LOCUS	LUNCH	LADDER	LARGOS	LAZING	LESSON
LODEN	LUNGE	LADDIE	LARIAT	LEADEN	LESSOR
LODES	LUNGS	LA-DI-DA	LARINE	LEADER	LETHAL
LODGE	LUPIN	LADIES	LARKED	LEAD-IN	LETTER
LOESS	LUPUS	LADING	LARKER	LEAGUE	LETUPS
LOFTS	LURCH	LADINO	LARNAX	LEAKED	LEVANT
LOFTY	LURED	LADLED	LARVAE	LEAKER	LEVEES
LOGIC	LURER	LADLER	LARVAL	LEANED	LEVELS
LOGOS	LURES	LADLES	LARYNX	LEANER	LEVERS
LOINS	LUREX	LAGENA	LASCAR	LEAN-TO	LEVIED
LOIRE	LURGY	LAGERS	LASERS	LEAPED	LEVIER
LOLLY	LURID	LAGGED	LASHED	LEAPER	LEVIES
LONER	LUSTS	LAGOON	LASHER	LEARNT	LEVITY
LOOKS	LUSTY	LAHORE	LASHES	LEASED	LEWDLY
LOOMS	LUTES	LAICAL	LASH-UP	LEASER	LIABLE
LOONS	LUXOR	LAIRDS	LASKET	LEASES	LIAISE
LOONY	LUZON	LALANG	LASSES	LEAVED	LIBBER
LOOPS	LYCEE	LAMBDA	LASSOS	LEAVEN	LIBELS
LOOPY	LYING	LAMBED	LASTED	LEAVER	LIBIDO
LOOSE	LYMPH	LAMELY	LASTER	LEAVES	LIBRAN
LOPED	LYNCH	LAMENT	LASTLY	LECHER	LIBYAN
LOPER	LYRES	LAMEST	LATEEN	LECTOR	LICHEN
LORAN	LYRIC	LAMINA	LATELY	LEDGER	LICKED
LORDS	LYSIN	LAMING	LATENT	LEDGES	LICKER
LORIS	LYSIS	LAMMAS	LATEST	LEERED	LIDDED
LORRY	LYSOL	LAMPAS	LATHER	LEEWAY	LIEGES
LOSER	LYTIC	LANATE	LATHES	LEGACY	LIE-INS
LOSSY	LYTTA	LANCED	LATINS	LEGATE	LIENAL
LOTIC		LANCER	LATISH	LEGATO	LIERNE
LOTUS		LANCES	LATIUM	LEGEND	LIFERS
LOUGH		LANCET	LATRIA	LEGERS	LIFTED
LOUPE		LANDAU	LATTEN	LEGGED	LIFTER
LOUSE		LANDED	LATTER	LEGION	LIGAND
LOUSY		LANDES	LATVIA	LEGIST	LIGATE
LOUTS		LANGUE	LAUDED	LEGUME	LIGHTS

LIGNIN	LITHIC	LONERS	LUDLOW	LACTOSE	LARGESS
LIGULA	LITMUS	LONGAN	LUFFED	LACUNAE	LARGEST
LIGULE	LITRES	LONGED	LUGGED	LACUNAR	LARGISH
LIKASI	LITTER	LONGER	LUGGER	LACUNAS	LARIATS
LIKELY	LITTLE	LOOFAH	LULLED	LADDERS	LARKING
LIKING	LIVE-IN	LOOKED	LUMBAR	LADDIES	LASAGNA
LILACS	LIVELY	LOOK-IN	LUMBER	LADLING	LASAGNE
LILIES	LIVERS	LOOMED	LUMMOX	LAGGARD	LASCAUX
LIMBER	LIVERY	LOONEY	LUMPED	LAGGING	LASHING
LIMBIC	LIVING	LOOPED	LUMPEN	LAGOONS	LASH-UPS
LIMBOS	LIZARD	LOOPER	LUNACY	LAICISM	LASSOED
LIMBUS	LLAMAS	LOOSED	LUNATE	LAICIZE	LASSOER
LIMEYS	LOADED	LOOSEN	LUNGED	LALLANS	LASTING
LIMIER	LOADER	LOOSER	LUNGER	LAMAISM	LATCHED
LIMING	LOAFER	LOOSES	LUNGES	LAMAIST	LATCHES
LIMITS	LOANED	LOOTED	LUNULA	LAMBERT	LATCHET
LIMNED	LOANER	LOOTER	LUPINE	LAMBING	LATENCY
LIMNER	LOATHE	LOPING	LUPIMS	LAMELLA	LATERAL
LIMPED	LOAVES	LOPPED	LURING	LAMENTS	LATRINE
LIMPER	LOBATE	LOPPER	LURKED	LAMINAR	LATTICE
LIMPET	LOBBED	LOQUAT	LURKER	LAMPERN	LATVIAN
LIMPID	LOBITO	LORDED	LUSAKA	LAMPOON	LAUDING
LIMPLY	LOBULE	LORDLY	LUSHES	LAMPERY	LAUGHED
LINAGE	LOCALE	LORICA	LU-SHUN	LANCERS	LAGHTER
LINDEN	LOCALS	LOSERS	LUSTED	LANCETS	LAUNDER
LINEAL	LOCATE	LOSING	LUSTRE	LANCHO	LAUNDRY
LINEAR	LOCHIA	LOSSES	LUTEAL	LANCING	LAURELS
LINERS	LOCKED	LOTION	LUXATE	LANDAUS	LAWLESS
LINEUP	LOCKER	LOTTED	LUXURY	LANDING	LAWSUIT
LINGER	LOCKET	LOUDEN	LYCEES	LANDTAG	LAWYERS
LINGUA	LOCKUP	LOUDER	LYCEUM	LANGRES	LAXNESS
LINING	LOCULE	LOUDLY	LYCHEE	LANGUID	LAYERED
LINKED	LOCUMS	LOUGHS	LYNXES	LANGUOR	LEYETTE
LINKUP	LOCUST	LOUISE	LYRATE	LANIARY	LEY-OFFS
LINNET	LODGED	LOUNGE	LYRICS	LANKEST	LEYOUTS
LINTEL	LODGER	LOURED	LYRIST	LANKIER	LAZIEST
LINTER	LODGES	LOUSED	LYSINE	LANKILY	L-DRIVER
LIPASE	LOFTED	LOUVAR		LANOLIN	LEACHED
LIPIDS	LOFTER	LOUVRE		LANSING	LEACHER
LIPOID	LOGGED	LOVAGE	**7 LETTERS**	LANTANA	LEADING
LIPOMA	LOGGER	LOVELY	LABELED	LANTERN	LEAD-INS
LIQUID	LOGGIA	LOVERS	LABIALS	LANYARD	LEAFAGE
LIQUOR	LOGIER	LOVING	LABIATE	LAOTAIN	LEAFIER
LISBON	LOGION	LOWEST	LABOURS	LAPDOGS	LEAFLET
LISPED	LOGJAM	LOWING	LABROID	LAPLACE	LEAGUED
LISPER	LOGLOG	LOW-KEY	LACIEST	LAPLAND	LEAGUES
LISSOM	LORIET	LOYANG	LACKEYS	LAPPING	LEAKAGE
LISTED	LOITER	LOZERE	LACKING	LAPSING	LEAKIER
LISTEN	LOLLED	L-PLATE	LACONIC	LAPWING	LEAKING
LITANY	LOLLER	LUANDA	LACQUER	LARCENY	LEANEST
LITCHI	LOLLOP	LUBBER	LACTASE	LARCHES	LEANING
LITERS	LOMENT	LUBECK	LACTATE	LARDERS	LEAN-TOS
LITHER	LONDON	LUBLIN	LACTEAL	LARDING	LEAPING
LITHIA	LONELY	LUCENT	LACTONE	LARGELY	LEARNED

LEARNER	LEONINE	LIGURIA	LITCHIS	LOGGIAS	LOWDOWN
LEASHES	LEOPARD	LIKABLE	LITERAL	LOGGING	LOWERED
LEASING	LEOTARD	LIKENED	LITHELY	LOGICAL	LOWLAND
LEATHER	LEPORID	LIKINGS	LITHEST	LOGIEST	LOWLIER
LEAVENS	LEPROSE	LILTING	LITHIUM	LOGJAMS	LOW LIFE
LEAVING	LEPROSY	LIMACON	LITHOID	LOGWOOD	LOWNESS
LEBANON	LEPROUS	LIMBATE	LITOTES	LOLLARD	LOW-RISE
LECHERS	LERWICK	LIMBURG	LITTERS	LOLLIES	LOW TIDE
LECHERY	LESBIAN	LIMEADE	LITURGY	LOLLING	LOYALLY
LECTERN	LESIONS	LIMIEST	LIVABLE	LOMBARD	LOYALTY
LECTION	LESOTHO	LIMINAL	LIVENED	LONGBOW	LOZENGE
LECTURE	LESSEES	LIMITED	LIVENER	LONGEST	L-PLATES
LEDGERS	LESSONS	LIMITER	LIVIDLY	LONGING	LUBBOCK
LEECHES	LESSORS	LIMNING	LIVINGS	LONGISH	LUCERNE
LEERIER	LETDOWN	LIMOGES	LIVONIA	LONG TON	LUCIDLY
LEERING	LETTERS	LIMPEST	LIVORNO	LOOFAHS	LUCIFER
LEE TIDE	LETTING	LIMPETS	LIZARDS	LOOKERS	LUCKIER
LEEWARD	LETTUCE	LIMPIMG	LOADING	LOOKING	LUCKILY
LEFTIES	LEUCINE	LIMPKIN	LOAFERS	LOOKOUT	LUCKNOW
LEFTISM	LEUCITE	LIMPOPO	LOAFING	LOOMING	LUDDITE
LEFTIST	LEUCOMA	LIMULUS	LOANING	LOONIER	LUFFING
LEGALLY	LEVATOR	LINABLE	LOATHED	LOONIES	LUGANDA
LEGATEE	LEVELED	LINCTUS	LOATHER	LOOPING	LUGGAGE
LEGATES	LEVERED	LINDANE	LOATHLY	LOOSELY	LUGGERS
LEGATOR	LEVERET	LINDENS	LOBBIED	LOOSEST	LUGGING
LEGENDS	LEVYING	LINEAGE	LOBBIES	LOOSING	LUGHOLE
LEGGIER	LEXICAL	LINEATE	LOBBING	LOOTERS	LUGSAIL
LEGGING	LEXICON	LINEMAN	LOBBYER	LOPPING	LUGWORM
LEGHORN	LIAISED	LINEMEN	LOBELIA	LOQUATS	LULLABY
LEGIBLE	LIAISON	LINE-OUT	LOBSTER	LORDING	LULLING
LEGIBLY	LIANOID	LINEUPS	LOBULAR	LORELEI	LUMBAGO
LEGIONS	LIASSIC	LINGCOD	LOCALES	LORGNON	LUMENAL
LEGLESS	LIBBERS	LINGOES	LOCALLY	LORRIES	LUMPIER
LEG-PULL	LIBELED	LINGUAL	LOCATED	LOSABLE	LUMPILY
LEGROOM	LIBERAL	LININGS	LOCATER	LOSINGS	LIUMPING
LEG SIDE	LEBERIA	LINKAGE	LOCHIAL	LOTIONS	LUMPISH
LEGUMES	LIBERTY	LIMKING	LOCKAGE	LOTTERY	LUMP SUM
LEGUMIN	LIBIDOS	LINKMAN	LOCKERS	LOTTING	LUNATIC
LEGWORK	LIBRARY	LINKUPS	LOCKETS	LOUSES	LUNCHED
LE HAVRE	LIBRATE	LINNETS	LOCKING	LOUDEST	LUNCHER
LEIPZIG	LICENCE	LINOCUT	LOCKJAW	LOUNGED	LUNCHES
LEISTRE	LICENSE	LINSANG	LOCKNUT	LOUNER	LUNETTE
LEISURE	LICKING	LINSEED	LOCKOUT	LOUNGES	LUNGING
LEITRIM	LIE-DOWN	LINTELS	LOCKUPS	LOURDES	LUPULIN
LEMMING	LIFTING	LIONESS	LOCOISM	LOURING	LURCHED
LENDERS	LIFT-OFF	LIONIZE	LOCULAR	LOUSIER	LURCHER
LEISURE	LIGHTED	LIPETSK	LOCUSTS	LOUSILY	LURCHES
LEITRIM	LIGHTEN	LIPREAD	LODGERS	LOUSING	LURGIES
LEMMING	LIGHTER	LIQUATE	LODGING	LOUTISH	LURIDLY
LENDERS	LIGHTLY	LIQUEFY	LOFTIER	LOUVIAN	LURKING
LENGTHY	LIGNIFY	LIQUER	LOFTILY	LOUVRES	LUSATIA
LENIENT	LIGNITE	LIQUIDS	LOFTING	LOVABLE	LUSTFUL
LENTIGO	LIGROIN	LISPING	LOGBOOK	LOWBORN	LUSTILY
LENTILS	LIGULAR	LISTING	LOGGERS	LOWBROW	LUSTING

LUSTRAL
LUSTRES
LUTEOUS
LYCHEES
LYCHNIS
LYCOPOD
LYDDITE
LYING-IN
LYNCHED
LYNCHER
LYRICAL

8 LETTERS
LABDANUM
LABELING
LABELLED
LABELLER
LABELLUM
LABILITY
LABOURED
LABOURER
LABRADOR
LABURNUM
LACERANT
LACERATE
LACEWING
LACINESS
LA CORUNA
LACRIMAL
LACROSSE
LACTONIC
LACUNOSE
LADDERED
LADYBIRD
LADYLIKE
LADYSHIP
LAEVULIN
LAGGARDS
LAH-DI-DAH
LAID-BACK
LAMASERY
LAMBASTE
LAMBDOID
LAMBENCY
LAMBSKIN
LAME DUCK
LAMELLAR
LAMENESS
LAMENTED
LAMENTER
LAMINATE
LAMPOONS
LAMPPOST

LAMPREYS
LANCELET
LANDFALL
LANDFORM
LANDINGS
LANDLADY
LANDLORD
LANDMARK
LANDMASS
LANDMINE
LANDRACE
LANDSLIP
LANDWARD
LANDLAUF
LANGUAGE
LANGUISH
LANKIEST
LANKNESS
LANNERET
LANTERNS
LANYARDS
LAP-CHART
LAPELLED
LAPIDARY
LAPILLUS
LAPPETED
LAPSABLE
LAPWINGS
LARBOARD
LARGESSE
LARKSOME
LARKSPUR
LARRIGAN
LARYNGES
LARYNXES
LASHINGS
LA SPEZIA
LASSOING
LAST PORT
LAST WORD
LAS VEGAS
LATCHING
LATCHKEY
LATENESS
LATERALS
LATERITE
LATHERED
LATINATE
LATINISM
LATINIST
LATINITY
LATINIZE
LATITUDE
LATRINES

LATTERLY
LATTICES
LAUDABLE
LAUDABLY
LAUDANUM
LAUGHING
LAUGHTER
LAUNCHED
LAUNCHER
LAUNCHES
LAUREATE
LAUSANNE
LAVATORY
LAVENDER
LAVISHED
LAVISHER
LAVISHLY
LAWGIVER
LAWSUITS
LAXATION
LAXATIVE
LAYABOUT
LAYERING
LAYETTES
LAYSHAFT
LAYWOMAN
LATWOMEN
LAZINESS
LAZULITE
L-DRIVERS
LEACHING
LEADSMAN
LEAD TIME
LEADWORT
LEAFIEST
LEAF-LARD
LEAFLETS
LEAGUING
LEAKAGES
LEAKIEST
LEANINGS
LEANNESS
LEAPFROG
LEAP YEAR
LEARNERS
LEARNING
LEASABLE
LEATHERY
LEAVENED
LEAVINGS
LECITHIN
LECTERNS
LECTURED
LECTURER

LECTURES
LEEBOARD
LEERIEST
LEE SHORE
LEE TIDES
LEFT-HAND
LEFTISTS
LEFTOVER
LEFTWARD
LEFTWING
LEGACIES
LEGAL AID
LEGALESE
LEGALISM
LEGALIST
LEGALITY
LEGALIZE
LEGATEES
LEGATINE
LEGATION
LEGENDRY
LEGGIEST
LEGGINGS
LG-PULLS
LEG-SIDES
LEINSTER
LEISURED
LEMMINGS
LEMONADE
LEMUROID
LENGTHEN
LENIENCY
LENINISM
LENINIST
LENITIVE
LENTICEL
LEOPARDS
LEOTARDS
LEPIDOTE
LEPORINE
LESBIANS
LESSENED
LETDOWNS
LETHALLY
LETHARGY
LETRASET
LETTERED
LETTERER
LETTINGS
LETTUCES
LEUCITIC
LEUKEMIA
LEVANTER
LEVELING

LEVELLED
LEVELLER
LEVRAGE
LEVERETS
LEVERING
LEVIABLE
LEVIGATE
LEVITATE
LEWDNESS
LEWISITE
LEXICONS
LIAISING
LIAISONS
LIAONING
LIAOTUNG
LIAOYANG
LIBATION
LIBECCIO
LIBELLING
LIBELLED
LIBELLER
LIBERALS
LIBERATE
LIBERIAN
LIBRETTI
LIBRETTO
LICENCES
LICENSED
LICENSEE
LICENSER
LITCHENIN
LICKINGS
LICORICE
LIE-DOWNS
LIENTERY
LIFE BELT
LIFEBOAT
LIFE BUOY
LIFELESS
LIFELIKE
LIFELINE
LIFELONG
LIFE PEER
LIFE SIZE
LIFESPAN
LIFETIME
LIFE WORK
LIFTABLE
LIFT-OFFS
LIGAMENT
LIGATION
LIGATIVE
LIGATURE
LIGHT ALE

LIGHTERS	LISTENED	LOGBOOKS	LORIKEET	LUSHNESS
LIGHTEST	LISTENER	LOGCABIN	LORRAINE	LUSTRATE
LIGHTING	LISTLESS	LOGICIAN	LOTHARIO	LUSTROUS
LIGNEOUS	LITANIES	LOGICISM	LOUDNESS	LUTANIST
LIGNITIC	LITERACY	LOGISTIC	LOUNGERS	LUTENIST
LIGULATE	LITERALS	LOGOGRAM	LOUNGING	LUTEOLIN
LIGULOID	LITERARY	LOGOTYPE	LOUSIEST	LUXURIES
LIGURIAN	LITERATE	LOGOTYPY	LOVEBIRD	LYALLPUR
LIKELIER	LITERATI	LOITERED	LOVELESS	LYCHGATE
LIKENESS	LITHARGE	LOITERER	LOVELIER	LYINGS-IN
LIKENING	LITIGANT	LOLLARDY	LOVELIES	LYMPHOID
LIKEWISE	LITIGATE	LOLLIPOP	LOVELORN	LYMPHOMA
LIMA BEAN	LITTERED	LOLLOPED	LOVESICK	LYNCHING
LIMACINE	LITTORAL	LOMBARDY	LOVINGLY	LYNCH LAW
LIMASSOL	LIVELIER	LONDONER	LOWBROWS	LYONNAIS
LIMBLESS	LIVELONG	LONDRINA	LOWERING	LYRE BIRD
LIMEKILN	LIVENING	LONELIER	LOWLANDS	LYRICISM
LIMERICK	LIVERIED	LONESOME	LOWLIEST	LYRICIST
LIMINESS	LIVERIES	LONE WOLF	LOW-LYNG	LYSOSOME
LIMITARY	LIVERISH	LONGBOAT	LOW TIDES	LYSOZYME
LIMITING	LIVETRAP	LONGBOWS	LOW WATER	
LIMNETIC	LIVEWARE	LONGERON	LOYALISM	
LIMONENE	LIVEWIRE	LONG FACE	LOYALIST	**9 LETTERS**
LIMONITE	LIVONIAN	LONGHAND	LOZENGES	LABELLING
LIMOUSIN	LIXIVIUN	LONG-HAUL	LUCIDITY	LABELLOID
LIMPIDLY	LOADINGS	LONGHORN	LUCKIEST	LABIALISM
LIMPNESS	LOADSTAR	LONGINGS	LUCKLESS	LIABILITY
LINALOOL	LOANABLE	LONGJUMP	LUCKY DIP	LABIALIZE
LINCHPIN	LOANWORD	LONG-LIFE	LUDDITES	LABORIOUS
LINEAGES	LOATHING	LONGSHIP	LUDHIANA	LABOUR DAY
LINEALLY	LOBBYING	LONGSHOT	LUGHOLES	LABOURERS
LINESMAN	LOBBYISM	LONG SUIT	LUGSAILS	LABOURING
LINESMEN	LOBBYIST	LONG-TERM	LUGWORMS	LABOURISM
LINGERED	LOBELINE	LONG TONS	LUKEWARM	LABOURIST
LINGERER	LOBLOLLY	LONGUEUR	LUMBERED	LABRADORS
LINGERIE	LOBOTMY	LONG WAVE	LUMBERER	LABURNUMS
LINGUIST	LOBSTERS	LONGWAYS	LUMINARY	LABYRINTH
LINIMENT	LOCALISM	LOOKER-ON	LUMINOUS	LACCOLITH
LINKABLE	LOCALIST	LOOKOUTS	LUMPFISH	LACERABLE
LINKAGES	LOCALITY	LOONIEST	LUMPIEST	LACERATED
LINKWORK	LOCALIZE	LOONY BIN	LUMP SUMS	LACERTIAN
LINOCUTS	LOCATING	LOOPHOLE	LUNATICS	LACHRYMAL
LINOLEUM	LOCATION	LOOSEBOX	LUNATION	LACINIATE
LINOTYPE	LOCATIVE	LOOSE END	LUNCHEON	LACQUERED
LINOSTOCK	LOCKABLE	LOOSENED	LUNCHING	LACQUERER
LIONFISH	LOCKOUTS	LOOSENER	LUNEBURG	LACTATION
LIONIZED	LOCOWEED	LOP-EARED	LUNGFISH	LADDERING
LIONIZER	LOCUTION	LOP-SIDED	LUNGWORM	LADIES' MAN
LIPOIDAL	LODESTAR	LOQUITER	LUNGWORT	LADIES' MEN
LIPSTICK	LODGINGS	LORDLIER	LUNULATE	LADYBIRDS
LIQUENCE	LODGMENT	LORDOSIS	LURCHING	LAEVULOSE
LIQUERS	LODICULE	LORDOTIC	LURINGLY	LAGOMORPH
LISSOMLY	LOESSIAL	LORDSHIP	LUSATION	LALLATION
LISTABLE	LOFTIEST	LORICATE	LUSCIOUS	LAMAISTIC

LAMBASTED	LATECOMER	LEGENDARY	LICHENOID	LIPSTICKS
LAMBSKINS	LATERALLY	LEGGINESS	LIENTERIC	LIQUIDATION
LAME DUCKS	LATERITIC	LEGGINGED	LIFE BELTS	LIQUIFIED
LAMENTING	LATHERING	LEGIONARY	LIFEBLOOD	LIQUEFIER
LAMINABLE	LATIMERIA	LEGISLATE	LIFEBOATS	LIQUIDATE
LAMINARIA	LATINZERS	LEG-WARMER	LIFE BUOYS	LIQUIDITY
LAMINATED	LATITUDES	LEICESTER	LIFE CYCLE	LIQUIDIZE
LAMINATES	LATTER-DAY	LEISURELY	LIFEGUARD	LIQUORICE
LAMINATOR	LAUDATION	LEITMOTIV	LIFELINES	LISPINGLY
LAMINITIS	LAUDATORY	LEMNISCUS	LIFE PEERS	LISTENERS
LAMP-BLACK	LAUGHABLE	LEMON CURD	LIFE-SAVER	LISTENING
LAMPOONED	LAUGHABLY	LEMON SOLE	LIFESPANS	LIST PRICE
LAMPOONER	LAUNCHING	LEND-LEASE	LIFE STORY	LITERALLY
LAMPPOSTS	LAUNCH PAD	LENGTHIER	LIFESTYLE	LITERATIM
LAMPSHADE	LAUNDERED	LENGTHILY	LIFETIMES	LITHENESS
LANCASTER	LAUNDERER	LENIENTLY	LIGAMENTS	LITHIASIS
LANCEWOOD	LAUNRESS	LENINAKAN	LIGATURES	LITHOLOGY
LANCINATE	LAUNDRIES	LENINGRAD	LIGHT BULB	LITHOPONE
LAND AGENT	LAUREATES	LEPONTINE	LIGHTENED	LITHOTOMY
LANDAULET	LAVISHING	LEPTOSOME	LIGHT-FAST	LITHUANIA
LANDFALLS	LAWGIVING	LEPTOTENE	LIGHTNESS	LITIGABLE
LANDLORDS	LAWLESSLY	LESSENING	LIGHTNING	LITIGANTS
LANDMARKS	LAWNMOWER	LETHALITY	LIGHTSHIP	LITIGATED
LANDMINES	LAWN PARTY	LETHARGIC	LIGHTS-OUT	LITIGATOR
LANDOWNER	LAXATIVES	LETTERBOX	LIGHT YEAR	LITIGIOUS
LAND ROVER	LAYABOUTS	LETTERING	LIGNIFORM	LITTERBIN
LANDSCAPE	LAY FIGURE	LEUCOTOMY	LIKELIEST	LITTERING
LANDSLIDE	LAYPERSON	LEUCAEMIA	LILY-WHITE	LITTORIALS
LANDSLIPS	LAY READER	LEVANTINE	LIMA BEANS	LITURGICS
LANDWARDS	LAY SISTER	LEVELLERS	LIMELIGHT	LITURGIES
LANGOUSTE	LAZARETTO	LEVELLING	LIMERICKS	LITURGISM
LANGUAGES	LAZYBONES	LEVIATHAN	LIMESTONE	LITURGIST
LANGUEDOC	LEAD TIMES	LEVIGATOR	LIMEWATER	LIVELIEST
LANGUIDLY	LEAFINESS	LEVITATOR	LIMITABLE	LIVERPOOL
LANKINESS	LEAF MOULD	LEXICALLY	LIMITLESS	LIVERWORT
LANOLATED	LEAF STALK	LIABILITY	LIMNOLOGY	LIVERYMAN
LANTHANUM	LEAKINESS	LIBATIONS	LIMOUSINE	LIVERYMEN
LAODICEAN	LEAP YEARS	LIBELLANT	LIMPIDITY	LIVESTOCK
LAPLANDER	LEARNABLE	LIBELLING	LIMPINGLY	LIVE WIRES
LARCENIES	LEARNEDLY	LIBELLOUS	LINCHPINS	LIVIDNESS
LARCENIST	LEASEBACK	LIBERALLY	LINEAMENT	LJUBLJANA
LARCENOUS	LEASEHOLD	LIBERATED	LINEARITY	LOADSTARS
LARGENESS	LEASTWAYS	LIBERATOR	LINEATION	LOADSTONE
LARGHETTO	LEAVENING	LIBERTIES	LINEOLATE	LOAMINESS
LARKSPURS	LECHEROUS	LIBERTINE	LINGERERS	LOANWORDS
LARVICIDE	LECTORATE	LIBIDINAL	LINGUISTS	LOATHSOME
LARYNGEAL	LECTURERS	LIBRARIAN	LINGULATE	LOBECTOMY
LASHINGLY	LECTURING	LIBRARIES	LINKOPING	LOCALIZED
LAS PALMAS	LEERINGLY	LIBRATION	LINOLEATE	LOCALIZER
LASSITUDE	LEE SHORES	LIBRATORY	LINOTYPER	LOCAL TIME
LAST-DITCH	LEFTOVERS	LIBRETTOS	LIONIZING	LOCATABLE
LASTINGLY	LEFWARDS	LIBRIFORM	LIPOLYSIS	LOCATIONS
LAST STRAW	LEGALIZED	LICENSEES	LIPOLYTIC	LOCHSMITH
LATCHKEYS	LEGATIONS	LICENSING	LIP-READER	LOCOMOTOR

LOCUTIONS	LOUDMOUTH	LYCHGATES	LANDLUBBER
LODESTAR	LOUISBURG	LYMINGTON	LANDMASSES
LODESTONE	LOUISIANA	LYMPHATIC	LAND ROVERS
LODGEABLE	LOUNGE BAR	LYONNAISE	LANDSCAPED
LOFTINESS	LOUSEWORT	LYOPHILIC	LANDSCAPES
LOGAOEDIC	LOUSINESS	LYOPHOBIC	LANDSLIDES
LOGARITHM	LOVEBIRDS	LYREBIRDS	LANGLAUFER
LOG CABINS	LOVECHILD	LYRICALLY	LANGUISHED
LOGICALLY	LOVELIEST	LYRICISMS	LANGUISHER
LOGICIANS	LOVING CUP	LYRICISTS	LANIFEROUS
LOGISTICS	LOW COMEDY	LYSIMETER	LANTHANIDE
LOGOGRIPH	LOWERABLE	LYSOSOMAL	LAPAROTOMY
LOGOMACHY	LOWER CASE		LAPIDARIAN
LOINCLOTH	LOWERMOST		LAPIDARIES
LOITERERS	LOWESTOFT	**10 LETTERS**	LARGE-SCALE
LOITERING	LOWLANDER	LABORATORY	LARVICIDAL
LOLLINGLY	LOWLINESS	LABOUR DAYS	LARYNGITIC
LOLLIPOPS	LOW-MINDED	LABOUREDLY	LARYNGITIS
LOLLOPING	LOW-NECKED	LABYRINTHS	LASCIVIOUS
LOMBARDIC	LOW SEASON	LACERATING	LAST MINUTE
LONELIEST	LOYALISTS	LACERATION	LATECOMERS
LONE WOLF	LOYALTIES	LACERATIVE	LATENT HEAT
LONG BOATS	LUBRICANT	LACHRYMOSE	LATTERMOST
LONGCLOTH	LUBRICATE	LACKLUSTRE	LAUGHINGLY
LONGEVITY	LUBRICITY	LACQUERING	LAUNCH PADS
LONGEVOUS	LUBRICOUS	LACRIMATOR	LAUNDERING
LONG FACES	LUCIFERIN	LACTESCENT	LAUNDRYMAN
LONGICORN	LUCKINESS	LACTIC ACID	LAURACEOUS
LONGINGLY	LUCKY DIPS	LACTOGENIC	LAUREATION
LONGITUDE	LUCRATIVE	LACTOMETER	LAURENTIAN
LONG JOHNS	LUCUBRATE	LACTOSCOPE	LAVATIONAL
LONG-LIVED	LUDICROUS	LACUNIOSITY	LAVATORIAL
LONG-RANGE	LUFTWAFFE	LACUSTRINE	LAVATORIES
LONGSHIPS	LULLABIES	LADY-KILLER	LAVISHNESS
LONGSHORE	LULLINGLY	LADY'S-SMOCK	LAW-ABIDING
LONG SHOTS	LUMBERING	LAMARCKIAN	LAW-BREAKER
LONGUEUIL	LUMBERMAN	LAMASERIES	LAWFULNESS
LONGUEURS	LUMBERMEN	LAMBASTING	LAWNMOWERS
LOOK-ALIKE	LUMBRICAL	LAMBDACISM	LAWN TENNIS
LOOM-STATE	LUMINANCE	LAMBREQUIN	LAWRENCIUM
LOONINESS	LUMINESCE	LAMELLATED	LAY BROTHERS
LOONY BINS	LUMPINESS	LAMENTABLE	LAY FIGURES
LOOPHOLES	LUNATICAL	LAMENTABLY	LAYPERSONS
LOOSE ENDS	LUNISOLAR	LAMINATING	LAY READERS
LOOSE-LEAF	LUNITIDAL	LAMINATION	LAY SISTERS
LOOSENESS	LURIDNESS	LAMPOONERY	LEADERSHIP
LOOSENING	LURKINGLY	LAMPOONING	LEAF-HOPPER
LOQUACITY	LUSTFULLY	LAMPSHADES	LEAFLETING
LORDLIEST	LUSTINESS	LANCASHIRE	LEASEBACKS
LORDSHIPS	LUTANISTS	LANCEOLATE	LEAVENINGS
LORGNETTE	LUTHERISM	LAND AGENTS	LEBENSRAUM
LORRY PARK	LUXURIANT	LANDING NET	LECTIONARY
LOST CAUSE	LUXURIATE	LANDLADIES	LECTORSHIP
LOTTERIES	LUXURIOUS	LANDLOCKED	LEFT-HANDED

LEFT-HANDER	LIBERATING	LIST PRICES	LONGWINDED
LEFT-WINGER	LIBERATION	LITERALISM	LOOK-ALIKES
LEGALISTIC	LIBERATORS	LITERALIST	LOQUACIOUS
LEGALIZING	LIBERTINES	LITERARILY	LORDLINESS
LEGATESHIP	LIBIDINOUS	LITERATELY	LORGNETTES
LEGATORIAL	LIBRARIANS	LITERATION	LORRY PARKS
LEGIBILITY	LIBRETTIST	LITERATURE	LOS ANGELES
LEGISLATED	LIBREVILLE	LITHOGRAPH	LOSS LEADER
LEGISLATOR	LICENSIBLE	LITHOLOGIC	LOST CAUSES
LEGITIMACY	LICENTIATE	LITHOPHYTE	LOTUS-EATER
LEGITIMATE	LICENTIOUS	LITHOTOMIC	LOUDHAILER
LEGITIMISM	LIEUTENANT	LITHOTRITY	LOUDMOUTHS
LEGITIMIST	LIFE CYCLES	LITHUANIAN	LOUNGE BARS
LEGITIMIZE	LIFEGUARDS	LITIGATING	LOUNGE SUIT
LEGUMINOUS	LIFE JACKET	LITIGATION	LOVABILITY
LEG-WARMERS	LIFELESSLY	LITTERBINS	LOVE AFFAIRS
LEISHMANIA	LIFE-SAVING	LITTERLOUT	LOVELINESS
LEITMOTIVS	LIFESTYLES	LITURGICAL	LOVEMAKING
LEMNISCATE	LIGHT BULBS	LIVABILITY	LOVING CUPS
LEMON SOLES	LIGHTENING	LIVELIHOOD	LOWER CLASS
LENGTHENED	LIGHTRAGE	LIVELINESS	LOWER HOUSE
LENGTHENER	LIGHTHOUSE	LIVING ROOM	LOWERINGLY
LENGTHIEST	LIGHTNINGS	LIVING WAGE	LOWLANDERS
LENGTHWAYS	LIGHTSHIPS	LOADSTONES	LOW-PITCHED
LENTAMENTE	LIGHT YEARS	LOBOTOMIES	LOW PROFILE
LENTICULAR	LIGNOCAINE	LOBSTER POT	LOW-TENSION
LENTISSIMO	LIKELIHOOD	LOBULATION	LUBRICANTS
LEOPARDESS	LIKE-MINDED	LOCAL DERBY	LUBRICATED
LEPIDIOLITE	LIKENESSES	LOCALISTIC	LUBRICATOR
LEPRECHAUN	LILIACEOUS	LOCALITIES	LUBRICIOUS
LEPTOSOMIC	LIMICOLINE	LOCALIZING	LUGGAGE VAN
LESBIANISM	LIMICOLOUS	LOCKER ROOM	LUGUBRIOUS
LESSEESHIP	LIMITARIAN	LOCK KEEPER-	LUMBERJACK
LETTER BOMB	LIMITATION	LOCKSMITHS	LUMBER-ROOM
LETTERHEAD	LIMOUSINES	LOCKSTITCH	LUMBERYARD
LEUCOCYTES	LINEAMENTS	LOCOMOTION	LUMINARIES
LEUCOCYTIC	LINECASTER	LOCOMOTIVE	LUMINOSITY
LEUCODERMA	LINGUIFORM	LOCULATION	LUMINOUSLY
LEUCOMAINE	LINGUISTIC	LODESTONES	LUNAR MONTH
LEUCOPENIA	LINSEED OIL	LOGANBERRY	LURCHINGLY
LEUCOPENIC	LIPOMATOUS	LOGARITHMS	LUSCIOUSLY
LEUCOPLAST	LIPOPHILIC	LOGGERHEAD	LUSTRATION
LEVERKUSEN	LIP-READING	LOGICALITY	LUSTRATIVE
LEVIATHANS	LIP SERVICE	LOGISTICAL	LUSTREWARE
LEVIGATION	LIQUEFYING	LOGOGRAPHY	LUSTROUSLY
LEVIGATING	LIQUESCENT	LOGOPAEDIC	LUTINE BELL
LEVITATION	LIQUIDATED	LOGROLLING	LUXEMBOURG
LEXICALITY	LIQUIDATOR	LOINCLOTHS	LUXURIANCE
LEXICOLOGY	LIQUIDIZED	LOIR-ET-CHER	LUXURIATED
LIBATIONAL	LIQUIDIZER	LONELINESS	LYCOPODIUM
LIBERALISM	LIQUORICES	LONGHAIRED	LYMPHOCYTE
LIBERALIST	LISSOMNESS	LONG-HEADED	LYOPHILIZE
LIBERALITY	LISTENABLE	LONGITUDES	
LIBERALIZE	LISTLESSLY	LONG-JUMPER	

11 LETTERS

11 LETTERS

LABIODENTAL
LABORIOUSLY
LABOR UNIONS
LABOURINGLY
LABOUR PARTY
LABRADORITE
LACCOLITHIC
LACERATIONS
LACERTILIAN
LACINIATION
LACONICALLY
LACRMATION
LACONICALLY
LACRIMATION
LACRIMATORY
LACTALBUMIN
LACTATIONAL
LACTESCENCE
LACTIFEROUS
LADY-KILLERS
LAEVOGYRATE
LAGOMORPHIC
LAICIZATION
LAMELLATION
LAMELLICORN
LAMELLIFORM
LAMELLOSITY
LAMENTATION
LAMENTINGLY
LAMINAR FLOW
LAMPROPHYRE
LANCASTRIAN
LANCINATION
LANDING GEAR
LANDING NETS
LANDLUBBERS
LANDSCAPING
LANDSCAPIST
LANGUISHING
LAPAROSCOPY
LAPIS LAZULI
LARGE-MINDED
LARKISHNESS
LARYNGOLOGY
LARYLOTOMY
LATITUDINAL
LAUDABILITY
LAUGHING GAS
LAUNDERETTE
LAURUSTINUS
LAW-BREAKING
LAWLESSNESS
LAWN PARTIES

LAY BROTHERS
LEADING LADY
LEAF-CLIMBER
LEAP FROGGED
LEARNEDNESS
LEASE HOLDER
LEATHERBACK
LEATHERETTE
LEATHERWOOD
LEAVE TAKING
LECHEROUSLY
LECITHINASE
LECTURESHIP
LEFT-HANDERS
LEFT-WINGERS
LEGAL TENDER
LEGATIONARY
LEGERDEMAIN
LEGIONARIES
LEGIONNAIRE
LEGISLATING
LEGISLATION
LEGISLATIVE
LEGISLATORS
LEGISLATURE
LEGITIMIZED
LEMON SQUASH
LENGTHENING
LENGTHINESS
LENTIGINOUS
LEPIDOSIREN
LEPRECHAUNS
LEPROSARIUM
LEPTORRHINE
LESE-MAJESTY
LETTER BOMBS
LETTERBOXES
LETTERHEADS
LETTERPRESS
LEUCOCRATIC
LEUCODERMAL
LEUCORRHOEA
LEUCOTOMIES
LEVEL-HEADED
LIABILITIES
LIBELLOUSLY
LIBERAL ARTS
LIBERALIZED
LIBERALIZER
LIBERALNESS
LIBERTARIAN
LIBERTICIDE
LIBERTINISM
LIBERATIONAL

LIBRETTISTS
LICENTIATES
LICKSPITTLE
LIE DETECTOR
LIEUTENANCY
LIEUTENANTS
LIFE JACKETS
LIFE OF RILEY
LIFE STORIES
LIGAMENTOUS
LIGHT-FOOTED
LIGHT-HEADED
LIGHTHOUSES
LIGHTWEIGHT
LIKABLENESS
LILLIPUTIAN
LILY-LIVERED
LIMITATIONS
LIMITLESSLY
LIMNOLOGIST
LIMP-WRISTED
LINDISFARNE
LINEAMENTAL
LINE DRAWING
LINEN BASKET
LINE OF SIGHT
LINE PRINTER
LINERTRAINS
LINGERINGLY
LINGUISTICS
LION-HEARTED
LIONIZATION
LIPOPROTEIN
LIQUEFIABLE
LIQUESCENCE
LIQUIDAMBAR
LIQUIDATING
LIQUIDATION
LIQUIDATORS
LIQUIDIZERS
LIQUIDIZING
LITERALNESS
LITERATURES
LITHOGRAPHS
LITHOGRAPHY
LITHOLOGIST
LITHOMETEOR
LITHOPHYTIC
LITHOSPHERE
LITHOTOMIST
LITTERATEUR
LITTERLOUTS
LITTLE WOMAN
LITURGISTIC

LIVABLENESS
LIVELIHOODS
LIVING ROOMS
LO AND BEHOLD
LOATHSOMELY
LOBSTERPOTS
LOCAL COLOUR
LOCALIZABLE
LOCAL OPTION
LOCKER ROOMS
LOCK KEEPERS
LOCOMOTIVES
LOCUM TENENS
LOGARITHMIC
LOGGERHEADS
LOGISTICAIN
LOGOGRAPHER
LOGOGRIPHIC
LOGOMACHIST
LOGOPAEDICS
LOITERINGLY
LOLLIPOP MAN
LOLLIPOP MEN
LONDON DERRY
LONG JUMPERS
LONGSIGHTED
LONGWEARING
LOOSE CHANGE
LOOSE STRIFE
LOPHO BRANCH
LORD'S PRAYER
LOSS LEADERS
LOTUS-EATERS
LOUDHAILERS
LOUDMOUTHES
LOUNGE SUITS
LOUTISHNESS
LOVE AFFAIRS
LOW COMEDIES
LOW-PRESSURE
LOW PROFILES
LOW SPIRITED
LOXODROMICS
LUBRICATING
LUBRICATION
LUBRICATIVE
LUBRICATORS
LUDICROUSLY
LUGGAGE RACK
LUGGAGE VANS
LUMBERINGLY
LUMBER JACKS
LUMBER-ROOMS
LUMBERYARDS

525

LUMBRICALIS
LUMINESCENT
LUNAR MONTHS
LUSTFULNESS
LUTHERANISM
LUXURIANTLY
LUXURIATING
LUXURIATION
LUXURIOUSLY
LYMPHOBLAST
LYMPHOCYTIC

12 LETTERS
LABORATORIES
LABOUR MARKET
LABOUR OF LOVE
LABOUR SAVING
LABYRINTHINE
LACERABILITY
LACHRYMOSITY
LACTOPROTEIN
LAISSEZ FAIRE
LAMENTATIONS
LANDING CRAFT
LANDING FIELD
LANDING STAGE
LANDING STRIP
LANDLUBBERLY
LANGUISHMENT
LANGUOROUSLY
LANTERN-JAWED
LANTERNSLIDE
LAPIS LAZULIS
LARYNGOSCOPE
LARYNGOSCOPY
LASCIVIOUSLY
LASER PRINTER
LANTEENRIGGED
LATINIZATION
LAUNDERETTES
LAUNDRYWOMAN
LAUREATESHIP
LEADING LIGHT
LEAPFROGGING
LEASEHOLDERS
LEATHERINESS
LEAVE TAKINGS
LECTURESHIPS
LEGALIZATION
LEGIONNAIRES
LEGISLATURES
LEGITIMATELY
LEGITIMATION

LEGITIMATIZE
LEGITIMISTIC
LEGITIMIZING
LENTICELLATE
LEOPARD'S-BANE
LETTER OPENER
LEXICOGRAPHY
LEXICOLOGIST
LIBERALISTIC
LIBERALITIES
LIBERALIZING
LIBERAL PARTY
LIBERTARIANS
LIBERTICIDAL
LIBIDINOUSLY
LICENCE PLATE
LICENTIATION
LICENTIOUSLY
LIE DETECTORS
LIFELESSNESS
LIGHT-HEARTED
LIGHTWEIGHTS
LIMNOLOGICAL
LINE DRAWINGS
LINE-ENGRAVER
LINEN BASKETS
LINE PRINTERS
LINE PRINTING
LINES OF SIGHT
LINGUA FRANCA
LIQUEFACIENT
LIQUEFACTION
LIQUEFACTIVE
LISTLESSNESS
LITERALISTIC
LITERARINESS
LITERATENESS
LITHOGRAPHER
LITHOGRAPHIC
LITTERATEURS
LITTLE FINGER
LITTLE PEOPLE
LITURGICALLY
LIVERPUDLIAN
LIVER SAUSAGE
LIVERY STABLE
LIVING FOSSIL
LOCAL DERBIES
LOCALIZATION
LOCKSMITHERY
LOCKSTITCHES
LODGING HOUSE
LOGANBERRIES
LOGISTICALLY

LONELY HEARTS
LONESOMENESS
LONG-DISTANCE
LONG-DIVISION
LONGITUDINAL
LONGSHOREMAN
LONGSHOREMEN
LONG-STANDING
LONG VACATION
LONG WINDEDLY
LOOKING GLASS
LOOSE JOINTED
LOOSE-TONGUED
LOQUACIOUSLY
LOSS ADJUSTER
LOST PROPERTY
LOUDSPEAKERS
LOUGHBOROUGH
LOVECHILDREN
LOWERCLASSES
LUGGAGE RACKS
LUGUBRIOUSLY
LUMBERJACKET
LUMINESCENCE
LUNCHEONETTE
LUSCIOUSNESS
LYMPHANGITIC
LYMPHANGITIS
LYMPHOMATOID
LYSERGIC ACID

13 LETTERS
LABIALIZATION
LABORIOUSNESS
LABOURS OF LOVE
LACKADAISICAL
LACTOBACILLUS
LADY-IN-WAITING
LAEVOROTATION
LAEVOROTATORY
LAMELLIBRANCH
LANCE CORPORAL
LANDING FIELDS
LANDING STAGES
LANDING STRIPS
LANDOWNERSHIP
LANTERNSLIDES
LAPAROSCOPIES
LARYNGOLOGIST
LARYNGOSCOPIC
LASER PRINTERS
LATCHKEY CHILD
LATIN AMERICAN
LAUGHING STOCK

LAUNDRY BASKET
LEADING LADIES
LEADING LIGHTS
LEATHERJACKET
LECHEROUSNESS
LEGISLATORIAL
LEISHMANIASIS
LEISURELINESS
LEPIDOPTERIST
LEPIDOPTEROUS
LETHARGICALLY
LETTERPRESSES
LEVEL CROSSING
LEXICOGRAPHER
LEXICOGRAPHIC
LEXICOLOGICAL
LIBRARIANSHIP
LICENSE PLATES
LICENSING LAWS
LIFE PRESERVER
LIGHT AIRCRAFT
LIGHT-FINGERED
LIGHT-HEADEDLY
LIGNIFICATION
LIMITLESSNESS
LINE-ENGRAVING
LITHOGRAPHING
LITIGIOUSNESS
LITTLE FINGERS
LIVERY COMPANY
LIVERY STABLES
LIVING FOSSILS
LOATHSOMENESS
LONGSUFFERING
LONG VACATIONS
LOSS ADJUSTERS
LOWER EAST SIDE
LOW-PASS FILTER
LUBRICATIONAL
LUDICROUSNESS
LUNATIC FRINGE
LUNCHEONETTES
LYMPHADENITIS
LYMPHATICALLY
LYMPHOBLASTIC
LYMPHOCYTOSIS
LYMPHOCYTOTIC
LYMPHOPOIESIS
LYMPHOPOIETIC

3 LETTERS	MANX	MIRE	**5 LETTERS**	MARRY	METED
MAC	MANY	MIRY	MACAO	MARSH	METER
MAD	MAPS	MISS	MACEW	MASAI	METHS
MAG	MARE	MIST	MACES	MASAN	METOL
MAM	MARK	MITE	MACHO	MASER	ME-TOO
MAN	MARL	MITT	MACLE	MASKS	METRE
MAP	MARS	MOEN	MACON	MASON	METRO
MAR	MASH	MIBS	MADAM	MASTS	MEUSE
MAS	MASS	MOCK	MADLY	MATCH	MEWED
MAT	MAST	MODE	MAFIA	MATED	MEZZO
MAW	MATE	MODS	MAGIC	MATER	MIAMI
MAY	MATS	MOKE	MAGMA	MATES	MIAOW
MEN	MATT	MOLD	MAGUS	MATEY	MICKS
MET	MAUL	MOLE	MAIDS	MATIN	MICRO
MEW	MAWS	MOLL	MAINE	MATTE	MIDDY
MID	MAYA	MOLT	MAINS	MAUVE	MIDGE
MIX	MAYS	MOMS	MAINZ	MAXIM	MID-ON
MOB	MAZE	MONK	MAIZE	MAYAN	MIDST
MOD	MAZY	MONO	MAJOR	MAYBE	MIENS
MOM	MEAD	MOOD	MAKER	MAYN'T	MIFFY
MOO	MEAL	MOON	MAKES	MAYOR	MILES
MOP	MEAN	MOOR	MALAR	MAYST	MILKY
MOS	MEAT	MOOS	MALAY	MAZES	MILLS
MOT	MEEK	MOOT	MALES	MEADS	MIMED
MOW	MEET	MOPE	MALLS	MEALS	MIMER
MPS	MEGA-	MOPS	MALMO	MEALY	MIMES
MRS	MELT	MORE	MALTA	MEANS	MIMIC
MTV	MEMO	MORN	MALTY	MEANT	MINCE
MUD	MEND	MOSS	MAMAS	MEATH	MINDS
MUG	MENU	MOST	MAMBA	MEATY	MINED
MUM	MEOW	MOTE	MAMBO	MECCA	MINER
	MERE	MOTH	MAMEY	MEDAL	MINES
	MESH	MOTS	MAMMA	MEDAN	MINGY
4 LETTERS	MESS	MOVE	MAMMY	MEDIA	MINIM
MA'AM	METE	MOWN	MANDE	MEDIC	MINUS
MACE	MEWS	MUCH	MANED	MEDOC	MINOR
MACH	MICA	MUCK	MANES	MEETS	MINSK
MACS	MICE	MUFF	MANGE	MELEE	MINTS
MADE	MICK	MUGS	MANGO	MELON	MINUS
MAGI	MIDI	MULE	MANGY	MEMOS	MIRED
MAGS	MIEN	MULL	MANIA	MENAI	MIRES
MAID	MIKE	MUMS	MANIC	MENDS	MIRTH
MAIL	MILD	MUON	MANLY	MENUS	MISER
MAIM	MILE	MURK	MANNA	MEOWS	MISSY
MAIN	MILK	MUSE	MANOR	MERCY	MISTS
MAKE	MILL	MUSH	MANSE	MERES	MISTY
MALE	MILT	MUSK	MANTA	MERGE	MITES
MALI	MIME	MUSS	MANUS	MERIT	MITIS
MALL	MIND	MUST	MAORI	MERRY	MITRE
MALM	MINE	MUTE	MAPLE	MESIC	MITTS
MALT	MINI	MUTT	MARCH	MESNE	MIXED
MAMA	MINK	MYNA	MARES	MESON	MIXER
MAMS	MINT	MYTH	MARKS	MESSY	MIXES
MANE	MINX		MARNE	METAL	MIX-UP

MIZAR	MOSUL	MUTED	MALATE	MARKER	MAZILY
MOANS	MOTEL	MUTES	MALAWI	MARKET	MEADOW
MOATS	MOTES	MUTTS	MALAYA	MARKKA	MEAGRE
MOCHA	MOTET	MUZAK	MALEIC	MARKUP	MEANER
MOCKS	MOTHS	MUZZY	MALICE	MARLIN	MEANLY
MODAL	MOTHY	MYNAH	MALIGN	MARMOT	MEATUS
MODEL	NOTIF	MYOMA	MALLEE	MAROON	MECCAS
MODEM	MOTOR	MUOPE	MALLET	MARQUE	MEDALS
MODES	MOTTO	MYRRH	MALLOW	MARRED	MEDDLE
MOGGY	NOULD	MYTHS	MALTED	MARRER	MEDIAL
MOGUL	MOULT		MALTHA	MARRON	MEDIAN
MOIRE	MOUND		MAMBAS	MARROW	MEDICK
MOIST	MOUNT	**6 LETTERS**	MAMMAL	MARSHY	MEDICO
MOKES	MOURN	MACACO	MAMMON	MARTEN	MEDICS
MOKPO	MOUSE	MACAWS	MANAGE	MARTIN	MEDINA
MOLAL	MOUSY	MACEIO	MANAMA	MARTYR	MEDIUM
MOLAR	MOUTH	MACKLE	MANANA	MARVEL	MEDLAR
MOLDS	MOVED	MACRON	MANAUS	MASCLE	MEDLEY
MOLDY	MOVER	MACULA	MANCHE	MASCON	MEEKER
MOLES	MOVES	MADAME	MANCHU	MASCOT	MEEKLEY
MOLLS	MOVIE	MADAMS	MANEGE	MASERS	MEERUT
MOLLY	MOWED	MADCAP	MANFUL	MASERU	MEETER
MOLTO	MOWER	MADDEN	MANGER	MASHED	MEGILP
MOLTS	MUCIN	MADDER	MANGLE	MASHER	MEGOHM
MOMMA	MUCKY	MADE-UP	MANGOS	MASHES	MEKNES
MOMMY	MUCRO	MADMAN	MANIAC	MASHIE	MEKONG
MONAD	MUCUS	MADMEN	MANIAS	MASJID	MELEES
MONAL	MUDDY	MADRAS	MANILA	MASKED	MELLOW
MONEY	MUFFS	MADRID	MANNED	MASKER	MELODY
MOKES	MUFTI	MADURO	MANNER	MASONS	MELOID
MONTH	MUGGY	MAENAD	MANORS	MASQUE	MELONS
MONZA	MULTCH	MAGGOT	MANQUE	MASSED	MELTED
MOOCH	MULCH	MAGIAN	MANTEL	MASSES	MELTER
MOODS	MULCT	MAGNET	MANTIC	MASSIF	MELTON
MOODY	MULES	MAGNUM	MANTIS	MASTER	MEMBER
MOOED	MULEY	MAGPIE	MANTLE	MASTIC	MEMOIR
MOONS	MULGA	MAGUEY	MANUAL	MARADI	MEMORY
MOONY	MULLS	MAGYAR	MANURE	MATING	MENACE
MOORS	MULTI	MAHOUT	MAOISM	MATINS	MENADO
MOOSE	MUMMY	MAIDEN	MAOIST	MATRIX	MENAGE
MOPED	MUMPS	MAIKOP	MAPLES	MATRON	MENDED
MOPER	MUNCH	MAILED	MAPPED	MATTED	MENDER
MOP-UP	MUNGO	MAILER	MAQUIS	MATTER	MENHIR
MORAL	MURAL	MAIMED	MARACA	MATURE	MENIAL
MORAY	MUREX	MAIMER	MARAUD	MAULED	MENSES
MOREL	MURKY	MAINLY	MARBLE	MAULER	MENTAL
MORES	MUSED	MAJORS	MARBLY	MAUNDY	MENTON
MORNS	MUSER	MAKALU	MARCHE	MAUSER	MENTOR
MORON	MUSES	MAKERS	MARGAY	MAXIMA	MEOWED
MORPH	MUSHY	MAKE-UP	MARGIN	MAXIMS	MERCER
MOSEY	MUSIC	MAKING	MARIAN	MAY DAY	MERELY
MOSSI	MUSKY	MALADY	MARINA	MAYFLY	MERGED
MOSSO	MUSTH	MALAGA	MARINE	MAYHEM	MERGER
MOSSY	MUSTY	MALANG	MARKED	MAYORS	MERINO

MERITS	MILIUM	MITRES	MOPEDS	MUCKED	MUZZLE
MERLIN	MILKED	MITTEN	MOPING	MUCKER	MYELIN
MERLON	MILKER	MIXERS	MOPOKE	MUCOID	MYNAHS
MERMAN	MILLED	MIXING	MOPPED	MUCOUS	MYOPIA
MERSIN	MILLER	MIX-UPS	MOPPET	MUDCAT	MYOPIC
MERCAL	MILLET	MIZZEN	MORALE	MUDDED	MYOSIN
MESHED	MILORD	MOANED	MORALS	MUDDLE	MYRIAD
MESHES	MILTER	MOANER	MORASS	MUD PIE	MYRICA
MESSED	MIMICS	MOATED	MORBID	MUESLI	MYRTLE
MESSES	MIMING	MOBBED	MOREEN	MUFFED	MYSELF
MESS-UP	MIMOSA	MOBBER	MORGUE	MUFFIN	MYSORE
METAGE	MINCED	MOBILE	MORION	MUFFLE	MYSTIC
METALS	MINCER	MOCKED	MORMON	MUFTIS	MYTHOS
METEOR	MINDED	MOCK-UP	MORNAY	MUGGED	MYXOMA
METERS	MINDEL	MOD CON	MORONS	MUGGER	
METHOD	MINDER	MODELS	MOROSE	MUKLUK	
METHYL	MINERS	MODEMS	MORROW	MULISH	**7 LETTERS**
METIER	MINGLE	MODENA	MORSEL	MULLAH	MACABRE
METING	MINIFY	MODERN	MORTAL	MULLED	MACADAM
METOPE	MINIMA	MODEST	MORTAR	MULLER	MACAQUE
METRES	MINIMS	MODIFY	MORULA	MULLET	MACEDON
METRICS	MINING	MODISH	MOSAIC	MULTAN	MACHETE
METROS	MINION	MODULE	MOSCOW	MUMBLE	MACHINE
METTLE	MINIUM	MOGULS	MOSLEM	MUMMER	MACRAINE
MEWING	MINNOW	MOHAIR	MOSQUE	MUNICH	MACRAME
MEWLER	MINOAN	MOHAWK	MOSTLY	MURALS	MACULAR
MEXICO	MINORS	MOHOLE	MOTELS	MURDER	MADDEST
MEZZOS	MINTED	MOIETY	MOTETS	MURINE	MADERIA
MIAOWS	MINTER	MOLARS	MOTHER	MURMUR	MADISON
MIASMA	MINUET	MOLDED	MOTIFS	MUSCAT	MADNESS
MICKEY	MINUTE	MOLDER	MOTILE	MUSCID	MADONNA
MICMAC	MINXES	MOLEST	MOTION	MUSCLE	MADRONA
MICRON	MIOSIS	MOLISE	MOTIVE	MUSCLY	MADURAI
MICROS	MIOTIC	MOLOCH	MOTLEY	MUSEUM	MADWORT
MIDIAR	MIRAGE	MOLTED	MOTMOT	MUSHES	MAENADS
MIDDAY	MIRING	MOLTEN	MOTORS	MUSING	MAESTRI
MIDDEN	MIRROR	MOMENT	MOTOWN	MUSKET	MAESTRI
MIDDLE	MISCUE	MOMISM	MOTTLE	MUSLIM	MAESTRO
MIDGES	MISERE	MOMMAS	MOTTOS	MUSLIN	MAFIOSO
MIDGET	MISERS	MONACO	MOULDS	MUSSED	MAGENTA
MIDGUT	MISERY	MONDAY	MOULDY	MUSSEL	MAGGOTS
MID-OFF	MISFIT	MONEYS	MOULIN	MUSTEE	MAGGOTY
MIDRIB	MISHAP	MONGER	MOULTS	MUSTER	MADHREB
MIDSTS	MISLAY	MONGOL	MOUNDS	MUSTN'T	MAGICAL
MIDWAY	MISLED	MONIES	MOUNTS	MUTANT	MAGNATE
MIFFED	MISSAL	MONISM	MOUSER	MUTATE	MAGNETO
MIGHTY	MISSED	MONIST	MOUSSE	MUTELY	MAGNETS
MIKADO	MISSES	MONKEY	MOUTHS	MUTING	MAGGNIFY
MILADY	MISSIS	MONTHS	MOUTON	MUTINY	MAGNUMS
MILDER	MISSUS	MOOING	MOVERS	MUTISM	MAGPIES
MILDEW	MISTED	MOONED	MOVIES	MUTTER	MAHATMA
MILDLY	MISTER	MOORED	MOVING	MUTTON	MAHIAN
MILERS	MISUSE	MOOTED	MOWERS	MUTUAL	MAH-JONG
MILIEU	MITRAL	MOOTER	MOWING	MUTULE	MAHONIA

529

MAHOUTS	MANHUNT	MARLITE	MAULING	MEMOIRS	MICRONS
MAIDENS	MANIACS	MARMITE	MAUNDER	MEMPHIS	MIDDENS
MAILBAG	MANIKIN	MARMOTS	MAWKISH	MENACED	MIDDLE C
MAILBOX	MANIPUR	MAROONS	MAXILLA	MENACER	MIDGETS
MAILING	MAN JACK	MARQUEE	MAXIMAL	MENACES	MIDIRON
MAILMAN	MANKIND	MARQUIS	MAXIMIN	MENAGES	MIDLAND
MAILMAN	MANLIER	MARRIED	MAXIMUM	MENDERS	MIDIRON
MAIMING	MANLIKE	MARRIER	MAXIMUS	MENDING	MIDLAND
MAINTOP	MAN-MADE	MARRING	MAXWELL	MENDIPS	MIDMOST
MAJESTY	MANNERS	MARROPS	MAY DAYS	MENDOZA	MIDRIFF
MAJORCA	MANNING	MARSALA	MAYENNE	MENFOLK	MIDTERM
MAJORED	MANNISH	MARSHAL	MAYFAIR	MENIALS	MIDWEEK
MAKASAR	MANNITE	MARSHES	MAYORAL	MENTHOL	MIDWEST
MAKINGS	MANNOSE	MARTENS	MAYPOLE	MENTION	MIDWIFE
MALABAR	MANNOSE	MARTIAL	MAYWEED	MENTORS	MIDYEAR
MALACCA	MANROPE	MARTIAN	MAZRAKA	MEOWING	MIGHTN'T
MALAISE	MANSARD	MARTINI	MAZZARD	MERCIES	MIGRANT
MALARIA	MANSION	MARTINS	MEADOWS	MERCURY	MIKADOS
MALATYA	MANTLED	MARTYRS	MEALIER	MERGERS	MILDEST
MALAYAN	MANTLES	MARTYRY	MEANDER	MERGING	MILDEWY
MALEATE	MANUALS	MARVELS	MEANEST	MERITED	MILEAGE
MALEFIC	MANUKAU	MARXISM	MEANING	MERMAID	MILIARY
MALINES	MANURED	MARXIST	MEASLES	MERRIER	MILIEUS
MALINKE	MANURER	MASBATE	MEASURE	MERRILY	MILIEUX
MALLARD	MANX CAT	MASCARA	MEATIER	MESARCH	MILITIA
MALLETS	MANXMAN	MASCOTS	MEATILY	MESHING	MILKERS
MALLEUS	MAOISTS	MASHHAD	MEDDLED	MESSAGE	MILKIER
MALLOWS	MAPPING	MASHING	MEDIACY	MESSIAH	MILKILY
MALMSEY	MARABOU	MASKING	MEDIANS	MESSIER	MILKING
MALTASE	MARACAS	MASONIC	MEIANT	MESSILY	MILKMAN
MALTESE	MARACAY	MASONRY	MEDIATE	MESSINA	MILK RUN
MALTING	MARASCA	MASQUES	MEDICAL	MESSING	MILKSOP
MALTOSE	MARATHA	MASSAGE	MEDICOS	MESS-UPS	MILLDAM
MAMILLA	MARITHI	MASSUER	MEDIUMS	MESTIZA	MILLERS
MAMMALS	MARBLED	MASSIFS	MEDLARS	MESTIZO	MILLINE
MAMMARY	MARBLES	MASSING	MEDLEYS	METALED	MILLING
MAMMIES	MARCHED	MASSIVE	MEDULLA	METAMER	MILLION
MAMMOTH	MARCHER	MASTERS	MEEKEST	METEORS	MILLRUN
MANACLE	MARCHES	MASTERY	MEEKRAT	METERED	MIMESIS
MANAGED	MAREMMA	MASTIFF	MEETING-	METHANE	MIMETIC
MANAGER	MARGAUX	MASTOID	MEGATION	METHODS	MIMICRY
MANAGUA	MARGINS	MASURIA	MEIOSIS	METIERS	MINABLE
MANAKIN	MARIMBA	MATADOR	\MEIOTIC	METONYM	MINARET
MANATEE	MARINAS	MATCHED	MEISSEN	METOPIC	MINCERS
MANDATE	MARINER	MATCHES	MELANGE	METRICS	MINCING
MANDREL	MARINES	MATHURA	MELANIC	METREFY	MINDERS
MANGERS	MARITAL	MATINEE	MELANIN	METRIST	MINDFUL
MANGIER	MARKERS	MATRONS	MELILOT	MEXICAN	MINDING
MANGILY	MARKETS	MATTERS	MELISMA	MIAWED	MINERAL
MANGLED	MARKHOR	MATTING	MELODIC	MIASMAL	MINGIER
MANGOES	MARKING	MATYTINS	MELTAGE	MIASMAS	MINGLED
MANHOLE	MARKUPS	MATTOCK	MELTING	MICELLE	MINIBUS
MANHOOD	MARLINE	MATURED	MEMBERS	MICKEYS	MINICAB
MANHOUR	MARLINS	MAUDLIN	MEMENTO	MICROBE	MINIMAL

MINIMAX	MITOSIS	MONKEYS	MOSQUES	MUGGING	MUZZLES
MINIMUM	MITOTIC	MONKISH	MOSSIER	MIGGINS	MYALGIA
MINIMUS	MITTENS	MONOCLE	MOTHERS	MUGSHOT	MYALGIC
MINIONS	MITZVAH	MONOMER	MOTIONS	MUGWORT	MYCENAE
MINIVER	MIXABLE	MONSOON	MOTIONS	MUGWUMP	MYCOSIS
MINIVET	MIXED UP	MONSTER	MOTIVES	MULATTO	MYCOTIC
MINNOWS	MIXTURE	MONTAGE	MOTORED	MULCHED	MYELOID
MINORCA	MIZORAM	MONTANA	MOTTLED	MULCTED	MYELOMA
MINSTER	MOANERS	MONTANE	MOTTOES	MULLAHS	MYIASIS
MINTAGE	MOANING	MONTHLY	MOUFLON	MULLEIN	MYNHEER
MINTING	MOBBING	MOOCHED	MOUILLE	MUMBLED	MYOLOGY
MINUETS	MOBILES	MOOCHER	MOULDED	MUMBLER	MYOTOME
MINUSES	MOBSTER	MOODIER	MOULDER	MUMMERS	MYRAIDS
MINUTED	MOCKERS	MOODILY	MOUNTED	MUMMERY	MYRTLES
MINUTES	MOCKERY	MOONEYE	MOULTER	MUMMIES	MYSTERY
MINXISH	MOCKING	MOONILY	MOUNTED	MUMMIFY	MYSTICS
MIOCENE	MOCK-UPS	MOONING	MOUNTER	MUMMING	MYSTIFY
MIRACLE	MODALLY	MOONLIT	MOUNTILE	MUNCHED	
MIRADOR	MODCONS	MOONSET	MOURNED	MUNCHER	
MIRAGES	MODELED	MOORAGE	MOURNER	MUNDANE	**8 LETTERS**
MIRRORS	MODERAS	MOORHEN	MOUSERS	MUNSTER	MACADMIA
MISCALL	MODERNS	MOORING	MOUSIER	MUNTJAC	MACARONI
MISCAST	MODESTY	MOORISH	MOUSING	MURDERS	MACAROON
MISDEAL	MODICUM	MOOTING	MOUSSES	MURKIER	MACERATE
MISDEED	MODISTE	MOPPETS	MOUTHED	MURKILY	MACHETES
MISERLY	MODULAR	MOPPNG	MOUTHER	MURMURS	MACHINES
MISFILE	MODULES	MORAINE	MOVABLE	MURRAIN	MACHINES
MISFIRE	MODULUS	MORALLY	MOVABLY	MUSCLED	MACHISMO
MISFITS	MOFETTE	MORAVIA	MOVIOLA	MUSCLES	MACKERAL
MISHAPS	MOGADOR	MORCEAU	MUCKIER	MUSEFUL	MACRURAL
MISHEAR	MOGGIES	MORDANT	MUCKILY	MUSEUMS	MADDENED
MISKOLC	MOGILEV	MORDENT	MUCKING	MUSHIER	MADHOUSE
MISLAID	MOHICAN	MORDVIN	MUD BATH	MUSHILY	MADONNAS
MISLEAD	MOIDORE	MOREISH	MUDDIED	MUSICAL	MADRIGAL
MISPLAY	MOISTEN	MORELLA	MUDDIER	MUSKETS	MADURESE
MISREAD	MOISTLY	MORELLO	MUDDING	MUSKIER	MAEBASHI
MISRULE	MOLDER	MORELOS	MUDDLED	MUSKRAT	MAENADIC
MISSALS	MOLDING	MORGUES	MUDDLER	MUSLIMS	MAESTROS
MISSIES	MOLLIFY	MORMONS	MUDDLES	MUSSELS	MAGAZINE
MISSILE	MOLLUSC	MORNING	MUDFISH	MUSSING	MAGELLAN
MISSING	MOLTING	MOROCCO	MUDFLAP	MUSTANG	MAGHREBI
MISSION	MOMBASA	MORONIC	MUDFLAT	MUSTARD	MAGIC EYE
MISSIVE	MOMENTA	MORROWS	MUDPACK	MUSTERS	MAGICIAN
MISTAKE	MOMENTS	MORSELS	MUDFLAT	MUSTIER	MAGNATES
MISTERS	MOMMIES	MORTALS	MUDPACK	MUSTILY	MAGNESIA
MISTILY	MONACAN	MORTARS	MUD PIES	MUTABLE	MAGNETIC
MISTIME	MONADIC	MORTIFY	MUEZZIN	MUTABLY	MAGNETOS
MISTING	MONARCH	MORTISE	MUFFING	MUTAGEN	MAGNOLIA
MISTOOK	MONARDA	MORULAR	MUFFINS	MUTANTS	MAHARAJA
MISTRAL	MONDAYS	MOSAICS	MUFFLED	MUTTONY	MAHARANI
MISUSED	MONEYED	MOSELLE	MUFFLER	MUZZIER	MAHATMAS
MISUSER	MONGOLS	MOSEYED	MUGGERS	MUZZILY	MAHOGANY
MISUSES	MONGREL	MOSLEMS	MUGGIER	MUZZLED	MAIDENLY
MITHRAS	MONITOR	MOSOTHO	MUGGILY	MUZZLER	MAIEUTIC

MAILABLE	MANGANIC	MARINADE	MATERIAL	MEGALITH
MAILBAGS	MANGANIN	MARINATE	MATERNIE	MEGATONS
MAILSHOT	MANGIEST	MARINERS	MATERNAL	MEGAVOLT
MAINLAND	MANGLING	MARIPOSA	MATINEES	MEGAWATT
MAIN LINE	MANGONEL	MARITIME	MATRICES	MELAMINE
MAINMAST	MANGROVE	MARJORAM	MATRIXES	MELANGES
MAINSAIL	MANHOLES	MARKDOWN	MATRONAL	MELANISM
MAINSTAY	MANHOURS	MARKEDLY	MATRONLY	MELANIST
MAINTAIN	MANHUNTS	MARKETED	MATTERED	MELANITE
MAJESTIC	MANIACAL	MARKETER	MATTRESS	MELANOID
MAJOLICA	MANICURE	MARKINGS	MATURATE	MELANOMA
MAJORING	MANIFEST	MARKSMAN	MATURELY	MELANOUS
MAJORITY	MANIFOLD	MARKSMEN	MATURING	MELINITE
MALADIES	MANIKINS	MARMOSET	MATURITY	MELLOWED
MALAGASY	MANITOBA	MAROONED	MAVERICK	MELLOWER
MALAISES	MANILEST	MAROQUIN	MAXILLAR	MELLOWLY
MALAPROP	MANNERED	MARQUEES	MAXIMIZE	MELODEON
MALARIAL	MANNERLY	MARQUESS	MAXIMUMS	MELODIES
MALARKEY	MANNHEIM	MARQUAISE	MAYORESS	MELODIST
MALAYSIA	MANNITIC	MARRIAGE	MAYPOLES	MELODIZE
MAL DE MER	MANNITOL	MARRIEDS	MAZATLAN	MELTABLE
MALDIVES	MAN-OF-WAR	MARRYING	MAZURKAS	MELTDOWN
MALENESS	MANORIAL	MARSHALS	MEA CULPA	MEMBRANE
MALIGNED	MANPOWER	MARSH GAS	MEAGRELY	MEMENTOS
MALIGNER	MANSARDS	MARTAGON	MEALIEST	MEMORIAL
MALIGNLY	MANSIONS	MARTELLO	MEALWORM	MEMORIES
MALINGER	MAN-SIZED	MARTIANS	MEANINGS	MEMORIZE
MALLARDS	MANTILLA	MARTINET	MEANNESS	MEMSAHIB
MALPOSED	MANTISES	MARTINIS	MEANTIME	MENACING
MALTREAT	MANTISSA	MARTYRED	MEASURED	MENARCHE
MALTSTER	MANTLING	MARVELED	MEASURER	MENDABLE
MALVASIA	MAN-TO-MAN	MARXISTS	MEASURES	MENHADEN
MAMA'S BOY	MANUALLY	MARYLAND	MEATBALL	MENIALLY
MAMMOTHS	MANURING	MARZIPAN	MEATIEST	MENINGES
MANACLED	MANX CATS	MASSACRE	MECHANIC	MEN-OF-WAR
MANACLES	MAPPABLE	MASSAGED	MECONIUM	MENOLOGY
MANAGERS	MAPPINGS	MASSAGER	MEDALLIC	MEN'S ROOM
MANAGING	MAQUETTE	MASSAGES	MEDDLERS	MENSURAL
MANATOID	MARABOUS	MASSEDLY	MEDDLING	MENSWEAR
MANCIPLE	MARANHAO	MASSETER	MEDELLIN	MENTALLY
MANDALAY	MARASMIC	MASSEURS	MEDIALLY	MENTIONS
MANDAMUS	MARASMUS	MASSICOT	MEDIATED	MEPHITIC
MANDARIN	MARATHON	MASTERED	MEDIATOR	MEPHITIS
MANDATED	MARAUDER	MASTERLY	MEDICAID	MERCHANT
MANDATES	MARBLING	MASTHEAD	MEDICALS	MERCIFUL
MANDIBLE	MARCHERS	MASTIFFS	MEDICARE	MERCURIC
MANDOLIN	MARCHESA	MASTITIS	MEDICATE	MERGENCE
MANDORLA	MARCHESE	MASTODON	MEDICINE	MERIDIAN
MANDRAKE	MARCHING	MASTOIDS	MEDIEVAL	MERINGUE
MANDRILL	MARGARIC	MASURIAN	MEDICRE	MERISTEM
MAN-EATER	MARGINAL	MATABELE	MEDITATE	MERISTIC
MANEUVER	MARIANAO	MATADORS	MEDUSOID	MERITING
MANFULLY	MARIGOLD	MATCHBOX	MEEKNESS	MERMAIDS
MANGABEY	MARIMBAS	MATCHING	MEETINGS	MERRIEST

MESCALIN	MIGRANTS	MINUTING	MOBSTERS	MONKHOOD
MESDAMES	MIGRATED	MIRACLES	MOCCASIN	MONOACID
MESMERIC	MIGRATOR	MIREPOIX	MOCKABLE	MONOCARP
MESOCARP	MILANESE	MIRRORED	MODALITY	MONOCLES
MESODERM	MILCH COW	MIRTHFUL	MODELING	MONOCRAT
MESOGLEA	MILDEWED	MISAPPLY	MODELLED	MONOCYTE
MESOZOIC	MILDNESS	MISCARRY	MODELLER	MONOGAMY
MESQUITE	MILEAGES	MISCHIEF	MODERATE	MONOGENY
MESSAGES	MILEPOST	MISCIBLE	MODERATO	MONOGRAM
MESSANIA	MILIARIA	MISCOUNT	MODESTLY	MONOGYNY
MESSIAHS	MILITANT	MISDEEDS	MODIFIED	MONOHULL
MESSIEST	MILITARY	MISERERE	MODIFIER	MONOLITH
MESSMATE	MILITATE	MISFIRED	MODIOLUS	MONOLOGY
MESSUAGE	MILITIAS	MISFIRES	MODISHLY	MONOMIAL
MESTIZOS	MILKFISH	MISGUIDE	MODULATE	MONOPOLY
METALING	MILKIEST	MISHEARD	MOHAMMED	MONORAIL
METALLED	MILKMAID	MISHMASH	MOIETIES	MONOSEMY
METALLIC	MILK RUNS	MISJUDGE	MOISTURE	MONOSOME
METAMALE	MILKSOPS	MISLAYER	MOLALITY	MONOTONE
METAMERE	MILKWEED	MISNOMER	MOLASSES	MONOTONY
METAMORE	MILKWORT	MISOGAMY	MOLDAVIA	MONOTYPE
METAPHOR	MILKY WAY	MISOGYNY	MOLDERED	MONOXIDE
METAZOAN	MILLABLE	MISOLOGY	MOLDIEST	MONROVIA
METAZOIC	MILLIARD	MISPLACE	MOLDINGS	MONSIEUR
METEORIC	MILLIARY	MISPLEAD	MOLECULE	MONSOONS
METERING	MILLIBAR	MISPRINT	MOLEHILL	MONSTERS
METHANOL	MIILLINER	MISQUOTE	MOLESKIN	MONTAGES
METHYLAL	MILLIONS	MISSHAPE	MOLESTED	MONTEITH
METHYLIC	MILLPOND	MISSILES	MOLESTER	MONTREAL
METONYMY	MILLRACE	MISSIONS	MOLLUSCS	MONTUENT
METRICAL	MILTONIC	MISSIVES	MOLYBDIC	MOOCHING
METRISTIS	MIMETITE	MISSOURI	MOMENTUM	MOODIEST
MEUNIERE	MIMICKED	MISSPELL	MONACHAL	MOONBEAM
MEXICALI	MIMICKER	MISSPELT	MONADISM	MOONCALF
MEZEREON	MINARETS	MISSPEND	MONANDRY	MOONFISH
MEZEREUM	MINATORY	MISSPENT	MONARCHS	MOONLESS
MEZIERES	MINCEPIE	MISTATES	MONARCHY	MOONRISE
MIAOWING	MINDLESS	MISTAKEN	MONASTIC	MOONSHED
MICELLAR	MIND'S EYE	MISTAKES	MONAURAL	MOON SHOT
MICHIGAN	MINERALS	MISTIMED	MONAZITE	MOONWORT
MICROBES	MINGIEST	MISTREAT	MONETARY	MOORCOCK
MICRODOT	MINGLING	MISTRESS	MONETIZE	MOORHENS
MIDBRAIN	MINI CABS	MISTRIAL	MONEBOX	MOORINGS
MIDDLE CS	MINIMIZE	MISTRUST	MONGOLIA	MOORLAND
MIDDLING	MINIMUMS	MISUSAGE	MONGOLIC	MOORWORT
MIDFIELD	MINISTER	MISUSING	MONGOOSE	MOPINGLY
MIDLANDS	MINISTRY	MITICIDE	MONGRELS	MOQUETTE
MIDNIGHT	MINORCAN	MITIGATE	MONISTIC	MORAINAL
MIDPOINT	MINORITY	MITTIMUS	MONITION	MORAINES
MIDRIIFFS	MINOTAUR	MIXED BAG	MONITORS	MORALISM
MIDWIVES	MINISTERS	MIXTURES	MONITORY	MORALIST
MIGHTIER	MINSTRAL	MNEMONIC	MONKEYED	MORALITY
MIGHTILY	MINUTELY	MOBILIZE	MONKFISH	MORALIZE
MIGRAINE	MINITIAE	MOBOCRAT	MON-KHMER	MORASSES

MORATORY	MOUTHFUL	MUSHIEST	MACHINERY	MAJORETTE
MORAVIAN	MOUTHING	MUSHROOM	MACHINING	MAJOR SUIT
MORBIDLY	MOVABLES	MUSICALE	MACHMETER	MAJUSCULE
MORBIFIC	MOVEMENT	MUSICALS	MACKERELS	MAKESHIFT
MORBIHAN	MOVINGLY	MUSICIAN	MACROCOSM	MAKEYEVKA
MORDANCY	MOZZETTA	MUSINGLY	MACROCYST	MALACHITE
MOREOVER	MUCHNESS	MUSKETRY	MACROCYTE	MALADROIT
MORESQUE	MUCILAGE	MUSKIEST	MACRUOID	MALAGUENA
MORIBUND	MUCINOUS	MUSQUASH	MACRUROUS	MALADERS
MORNINGS	MUCKHEAP	MUSTACHE	MADDENING	MALATHION
MOROCCAN	MUCKIEST	MUSTANGS	MADELEINE	MALAYALAM
MORONISM	MUCKWORM	MUSTERED	MADHOUSES	MALAYSIAN
MOROSELY	MUCOSITY	MUSTIEST	MADREPORE	MALDIVIAN
MORPHEME	MUD BATHS	MUTATION	MADRIGALS	MALFORMED
MORPHEUS	MUDDIEST	MUTENESS	MAELSTROM	MALGRE LUI
MORPHINE	MUDDLING	MUTICOUS	MAGAZINES	MALIC ACID
MORTALLY	MUDDYING	MUTILATE	MAGDEBURG	MALICIOUS
MORTGAGE	MUDFLATS	MUTINEER	MAGICALLY	MALIGNANT
MORTISER	MUDGUARD	MUTINIES	MAGIC EYES	MALIGNING
MORTISES	MUDPACKS	MUTINOUS	MAGICIANS	MALIGNITY
MORTMAIN	MUDSTONE	MUTINIED	MAGIC WAND	MALLEABLE
MORTUARY	MUENSTER	MUTTERED	MAGISTERY	MALLEMUCK
MOSEYING	MUEZZINS	MUTTERER	MAGISTRAL	MALLEOLAR
MOSQUITO	MUFFLERS	MUTUALLY	MAGMATISM	MALLEOLUS
MOSSIEST	MUFFLING	MUZZIEST	MAGNESIAN	MALTINESS
MOTHBALL	MUGGINGS	MUZZLING	MAGNESITE	MALTSTERS
MOTHERED	MUG'S GAME	MYCELIAL	MAGNESUIM	MALVOISIE
MOTHERLY	MUGSHOTS	MYCELIUM	MAGNETICS	MAMA'S
MOTILITY	MUGWUMPS	MYCELOID	MAGNETISM	BOYS
MOTIONED	MULATTOS	MYCETOMA	MAGNETITE	MAMILLARY
MOTIONER	MULBERRY	MYCOLOGY	MAGNETIZE	MAMILLATE
MOTIVATE	MULCHING	MYELINIC	MAGNETRON	MAMMALIAN
MOTIVITY	MULCTING	MYELITIS	MAGNIFICO	MAMMALOGY
MOT JUSTE	MULETEER	MYLONITE	MAGNIFIED	MAMMONISM
MOTORBUS	MULHOUSE	MYOGENIC	MAGNIFIER	MAMMONIST
MOTORCAR	MULISHLY	MYOGRAPH	MAGNITUDE	MANACLING
MOTORING	MULLIONS	MYOLOGIC	MAGNOLIAS	MANCHURIA
MOTORIST	MULTIFID	MYOSOTIS	MAHARAJAH	MANDARINS
MOTORIZE	MULTIPED	MYOTONIA	MAHARAJAS	MANDATARY
MOTORMAN	MULTIPLE	MYOTONIC	MAHARANIES	MANDATING
MOTORMEN	MULTIPLY	MYRIAPOD	MAILBOXES	MANDATORY
MOTORWAY	MUMBLING	MYSTICAL	MAILCOACH	MANDIBLES
MOULDIER	MUNCHING	MYSTIQUE	MAIL ORDER	MANDOLINS
MOULDING	MUNIMENT	MYTHICAL	MAILSHOTS	MANDRAKES
MOULMIEN	MUNITION		MAINFRAME	MANDRILLS
MOULTING	MURALIST		MAINLINED	MAN-EATERS
MOUNTAIN	MURDERED	**9 LETTERS**	MAIN LINES	MAN-EATING
MOUNTIES	MURDERER	MACARONIC	MAINMASTS	MANEUVERS
MOUNTING	MURRAINS	MACAROONS	MAINSAILS	MAN FRIDAY
MOURNERS	MURRELET	MACCABEES	MAINSHEET	MANGALORE
MOURNFUL	MURRHINE	MACEDOINE	MAINSTAYS	MANGANATE
MOURNING	MUSCATEL	MACERATED	MAJESTICS	MANGANITE
MOUSIEST	MUSCLING	MACERATER	MAJESTIES	MANGANOUS
MOUSSAKA	MUSCULAR	MACHINATE	MAJORDOMO	MANGETOUT

MANGINESS	MARSUPIAL	MAYORALITY	MEMBRANES	MESOPHYLL
MANGROVES	MARSUPIUM	MAYORSHIP	MEMORABLE	MESOPHYTE
MANHANDLE	MARTINETS	MEANDERED	MEMORABLY	MESSALINE
MANHATTAN	MARTINMAS	MEANDERER	MEMORANDA	MESSENGER
MANHUNTER	MARTYRDOM	MEANDROUS	MEMORIALS	MESSIANIC
MANICURED	MARTYRING	MEANS TEST	MEMORIZED	MESSIEURS
MANIFESTO	MARVELING	MEANTIMES	MEMORIZER	MESSINESS
MANIFOLDS	MARZIPANS	MEANWHILE	MEMSAHIBS	MESTRANOL
MANIZALES	MASCULINE	MEASURING	MENADIONE	METABOLIC
MANILINESS	MASOCHISM	MEATBALLS	MENAGERIE	METALLINE
MANNEQUIN	MASOCHIST	MEATINESS	MEN-AT-ARMS	METALLING
MANNERISM	MASSACRED	MECHANICS	MENDACITY	METALLIOD
MANNERIST	MASSACRER	MECHANISM	MENDELIAN	METALWORK
MANNISHLY	MASSACRES	MECHANIST	MENDELISM	METAMERAL
MANOEUVRE	MASSAGING	MECHANIZE	MENDICANT	METAPHASE
MANOMETER	MASSIVELY	MEDALLION	MENISCOID	METAPLASM
MANOMETRY	MASS MEDIA	MEDALLIST	MENOPAUSE	METAXYLEM
MANTILLAS	MASTERDOM	MEDIAEVAL	MEN'S ROOMS	METEORITE
MANUBRIAL	MASTERFUL	MEDIATING	MENSTRUAL	METEOROID
MANUBRIUM	MASTERING	MEDIATION	MENSTRUUM	METHADONE
MANY-SIDED	MASTER KEY	MEDIATIVE	MENTAL AGE	METHODISM
MARACAIBO	MASTHEADS	MEDIATIZE	MENTALISM	METHODIST
MARATHONS	MASTICATE	MEDIATORS	MENTALITY	METHODIZE
MARAUDERS	MASTODONS	MEDICABLE	MENTIONED	METHOXIDE
MARAUDING	MATAMOROS	MEDICABLY	MENTIONER	METHYLATE
MARCASITE	MATCHLESS	MEDICALLY	MENTORIAL	METHYLENE
MARCH-PAST	MATCHMARK	MEDICATED	MEPACRINE	METRELGIA
MARDI GRAS	MATCHWOOD	MEDICINAL	MERBROMIN	METRICIZE
MARE'S NEST	MATELASSE	MEDICINES	MERCAPTAN	METRIC TON
MARGARINE	MATERIALS	MEDITATED	MERCENARY	METRIFER
MARGARITA	MATERNITY	MEDITATOR	MERCERIZE	METROLOGY
MARGARITE	MATEYNESS	MEDULLARY	MERCHANTS	METRONOME
MARGINATE	MATRIARCH	MEGACYCLE	MERCILESS	MEZZANINE
MARIGOLDS	MATRICIDE	MEGADEATH	MERCURATE	MEZZOTINT
MARIJUANA	MATRIMONY	MEGAHERTZ	MERCURIAL	MICACEOUS
MARINADES	MATRONAGE	MEGALITHS	MERCUROUS	MICHOACAN
MARINATED	MATSUMOTO	MEGAPHONE	MERGANSER	MICROBIAL
MARITALLY	MATSUYAMA	MEGASPORE	MERIDIANS	MICROCHIP
MARKDOWNS	MATTERING	MELANESIA	MERINGUES	MICROCOPY
MARKETEER	MATUTINAL	MELANOSIS	MERITEDLY	MICROCOSM
MARKETERS	MAULSTICK	MELATONIN	MERITLESS	MICROCYTE
MARKETING	MAUNDERED	MELBOURNE	MEROCRINE	MICRODONT
MARMALADE	MAUNDERER	MELIORATE	MREOZOITE	MICROFILM
MARMOREAL	MAURITIAN	MELIORISM	MERRIMENT	MICROMESH
MARMOSETS	MAURITIUS	MELITOPOL	MERRINESS	MICROPYLE
MAROONING	MAUSOLEAN	MELLOWEST	MERSEBURG	MICROSOME
MARQUETRY	MAUSOLEUM	MELLOWING	MESCALINE	MICROTOME
MARQUISES	MAVERICKS	MELODIOUS-	MESENTARY	MICROTOMY
MARRAKECH	MAWKISHLY	MELODIZER	MESICALLY	MICROTONE
MARRIAGES	MAXILLARY	MELODRAMA	MESMERISM	MICROWAVE
MARROWFAT	MAXIMALLY	MELTDOWNS	MESMERIST	MIDDLE AGE
MARSEILLES	MAXIMIZED	MELTINGLY	MESMERIZE	MIDDLEMAN
MARSHALCY	MAXIMZER	MELTWATER	MESOMORPH	MIDDLEMEN
MARSHALED	MAYFLOWER	MELUNGEON	MESOPAUSE	MIDDLESEX

MIDHEAVEN	MINISKIRT	MITREWORT	MONITORED	MOONSHINE
MIDNIGHTS	MINITRACK	MNEMONICS	MONITRESS	MOON SHOTS
MIDPOINTS	MINISTERS	MOANINGLY	MONKEYING	MOONSTONE
MIDSUMMER	MINITRACK	MOBILIZED	MONKEY NUT	MOOT POINT
MID-WICKET	MINNESOTA	MOBOCRACY	MONKSHOOD	MORACEOUS
MIDWIFERY	MINOR SUIT	MOCCASINS	MONOBASIC	MORADABAD
MIDWINTER	MINSTRELS	MOCKERIES	MONOCHORD	MORALISTS
MIDFITNESS	MINT JULEP	MOCKINGLY	MONOCLINE	MORALIZED
MIGHTIEST	MINUSCULE	MODELLING	MONOCOQUE	MORALIZER
MIGRAINES	MIRRORING	MODERATED	MONOCRACY	MORATORIA
MIGRATING	MIRTHLESS	MODERATES	MONOCULAR	MORBIDITY
MIGRATION	MISADVISE	MODERATOR	MONOCYTIC	MORDACITY
MIGRATORY	MISBEHAVE	MODERATOS	MONODRAMA	MORDANTLY
MILCH COWS	MISBELIEF	MODERNISM	MONOGENIC	MORGANITE
MILESTONE	MISCHANCE	MODERNIST	MONOGRAMS	MORMONISM
MILITANCY	MISCHIEFS	MODERNITY	MONOGRAPH	MORPHEMES
MILITANTS	MISCOUNTS	MODERNIZE	MONOLATER	MORPHEMIC
MILITATED	MISCREANT	MODIFIERS	MONOLATRY	MORPHOSIS
MILK FLOAT	MISCREATE	MODIFYING	MONOLITHS	MORSE CODE
MILKINESS	MISDEALER	MODILLION	MONOLOGIC	MORTALITY
MILKMAIDS	MISDIRECT	MODULATED	MONOLOGUE	MORTAL SIN
MILK SHAKE	MISERABLE	MODULATOR	MONOMANIA	MORTGAGED
MILK TOOTH	MISERABLY	MOISTENED	MONOMERIC	MORTGAGEE
MILLBOARD	MISFIRING	MOISTENER	MONOMETER	MORTGAGES
MILLENARY	MISGIVING	MOISTNESS	MONOPHAGY	MORTGAGOR
MILLENNIA	MISGOVERN	MOLDAVIAN	MONOPHONY	MORTICIAN
MILLEPEDE	MISGUIDED	MOLDAVITE	MONOPLANE	MORTIFIED
MILLEPORE	MISGUIDER	MOLDERING	MONOPSONY	MORTIFIER
MILLERITE	MISHANDLE	MOLDINESS	MONORAILS	MOSAICIST
MILLIBARS	MISINFORM	MOLECULAR	MONOSOMIC	MOSCHATEL
MILLIGRAM	MISJUGDED	MOLECULES	MONOSTICH	MOSQUITOS
MILLINERS	MISJUGDER	MOLEHILLS	MONOSTOME	MOSSINESS
MILLINERY	MISLAYING	MOLESKINS	MONOTONIC	MOTHBALLS
MILLIONTH	MISLEADER	MOLESTERS	MONOTREME	MOTH-EATEN
MILLIPEDE	MISMANAGE	MOLESTING	MONOTYPER	MOTHERING
MILLPONDS	MISNOMER	MOLLIFIED	MONOTYPIC	MOTHPROOF
MILLSTONE	MISONEISM	MOLLIFIER	MONOXIDES	MOTIONING
MILLWHEEL	MISONEIST	MOLLUSCAN	MONSIGNOR	MOTIVATED
MILOMETER	MISPLACED	MOLYBDATE	MONSTROUS	MOTOCROSS
MILWAUKEE	MISPRINTS	MOMENTARY	MONTAUBAN	MOTORBIKE
MIMICKING	MISQUOTED	MOMENTOUS	MONT BLANC	MOTORBOAT
MINARETED	MISREPORT	MOMENTUMS	MONTERREY	MOTORCADE
MINCEMEAT	MISSHAPEN	MONACHISM	MONTHLIES	MOTORCARS
MINCE PIES	MISSILERY	MONARCHAL	MONITCULE	MOTORISTS
MINCINGLY	MISSTATED	MONASTERY	MONTRUELL	MOTORIZED
MINEFIELD	MISTAKING	MONATOMIC	MONUMENTS	MOTORWAYS
MINELAYER	MISTIMING	MONEYBAGS	MONZONITE	MOULDABLE
MINIATURE	MISTINESS	MONEYLESS	MOODINESS	MOULDERED
MINIBUSES	MISTLETOE	MONEYWORT	MOONBEAMS	MOULDIEST
MINIDRESS	MISTRIALS	MONGERING	MOON-FACED	MOULDINGS
MINIMALLY	MITICIDAL	MONGOLIAN	MOONINESS	MOUNTABLE
MINIMIZED	MITIGABLE	MONGOLISM	MOONLIGHT	MOUNTAINS
MINIMIZER	MITIGATED	MONGOLOID	MOONRAKER	MOUSETAIL
MINISCULE	MITIGATOR	MONGOOSES	MOONSCAPE	MOUSETRAP

MOUSINESS	MUSIC HALL	MACROCOSMS	MALTHUSIAN
MOUSTACHE	MUSICIANS	MACROCYTIC	MALTREATED
MOUTHFULS	MUSKETEER	MACROGRAPH	MALTREATER
MOUTHPART	MUSKINESS	MACROPHAGE	MALVACEOUS
MOUTHWASH	MUSKMELON	MACROSPORE	MANAGEABLE
MOVEABLES	MUSLIMISM	MACULATION	MANAGEABLY
MOVEMENTS	MUSTACHES	MADAGASCAN	MANAGEMENT
MOVIE STAR	MUSTACHIO	MADAGASCAR	MANAGERESS
MOVIETONE	MUSTERLINE	MADREPORAL	MANAGERIAL
MOVING VAN	MUSTERING	MAELSTROMS	MANCHINEEL
MUCIC ACID	MUSTINESS	MAGIC WANDS	MANCHURIAN
MUCKHEAPS	MUTAGENIC	MAIGISTRACY	MANCUNIANS
MUCKINESS	MUTATIONS	MAGISTRATE	MANEUVERED
MUCKRAKER	MUTILATED	MAGNA CARTA	MAN FRIDAYS
MUCRONATE	MUTILATOR	MAGNETITIC	MANFULNESS
MUDDINESS	MUTINEERS	MAGNETIZED	MANGOSTEEN
MUDGUARDS	MUTINYING	MAGNETIZER	MANHANDLED
MUGGINESS	MUTTERERS	MAGNIFIERS	MANIACALLY
MUGGINSES	MUTTERING	MAGNIFYING	MANICURING
MULATTOES	MUTUALITY	MAGNITUDES	MANICURIST
MULATEERS	MUTUALIZE	MAGNUM OPUS	MANIFESTED
MULLIONED	MUZZINESS	MAIDENHAIR	MANIFESTLY
MULTICIDE	MYCENAEAN	MAIDENHEAD	MANIFESTOS
MULTIFOIL	MYDRIASIS	MAIDENHOOD	MANIFOLDER
MULTIFOLD	MYDREATIC	MAIDEN NAME	MANIPULATE
MULTIFORM	MYOGLOBIN	MAIN CHANCE	MANEQUINS
MULTIHULL	MYOGRAPHY	MAIN CLAUSE	MANNERISMS
MULTIPARA	MYOLOGIST	MAIN FRAMES	MANOEUVRED
MULTIPLES	MYROBALAN	MAINLINING	MANOEUVRER
MULTIPLET	MYSTAGOGY	MAINSPRING	MANOEUVRES
MULTIPLEX	MYSTERIES	MAINSTREAM	MAN OF STRAW
MUTLITUDE	MYSTICISM	MAINTAINED	MANOMETERS
MUMMIFIED	MYSTIFIER	MAINTAINER	MANOR HOUSE
MUNDANELY	MYSTIQUES	MAISONETTE	MANSERVANT
MUNICIPAL	MYTHICIZE	MAJOR-DOMOS	MANTELTREE
MUNIMENTS	MYTHOLOGY	MAJORETTES	MANTICALLY
MUNITIONS	MYXOEDEMA	MAJORITIES	MANUSCRIPT
MURDERERS	MYXOVIRUS	MAJUSCULAR	MANZANILLA
MURDERESS		MAKESHIFT	MARASCHINO
MURDERING		MAKEWEIGHT	MARCESCENT
MURDEROUS	**10 LETTERS-**	MALACOLOGY	MARCH-PASTS
MURKINESS	MAASTRICHT	MALADDRESS	MARCONI RIG
MURMURING	MACADAMIZE	MALAPROPOS	MARE'S NESTS
MUSACEOUS	MACEBEARER	MALCONTENT	MARGARITAS
MUSCADINE	MACEDONIAN	MALEFACTOR	MARGINALIA
MUSCARINE	MACERATING	MALEFICENT	MARGINALLY
MUSCATELS	MACERATION	MALEVOLENT	MARGUERITE
MUSCLEMAN	MACERATIVE	MALFEASANT	MARINATING
MUSCLEMEN	MACHINABLE	MALIGNANCY	MARINATION
MUSCOVADO	MACHINATOR	MALINGERED	MARIONETTE
MUSCOVITE	MACHINE GUN	MALINGERER	MARKEDNESS
MUSHINESS	MACHINISTS	MALODOROUS	MARKETABLE
MUSHROOMS	MACH NUMBER	MALPIGHIAN	MARKETABLY
MUSICALLY	MACKINTOSH	MALTED MILK	MARKETEERS

537

MARKET TOWN	MATURATION	MELODRAMAS	METAPHRASE
MARKSWOMAN	MATURATIVE	MELTING POT	METAPHRAST
MARLACIOUS	MAUDLINISM	MEMBERSHIP	METAPHYSIC
MARQUISATE	MAUNDERING	MEMBRANOUS	METAPLASIA
MARROWBONE	MAURITANIA	MEMORANDUM	METASTABLE
MARSHALING	MAUSOLEUMS	MEMORIZING	METASTASIS
MARSHALLED	MAXILLIPED	MENACINGLY	METASTATIC
MARSHALLER	MAXIMALIST	MENAGERIES	METATARUS
MARSHINESS	MAXIMIZING	MENARCHEAL	METATHEORY
MARSUPIALS	MAXISINGLE	MENDACIOUS	METATHESIS
MARTELLATO	MAYONNAISE	MENDICANCY	METATHETIC
MARTENSITE	MAYORESSES	MENDICANTS	METATHORAX
MARTIAL ART	MEADOWLARK	MENINGITIC	METEORITES
MARTIALISM	MEAGRENESS	MENINGITIS	METEORITIC
MARTIALIST	MEANDERING	MEN OF STRAW	METHIONINE
MARTIAL LAW	MEANINGFUL	MENOPAUSAL	METHODICAL
MARTINGALE	MEANS TESTS	MENOPAUSIC	METHODISTS
MARTINICAN	MEASLINESS	MENSTRUATE	METHODIZER
MARTINIQUE	MEASURABLE	MENSTRUOUS	METHUSELAH
MARVELLING	MEASURABLY	MENSURABLE	METHYLATOR
MARVELLOUS	MEASUREDLY	MENTAL AGES	METHYLDOPA
MARVELMENT	MECHANICAL	MENTAL NOTE	METICULOUS
MARXIANISM	MECHANISMS	MENTIONING	METOESTRUS
MASOCHISTS	MECHANIZED	MERCANTILE	METRICALLY
MASQUERADE	MECHANIZER	MERCAPTIDE	METRICIZED
MASSACRING	MEDALLIONS	MERIDIONAL	METRIC TONS
MASSASAUGA	MEDALLISTS	MERRYMAKER	METRONOMES
MASSETERIC	MEDDLESOME	MERSYSIDE	METRONOMIC
MASTECTOMY	MEDDLINGLY	MESENCHYME	METRONYMIC
MASTER CARD	MEDICAMENT	MESENTERIC	METROPOLIS
MASTERHOOD	MEDICATION	MESENTERON	METTLESOME
MASTERKEYS	MEDICATIVE	MESITYLENE	MEZZANINES
MASTERMIND	MEDIOCRITY	MESMERISTS	MEZZOTINTS
MASTERSHIP	MEDITATING	MESMERIZED	MICHELMAS
MASTERWORK	MEDITATION	MESMERIZER	MICKEY FINN
MASTICABLE	MEDIUM WAVE	MESOCRATIC	MICROCHIPS
MASTICATED	MEDULLATED	MESODERMAL	MICROCLINE
MASTICATOR	MEERSCHAUM	MESOLITHIC	MICROCOSMS
MASTURBATE	MEGAGAMETE	MESOMORPHY	MICROCYTIC
MATCHBOARD	MEGALITHIC	MESOPHYTIC	MICROFICHE
MATCHBOXES	MEGAPHONES	MESOSPHERE	MICROFILMS
MATCHMAKER	MEGAPHONIC	MESOTHORAX	MICROGRAPH
MATCH POINT	MEGASPORIC	MESSENGERS	MICROMETER
MATCHSTICK	MELANCHOLY	METABOLISM	MICROMETRY
MATERIALLY	MELANESIAN	METABOLITE	MICROPHONE
MATERNALLY	MELANISTIC	METABOLIZE	MICROPHYTE
MATO GROSSO	MELANOCYTE	METACARPAL	MICROPRINT
MATRIARCHS	MELANOSITY	METACARPUS	MICROPYLAR
MATRIARCHY	MELBURNIAN	METACENTRE	MICROSCOPE
MATRICIDAL	MELIACEOUS	METAFEMALE	MICROSCOPY
MATRICIDES	MELIORABLE	METAGALAXY	MICROSEISM
MATRILOCAL	MELISMATIC	METALLURGY	MICROSOMAL
MATTERHORN	MELLOPHONE	METAMERISM	MICROSPORE
MATTRESSES	MELLOWNESS	METAPHORIC	MICROTOMIC

MICROTONAL	MINISTERED	MISTAKENLY	MONOCARPIC
MICROWAVES	MINISTRAINT	MISTRESSES	MONOCHROME
MIDDLE-AGED	MINISTRIES	MISTRUSTED	MONOCLINAL
MIDDLE AGES	MINNESOTAN	MISTRUSTER	MONOCLINIC
MIDDLEBROW	MINORITIES	MITIGATING	MONOCRATIC
MIDDLE EAST	MINOR SUITS	MITIGATION	MONOCYCLIC
MIDDLE NAME	MINSTRELSY	MITIGATIVE	MONOCYTOID
MIDDLE WEST	MINT JULEPS	MIXABILITY	MONOECIOUS
MIDLOTHIAN	MINISCULAR	MIXED GRILL	MONOGAMIST
MIDSECTION	MINUTENESS	MIXOLYDIAN	MONOGAMOUS
MIDSHIPMAN	MIRACIDIAL	MIZZENMAST	MONOGENOUS
MIDSHIPMEN	MIRACIDIUM	MOBILE HOME	MONOGRAPHS
MIGHTINESS	MIRACULOUS	MOBILIZING	MONOGYNIST
MIGNONETTE	MIRTHFULLY	MOBOCRATIC	MONOGYNOUS
MIGRAINOID	MISAPPLIED	MOCK-HEROIC	MONOHYBRID
MIGRATIONS	MISBEHAVED	MODERATELY	MONOLITHIC
MILOMETER	MISBEHAVER	MODERATING	MONOLOGIST
MILESTONES	MISCALLING	MODERATION	MONOLOGUES
MILITANTLY	MISCARRIED	MODERATORS	MONOMANIAC
MILITARILY	MISCASTING	MODERNISMS	MONOMEROUS
MILITARISM	MISCELLANY	MODERNIST	MONOPHOBIA
MILITARIST	MISCHANCES	MODERNIZED	MONOPHOBIC
MILITARIZE	MISCH METAL	MODERNIZER	MONOPHONIC
MILITATING	MISCONDUCT	MODERNNESS	MONOPLANES
MILITATION	MISCOUNTED	MODIFIABLE	MONOPLEGIA
MILITIAMEN	MISCREANTS	MODISHNESS	MONOPLEGIC
MILK FLOATS	MISERICORD	MODULATING	MONOPODAIL
MILK SHAKES	MISFORTUNE	MODULATION	MONOPODUIM
MILLENNIAL	MISGIVINGS	MODULATIVE	MONOPOLIES
MILLENNIUM	MISHANDLED	MOGADISCIO	MONOPOLISM
MILLEPEDES	MISHEARING	MOHAMMEDAN	MONOPOLUST
MILLESIMAL	MISJOINDER	MOISTENING	MONOPOLIZE
MILLIGRAMS	MISJUDGING	MOISTURIZE	MONOPTEROS
MILLILITRE	MISLEADING	MOLLIFYING	MONOTHEISM
MILLIMETRE	MISMANAGED	MOLLUSCOID	MONOTHEIST
MILLIONTHS	MISMANAGER	MOYLBDENUM	MONOTONOUS
MILLIPEDES	MISMATCHED	MONADISTIC	MONOVALENT
MILLSTONES	MISMATHCES	MONADOLOGY	MONSIGNORS
MILLSTREAM	MISOGAMIST	MONANDROUS	MONSTRANCE
MILLWHEELS	MISOGYNIST	MONANTHOUS	MONTE CARLO
MILLWRIGHT	MISOGYNOUS	MONARCHIES	MONTENEGRO
MILOMETERS	MISOLOGIST	MONARCHIST	MONTEVIDEO
MIMEOGRAPH	MISPLACING	MONEGASQUE	MONTGOMERY
MINATORILY	MISPRINTED	MONETARISM	MONTMARTE
MINDLESSLY	MISPRISION	MONETARIST	MONUMENTAL
MIND READER	MISQUOTING	MONEYBOXES	MONZONITIC
MINEFIELDS	MISREADING	MONEYMAKER	MOONFLOWER
MINERALIZE	MISSIONARY	MONEY ORDER	MOONSCAPES
MINEROLOGY	MISSOURIAN	MONGRELISM	MOONSTONES
MINERAL OIL	MISSPELLED	MONGRELIZE	MOONSTRUCK
MINESTONE	MISSTATING	MONILIFORM	MOOT POINTS
MINATURES	MISSUPPOSE	MONITORIAL	MORALISTIC
MINIMALIST	MISTAKABLE	MONITORING	MORALITIES
MINIMIZING	MISTAKABLY	MONKEY NUTS	MORALIZERS

MORALIZING
MORATORIUM
MORBIDNESS
MORDACIOUS
MORDVINIAN
MORGANATIC
MOROSENESS
MORPHEUSES
MORPHINISM
MORPHOLOGY
MORTAL SINS
MORTGAGES
MORTGAGING
MORTGAGORS
MORTICIANS
MORTIFYING
MORTUARIES
MOSQUITOES
MOTHERHOOD
MOTHERLESS
MOTHER'S BOY
MOTHER'S DAY
MOTHER-TO-BE
MOTHERWORT
MOTIONLESS
MOTIVATING
MOTIVATION
MOTIVATIVE
MOTIVELESS
MOTONEURON
MOTORBIKES
MOTORCADES
MOTORCYCLE
MOTORIZING
MOTOR LODGE
MOTS JUSTES
MOULDBOARD
MOULDERING
MOULDINESS
MOUNTEBANK
MOURNFULLY
MOUSETRAPS
MOUSSELINE
MOUSTACHES
MOUTH ORGAN
MOUTHPIECE
MOVABILITY
MOVIE STARS
MOVING VANS
MOZAMBIQUE
MOZZARELLA
MUCKRAKERS
MUCKRAKING
MUDDLINGLY

MIDSKIPPER
MUDSLINGER
MUHAMMADAN
MULBERRIES
MULIEBRITY
MULISHNESS
MULTIBIRTH
MULTIMEDIA
MULTIPLANE
MULTIPLIED
MULTIPLIER
MULTISTAGE
MULTITUDES
MUMBLINGLY
MUMBO JUMBO
MUMMIFYING
MUNIFICENT
MURPHY'S LAW
MUSCOVITES
MUSCULARLY
MUSHROOMED
MUSICAL BOX
MUSIC HALLS
MUSICOLOGY
MUSKETEERS
MUSKETRIES
MUSTARD GAS
MUTABILITY
MUTATIONAL
MUTILATING
MUTILATION
MUTILATIVE
MUTINOUSLY
MUTUAL FUND
MYASTHENIA
MYASTHENIC
MYCETOZOAN
MYCOLOGIST
MYCORRHIZA
MYCOSTATIN
MYOCARDIAL
MYOCARDIUM
MYOGRAPHIC
MYOPICALLY
MYRIAPODAN
MYRTACEOUS
MYSTAGOGIC
MYSTAGOGUE
MYSTERIOUS
MYSTICALLY
MYSTIFYING
MYTHICIZER
MYTHOMANIA
MYTHOPOEIA

MYTHOPOEIC
MYXOEDEMIC
MYXOMATOUS
MYXOMYCETE

11 LETTERS
MACADAMIZER
MACHICOLATE
MACHINATION
MACHINE CODE
MACHINE GUNS
MACHINE TOOL
MACROBIOTIC
MACROCOSMIC
MACROGAMETE
MACROPHAGIC
MACROSCOPIC
MADDENINGLY
MADEIRA CAKE
MADRIGALIAN
MAGGOTINESS
MAGISTERIAL
MAGISTRALLY
MAGISTRATES
MAGLEMOSIAN
MAGNANIMITY
MAGNANIMITY
MAGNANIMOUS
MAGNETIZING
MAGNIFIABLE
MAGNIFICENT
MAHARASHTRA
MAIDENHEADS
MAIDEN NAMES
MAIDSERVANT
MAILING LIST
MAIN CLAUSES
MAINSPRINGS
MAINTAINING
MAINTENANCE
MAIN-TOPMAST
MAINTOPSAIL
MASONETTES
MAKE-BELIEVE
MAKHACHKALA
MALADJUSTED
MALADROITLY
MALAPROPIAN
MALAPROPISM
MALCONTENTS
MALEDICTION
MALEDICTIVE
MALEFACTION

MALEFACTORS
MALEFICENCE
MALFEASANCE
MALFUNCTION
MALICIOUSLY
MALIGNANTLY
MALINGERERS
MALINGERING
MALOCCLUDED
MALONIC ACID
MALPOSITION
MALPRACTICE
MALTED MILKS
MALTREATING
MAMMALOGIST
MAMMIFEROUS
MAMMONISTIC
MANAGEMENTS
MANDATORILY
MANDOLINIST
MANEUVERING
MANHANDLING
MANICHAEISM
MANICURISTS
MANIFESTING
MANIFESTOES
MANIPULATED
MANIPULATOR
MANNERISTIC
MANNISHNESS
MANOEVERING
MANOR HOUSES
MANSERVANTS
MANTELPIECE
MANTELSHELF
MANTOUX TEST
MANUFACTORY
MANUFACTURE
MANUSCRIPTS
MARASCHINOS
MARCESCENCE
MARCHIONESS
MARE CLAUSUM
MARE LIBERUM
MARGINALITY
MARGINATION
MARICULTURE
MARINE CORPS
MARIONETTES
MARKETPLACE
MARKET PRICE
MARKET TOWNS
MARKOV CHAIN
MARLBOROUGH

MARQUESSATE	MEANDERINGS	MERCENARILY	MICROFILMED
MARQUISETTE	MEANINGLESS	MERCHANDISE	MICROAMETE
MARAM GRASS	MEASUREMENT	MERCHANTMAN	MICROGRAPHY
MARROW BONES	MECHANICIAN	MERCILESSLY	MICROGROOVE
MARSHALLING	MECHANISTIC	MERCURATION	MICROMETERS
MARSHMALLOW	MACHANIZING	MERCURIALLY	MICROMETRIC
MARTENSITIC	MACKLENBURG	MERITOCRACY	MICROPHONES
MARTIAL ARTS	MADIASTINAL	MERITORIOUS	MICROPHONIC
MARTINETISH	MADIASTINUM	MEROBLASTIC	MICROPHYTIC
MARTINETIM	MEDICAMENTS	MERRYMAKERS	MICROREADER
MARTYROLOGY	MEDICATIONS	MERRYMAKING	MICROSCOPES
MASCULINITY	MEDICINE MAN	MESALLIANCE	MICROSCOPIC
MASKING TAPE	MEDICINE EN	MESENCHYMAL	MICROSECOND
MASOCHISTIC	MEDIEVALISM	MESMERIZING	MICROSPORIC
MASONICALLY	MEDIEVALIST	MESOBENTHOS	MICROTOMIST
MASQUERADED	MEDITATIONS	MESOCEPHALY	MIDDLEBROWS
MASQUERADER	MEERSCHAUMS	MESOGASTRIC	MIDDLECLASS
MASQUERADES	MEGACEPHALY	MESOMORPHIC	MIDDLENAMES
MASSACHUSET	MEGALOBLAST	MESONEPHRIC	MIDDLE-SIZED
MASSIVENESS	MEGALOMANIA	MESONEPHROS	MIDNIGHT SUN
MASS-PRODUCE	MEGALOPOLIS	MESOPHYLLIC	MIGRATIONAL
MASTER CARDS	MEITOTICALLY	MESOPOTOMIA	MILITARISTS
MASTERFULLY	MELANCHOLIA	MESOSPHERIC	MILITARIZED
MASTER MINDS	MELANCHOLIC	MESOTHELIAL	MILLEFLEURS
MASTER PIECE	MELIORATION	MESOTHELIUM	MILLENARIAN
MASTER WORKS	MELIORATIVE	MESOTHORIUM	MILLILITRES
MASTICATING	MELLIFEROUS	METABOLISMS	MILLIMETRES
MASTICATION	MELLIFLUOUS	METACETRIC	MILLIMICRON
MASTICATORY	MELODICALLY	METAGENESIS	MILLIONAIRE
MASTOIDITIS	MELODIOUSLY	METAGENETIC	MILLISECOND
MASTURBATED	MELTABILITY	METALLOCENE	MIMEOGRAPHS
MATCHLESSLY	MELTING POTS	METALLOIDAL	MIMETICALLY
MATCHMAKERS	MEMBERSHIPS	METALLURGIC	MIMOSACEOUS
MATCHMAKING	MEMORABILIA	METALWORKER	MINAS GERAIS
MATCH POINTS	MEMORANDUMS	METAMORPHIC	MIND-BENDING
MATCH STICKS	MEMORIALIST	METANEPHROS	MIND-BLOWING
MATERIALIM	MEMORIALIZE	METAPHYSICS	MINDFULNESS
MATERIALIST	MEMORIZABLE	METAPLASMIC	MIND READERS
MATERIALITY	MENAQUINONE	METASTASIZE	MIND READING
MATERIALIZE	MENDELIVIUM	METATHERIAN	MINERALIZER
MATERNALISM	MENDEL'S LAWS	METATHESIZE	MINERAL OILS
MATHEMATICS	MENORRHAGIA	METEMPIRICS	MIESWEEPER
MATINEE IDOL	MENORRHAGIC	METEOOLOGY	MINIATURIST
MATRIARCHAL	MENSTRUATED	METHODOLOGY	MINIATURIZE
MATRICULANT	MENSURATION	METHYLAMINE	MINIMUM WAGE
MATRICULATE	MENSURATIVE	METHYLATION	MINISTERIAL
MATRILINEAL	MENTALISTIC	METONYMICAL	MINISTERING
MATRIMONIAL	MENTALITIES	METRICATION	MINISTERIUM
MAUDLINNESS	MENTAL NOTES	METRICIZING	MINISTRANTS
MAUNDY MONEY	MENTHACEOUS	METROLOGIST	MINOR PLANET
MAURITANIAN	MENTHOLATED	MICKEY MOUSE	MINUTE STEAK
MAWKISHNESS	MENTIONABLE	MICROCCOCUS	MIRACLE PLAY
MAYONNAISES	MEPROBAMATE	MICROCOSMIC	MIRTHLESSLY
MEADOWSWEET	MERCENARIES	MICROFICHES	MISALLIENCE

MISANTHROPE	MOLYBDENITE	MORTALITIES	MYELOMATOID
MISANTHROPY	MOLYBDENOUS	MORTARBOARD	MYOCARDITIS
MISAPPLYING	MOMENTARILY	MORTISE LOCK	MYRIAPODOUS
MISBEGOTTEN	MONARHICAL	MOSQUITO NET	MYRMECOLOGY
MISBEHAVING	MONARCHISTS	MOTHER-IN-LAW	MYSTERY PLAY
MISCARRIAGE	MONEYLENDER	MOTHER'S BOYS	MYSTERY TOUR
MISCARRYING	MONEYMAKERS	MOTHER'S RIUN	MYSTIFIEDLY
MISCELLANEA	MONEYMAKING	MOTHERS-TO-BE	MYTHOLOGIES
MISCHIEVOUS	MONEY ORDERS	MOTHPROOFED	MYTHOLOGIST
MISCIBILITY	MONEY SUP[PLY	MOTORCYCLES	MTHOLOGIST
MISCONCEIVE	MONITORSHIP	MOTORLODGES	MYTHOLOGIZE
MISCONSTRUE	MONOCHASIAL	MOUNTAINEER	MYTHOMANIAC
MISCOUNTING	MONOCHASIUM	MOUNTAINOUS	MYTHOPOEISM
MISCREATION	MONOCHROMAT	MOUNTAINTOP	MYTHOPOEIST
MISDIRECTED	MONOCHROMIC	MOUNTEBANKS	MYOXMATOSIS
MISE-EN SCENE	MONOCLINISM	MOUTHORGANS	
MISERLINESS	MONOCLINOUS	MOUTHPIECES	
MISFEASANCE	MONOCULTURE	MOUTHWASHES	**12 LETTERS**
MISFORTUNES	MONOGENESIS	MUCOPROTEIN	MACHINATIONS
MISGOVERNOR	MONOGENETIC	MUDDLEDNESS	MACHINE CODES
MISGUIDANCE	MONOGRAMMED	MUDSLINGING	MACHINE TOOLS
MISGUIDEDLY	MONOGRAPHER	MUHAMMADANS	MACKINTOSHES
MISHANDLING	MONOGRAPHIC	MULTANGULAR	MACROCLIMATE
MISINFORMED	MONOHYDRATE	MULTNOMINAL	MACROCYTOSIS
MISJUDGMENT	MONOLATROUS	MULTIPARITY	MACROGRAPHIC
MISMANAGING	MONOLINGUAL	MULTIPAROUS	MACRONUCLEUS
MISMATCHING	MONOMANIACS	MULTIPLEXER	MACROPHYSICS
MISOGYNISTS	MONOMORPHIC	MULTIPLYING	MACROPTEROUS
MISONEISTIC	MONONUCLEAR	MULTIRACIAL	MADEMOISELLE
MISPRINTING	MOOPHAGOUS	MULTISCREEN	MAGIC LANTERN
MISREMEMBER	MONOPHTHONG	MULTISTOREY	MAGISTRACIES
MISREPORTED	MONOPOLISTS	MULTIVALENT	MAGISTRATURE
MISSING LINK	MONOPOLIZED	MUDANENESS	MAGNETICALLY
MISSISSAUGA	MONOPOLIZER	MUNICIPALLY	MAGNETIC HEAD
MISSISSIPPI	MONOSTICHIC	MUNIFICENCE	MAGNETIC POLE
MISSPELLING	MOONOSTRPHE	MURDERESSES	MAGNETIC TAPE
MISSPENDING	MONOSTYLOUS	MURDEROUSLY	MAGNETIZABLE
MISTRUSTFUL	MONOTHEISTS	MURMURINGLY	MAGNETOGRAPH
MISTRUSTING	MONOVALENCE	MUSCLE-BOUND	MAGNETOMETER
MITHRIDATIC	MONSEIGNEUR	MUSCOVY DUCK	MAGNETOMETRY
MIXED GRILLS	MONSTRANCES	MUSCULARITY	MAGNIFICENCE
MOBILE HOMES	MONSTROSITY	MUSCULATURE	MAGNILOQUENT
MOBILE PHONE	MONSTROUSLY	MUSEUM PIECE	MAGNITOGORSK
MOBILIZABLE	MONS VENERIS	MUSHROOMING	MAGNIM OPUSES
MOCKING BIRD	MONTENEGRAN	MUSICALNESS	MAIDENLINESS
MODERNISTIC	MONTPELLIER	MUSIC CENTRE	MAID OF HONOUR
MODERNIZING	MOONLIGHTER	MUSKELLUNGE	MAID SERVANTS
MODULATIONS	MORAVIANISM	MUSTACHIOED	MAILING LISTS
MOHAMMEDANS	MORIBUNDITY	MUTILATIONS	MAINTAINABLE
MOISTURIZED	MORNING COAT	MUTTERINGLY	MAITRE D'HOTEL
MOISTURIZER	MORNING STAR	MUTTONCHOPS	MAJESTICALLY
MOLESTATION	MORONICALLY	MUTUAL FUNDS	MAJOR GENERAL
MOLLIFIABLE	MORPHOLOGIC	MYCOLOGICAL	MALACOLOGIST
MOLLYCODDLE	MORRIS DANCE	MYCORRHIZAL	MALAPROPISMS

MALEDICTIONS	MASTERLINESS	MERCHANT NAVY	MICROFILMING
MALEFACTRESS	MASTERMINDED	MERCIFULNESS	MICROGRAPHER
MALEVOLENTLY	MASTER OF ARTS	MERCURIALIZE	MICROGRAPHIC
MALFEASANCES	MASTERPIECES	MERCY KILLING	MICROHABITAT
MALFORMATION	MASTERSTROKE	MERETRICIOUS	MICRONUCLEUS
MALFUNCTIONS	MASTIGOPHORE	MERISTEMTIC	MICROPHYSICS
MALIGNANCIES	MASTURBATING	MEROPLANKTON	MICROSCOPIST
MALIMPRINTED	MASTURBATION	MERRY-GO-ROUND	MICROSECONDS
MALLEABILITY	MATERIALISTS	MESENTERITIS	MICROSEISMIC
MALNOURISED	MATERIALIZED	MESENTERONIC	MICROSTOMOUS
MALNUTRITION	MATERIALIZER	MESMERICALLY	MIDDLE COURSE
MALOCCLUSION	MATHEMATICAL	MESOCEPHALIC	MIDDLE FINGER
MALPRACTICES	MATINEE IDOLS	MESOGASTRIUM	MIDDLE SCHOOL
MALTESE CROSS	MATRICARCHIES	MESOGNATHISM	MIDDLE WEIGHT
MALTREATMENT	MATRICLINOUS	MESOGNATHOUS	MIDSUMMER DAY
MAMMALOGICAL	MATRICULATED	MEOSMORPHISM	MIDWESTERNER
MANAGERESSES	MATRICULATOR	MESOMORPHOUS	MILITARISTIC
MANAGERIALLY	MATRONLINESS	MESOPOTAMIAN	MILITARIZING
MANDARIN DUCK	MATTER-OF-FACT	MESOTHORACIC	MILLEFEUILLE
MANEUVERABLE	MATURATIONAL	METAGALACTIC	MILLENARIANS
MANGEL-WURZEL	MAXIMIZATION	METAGNATHISM	MILLIONAIRES
MANIFESTABLE	MEALY-MOUTHED	METAGNATHOUS	MILTON KEYNES
MANIPULATING	MEANDERINGLY	METALANGUAGE	MIMEOGRAPHED
MANIPULATION	MEANINGFULLY	METALLICALLY	MIND-BOGGLING
MANIPULATIVE	MEASUREMENTS	METALLURGIST	MINDLESSNESS
MANIPULATORY	MECAMYLAMINE	METALWORKERS	MINE DETECTOR
MANNERLINESS	MECHANICALLY	METALWORKING	MINERALOGIST
MANOEUVRABLE	MEDALLIONIST	METAMORPHISM	MINERAL WATER
MAN OF LETTERS	MEDICAMENTAL	METAMORPHOSE	MINESWEEPERS
MANSLAUGHTER	MEDIOCRITIES	METAPHORICAL	MINESWEEPING
MANTELPIECES	MEDITATINGLY	METAPHRASTIC	MINIATURISTS
MANUFACTURAL	MEDITATIVELY	METAPHYSICAL	MINICOMPUTER
MANUFACTURED	MEETING HOUSE	METASOMATISM	MINIFICATION
MANUFACTURER	MEGACEPHALIC	METATHORACIC	MINIMIZATION
MARCASITICAL	MEGALOCARDIA	METEMPIRICAL	MINIMUM WAGES
MARITIME ALPS	MEGALOMANIAC	METEORICALLY	MINISTRATION
MARKET FORCES	MELANCHOLILY	METEOROGRAPH	MINISTRATIVE
MARKET GARDEN	MELODRAMATIC	METHACRYLATE	MINOR PLANETS
MARKET PRICES	MELTING POINT	METHODICALLY	MINUTE STEAKS
MARKSMANSHIP	MEMORABILITY	METHOTREXATE	MIRACLE PLAYS
MARLINESPIKE	MEMORIALIZER	METICULOUSLY	MIRROR IMAGES
MARRIAGEABLE	MEMORIZATION	METONIC CYCLE	MIRTHFULNESS
MARSEILLAISE	MENAGE A TROIS	METROLOGICAL	MISADVENTURE
MARSHALL PLAN	MENDACIOUSLY	METROPOLISES	MISALIGNMENT
MARSHMALLOWS	MEN OF LETTERS	METROPOLITAN	MISALLIANCES
MARSUPIALIAN	MENSTRUATING	METRORRHAGIA	MISANTHROPES
MARVELLOUSLY	MENSTRUATION	MEZZO-RELIEVO	MISANTHROPIC
MASQUERADERS	MEPHITICALLY	MEZZO-SOPRANO	MISAPPREHEND
MASQUERADING	MERCHANTILISM	MICROANALYST	MISBEHAVIOUR
MASSOTHERAPY	MERCHANTILIST	MICROBALANCE	MISCALCULATE
MASS-PRODUCED	MERCHANDISED	MICROBIOLOGY	MISCARRIAGES
MASS-PRODUCER	MERCHANDISER	MICROCEPHALY	MISCEGENETIC
MASTECTOMIES	MERCHANTABLE	MICROCIRCUIT	MISCELLANIES
MASTER-AT-ARMS	MERCHANT BANK	MICROCLIMATE	MISCELLANIST

MISCONCEIVED
MISCONCEIVER
MISCONDUCTED
MISCONSTRUED
MISDEMEANOUR
MISDIRECTING
MISDIRECTION
MISINFORMANT
MISINFORMING
MISINTERPRET
MISJUDGEMENT
MISJUDGMENTS
MISLEADINGLY
MISPLACEMENT
MISPRONOUNCE
MISQUOTATION
MISREPORTING
MISREPRESENT
MISSING LINKS
MISSIONARIES
MISSPELLINGS
MISSTATEMENT
MISTREATMENT
MIXED-ABILITY
MIXED DOUBLES
MIXED ECONOMY
MIXED FARMING
MNEMONICALLY
MOBILIZATION
MOCKING BIRDS
MODERATENESS
MODIFICATION
MODIFICATORY
MODULABILITY
MODUS VIVENDI
MOHAVE DESERT
MOISTURIZING
MOLLIFYINGLY
MOLLYCODDLED
MONADELPHOUS
MONARCHISTIC
MONASTICALLY
MONETIZATION
MONEYCHANGER
MONEY-GRABBER
MONEYLENDERS
MONEYLENDING
MONEY-SPINNER
MONISTICALLY
MONKEY-PUZZLE
MONKEY WRENCH
MONOCHLORIDE
MONOCHROMIST
MONODRAMATIC

MONOFILIMENT
MONOGAMISTIC
MONOGAMOUSLY
MONOMANIACAL
MONOMETALLIC
MONOMETRICAL
MONOMORPHISM
MONOPETALOUS
MONOPHTHONGS
MONOPHYLETIC
MONOPHYLLOUS
MONOPOLISTIC
MONOPOLIZING
MONOSEPALOUS
MONOSPERMOUS
MONOSTROPHIC
MONOSYLLABIC
MONOSYLLABLE
MONOTHEISTIC
MONOTONOUSLY
MONOTRICHOUS
MONTPARNESSE
MONUMENTALLY
MOONLIGHTERS
MOONLIGHTING
MORALITY PLAY
MORALIZATION
MORALIZINGLY
MORBIFICALLY
MORNING COATS
MORNING DRESS
MORNING GLORY
MORPHOLOGIES
MORPHOLOGIST
MORRIS DANCER
MORRIS DANCES
MORTAR BOARDS
MORTGAGEABLE
MORTIFYINGLY
MORTISE LOCKS
MOSQUITO NETS
MOTHERLINESS
MOTHER NATURE
MOTHERS-IN-LAW
MOTHER TONGUE
MOTHPROOFING
MOTIONLESSLY
MOTIVATIONAL
MOTORCYCLIST
MOTORIZATION
MOTOR SCOOTER
MOULDABILITY
MOUNTAINEERS
MOUNTAIN LION

MOUNTAINSIDE
MOUNTAINTOPS
MOURNFULNESS
MOUTHBROODER
MOUTH-TO-MOUTH
MOVABLE FEAST
MUCILAGINOUS
MUCOPURULENT
MUDDLE-HEADED
MULLIGATAWNY
MULTICHANNEL
MULTIFACETED
MULTIFARIOUS
MULTIFOLIATE
MULTIFORMITY
MULTIGRAVIDA
MULTILAMINAR
MULTILATERAL
MULTILINGUAL
MULTINUCLEAR
MULTIPARTITE
MULTIPLIABLE
MULTIPLICAND
MULTIPLICATE
MULTIPLICITY
MULTIPURPOSE
MULTIVALENCY
MUNICIPALITY
MUNICIPALIZE
MUNIFICENTLY
MUSEUM PIECES
MUSICAL BOXES
MUSIC CENTRES
MUSICIAN SHIP
MUSICOLOGIST
MYRMECOPHILE
MYSTERIOUSLY
MYSTERY PLAYS
MYSTERY TOURS
MYSTIFYINGLY
MYTHOLOGICAL
MYTHOLOGISTS
MYTHOLOGIZER
MYXOMYCETOUS

13 LETTERS
MACARONICALLY
MACHIAVELLIAN
MACHICOLATION
MACHINABILITY
MACHINEGUNNED
MACRENCEPHALY

MACROCLIMATIC
MACROECONOMIC
MACROMOLECULE
MACRONUTRIENT
MADRIGALESQUE
MAGIC LANTERNS
MAGISTERIALLY
MAGNANIMOUSLY
MAGNETIC FIELD
MAGNETIC HEADS
MAGNETIC NORTH
MAGNETIC POLES
MAGNETIC TAPES
MAGNETIZATION
MAGNETOMETRIC
MAGNETOMOTIVE
MAGNETOSPHERE
MAGNIFICATION
MAGNIFICENTLY
MAGNILOQUENCE
MAGNITUDINOUS
MAIDS OF HONOUR
MAJOR GENERALS
MALADJUSTMENT
MALADMINISTER
MALADROITNESS
MALFORMATIONS
MALFUNCTIONED
MALICIOUSNESS
MANAGEABILITY
MANDARIN DUCKS
MANIFESTATION
MANIPULATABLE
MANIPULATIONS
MANTELSHELVES
MANUFACTURERS
MANUFACTURING
MARCHIONESSES
MARKETABILITY
MARRIAGE LINES
MARTYRIZATION
MARTYROLOGIST
MASSIF CENTRAL
MASS-PRODUCING
MASTERFULNESS
MASTERMINDING
MASTERS-AT-ARMS
MASTERS OF ARTS
MASTERSTROKES
MATCHLESSNESS
MATERIALISTIC
MATERIALIZING
MATERNALISTIC
MATHEMATICIAN

MATRICULATING	MICROCOMPUTER	MONEY-SPINNERS
MATRICULATION	MICRODETECTOR	MONKEY-PUZZLES
MATURE STUDENT	MICRONUTRIENT	MONOCHROMATIC
MEANINGLESSLY	MICROORGANISM	MONOGRAMMATIC
MEASURABILITY	MICROPARASITE	MONOMOLECULAR
MECHANIZATION	MICROPHYSICAL	MONONUCLEOSIS
MEDIATIZATION	MIDDLE EASTERN	MONOSYLLABISM
MEDIATORIALLY	MIDDLE SCHOOLS	MONOSYLLABLES
MEDIEVALISTIC	MIDDLEWEIGHTS	MONOTREMATOUS
MEDITERRANEAN	MID-LIFE CRISIS	MONSTROSITIES
MEETINGHOUSES	MILK CHOCOLATE	MONUMENTALITY
MEGALOBLASTIC	MILLENNIALIST	MOONLIGHT FLIT
MEGALOMANIACS	MILLIONAIRESS	MORALITY PLAYS
MEGALOPOLITAN	MINE DETECTORS	MORAL MAJORITY
MELODIOUSNESS	MINERALOGICAL	MORNING PRAYER
MELODRAMATIST	MINERALOGISTS	MORRIS DANCERS
MELTING POINTS	MINERAL WATERS	MORTIFICATION
MENSTRUATIONS	MINICOMPUTERS	MOTHER COUNTRY
MERCENARINESS	MINISTERIALLY	MOTHER-OF-PEARL
MERCERIZATION	MIRABILE DICTU	MOTION PICTURE
MERCHANDISING	MIRTHLESSNESS	MOTOR CYCLISTS
MERCHANT BANKS	MISADVENTURES	MOTOR SCOOTERS
MERCILESSNESS	MISCALCULATED	MOUNTAIN LIONS
MERCURIALNESS	MISCEGENATION	MOUNTAINSIDES
MERCUROCHROME	MISCELLANEOUS	MOUTH-WATERING
MERCY KILLINGS	MISCHIEVOUSLY	MOVABLE FEASTS
MERITOCRACIES	MISCONCEIVING	MOVING PICTURE
MERITORIOUSLY	MISCONCEPTION	MULTICELLULAR
MERRY-GO-ROUNDS	MISCONDUCTING	MULTICOLOURED
MESENCEPHALIC	MISCONSTRUING	MULTINATIONAL
MESENCEPHALON	MISDEMEANOURS	MULTIPLE STORE
MESMERIZATION	MISERABLENESS	MULTITUDINOUS
MESSIANICALLY	MISGOVERNMENT	MUMMIFICATION
METABOLICALLY	MISJUDGEMENTS	MURDEROUSNESS
METABOLIZABLE	MISMANAGEMENT	MUSICAL CHAIRS
METALLIFEROUS	MISPROPORTION	MUSICOLOGICAL
METALLIZATION	MISQUOTATIONS	MYCOBACTERIUM
METALLOGRAPHY	MISSTATEMENTS	MYSTIFICATION
METALLURGICAL	MISTRUSTFULLY	MYTHICIZATION
METALLURGISTS	MISTRUSTINGLY	
METAMERICALLY	MISUNDERSTAND	
METAMORPHOSED	MISUNDERSTOOD	
METAMORPHOSES	MIXED BLESSING	
METAMORPHOSIS	MIXED METAPHOR	
METAPHOSPHATE	MOBILIZATIONS	
METEOROLOGIST	MODERNIZATION	
METHODIZATION	MODIFIABILITY	
METHODOLOGIES	MODIFICATIONS	
METHODOLOGIST	MOLLIFICATION	
METHYL ALCOHOL	MOLLYCODDLING	
METROPOLITANS	MOMENT OF TRUTH	
MICROANALYSIS	MONEY CHANGERS	
MICROANALYTIC	MONEY-GRUBBERS	
MICROCHEMICAL	MONEY-GRUBBING	

3 LETTERS	NIBS	NARES	NIPPY	6 LETTERS	NECTAR
NAB	NICE	NARKS	NITRE	NAFFIS	NEEDED
NAG	NICK	NARKY	NITTY	NABBED	NEARER
NAP	NIFF	NASAL	NIVAL	NABLUS	NEARLY
NAY	NIGH	NASTY	NIXED	NABOBS	NEATEN
NCO	NINE	NATAL	NOBLE	NACHOS	NEATER
NEE	NIPS	NATES	NOBLY	NACRED	NEATLY
NET	NISI	NATTY	NODAL	NADIRS	NEBULA
NEW	NITS	NAURU	NODDY	NAEVUS	NECKED
NHS	NOBS	NAVAL	NODES	NAGANA	NECTAR
NIB	NIDE	NAVAR	NODUS	NAGANO	NEEDED
NIL	NODS	NAVEL	NITRE	NAGGED	NEEDLE
NIP	NOEL	NAVES	NITTY	NAGGER	NEEDN'T
NIT	NOES	NAVVY	NIVAL	NAGOYA	NEGATE
NIX	NONE	NAZIS	NIXED	NAGPUR	NEIGHS
NOB	NON-U	NEATH	NOBLE	NAIADS	NEKTON
NOD	NOOK	NECKS	NOBLY	NAILED	NELSON
NON-	NOON	NEEDS	NODAL	NAILER	NEPALI
NOR	NOPE	NEEDY	NODDY	NAMELY	NEPHEW
NOT	NORM	NEGEV	NODES	NAMING	NEREID
NOW	NOSE	NEGRO	NODUS	NANTES	NEREIS
NUB	NOSH	NEGUS	NOHOW	NAPALM	NERVED
NUN	NOSY	NEIGH	NOISE	NAPKIN	NERVES
NUT	NOTE	NELLY	NOISY	NAPLES	NESTED
	NOUN	NEPAL	NOMAD	NAPPED	NESTER
	NOUS	NEPER	NONCE	NAPPER	NESTLE
4 LETTERS	NOVA	NERDS	NOOKS	NARIAL	NETHER
NAFF	NUBS	NERVE	NO ONE	NARKED	NETTED
NAGS	NUDE	NERVY	NOOSE	NARROW	NETTLE
NAIL	NUKE	NESTS	NOPAL	NARVIK	NETTLY
NAME	NULL	NEURO-	NO-PAR	NASALS	NEURAL
NAPE	NUMB	NEUSS	NORMS	NASIAL	NEURON
NAPS	NUNS	NEVER	NORSE	NASION	NEUTER
NARK	NUTS	NEWEL	NORTH	NASSAU	NEVADA
NASA		NEWER	NOSED	NATANT	NEWARK
NATO		NEWLY	NOSES	NATION	NEWEST
NAVE	5 LETTERS	NEWSY	NOTCH	NATIVE	NEWISH
NAVY	NAAFI	NEWTS	NOTED	NATRON	NEWTON
NAYS	NABOB	NEXUS	NOTES	NATTER	NIBBLE
NAZI	NACRE	NICER	NOTUM	NATURE	NICELY
NCOS	NADIR	NICHE	NOUNS	NAUGHT	NICEST
NEAR	NAIAD	NICKS	NOVAE	NAUSEA	NICETY
NEAT	NAILS	NIDAL	NOVAS	NAUTCH	NICHES
NECK	NAIVE	NIDUS	NOVEL	NAVAHO	NIBBLE
NEED	NAKED	NIECE	NO WAY	NAVELS	NICELY
NE'ER	NAMED	NIFFY	NUCHA	NAVIES	NICEST
NEON	NAMES	NIFTY	NUDGE	NAZISM	NICETY
NERD	NAMUR	NIGHT	NUKED	NEARBY	NICHES
NEST	NANCY	NIHIL	NURSE	NEARED	NICKED
NETS	NANNY	NIMBI	NUTTY	NEARER	NICKEL
NETT	NAPES	NIMES	NYALA	NEATLY	NICKER
NEWS	NAPPA	NINES	NYLON	NEBULA	NIDIFY
NEWT	NAPPE	NINNY	NYMPH	NECKED	NIECES
NEXT	NAPPY	NINTH		NECKER	NIELLO

NIEVRE	NOTING	NAIVELY	NEGLECT	NIBBLER	NOMADIC
NIGGLE	NOTION	NAKEDLY	NEGRESS	NIBBLES	NOMBRILL
NIGHTS	NOUGAT	NALCHIK	NEGRITO	NICKELS	NOMINAL
NILGAI	NOUGHT	NAMABLE	NEGROES	NICKING	NOMINEE
NIMBLE	NOUNAL	NAME DAY	NEGROID	NICOBAR	NONAGON
NIMBLY	NOVARA	NAMIBIA	NEIGHED	NICOSIA	NON-IRON
NIMBUS	NOVELS	NANKEEN	NEITHER	NIFTIER	NONPLUS
NINETY	NOVICE	NANKING	NELLIES	NIFTILY	NON-PROS
NINGPO	NOWISE	NANNIES	NELUMBO	NIGERIA	NONSTOP
NINTHS	NOZZLE	NANNING	NEMATIC	NIGGARD	NONSUIT
NIOBIC	NUANCE	NANTUNG	NEMESIS	NIGGERS	NOODLES
NIPPED	NUBBLE	NAPHTHA	NEOCENE	NIGGLED	NONDAY
NIPPER	NUBBLY	NAPKINS	NEOGENE	NIGGLER	NO-PLACE
NIPPLE	NUBILE	NAPPIES	NEOLITH	NIGHTIE	NORFOLK
NIPPON	NUCHAL	NAPPING	NEONATE	NIGHTLY	NORMANS
NITRIC	NUCLEI	NARKIER	NEOTENY	NILOTIC	NORWICH
NITWIT	NUDGED	NARKING	NEOTYPE	NIMBLER	NOSEBAG
NIXING	NUDGER	NARRATE	NEOZOIC	NINEPIN	NOSEGAY
NO BALL	NUDGES	NARROWS	NEPHEWS	NINNIES	NOSHING
NOBBLE	NUDISM	NARTHEX	NEPHRON	NIOBITE	NOSIEST
NOBLER	NUDIST	NARWHAL	NEPOTIC	NIOBIUM	NOSTRIL
NOBLES	NUDIST	NASALLY	NEPTUNE	NIOBOUS	NOSTRUM
NOBODY	NUDITY	NASCENT	NEREIDS	NIPPERS	NOTABLE
NODDED	NUGGET	NASTIER	NERITIC	NIPPIER	NOTABLY
NODDLE	NUKING	NASTILLY	NERVATE	NIPPILY	NOTCHED
NODOSE	NUMBAT	NATIONS	NERVIER	NIPPING	NOTCHES
NODULE	NUMBED	NATIVES	NERVILY	NIPPLES	NOTELET
NOESIS	NUMBER	NATTIER	NERVINE	NIRVANA	NOTEPAD
NOETIC	NUMBLY	NATTILY	NERVING	NITRATE	NOTHING
NOGGIN	NUNCIO	NATURAL	NERVOUS	NITRIDE	NOTICED
NOISES	NURSED	NATURES	NERVURE	NITRIFY	NOTICES
NOMADS	NURSES	NAUGHTY	NESTEGG	NITRILE	NOTIONS
NOMISM	NUTANT	NAURUAN	NESTLING	NITRITE	NO-TRUMP
NONAGE	NUTLET	NAVARRE	NESTLED	NITROSO	NOUGATS
NONCES	NUTMEG	NAVVIES	NESTLER	NITROUS	NOUGHTS
NONEGO	NUTRIA	NAYARIT	NETBALL	NITWITS	NOURISH
NOODLE	NUTTED	NEAREST	NETSUKE	NIVEOUS	NOVELLA
NOOSES	NUTTER	NEARING	NETTING	NO BALLS	NOVELLE
MORDIC	NUZZLE	NEATEST	NETTLED	NOBBLED	NOVELTY
NORITE	NYLONS	NEBULAE	NETTLES	NOBBLER	NOVICES
NORMAL	NYMPHA	NEBULAR	NETWORK	NOBLEST	NOWHERE
NORMAN	NYMPHS	NEBULAS	NEUROMA	NOCTUID	NOXIOUS
NORTHS		NECKING	NEUTRAL	NOCTULE	NOZZLES
NORWAY		NECKET	NEUTRON	NOCTURN	NUANCES
NOSHED	**7 LETTERS**	NECKTIE	NEWBORN	NODDING	NUCLEAR
NOSH-UP	NABBING	NECROSE	NEW DEAL	NODDLES	NUCLEIN
NO-SIDE	NACELLE	NECTARY	NEW MOON	NODICAL	NUCLEON
NOSIER	NAEVOID	NEEDFUL	NEWNESS	NODULAR	NUCLEUS
NOSILY	NAGGERS	NEEDIER	NEW TOWN	NODULES	NUCLIDE
NOSING	NAGGING	NEEDING	NEW WAVE	NOGGING	NUDGING
NOSTOC	NAHUATL	NEEDLED	NEW YEAR	NOGGINS	NUDISTS
NOTARY	NAIADES	NEEDLES	NEXUSES	NOISIER	NUGGETS
NOTICE	NAILING	NEGATED	NIAGARA	NOISILY	NUGGETY
NOTIFY	NAIROBI	NEGATOR	NIBBLED	NOISOME	NULLIFY

NULL SET	NASCENCE	NEOPRENE	NIHILITY	NOSINESS
NUMBERS	NASTIEST	NEOTERIC	NIJMEGEN	NOSOLOGY
NUMBING	NATATION	NEPALESE	NIMBLEST	NOSTRILS
NUMERAL	NATIONAL	NEPHRITE	NIMBUSES	NOSTRUMS
NUMMERY	NATIVISM	NEPHRITE	NINEFOLD	NOTA BENE
NUNATAK	NATIVIST	NEPOTISM	NINEPINS	NOTABLES
NUNNERY	NATIVITY	NEPOTIST	NINETEEN	NOTORIAL
NUPTIAL	NATTERED	NERVIEST	NINTIES	NOTARIES
NURSERY	NATTIEST	NESICENT	NIPPIEST	NOTARIES
NURSING	NATURALS	NEST EGGS	NIRVANAS	NOTATION
NURTURE	NATURISM	NESTLING	NIRVANIC	NOCHING
NUTCASE	NATURIST	NETTLING	NITRATES	NOTEBOOK
NUTGALL	NAUPLIUS	NETWOORKS	NITROGEN	NOTECASE
NUTMEGS	NAVICERT	NEURITIC	NITROSYL	NOTELETS
NUTRIAS	NAVIGATE	NEUROSES	NIVATION	NOTEPADS
NUTTIER	NAVY BLUE	NEUROSIS	NOBBLING	NOTICING
NUTTILY	NAZARENE	NEUROTIC	NOBELIUM	NOTIFIER
NUTTING	NAZARETH	NEUTERED	NOBILITY	NOTIONAL
NUTWOOD	NEAP TIDE	NEUTRALS	NOBLEMAN	NOTOGAEA
NUZZLED	NEARCTIC	NEUTRONS	NOBLEMEN	NOTORNIS
NYMPHAL	NEAR EAST	NEW BLOOD	NOBODIES	NOVATION
NYMPHET	NEAR MISS	NEW BROOM	NOCTURNE	NOVELIST
	NEARNESS	NEWCOMER	NODALITY	NOVELLAS
	NEARSIDE	NEW DEALS	NODASITY	NOVEMBER
8 LETTERS	NEATNESS	NEWLYWED	NO-GO AREA	NOVGOROD
NABOBERY	NEBRASKA	NEW MOONS	NOISIEST	NOWADAYS
NACELLES	NEBULIZE	NEWSCAST	NOMADISM	NUBECULA
NACREOUS	NEBULOUS	NEWSPEAK	NOMINATE	NUBILITY
NAGALAND	NECKBAND	NEWSREEL	NOMINEES	NUCELLAR
NAGASAKI	NECKLACE	NEWSROOM	NOMISTIC	NUCELLUS
NAIL FILE	NECKLETS	NEW TOWNS	NOMOLOGY	NUCLEASE
NAIL HEAD	NECKLINE	NEW WAVES	NONESUCH	NUCLEATE
NAINSOOK	NECKTIES	NEW WORLD	NON-EVENT	NUDENESS
NAISSANT	NECROSIS	NEXT-DOOR	NONJUROR	NUDICAUL
NAMANGAN	NECROTIC	NIBBLING	NON LICET	NUGATORY
NAME DAYS	NEEDIEST	NICENESS	NONMENTAL	NUISANCE
NAMEDROP	NEEDLESS	NICETIES	NONSENSE	NULLSETS
NAMELESS	NEEDLING	NICHROME	NONSTICK	NUMBERED
NAMESAKE	NEGATING	NICKELED	NONTOXIC	NUMBFISH
NAMIBIAN	NEGATION	NICKELIC	NONUNION	NUMBNESS
NAPHTHOL	NEGATIVE	NICKNACK	NONVOTER	NUMERACY
NAPHTHYL	NEGLIGEE	NICKNAME	NONWHITE	NUMERALS
NAPIFORM	NEGRILLO	NICOTINE	NOONTIME	NUMERARY
NARCEINE	NEGRITIC	NIELLIST	NORMALLY	NUMERATE
NARCISSI	NEGROISM	NIFTIEST	NORMANDY	NUMEROUS
NARCOSIS	NEIGHING	NIGERIAN	NORSEMAN	NUMINOUS
NARCOTIC	NEKTONIC	NIGGARDS	NORSEMEN	NUMMULAR
NARKIEST	NEMATODE	NIGGLERS	NORTHERN	NUMSKULL
NARRATED	NEMBUTAL	NIGGLING	NORTHING	NUPTIALS
NARRATOR	NEOGAEAN	NIGHTCAP	NOSEBAGS	NURISTAN
NARROWED	NEOMYCIN	NIGHTJAR	NOSEBAND	NURSLING
NARROWLY	NEONATAL	NIGHT OWL	NOSECONE	NURTURED
NASALITY	NEOPHYTE	MIHILISM	NOSEDIVE	NUTURER
NASALIZE	NEOPLASM	NIHILIST	NOSEGAYS	NUTATION

NUT-BROWN	NECESSARY	NEUROPATH	NITRATION	NOVELETTE
NUTCASES	NECESSITY	NEUROTICS	NITRIDING	NOVELISTS
NUTHATCH	NECKCLOTH	NEUROTOMY	NIVERNIAS	NOVELTIES
NUTHOUSE	NECKLACES	NEUTERING	NO-ACCOUNT	NOVEMBERS
NUTRIENT	NECKLINES	NEUTRALITY	NOBILIARY	NOVITIATE
NUTSHELL	NECKPIECE	NEUTRETTO	NOBLENESS	NOVOCAINE
NUTTIEST	NECROLOGY	NEVERMORE	NOCTILUCA	NOXIOUSLY
NUZZLING	NECROTOMY	NEW BROOMS	NOCTURNAL	NUCLEATOR
NYMPHETS	NECTARIAL	NEWCOMERS	NOCTURNES	NUCLEOLAR
NYSTATIN	NECTARINE	NEWLYWEDS	NO-GO AREAS	NUCLEOLUS
	NEEDFULLY	NEWSAGENT	NOISINESS	NUCLEONIC
	NEEDINESS	NEWSHOUND	NOMINALLY	NUEVO LEON
9 LETTERS	NEFARIOUS	NEWSINESS	NOMINATED	NUISANCES
NAHUATLAN	NEGATIONS	NEWSPAPER	NOMINATOR	NULLIFIED
NAILBRUSH	NEGATIVED	NEWSPRINT	NOMOCRACY	NULLIFIER
NAIL FILES	NEGATIVES	NEWSREELS	NOMOGRAPH	NULLIPARA
NAIVENESS	NEGLECTED	NEWSROOMS	NONAGONAL	NULLIPORE
NAIVEITIES	NEGLECTER	NEWSSHEET	NONEDIBLE	NULLITIES
NAKEDNESS	NEGLIGEES	NEWSSTAND	NONENTITY	NUMBERING
NAMEPLATES	NEGLIGENT	NEWTONIAN	NON-EVENTS	NUMBER ONE
NAMESAKES	NEGOTIANT	NICARAGUA	NON-FINITE	NUMBER TEN
NANNY GOAT	NEGOTIATE	NICCOLITE	NONILLION	NUMBSKULL
NANOMETER	NEGRITUDE	NICKELING	NONPAREIL	NUMERABLE
NANTUCKET	NEIGHBOUR	NICKELLED	NONPAROUS	NUMERATOR
NAPHTHENE	NEMERTEAN	NICKELOUS	NONSMOKER	NUMERICAL
NAPPINESS	NEODYMIUM	NICKNACKS	NONVERBAL	NUMMULITE
NARCISSUS	NEOLITHIC	NICKNAMED	NONWHITES	NUMSKULLS
NARCOTICS	NEOLOGISM	NICOTANIA	NORMALITY	NUNNERIES
NARCOTISM	NEOLOGIST	NICOTINIC	NORMALIZE	NUREMBERG
NARCOTIZE	NEOLOGIZE	NICTITATE	NORMATIVE	NURSELING
NARRATING	NEON LIGHT	NIFTINESS	NORTHEAST	NURSEMAID
NARRATION	NEOPHYTES	NIGGARDLY	NORTHERLY	NURSERIES
NARRATIVE	NEOPHYTIC	NIGHTCAPS	NORTH POLE	NURSELINGS
NARRATORS	NEOPLASTY	NIGHTCLUB	NORTHWARD	NURTURING
NARROWING	NEOTENOUS	NIGHTFALL	NORTHWEST	NUTHOUSES
NASHVILLE	NEPHELENE	NIGHTGOWN	NORWEGIAN	NUTRIENTS
NASTINESS	NEPHOGRAM	NIGHTHAWK	NOSEBLEED	NUTRIMENT
NATIONALS	NEPHOLOGY	NIGHTLIFE	NOSECONES	NUTRITION
NATROLITE	NEPHRITIC	NIGHTLONG	NOSEDIVED	NUTRITIVE
NATTERING	NEPHRITIS	NIGHTMARE	NOSTALGIA	NUTSHELLS
NATTINESS	NEPHROSIS	NIGHT OWLS	NOSTALGIC	NUTTINESS
NATURALLY	NEPHROTIC	NIGHT SOIL	NOSTOLOGY	NYASALAND
NATURISTS	NEPTUNIAN	NIGHTTIME	NOTARIZED	NYMPHALID
NAUGHTIER	NEPTUNIUM	NIGHTWEAR	NOTATIONS	NYSTAGMIC
NAUSEATED	NERVELESS	NIGROSINE	NOTEBOOKS	NYSTAGMUS
NAUTILOID	NERVOUSLY	NIHILISTS	NOTEPAPER	NAIL -BITING
NAVICULAR	NESCIENCE	NINETEENS	NOTIFYING	
NAVIGABLE	NESTLINES	NINETIETH	NO-TILLAGE	
NAVIGABLY	NETWORKED	NIPPINESS	NOTOCHORD	
NAVIGATED	NEUCHATEL	NIPPONESE	NOTOGAEAN	
NAVIGATOR	NEURALGIA	NISI PRIUS	NOTORIETY	
NEAP TIDES	NEURALGIC	NISSEN HUT	NOTORIOUS	
NEAR THINGS	NEUROGLIA	NITPICKER	NOURISHED	
NEBULIZER	NEUROLOGY	NITRAMINE	NOURISHER	

10 LETTERS

NAMBY-PAMBY	NEGLECTING	NICKNAMING	NONTYPICAL
NAMEPLATES	NEGLIGENCE	NICOTINISM	NONVIOLENT
NANNY GOAT	NEGLIGIBLE	NIDICOLOUS	NORMALIZED
NANOSECOND	NEGLIGIBLY	NIDIFUGOUS	NORRKOPING
NAPKIN RING	NEGOTIABLE	NIGHTCLUBS	NORTHBOUND
NAPOLEONIC	NEGOTIATED	NIGHTDRESS	NORTHENER
NARCISSISM	NEGOTIATOR	NIGHTLIGHT	NORTH POLES
NARCISSIST	NEIGHBOURS	NIGHTMARES	NORTHWARDS
NARCOLEPSY	NEMATOCYST	NIGHTSHADE	NOSEBLEEDS
NARRATABLE	NEOLOGICAL	NIGHT SHIFT	NOSEDIVING
NARRATIONS	NEOLOGISMS	NIGHTSHIRT	NOSOGRAPHY
NARRATIVES	NEON LIGHTS	NIGHTSTICK	NOSY PARKER
NARROW BOAT	NEOPLASTIC	NIHILISTIC	NOTABILITY
NARROWNESS	NEPENTHEAN	NIMBLENESS	NOTARIZING
NASTURTIUM	NEPHOGRAPH	NINCOMPOOP	NOTATIONAL
NATATIONAL	NEPHOSCOPE	NINETEENTH	NOTEWORTHY
NATIONALLY	NEPHRALGIA	NINITIETHS	NOTICEABLE
NATIONHOOD	NEPHRALGIC	NINETY-NINE	NOTICEABLY
NATIONWIDE	NEPHRIDIAL	NISSEN HUTS	NOTIFIABLE
NATIVISTIC	NEPHRIDIUM	NITPICKERS	NOTINGHAM
NATIVITIES	NEPHROTOMY	NITPICKING	NOURISHING
NATTERJACK	NEPOTISTIC	NITRIC ACID	NOVACULITE
NATURAL GAS	NETHERMOST	NITROMETER	NOVA SCOTIA
NATURALISM	NETTLE FISH	NO-ACCOUNTS	NOVELETTES
NATURALIST	NETTLESOME	NOBEL PRIZE	NOVELISTIC
NATURALIZE	NETWORKING	NOBILITIES	NOVITIATES
NATUROPATH	NEURECTOMY	NO-MAN'S-LAND	NUCLEATION
NAUGHTIEST	NEUROBLAST	NOMINALISM	NUCLEONICS
NAUSEATING	NEUROCOELE	NOMINALIST	NUCLEOSIDE
NAUSEATION	NEUROGENIC	NOMINATING	NUCLEOTIDE
NAUSEOULSY	NEUROLEMMA	NOMINATION	NUDIBRANCH
NAUTICALLY	NEUROPATHY	NOMINATIVE	NULLIFYING
NAVIGATING	NEUTRALISM	NOMOGRAPHY	NUMBERLESS
NAVIGATION	NEUTRALIST	NOMOLOGIST	NUMBSKULLS
NAVIGATORS	NEUTRALITY	NOMOTHETIC	NUMERATION
NEAPOLITAN	NEUTRALIZE	NONALIGNED	NUMERATIVE
NEAR MISSES	NEUTROPHIL	NONCHALANT	NUMERATORS
NEAR THINGS	NEVER-NEVER	NONDRINKER	NUMEROLOGY
NEBULOSITY	NEWFANGLED	NONESUCHES	NUMEROUSLY
NEBULOUSLY	NEWS AGENCY	NONETHICAL	NUMISMATIC
NECROLATRY	NEWSAGENTS	NONFACTUAL	NUMMULITIC
NECROMANCY	NEWSCASTER	NONFERROUS	NUNCIATURE
NECROPHOBE	NEWSHOUNDS	NONFICTION	NURSELINGS
NECROPOLIS	NEWSLETTER	NONJOINDER	NURSEMAIDS
NEEDLEFISH	NEWSPAPERS	NONMEDICAL	NURSERYMAN
NEEDLESSLY	NEWSREADER	NO-NONSENSE	NURSERYMEN
NEEDLEWORK	NEWSSHEETS	NONPAREILS	NURTURABLE
NE'ER-DO-WELL	NEWSSTAND	NONPAYMENT	NUTATIONAL
NEGATIVELY	NEWSVENDOR	NONPLUSSED	NUTCRACKER
NEGATIVING	NEWSWORTHY	NONSMOKERS	NUTRITIOUS
NEGATIVISM	NEWTON'S LAW	NONSMOKING	NYCTALOPIA
NEGATIVIST	NEW ZEALAND	NONSTARTER	NYCTINASTY
NEGLECTFUL	NICURAGUAN	NONSTATIVE	NYMPHOLEPT
	NICKELLING	NON-STRIKER	

11 LETTERS
NAILBRUSHES
NAIL VARNISH
NAKHICHEVAN
NAMEDROPPED
NAMEDROPPER
NAPHTHALENE
NAPKIN RINGS
NARAYANGANJ
NARCISSISTS
NARCISSUES
NARCOLEPTIC
NARROW BOATS
NARROW GAUG
NASOFRONTAL
NASOPHARYNX
NASTURTIUMS
NATIONALISM
NATIONALIST
NATIONALITY
NATIONALIZE
NATION STATE
NATURALISTS
NATURALIZED
NATURALNESS
NEANDERTHAL
NEAR EASTERN
NEARSIGHTED
NECESSARIES
NECESSARILY
NECESSITATE
NECESSITIES
NECESSITOUS
NECKERCHIEF
NECROBIOSIS
NECROBIOTIC
NECROLOGIST
NECROMANCER
NECROMANTIC
NECROPHILIA
NECROPHILIC
NECROPHOBIA
NECROPHOBIC
NEEDFULNESS
NEEDLEPOINT
NEEDLEWOMAN
NEEDLEWOMEN
NE'ER-DO-WELLS
NEFARIOUSLY
NEGLIGENTLY
NEGOTIATING
NEGOTIATION
NEGOTIATORS
NEIGHBOURLY

NEOCOLONIAL
NEOLOGISTIC
NEOHELINITE
NEPHOLOGIST
NEPHRECTOMY
NE PLUS ULTRA
NERVE CENTRE
NERVELESSLY
NERVOUSNESS
NETHERLANDS
NEUROFIBRIL
NEUROLOGIST
NEUROMATOUS
NEUROPATHIC
NUROPTERAN
NEUROTICISM
NEUROTOMIST
NEUTRALIZED
NEUTRALIZER
NEUTRON BOMB
NEVER-NEVERS
NEWSCASTERS
NEWS LETTERS
NEWS READERS
NEWS VENDORS
NEW YEAR'S DAY
NEW YEAR'S EVE
NICENE CREED
NICKELODEON
NICTITATION
NIETZSCHEAN
NIGHTINGALE
NIGHTLIGHTS
NIGHTMARISH
NIGHTSCHOOL
NIGHTSHADES
NIGHTSHIFTS
NIGHTSHIRTS
NIGHTSTICKS
NIGRESCENCE
NINCOMPOOPS
NINETEENTHS
NINETY-NINES
NITRIFIABLE
NITROGENIZE
NITROGENIZE
NITROGENOUS
NITROMETRIC
NITROSAMINE
NITTY-GRITTY
NOBEL PRIZES
NOCICEPTIVE
NOCILUCENT
NOCTURNALLY

NOISELESSLY
NOISOMENESS
NOMADICALLY
NO-MAN'S-LAND
NOMENCLATOR
NOMINATIONS
NOMINATIVES
NOMOGRAPHER
NOMOGRAPHIC
NOMOLOGICAL
NOMS DE PLUME
NONCHALANCE
NONCREATIVE
NONDESCRIPT
NONENTITIES
NONETHELESS
NONEXISTENT
NONFEASANCE
NONHARMONIC
NONILLIONTH
NONIRRITANT
NONMETALLIC
NONOPERABLE
NONPARTISAN
NONPLUSSING
NONRESIDENT
NONSENSICAL
NON SEQUITUR
NONSTANDARD
NON STARTERS
NON VERBALLY
NONVIOLENCE
NORMALIZING
NORTHAMPTON
NORTHEASTER
NORTHERNERS
NORTHUMBRIA
NORTHWESTER
NOSOGRAPHER
NOSOGRAPHIC
NOSOLOGICAL
NOSY PARKERS
NOTABLENESS
NOTHINGNESS
NOTICE BOARD
NOTOCHORDAL
NOTORIOUSLY
NOTOTHERIUM
NOURISHMENT
NOXIOUSNESS
NUCLEAR-FREE
NUCLEIC ACID
NUCLEOPLASM
NULL AND VOID

NULLIFIDIAN
NULLIPAROUS
NUMBERPLATE
NUMBERATIONS
NUMERICALLY
NUMISMATICS
NUMISMATIST
NUNCUPATIVE
NURSING HOME
NUT CRACKERS
NUTRITIONAL
NYCTINASTIC
NYCTITROPIC
NYCTOPHOBIA
NYCTOPHOBIC
NYMPHOMANIA

12 LETTERS
NAIL SCISSORS
NAMBY-PAMBIES
NAMEDROPPERS
NAMEDROPPING
NANOPLANKTON
NANSEN BOTTLE
NARCISSISTIC
NARCOTICALLY
NARROW GAUGES
NARROW-MINDED
NARROW SQUEAK
NASALIZATION
NATIONAL DEBT
NATIONALISTS
NATIONALIZED
NATION STATES
NATIVITY PLAY
NATURALISTIC
NATURALIZING
NATUROPATHIC
NAUSEATINGLY
NAUSEOUSNESS
NAUTICAL MILE
NAVIGABILITY
NAVIGATIONAL
NEANDERTHALS
NEBULIZATION
NEBULOUSNESS
NECESSITATED
NECKERCHIEFS
NECROLOGICAL
NECROMANCERS
NECROPHILIAC
NECROPHILISM
NECROPOLISES

NEEDLESSNESS	NONCHALANTLY	**13 LETTERS**	NONCOMPLIANCE
NEGATIVENESS	NONCOMBATANT	NARCOANALYSIS	NONCONCURRENT
NEGATIVE POLE	NONCOMMITAL	NARCOTIZATION	NONCONDUCTORS
NEGATIVISTIC	NONCONDUCTOR	NARROW SQUEAKS	NONCONFORMISM
NEGLECTFULLY	NONCORRODING	NATIONAL DEBTS	NONCONFORMIST
NEGOTIATIONS	NONESSENTIAL	NATIONALISTIC	NONCONFORMITY
NEIGHBOURING	NONEXISTENCE	NATIONALITIES	NONCONTAGIOUS
NEMATOCYSTIC	NONEXPLOSIVE	NATIONALIZING	NONCOOPERATOR
NEOANTHROPIC	NONFICTIONAL	NATIONAL PARKS	NONINDUSTRIAL
NEOCLASSICAL	NONFLAMMABLE	NATIONAL TRUST	NONINFECTIOUS
NEOLOGICALLY	NONIDENTICAL	NATIVITY PLAYS	NONPRODUCTIVE
NEOTERICALLY	NONIDIOMATIC	NAUTICAL MILES	NONRETURNABLE
NEPHELOMETER	NONMALIGNANT	NEARSIGHTEDLY	NONSENSICALLY
NEPHOLOGICAL	NONOPERATIVE	NECESSARY EVIL	NORADRENALINE
NERVE CENTRES	NONPOISONOUS	NECESSITARIAN	NORFOLK JACKET
NERVE-RACING	NONPOLITICAL	NECESSITATING	NORMALIZATION
NETHER LANDER	NONRESIDENCE	NECESSITATION	NORTHEASTERLY
NETTLE RASHES	NONRESIDENTS	NECESSITATIVE	NORTHEASTWARD
NEURASTHENIA	NONRESISTANT	NECESSITOUSLY	NORTH OSSETIAN
NEURASTHENIC	NONSCHEDULED	NECKERCHIEVES	NORTHWESTERLY
NEUROLOGICAL	NONSECTARIAN	NECROPHILIACS	NORTHWESTWARD
NEUROLOGISTS	NON SEQUITURS	NEFARIOUSNESS	NOSOLOGICALLY
NEUROPTEROUS	NONSTRATEGIC	NEGATIVE POLES	NOSTALGICALLY
NEUROSURGEON	NONTECHNICAL	NEGLIGIBILITY	NOTICEABILITY
NEUROSURGERY	NONVIOLENTLY	NEGOTIABILITY	NOTIFICATIONS
NEUROTICALLY	NORTHEASTERN	NEIGHBOURHOOD	NOTORIOUSNESS
NEUROTOMICAL	NORTHEASTERS	NEOCLASSICISM	NUCLEAR ENERGY
NEUTRALIZNG	NORTHERNMOST	NEOCLASSICIST	NUCLEAR FAMILY
NEUTRON BOMBS	NORTHUMBRIAN	NEOPLASTICISM	NUCLEAR WINTER
NEVERTHELESS	NORTH WESTERN	NERVELESSNESS	NUCLEONICALLY
NEW BRUNSWICK	NOTE WORTHILY	NERVOUS SYSTEM	NUCLEOPLASMIC
NEWFOUNDLAND	NOTICE BOARDS	NEUROFIBRILLAR	NUCLEOPROTEIN
NEWS AGENCIES	NOTIFICATION	NEUROMUSCULAR	NUISANCE VALUE
NEWSPAPERMAN	NOURISHINGLY	NEUROSURGICAL	NULLIFICATION
NEW TESTAMENT	NOUVEAU RICHE	NEUROVASCULAR	NUMEROLOGICAL
NEW ZEALANDER	NUBIAN DESERT	NEW TECHNOLOGY	NUMISMATOLOGY
NICOTINAMIDE	NUCLEOPHILIC	NICKELIFEROUS	NURSERY RHYMES
NIDIFICATION	NUMBER PLATES	NIGGARDLINESS	NURSERY SCHOOL
NIETZSCHISM	NUMEROUSNESS	NIGHTCLUBBING	NYMPHAEACEOUS
NIGHTDRESSES	NUMINOUSNESS	NIGHTMARISHLY	NYMPHOMANIACS
NIGHTINGALES	NUMISMATISTS	NIGHT WATCHMAN	
NIMBOSTRATUS	NURSERY RHYME	NITRIFICATION	
NITROBENZENE	NURSING HOMES	NITROBACTERIA	
NITROMETHANE	NUTRITIONIST	NITROGLYCERIN	
NO-CLAIM BONUS	NUTRITIOUSLY	NITROPARAFFIN	
NOCTAMBULISM	NUTS AND BOLTS	NOISELESSNESS	
NOCTAMBULIST	NYCTITROPISM	NOMENCLATURES	
NOCTILUCENCE	NYMPHOLEPTIC	NOMOGRAPHICAL	
NOCTURNALITY	NYMPHOMANIAC	NOMOLOGICALLY	
NOLENS VOLENS		NONAGENARIANS	
NOMENCLATURE		NONAGGRESSION	
NOMINALISTIC		NONAPPEARANCE	
NONAGENARIAN		NONATTENDANCE	
NONALIGNMENT		NONCOMBATANTS	

3 LETTERS	4 LETTERS	5 LETTERS	6 LETTERS

3 LETTERS

OAF	ONLY	ODOUR	OUGHT	OCTANE	ONRUSH
OAK	ONTO	OFFAL	OUIJA	OCTANT	ONSIDE
OAP	ONUS	OFFER	OUJDA	OCTAVE	ONWARD
OAR	ONYX	OFTEN	OUNCE	OCTAVO	OOCYTE
ODD	OOPS	OGIVE	OUTDO	OCTETS	OODLES
ODE	OOZE	OGLED	OUTER	OCTOPI	OOGAMY
O'ER	OOZY	OGLER	OUTGO	OCULAR	OOLITE
OFF	OPAL	OGRES	OUTRE	ODDEST	OOLOGY
OFT	OPEC	OILED	OUZEL	ODDITY	OOLONG
OHM	OPEN	OILER	OVALS	ODDS-ON	OOZIER
OHO	OPUS	OINKS	OVARY	ODENSE	OOZILY
OHP	ORAL	OKAPI	OVATE	ODESSA	OOZING
OIL	ORAN	OKAYS	OVENS	ODIOUS	OPAQUE
OLD	ORBS	OLDEN	OVERS	ODOURS	OPENED
ONE	ORES	OLDER	OVERT	OEDEMA	OPENER
OOF	ORGY	OLEUM	OVINE	OEUVRE	OPENLY
OPS	ORLY	OLIVE	OVOID	OFFEND	OPERAS
OPT	ORYX	OMAHA	OVOLO	OFFERS	OPERON
ORB	OSLO	OMEGA	OVULE	OFFICE	OPHITE
ORE	OUCH	OMENS	OWING	OFFING	OPINED
OUR	OURS	OMUTA	OWLET	OFFSET	OPORTO
OUT	OUST	ON-AIR	OWNED	OGDOAD	OPPOSE
OVA	OUZO	ONION	OWNER	OGIVAL	OPPUGN
OWE	OVAL	ONSET	OXBOW	OGRESS	OPTICS
OWL	OVEN	OOPMH	OXEYE	OHMAGE	OPTING
OWN	OVER	OOTID	OXFAM	OIDIUM	OPTION
	OVUM	OOZED	OXIDE	OILCAN	OPUSES
	OWED	OPALS	OXIME	OILCUP	ORACLE
	OWLS	OP ART	OXLIP	OILIER	ORADEA
4 LETTERS	OXEN	OPERA	OZONE	OILILY	ORALLY
OAFS	OYEZ	OPINE		OILING	ORANGE
OAKS		OPIUM		OILMAN	ORATOR
OAPS		OPTED	**6 LETTERS**	OILMEN	ORBITS
OARS	**5 LETTERS**	OPTIC	OAFISH	OILRIG	ORCEIN
OATH	OAKEN	ORACH	OAXACA	OINKED	ORCHID
OATS	OAKUM	ORATE	OBELUS	OKAYED	ORCHIL
OBEY	OARED	ORBIT	OBEYED	OLD AGE	ORCHIS
OBOE	OASES	ORDER	OBEYER	OLD BOY	ORDAIN
ODDS	OASIS	ORGAN	OBJECT	OLDEST	ORDEAL
ODES	OATEN	ORIBI	OBLAST	OLD HAT	ORDERS
OGLE	OATHS	ORIEL	OBLATE	OLDISH	ORDURE
OGRE	OBESE	ORION	OBLIGE	OLD LAG	OREBRO
OHIO	OBOES	ORIYA	OBLONG	OLD MAN	OREGON
OHMS	OCCUR	ORLON	OBOIST	OLEATE	ORGANS
OILS	OCEAN	ORLOP	OBSESS	O LEVEL	ORGEAT
OILY	OCHRE	ORMER	OBTAIN	OLIVES	ORIENT
OINK	OCREA	ORRIS	OBTECT	OMASUM	ORIGAN
OKAY	OCTAD	ORURO	OBTUSE	OMEGAS	ORIGIN
OKRA	OCTAL	OSAKA	OBVERT	ONAGER	ORIOLE
OMEN	OCTET	OSCAR	OCCULT	ONCOST	ORISON
OMIT	ODDER	OSIER	OCCUPY	ONE-OFF	ORISSA
OMNI-	ODDLY	OSMIC	OCEANS	ONE-WAY	ORMOLU
ONCE	ODEUM	OTHER	OCELOT	ONIONS	ORNATE
ONES	ODIUM	OTTER	O'CLOCK	ONLINE	ORNERY

OROIDE	OXALIS	OCTOBER	OMNIBUS	ORDERLY	OUSTING
ORPHAN	OXCART	OCTOPOD	ONESELF	ORDINAL	OUTBACK
ORPINE	OXIDES	OCTOPUS	ONE-STAR	ORECTIC	OUTCAST
ORRERY	OXTAIL	OCTUPLE	ONE-STEP	OREGANO	OUTCOME
OSCARS	OXYGEN	OCULIST	ONETIME	ORGANIC	OUTCROP
OSCINE	OYSTER	ODDBALL	ON-GLIDE	ORGANON	OUTDATE
OSIERS	OZALID	ODDMENT	ONGOING	ORGANUM	OUTDONE
OSMIUM		ODDNESS	ONSHORE	ORGANZA	OUTDOOR
OSMOSE		ODOROUS	ONTARIO	ORGASAM	OUTFACE
OSMOUS	**7 LETTERS**	ODYSSEY	ONWARDS	ORIENTE	OUTFALL
OSPREY	OAKLAND	OEDIPAL	OOLITIC	ORIFICE	OUTFITS
OSSIEN	OARFISH	OERSTED	OOPHYTE	ORIGAMI	OUFLOW
OSSIFY	OARLOCK	OESTRUS	OOSPERM	ORIGINS	OUTGREW
OSTEAL	OARSMAN	OFFBEAT	OOSPORE	ORINOCO	OUTGROW
OSTEND	OARSMEN	OFFENCE	OOTHECA	ORISONS	OUTHAUL
OSTIUM	OATCAKE	OFFERED	OOZIEST	ORKNEYS	OUTINGS
OSTLER	OATMEAL	OFFERER	OPACITY	ORLEANS	OUTLAST
OTHERS	OBCONIC	OFFHAND	OPALINE	OROGENY	OUTLAWS
OTIOSE	OBELISK	OFFICER	OPEN-AIR	OROLOGY	OUTLAYS
OTITIS	OBELIZE	OFFICES	OPENERS	OROTUND	OUTLETS
OTTAVA	OBESITY	OFFINGS	OPENING	ORPHANS	OUTLIER
OTTAWA	OBEYING	OFF-LOAD	OPERAND	ORPHREY	OUTLINE
OTTERS	OBJECTS	OFF-PEAK	OPERANT	ORTOLAN	OUTLIVE
OUNCES	OBLIGED	OFFSIDE	OPERATE	OSCULAR	OUTLOOK
OUSTED	OBLIGEE	OGREISH	OPHITIC	OSCULUM	OUTMOST
OUSTER	OBLIGER	OILBIRD	OPIATES	OSHOGBO	OUTPLAY
OUTAGE	OBLIGOR	OILIEST	OPINING	OSMIOUS	OUTPORT
OUTBID	OBLIQUE	OILRIGS	OPINION	OSMOSIS	OUTPOST
OUTCRY	OBLONGS	OILSKIN	OPOSSUM	OSMOTIC	OUTPOUR
OUTDID	OBLOQUY	OILWELL	OPPOSED	OSMUNDA	OUTPUTS
OUTFIT	OBOISTS	OINKING	OPPOSER	OSPREYS	OUTRAGE
OUTFOX	OBOVATE	OKAYAMA	OPPRESS	OSSEOUS	OUTRANK
OUTGAS	OBOVOID	OKAYING	OPSONIC	OSSETIA	OUTRIDE
OUTING	OBSCENE	OKINAWA	OPSONIN	OSSETIC	OUTODE
OUTLAW	OBSCURE	OLD BOYS	OPTICAL	OSSICLE	OUTSELL
OUTLAY	OBSERVE	OLD HAND	OPTIMAL	OSSUARY	OUTSIDE
OUTLET	OBTRUDE	OLD LADY	OPTIMUM	OSTEOID	OUTSIZE
OUTMAN	OBVERSE	OLD LAGS	OPTIONS	OSTEOMA	OUTSOLD
OUTPUT	OBVIATE	OLD MAID	OPULENT	OSTIOLE	OUTSOLE
OUTRAN	OBVIOUS	OLD NICK	OPUNTIA	OSTLERS	OUTSTAY
OUTRUN	OCARINA	OLDSTER	OQUASSA	OSTMARK	OUT-TAKE
OUTSET	OCCIPUT	OLDTIME	ORACLES	OSTOSIS	OUTTALK
OUTWIT	OCCLUDE	OLDUVAI	ORANGES	OSTRAVA	OUTVOTE
OVERDO	OCEANIA	OLEFINE	ORATION	OSTRICH	OUTWARD
OVERLY	OCEANIC	O LEVELS	ORATORS	OTOCYST	OUTWASH
OVIEDO	OCELLAR	OLIVERY	ORATORY	OTOLITH	OUTWEAR
OVISAC	OCELLUS	OLIVINE	ORBITAL	OTOLOGY	OUTWORK
OVOIDS	OCELOTS	OLYMPIC	ORBITED	OTTOMAN	OUTWORN
OVULAR	OCHROID	OLYMPUS	ORCHARD	OUABAIN	OVARIAN
OWELTY	OCREATE	OMENTUM	ORCHIDS	OUGHTN'T	OVARIES
OWLETS	OCTADIC	OMICRON	ORCINOL	OUR LADY	OVATION
OWLISH	OCTAGON	OMINOUS	ORDEALS	OUR LORD	OVERACT
OWNERS	OCTANES	OMITTED	ORDERED	OURSELF	OVERAGE
OWNING	OCTAVES	OMITTER	ORDERER	OUSTERS	OVERALL

OVERARM	OBJECTED	OFF-GLIDE	ON-SCREEN	ORDAINED
OVERAWE	OBJECTOR	OFFICERS	ONSTREAM	ORDAINER
OVERBID	OBLATION	OFFICIAL	ONTOGENY	ORDERING
OVERDID	OBLATORY	OFFPRINT	ONTOLOGY	ORDINALS
OVERDUE	OBLIGATE	OFFSHOOT	OOGAMOUS	ORDINAND
OVERFLY	OBLIGING	OFFSHORE	OOGONIAL	ORDINARY
OVERJOY	OBLIQUES	OFFSTAGE	OOGONIUM	ORDINATE
OVERLAP	OBLIVION	OFF-WHITE	OOLOGIST	ORDNANCE
OVERLAY	OBSCURED	OHMMETER	OOPHYTIC	ORENBURG
OVERLIE	OSERVED	OILCLOTH	OOSPHERE	ORGANDIE
OVERMAN	OBSERVER	OILFIELD	OOSPORIC	ORGANISM
OVERPAY	OBSESSED	OIL-FIRED	OOTHECAL	ORGANIST
OVERRAN	OBSIDIAN	OILINESS	OOZINESS	ORGANIZE
OVERRUN	OBSOLETE	OIL PAINT	OPALESCE	ORGASMIC
OVERSAW	OBSTACLE	OILSKINS	OPAQUELY	ORIENTAL
OVERSEE	OBSTRUCT	OIL SLICK	OPENCAST	ORINASAL
OVERSET	OBTAINED	OILSTONE	OPEN-EYED	ORNAMENT
OVERSEW	OBTAINER	OIL WELLS	OPENINGS	ORNATELY
OVERTAX	OBTRUDED	OINTMENT	OPENNESS	ORNITHIC
OVERTLY	OBTRUDER	OKLAHOMA	OPEN-PLAN	OROGENIC
OVERTOP	OBTUSELY	OLD FLAME	OPEN-SHOP	OROMETER
OVERUSE	OBVIATED	OLD GUARD	OPENWORK	ORPHANED
OVIDUCT	OBVOLUTE	OLD HANDS	OPERABLE	ORPIMENT
OVIFORM	OCARINAS	OLD MAIDS	OPERABLY	ORRERIES
OVULATE	OCCASION	OLDSTERS	OPERATED	ORTHODOX
OWN GOAL	OCCIDENT	OLD-TIMER	OPERATIC	ORTHOEPY
OXALATE	OCCLUSAL	OLD WOMAN	OPERATOR	OSCITANT
OXAZINE	OCCUPANT	OLD WOMEN	OPERETTA	OSCULANT
OXBLOOD	OCCUPIED	OLD WORLD	OPHIDIAN	OSCULATE
OXCARTS	OCCUPIER	OLEANDER	OPINICUS	OSNABURG
OXHEART	OCCURRED	OLEASTER	OPINIONS	OSSIFIED
OXIDANT	OCEANIAN	OLEFINIC	OPIUMISM	OSSIFIER
OXIDASE	OCHREOUS	OLIBANUM	OPOSSUMS	OSTEITIC
OXIDATE	OCOTILLO	OLIGARCH	OPPILATE	OSTEITIS
OXIDIZE	OCTAGONS	OLIGURIA	OPPONENT	OSTINATO
OXONIAN	OCTARCHY	OLYMPIAD	OPPOSING	OSTIOLAR
OXYACID	OCTOBERS	OLYMPIAN	OPPOSITE	OSTRACOD
OXYSALT	OCTOROON	OMDURMAN	OPPUNGER	OTIOSITY
OXYTONE	OCULISTS	OMELETTE	OPSONIZE	OTOSCOPE
OYSTERS	ODDBALLS	OMISSION	OPTATIVE	OTTOMANS
OZONIZE	ODDITIES	OMITTING	OPTICIAN	OUTBLUFF
	ODDMENTS	OMNIVORE	OPTIMISM	OUTBOARD
	ODIOUSLY	OMPHALOS	OPTIMIST	OUTBOUND
8 LETTERS	ODOMETER	ONCE-OVER	OPTIMIZE	OUTBRAVE
OAFISHLY	ODONTOID	ONCOLOGY	OPTIONAL	OUTBREAK
OARLOCKS	ODYSSEYS	ONCOMING	OPULENCE	OUTBREED
OATCAKES	OENOLOGY	ONDOGRAM	ORACULAR	OUTBURST
OBDURACY	OESTRIOL	ONE-HORSE	ORANGERY	OUTCASTE
OBDURATE	OESTRONE	ONE-PIECE	ORATIONS	OUTCASTS
OBEDIENT	OESTROUS	ONE-SIDED	ORATORIO	OUTCLASS
OBEISANT	OFFENCES	ONE-TO-ONE	ORBITING	OUTCOMES
OBELISKS	OFFENDED	ONE-TRACK	ORCHARDS	OUTCRIES
OBERLAND	OFFENDER	ONLOOKER	ORCHITIC	OUTCROPS
OBITUARY	OFFERING	ONRUSHES	ORCHITIS	OUTCROSS

555

OUTDATED	OVERBIDS	OVERSTEP	OBSCURELY	OFFERINGS
OUTDOING	OVERBOOK	OVERTAKE	OBSCURING	OFFERTORY
OUTDOORS	OVERBORE	OVERTIME	OBSCURITY	OFFHANDED
OUTFACED	OVERCALL	OVERTIRE	OBSEQUENT	OFFICE BOY
OUTFALLS	OVERCAME	OVERTONE	OBSEQUIES	OFFICIALS
OUTFIELD	OVERCAST	OVERTOOK	OBSERVANT	OFFICIANT
OUTFLIGHT	OVERCOAT	OVERTURE	OBSERVERS	OFFICIARY
OUTFLANK	OVERCOME	OVERTURN	OBSERVING	OFFICIATE
OUFLOWS	OVERCOOK	OVERVIEW	OBSESSING	OFFICIOUS
OUTFOXED	OVERCROP	OVERWIND	OBSESSION	OFF-LOADED
OUTGOING	OVERDONE	OVERWORK	OBSESSIVE	OFFSHOOTS
OUT-GROUP	OVERDOSE	OVIDUCAL	OBSOLESCE	OFFSPRING
OUTGROWN	OVERDRAW	OVIPOSIT	OBSTACLES	OFF-STREET
OUTHOUSE	OVERDREW	OVULATED	OBSTETRIC	OILFIELDS
OUTLAWED	OVERFLEW	OWLISHLY	OBSTINANCY	OIL PAINTS
OUTLAWRY	OVERFLOW	OWN GOALS	OBSTINATE	OIL SLICKS
OUTLINED	OVERGROW	OXBRIDGE	OBSTRUENT	OIL TANKER
OUTLINES	OVERHAND	OXIDASIC	OBTAINING	OINTMENT
OUTLIVED	OVERHANG	OXIDIZED	OBTRUDING	OKLAHOMAN
OUTLOOKS	OVERHAUL	OXIDIZER	OBTRUSIVE	OLD FLAMES
OUTLYING	OVERHEAD	OXPECKER	OBVERSION	OLD MASTER
OUTMODED	OVERHEAR	OXTONGUE	OBVIATING	OLD SCHOOL
OUTPOINT	OVERHEAT	OXYGENIC	OBVIATION	OLD-TIMES
OUTPOSTS	OVERHUNG	OXYMORON	OBVIOUSLY	OLEACEOUS
OUTRAGED	OVERKILL	OXYTOCIC	OCCASIONS	OLEANDERS
OUTRAGES	OVERLAID	OXYTOCIN	OCCIPITAL	OLECRANAL
OUTREACH	OVERLAIN	OZONIZER	OCCLUDENT	OLECRANON
OUTRIDER	OVERLAND		OCCLUSION	OLEOGRAPH
OUTRIGHT	OVERLAPS		OCCULTISM	OLEORESIN
OUTRIVAL	OVERLAYS	**9 LETTERS**	OCCULTIST	OLFACTION
OUTSHINE	OVERLEAF	OAST HOUSE	OCCUPANCY	OLFACTORY
OUTSHONE	OVERLOAD	OBBLIGATO	OCCUPANTS	OLIGARGHY
OUTSHOOT	OVERLONG	OBCORDATE	OCCUPIERS	OLIGOCENE
OUTSIDER	OVERLOOK	OBEDIANCE	OCCUPYING	OLIGOPOLY
OUTSIDES	OVERLORD	OBEISANCE	OCCURRENT	OLIVE DRAB
OUTSMART	OVERMUCH	OBELISCAL	OCCURRING	OLIVENITE
OUTSTAND	OVERPAID	OBFUSCATE	OCELLATED	OLYMPIADS
OUTSTARE	OVERPASS	OBJECTIFY	OCTAGONAL	OLYMPIANS
OUTSTRIP	OVERPLAY	OBJECTING	OCTAMETER	OMBUDSMAN
OUTSWING	OVERRATE	OBJECTION	OCTENNIAL	OMBUDSMEN
OUT-TAKES	OVERRIDE	OBJECTIVE	OCTILLION	OMELETTES
OUTVOTED	OVERRIPE	OBJECTORS	OCTOPUSES	OMINOUSLY
OUTWARDS	OVERRODE	OBJURGATE	ODALISQUE	OMISSIBLE
OUTWEIGH	OVERRULE	OBLATIONS	ODD-JOB MAN	OMISSIONS
OUTWORKS	OVERSEAS	OBLIGABLE	ODD MAN OUT	OMNIBUSES
OVALNESS	OVERSEEN	OBLIGATED	ODD MEN OUT	OMNIRANGE
OVARITUS	OVERSEER	OBLIGATOR	ODOMETERS	OMOPHAGIA
OVATIONS	OVERSELL	OBLIQUITY	ODOURLESS	OMOPHAGIC
OVENBIRD	OVERSHOE	OBLIVIOUS	OESTROGEN	ONCE-OVERS
OVENWARE	OVERSHOT	OBNOXIOUS	OFF COLOUR	ONDOGRAPH
OVERALLS	OVERSIDE	OBREPTION	OFFENBACH	ONDOMETER
OVERARCH	OVERSIZE	OBSCENELY	OFFENDERS	ONEROUSLY
OVERAWED	OVERSOLD	OBSCENITY	OFFENDING	ONIONSKIN
OVERBEAR	OVERSTAY	OBSCURANT	OFFENSIVE	ONLOOKERS

ONLOOKING	ORIGINALS	OUTLIVING	OVERNIGHT
ONOMASTIC	ORIGINATE	OUTNUMBER	OVERPOWER
ONRUSHING	ORNAMENTS	OUT-OF-DATE	OVERPRINT
ONSLAUGHT	ORNITHINE	OUTPLAYED	OVERPROOF
ONTOGENIC	OROGRAPHY	OUTRAGING	OVERRATED
OOGENESIS	OROLOGIST	OUTRANKED	OVERREACH
OOGENETIC	ORHPANAGE	OUTRIDDEN	OVERREACT
OOLOGICAL	ORPHANING	OUTRIDERS	OVERRIDER
OPEN-ENDED	ORTHODOXY	OUTRIDING	OVERRULED
OPEN-FACED	ORTHOEPIC	OUTRIGGER	OVERSCORE
OPEN HOUSE	ORTHOPTER	OUTRUNNER	OVERSEER
OPEN SHOPS	ORTHOPTIC	OUTSIDES	OVERSEXED
OPERATING	OSCILLATE	OUTSKIRTS	OVERSHOES
OPERATION	OSCITANCY	OUTSPOKEN	OVERSHOOT
OPERATIVE	OSMOMETER	OUTSPREAD	OVERSIGHT
OPERATORS	OSMOMETRY	OUTSTARED	OVERSIZES
OPERCULAR	OSNABRUCK	OUTSTAYED	OVERSKIRT
OPERETTAS	OSSICULAR	OUTTALKED	OVERSLEEP
OPHIOLOGY	OSSIFRAGE	OUTVOTING	OVERSLEPT
OPPONENCY	OSSIFYING	OUTWARDLY	OVERSPEND
OPPONENTS	OSTENSIVE	OUTWITTED	OVERSPILL
OPPORTUNE	OSTEOLOGY	OUTWORKER	OVERSTATE
OPPOSABLE	OSTEOPATH	OVATIONAL	OVERSHOCK
OPPOSABLY	OSTEOTOME	OVEN-READY	OVERTAKEN
OPPOSITES	OSTEOTOMY	OVERACTED	OVERTAXED
OPPRESSED	OSTRACISM	OVERAWING	OVERTHREW
OPPRESSOR	OSTRACIZE	OVERBLOWN	OVERTHROW
OPTICALLY	OSTRICHES	OVERBORNE	OVERTONES
OPTICIANS	OTHERNESS	OVERBUILD	OVERTRADE
OPTIMISTS	OTOCYSTIC	OVERCHECK	OVERTRICK
OPTIMIZER	OTOLITHIC	OVERCLOUD	OVERTRUMP
OPTOMETER	OTOLOGIST	OVERCOATS	OVERTURES
OPTOMETRY	OTOSCOPIC	OVERCROWD	OVERVIEW
OPULENTLY	OUBLIETTE	OVERDOING	OVERWEIGH
ORANGEADE	OUR FATHER	OVERDOSED	OVERWHELM
ORANGEISM	OURSELVES	OVERDOSES	OVERWRITE
ORANGEMAN	OUT-AND-OUT	OVERDRAFT	OVIFEROUS
ORANG-UTAN	OUTBRAVED	OVERDRAWN	OVIPAROUS
ORATORIES	OUTBREAKS	OVERDRESS	OVOTESTIS
ORATORIOS	OUTBURSTS	OVERDRIVE	OVULATION
ORBICULAR	OUTCASTES	OVERFLOWN	OWNERSHIP
OCHESTRA	OUTERMOST	OVERFLOWS	OXIDATION
ORDAINING	OUTFACING	OVERGLAZE	OXIDATIVE
ORDERLIES	OUTFITTED	OVERGROWN	OXIDIZING
ORDINANCE	OUTFITTER	OVERHANGS	OXYGENATE
ORGANELLE	OUTFOUGHT	OVERHAULS	OXYGENIZE
ORGANISMS	OUTFOXING	OVERHEADS	OYSTER BED
ORGANISTS	OUTGOINGS	OVERHEARD	OZOCERITE
ORGANIZED	OUTGROWTH	OVERISSUE	
ORGANIZER	OUTHOUSES	OVERJOYED	**10 LETTERS**
ORGANZINE	OUTLASTED	OVERLADEN	OAFISHNESS
ORGANISTIC	OUTLAWING	OVERLOAD	OAST HOUSES
ORIENTALS	OUTLAYING	OVERLORDS	OBDURATELY
ORIENTATE	OUTLINING	OVERLYING	OBEDIENTLY

O

10 LETTERS

OBEISANCES	OENOLOGIST	OPPILATION	OSTENSIBLY
OBELISKOID	OESOPHAGUS	OPPOSINGLY	OSTOEBLAST
OBERHAUSEN	OESTRADIOL	OPPOSITION	OSTEOCLAST
OBFUSCATED	OFFENSIVES	OPPRESSING	OSTEOPATHS
OBITUARIES	OFFICE BOYS	OPPRESSION	OSTEOPATHY
OBITUARIST	OFFICIALLY	OPPRESSIVE	OSTEOPHYTE
OBJECTIONS	OFFICIATED	OPPRESSORS	OSTRACIZED
OBJECTIVES	OFFICIATOR	OPPOBRIUM	OSTRACIZER
OBJECTS D'ART	OFF-LICENCE	OPTICAL ART	OSTRACODAN
OBJURGATOR	OFF-LOADING	OPTIMISTIC	OTOLOGICAL
OBLIGATING	OFF-PUTTING	OPTIMIZING	OUBLIETTES
OBLIGATION	OFFSETTING	OPTIONALLY	OUIJA BOARD
OBLIGATIVE	OFF-THE-WALL	OPTOMETRIC	OUTBALANCE
OBLIGATORY	OIL-BEARING	ORANGEWOOD	OUTBIDDING
OBLIGINGLY	OIL TANKERS	ORANGUTANG	OUTBRAVING
OBLITERATE	OLDE WORLDE	ORATORICAL	OUTCLASSED
OBSEQUIOUS	OLD MAIDISH	ORCHESTRAL	OUTFIELDER
OBSERVABLE	OLD MASTERS	ORCHESTRAS	OUTFITTERS
OBSERVABLY	OLD SCHOOLS	ORDER PAPER	OUTFITTING
OBSERVANCE	OLEAGINOUS	ORDINANCES	OUTFLANKED
OBSESSIONS	OLEOGRAPHY	ORDINARILY	OUGENERAL
OBSESSIVES	OLIGARCHIC	ORDINATION	OUTGROWING
OBSTETRICS	OLIGOCLASE	ORDONNANCE	OUTGROWTHS
OBSTRUCTED	OLIGOPSONY	ORDIVICIAN	OUTLANDISH
OBSTRUCTER	OLIGURETIC	ORGANICISM	OUTLASTING
OBTAINABLE	OLIVACEOUS	ORGANICIST	OUT OF DOORS
OBTAINMENT	OMMATIDIAL	ORGANISMAL	OUTPATIENT
OBTUSENESS	OMMATIDIUM	ORGANIZERS	OUTPLAYING
OBVOLUTION	OMNIPOTENT	ORGANIZING	OUTPOINTED
OBVOLUTIVE	OMNISCIENT	ORGANOLOGY	OUTPOURING
OCCASIONAL	OMNIVOROUS	ORIENTATED	OUTRAGEOUS
OCCASIONED	ONCOLOGIST	ORIGINALLY	OUTRANKING
OCCIDENTAL	ONE ANOTHER	ORIGINATED	OUTRIGGERS
OCCUPATION	ONE-MAN BAND	ORIGINATOR	OUTRIVALED
OCCURRENCE	ONE-SIDEDLY	ORNAMENTAL	OUTRUNNING
OCEANARIUM	ONOMASTICS	ORNAMENTED	OUTSELLING
OCEANGOING	ONSLAUGHTS	ORNATENESS	OUTSHINING
OCEANOLOGY	OOPHORITIC	ORINTHOPOD	OUTSMARTED
OCELLATION	OOPHORITIS	ORNITHOSIS	OUTSTARING
OCHLOCRACY	OOPS-A-DAISY	OROGAPHER	OUTSTATION
OCTAHEDRAL	OPALESCENT	OROGRAPHIC	OUTSTAYING
OCTAHEDRON	OPAQUENESS	OROLOGICAL	OUTSTRETCH
OCTAMEROUS	OPEN-HANDED	ORPHANAGES	OUTSWINGER
OCTANGULAR	OPEN LETTER	ORTHOCLASE	OUTTALKING
OCTAVALENT	OPEN-MINDED	ORTHOGENIC	OUTWEIGHED
OCTODECIMO	OPEN SEASON	ORTHOGONAL	OUTWITTING
OCULOMOTOR	OPEN SECRET	OSCILLATED	OUTWORKERS
ODALISQUES	OPEN SESAME	OSCILLATOR	OVARIOTOMY
ODD-PINNATE	OPERATIONS	OSCILATION	OVERACTING
ODIOUSNESS	OPERATIVES	OSCULATORY	OVERACTIVE
ODONTALGIA	OPERETTIST	OSMERIDIUM	OVERARCHED
ODONTALGIC	OPHICLEIDE	OSMOMETRIC	OVERBOOKED
ODONTOLOGY	OPHTHALMIA	OSSIFEROUS	OVERBURDEN
OEDEMATOUS	OPHTHALMIC	OSTENSIBLE	OVERCHARGE

OVERCOMING	**11 LETTERS**	OFFICIALESE	ORIENTALIZE
OVERDOSAGE	OARSMANSHIP	OFFICIATING	ORIENTATING
OVERDOSING	OBFUSCATING	OFFICIATION	ORIENTATION
OVERDRAFTS	OBFUSCATION	OFFICIOUSLY	ORIGINALITY
OVEREXPOSE	OBJECTIVELY	OFF-LICENCES	ORIGINAL SIN
OVERFLIGHT	OBJECTIVISM	OIL PAINTING	ORIGINATING
OVERFLOWED	OBJECTIVIST	OLD-WOMANISH	ORIGINATION
OVERFLYING	OBJECTIVITY	OLEOGRAPHIC	ORIGINATORS
OVERHAULED	OBJURGATION	OLIGARCHIES	ORNAMENTING
OVERLAPPED	OBJURGTORY	OLIGOCHAETE	ORNITHOLOGY
OVERLAYING	OBLIGATIONS	OLIGOTROPHY	ORNITHOPTER
OVERLOADED	OBLIQUITOUS	OLIVE BRANCH	ORTHOCNTRE
OVERLOOKED	OBLITERATED	OMINOUSNESS	ORTHODONTIC
OVERMANNED	OBLITERATOR	OMMATOPHORE	ORTHOGRAPHY
OVERMASTER	OBLIVIOUSLY	OMNIFAROUS	ORTHOPAEDIC
OVERMATTER	OBNOXIOUSLY	OMNIPOTENCE	ORTHOPTERAN
OVERPASSES	OBSCENITIES	OMNIPRESENT	ORTHOSCOPIC
OVERPLAYED	OBSCURATION	OMNISCIENCE	ORTHOSTICHY
OVERRATING	OBSCURITIES	ONAGRACEOUS	ORTHOTROPIC
OVERRIDDEN	OBSERVANCES	ONCOLOGICAL	OSCILLATING
OVERRIDING	OBSERVATION	ONE-MAN BANDS	OSCILLATION
OVERRULING	OBSERVATORY	ONEROUSNESS	OSCILLATORS
OVERSEEING	OBSESSIONAL	ONTOLOGICAL	OSCILLATORY
OVERSHADOW	OBSOLESCENT	OPALESCENCE	OSCILLOGRAM
OVERSIGHTS	OBSTINATELY	OPEN-AND-SHUT	OSMOTICALLY
OVERSPILLS	OBSTIPATION	OPENHEARTED	OSTENTATION
OVERSTATED	OBSTRUCTING	OPENING TIME	OSTEOCLASIS
OVERSTAYING	OBSTRUCTION	OPEN LETTERS	OSTEOLOGIST
OVERSTRUNG	OBSTRUCTIVE	OPEN-MOUTHED	OSTEOPATHIC
OVERTAXING	OBTRUSIVELY	OPEN SEASONS	OSTEOPHYTIC
OVERTHROWN	OBVIOUSNESS	OPEN SECRETS	PSTEOPLASTY
OVERTHROWS	OCCASIONING	OPEN SESAMES	OSTRACIZING
OVERTHRUST	OCCIDENTALS	OPEN VERDICT	OSTRACODERM
OVERTOPPED	OCCULTATION	OPERABILITY	OSTRACODOUS
OVERTURNED	OCCUPATIONS	OPERATIONAL	OUIJA BOARDS
OVERWEIGHT	OCCURRENCES	OPHIOLOGIST	OUTBALANCED
OVERWORKER	OCHLOCRATIC	OPHTHALMIAC	OUTBUILDING
OVIPOSITOR	OCHLOPHOBIA	OPINIONATED	OUTCLASSING
OVULATIONS	OCTAHEDRITE	OPINION POLL	OUTDISTANCE
OXIDIMETRY	OCTILLIONTH	OPPORTUNELY	OUTFIELDERS
OXYCEPHALY	ODDS AND ENDS	OPPORTUNISM	OUTFIGHTING
OXYGENATED	ODONTOBLAST	OPPORTUNIST	OUTFLANKING
OXYGENIZER	ODONTOGRAPH	OPPOSITIONS	OUTNUMBERED
OXYGEN MASK	ODONTOPHORE	OPPROBRIOUS	OUT-OF-THE-WAY
OXYGEN TENT	ODORIFEROUS	OPTOMETRIST	OUTPATIENTS
OYSTER BEDS	ODOROUSNESS	ORANGUTANGS	OUTPOINTING
	OENOLOGICAL	ORCHESTRATE	OUTPOURINGS
	OESOPHAGEAL	ORDERLINESS	OUTRIVALING
	OESTROGENIC	ORDER PAPERS	OUTRIVALLED
	OFFENSIVELY	ORDINATIONS	OUTSMARTING
	OFFERTORIES	ORGANICALLY	OUTSPOKENLY
	OFFHANDEDLY	ORIEL WINDOW	OUTSTANDING
	OFFICE BLOCK	ORIENTALISM	OUTSTRIPPED
	OFFICIALDOM	ORIENTALIST	OUTWEIGHING

OVERACHIEVE
OVERANXIOUS
OVERARCHING
OVERBALANCE
OVERBEARING
OVERBIDDING
OVERBOOKING
OVERCHARGED
OVERCHARGES
OVERCLOUDED
OVERCROPPED
OVERCROWDED
OVERDEVELOP4
OVERDRAUGHT
OVERDRAWING
OVERDRESSED
OVEREXPOED
OVERFLOWING
OVERGARMENT
OVERHAULING
OVERHEARING
OVERINDULGENCE
OVERLAPPING
OVERLOADING
OVERLOOKING
OVERMANNING
OVERPLAYING
OVERPOWERED
OVERPRODUCE
OVERPROTECT
OVERREACHED
OVERREACTED
OVERRUNNING
OVERSELLING
OVERSTAFFED
OVERSTATING
OVERSTAYING
OVERSTEPPED
OVERSHOCKED
OVERSTUFFED
OVERTOPPING
OVERTURNING
OVERWEENING
OVERWHELMED
OVERWORKING
OVERWROUGHT
OVIPOSITION
OWNER-DRIVER
OXIDATIONAL
OXIDIMETRIC
OXIDIZATION
OXYCEPHALIC
OXYGENATING
OXYGENATION

OXYGEN MASKS
OXYGEN TENTS\
OXYHYDROGEN
OXYSULPHIDE
OZONIFEROUS
OZONIZATION
OZONOSPHERE

12 LETTERS
OBJECT LESSON
OBLIGATIONAL
OBLIGATORILY
OBLITERATING
OBLITERATION
OBLITERATIVE
OBSCURANTISM
OBSCURANTIST
OBSEQUIOUSLY
OBSERVATIONS
OBSOLESCENCE
OBSOLETENESS
OBSTETRICIAN
OBSTREPEROUS
OBSTRUCTIONS
OCCASIONALLY
OCCUPATIONAL
OCEANOGRAPHY
OCTOGENARIAN
OCTOSYLLABIC
OCTOSYLLABLE
ODONTOGRAPHY
ODONTOLOGIST
ODONTOPHORAL
OESOPHAGUSES
OFFICE BLOCKS
OFFICE HOLDER
OIL PAINTINGS
OLD-FASHIONED
OLD SCHOOL TIE
OLD TESTAMENT
OLD WIVES' TALE
OLEORESINOUS
OLIGOTROPHIC
OLYMPIC GAMES
OMNIPRESENCE
ONE-SIDEDNESS
ONE-TRACK MIND
ONE-UPMANSHIP
ONOMATOPOEIA
ONOMATOPOETIC
ONYCHOPHORAN
OOPHORECTOMY
OPEN-HANDEDLY

OPENING TIMES
OPEN-MINDEDLY
OPEN SANDWICH
OPEN VERDICTS
OPERA GLASSES
OPERATICALLY
OPHTHALMITIS
OPINION POLLS
OPPORTUNISTS
OPPOSABILITY
OPPOSITENESS
OPPOSITIONAL
OPPRESSINGLY
OPPRESSIVELY
OPTIMIZATION
ORATORICALLY
ORBICULARITY
ORCHESTRA PIT
ORCHESTRATED
ORCHIDACEOUS
ORDINARINESS
ORGAN GRINDER
ORGANICISTIC
ORGANIZATION
ORGANOGRAPHY
ORGANOLEPTIC
ORGANOLOGIST
ORIEL WINDOWS
ORIENTALISTS
ORIENTATIONS
ORIENTEERING
ORNAMENTALLY
OROGENICALLY
OROLOGICALLY
ORTHOCEPHALY
ORTHODONTICS
ORTHOGENESIS
ORTHOGENETIC
ORTHOGRAPHER
ORTHOGRAPHIC
ORTHOMORPHIC
ORTHOPAEDICS
ORTHOPAEDIST
ORTHOPTEROUS
ORTHORHOMBIC
ORHOTROPISM
OSCILLATIONS
OSCILLOGRAPH
OSCILLOSCOPE
OSSIFICATION
OSTENTATION
OSTENTATIOUS
OSTEOBLASTIC
OSTEOCLASTIC

OSTEOLOGICAL
OSTEOMALACIA
OSTEOPLASTIC
OSTRACIZABLE
OTHER WORLDLY
OUTBALANCING
OUTBUILDINGS
OUTDISTANCED
OUTGENERALED
OUTLANDISHLY
OUTMANOEUVRE
OUTNUMBERING
OUTRAGEOUSLY
OUTRIVALLING
OUTSTRETCHED
OUTSTRIPPING
OVERBALANCED
OVERBURDENED
OVERCAPACITY
OVERCAUTIOUS
OVERCHARGING
OVERCLOUDING
OVERCRITICAL
OVERCROPPING
OVERCROWDING
OVERDRESSING
OVEREMPHATIC
OVERESTIMATE
OVEREXPOSING
OVERGENEROUS
OVERINDULGED
OVERMASTERED
OVERPOPULATE
OVERPOWERING
OVERREACHING
OVERREACTING
OVERREACTION
OVERSHADOWED
OVERSHOOTING
OVERSIMPLIFY
OVERSLEEPING
OVERSTEPPING
OVERSTOCKING
OVERTHROWING
OVERWHELMING
OWNER-DRIVERS
OXYACETYLENE
OXYGENIZABLE

13 LETTERS

OBJECTIONABLE
OBJECTIONABLY
OBJECTIVENESS
OBJECTIVISTIC
OBJECT LESSONS
OBLATE SPHERES
OBLIVIOUSNESS
OBNOXIOUSNESS
OBSERVATIONAL
OBSERVATORIES
OBSESSIVENESS
OBSTETRICALLY
OBSTETRICIANS
OBSTRUCTIONAL
OBSTRUCTIVELY
OBTAINABILITY
OBTRUSIVENESS
OCCASIONALISM
OCCIDENTALISM
OCCIDENTALIST
OCCIDENTALIZE
OCCLUSIVENESS
OCEANOGRAPHER
OCEANOGRAPHIC
OCTOGENARIANS
ODONTOBLASTIC
ODONTOGLOSSUM
ODONTOGRAPHIC
ODONTOLOGICAL
OFFENSIVENESS
OFFHANDEDNESS
OFFICEHOLDERS
OFFICIOUSNESS
OLD AGE PENSION
OLD-BOY NETWORK
OLD SCHOOL TIES
OLD WIVES' TALES
OLIGOPOLISTIC

OLIVE BRANCHES
OMMATOPHOROUS
ONE-NIGHT STAND
ONE-TRACK MINDS
ONTOGENICALLY
ONTOLOGICALLY
OPENHEARTEDLY
OPERATIONALLY
OPERATIVENESS
OPTHALMOLOGY
OPPORTUNENESS
OPPORTUNISTIC
OPPORTUNITIES
OPPOSITIONIST
OPPROBRIOUSLY
ORCHESTRA PITS
ORCHESTRATING
ORCHESTRATION
ORDINARY LEVEL
ORGAN GRINDERS
ORGANIZATIONS
ORGANOGENESIS
ORGANOGENETIC
ORGANOGRAPHIC
ORGANOLOGICAL
ORGANOTHERAPY
ORIENTALISTIC
ORIENTATIONAL
ORNAMENTATION
ORNITHISCHIAN
ORNITHOLOGIST
ORTHOCEPHALIC
ORTHOEPICALLY
ORTHOGANTHISM
ORTHOGNATHOUS
ORTHOHYDROGEN
ORTHOSTICHOUS
OSCILLOGRAPHY
OSTENSIBILITY

OSTEOMALACIAL
OSTEOMYELITIS
OTHER-DIRECTED
OUTBOARD MOTOR
OUTDISTANCING
OUTGENERALING
OUTGENERALLED
OUTMANOEUVRED
OUTSPOKENNESS
OUTSTANDINGLY
OVERABUNDANCE
OVERAMBITIOUS
OVERBALANCING
OVERBEARINGLY
OVERBURDENING
OVERCONFIDENT
OVERCRITICIZE
OVERCULTIVATE
OVERDEVELOPED
OVERELABORATE
OVEREMPHASIZE
OVERESTIMATED
OVERESTIMATES
OVERINDULGING
OVERMASTERING
OVERPOPULATED
OVERREACTIONS
OVERSHADOWING
OVERSTATEMENT
OVERSUBSCRIBE
OVERWEENINGLY
OVOVIVIPAROUS
OWNER-OCCUPIED
OWNER-OCCUPIER
OYSTER CATCHER

P
3 LETTERS to 5 LETTERS

3 LETTERS	4 LETTERS				
PAD	PACE	PHEW	PUPS	PARCH	PEONY
PAL	PACK	PHON	PURE	PARED	PERAK
PAN	PACT	PHOT	PURL	PARER	PERCH
PAP	PADS	PHUT	PURR	PARIS	PERIL
PAR	PAGE	PICA	PUSH	PARKA	PERKS
PAS	PAID	PICK	PUSS	PARKS	PERKY
PAT	PAIL	PIED	PUTT	PARKY	PERRY
PAW	PAIN	PIER	PYRE	PARMA	PER SE
PAY	PAIR	PIGS		PAROL	PESKY
PCS	PALE	PIKE		PARRY	PESOS
PEA	PALL	PILE	5 LETTERS	PARSE	PESTS
PEE	PALM	PILL	PACED	PARTS	PETAL
PAG	PALP	PIMP	PACER	PARTY	PETER
PEN	PALS	PINE	PACES	PASHA	PETIT
PEP	PANE	PING	PACKS	PASSE	PETTY
PER	PANT	PINK	PACTS	PASTA	PEWEE
PET	PAPA	PINS	PADDY	PASTS	PEWIT
PEW	PARA-	PINT	PADRE	PASTY	PHASE
PHD	PARE	PINY	PADUA	PATCH	PHIAL
PHS	PARK	PIPE	PAEAN	PATEN	PHLOX
PIE	PARS	PIPS	PAEON	PATER	PHONE
PIG	PART	PIPA	PAGAN	PATES	PHOTO
PIN	PASS	PISH	PAGED	PATHS	PHUTS
PIP	PAST	PITH	PAGES	PATIO	PHYLA
PIS	PATE	PITS	PAILS	PATNA	PHYLE
PIT	PATH	PITY	PAINS	PATTY	PIANO
PIX	PATS	PLAN	PAINT	PAUSE	PICKS
PLC	PAVE	PLAY	PAIRS	PAVED	PICKY
PLY	PAWL	PLEA	PALEA	PAWED	PICOT
PMS	PAWN	PLEB	PALED	PAWKY	PIECE
POD	PAWS	PLED	PALER	PAWNS	PIERS
POP	PAYE	PLOD	PALES	PAYEE	PIETA
POT	PEAK	PROF	PALLS	PEACE	PIETY
POW	PEAL	PROM	PALLY	PEACH	PIGGY
POX	PEAR	PROP	PALMA	PEAKS	PIGMY
PPS	PEAS	PROS	PALMS	PEAKY	PIING
PRE-	PEAT	PROW	PALMY	PEARL	PIKES
PRO	PECK	PSST	PALSY	PEARS	PILAF
PRY	PEED	PUBS	PANDA	PEATS	PILED
PTA	PEEK	PUCE	PANEL	PEATY	PILES
PTO	PEEL	PUCK	PANES	PECAN	PILLS
PUB	PEEP	PUDS	PANGS	PECKS	PILOT
PUD	PEER	PUFF	PANIC	PEDAL	PIMPS
PUG	PEGS	PUGS	PANNE	PEEPS	PINCH
PUN	PELT	PUKE	PANSY	PEERS	PINED
PUP	PENS	PULL	PANTS	PEEVE	PINES
PUS	PERK	PULP	PANTY	PEKOE	PINEY
PUT	PERM	PUMA	PAPAL	PELTS	PINGO
PVC	PERT	PUMP	PAPAS	PENAL	PINKO
PYX	PERU	PUNK	PAPAW	PENCE	PINKS
	PEST	PUNS	PAPER	PENIS	PINNA
	PETS	PUNT	PAPPY	PENNA	PINNY
	PEWS	PUNY	PAPUA	PENNY	PINTA
		PUPA	PARAS	PENZA	PINTO

PINTS	PODIA	POWAN	PSYCH	PADDED	PAPYRI
PINUP	POEMS	POWER	PUBIC	PADDLE	PARADE
PIOUS	POESY	POXES	PUBIS	PADRES	PARAMO
PIPAL	POETS	PRANK	PUCKS	PAEANS	PARANA
PIPED	POGGE	PRATE	PUDGY	PAELLA	PARANG
PIPER	POINT	PRATO	PUFFS	PAEONY	PARAPH
PIPES	POISE	PRATS	PUFFY	PAGANS	PARCEL
PIPIT	POKED	PRAWN	PUKED	PAGODA	PARDON
PIQUE	POKER	PREEN	PUKKA	PAHING	PARENT
PISTE	POKES	PREPS	PULER	PAID-UP	PARGET
PITCH	POLAR	PRESA	PULLS	PAINED	PARIAH
PITHY	POLED	PRESS	PULPS	PAINTS	PARIAN
PITON	POLES	PRICE	PULPY	PAIRED	PARIES
PIURA	POLIO	PRICK	PULSE	PAJAMA	PARING
PIVOT	POLJE	PRICY	PUMAS	PALACE	PARISH
PIXEL	POLKA	PRIDE	PUMPS	PALAIS	PARITY
PIXIE	POLLS	PRIER	PUNCH	PALATE	PARKAS
PIZZA	POLYP	PRING	PUNKA	PALELY	PARKED
PLACE	POLYS	PRILL	PUNKS	PALEST	PARKIN
PLAID	POMMY	PRIME	PUNTS	PALING	PARLEY
PLAIN	PONCE	PRIMO	PUNTY	PALISH	PARODY
PLAIT	PONCY	PRIMP	PUPAE	PALLAS	PAROLE
PLANE	PONDS	PRINK	PUPAL	PALLED	PARREL
PLANK	PONGS	PRINT	PUPAS	PALLET	PARROT
PLANS	PONGY	PRIOR	PUPIL	PALLIS	PARSEC
PLANT	POOCH	PRISE	PUPPY	PALLOR	PARSED
PLASH	POOLE	PRISM	PUREE	PALMAR	PARSEE
PLASM	POOLS	PRIVY	PURER	PALMED	PARSER
PLATE	POONA	PRIZE	PURGE	PALMED	PARSON
PLATY	POOPS	PRO-AM	PURRS	PALTER	PARTED
PLAYS	POPES	PROBE	PURSE	PALTRY	PARTLY
PLAZA	POPPA	PRODS	PUSAN	PAMPAS	PARTON
PLEAD	POPPY	PROEM	PUSHY	PAMPER	PARURE
PLEAS	POPSY	PROFS	PUT-ON	PANADA	PASHTO
PLEAT	POP-UP	PROLE	PUTTO	PANAMA	PASSED
PLEBS	PORCH	PROMO	PUTTS	PANDAS	PASSES
PLICA	PORED	PROMS	PUTTY	PANDER	PASSIM
PLIED	PORES	PRONE	PYGMY	PANDIT	PASTED
PLIER	PORGY	PRONG	PYLON	PANELS	PASTEL
PLONK	PORKY	PROOF	PYOID	PANICS	PASTES
PLOTS	PORNO	PROPS	PYRAN	PANNED	PASTOR
PLOWS	PORTS	PROSE	PYRES	PANTED	PASTRY
PLOYS	POSED	PROSY	PYREX	PANTRY	PATCHY
PLUCK	PODER	PROTO	PYXES	PANZER	PATENT
PLUGS	PODES	PROUD	PYXIE	PAOTOW	PATERS
PLUMB	POSIT	PROVE		PAPACY	PATHAN
PLUME	POSSE	PROWL		PAPAIN	PATHOS
PLUMS	POSTS	PROWS	**6 LETTERS**	PAPAYA	PATINA
PLUMY	POTTO	PROXY	PACIFY	PAPERS	PATIOS
PLUNK	POTTY	PRUDE	PACING	PAPERY	PATOIS
PLUSH	POUCH	PRUNE	PACKED	PAPIST	PATRAS
PLUTO	POULT	PSALM	PACKER	PAPPUS	PATROL
POACH	POUND	PSEUD	PACKET	PAPUAN	PATRON
PODGY	POUTS	PSOAS	PADAUK	PAPULE	PATTED

PATTEN	PELMET	PETALS	PIGEON	PITCHY	PLIGHT
PATTER	PELOTA	PETARD	PIGGED	PITHOS	PLINTH
PAUCAL	PELTED	PETERS	PIGGIN	PITIED	PLISSE
PAUNCH	PELTER	PETITE	PIGLET	PITIES	PLOUGH
PAUPER	PELTRY	PETREL	PIGNUS	PITMAN	PLOVER
PAUSED	PELVES	PETROL	PIGNUT	PITMEN	PLOWED
PAUSER	PELVIC	PETTED	PIGSTY	PIESAW	PLUCKS
PAUSES	PELVIS	PETTER	PILEUM	PITTED	PLUCKY
PAVANE	PENCHI	PEWITS	PILEUP	PIVOTS	PLUMED
PAVING	PENCIL	PEWTER	PILEUS	PIXELS	PLUMES
PAWING	PENMAN	PHASED	PILFER	PIXIES	PLUMMY
PAWNED	PENNED	PHASES	PILING	PIZZAS	PLUNGE
PAWPAW	PENNON	PHASIC	PILLAR	PLACED	PLURAL
PAXWAX	PEN PAL	PHENOL	PILLOW	PLACER	PLUSES
PAYBED	PENTAD	PHENYL	PILOSE	PLACES	PLUTON
PAYDAY	PENT UP	PHIALS	PILOTS	PLACET	PLYING
PAYEES	PENTYL	PHILAE	PILULE	PLACID	PNEUMA
PAYING	PENULT	PHIZOG	PIMPED	PLAGAL	POCKED
PAYOFF	PENURY	PHLEGM	PIMPLE	PLAGUE	POCKET
PAYOLA	PEOPLE	PHLOEM	PIMPLY	PLAGUY	PODDED
PAYOUT	PEORIA	PHOBIA	PINCER	PLAICE	PODIUM
PEACES	PEPLUM	PHOBIC	PINEAL	PLAIDS	PODZOL
PEACHY	PEPPED	PHOBOS	PINENE	PLAINS	POETIC
PEAHEN	PEPPER	PHOEBE	PINERY	PLAINT	POETRY
PEAKED	PEPSIN	PHONED	PINGED	PLANAR	POGROM
PEALED	PEPTIC	PHONES	PINIER	PLANED	POINTE
PEANUT	PERILS	PHONEY	PINING	PLANER	POINTS
PEARLS	PERIOD	PHONIC	PINION	PLANES	POISED
PEARLY	PERISH	PHONON	PINITE	PLANET	POISON
PEBBLE	PERKED	PHOOEY	PINKED	PLANKS	POKERS
PEBBLY	PERLIS	PHOTIC	PINKER	PLANTS	POKILY
PECANS	PERMED	PHOTON	PINKIE	PLAQUE	POKING
PECKED	PERMIT	PHOTOS	PINKOS	PLASHY	POLAND
PECTEN	PERNOD	PHRASE	PINNED	PLASMA	POLDER
PECTIC	PERRON	PHYLUM	PINNER	PLATAN	POLICE
PECTIN	PERSIA	PHYSIC	PINTAS	PLATER	POLICY
PEDALS	PERSON	PHYSIO	PINTLE	PLATES	POLING
PEDANT	PERTLY	PHYTON	PINUPS	PLAYED	POLISH
PEDATE	PERUKE	PIAFFE	PIPAGE	PLAYER	POLITE
PEDDLE	PERUSE	PIANOS	PIPALS	PLAZAS	POLITY
PEDLER	PESADE	PIAZZA	PIPERS	PLEACH	POLKAS
PEEPBO	PESTER	PICKED	PIPING	PLEASE	POLLAN
PEEPED	PESTLE	PICKER	PIPITS	PLEATS	POLLED
PEEPER	PETALS	PICKET	PIPKIN	PLEBBY	POLLEN
PEEPUL	PATARD	PICKLE	PIPPED	PLEDGE	POLLEX
PEERED	PATERS	PICK-UP	PIPPIN	PLEIAD	POLLUX
PEEVED	PATITE	PICNIC	PIQUED	PLENTY	POLONY
PEEWIT	PETRAL	PIDDLE	PIQUES	PLENUM	POLYPS
PEGGED	PETROL	PIDGIN	PIQUET	PLEURA	POMACE
PEG LEG	PETTED	PIECED	PIRACY	PLEXOR	POMADE
PEKING	PETTER	PIECER	PISCES	PLEXUS	POMMEL
PELAGE	PESETA	PIECES	PISTIL	PLIANT	POMPOM
PELITE	PESTER	PIERCE	PISTOL	PLICAL	POMPON
PELLET	PESTLE	PIFFLE	PISTON	PLIERS	PONCES

PONCEY	POTTER	PROBES	PUMMEL	PUZZLE	PALMYRA
PONCHO	POUNCE	PROFIT	PUMPED	PYLONS	PALPATE
PONDER	POUNDS	PROJET	PUNCHY	PYRENE	PALSIED
PONGED	POURER	PROLEG	PUNDIT	PYRITE	PAMPEAN
PONGEE	POUTED	PROLES	PUNIER	PYTHON	PANACEA
PONGID	POWDER	PROLIX	PUNISH		PANACHE
PONIES	POWERS	PROLOG	PUNJAB		PANAMAS
PONTIC	POWWOW	PROMOS	PUNKAH	**7 LETTERS**	PAN-ARAB
PONTIL	PRAGUE	PROMPT	PUNNED	PACIFIC	PANCAKE
POODLE	PRAISE	PRONGS	PUNNET	PACKAGE	PANCHAX
POOPED	PRANCE	PRONTO	PUNTED	PACKERS	PANDECT
POOPER	PRANKS	PROOFS	PUNTER	PACKETS	PAMDITS
POORER	PRATED	PROPEL	PUPATE	PACK ICE	PANDORE
POORLY	PRATER	PROPER	PUPILS	PACKING	PANELED
POP ART	PRAWNS	PROPYL	PUPPED	PADDIES	PANGAEA
POPERY	PRAXIS	PROSES	PUPPET	PADDING	PANICKY
POPGUN	PRAYED	PROTEA	PUPPIS	PADDLED	PANICLE
POPISH	PRAYER	PRO TEM	PURDAH	PADDLER	PANNIER
POPLAR	PREACH	PROTON	PUREED	PADDLES	PANNING
POPLIN	PRECIS	PROVED	PUREES	PADDOCK	PANOCHA
POPPAS	PREFAB	PROVEN	PURELY	PADLOCK	PANOPLY
POPPED	PREFER	PROWLS	PUREST	PADRONE	PANSIES
POPPER	PREFIX	PRUDES	PURFLE	PAGEANT	PANTHER
POPPET	PREPAY	PRUNED	PURGED	PAGEBOY	PANTIES
POPPLE	PREPPY	PRUNER	PURGER	PAGINAL	PANTILE
PORING	PRESET	PRUNES	PURGES	PAGODAS	PANTING
PORISM	PRESTO	PRYING	PURIFY	PAINFUL	PANTOUM
PORKER	PRETTY	PSALMS	PURINE	PAINING	PANZERS
POROUS	PREYED	PSEUDO-	PURISM	PAINTED	PAPAYAS
PORTAL	PREYER	PSEUDS	PURIST	PAINTER	PAPERED
PORTED	PRICED	PSEUDY	PURITY	PAIRING	PAPERER
PORTER	PRICES	PSYCHE	PURLED	PAIR-OAR	PAPILLA
PORTLY	PRICEY	PSYCHO-	PURLER	PAISLEY	PAPISTS
POSERS	PRICKS	PTOSIS	PURLIN	PAJAMAS	PAPOOSE
POSEUR	PRIDED	PUBLIC	PURPLE	PALACES	PAPRIKA
POSHER	PRIDES	PUCKER	PURRED	PALADIN	PAPYRUS
POSIES	PRIMER	PUDDLE	PURSED	PALATAL	PARABLE
POSSES	PRIMES	PUDDLY	PURSER	PALATES	PARADED
POSSET	PRIMLY	PUFFED	PURSES	PALAVER	PARADER
POSSUM	PRIMUS	PUFFER	PURSUE	PALE ALE	PARADES
POSTAL	PRINCE	PUFFIN	PURVEY	PALERMO	PARADOX
POSTED	PRINTS	PUGGED	PUSHED	PALETTE	PARAGON
POSTER	PRIORS	PUKING	PUSHER	PALFREY	PARAPET
POSTIE	PRIORY	PULLED	PUSHES	PALINGS	PARASOL
POTAGE	PRISED	PULLET	PUSH-UP	PALLETS	PARBOIL
POTASH	PRISMS	PULLEY	PUSSES	PALLIER	PARCELS
POTATO	PRISON	PULL-IN	PUTLOG	PALLING	PARCHED
POTBOY	PRISSY	PULL-ON	PUT-OFF	PALLIUM	PARDONS
POTEEN	PRIVET	PULPED	PUT-ONS	PALMATE	PAREIRA
POTENT	PRIZED	PULPIT	PUTRID	PALMIER	PARENTS
POTFUL	PRIZES	PULSAR	PUTSCH	PALMING	PARESIS
POTHER	PRO-AMS	PULSED	PUTTED	PALMIRA	PARETIC
POTION	PROBED	PULSES	PUTTEE	PALMIST	PARFAIT
POTTED	PROBER	PUMICE	PUTTER	PALM OIL	PARIAHS

PARINGS	PATELLA	PECTATE	PEOPLED	PERUGIA
PARKIER	PATENCY	PECTIZE	PEOPLES	PERUSAL
PARKING	PATENTS	PEDALED	PEPPERS	PERUSED
PARKWAY	PATHANS	PEDANTS	PEPPERY	PERUSER
PARLEYS	PATHWAY	PEDDLED	PEP PILL	PERVADE
PARLOUR	PATIALA	PEDDLER	PEPPING	PERVERT
PARLOUS	PATIENT	PEDICLE	PEP TALK	PESCARA
PARODIC	PATRIAL	PEDLARS	PEPTIDE	PESETAS
PAROLED	PATRIOT	PEDOCAL	PEPTIZE	PESKIER
PAROLES	PATROLS	PEEKING	PEPTONE	PESSARY
PARONYM	PATRONS	PEELING	PERACID	PESTLES
PAROTIC	PATTENS	PEEPERS	PERCALE	PETARDS
PAROTID	PATTERN	PEEPING	PER CENT	PETCOCK
PARQUET	PATTERS	PEERAGE	PERCEPT	PETIOLE
PARRIED	PATTIES	PEERESS	PERCHED	PET NAME
PARRIES	PATTING	PEERING	PERCHER	PETRELS
PARROTS	PAUCITY	PEEVING	PERCHES	PETRIFY
PARSEES	PAULINE	PEEVISH	PERCOID	PETROUS
PARSERS	PAULIST	PEEWTS	PERCUSS	PETTIER
PARSING	PAUNCHY	PEGGING	PER DIEM	PETTILY
PARSLEY	PAUPERS	PEGLEGS	PEREIRA	PETTING
PARSNIP	PAUSING	PELAGIC	PERFECT	PETTISH
PARSONS	PAVANES	PELICAN	PERFIDY	PETUNIA
PARTAKE	PAVINGS	PELITIC	PERFORM	PHAETON
PARTIAL	PAVIOUR	PELLETS	PERFUME	PHALANX
PARTIED	PAWKIER	PELMETS	PERFUSE	PHALLIC
PARTIES	PAWKILY	PELORIA	PERGOLA	PHALLUS
PARTING	PAWNAGE	PELORUS	PERHAPS	PHANTON
PARTITA	PAWNING	PELOTAS	PERIDOT	PHARAOH
PARTITE	PAWPAWS	PELTATE	PERIGEE	PHARYNX
PARTNER	PAYABLE	PELTING	PERIGON	PHASING
PARTOOK	PAYBEDS	PENALLY	PERIODS	PHASMID
PARVENU	PAY DIRT	PENALTY	PERIQUE	PHELLEM
PASCHAL	PAYLOAD	PENANCE	PERIWIG	PHILTRE
PASSADE	PAYMENT	PENDANT	PERJURE	PHIZOGS
PASSAGE	PAYOUTS	PENDENT	PERJURY	PHLOXES
PASSANT	PAYROLL	PENDING	PERKIER	PHOBIAS
PAS SEUL	PAYSLIP	PENGUIN	PERKILY	PHOBICS
PASSING	PEACHES	PENISES	PERKING	PHOCINE
PASSION	PEACOCK	PEN NAME	PERLITE	PHOENIX
PASSIVE	PEAFOWL	PENNANT	PERMIAN	PHONATE
PASSKEY	PEAHENS	PENNATE	PERMING	PHONE-IN
PASTELS	PEAKIER	PENNIES	PERMITS	PHONEME
PASTERN	PEAKING	PENNING	PERMUTE	PHONEYS
PASTE-UP	PEALING	PENNONS	PERPEND	PHONICS
PASTIER	PEANUTS	PEN PALS	PERPLEX	PHONIER
PASTIES	PEARLER	PENSILE	PERSEID	PHONING
PASTILY	PEASANT	PENSION	PERSIAN	PHRASAL
PASTIME	PEBBLES	PENSIVE	PERSIST	PHRASED
PASTORS	PECCANT	PENTANE	PERSONA	PHRASES
PASTURE	PECCARY	PENTENE	PERSONS	PHRATRY
PATCHED	PECKERS	PENTODE	PERSPEX	PHRENIC
PATCHER	PECKING	PENTOSE	PERTAIN	PHYSICS
PATCHES	PECTASE	PEONIES	PERTURB	PHYSIOS

PIANISM	PILLAGE	PISCARY	PLATOON	PLUNGER
PIANIST	PILLARS	PISCINA	PLATTER	PLURALS
PIANOLA	PILLBOX	PISCINE	PLAUDIT	PLUSHER
PIASTRE	PILLION	PISTILS	PLAY-ACT	PLUVIAL
PIAZZAS	PILLOCK	PISTOLS	PLAYBOY	PLYWOOD
PIBROCH	PILLORY	PISTONS	PLAYERS	POACHED
PICADOR	PILLOWS	PIT-A-PAT	PLAYFUL	POACHER
PICARDY	PILOTED	PITCHED	PLAYING	PO BOXES
PICCOLO	PILSNER	PITCHER	PLAYLET	POCHARD
PICEOUS	PILULAR	PITCHES	PLAY-OFF	POCKETS
PICKAXE	PIMENTO	PITEOUS	PLAYPEN	PODAGRA
PICKERS	PIMPING	PITFALL	PLEADED	PODDING
PICKETS	PIMPLED	PITHEAD	PLEADER	PODESTA
PICKIER	PIMPLES	PITHIER	PLEASED	PODGIER
PICKING	PINBALL	PITHILY	PLEASER	PODGILY
PICKLED	PINCERS	PITIFUL	PLEATED	PODIUMS
PICKLER	PINCHED	PIT PONY	PLEATER	POETESS
PICKLES	PINCHES	PIT DROP	PLEDGED	POETICS
PICK-UPS	PINETUM	PITTING	PLEDGER	PO-FACED
PICNICS	PINFISH	PITYING	PLEDGES	POGONIA
PICOTEE	PINFOLD	PIVOTAL	PLEDGET	POGROMS
PICRATE	PINGING	PIVOTED	PLENARY	POINTED
PICRITE	PINGUID	PIZZAZZ	PLEURAL	POISING
PICTISH	PINHEAD	PLACARD	PLEURON	POISONS
PICTURE	PINHOLE	PLACATE	PLIABLE	POKIEST
PIDDLED	PINIEST	PLACEBO	PLIANCY	POLARIS
PIDDOCK	PINIONS	PLACING	PLICATE	POLEAXE
PIDGIND	PINKIEST	PLACKET	PLIGHTS	POLECAT
PIEBALD	PINKEYE	PLACOID	PLINTHS	POLEMIC
PIECING	PINK GIN	PLAGUED	PLODDED	POLICED
PIE-EYED	PINKIES	PLAGUER	PLODDER	POLITIC
PIERCED	PINKING	PLAGUES	PLONKED	POLLACK
PIERCER	PINKISH	PLAINER	PLOPPED	POLLARD
PIETIES	PINKOES	PLAINLY	PLOSION	POLLING
PIGEONS	PINNACE	PLAINTS	PLOSIVE	POLL TAX
PIGFISH	PINNATE	PLAITED	PLOTTED	POLLUTE
PIGGERY	PINNIES	PLANETS	PLOTTER	POLTAVA
PIGGIER	PINNING	PLANING	PLOUGHS	POLYGON
PIGGIES	PINNULE	PLANISH	PLOVERS	POLMER
PIGGING	PINTAIL	PLANNED	PLOWING	POLYNYA
PIGGISH	PINWORK	PLANNER	PLUCKED	POLYPOD
PIG IRON	PINWORM	PLANNER	PLUCKER	POLYPUS
PIGLETS	PIONEER	PLANTED	PLUGGED	POMMELS
PIGMENT	PIOUSLY	PLANTER	PLUMAGE	POMMIES
PIGMIES	PIPETTE	PLANULA	PLUMATE	POMPANO
PIGSKIN	PIPPING	PLAQUES	PLUMBED	POMPEII
PIGTAIL	PIPPINS	PLASMIN	PLUMBER	POMPOMS
PIGWEED	PIQUANT	PLASMON	PLUMBIC	POMPOUS
PIKE MAN	PIQUING	PLASTER	PLUMING	PONCHOS
PIKEMEN	PIRAEUS	PLASTIC	PLUMMET	PONGIER
PILEATE	PIRANHA	PLASTID	PLUMPER	PONGING
PILEOUS	PIRATED	PLATEAU	PLUMULE	PONIARD
PILEUPS	PIRATES	PLATINA	PLUNDER	PONTIFF
PILGRIM	PIRATIC	PLATING	PLUNGED	PONTINE

PONTOON	POTENCY	PREEMPT	PRINTED	PROSAIC
POOCHES	POTFULS	PREENED	PRINTER	PROSIER
POODLES	POTHEEN	PREENER	PRISING	PROSILY
POOFIER	POTHERB	PREFABS	PRISOND	PROSODY
POOH-BAH	POTHOLE	PREFACE	PRITHEE	PROSPER
POOLING	POTHOOK	PREFECT	PRIVACY	PROTEAN
POOPERS	POTICHE	PREHEAT	PRIVATE	PROTECT
POOREST	POTIONS	PRELACY	PRIVIER	PROTEGE
POOR LAW	POTLUCK	PRELATE	PRIVIES	PROTEIN
POPADUM	POTOMAC	PRELIMS	PRIVILY	PROTEST
POPCORN	POTSHOT	PRELUDE	PRIVITY	PROTIST
POPEDOM	POTTAGE	PREMIER	PRIZING	PROTIUM
POP-EYED	POTTERS	PREMISE	PROBANG	PROTONS
POPGUNS	POTTERY	PREMISS	PROBATE	PROTYLE
POPLARS	POTTIER	PREMIUM	PROBING	PROUDER
POPOVER	POTTIES	PREPACK	PROBITY	PROUDLY
POPPERS	POTTING	PREPAID	PROBLEM	PROVERB
POPPETS	POUCHED	PREPARE	PROCARP	PROVIDE
POPPIES	POUCHES	PREPUCE	PROCEED	PROVING
POPPING	POULARD	PRESAGE	PROCESS	PROVISO
POPULAR	POULTRY	PRESENT	PROCTOR	PROVOKE
PORCHES	POUNCED	PRESIDE	PROCURE	PROVOST
PORCINE	POUNCES	PRESSED	PRODDED	PROWESS
PORKERS	POUNDAL	PRESSES	PRODDER	PROWLED
PORKIER	POUNDED	PRESSOR	PRODIGY	PROWLER
PORK PIE	POUNDER	PRESS-UP	PRODUCE	PROXIES
PORTAGE	POURING	PRESTOS	PRODUCT	PROXIMA
PORTALS	POUTING	PRESUME	PROFANE	PRUDENT
PORTEND	POVERTY	PRETEND	PROFESS	PRUDERY
PORTENT	POWDERS	PRETEST	PROFFER	PRUDISH
PORTERS	POWDERY	PRETEXT	PROFILE	PRUNING
PORTICO	POWERED	PRETZEL	PROFITS	PRURIGO
PORTING	POWWOWS	PREVAIL	PRO-FORM	PRUSSIA
PORTION	PRAIRIE	PREVENT	PROFUSE	PSALMIC
PORTRAY	PRAISED	PREVIEW	PROGENY	PSALTER
POSEURS	PRAISER	PREYING	PROGRAM	PSYCHED
POSHEST	PRAISES	PREZZIE	PROJECT	PSYCHES
POSITED	PRALINE	PRICIER	PROLATE	PSYCHIC
POSSESS	PRANCED	PRICING	PRO-LIFE	PSYLLID
POSSETS	PRANCER	PRICKED	PROLINE	PTERYLA
POSSUMS	PRATING	PRICKER	PROLONG	PTYALIN
POSTAGE	PRATTLE	PRICKET	PROMISE	PUBERTY
POSTBAG	PRAWNER	PRICKLY	PROMOTE	PUBLISH
POSTBOX	PRAYERS	PRICING	PROMPTS	PUCCOON
POSTERN	PRAYING	PRIESTS	PRONATE	PUCKERS
POSTERS	PREBEND	PRIMARY	PRONOUN	PUCKING
POSTFIX	PRECAST	PRIMATE	PROOFED	PUDDING
POSTIES	PRECEDE	PRIMERS	PROPANE	PUDDLED
POSTING	PRECEPT	PRIMINE	PROPEND	PUDDLER
POSTMAN	PRECESS	PRIMING	PROPENE	PUDDLES
POSTMEN	PRECISE	PRIMMER	PROPHET	PUDENDA
POSTURE	PRECOOK	PRIMULA	PROPOSE	PUDGIER
POSTWAR	PREDATE	PRINCES	PROPPED	PUDGILY
POTABLE	PREDICT	PRINKER	PRO RATA	PUERILE

PUFFIER	PUSHIER	PAINTERS	PANORAMA	PARMESAN
PUFFILY	PUSHILY	PAINTING	PANPIPES	PARODIED
PUFFING	PUSHING	PAKISTAN	PANSOPHY	PARODIES
PUFFINS	PUSHROD	PALADINS	PANTHEON	PARODIST
PUGGING	PUSH-UPS	PALATALS	PANTHERS	PAROLING
PULLETS	PUSTULE	PALATIAL	PANTILES	PARATOID
PULLEYS	PUTAMEN	PALATINE	PANTRIES	PAROXYSM
PULLING	PUT-DOWN	PALAVERS	PAPACIES	PARROTED
PULL-INS	PUT-OFFS	PALEFACE	PAPERBOY	PARRYING
PULLMAN	PUTREFY	PALENESS	PAPERING	PARSABLE
PULLOUT	PUTTERS	PALETTES	PAPILLON	PARSNIPS
PULPIER	PUTTING	PALFREYS	PAPISTRY	PARTAKEN
PULPING	PUT-UPON	PALINODE	PAPOOSES	PARTAKER
PULPITS	PUZZLED	PALISADE	PARABLES	PARTERRE
PULSARS	PUZZLER	PALLADIC	PARABOLA	PARTHIAN
PULSATE	PUZZLES	PALLIATE	PARADIGM	PARTIBLE
PULSING	PYAEMIA	PALLIDLY	PARADING	PARTICLE
PUMPKIN	PYAEMIC	PALLIEST	PARADISE	PARTINGS
PUNCHED	PYGMIES	PALL MALL	PARADROP	PARTISAN
PUNCHER	PYJAMAS	PALMETTE	PARAFFIN	PARTNERS
PUNCHES	PYLORUS	PALMETTO	PARAGOGE	PARTSONG
PUNCH-UP	PYRALID	PALMIEST	PARAGONS	PART-TIME
PUNDITS	PYRAMID	PALMISTS	PARAGUAY	PART WORK
PUNGENT	PYRETIC	PALMITIN	PARAKEET	PARTYING
PUNIEST	PYREXIA	PALOMINO	PARALLAX	PAR VALUE
PUNJABI	PYRITES	PALPABLE	PARALLEL	PARVENUS
PUNKAHS	PYRITIC	PALPABLY	PARALYSE	PASSABLE
PUNNETS	PYROGEN	PALPATED	PARAMENT	PASSABLY
PUNNING	PYROSIS	PALTERER	PARAMOUR	PASSAGES
PUNSTER	PYRRHIC	PALTRIER	PARANOIA	PASSBOOK
PUNTERS	PYRROLE	PALTRILY	PARANOID	PASSERBY
PUNTING	PYTHONS	PAMPERED	PARAPETS	PASSIBLE
PUPPETS		PAMPERER	PARAQUAT	PASSIONS
PUPPIES		PAMPHLET	PARASITE	PASSKEYS
PUPPING	**8 LETTERS**	PAMPLONA	PARASOLS	PASSOVER
PURGING	PACIFIED	PANACEAN	PARAVANE	PASSPORT
PURISTS	PACIFIER	PANACEAS	PAR AVION	PASSWORD
PURITAN	PACIFISM	PANATELA	PARAZOAN	PASTERNS
PURLIEU	PACIFIST	PANCAKES	PARCELLED	PASTE-UPS
PURLING	PACKABLE	PANCREAS	PARCENER	PASTICHE
PURLOIN	PACKAGED	PANDA CAR	PARCHING	PASTIEST
PURPLES	PACKAGER	PANDANUS	PARDONED	PASTILLE
PURPORT	PACKAGES	PANDEMIC	PARDONER	PASTIMES
PURPOSE	PADDLING	PANDERED	PARENTAL	PASTINGS
PURPURA	PADDOCKS	PANDERER	PARISHES	PASTORAL
PURPURE	PADLOCKS	PANELING	PARISIAN	PASTRAMI
PURRING	PAEONIES	PANELLED	PARKIEST	PASTRIES
PURSERS	PAGANISM	PANGOLIN	PARKLAND	PASTURES
PURSING	PAGANIST	PANICKED	PARKWAYS	PATAGIUM
PURSUED	PAGANIZE	PANICLED	PARLANCE	PATCHIER
PURSUER	PAGEANTS	PANMIXIA	PARLANDO	PATCHILY
PURSUIT	PAGINATE	PANNIERS	PARLAYED	PATCHING
PURVIEW	PAGURIAN	PANNIKIN	PARLAYER	PATELLAR
PUSHERS	PAINLESS	PANOPTIC	PARLOURS	PATTELAS

PATENTED	PEDIFORM	PERFUMES	PETTIEST	PICKEREL
PATENTEE	PEDIGREE	PERGOLAS	PETTIFOG	PICKETED
PATENTLY	PEDIMENT	PERIANTH	PETULANT	PICKETER
PATENTOR	PEDIPALP	PERIBLEM	PETUNIAS	PICKIEST
PATERNAL	PEDOLOGY	PERICARP	PETUNTSE	PICKINGS
PATHETIC	PEDUNCLE	PERIDERM	PEWTERER	PICKLING
PATHLESS	PEEKABOO	PERIDIUM	PFENNIGS	PICKLOCK
PATHOGEN	PEELINGS	PERIGEAN	PHAETONS	PICK-ME-UP
PATHWAYS	PEEPHOLE	PERIGEES	PHANTOMS	PICOLINE
PATIENCE	PEEPSHOW	PERIGYNY	PHARAOHS	PICTURED
PATIENTS	PEERAGES	PERILOUS	PHARISEE	PICTURES
PARTIALS	PEERLESS	PERILUNE	PHARMACY	PIDDLING
PATRIOTS	PEGBOARD	PERINEUM	PHASE-OUT	PIEBALDS
PATRONAL	PEIGNOR	PERIODIC	PHEASANT	PIE CHART
PATTENED	PEKINESE	PERIOTIC	PHENETIC	PIECRUST
PATTERNS	PELICANS	PERISHED	PHENOLIC	PIEDMONT
PATULOUS	PELLAGRA	PERISHER	PHILTRES	PIERCING
PAUNCHES	PELLICLE	PERIWIGS	PHIMOSIS	PIFFLING
PAVEMENT	PELL-MELL	PERJURED	PHONE BOX	PIGGIEST
PAVILION	PELLUCID	PURJURER	PHONE-INS	PIGMENTS
PAVONINE	PELVISES	PERKIEST	PHONEMES	PIGSKINS
PAWKIEST	PEMMICAN	PERLITIC	PHONEMIC	PIGSTICK
PAWNSHOP	PENALIZE	PERMEANT	PHONETIC	PIGSTIES
PAYCHECK	PENANCES	PERMEATE	PHONIEST	PIGSWILL
PAYLOADS	PENCHANT	PERMUTED	PHOSGENE	PIGTAILS
PAYMENTS	PENCILED	PERONEAL	PHOSPHOR	PILASTER
PAY PHONE	PENDANTS	PERORATE	PHOTOFIT	PILCHARD
PAYROLLS	PENDULUM	PEROXIDE	PHOTOMAP	PILEWORT
PAYSLIPS	PENGUINS	PERSONAL	PHOTOPIA	PILFERED
PEACEFUL	PENITENT	PERSONAS	PHOTOPIC	PILFERER
PEACOCKS	PENKNIFE	PERSPIRE	PHOTOSET	PILGRIMS
PEAFOWLS	PEN NAMES	PERSUADE	PHRASING	PILIFORM
PEA GREEN	PENNANTS	PERTNESS	PHRATRIC	PILLAGED
PEAKIEST	PENNINES	PERUSALS	PHREATIC	PILLAGER
PEARLIER	PENOLOGY	PERUSING	PHTHALIC	PILLIONS
PEARLITE	PENSIONS	PERUVIAN	PHTHASIC	PILLOCKS
PEARMAIN	PENSTOCK	PERVADED	PHTHASIS	PILLOWED
PEASANTS	PENTACLE	PERVADER	PHYLETIC	PILOTAGE
PEBBLING	PENTAGON	PERVERSE	PHYLLITE	PILOTING
PECCABLE	PENTOMIC	PERVERTS	PHYLLODE	PIMENTOS
PECCANCY	PENTOSAN	PERVIOUS	PHYLLOID	PIMIENTO
PECTORAL	PENUMBRA	PESHAWAR	PHYLLOME	PINAFORE
PECULATE	PENZANCE	PESKIEST	PHYSICAL	PINASTER
PECULIAR	PEOPLING	PESTERED	PHYSIQUE	PINCE-NEZ
PEDAGOGY	PEPPERED	PESTERER	PIACENZA	PINCHING
PEDALING	PEP PILLS	PESTHOLE	PIACULAR	PINETREE
PEDALLED	PEP TALKS	PETALINE	PIANISTS	PINEWOOD
PEDANTIC	PEPTIZER	PETALODY	PIANOLAS	PING-PONG
PEDANTRY	PER ANNUM	PETALOID	PIASSACA	PINHEADS
PEDDLERS	PERCEIVE	PETECHIA	PIASTRES	PINIONED
PEDDLING	PERCHING	PETITION	PICADORS	PINK GINS
PEDERAST	PERFORCE	PETIT MAL	PICCOLOS	PINKROOT
PEDESTAL	PERFUMED	PET NAMES	PICKABLE	PIN MONEY
PEDICURE	PURFUMER	PETROLIC	PICKAXES	PINNACES

PINNACLE	PLASTICS	PLUMBERY	POLONIUM	PORTIERE
PINNIPED	PLASTRAL	PLUMBING	POLTROON	PORTIONS
PINOCHILE	PLASTRON	PLUMBISM	POLYGALA	PORTLIER
PINPOINT	PLATELET	PLUMBOUS	POLYGAMY	PORTRAIT
PINPRICK	PLATFORM	PLUMMIER	POLYGENE	PORT SAID
PINTABLE	PLATINIC	PLUMPEST	POLYGLOT	PORTUGAL
PINT-SIZE	PLATOONS	PLUMPING	POLYGONS	POSITING
PINWHEEL	PLATTERS	PLUNGERS	POLYGYNY	POSITION
PIONEERS	PLATYPUS	PLUNGING	POLYMATH	POSITIVE
PIPECLAY	PLAUDITS	PLUSHEST	POLYMERS	POSITRON
PIPEFISH	PLAUSABLE	PLUTONIC	POLYPARY	POSOLOGY
PIPELINE	PLAYBACK	PLUVIOUS	POLYPODY	POSSIBLE
PIPE RACK	PLAYBILL	PLYMOUTH	POLYPOID	POSSIBLY
PIPERINE	PLAYBOYS	POACEOUS	POLYPOUS	POSTBAGS
PIPETTES	PLAYGOER	POACHERS	POLYSEMY	POST CARD
PIPEWORT	PLAYMATE	POACHING	POLYURIA	POST CAVA
PIRACIES	PLAY-OFFS	POCKETED	POLYURIC	POST CODE
PIRHANAS	PLAYPENS	POCKMARK	POLYZOAN	POST DATE
PIRATING	PLAYROOM	PODAGRAL	POLYZOIC	POST-FREE
PISIFORM	PLAYSUIT	PODGIEST	POMANDER	POST HORN
PISOLITE	PLAYTIME	PODIATRY	POMOLOGY	POSTICHE
PITCHERS	PLEADING	PODZOLIC	PONDERED	POSTINGS
PITCHING	PLEASANT	POETICAL	PONDERER	POSTLUDE
PITFALLS	PLEASING	POIGNANT	PONDWEED	POSTMARK
PITHEADS	PLEASURE	POINTERS	PONGIEST	POST-OBIT
PITHIEST	PLEATING	POINTING	PONIARDS	POSTPAID
PITIABLE	PLEBBIER	POISONED	PONTIFEX	POSTPONE
PITIABLY	PLEBEIAN	POISONER	PONTIFFS	POSTURAL
PITILESS	PLECTRUM	POKEWEED	PONTOONS	POSTURED
PIT PROPS	PLEDGING	POKINESS	PONYTAIL	POSTURER
PITTANCE	PLEIADES	POLARITY	POOFIEST	POSTURES
PIVOTING	PLEIN-AIR	POLARIZE	POOH-POOH	POTASSIC
PIZZERIA	PLETHORA	POLAROID	POOR LAWS	POTATION
PLACABLE	PLEURISY	POLEAXED	POORLIER	POTATOES
PLACARDS	PLIANTLY	POLECATS	POORNESS	POTBELLY
PLACATED	PLIGHTED	POLEMICS	POPADUMS	POTBOUND
PLACEBOS	PLIGHTER	POLE STAR	POPINJAY	POTENTLY
PLACE MAT	PLIMSOLL	POLICIES	POPOVERS	POTHOLER
PLACENTA	PLIOCENE	POLICING	POPPADOM	POTHOLES
PLACIDLY	PLODDERS	POLISHED	POPSICLE	POTLUCKS
PLAGUILY	PLODDING	POLISHER	POPULATE	POT PLANT
PLAGUING	PLONKING	POLISHES	POPULISM	POTSHOTS
PLAINEST	PLOPPING	POITELY	POPULIST	POTSTONE
PLAITING	PLOSIVES	POLITICO	POPULOUS	POTTERED
PLANCHET	PLOTTING	POLITICS	PORKIEST	POTTERER
PLANFORM	PLOUGHED	POLITIES	PORK PIES	POTTIEST
PLANGENT	PLOUGHER	POLKA DOT	POROSITY	POULTICE
PLANKING	PLUCKIER	POLLARDS	PORPHYRY	POUNCING
PLANKTON	PLUCKILY	POLLICAL	PORPOISE	POUNDAGE
PLANNERS	PLUCKING	POLLINIC	PORRIGE	POUNDING
PLANNING	PLUGGING	POLLSTER	PORTABLE	POWDERED
PLANOSOL	PLUGHOLE	POLLUTED	PORTENTS	POWDERER
PLANTAIN	PLUMBAGO	POLLUTER	PORTHOLE	POWERFUL
PLANTERS	PLUMBERS	POLO NECK	POTICOS	POWERING

PRACTICE	PRESENTS	PRISONER	PROPHAGE	PSALMODY
PRACTISE	PRESERVE	PRISSIER	PROPHASE	PSALTERS
PRAEDIAL	PRESIDED	PRISSILY	PROPHECY	PSALTERY
PRAESEPE	PRESIDER	PRISTINE	PROPHESY	PSEPHITE
PRAIRIES	PRESIDIA	PRIVATES	PROPHETS	PSORALEA
PRAISING	PRESIDIO	PRIVIEST	PROPOLIS	PSYCHICS
PRALINES	PRESS BOX	PRIZE DAY	PROPOSAL	PSYCHING
PRANCING	PRESSING	PROBABLE	PROPOSED	PTEROPOD
PRANDIAL	PRESSMAN	PROBABLY	PROPOSER	PTOMAINE
PRANKISH	PRESSMEN	PROBATED	PROPOUND	PTYALISM
PRATIQUE	PRESS-UPS	PROBATES	PROPPING	PUB-CRAWL
PRATTLED	PRESSURE	PROBLEMS	PROROGUE	PUBLICAN
PRATTLER	PRESSURE	PROCAINE	PROSAISM	PUBLICLY
PREACHED	PRESTIGE	PROCEEDS	PROSIEST	PUCKERED
PREACHER	PRESUMED	PROCLAIM	PROSODIC	PUDDINGS
PREAMBLE	PRESUMER	PROCTORS	PROSPECT	PUDDLING
PREAXIAL	PRETENCE	PROCURED	PROSTATE	PUDENDUM
PREBENDS	PRETEXTS	PROCURER	PROSTYLE	PUDGIEST
PRECEDED	PRETORIA	PRODDING	PROTASIS	PUFFBALL
PRECEPTS	PRETTIER	PRODIGAL	PROTEGEE	PUFFBIRD
PRECINCT	PRETTIFY	PRODROME	PROTEGES	PUFFIEST
PRECIOUS	PRETTILY	PRODUCED	PROTEINS	PUGILISM
PRECLUDE	PRETZELS	PRODUCER	PROTEOSE	PUGILIST
PREDATED	PREVIEWS	PRODUCTS	PROTESTS	PUISSANT
PREDATOR	PREVIOUS	PROEMIAL	PROTOCOL	PULLMANS
PREDELLA	PREZZIES	PROFANED	PROTOZOA	PULLOUTS
PREENING	PRIAPISM	PROFANER	PROTRACT	PULLOVER
PRE-EXIST	PRICE TAG	PROFILED	PROTRUDE	PULMONIC
PREFACED	PRICIEST	PROFILES	PROUDEST	PULMOTOR
PREFACER	PRICKING	PROFITED	PROVABLE	PULPIEST
PREFACES	PRICKLED	PROFITER	PROVABLY	PULPWOOD
PREFECTS	PRICKLES	PRO FORMA	PROVENCE	PULSATED
PREFIXAL	PRIDEFUL	PROFOUND	PROVENLY	PULSATOR
PREFIXED	PRIESTLY	PROGRAMS	PROVERBS	PULSEJET
PREFIXES	PRIGGERY	PROGRESS	PROVIDED	PULVINIS
PREGNANT	PRIGGISH	PROHIBIT	PROVIDER	PUMMELED
PREJUDGE	PRIGGISM	PROJECTS	PROVINCE	PUMPKINS
PRELATES	PRIMATES	PROLAPSE	PROVISOS	PUMP ROOM
PRELATIC	PRIMEVAL	PROLIFIC	PROVOKED	PUNCHEON
PRELUDER	PRIMMEST	PROLOGUE	PROVOSTS	PUNCHIER
PRELUDES	PRIMNESS	PROMISED	PROWL CAR	PUNCHING
PREMIERE	PRIMROSE	PROMISER	PROWLERS	PUNCH-UPS
PREMIERS	PRIMULAS	PROMISES	PROWLING	PUNCTATE
PREMISES	PRIMUSES	PROMISOR	PROXIMAL	PUNCTUAL
PREMIUMS	PRINCELY	PROMOTED	PRUDENCE	PUNCTURE
PREMOLAR	PRINCESS	PROMOTER	PRUINOSE	PUNGENCY
PREMORSE	PRINTERS	PROMPTED	PRUNABLE	PUNINESS
PRENATAL	PRINTING	PROMPTER	PRUNELLA	PUNISHED
PREPARED	PRINTOUT	PROMPTLY	PRUNELLE	PUNISHER
PREPENSE	PRIORATE	PRONATOR	PRURIENT	PUNITIVE
PRESAGED	PRIORESS	PRONOUNS	PRURITIC	PUNSTERS
PRESAGER	PRIORIES	PROOFING	PRURITUS	PUPARIAL
PRESAGES	PRIORITY	PROPERLY	PRUSSIAN	PUPARIUM
PRESENCE	PRISMOID	PROPERTY	PSALMIST	PUPATION

PUPPETRY	PYROSTAT	PANATELAS	PARAPLASM	PASSERINE
PUPPY FAT	PYROXENE	PANDA CARS	PARASITES	PASSERBY
PUPPYISH	PYRROLIC	PANDEMICS	PARASITIC	PASSIONAL
PURBLIND	PYRRUVIC	PANDERING	PARATAXIS	PASSIVELY
PURCHASE	PYTHONIC	PANDURATE	PARATHION	PASSIVISM
PUREBRED	PYXIDIUM	PANEGYRIC	PARBOILED	PASSIVIST
PUREEING		PANELLING	PARBUCKLE	PASSIVITY
PURENESS	**9 LETTERS**	PANELLIST	PARCELING	PASSOVERS
PURFLING	PACEMAKER	PANHANDLE	PARCELLED	PASSPORTS
PURIFIED	PACHYDERM	PANICKING	PARCENARY	PASSWORDS
PURIFIER	PACHYTENE	PANNIKINS	PARCHMENT	PASTICHES
PURISTIC	PACIFIERS	PANOPILED	PARDONERS	PASTILLES
PURITANS	PACIFISTS	PANORAMAS	PARDONING	PASTINESS
PURLIEUS	PACIFYING	PANORAMIC	PAREGORIC	PASTORALE
PURPLISH	PACKAGERS	PANOSOPHIC	PARENTAGE	PASTORALS
PURPOSED	PACKAGING	PANTHEISM	PARENTING	PASTORATE
PURPOSES	PACKED-OUT	PANTHEIST	PARGETING	PASTURAGE
PURPURIN	PACKHORSE	PANTHEONS	PARHELION	PASTURING
PURSLANE	PADLOCKED	PANTOMIME	PARI PASSU	PATAGONIA
PURSUANT	PAEDERAST	PANTY HOSE	PARISIANS	PATCHABLE
PURSUERS	PAEDOLOGY	PAPARAZZI	PARLEYING	PATCHIEST
PURSUING	PAGANIZER	PAPARAZZO	PARNASSUS	PATCHOULI
PURSUITS	PAGEANTRY	PAPERBACK	PAROCHIAL	PATCHWORK
PURULENT	PAILLASSE	PAPERBOYS	PARODISTS	PATELLATE
PURVEYED	PAILLETTE	PAPER CLIP	PARODYING	PATENTEES
PURVEYOR	PAINFULLY	PAPERWORK	PAROICOUS	PATENTING
PUSHBIKE	PAINTERLY	PAPATERIE	PAROLABLE	PATERNITY
PUSHCART	PAINTINGS	PAPILLARY	PARONYMIC	PATHOLOGY
PUSHIEST	PAINTWORK	PAPILLOMA	PAROTOSIS	PATRIARCH
PUSHOVER	PAKISTANI	PAPILOTTE	PAROXYSMS	PATRICIAN
PUSH-PULL	PALANQUIN	PAPYRUSES	PARQUETRY	PATRICIDE
PUSTULAR	PALATABLE	PARABLAST	PARRICIDE	PATRIMONY
PUSTULES	PALATABLY	PARABOLAS	PARROTING	PATRIOTIC
PUTACTIVE	PALEFACES	PARABOLIC	PARSIMONY	PATRISTIC
PUT-DOWNS	PALEMBANG	PARACHUTE	PARSONAGE	PATROL CAR
PUTCHES	PALESTINE	PARADIGMS	PARTAKING	PATROLLED
PUTTERED	PALISADES	PARADISES	PARTERRES	PATROLLER
PUT-UP JOB	PALLADIAN	PARADOXES	PARTHENON	PATROLMAN
PUZZLERS	PALLADIUM	PARADOGIC	PARTIALLY	PATROLMEN
PUZZLING	PALLADOUS	PARAGRAPH	PARTICLES	PARTONAGE
PYELITIC	PALLIASSE	PARAKEETS	PARTI PRIS	PATRONESS
PYELITIS	PALLIATED	PARALLELS	PARTISANS	PATRONIZE
PYGIDIAL	PALLIATOR	PARALYSED	PARTITION	PATTERING
PYGIDIUM	PALMATION	PARALYSER	PARTITIVE	PATTERNED
PYODERMA	PALMETTOS	PARALYSES	PARTNERED	PAULOWNIA
PYOGENIC	PALMISTRY	PARALYSIS	PARTBRIDGE	PAUPERISM
PYRAMIDS	PALOMINOS	PARALYTIC	PART-SONGS	PAUPERIZE
PYRAZOLE	PALPATING	PARRAMATTA	PART WORKS	PAUSINGLY
PYRENEAN	PALPATION	PARAMEDIC	PARTY LINE	PAVEMENTS
PYRENEES	PALPEBRAL	PARAMETER	PARTY WALL	PAVILLIONS
PYRENOID	PALPITATE	PARAMORPH	PAS DE DEUX	PAWKINESS
PYREXIAL	PALTRIEST	PARAMOUNT	PASO DOBLE	PAWNSHOPS
PYRIDINE	PAMPERING	PARAMOURS	PASSBOOKS	PAYCHECKS
PYRIFORM	PAMPHLETS	PARANOIAC	PASSENGER	PAYMASTER

PAY PACKET	PENNILESS	PERINATAL	PETAL-LIKE	PHONOTYPE
PAY PHONE	PENNINITE	PERIODATE	PETALODIC	PHONOTYPY
PEACEABLE	PENNY-WISE	PERIPHERY	PETECHIAL	PHOSPHATE
PEACE PIPE	PENNYWORT	PERISCOPE	PETERSHAM	PHOSPHENE
PEACETIME	PEN PUSHER	PERISHERS	PETIOLATE	PHOSPHIDE
PEARLIEST	PENSILITY	PERISHING	PETIT FOUR	PHOSPHITE
PEARMAINS	PENSIONED	PERISPERM	PETITIONS	PHOTOCELL
PEASANTRY	PENSIONER	PERISTOME	PETRIFIED	PHOTOCOPY
PEA SOUPER	PENSIVELY	PERISTYLE	PETRIFIER	PHOTOGRAM
PECCARIES	PENTAGONS	PERITONIA	PETROLEUM	PHOTOSTAT
PECTINATE	PENTAGRAM	PERITRACK	PETROLOGY	PHOTOTUBE
PECULATED	PENTARCHY	PERJURERS	PETTICOAT	PHOTOTYPE
PECULATOR	PENTECOST	PERJURIES	PETTINESS	PHRENETIC
PECUNIARY	PENTHOUSE	PERKINESS	PETTISHLY	PHRENITIS
PEDAGOGIC	PENTOXIDE	PERMALLOY	PETTY CASH	PHTHALEIN
PEDAGOGUE	PENUMBRAL	PERMANENT	PETULANCE	PHYCOLOGY
PEDALLING	PENUMBRAS	PERMEABLE	PHAGOCYTE	PHYLLITIC
PEDATIFID	PENURIOUS	PERMEANCE	PHALANGER	PHYLLOMIC
PEDERASTS	PEPPERING	PERMEATED	PHALANGES	PHYLOGENY
PEDERASTY	PEPPER POT	PERMEATOR	PHALANXES	PHYSICALS
PEDESTALS	PEPSINATE	PER MENSEM	PHALAROPE	PHYSICIAN
PEDICULAR	PEPTIDASE	PERMITTED	PHALLUSES	PHYSICIST
PEDICURES	PEPTONIZE	PERMITTER	PHANTASMS	PHYSIQUES
PEDIGREED	PERBORATE	PERMUTING	PHARISAIC	PHYTOTRON
PEDIGREES	PERCALINE	PERPETUAL	PHARISEES	PIANISTIC
PEDIMENTS	PER CAPITA	PERPIGNAN	PHARYNXES	PICKETING
PEDUNCLED	PERCEIVED	PERPLEXED	PHASE-OUTS	PICKINESS
PEEPHOLES	PERCEIVER	PERSECUTE	PHEASANTS	PICK-ME-UPS
PEERESSES	PERCHANCE	PERSEVERE	PHELLOGEN	PICNICKED
PEEVISHLY	PERCHERON	PERSIMMON	PHENACITE	PICNICKER
PEGMATITE	PERCOLATE	PERSISTED	PHENAZINE	PICOLINIC
PEKINESES	PERCUSSOR	PERSISTER	PHENETOLE	PICTORIAL
PEKINGESE	PERDITION	PERSONAGE	PHENOCOPY	PICTURING
PELLITORY	PEREGRINE	PERSONALS	PHENOLATE	PIECE-DYED
PELMANISM	PERENNATE	PERSONATE	PHENOLOGY	PIECEMEAL
PELTATION	PERRENIAL	PERSONIFY	PHENOMENA	PIECEWORK
PEMPHIGUS	PERFECTED	PERSONNEL	PHENOTYPE	PIE CHARTS
PENALIZED	PERFECTER	PERSPIRED	PHENOXIDE	PIECRUSTS
PENALTIES	PERFECTLY	PERSUADED	PHEROMONE	PIERCABLE
PENCHANTS	PERFIDIES	PERSUADER	PHILANDER	PIERIDINE
PENCILING	PERFORATE	PERTAINED	PHILATELY	PIGGERIES
PENCILLED	PERFORMED	PERTINENT	PHILIPPIC	PIGGISHLY
PENCILLER	PERFORMER	PERTURBED	PHILOLOGY	PIGGYBACK
PENDRAGON	PERFUMERY	PERTUSSIS	PHLEBITIC	PIGGYBANK
PENDULOUS	PERFUMING	PERVADING	PHLEBITIS	PIGHEADED
PENDULUMS	PERFUSION	PERVASIVE	PHLYCTENA	PIGTAILED
PENEPLAIN	PERFUSIVE	PERVERTED	PHOENECIA	PIKEPERCH
PENETRANT	PERICLASE	PERVERTER	PHOENIXES	PIKESTAFF
PENETRATE	PERICLINE	PESSARIES	PHONATION	PILASTERS
PEN FRIEND	PERICYCLE	PESSIMISM	PHONATORY	PICHARDS
PENINSULA	PEROLYMPH	PESSIMIST	PHONINESS	PILFERERS
PENITENCE	PERIMETER	PESTERING	PHONOGRAM	PILFERING
PENITENTS	PERIMETRY	PESTICIDE	PHONOLITE	PILLAGERS
PENINIVES	PERIMORPH	PESTILENT	PHONOLOGY	PILLAGING

PILLAR BOX	PLACENTAE	PRECONIZE	PRESERVES	PRISONERS
PILLBOXES	PLACENTAL	PRECOOKED	PRESETTER	PRISSIEST
PILLORIED	PLACENTAS	PRECURSOR	PRESHRUNK	PRIVATEER
PILLORIES	PLACIDITY	PREDATING	PRESIDENT	PRIVATELY
PILLOWING	PLACODERM	PREDATORS	PRESIDING	PRIVATION
PIMPERNEL	PLAIN-LAID	PREDATORY	PRESIDIUM	PRIVATIVE
PINACEOUS	PLAINNESS	PREDICANT	PRESSGANG	PRIVATIZE
PINAFORES	PLAINSMAN	PREDICATE	PRESSINGS	PRIVILEGE
PINCHBECK	PLAINSONG	PREDICATED	PRESSMARK	PRIZE DAYS
PINCHCOCK	PLAINTIFF	PREDICATOR	PRESSROOM	PROACTIVE
PINEAPPLE	PLAINTATIVE	PREDIGEST	PRESS-STUD	PROBABLES
PINETREES	PLANARIAN	PRE-EMPTED	PRESSURED	PROBATING
PINEWOODS	PLANATION	PRE-EMPTOR	PRESSURES	PROBATION
PINIONING	PLANETARY	PREFACING	PRESSWORK	PROBATIVE
PINNACLES	PLANETOID	PREFATORY	PRESTIGES	PROBEABLE
PINNATION	PLANE TREE	PREFERRED	PRESTRESS	PROBINGLY
PINPOINTS	PLANGENCY	PREFIGURE	PRESUMING	PROBISCIS
PINPRICKS	PLANISHER	PREFIXING	PRETENCES	PROCEDURE
PINSTRIPE	PLANTABLE	PREFLIGHT	PRETENDED	PROCEEDED
PINTABLES	PLANTAINS	PREGNABLE	PRETENDER	PROCEEDER
PINTADERA	PLASMAGEL	PREGNANCY	PRETERITE	PROCESSED
PINWHEELS	PLAMASOL	PREHEATED	PRETTIEST	PROCESSOR
PIONEERED	PLASTERED	PREJUDGED	PREVAILED	PROCLITIC
PIOUSNESS	PLASTERER	PREJUDGER	PREVAILER	PROCONSUL
PIPE DREAM	PLATELETS	PREJUDICE	PREVALENT	PROCREANT
PIPELINES	PLATE RACK	PRELATISM	PREVENTED	PROCREATE
PIPE RACKS	PLATFORMS	PRELATIST	PREVENTER	PROCTORED
PIPERONAL	PLATANIZE	PRELATURE	PREVIEWED	PROCURERS
PIPESTONE	PLATANOID	PRELUDIAL	PREVISION	PROCURING
PIPSQUEAK	PLATINOUS	PRELUSION	PRICELESS	PRODIGALS
PIQUANTLY	PLATITUDE	PRELUSIVE	PRICE TAGS	PRODIGIES
PIRATICAL	PLAUSIBLE	PREMATURE	PRICINESS	PRODROMAL
PIROUETTE	PLAUSIBLY	PREMIERED	PRICKLIER	PRODUCERS
PISS-TAKES	PLAY-ACTED	PREMIERES	PRICKLING	PRODUCING
PISTACHIO	PLAYBACKS	PREOCCUPY	PRIESTESS	PROFANELY
PITCH-DARK	PLAY DOUGH	PREORDAIN	PRIMAEVAL	PROFANING
PITCHFORK	PLAYED-OUT	PREPACKED	PRIMARIES	PROFANITY
PITEOUSLY	PLAYFULLY	PREPARING	PRIMARILY	PROFESSED
PITHNESS	PLAYGOERS	PREPAYING	PRIMATIAL	PROFESSOR
PITOT TUBE	PLAYGROUP	PREPOTENT	PRIME COST	PROFFERED
PIT PONIES	PREBENDAL	PREPUTIAL	PRIMENESS	PROFFERER
PITTANCES	PRECANCEL	PRERECORD	PRIME RATE	PROFILING
PITUITARY	PRECEDENT	PRESAGING	PRIME TIME	PROFITEER
PITYINGLY	PRECEDING	PRESBYTER	PRIMIPARA	PROFITING
PIZZICATO	PRECENTOR	PRESCHOOL	PRIMITIVE	PROFLUENT
PLACARDED	PRECEPTOR	PRESCIENT	PRIMROSES	PROFUSELY
PLACATING	PRECINCTS	PRESCRIBE	PRINCEDOM	PROFUSION
PLACATED	PRECIPICE	PRESCRIPT	PRINCETON	PROGESTIN
PLACATION	PRECISELY	PRESENCES	PRINCIPAL	PROGNOSES
PLACATORY	PRECISIAN	PRESENTED	PRINCIPLE	PROGNOSIS
PLACEBOES	PRECISION	PRESENTEE	PRINTABLE	PROGRAMED
PLACE CARD	PRECLUDED	PRESENTER	PRINTINGS	PROGRAMER
PLACE MATS	PRECOCIAL	PRESENTLY	PRINTOUTS	PROGRAMME
PLACEMENT	PRECOCITY	PRESERVED	PRISMATIC	PROJECTED

575

P

9 LETTERS to 10 LETTERS

PROJECTOR	PROTAMINE	PUBESCENT	PUPPY LOVE	**10 LETTERS**
PROLACTIN	PROTANDRY	PUBLICANS	PURCHASED	PACE
PROLAMINE	PROTECTED	PUBLIC BAR	PUCHASER	BOWLER
PROLAPSED	PROTECTOR	PUBLICIST	PURCHASES	PACEMAK-
PROLAPSES	PROTESTER	PUBLICITY	PUREBREDS	ERS
PROLEPSIS	PROTHESIS	PUBLICIZE	PURGATION	PACHY-
PROLEPTIC	PROTHETIC	PUBLISHED	PURGATIVE	DERMS
PROLIXITY	PROTHORAX	PUBLISHER	PURGATORY	PACK ANIMAL
PROLOGUES	PROTOCOLS	PUCKERING	PURIFIERS	PACKSADDLE
PROLONGED	PROTOGYNY	PUCKISHLY	PURIFYING	PACKTHREAD
PROLONGER	PROTONEMA	PUDGINESS	PULOINED	PADDLEFISH
PROLUSION	PROTOSTAR	PUERILISM	PULOINER	PADLOCKING
PROLUSORY	PROTOTYPE	PUERILITY	PUPORTED	PAEDERASTS
PROMENADE	PROTOXIDE	PUERPERAL	PURPOSELY	PAEDERASTY
PROMINENT	PROTOZOAN	PUFFINESS	PURPOSING	PAEDIATRIC
PROMISING	PROTRUDED	PUGILISTS	PURPOSIVE	PAGANISTIC
PROMOTERS	PROUDNESS	PUGNACITY	PURSUANCE	PAGINATION
PROMOTING	PROUSTITE	PUISSANCE	PURULENCE	PAILLASSES
PROMOTION	PROVENCAL	PULLOVERS	PURVEYING	PAINKILLER
PROMOTIVE	PROVENDER	PULLULATE	PURVEYORS	PAINLESSLY
PROMPTING	PROVIDENT	PULMONARY	PUSHBIKES	PAINTBRUSH
PRONATION	PROVIDERS	PULMONATE	PUSHCARTS	PAKISTANIS
PRONENESS	PROVIDING	PULPINESS	PUSHCHAIR	PALAEOCENE
PRONGHORN	PROVINCES	PULSATILE	PUSHINESS	PALAEOGENE
PRONOUNCE	PROVISION	PULSATING	PUSHINGLY	PALAEOLITH
PROOFREAD	PROVISORY	PULSATION	PUSSYFOOT	PALAEOZOIC
PROPAGATE	PROVOKING	PULSATIVE	PUSTULANT	PALANQUINS
PROPAGULE	PROVOLONE	PULSATORY	PUTREFIED	PALATALIZE
PRO PATRIA	PROWESSES	PULVERIZE	PUTREFIER	PALATIALLY
PROPELLED	PROWL CARS	PULVILLUS	PUTRIDITY	PALATINATE
PROPELLER	PROXIMATE	PULVINATE	PUTTERING	PALEACEOUS
PROPHETIC	PROXIMITY	PUMICEOUS	PUTTYROOT	PALIMPSEST
PROPONENT	PRUDENTLY	PUMMELING	PUT-UP JOBS	PALINDROME
PROPOSALS	PRUDISHLY	PUMMELLED	PYCNIDIUM	PALLBEARER
PROPRIETY	PRURIENCE	PUMP ROOMS	PYONGYANG	PALLIASSES
PROPTOSIS	PRUSSIATE	PUNCH BALLS	PYORRHOEA	PALLIATING
PROPYLITE	PRYTANEUM	PUNCH BOWL	PYRAMIDAL	PALLIATION
PROROGUED	PSALMISTS	PUNCHIEST	PYRETHRIN	PALLIATIVE
PROSCRIBED	PSALMODIC	PUNCH LINE	PYRIDOXAL	PALLIDNESS
PROSECTOR	PSEUDONYM	PUNCTILLO	PYROGENIC	PALMA-
PROSECUTE	PSORIASIS	PUNCTUATE	PYROLITIC	CEOUS
PROSELYTE	PSORIATIC	PUNCTURED	PYROLYSIS	PALMETTOES
PROSIMIAN	PSYCHICAL	PUNCTURER	PYROMANCY	PALM SUN-
PROSINESS	PSYCHOSES	PUNCTURES	PYROMANIA	DAY
PROSODIST	PSYCHOSIS	PUNGENTLY	PYROMETER	PALPATATION
PROSPECTS	PSYCHOTIC	PUNISHING	PYROMETRY	PALPEBRATE
PROSPERED	PTARMIGAN	PUPILLAGE	PYROXENIC	PALPITATED
PROSTATES	PTERYGOID	PUPILLARY	PYROXYLIN	PALSY-
PROSTATIC	PTOLEMAIC	PUPPETEER		WALSY
PROSTRATE	PUB-CRAWLS	PUPPYHOOD		PALTRINESS

PALYNOLOGY	PARAPLEGIA	PATHFINDER	PENALIZING
PANAMANIAN	PARAPLEGIC	PATHOGENIC	PENCILLING
PAN-ARABISM	PARAPODIUM	PATISSERIE	PENDENTIVE
PANCAKE DAY	PARAPRAXIS	PATRIARCHS	PENETRABLE
PANCREASES	PARASELENE	PATRIARCHY	PENETRALIA
PANCREATIC	PARASITISM	PATRICIDAL	PENETRANCE
PANCREATIN	PARASITIZE	PATRICIDES	PENETRATED
PANEGYRICS	PARASTICHY	PATRILOCAL	PENETRATOR
PANEGYRIST	PARASTATIC	PATRIOTISM	PEN FRIENDS
PANEGYRIZE	PARATROOPS	PATROL CARS	PENICILLIN
PANELLISTS	PARBOILING	PATROLLING	PENINSULAR
PANGENESIS	PARCELLING	PATRONIZED	PENINSULAS
PANGENETIC	PARCEL POST	PATRONIZER	PENITENTLY
PANHANDLED	PARCHMENTS	PATRONYMIC	PENMANSHIP
PANHANDLER	PARDONABLE	PATTERNING	PENNYCRESS
PANHANDLES	PARDONABLY	PAWNBROKER	PENNYROYAL
PANICULATE	PARENCHYMA	PAYMASTERS	PENNYWORTH
PANJANDRUM	PARENTERAL	PAY PACKETS	PENOLOGIST
PANTALOONS	PARENTHOOD	PAY STATION	PEN PUSHERS
PANTHEISTS	PARI-MUTUEL	PEACE CORPS	PENSIONARY
PANTOGRAPH	PARISH-PUMP	PEACEFULLY	PENSIONERS
PANTOMIMES	PARKING LOT	PEACEMAKER	PENSIONING
PANTOMIMIC	PARK KEEPER	PEACE PIPES	PENTAGONAL
PAPAVERINE	PARLIAMENT	PEACHINESS	PENTAGRAMS
PAPERBACKS	PARLOR CARS	PEACH MELBA	PENTAMETER
PAPERBOARD	PARONYMOUS	PEARL DIVER	PENTAQUINE
PAPER CHASE	PAROXYSMAL	PEARLINESS	PENTASTICH
PAPERINESS	PARRICIDAL	PEAR-SHAPED	PENTATEUCH
PAPER KNIFE	PARROTFISH	PEASHOOTER	PENTATHLON
PAPER MONEY	PARSONAGES	PEA SOUPERS	PENTHOUSES
PAPER TIGER	PARTIALITY	PEBBLEDASH	PENTIMENTO
PAPISTICAL	PARTICULAR	PECCADILLO	PENTSTEMON
PARABIOSIS	PARTITIONS	PECTIZABLE	PEPPERCORN
PARABIOTIC	PARTITIVES	PECULATING	PEPPER MILL
PARABOLIST	PARTNERING	PECULATION	PEPPERMINT
PARABOLIZE	PARTRIDGES	PECULIARLY	PEPPER POTS
PARABOLOID	PARTURIENT	PEDAGOGISM	PEPPERWORT
PARACHUTED	PARTY LINES	PEDAGOGUES	PEPSINOGEN
PARACHUTES	PARTY PIECE	PEDANTRIES	PEPTIZABLE
PARAGRAPHS	PARTY WALLS	PEDERASTIC	PEPTONIZER
PARAGUAYAN	PASQUINADE	PEDESTRIAN	PERACIDITY
PARALLELED	PASSAGEWAY	PEDIATRICS	PERCIEVING
PARALOGISM	PASSENGERS	PEDICULATE	PERCENTAGE
PARALYSING	PASSIONATE	PEDICULOUS	PERCENTILE
PARALYTICS	PASTEBOARD	PEDICURIST	PERCEPTION
PARAMECIUM	PASTELLIST	PEDOMENTAL	PERCEPTIVE
PARAMEDICS	PASTUERISM	PEDIOLOGIST	PERCEPTUAL
PARAMETERS	PASTUERIZE	PEEPING TOM	PERCIPIENT
PARAMETRIC	PAST MASTER	PEGMATITIC	PERCOLATED
PARAMNESIA	PASTY-FACED	PEJORATION	PERCOLATOR
PARANOIACS	PATCHINESS	PEJORATIVE	PERCUSSION
PARANORMAL	PATCHWORKS	PELLAGROUS	PERCUSSIVE
PARAPHRASE	PATENTABLE	PELLICULAR	PEREMPTORY
PARAPHYSIS	PATERNALLY	PELLUCIDLY	PERENNIALS

P 10 LETTERS

PERFECTING	PERPETUITY	PHARISAISM	PHRASEBOOK
PERFECTION	PERPLEXING	PHARMACIES	PHRENOLOGY
PERFECTIVE	PERPLEXITY	PHARMACIST	PHTHISICAL
PERFIDIOUS	PERQUISITE	PHARYNGEAL	PHYLACTERY
PERFOLIATE	PERSECUTED	PHELLODERM	PHYLLODIAL
PERFORABLE	PERSECUTOR	PHENACAINE	PHYLLOXERA
PERFORATED	PERSEVERED	PHENACETIN	PHYLOGENIC
PERFORATOR	PERSIAN CAT	PHENAFORMIN	PHYSIATRIC
PERFORMERS	PERSIENNES	PHENOCRYST	PHYSICALLY
PERFORMING	PERSIFLAGE	PHENOMENAL	PHYSICIANS
PERICLINAL	PERSIMMONS	PHENOMENON	PHYSICISTS
PERICYCLIC	PERSISTENT	PHENOTYPIC	PHYSIOCRAT
PERIDERMAL	PERSISTING	PHILATELIC	PHYSIOLOGY
PERIDOTITE	PERSONABLE	PHILIPPICS	PHYTOGENIC
PERIGYNOUS	PERSONABLY	PHILIPPINE	PHYTOPHAGY
PERIHELION	PERSONAGES	PHILISTINE	PHYTOTOXIN
PERILOUSLY	PERSONALLY	PHILOSOPHY	PIANISSIMO
PERIMETERS	PERSONALITY	PHLEBOTOMY	PIANOFORTE
PERIMETRIC	PERSONATOR	PHLEGMATIC	PICARESQUE
PERIMYSIUM	PERSPIRING	PHLOGISTICS	PICCADILLY
PERIODICAL	PERSUADING	PHLOGISTON	PICCALILLI
PERIOSTEUM	PERSUASION	PHLOGOPHITE	PICANINNY
PERIPETEIA	PERSUASIVE	PHOCOMELIA	PICHICIEGO
PERIPHERAL	PERTAINING	PHOENECIAN	PICKPOCKET
PERIPHYTON	PERTINENCE	PHONE BOOKS	PICNICKERS
PERIPTERAL	PERTURBING	PHONE BOXES	PICNICKING
PERISARCAL	PERVERSELY	PHONEYNESS	PICRIC ACID
PERISCOPES	PERVERSION	PHONEY WARS	PICROTOXIC
PERISCOPIC	PERVERSITY	PHONICALLY	PICROTOXIN
PERISHABLE	PERVERTING	PHONOGRAPH	PICTOGRAPH
PERISTOMAL	PESSIMISTS	PHONOLITIC	PIED-A-TERRE
PERISTYLER	PESTICIDAL	PHONOMETER	PIERCINGLY
PERISTYLES	PESTICIDES	PHONOSCOPE	PIGEONHOLE
PERITONEAL	PESTILENCE	PHONOTYPIC	PIGEON-TOED
PERITONEUM	PETIT FOURS	PHOSGENITE	PIGGYBACKS
PERITRICHA	PETITIONED	PHOSPHATES	PIGGYBANKS
PREIWINKLE	PETITIONER	PHOSPHATIC	PIGMENTARY
PERMAFROST	PETIT POINT	PHOSPHORUS	PIGSTICKER
PERMANENCE	PETITS POIS	PHOTOFLOOD	PIKESTAFFS
PERMANENCY	PETRIFYING	PHOTOGENIC	PILE DRIVER
PERMANENTS	PETROGRAPH	PHOTOGRAPH	PILGRIMAGE
PERMEATING	PETROLATUM	PHOTOLYSIS	PILIFEROUS
PERMEATION	PETROPOLIS	PHOTOLYTIC	PILLORYING
PERMEATIVE	PETTICOATS	PHOTOMETER	PILLOWCASE
PERMISSION	PETULANTLY	PHOTOMETRY	PILLOW TALK
PERMISSIVE	PHAGOCYTES	PHOTOMURAL	PILOT LIGHT
PERMITTING	PHAGOCYTIC	PHOTONASTY	PIMPERNELS
PERNAMBUCO	PHAGOMANIA	PHOTOPHILY	PIMPLINESS
PERNICIOUS	PHALANGEAL	PHOTOPHORE	PINA COLADA
PERNICKETY	PHALLICISM	PHOTOSTATS	PINCERLIKE
PERORATION	PHALLICIST	PHOTOTAXIS	PINCHPENNY
PEROXIDASE	PHANEROGAM	PHOTOTONIC	PINCUSHION
PERPETRATE	PHANTASIES	PHOTOTONUS	PINEAPPLES
PERPETUATE	PHANTASMAL	PHOTOTYPIC	PINE MARTEN

PINFEATHER	PLASTICINE	POLAR BEARS	POOH-POOHED
PINGUIDITY	PLASTICITY	POLARITIES	POORHOUSES
PINNATIFID	PLASTICIZE	POLARIZING	POOR WHITES
PINNATIPED	PLAT DU JOUR	POLEMICIST	POPE'S NOSES
PINPOINTED	PLATE GLASS	POLE VAULTS	POPISHNESS
PINSTRIPED	PLATELAYER	POLITBUROS	POPULARITY
PINSTRIPES	PLATE RACKS	POLITENESS	POPULARIZE
PIONEERING	PLATITUDES	POLITICIAN	POPULATING
PIPED MUSIC	PLATYPUSES	POLITICIZE	POPULATION
PIPE DREAMS	PLAY-ACTING	POLLARDING	PORCUPINES
PIPERAZINE	PLAYFELLOW	POLLINATED	PORIFEROUS
PIPERIDINE	PLAYGROUND	POLLINATOR	PORK BARREL
PIPSISSEWA	PLAYGROUPS	POLLINOSIS	PORNOCRACY
PIPSQUEAKS	PLAYHOUSES	POLLUTANTS	POROUSNESS
PIROUETTES	PLAYSCHOOL	POLONAISES	PORPHYROID
PISTACHIOS	PLAYTHINGS	POLYANTHUS	PORTAMNETO
PISTILLATE	PLAYWRIGHT	POLYATOMIC	PORTCULLIS
PISTON RING	PLEASANTER	POLYBASITE	PORTENDING
PITCH-BLACK	PLEASANTLY	POLYCARPIC	PORTENTOUS
PITCHFORK	PLEASANTRY	POLYCHEATE	PORTFOLLIOS
PITCHINESS	PLEASINGLY	POLYCHROME	PORTIONING
PIRCHSTONE	PLEBISCITE	POLYCHROMY	PORTLINESS
PITH HELMET	PLEONASTIC	POLYCLINIC	PORT OF CALL
PITILESSLY	PLESIOSAUR	POLYCYCLIC	PORTRAYALS
PITOT TUBES	PLEURODONT	POLYDACTYL	PORTRAYING
PITTSBURGH	PLEUROTOMY	POLYDIPSIA	PORTUGUESE
PITYRIASIS	PLEXIGLASS	POLYDIPSIC	POSITIONAL
PLACARDING	PLIABILITY	POLYGAMIST	POSITIONED
PLACE CARDS	PLODDINGLY	POLYGAMOUS	POSITIVELY
PLACEMENTS	PLOUGHBOYS	POLYGRAPHS	POSITIVISM
PLAGIARISM	PLUCKINESS	POLYGYNIST	POSITIVIST
PLAGIARIST	PLUMB LINES	POLYGYNOUS	POSSESSING
PLAIGARIZE	PLUMMETING	POLYHEDRAL	POSSESSION
PLAINCHANT	PLUNDERERS	POLYHEDRON	POSSESSIVE
PLAIN FLOUR	PLUNDERING	POLYMATHIC	POSSESSORS
PLAINTIFFS	PLUNDEROUS	POLYMERISM	POSSESSORY
PLANCHETTE	PLUPERFECT	POLYMERIZE	POST-BELLUM
PLANETARIA	PLURALISTS	POLYMEROUS	POST-CYCLIC
PLANE TREES	PLURALIZER	POLYNESIAN	POSTDATING
PLANGENTLY	PLUTOCRACY	PLYNOMIAL	POSTERIORS
PLANIMETER	PLUTOCRATS	POLYPHAGIA	POSTHUMOUS
PLANIMETRY	PNEUMATICS	POLYPHONIC	POSTILIONS
PLANK-SHEER	POCKETABLE	POLYPODOUS	POSTLIMINY
PLANKTONIC	POCKETBOOK	POLYRHYTHM	POSTMARKED
PLANOMETER	POCKETFULS	POLYSEMOUS	POSTMASTER
PLANOMETRY	POCKMARKED	POLYTHEISM	POSTMORTEM
PLANTATION	PODIATRIST	POLYTHEIST	POST OFFICE
PLASMAGENE	POETASTERS	POLYVALENT	POSTPARTUM
PLASMODIUM	POETICALLY	POMERANIAN	POSTPONING
PLASMOLYSE	POGO STICKS	POMIFEROUS	POSTSCRIPT
PLASMOSOME	POIGNANTLY	POMOLOGIST	POSTULANCY
PLASTERERS	POINSETTIA	PONDERABLE	POSTULANTS
PLASTERING	POINT-BLANK	POND-SKATER	POSTULATED
PLASTIC ART	POKER-FACED	PONTIFICAL	POSTULATES

POSTULATOR	PRECISIONS	PREPOSSESS	PRIMA DONNA
POTABILITY	PRECLUDNG	PREPOTENY	PRIMA FACIE
POTATO CHIP	PRECLUSION	PREP SCHOOL	PRIMAQUINE
POTBELLIED	PRECLUSIVE	PRESAGEFUL	PRIME MOVER
POTBELLIES	PRECOCIUOS	PRESBYOPIA	PRIME RATES
POTBOILERS	PRECONCERT	PRESBYOPIC	PRIMITIVES
POTENTATES	PRECOOKING	PRESBYTERY	PREMORDIAL
POTENTIATE	PRECURSORS	PRESCHOOLS	PREMORDIUM
POTENTILLA	PRECURSORY	PRESCIENCE	PRINCEDOMS
POTENTNESS	PREDAACIOUS	PRESCRIBED	PRINCELING
POTHUNTERS	PREDECEASE	PRESCRIBER	PRINCESES
POTPOURRIS	PREDESTINE	PRESCRIPTS	PRINCIPALS
POULTERERS	PREDICABLE	PRESENT-DAY	PRINCIPIUM
POULTRYMAN	PREDICATED	PRESENTERS	PRINCIPLED
POURPARLER	PREDICATES	PRESENTING	PRINCIPLES
POWDER KEGS	PREDICTING	PRESERVERS	PRINTMAKER
POWDER PUFF	PREDICTION	PRESERVING	PRIORITIES
POWDER ROOM	PREDICTIVE	PRESETTING	PRIORITIZE
POWER BASES	PREDISPOSE	PRESIDENCY	PRISMATOID
POWERBOATS	PRE-EMINENT	PRESIDENTS	PRISMOIDAL
POWER DIVES	PRE-EMPTING	PREIDIUMS	PRISONCAMP
POWERFULLY	PRE-EMPTION	PRESIGNIFY	PRISSINESS
POWERHOUSE	PRE-EMPTIVE	PRESS AGENT	PRIVATEERS
POWER PLANT	PRE-EMPTORY	PRESS BARON	PRIVATIONS
POWER POINT	PREEXISTED	PRESS BOXES	PRIVATIZED
POZZUOLANA	PREFECTURE	PRESSGANGS	PRIVILEGES
PRACTICALS	PREFERABLE	PRESSINGLY	PRIVY PURSE
PACTISING	PREFERABLY	PRESS-STUDS	PRIZE FIGHT
PORAESIDIUM	PREFERENCE	PRESSURING	PROCAMIAL
PRAGMATICS	PREFERMENR	PRESSURIZE	PROCAMBIUM
PRAGMATISM	PREFERRING	PRESUMALE	PROCEDURAL
PRAGMATIST	PREFIGURED	PRESMABLY	PROCEDURES
PRAIRIE DOG	PREFRONTAL	PRESUMEDLY	PROCEEDING
PRANCINGLY	PREGLACIAL	PRESUPPOSE	PROCESSING
PRANKSTERS	PREGNANTLY	PRETENDERS	PROCESSION
PRASELENIC	PREHEATING	PRETENDING	PROCESSORS
PRATINCOLE	PREHENSILE	PRETENSION	PROCLAIMED
PRAYER RUGS	PREHENSION	PRETTIFIED	PROCLIVITY
PREACHMENT	PREHISTORY	PRETTINESS	PROCONSULS
PREADMITE	PREHOMIDNID	PREVAILING	PROCREATED
PREAMBULAR	PREJUDGING	PREVALENCE	PROCREATOR
PREARRANGE	PREJUDICED	PREVENIENT	PROCRYPTIC
PREBENDARY	PREJUDICES	PREVENTING	PROCTOLOGY
PRECARIOUS	PRELEXICAL	PREVENSION	PROCTORIAL
PRECAUTION	PREMARITAL	PREVENTIVE	PROCUMBENT
PRECEDENCE	PREMAXILLA	PREVIEWING	PROCURATOR
PRECEDENTS	PREMEDICAL	PREVIOUSLY	PRODIGALLY
PRECENTORS	PRENATALLY	PREVISIONS	PRODIGIOUS
PRECEPTIVE	PRENOMINAL	PREVOCALIC	PRODUCIBLE
PRECESSION	PREPACKAGE	PRICKLIEST	PRODUCTION
PRECIOUSLY	PREPACKING	PRIEST-HOLE	PRODUCTIVE
PRECIPICED	PREPAREDLY	PRIESTHOOD	PROFESSING
PRECIPICES	PREPAYABLE	PRIESTLIER	PROFESSION
PRECIPITIN	PREPAYMENT	PRIGGISHLY	PROFESSORS

PROFFERING	PROPELLENT	PROTHALLIC	PUISSANCES
PROFICIENT	PROPELLERS	PROTHALLUS	PULLULATED
PROFITABLE	PROPELLING	PROTOHUMAN	PULSATIONS
PROFITABLY	PROPENCITY	PROTONEMAL	PULSIMETER
PROFITEERS	PROPERNESS	PROTOPATHY	PULVERABLE
PROFITLESS	PROPER NOUN	PROTOPLASM	PULVERIZED
PROFLIGACY	PROPERTIED	PROTOPLAST	PULVERIZER
PROFLIGATE	PROPERTIES	PROTOSTELE	PUMMELLING
PROFOUNDLY	PROPHECIES	PROTOTYPAL	PUNCH BALLS
PROFUNDITY	PROPHESIER	PROTOTYPES	PUNCHBOARD
PROGENITOR	PROPHESIED	PROTOXYLEM	PUNCH BOWLS
PROGLLOTIS	PROPHESIES	PROTOZOANS	PUNCH-DRUNK
PROGNOSTIC	PROPIONATE	PROTRACTED	PUNCHINESS
PROGRAMERS	PROPITIATE	PROTRACTOR	PUNCH LINES
PROGRAMING	PROPTIOUS	PROTRUDENT	PUNCTUATION
PROGRAMMED	PROPONENTS	PROTRUDING	PUNCTILIOS
PROGRAMMER	PROPORTION	PROTRUSILE	PUNCTUALLY
PROGRAMMES	PROPOSABLE	PROTRUSION	PUNCTUATED
PROGRESSED	PROPOSITUS	PROTRUSIVE	PUNCTUATOR
PROGRESSES	PROPOUNDED	PROVENANCE	PUNCTURING
PROHIBITED	PROPOUNDER	PROVENCALE	PUNISHABLE
PROHIBITER	PROPRIETOR	PROVERBIAL	PUNSHMENT
PROJECTILE	PROPULSION	PROVIDENCE	PUNITIVELY
PROJECTING	PROPULSIVE	PROVINCIAL	PUPIPAROUS
PROJECTIVE	PROPYLAEUM	PROVISIONS	PUPPETEERS
PROJECTORS	PROROGUING	PROVITAMIN	PURCHASERS
PROLAPSING	PROSCENIUM	PRUDENTIAL	PURCHASING
PROLOCUTOR	PROSCRIBED	PRURIENTLY	PURGATIVES
PROLONGING	PROSECUTED	PSALMODIST	PURITANISM
PROMENADED	PROSECUTOR	PSALTERIES	PURLOINING
PROMENADER	PROSELYTES	PSALTERIUM	PURPLENESS
PROMENADES	PROSELYTIC	PSEPHOLOGY	PURPORTING
PROMETHIUM	PROSPECTED	PSESPHITIC	PURPOSEFUL
PROMINENCE	PROSPECTOR	PSEUDOCARP	PURSUANCES
PROMISSORY	PROSPECTUS	PSEUDONYMS	PURSUIVANT
PROMONTORY	PROSPERING	PSILOCYBIN	PURVEYANCE
PROMOTABLE	PROSPERITY	PSITTACINE	PUSH-BUTTON
PROMOTIONS	PROSPEROUS	PSYCHIATRY	PUSHCHAIRS
PROMPTBOOK	PROSTHESIS	PSYCHOLOGY	PUTREFYING
PROMPTNESS	PROSTHETIC	PSYCOPATH	PUTRESCENT
PROMULGATE	PROSTITUTE	PSYCOTICS	PUTRESCINE
PRONEPHRIC	PROSTOMIUM	PTOLEMAIST	PUZZLEMENT
PRONEPHROS	PROSTRATED	PUB-CRAWLED	PUZZLINGLY
PRONOMINAL	PROTANOPIA	PUBERULENT	PYCNOMETER
PRONOUNCED	PROTANOPIC	PUBESCENE	PYOGENESIS
PRONOUNCER	PROTECTING	PUBLIC BARS	PYORRHOEAL
PRONUCLEAR	PROTECTION	PUBLICISTS	PYRACANTHA
PRONUCLEUS	PROTECTIVE	PUBLICIZED	PYRIDOXINE
PEO-OESTRUS	PROTECTORS	PUBLISHERS	PYROGALLIC
PROPAGABLE	PROTECTORY	PUBLISHING	PYROGALLOL
PROPAGANDA	PROTEINASE	PUERPERIUM	PYROGRAPHY
PROPAGATED	PRO TEMPORE	PUERTO RICO	PYROLUSITE
PROPAGATOR	PROTESTANT	PUGILISTIC	PYROMANCER
PROPELLANT	PROTESTERS	PUGNACIOUS	PYROMANIAC

PYROMANTIC
PYROMETRIC
PYROPHORIC
PYROSTATIC
PYROXENITE
PYRRHOTITE
PYTHAGORAS

11 LETTERS
PACE BOWLERS
PACIFICALLY
PACKAGE DEAL
PACKAGE TOUR
PACK ANIMALS
PACKING CASE
PAEDIATRICS
PAEDOLOGIST
PAINFULNESS
PAINKILLERS
PAINSTAKING
PALAEARCTIC
PALATINATES
PALEOGRAPHY
PALEOLITHIC
PALESTINIAN
PALINPSESTS
PALINDROMES
PALINDROMIC
PALLBEARERS
PALLIATIVES
PALPABILITY
PALPITATING
PALPITATION
PAMPAS GRASS
PAMPHLETEER
PAN-AMERICAN
PANCAKE ROLL
PANCHEN LAMA
PANDEMONIAC
PANDEMONIUM
PANDORA'S BOX
PANEGYRICAL
PANHANDLERS
PANHANDLING
PANHELLENIC
PANJANDRUMS
PANTHEISTIC
PANTOGRAPHS
PANTOGRAPHY
PANTOMIMIST
PAPER CHASES
PAPER-CUTTER
PAPER HANGER

PAPER KNIVES
PAPER TIGERS
PAPERWEIGHT
PAPIER-MACHE
PAPYRACEEOUS
PARABLASTIC
PARACETAMOL
PARACHUTING
PARACHUTIST
PARADOXICAL
PARAGENESIS
PARAGENETIC
PARAGRAPHIA
PARAGRAPHIC
PARALDEHYDE
PARALEIPSIS
PARALLACTIC
PARALLELING
PARALLELISM
PARALLELIST
PARALLELLED
PARAMEDICAL
PARAMORPHIC
MARAMOUNCY
PARAPHRASED
PARAPHRASES
PARAPLASTIC
PARAPLEGICS
PARATHYROID
PARATROOPER
PARATHYPOID
PARENTHESES
PARENTHESIS
PARENTHETIC
PARESTHESIA
PARESTHETIC
PARI-MUTUELS
PARIPINNATE
PARISH-CLERK
PARISHONER
PARKING LOTS
PARK KEEPERS
PARLIAMENTS
PARLOUR GAME
PAROCHIALLY
PARONOMASIA
PARSON'S NOSE
PARTIALNESS
PARTICIPANT
PARTICIPATE
PARTICIPIAL
PARTCIPLES
PARTICULARS
PARTICULATE

PARTING SHOT
PARTITIONED
PARTIRTIONER
PARTITIVELY
PARTENERSHIP
PARTURIENCY
PARTURITION
PARTY PIECES
PARTY POOPER
PAS-DE-CALAIS
PASQUINADER
PASSIBILITY
PASSIONLESS
PASSION PLAY
PASSIONTIDE
PASSIVENESS
PASTEBOARDS
PASTEURIZED
PASTEURIZER
PAST MASTERS
PAST PERFECT
PATCH POCKET
PATELLIFORM
PATERNALISM
PATERNALIST
PATERNOSTER
PATHFINDERS
PATHFINDING
PATHOLOGIST
PATISSERIES
PATRIARCHAL
PATRILINEAL
PATRIMONIAL
PATROL WAGON
PATRONIZING
PATRON SAINT
PATRONYMICS
PAUNCHINESS
PAVING STONE
PAWNBROKERS
PAWNBROKING
PAY ENVELOPE
PAY STATIONS
PEACH MELBAS
PEACOCK BLUE
PEARL DRIVERS
PEARLY GATES
PEASHOOTERS
PECCABILITY
PECCADILLOS
PECTINATION
PECTIZATION
PECULATIONS
PECULIARITY

PECUNILARILY
PEDESTRIANS
PEDICULOSIS
PEDICURISTS
PEDOLOGICAL
PEDUNCULATE
PEEPING TOMS
PEEVISHNESS
PELARGONIUM
PELLUCIDITY
PELOPONESE
PENALTY AREA
PENDULOUSLY
PENETRALIAN
PENETRATING
PENETRATION
PENETRATIVE
PENICILLATE
PENICILLIUM
PENITENTIAL
PENNY WEIGHT
PENNY WORTHS
PENOLOGICAL
PENSIVENESS
PENTADACTYL
PENTAHEDRON
PENTAMEROUS
PENTAMETERS
PENTANGULAR
PENTATHLONS
PENTAVALENT
PENTECOSTAL
PENTLANDITE
PENULTIMATE
PENURIOUSLY
PEPPERCORNS
PEPPER MILLS
PEPPERMINTS
PEPETIC ULCER
PEPTIZATION
PERAMBULATE
PERECEIVABLE
PERCENTAGES
PERCEPTIBLE
PERCEPTIBILY
PERCHLORATE
PERCHLORIDE
PERCIPIENCE
PERCOLATING
PERCOLATION
PERCOLATIVE
PERCOLATORS
PEREGRINATE
PERENNIALLY

PERFECTIBLE	PERSONALIST	PHOSPHOROUS	PILOCARPINE
PERFORATING	PERSONALITY	PHOTOACTIVE	PILOT LIGHTS
PERFORATION	PERSONALIZE	PHOTOCOPIED	PINA COLADAS
PERFORATIVE	PERSONATION	PHOTOCOPIER	PINCUSHIONS
PERFORMABLE	PERSONATIVE	PHOTOCOPIES	PINEAL GLAND
PERFORMANCE	PERSONIFIED	PHOTO FINISH	PINE MARTENS
PERFUNCTORY	PERSECTIVE	PHOTOGRAPHS	PINNATISECT
PERICARDIUM	PERSPICUITY	PHOTOGRAPHY	PINPOINTING
PERIDOTITIC	PERSPICUOUS	PHOTOMETRIC	PIPE CLEANER
PERIGORDIAN	PERSUADABLE	PHOTONASTIC	PIPE OF PEACE
PERIHELIONS	PERSUASIONS	PHOTO-OFFSET	PIPERACEOUS
PERIMORPHIC	PERTINACITY	PHOTOPERIOD	PIPISTRELLE
PERINEURIUM	PERTINENTLY	PHOTOPHOBIA	PIRATICALLY
PERIODICALS	PERTURBABLE	PHOTOPHOBIC	PIROUETTING
PERIODICITY	PERTURBABLY	PHOTOSETTER	PISCATORRIAL
PERIODONTAL	PERVASIVELY	PHOTOSPHERE	PISCIVOROUS
PERIODONTIC	PERVERSIONS	PHOTOSTATIC	PISTON RINGS
PERIPETEIAN	PERVERTEDLY	PHOTOTACTIC	PITCHBLENDE
PERIPHERALS	PERVERTIBLE	PHOTOTROPIC	PITCHFORKED
PERIPHERIES	PESSIMISTIC	PHRASAL VERB	PITCHOMETER
PERIPHRASES	PESTERINGLY	PHRASEBOOKS	PITEOUSNESS
PERIPHRASIS	PESTIFEROUS	PHRASEOGRAM	PITH HELMETS
PERISHABLES	PESTILENCES	PHRASEOLOGY	PITIFULNESS
PERISHINGLY	PETITIONARY	PHTHIRIASIS	PITUITARIES
PERISPERMAL	PETITIONERS	PHYCOLOGIST	PLACABILITY
PERISTALSIS	PETITIONING	PHYCOMYCETE	PLAGIARISMS
PERISTALTIC	PETRODOLLAR	PHYLLOCLADE	PLAGIARISTS
PERITHECIUM	PETROGRAPHY	PHYLLOTAXIS	PLAGIARIZED
PERITONEUMS	PETROLOGIST	PHYLOTACTIC	PLAGIARIZER
PERITONITIC	PETIFOGGER	PHYSIATRICS	PLAGIOCLASE
PERITONITIS	PETTISHNESS	PHYSICALISM	PLAINSPOKEN
PERIWINKLES	PHAGOMANIAC	PHYSICALIST	PLAINTIVELY
PERLOCUTION	PHAGOPHOBIA	PHYSIOGNOMY	PLANETARIUM
PERMANENTLY	PHAGOPHOBIC	PHYTOGRAPHY	PLANETOIDAL
PERMISSIBLE	PHALANSTERY	PICKPOCKETS	PLANIMETRIC
PERMISSIBLY	PHANEROZOIC	PICKWICKIAN	PLANISPERE
PERMUTATION	PHARMACISTS	PICTORIALLY	PLANO-CONVEX
PERORATIONS	PHARYNGITIS	PICTURE BOOK	PLANOGAMETE
PERPETRATED	PHILANDERER	PICTURE CARD	PLANOGRAPHY
PERPETRATOR	PHILATELIST	PICTURESQUE	PLANOMETRIC
PERPETUALLY	PHILHELLENE	PIECE OF CAKE	PLANTAGENET
PERPETUATED	PHILIPPINES	PIECE OF WORK	PLANTATIONS
PERPLEXEDLY	PHILOLOGIST	PIEDMONTEITE	PLANTIGRADE
PERQUISITES	PHILOSOPHER	PIEDS-A-TERRE	PLASMAGNETIC
PERSECUTING	PHLEBOTOMIC	PIEZOMETRIC	PLASMODESMA
PERSECUTION	PHONOGRAPHS	PIGEONHOLED	PLASMOLYSIS
PERSECUTIVE	PHONOGRAPHY	PIGEONHOLES	PLASMOLYTIC
PERSECUTORS	PHONOLOGIST	PIGGISHNESS	PLASTER CAST
PERSEVERANT	PHONOMETIC	PIGHEADEDLY	PLASTICALLY
PERSEVERING	PHONOTYPIST	PIGSTICKING	PLASTIC ARTS
PERSIAN CATS	PHOSPHATASE	PILE DRIVERS	PLASTICIZER
PERSISTENCE	PHOSPHATIZE	PILGRAMAGES	PLATOMETER
PERSNICKETY	PHOSPHORATE	PILLAR BOXES	PLASTOMETRY
PERSONALISM	PHOSPHORITE	PILLOW CASES	PLATELAYERS

PLATINOTYPE	POLEMICALLY	PORTS OF CALL	PRECLUDABLE
PLATS DE JOUR	POLE VAULTED	POSITIONING	PRECONCEIVE
PLATYRRHINE	POLE VAULTER	POSITIVISTS	PRECONTRACT
PLAYER PIANO	POLICE STATE	POSITIONING	PRECRITICAL
PLAYFELLOWS	POLICE WOMAN	POSITIVISTS	PREDATORILY
PLAYFULNESS	POLICE WOMEN	POSITRONIUM	PREDECEASED
PLAYGROUNDS	POLITICALLY	POSSESSIONS	PREDECESOR
PLAYING CARD	POLITICIANS	POSSESSIVES	PREDESTINED
PLAY ON WORDS	POLITICIZED	POSSIBILITY	PREDICAMENT
PLAYSCHOOLS	POLITICKING	POSTAL ORDER	PREDICATING
PLAYWRIGHTS	POLLEN COUNT	POSTERITIES	PREDICATION
PLEASANTEST	POLLINATING	POSTER PAINT	PREDICATIVE
PLEASURABLE	POLLINATION	POSTGLACIAL	PREDICATORY
PLEASURABLY	POLTERGEIST	POSTMARKING	PREDICTABLE
PLEASUREFUL	POLYANDROUS	POSTMASTERS	PREDICTABLY
PLEBEIANISM	POLYCHASIUM	POSTMORTEMS	PREDICTIONS
PLEBISCITES	POLYGAMISTS	POSTNUPTIAL	PREDIGESTED
PLECTOGNATH	POLY GENESIS	POST OFFICES	PREDISPOSAL
PLEISTOCENE	POLY GENETIC	POSTPONABLE	PREDISPOSED
PLENTEOUSLY	POLY GLOTISM	POSTSCRIPTS	PREDOMINANT
PLENTIFULLY	POLYGRAPHIC	POSTULATING	PREDOMINATE
PLEOCHROISM	POLYHYDROXY	POSTULATION	PRE-EMINENCE
PLEOMORPHIC	POLYNUCLEAR	POTATO CHIPS	PRE-EXISTENT
PLICATENESS	POLYPEPTIDE	POTATO CRISP	PRE-EXISTING
PLOUGHSHARE	POLYPHONOUS	POTENTIALLY	PREFACTORILY
PLOUGHSTAFF	POLYPLOIDAL	POTTING SHED	PREFECTURAL
PLUM PUDDING	POLYSTERENE	POVERTY TRAP	PREFECTURES
PLUNDERABLE	POLYTECHNIC	POWDER PUFFS	PREFERENCES
PLURALISTIC	POLYTHEISTS	POWDER ROOMS	PREFIGURING
PLURALITIES	POLYTOPHIC	POWER BROKER	PREGNANCIES
PLUTOCRATIC	POLYVALENCY	POWER HOUSES	PREHISTORIC
PLUVIOMETER	POLYZOARIUM	POWERLESSLY	PRE-IGNITION
PLUVIOMETRY	POMEGRANATE	POWERPLANTS	PREJUDMENT
PNEUMECTOMY	POMICULTURE	POWER POINTS	PREJUDICIAL
PNEUMOGRAPH	POMOLOGICAL	PRACTICABLE	PREJUDICING
POCKET BOOKS	POMPOUSNESS	PRACTICABLY	PRELIMINARU
POCKET KNIFE	PONDEROUSLY	PRACTICALLY	PRELITERACY
POCKET MONEY	PONDICHERRY	PRAEDIALITY	PRELITERATE
POCOCURANTE	PONTIFICALS	PRAESIDIUMS	PREMATURELY
POCTOSCOPIC	PONTIFICATE	PRAGMATISTS	PREMEDIATE
PODIATRISTS	POOH-POOHING	PRARIE DOGS	PREMIERSHIP
PODOPHYLLIN	POPULARIZED	PRATTLINGLY	PREMIUM BOND
POINSETTIAS	POPULARIZER	PRAYER WHEEL	PREMONITION
POINTEDNESS	POPULATIONS	PREARRANGED	PREMUNITION
POINTE-NOIRE	PORK BARRELS	PREARRANGER	PREOCCUPIED
POINTILLISM	PORNOGRAPHY	PRECAMBRIAN	PREORDAINED
POINTILLIST	PORPHYRITIC	PRECAUTIONS	PREPARATION
POINTLESSLY	PORTABILITY	PRECAUTIOUS	PREPARITIVE
POINT OF VIEW	PORTER HOUSE	PRECESSIONS	PREPARATORY
POISONOUSLY	PORTMANTEAU	PRECIPITANT	PREPOSITION
POLARMETER	PORT OF ENTRY	PRECIPITATE	PREPOSITIVE
POLARMETRY	PORTRAITIST	PRECIPITOUS	PREP SCHOOLS
POLARISCOPE	PORTRAITURE	PRECISENESS	PRERECORDED
POLARIZABLE	PORTRAYABLE	PRECLINICAL	PREROGATIVE

PRESBYTERAL	PROBATIONAL	PROMINENTLY	PROTAGONISM
PRESCRIBING	PROBATIONER	PROMISCUITY	PROTAGONIST
PRESENTABLE	PROBLEMATIC	PROMISCUOUS	PROTANDROUS
PRESENTABLY	PROBOSCISES	PROMISINGLY	PROTECTIONS
PRESENTIMENT	PROCEEDINGS	PROMOTIONAL	PROTECTORAL
PRESERVABLE	PROCEPHALIC	PROMPTITUDE	PROTECTRESS
PRESS AGENCY	PROCESSIONS	PROMULGATED	PROTEOLYSIS
PRESS AGENTS	PROCHRONISM	PROMULGATOR	PROTEOLYTIC
PRESS BARONS	PROCLAIMING	PROMYCELIUM	PROTEROZOIC
PRESSGANGED	PROCONSULAR	PRONOUNCING	PROTESTANTS
PRESSURIZED	PROCREATING	PROOFREADER	PROTHROMBIN
PRESSURIZER	PROCREATION	PROOF SPIRIT	PROTOGYNOUS
PRESTIGIOUS	PROCRUSTEAN	PROPAGATING	PROTOLITHIC
PRESTISSIMO	PROCTOSCOPE	PROPAGATION	PROTOPATHIC
PRESTRESSED	PROCTOSCOPY	PROPAGATIVE	PROTOSTELIC
PRESUMINGLY	PROCURATION	PROPAGATORS	PROTRACTILE
PRESUMPTION	PROCUREMENT	PROPELLANTS	PROTRACTING
PRESUMPTIVE	PRODIGALITY	PROPER NOUNS	PROTRACTION
PRESUPPOSED	PRODUCTIONS	PROPHESYING	PROTRACTIVE
PRETENDEDLY	PROFANATION	PROPHYLAXES	PROTRACTORS
PRETENTIONS	PROFANATORY	PROPHYLAXIS	PROTRUDABLE
PRETENTIOUS	PROFANENESS	PROPINQUITY	PROTRUSIONS
PRETERITION	PROFANITIES	PROPITABLE	PROTUBERANT
PRETERITIVE	PROFESSEDLY	PROPITIATED	PROVABILITY
PRETTIFYING	PROFESSIONS	PROPITIATOR	PROVIDENCES
PRETTY PENNY	PROFICIENCY	PROPORTIONS	PROVIDENTLY
PREVALENTLY	PROFITEERED	PROPOSITION	PROVINSIALS
PREVARICATE	PROFITEROLE	PROPOUNDING	PROVISIONAL
PREVENTABLE	PROFLIGATES	PROPANOLOL	PROVISIONED
PREVENTABLY	PROFUSENESS	PROPRIETARY	PROVISIONER
PREVENTATIVE	PROGENITIVE	PROPRIETIES	PROVISORILY
PRICKLINESS	PROGENITORS	PROPRIETORS	PROVOCATION
PRICKLY HEAT	PROGNATHISM	PROROGATION	PROVOCATIVE
PRICKLY PEAR	PROGNATHOUS	PROSAICALLY	PROVOKINGLY
PRIESTCRAFT	PROGRAMMERS	PROSAICNESS	PROXIMATELY
PRIESTLIEST	PROGRAMMING	PROS AND CONS	PROXIMATION
PRIMA DONNAS	PROGRESSING	PROSCENIUMS	PRUDENTNESS
PRIMATOLOGY	PROGRESSION	PROSCRIBING	PRUDISHNESS
PRIME MOVERS	PROGRESSIVE	PROSECUTING	PRUSSIC ACID
PRIME NUMBER	PROHIBITING	PROSECUTION	PSEUDOMORPH
PRIMIPARITY	PROHIBITION	PROSECUTORS	PSILOMELANE
PRIMIPAROUS	PROHIBITORY	PROSELYTISM	PSITTACOSIS
PRIMITIVELY	PROJECTILES	PROSELYTIZE	PSYCHEDELIA
PRIMITIVISM	PROJECTIONS	PROSENCHYMA	PSYCHEDELIC
PRIMITIVIST	PROKOPYEVSK	PROSPECTING	PSYCHIATRIC
PRINCIPALLY	PROLATENESS	PROSPECTIVE	PSYCHICALLY
PRINTING INK	PROLEGOMENA	PROSPECTORS	PSYCHODRAMA
PRIORITIZED	PROLETARIAN	PROSTATITIS	PSYCHOGENIC
PRISON CAMPS	PROLETARIAT	PROSTHETICS	PSYCHOGRAPH
PRIVATIZING	PROLIFERATE	PROSTITUTED	PSYCHOMETRY
PRIZEFIGHTS	PROLIFEROUS	PROSTITUTES	PSYCHOMOTOR
PROBABILISM	PROLONGMENT	PROSTITUTOR	PSYCHOPATHS
POBABILIST	PROMENADING	PROSTRATING	PSYCHOPATHY
PROBABILITY	PROMINENCES	PROSTRATION	PTERIDOLOGY

	12 LETTERS	PARAMAGNETIC	PEASE PUDDING
PTERODACTYL	PACIFICATION	PARAMILITARY	PECCADILLOES
PTOCHOCRACY	PACKAGE DEALS	PARAMORPHISM	PECKING ORDER
PUB-CRAWLING	PACKAGE TOURS	PARAPHRASING	PEDANTICALLY
PUBLICATION	PACKING CASES	PARAPHRASTIC	PEDIATRICIAN
PUBLIC-HOUSE	PADDLING POOL	PARASITICIDE	PEJORATIVELY
PUBLICIZING	PAEDOGENESIS	PARASITOLOGY	PANALIZATION
PUBLIC WORKS	PAEDOGENETIC	PARATHYROIDS	PENALTY AREAS
PUBLISHABLE	PAEDOLOGICAL	PARATROOPERS	PENDENTE LITE
PUCKISHNESS	PAGANIZATION	PARENTHESIZE	PENITENTIARY
PUERTO RICAN	PAINT BRUSHES	PARISH CLERKS	PENNSYLVANIA
PULCHRITUDE	PALAEOBOTANY	PARISHIONERS	PENNULTIMATE
PULLULATING	PALAEOGRAPHY	PARISYLLABIC	PENNY PINCHER
PULLULATION	PALAEOLITHIC	PARKING LIGHT	PENNY WHISTLE
PULSATILITY	PALATABILITY	PARKING METER	PENTARCHICAL
PULVERIZING	PALATIALNESS	PARLOUR GAMES	PEPTIC ULCERS
PULVERULENT	PALEOGRAPHER	PAROCHIALISM	PERADVENTURE
PUMPKINSEED	PALEONTOLOGY	PARSIMONIOUS	PERAMBULATED
PUNCHED CARD	PALETTE KNIFE	PARSON'S NOSES	PERAMBULATOR
PUNCTILIOUS	PALINGENESIS	PART EXCHANGE	PERCEPTIONAL
PUNCTUALITY	PALINGENETIC	PARTIALITIES	PERCEPTIVELY
PUNTUATION	PALPITATIONS	PARTICIPANTS	PERCEPTIVITY
PUNCTURABLE	PALYNOLOGIST	PARTICIPATED	PERCOLATIONS
PUNISHINGLY	PAMPHLETEERS	PARTICIPATOR	PERCUTANEOUS
PUNISHMENTS	PANCAKE ROLLS	ARTICULARLY	PEREGRINATOR
PURCHASABLE	PANCHROMATIC	PARTING SHOTS	PEREMPTORILY
PURCHASE TAX	PANDANACEOUS	PARTISANSHIP	PERFIDIOUSLY
PUREBLOODED	PANDEMONIUMS	PARTITIONING	PERFOLIATION
PURGATORIAL	PANHELLENISM	PARTNERSHIPS	PERFORATIONS
PURIFICATOR	PANHELLENIST	PART OF SPEECH	PERFORMANCES
PURITANICAL	PANOPTICALLY	PARTY POOPERS	PERFORMATIVE
PURPLE HEART	PANTECHNICON	PASQUEFLOWER	PERICARDITIC
PURPOSELESS	PANTISOCRACY	PASSE-PARTOUT	PERICARDITIS
PUSHINGNESS	PANTOGRAPHER	PASSIONATELY	PERICYNTHION
PUSSYFOOTED	PANTOGRAPHIC	PASSION PLAYS	PERILOUSNESS
PUSSY WILLOW	PAPERHANGERS	PASTEURIZING	PERIMORPHISM
PUSTULATION	PAPERHANGING	PAST PERFECTS	PERINEPHRIUM
PUTREFIABLE	PAPERWEIGHTS	PATCH POCKETS	PERINEURITIC
PUTRESCENCE	PAPULIFEROUS	PATERNALISTS	PERINEURITIS
PYCNOMETRIC	PARABOLOIDAL	PATERNOSTERS	PERIODICALLY
PYELOGRAPHY	PARACHRONISM	PATHETICALLY	PERIODONTICS
PYLORECTOMY	PARACHUTISTS	PATHOGENESIS	PERIOD PIECES
PYRANOMETER	PARADE GROUND	PATHOGENETIC	PERIONYCHIUM
PYRARGYRITE	PARADIGMATIC	PATHOLOGICAL	PERIPHERALLY
PYROCLASTIC	PARADISIACAL	PATHOLOGISTS	PERIPHRASTIC
PYROGALLATE	PARAESTHESIA	PATRIARCHATE	PERITRICHOUS
PYROGRAPHER	PARAESTHETIC	PATRIARCHIES	PERMANENT WAY
PYROGRAPHIC	PARAHYDROGEN	PATRICLINOUS	PERMANGANATE
PYROMANIACS	PARALANGUAGE	PATROL WAGONS	PERMEABILITY
PYROTECHNIC	PARALLEL BARS	PATRON SAINTS	PERMISSIVELY
PYRRHULOXIA	PARALLELISMS	PAVING STONES	PERMITTIVITY
PYRROLIDINE	PARALLELLING	PAY ENVELOPES	PERMUTATIONS
PYTHAGOREAN	PARALOGISTIC	PEACEFULNESS	PERNICIOUSLY
	PARALYSATION	PEANUT BUTTER	PERPETRATING

PERPETRATION	PHILISTENISM	PHYSIOCRATIC	PLIMSOLL LINE
PERPETRATORS	PHILODENDRON	PHYSIOGNOMIC	PLODDINGNESS
PERPETUATING	PHILOLOGICAL	PHYSIOGRAPHY	PLOUGHSHARES
PERPETUATION	PHILOLOGISTS	PHYSIOLOGIES	PLUMBIFEROUS
PERPETUITIES	PHILOSOPHERS	PHYSIOLOGIST	PLUM PUDDINGS
PERPLEXITIES	PHILOSOHIES	PHYSOSTOMOUS	PLUTOCRACIES
PERSECUTIONS	PHILOSOPHIZE	PHYTOGENESIS	PLUVIOMETRIC
PERSEVERANCE	PHLEBOTOMIST	PHYTOGENETIC	PNEUMOCOCCUS
PERSISTENTLY	PHONEMICALLY	PHYTOHORMONE	PNEUMOTHORAX
PERSONA GRATA	PHONE-TAPPING	PHYTOPHAGOUS	POET LAUREATE
PERSONALIZED	PHONETICALLY	PICCANINNIES	POINTILLISTS
PERSONIFYING	PHONETICIANS	PICKERELWEED	POINT OF ORDER
PERSPECIVES	PHONOGRAPHER	PICTURE BOOKS	POINTS OF VIEW
PERSPICACITY	PHONOLLOGICAL	PICTURE CARDS	POINT-TO-POINT
PERSPIRATION	PHONOLLOGISTS	PIECE OF EIGHT	POLARIMETRIC
PERSPIRATORY	PHONOTACTICS	PIECES OF WORK	POLARIZATION
PERSPIRINGLY	PHOSPHATURIA	PIGEONHOLING	POLAROGRAPHY
PERSUASIVELY	PHOSPHATURIC	PIGMENTATION	POLE POSITION
PERTINACIOUS	PHOSPHOLIPID	PILOT OFFICER	POLE VAULTERS
PERTURBATION	PHOSPHORESCE	PINEAL GLANDS	POLE VAULTING
PERTURBINGLY	PHOSPHORITIC	PINK ELEPHANT	PLICE STATES
PERVERSENESS	PHOTOACTINIC	PIPE CLEANERS	POLICYHOLDER
PESTILENTIAL	PHOTOCATHODE	PIPES OF PEACE	POLITICIZING
PETALIFEROUS	PHOTOCHEMIST	PISCICULTURE	POLLEN COUNTS
PETERBOROUGH	PHOTOCOMPOSE	PITCHFORKING	POLLING BOOTH
PETIT LARCENY	PHOTOCOPIERS	PITIABLENESS	POLTER GEISTS
PETRIFACTION	PHOTOCOPYING	PITILESSNESS	POLYANTHUSES
PETRODOLLARS	PHOTOCURRENT	PITTER-PATTER	POLYCENRISM
PETROGRAPHER	PHOTODYNAMIC	PLACENTATION	POLYCHAETOUS
PETROGRAPHIC	PHOTOENGRAVE	PLACE SETTING	POLYCYTHEMIA
PETROLOGICAL	PHOTOGEOLOGY	PLAGIARISTIC	POLYMBRYONY
PETROLOGISTS	PHOTOGRAPHED	PLAGIARIZING	POLYETHYLENE
PETROZAVODSK	PHOTOGRAPHER	PLAGIOCLIMAX	POLYISOPRENE
PETTIFOGGING	PHOTOGRAPHIC	PLAIN-CLOTHES	POLYMORPHISM
PETTY LARCENY	PHOTOGRAVURE	PLAIN SAILING	POLYPETALOUS
PETTY OFFICER	PHOTOKENESIS	PLANETARIUMS	POLYPHYLETIC
PHAGOCYTOSIS	PHOTOKINETIC	PLANETESIMAL	POLYPHYODONT
PHANEROGAMIC	PHOTOMETRIST	PLANISPHERIC	POLYRHYTHMIC
PHANEROPHYTE	POTOMONTAGE	PLANO-CONCAVE	POLYSEPALOUS
PHARMACOLOGY	POTONEUTRON	PLANOGRAPHIC	POLYSULPHIDE
PHARYNGOLOGY	PHOTONUCLEAR	PLASTERBOARD	POLYSYLLABIC
PHARYNGOTOMY	PHOTOPHILOUS	PLASTER CASTS	POLYSYLLABLE
PHELLODERMAL	PHOTOPOLYMER	PLASTOMETRIC	POLYSYNDETON
PHENANTHRENE	PHOTOSPHERIC	PLATONICALLY	POLYTECHNICS
PHENOLOGICAL	PHOTOSTATTED	PLAUSIBILITY	POLYTHEISTIC
PHENOMENALLY	PHOTOTHERAPY	PLAYER PIANOS	POLYTONALIST
PHI BETA KAPPA	PHOTOTHERMIC	PLAYING CARDS	POLYTONALITY
PHILADELPHIA	PHOTOTROPISM	PLAYING FIELD	POLYURETHANE
PHILADELPHUS	PHRASAL VERBS	PLAYS ON WORDS	POMEGRAN-
PHILANDERERS	PHRASEOGRAPH	PLEASANTNESS	ATTES
PHILANDERING	PHRENOLOGIST	PLEASANTRIES	PONS ASINORUM
PHILANTHROPY	PHYCOLOGICAL	PLEASINGNESS	PONTIFICATED
PHILATELISTS	PHYLETICALLY	PLEIOTROPISM	PONTIFICATES
PHILHARMONIC	PHYSICALNESS	PLEOMORPHISM	PONY-TREKKING

POOR RELATION
POOR-SPIRITED
POPOCATEPETL
POPULARIZING
POPULOUSNESS
PORNOGRAPHER
PORNOGRAPHIC
PORPHYROPSIN
PORT-AU-PRINCE
PORTCULLISES
PORTE-COCHERE
PORTENTOUSLY
PORTERHOUSES
PORT HARCOURT
PORTMANTEAUS
PORTMANTEAUX
PORTS OF ENTRY
POSITIVENESS
POSITIVE POLE
POSITIVISTIC
POSSESSIVELY
POSTAGE STAMP
POSTAL ORDERS
POSTDILUVIAL
POSTDILUVIAN
POSTDOCTORAL
POSTER COLOUR
POSTER PAINTS
POSTGRADUATE
POSTHUMOUSLY
POSTMERIDIEM
POSTPONEMENT
POSTPOSITION
POSTPOSITIVE
POSTPRANDIAL
POTATO BEETLE
POTATO CRISPS
POTENTIALITY
POTTER'S WHEEL
POTTING SHEDS
POTTY-TRAINED
POVERTY TRAPS
POWER BROKERS
POWERFULNESS
POWER STATION
PRACTICALITY
PRACITIONER
PRAGMATISTIC
PRAISEWORTHY
PRASEODYMIUM
PRAYER WHEELS
PREAMPLIFIER
PREARRANGING
PREBENDARIES

PRECARIOUSLY
PRECEDENTIAL
PRECENTORIAL
PRECEPTORATE
PRECEPTORIAL
PRECIOUSNESS
PRECIPITANCE
PRECIPITATED
PRECIPITATES
PRECIPITATOR
PRECISIANISM
PRECISIONISM
PRECISIONIST
PRECOCIOUSLY
PRECOGNITION
PRECOGNITIVE
PRECONCIEVED
PRECONDITION
PRECONSCIOUS
PREDECEASING
PREDECESSORS
PREDESTINATE
PREDESTINING
PREDETERMINE
PREDICAMENTS
PREDICTIVELY
PREDIGESTING
PREDIGESTION
PREDILECTION
PREDISPOSING
PREDOMINANCE
PREDOMINATED
PREDOMINATOR
PRE-ECLAMPSIA
PRE-EMINENTLY
PRE-EMPTIVELY
PRE-EXISTENCE
PREFABRICATE
PREFECTORIAL
PREFORMATION
PREGNABILITY
PREJUDGEMENT
PREJUDGMENTS
PREMARITALLY
PREMAXILLARY
PREMEDITATED
PREMEDITATOR
PREMENSTRUAL
PREMIERSHIPS
PREMIUM BONDS
PREMONITIONS
PREOCCUPYING
PREORDAINING
PREPARATIONS

PREPAREDNESS
PREPONDERATE
PREPOSITIONS
PREPOSSESSED
PREPOSTEROUS
PRERECORDING
PREREQUISITE
PREROGATIVES
PRESBYTERATE
PRESBYTERIAL
PRESBYTERIAN
PRESBYTERIES
PRESCRIPTION
PRESCRIPTIVE
PRESENTATION
PRESENTATIVE
PRESENTIMENT
PRESERVATION
PRESERVATIVE
PRESIDENCES
PRESINDENTIAL
PRESS CUTTING
PRESS GALLERY
PRESSGANGING
PRESSINGNESS
PRESS RELEASE
PRESSURIZING
PRESUMPTIOUS
PRESUMPTUOUS
PRESUPPOSING
PRETTY-PRETTY
PREVAILINGLY
PREVIOUSNESS
PRICKLY PEARS
PRIDE OF PLACE
PRIESTLINESS
PRIEST-RIDDEN
PRIGGISHNESS
PRIME NUMBERS
PRIMOGENITOR
PRIMORDIALLY
PRIMULACEOUS
PRIMUM MOBILE
PRINCELINESS
PRINCIPAL BOY
PRINCIPALITY
PRINTABILITY
PRIORITIZING
PRIZMATOIDAL
PRIVATE PARTS
PRIVY COUNSIL
PRIZEFIGHTER
PROBATIONARY
PROBATIONERS

PROBOSCIDEAN
PROCATHEDRAL
PROCESSIONAL
PROCLAMATION
PROCLIVITIES
PROCONSULATE
PROCOLOGIST
PRODIGIOUSLY
PRODUCTIONAL
PRODUCTIVELY
PRODUCTIVITY
PROFANATIONS
PROFESSIONAL
PROFICIENTLY
PROFITEERING
PROFITLESSLY
PROFIT MARGIN
PROFOUNDNESS
PROFUNDITIES
PROGESTERONE
PROGRAMMABLE
PROGRAMMATIC
PROGRESSIONS
PROGRESSIVES
PROHIBITIONS
PROJECTIONAL
PROLEGOMENAL
PROLEGOMENON
PROLETARIANS
PROLIFERATED
PROLIFICALLY
PROLIFICNESS
PROLONGATION
PROMISED LAND
PROMONTORIES
PROMULGATING
PROMULGATION
PROMULGTAORS
PRONOMINALLY
PRONOUNCEDLY
PROOFREADERS
PROOFREADING
PROPAEDEUTIC
PROPAGANDISM
PROPAGANDIST
PROPAGANDIZE
PROPENSITIES
PROPHESIABLE
PROPHYLACTIC
PROPITIATING
PROPITIATION
PROPITIATIVE
PROPITIATORY
PROPITIOUSLY

PROPORTIONAL
PROPORTIONED
PROPOSITIONS
PROROGATIONS
PROSCRIPTION
PROSCRIPTIVE
PROSECUTABLE
PROSECUTIONS
PROSELYTIZED
PROSELYTIZER
PROSOPOPOEIA
PROSPECTUSES
PROSPEROUSLY
PROSTITUTING
PROSTITUTION
PROSTRATIONS
PROTACTINIUM
PROTAGONISTS
PROTECTIVELY
PROTECTORATE
PROTESTATION
PROTESTINGLY
PROTHALAMION
PROTHONOTARY
PROTOHISTORY
PROTOMORPHIC
PROTOPLASMIC
PROTOPLASTIC
PROTOSEMITIC
PROTOTHERIAN
PROTOTROPHIC
PROTOZOOLOGY
PROTRACTEDLY
PROTUBERANCE
PROVERBIALLY
PROVIDENTIAL
PROVINCIALLY
PROVISIONING
PROVOATIONS
PRUDENTIALLY
PRUSSIAN BLUE
PSEPHOLOGIST
PSEUDONYMITY
PSEUDONYMOUS
PSEUDOPODIUM
PSYCHIATRIST
PSYCOACTIVE
PSYCHOBABBLE
PSYCHOGNOSIS
PSYCHOGRAPHY
PSYCHOLOGIES
PSYCHOLOGISM
PSYCHOLOGIST
PSYCHOLOGIZE

PSYCHOMETRIC
PSYCHOPATHIC
PSYCHOSOCIAL
PSYCHROMETER
PTERIDOPHYTE
PTERIDOSPERM
PTERODACTYLS
PUBLICATIONS
PUBLLIC HOUSES
PUBLIC SCHOOL
PUBLIC SECTOR
PUBLIC SPIRIT
PUGNACIOUSLY
PULVERULENCE
PUMPERNICKEL
PUNCHED CARDS
PUNITIVENESS
PURIFICATION
PURIFICATORY
PURISTICALLY
PURPLE HEARTS
PURPOSE-BUILT
PURPOSEFULLY
PURSE STRINGS
PUSSYFOOTING
PUSSY WILLOWS
PUTREFACTION
PUTREFACTIVE
PYELOGRAPHIC
PYRIDOXAMINE
PYROCHEMICAL
PYROELECTRIC
PYROGNOSTICS
PTROLIGNEOUS
PYROMANIACAL
PYROPHYLLITE
PYROSULPHATE
PYROTECHNICS

13 LETTERS
PADDLE STEAMER
PADDLING POOLS
PAEDIATRICIAN
PAINSTAKINGLY
PALAEOGRAPHIC
PALAEONTOLOGY
PALAEOZOOLOGY
PALEOGRAPHERS
PALETTE KNIVES
PALYNOLOGICAL
PANCHROMATISM
PANDORA'S BOXES
PANIC STATIONS

589

PANIC-STRICKEN
PANORAMICALLY
PANSOPHICALLY
PANTECHNICONS
PAPAVERACEOUS
PAPILLOMATOUS
PARABOLICALLY
PARADE GROUNDS
PARADOXICALLY
PARAGOGICALLY
PARALLELOGRAM
PARALYTICALLY
PARAMAGNETISM
PARANOIACALLY
PARAPHERNALIA
PARASITICALLY
PARASITICIDAL
PARASYNTHESIS
PARASYNTHETON
PARENT COMPANY
PARENTHETICAL
PAR EXCELLENCE
PARKING GARAGE
PARKING LIGHTS
PARKING METERS
PARKINSON'S LAW
PARLIAMENTARY
PARROT-FASHION
PART EXCHANGES
PARTHENOCARPY
PARTICIPATING
PARTICIPATION
PARTICIPIALLY
PARTI-COLOURED
PARTICULARISM
PARTICULARIST
PARTICULARITY
PARTICULARIZE
PARTS OF SPEECH
PASSEMENTERIE
PASSIONFLOWER
PASSIONLESSLY
PASSIVIZATION
PATENT LEATHER
PATERFAMILIAS
PATERNALISTIC
PATHOGNOMONIC
PATRIOTICALLY
PATRISTICALLY
PATRONIZINGLY
PEACEABLENESS
PEACE OFFERING
PECKING ORDERS
PECTORAL CROSS

PECULIARITIES
PEDAGOGICALLY
PEDESTRIANIZE
PEDIATRICIANS
PEDUNCULATION
PELOPONNESIAN
PELTIER EFFECT
PENEPLANATION
PENETRABILITY
PENETRATINGLY
PENETRATIVELY
PENICILLATION
PENITENTIALLY
PENNILESSNESS
PENNSYLVANIAN
PENNY-DREADFUL
PENNY-FARTHING
PENNY-PINCHERS
PENNY-PINCHING
PENNY WHISTLES
PENTANOIC ACID
PEPPER-AND-SALT
PEPTONIZATION
PERAMBULATING
PERAMBULATION
PERAMBULATORS
PERAMBULATORY
PERCUSSION CAP
PERCUSSIONIST
PEREGRINATION
PERFECTIONISM
PERFECTIONIST
PERFUNCTORILY
PERICARPOIDAL
PERICHONDRIUM
PERIODIC TABLE
PERISHABILITY
PERISODACTYL
PERMANENT WAVE
PERMANENT WAYS
PERMUTATIONAL
PERPENDICULAR
PERSEVERATION
PERSONALISTIC
PERSONALITIES
PERSONALIZING
PERSONIFIABLE
PERSPECTIVISM
PERSPICACIOUS
PERVASIVENESS
PERVERTEDNESS
PETROCHEMICAL
PETROL STATION
PETROPAVLOVSK

PETTY OFFICERS
PHARMACEUTICS
PHARMACOGNOSY
PHARMACOPOEIA
PHARYNGOSCOPE
PHARYNGOSCOPY
PHELLOGENETIC
PHENOMENALISM
PHENOMENALIST
PHENOMENOLOGY
PHENOTHIAZINE
PHENYLALANINE
PHI BETA KAPPAS
PHILANTHROPIC
PHILHELLENISM
PHILOSOPHICAL
PHILOSOPHIZED
PHILOSOPHIZER
PHI-PHENOMENON
PHOSPHORYLASE
PHOTOCHEMICAL
PHOTOCOMPOSER
PHOTODYNAMICS
PHOTOELECTRIC
PHOTOELECTRON
PHOTOEMISSION
PHOTOEMISSIVE
PHOTOENGRAVER
PHOTO FINISHES
PHOTOGRAPHERS
PHOTOGRAPHING
PHOTOPERIODIC
PHOTORECEPTOR
PHOTOSTATTING
PHRASEOGRAPHY
PHRASEOLOGIST
PHRENOLOGICAL
PHYCOMYCETOUS
PHYLLOQUINONE
PHYSICALISTIC
PHYSICAL JERKS
PHYSIOGNOMIES
PHYSIOGNOMIST
PHYSIOGRAPHER
PHYSIOGRAPHIC
PHYSIOLOGICAL
PHYSIOLOGISTS
PHYSIOTHERAPY
PHYSOCLISTOUS
PHYSOSTIGMINE
PHYTOPLANKTON
PICTURESQUELY
PICTURE WINDOW
PIECES OF EIGHT

PIEZOELECTRIC
PIGEON-CHESTED
PIGHEADEDNESS
PILOT OFFICERS
PINK ELEPHANTS
PINKING SHEARS
PISCICULTURAL
PITCHED BATTLE
PLACE SETTINGS
PLAGIOTROPISM
PLAINTIVENESS
PLASTIC BULLET
PLATINIFEROUS
PLATINIRIDIUM
PLATINIZATION
PLATINUM-BLOND
PLATITUDINIZE
PLATITUDINOUS
PLATYHELMINTH
PLAYING FIELDS
PLENTEOUSNESS
PLENTIFULNESS
PLIMSOLL LINES
PLOUGHMANSHIP
PLURALIZATION
PNEUMATICALLY
PNEUMATOLYSIS
PNEUMATOMETER
PNEUMATOMETRY
PNEUMATOPHORE
PNEUMOGASTRIC
PNEUMONECTOMY
POETIC JUSTICE
POETIC LICENCE
POETS LAUREATE
POINTLESSNESS
POINTS OF ORDER
POINT-TO-POINTS
POISONOUSNESS
POLE POSITIONS
POLICE OFFICER
POLICE STATION
POLIOMYELITIS
POLLING BOOTHS
POLLINIFEROUS
POLYADELPHOUS
POLYCHROMATIC
POLYCOTYLEDON
POLYDACTYLOUS
POLYEMBRYONIC
POLYGALACEOUS
POLYGONACEOUS
POLYPROPYLENE
POLYPROTODONT

POLYSYLLABLES
POLYSYLLOGISM
POLYSYNTHESIS
PONDERABILITY
PONDEROUSNESS
PONTIFICATING
POOR RELATIONS
PORCELLANEOUS
PORNOGRAPHERS
POSITIVE POLES
POSSIBILITIES
POSTAGE STAMPS
POSTER COLOURS
POSTE RESTANTE
POSTGRADUATES
POSTMAN'S KNOCK
POST OFFICE BOX
POSTOPERATIVE
POSTPONEMENTS
POTATO BEETLES
POTENTIOMETER
POTTER'S WHEELS
POTTY-TRAINING
POWERLESSNESS
POWER POLITICS
POWER STATIONS
POWER STEERING
PRACTICAL JOKE
PRACTITIONERS
PRAGMATICALLY
PRAYER MEETING
PRAYING MANTIS
PREADAPTATION
PREADOLESCENT
PRECAUTIONARY
PRECEPTORSHIP
PRECIOUS METAL
PRECIOUS STONE
PRECIPITATELY
PRECIPITATING
PRECIPITATION
PRECIPITATIVE
PRECIPITOUSLY
PRECONCEPTION
PRECONDITIONS
PRECONIZATION
PREDATORINESS
PREDETERMINED
PREDETERMINER
PREDICABILITY
PREDICATIVELY
PREDILECTIONS
PREDOMINANTLY
PREDOMINATING

PREDOMINATION
PREFABRICATED
PREFABRICATOR
PREFERABILITY
PREJUDGEMENTS
PRELIMINARIES
PRELIMINARILY
PREMATURENESS
PREMEDICATION
PREMEDITATIVE
PREOCCUPATION
PREORDINATION
PREPARATORILY
PREPONDERANCE
PREPONDERATED
PREPOSITIONAL
PREPOSSESSING
PREPOSSESSION
PRE-RAPHAELITE
PREREQUISITES
PRESBYTERIANS
PRESCRIPTIBLE
PRESCRIPTIONS
PRESENTATIONS
PRESENTIMENTS
PRESERVATIVES
PRESS AGENCIES
PRESS CUTTINGS
PRESS RELEASES
PRESSURE GROUP
PRESSURE POINT
PRESUMPTIVELY
PRETENTIOUSLY
PRETERNATURAL
PREVARICATING
PREVARICATION
PREVARICATORS
PRICELESSNESS
PRIMARY COLOUR
PRIMARY SCHOOL
PRIMARY STRESS
PRIME MERIDIAN
PRIME MINISTER
PRIMITIVENESS
PRIMOGENITURE
PRINCE CONSORT
PRINCIPAL BOYS
PRINTED MATTER
PRINTING PRESS
PRISONER OF WAR
PRISON VISITOR
PRIVATE MEMBER
PRIVATE SCHOOL
PRIVATE SECTOR

PRIVATIZATION	PRONOUNCEABLE	PROXIMATENESS
PRIZEFIGHTERS	PRONOUNCEMENT	PSEUDOMORPHIC
PRIZEFIGHTING	PRONUNCIATION	PSYCHIATRISTS
PROBABILISTIC	PROPAGABILITY	PSYCHOANALYSE
PROBABILITIES	PROPAGANDISTS	PSYCHOANALYST
PROCESS-SERVER	PROPAGANDIZED	PSYCHOANALYZE
PROCLAMATIONS	PROPAGATIONAL	PSYCHOBIOLOGY
PROCONSULATES	PROPAROXYTONE	PSYCHODYNAMIC
PROCRASTINATE	PROPHETICALLY	PSYCHOGENESIS
PROCTOLOGICAL	PROPHYLACTICS	PSYCHOGENETIC
PRODUCIBILITY	PROPITAITIOUS	PSYCHOGNOSTIC
PROFESSIONALS	PROPORTIONATE	PSYCHOGRAPHIC
PROFESSORIATE	PROPORTIONING	PSYCHOHISTORY
PROFESSORSHIP	PROPOSITIONAL	PSYCHOKINESIS
PROFITABILITY	PROPOSITIONED	PSYCHOKINETIC
PROFIT MARGINS	PROPRIETARILY	PSYCHOLOGICAL
PROFIT SHARING	PROPRIETORIAL	PSYCHOLOGISTS
PROGNOSTICATE	PROSCRIPTIONS	PSYCHOMETRICS
PROGRESSIONAL	PROSELYTIZERS	PSYCHOPHYSICS
PROGRESSIVELY	PROSELYTIZING	PSYCHOSOMATIC
PROGRESSIVISM	PROSTAGLANDIN	PSYCHOSURGERY
PROGRESSIVIST	PROSTATECTOMY	PSYCHOTHERAPY
PROHIBITIVELY	PROTECTIONISM	PSYCHOTICALLY
PROJECTIONIST	PROTECTIONIST	PSYCHROPHILIC
PROLEPTICALLY	PROTECTORATES	PUBLIC COMPANY
PROLIFERATING	PROTEINACEOUS	PUBLIC SCHOOLS
PROLIFERATION	PROTESTANTISM	PULVERIZATION
PROLIFERATIVE	PROTESTATIONS	PUNCTILIOUSLY
PROLONGATIONS	PROTHETICALLY	PUNISHABILITY
PROMENADE DECK	PROTUBERANCES	PURITANICALLY
PROMINENTNESS	PROTUBERANTLY	PURPLE PASSAGE
PROMISCUOUSLY	PROVINCIALISM	PURPOSELESSLY
PROMISED LANDS	PROVINCIALITY	PURPOSIVENESS
PROMISINGNESS	PROVING GROUND	PUSILLANIMITY
PROMOTIVENESS	PROVISIONALLY	PUSILLANIMOUS
PRONOMINALIZE	PROVOCTIVELY	PYROPHOSPHATE

4 LETTERS	6 LETTERS	7 LETTERS	QUIETER
QUAD	QATARI	Q-FACTOR	QUIETUS
QUAY	QINTAR	QUACKED	QUILMES
QUID	QUACKS	QUADRAT	QUILTED
QUIN	QUAGGA	QUADRIC	QUILTER
QUIP	QUAGGY	QUAFFER	QUINARY
QUIT	QUAHOG	QUAILED	QUINATE
QUIZ	QUAILS	QUAKERS	QUINCES
QUOD	QUAINT	QUAKILY	QUININE
	QUAKED	QUALIFY	QUINONE
	QUAKER	QUALITY	QUINTAL
5 LETTERS	QUAKES	QUANGOS	QUINTAN
QATAR	QUALMS	QUANTAL	QUINTET
QUACK	QUANGO	QUANTIC	QUINTIC
QUADS	QUANTA	QUANTUM	QUIPPED
QUAFF	QUARKS	QUARREL	QUITTED
QUAIL	QUARRY	QUARTAN	QUITTER
QUAKE	QUARTO	QUARTER	QUITTOR
QUAKY	QUARTS	QUARTET	QUIVERS
QUALE	QUARTZ	QUARTIC	QUIVERY
QUALM	QUASAR	QUANTAL	QUI VIVE
QUANT	QUAVER	QUANTIC	QUIZZED
QUARK	QUEASY	QUANTUM	QUIZZER
QUART	QUEBEC	QUARREL	QUIZZES
QUASH	QUEENS	QUARTAN	QUONDAM
QUASI-	QUENCH	QUARTER	QUORATE
QUAYS	QUESTS	QUARTET	QUORUMS
QUEEN	QUEUED	QUARTIC	QUOTHED
QUEER	QUEUES	QUARTOS	QUOTING
QUELL	QUICHE	QUASARS	
QUERN	QUIFFS	QUAVERY	
QUERY	QUILLS	QUAYAGE	8 LETTERS
QUEST	QUILTS	QUECHUA	QUACKERY
QUEUE	QUINCE	QUEENED	QUACKING
QUICK	QUINOL	QUEENLY	QUADRANT
QUIET	QUINSY	QUEERED	QUADRATE
QUIFF	QUIRES	QUEERER	QUADROON
QUILL	QUIRKS	QUEERLY	QUAGMIRE
QUILT	QUIRKY	QUELLED	QUAILING
QUINS	QUIVER	QUELLER	QUAINTLY
QUINT	QUOITS	QUERIED	QUALMISH
QUIPS	QUORUM	QUERIES	QUANDARY
QUIRE	QUOTAS	QUERIST	QUANDONG
QUIRK	QUOTED	QUESTED	QUANTIFY
QUITE	QUOTES	QUESTER	QUANTITY
QUITO	QWERTY	QUETZAL	QUANTIZE
QUITS		QUEUING	QUARRELS
QUOIN		QUIBBLE	QUARRIED
QUOIT		QUICHES	QUARRIER
QUOTA		QUICKEN	QUARRIES
QUOTE		QUICKER	QUARTEN
QUOTH		QUICKIE	QUARTERS
QUR'AN		QUICKLY	QUARTLET
		QUIETEN	QUARTILE

	9 LETTERS		QUIZMASTER
QUASHING	**9 LETTERS**	QUIXOTISM	QUOTATIONS
QUATRAIN	QUADRANTS	QUIZZICAL	
QUAVERED	QUADRATIC	QUODLIBET	
QUAVERER	QUADRIFIED	QUOTATION	
QUEASIER	QUADRILLE	QUOTIDIAN	**11 LETTERS**
QUEASILY	QUADRUPED	QUOTIENTS	QUADRANGLES
QUEENDOM	QUADRUPLE		QUADRENNIAL
QUEENING	QUADRUPLY		QUADRENNIUM
QUEEREST	QUAGMIRES	**10 LETTERS**	QUADRILLION
QUEERING	QUAKERISM	QUADRANGLE	QUADRUPEDAL
QUELLING	QUAKINESS	QUADRANTAL	QUADRUPLETS
QUENCHED	QUALIFIED	QUADRATICS	QUADRUPLING
QUENCHER	QUALIFIER	QUADRATURE	QUALIFIABLE
QUERCINE	QUALITIES	QUADRICEPS	QUALITATIVE
QUERYING	QUARRELED	QUADRILLES	QUANTIFIERS
QUESTING	QUARRYING	QUADRISECT	QUANTIFYING
QUESTION	QUATERED	QUADRIVIAL	QUANTUM LEAP
QUIBBLED	QUARTERLY	QUADRUPEDS	QUARANTINED
QUIBBLER	QUARTZINE	QUADRUPLED	QUARRELLING
QUIBBLES	QUATRAINS	QUADRUPLET	QUARRELSOME
QUIBERON	QUAVERING	QUADRUPLEX	QUARTER DAYS
QUICKEST	QUEASIEST	QUAINTNESS	QUARTERDECK
QUICKIES	QUEBECOIS	QUALIFIERS	QUARTER HOUR
QUICKSET	QUEBRACHO	QUALIFYING	QUARTERLIES
QUIDDITY	QUEERNESS	QUANDARIES	QUARTER NOTE
QUIDNUNC	QUENCHING	QUANTIFIED	QUAVERINGLY
QUIETEST	QUERCETIN	QUANTIFIER	QUEENLINESS
QUIETISM	QUERETARO	QUANTITIES	QUEEN MOTHER
QUIETIST	QUERULOUS	QUARANTINE	QUEEN'S BENCH
QUIETUDE	QUESTIONS	QUARRELING	QUERULOUSLY
QUILTING	QUEUE-JUMP	QUARRELLED	QUESTIONARY
QUINTETS	QUIBBLERS	QUARRELLER	QUESTIONERS
QUINTILE	QUIBBLING	QUARTERAGE	QUESTIONING
QUIPPING	QUICKENED	QUARTERDAY	QUESTION TAG
QUIPSTER	QUICKLIME	QUARTERING	QUEUE-JUMPED
QUIRKIER	QUICKNESS	QUARTERSAW	QUEUE-JUMPER
QUIRKILY	QUICKSAND	QUATERNARY	QUIBBLINGLY
QUISLING	QUICKSTEP	QUATERNION	QUICK CHANGE
QUITTERS	QUIESCENT	QUATREFOIL	QUICK-FREEZE
QUITTING	QUIETENED	QUEASINESS	QUICKSILVER
QUIVERED	QUIETIST	QUEENSLAND	QUICK-WITTED
QUIVERER	QUIETNESS	QUENCHABLE	QUID PRO QUOS
QUIXOTIC	QUIETUSES	QUESTINGLY	QUIESCENTLY
QUIZZING	QUILLWORT	QUESTIONED	QUINCUNCIAL
QUOTABLE	QUINIDINE	QUESTIONER	QUINDECAGON
QUOTHING	QUINOLINE	QUICKENING	QUINTILLION
QUOTIENT	QUINONOID	QUICKSANDS	QUINTUPLETS
	QUINTUPLE	QUICKSTEPS	QUIVERINGLY
	QUIRKIEST	QUID PRO QUO	QUIZMASTERS
	QUISLINGS	QUIESCENCE	QUIZZICALLY
	QUITCLAIM	QUIETENING	QUONSER HUTS
	QUITTANCE	QUINTUPLET	QUOTABILITY
	QUIVERFUL	QUIRKINESS	
	QUIVERING	QUITTANCES	

12 LETTERS
QUADRAGESIMA
QUADRANGULAR
QUADROPHONIC
QUADRILLIONS
QUADRINOMIAL
QUADRIPLEGIA
QUADRIPLEGIC
QUADRIVALENT
QUADRUMANOUS
QUALIFYINGLY
QUANTIFIABLE
QUANTITATIVE
QUANTIZATION
QUANTUM LEAPS
QUAQUAVERSAL
QUARANTINING
QUARTER-BOUND
QUARTER FINAL
QUARTER NOTES
QUARTERSTAFF
QUEEN CONSORT
QUEEN MOTHERS
QUELQUECHOSE

QUESTIONABLE
QUESTIONABLY
QUESTION MARK
QUESTION TAGS
QUESTION TIME
QUEUE-JUMPERS
QUEUE-JUMPING
QUINDECAPLET
QUINQUENNIAL
QUINQUENNIUM
QUINTESSENCE
QUIXOTICALLY
QUIZZICALITY

13 LETTERS
QUADRICIPITAL
QUADRILATERAL
QUADRILLIONTH
QUADRIPARTITE
QUADRISECTION
QUADRIVALENCY
QUADRUPLICATE
QUADRUPLICITY

QUALIFICATION
QUALIFICATORY
QUALITATIVELY
QUANTUM THEORY
QUARTERFINALS
QUARTERMASTER
QUARTERSTAFFS
QUARTERSTAVES
QUARTZIFEROUS
QUEENS CONSORT
QUEEN'S COUNSEL
QUEEN'S ENGLISH
QUERULOUSNESS
QUESTIONINGLY
QUESTION MARKS
QUESTIONNAIRE
QUICK-TEMPERED
QUINDECENNIAL
QUINQUAGESIMA
QUINQUEVALENT
QUINTILLIONTH
QUINTUPLICATE
QUODLIBETICAL
QUOTATION MARK

R 3 LETTERS to 5 LETTERS

3 LETTERS	RANT	RISK	5 LETTERS	RAVEL	RERUN
RAF	RAPE	RITE	RABAT	RAVEN	RESAT
RAG	RAPS	RIVE	RABBI	RAVER	RESET
RAJ	RAPT	ROAD	RABIC	RAWER	RESIN
RAM	RARE	ROAM	RABID	RAWLY	RESIT
RAN	RASH	ROAN	RACED	RAYON	RESTS
RAP	RASP	ROAR	RACER	RAZED	RETCH
RAT	RATE	ROBE	RACES	RAZER	RETRO-
RAW	RATS	ROCK	RACKS	RAZOR	RETRY
RAY	RAVE	ROCS	RADAR	REACH	REUSE
RED	RAYS	RODE	RADII	REACT	REVEL
REF	RAZE	RODS	RADIO	READY	REVET
REP	READ	ROES	RADIX	REALM	REVUE
REV	REAL	ROLE	RADOM	REAMS	REXES
REX	REAM	ROLL	RADON	REARM	RHEAS
RIB	REAP	ROMP	RAFTS	REARS	RHEUM
RIG	REAR	ROMS	RAGAS	REBEL	RHINE
RIM	RECK	ROOD	RAGED	REBUS	RHINO
RIP	REDO	ROOF	RAGES	REBUT	RHONE
RNA	REDS	ROOK	RAIDS	RECAP	RHUMB
ROB	REED	ROOM	RAILS	RECTO	RHYME
ROC	REEF	ROOT	RAINS	RECUR	RIALS
ROD	REEK	ROPE	RAINY	REDAN	RICIN
ROE	REEL	ROPY	RAISE	REDIA	RICKS
ROM	REFS	ROSE	RAJAH	REDID	RIDER
ROT	REIN	ROSY	RAKED	REDDS	RIDES
ROW	RELY	ROTA	RAKER	REDDY	RIDGE
RUB	REND	ROTE	RALLY	REEFS	RIDGY
RUE	RENT	ROTS	RAMIE	REEKS	RIFFS
RUG	REPS	ROUE	RAMPS	REELS	RIFLE
RUM	REST	ROUT	RAMUS	REEVE	RIFTS
RUN	REVS	ROUX	RANCE	REFER	RIGHT
RUT	RHEA	ROVE	RANCH	REFIT	RIGID
RYE	RIAL	ROWS	R AND B	REGAL	RIGOR
	RIBS	RUBS	R AND D	REICH	RILED
	RICE	RUBY	RANDY	REIFY	RILEY
4 LETTERS	RICH	RUCK	RANEE	REIGN	RILLS
RACE	RICK	RUDE	RANGE	REIMS	RINDS
RACK	RIDE	RUED	RANGY	REINS	RINGS
RACY	RIFE	RUFF	RANKS	REJIG	RINKS
RAFT	RIFT	RUGS	RAPED	RELAX	RINSE
RAGA	RIGS	RUHR	RAPES	RELAY	RIOTS
RAGE	RILE	RUIN	RAPHE	RELIC	RIPEN
RAGS	RILL	RULE	RAPID	REMIX	RIPER
RAID	RIME	RUMP	RARER	REMIT	RISEN
RAIL	RIMS	RUMS	RASHT	RENAL	RISER
RAIN	RIMY	RUNE	RASPS	RENEW	RISES
RAKE	RIND	RUNG	RATAL	RENIN	RISKS
RAMP	RING	RUNS	RATED	RENTE	RISKY
RAMS	RINK	RUNT	RATEL	RENTS	RITES
RAND	RIOT	RUTS	RATES	REPAY	RITZY
RANG	RIPE	RYES	RATIO	REPEL	RIVAL
RANI	RIPS		RATTY	REPLY	RIVEN
RANK	RISE		RAVED	RERAN	RIVER

RIVET	RUFFS	RADIUS	RAPINE	REASON	REFUEL
RIYAL	RUGBY	RADOME	RAPING	REBATE	REFUGE
ROACH	RUING	RADULA	RAPIST	REBELS	REFUND
ROADS	RUINS	RAFFIA	RAPPED	REBIND	REFUSE
ROANS	RULED	RAFFLE	RAPPEL	REBORN	REFUTE
ROARS	RULER	RAFTED	RAPPER	REBUFF	REGAIN
ROAST	RULES	RAFTER	RAPTOR	REBUKE	REGALE
ROBED	RUMBA	RAGBAG	RAREFY	RECALL	REGARD
ROBES	RUMEN	RAGGED	RARELY	RECANT	REGENT
ROBIN	RUMMY	RAGING	RAREST	RECAPS	REGGAE
ROBLE	RUMPS	RAGLAN	RARING	RECAST	REGIME
ROBOT	RUNES	RAGMAN	RARITY	RECEDE	REGINA
ROCKS	RUNGS	RAGOUT	RASCAL	RECENT	REGION
ROCKY	RUNIC	RAGTAG	RASHER	RECEPT	REGLET
RODEO	RUN-IN	RAIDED	RASHES	RECESS	REGRET
ROMPS	RUNNY	RAIDER	RASHLY	RECIFE	REGULO
RONDO	RUNTS	RAILED	RASPED	RECIPE	REHASH
ROODS	RUNTY	RAILER	RASPER	RECITE	REHEAR
ROOFS	RUN-UP	RAILEX	RATBAG	RECKED	REHEAT
ROOKS	RUPEE	RAINED	RATHER	RECKON	REIGNS
ROOMS	RURAL	RAISED	RATIFY	RECOIL	REINED
ROOMY	RUSES	RAISER	RATINE	RECORD	REJECT
ROOST	RUSHY	RAISES	RATING	RECOUP	REJIGS
ROOTS	RUSKS	RAISIN	RATION	RECTAL	REJOIN
ROPED	RUSSO-	RAJAHS	RATIOS	RECTOR	RELAID
ROPES	RUSTY	RAJKOT	RATITE	RECTOS	RELATE
ROPEY	RUTTY	RAJPUT	RATLAM	RECTUM	RELAYS
ROSES		RAKING	RATOON	RECTUS	RELENT
ROSIN		RAKISH	RATTAN	REDACT	REMAKE
ROTAS	**6 LETTERS**	RAMBLE	RAT-TAT	REDBUD	REMAND
ROTOR	RABATO	RAMIFY	RATTED	REDCAP	REMARK
ROUEN	RABBIS	RAMJET	RATTER	REDDEN	REMEDY
ROUES	RABBIT	RAMMED	RATTLE	REDDER	REMIND
ROUGE	RABBLE	RAMMER	RATTLY	REDEEM	REMISE
ROUGH	RABIES	RAMOSE	RAVAGE	REDFIN	REMISS
ROUND	RACEME	RAMPUR	RAVENS	RED-HOT	REMORA
ROUPY	RACERS	RAMROD	RAVERS	REDONE	REMOTE
ROUSE	RACHIS	RAMTIL	RAVE-UP	REDOWA	REMOVE
ROUST	RACIAL	RANCHI	RAVINE	REDUCE	RENAME
ROUTE	RACIER	RANDAN	RAVING	REECHO	RENDER
ROVED	RACILY	RANDOM	RAVISH	REEFED	RENEGE
ROVER	RACING	RANEES	RAWEST	REEFER	RENNES
ROWAN	RACISM	RANGED	RAZING	REEKED	RENNET
ROWDY	RACIST	RANGER	RAZORS	REELED	RENNIN
ROWED	RACKED	RANGES	RAZZLE	REELER	RENOWN
ROWEL	RACKER	RANKED	READER	REEVES	RENTAL
ROWER	RACKET	RANKER	REALLY	REFACE	RENTED
ROYAL	RACOON	RANKLE	REALMS	REFILL	RENTER
RUBLE	RADDLE	RANKLY	REAMED	REFINE	RENVOI
RUCHE	RADIAL	RANSOM	REAMER	REFITS	REOPEN
RUCKS	RADIAN	RANTED	REAPED	REFLET	REPAID
RUDDY	RADIOS	RANTER	REAPER	REFLEX	REPAIR
RUDER	RADISH	RAPIDS	REARED	REFLUX	REPAND
RUFFE	RADIUM	RAPIER	REARER	REFORM	REPAST

REPEAL	REVIEW	RILLET	ROMANO	RUBLES
REPEAT	REVILE	RIMINI	ROMANS	RUBRIC
REPENT	REVISE	RIMMED	ROMANY	RUCKED
REPINE	REVIVE	RIMOSE	ROMEOS	RUCKUS
REPLAN	REVOKE	RINGED	ROMPED	RUDDER
REPLAY	REVOLT	RINGER	RONDEL	RUDDLE
REPONE	REVUES	RINSED	RONDOS	RUDELY
REPORT	REVVED	RINSER	ROOFED	RUDEST
REPOSE	REWARD	RINSES	ROOKED	RUEFUL
REPUTE	REWIND	RIOTED	ROOKIE	RUFFLE
REREAD	REWIRE	RIOTER	ROOMED	RUFFLY
RERUNS	REWORD	RIPEST	ROOMER	RUFOUS
RESALE	REWORK	RIP-OFF	ROOSTS	RUGGED
RESCUE	RHEBOK	RIPPED	ROOTED	RUGOSE
RESEAT	RHESUS	RIPPER	ROOTER	RUINED
RESEAU	RHEUMY	RIPPLE	ROPIER	RUINER
RESECT	RHEYDT	RIPPLY	ROPILY	RULERS
RESEDA	RHINAL	RIPSAW	ROPING	RULING
RESENT	RHODIC	RISERS	ROQUET	RUMBAS
RESHIP	RHYMED	RISING	ROSARY	RUMBLE
RESIDE	RHYMES	RISKED	ROSIER	RUMBLY
RESIGN	RHYTHM	RISKER	ROSILY	RUMMER
RESILE	RHYTON	RISQUE	ROSINY	RUMOUR
RESINS	RIALTO	RITUAL	ROSTER	RUMPLE
RESIST	RIBALD	RIVALS	ROSTOV	RUMPLY
RESITS	RIBBED	RIVERS	ROSTRA	RUMPUS
RESORB	RIBBON	RIVETS	ROTARY	RUNDLE
RESORT	RIBOSE	RIYADH	ROTATE	RUNNEL
RESTED	RICHER	RIYALS	ROTGUT	RUNNER
RESTER	RICHES	ROAMED	ROTORS	RUN-OFF
RESULT	RICHLY	ROAMER	ROTTED	RUN-OUT
RESUME	RICKED	ROARER	ROTTEN	RUNWAY
RETAIL	RICTAL	ROASTS	ROTTER	RUPEES
RETAIN	RICTUS	ROBALO	ROTUND	RUPIAH
RETAKE	RIDDED	ROBAND	ROUBLE	RUSHED
RETARD	RIDDEN	ROBBED	ROUGED	RUSHER
RETELL	RIDDER	ROBBER	ROUNDS	RUSHES
RETENE	RIDDLE	ROBBIN	ROUSER	RUSSET
RETIAL	RIDERS	ROBING	ROUTED	RUSSIA
RETINA	RIDGED	ROBINS	ROUTER	RUSTED
RETIRE	RIDGES	ROBOTS	ROUTES	RUSTIC
RETOLD	RIDING	ROBUST	ROVERS	RUSTLE
RETOOK	RIFFLE	ROCHET	ROVING	RUTILE
RETOOL	RIFLED	ROCKED	ROWANS	RUTTED
RETORT	RIFLER	ROCKER	ROWERS	RWANDA
RETURN	RIFLES	ROCKET	ROWING	RYAZAN
RETUSE	RIGGED	ROCOCO	ROYALS	
REUSED	RIGGER	RODENT	ROZZER	
REVAMP	RIGHTS	RODEOS	RUBATO	
REVEAL	RIGOUR	ROGUES	RUBBED	
REVERE	RIG-OUT	ROLLED	RUBBER	
REVERS	RIJEKA	ROLLER	RUBBLE	
REVERT	RILEYS	ROLL-ON	RUBBLY	
REVEST	RILING	ROMAIC	RUBIES	

7 LETTERS	RALLINE	RATTIER	REBIRTH	REDUCER
RABBITS	RAMADAN	RATTILY	REBOUND	REDWING
RABBLER	RAMBLED	RATTING	REBUFFS	REDWOOD
RABBLES	RAMBLER	RATTISH	REBUILD	REEDIER
RACCOON	RAMBLES	RATTLED	REBUILT	REEDING
RACEMIC	RAMEKIN	RATTLES	REBUKED	REEFERS
RACHIAL	RAMMING	RAT TRAP	REBUKER	REEFING
RACIEST	RAMMISH	RAUCOUS	REBUKES	REEKING
RACISTS	RAMPAGE	RAUNCHY	REBUSES	RE-ELECT
RACKETS	RAMPANT	RAVAGED	RECALLS	REELLING
RACKETY	RAMPART	RAVAGER	RECAPED	RE-ENTER
RACOONS	RAMPION	RAVAGES	RECEDED	RE-ENTRY
RACQUET	RAMRODS	RAVELED	RECIEPT	REFACED
RADIALS	RAMSONS	RAVELIN	RECIEVE	REFEREE
RADIANT	RANCHES	RAVELLY	RECIPES	REFILLS
RADIATE	RANCHES	RAVENER	RECITAL	REFINED
RADICAL	RANCOUR	RAVENNA	RECITED	REFINER
RADICEL	RANDIER	RAVE-UPS	RECITER	REFLATE
RADICES	RANDOMS	RAVINES	RECKING	REFLECT
RADICLE	RANGERS	RAVINGS	RECLAIM	REFORMS
RADIOED	RANDILY	RAVIOLI	RECLINE	REFRACT
RADULAR	RANGING	RAW DEAL	RECLUSE	REFRAIN
RAFFISH	RANGGON	RAW HIDE	RECORDS	REFRESH
RAFFLED	RANKERS	RAWNESS	RECOUNT	REFUGEE
RAFFLER	RANKING	RAZZLES	RECOVER	REFUGES
RAFFLES	RANKLED	REACHED	RECRUIT	REFUNDS
RAFTERS	RANSACK	REACHER	RECTIFY	REFUSAL
RAFTING	RANSOMS	REACHES	RECTORS	REFUSED
RAGBAGS	RANTERS	REACTED	RECTORY	REFUSER
RAGGING	RANTING	REACTOR	RECTRIX	REFUTED
RAGOUTS	RAPHIDE	READERS	RECTUMS	REFUTER
RAGTIME	RAPIDLY	READIED	RECURVE	REGALIA
RAGWEED	RAPIERS	READIER	RECYCLE	REGALLY
RAGWORM	RAPISTS	READIES	REDCOAT	REGARDS
RAGWORT	RAPPING	READILY	RED DEER	REGATTA
RAIDERS	RAPPORT	READING	REDDEST	REGENCY
RAIDING	RAPTURE	READOUT	REDDISH	REGENTS
RAILING	RAREBIT	REAGENT	RED FISH	REGIMEN
RAILWAY	RASBORA	REALGAR	RED FLAG	REGIMES
RAIMENT	RASCALS	REALIGN	RED HEAD	REGINAS
RAINBOW	RASHERS	REALISM	REDHEAD	REGIONS
RAINIER	RASHEST	REALIST	RED MEAT	REGNANT
RAINILY	RASPING	REALITY	REDNECK	REGOSOL
RAINING	RATABLE	REALIZE	REDNESS	REGRATE
RAINOUT	RATABLY	REALTOR	REDOING	REGRESS
RAISERS	RATAFIA	REAMERS	REDOUBT	REGRETS
RAISING	RAT-A-TAT	REAMING	REDOUND	REGROUP
RAISINS	RATBAGS	REAPERS	REDPOLL	REGULAR
RAISINY	RATCHET	REAPING	REDRAFT	REGULOS
RAKE-OFF	RATE-CAP	REARING	REDRESS	REGULUS
RALEIGH	RATINGS	REARMED	REDROOT	REHOUSE
RALLIED	RATIONS	REASONS	REDSKIN	REIFIER
RALLIER	RATLINE	REBATER	RED TAPE	REIGNED
RALLIES	RAT RACE	REBATES	REDUCED	REINING

REISSUE	REPLIES	RETINAL	RHODIUM	RIPTIDE
REJECTS	REPORTS	RETINAS	RHOMBUS	RISIBLE
REJOICE	REPOSAL	RETINOL	RHONDDA	RISIBLY
RELAPSE	REPOSED	RETINUE	RHUBARB	RISINGS
RELATED	REPOSER	RETIRED	RHYMING	RISKIER
RELATOR	REPOSIT	RETIRER	RHYTHMS	RISKILY
RELATUM	REPRESS	RETORTS	RIBBAND	RISKING
RELAXED	REPRINT	RETOUCH	RIBBING	RISOTTO
RELAXER	REPRISE	RETRACE	RIBBONS	RISSOLE
RELAXIN	REPROOF	RETRACT	RIB CAGE	RITUALS
RELAYED	REPROVE	RETREAD	RIBWORT	RIVALED
RELEASE	REPTANT	RETREAT	RICHEST	RIVALRY
RELIANT	REPTILE	RETRIAL	RICKETS	RIVETED
RELYING	REPULSE	RETSINA	RICKETY	RIVETER
REMAINS	REPUTED	RETURNS	RICKING	RIVIERA
REMAKES	REQUEST	REUNIFY	RIDDLED	RIVIERE
REMANDS	REQUIEM	REUNION	RIDDLER	RIVULET
REMARKS	REQUIRE	REUNITE	RIDDLES	ROACHES
REMARRY	REQUITE	REUSING	RIDGING	ROADBED
REMATCH	REREDOS	REVALUE	RIDOTTO	ROAD HOG
REMNANT	RESCIND	REVELED	RIFFLED	ROADMAN
REMODEL	RESCUED	REVELRY	RIFFLER	ROADMEN
REMORSE	RESCUER	REVENGE	RIFLERY	ROAD TAX
REMOTER	RESCUES	REVENUE	RIFLING	ROADWAY
REMOULD	RESERVE	REVERED	RIGGING	ROAMERS
REMOUNT	RESHAPE	REVERER	RIGHTED	ROAMING
REMOVAL	RESIDED	REVERIE	RIGHTER	ROARING
REMOVED	RESIDER	REVERSE	RIGHTLY	ROASTED
REMOVER	RESIDUE	REVIEWS	RIGIDLY	ROASTER
REMOVES	RESOLVE	REVILED	RIG-OUTS	ROBBERS
RENAMED	RESORTS	REVILER	RIM-FIRE	ROBBERY
RENDING	RESOUND	REVISAL	RIMLESS	ROBBING
RENEGED	RESPECT	REVISED	RIMMING	ROCKERS
RENEGER	RESPIRE	REVISER	RIMROCK	ROCKERY
RENEWAL	RESPITE	REVIVAL	RINGENT	ROCKETS
RENEWED	RESPOND	REVIVED	RINGERS	ROCKIER
RENEWER	RESTATE	REVIVER	RINGING	ROCKIES
RENTALS	RESTFUL	REVOICE	RINGLET	ROCKING
RENT BOY	RESTING	REVOKED	RINSING	ROCKOON
RENTERS	RESTIVE	REVOKER	RIOT ACT	RODENTS
RENTIER	RESTOCK	REVOLTS	RIOTERS	RODLIKE
RENTING	RESTORE	REVOLVE	RIOTING	ROWBUCK
REORDER	RESTYLE	REVVING	RIOTOUS	ROE DEER
REPAIRS	RESULTS	REWARDS	RIPCORD	ROGUERY
REPASTS	RESUMED	REWIRED	RIPENED	ROGUISH
REPEATS	RESUMES	REWRITE	RIPENER	ROISTER
REPINED	RETABLE	REWROTE	RIP-OFFS	ROLL BAR
REPLACE	RETAKEN	REYNOSA	RIPOSTE	ROLLERS
REPLAYS	RETAKER	RHAETIC	RIPPING	ROLLICK
REPLETE	RETAKES	RHATENY	RIPPLED	ROLLING
REPLEVY	RETCHED	RHENIUM	RIPPLER	ROLLMOP
REPLICA	RETHINK	RHEUMIC	RIPPLES	ROLL-ONS
REPLIED	RETICLE	RHEIZOID	RIPPLET	ROLL-TOP
REPLIER	RETINAE	RHIZOME	RIPSAWS	ROLLWAY

ROMAGNA	ROUNDUP	RUSHING	RAMENTUM	REACTORS
ROMANCE	ROUSING	RUSSIAN	RAMIFIED	READABLE
ROMPERS	ROUTINE	RUSTICS	RAMOSITY	READABLY
ROMPING	ROUTING	RUSTIER	RAMPAGED	READIEST
RONDEAU	ROWDIER	RUSTILY	RAMPAGER	READINGS
RONDURE	ROWDILY	RUSTING	RAMPANCY	READJUST
RONTGEN	ROWLOCK	RUSTLED	RAMPARTS	READOUTS
ROOFING	ROYALLY	RUSTLER	RAMULOSE	READYING
ROOFTOP	ROYALTY	RUTTING	RANCHERS	READY-MIX
ROOKERY	ROZZERS	RUTTISH	RANDIEST	REAFFIRM
ROOKIES	RUBBERS	RYBINSK	RANDOMLY	REAGENTS
ROOKING	RUBBERY		RANKLING	REALISTS
ROOMERS	RUBBING		RANKNESS	REALIZED
ROOMFUL	RUBBISH	**8 LETTERS**	RANSOMED	REALIZER
ROOMIER	RUBDOWN	RABBITED	RANSOMER	REALNESS
ROOMILY	RUBELLA	RABBITER	RAPACITY	REAL-TIME
ROOMING	RUBEOLA	RABBITRY	RAPESEED	REALTORS
ROOSTED	RUBICON	RABIDITY	RAPIDITY	REAPABLE
ROOSTER	RUBIDIC	RACCOONS	RAPTNESS	REAPPEAR
ROOTAGE	RUBIOUS	RACEMISM	RAPTURES	REARMING
ROOTING	RUBRICS	RACEMOSE	RARA AVIS	REARMOST
ROOTLET	RUCHING	RACIALLY	RAREFIED	REARWARD
ROPIEST	RUCKING	RACINESS	RAREFIER	REASONED
RORQUAL	RUCTION	RACK-RENT	RARENESS	REASONER
ROSARIO	RUDDERS	RAQUENTS	RARITIES	REASSURE
ROSEATE	RUDDIER	RADIALLY	RASCALLY	REAWAKEN
ROSEBUD	RUDDILY	RADIENCE	RASHNESS	REBELLED
ROSE HIP	RUDERAL	RADIATED	RASORIAL	REBOUNDS
ROSELLA	RUFFIAN	RADIATOR	RASPINGS	REBUFFED
ROSEOLA	RUFFLED	RADICALS	RATCHETS	REBUKING
ROSETTE	RUFFLER	RADICAND	RATIFIED	REBUTTAL
ROSIEST	RUFFLES	RADIOING	RATIFIER	REBUTTED
ROSINED	RUINING	RADISHES	RATIONAL	REBUTTER
ROSTERS	RUINOUS	RAFFLING	RATIONED	RECALLED
ROSTOCK	RULABLE	RAGGEDLY	RATSBANE	RECANTED
ROSTRAL	RULINGS	RAG TRADE	RATTIEST	RECANTER
ROSTRUM	RUMANIA	RAILHEAD	RATTLING	RECAPPED
ROTATED	RUMBLED	RAILINGS	RAT TRAPS	RECEDING
ROTATOR	RUMBLER	RAILLERY	RAVAGING	RECIEPTS
ROTIFER	RUMBLES	RAILROAD	RAVELLED	RECIEVED
ROTTERS	RUMMAGE	RAILWAYS	RAVELLER	RECIEVER
ROTTING	RUMMEST	RAILBAND	RAVENING	RECENTLY
ROTUNDA	RUMOURS	RAINBOWS	RAVENOUS	RECEPTOR
ROUBAIX	RUMPLED	RAINCOAT	RAVISHED	RECESSED
ROUBLES	RUNAWAY	RAINDROP	RAVISHER	RECESSES
ROUGHEN	RUN-DOWN	RAINFALL	RAW-BONED	RECHARGE
ROUGHER	RUNNELS	RAINIEST	RAW DEALS	RECISION
ROUGHLY	RUNNERS	RAINLESS	RAWHIDES	RECITALS
ROUGING	RUNNIER	RAISABLE	RAZOR-CUT	RECITERS
ROULEAU	RUNNING	RAKE-OFFS	REACHING	RECITING
ROUNDED	RUN-OFFS	RAKISHLY	REACTANT	RECKLESS
ROUNDEL	RUNTISH	RALLYING	REACTING	RECKONED
ROUNDER	RUNWAYS	RAMBUTAN	REACTION	RECKONER
ROUNDLY	RUPTURE	RAMEKINS	REACTIVE	RECLINED

R 8 LETTERS

RECLINER	REFEREED	REINVEST	REMOULDS	REPRIEVE
RECLUSES	REFEREES	REISSUED	REMOUNTS	REPRINTS
RECOILED	REFERENT	REISSUER	REMOVALS	REPRISAL
RECOMMIT	REFERRAL	REISSUES	REMOVERS	REPRISES
RECORDED	REFERRED	REJECTED	REMOVING	REPROACH
RECORDER	REFERRER	REJECTER	RENAMING	REPROOFS
RECOUNTS	REFILLED	REJIGGED	RENDERED	REPROVAL
RECOUPED	REFINERY	REJOICED	RENDERER	REPROVED
RECOURSE	REFINING	REJOICER	RENDIBLE	REPROVER
RECOVERY	REFINISH	REJOINED	RENDZINA	REPTILES
RECREANT	REFITTED	REKINDLE	RENEGADE	REPUBLIC
RECREATE	REFLATED	RELAPSED	RENEGING	REPULSED
RECRUITS	REFLEXES	RELAPSES	RENEWALS	REPULSER
RECTALLY	REFOREST	RELATING	RENEWING	REPULSES
RECURRED	REFORMED	RELATION	RENIFORM	REQUESTS
RECUSANT	REFORMER	RELATIVE	RENOUNCE	REQUIEMS
RECYCLED	REFRAINS	RELAXANT	RENOVATE	REQUIRER
REDACTOR	REFUELED	RELAXING	RENOWNED	REQUITAL
RED ALERT	REFUGEES	RELAYING	RENTABLE	REQUITED
REDBRICK	REFUGIUM	RELEASED	RENT BOYS	REQUITER
REDCOATS	REFUNDED	RELEASER	RENT-FREE	RESCRIPT
RED CROSS	REFUNDER	RELEASES	RENTIERS	RESCUERS
REDDENED	REFUSALS	RELEGATE	RENT-ROLL	RESCUING
REDEEMED	REFUSING	RELEVANT	REOPENED	RESEARCH
REDEEMER	REFUTING	RELIABLE	REPAIRED	RESEMBLE
REDEMAND	REGAINED	RELIABLY	REPAIRER	RESENTED
REDEPOLY	REGAINER	RELIANCE	REPARTEE	RESERVED
REDESIGN	REGALITY	RELIEVED	REPAYING	RESERVER
RED-FACED	REGARDED	RELIEVER	REPEALED	RESERVES
RED FLAGS	REGATTAS	RELIGION	REPEALER	RESETTER
RED GIANT	REGELATE	RELINING	REPEATED	RESETTLE
RED HEADS	REGENTAL	RELISHED	REPEATER	RESIDENT
REDIRECT	REGICIDE	RELISHES	REPELLED	RESIDING
RED LIGHT	REGIMENS	RELIVING	REPELLER	RESIDUAL
REDNECKS	REGIMENT	RELOADED	REPENTED	RESIDUES
REDOLENT	REGIONAL	RELOCATE	REPEATED	RESIDUUM
REDOUBLE	REGISTER	REMAINED	REPEATER	RESIGNED
REDOUBTS	REGISTERY	REMAKING	REPELLED	RESIGNER
REDSHANK	REGRATER	REMANDED	REPENTED	RESINATE
REDSKINS	REGROWTH	REMARKED	REPENTER	RESINOID
REDSTART	REGULARS	REMARKER	REPEOPLE	RESINOUS
REDUCING	REGULATE	REMARQUE	REPETEND	RESISTED
REDUVIID	REGULINE	REMEDIAL	REPHRASE	RESISTER
REDWOODS	REHASHED	REMEDIED	REPINING	RESISTOR
RE-ECHOED	REHASHES	REMEDIES	REPLACED	RESOLUTE
REEDBUCK	REHEARSE	REMEMBER	REPLACER	RESOLVED
REEDIEST	REHEATER	REMIGIAL	REPLAYED	RESOLVER
REEDLING	REHOBOAM	REMINDED	REPLEVIN	RESOLVES
REEF KNOT	REHOUSED	REMINDER	REPLICAS	RESONATE
REELABLE	REIGNING	REMITTED	REPLYING	RESORTED
REELABLY	REIMPORT	REMITTER	REPORTED	RESORTER
RE-EMPLOY	REIMPOSE	REMNANTS	REPORTER	RESOURCE
RE-EXPORT	REINDEER	REMOTELY	REPOSING	RESPECTS
REFACING	REINSURE	REMOTEST	REPOUSSE	RESPIRED

RESPITES	REVENGED	RHYTHMIC	RIVALLED	ROOSTING
RESPONSE	REVENGER	RIBALDRY	RIVERBED	ROOT BEER
RESTATED	REVENUED	RIB CAGES	RIVERINE	ROOT CROP
REST CURE	REVEREND	RICOSOME	RIVITERS	ROOTLESS
REST HOME	REVERENT	RICE BIRD	RIVETING	ROOTLIKE
RESTLESS	REVERIES	RICHNESS	RIVIERAS	ROPEWALK
RESTORED	REVERING	RICKRACK	RIVULETS	ROPINESS
RESTORER	REVERSAL	RICKSHAW	ROAD HOGS	ROSARIAN
RESTRAIN	REVERSED	RICOCHET	ROAD SHOW	ROSARIES
RESTRICT	REVERSER	RIDDANCE	ROADSIDE	ROSEBUSH
REST ROOM	REVERSES	RIDDLING	ROADSTER	ROSEFISH
RESULTED	REVERTED	RIDICULE	ROAD TEST	ROSE HIPS
RESUMING	REVERTER	RIESLING	ROAD WORK	ROSEMARY
RETAILED	REVIEWAL	RIFENESS	ROASTERS	ROSEOLAR
RETAILER	REVIEWED	RIFFLING	ROASTING	ROSE-ROOT
RETAINED	REVIEWER	RIFFRAFF	ROBOTICS	ROSETTES
RETAINER	REVILERS	RIFLEMAN	ROBOTISM	ROSEWOOD
RETAKING	REVILING	RIGADOON	ROBUSTLY	ROSINESS
RETARDED	REVISERS	RIGATONI	ROCAILLE	ROSINING
RETARDER	REVISING	RIGHTFUL	ROCK CAKE	ROSTRUMS
RETCHING	REVISION	RIGHTING	ROCK DASH	ROTARIAN
RETICENT	REVISORY	RIGHTISM	ROCKETED	ROTATING
RETICULE	REVIVALS	RIGHTIST	ROCKETRY	ROTATION
RETINENE	REVIVING	RIGIDITY	ROCKFALL	ROTATIVE
RETINITE	REVOKING	RIGORISM	ROCKFISH	ROTATORY
RETINUED	REVOLTED	RIGORIST	ROCKIEST	ROTENONE
RETINUES	REVOLTER	RIGOROUS	ROCKLING	ROTTENLY
RETIRING	REVOLUTE	RIMOSITY	ROCKROSE	ROTUNDAS
RETORTED	REVOLVED	RINGBOLT	ROCKSALT	ROUGHAGE
RETORTER	REVOLVER	RINGBONE	ROCKWEED	ROUGH-DRY
RETRACED	REWARDED	RINGDOVE	ROEBUCKS	ROUGHEST
RETREADS	REWARDER	RING-DYKE	ROENTGEN	ROUGH-HEW
RETREATS	REWINDER	RINGHALS	ROGATION	ROUGHING
RETRENCH	REWIRING	RINGLETS	ROGATORY	ROULETTE
RETRIALS	REWORDED	RING ROAD	ROLE PLAY	ROUND-ARM
RETRIEVE	REWORKED	RINGSIDE	ROLLAWAY	ROUNDELS
RETROACT	REWRITES	RINGWORM	ROLL BARS	ROUNDERS
RETROFIT	RHAETIANS	RINSABLE	ROLL CALL	ROUNDEST
RETRORSE	RHAPSODY	RIOT ACTS	ROLLMOPS	ROUNDING
RETURNED	RHEOBASE	RIPARIAN	ROLY-POLY	ROUNDISH
RETURNER	RHEOLOGY	RIPCORDS	ROMANCED	ROUND-UPS
REUNIONS	RHEOSTAT	RIPENESS	ROMANCES	ROUTINES
REUNITED	RHETORIC	RIPENING	ROMAN LAW	ROVEOVER
REUNITER	RH FACTOR	RIPOSTED	ROMANSCH	ROWDIEST
REUSABLE	RHINITIS	RIPOSTES	ROMANTIC	ROWDYISM
REVALUED	RHIZOMES	RIPPABLE	RONDELET	ROWHOUSE
REVAMPED	RHIZOPOD	RIPPLING	RONTGENS	ROWLOCKS
REVAMPER	RHIZOPUS	RIPTIDES	ROOFLESS	ROYALISM
REVEALED	RHODESIA	RISKIEST	ROOF RACK	ROYALIST
REVEALER	RHODINAL	RISOTTOS	ROOFTOPS	ROYALIST
REVEILLE	RHOMBOID	RISSOLES	ROOFTREE	RUBBINGS
REVELING	RHONCHAL	RITENUTO	ROOMIEST	RUBBISHY
REVELLED	RHONCHUS	RITUALLY	ROOMMATE	RUBDOWNS
REVELLER	RHUBARBS	RIVALING	ROOSTERS	RUBELITE
				RUBEOLAR

603

R

RUBICONS	RACONTEUR	RATTLEBOX	RECLAIMED	RED LIGHTS
RUBICUND	RADIAL-PLY	RAUCOUSLY	RECLINATE	REDOLENCE
RUBIDIUM	RADIANCES	RAUNCHIER	RECLINING	REDOUBLED
RUBRICAL	RADIANTLY	RAUNCHILY	RECLUSION	REDOUNDED
RUCKSACK	RADIATING	RAUWOLFIA	RECLUSIVE	RED-PENCIL
RUCKUSES	RADIATION	RAVELLING	RECOGNIZE	RED PEPPER
RUDDIEST	RADIATIVE	RAVISHING	RECOILING	REDRESSED
RUDENESS	RADIATORS	RAZORBACK	RECOLLECT	REDRESSER
RUDIMENT	RADICALLY	RAZORBILL	RECOMMEND	REDUCIBLE
RUEFULLY	RADIOGRAM	REACHABLE	RECOMPOSE	REDUCTASE
RUFFIANS	RADIOLOGY	REACTANCE	RECONCILE	REDUCTION
RUFFLING	RAFFINOSE	REACTIONS	RECONDITE	REDUNDANT
RUGGEDLY	RAFFISHLY	READDRESS	RECONVERT	RE-ECHOING
RUGOSITY	RAFFLESIA	READINESS	RECORDERS	REEDINESS
RUINABLE	RAILHEADS	READY-MADE	RECORDING	RE-EDUCATE
RULEBOOK	RAILROADS	REALIGNED	RECOUNTAL	REEF KNOTS
RUMANIAN	RAIN CHECK	REALISTIC	RECOUNTED	REEKINGLY
RUMBLING	RAINCOATS	REALITIES	RECOUPING	RE-ELECTED
RUMINANT	RAINDROPS	REALIZING	RE-COVERED	RE-ENFORCE
RUMMAGED	RAINFALLS	REANIMATE	RECOVERER	RE-ENTRANT
RUMMAGER	RAIN GAUGE	REAPPOINT	RECREANTS	RE-ENTRIES
RUMMAGES	RAININESS	REARGUARD	RECREATED	RE-EXAMINE
RUMOURED	RAINMAKER	REARRANGE	RE-CREATOR	REFECTION
RUMPLING	RAINPROOF	REARWARDS	RECREMENT	REFECTORY
RUN-ABOUT	RAINSTORM	REASONING	RECRUITED	REFERABLE
RUNAWAYS	RAINWATER	REASSURED	RECRUITER	REFERENCE
RUNDOWNS	RAJASTHAN	REASSURER	RECTANGLE	REFERENDA
RUNNER-UP	RAMIFYING	REBATABLE	RECTIFIED	REFERRALS
RUNNIEST	RAMPAGING	REBELLING	RECTIFIER	REFERRING
RUPTURED	RAMPANTLY	REBELLION	RECTITUDE	REFILLING
RUPTURES	RANCIDITY	REBINDING	RECTOCELE	REFINABLE
RURALISM	RANCOROUS	REBOUNDED	RECTORATE	REFINANCE
RURALIST	RANDINESS	REBUFFING	RECTORIAL	REFITTING
RURALITY	RANDOMIZE	REBUKABLE	RECTORIES	REFLATING
RURALIZE	RANGINESS	REBUTTALS	RECUMBENT	REFLATION
RUSH HOUR	RANSACKED	REBUTTING	RECURRENT	REFLECTED
RUSTICAL	RANSACKER	RECALLING	RECURRING	REFLECTOR
RUSTIEST	RANSOMERS	RECANTING	RECUCANCY	REFLEXIVE
RUSTLERS	RANSOMING	RECAPPING	RECUSANTS	REFORMERS
RUSTLING	RANTINGLY	RECAPTION	RECYCLING	REFORMING
RUTABAGA	RAPACIOUS	RECAPTURE	REDACTION	REFORMISM
RUTHENIC	RAPID-FIRE	RECASTING	RED ALERTS	REFORMIST
RUTHLESS	RAPIDNESS	RECEIVERS	REDBREAST	REFRACTED
	RAPTORIAL	RECENSION	REDBRICKS	REFRACTOR
	RAPTUROUS	RECEPTIVE	RED CARPET	REFRAINED
9 LETTERS	RARE EARTH	RECESSING	REDDENING	REFRAINER
RABBINATE	RASCALITY	RECESSION	REDEEMERS	REFRESHED
RABBITING	RASPBERRY	RECESSIVE	REDEEMING	REFRESHER
RABBITTED	RASPINGLY	RECHARGED	REDELIVER	REFUELING
RACEHORSE	RATEPAYER	RECHAUFFE	REDEVELOP	REFUELLED
RACETRACK	RATIFYING	RECHERCHE	RED GIANTS	REFULGENT
RACIALISM	RATIONALE	RECIPIENT	RED-HANDED	REFUNDING
RACIALIST	RATIONING	RECITABLE	RED-HEADED	REFURBISH
RACKETEER	RATTINESS	RECKONING	RED INDIAN	REFUSABLE

REFUTABLE	RELIGIONS	REPENTANT	RESCINDED	RESTRAINT
REGAINING	RELIGIOSE	REPENTING	RESCINDER	REST ROOMS
REGARDANT	RELIGIOUS	REPERTORY	RESCUABLE	RESULTANT
REGARDFUL	RELIQUARY	REPHRASED	RESECTION	RESULTING
REGENCIES	RELISHING	REPLACING	RESEMBLED	RESUMABLE
REGICIDAL	RELIVABLE	REPLAYING	RESEMBLER	RESURFACE
REGICIDES	RELOADING	REPLEADER	RESENTFUL	RESURGENT
REGIMENTS	RELOCATED	REPLENISH	RESENTING	RESURRECT
REGISTERS	RELUCTANT	REPLETION	RESERPINE	RETAILERS
REGISTRAR	REMAINDER	REPLETIVE	RESERVING	RETAILING
REGRESSED	REMAINING	REPLICATE	RESERVIST	RETAINING
REGRESSOR	REMANDING	REPLY-PAID	RESERVOIR	RETALIATE
REGRETFUL	REMANENCE	REPORTAGE	RESETTING	RETARDANT
REGRETTED	REMARKING	REPORTERS	RESETTLED	RETARDATE
REGRETTER	REMARRIED	REPORTING	RESHUFFLE	RETARDING
REGROUPED	REMEDYING	REPOSEDLY	RESIDENCE	RETELLING
REGULABLE	REMINDERS	REPOSEFUL	RESIDENCY	RETENTION
REGULARLY	REMINDFUL	REPOSSESS	RESIDENTS	RETENTIVE
REGULATED	REMINDING	REPREHEND	RESIDUARY	RETHOUGHT
REGULATOR	REMINISCE	REPRESENT	RESIGNING	RETICENCE
REHASHING	REMISSION	REPRESSED	RESILIENT	RETICULES
REHEARSAL	REMISSIVE	REPRESSER	RESINATED	RETICULUM
REHEARSED	REMITTING	REPRIEVED	RESISTANT	RETINITIS
REHEARSER	REMODELED	REPRIEVER	RESISTERS	RETORSION
REHOUSING	REMONTANT	REPRIEVES	RESISITING	RETORTING
REIMBURSE	REMONTOIR	REPRIMAND	RESISTORS	RETORTION
REINFORCE	REMOULDED	REPRINTED	RESITTING	RETOUCHED
REINSTALL	REMOUNTED	REPRINTER	RESNATRON	RETOUCHER
REINSTATE	REMOVABLE	REPRISALS	RESOLUBLE	RETRACING
REINSURED	REMOVABLY	REPROBACY	RESOLVENT	RETRACTED
REINSURER	REMSCHEID	REPROBATE	RESOLVING	RETRACTOR
REISSUING	RENASCENT	REPROCESS	RESONANCE	RETREADED
REITERATE	RENDERING	REPRODUCE	RESONATED	RETREATAL
REJECTING	RENDITION	REPROVING	RESONATOR	RETREATED
REJECTION	RENEGADES	REPTILIAN	RESORBENT	RETRIEVAL
REJECTIVE	RENEWABLE	REPTILOID	RESORTING	RETRIEVED
REJIGGING	RENEWEDLY	REPUBLICS	RESOUNDED	RETRIEVER
REJOICING	RENOUNCED	REPUBLISH	RESOURCES	RETROCEDE
REJOINDER	RENOUNCER	REPUDIATE	RESPECTED	RETROFIRE
REJOINING	RENOVATED	REPUGNANT	RESPECTER	RETROFLEX
REKINDLED	RENOVATOR	REPULSING	RESPIRING	RETROPACK
RELAPSING	REOPENING	REPULSION	RESPONDED	RETROUSSE
RELATABLE	REPAIRING	REPULSIVE	RESPONDER	RETURNING
RELATIONS	REPAIRMAN	REPUTABLE	RESPONSER	REUNITING
RELATIVES	REPARABLE	REPUTABLY	RESPONSES	REUTILIZE
RELAXABLE	REPARABLY	REPUTEDLY	RESTATING	REVALUING
RELAXEDLY	REPARTEES	REQUESTED	REST CURES	REVAMPING
RELEASING	REPAYABLE	REQUESTER	RESTFULLY	REVEALING
RELEGATED	REPEALING	REQUIRING	REST HOMES	REVELATOR
RELENTING	REPEATERS	REQUISITE	RESTIFORM	REVELLING
RELEVANCE	REPEATING	REQUITING	RESTIVELY	REVELMENT
RELEVANCY	REPECHAGE	REREDOSES	RESTOCKED	REVELROUS
RELIEF MAP	REPELLANT	RERUNNING	RESTORERS	REVENGING
RELIEVING	REPELLING	RESALABLE	RESTORING	REVERABLE

REVERENCE
REVERENDS
REVERSALS
REVERSING
REVERSION
REVERTING
REVERTIVE
REVETMENT
REVIEWERS
REVIEWING
REVISABLE
REVISIONS
REVIVABLE
REVIVABLY
REVOCABLE
REVOACBLY
REVOKABLE
REVOKABLY
REVOLTING
REVOLVERS
REVOLVING
REVULSION
REVULSING
REWARDING
REWIRABLE
REWORDING
REWORKING
REWRITING
REYKJAVIK
RHAPSODIC
RHEOMETER
RHEOMETRY
RHEOSTATS
RHEOTAXIS
RHEUMATIC
RH FACTORS
RHIGOLENE
RHINELAND
RHINOLOGY
RHIZOBIUM
RHIZOIDAL
RHIZOTOMY
RHODAMINE
RHODESIAN
RHODOLITE
RHODONITE
RHODOPSIN
RHOMBOIDS
RHOMBUSES
RHOTACISM
RHOTACIST
RHYMESTER
RHYOLITIC
RHYTHMICS

RIBOSOMAL
RICE PADDY
RICE PAPER
RICKSHAWS
RICOCHETS
RIDDANCES
RIDERLESS
RIDGELING
RIDGEPOLE
RIDICULED
RIDICULER
RIFLEBIRD
RIGHTEOUS
RIGHT-HAND
RIGHTISTS
RIGHTNESS
RIGHTWARD
RIGHT WING
RIGMAROLE
RING ROADS
RIO GRANDE
RIOTOUSLY
RIPOSTING
RISKINESS
RITUALISM
RITUALIST
RITUALIZE
RIVALLING
RIVALRIES
RIVALROUS
RIVERBEDS
RIVERHEAD
RIVERSIDE
ROADBLOCK
ROADHOUSE
ROADSHOWS
ROADSTEAD
ROADSTERS
ROAD TAXES
ROAD TESTS
ROAD WORKS
ROASTINGS
ROBBERIES
ROBOT-LIKE
ROCKBOUND
ROCKCAKES
ROCKERIES
ROCKETEER
ROCKETING
ROCKFALLS
ROCKINESS
ROCK'N'ROLL
ROCK PLANT
ROCKSHAFT

ROENTGENS
ROGUERISH
ROISTERER
ROLE MODEL
ROLE PLAYS
ROLL CALLS
ROLLINGLY
ROMANCING
ROMAN NOSE
ROMANTICS
ROMPINGLY
ROOF RACKS
ROOKERIES
ROOMINESS
ROOMMATES
ROOTCROPS
ROOTSTOCK
ROQUEFORT
ROSACEOUS
ROSEWATER
ROSINWEED
ROSTELLUM
ROTAMETER
ROTARIANS
ROTATABLE
ROTATIONS
ROTIFERAL
ROTOVATOR
ROTTERDAM
ROTUNDITY
ROUGHCAST
ROUGHENED
ROUGH-HEWN
ROUGHNECK
ROUGHNESS
ROUGHSHOD
ROUNDELAY
ROUNDNESS
ROUNDSMAN
ROUNDSMEN
ROUND-TRIP
ROUNDWORM
ROUTINELY
ROUTINISM
ROUTINIST
ROVING EYE
ROWDINESS
ROW HOUSES
ROYAL BLUE
ROYALISTS
ROYALTIES
RUBBERIZE
RUBBISHED
RUBESCENT

RUBRICATE
RUBRICIAN
RUCKSACKS
RUDACEOUS
RUDBECKIA
RUDDINESS
RUDIMENTS
RUFESCENT
RUFFIANLY
RUINATION
RUINOUSLY
RULEBOOKS
RUMBLINGS
RUMINANTS
RUMINATED
RUMINATOR
RUMMAGING
RUN-ABOUTS
RUN-AROUND
RUNCINATE
RUNNERS-UP
RUNNER-UP
RUNNYMEDE
RUNTINESS
RUPTURING
RUSH HOURS
RUSHINESS
RUSHINGLY
RUSHLIGHT
RUSSETISH
RUSTICATE
RUSTICITY
RUSTINESS
RUSTPROOF
RUTABAGAS
RUTACEOUS
RUTHENIUM
RUTILATED
RUTTINESS

10 LETTERS
RABBINICAL
RABBITFISH
RABBITTING
RACECOURSE
RACEHORSES
RACETRACKS
RACHMANISM
RACIALISTS
RACKETEERS
RACK-RENTER
RACONTEURS
RADARSCOPE

RADIATIONS	REAFFOREST	RECORDABLE	REFLECTIVE
RADICALISM	REAL ESTATE	RECORDINGS	REFLECTORS
RADIO ALARM	REALIGNING	RECOUNTING	REFLEXIVES
RADIOGENIC	REALIZABLE	RECOUPABLE	REFORESTED
RADIOGRAMS	REALIZABLY	RECOUPMENT	REFRACTING
RADIOGRAPH	REALLOCATE	RECOVERIES	REFRACTION
RADIOLYSIS	REANIMATED	RE-COVERING	REFRACTIVE
RADIOMETER	REAPPEARED	RECREATING	REFRACTORY
RADIOMETRY	REAPPRAISE	RECREATION	REFRAINING
RADIOPAQUE	REARGUARDS	RECRUDESCE	REFRESHFUL
RADIOPHONY	REARMAMENT	RECRUITING	REFRESHING
RADIOSCOPE	REARRANGED	RECTANGLES	REFRINGENT
RADIOSCOPY	REARRANGER	RECTIFIERS	REFUELLING
RADIOSONDE	REASONABLE	RECTIFYING	REFUGEEISM
RADIOTOXIN	REASONABLY	RECUMBENCE	REFULGENCE
RAGAMUFFIN	REASSEMBLE	RECUPERATE	REFUNDABLE
RAGGEDNESS	REASSURING	RECURRENCE	REGALEMENT
RAILROADED	REBELLIONS	RED ADMIRAL	REGARDABLE
RAIN CHECKS	REBELLIOUS	RED-BLOODED	REGARDLESS
RAIN FOREST	REBOUNDING	REDBREASTS	REGELATION
RAIN GAUGES	REBUILDING	REDCURRANT	REGENERACY
RAINMAKING	REBUKINGLY	REDECORATE	REGENERATE
RAINSTORMS	REBUTTABLE	REDEEMABLE	REGENSBURG
RAJYA SABHA	RECALLABLE	REDEEMABLY	REGENTSHIP
RAKISHNESS	RECAPTURED	REDELIVERY	REGIMENTAL
RAMPAGEOUS	RECEIVABLE	REDEMPTION	REGIMENTED
RAMSHACKLE	RECENTNESS	REDEPLOYED	REGIONALLY
RANCH HOUSE	RECEPTACLE	RED HERRING	REGISTERED
RANCIDNESS	RECEPTIONS	RED INDIANS	REGISTERER
RANDOMNESS	RECESSIONS	REDIRECTED	REGISTRANT
RANSACKING	RECHARGING	REDISCOUNT	REGISTRARS
RANUNCULUS	RECHRISTEN	REDOUBLING	REGISTRIES
RAPPORTEUR	RECIDIVISM	REDOUNDING	REGRESSING
RARE EARTHS	RECIDIVIST	RED PEPPERS	REGRESSION
RAREFIABLE	RECIPIENCE	REDRESSING	REGRESSIVE
RATIONALES	RECIPIENTS	REDUCTIONS	REGRETTING
RATIONALLY	RECIPROCAL	REDUNDANCY	REGROUPING
RATTLETRAP	RECITATION	RE-EDUCATED	REGULARITY
RAUNCHIEST	RECITATIVE	RE-ELECTING	REGULARIZE
RAVAGEMENT	RECKLESSLY	RE-ELECTION	REGULATING
RAVENOUSLY	RECKONINGS	RE-ENFORCER	REGULATIONS
RAVISHMENT	RECLAIMANT	RE-ENTRANCE	REGULATIVE
RAWALPINDI	RECLAIMING	RE-EXAMINER	REGULATORS
RAWINSONDE	RECLINABLE	RE-EXPORTER	REGULATORY
RAZZMATAZZ	RECOGNIZED	REFEREEING	REHEARSALS
REACTIONAL	RECOGNIZEE	REFERENCER	REHEARSING
REACTIVATE	RECOGNIZER	REFERENCES	REIMBURSED
REACTIVELY	REGOGNIZOR	REFERENDUM	REIMBURSER
REACTIVITY	RECOILLESS	REFILLABLE	REINFORCED
READERSHIP	RECOMMENCE	REFINEMENT	REINSTATED
READJUSTED	RECOMPENSE	REFINERIES	REINSTATOR
READJUSTER	RECONCILED	REFINISHER	REINSURING
READY MONEY	RECONCILER	REFLECTING	REISSUABLE
REAFFIRMED	RECONSIDER	REFLECTION	REITERATED

REJECTABLE	REMOVAL VAN	REPUTATION	RESTAURANT
REJECTIONS	REMUNERATE	REQUESTING	RESTHARROW
REJOINDERS	RENDERABLE	REQUIESCAT	RESTLESSLY
REJUVENATE	RENDERINGS	REQUIRABLE	RESTOCKING
REKINDLING	RENDEZVOUS	REQUISITES	RESTORABLE
RELATIONAL	RENDITIONS	REQUITABLE	RESTRAINED
RELATIVELY	RENOUNCING	RESCHEDULE	RESTRAINER
RELATIVISM	RENOVATING	RESCINDING	RESTRAINTS
RELATIVIST	RENOVATION	RESCISSION	RESTRICTED
RELATIVITY	RENOVATIVE	RESCISSORY	RESUMPTION
RELAXATION	RENOWNEDLY	RESEARCHED	RESUMPTIVE
RELEGATING	RENT STRIKE	RESEARCHER	RESUPINATE
RELEGATION	REORGANIZE	RESEARCHES	RESURFACED
RELENTLESS	REPAIRABLE	RESEMBLANT	RESURGENCE
RELATIVITY	REPERATION	RESEMBLING	RETAINABLE
RELAXATION	REPARITIVE	RESENTMENT	RETAINMENT
RELEGATING	REPATRIATE	RESERVABLE	RETALIATED
RELEGATION	REPAYMENTS	RESERVEDLY	RETALIATOR
RELENTLESS	REPEALABLE	RESERVISTS	RETHINKING
RELEVANTLY	REPEATABLE	RESERVOIRS	RETICENTLY
RELIEF MAPS	REPEATEDLY	RESETTLING	RETICULATE
RELIEF ROAD	REPELLENCE	RESHIPMENT	RETIREMENT
RELIEVABLE	REPELLENTS	RESHUFFLED	RETOUCHING
RELINQUISH	REPENTANCE	RESHUFFLES	RETRACTILE
RELISHABLE	REPERTOIRE	RESIDENCES	RETRACTING
RELOCATING	REPETITION	RESIGNEDLY	RETRACTION
RELOCATION	REPETITIVE	RESILEMENT	RETRACTIVE
RELUCTANCE	REPHRASING	RESILIENCE	RETREADING
REMAINDERS	REPLICATED	RESILIENCY	RETREATING
REMAINMENT	REPORTABLE	RESISTANCE	RETRENCHED
REMARKABLE	REPORTEDLY	RESISTIBLY	RETRIEVERS
REMARKABLY	REPOSITION	RESISTLESS	RETRIEVING
REMARRYING	REPOSITORY	RESOLUTELY	RETROCHOIR
REMEDIABLE	REPRESSING	RESOLUTION	RETROGRADE
REMEDIABLY	REPRESSION	RESOLVABLE	RETROGRESS
REMEDIALLY	REPRESSIVE	RESONANCES	RETROSPECT
REMEDILESS	REPRIEVING	RESONANTLY	RETROVERSE
REMEMBERED	REPRIMANDS	RESONATING	RETURNABLE
REMEMBERER	REPRINTING	RESONATION	REUNIONISM
REMINISCED	REPROACHED	RESONATORS	REUNIONIST
REMISSIBLE	REPROACHER	RESORCINOL	REUNITABLE
REMISSIONS	REPROACHES	RESORPTION	REVANCHISM
REMISSNESS	REPROBATER	RESORPTIVE	REVANCHIST
REMITTABLE	REPROBATES	RESOUNDING	REVEALABLE
REMITTANCE	REPRODUCED	RESPECTERS	REVEALEDLY
REMITTENCE	REPRODUCER	RESPECTFUL	REVEALMENT
REMODELING	REPROVABLE	RESPECTING	REVEGETATE
REMODELLED	REPTILIANS	RESPECTIVE	REVELATION
REMODELLER	REPUBLICAN	RESPIRABLE	REVENGEFUL
REMONETIZE	REPUDIABLE	RESPIRATOR	REVERENCED
REMORSEFUL	REPUDIATED	RESPONDENT	REVERENCER
REMOTENESS	REPUDIATOR	RESPONDING	REVERENCES
REMOULDING	REPUGNANCE	RESPONSIVE	REVERENTLY
REMOUNTING	REPULSIONS	RES PUBLICA	REVERSIBLE

REVERTIBLE	RIGOROUSLY	ROUNDABOUT	**11 LETTERS**
REVETMENTS	RINDERPEST	ROUNDHEADS	RABBIT HUTCH
REVIEWABLE	RING BINDER	ROUNDHOUSE	RABBIT PUNCH
REVILEMENT	RING FINGER	ROUND ROBIN	RABELAISIAN
REVILINGLY	RINGLEADER	ROUND-TABLE	RACE COURSES
REVISIONAL	RINGMASTER	ROUND TRIPS	RACE MEETING
REVITALIZE	RING-NECKED	ROUSEDNESS	RACQUETBALL
REVIVALISM	RING-TAILED	ROUSSILLON	RADIATIONAL
REVIVALIST	RIPPLINGLY	ROUSTABOUT	RADICALNESS
REVIVIFIED	RIP-ROARING	ROUTE MARCH	RADIO ACTIVE
REVIVINGLY	RISIBILITY	ROWING BOAT	RADIO ALARMS
REVOCATION	RISING DAMP	ROYAL FLUSH	RADIO BEACON
REVOCATIVE	RITARDANDO	ROYALISTIC	RADIOCARBON
REVOKINGLY	RITORNELLO	RUB AL' KHALI	RADIOGRAPHY
REVOLUTION	RIVER BASIN	RUBBER BAND	RADIOLARIAN
REVOLVABLE	ROAD BLOCKS	RUBBERNECK	RADIOLOGIST
RHAPSODIES	ROADHOUSES	RUBBER TREE	RADIOLUCENT
RHAPSODIST	ROAD RUNNER	RUBBISH BIN	RADIOMETRIC
RHAPSODIZE	ROAD-TESTED	RUBBISHING	RADIOPACITY
RHEOLOGIST	ROAD-WORTHY	RUBLEWORK	RADIOPHONIC
RHEOMETRIC	ROBUSTNESS	RUBESCENCE	RADIOSCOPIC
RHEOSTATIC	ROCK BOTTOM	RUBIACEOUS	RADIOTHERMY
RHEOTACTIC	ROCK GARDEN	RUBIGINOUS	RAFFISHNESS
RHEOTROPIC	ROCK PLANTS	RUBRICATOR	RAGAMUFFINS
RHETORICAL	ROCK SALMON	RUDDERHEAD	RAILROADING
RHEUMATICS	ROISTERERS	RUDDERLESS	RAIN FORESTS
RHEUMATISM	ROISTEROUS	RUDDERPOST	RAISON D'ETRE
RHEUMATOID	ROLE MODELS	RUEFULNESS	RALLENTANDO
RHINESTONE	ROLE-PLAYED	RUFESCENCE	RAMAN EFFECT
RHINOCEROS	ROLLED GOLD	RUFFIANISM	RAMBOUILLET
RHINOSCOPY	ROLLICKING	RUGGEDNESS	RANCH HOUSES
RHIZOMORPH	ROLLING PIN	RUMBLINGLY	RANCOROUSLY
RHIZOPODAN	ROLY-POLIES	RUMINATING	RANGE FINDER
RHOMBOIDAL	ROMANESQUE	RUMINATION	RANK AND FILE
RHUMBATRON	ROMAN NOSES	RUMINATIVE	RAPACIOUSLY
RHYMESTERS	ROOD SCREEN	RUMPUS ROOM	RAPSCALLION
RHYTHMICAL	ROOF GARDEN	RUNNER BEAN	RAPTUROUSLY
RIBBONFISH	ROPE LADDER	RUN-OF-PAPER	RAREFACTION
RIBOFLAVIN	ROSANILINE	RUN-THROUGH	RASPBERRIES
RICKETTSIA	ROSEMALING	RUPTURABLE	RASTAFARIAN
RICOCHETED	ROSE WINDOW	RURITANIAN	RATE-CAPPING
RIDGEPOLES	ROSTELLATE	RUSHLIGHTS	RATIOCINATE
RIDICULING	ROTARY CLUB	RUSSOPHILE	RATIONALISM
RIDICULOUS	ROTATIONAL	RUSSOPHOBE	RATIONALIST
RIEMANNIAN	ROTISSERIE	RUSTICATED	RATIONALITY
RIFLE RANGE	ROTOVATORS	RUSTICATOR	RATIONALIZE
RIFT VALLEY	ROTTENNESS	RUSTLINGLY	RATTLESNAKE
RIGHTABOUT	ROTTWEILLER	RUTHENIOUS	RATTLETRAPS
RIGHT ANGLE	ROUGHENING	RUTHERFORD	RAUCOUSNESS
RIGHTFULLY	ROUGHHOUSE	RUTHLESSLY	RAVEN-HAIRED
RIGHT OF WAY	ROUGHNECKS		RAVISHINGLY
RIGHTWARDS	ROUGH PAPER		REACH-ME-DOWN
RIGMAROLES	ROUGHRIDER		REACTIONARY
RIGORISTIC	ROUGH STUFF		REACTIONISM

REACTIVATED	RECRIMINATE	REGIMENTING	REORGANIZER
READABILITY	RECRUITABLE	REGIONALISM	REPARATIONS
READDRESSED	RECRUITMENT	REGIONALIST	REPARTITION
READERSHIPS	RECTANGULAR	REGISTERING	REPATRIATED
READJUSTING	RECTIFIABLE	REGISTRABLE	REPELLINGLY
READ-THROUGH	RECTILINEAR	REGRETFULLY	REPERTOIRES
READY-TO-WEAR	RECUPERATED	REGRETTABLE	REPETITIONS
READY-KNITTED	RECUPERATOR	REGRETTABLY	REPETITIOUS
REAFFIRMING	RECURRENCES	REGULARIZED	REPLACABLE
REALIGNMENT	RECURRENTLY	REGULATIONS	REPLACEMENT
REALIZATION	RECURRINGLY	REGURGITANT	REPLENISHED
REALPOLITIK	REDACTIONAL	REGURGITATE	REPLENISHER
REANIMATING	RED ADMIRAL	REIFICATION	REPLETENESS
REANIMATION	RED CRESCENT	REIMBURSING	REPLEVIABLE
REAPPEARING	RED CURRANTS	REINCARNATE	REPLICATING
REAPPORTION	REDECORATED	REINFORCING	REPLICATION
REAPPRAISAL	REDEPLOYING	REINSTATING	REPLICATIVE
REAPPRAISED	REDEVELOPED	REINSURANCE	REPOSSESSED
REAR ADMIRAL	REDEVELOPER	REINTRODUCE	REPOSSESSOR
REARRANGING	RED HERRINGS	REITERATING	REPREHENDED
REASSURANCE	REDIFFUSION	REITERATION	REPREHENDER
REASSUREDLY	REDIRECTING	REITERATIVE	REPRESENTED
REBARBATIVE	REDIRECTION	REJUVENATED	REPRESSIBLE
RECALESCENT	·REDOUBTABLE	REJUVENATOR	REPRESSIONS
RECANTATION	REDOUBTABLY	RELATEDNESS	REPRIEVABLE
RECAPTURING	REDRESSABLE	RELAXATIONS	REPRIMANDED
RECEIVABLES	REDUCTIONAL	RELIABILITY	REPRIMANDER
RECEPTABLES	REDUNDANTLY	RELIEF ROADS	REPROACHFUL
RECEPTIVELY	REDUPLICATE	RELIGIONISM	REPROACHING
RECEPTIVITY	RE-EDUCATING	RELIGIOSITY	REPROBATION
RECESSIONAL	RE-EDUCATION	RELIQUARIES	RETROBATIVE
RECIDIVISTS	RE-ELECTIONS	RELISHINGLY	REPROCESSED
RECIPROCATE	REFECTORIES	RELUCTANTLY	REPRODUCERS
RECIPROCITY	REFERENDUMS	RELUCTIVITY	REPRODUCING
RECITATIONS	REFERENTIAL	REMAINDERED	REPROGRAPHY
RECITATIVES	REFINEMENTS	REMEMBERING	REPROVINGLY
RECLAIMABLE	REFLECTANCE	REMEMBRANCE	REPUBLICANS
RECLAMATION	REFLECTIONS	REMINISCENT	REPUBLISHER
RECLINATION	REFORESTING	REMINISCING	REPUDIATING
RECOGNITION	REFORMATION	REMITTANCES	REPUDIATION
RECOGNIZING	REFORMATIVE	REMODELLING	REPUDIATIVE
RECOILINGLY	REFORMATORY	REMONSTRANT	REPUDIATORY
RECOLLECTED	REFRACTABLE	REMONSTRATE	REPULSIVELY
RECOMMENDED	REFRAINMENT	REMORSELESS	REPUTATIONS
RECOMMENDER	REFRANGIBLE	REMOVAL VANS	REQUEST STOP
RECOMPENSED	REFRESHMENT	REMUNERABLE	REQUIREMENT
RECOMPENSER	REFRIGERANT	REMUNERATED	REQUISITION
RECONCILING	REFRIGERATE	REMUNERATOR	REQUITEMENT
RECONDITION	REFRINGENCY	RENAISSANCE	RERADIATION
RECONNOITRE	REFURBISHED	RENOGOTIATE	RESCHEDULED
RECONSTRUCT	REFUTATIONS	RENOVATIONS	RESCINDABLE
RECOVERABLE	REGENERABLE	RENTABILITY	RESCINDMENT
RECREATIONS	REGENERATED	RENT STRIKES	RESCISSIBLE
RECREMENTAL	REGIMENTALS	REORGANIZED	RESEARCHERS

RESEARCHING	RTINOSCOPY	RICOCHETTED	ROUGH-SPOKEN
RESECTIONAL	RETIREMENTS	RIFLE RANGES	ROUNDABOUTS
RESEMBLANCE	RETOUCHABLE	RIFT VALLEYS	ROWING BOATS
RESENTFULLY	RETRACEABLE	RIGHT-ANGLED	RUBBER BANDS
RESERVATION	RETRACEMENT	RIGHT ANGLES	RUBBER PLANT
RESHUFFLING	RETRACTABLE	RIGHTEOUSLY	RUBBER STAMP
RESIDENTIAL	RETRACTIONS	RIGHT-HANDED	RUBBER TREES
RESIGNATION	RETRENCHING	RIGHT-HANDER	RUBBISH BINS
RESILIENTLY	RETRIBUTION	RIGHT-MINDED	RUBEFACIENT
RESISTANCES	RETRIBUTIVE	RIGHTS ISSUE	RUBEFACTION
RESISTENCIA	RETROLENTAL	RIGHTS OF WAY	RUBICANDITY
RESISTINGLY	RETRO-ROCKET	RIGHT-WINGER	RUBRICATION
RESISTIVITY	RETROVERTED	RIGOR MORTIS	RUDESHEIMAR
RESOLUTIONS	REUPHOLSTER	RING BINDERS	RUDIMENTARY
RESOURCEFUL	REUSABILITY	RING FINGERS	RULE OF THUMB
RESPECTABLE	REVALUATION	RINGLEADERS	RUMBUSTIOUS
RESPECTABLY	REVELATIONS	RINGMASTERS	RUMINATIONS
RESPIRATION	REVENGINGLY	RINSABILITY	RUMMAGE SALE
RESPIRATORS	REVERBERANT	RIOTOUSNESS	RUMPUS ROOM
RESPIRATORY	REVERBERATE	RITUALISTIC	RUNNER BEANS
RESPLENDENT	REVERENCING	RIVER BASINS	RUNNING JUMP
RESPONDENCE	REVERENTIAL	ROAD HOLDING	RUNNING MATE
RESPONDENTS	REVERSIONER	ROAD MANAGER	RUN-THROUGHS
RESPONSIBLE	REVISIONISM	ROAD ROLLERS	RUNTISHNESS
RESPONSIBLY	REVISIONIST	ROAD TESTERS	RUSSOPHOBIA
RESPONSIONS	REVITALIZED	ROCK-AND-ROLL	RUSSOPHOBIC
RESTATEMENT	REVITALISTS	ROCK GARDENS	RUSTICATING
RESTAURANTS	REVIVIFYING	RODENTICIDE	RUSTICATION
RESTFULNESS	REVOCATIONS	RODOMONTADE	RUSTPROOFED
RESTITUTION	REVOLTINGLY	ROGUISHNESS	RUTTISHNESS
RESTITUTIVE	REVOLUTIONS	ROLE PLAYING	
RESTIVENESS	REVOLVINGLY	ROLLER BLIND	
RESTORATION	RHABDOMANCY	ROLLER SKATE	**12 LETTERS**
RESTORATIVE	RHABDOMYOMA	ROLLER TOWEL	RABBIT WARREN
RESTRAINING	RHAMNACEOUS	ROLLICKINGS	RABBLE-ROUSER
RESTRICTING	RHAPSODIZED	ROLLICKSOME	RACE MEETINGS
RESTIRICTION	RHEOLOGICAL	ROLLING MILL	RACEMIZATION
RESTRICTIVE	RHEOTROPISM	ROLLING PINS	RADICALISTIC
RESTRUCTURE	RHETORICIAN	ROLLTOP DESK	RADIO BEACONS
RESURFACING	RHEUMATICKY	ROMAN CANDLE	RADIOBIOLOGY
RESURRECTED	RHINESTONES	ROMANTICISM	RADIOCHEMIST
RESUSCITATE	RHINOLOGIST	ROMANTICIST	RADIOELEMENT
RETALIATING	RHINOPLASTY	ROMANTICIZE	RADIOGRAPHER
RETALIATION	RHINOSCOPIC	ROOD SCREENS	RADIOGRAPHIC
RETALIATIVE	RHIZOMATOUS	ROOF GARDENS	RADIOISOTOPE
RETALITORY	RHIZOPODOUS	ROOM SERVICE	RADIOLOGICAL
RETARDATION	RHIZOSPHERE	ROPE LADDERS	RADIOLOGISTS
RETARDATIVE	RHODE ISLAND	ROSE WINDOWS	RADIONUCLIDE
RETARDINGLY	RHOTACISTIC	ROTARIANISM	RADIOTHERAPY
RETENTIVELY	RHYTHMICITY	ROTISSERIES	RAISON D'ETRES
RETENTIVITY	RICE PADDIES	ROTOGRAVURE	RALLENTANDOS
RETICULATED	RICKETINESS	ROTTENSTONE	RAMBUNCTIOUS
RETINACULAR	RICKETTSIAL	ROTUNDITIES	RAMENTACEOUS
RETINACULUM	RICOCHETTING	ROUGHCASTER	RAMIFICATION

R 12 LETTERS

RANGE FINDERS
RANKINE SCALE
RAPHAELESQUE
RAPSCALLIONS
RASTAFARIANS
RATIFICATION
RATIOCINATOR
RATIONALISTS
RATIONALIZED
RATIONALIZER
RATTLESNAKES
RAVENOUSNESS
RAYLEIGH DISC
RAZZLE-DAZZLE
REACTIVATING
REACTIVATION
REACTIVENESS
READRESSING
READJUSTABLE
READJUSTMENT
REAFFIRMANCE
REAFFORESTED
REALIGNMENTS
REALIZATIONS
REALLOCATION
REAL PROPERTY
REAPPEARANCE
REPAPPRAISALS
REAPPRAISING
REAR ADMIRALS
REASSURANCES
REASSURINGLY
REAUMUR SCALE
REBELLIOUSLY
RECALCITRANT
RECALESCENCE
RECANTATIONS
RECAPITALIZE
RECAPITULATE
RECEIVERSHIP
RECEPTIONIST
RECESSIONALS
RECIDIVISTIC
RECIPROCALLY
RECIPROCATED
RECIPROCATOR
RECKLESSNESS
RECOGNITIONS
RECOGNIZABLE
RECOGNIZABLY
RECOGNIZANCE
RECOLLECTING
RECOLLECTION
RECOLLECTIVE

RECOMMENDING
RECOMMITMENT
RECOMPENSING
RECONCILABLE
RECONCILABLY
RECONNOITRED
RECONNOITRER
RECONSIDERED
RECONSTITUTE
RECONVERSION
RECORDPLAYER
RECREATIONAL
RECRIMINATED
RECRIMINATOR
RECUPERATING
RECUPERATION
RECUPERATIVE
RED BLOOD CELLS
REDECORATING
REDEMANDABLE
REDEMPTIONAL
REDEPLOYMENT
REDEVELOPING
REDINTEGRATE
REDISTRIBUTE
RED-LETTER DAY
REDUCIBILITY
REDUNDANCIES
REDUPLICATED
REEFER JACKET
RE-EMPLOYMENT
RE-EXAMINABLE
REFLATIONARY
REFLECTINGLY
REFLECTIONAL
REFRACTORILY
REFRESHINGLY
REFRESHMENTS
REFRIGERANTS
REFRIGERATED
REFRIGERATOR
REFURBISHING
REFUTABILITY
REGENERATING
REGENERATION
REGENERATIVE
REGISTRATION
REGULARIZING
REGURGITATED
REHABILITATE
REIMBURSABLE
REIMPOSITION
REIMPRESSION
REINCARNATED

REINVESTMENT
REITERATIONS
REJUVENATING
REJUVENATION
RELATIONSHIP
RELATIVISTIC
RELENTLESSLY
RELINQUISHED
RELINQUISHER
REMAINDERING
REMAINDERMAN
REMEMBRANCER
REMEMBRANCES
REMINISCENCE
REMONSTRANCE
REMONSTRATED
REMONSTATOR
REMORSEFULLY
REMOVABILITY
REMUNERATING
REMUNERATION
REMUNERATIVE
RENAISSANCES
RENEGOTIABLE
RENEWABILITY
RENOUNCEMENT
RENUNCIATION
RENUNCIATIVE
REORGANIZING
REPARABILITY
REPATRIATION
REPERCUSSION
REPERCUSSIVE
REPLACEMENTS
REPLENISHING
REPLICATIONS
REPOSITORIES
REPOSSESSING
REPOSSESSION
REPREHENDING
REPREHENSION
REPREHENSIVE
REPREHONSORY
REPRESENTING
REPRESSIVELY
REPRIMANDING
REPROACHABLE
REPROACHABLY
REPROCESSING
REPRODUCIBLE
REPROGRAPHIC
REPUTABILITY
REQUEST STOPS
REQUIREMENTS

REQUISITIONS
RESCHEDULING
RESEARCHABLE
RESEMBLANCES
RESERVATIONS
RESERVEDNESS
RESETTLEMENT
RESIDENTIARY
RESIDENTSHIP
RESIGNATIONS
RESIGNEDNESS
RESINIFEROUS
RESINOUSNESS
RESOLUTIONER
RESOLVEDNESS
RESOUNDINGLY
RESOURCELESS
RESPECTFULLY
RESPECTIVELY
RESPLENDENCE
RESPONSIVELY
RESTATEMENTS
RESTAURATEUR
RESTLESSNESS
RESTORATIONS
RESTORATIVES
RESTRAINABLE
RESTRAINEDLY
RESTRICTEDLY
RESTRICTIONS
RESTRUCTURED
RESUPINATION
RESURRECTING
RESURRECTION
RESUSCITABLE
RESUSCITATED
RESUSCITATOR
RETICULATION
RETINOSCOPIC
RETRACTILITY
RETRENCHABLE
RETRENCHMENT
RETROCESSION
RETROCESSIVE
RETROFLEXION
RETROGRESSED
RETRO-ROCKETS
RETROVERSION
REUNIONISTIC
REVALUATIONS
REVEGETATION
REVELATIONAL
REVERBERATED
REVERBERATOR

REVERENDSHIP
REVERENTNESS
REVERSIONARY
REVISABILITY
REVISIONISTS
REVITALIZING
REVIVABILITY
REVIVALISTIC
REVOCABILITY
REVOKABILITY
REVULSIONARY
RHAPSODISTIC
RHAPSODIZING
RHESUS FACTOR
RHETORICALLY
RHETORICIANS
RHINOCEROSES
RHINOCEROTIC
RHINOLOGICAL
RHINOPLASTIC
RHIZOCARPOUS
RHODODENDRON
RHOMBOHEDRAL
RHOMBOHEDRON
RHYMING SLANG
RHYTHMICALLY
RHYTHM METHOD
RIBONUCLEASE
RICHTER SCALE
RICOCHETTING
RIDICULOUSLY
RIGHTFULNESS
RIGHT-HANDERS
RIGHT-HAND MAN
RIGHT-HAND MEN
RIGHTS ISSUES
RIGHT-WINGERS
RIGOROUSNESS
RING-STREAKED
RIO DE JANEIRO
ROAD MANAGERS
ROCKING CHAIR
ROCKING HORSE
ROLLER BLINDS
ROLLER SKATED
ROLLER-SKATER
ROLLER SKATES
ROLLER TOWELS
ROLLICKINGLY
ROLLING MILLS
ROLLING STOCK
ROLLING STONE
ROLL OF HONOUR
ROLLTOP DESKS

ROMAN CANDLES
ROMAN NUMERAL
ROMANTICALLY
ROMANTICISTS
ROMANTICIZED
ROOMING HOUSE
ROOTLESSNESS
ROSE-COLOURED
ROTARY TILLER
ROUGH DIAMOND
ROUND BRACKET
ROUTE MARCHES
ROYAL FLUSHES
RUBBER DINGHY
RUBBER NECKED
RUBBER PLANTS
RUBBER STAMPS
RULES OF THUMB
RUMINATINGLY
RUMINATIVELY
RUMMAGE SALES
RUMOURMONGER
RUNNING JUMPS
RUNNING MATES
RUN-OF-THE-MILL
RURALIZATION
RUSTPROOFING
RUTHLESSNESS

13 LETTERS

RABBIT HUTCHES
RABBIT PUNCHES
RABBIT WARRENS
RABBLE-ROUSING
RACK-AND-PINION
RADIOACTIVATE
RADIOACTIVITY
RADIOCHEMICAL
RADIOGRAPHERS
RADIOSOTOPIC
RADIOTELEGRAM
RADIOTELETYPE
RAG-AND-BONE-MAN
RAMIFICATIONS
RANCOROUSNESS
RANDOMIZATION
RAPPROCHEMENT
RAPTUROUSNESS
RAREFACTIONAL
RATEABLE VALUE
RATIOCINATION
RATIONALISTIC
RATIONALIZING

REACTIONARIES
READJUSTMENTS
READ-WRITE HEAD
REAFFIRMATION
REAFFORESTING
REALISTICALLY
REAPPOINTMENT
REARRANGEMENT
RECALCITRANCE
RECAPITULATED
RECEPTIONISTS
RECEPTION ROOM
RECESSIVENESS
RECIPROCALITY
RECIPROCATING
RECIPROCATION
RECIPROCATIVE
RECOGNITIONAL
RECOLLECTIONS
RECOMBINATION
RECOMMENDABLE
RECOMPENSABLE
RECOMPOSITION
RECONCILEMENT
RECONCILINGLY
RECONDITENESS
RECONDITIONED
RECONDITIONER
RECONNOITRING
RECONSIDERING
RECONSTITUENT
RECONSTITUTED
RECONSTRUCTED
RECONSTRUCTOR
RECORD-CHANGER
RECORD LIBRARY
RECORD PLAYERS
RECRIMINATING
RECRIMINATION
RECRIMINATIVE
RECRIMINATORY
RECRUDESCENCE
RECRYSTALLIZE
RECTIFICATION
RED BLOOD CELLS
REDEEMABILITY
REDEVELOPMENT
REDISTRIBUTED
RED-LETTER DAYS
REDUPLICATING
REDUPLICATION
REDUPLICATIVE
REEFER JACKETS
RE-ENFORCEMENT

RE-EXAMINATION
RE-EXPORTATION
REFERENCE BOOK
REFLEXIVENESS
REFORESTATION
REFORMATIONAL
REFORMATORIES
REFRACTOMETER
REFRACTOMETRY
REFRIGERATING
REFRIGERATION
REFRIGERATIVE
REFRIGERATORS
REFURBISHMENT
REGARDFULNESS
REGIMENTATION
REGISTRARSHIP
REGISTRATIONS
REGRETFULNESS
REGURGITATING
REGURGITATION
REHABILITATED
REIGN OF TERROR
REIMBURSEMENT
REIMPORTATION
REINCARNATING
REINCARNATION
REINFORCEMENT
REINSTATEMENT
REJUVENESCENT
RELATIONSHIPS
RELIGIOUSNESS
RELINQUISHING
REMINISCENCES
REMISSIBILITY
REMONSTRANCES
REMONSTRATING
REMONSTRATION
REMONSTRATIVE
REMORSELESSLY
REMOTE CONTROL
RENEGOTIATION
RENSSELAERITE
RENUNCIATIONS
REPEATABILITY
REPELLINGNESS
REPERCUSSIONS

REPLENISHMENT
REPOSEFULNESS
REPREHENDABLE
REPREHENSIBLE
REPREHENSIBLY
REPRESENTABLE
REPROACHFULLY
REPROACHINGLY
REPRODUCTIONS
REPUBLICANISM
REPUBLICANIZE
REPUBLICATION
REPUBLISHABLE
REPULSIVENESS
REQUISITIONED
REQUISITIONER
RESENTFULNESS
RESISTIBILITY
RESISTIVENESS
RESOLVABILITY
RESOURCEFULLY
RESPIRABILITY
RESPIRATIONAL
RESPLENDENTLY
RESTAURANT CAR
RESTAURATEURS
RESTRAININGLY
RESTRICTIVELY
RESTRUCTURING
RESURRECTIONS
RESUSCITATING
RESUSCITATION
RESUSCITATIVE
RETAINABILITY
RETENTIVENESS
RETICULATIONS
RETINOSCOPIST
RETROACTIVELY
RETROACTIVITY
RETROGRESSING
RETROGRESSION
RETROGRESSIVE
RETROSPECTION
RETROSPECTIVE
RETURNABILITY
REUNIFICATION
REUTILIZATION

REVEALABILITY
REVELATIONIST
REVERBERATING
REVERBERATION
REVERBERATIVE
REVERBERATORY
REVERENTIALLY
REVERSIBILITY
REVOLUTIONARY
REVOLUTIONIST
REVOLUTIONIZE
RHABDOMANTIST
RHAPSODICALLY
RHIZOCEPHALAN
RHIZOMORPHOUS
RHODOCHROSITE
RHODODENDRONS
RIBEIRAO PRETO
RIGHTEOUSNESS
RIGHT TRIANGLE
ROCK-AND-ROLLER
ROCKING CHAIRS
ROCKING HORSES
ROGUES' GALLERY
ROLLER COASTER
ROLLER-SKATERS
ROLLER SKATING
ROLLING STONES
ROLL OF HONOURS
ROLL-ON ROLL-OFF
ROMAN CATHOLIC
ROMAN NUMERALS
ROMANTICIZING
ROOMING HOUSES
RORSCHACH TEST
ROTARY TILLERS
ROTTEN BOROUGH
ROUGH-AND-READY
ROUGH DIAMONDS
ROUND BRACKETS
ROUND-THE-CLOCK
ROYAL HIGHNESS
RUBBERNECKING
RUBBER-STAMPED
RUMOUR MONGERS

3 LETTERS	SAGA	SETS	SLAB	SOON	SUEZ
SAC	SAGE	SEWN	SLAG	SOOT	SUIT
SAD	SAGO	SEXY	SLAM	SOPS	SULK
SAE	SAID	SHAD	SLAP	SORE	SUMP
SAG	SAIL	SHAG	SLAT	SORT	SUMS
SAP	SAKE	SHAH	SLAV	SO-SO	SUNG
SAT	SALT	SHAT	SLAY	SOTS	SUNK
SAW	SAME	SHED	SLED	SOUL	SUNS
SAY	SAN'A	SHEW	SLEW	SOUP	SUPS
SDI	SAND	SHIM	SLID	SOUR	SURD
SDP	SANE	SHIN	SLIM	SOWN	SURE
SEA	SANG	SHIP	SLIP	SOWS	SURE
SEC	SANK	SHOA	SLIT	SPAM	SURF
SEE	SAPS	SHOD	SLOB	SPAN	SUSS
SET	SARI	SHOE	SLOE	SPAR	SWAB
SEW	SASH	SHOO	SLOG	SPAS	SWAG
SEX	SASS	SHOP	SLOP	SPAT	SWAM
SHE	SATE	SHOT	SLOT	SPAY	SWAN
SHY	SAVE	SHOW	SLOW	SPEC	SWAP
SIC	SAWN	SHUN	SLUB	SPED	SWAT
SIN	SAWS	SHUN	SLUE	SPEW	SWAY
SIP	SAYS	SHUT	SLUG	SPIC	SWIG
SIR	SCAB	SIAN	SLUM	SPIK	SWIN
SIS	SCAG	SICK	SLUR	SPIN	SWOP
SIT	SCAM	SIDE	SLUT	SPIT	SWOT
SIX	SCAN	SIFT	SMOG	SPIV	SWUN
SKI	SCAR	SIGH	SMUG	SPOT	SYNC
SLY	SCAT	SIGN	SMUT	SPOR	
SOB	SCUD	SIKH	SNAG	SPUD	
SOD	SCUM	SILK	SNAP	SPUN	5 LETTERS
SOH	SEAL	SILL	SNIP	SPUR	SABAH
SOL	SEAM	SILO	SNOB	STAB	SABER
SON	SEAR	SILT	SNOG	STAG	SABIN
SOP	SEAS	SIDE	SNOT	STAR	SABLE
SOS	SEAT	SINE	SNOW	STAY	SABOT
SOT	SECS	SING	SNUB	STEM	SABRA
SOU	SECT	SINH	SNUG	STEP	SABRE
SOW	SEED	SINK	SOAK	STET	SACKS
SOX	SEEK	SINO-	SOAP	STEW	SADHU
SOY	SEEM	SINS	SOAR	STIR	SADLY
SPA	SEEN	SIPS	SOBS	STOL	SAFER
STD	SEEP	SIRE	SOCK	STOP	SAFES
STY	SEER	SIRS	SODA	STOW	SAGAS
SUB	SEES	SITE	SODA	STUB	SAGES
SUE	SELF	SIZE	SOFA	STUD	SAGGY
SUM	SELL	SKEW	SOFT	STUM	SAHIB
SUN	SEME	SKID	SOIL	STUN	SAIGA
SUP	SEMI	SKIM	SOLD	SUBS	SAILS
	SEND	SKIN	SOLE	SUCH	SAINT
	SENT	SKIP	SOLO	SUCK	SAKAI
4 LETTERS	SERA	SKIS	SOMA	SUDS	SAKER
SACK	SERE	SKIT	SOME	SUED	SAKES
SACS	SERF	SKUA	SONG	SUER	SALAD
SAFE	SETA	SKYE	SONS	SUET	SALEM

SALEP	SCALP	SEDUM	SHARD	SHRUG	SIZED
SALES	SCALY	SEEDS	SHARE	SHUCK	SIZES
SALIC	SCAMP	SEEDY	SHARP	SHUNT	SKATE
SALLY	SCAMS	SEERS	SHAVE	SHUSH	SKEET
SALOL	SCANS	SEGNO	SHAWL	SHYED	SKEIN
SALON	SCANT	SEINE	SHEAF	SHYER	SKELP
SALOP	SCAPE	SEISE	SHEAR	SHYLY	SKEWS
SALPA	SCARE	SEIZE	SHEDS	SIBIU	SKIDS
SALTA	SCARF	SELVA	SHEEN	SIBYL	SKIED
SALTS	SCARP	SEMEN	SHEEP	SIDED	SKIER
SALTY	SCARS	SEMIS	SHEER	SIDES	SKIES
SALVE	SCARY	SENNA	SHEET	SIDLE	SKIFF
SALVO	SCAUP	SENOR	SHEIK	SIEGE	SKILL
SAMBA	SCEND	SENSE	SHELF	SIENA	SKIMP
SAMEY	SCENE	SENZA	SHELL	SIEVE	SKINK
SAMOA	SCENT	SEOUL	SHERD	SIGHS	SKINS
SANDS	SCHWA	SEPAL	SHEWN	SIGHT	SKINT
SANDY	SCION	SEPIA	SHIED	SIGLA	SKIPS
SANER	SCOFF	SEPOY	SHIER	SIGMA	SKIRL
SAPID	SCOLD	SERAC	SHIES	SIGNS	SKIRT
SAPPY	SCONE	SERFS	SHIFT	SIKHS	SKITS
SARAN	SCOOP	SERGE	SHILY	SILEX	SKIVE
SARGE	SCOOT	SERIF	SHINE	SILKS	SKUAS
SARIS	SCOPE	SERIN	SHINS	SILKY	SKULK
SARKY	SCORE	SEROW	SHINY	SILLS	SKULL
SAROS	SCORN	SERUM	SHIPS	SILLY	SKUNK
SASSY	SCOTS	SERVE	SHIRE	SILOS	SLABS
SATAN	SCOUR	SERVO	SHIRK	SILTY	SLACK
SATED	SCOUT	SETAL	SHIRR	SINAI	SLAIN
SATEM	SCOWL	SET-TO	SHIRT	SINCE	SLAKE
SATIN	SCRAG	SET-UP	SHIVE	SINES	SLANG
SATYR	SCRAM	SEVEN	SHLUH	SINEW	SLANT
SAUCE	SCRAP	SEVER	SHOAL	SINGE	SLAPS
SAUCY	SCREE	SEWED	SHOAT	SINKS	SLASH
SAUNA	SCREW	SEWER	SHOCK	SINUS	SLATE
SAUNA	SCRIM	SEXED	SHOED	SIOUX	SLATS
SAURY	SCRIP	SEXES	SHOES	SIRED	SLATY
SAUTE	SCRUB	SHACK	SHONA	SIREN	SLAVE
SAVED	SCRUM	SHADE	SHONE	SIRES	SLAVS
SAVER	SCUBA	SHADY	SHOOK	SISAL	SLEDS
SAVES	SCUFF	SHAFT	SHOOT	SISSY	SLEEK
SAVIN	SCULL	SHAHS	SHOPS	SITAR	SLEEP
SAVOY	SCURF	SHAKE	SHORE	SITED	SLEET
SAVVY	SCUTE	SHAKO	SHORN	SITES	SLEPT
SAWED	SEALS	SHAKY	SHORT	SIT-IN	SLEWS
SAWER	SEAMS	SHALE	SHOTS	SIT-UP	SLICE
SAXON	SEAMY	SHALL	SHOTT	SITUS	SLICK
SAYER	SEATS	SHALT	SHOUT	SIVAS	SLIDE
SAY-SO	SEBUM	SHALY	SHOVE	SIXES	SLILY
SCABS	SECCO	SHAME	SHOWN	SIXMO	SLIME
SCADS	SECTS	SHAMS	SHOWS	SIXTE	SLIMY
SCALD	SEDAN	SHANK	SHRED	SIXTH	SLING
SCALE	SEDGE	SHAN'T	SHREW	SIXTY	SLINK
SCALL	SEDGY	SHAPE	SHRUB	SIZAR	SLIPS

SLOBS	SNIPS	SOUND	SPOIL	STEAM	STRUT
SLOES	SNOBS	SOUPS	SPOKE	STEED	STUBS
SLOGS	SNOGS	SOUPY	SPOOL	STEEL	STUCK
SLOOP	SNOOD	SOUSE	SPOON	STEEP	STUDS
SLOPE	SNOOK	SOUTH	SPOOR	STEER	STUDY
SLOPS	SNOOP	SOWED	SPORE	STEIN	STUFF
SLOSH	SNORE	SOWER	SPORT	STELE	STULL
SLOTH	SNORT	SOYUZ	SPOTS	STEMS	STUNG
SLUED	SNOUT	SPACE	SPOUT	STEPS	STUNK
SLUGS	SNOWS	SPADE	SPRAG	STERE	STUNT
SLUMS	SNOWY	SPAIN	SPRAT	STEWS	STUPE
SLUNG	SNUBS	SPALL	SPRAY	STICH	STYLE
SLUNK	SOAKS	SPANK	SPREE	STICK	SUAVE
SLURP	SOAPS	SPARS	SPRIG	STIES	SUDAN
SLURS	SOAPY	SPASM	SPRIT	STIFF	SUDOR
SLUSH	SOBER	SPATE	SPRUE	STILE	SUDSY
SLYER	SOCHE	SPATS	SPUDS	STILL	SUEDE
SLYPE	SOCHI	SPAWN	SPUME	STILT	SUETY
SMACK	SOCIO-	SPEAK	SPUNK	STING	SUGAR
SMALL	SOCKS	SPEAR	SPURN	STINK	SUING
SMALT	SOCLE	SPECK	SPURS	STINT	SUINT
SMARM	SODAS	SPECS	SPURT	STIPE	SUITE
SMART	SOFAR	SPEED	SQUAB	STIRK	SUITS
SMASH	SOFAS	SPELL	SQUAD	STIRS	SULKS
SMEAR	SOFIA	SPELT	SQUAT	STOAT	SULKY
SMELL	SOFTA	SPEND	SQUAW	STOCK	SULLY
SMELT	SOFTY	SPENT	SQUIB	STOIC	SUMPS
SMILE	SOGGY	SPERM	SQUID	STOKE	SUNNI
SMIRK	SOILS	SPICA	STABS	STOLE	SUNNY
SMITE	SOLAR	SPICE	STACK	STOMA	SUN-UP
SMITH	SOLED	SPICS	STAFF	STOMP	SUPER
SMOCK	SOLES	SPICY	STAGE	STONE	SUPRA
SMOKE	SOL-FA	SPIED	STAGS	STONY	SURAH
SMOKY	SOLID	SPIEL	STAGY	STOOD	SURAL
SMOLT	SOLOS	SPIES	STAID	STOOK	SURAT
SMOTE	SOLUM	SPIKE	STAIN	STOOL	SURDS
SMUTS	SOLVE	SPIKS	STAIR	STOOP	SURER
SNACK	SOMME	SPIKY	STAKE	STOPE	SURFY
SNAFU	SONAR	SPILE	STALE	STOPS	SURGE
SNAGS	SONDE	SPILL	STALK	STORE	SURLY
SNAIL	SONGS	SPILT	STALL	STORK	SUSHI
SNAKE	SONIC	SPINE	STAMP	STORM	SWABS
SNAKY	SONNY	SPINS	STAND	STORY	SWAGE
SNAPS	SOOTY	SPINY	STANK	STOSS	SWAIN
SNARE	SOPOR	SPIRE	STARE	STOUP	SWAMI
SNARL	SOPPY	SPIRY	STARK	STOUT	SWAMP
SNATH	SORES	SPITE	STARS	STOVE	SWANK
SNEAK	SORGO	SPITS	START	STRAP	SWANS
SNECK	SORRY	SPITZ	STATE	STRAW	SWAPS
SNEER	SORTS	SPIVS	STAVE	STREW	SWARD
SNICK	SORUS	SPLAT	STAYS	STRIA	SWARF
SNIDE	SOTHO	SPLAY	STEAD	STRIP	SWARM
SNIFF	SOUGH	SPLIT	STEAK	STROP	SWASH
SNIPE	SOULS	SPODE	STEAL	STRUM	SWATH

S
5 LETTERS to 6 LETTERS

SWATS	SAFEST	SANTOS	SCARPS	SCUBAS	SELECT
SWAZI	SAFETY	SAPELE	SCATTY	SCUFFS	SELLER
SWEAR	SAGELY	SAPOTA	SCENES	SCULPT	SELVES
SWEAT	SAGGAR	SAPPED	SCENIC	SCUMMY	SEMEME
SWEDE	SAGGED	SAPPER	SCENTS	SCURFY	SEMITE
SWEEP	SAHARA	SARGES	SCHEMA	SCURRY	SEMPRE
SWEET	SAHIBS	SARNIE	SCHEME	SCURVY	SENARY
SWELL	SAIGON	SARONG	SCHISM	SCUTCH	SENATE
SWEPT	SAILED	SARTHE	SCHIST	SCUTUM	SENDAI
SWIFT	SAILOR	SASEBO	SCHELP	SCUZZY	SENDER
SWIGS	SAINTS	SASHAY	SCHOOL	SCYTHE	SEND-UP
SWILLS	SAITHE	SASHES	SCHORL	SEABED	SENECA
SWIMS	SALAAM	SASSED	SCHUSS	SEA DOG	SENEGA
SWINE	SALADS	SASSES	SCHWAS	SEALED	SENILE
SWING	SALAMI	SATEEN	SCHWYZ	SEALER	SENIOR
SWIPE	SALARY	SATING	SCILLS	SEAMAN	SENNAR
SWIRL	SALIFY	SATINY	SCIONS	SEAMEN	SENNIT
SWISH	SALINE	SATIRE	SCLAFF	SEAMER	SENORA
SWISS	SALIVA	SATURN	SCLERA	SEANCE	SENORS
SWOON	SALLEE	SATYRS	SCOFFS	SEARCH	SENSED
SWOOP	SALLOW	SAUCED	SCOLDS	SEARED	SENSES
SWOPS	SALMON	SAUCER	SCOLEX	SEASON	SENSOR
SWORD	SALONS	SAUCES	SCONCE	SEATED	SENTRY
SWORE	SALOON	SAUGER	SCONES	SEATER	SEPALS
SWORN	SALOOP	SAUNAS	SCOOPS	SEAWAY	SEPSIS
SWOTS	SALTED	SAVAGE	SCORCH	SECANT	SEPTAL
SWUNG	SALTER	SAVANT	SCORED	SECEDE	SEPTET
SYLPH	SALTUS	SAVERS	SCORER	SECOND	SEPTIC
SYLVIA	SALUKI	SAVING	SCORIA	SECRET	SEPTUM
SYNOD	SALUTE	SAVOIE	SCORNS	SECTOR	SEQUEL
STRIS	SALVED	SAVORY	SCOTCH	SECUND	SEQUIN
SYRUP	SALVER	SAVOUR	SCOTER	SECURE	SERAPH
	SALVES	SAVOYS	SCOTIA	SEDANS	SERBIA
	SALVIA	SAWFLY	SCOUSE	SEDATE	SEREIN
6 LETTERS	SALVOR	SAWING	SCOUTS	SEDILE	SERENE
SABBAT	SALVOS	SAWYER	SCOWLS	SEDUCE	SERIAL
SABERS	SALYUT	SAXONS	SCRAPE	SEEDED	SERIES
SABLES	SAMARA	SAXONY	SCRAPS	SEEDER	SERIFS
SABRAS	SAMBAR	SAYING	SCRAWL	SEEING	SERINE
SABRES	SAMBAS	SCABBY	SCREAM	SEEKER	SERMON
SACHET	SAMITE	SCALAR	SCREED	SEEMED	SEROSA
SACKED	SAMOAN	SCALDS	SCREEN	SEEMER	SEROUS
SACKER	SAMOSA	SCALED	SCREWS	SEEMLY	SERUMS
SACRAL	SAMPAN	SCALER	SCREWY	SEEPED	SERVAL
SACRED	SAMPLE	SCALES	SCRIBE	SEESAW	SERVED
SACRUM	SAMSUN	SCALPS	SCRIMP	SEETHE	SERVER
SADDEN	SANDAL	SCAMPI	SCRIPT	SEICHE	SERVES
SADDER	SANDED	SCAMPS	SCROLL	SEINES	SERVOS
SADDLE	SANDER	SCANTY	SCROOP	SEISER	SESAME
SADHUS	SANDHI	SCARAB	SCROTA	SEISIN	SESTET
SADISM	SANELY	SCARCE	SCRUBS	SEIZED	SET-OFF
SADIST	SANEST	SCARED	SCRUFF	SEIZER	SETOSE
SAFARI	SANIES	SCARER	SCRUMP	SEJANT	SETTEE
SAFELY	SANITY	SCARFS	SCRUMS	SELDOM	SETTER

SETTLE	SHEIKH	SHRIMP	SIMMER	SKINNY	SLOSHY
SET-UPS	SHEILA	SHRINE	SIMNEL	SKIRTS	SLOTHS
SEVENS	SHEKEL	SHRINK	SIMONY	SKIVED	SLOUCH
SEVERE	SHELLS	SHRIVE	SIMOOM	SKIVER	SLOUGH
SEVRES	SHELVE	SHROUD	SIMPER	SKIVVY	SLOVAK
SEWAGE	SHENSI	SHRUBS	SIMPLE	SKOPLE	SLOVEN
SEWERS	SHERDS	SHRUGS	SIMPLY	SKULLS	SLOWED
SEWING	SHERIA	SHRUNK	SINGHI	SKUNKS	SLOWER
SEXIER	SHERPA	SHUCKS	SINEWS	SKYCAP	SLOWLY
SEXILY	SHERRY	SHUFTI	SINEWY	SKYLAB	SLUDGE
SEXING	SHEWED	SHUFTY	SINGED	SLACKS	SLUDGY
SEXISM	SHIELD	SHUNTS	SINGER	SLAGGY	SLUICE
SEXIST	SHIEST	SHYEST	SINGES	SLAKED	SLUING
SEXPOT	SHIFTS	SYING	SINGLE	SLAKER	SLUMMY
SEXTET	SHIFTY	SIALIC	SINGLY	SLALOM	SLUMPS
SEXTON	SHIITE	SIBYLS	SINING	SLANGY	SLURRY
SEXUAL	SHINER	SICILY	SINKER	SLANTS	SLUSHY
SHABBY	SHINNY	SICKED	SINNED	SLAP-UP	SLYEST
SHACKS	SHINTO	SICKEN	SINNER	SLATED	SMACKS
SHADED	SHIRAZ	SICKER	SINTER	SLATER	SMALLS
SHADES	SHIRES	SICKLE	SIOUAN	SLATES	SMALTO
SHADOW	SHIRTS	SICKLY	SIPHON	SLAVED	SMARMY
SHAFTS	SHIRTY	SIDE-ON	SIPPED	SLAVER	SMEARS
SHAGGY	SHIVER	SIDING	SIPPER	SLAVES	SMEARY
SHAKEN	SHOALS	SIDLED	SIPPET	SLAVIC	SMEGMA
SHAKER	SHOCKS	SIDLER	SIRENS	SLAYER	SMELLS
SHAKES	SHODDY	SIECLE	SIRING	SLEAVE	SMELLY
SHALOM	SHOGUN	SIEGES	SIRIUS	SLEAZY	SMELTS
SHAMAN	SHOOED	SIENNA	SIRRAH	SLEDGE	SMILAX
SHAMED	SHOOTS	SIERRA	SISKIN	SLEEPY	SMILED
SHAMMY	SHORAN	SIESTA	SISTER	SLEETY	SMILER
SHANDY	SHORED	SIEVED	SITARS	SLEEVE	SMILES
SHANKS	SHORES	SIEVES	SITCOM	SLEIGH	SMIRCH
SHANNY	SHORTS	SIFAKA	SITING	SLEUTH	SMIRKS
SHANSI	SHORTY	SIFTED	SIT-INS	SLEWED	SMITER
SHANTY	SHOULD	SIFTER	SITTER	SLICED	SMITHS
SHAPED	SHOUTS	SIGHED	SIT-UPS	SLICER	SMITHY
SHAPES	SHOVED	SIGHER	SIXTHS	SLICES	SMOCKS
SHARDS	SHOVEL	SIGHTS	SIZING	SLICKS	SMOGGY
SHARED	SHOVER	SIGNAL	SIZZLE	SLIDES	SMOKED
SHARER	SHOVES	SIGNED	SKATED	SLIGHT	SMOKER
SHARES	SHOWED	SIGNER	SKATER	SLIMLY	SMOKES
SHARIA	SHOWER	SIGNET	SKATES	SLINGS	SMOOCH
SHARKS	SHRANK	SIGNOR	SKEINS	SLINKY	SMOOTH
SHARPS	SHREDS	SIKKIM	SKELLY	SLIP-ON	SMUDGE
SHAVED	SHREWD	SILAGE	SKETCH	SLIPPY	SMUDGY
SHAVEN	SHREWS	SILENT	SKEWED	SLIP-UP	SMUTCH
SHAVER	SHRIEK	SILICA	SKEWER	SLIVER	SMUTTY
SHAVES	SHRIFT	SILKEN	SKIBOB	SLOGAN	SNACKS
SHAWLS	SHRIKE	SILTED	SKIERS	SLOOPS	SNAFUS
SHEARS	SHRILL	SILVAN	SKIFFS	SLOPED	SNAGGY
SHEATH	SHRIMP	SILVER	SKIING	SLOPER	SNAILS
SHEAVE	SHRINE	SIMIAN	SKILLS	SLOPES	SNAKED
SHEETS	SHRILL	SIMILE	SKIMPY	SLOPPY	SNAKES

SNAPPY	SOFFIT	SPADES	SPOILS	SQUILL	STEAKS
SNARED	SOFTEN	SPADIX	SPOILT	SQUINT	STEAMY
SNARER	SOFTER	SPANKS	SPOKEN	SQUIRE	STEEDS
SNARES	SOFTIE	SPARED	SPOKES	SQUIRM	STEELS
SNARLS	SOFTLY	SPARER	SPONGE	SQUIRT	STEELY
SNARLY	SOIGNE	SPARES	SPONGY	SQUISH	STEERS
SNATCH	SOILED	SPARID	SPOOFS	STABLE	STEEVE
SNAZZY	SOIREE	SPARKS	SPOOKS	STABLY	STEINS
SNEAKS	SOLACE	SPARRY	SPOOKY	STACKS	STELAR
SNEAKY	SOLDER	SPARSE	SPOOLS	STADIA	STENCH
SNEERS	SOLELY	SPASMS	SPOONS	STAFFS	STEPPE
SNEEZE	SOLEMN	SPATHE	SPOORS	STAGED	STEREO
SNEEZY	SOLIDI	SPAVIN	SPORES	STAGER	STERIC
SNICKS	SOLIDS	SPAYED	SPORTS	STAGES	STERNA
SNIDER	SOLING	SPEARS	SPORTY	STAGEY	STERNS
SNIFFS	SOLUTE	SPECIE	SPOT-ON	STAINS	STEROL
SNIFFY	SOLVED	SPECKS	SPOTTY	STAIRS	STEWED
SNIPED	SOLVER	SPEECH	SPOUSE	STAKED	STICKS
SNIPER	SOMANI	SPEEDS	SPOUTS	STAKES	STICKY
SNIPES	SOMBRE	SPEEDY	SPRAIN	STALAG	STIFFS
SNIPPY	SOMITE	SPEISS	SPRANG	STALED	STIFLE
SNITCH	SONANT	SPELLS	SPRATS	STALER	STIGMA
SNIVEL	SONATA	SPERMS	SPRAWL	STALKS	STILES
SNOOPS	SONNET	SPEWED	SPRAYS	STALKY	STILLS
SNOOPY	SONORA	SPEWER	SPREAD	STALLS	STILLY
SNOOTY	SOONER	SPHENE	SPREES	STAMEN	STILTS
SNOOZE	SOOTHE	SPHERE	SPRIER	STAMPS	STINGS
SNORED	SOPPED	SPHINX	SPRIGS	STANCE	STINGY
SNORER	SORBET	SPICED	SPRING	STANCH	STINKS
SNORES	SORBIC	SPICER	SPRINT	STANDS	STINTS
SNORTS	SORDID	SPICES	SPRITE	STANZA	STIPEL
SNOTTY	SORELY	SPIDER	SPROUT	STAPES	STIPES
SNOUTS	SORREL	SPIELS	SPRUCE	STAPLE	STIRPS
SNOWED	SORROW	SPIGOT	SPRUNG	STARCH	STITCH
SNUBBY	SORTED	SPIKED	SPRYLY	STARED	STOATS
SNUFFY	SORTER	SPIKES	SPUNKY	STARER	STOCKS
SNUGLY	SORTIE	SPILLS	SPURGE	STARES	STOCKY
SOAKED	SOTHIC	SPINAL	SPURRY	STARRY	STODGE
SOAKER	SOUGH	SPINEL	SPURTS	STARST	STODGY
SOAPED	SOUGHT	SPINES	SPUTUM	STARVE	STOICS
SOARED	SOUNDS	SPINET	SPYING	STASIS	STOKED
SOARER	SOURCE	SPIRAL	SQUABS	STATED	STOKER
SOBBED	SOURED	SPIRES	SQUADS	STATER	STOKES
SOBBER	SOURER	SPIRIT	SQUALL	STATES	STOLEN
SOCAGE	SOURLY	SPITAL	SQUAMA	STATIC	STOLES
SOCCER	SOUSED	SPITED	SQUARE	STATOR	STOLID
SOCIAL	SOVIET	SPAKES	SQUASH	STATUE	STOLON
SOCKED	SOWERS	SPLASH	SQUATS	STATUS	STONED
SOCKET	SOWETO	SPLEEN	SQUAWK	STAVED	STONER
SOCMAN	SOWING	SPLICE	SQUAWS	STAVES	STONES
SODDEN	SPACED	SPLINE	SQUEAK	STAYED	STOOGE
SODIUM	SPACER	SPLINT	SQUEAL	STAYER	STOOLS
SODOMY	SPACES	SPLITS	SQUIBS	STEADS	STOP-GO
SOEVER	SPADER	SPLOSH	SQUIDS	STEADY	STORAX

STORED	STUNTS	SUNDEW	SWEETS	SAILORS	SAN JOSE
STORES	STUPID	SUNDRY	SWELLS	SAINTED	SAN JUAN
STOREY	STUPOR	SUNGOD	SWERVE	SAINTLY	SANTA FE
STORKS	STURDY	SUNKED	SWIFTS	SALAAMS	SAO LUIS
STORMS	STYLAR	SUNLIT	SWILLS	SALABLE	SAPHENA
STORMY	STYLED	SUNNED	SWINES	SALERNO	SAPIENT
STOUPS	STYLER	SUNNIS	SWINGE	SALICIN	SAPLESS
STOVER	STYLES	SUNRAY	SWINGS	SALIENT	SAPLING
STOVES	STYLET	SUNSET	SWIPED	SALLIED	SAPONIN
STOWED	STYLUS	SUNTAN	SWIPES	SALLIER	SAPPERS
STRAFE	STYMIE	SUPERB	SWIRLS	SALLIES	SAPPIER
STRAIN	STYRAX	SUPINE	SWIRLY	SALLOWS	SAPPILY
STRAIT	STYRIA	SUPPED	SWITCH	SALMONS	SAPPING
STRAKE	SUABLE	SUPPER	SWIVEL	SALOONS	SAPPORO
STRAND	SUBBED	SUPPLE	SWOONS	SALPINX	SAPROBE
STRAPS	SUBDUE	SUPPLY	SWOOPS	SALISFY	SAPSAGO
STRATA	SUBITO	SURELY	SWOOSH	SALTANT	SAPWOOD
STRAWS	SUBLET	SUREST	SWORDS	SALTBOX	SARACEN
STRAYS	SUBMIT	SURETY	SYDNEY	SALTERN	SARANSK
STREAK	SUBORN	SURFED	SYLVAN	SALTIER	SARATOV
STREAM	SUBSET	SURFER	SYMBOL	SALTILY	SARAWAK
STREET	SUBTLE	SURGED	SYNCOM	SALTING	SARCASM
STRESS	SUBTLY	SURGER	SYNDIC	SALTIRE	SARCOID
STREWN	SUBURB	SURGES	SYNODS	SALTPAN	SARCOMA
STRICK	SUBWAY	SURREY	SYNTAX	SALTPOT	SARCOUS
STRICT	SUCHOU	SURTAX	SYPHER	SALUTED	SARDINE
STRIDE	SUCKED	SURVEY	SYPHON	SALUTER	SARDIUS
STRIFE	SUCKER	SUSLIK	SYRIAN	SALUTES	SARKIER
STRIKE	SUCKLE	SUSSED	SYRINX	SALVAGE	SARDINE
STRING	SUDDEN	SUTTEE	SYRUPY	SALVERS	SARDIUS
STRIPE	SUFFER	SUTURE	SYSTEM	SALVING	SARKIER
STRIPS	SUFFIX	SVELTE	SYZRAN	SALVOES	SARNIES
STRIPY	SUGARS	SWABIA	SYZYGY	SAMISEN	SARONGS
STRIVE	SUGARY	SWAGER	SZEGED	SAMOSAS	SARONIC
STROBE	SUITED	SWAINS		SAMOVAR	SASSABY
STRODE	SUITES	SWAMIS		SAMOYED	SASSARI
STROKE	SUITOR	SWAMPS	**7 LETTERS**	SAMPANS	SASSIER
STROLL	SULCUS	SWAMPY	SABBATH	SAMPLED	SASSING
STROMA	SULKED	SWANKS	SACATON	SAMPLER	SATANIC
STRONG	SULKER	SWANKY	SACCATE	SAMPLES	SATCHEL
STROPS	SULLEN	SWARDS	SACCULE	SAMURAI	SATIATE
STROUD	SULTAN	SWARMS	SACHETS	SANCTUM	SATIETY
STROVE	SULTRY	SWATCH	SACKING	SANCTUS	SATINET
STRUCK	SUMACH	SWATHE	SADDEST	SANDALS	SATIRES
STRUMA	SUMMAT	SWATHS	SADDLED	SANDBAG	SATISFY
STRUNG	SUMMED	SWATOW	SADDLER	SANDBAR	SATSUMA
STRUTS	SUMMER	SWAYED	SADDLES	SANDBOX	SATYRIC
STUBBY	SUMMIT	SWAYER	SADIRON	SANDERS	SATYRID
STUCCO	SUMMON	SWEATS	SAFROLE	SAND FLY	SAUCERS
STUDIO	SUNBED	SWEATY	SAGGIER	SANDIER	SAUCIER
STUFFY	SUNBOW	SWEDEN	SAGGING	SANDING	SAUCILY
STUMER	SUNDAE	SWEDES	SAGUARO	SANDPIT	SAUCING
STUMPS	SUNDAY	SWEENY	SAHARAN	SANGRIA	SAUNTER
STUMPY	SUNDER	SWEEPS	SAILING	SANICLE	SAURIAN

SAUSAGE	SCHISMS	SCRUBBY	SECRETS	SEPTATE	SFUMATO
SAUTEED	SCHMUCK	SCRUFFS	SECTARY	SEPTETS	SHACKED
SAVABLE	SCHOLAR	SCRUFFY	SECTILE	SEPTIME	SHACKLE
SAVAGED	SCHOOLS	SCRUMPY	SECILON	SEQUELA	SHADIER
SAVAGES	SCIATIC	SCRUNCH	SECTORS	SEQUELS	SHADILY
SAVANNA	SCIENCE	SCRUPLE	SECULAR	SEQUENT	SHADING
SAVANTA	SCISSOR	SCUDDED	SECURED	SEQUINS	SHADOOF
SAVE-ALL	SCOFFED	SCUFFED	SECURER	SEQUOIA	SHADOWS
SAVINGS	SCOFFER	SCUFFLE	SEDATED	SERAPHS	SHADOWY
SAVIOUR	SCOLDED	SCULLED	SEDILIA	SERBIAN	SHAFTED
SAVOURY	SCOLDER	SCULLER	SEDUCED	SERFDOM	SHAHDOM
SAWBILL	SCOLLOP	SCULPIN	SEDUCER	SERGIPE	SHAKERS
SAWDUST	SCONCES	SCUMBLE	SEEDBED	SERIALS	SHAKE-UP
SAWFISH	SCOOPED	SCUMMER	SEEDIER	SERIATE	SHAKHTY
SAWMILL	SCOOPER	SCUPPER	SEEDILY	SERICIN	SHAKIER
SAWN-OFF	SCOOTED	SCUTATE	SEEDING	SERIEMA	SHAKILY
SAXHORN	SCOOTER	SCUTTLE	SEEKERS	SERINGA	SHAKING
SAXTUBA	SCOPULA	SCYTHED	SEEKING	SERIOUS	SHALLOP
SAYINGS	SCORERS	SCYTHES	SEEMING	SERMONS	SHALLOT
SCABBLE	SCORIFY	SEABIRD	SEEPAGE	SERPENT	SHALLOW
SCABIES	SCORING	SEACOCK	SEEPING	SERPIGO	SHAMANS
SCALERS	SCORNED	SEA DOGS	SEESAWS	SERRATE	SHAMBLE
SCALDED	SCORNER	SEAFOOD	SEETHED	SERRIED	SHAMING
SCALENE	SCORPER	SEAGRIT	SEGMENT	SERUMAL	SHAMMED
SCALIER	SCORPIO	SEAGULL	SEISMIC	SERVANT	SHAMMER
SCALING	SCOTOMA	SEA-LANE	SEIZING	SERVERS	SHAMPOO
SCALLOP	SCOURER	SEALANT	SEIZURE	SERVERY	SHANNON
SCALPED	SCOURGE	SEA LEGS	SEKONDI	SERVICE	SHAPELY
SCALPER	SCOUSES	SEALERS	SELENIC	SERVILE	SHAPING
SCAMPER	SCOUTED	SEALING	SELFISH	SERVING	SHARERS
SCANDAL	SCOUTER	SEA LION	SELLERS	SESOTHO	SHARING
SCANDIC	SCOWLED	SEAMARK	SELLING	SESSILE	SHARPEN
SCANNED	SCOWLER	SEAMIER	SELL-OUT	SESSION	SHARPER
SCANNER	SCRAGGY	SEA MILE	SELTZER	SESTINA	SHARPLY
SCAPOSE	SCRAPED	SEA MIST	SELVAGE	SETBACK	SHATTER
SCAPULA	SCRAPER	SEANCES	SEMATIC	SETLINE	SHAVERS
SCARABS	SCRAPES	SEAPORT	SEMINAL	SETTEES	SHAVING
SCARIER	SCRAPPY	SEARING	SEMINAR	SETTERS	SHAWNEE
SCARIFY	SCRATCH	SEASICK	SEMITIC	SETTING	SHEARED
SCARING	SCRAWLS	SEASIDE	SENATES	SETTLED	SHEARER
SCARLET	SCRAWLY	SEASONS	SENATOR	SETTLER	SHEATHE
SCARPER	SCRAWNY	SEATING	SENDERS	SETTLES	SHEATHS
SCARRED	SCREAMS	SEATTLE	SENDING	SEVENTH	SHEAVES
SCARVES	SCREECH	SEAWALL	SEND-OFF	SEVERAL	SHEBANG
SCATTED	SCREEDS	SEAWARE	SEND-UPS	SEVERED	SHEBEEN
SCATTER	SCREENS	SEAWAYS	SENEGAL	SEVILLE	SHEDDER
SCENERY	SCREWED	SEAWEED	SENOIRS	SEXIEST	SHEERER
SCENTED	SCREWER	SECEDED	SENORAS	SEXISTS	SHIEKHS
SCEPTIC	SCRIBAL	SECEDER	SENSATE	SEXLESS	SHEILAS
SCEPTRE	SCRIBES	SECLUDE	SENSING	SEXPOTS	SHEKELS
SCHEMED	SCRIMPY	SECONDO	SENSORS	SEXTANT	SHELLAC
SCHEMER	SCRIPTS	SECONDS	SENORAS	SEXTETS	SHELLED
SCHEMES	SCROLLS	SECRECY	SENSORY	SEXTILE	SHELTER
SCHERZO	SCROOGE	SECRETE	SENSUAL	SEXTONS	SHELVED

SHELVER	SHRIEKS	SIGNALS	SITCOMS	SKYSAIL	SLIP-UPS
SHELVES	SHRIFTS	SIGNETS	SIT-DOWN	SLACKED	SLPWAY
SHERBET	SHRIKES	SIGNIFY	SITTERS	SLACKEN	SLITHER
SHERIFF	SHRILLY	SIGNING	SITTING	SLACKER	SLITTED
SHERPAS	SHRIMPS	SIGNORA	SITUSTE	SLACKLY	SLIVERS
SHEWING	SHRINES	SIGNORE	SIXFOLD	SLAGGED	SLOBBER
SHIELDS	SHRINKS	SIGNORS	SIX-PACK	SLAKING	SLOGANS
SHIFTED	SHRIVEL	SILENCE	SIXTEEN	SLALOMS	SLOGGED
SHIFTER	SHRIVER	SILINTS	SIXTIES	SLAMMED	SLOGGER
SHIITES	SHOUDES	SILESIA	SIZABLE	SLANDER	SLOPING
SHIKOKU	SHRUBBY	SILICLE	SIZZLED	SLANGED	SLOPPED
SHIMMER	SHUCKED	SILICON	SIZZLER	SLANTED	SLOSHED
SHINDIG	SHUCKER	SILIQUA	SKATING	SLAPPED	SLOTTED
SHINGLE	SHUDDER	SILKIER	SKATOLE	SLAPPER	SLOTTER
SHINGLY	SHUFFLE	SILKILY	SKEPTIC	SLASHED	SLOUCHY
SHINIER	SHUNNED	SILLIER	SKETCHY	SLASHER	SLOVENE
SHINING	SHUNNER	SILLIES	SKEWERS	SHASHES	SLOWEST
SHINNED	SHUNTED	SILTING	SKEWING	SLATING	SLOWING
SHIPPED	SHUNTER	SILURID	SKIABLE	SLATTED	SLUGGED
SHIPPER	SHUSHED	SILVERS	SKIBOBS	SLAVERS	SLUICED
SHIPWAY	SHUT-EYE	SILVERY	SKIDDED	SLAVERY	SLUICES
SHIRKED	SHUT-OFF	SIMIANS	SKIDPAN	SLAVING	SLUMBER
SHIRKER	SHUTOUT	SIMILAR	SKID ROW	SLAVISH	SLUMMED
SHIVERS	SHUTTER	SIMILIES	SKIFFLE	SLAYERS	SLUMMER
SHIVERY	SHUTTLE	SIMIOUS	SKI JUMP	SLAYING	SLUMPED
SHCKED	SHYNESS	SIMPERS	SKILFUL	SLEDDED	SLURRED
SHOCKER	SHYSTER	SIMPLER	SKI LIFT	SLEDDER	SLYNESS
SHOEING	SIALKOT	SIMPLEX	SKILLED	SLEDGED	SMACKED
SHOGUNS	SIALOID	SIMULAR	SKILLET	SLEDGES	SMACKER
SHOOING	SIAMANG	SINOLA	SKIMMED	SLEEKED	SMALL AD
SHOOTER	SIAMESE	SINCERE	SKIMMIA	SLEEKER	SMALLER
SHOPPED	SIBERIA	SINE DIE	SKIMPED	SLEEKLY	SMARTED
SHOPPER	SIBLING	SINGING	SKINFUL	SLEEPER	SMARTEN
SHORING	SICKBAY	SINGLED	SKINNED	SLEETED	SMARTER
SHORTED	SICKBED	SINGLES	SKINNER	SLEEVES	SMARTLY
SHORTEN	SICKEST	SINGLET	SKI POLE	SLEIGHS	SMASHED
SHORTER	SICKING	SINITIC	SKIPPED	SLEIGHT	SMASHER
SHORTILE	SICKLES	SINKERS	SKIPPER	SLENDER	SMASHES
SHORTLY	SICK PAY	SINKING	SKIPPET	SLEUTHS	SMASH-UP
SHOTGUN	SIDE ARM	SINLESS	SKIRRET	SLEWING	SMATTER
SHOT PUT	SIDECAR	SINNERS	SKIRTED	SLICING	SMEARED
SHOTTEN	SIDINGS	SINNING	SKITTER	SLICKED	SMEARER
SHOUTED	SIEMENS	SINUATE	SKITTLE	SLICKER	SMECTIC
SHOUTER	SIERRAN	SINUJU	SKIVERS	SLICKLY	SMELLED
SHOVELS	SIERRAS	SINOUS	SKIVING	SLIDING	SMELTED
SHOVING	SIESTAS	SINUSES	SKULKED	SLIGHTS	SMELTER
SHOWERS	SIEVING	SIPHONS	SKULKER	SLIMIER	SMIGING
SHOWERY	SIFTERS	SIPPING	SKY-BLUE	SLIMILY	SMILING
SHOWIER	SIGHING	SIRLOIN	SKYCAPS	SLIMMED	SMIRKED
SHOWILY	SIGHTED	SIROCCO	SKYDIVE	SLIMMER	SMIRKER
SHOWING	SIGHTER	SIRRAHS	SKY-HIGH	SLINGER	SMITING
SHOWMAN	SIGHTLY	SISSIER	SKYJACK	SLIP-ONS	SMITTEN
SHOWMEN	SIGMATE	SISSIES	SKYLARK	SLIPPED	SMOKERS
SHOW-OFF	SIGMOID	SISTERS	SKYLINE	SLIPPER	SMOKIER

SMOKILY	SNUBBED	SOMEDAY	SPANIEL	SPILLER	SPOTTED
SMOKING	SNUBBER	SOMEHOW	SPANISH	SPINACH	SPOTTER
SMOLDER	SNUFFED	SOMEONE	SPANKED	SPINDLE	SPOUSAL
SMOTHER	SNUFFER	SOMEWAY	SPANKER	SPINDLE	SPOUSES
SMUDGED	SNUFFLE	SOMITAL	SPANNED	SPINDLY	SPOUTED
SMUDGES	SNUFFLY	SONANCE	SPANNER	SPIN-DRY	SPOUTER
SMUGGER	SNUGGLE	SONATAS	SPARING	SPINETS	SPRAINS
SMUGGLE	SOAKAGE	SONDAGE	SPARKED	SPINNER	SPRAWLS
SMUTCHY	SOAKING	SONGFUL	SPARKLE	SPINNEY	SPRAWLY
SNACKED	SO-AND-	SONNETS	SPARRED	SPIN-OFF	SPRAYED
SNAFFLE	SO	SOOCHOW	SPARROW	SPINOSE	SPRAYER
SNAGGED	SOAPBOX	SOOTHED	SPARSER	SPINOUS	SPREADS
SNAKILY	SOAPIER	SOOTHER	SPARTAN	SPINULE	SPRIEST
SNAKING	SOAPILY	SOOTIER	SPASTIC	SPIRAEA	SPRIGGY
SNAPPED	SOAPING	SOOTILY	SPATHIC	SPIRALS	SPRINGE
SNAPPER	SOARING	SOPHISM	SPATIAL	SPIRANT	SPRINGS
SNARING	SOBBING	SOPHIST	SPATTER	SPIREME	SPRINGY
SNARLED	SOBERED	SOPPIER	SPATULA	SPIRITS	SPRINTS
SNARL-UP	SOBERLY	SOPPILY	SPAWNED	SPIROID	SPRITES
SNATCHY	SOCAGER	SOPPING	SPAWNER	SPIRULA	SPROUTS
SNEAKED	SOCIALS	SOPRANO	SPAYING	SPITING	SPRUCED
SNEAKER	SOACIETY	SORBETS	SPEAKER	SPITING	SPRUCES
SNEERED	SOCKETS	SORBOSE	SPEARER	SPITTER	SPUMONE
SNEERER	SOCKEYE	SORCERY	SPECIAL	SPITTLE	SPUMOUS
SNEEZES	SOCKING	SORDINO	SPECIES	SPLASHY	SPURNED
SNICKED	SODDING	SORGHUM	SPECIFY	SPLAYED	SPURNER
SNICKER	SOD'S	SORTIES	SPECKLE	SPLEENS	SPURRED
SNIDELY	LAW	SOROSIS	SPECTRA	SPLENIC	SPURTED
SNIDEST	SOFTEST	SORRIER	SPECTRE	SPLICED	SPUTNIK
SNIFFED	SOFTIES	SORRILY	SPEEDED	SPLICER	SPUTTER
SNIFFER	SOGGIER	SORROWS	SPEEDER	SPLICES	SQUABBY
SNIFFLE	SOGGILY	SORTIES	SPELLED	SPLINTS	SQUACCO
SNIFTER	SOILAGE	SORTING	SPELLER	SPLODGE	SQUALID
SNIGGLE	SOILING	SORT-OUT	SPELTER	SPLODGY	SQUALLS
SNIPERS	SOIREES	SOTTISH	SPENCER	SPLURGE	SQUALLY
SNIPING	SOJOURN	SOUFFLE	SPENDER	SPOILED	SQUALOR
SNIPPED	SOLACED	SOUGHED	SPEWING	SPOILER	SQUARED
SNIPPET	SOLACER	SOULFUL	SPHENIC	SPOKANE	SQUARER
SNOGGED	SOLACES	SOUNDED	SPHERAL	SPONDEE	SQUARES
SNOOKER	SOLANUM	SOUNDER	SPHERES	SPONGED	SQUASHY
SNOOPED	SOLARIA	SOUNDLY	SPICATE	SPONGER	SQUAWKS
SNOOPER	SOLDIER	SOUPCON	SPICERY	SPONGES	SQUEAKS
SNOOZED	SOLICIT	SOUPFIN	SPICIER	SPONGIN	SQUEAKY
SNORERS	SOLIDLY	SOURCES	SPICILY	SPONSON	SQUEALS
SNORING	SOLIDUS	SOUREST	SPICING	SPONSOR	SQUEEZE
SNORKEL	SOLOIST	SOURING	SPICULE	SPOOFER	SQUELCH
SNORTED	SOLOMON	SOURSOP	SPIDERS	SPOOKED	SQUIDGY
SNORTER	SOLUBLE	SOUSING	SPIDERY	SPOONED	SQUIFFY
SNOWCAP	SOLVATE	SOUTANE	SPIGNEL	SPOORER	SQUILLA
SNOWIER	SOLVENT	SOUTHER	SPIGOTS	SPORRAN	SQUINCH
SNOWILY	SOLVERS	SOVIETS	SPIKIER	SPORTED	SQUINTS
SNOWING	SOLVING	SOVKHOZ	SPIKILY	SPORTER	SQUINTY
SNOWMAN	SOMALIA	SOZZLED	SPIKING	SPORULE	SQUIRES
SNOWMEN	SOMATIC	SPACING	SPILLED	SPOTLIT	SQUIRMS

SQUIRMY	STARVER	STICHIC	STOWAGE	STUFFED	SUCCUBI
SQUIRTS	STASHED	STICKER	STOWING	STUFFER	SUCCUMB
SQUISHY	STASHES	STICKLE	STRAFED	STUMBLE	SUCCUSS
STABBED	STATENT	STICK-ON	STAFTER	STUMPED	SUCKERS
STABBER	STATELY	STICK-UP	STRAINS	STUMPER	SUCKING
STABILE	STATICS	STIFFEN	STRAITS	STUNNED	SUCKLED
STABLED	STATING	STIFFER	STRANDS	STUNNER	SUCKLER
STABLES	STATION	STIFFLY	STRANGE	STUNTED	SUCRASE
STACKER	STATISM	STIFLED	STRATAL	STUPEFY	SUCROSE
STADDLE	STATIST	STIFLER	STRATAS	STUPORS	SUCTION
STADIUM	STATIVE	STIGMAS	STRATUM	STUTTER	SUDANIC
STAFFED	STATUED	STILLED	STRATUS	STYGAIN	SUDETES
STAFFER	STATUTE	STILLER	STRAYED	STYLING	SUFFICE
STAGIER	STAUNCH	STILTED	STRAYER	STYLISH	SUFFUSE
STAGILY	STAVING	STILTON	STREAKS	STYLIST	SUGARED
STAGING	STAYERS	STIMULI	STREAKY	STYLIZE	SUGGEST
STAIDLY	STAYING	STINGER	STREAMS	STYLOID	SUICIDE
STAINED	STEALER	STINKER	STREETS	STYLOPS	SUITING
STAINER	STEALTH	STINTED	STREACH	STYMIED	SUITORS
STAKING	STEAMED	STINTER	STRETTA	STYPSIS	SUKHUMI
STALEST	STEAMER	STIPEND	STRETTO	STYPTIC	SULCATE
STALING	STEARIC	STIPPLE	STREWED	STYRENE	SULKIER
STALKED	STEARIN	STIPULE	STREWER	SUAVELY	SULKILY
STALKER	STEELED	STIR-FRY	STREWTH	SUAVITY	SULKING
STALLED	STEEPED	STIRRED	STRIATE	SUBACID	SULLAGE
STAMBUL	STEEPEN	STIRRER	STRIDES	SUBBASE	SULLIED
STAMENS	STEEPER	STIRRUP	STRIDOR	SUBBASS	SULPHUR
STAMINA	STEEPLE	STOCKED	STRIIKER	SUBBING	SULTANA
STAMMEL	STEERER	STOCKER	STRIKES	SUBDUAL	SULTANS
STAMMER	STELLAR	STOCIAL	STRINGS	SUBDUCT	SUMATRA
STAMPED	STEMMED	STOCKERS	STRINGY	SUBDUED	SUMMAND
STAMPER	STEMMER	STOCKING	STRINGY	SUBEDIT	SUMMERY
STANCES	STEMSON	STOMACH	STRIPED	SUBERIN	SUMMING
STANDBY	STENCIL	STOMPED	STRIPER	SUBFUSC	SUMMITS
STANDER	STEN GUN	STOMPER	STRIPES	SUBJECT	SUMMONS
STAND-IN	STENTOR	STONIER	STRIPEY	SUBJOIN	SUNBEAM
STAND-UP	STEPPED	STONILY	STRIVEN	SUBLIME	SUNBEDS
STANNIC	STEPPER	STONING	STRIVER	SUBPLOT	SUNBELT
STANZAS	STEPPES	STOOGES	STROBIC	SUB ROSA	SUNBIRD
STAPLED	STEPSON	STOOKER	STROKED	SUBSETS	SUNBURN
STAPLER	STEREOS	STOOPED	STROKES	SUBSIDE	SUNDAES
STAPLES	STERILE	STOOPER	STROLLS	SUBSIDY	SUNDAYS
STARCHY	STERLET	STOPGAP	STROPHE	SUBSIST	SUNDIAL
STARDOM	STERNAL	STOPING	STROPPY	SUBSOIL	SUNDOWN
STARING	STERNER	STOPPED	STRUDEL	SUBSUME	SUNFISH
STARKER	STERNLY	STOPPER	STUBBED	SUBTEND	SUNGLOW
STARKLY	STERNUM	STORAGE	STUBBLE	SUBTLER	SUN GODS
STARLET	STEROID	STOREYS	STUBBLY	SUBTYPE	SUNLAMP
STARLIT	STERTOR	STORIED	STUCK-UP	SUBURBS	SUNLESS
STARRED	STETSON	STORIES	STUDDED	SUBVERT	SUNNIER
STARTED	STEWARD	STORING	STUDENT	SUBWAYS	SUNNILY
STARTER	STEWING	STORMED	STUDIED	SUCCEED	SUNNING
STARTLE	STHENIC	STOUTER	STUDIES	SUCCESS	SUNRISE
STARVED	STIBINE	STOUTLY	STUDIOS	SUCCOUR	SUNROOF

SUNSETS	SWATTED	SYNGAMY	SALIVATE	SANTONIN
SUNSPOT	SWATTER	SYNODAL	SALLYING	SAO PAULO
SUNSTAR	SWAYING	SYNODIC	SALPICON	SAPIDITY
SUNTANS	SWEARER	SYNONYM	SALTBUSH	SAPIENCE
SUNTRAP	SWEATED	SYNOVIA	SALTIEST	SAPLINGS
SUNWISE	SWEATER	SYPHONS	SALTILLO	SAPONIFY
SUPPERS	SWEDISH	SYRINGA	SALTLICK	SAPONITE
SUPPING	SWEEPER	SYRINGE	SALTNESS	SAPPHIRE
SUPPLER	SWEETEN	SYRPHID	SALTPANS	SAPPIEST
SUPPORT	SWEETER	SYSTEMS	SALTWORT	SAPROBIC
SUPPOSE	SWEETIE	SYSTOLE	SALUTARY	SAPROPEL
SUPREME	SWEETLY		SALUTING	SARABAND
SUPREMO	SWELLED		SALVABLE	SARACENS
SURBASE	SWELTER	**8 LETTERS**	SALVABLY	SARAJEVO
SURCOAT	SWERVED	SAARLAND	SALVADOR	SARDINES
SURFACE	SWERVER	SABADELL	SALVAGED	SARDINIA
SURFEIT	SWERVES	SABBATIC	SALVAGER	SARDONIC
SURFERS	SWIFTER	SABOTAGE	SALZBURG	SARDONYX
SURFING	SWIFTLY	SABOTEUR	SAMARIUM	SARGASSO
SURGEON	SWIGGED	SABULOUS	SAMENESS	SARKIEST
SURGERY	SWIGGER	SACKLIKE	SAMIZDAT	SASHAYED
SURGING	SWILLED	SACK RACE	SAMOVARS	SASSIEST
SURINAM	SWILLER	SACREDLY	SAMPHIRE	SASTRUGA
SURLIER	SWIMMER	SACRISITY	SAMPLERS	SATANISM
SURLILY	SWINDLE	SADDENED	SAMPLING	SATANIST
SURMISE	SWINGER	SADDLERS	SAMURAIS	SATCHELS
SURNAME	SWINGLE	SADDLERY	SANCTIFY	SATIABLE
SURPASS	SWINISH	SADDLING	SANCTION	SATIABLY
SURPLUS	SWIPING	SADISTIC	SANCTITY	SATIATED
SURREAL	SWIPPLE	SAFENESS	SANCTUMS	SATIRIST
SURREYS	SWIRLED	SAFETIES	SANDARAC	SATIRIZE
SURVEYS	SWISHED	SAGACITY	SANDBAGS	SATSUMAS
SURVIVE	SWISHER	SAGGIEST	SANDBANK	SATURANT
SUSPECT	SWISHES	SAGITTAL	SANDBARS	SATURATE
SUSPEND	SWIVELS	SAILABLE	SAND-CAST	SATURDAY
SUSSING	SWIZZLE	SAILFISH	SAND DUNE	SAUCEPAN
SUSTAIN	SWOLLEN	SAILINGS	SAN DIEGO	SAUCIEST
SUSTRES	SWOONED	SAILORLY	SANDIEST	SAUNTERS
SWABBED	SWOOPED	SAINFOIN	SANDPITS	SAUROPOD
SWABBER	SWOPPED	SAKHALIN	SANDSHOE	SAUSAGES
SWABIAN	SWOTTED	SALAAMED	SANDSOAP	SAUTEING
SWADDLE	SYENITE	SALACITY	SAND TRAP	SAVAGELY
SWAGGER	SYLLABI	SALARIED	SANDWICH	SAVAGERY
SWAHALI	SYLPHIC	SALARIES	SANDWORM	SAVAGING
SWALLOW	SYLPHID	SALEABLE	SANDWORT	SAVANNAH
SWAMPED	SYLVITE	SALEABLY	SANENESS	SAVANNAS
SWANKED	SYMBOLS	SALEROOM	SANGAREE	SAVIOURS
SWANNED	SYMPTOM	SALESMAN	SANGUINE	SAVORIES
SWANSEA	SYNAPSE	SALESMEN	SANITARY	SAVOROUS
SWAMPED	SYNCARP	SALES TAX	SANITIZE	SAVOURED
SWAPPER	SYNCHRO	SALIENCE	SANSKRIT	SAVOYARD
SWARMED	SYNCOPE	SALIENTS	SANTA ANA	SAWBONES
SWARTHY	SYNERGY	SALINITY	SANTAREM	SAWHORSE
SWATHED	SYNESIS	SALIVARY	SANTIAGO	SAWMILLS

SAWTOOTH	SCHNAPPS	SCRAPERS	SEGMENTS	SERAGLIO
SCABBARD	SCHOLARS	SCRAPING	SEIGNEUR	SERAPHIC
SCABBIER	SCHOLIUM	SCRAPPED	SEISABLE	SERAPHIM
SCABBILY	SCHOOLED	SCRATCHY	SEISMISM	SERENADE
SCABIOUS	SCHOONER	SCRAWLED	SEIZABLE	SERENATA
SCABROUS	SCHWERIN	SCRAWLER	SEIZURES	SERENELY
SCAFFOLD	SCIATICA	SCREAMED	SELANGOR	SERENITY
SCALABLE	SCIENCES	SCREAMER	SELECTED	SERGEANT
SCALABLY	SCILICET	SCREECHY	SELECTOR	SERIALLY
SCALAWAG	SCIMITAR	SCREENED	SELENATE	SERIATIM
SCALDING	SCINCOID	SCREWIER	SELENITE	SERMONIC
SCALENUS	SCIRRHUS	SEASCAPE	SELENIUM	SEROLOGY
SCALIEST	SCISSILE	SEASHELL	SELFHELP	SEROSITY
SCALLION	SCISSION	SEASHORE	SELFHOOD	SEROTINE
SCALLOPS	SCISSORS	SEASONAL	SELFLESS	SERPENTS
SCALPELS	SCIURINE	SEASONED	SELF-MADE	SERPULID
SCALPERS	SCIUROID	SEASONER	SELF-PITY	SERRANID
SCALPING	SCLAFFER	SEAT BELT	SELF-RULE	SERRATED
SCAMMONY	SCLERITE	SEAWALLS	SELFSAME	SERVABLE
SCAMPISH	SCLEROMA	SEAWARDS	SELF-WILL	SERVANTS
SCANDALS	SCLEROUS	SECEDING	SELL-OUTS	SERVICED
SCANDIUM	SCOFFING	SECLUDED	SELVAGES	SERVICES
SCANNERS	SCOLDING	SECONDED	SEMANTIC	SERVINGS
SCANNING	SCOLLOPS	SECONDER	SEMARANG	SERVITOR
SCANSION	SCOOPING	SECONDLY	SEMESTER	SESAMOID
SCANTIER	SCOOTERS	SECRETED	SEMIARID	SESSIONS
SCANTILY	SCOOTING	SECRETIN	SEMIDOME	SETBACKS
SCAPULAR	SCORCHED	SECRETLY	SEMINARS	SETIFORM
SCAPULAS	SCORCHER	SECTIONS	SEMINARY	SET PIECE
SCARCELY	SCORCHES	SECTORIAL	SEMIOTIC	SETSCREW
SCARCEST	SCORNFUL	SECURELY	SEMITICS	SETTINGS
SCARCITY	SCORNING	SECUREST	SEMITIST	SETTLERS
SCARIEST	SCORPION	SECURING	SEMITONE	SETTLING
SCARIOUS	SCORPIUS	SECURITY	SEMOLINA	SEVENTHS
SCARRING	SCOTCHED	SEDATELT	SEMPLICE	SEVERELY
SCATHING	SCOT-FREE	SEDATING	SEMATORS	SEVERING
SCATTIER	SCOTLAND	SEDATION	SENDABLE	SEVERITY
SCATTILY	SCOTOPIA	SEDATIVE	SEND-OFFS	SEWERAGE
SCATTING	SCOTOPIC	SEDIMENT	SENILITY	SEXINESS
SCAVENGE	SCOTSMAN	SEDITION	SENORITA	SEXOLOGY
SCENARIO	SCOTTISH	SEDUCERS	SENSIBLE	SEX ORGAN
SCENTING	SCOURERS	SEDUCING	SENSIBLY	SEXTANTS
SCEPTICS	SCOURGED	SEDULITY	SENSUOUS	SEXTUPLE
SCEPTRES	SCOURGER	SEDULOUS	SENTENCE	SEXUALITY
SCHEDULE	SCOURGES	SEEDBEDS	SENTNENT	SHABBIER
SCHEMATA	SCOURING	SEEDCASE	SENTINEL	SHABBILY
SCHEMERS	SCOUTING	SEEDCORN	SENTRIES	SHACKING
SCHEMING	SCOWLING	SEEDIEST	SEPALLED	SHACKLED
SCHERZOS	SCRABBLE	SEEDLESS	SEPALOID	SHACKLER
SCHILLER	SCRAGGED	SEEDLING	SEPERATE	SHACKLES
SCHIZOID	SCRAGGLY	SEEDSMAN	SEPHARDI	SHADDOCK
SCHIZONT	SCRAMBLE	SEEDSMEN	SEPTUPLE	SHADIEST
SCHMULTZ	SCRAMMED	SEESAWED	SEQUINED	SHADINGS
SCHMUCKS	SCRANTON	SEETHING	SEQUOIAS	SHADOWED

SHADOWER	SHERBETS	SHORTEST	SIBLINGS	SIMONIST
SHAFTING	SHERIFFS	SHORTIES	SICILIAN	SIMPERED
SHAGBARK	SHEILDED	SHORTING	SICKBAYS	SIMPERER
SHAGGIER	SHEILDER	SHOTGUNS	SICKBEDS	SIMPLEST
SHAGGILY	SHIELING	SHOULDER	SICK CALL	SIMPLIFY
SHAGREEN	SHIFTIER	SHOULDN'T	SICKENED	SIMPLISM
SHAKABLE	SHIFTILY	SHOUTING	SICKENER	SINCIPUT
SHAKEOUT	SHIFTING	SHOVELED	SICKLIER	SINECURE
SHAKE-UPS	SHIFT KEY	SHOVELER	SICKNESS	SINFONIA
SHAKIEST	SHILLING	SHOWBOAT	SICKROOM	SINFULLY
SHALLOON	SHIMMERY	SHOWCASE	SIDEARMS	SINGABLE
SHALLOTS	SHIN BONE	SHOWDOWN	SIDEBAND	SINGEING
SHALLOWS	SHINDIGS	SHOWERED	SIDECARS	SINGLETS
SHAMABLE	SHINGLER	SHOWGIRL	SIDE DISH	SINGLING
SHAMBLED	SHINGLES	SHOWIEST	SIDEKICK	SINGSONG
SHAMBLES	SHINIEST	SHOWINGS	SIDELINE	SINGULAR
SHAMEFUL	SHINNIED	SHOW-OFFS	SIDELONG	SINISTER
SHAMMIES	SHINNING	SHOWROOM	SIDEREAL	SINKABLE
SHAMMING	SHIPABLE	SHRAPNEL	SIDERITE	SINKHOLE
SHAMPOOS	SHIPLOAD	SHREDDED	SIDESHOW	SINN FEIN
SHAMROCK	SHIPMATE	SHREDDER	SIDESLIP	SINOLOGY
SHANDIES	SHIPMENT	SHREWDER	SIDESMAN	SINUSOID
SHANGHAI	SHIPPERS	SHREWDLY	SIDESTEP	SIPHONAL
SHANTIES	SHIPPING	SHREWISH	SIDEWALK	SIPHONED
SHANTUNG	SHIPWORM	SHRIEKISH	SIDEWALL	SIRENIAN
SHAPABLE	SHIPYARD	SHRIEKED	SIDEWAYS	SIRLOINS
SHARABLE	SHIRKERS	SHRIEKER	SIFTINGS	SIROCCOS
SHARE-OUT	SHIRKING	SHRIEVAL	SIGHTINGS	SISSIEST
SHARP END	SHIRRING	SHRILLER	SIGHTING	SISSYISH
SHARPEST	SHIRTIER	SHRIMPER	SIGHTSEE	SISTERLY
SHARPISH	SHIRTING	SHRINKER	SIGNALED	SISTROID
SHARP-SET	SHIVERED	SHROUDED	SIGNALLY	SITARIST
SHAVABLE	SHIVERER	SHRUGGED	SIGNINGS	SIT-DOWNS
SHAVINGS	SHIZUOKA	SHRUNKEN	SIGNORAS	SITOLOGY
SHEADING	SHOCKERS	SHUCKING	SIGNPOST	SITTINGS
SHEARING	SHOCKING	SHUDDERS	SILASTIC	SITUATED
SHEATHED	SHODDIER	SHUDDERY	SILENCED	SITZMARK
SHEBEENS	SHODDILY	SHUFFLED	SILENCER	SIX-PACKS
SHEDABLE	SHOEBILL	SHUFFLER	SILENCES	SIXPENCE
SHEDDING	SHOEHORN	SHUFFLES	SILENTLY	SIXPENNY
SHEEPDIP	SHOELACE	SHUNNING	SILICATE	SIXTEENS
SHEEPDOG	SHOETREE	SHUNTERS	SILICIDE	SIXTIETH
SHEEPISH	SHOLAPUR	SHUNTING	SILICIFY	SIZEABLE
SHEEREST	SHOOTERS	SHUSHING	SILICONE	SIZZLERS
SHEERING	SHOOTING	SHUTDOWN	SILKIEST	SIZZLING
SHEETING	SHOOT-OUT	SHUTTERS	SILKWORM	SKELETAL
SHEIKDOM	SHOPGIRL	SHUTTING	SILLABUB	SKELETON
SHELDUCK	SHOPLIFT	SHUTTLED	SILLIEST	SKEPTICS
SHELLING	SHOPPERS	SHUTTLES	SILOXANE	SKEPTISM
SHELTERS	SHOPPING	SHYSTERS	SILURIAN	SKETCHED
SHELVING	SHOPTALK	SIANGTAN	SILVERED	SKETCHER
SHENYANG	SHORTAGE	SIBERIAN	SIVERER	SKETCHES
SHEPHERD	SHORT CUT	SIBILANT	SIMMERED	SKEWBACK
SHERATON	SHORT-DAY	SIBILATE	SIMONIAC	SKEWBALD

SKEWERED	SLEAZILY	SLOVAKIA	SMUGGEST	SNOTTIER
SKIDDING	SLEDDING	SLOVENIA	SMUGGLER	SNOWBALL
SKIDPANS	SLEDGING	SLOVENLY	SMUGNESS	SNOWBIRD
SKIJORER	SLEEKEST	SLOWDOWN	SMUTTIER	SNOWDROP
SKI JUMPS	SLEEKING	SLOWNESS	SMUTTILY	SNOWFALL
SKI LIFTS	SLEEPERS	SLOWWORM	SNACK BAR	SNOWIEST
SKILLETS	SLEEPIER	SLUDGIER	SNACKING	SNOWLINE
SKIMMERS	SLEEPILY	SLUGGARD	SNAFFLED	SNOWSHED
SKIMMING	SLEEPING	SLUGGING	SNAFFLES	SNOWSHOE
SKIMPIER	SLEETING	SLUGGISH	SNAGGING	SNUBBING
SKIMPILY	SLEEVING	SLUICING	SNAPBACK	SNUFFBOX
SKIMPING	SLEIGHER	SLUMMING	SNAPPERS	SNUFFERS
SKIN-DEEP	SLICKERS	SLUMPING	SNAPPIER	SNUFFING
SKIN-DIVE	SLICKEST	SLURPING	SNAPPILY	SNUFFLED
SKINHEAD	SLICKING	SLURRING	SNAPPING	SNUFFLER
SKINLESS	SLIDABLE	SLUSHIER	SNAPPISH	SNUFFLES
SKINNIER	SLIGHTED	SLUTTISH	SNAPSHOT	SNUGGERY
SKINNING	SLIGHTER	SMACKERS	SNARLING	SNUGGLED
SKIPJACK	SLIGHTLY	SMACKING	SNARL-UPS	SNUGNESS
SKI PLANE	SLIMIEST	SMALL ADS	SNATCHED	SO-AND-SOS
SKI POLES	SLIMMERS	SMALLEST	SNATCHER	SOAPBARK
SKIPPERS	SLIMMEST	SMALL FRY	SNATCHES	SOAPIEST
SKIPPING	SLIMNESS	SMALLISH	SNAZZIER	SOAPLESS
SKIRMISH	SLINGING	SMALL POX	SNAZZILY	SOAPSUDS
SKIRTING	SLINKIER	SMALLITE	SNEAKERS	SOAPWORT
SKITTISH	SLINKILY	SMARMIER	SNEAKILY	SOBERING
SKITTLES	SLINKING	SMARTEST	SNEAKING	SOBRIETY
SKIVVIED	SLIPCASE	SMARTING	SNEERING	SOB STORY
SKIVVIES	SLIPKNOT	SMASHIERS	SNEEZING	SO-CALLED
SKULKING	SLIPPAGE	SMASHING	SNICKERS	SOCIABLE
SKULLCAP	SLIPPERS	SMASH-UPS	SNIFFLED	SOCIABLY
SKYDIVER	SLIPPERY	SMEARING	SNIFFLER	SOCIALLY
SKYLARKS	SLIPPIER	SMELLIER	SNIFFLES	SOCIETAL
SKYLIGHT	SLIPPING	SMELLING	SNIFTERS	SOCRATIC
SKYLINES	SLIPROAD	SMELTING	SNIGGERS	SODALITE
SKYWARDS	SLIPSHOD	SMIRCHED	SNIGGLER	SODAMIDE
SLACKEST	SLIPWAYS	SMIRCHER	SNIPPETS	SODAMITE
SLACKING	SLITHERY	SMIRKING	SNIPPILY	SOFTBALL
SLAGGING	SLITTING	SMITHERY	SNIPPING	SOFTCOPY
SLAGHEAP	SLIVERER	SMITHIES	SNITCHED	SOFTENED
SLAKABLE	SLOBBERY	SMOCKING	SNITCHES	SOFTNER
SLANDERS	SLOE-EYED	SMOKABLE	SNIVELED	SOFTNESS
SLANGING	SLOGGERS	SMOKIEST	SNIVELLY	SOFT SELL
SLANTING	SLOGGING	SMOLENSK	SNOBBERY	SOFT SOAP
SLAP-BANG	SLOPPIER	SMOOCHED	SNOBBISH	SOFT SPOT
SLAPDASH	SLOPPILY	SMOOTHED	SNOGGING	SOFTWARE
SLAPPING	SLOPPING	SMOOTHEN	SNOOPERS	SOFTWOOD
SLASHING	SLOPWORK	SMOOTHER	SNOOPING	SOGGIEST
SLATTERN	SLOSHING	SMOOTHIE	SNOOTIER	SOJOURNS
SLAVERED	SLOTHFUL	SMOOTHLY	SNOOTILY	SOLACING
SLAVERER	SLOTTING	SMOTHERY	SNOOZING	SOLANDER
SLAVONIA	SLOUCHED	SMOULDER	SNORKELS	SOLARIUM
SLAVONIC	SLOUCHER	SMUDGILY	SNORTERS	SOLARIZE
SLEAZIER	SLOUGHED	SMUDGING	SNORTING	SOLDERED

SOLDERER	SORORATE	SPECKLED	SPLENDID	SPRUCING
SOLDIERS	SORORITY	SPECKLES	SPLENIAL	SPRYNESS
SOLDIERY	SORPTION	SPECTATE	SPLENIUS	SPUNKIER
SOLECISM	SORRIEST	SPECTRAL	SPLICERS	SPUNKILY
SOLECIST	SORROWED	SPECTRES	SPLICING	SPURIOUS
SOLEMNLY	SORROWER	SPECTRUM	SPLINTER	SPURNING
SOLENOID	SORTABLE	SPECULAR	SPLIT END	SPURTING
SOLIDAGO	SOUCHONG	SPECULUM	SPLIT PEA	SPUTTERS
SOLIDARY	SOUFFLES	SPEECHES	SPLITTER	SPYGLASS
SOLIDIFY	SOUGHING	SPEEDIER	SPLODGES	SQUABBLE
SOLIDITY	SOULLESS	SPEEDILY	SPLOSHED	SQUAD CAR
SOLIHULL	SOUNDBOX	SPEEDING	SPLOSHES	SQUADRON
SOLINGEN	SOUNDING	SPEEDWAY	SPLURGED	SQUALENE
SOLITARY	SOURDINE	SPELAEAN	SPLURGES	SQUALLED
SOLITUDE	SOURNESS	SPELLING	SPLUTTER	SQUALLER
SOLOISTS	SOURPUSS	SPENDERS	SPOILAGE	SQUAMATE
SOLONETZ	SOUTACHE	SPENDING	SPOILERS	SQUAMOUS
SOLSTICE	SOUTHERN	SPERMARY	SPOILING	SQUANDER
SOLUTION	SOUTHING	SPERMINE	SPOILATE	SQUARELY
SOLVABLE	SOUTHPAW	SPERMOUS	SPONDAIC	SQUAREST
SOLVENCY	SOUVENIR	SPHAGNUM	SPONDEES	SQUARING
SOLVENTS	SOWBREAD	SPHENOID	SPONGERS	SQUARISH
SOMALIAN	SOYA BEAN	SPHERICS	SPONGIER	SQUASHED
SOMBRELY	SOY SAUCE	SPHEROID	SPONGILY	SQUASHER
SOMBRERO	SPACE-AGE	SPHERULE	SPONGING	SQUASHES
SOMBROUS	SPACE-BAR	SPHINXES	SPONSION	SQUATTED
SOMEBODY	SPACEMAN	SPHYGMIC	SPONSORS	SQUATTER
SOMERSET	SPACEMEN	SPICCATO	SPOOKIER	SQUARKE
SOMETIME	SPACIOUS	SPICIEST	SPOOKILY	SQUARKER
SOMEWHAT	SPANDREL	SPICULUM	SPOOKING	SQUEAKED
SONANTAL	SPANGLED	SPIKELET	SPOOKISH	SQUEAKER
SONATINA	SPANGLES	SPIKIEST	SPOON-FED	SQUEALED
SONGBIRD	SPANIARD	SPILLAGE	SPOONFUL	SQUEALER
SONGBOOK	SPANIELS	SPILLING	SPORTIER	SQUELCHY
SONGSTER	SPANKING	SPILLWAY	SPORTILY	SQUEEZED
SON-IN-LAW	SPARKLED	SPINDLES	SPORTING	SQUEEZER
SONOBUOY	SPARKLER	SPINIFEX	SPOT-WELD	SQUEEZES
SORORANT	SPARKLES	SPINNERS	SPOUTERS	SQUIGGLE
SONORITY	SPARLING	SPINNEYS	SPOUTING	SQUIGGLY
SONOROUS	SPARRING	SPINNING	SPRAINED	SQUINTED
SOOTHING	SPARROWS	SPIN-OFFS	SPRAWLED	SQUINTER
SOOTHSAY	SPARSELY	SPINSTER	SPRAWLER	SQUIRMED
SOOTIEST	SPARSEST	SPIRACLE	SPRAYERS	SQUIRMER
SOPHISMS	SPASTICS	SPIRALED	SPRAY GUN	SQUIRREL
SOPHISTS	SPATTERS	SPIRITED	SPRAYING	SQUIRTED
SOPRANOS	SPATULAR	SPITEFUL	SPREADER	SQUIRTER
SORBITOL	SPAWNING	SPITFIRE	SPRIGGER	SQUISHED
SORBONNE	SPEAKERS	SPITTING	SPRINGER	SRI LANKA
SORCERER	SPEAKING	SPITTOON	SPRINKLE	SRINAGAR
SORDIDLY	SPEARING	SPLASHED	SPRINTED	STABBERS
SOREDIUM	SPECIALS	SPLASHER	SPRINTER	STABBING
SORENESS	SPECIFIC	SPLATTED	SPROCKET	STABLING
SORICINE	SPECIMEN	SPLATTER	SPROUTED	STACCATO
SOROCABA	SPECIOUS	SPLAYING	SPRUCELY	STACKING

STADIUMS	STARVING	STICKFUL	STONE AGE	STRINDER
STAFFING	STAR WARS	STICKIER	STONEFLY	STRIPIER
STAFFMAN	STARWORT	STICKILY	STONIEST	STRIPPED
STAGGARD	STASHING	STICKING	STOOPING	STRIPPER
STAGGERS	STATABLE	STICKLER	STOP COCK	STROBILA
STAGINGS	STATICAL	STICKPIN	STOPGAPS	STROKING
STAGNANT	STATIONS	STICK-UPS	STOPOVER	STROLLED
STAGNATE	STATUARY	STIFFEST	STOPPAGE	STROLLER
STAINING	STATURES	STIFLING	STOPPERS	STRONGER
STAIRWAY	STATUSES	STIGMATA	STOPPING	STRONGLY
STALKERS	STATUES	STILBENE	STORABLE	STROPHES
STALKILY	STAYSAIL	STILBITE	STOREYED	STROPHIC
STALKING	STEADIES	STILETTO	STORMIER	STRUDELS
STALLING	STEADIER	STILLEST	STORMILY	STRUGGLE
STALLION	STEADILY	STILLING	STORMING	STRUMMED
STALWART	STEALING	STIMULUS	STOUTEST	STRUMMER
STAMFORD	STEALTHY	STINGERS	STOWAWAY	STRUMPET
STAMINAL	STEAMERS	STINGIER	STRADDLE	STRUNG-UP
STAMMERS	STEAMIER	STINGILY	STRAFING	STRUTTED
STAMPEDE	STEAMILY	STINGING	STRAGGLE	STRUTTER
STAMPING	STEAMING	STINGRAY	STAGGILY	STUBBIER
STANCHED	STEAPSIN	STINKERS	STRAIGHT	STRUBBILY
STANCHER	STEARATE	STINKING	STRAINED	STRUBBING
STANDARD	STEATITE	STINTING	STRAINER	STRUBBLED
STANDBYS	STEELIER	STIPENDS	STRAITEN	STUBBORN
STANDING	STEEPEST	STIPPLED	STRABDED	STUCCOED
STAND-INS	STEEPING	STIPPLER	STRANGER	STUDBOOK
STANDISH	STEEPLES	STIPULAR	STRANGLE	STUDDING
SYANNARY	STEERAGE	STIRRERS	STRAPPED	STUDENTS
STANNITE	STEERING	STIRRING	STRATEGY	STUDIOUS
STANNOUS	STEINBOK	STIRRUPS	STRATIFY	STUDWORK
STANZAIC	STELLATE	STITCHED	STRAW MAN	STUDYING
STAPELIA	STELLIFY	STITCHER	STRAW MEN	STUFFIER
STAPLERS	STELLITE	STITCHES	STRAYING	STUFFING
STAPLING	STEMHEAD	STOCKADE	STREAKED	STULTIFY
STARCHED	STEMMING	STOCKCAR	STREAKER	STUMBLED
STARCHER	STENCHES	STOCKIER	STREAMED	STUMBLER
STARCHES	STENCILS	STOCKILY	STREAMER	STUMBLES
STAR DUST	STEN GUNS	STOCKING	STRENGTH	STUMPIER
STAR FISH	STENOSIS	STOCKIST	STRESSED	STUMPING
STARGAZE	STENOTIC	STOCKMAN	STRESSES	STUNNERS
STARKERS	STEPPING	STOCKMEN	STRETCHY	STUNNING
STARKEST	STEPWISE	STOCKPOT	STREUSEL	STUNTING
STARLESS	STERIGMA	STOCKTON	STREWING	STUNT MAN
STARLIKE	STERLING	STODGIER	STRIATED	STUNT MEN
STARLING	STERNEST	STODGILY	STRICKEN	STUPIDER
STARRIER	STERNSON	STOICISM	STRICKLE	STUPIDLY
STARRILY	STERNUMS	STOLIDLY	STRICTER	STURDIER
STARRING	STERNWAY	STOMACHS	STRICTLY	STURDILY
STAR SIGN	STEROIDS	STOMACHY	STRIDDEN	STURGEON
STARTERS	STETSONS	STOMATAL	STRIDENT	STUTTERS
STARTING	STEWARDS	STOMATIC	STRIGOSE	STYLISTS
STARTLED	STIBNITE	STOMPING	STRIKERS	STYLIZED
STARTLER	STICKERS	STONABLE	STRIKING	STYLIZER

STYLUSES	SUFFUSED	SUPINATE	SWANNING	SYLLABUS
STYMYING	SUGARING	SUPINELY	SWANSKIN	SYLVATIC
STYPTICS	SUICIDAL	SUPPLANT	SWANSONG	SYMBIONT
SUBACUTE	SUICIDES	SUPPLEST	SWAP MEET	SYMBOLIC
SUBAGENT	SUITABLE	SUPPLIED	SWAPPING	SYMMETRY
SUBCLASS	SUITABLY	SUPPLIER	SWARMING	SYMPATHY
SUBDUING	SUITCASE	SUPPLIES	SWASTIKA	SYMPHILE
SUBERIZE	SULKIEST	SUPPORTS	SWATCHES	SYMPHONY
SUBEROSE	SULLENER	SUPPOSED	SWATHING	SYMPOSIA
SUBFLOOR	SULLENLY	SUPPOSER	SWATTERS	SYMPTOMS
SUBGENUS	SULLYING	SUPPRESS	SWATTING	SYNAPSIS
SUBGROUP	SULPHATE	SUPREMOS	SWAYABLE	SYNAPTIC
SUBHUMAN	SULPHIDE	SURABAYA	SWAY-BACK	SYNARCHY
SUBJECTS	SULPHITE	SURCOATS	SWEARING	SYNCARPY
SUBLEASE	SULPHONE	SUREFIRE	SWEATBOX	SYNCLINE
SUBMERGE	SULTANAS	SURENESS	SWEATERS	SYNCOPIC
SUBORDER	SULTANIC	SURETIES	SWEATIER	SYNDESIS
SUBORNED	SULTRIER	SURFABLE	SWEATILY	SYNDETIC
SUBORNER	SULTRILY	SURFACER	SWEATING	SYNDETON
SUBOXIDE	SUMATRAN	SURFACES	SWEEPERS	SYNDICAL
SUBPLOTS	SUMMERED	SURFBIRD	SWEEPING	SYNDROME
SUBPOENA	SUMMITAL	SURFBOAT	SWEETEST	SYNERGIC
SUBSERVE	SUMMONED	SURFLIKE	SWEETIES	SYNGAMIC
SUBSHRUB	SUM TOTAL	SURGEONS	SWEET PEA	SYNONYMS
SUBSIDED	SUNBAKED	SURGICAL	SWEETSOP	SYNONYMY
SUBSIDER	SUNBATHE	SURICATE	SWELLING	SYNOPSES
SUBSOLAR	SUNBEAMS	SURLIEST	SWERVING	SYNOPTIC
SUBSONIC	SUNBELTS	SURMISED	SWIFTEST	SYNOVIAL
SUBSTAGE	SUNBURNT	SURMISER	SWIGGING	SYNTONIC
SUBSUMED	SUNDERED	SURMISES	SWILLING	SYPHILIS
SUBTITLE	SUNDIALS	SURMOUNT	SWIMMERS	SYPHONED
SUBTLEST	SUNDRIES	SURNAMES	SWIMMING	SYRACUSE
SUBTLETY	SUNGLASS	SURPLICE	SWIMSUIT	SYRINGED
SUBTONIC	SUNLAMPS	SURPRINT	SWINDLED	SYRINGES
SUNTOTAL	SUNLIGHT	SURPRISE	SWINDLER	SYSTEMIC
SUBTRACT	SUNNIEST	SURROUND	SWINDLES	SYSTOLIC
SUBULATE	SUNRISES	SURVEYED	SWINEPOX	
SUBURBAN	SUNROOFS	SURVEYOR	SWINGERS	
SUBURBIA	SUNSHADE	SURVIVAL	SWINGING	**9 LETTERS**
SUCCINCT	SUNSHINE	SURVIVED	SWIRLING	SABADILLA
SUCCINIC	SUNSHINY	SURVIVOR	SWISHEST	SABOTAGED
SUCCUBUS	SUNSPOTS	SUSPECTS	SWISHING	SABOTEURS
SUCHLIKE	SUNTRAPS	SUSPENSE	SWITCHED	SACCHARIN
SUCKLING	SUN VISOR	SUTURING	SWITCHER	SACCULATE
SUDANESE	SUNWARDS	SUZERAIN	SWITCHES	SACKCLOTH
SUDATORY	SUPERBLY	SVALBARD	SWIVELED	SACK RACES
SUDDENLY	SUPEREGO	SWABBING	SWOONING	SACRAMENT
SUFFERED	SUPERFIX	SWADDLED	SWOOPING	SACRARIUM
SUFFERER	SUPERIOR	SWALLOWS	SWOTTING	SACRED COW
SUFFICED	SUPERMAN	SWAMPING	SYBARITE	SACRIFICE
SUFFICER	SUPERMEN	SWANKIER	SYCAMINE	SACRILEGE
SUFFIXIAL	SUPERNAL	SWANKILY	SYCAMORE	SACRISTAN
SUFFIXES	SUPERSEX	SWANKING	SYCONIUM	SADDENING
SUFFRAGE	SUPERTAX	SWANNERY	SYLLABLE	SADDLEBAG

SADDLEBOW	SANDINESS	SATURNISM	SCHIZOPOD	SCRAMMING
SAFEGUARD	SANDPAPER	SAUCEPANS	SCHLEPPED	SCRAPBOOK
SAFE HOUSE	SANDPIPER	SAUCINESS	SCHLIERIC	SCRAP HEAP
SAFELIGHT	SANDSHOES	SAUNTERED	SCHMALTZY	SCRAPINGS
SAFETY NET	SANDSTONE	SAUNTERER	SCHNAUZER	SCRAPPIER
SAFETY PIN	SANDSTORM	SAUTERNES	SCHNITZEL	SCRAPPILY
SAFFLOWER	SANDTRAPS	SAVOURING	SCHOLARLY	SCRAPPING
SAFRANIZE	SANFORIZE	SAXIFRAGE	SCHOLIAST	SCRATCHED
SAGAGIOUS	SANGFROID	SAXOPHONE	SCHOOLBOY	SCRATCHER
SAGEBRUSH	SANITARIA	SCABBARDS	SCHOOLING	SCRATCHES
SAGITTATE	SANITIZED	SCABBIEST	SCHOONERS	SCRAWLING
SAILBOARDS	SAN MARINO	SCABIETIC	SCIENTISM	SCRAWNIER
SAILCLOTH	SANS SERIF	SCAFFOLDS	SCIENTIST	SCRAWNILY
SAILPLANE	SANTA CRUZ	SCAGLIOLA	SCIMITARS	SCREAMING
SAINTHOOD	SANTANDER	SCALAWAGS	SCINTILLA	SCREECHED
SAINTLILY	SANTONICA	SCALDFISH	SCIOMANCY	SCREECHER
SAINT PAUL	SAPHENOUS	SCALDINESS	SCIRRHOID	SCREECHES
SAINT'S DAY	SAPIENTLY	SCALLIONS	SCIRRHOUS	SCREENING
SALAAMING	SAPODILLA	SCALLOPED	SCLERITIC	SCREWBALL
SALACIOUS	SAPPHIRES	SCALLOPER	SCLERITIS	SCREWIEST
SALAD DAYS	SAPRAEMIA	SCALLYWAG	SCLEROSAL	SCREW TOPS
SALAMANCA	SAPRAEMIC	SCAMPERED	SCLEROSED	SCRIBBLED
SALERATUS	SAPROLITE	SCAMPERER	SCLEROSES	SCRIBBLER
SALEROOMS	SAPROZOIC	SCANITEST	SCLEROSIS	SCRIBBLES
SALESGIRL	SAPSUCKER	SCANTLING	SCLEROTIC	SCRIMMAGE
SALESROOM	SARABANDS	SCANTNESS	SCOLDABLE	SCRIMPILY
SALES SLIP	SARACENIC	SCAPA FLOW	SCOLDINGS	SCRIMPING
SALES TALK	SARCASTIC	SCAPEGOAT	SCOLECITE	SCRIMSHAW
SALIMETER	SARCOCARP	SCAPHOPOD	SCOLIOSIS	SCRIPTURE
SALAMETRY	SARDINIAN	SCAPOLITE	SCOLIOTIC	SCROLLING
SALISBURY	SARGASSUM	SCARABOID	SCOLLOPED	SCROUNGED
SALIVATED	SARTORIAL	SCARECROW	SCOMBROID	SCROUNGER
SALMONOID	SARTORIUS	SCARFSKIN	SCOPOLINE	SCRUBBERS
SALOON BAR	SASHAYING	SCARIFIED	SCOPULATE	SCRUBBIER
SALPIFORM	SASKATOON	SCARIFIER	SCORBUTIC	SCRUBBING
SALTINESS	SASSAFRAS	SCARINGLY	SCORCHERS	SCRUBLAND
SALTLICKS	SASSENACH	SCARPERED	SCORCHING	SCRUFFIER
SALTPETRE	SATANINSTS	SCATOLOGY	SCORECARD	SCRUMHALF
SALTWATER	SATELLITE	SCATTERED	SCORIFIER	SCRUMMAGE
SALTWORKS	SATIATING	SCATTERER	SCORPIOID	SCRUMPING
SALVAGING	SATIATION	SCATTIEST	SCORPIONS	SCRUNCHED
SALVATION	SATINWOOD	SCAVENGED	SCOTCH EGG	SCRUPLING
SAMARITAN	SATIRICAL	SACVENGER	SCOTCHING	SCUFFLING
SAMARKAND	SATIRIZED	SCENARIOS	SCOUNDREL	SCULLIONS
SANATORIA	SATIRIZER	SCENARIST	SCOURGING	SCULPTORS
SANCTIONS	SATISFIED	SCENTLESS	SCOURINGS	SCULPTURE
SANCTUARY	SATISFIER	SCEPTICAL	SCRABBLED	SCUPPERED
SANDALLED	SATURABLE	SCHEDULAR	SCRABBLER	SCURRYING
SANDBANKS	SATURATED	SCHEDULED	SCRAGGIER	SCUTATION
SANDBLAST	SATURATER	SCHEDULES	SCRAGGILY	SCUTCHEON
SAND-BLIND	SATURDAYS	SCHEELITE	SCRAGGING	SCUTELLAR
SANDBOXES	SATURNIAN	SCHEMATIC	SCRAMBLED	SCUTELLUM
SAND DUNES	SATURNIID	SCHILLING	SCRAMBLER	SCUTIFORM
SAND FLIES	SATURINE	SCHISTOSE	SCRAMBLES	SCUTTLING

633

SEABOARDS	SELACHIAN	SEPTEMBER	SFORZANDO	SHIFT KEYS
SEA BREEZE	SELECTING	SEPTENARY	SGRAFFITO	SHIFTLESS
SEA CHANGE	SELECTION	SEPTICITY	SHABBIEST	SHILLINGS
SEAFARING	SELECTIVE	SEPTUPLET	SHACKLING	SHIMMERING
SEAFRONTS	SELECTORS	SEPULCHRE	SHADINESS	SHINBONES
SEAHORSES	SELENIOUS	SEPULTURE	SHADOW-BOX	SHININESS
SEAL-POINT	SELF-ABUSE	SEQUACITY	SHADOWIER	SHINNYING
SEALYHAMS	SELF-DOUBT	SEQUENCER	SHADOWING	SHIPBOARD
SEAMINESS	SELF-DRIVE	SEQUENCES	SHAGGIEST	SHIPMATES
SEAPLANES	SELFISHLY	SEQUESTER	SHAKEDOWN	SHIPMENTS
SEA POWERS	SELLOTAPE	SERAGLIOS	SHAKEOUTS	SHIPOWNER
SEARCHING	SEMANTICS	SERENADED	SHAKINESS	SHIPSHAPE
SEASCAPES	SEMAPHORE	SERENADER	SHALLOWED	SHIPWRECK
SEASHELLS	SEMBLANCE	SERENADES	SHALLOWER	SHIPYARDS
SEASONING	SEMESTERS	SERGEANCY	SHALLOWLY	SHIRTIEST
SEAT BELTS	SEMESTRAL	SERGEANTS	SHAMANISM	SHIRTTAIL
SEA URCHIN	SEMI-BANTU	SERIALISM	SHAMANIST	SHITTIEST
SEAWORTHY	SEMIBREVE	SERIALIZE	SHAMATEUR	SHIVERING
SEBACEOUS	SEMICOLON	SERICIOUS	SHAMBLING	SHOCKABLE
SECATEURS	SEMIFINAL	SERIGRAPH	SHAMBOLIC	SHODDIEST
SECESSION	SEMIFLUID	SERIOUSLY	SHAMELESS	SHOEHORNS
SECLUDING	SEMILUNAR	SERMONIZE	SHAMPOOED	SHOELACES
SECLUSION	SEMIOTICS	SEROLOGIC	SHAMPOOER	SHOEMAKER
SECLUSIVE	SEMIRIGID	SEROTINAL	SHANGRI-LA	SHOESHINE
SECONDARY	SEMISOLID	SEROTONIN	SHAPELESS	SHOETREES
SECONDERS	SEMITONES	SERRATION	SHAPELIER	SHOOTINGS
SECONDING	SEMITONIC	SERRIFORM	SHARECROP	SHOOT-OUTS
SECRETARY	SEMIVOCAL	SERRULATE	SHARKSKIN	SHOP FLOOR
SECRETING	SEMIVOWEL	SERVERIES	SHARPENED	SHORELESS
SECRETION	SENESCENT	SERVICING	SHARPENER	SHORELINE
SECRETIVE	SENESCHAL	SERVIETTE	SHARP-EYED	SHORTAGES
SECRETORY	SENIORITY	SERVILELY	SHARPNESS	SHORTCAKE
SECTARIAN	SENORITAS	SERVILITY	SHATTERED	SHORT CUTS
SECTILILTY	SENSATION	SERVITORS	SHATTERER	SHORTENED
SECTIONAL	SENSELESS	SERVITUDE	SHEARLING	SHORTENER
SECTIONED	SENSILLUM	SESSILITY	SHEATFISH	SHORTFALL
SECTORIAL	SENSITIVE	SESSIONAL	SHEATHING	SHORTHAND
SECUNDINE	SENSITIZE	SETACEOUS	SHEEPDIPS	SHORT-HAUL
SECURABLE	SENSORIUM	SET PIECES	SHEEPDOGS	SHORTHORN
SEDATIVES	SENTENCED	SETSQUARE	SHEEPFOLD	SHORT LIST
SEDENTARY	SENTENCES	SET THEORY	SHEEPSKIN	SHORTNESS
SEDIMENTS	SENITENCE	SETTLINGS	SHEEPWALK	SHORT-TERM
SEDITIOUS	SENTIMENT	SEVENFOLD	SHEERLEGS	SHORT TIME
SEDUCIBLE	SENTINELS	SEVENTEEN	SHEERNESS	SHORT WAVE
SEDUCTION	SENTRY BOX	SEVENTIES	SHEIKHDOM	SHOULDERS
SEDUCTIVE	SEPARABLE	SEVERABLE	SHELDUCKS	SHOVELING
SEEDINESS	SEPARABLY	SEVERALLY	SHELF LIFE	SHOVELLED
SEEDLINGS	SEPARATED	SEVERANCE	SHELLFIRE	SHOWCASES
SEEMINGLY	SEPARATES	SEX APPEAL	SHELLFISH	SHOWDOWNS
SEESAWING	SEPARATOR	SEXENNIAL	SHELTERED	SHOWERING
SEGMENTAL	SEPHARDIC	SEX OBJECTS	SHELTERER	SHOWGIRLS
SEGMENTED	SEPIOLITE	SEXORGANS	SHEPHERDS	SHOWINESS
SEGREGATE	SPEPTARIAN	SEXTUPLET	SHEILDING	SHOWPIECE
SEIGNEURS	SEPTARIUM	SEXUALITY	SHIFTIEST	SHOWPLACE

SHOWROOMS	SIGNALING	SIX-FOOTER	SLAPHAPPY	SMARMIEST
SHOW TRIALS	SIGNALIZE	SIXPENCES	SLAPSTICK	SMARTENED
SHREDDERS	SIGNALLED	SIXTEENMO	SLATINESS	SMASHABLE
SHREDDING	SIGNALLER	SIXTEENTH	SLATTERNS	SMATTERER
SHREWDEST	SIGNALMAN	SIXTH FORM	SLAUGHTER	SMEAR TEST
SHREIKING	SIGNALMEN	SIXTIETHS	SLAVERING	SMELLIEST
SHRILLEST	SIGNATORY	SIZARSHIP	SLAVISHLY	SMILLINGLY
SHRINKAGE	SIGNATURE	SKAGERRAK	SLAVONIAN	SMIRCHING
SHRINKING	SIGNBOARD	SKEDDADLE	SLEAZIEST	SMOKELESS
SHRIVELED	SIGNIFIED	SKELETONS	SLEEKNESS	SMOLDERED
SHROUDING	SIGNIFIER	SKEPTICAL	SLEEPIEST	SMOOCHING
SHRUBBERY	SIGNORINA	SKETCHERS	SLEEPLESS	SMOOTHEST
SHRUGGING	SIGNPOSTS	SKETCHIER	SLEEPWALK	SMOOTHIES
SHUDDERED	SIKKIMESE	SKETCHILY	SLICEABLE	SMOOTHING
SHUFBOARD	SILENCERS	SKETCHING	SLICKNESS	SMOTHERED
SHUFFLERS	SILENCING	SKETCHPAD	SLIDE RULE	SMUGGLERS
SHUFFLING	SILICATES	SKEWBALL	SLIGHTEST	SMUGGLING
SHUNNABLE	SILICEOUS	SKEWERING	SLIGHTING	SMUTTIEST
SHUTDOWNS	SILICOSIS	SKEW-WHIFF	SLIMNESS	SNACK BARS
SHUTTERED	SILIQUOSE	SKAISCOPE	SLINGSHOT	SNAFFLING
SHUTTERING	SILKALINE	SKIASCOPY	SLINKIEST	SNAKE BITE
SIBILANCE	SILKINESS	SKIDPROOF	SLIPCASES	SNAKEROOT
SIBILANTS	SILKWORMS	SKIJORING	SLIPKNOTS	SNAKESKIN
SIBYLLINE	SILTATION	SKILFULLY	SLIPNOOSE	SNAKINESS
SICCATIVE	SILVERING	SKIMMINGS	SLIPPAGES	SNAPPABLE
SICKENING	SIMAROUBA	SKIMPIEST	SLIPPIEST	SNAPPIEST
SICK LEAVE	SIMILARLY	SKIN-DIVED	SLIP ROADS	SNAPSHOTS
SICKLIEST	SIMMERING	SKIN DIVER	SLIPSHEET	SNARE DRUM
SICKROOMS	SIMPATICO	SKIN FLICK	SLITHERED	SNARINGLY
SIC PASSIM	SIMPERING	SKINFLINT	SLIVOVITZ	SNATCHING
SIDEBOARD	SIMPLETON	SKIN GRAFT	SLOBBERED	SNAZZIEST
SIDE-DRESS	SIMULACRA	SKINHEADS	SLOBBERER	SNEAKIEST
SIDE ISSUE	SIMULATED	SKINNIEST	SLOPINGLY	SNIGGERED
SIDEKICKS	SIMULATOR	SKIN-TIGHT	SLOPPIEST	SNIPEFISH
SIDELIGHT	SINCERELY	SKI PLANES	SLOUCH HAT	SNITCHING
SIDELINED	SINCERITY	SKIPPERED	SLOUCHILY	SNIVELING
SIDELINES	SINECURES	SKITTERED	SLOUCHING	SNIVELLED
SIDE ORDER	SINGAPORE	SKIVVYING	SLOUGHING	SNIVELLER
SIDERITIC	SINGINGLY	SKULLCAPS	SLOVAKIAN	SNOOKERED
SIDEROSIS	SINGLETON	SKYDIVERS	SLOVENIAN	SNOOTIEST
SIDEROTIC	SINGSONGS	SKYDIVING	SLOWCOACH	SNOTTIEST
SIDESHOWS	SINGULARS	SKYJACKED	SLOWDOWNS	SNOWBALL
SIDESLIPS	SINGULTUS	SKYJACKER	SLOWWORMS	SNOWBERRY
SIDESTEPS	SINHALESE	SKYLARKED	SLUDGIEST	SNOW-BLIND
SIDESWIPE	SINISTRAL	SKYLARKER	SLUGGARDS	SNOWBLINK
SIDETRACK	SINOLOGUE	SKYLIGHTS	SLUMBERED	SNOWBOUND
SIDEWARDS	SINOUSITY	SKYROCKET	SLUMBERER	SNOWDONIA
SIGHTABLE	SINUSITIS	SKYWRITER	SLUSH FUND	SNOWDRIFT
SIGHTINGS	SIPHONAGE	SLACKENED	SLUSHIEST	SNOWDROPS
SIGHTLESS	SIPHONING	SLACKNESS	SMALL ARMS	SNOWFALLS
SIGHT-READ	SISYPHEAN	SLAGHEAPS	SMALL BEER	SNOWFIELD
SIGHTSEER	SITUATING	SLANDERED	SMALLNESS	SNOWFLAKE
SIGMATION	SITUATION	SLANDERER	SMALL TALK	SNOWINESS
SIGNAL BOX	SITZKREIG	SLANTWISE	SMALL-TIME	SNOWSHOER

SNOWSHOES	SOLSTICES	SOUVENIRS	SPEEDWELL	SPLENETIC
SNOWSTORM	SOLUTIONS	SOU'WESTER	SPELLABLE	SPLENITIS
SNOW-WHITE	SOLUTREAN	SOVEREIGN	SPELLBIND	SPLINTERS
SNUB-NOSED	SOLVATION	SOVIETISM	SPELLINGS	SPLINTERY
SNUFFLING	SOMBREROS	SOVIETIST	SPELUNKER	SPLIT ENDS
SNUGGLING	SOMEPLACE	SOVIETIZE	SPENDABLE	SPLIT PEAS
SOAKINGLY	SOMETHING	SOYA BEANS	SPERMATIC	SPLIT RING
SOAPBERRY	SOMETIMES	SPACEBAND	SPERMATID	SPLITTING
SOAPBOXES	SOMEWHERE	SPACED OUT	SPHAGNOUS	SPLOSHING
SOAPINESS	SOMMELIER	SPACELESS	SPHAGNUMS	SPLURGING
SOAP OPERA	SOMNOLENT	SPACEPORT	SPHENODON	SPLUTTERS
SOAPSTONE	SONGBIRDS	SPACESHIP	SPHERICAL	SPODUMENE
SOAPSUDSY	SONGBOOKS	SPACESUIT	SPHEROIDS	SPOKEN FOR
SOARINGLY	SONGSTERS	SPACE-TIME	SPHERULAR	SPOKESMAN
SOBBINGLY	SONIC BOOM	SPACEWALK	SPHINCTER	SPONGE BAG
SOBERNESS	SONNETEER	SPADEFISH	SPHYGMOID	SPONGIEST
SOBRIQUET	SON-OF-A GUN	SPADEWORK	SPICINESS	SPONSORED
SOCIALISM	SONS-IN-LAW	SPAGHETTI	SPICULATE	SPOOKIEST
SOCIALIST	SOOTINESS	SPANGLING	SPIDERMAN	SPOONBILL
SOCIALITE	SOPHISTER	SPANIARDS	SPIDERWEB	SPOON-FED
SOCIALITY	SOPHISTIC	SPANKINGS	SPIKENARD	SPOONFULS
SOCIALIZE	SOPHISTRY	SPARENESS	SPIKE-RUSH	SPOONSFUL
SOCIETIES	SOPHOMORE	SPARE PART	SPIKINESS	SPOROCYTE
SOCIOLOGY	SOPORIFIC	SPARERIBS	SPILLIKIN	SPOROGONY
SOCIOPATH	SOPPINESS	SPARE TYRE	SPILLWAYS	SPOROZOAN
SODA WATER	SOPRANINO	SPARINGLY	SPINDLER	SPORTIEST
SODOMITES	SORCERERS	SPARKLERS	SPIN-DRIED	SPORTSCAR
SOFTENING	SORCERESS	SPARKLING	SPINDRIFT	SPORTSMAN
SOSFT FRUIT	SORCEROUS	SPARK PLUG	SPIN-DRYER	SPORTSMEN
SOFT-PEDAL	SORRINESS	SPASMODIC	SPINELESS	SPORULATE
SOFT SPOTS	SORRROWFUL	SPATIALLY	SPININESS	SPOT CHECK
SOFTWOODS	SORROWING	SPATTERED	SPINNAKER	SPOTLIGHT
SOGGINESS	SORTILEGE	SPATULATE	SPINNERET	SPOTTABLE
SOJOURNED	SORTITION	SPEAKABLE	SPINOSITY	SPOTTIEST
SOLAR CELL	SOSTENUTO	SPEAKEASY	SPINSTERS	SPRAINING
SOLARIUMS	SOTTO VOCE	SPEARHEAD	SPINULOSE	SPRAWLING
SOLAR YEAR	SOUBRETTE	SPEARMINT	SPIRALING	SPRAY GUNS
SOLDERING	SOULFULLY	SPEARWORT	SPIRALLED	SPREADING
SOLDIERED	SOUL MUSIC	SPECIALLY	SPIRILLAR	SPRIGHTLY
SOLDIERLY	SOUNDABLE	SPECIALTY	SPIRILLUM	SPRINGBOK
SOLOCISMS	SOUNDINGS	SPECIFICS	SPIRITING	SPRINGIER
SOLEMNIFY	SOUNDLESS	SPECIFIED	SPIRITOSO	SPRINGING
SOLEMNITY	SOUNDNESS	SPECIFIER	SPIRITUAL	SPRINKLED
SOLEMNIZE	SOUNDPOST	SPECIMENS	SPIROGYRA	SPRINKLER
SOLFATARA	SOUP SPOON	SPECTACLE	SPITFIRES	SPRINKLES
SOLFERINO	SOUR CREAM	SPECTATED	SPITTOONS	SPRINTING
SOLICITED	SOUTHDOWN	SPECULATE	SPLASHIER	SPRITSALL
SOLIDNESS	SOUTHEAST	SPEECH DAY	SPLASHILY	SPROCKETS
SOLILOQUY	SOUTHERLY	SPEECHIFY	SPLASHING	SPROUTING
SOLIPSISM	SOUTHPAWS	SPEEDBOAT	SPLATTING	SPUNKIEST
SOLIPSIST	SOUTH POLE	SPEEDIEST	SPLAYFOOT	SPUTTERED
SOLITAIRE	SOUTHWARD	SPEEDSTER	SPLEENFUL	SPUTTERER
SOLONCHAK	SOUTHWARK	SPEED TRAP	SPLEENISH	SQUABBLED
SOLOTHURN	SOUTHWEST	SPEEDWAYS	SPLENDOUR	SQUABBLER

SQUABBLES	STAINLESS	STAVROPOL	STINKHORN	STORYBOOK
SQUAD CARS	STAIRCASE	ST BERNARD	STINKWEED	STORY LINE
SQUADRONS	STAIRHEAD	STEADFAST	STINKWOOD	STOUTNESS
SQUALIDLY	STAIRWELL	STEADIEST	STIPIFORM	STOVEPIPE
SQUALLIER	STALEMATE	STEADYING	STIPITATE	STOWAWAYS
SQUALLING	STALINISM	STEAMBOAT	STIPPLING	STRADDLED
SQUAMOSAL	STALINIST	STEAMED-UP	STIPULATE	STRADDLER
SQUARE ONE	STALL-FEED	STEAMIEST	STIR-FRIED	STRAGGLED
SQUARROSE	STALLIONS	STEAM IRON	STIRRABLE	STRAGGLER
SQUASHIER	STALWARTS	STEAMSHIP	STICHING	STRAIGHTS
SQUASHILY	STAMINATE	STEATITIC	STOCKADED	STRAINERS
SQUASHING	STAMINODE	STEEL BAND	STOCKADES	STRAINING
SQUATNESS	STAMINODY	STEELHEAD	STOCKCARS	STRANGELY
SQUATTERS	STAMMERED	STEELIEST	STOCK CUBES	STRANGLES
SQUATTEST	STAMMERER	STEELWORK	STOCKFISH	STRANGURY
SQUATTING	STAMPEDED	STEELYARD	STOCKHOLM	STRAPLESS
SQUAWKERS	STAMPEDER	STEEPENED	STOCKIEST	STRAPPING
SQUAWKING	STAMPEDES	STEEPNESS	STOCKINET	STRATAGEM
SQUEAKERS	STANCHING	STEERABLE	STOCKINGS	STRATEGIC
SQUEAKIER	STANCHION	STEERSMAN	STOCKISTS	STRAW POLL
SQUEAKING	STANDARDS	STEERSMEN	STOCKPILE	STREAKERS
SQUEALERS	STANDPIPE	STELLULAR	STOCKPOTS	STREAKIER
SQUEALING	STAPEDIAL	STENCILED	STOCKROOM	STREAKILY
SQUEAMISH	STAR-APPLE	STENOTYPE	STOCKYARD	STREAKING
SQUEEGEES	STARBOARD	STENOTYPY	STODGIEST	STREAMERS
SQUEEZING	STARCHIER	STEPCHILD	STOICALLY	STREAMING
SQUELCHED	STARCHILY	STERADIAN	STOKEHOLD	STREETCAR
SQUELCHER	STARCHING	STERILANT	STOKEHOLE	STRENGTHS
SQUIDGIER	STARGAZER	STERILITY	STOLIDITY	STRENUOUS
SQUIFFIER	STARKNESS	STERILIZE	STOMACHED	STRESSFUL
SQUIGGLER	STARLIGHT	STERNMOST	STOMACHIC	STRESSING
SQUIGGLES	STARLINGS	STERNNESS	STONECHAT	STRETCHED
SQUINTING	STARRIEST	STERNPOST	STONE-COLD	STRETCHER
SQUIRMING	STAR SIGNS	STEVEDORE	STONECROP	STRETCHES
SQUIRRELS	STARTLING	STICKIEST	STONE-DEAD	STRIATION
SQUIRTERS	STATEHOOD	STICKLERS	STONE-DEAF	STRICTEST
SQUIRTING	STATELESS	STICKPINS	STONEFISH	STRICTURE
SQUISHIER	STATEMENT	STICKSEED	STONELESS	STRIDENCE
SQUISHING	STATEROOM	STICKWEED	STONE-LILY	STRIDENCY
STABILITY	STATESIDE	STICKY END	STONEWALL	STRIKE PAR
STABILIZE	STATESMAN	STIFFENED	STONEWARE	STRINGENT
STABLE BOY	STATESMEN	STIFFENER	STONEWORK	STRINGIER
STAGE DOOR	STATIONED	STIFFNESS	STONEWORT	STRINGILY
STAGEHAND	STATIONER	STIGMATIC	STONINESS	STRINGING
STAGE NAME	STATISTIC	STILETTOS	STOPCOCKS	STRIP CLUB
STAGGERED	STATOCYST	STILLBORN	STOPLIGHT	STRIPIEST
STAGGERER	STATOLITH	STILL LIFE	STOPOVERS	STRIPLING
STAGHOUND	STATUETTE	STILLNESS	STOPPABLE	STRIPPERS
STAGINESS	STATUS QUO	STILTEDLY	STOPPAGES	STRIPPING
STAGNANCY	STATUTORY	STIMULANT	STOPPERED	STROBILUS
STAGNATED	STAUNCHED	STIMULATE	STOP PRESS	STROLLERS
STAG PARTY	STAUNCHER	STINGIEST	STOPWATCH	STROLLING
STAIDNESS	STAUNCHLY	STINGRAYS	STOREROOM	STROMATIC
STAINABLE	STAVANGER	STINK-BOMB	STORMIEST	STRONGARM

STRONGBOX	SUBEDITED	SUCCESSOR	SUNSHADES	SURVIVING
STRONGEST	SUBEDITOR	SUCCINATE	SUNSTROKE	SURVIVORS
STRONGYLE	SUBFAMILY	SUCCOURED	SUNTANNED	SUSPECTED
STRONTIAN	SUBJACENT	SUCCOURER	SUN VISORS	SUSPECTOR
STRONTIUM	SUBJECTED	SUCCULENT	SUPERABLE	SUSPENDED
STROPPER	SUBJOINED	SUCCUMBED	SUPERCOOL	SUSPENSOR
STRUCTURE	SUBJUGATE	SUCCUMBER	SUPEREGOS	SUSPICION
STRUGGLED	SUBLEASED	SUCKLINGS	SUPERFINE	SUSTAINED
STRUGGLER	SUBLEASES	SUCTIONAL	SUPERHEAT	SUSTAINER
STRUGGLES	SUBLESSEE	SUCTORIAL	SUPERIORS	SUSSURANT
STRUMATIC	SUBLESSOR	SUDORIFIC	SUPERNOVA	SUSSURATE
STRUMMING	SUBLIMATE	SUFFERERS	SUPERPOSE	SUZERIANS
STRUMPETS	SUBLIMELY	SUFFERING	SUPERSEDE	SWADDLING
STRUNG-OUT	SUBLIMITY	SUFFICING	SUPERSTAR	SWAGGERED
STRUTTING	SUBLUNARY	SUFFIXION	SUPERVENE	SWAGGERER
STRYCHNIC	SUBMARINE	SUFFOCATE	SUPERVISE	SWAHILIAN
STUBBIEST	SUBMENTAL	SUFFRAGAN	SUPINATOR	SWALLOWED
STUDBOOKS	SUBMERGED	SUFFUSING	SUPPERADD	SWALLOWER
STUDHORSE	SUBMITTAL	SUFFUSION	SUPPLIANT	SWAMPLAND
STUFFIEST	SUBMITTED	SUFFUSIVE	SUPPLIERS	SWANKIEST
STUMBLING	SUBMITTER	SUGAR BEET	SUPPLYING	SWAN'S DOWN
STUMPIEST	SUBMUCOSA	SUGARCANE	SUPPORTED	SWANSONG
STUPIFIED	SUBNORMAL	SUGGESTED	SUPPORTER	SWAP MEETS
STUPIFIER	SUBORNING	SUGGESTER	SUPPOSING	SWARTHIER
STUPIDEST	SUBPHYLAR	SUITCASES	SUPPURATE	SWARTHILY
STUPOROUS	SUBPHYLUM	SULCATION	SUPREMACY	SWASITIKAS
STURDIEST	SUBPOENAS	SULKINESS	SUPREMELY	SWATHABLE
STURGEONS	SUBREGION	SULLENEST	SUPREMITY	SWAYINGLY
STUTTERED	SUBROGATE	SULLIABLE	SURAKARTA	SWAZILAND
STUTTERER	SUBSCRIBE	SULPHATES	SURCHARGE	SWEARWORD
STUTTGART	SUBSCRIPT	SULPHIDES	SURCINGLE	SWEATBAND
STYLEBOOK	SUBSIDIES	SULPHITIC	SURE THING	SWEATIEST
STYLELESS	SUBSIDING	SULPHURET	SURFACING	SWEATSHOP
STYLIFORM	SUBSIDIZE	SULPHURYL	SURFBOARD	SWEEPBACK
STYLISHLY	SUBSISTED	SULTANATE	SURFEITED	SWEEPINGS
STYLISTIC	SUBSISTER	SULTRIEST	SURFEITER	SWEET CORN
STYLIZING	SUBSOCIAL	SUMMARIES	SURFPERCH	SWEETENER
STYLOBATE	SUBSOILER	SUMMARILY	SURGEONCY	SWEETMEAT
STYLOLITE	SUBSTANCE	SUMMARIZE	SURGERIES	SWEETNESS
STYLOPIZE	SUBSTRATA	SUMMATION	SURLINESS	SWEET PEAS
STYPTICAL	SUBSTRATE	SUMMERING	SURMISING	SWEET TALK
STYROFOAM	SUBSUMING	SUMMING-UP	SURPASSED	SWELLFISH
SUABILITY	SUBTENANT	SUMMONING	SURPLICES	SWELLINGS
SUAVENESS	SUBTENDED	SUMMONSED	SURPLUSES	SWELTERED
SUBALPINE	SUBTILIZE	SUMMONSES	SURPRISED	SWEPT-BACK
SUBALTERN	SUBTITLED	SUMPTUARY	SURPRISER	SWEPTWING
SUBARCTIC	SUBTITLES	SUMPTUOUS	SURPRISES	SWERVABLE
SUBATOMIC	SUBTOTALS	SUNBATHED	SURRENDER	SWIFTNESS
SUBCLIMAX	SUBVERTED	SUNBATHER	SURROGACY	SWIMMABLE
SUBCORTEX	SUBVERTER	SUNBURNED	SURROGATE	SWIMMERET
SUBDEACON	SUCCEEDED	SUNDERING	SURROUNDS	SWINDLERS
SUBDIVIDE	SUCCEEDER	SUNFLOWER	SURVEYING	SWINDLING
SUBDUABLE	SUCCENTOR	SUN LOUNGE	SURVEYORS	SWINEHERD
SUBDUEDLY	SUCCESSES	SUNNINESS	SURVIVALS	SWINGEING

SWING-WING
SWINISHLY
SWITCHING
SWIVELING
SWIVELLED
SWORDBILL
SWORDFISH
SWORDPLAY
SWORDSMAN
SWORDSMEN
SWORDTAIL
SYBARITES
SYBARITIC
SYCAMORES
SYCOPHANT
SYKTYVKAR
SYLLABARY
SYLLABIFY
SYLLABISM
SYLLABLES
SYLLABUBS
SYLLEPSIS
SYLLEPTIC
SYLLOGISM
SYLLOGIZE
SYLPHLIKE
SYLVANITE
SYMBIOSIS
SYMBIOTIC
SYMBOLISM
SYMBOLIST
SYMBOLIZE
SYMBOLOGY
SYMPATHIN
SYMPATRIC
SYMPHONIC
SYMPHYSIS
SYMPODIAL
SYMPODIUM
SYMPOSAIC
SYMPOSIUM
SYNAGOGUE
SYNALEPHA
SYNCLINAL
SYNCOPATE
SYNCRETIC
SYNCYTIUM
SYNDACTYL
SYNDICATE
SYNDROMES
SYNDROMIC
SYNECTICS
SYNERESIS
SYNERGISM

SYNERGIST
SYNIZESIS
SYNKARYON
SYNOEKETE
SYNONYMIC
SYNOVITIC
SYNOVITIS
SYNTACTIC
SYNTHESES
SYNTHESIS
SYNTHETIC
SYPHERING
SYPHILOID
SYPHILOMA
SYPHONING
SYRINGEAL
SYRINGING
SYSTALTIC

10 LETTERS
SABBATICAL
SABOTAGING
SABULOSITY
SACCHARASE
SACCHARATE
SACCHARIDE
SACCHARIFY
SACCHARINE
SACCHAROID
SACCHAROSE
SACERDOTAL
SACRAMENTO
SACRAMENTS
SACRED COWS
SACREDNESS
SACRIFICED
SACRIFICER
SACRIFICES
SACRILEGES
SACRISTANS
SACRISTIES
SACROILIAC
SACROSANCT
SADDLEBACK
SADDLEBAGS
SADDLEBILL
SADDLERIES
SADDLE-SORE
SADDLETREE
SAFARI PARK
SAFEGUARDS
SAFE HOUSES
SAFETY BELT

SAFETY LAMP
SAFETY NETS
SAFETY PINS
SAHARANPUR
SAILBOARDS
SAILOR SUIT
SAILPLANES
SAINT LOUIS
SAINT'S DAYS
SALABILITY
SALAD CREAM
SALA MANDER
SALES CLERK
SALES GIRLS
SALES PITCH
SALES SLIPS
SALES TAXES
SALES WOMAN
SALICORNIA
SALICYLATE
SALIFEROUS
SALIFIABLE
SALIMETRIC
SALIVATING
SALIVATION
SALLOWNESS
SALMANAZAR
SALMONELLA
SALOON BARS
SALPINGIAN
SALTARELLO
SALTCELLAR
SALTIGRADE
SALT SHAKER
SALUBRIOUS
SALUTARILY
SALUTATION
SALUTATORY
SALVERFORM
SAMARITANS
SAMARSKITE
SAN ANTONIO
SANATORIUM
SANCTIFIED
SANCTIFIER
SANCTIMONY
SANCTIONED
SANCTIONER
SANCTITUDE
SANDALWOOD
SANDBAGGED
SANDBAGGER
SANDCASTLE
SANDERLING

SANDGROUSE
SANDPIPERS
SANDSTORMS
SANDWICHED
SANDWICHES
SANFORIZED
SANGUINARY
SANGUINELY
SANITARIAN
SANITARILY
SANITARIUM
SANITATION
SANITIZING
SANSKRITIC
SANTA CLARA
SANTA CLAUS
SANTA MARIA
SANTA MARTA
SAPIENTIAL
SAPONIFIER
SAPPANWOOD
SAPPHIRINE
SAPROGENIC
SAPROLITIC
SAPROPELIC
SAPROPHYTE
SARCOPHAGI
SARMENTOSE
SARRACENIA
SASH WINDOW
SATELLITES
SATINWOODS
SATIRIZING
SATISFYING
SATURATING
SATURATION
SATURNALIA
SATYRIASIS
SAUNTERING
SAUSAGE DOG
SAVAGENESS
SAVAGERIES
SAXICOLOUS
SAXOPHONES
SAXOPHONIC
SCABBINESS
SCAFFOLDER
SCALEBOARD
SCALLOPING
SCALLYWAGS
SCALOPPINE
SCALPELLIC
SCAMPERING
SCANDALIZE

SCANDALOUS	SCORPAENID	SCYPHIFORM	SELF-ACTION
SCANSORIAL	SCORPIONIC	SCYPHOZOAN	SELF-DENIAL
SCANTINESS	SCOTCH EGGS	SEA ANEMONE	SELF-ESTEEM
SCAPEGOATS	SCOTCH MIST	SEA BREEZES	SELF-FEEDER
SCAPEGRACE	SCOTCH TAPE	SEA CAPTAIN	SELFLESSLY
SCARABAEID	SCOTTICISM	SEA CHANGES	SELF-REGARD
SCARABAEUS	SCOUNDRELS	SEALED-BEAM	SELF-SEEKER
SCARCEMENT	SCOWLINGLY	SEALING WAX	SELF-STYLED
SCARCENESS	SCRAGGIEST	SEAMANLIKE	SELF-WILLED
SCARCITIES	SCRAMBLING	SEAMANSHIP	SELL-BY DATE
SCARECROWS	SCRAPBOOKS	SEAMSTRESS	SELLOTAPED
SCARDEY CAT	SCRAP HEAPS	SEARCHABLE	SEMAPHORES
SCARIFYING	SCRAP PAPER	SEASONABLE	SEMAPHORIC
SCARLATINA	SCRAPPIEST	SEASONABLY	SEMATOLOGY
SCARPERING	SCRATCHIER	SEASONEDLY	SEMIANNUAL
SCATHINGLY	SCRATCHILY	SEASONINGS	SEMIBREVES
SCATTER-GUN	SCRATCHING	SEA URCHINS	SEMICIRCLE
SCATTERING	SCRATCHPAD	SEBIFEROUS	SEMICOLONS
SCATTINESS	SCRAWNIEST	SEBORRHOEA	SEMIFINALS
SCAVENGERS	SCREECHING	SECOND BEST	SEMINALITY
SCAVENGING	SCREENABLE	SECOND-HAND	SEMINARIAL
SCENICALLY	SCREENINGS	SECONDMENT	SEMINARIAN
SCEPTICISM	SCREENPLAY	SECOND-RATE	SEMINARIES
SCHAERBEEK	SCREEN TEST	SECOND WIND	SEMIQUAVER
SCHEDULING	SCREWBALLS	SECRETAIRE	SEMIVOWELS
SCHEMATISM	SCRIBBLERS	SECRETIONS	SEMIWEEKLY
SCHEMATIZE	SCRIBBLING	SECTIONING	SENATORIAL
SCHEMINGLY	SCRIMMAGED	SECULARISM	SENEGALESE
SCHERZANDO	SCRIMMAGER	SECULARIST	SENEGAMBIA
SCHIPPERKE	SCRIMMAGES	SECULARITY	SENESCENCE
SCHISMATIC	SCRIPTURAL	SECULARIZE	SENSATIONS
SCHIZOCARP	SCROFULOUS	SECUNDINES	SENSE ORGAN
SCHIZOGONY	SCROLLWORK	SECUREMENT	SENSIBILIA
SCHLEPPING	SCROUNGERS	SECURENESS	SENSITIZED
SCHNITZELS	SCROUNGING	SECURITIES	SENSITIZER
SCHOLASTIC	SCRUBBIEST	SEDAN CHAIR	SENSUALISM
SCHOOLGIRL	SCRUFFIEST	SEDATENESS	SENSUALIST
SCHOOLMARM	SCRUMMAGED	SEDUCINGLY	SENSUALITY
SCHOOLMATE	SCRUMMAGER	SEDUCTRESS	SENSUOUSLY
SCHOOLWORK	SCRUMMAGES	SEDULOUSLY	SENTENCING
SCIENTIFIC	SCRUNCHING	SEEMLINESS	SENTENTIAL
SCIENTISTS	SCRUPULOUS	SEERSUCKER	SENTIMENTS
SCILLONIAN	SCRUTINEER	SEETHINGLY	SEPARATELY
SCIOMANCER	SCRUTINIES	SEE-THROUGH	SEPARATING
SCIOMANTIC	SCRUTINIZE	SEGMENTARY	SEPARATION
SCLEROTIUM	SCULLERIES	SEGMENTING	SEPARATISM
SCLEROTOMY	SCULPTRESS	SEGREGABLE	SEPARATIST
SCOFFINGLY	SCULPTURAL	SEGREGATED	SEPARATIVE
SCOLDINGLY	SCULPTURES	SEGREGATOR	SEPARATORS
SCOLLOPING	SCUPPERING	SEISMOLOGY	SEPARATRIX
SCOREBOARD	SCURRILITY	SELECTIONS	SEPTENNIAL
SCORECARDS	SCURRILOUS	SELECTNESS	SEPTICALLY
SCORNFULLY	SCURVINESS	SELENOLOGY	SEPTICIDAL
SCORNINGLY	SCUTELLATE	SELF-ACTING	SEPTIC TANK

SEPTILLION	SHAPELIEST	SHORT-RANGE	SIGNPOSTED
SEPULCHRAL	SHARPENERS	SHORT STORY	SILENTNESS
SEPULCHRES	SHARPENING	SHOULDERED	SILHOUETTE
SEQUACIOUS	SHATTERING	SHOVELHEAD	SILICULOSE
SEQUENCING	SHEARWATER	SHOVELLING	SILK SCREEN
SEQUENTIAL	SHEATHBILL	SHOVENOSE	SILVERFISH
SEQUESTRAL	SHEATHINGS	SHOW JUMPER	SILVERWARE
SEQUESTRUM	SHEEPISHLY	SHOWPIECES	SILVERWEED
SERENADING	SHEEP'S EYES	SHOW TRIALS	SIMFEROPOL
SERENENESS	SHEEPSHANK	SHREVEPORT	SIMILARITY
SERIALIZED	SHEEPSHEAD	SHREWDNESS	SIMILITUDE
SERIGRAPHY	SHEEPSKINS	SHREWSBURY	SIMONICAL
SERIOCOMIC	SHEET MUSIC	SHRIEVALTY	SIMPLE LIFE
SERMONICAL	SHEIKDOMS	SHRILLNESS	SIMPLENESS
SERMONIZED	SHELF LIVES	SHRINKABLE	SIMPLETONS
SERMONIZER	SHELLPROOF	SHRINK-WRAP	SIMPLICITY
SEROLOGIST	SHELLSHOCK	SHRIVELING	SIMPLIFIED
SERPENTINE	SHELTERING	SHRIVELLED	SIMPLIFIER
SERVICEMAN	SHENANIGAN	SHROUD-LAID	SIMPLISTIC
SERVICEMEN	SHERPHERDED	SHROVETIDE	SIMULACRUM
SERVIETTES	SHERARDIZE	SHUDDERING	SIMULATING
SERVOMOTOR	SHIBBOLETH	SHUNT-WOUND	SIMULATION
SETSQUARES	SHIFTINESS	SHUTTERING	SIMULATIVE
SETTLEABLE	SHIFTINGLY	SIALAGOGIC	SIMULATORS
SETTLEMENT	SHIFT STICK	SIALAGOGUE	SINCIPITAL
SEVASTOPOL	SHILLELAGH	SIAMESE CAT	SINECURISM
SEVENTIETH	SHIMMERING	SIBILIATION	SINECURIST
SEVERANCES	SHIPBOARDS	SICKLEBILL	SINE QUA NON
SEVERENESS	SHIPMASTER	SICKLINESS	SINEWINESS
SEVERITIES	SHIP-RIGGED	SICKNESSES	SINFULNESS
SEXAGENARY	SHIPWRECKS	SICK PARADE	SINGHALESE
SEXAGISIMA	SHIPWRIGHT	SIDEBOARDS	SINGLE FILE
SEXIVALENT	SHIRE HORSE	SIDE DISHES	SINGLENESS
SEX OBJECTS	SHIRT FRONT	SIDE EFFECT	SINGLETONS
SEXOLOGIST	SHIRT TAILS	SIDE ISSUES	SINGULARLY
SEXPARTITE	SHISH KEBAB	SIDELIGHTS	SINISTROUS
SEXTILLION	SHOALINESS	SIDELINING	SINN FEINER
SEXTUPLETS	SHOCKINGLY	SIDE ORDERS	SINOLOGIST
SEYCHELLES	SHOCKPROOF	SIDEROLITE	SINUSOIDAL
SHABBINESS	SHODDINESS	SIDEROSTAT	SISTERHOOD
SHADOWIEST	SHOEMAKING	SIDESADDLE	SITOSTEROL
SHAGGED OUT	SHOESHINES	SIDE STREET	SITUATIONS
SHAGGINESS	SHOESTRING	SIDESTROKE	SIX-FOOTERS
SHAKEDOWNS	SHOPKEEPER	SIDESWIPED	SIX-SHOOTER
SHALLOWEST	SHOPLIFTED	SIDESWIPER	SIXTEENTHS
SHALLOWING	SHOPLIFTER	SIDESWIPES	SIXTH FORMS
SHAMANISMS	SHOPSOILED	SIDETRACKS	SIXTH SENSE
SHAMANISTS	SHOPWALKER	SIDEWINDER	SKATEBOARD
SHAMATEURS	SHOREWARDS	SIGHTSEERS	SKEDADDLED
SHAMEFACED	SHORTBREAD	SIGNALIZED	SKETCHABLE
SHAMEFULLY	SHORTENING	SIGNALLING	SKETCHBOOK
SHAMPOOING	SHORTFALLS	SIGNATURES	SKETCHIEST
SHANGHAIED	SHORT LISTS	SIGNIFYING	SKETCHPADS
SHANTYTOWN	SHORT-LIVED	SIGNORINAS	SKIMPINESS

SKIN DIVERS	SLUSHINESS	SNOW-CAPPED	SOLITARIES
SKIN DIVING	SMALL HOURS	SNOWDRIFTS	SOLITARILY
SKIN FLICKS	SMALL PRINT	SNOWFIELDS	SOLSTITIAL
SKINFLINTS	SMALL-SCALE	SNOWFLAKES	SOLUBILITY
SKIN GRAFTS	SMALL TIMER	SNOWMOBILE	SOLUBILIZE
SKINNINESS	SMARAGDITE	SNOWPLOUGH	SOLVOLYSIS
SKIPPERING	SMART ALECK	SNOWSTORMS	SOMALILAND
SKIRMISHED	SMARTENING	SNUBBINGLY	SOMATOLOGY
SKIRMISHER	SMARTINGLY	SNUFFINESS	SOMATOTYPE
SKIRMISHES	SMATTERING	SNUFFINGLY	SOMBRENESS
SKITTERING	SMEARINESS	SOAP BUBBLE	SOMERSAULT
SKITTISHLY	SMEAR TESTS	SOAP OPERAS	SOMNOLENCE
SKYJACKERS	SMELLINESS	SOBERINGLY	SONGSTRESS
SKYJACKING	SMIRKINGLY	SOBRIQUETS	SONGWRITER
SKYLARKNG	SMOKEHOUSE	SOB STORIES	SONIC BOOMS
SKYROCKETS	SMOKESTACK	SOCIALISTS	SONIFEROUS
SKYSCRAPER	SMOLDERING	SOCIALITES	SONOROUSLY
SKYWRITING	SMOOTHABLE	SOCIALIZED	SONS-OF-GUNS
SLACKENING	SMOOTHBORE	SOCIALIZER	SOOTHINGLY
SLANDERERS	SMOOTHNESS	SOCIALNESS	SOOTHSAYER
SLANDERING	SMOTHERING	SOCIAL WORK	SOPHOMORES
SLANDEROUS	SMOULDERED	SOCIOMETRY	SORDIDNESS
SLANGINESS	SMUDGINESS	SOCIOPATHY	SORORICIDE
SLANTINGLY	SMUTTINESS	SODDENNESS	SORORITIES
SLASHINGLY	SNAIL'S PACE	SOFT-BOILED	SOUBRIQUET
SLATTERNLY	SNAKEMOUTH	SOFT-FINNED	SOULLESSLY
SLAVE TRADE	SNAPDRAGON	SOFT FRUITS	SOUNDPROOF
SLAVOPHILE	SNAPPINESS	SOFT-HEADED	SOUNDTRACK
SLEAZINESS	SNAPPINGLY	SOFT OPTION	SOUP SPOONS
SLEEPYHEAD	SNAPPISHLY	SOFT PALATE	SOUR GRAPES
SLEEVELESS	SNARE DRUMS	SOFT-SOAPED	SOURPUSSES
SLENDERIZE	SNARLINGLY	SOFT-SPOKEN	SOUSAPHONE
SLIDE RULES	SNAZZINESS	SOJOURNERS	SOUTHBOUND
SLIGHTNESS	SNEAKINESS	SOJOURNING	SOUTHERNER
SLINGSHOTS	SNEAKINGLY	SOLAR CELLS	SOUTHWARDS
SLINKINESS	SNEAK THIEF	SOLAR PANEL	SOU'WESTERS
SLINKINGLY	SNEERINGLY	SOLAR YEARS	SOVEREIGNS
SLIPPINESS	SNEEZEWORT	SOLDERABLE	SPACECRAFT
SLIPPINGLY	SNICKERING	SOLDIERING	SPACE PROBE
SLIPSTREAM	SNIFFINGLY	SOLECISTIC	SPACESHIPS
SLITHERING	SNIGGERING	SOLEMNIZED	SPACESUITS
SLOBBERING	SNIPPINESS	SOLEMNIZER	SPACEWOMAN
SLOPPINESS	SNIVELLERS	SOLEMNNESS	SPACIOUSLY
SLOPWORKER	SNIVELLING	SOLENOIDAL	SPALLATION
SLLOTHFULLY	SNOBBISHLY	SOLFATARIC	SPARE PARTS
SLOUCH HATS	SNOOKERING	SOLICITING	SPARE TYRES
SLOW MOTION	SNOOTINESS	SOLICITORS	SPARK PLUGS
SLOW-WITTED	SNORKELLED	SOLICITOUS	SPARSENESS
SLUGGISHLY	SNORTINGLY	SOLICITUDE	SPARTANISM
SLUICEGATE	SNOTTINESS	SOLIDARITY	SPATCHCOCK
SLUMBERERS	SNORKELLED	SOLIDIFIED	SPATIALITY
SLUMBERING	SNORTINGLY	SOLIDIFIER	SPATTERING
SLUMBEROUS	SNOTTINESS	SOLID-STATE	SPEARHEADS
SLUSH FUNDS	SNOWBALLED	SOLITAIRES	SPECIALISM

SPECIALIST	SPLEENWORT	SQUAMULOSE	STARVATION
SPECIALITY	SPLENDIDLY	SQUANDERED	STARVELING
SPECIALIZE	SPLINTERED	SQUANDERER	STATECRAFT
SPECIATION	SPLIT-LEVEL	SQUARE KNOT	STATEMENTS
SPECIFYING	SPLIT RINGS	SQAURE MEAL	STATEROOMS
SPECIOSITY	SPLUTTERED	SQUARENESS	STATIONARY
SPECIOUSLY	SPLUTTERER	SQUARE ROOT	STATIONERS
SPECTACLES	SPOILSPORT	SQUASHIEST	STATIONERY
SPECTATING	SPOKESHAVE	SQUEAKIEST	STATIONING
SPECTATORS	SPOLIATION	SQUEEZABLE	STATISTICS
SPECULATED	SPONGE BAGS	SQUEEZEBOX	STATOBLAST
SPECULATOR	SPONGE CAKE	SQUELCHIER	STATOSCOPE
SPEECH DAYS	SPONGINESS	SQUELCHING	STATUESQUE
SPEECHLESS	SPONSORIAL	SQUETEAGUE	STATUETTES
SPEEDBOATS	SPONSORING	SQUIDGIEST	STATUTABLE
SPEEDINESS	SPOOKINESS	SQUIFFIEST	STATUTE LAW
SPEED LIMIT	SPOONERISM	SQUISHIEST	STAUNCHEST
SPEED TRAPS	SPORANGIAL	STABILIZER	STAUNCHING
SPELEOLOGY	SPORANGIUM	STABILIZED	STAUROLITE
SPELLBOUND	SPORORHORE	STABLE BOYS	STAVESACRE
SPELUNKING	SPOROPHYLL	STABLENESS	STAY-AT-HOME
SPERMACETI	SPOROPHYTE	STAFF NURSE	ST BERNARDS
SPERMATIUM	SPOROZOITE	STAGE COACH	STEADINESS
SPERMICIDE	SPORTINESS	STAGECRAFT	STEAKHOUSE
SPERM WHALE	SPORTINGLY	STAGE DOORS	STEALTHIER
SPERRYLITE	SPORTIVELY	STAGEHANDS	STEALTHILY
SPHALERITE	SPORTS CARS	STAGE NAMES	STEAMBOATS
SPHENOIDAL	SPORTSWEAR	STAGGERING	STEAM-CHEST
SPHERICITY	SPOT CHECKS	STAGNANTLY	STEAMINESS
SPHEROIDAL	SPOTLESSLY	STAGNATING	STEAM IRONS
SPHERULITE	SPOTLIGHTS	STAGNATION	STEAMSHIPS
SPHINCTERS	SPOTTINESS	STAIRCASES	STEAMTIGHT
SPICEBERRY	SPREADABLE	STAIRWELLS	STEEL BANDS
SPIDERWEBS	SPRINGBOKS	STALACTITE	STEELINESS
SPIDERWORT	SPRINGHAAS	STALAGMITE	STEELWORKS
SPINAL CORD	SPRINGHEAD	STALEMATED	STEEPENING
SPINDLIEST	SPRINGIEST	STALEMATES	STELLIFORM
SPIN-DRYING	SPRING ROLL	STALKINESS	STEM-WINDER
SPINESCENT	SPRINGTAIL	STALWARTLY	STENCILING
SPINNAKERS	SPRING TIDE	STAMMERERS	STENCILLED
SPIRACULAR	SPRINGTIME	STAMMERING	STENCILLER
SPIRALLING	SPRINGWOOD	STAMPEDING	STENOGRAPH
SPIRITEDLY	SPRINKLERS	STANCHABLE	STENOTYPIC
SPIRITLESS	SPRINKLING	STANCHIONS	STENTORIAN
SPIRITUALS	SPRUCENESS	STANDPIPES	STEPFATHER
SPIROGRAPH	SPUMESCENT	STANDPOINT	STEPMOTHER
SPIROMETER	SPUNKINESS	STANDSTILL	STEPPARENT
SPIROMETRY	SPURIOUSLY	STARCHIEST	STEPSISTER
SPITEFULLY	SPUTTERING	STARFISHES	STEREOBATE
SPLANCHNIC	SPYGLASSES	STARFLOWER	STEREOGRAM
SPLASHBACK	SQUABBLING	STARGAZERS	STEREOPSIS
SPLASHDOWN	SQUALIDITY	STARGAZING	STEREOTOMY
SPLASHIEST	SQUALLIEST	STARRINESS	STEREOTYPE
SPLATTERED	SQUAMATION	STARRY-EYED	STEREOTYPY

STERICALLY	STONE FRUIT	STRINGENCY	SUBJUGABLE
STERILIZED	STONE HENGE	STRINGENDO	SUBJUGATED
STERNWARDS	STONEMASON	STRINGHALT	SUBJUGATOR
STERTOROUS	STONY BROKE	STRINGIEST	SUBKINGDOM
STEVEDORES	STOOPINGLY	STRIP CLUBS	SUBLEASING
STEWARDESS	STOPPERING	STRIPLINGS	SUBLETTING
STICKINESS	STOREHOUSE	STRIPTEASE	SUBLIMABLE
STICK SHIFT	STOREROOMS	STRONGHOLD	SUBLIMATED
STICK TIGHT	STORKSBILL	STRONGNESS	SUBLIMATES
STICKY ENDS	STORMBOUND	STRONG ROOM	SUBLIMINAL
STIFFENERS	STORM CLOUD	STROPPIEST	SUBLINGUAL
STIFFENING	STORMINESS	STRUCTURAL	SUBMARINER
STIFLINGLY	STORMPROOF	STRUCTURED	SUBMARINES
STIGMATISM	STORY LINES	STRUGGLING	SUBMEDIANT
STIGMATIST	STRABISMAL	STRUTHIOUS	SUBMERGING
STIGMATIZE	STRABISMUS	STRYCHNINE	SUBMERSION
STILLBIRTH	STRADDLING	STUBBINESS	SUBMISSION
STILL LIFES	STRAIGHTEN	STUBBORNER	SUBMISSIVE
STIMULABLE	STRAIGHTER	STUBBORNLY	SUBMITTING
STIMULANTS	STRAITENED	STUDIOUSLY	SUBMONTANE
STIMULATED	STRAITNESS	STUFFINESS	SUBOCEANIC
STIMULATOR	STRAMONIUM	STUNNINGLY	SUBORBITAL
STINGINESS	STRANGLERS	STUPEFYING	SUBORDINAL
STINGINGLY	STRANGLING	STUPENDOUS	SUBPOENAED
STINKBOMBS	STRASBOURG	STUPIDNESS	SUBREPTION
STINKINGLY	STRATAGEMS	STURDINESS	SUBROUTINE
STINKSTONE	STRATEGICS	STUTTERING	SUBSCRIBED
STIPELLATE	STRATEGIES	STYLISTICS	SUBSCRIBER
STIPULABLE	STRATEGIST	STYLOGRAPH	SUBSECTION
STIPULATED	STRATIFIED	STYLOLITIC	SUBSEQUENT
STIPULATOR	STRATIFORM	STYPTICITY	SUBSIDENCE
STIR-FRYING	STRATOCRAT	SUBACETATE	SUBSIDIARY
STIRRINGLY	STRAWBERRY	SUBACIDITY	SUBSIDIZED
STIRRUP CUP	STRAWBOARD	SUBALTERNS	SUBSIDIZER
STITCHWORT	STRAW POLLS	SUBAQUATIC	SUBSISTENT
STOCHASTIC	STREAKIEST	SUBAQUEOUS	SUBSISTING
STOCKADING	STREAMLINE	SUBCALIBRE	SUBSPIECES
STOCK CUBES	STREETCARS	SUNCLAVIAN	SUBSTANCES
STOCKINESS	STREETWISE	SUBCOMPACT	SUBSTATION
STOCKPILED	STRELITZIA	SUBCULTURE	SUBSTITUTE
STOCKPILER	STRENGTHEN	SUBDIVIDED	SUBSTRATUM
STOCKPILES	STRESS MARK	SUBDIVIDER	SUBSUMABLE
STOCKROOMS	STRETCHERS	SUBDUCTION	SUBTANGENT
STOCK-STILL	STRETCHIER	SUBEDITING	SUBTENANCY
STOCKYARDS	STRETCHING	SUBEDITORS	SUBTENANTS
STODGINESS	STRIATIONS	SUBGENERIC	SUBTENDING
STOKEHOLDS	STRICTNESS	SUBGLACIAL	SUBTERFUGE
STOMACHING	STRICTURES	SUBHEADING	SUBTILIZER
STOMATITIC	STRIDENTLY	SUBJACENCY	SUBTITULAR
STOMATITIS	STRIDULATE	SUBJECTIFY	SUBTLENESS
STOMATOPOD	STRIDULOUS	SUBJECTING	SUBTLETIES
STOMODAEAL	STRIGIFORM	SUBJECTION	SUBTRACTED
STOMODAEUM	STRIKINGLY	SUBJECTIVE	SUBTRACTER
STONE-BLIND	STRING BEAN	SUBJOINING	SUBTRAHEND

SUBTROPICS	SUNFLOWERS	SURGICALLY	SWEET TOOTH
SUBTYPICAL	SUNGLASSES	SURJECTION	SWELTERING
SUBVENTION	SUN LOUNGES	SURJECTIVE	SWERVINGLY
SUBVERSION	SUPERBNESS	SURMISABLE	SWIMMINGLY
SUBVERSIVE	SUPERCARGO	SURMISEDLY	SWINEHERDS
SUBVERTING	SUPERCLASS	SURMOUNTED	SWINGINGLY
SUCCEEDING	SUPERDUPER	SURMOUNTER	SWIRLINGLY
SUCCESSFUL	SUPERFLUID	SURPASSING	SWISHINGLY
SUCCESSION	SUPERGIANT	SURPLUSAGE	SWISS CHARD
SUCCESSIVE	SUPERGRASS	SURPRISING	SWITCHABLE
SUCCESSORS	SUPERHUMAN	SURREALISM	SWITCHBACK
SUCCINCTLY	SUPERLUNAR	SURREALIST	SWITCHED-ON
SUCCOURING	SUPERNOVAS	SURRENDERS	SWITCHGEAR
SUCCULENCE	SUPERORDER	SURROGATES	SWIVELLING
SUCCULENTS	SUPEROXIDE	SURROUNDED	SWOONINGLY
SUCCUMBING	SUPERPOWER	SURVEYABLE	SWORDCRAFT
SUCCUSSION	SUPERSEDED	SURVIVABLE	SWORD DANCE
SUCCUSSIVE	SUPERSEDER	SUSCEPTIVE	SWORDSTICK
SUCKERFISH	SUPERSONIC	SUSPECTING	SYCOPHANTS
SUDDENNESS	SUPERSTARS	SUSPENDERS	SYLLABUSES
SUFFERABLE	SUPERTONIC	SUSPENDING	SYLLOGISMS
SUFFERANCE	SUPERVENED	SUSPENSION	SYLLOGIZER
SUFFERINGS	SUPERVISOR	SUSPENSIVE	SYLPHIDINE
SUFFICIENT	SUPINENESS	SUSPENSOID	SYLVESTRAL
SUFFOCATED	SUPPLANTED	SUSPENSORY	SYMBIONTIC
SUFFRAGISM	SUPPLANTER	SUSPICIONS	SYMBOLIZED
SUFFRAGIST	SUPPLEJACK	SUSPICIOUS	SYMMETRIZE
SUGAR DADDY	SUPPLEMENT	SUSTAINING	SYMPATHIES
SUGARINESS	SUPPLENESS	SUSTENANCE	SYMPATHIZE
SUGGESTING	SUPPLETION	SUSTENTION	SYMPHONIES
SUGGESTION	SUPPLETIVE	SUZERAINTY	SYMPHONIST
SUGGESTIVE	SUPPLETORY	SVERDLOVSK	SYMPHYSIAL
SUICIDALLY	SUPPLIABLE	SWAGGERERS	SYMPHYSTIC
SULLENNESS	SUPPLIANCE	SWAGGERING	SYMPOSIUMS
SULPHA DRUG	SUPPLIANTS	SWALLOWING	SYNAGOGUES
SULPHATION	SUPPLICANT	SKANKINESS	SYNCARPOUS
SULPHONATE	SUPPLICATE	SWAN-UPPING	SYNCHRONIC
SULPHURATE	SUPPORTERS	SWARTHIEST	SYNCLASTIC
SULPHURIZE	SUPPORTING	SWASHINGLY	SYNCOPATED
SULPHUROUS	SUPPORTIVE	SWEARINGLY	SYNCOPATOR
SULTANATES	SUPPOSABLE	SWEARWORDS	SYNCRETISM
SULTRINESS	SUPPOSEDLY	SWEATBANDS	SYNCRETIST
SUMMARIZED	SUPPRESSED	SWEAT GLAND	SYNCRETIZE
SUMMARIZER	SUPPRESSOR	SWEATINESS	SYNDICATED
SUMMATIONS	SUPPURATED	SWEATSHIRT	SYNDICATES
SUMMERTIME	SUPRARENAL	SWEATSHOPS	SYNDICSHIP
SUMMERWOOD	SURCHARGED	SWEEPINGLY	SYNECDOCHE
SUMMINGS-UP	SURCHARGER	SWEEPSTAKE	SYNECOLOGY
SUMMONABLE	SURCHARGES	SWEETBREAD	SYNERGETIC
SUMMONISING	SUREFOOTED	SWEETBRIER	SYNOECIOUS
SUNBATHERS	SURFACTANT	SWEETENERS	SYNONYMITY
SUNBATHING	SURFBOARDS	SWEETENING	SYNONYMIZE
SUNDAY BEST	SURFCASTER	SWEETHEART	SYNONYMOUS
SUNDOWNERS	SURFEITING	SWEETMEATS	SYNTACTICS

645

SYNTHESIST
SYNTHESIZE
SYNTHETISM
SYNTHETIST
SYPHILITIC
SYSTEMATIC
SYSTEMIZER

11 LETTERS
SABBATICALS
SACCULATION
SACREMANTAL
SACRIFICIAL
SACRIFICING
SACRILEGIST
SACROILIACS
SADDENINGLY
SADDLECLOTH
SAFARI PARKS
SAFEBREAKER
SAFE-CONDUCT
SAFE-DEPOSIT
SAFEGUARDED
SAFEKEEPING
SAFETY BELTS
SAFETY CATCH
SAFETY-GLASS
SAFETY LAMPS
SAFETY MATCH
SAFETY RAZOR
SAFETY VALVE
SAGACIOUSLY
SAGITTARIAN
SAGITTARIUS
SAILING BOAT
SAILOR SUITS
SAINT GALLEN
SAINTLINESS
SALACIOUSLY
SALAMANDERS
SALEABILITY
SALESCLERKS
SALESPEOPLE
SALESPERSON
SALICACEOUS
SALIENTNESS
SALINOMETER
SALINOMETRY
SALMONBERRY
SALMON TROUT
SALPINGITIC
SALPINGITIS
SALTATORIAL

SALTCELLARS
SALT SHAKERS
SALUTATIONS
SALVABILITY
SALVADORIAN
SALVAGEABLE
SALVATIONAL
SANATORIUMS
SANCTIFYING
SANCTIONING
SANCTUARIES
SANDBAGGING
SANDBLASTED
SANDBLASTER
SAND-CASTING
SANDCASTLES
SANDPAPERED
SANDWICHING
SANGUINARIA
SANGUINEOUS
SANITARIUMS
SAN MARINESE
SAN SALVADOR
SANSEVIERIA
SANSKRITIST
SAPONACEOUS
SAPOTACEOUS
SAPROPHYTIC
SARCOMATOID
SARCOPHAGUS
SARDONICISM
SARTORIALLY
SASH WINDOWS
SATANICALLY
SATELLITIUM
SATIABILITY
SATIRICALLY
SATISFIABLE
SATURNALIAS
SAUDI ARABIA
SAURISCHIAN
SAUROPODOUS
SAUSAGE DOGS
SAUSAGE ROLL
SAVABLENESS
SAVING GRACE
SAVINGS BANK
SAVOIR-FAIRE
SAVOURINGLY
SAXOPHONIST
SCAFFOLDING
SCALARIFORM
SCAMMONIATE
SCANDALIZED

SCANDALIZER
SCANDINAVIA
SCARABAEOID
SCAREDY CATS
SCAREMONGER
SCARLATINAL
SCATOLOGIST
SCATTERABLE
SCENOGRAPHY
SCEPTICALLY
SCHEMATIZED
SCHISMATICS
SCHISTOSITY
SCHISTOSOME
SCHIZOPHYTE
SCHOLARSHIP
SCHOLASTIC
SCHOOLCHILD
SCHOOLHOUSE
SCHOOLMARMS
SCHOOLMATES
SCIENCE PARK
SCIENTISTIC
SCIENTOLOGY
SCINTILLATE
SCIRRHOSITY
SCLERODERMA
SCLEROMETER
SCLEROTIOID
SCOPOLAMINE
SCOREBOARDS
SCORIACEOUS
SCORAENOID
SCOTCH BROTH
SCOTCH MISTS
SCOTCH TAPED
SCOTOMATOUS
SCOURGINGLY
SCOUTMASTER
SCRAGGINESS
SCRAPPIEST
SCRATCHIEST
SCRATCHPADS
SCRAWNINESS
SCREAMINGLY
SCREENPLAYS
SCREEN TESTS
SCREW DRIVER
SCRIMMAGING
SCRIMPINESS
SCRIPTORIUM
SCRUBBINESS
SCRUMHALVES
SCRUMMAGING

SCRUMPTIOUS
SCRUTINEERS
SCRUTINIZED
SCRUTINIZER
SCULPTURING
SCYPHISTOMA
SEA ANEMONES
SEA CAPTAINS
SEARCHINGLY
SEARCHLIGHT
SEARCH PARTY
SEA SICKNESS
SEBORRHOEAL
SECESSIONAL
SECONDARILY
SECOND-CLASS
SECOND-GUESS
SECOND HANDS
SECONDMENTS
SECOND-RATER
SECOND SIGHT
SECRET AGENT
SECRETARIAL
SECRETARIAT
SECRETARIES
SECRETIVELY
SECULARIZED
SECULARIZER
SEDAN CHAIRS
SEDENTARILY
SEDIMENTARY
SEDITIOUSLY
SEDUCTIVELY
SEGREGATING
SEGREGATION
SEGREGATIVE
SEIGNIORAGE
SEISMICALLY
SEISMOGRAPH
SEISMOLOGIC
SEISMOSCOPE
SELAGINELLA
SELECTIVELY
SELECTIVITY
SELENOGRAPH
SELF-ASSURED
SELF-CENTRED
SELF-COMMAND
SELF-CONCEPT
SELF-CONTROL
SELF-DEFENCE
SELF-DENYING
SELF-EVIDENT
SELF-IMPOSED

SELF-INDUCED	SERENDIPITY	SHOPLIFTING	SIMMERINGLY
SELFISHNESS	SERIALIZING	SHOPSTEWARD	SIMPERINGLY
SELF-LOADING	SERPIGINOUS	SHOPWALKERS	SIMPLIFYING
SELF-LOCKING	SERRULATION	SHORT-CHANGE	SIMULACRUMS
SELF-PITYING	SERTULARIAN	SHORTCOMING	SIMULATIONS
SELF-RELIANT	SERVICABLE	SHORTHANDED	SINE QUA NONS
SELF-RESPECT	SERVICEABLY	SHORT-LISTED	SINFONIETTA
SELF-SEEKERS	SERVICE FLAT	SHORT SHRIFT	SINGAPOREAN
SELF-SEEKING	SERVICE ROAD	SHORT SPOKEN	SINGLE-BLIND
SELF-SERVICE	SERVO MOTORS	SHORT-WINDED	SINGLE-CROSS
SELF-STARTER	SESQUIOXIDE	SHOULDERING	SINGLE-PHASE
SELF-WINDING	SETTLEMENTS	SHOWERPROOF	SINGLE-SPACE
SELL-BY DATES	SEVENTEENTHS	SHOW JUMPERS	SINGLE-TRACK
SELLOTAPING	SEVENTIETHS	SHOWJUMPING	SINGULARITY
SEMANTICIST	SEXAGEISMAL	SHOWMANSHIP	SINGULARIZE
SEMASIOLOGY	SEXLESSNESS	SHOW OF HANDS	SINISTRORSE
SEMIAQUATIC	SEXOLOGISTS	SHOWSTOPPER	SINKING FUND
SEMIARIDITY	SEXTODECIMO	SHRINKINGLY	SINN FEINISM
SEMICIRCLES	SHADOW-BOXED	SHRIVELLING	SINOLOGICAL
SEMIDIURAL	SHADOWGRAPH	SHRUBBERIES	SINOLOGISTS
SEMIFLUIDIC	SHADOWINESS	SHRUBBINESS	SINO-TIBETAN
SEMIMONTHLY	SHAMANISTIC	SHUTTLECOCK	SINOUSITIES
SEMIOTICIAN	SHAMELESSLY	SIAMESE CATS	SINUOUSNESS
SEMIPALMATE	SHANK'S PONY	SIAMESE TWIN	SISTERHOODS
SEMIQUAVERS	SHANTYTOWNS	SICKENINGLY	SISTER-IN-LAW
SEMISKILLED	SHAPELESSLY	SIDE EFFECTS	SITTING DUCK
SEMIONALLY	SHAPELINESS	SIDESADDLES	SITTING ROOM
SEMITRAILER	SHAREHOLDER	SIDESLIPPED	SITUATIONAL
SEMITROPICS	SHARP-WITTED	SIDESTEPPED	SIX-SHOOTERS
SEMIVOLCALIC	SHAVING FOAM	SIDESTEPPER	SIXTH-FORMER
SEMIPITERNAL	SHEATH KNIFE	SIDE STREETS	SIZABLENESS
SENSATIONAL	SHEET ANCHOR	SIDESWIPING	SKATEBOARDS
SENSELESSLY	SHELLACKING	SIDETRACKED	SKEDADDLING
SENSE ORGANS	SHENANIGANS	SIDE-WHEELER	SKELETONIZE
SENSIBILITY	SHEPHERDESS	SIERRA LEONE	SKELETON KEY
SENSITIVELY	SHEPHERDING	SIERRA MADRE	SKEPTICALLY
SENSITIVITY	SHIBBOLETHS	SIGHT SCREEN	SKETCHINESS
SENSITIZING	SHIFTLESSLY	SIGHT SEEING	SKILFULNESS
SENSUALISTS	SHIFT STICKS	SIGNAL BOXES	SKIMMED MILK
SENSUALNESS	SHIMONOSEKI	SIGNALIZING	SKIRMISHERS
SENTENTIOUS	SHIP BISCUIT	SIGNATORIES	SKIRMISHING
SENTIMENTAL	SHIPBUILDER	SIGNIFIABLE	SKULDUGGERY
SENTRY BOXES	SHIPWRECKED	SIGNIFICANT	SKYJACKINGS
SEPARATIONS	SHIPWRIGHTS	SIGNPOSTING	SKYROCKETED
SEPARATISTS	SHIRE HORSES	SILHOUETTED	SKYSCRAPERS
SEPTAVALENT	SHIRT FRONTS	SILHOUETTES	SLAUGHTERED
SEPTICAEMIA	SHIRTSLEEVE	SILICON CHIP	SLAUGHTERER
SEPTICAEMIC	SHISH KEBABS	SILLIMANITE	SLAVE DRIVER
SEPTIC TANKS	SHIVERINGLY	SILLY SEASON	SLAVE LABOUR
SEPTIFRAGAL	SHOCKHEADED	SILVER BIRCH	SLAVISHNESS
SEPTIVALENT	SHOCK TROOPS	SILVER PAPER	SLEEPING BAG
SEQUESTERED	SHOESTRINGS	SILVER PLATE	SLEEPING CAR
SEQUESTERANT	SHOPKEEPERS	SILVERPOINT	SLEEPLESSLY
SEQUESTERATE	SHOPLIFTERS	SILVERSMITH	SLEEPWALKED

S

SLEEPWALKER	SOFT-SOAPING	SPECIALNESS	SPLUTTERING
SLEEPYHEADS	SOFT TOUCHES	SPECIFIABLE	SPOILSPORTS
SLENDERIZED	SOLANACEOUS	SPECIFICITY	SPOKESWOMAN
SLENDERNESS	SOLARIMETER	SPECTACULAR	SPONDYLITIS
SLEUTHHOUND	SOLAR PANELS	SPECTRALITY	SPONGE CAKES
SLICED BREAD	SOLAR PLEXUS	SPECTACULAR	SPONSORSHIP
SLICE OF LIFE	SOLAR SYSTEM	SPECTRALITY	SPONTANEITY
SLICKENSIDE	SOLEMNITIES	SPECULATING	SPONTANEOUS
SLIDE-ACTION	SOLEMNIZING	SPECULATION	SPOROGONIAL
SLIDING DOOR	SOLIDIFYING	SPECULATIVE	SPOROGONIUM
SLIGHTEDLY	SOLILOQUIES	SPECULATORS	SPOROPHYTIC
SLIPPED DISC	SOLILOQUIST	SPEECHIFIED	SPORTSWOMAN
SLIPSTREAMS	SOLILOQUIZE	SPEECHIFIER	SPORULATION
SLOOP-RIGGED	SOLIPSISTIC	SPEED LIMITS	SPOT CHECKED
SLOPINGNESS	SOLMIZATION	SPEEDOMETER	SPOTTED DICK
SLOT MACHINE	SOLUBLENESS	SPELLBINDER	SPREAD-EAGLE
SLOUCHINESS	SOLVABILITY	SPENDTHRIFT	SPREADSHEET
SLOUCHINGLY	SOMATICALLY	SPERMATHECA	SPRINGBOARD
SLOWCOACHES	SOMATOLOGIC	SPERMATOZOA	SPRING-CLEAN
SMALL CHANGE	SOMATOPLASM	SPERMICIDES	SPRINGFIELD
SMALLHOLDER	SOMERSAULTS	SPERMOPHILE	SPRINGINESS
SMALL-MINDED	SOMNOLENTLY	SPERM WHALES	SPRING ONION
SMALL SCREEN	SONGFULNESS	SPESSARTITE	SPRING ROLLS
SMALL-TIMERS	SOOTHSAYERS	SPHEROMETER	SPRING TIDES
SMART ALECKS	SOPHISTRIES	SPHERULITIC	SPRINKLINGS
SMART ALECKY	SORORICIDAL	SPHINCTERAL	SPUMESCENCE
SMARTY-PANTS	SORROWFULLY	SPHINGOSINE	SQUANDERERS
SMATTERINGS	SOTTISHNESS	SPHRAGISTIC	SQUANDERING
SMILINGNESS	SOUBRIQUETS	SPINA BIFIDA	SQUARE DANCE
SMITHEREENS	SOUGHT-AFTER	SPINAL CORDS	SQUARE KNOTS
SMITHSONITE	SOUL BROTHER	SPINELESSLY	SQUARE MEALS
SMOKESCREEN	SOULFULNESS	SPINESCENCE	SQUARE ROOTS
SMOKESTACKS	SOUNDLESSLY	SPINIFEROUS	SQUASHINESS
SMOOTHFACED	SOUNDTRACKS	SPINSTERISH	SQUEAMISHLY
SMORGASBORD	SOUP KITCHEN	SPINY-FINNED	SQUELCHIEST
SMOULDERING	SOUSAPHONES	SPIRACULATE	SQUIGGLIEST
SNAPDRAGONS	SOUTHAMPTON	SPIRIFEROUS	SQUIREARCHY
SNIPERSCOPE	SOUTHEASTER	SPIRIT LEVEL	SQUIRMINGLY
SNORKELLING	SOUTHERNERS	SPIRITUALLY	STABILIZERS
SNOWBALLING	SOUTHWESTER	SPIRKETTING	STABILIZING
SNOWMOBILES	SOVEREIGNTY	SPIROCHAETE	STADIOMETER
SNOWPLOUGHS	SOVIETISTIC	SPIROMETRIC	STAFF NURSES
SOAP BUBBLES	SPACE HEATER	SPITSTICKER	STAGE FRIGHT
SOCIABILITY	SPACE PROBES	SPLASHBOARD	STAGE MANAGE
SOCIALISTIC	SPARINGNESS	SPLASHDOWNS	STAGESTRUCK
SOCIALIZING	SPARROW HAWK	SPLASH GUARD	STAGGERBUSH
SOCIOLOGIST	SPASTICALLY	SPLASHINESS	STAGING POST
SOCIOMETRIC	SPATHACEOUS	SPLATTERING	STAG PARTIES
SOCIOPATHIC	SPEAKEASIES	SPLAYFOOTED	STAKEHOLDER
SOFTHEARTED	SPEAKERSHIP	SPLENDOROUS	STALACTITES
SOFT LANDING	SPEARHEADED	SPLENECTOMY	STALACTITIC
SOFT OPTIONS	SPECIALISMS	SPLENETICAL	STALAGMITES
SOFT PALATES	SPECIALISTS	SPLINTERING	STALAGMITIC
SOFT-PEDALED	SPECIALIZED	SPLIT SECOND	STALEMATING

STALLHOLDER	STEREOTYPES	STRAIGHT-OUT	STYLOSTIXIS
SRANDARDIZE	STEREOTYPIC	STRAIGHTWAY	SUBASSEMBLY
STANDOFFISH	STERILIZERS	STRAININGLY	SUBAUDITION
STANDPOINTS	STERILIZING	STRAITLACED	SUBAUXILLARY
STARA ZAGORA	STERNUTATOR	STRANGENESS	SUBBASEMENT
STAR CHAMBER	STETHOSCOPE	STRANGULATE	SUBCHLORIDE
STARCHINESS	STETHOSCOPY	STRAPHANGER	SUBCOMPACTS
STAR-CROSSED	STEWARDSHIP	STRATEGISTS	SUBCONTRACT
STAR-STUDDED	STICHICALLY	STRATHCLYDE	SUBCONTRARY
STARTLINGLY	STICHOMETRY	STRATIFYING	SUBCORTICAL
STARVELINGS	STICK INSECT	STRATOCRACY	SUBCULTURAL
STATELY HOME	STICKLEBACK	STRATOPAUSE	SUBCULTURES
STATESWOMAN	STICK SHIFTS	STRAWFLOWER	SUBDELIRIUM
STATISTICAL	STIFF-NECKED	STREAKINESS	SUBDIACONAL
STATOLITHIC	STIGMATICAL	STREAMLINED	SUBDIVIDING
STATUTE BOOK	STIGMATIZER	STREETLIGHT	SUBDIVISION
STATUTORILY	STILLBIRTHS	STREETVALUE	SUBDOMINANT
STAUNCHABLE	STILTEDNESS	STRENUOSITY	SUBDUEDNESS
STAUNCHNESS	STIMULATING	STRENUOUSLY	SUBHEADINGS
STAUROLITIC	STIMULATION	STRESS MARKS	SUBIRRIGATE
STAUROSCOPE	STIMULATIVE	STRETCHABLE	SUBJECTABLE
STAY-AT-HOMES	STIPENDIARY	STRETCHIEST	SUBJUGATING
STEADFASTLY	STIPULATING	STRETCHMARK	SUBJUGATION
STEALTHIEST	STIPULATION	STRIDULATED	SUBJUGATIVE
STEAM-BOILER	STIPULATORY	STRIDULATOR	SUBLIMATING
STEAM-ENGINE	STIRRUP CUPS	STRIKEBOUND	SUBLIMATION
STEAMROLLER	STIRRUP PUMP	STRING BEANS	SUBLITTORAL
STEAM SHOVEL	STOCKBROKER	STRINGBOARD	SUNMARGINAL
STEAROPTENE	STOCKHOLDER	STRINGENTLY	SUNMARINERS
STEATOLYSIS	STOCKJOBBER	STRINGINESS	SUBMERSIBLE
STEATOPYGIA	STOCK MARKET	STRINGPIECE	SUBMISSIONS
STEATOPYGIC	STOCK PILING	STRIP MINING	SUBMITTABLE
STEELWORKER	STOCK TAKING	STRIPTEASES	SUBMULTIPLE
STEEPLEJACK	STOICALNESS	STROBE LIGHT	SUBORDINARY
STEERAGEWAY	STOMACHACHE	STROBOSCOPE	SUBORDINATE
STELLARATOR	STOMACHICAL	STRONGBOXES	SUBORNATION
STENCILLING	STOMACH PUMP	STRONGHOLDS	SUBORNATIVE
STENOGRAPHY	STOMATOLOGY	STRONG POINT	SUBPOENAING
STENOHALINE	STONE CUTTER	STRONG ROOMS	SUBREGIONAL
STENOHAGUS	STONE FRUITS	STRUCTURING	SUBROGATION
STENOTROPIC	STONE GROUND	STRUCTURIST	SUBROUTINES
STENOTYPIST	STONEMASONS	STRUTTINGLY	SUBSCAPULAR
STEPBROTHER	STONE'S THROW	STUBBORNEST	SUBSCRIBERS
STEPHANOTIS	STONEWALLED	STUDENTSHIP	SUBSCRIBING
STEPLADDERS	STONEWALLER	STUDIDNESS	SUBSECTIONS
STEPPARENTS	STONEWORKER	STUDIOCOUCH	SUBSEQUENCE
STEPSISTERS	STOOLPIGEON	STULTIFYING	SUBSERVIENT
STEREOGRAPH	STOPWATCHES	STUMBLINGLY	SUBSIDENCES
STEREOMETRY	STOREHOUSES	STUNTEDNESS	SUBSIDIZERS
STEREOSCOPE	STOREKEEPER	STUPIDITIES	SUBSIDIZING
STEREOSCOPY	STORM LOUDS	STYLISHNESS	SUBSISTENCE
STEREOTAXIS	STORYTELLER	STYLIZATION	SUBSPECIFIC
STEREOTYPED	STRAGGLIEST	STYLOGRAPHY	SUBSTANDARD
STEREOTYPER	STRAIGHTEST	STYLOPODIUM	SUBSTANTIAL

SUBSTANTIVE
SUBSTATIONS
SUBSTITUENT
SUBSTITUTED
SUBSTITUTES
SUBSTRATIVE
SUBSUMPTION
SUBSUMPTIVE
SUBTERFUGES
SUBTRACTING
SUBTRACTION
SUBTRACTIVE
SUBTROPICAL
SUBURBANITE
SUBVENTIONS
SUBVERSIVES
SUCCEDANEUM
SUCCEEDABLE
SUCCESSIONS
SUCCESSORAL
SUCCOURABLE
SUCH AND SUCH
SUCKING PIGS
SUCTION PUMP
SUDETENLAND
SUFFERINGLY
SUFFICIENCY
SUFFOCATING
SUFFOCATIVE
SUFFRAGETTE
SUFFUMIGATE
SUGGESTIBLE
SUGGESTIONS
SUITABILITY
SULPHA DRUGS
SULPHUREOUS
SUMMARINESS
SUMMARIZING
SUMMATIONAL
SUMMER HOUSE
SUMMERINESS
SUMPTUOUSLY
SUNDRENCHED
SUNLESSNESS
SUNNY-SIDE UP
SUPERABOUND
SUPER CHARGE
SUPER FAMILY
SUPERFETATE
SUPERFICIAL
SUPERFLUITY
SUPERFLUOUS
SUPERIMPOSE
SUPERINDUCE

SUPERIORITY
SUPERJACENT
SUPERLATIVE
SUPERLUNARY
SUPERMARKET
SUPERNATANT
SUPERNORMAL
SUPERSCRIBE
SUPERSCRIPT
SUPERSEDEAS
SUPERSEDING
SUPERSEDURE
SUPERSONICS
SUPERSTRUCT
SUPERTANKER
SUPERVENING
SUPERVISING
SUPERVISION
SUPERVSORS
SUPERVISORY
SUPPLANTING
SUPPLEMENTS
SUPPLICANTS
SUPPLICATED
SUPPORTABLE
SUPPOSITION
SUPPOSITIVE
SUPPOSITORY
SUPPRESSING
SUPPRESSION
SUPPRESSIVE
SUPPRESSORS
SUPPURATING
SUPPURATION
SUPPURATIVE
SUPREMACIST
SUPREMATISM
SUPREMATIST
SUPREMENESS
SURBASEMENT
SURCHARGING
SURFCASTING
SURGEONFISH
SURMOUNTING
SURPASSABLE
SURPRISEDLY
SURREALISTS
SURREBUTTAL
SURREBUTTER
SURRENDERED
SURROGATION
SURROUNDING
SURVEILLANT
SURVIVAL KIT

SUSCEPTANCE
SUSCEPTIBLE
SUSPENSEFUL
SUSPENSIONS
SUSPICIONAL
SUSTAINABLE
SUSTAINEDLY
SUSTAINMENT
SUSURRATION
SWALLOWABLE
SWALLOW DIVE
SWALLOW TAIL
SWALLOWWORT
SWARTHINESS
SWEAT GLANDS
SWEATSHIRTS
SWEEPSTAKES
SWEETBREADS
SWEETHEARTS
SWEETPEPPER
SWEET POTATO
SWEET-TALKED
SWINDLINGLY
SWINISHNESS
SWISS CHEESE
SWITCHBACKS
SWITCH BLADE
SWITCHBOARD
SWITZERLAND
SWOLLEN HEAD
SWOLLENNESS
SWORD DANCER
SWORD DANCES
SWORD FISHES
SYCOPHANTIC
SYLLABOGRAM
SYLLOGISTIC
SYMBOLIZING
SYMBOLOGIST
SYMMETRICAL
SYMPATHETIC
SYMPATHIZED
SYMPATHIZER
SYMPETALOUS
SYMPHONOIUS
SYMPTOMATIC
SYNAGOGICAL
SYNCHOMESH
SYNCHONISM
SYNCHRONIZE
SYNCHROTRON
SYNCOPATING
SYNCOPATION
SYNDESMOSIS

SYNDESMOTIC
SYNDICALISM
SYNDICALIST
SYNDICATING
SYNDICATION
SYNECDOCHIC
SYNECOLOGIC
SYNKARYONIC
SYNTHESIZED
SYNTHESIZER
SYNTHETICAL
SYPHILITICS
SYPHILOLOGY
SYSSARCOSIS
SYSSARCOTIC
SYSTEMATICS
SYSTEMATISM
SYSTEMATIST
SYSTEMATIZE

12 LETTERS
SABBATARIANS
SACCHARINITY
SACRILEGIOUS
SADISTICALLY
SAFEBREAKERS
SAFEGUARDING
SAFETY ISLAND
SAFETY RAZORS
SAFETY VALVES
SAILING BOATS
SAINT-ETIENNE
SALAMANDRINE
SALESMANSHIP
SALES PITCHES
SALIFICATION
SALINOMETRIC
SALMON TROUTS
SALPIGLOSSIS
SALUTARINESS
SALUTATORILY
SALVATIONISM
SALVATIONIST
SAMARITANISM
SANCTIFIABLE
SANCTIONABLE
SANDBLASTING
SANDPAPERING
SAN FRANCISCO
SANGUINARILY
SANGUINENESS
SANGINOLENT
SANITARINESS

SAN SEBASTIAN
SANTALACEOUS
SANTO DOMINGO
SAONE-ET-LOIRE
SAPINDACEOUS
SAPONIFIABLE
SAPROPHAGOUS
SARCOMATOSIS
SARDONICALLY
SARSAPARILLA
SASKATCHEWAN
SATIRIZATION
SATISFACTION
SATISFACTORY
SATISFYINGLY
SATURABILITY
SAUDI ARABIAN
SAUSAGE ROLLS
SAVING GRACES
SAVINGS BANKS
SAXOPHONISTS
SCALABLENESS
SCANDALIZING
SCANDALOUSLY
SCANDINAVIAN
SCAREMONGERS
SCARIFICATOR
SCARLET FEVER
SCARLET WOMAN
SCARLET WOMEN
SCATOLOGICAL
SCATTER BRAIN
SCENESHIFTER
SCENOGRAPHER
SCENOGRAPHIC
SCHAFFHAUSEN
SCHEMATIZING
SCHIZOMYCETE
SCHIZOPHYTIC
SCHIZOTHYMIA
SCHIZOTHYMIC
SCHOLARSHIPS
SCHOLASTICAL
SCHOOLFELLOW
SCHOOLHOUSES
SCHOOL-LEAVER
SCHOOL MASTER
SCHORLACEOUS
SCIENCE PARKS
SCINTILLATED
SCINTILLATOR
SCLERENCHYMA
SCLEROMETRIC
SCOLOPENDRID

SCORNFULNESS
SCOTCH TAPING
SCOTCH WISKEY
SCOTLAND YARD
SCOUTMASTERS
SCRATCHINESS
SCRATCH PAPER
SCREWDRIVERS
SCRIPTWRITER
SCROBICULATE
SCRUPULOUSLY
SCRUTINIZING
SCURRILOUSLY
SCUTELLATION
SEAMSTRESSES
SEARCHLIGHTS
SEASONALNESS
SEASON TICKET
SECESSIONISM
SECESSIONIST
SECLUDEDNESS
SECOND COMING
SECOND COUSIN
SECOND-DEGREE
SECOND NATURE
SECOND PERSON
SECOND STRING
SECRET AGENTS
SECRETARIATS
SECRETIONARY
SECRET POLICE
SECTARIANISM
SECTIONALISM
SECTIONALIST
SECTIONALIZE
SECULARISTIC
SECULARIZING
SECURITY RISK
SEDULOUSNESS
SEGMENTATION
SEINE-ET-MARNE
SEISMOGRAPHS
SEISMOGRAPHY
SEISMOLOGIST
SEISMOSCOPIC
SELENOGRAPHY
SELENOLOGIST
SELF-ABSORBED
SELF-ANALYSIS
SELF-ASSEMBLY
SELF-CATERING
SELF-COLOURED
SELF-DESTRUCT
SELF-EDUCATED

SELF-EFFACING
SELF-EMPLOYED
SELF-INTEREST
SELFLESSNESS
SELF-PORTRAIT
SELF-RELIANCE
SELF-REPROACH
SELF-STARTERS
SELLING POINT
SEMANTICALLY
SEMICIRCULAR
SEMIDETACHED
SEMIDIAMETER
SEMIFINALIST
SEMIFLUIDITY
SEMINIFEROUS
SEMIOTICIANS
SEMIPRECIOUS
SEMPITERNITY
SENARMONTITE
SENSIBLENESS
SENSITOMETER
SENSITOMETRY
SENSORIMOTOR
SENSUOUSNESS
SEPARABILITY
SEPERATENESS
SEPARATISTIC
SEPTILATERAL
SEPTILLIONTH
SEPTUAGESIMA
SEPTUPLICATE
SEQUENTIALLY
SEQUESTRABLE
SEQUESTRATED
SEQUESTRATOR
SERIAL NUMBER
SERICULTURAL
SERVICEBERRY
SERVICE FLATS
SERVICE ROADS
SESQUIALTERA
SEVENTEENTHS
SEVENTY-EIGHT
SEVERANCE PAY
SEXAGENARIAN
SEXCENTENARY
SEXTILLIONTH
SEXTUPLICATE
SHADOW-BOXING
SHAHJAHANPUR
SHAMATEURISM
SHAMEFACEDLY
SHAMEFULNESS

SHARECROPPER
SHAREHOLDERS
SHARPSHOOTER
SHARP-SIGHTED
SHARP-TONGUED
SHATTERINGLY
SHATTERPROOF
SHAVING CREAM
SHEATH KNIVES
SHEEPISHNESS
SHEEPSHEARER
SHEET ANCHORS
SHELLACKINGS
SHELLSHOCKED
SHEPHERD'S PIE
SHETLAND PONY
SHIFTINGNESS
SHILLY-SHALLY
SHIMMERINGLY
SHIPBUILDERS
SHIPBUILDING
SHIPWRECKING
SHIRTSLEEVES
SHIRTWAISTER
SHOCKABILITY
SHOCKINGNESS
SHOCKING PINK
SHOOTING STAR
SHOP STEWARDS
SHORT-CHANGED
SHORT-CHANGER
SHORT CIRCUIT
SHORTCOMINGS
SHORT-LISTING
SHORTSIGHTED
SHORT STORIES
SHORT-WASTED
SHOW BUSINESS
SHOWSTOPPERS
SHOWSTOPPING
SHREWISHNESS
SHUDDERINGLY
SHUFFLEBOARD
SHUTTLECOCKS
SIAMESE TWINS
SICK HEADACHE
SIDESLIPPING
SIDESTEPPING
SIDETRACKING
SIDE-WHEELERS
SIGNIFICANCE
SIGN LANGUAGE
SILHOUETTING
SILICON CHIPS

S

12 LETTERS

SILVER FISHES	SNAKE CHARMER	SPECIFICALLY	SQUEEZE BOXES
SILVER MEDALS	SNAP FASTENER	SPECIOUSNESS	SQUELCHINGLY
SILVERSMITHS	SNAPPISHNESS	SPECTACULARS	SQUIRRELFISH
SIMILARITIES	SNEAKINGNESS	SPECTROGRAPH	STADDLESTONE
SIMPLE-MINDED	SNEAK PREVIEW	SPECTROMETER	STAFF OFFICER
SIMULTANEITY	SNEAK THIEVES	SPECTROMETRY	STAGE COACHES
SIMULTANEOUS	SNICKERINGLY	SPECTROSCOPE	STAGE-MANAGED
SINGLE-ACTING	SNIGGERINGLY	SPECTROSCOPY	STAGE MANAGER
SINGLE-ACTION	SNOBBISHESS	SPECULATIONS	STAGE WHISPER
SINGLE-DECKER	SOCIALIZABLE	SPEECHIFYING	STAGGERINGLY
SINGLE-HANDED	SOCIAL WORKER	SPEECHLESSLY	STAGING POSTS
SINGLE-MINDED	SOCIOLOGICAL	SPEEDOMETERS	STAINABILITY
SINGULARNESS	SOCIOLOGISTS	SPEEDWRITING	STAINED GLASS
SINISTERNESS	SODA FOUNTAIN	SPELLBINDERS	STAKE HOLDERS
SINKING FUNDS	SOFT LANDINGS	SPELLBINDING	STALL HOLDERS
SISTERLINESS	SOFT-PEDALING	SPENDTHRIFTS	STAMMERINGLY
SISTERS-IN-LAW	SOFT-PEDALLED	SPERMATHECAL	STANDARDIZED
SITTING DUCKS	SOLARIZATION	SPERMATOCYTE	STANDARDIZER
SITTING ROOMS	SOLAR SYSTEMS	SPERMATOZOAL	STANDARD LAMP
SKELETON KEYS	SOLICITATION	SPERMATOZOON	STANDARD TIME
SKIPPING-ROPE	SOLICITOUSLY	SPERMOGONIUM	STANDING ROOM
SKITTISHNESS	SOLIDIFIABLE	SPICK-AND-SPAN	STANDOFF HALF
SKYROCKETING	SOLILOQUIZED	SPINSTERHOOD	STAR CHAMBERS
SLANDEROUSLY	SOLITARINESS	SPIRITEDNESS	STAR-SPANGLED
SLAUGHTERING	SOLITUDINOUS	SPIRIT LEVELS	STARTING GATE
SLAUGHTEROUS	SOLVENT ABUSE	SPIRITUALISM	STATELY HOMES
SLAVE DRIVERS	SOMATOLOGIST	SPIRITUALIST	STATION BREAK
SLEDGEHAMMER	SOMERSAULTED	SPIRITUALITY	STATION HOUSE
SLEEPING BAGS	SOMNAMBULANT	SPIRITUALIZE	STATION WAGON
SLEEPING CARS	SOMNAMBULATE	SPIRITUOSITY	STATISTICIAN
SLEEPING PILL	SOMNAMBULISM	SPIROGRAPHIC	STAYING POWER
SLEEPWALKERS	SOMNAMBULIST	SPITEFULNESS	STEAK TARTARE
SLEEPWALKING	SONG AND DANCE	SPLASH GUARDS	STEALTHINESS
SLENDERIZING	SONOROUSNESS	SPLENDIDNESS	STEAMROLLERS
SLIDING DOORS	SOOTHINGNESS	SPLIT SECONDS	STEAM SHOVELS
SLIDING SCALE	SOPHISTICATE	SPOKESPEOPLE	STEEPLECHASE
SLIPPERINESS	SOUL BROTHERS	SPOKESPERSON	STEEPLEJACKS
SLIPPINGNESS	SOULLESSNESS	SPOON-FEEDING	STENOGRAPHER
SLIPSTREAMED	SOUND BARRIER	SPORADICALLY	STENOGRAPHIC
SLOTHFULNESS	SOUND EFFECTS	SPORTFULNESS	STENOTHERMAL
SLOT MACHINES	SOUNDPROOFED	SPORTIVENESS	STEPBROTHERS
SLOVENLINESS	SOUP KITCHENS	SPOT-CHECKING	STEPCHILDREN
SLUGGISHNESS	SOUTHEASTERN	SPOTLESSNESS	STEPDAUGHTER
SLUMBERINGLY	SOUTHERNMOST	SPOTLIGHTING	STEREOCHROME
SLUTTISHNESS	SOUTHERNWOOD	SPOTTED DICKS	STEREOCHROMY
SMALL FORTUNE	SOUTHWESTERN	SPREAD-EAGLED	STEREOGRAPHY
SMALL HOLDERS	SPACE HEATERS	SPREADSHEETS	STEREOMETRIC
SMALLHOLDING	SPACE SHUTTLE	SPRINGBOARDS	STEREOPHONIC
SMASH-AND-GRAB	SPACE STATION	SPRING ONIONS	STEREOSCOPIC
SMILACACEOUS	SPACIOUSNESS	SPURIOUSNESS	STEREOTYPING
SMOKESCREENS	SPEARHEADING	SQUAMOUSNESS	STEREOVISION
SMOOTH-SPOKEN	SPECIALISTIC	SQUARE DANCES	STERILIZABLE
SMORGASBORDS	SPECIALITIES	SQUARE-RIGGED	STERTOROUSLY
SNAGGLETOOTH	SPECIALIZING	SQAURE-RIGGER	STETHOSCOPES

STETHOSCOPIC	STRENGTHENED	SUBMAXILLARY	SUPERMINENT
STICK INSECTS	STRENGTHENER	SUBMERSIBLES	SUPERFICIARY
STICKLEBACKS	STREPTOCOCCI	SUBMISSIVELY	SUPERGLACIAL
STICKY WICKET	STREPTOMYCIN	SUBMITTINGLY	SUPERGRASSES
STIGMATIZING	STRETCHINESS	SUBNORMALITY	SUPERIMPOSED
STILETTO HEEL	STRETCHMARKS	SUBORDINATED	SUPERLATIVES
STINKINGNESS	STRIDULATING	SUBORDINATES	SUPERMARKES
STIPULATIONS	STRIDULATION	SUBPRINCIPAL	SUPERNATURAL
STIRRUP PUMPS	STRIDULATORY	SUBSCRIPTION	SUPERPOSABLE
STOCKBREEDER	STRIKINGNESS	SUBSCRIPTIVE	SUPERSEDABLE
STOCKBROKERS	STRIP CARTOON	SUBSEQUENTLY	SUPERSESSION
STOCKHOLDERS	STRIP MININGS	SUBSERVIENCE	SUPERSTITION
STOCK-IN-TRADE	STROBE LIGHTS	SUBSIDIARIES	SUPERSTRATUM
STOCKJOBBERS	STROBILATION	SUBSIDIARILY	SUPERTANKERS
STOCKJOBBERY	STROBOSCOPES	SUBSIDIZABLE	SUPERVENIENT
STOCK MARKETS	STROBOSCOPIC	SUBSISTINGLY	SUPPLEMENTAL
STOICHIOLOGY	STROMATOLITE	SUBSTANTIATE	SUPPLEMENTED
STOMACHACHES	STRONG-MINDED	SUBSTANTIVAL	SUPPLETORILY
STOMACH PUMPS	STRONG POINTS	SUBSTANTIVES	SUPPLICATING
STONECUTTING	STRONG WILLED	SUBSTITUTING	SUPPLICATION
STONEMASONRY	STROPHANTHIN	SUBSTITUTION	SUPPLICATORY
STONEWALLERS	STROPHANTHUS	SUBSTITUTIVE	SUPPOSITIONS
STONEWALLING	STRUCTURALLY	SUBSTRUCTURE	SUPPOSITIOUS
STONY-HEARTED	STRUGGLINGLY	SUBTEMPERATE	SUPPRESSABLE
STOOLPIGEONS	STRYCHNINISM	SUBTERRANEAN	SUPRAGLOTTAL
STOREKEEPERS	STUBBORNNESS	SUBTRACTIONS	SUPRALIMINAL
STOREKEEPING	STUDDINGSAIL	SUBURBANITES	SUPRAORBITAL
STORMTROOPER	STUDIOUSNESS	SUBVERSIVELY	SUPRAPROTEST
STORMY PETREL	STUFFED SHIRT	SUCCEDANEOUS	SUPREMACISTS
STORYTELLERS	STUPEFACIENT	SUCCEEDINGLY	SUPREME BEING
STORYTELLING	STUPEFACTION	SUCCESSFULLY	SUPREME COURT
STOUTHEARTED	STUPEFYINGLY	SUCCESSIONAL	SUREFOOTEDLY
STOVEPIPE HAT	STUPENDOUSLY	SUCCESSIVELY	SURFACE-TO-AIR
STRADIVARIUS	STUTTERINGLY	SUCCINCTNESS	SURMOUNTABLE
STRAGGLINGLY	STYLOGRAPHIC	SUCTION PUMPS	SURPASSINGLY
STRAIGHTAWAY	STYRACACEOUS	SUDORIFEROUS	SURPRISINGLY
STRAIGHTEDGE	SUBALTERNATE	SUFFRAGETTES	SURREALISTIC
STRAIGHTENED	SUBANTARCTIC	SUFFRUTICOSE	SURREJOINDER
STRAIGHTENER	SUBAURICULAR	SUGAR DADDIES	SURRENDERING
STRAIGHTNESS	SUBCELESTIAL	SUGGESTINGLY	SURROUNDEDLY
STRAINEDNESS	SUBCLIMACTIC	SUGGESTIVELY	SURROUNDINGS
STRAITJACKET	SUBCOMMITTEE	SUITABLENESS	SURVEILLANCE
STRANGLEHOLD	SUBCONSCIOUS	SULPHONAMIDE	SURVEYORSHIP
STRANGULATED	SUBCONTINENT	SULPHURATION	SURVIVAL KITS
STRAPHANGERS	SUBCONTRACTS	SUMMERIZABLE	SUSCEPTIVITY
STRAPHANGING	SUBCUTANEOUS	SUMMERHOUSES	SUSPICIOUSLY
STRATICULATE	SUBDIVISIONS	SUMMER SCHOOL	SUSTAININGLY
STRATIGRAPHY	SUBERIZATION	SUNDAY SCHOOL	SWAGGERINGLY
STRATOCRATIC	SUBINFEUDATE	SUPERABILITY	SWALLOW DIVES
STRATOSPHERE	SUBJECTIVELY	SUPERANNUATE	SWASH BUCKLER
STRAWBERRIES	SUBJECTIVISM	SUPERCHARGED	SWEEPINGNESS
STREAMLINING	SUBJECTIVIST	SUPERCHARGER	SWEET-AND-
STREET VALUES	SUBJECTIVITY	SUPERCILIARY	SOUR
STREET WALKER	SUBJUNCTIVES	SUPERCILIOUS	SWEET PEPPERS

SWEET-TALKING
SWEET WILLIAM
SWELTERINGLY
SWIMMING BATH
SWITCH BLADES
SWITCH BOARDS
SWIZZLE STICK
SWORD DANCERS
SYLLABICALLY
SYMBOLICALLY
SYMBOLOGICAL
SYMMETALLISM
SYMPATHIZERS
SYMPATHIZING
SYNAESTHESIA
SYNAESTHETIC
SYNAPTICALLY
SYNARTHROSIS
SYNCHROFLASH
SYNCHRONIZED
SYNCHRONIZER
SYNCHROSCOPE
SYNCLINORIUM
SYNDACTYLISM
SYNDECTICALLY
SYNDICALISTS
SYNDIOTACTIC
SYNONYMOUSLY
SYNOPTICALLY
SYNTHESIZERS
SYNTHESIZING
SYNTONICALLY
SYSTEMATIZED
SYSTEMATIZER
SYSTEMICALLY

13 LETTERS
SABRE-RATTLING
SACRIFICEABLE
SACRIFICIALLY
SACRIFICINGLY
SADOMASOCHISM
SADOMASOCHIST
SAFETY CATCHES
SAFETY CURTAIN
SAFETY ISLAND
SAFETY MATCHES
SAGACIOUSNESS
SAINT LAWRENCE
SALACIOUSNESS
SALAD DRESSING
SALVATION ARMY
SALVATIONISTS

SANCTIMONIOUS
SANDWICH BOARD
SANITARY TOWEL
SARCASTICALLY
SARCOPHAGUSES
SATANICALNESS
SATIRICALNESS
SATISFACTIONS
SATURNINENESS
SCANDALMONGER
SCARIFICATION
SCATTERBRAINS
SCENESHIFTERS
SCEPTICALNESS
SCHEMATICALLY
SCHIZOPHRENIA
SCHIZOPHRENIC
SCHOLARLINESS
SCHOLASTICATE
SCHOLASTICISM
SCHOOLFELLOWS
SCHOOL-LEAVERS
SCHOOLMASTERS
SCHOOLTEACHER
SCINTILLATING
SCINTILLATION
SCOLOPENDRINE
SCORCHED EARTH
SCORIFICATION
SCRIPTWRITERS
SCRIPTWRITING
SCULPTURESQUE
SEARCH PARTIES
SEARCH WARRANT
SEASON TICKETS
SEAWORTHINESS
SECLUSIVENESS
SECONDARINESS
SECOND COUSINS
SECOND-GUESSED
SECOND THOUGHT
SECRETARYSHIP
SECRETIVENESS
SECRET SERVICE
SECURITY RISKS
SEDENTARINESS
SEDIMENTARILY
SEDIMENTATION
SEDIMENTOLOGY
SEDITIOUSNESS
SEDUCTIVENESS
SEGREGATIONAL
SEISMOGRAPHER
SEISMOGRAPHIC

SEISMOLOGISTS
SELECTIVENESS
SELENOGRAPHER
SELENOGRAPHIC
SELF-ABASEMENT
SELF-ADDRESSED
SELF-ANNEALING
SELF-APPOINTED
SELF-ASSERTION
SELF-ASSERTIVE
SELF-ASSURANCE
SELF-CONFESSED
SELF-CONFIDENT
SELF-CONSCIOUS
SELF-CONTAINED
SELF-DECEPTION
SELF-DECEPTIVE
SELF-DEFEATING
SELF-EVIDENTLY
SELF-IMPORTANT
SELF-INDUCTION
SELF-INDUCTIVE
SELF-INDULGENT
SELF-INFLICTED
SELF-KNOWLEDGE
SELF-PITYINGLY
SELF-POSSESSED
SELF-PROPELLED
SELF-RESTRAINT
SELF-RIGHTEOUS
SELF-SACRIFICE
SELF-SATISFIED
SELLING-PLATER
SELLING POINTS
SEMIAUTOMATIC
SEMICONDUCTOR
SEMICONSCIOUS
SEMIDETACHEDS
SEMIFINALISTS
SEMIPARASITIC
SEMIPERMEABLE
SEMPER FIDELIS
SENIOR CITIZEN
SENSATIONALLY
SENSELESSNESS
SENSITIVENESS
SENSITIZATION
SENTENTIOUSLY
SENTIMENTALLY
SEQUENTIALITY
SERGEANT MAJOR
SERIALIZATION
SERIAL NUMBERS
SERVICE CHARGE

SEVENTH HEAVEN
SEWING MACHINE
SEXAGENARIANS
SEXPLOITATION
SHAKESPEAREAN
SHAMELESSNESS
SHAPELESSNESS
SHARP PRACTICE
SHARPSHOOTERS
SHEEPSHEARING
SHEPHERDESSES
SHIFTLESSNESS
SHIRTWAISTERS
SHOCK ABSORBER
SHOOTING MATCH
SHOOTING STARS
SHOOTING STICK
SHOP ASSISTANT
SHORT-CHANGING
SHORT CIRCUITS
SHORT-TEMPERED
SHOULDER BLADE
SHOULDER STRAP
SHROVE TUESDAY
SICK HEADACHES
SIDESPLITTING
SIERRA LEONEAN
SIGHTLESSNESS
SIGNATURE TUNE
SIGNIFICANTLY
SIGNIFICATION
SIGNIFICATIVE
SILENT PARTNER
SILVER BIRCHES
SILVER JUBILEE
SILVER MACHINE
SILVER-TONGUED
SILVER WEDDING
SIMPLE MACHINES
SINGLE-DECKERS
SINGULARITIES
SITTING TARGET
SIXTEENTH NOTE
SKEET SHOOTING
SKIRTING BOARD
SLAP AND TICKLE
SLEDGEHAMMERS
SLEEPING PILLS
SLEEPLESSNESS
SLEIGHT OF HAND
SLIDING SCALES
SLIPSTREAMING
SMALL FORTUNES
SMALLHOLDINGS

SMELLING SALTS
SMOOTH-TONGUED
SNAKE CHARMERS
SNAP FASTENERS
SNEAK PREVIEWS
SNOW BLINDNESS
SOCIAL CLIMBER
SOCIALIZATION
SOCIAL SCIENCE
SOCIAL SERVICE
SOCIAL WORKERS
SOCIOECONOMIC
SODA FOUNTAINS
SOFT-PEDALLING
SOLDERING IRON
SOLDIERLINESS
SOLICITATIONS
SOLICITORSHIP
SOLILOQUIZING
SOMERSAULTING
SOMNAMBULANCE
SOMNAMBULATOR
SOMNAMBULISTS
SOPHISTICALLY
SOPHISTICATED
SOPHISTICATES
SOPHISTICATOR
SOPORIFICALLY
SORROWFULNESS
SOUL-SEARCHING
SOUNDING BOARD
SOUNDLESSNESS
SOUNDPROOFING
SOUTHEASTERLY
SOUTHEASTWARD
SOUTHERLINESS
SOUTHWESTERLY
SOUTHWESTWARD
SPACE SHUTTLES
SPACE STATIONS
SPASMODICALLY
SPECIAL BRANCH
SPECIAL SCHOOL
SPECIFICATION
SPECTACULARLY
SPECTROGRAPHY
SPECTROMETRIC
SPECTROSCOPES
SPECTROSCOPIC
SPECULATIVELY
SPEECH THERAPY
SPENDING MONEY
SPERMATICALLY
SPERMATOPHORE

SPERMATOPHYTE
SPHERICALNESS
SPINE-CHILLING
SPINELESSNESS
SPINNING JENNY
SPINNING WHEEL
SPIRITUALISTS
SPIRITUALIZER
SPIT AND POLISH
SPITTING IMAGE
SPLAYFOOTEDLY
SPLENDIFEROUS
SPLINTER GROUP
SPONTANEOUSLY
SPORTSMANLIKE
SPORTSMANSHIP
SPREAD-EAGLING
SPRIGHTLINESS
SPRING CHICKEN
SPRING-CLEANED
SQUANDERINGLY
SQUARE-BASHING
SQUARE BRACKET
SQUEAMISHNESS
STABILIZATION
STAFF OFFICERS
STAFF SERGEANT
STAGE MANAGERS
STAGE-MANAGING
STAGE WHISPERS
STANDARDIZING
STANDARD LAMPS
STANDING ORDER
STANDOFFISHLY
STAPHYLOCOCCI
STARCH-REDUCED
STARTING BLOCK
STARTING GATES
STARTING PRICE
STATELESSNESS
STATE-OF-THE-ART
STATESMANLIKE
STATESMANSHIP
STATION BREAKS
STATION HOUSES
STATIONMASTER
STATION WAGONS
STATISTICALLY
STATISTICIANS
STEADFASTNESS
STEAMROLLERED
STEEPLECHASER
STEEPLECHASES
STEERING WHEEL

STENOGRAPHERS
STEPPING-STONE
STERCORACEOUS
STEREOGRAPHIC
STEREOSCOPIST
STEREOTYPICAL
STICKING POINT
STICK-IN-THE-MUD
STILETTO HEELS
STIMULATINGLY
STOCKBREEDERS
STOCKBREEDING
STOCK EXCHANGE
STORM TROOPERS
STORMY PETRELS
STOVEPIPE HATS
STRAIGHTEDGES
STRAIGHTENING
STRAIGHT-FACED
STRAIGHT FIGHT
STRAITJACKETS
STRANGLEHOLDS
STRANGULATING
STRANGULATION
STRATEGICALLY
STRATOCUMULUS
STRATOSPHERIC
STRAW-COLOURED
STREETWALKERS
STRENGTHENING
STRENUOUSNESS
STREPTOCOCCAL
STREPTOCOCCUS
STREPTOKINASE
STRIKEBREAKER
STRIP CARTOONS
STRIP LIGHTING
STRUCTURALISM
STRUCTURALIST
STUDENTS' UNION
STUDIO COUCHES
STUFFED SHIRTS
STYLISTICALLY

SUBCOMMITTEES
SUBCONTINENTS
SUBCONTRACTED
SUBCONTRACTOR
SUBDIVISIONAL
SUBEQUATORIAL
SUBJECT MATTER
SUBMACHINE GUN
SUBORDINATING
SUBORDINATION
SUBORDINATIVE
SUBPOPULATION
SUBSCRIPTIONS
SUBSERVIENTLY
SUBSIDIZATION
SUBSTANTIALLY
SUBSTANTIATED
SUBSTANTIATOR
SUBSTANTIVELY
SUBSTANTIVIZE
SUBSTITUTABLE
SUBSTITUTIONS
SUBSTRUCTURAL
SUBSTRUCTURES
SUFFICIENCIES
SUFFOCATINGLY
SUFFRAGANSHIP
SUFFRAGETTISM
SUFFUMIGATION
SULPHURIC ACID
SUMMARIZATION
SUMMER SCHOOLS
SUMPTUOUSNESS
SUNDAY SCHOOLS
SUPERABUNDANT
SUPERADDITION
SUPERANNUATED
SUPERCHARGES
SUPERCHARGING
SUPERCOLUMNAR
SUPEREMINENCE
SUPERFICIALLY
SUPERFLUIDITY

SUPERFLUOUSLY
SUPERHUMANITY
SUPERIMPOSING
SUPERINTENDED
SUPERLATIVELY
SUPERNATATION
SUPERNUMERARY
SUPERORDINATE
SUPERPHYSICAL
SUPERPOSITION
SUPERSENSIBLE
SUPERSTITIONS
SUPERSTITIOUS
SUPPLANTATION
SUPPLEMENTARY
SUPPLEMENTING
SUPPLICATIONS
SUPPLY TEACHER
SUPPOSITIONAL
SUPPOSITORIES
SUPERNATIONAL
SURREPTITIOUS
SURROGATESHIP
SURVIVABILLITY
SWASHBUCKLING
SWEET NOTHINGS
SWIMMING BATHS
SWIMMING POOLS
SWIZZLE STICKS
SWOLLEN HEADED
SWORDSMANSHIP
SYMBOLIZATION
SYMMETRICALLY
SYMPATHECTOMY
SYMPHONICALLY
SYNCHRONISTIC
SYNCHRONIZING
SYNTHETICALLY
SYSTEMATIZING
SYSTEMATOLOGY
SYSTEMIZATION

3 LETTERS	4 LETTERS			5 LETTERS	
3 LETTERS	TAPE	TILE	TRIS	TAMED	TEMPI
TAB	TAPS	TILL	TROD	TAMER	TEMPO
TAG	TARE	TILT	TROT	TAMMY	TEMPS
TAN	TARN	TIME	TRUE	TAMPA	TEMPT
TAP	TARO	TINE	TRUG	TANGO	TENCH
TAR	TARS	TING	TSAR	TANGY	TENET
TAT	TART	TINS	TUBA	TANKS	TENON
TAX	TASK	TINT	TUBE	TANSY	TENOR
TEA	TA-TA	TINY	TUBS	TANTA	TENSE
TEE	TATS	TIPS	TUCK	TANTO	TENTH
TEN	TAUT	TIRE	TUFT	TAPED	TENTS
THE	TAXI	TIRO	TUGS	TAPER	TEPEE
THY	TEAK	TOAD	TUNA	TAPES	TEPIC
TIC	TEAL	TO-DO	TUNE	TAPIR	TEPID
TIE	TEAM	TODS	TURD	TAPIS	TERMS
TIN	TEAR	TOED	TURF	TARDY	TERNE
TIP	TEAS	TOES	TURN	TARES	TERNI
TIT	TEAT	TOFF	TUSH	TARNS	TERNS
TNT	TEED	TOGA	TUTU	TAROS	TERRA
TOD	TEEM	TOGO	TWEE	TAROT	TERRY
TOE	TEES	TOGS	TWIG	TARRY	TERSE
TOG	TELE-	TOIL	TWIN	TARSI	TESLA
TON	TELL	TOLD	TWIT	TARTS	TESOL
TOO	TEMP	TOLL	TWOS	TASKS	TESTA
TOP	TEND	TOMB	TYPE	TASTE	TESTS
TOR	TENS	TOME	TYRE	TASTY	TESTY
TOT	TENT	TONE	TYRO	TATAR	TETRA
TOW	TERM	TONS	TZAR	TATRA	TEXAS
TOY	TERN	TOOK		TATTY	TEXTS
TRY	TEST	TOOL		TAUNT	THANE
TUB	TEXT	TOOT	**5 LETTERS**	TAUPE	THANK
TUT	THAN	TOPS	TABBY	TAWER	THAWS
TVS	THAT	TOE	TABES	TAWNY	THECA
TWO	THAW	TORS	TABLE	TAXED	THEFT
	THEE	TORT	TABOO	TAXER	THEGN
	THEM	TORY	TABOR	TAXES	THEIR
4 LETTERS	THEN	TOSS	TACET	TAXIS	THEME
TABS	THEO-	TOTE	TACIT	TAXON	THERE
TACK	THEY	TOTO	TACKS	TAYRA	THERM
TACO	THIN	TOTS	TACKY	TAZZA	THESE
TACT	THIS	TOUR	TACOS	T-BONE	THETA
TAGS	THOU	TOUT	TAEGU	TEACH	THEWS
TAIL	THRU	TOWN	TAFFY	TEAKS	THICK
TAKE	THUD	TOWS	TAIGA	TEAMS	THIEF
TALC	THUG	TOYS	TAILS	TEARS	THIGH
TALE	THUS	TRAD	TAINT	TEASE	THINE
TALK	TICK	TRAM	TAKEN	TEATS	THING
TALL	TICS	TRAP	TAKER	TECHY	THINK
TAME	TIDE	TRAY	TAKES	TEENS	THIOL
TAMP	TIDY	TREE	TALES	TEENY	THIRD
TANG	TIED	TREK	TALKS	TEETH	THOLE
TANH	TIER	TRIM	TALLY	TELEX	THONG
TANK	TIES	TRIO	TALON	TELIC	THORN
TANS	TIFF	TRIP	TALUS	TELLY	THOSE

THREE	TOAST	TOWED	TROTS	TWAIN	TALKED
THREW	TODAY	TOWEL	TROUT	TWANG	TALKER
THROB	TODDY	TOWER	TROVE	TWEAK	TALKIE
THROW	TO-DOS	TOWNS	TRUCE	TWEED	TALLER
THRUM	TOE-IN	TOXIC	TRUCK	TWEEN	TALLOW
THUDS	TOFFS	TOXIN	TRUER	TWEET	TALMUD
THUGS	TOGAS	TOYED	TRUES	TWERP	TALONS
THUJA	TOILE	TOYER	TRUGS	TWICE	TAMELY
THUMB	TOILS	TRACE	TRULY	TWIGS	TAMERS
THUMP	TOKAY	TRACK	TRUMP	TWILL	TAMEST
THYME	TOKEN	TRACT	TRUNK	TWINE	TAMPED
TIARA	TOKYO	TRADE	TRURO	TWINS	TAMPER
TICAL	TOLAN	TRAIL	TRUSS	TWIRL	TAMPON
TICKS	TOLLS	TRAIN	TRUST	TWIRP	TANDEM
TIDAL	TOMBS	TRAIT	TRUTH	TWIST	TANGLE
TIDED	TOMES	TRAMP	TRYMA	TWITE	TANGLY
TIDES	TOMMY	TRAMS	TRY-ON	TWITS	TANGOS
TIE-ON	TONAL	TRANS-	TRYST	TWIXT	TANKER
TIERS	TONDO	TRAPS	TSARS	TYPING	TANNED
TIE-UP	TONED	TRASH	TUBAL	TYPED	TANNER
TIFFS	TONER	TRASS	TUBAS	TYRES	TANNIC
TIGER	TONES	TRAVE	TUBBY	TYROL	TANNIN
TIGHT	TONGA	TRAWL	TUBER	TYROS	TANNOY
TIGON	TONGS	TRAYS	TUBES	TZARS	TAOISM
TIGRE	TONIC	TREAD	TUCKS		TAOIST
TILDE	TONNE	TREAT	TUDOR		TAPERS
TILED	TON-UP	TREEN	TUFTS	**6 LETTERS**	TAPING
TILER	TONUS	TREES	TUFTY	TABARD	TAPIERS
TILES	TOOLS	TREKS	TULIP	TABBED	TAPPED
TILLS	TOOTH	TREND	TULLE	TABLED	TAPPET
TILTH	TOOTS	TRESS	TULSA	TABLES	TARGET
TILTS	TOPAZ	TREWS	TUMID	TABLET	TARIFF
TIMED	TOPEE	TRIAD	TUMMY	TABOOS	TARMAC
TIMER	TOPER	TRIAL	TUNAS	TABRIZ	TAROTS
TIMES	TOPIC	TRIBE	TUNED	TACKED	TARPAN
TIMID	TOPOS	TRICE	TUNER	TACKER	TARPON
TINEA	TOQUE	TRICK	TUNES	TACKLE	TARRED
TINES	TORAH	TRIED	TUNIC	TACOMA	TARSAL
TINGE	TORCH	TRIER	TUNIS	TACTIC	TARSUS
TINGS	TORIC	TRIES	TUNNY	TAEJON	TARTAN
TINNY	TORSK	TRIKE	TURDS	TAGGED	TARTAR
TINTS	TORSO	TRILL	TURFS	TAHITI	TARTLY
TIPSY	TORTS	TRIMS	TURFY	TAILED	TASKER
TIRED	TORUN	TRINE	TURIN	TAILOR	TASMAN
TIRES	TORUS	TRIOL	TURKI	TAINAN	TASSEL
TIROS	TOTAL	TRIOS	TURKU	TAIPAN	TASTED
TITAN	TOTED	TRIPE	TURNS	TAIPEI	TASTER
TITHE	TOTEM	TRIPS	TURPS	TAIWAN	TASTES
TITLE	TOTER	TRITE	TUSKS	TAKERS	TATARY
TITRE	TOTES	TROLL	TUTEE	TAKEUP	TATTED
TITTY	TOUCH	TRONA	TUTOR	TAKING	TATTLE
TIZZY	TOUGH	TROOP	TUTTI	TALCUM	TATTOO
TOADS	TOURS	TROPE	TUTTY	TALENT	TAUGHT
TOADY	TOUTS	TROTH	TUTUS	TALION	TAUNTS

TAURUS	TENREC	THIEVE	TIE-DYE	TITCHY	TORERO
TAUTEN	TENSED	THIGHS	TIE-INS	TITFER	TORIES
TAUTER	TENSER	THINGS	TIEPIN	TITHER	TOROID
TAUTLY	TENSES	THINLY	TIERCE	TITHES	TOROSE
TAUTOG	TENSOR	THIRDS	TIE-UPS	TITLED	TORPID
TAVERN	TENTER	THIRST	TIFFIN	TITLES	TORPOR
TAWDRY	TENTHS	THIRTY	TIFLIS	TITTER	TORQUE
TAXEME	TENURE	THOLOS	TIGERS	TITTLE	TORRID
TAXIED	TENUTO	THONGS	TIGHTS	TITTUP	TORSOS
TAXING	TEPEES	THORAX	TIGRIS	THEMIS	TOSSED
TAXMAN	TEPEFY	THORIC	TILDES	TOASTS	TOSSES
TAXMEN	TERBIC	THORNS	TILERS	TOBAGO	TOSS-UP
T-BONES	TERCEL	THORNY	TILING	TOBRUK	TOTALS
TEABAG	TERCET	THORON	TILLED	TOCSIN	TOTEMS
TEACUP	TEREDO	THOUGH	TILLER	TODDLE	TOTING
TEAMED	TERETE	THRALL	TILTED	TOE CAP	TOTTED
TEAPOT	TERGAL	THRASH	TILTER	TOEING	TOTTER
TEAPOY	TERGUM	THREAD	TIMBAL	TOFFEE	TOUCAN
TEARER	TERMED	THREAT	TIMBER	TOGGED	TOUCHE
TEASED	TERMLY	THREES	TIMBRE	TOILED	TOUCHY
TEASEL	TERMOR	THRESH	TIMELY	TOILER	TOULON
TEASER	TERRET	THRICE	TIMERS	TOILET	TOUPEE
TEASES	TERROR	THRIFT	TIMING	TOKENS	TOURED
TEDDER	TESTED	THRILL	TINCAL	TOLLED	TOURER
TEDIUM	TESTER	THRIPS	TINDER	TOLUCA	TOUSLE
TEEING	TESTES	THRIVE	TINEAL	TOLUYL	TOUTED
TEEMED	TESTIS	THROAT	TINEID	TOMATO	TOWAGE
TEEPEE	TETCHY	THROBS	TINGED	TOMBAC	TOWBAR
TEETER	TETHER	THROES	TINGLE	TOMBOY	TOWELS
TEETHE	TETRAD	THRONE	TINGLY	TOMCAT	TOWERS
TEFLON	TETRYL	THRONG	TIN GOD	TOM-TOM	TOWHEE
TEGMEN	TETTER	THROVE	TIN HAT	TONGAN	TOWING
TELEDU	TETUAN	THROWN	TINIER	TONGUE	TOWNEE
TELIAL	TEUTON	THROWS	TINKER	TONICS	TOXINS
TELIUM	THAMES	THRUSH	TINKLE	TONING	TOXOID
TELLER	THANES	THRUST	TINKLY	TONKIN	TOYAMA
TELPAL	THANKS	THUMBS	TINNED	TONNES	TOYINGT
TELSON	THATCH	THUMPS	TIN-POT	TONSIL	TRACED
TEMPED	THAWED	THWACK	TINSEL	TOOLED	TRACER
TEMPER	THAWER	THWART	TINTED	TOOLER	TRACES
TEMPLE	THECAL	THYMIC	TIP-OFF	TOOTED	TRACKS
TEMPOS	THEFTS	THYMOL	TIPPED	TOOTER	TRACTS
TEMUCO	THEGNS	THYMUS	TIPPER	TOOTHY	TRADED
TENACE	THEINE	THYRSE	TIPPET	TOOTLE	TRADER
TENANT	THEIRS	TIARAS	TIPPLE	TOP DOG	TRADES
TENDED	THEISM	TIBIAE	TIPTOE	TOPEES	TRAGAL
TENDER	THEIST	TIBIAS	TIP-TOP	TOPEKA	TRAGIC
TENDON	THEMES	TICINO	TIRADE	TOP HAT	TRAGUS
TENETS	THENAR	TICKER	TIRANA	TOPHUS	TRAILS
TENNER	THENCE	TICKET	TIRING	TOPICS	TRAINS
TENNIS	THEORY	TICKLE	TISANE	TOPPED	TRAITS
TENONS	THERMS	TIDBIT	TISSUE	TOPPER	TRAMPS
TENORS	THESIS	TIDDILY	TITANS	TOPPLE	TRANCE
TENPIN	THETIC	TIDING	TITBIT	TORBAY	TRANNY

TRASHY	TROTHS	TUPELO	TWO-PLY	TALCOSE	TAPROOM
TRAUMA	TROTYL	TUPPED	TWO-WAY	TALENTS	TAPROOT
TRAVEL	TROUGH	TURBAN	TYCOON	TALIPED	TARANTO
TRAWLS	TROUPE	TURBID	TYNPAN	TALIPES	TARDIER
TREADS	TROUTS	TURBIT	TYPHUS	TALIPOT	TARDILY
TREATS	TROVER	TURBOT	TYPIFY	TALKERS	TARGETS
TREATLY	TROVES	TUREEN	TYPING	TALKIES	TARIFFS
TREBLE	TROWEL	TURFED	TYPIST	TALKING	TARMACS
TREBLY	TRUANT	TURGID	TYRANT	TALLAGE	TARNISH
TREMOR	TRUCES	TURGOR	TYRONE	TALLBOY	TARRASA
TRENCH	TRUCKS	TURION	TYUMEN	TALLEST	TARRIED
TRENDS	TRUDGE	TURKEY		TALLIED	TARRING
TRENDY	TRUEST	TURKIC		TALLIER	TARSIER
TREPAN	TRUISM	TURNED	**7 LETTERS**	TALLIES	TARATANS
TRESSY	TRUMPS	TURNER	TABANID	TALLINN	TARTARS
TRIADS	TRUNKS	TURNIP	TABASCO	TALLISH	TASSELS
TRIALS	TRUSTS	TURN-ON	TABBIES	TALLYHO	TASTIER
TRIBAL	TRUSTY	TURN-UP	TABBING	TAMABLE	TASTILY
TRIBES	TRUTHS	TURRET	TABLEAU	TAMARAU	TASTING
TRICES	TRYING	TURTLE	TABLING	TAMARIN	TATOUAY
TRICKS	TRY-OUT	TURVES	TABLOID	TAMBOUR	TATTERS
TRICKY	TRYISTS	TUSCAN	TABORET	TAMPERE	TATTIER
TRICOT	T-SHIRT	TUSCHE	TABORIN	TAMPICO	TATTING
TRIERS	TSINAN	TUSHES	TABULAR	TAMPING	TATTLED
TRIFID	TSINGA	TUSKER	TACHYON	TAMPONS	TATTLER
TRIFLE	TSWANA	TUSSAH	TACITLY	TANAGER	TATTOOS
TRIGER	TUAREG	TUSSIS	TACKIER	TANBARK	TAUNTED
TRIKES	TUBBED	TUSSLE	TACKILY	TANDEMS	TAUNTER
TRILBY	TUBERS	TUTORS	TACKING	TANGELO	TAUREAN
TRILLS	TUBING	TUTSAN	TACKLED	TANGENT	TAURINE
TRIMER	TUBULE	TUT-TUT	TACKLER	TANGIER	TAUTEST
TRIMLY	TUCKED	TUXEDO	TACKLES	TANGLED	TAVERNS
TRINAL	TUCKER	TUYERE	TACNODE	TANGLER	TAXABLE
TRIODE	TUCK-IN	TWANGS	TACTFUL	TANGLES	TAX-FREE
TRIOSE	TUCSON	TWANGY	TACTICS	TANGOED	TAXICAB
TRIPLE	TUFFET	TWEAKS	TACTILE	TANGRAM	TAXIING
TRIPOD	TUFTED	TWEEDS	TACTUAL	TANKAGE	TAXIWAY
TRIPOS	TUFTER	TWEEDY	TADPOLE	TANKARD	TBILIZI
TRITON	TUGGED	TWEETS	TADZHIK	TANKERS	TEABAGS
TRIUNE	TUGGER	TWELVE	TAFFETA	TANNAGE	TEACAKE
TRIVET	TULIPS	TWENTY	TAFFIES	TANNATE	TEACHER
TRIVIA	TUMBLE	TWERPS	TAGGERS	TANNERS	TEACHIN
TROCAR	TUMEFY	TWIGGY	TAGGING	TANNERY	TEACOSY
TROCHE	TUMOUR	TWILIT	TAGMEME	TANNING	TEACUPS
TROGAN	TUMULI	TWINED	TAIL END	TANTRUM	TEALEAF
TROIKA	TUMULT	TWINER	TAILING	TAOISTS	TEAMING
TROJAN	TUNDRA	TWINGE	TAILORS	TAPERED	TEAPOTS
TROLLS	TUNERS	TWIRLS	TAINTED	TAPERER	TEARFUL
TROMPE	TUNE-UP	TWIRLY	TAIYUAN	TAPETAL	TEARGAS
TROOPS	TUNGUS	TWIRPS	TAKABLE	TAPETUM	TEARING
TROPES	TUNICA	TWISTS	TAKEOFF	TAPHOLE	TEAROOM
TROPHY	TUNICS	TWISTY	TAKEOUT	TAPIOCA	TEASELS
TROPIC	TUNING	TWITCH	TAKEUPS	TAPPETS	TEASERS
TROPPO	TUNNEL	TWO-BIT	TAKINGS	TAPPING	TEASHOP

TEASING	TERMING	THICKER	TIDDLER	TIRADES	TOOTING
TECHILY	TERMINI	THICKET	TIDEWAT	TIREDLY	TOOTLED
TECHNIC	TERMITE	THICKLY	TIDIEST	TISSUES	TOOTLER
TECTRIC	TERNSRY	THIEVED	TIDINGS	TITANIA	TOOTLES
TEDIOUS	TERNATE	THIEVES	TIDYING	TITANIC	TOOTSIE
TEEMING	TERPENE	THIMBLE	TIE-DIED	TITBITS	TOPARCH
TEENAGE	TERRACE	THIN AIR	TIEPINS	TITFERS	TOPAZES
TEEPEES	TERRAIN	THINNED	TIFFANY	TITHING	TOPCOAT
TEGULAR	TERRANE	THINNER	TIGHTEN	TITMICE	TOP DOGS
TEHERAN	TERRENE	THIONIC	TIGHTER	TITOISM	TOP HATS
TEKTITE	TERRIER	THIONYL	TIGHTLY	TITOIST	TOPIARY
TELAMON	TERRIFY	THIRSTS	TIGRESS	TITRANT	TOPICAL
TEL AVIV	TERRINE	THIRSTY	TILAIPIA	TITRATE	TOPKNOT
TELEOST	TERRORS	THITHER	TILBURG	TITTERS	TOPLESS
TELERAN	TERSELY	THORITE	TILLAGE	TITTIES	TOPMAST
TELESIS	TERTIAL	THORIUM	TILLERS	TITULAR	TOPMOST
TELEXED	TERTAIN	THOUGHT	TILLING	TIZZIES	TOPONYM
TELEXES	TESSERA	THRALLS	TILTING	TOADIED	TOPPERS
TELLERS	TESTACY	THREADS	TIMBALE	TOADIES	TOPPING
TELLIES	TESTATE	THREADY	TIMBERS	TOASTED	TOPPLED
TELLING	TEST BAN	THREATS	TIMBRAL	TOASTER	TOPSOIL
TELPHER	TESTERS	THRIFTS	TIMBRES	TOBACCO	TOPSPIN
TELSTAR	TESTIER	THRIFTY	TIME LAG	TOBY JUG	TORCHES
TEMPERA	TESTIFY	THRILLS	TIMIDLY	TOCCATA	TORMENT
TEMPERS	TESTILY	THRIVED	TIMPANI	TOCSINS	TORNADO
TEMPEST	TESTING	THROATS	TINAMOU	TODDLES	TORONTO
TEMPING	TETANIC	THROATY	TINFOIL	TODDLED	TORPEDO
TEMPLES	TETANUS	THRONES	TINGING	TODDLER	TORQUAY
TEMPTED	TETHERS	THRONGS	TINGLED	TOE CAPS	TORQUES
TEMPTER	TETRODE	THROUGH	TINGLER	TOEHOLD	TORREFY
TENABLE	TEXTILE	THROWER	TIN GODS	TOENAIL	TORRENT
TENANCY	TEXTUAL	THROW-IN	TIN HATS	TOFFEES	TORREON
TENANTS	TEXTURE	THRUSTS	TINIEST	TOGGING	TORSADE
TENCHES	THALLIC	THRUWAY	TINKERS	TOGGLES	TORSION
TENDERS	THALLUS	THUDDED	TINKLED	TOHEROA	TORTONI
TENDING	THANKED	THULIUM	TINKLES	TOILETS	TORTURE
TENDONS	THAWING	THUMBED	TINNIER	TOILING	TORYISM
TENDRILL	THEATRE	THUMPED	TINNILY	TOLLING	TOSSING
TENFOLD	THEISTS	THUMPER	TINNING	TOLUATE	TOSS-UPS
TENNERS	THEORUM	THUNDER	TINTACK	TOLUENE	TOTALED
TENONER	THERAPY	THURGAU	TINTING	TOMBOLA	TOTALLY
TENPINS	THEREAT	THWACKS	TINTYPE	TOMBOYS	TOTE BAG
TENSELY	THEREBY	THYMINE	TINWARE	TOMCATS	TOTEMIC
TENSEST	THEREIN	THYROID	TINWORK	TOMFOOL	TOTTERY
TENSILE	THEREOF	THYRUS	TIPOFFS	TOM-TOMS	TOTTING
TENSING	THEREON	THYSELF	TIPPERS	TONETIC	TOUCANS
TENSION	THERETO	TIBETAN	TIPPING	TONGUES	TOUCHED
TENSIVE	THERMAL	TICKERS	TIPPLER	TONIGHT	TOUCHER
TENTAGE	THERMIC	TICKETS	TIPPLES	TONNAGE	TOUCHES
TENUITY	THERMIT	TICKING	TIPSIER	TONNEAU	TOUGHEN
TENUOUS	THERMOS	TICKLED	TIPSILY	TONSILS	TOUGHER
TEPIDLY	THEROID	TICKLER	TIPSTER	TONSURE	TOUGHLY
TEQUILA	THEURGY	TICKLES	TIPTOED	TONTINE	TOUPEES
TERBIUM	THICKEN	TIDBITS	TIPTOES	TOOLING	TOURACO

T

7 LETTERS to 8 LETTERS

TOURING	TRAWLER	TRIPPET	TRUSTER	TURN-OFF	TYPISTS
TOURISM	TREACLE	TRIPURA	TRYPSIN	TURN-ONS	TYRANNY
TOURIST	TREACLY	TRIREME	TRYPTIC	TURNOUT	TYRANTS
TOURNEY	TREADER	TRISECT	TRYSAIL	TURN-UPS	TYROONIC
TOUSLED	TREADLE	TRISMIC	TRYSTER	TURPETH	TZARINA
TOUTING	TREASON	TRISMUS	TSARDOM	TURRETS	
TOWARDS	TREATED	TRISOME	TSARINA	TURTLER	
TOWBOAT	TREATER	TRITELY	TSARIST	TURTLES	**8 LETTERS**
TOWELED	TREBLED	TRITIUM	T-SHIRTS	TUSCANY	TABLEAUS
TOWERED	TREBLES	TRITONE	T-SQUARE	TUSKERS	TABLEAUX
TOWHEAD	TREFOIL	TRIUMPH	TSUNAMI	TUSSIVE	TABLEMAT
TOWLINE	TREHALA	TRIVETS	TUATARA	TUSSLED	TABLOIDS
TOWPATH	TREKKED	TRIVIAL	TUBBIER	TUSSLES	TABULATE
TOWROPE	TREKKER	TROCHAL	TUBBING	TUSSOCK	TACITURN
TRACERS	TRELLIS	TROCHEE	TUBIFEX	TUTORED	TACKIEST
TRACERY	TREMBLE	TRODDEN	TUBULAR	TUXEDOS	TACKLING
TRACHEA	TREMBLY	TROIKAS	TUCKING	TWADDLE	TACONITE
TRACING	TREMOLO	TROJANS	TUCUMAN	TWANGED	TACTICAL
TRACKED	TREMORS	TROLLED	TUESDAY	TWEAKED	TACTLESS
TRACKER	TRENTON	TROLLEY	TUGGING	TWEETED	TADPOLES
TRACTOR	TREPANG	TROLLOP	TUITION	TWEETER	TAFFRAIL
TRADE-IN	TRESSES	TROMMEL	TUMBLED	TWELFTH	TAGMEMIC
TRADERS	TRESTLE	TROOPED	TUMBLER	TWELVES	TAHITIAN
TRADING	TRIABLE	TROOPER	TUMBLES	TWIDDLE	TAICHUNG
TRADUCE	TRIACID	TROPHIC	TUMBREL	TWIDDLY	TAILBACK
TRAFFIC	TRIADIC	TROPICS	TUMMIES	TWIGGED	TAILCOAT
TRAGEDY	TRIBADE	TROPISM	TUMOURS	TWIN BED	TAIL ENDS
TRAILED	TRIBUTE	TROTTED	TUMULAR	TWINGES	TAILGATE
TRAILER	TRICEPS	TROTTER	TUMULTS	TWINING	TAILINGS
TRAINED	TRICKLE	TROUBLE	TUMULUS	TWINKLE	TAILLESS
TRAINEE	TRICKLY	TROUGHS	TUNABLE	TWINNED	TAILORED
TRAINER	TRICKSY	TROUNCE	TUNEFUL	TWIN SET	TAIL PIPE
TRAIPSE	TRICORN	TROUPER	TUNICLE	TWIRLED	TAIL RACE
TRAITOR	TRIDENT	TROUPES	TUNISIA	TWIRLER	TALESKID
TRAJECT	TRIESTE	TROUSER	TUNNELS	TWISTED	TAILSPIN
TRAMCAR	TRIFLED	TROWELS	TUNNIES	TWISTER	TAILWIND
TRAMMEL	TRIFLER	TRUANCY	TUPPING	TWITTER	TAINTING
TRAMPED	TRIFLES	TRUANTS	TURBANS	TWOFOLD	TAKEAWAY
TRAMPER	TRIGGER	TRUCKED	TURBARY	TWOSOME	TAKEOFFS
TRAMPLE	TRILLED	TRUCKLE	TURBINE	TWO-STAR	TAKEOUTS
TRAMWAY	TRILOGY	TRUDGED	TURBOTS	TWO-STEP	TAKEOVER
TRANCES	TRIMMED	TRUDGEN	TURBINE	TWO-TIME	TAKORADI
TRANSIT	TRIMMER	TRUDGER	TUREENS	TWO-TONE	TALAPOIN
TRANSOM	TRINARY	TRUDGES	TURFING	TYCHISM	TALENTED
TRAPEZE	TRINITY	TRUFFLE	TURGITE	TYCOONS	TALESMAN
TRAPPED	TRINKET	TRUISMS	TURKEYS	TYLOSIS	TALISMAN
TRAPPED	TRIOLET	TRUMPED	TURKISH	TYMPANA	TALKABLE
TRAPPER	TRIPLET	TRUMPET	TURKMEN	TYNWALD	TALK
TRASHED	TRIPLEX	TRUNDLE	TURMOIL	TYPEBAR	SHOW
TRAUMAS	TRIPODS	TRUSSED	TURNERS	TYPESET	TALL BOYS
TRAVAIL	TRIPODY	TRUSSER	TURNERY	TYPHOID	TALLNESS
TRAVELS	TRIPOLY	TRUSSES	TURNING	TYPHOON	TALLYING
TRAVOIS	TRIPPED	TRUSTED	TURNIPS	TYPHOUS	TALLYMAN
TRAWLED	TRIPPER	TRUSTEE	TURNKEY	TYPICAL	TALMUDIC

662

TAMANDUA	TATTLERS	TELLABLE	TESSERAL	THIAZOLE
TAMARACK	TATTLING	TELLTALE	TESTABLE	THICKEST
TAMARIND	TATTOOED	TELLURIC	TESTATOR	THICKETS
TAMARISK	TATTOOER	TELSONIC	TEST BANS	THICKSET
TAMBOURS	TAUNTING	TEMPERITY	TEST CARD	THIEVERY
TAMEABLE	TAUTENED	TEMPERED	TEST CASE	THIEVING
TAMENESS	TAUTOMER	TEMPERER	TESTICLE	THIEVISH
TAMPERED	TAVERNER	TEMPESTS	TESTIEST	THIMBLES
TAMPERER	TAWDRILLY	TEMPLATE	TEST TUBE	THIN-FILM
TANDOORI	TAXATION	TEMPORAL	TETANIZE	THINKING
TANGENCI	TAX HAVEN	TEMPTERS	TETCHIER	THINNESS
TANGENTS	TAXINGLY	TEMPTING	TETCHILY	THINNEST
TANGIBLE	TAXI RANK	TENACITY	TETHERED	THINNING
TANGIBLY	TAXONOMY	TENANTRY	TETRACID	THIONINE
TANGIEST	TAXPAYER	TENDENCY	TETRAPOD	THIOUREA
TANGLING	TEABERRY	TENDERED	TETRARCH	THIRTEEN
TANGOING	TEA BREAK	TENDERER	TEUTONIC	THIRTLES
TANGOIST	TEA CADDY	TENDERLY	TEXTBOOK	THISTLES
TANGSHAN	TEA CAKES	TENDRILLS	TEXTILES	THORACES
TANKARDS	TEACHERS	TENEMENT	TEXTUARY	THORACIC
TANKED UP	TEA CHEST	TENESMIC	TEXTURAL	THORAXES
TANTALIC	TEACHING	TENESMUS	TEXTURES	THORNIER
TANTALUM	TEACH-INS	TENORITE	THAILAND	THORNILY
TANTALUS	TEA CLOTH	TENOTOMY	THALAMIC	THOROUGH
TANTRUMS	TEAHOUSE	TENSED UP	THALAMUS	THOUGHTS
TANZANIA	TEA-MAKER	TENSIBLE	THALLOID	THOUSAND
TAP DANCE	TEAM-MATE	TENSIONS	THALLOUS	THRALDOM
TAPE DECK	TEAMSTER	TENTACLE	THANKFUL	THRASHED
TAPERING	TEA PARTY	TENURIAL	THANKING	THRASHED
TAPE WORM	TEARABLE	TEOCALLI	THANK YOU	THRASHER
TAPPABLE	TEARAWAY	TEOSINTE	THATCHED	THREADED
TAPROOTS	TEARDROP	TEPHRITE	THATCHER	THREADER
TARBRUSH	TEAROOMS	TEPIDITY	THATCHES	THREATEN
TARDIEST	TEASPOON	TERATISM	THEARCHY	THREE-PLY
TARGETED	TEA TOWEL	TERATOID	THEATRES	THRENODY
TARLATAN	TECHNICS	TERATOMA	THEBAINE	THRESHED
TARRADON	TECTONIC	TEREBENE	THEISTIC	THRESHER
TARRYING	TEDDY BOY	TERESINA	THEMATIC	THRESHES
TARTARIC	TEENAGER	TERMINAL	THEOCRAT	THRILLED
TARTNESS	TEE SHIRT	TERMINUS	THEOLOGY	THRILLER
TARTRATE	TEESSIDE	TERMITES	THEOREMS	THRIVING
TASHKENT	TEETERED	TERMITIC	THEORIES	THROBBED
TASKWORK	TEETHING	TERMLESS	THEORIST	THROMBIN
TASMANIA	TEETOTAL	TERPENIC	THEORIZE	THROMBUS
TASSELED	TEGMINAL	TERRACES	THEREMIN	THRONGED
TASSELLY	TELECAST	TERRAPIN	THERMALS	THROTTLE
TASTABLE	TELEGONY	TERRAZO	THERMION	THROWING
TASTE BUD	TELEGRAM	TERRIBLE	THERMITE	THROW-INS
TASTEFUL	TELEMARK	TERRIBLY	THEROPOD	THRUMMED
TASTIEST	TELEPLAY	TERRIERS	THESPIAN	THRUMMER
TATARIAN	TELETEXT	TERRIFIC	THESSALY	THRUSHES
TATTERED	TELETYPE	TERTIARY	THEURGIC	THRUSTER
TATTIEST	TELEVISE	TERYLENE	THIAMINE	THRUWAYS
TATTLERS	TELEXING	TERZETTO	THIAZINE	THUDDING

T 8 LETTERS

THUGGERY	TIPPLERS	TONE POEM	TOURAINE	TRANSEPT
THUMBING	TIPSIEST	TONICITY	TOURISTS	TRANSFER
THUMBNUT	TIPSTAFF	TONNAGES	TOURISTY	TRANSFIX
THUMPING	TIPSTERS	TONSURES	TOURNEYS	TRANSITS
THUNDERS	TIRESOME	TOOTHIER	TOUSLING	TRANSMIT
THUNDERY	TITANATE	TOOTHILY	TOWELING	TRANSOMS
THURIBLE	TITANISM	TOOTLING	TOWELLED	TRANSUDE
THURIFER	TITANITE	TOOTSIES	TOWERING	TRAPDOOR
THURSDAY	TITANIUM	TOPARCHY	TOWN HALL	TRAPEZES
THWACKED	TITANOUS	TOP BRASS	TOWNSHIP	TRAPEZIA
THWACKER	TITCHIER	TOP COATS	TOWNSMAN	TRAPPERS
THWARTED	TITHABLE	TOP-DRESS	TOWNSMEN	TRAPPING
THWARTER	TITIVATE	TOP-HEAVY	TOWPATHS	TRAPPIST
THYROIDS	TITMOUSE	TOPKNOTS	TOWROPES	TRAPUNTO
TIA MARIA	TITOGRAD	TOP-LEVEL	TOXAEMIA	TRASHCAN
TICKETED	TITTERED	TOP-NOTCH	TOXAEMIC	TRASHIER
TICKLING	TITTERER	TOPOLOGY	TOXICANT	TRASHILY
TICKLISH	TOADFISH	TOPONYMY	TOXICITY	TRASHING
TICK TACK	TOADFLAX	TOPOTYPE	TRACHEAL	TRAVELED
TICK TOCK	TOADYING	TOPPINGS	TRACHEAS	TRAVERSE
TIDDLERS	TOADYISM	TOPPLING	TRACHIED	TRAVESTY
TIDEMARK	TOADYIST	TOP-SHELL	TRACHOMA	TRAWLERS
TIDEWAYS	TO-AND-FRO	TORCHERE	TRACHYTE	TRAWLING
TIDINESS	TOASTERS	TORCHIER	TRACINGS	TREADING
TIE-DYING	TOASTING	TOREADOR	TRACKING	TREADLER
TIENTSIN	TOBACCOS	TOREUTIC	TRACTITE	TREADLES
TIGHTEST	TOBOGGAN	TORNADOS	TRACTILE	TREASURE
TILEFISH	TOBY JUGS	TOROIDAL	TRACTION	TREASURY
TILLABLE	TOCCATAS	TORPIDLY	TRACTIVE	TREATIES
TILLICUM	TOCOLOGY	TORQUATE	TRACTORS	TREATING
TIMBRELS	TODDLERS	TORRANCE	TRADABLE	TREATISE
TIMBUKTU	TODDLING	TORRENTS	TRADE GAP	TREATIZE
TIME BOMB	TOENAILS	TORRIDLY	TRADE-OFF	TREBLING
TIMECARD	TOGETHER	TORTILLA	TRAD JAZZ	TREE FERN
TIME LAGS	TOGOLESE	TORTIOUS	TRADUCED	TREELESS
TIMELESS	TOILETRY	TORTOISE	TRADUCER	TREELINE
TIMELIER	TOILETTE	TORTUOUS	TRAGOPAN	TREENAIL
TIMEWORK	TOILSOME	TORTURED	TRAILERS	TREFOILS
TIMEWORN	TOKENISM	TORTURER	TRAILING	TREKKING
TIME ZONE	TOLERANT	TORTURES	TRAINEES	TREMBLED
TIMIDITY	TOLERATE	TOTALLING	TRAINERS	TREMBLER
TIMOROUS	TOLIDINE	TOTALITY	TRAINING	TREMBLES
TINCTURE	TOLL-FREE	TOTALIZE	TRAINSET	TREMOLOS
TINGLING	TOLLGATE	TOTALLED	TRAIPSED	TRENCHER
TINKERED	TOMAHAWK	TOTE BAGS	TRAITORS	TRENCHES
TINKERER	TOMATOES	TOTEMISM	TRAMLINE	TRENDIER
TINKLING	TOMBLIKE	TOTEMIST	TRAMMELS	TRENDIES
TINNIEST	TOMENTUM	TOTTERED	TRAMPING	TRENDILY
TINNITUS	TOMMY GUN	TOTTERER	TRAMPLED	TREPHINE
TINPLATE	TOMMY ROT	TOUCHIER	TRAMPLER	TRESPASS
TINSELLY	TOMORROW	TOUCHILY	TRANNIES	TRESSURE
TINSMITH	TONALITY	TOUCHING	TRANQUIL	TRESTLES
TINTACKS	TONE-DEAF	TOUGHEST	TRANSACT	TRIADISM
TIPPABLE	TONELESS	TOULOUSE	TRANSECT	TRAIL RUN

				9 LETTERS
TRIANGLE	TRISOMIC	TRUSTIES	TUTELARY	TABESCENT
TRIARCHY	TRISTICH	TRUSTILY	TUTORAGE	TABLATURE
TRIASSIC	TRITICUM	TRUSTING	TUTORIAL	TABLEHAND
TRIAXIAL	TRIUMPHS	TRUTHFUL	TUTORING	TABLEMATS
TRIAZINE	TRIUNITY	TSARINAS	TV DINNER	TABLEWARE
TRIAZOLE	TROCHAIC	T-SQUARES	TWADDLER	TABLE WINE
TRIBADIC	TROCHEES	TUBBIEST	TWANGING	TABULABLE
TRIBASIC	TROCHLEA	TUBELESS	TWEAKING	TABULATED
TRIBRACH	TROCHOID	TUBERCLE	TWEETERS	TABULATOR
TRIBUNAL	TROLLEYS	TUBEROSE	TWEETING	TACHYLYTE
TRIBUNES	TROLLING	TUBEROUS	TWEEZERS	TACITNESS
TRICHINA	TROLLOPS	TUBIFORM	TWELFTHS	TACKINESS
TRICHITE	TROMBONE	TUBULATE	TWENTIES	TACTFULLY
TRICHOID	TROOPERS	TUBULOUS	TWIDDLED	TACTICIAN
TRICHOME	TROOPING	TUCKERED	TWIDDLER	TACTICALLY
TRICKERY	TROPHIES	TUESDAYS	TWIDDLES	TAENIAISIS
TRICKIER	TROCHOID	TUG-OF-WAR	TWILIGHT	TAGMEMICS
TRICKILY	TROLLEYS	TUMBLERS	TWIN BEDS	TAILBACKS
TRICKING	TROLLING	TUMBLING	TWINKLED	TAILBOARD
TRICKLED	TROLLOPS	TUMBRELS	TWINKLER	TAILCOATS
TRICTRAC	TROMBONE	TUMIDITY	TWINNING	TAILGATED
TRICYCLE	TROPERS	TUMOROUS	TWIN SETS	TAILLIGHT
TRIDENTS	TROOPING	TUMULOSE	TWIRLERS	TAILORING
TRIFLING	TROPHIES	TUNELESS	TWIRLING	TAILPIECE
TRIFOCAL	TROPICAL	TUNGSTEN	TWISTERS	TAIL PIPES
TRIGGERS	TROTLINE	TUNICATE	TWISTING	TAILPLANE
TRIGLYPH	TROTTERS	TUNISIAN	TWITCHED	TAILSPINS
TRIGONAL	TROTTING	TUNNELED	TWITCHER	TAILSTOCK
TRIGRAPH	TROUBLED	TUNNELER	TWITCHES	TAILWINDS
TRILBIES	TROUBLER	TUPPENCE	TWITTERS	TAIWANESE
TRILEMMA	TROUBLES	TUPPENNY	TWITTERY	TAKEAWAYS
TRILLING	TROUNCED	TURBANED	TWITTING	TAKEOVERS
TRILLION	TROUPERS	TURBINES	TWO-EDGED	TALIGRADE
TRILLIUM	TROUPIAL	TURBOCAR	TWO-FACED	TALISMANS
TRIMETER	TROUSERS	TURBOFAN	TWOPENCE	TALKATIVE
TRIMMERS	TRUCKERS	TURBOJET	TWOPENNY	TALKING-TO
TRIMMEST	TRUCKING	TURGIDLY	TWO-PHASE	TALK SHOW
TRIMMING	TRUDGING	TURKOMAN	TWO-PIECE	TALL ORDER
TRIMNESS	TRUE-BLUE	TURMERIC	TWO-SIDED	TALL STORY
TRIMORPH	TRUEBORN	TURNABLE	TWOSOMES	TALMUDISM
TRINIDAD	TRUE-LIFE	TURNCOAT	TWO-STEPS	TALMUDIST
TRIOXIDE	TRUELOVE	TURNINGS	TWO-TIMED	TAMARINDS
TRIPLANE	TRUENESS	TURNKEYS	TWO-TIMER	TAMPERING
TRIPLETS	TRUFFLES	TURN-OFFS	TYMPANIC	TANDOORIS
TRIPLING	TRUISTIC	TURNOUTS	TYMPANUM	TANGERINE
TRIPLOID	TRUMPERY	TURNOVER	TYNESIDE	TANNERIES
TRIPODAL	TRUMPETS	TURNPIKE	TYPECAST	TANTALATE
TRIPOSES	TRUMPING	TURNSOLE	TYPEFACE	TANTALITE
TRIPPERS	TRUNCATE	TURRETED	TYPE-HIGH	TANTALIZE
TRIPPERS	TRUNDLED	TUSKLIKE	TYPHOONS	TANTALOUS
TRIPPING	TRUSSING	TUSSLING	TYPIFIED	TANZANIAN
TRIPTANE	TRUSTEES	TUSSOCKS	TYPIFIER	TAP DANCER
TRIPTYCH	TRUSTFUL	TUSSOCKY	TYPOLOGY	TAP DANCES
TRIPWIRE	TRUSTIER	TUTELAGE	TZARINAS	

665

T
9 LETTERS

TAPE DECKS	TEDDY BOYS	TENTACLES	THECODONT	THRILLING
TAPEWORMS	TEDIOUSLY	TENTATION	THEME PARK	THROATER
TARANATISM	TEENAGERS	TENTATIVE	THEME SONG	THROATILY
TARANTULA	TEE SHIRTS	TENUOUSLY	THEOCRACY	THROBBING
TARAXACUM	TEETERING	TEPHRITIC	THEOCRASY	THRONGED
TARDINESS	TELECASTS	TEREBINTH	THEOMANIA	THROTTLED
TARGETING	TELEGENIC	TERMAGANT	THEORISTS	THROTTLER
TARMACKED	TELEGONIC	TERMINALS	THEORIZED	THROTTLES
TARNISHED	TELEGRAMS	TERMINATE	THEORIZER	THROWAWAY
TARNISHER	TELEGRAPH	TERPINEOL	THEOSOPHY	THROWBACK
TARPAULIN	TELEMETER	TERRAPINS	THERAPIES	THROWSTER
TARTARIZE	TELEMETRY	TERRARIUM	THERAPIST	THRUMMING
TARTAROUS	TELEOLOGY	TERRIFIED	THERAPSID	THRUSTERS
TASIMETER	TELEPATHY	TERRIFIER	THEREFORE	THUMBNAIL
TASIMETRY	TELEPHONE	TERRITORY	THEREINTO	THUMBTACK
TASK FORCE	TELEPHONY	TERRORFUL	THEREUPON	THUNDERED
TASMANIAN	TELESCOPE	TERRORISM	THEREWITH	THUNDERER
TASTEBUDS	TELESCOPY	TERRORIST	THERMOSES	THURINGIA
TASTELESS	TELEVISED	TERRORIZE	THESAURUS	THURSDAYS
TASTINESS	TELLINGLY	TERSENESS	THESPIANS	THWACKING
TATTOOING	TELLTALES	TERVALENT	THEURGIST	THWARTING
TATTOOIST	TELLURATE	TESSERACT	THICKENED	THYLACINE
TAUTENING	TELLURIAN	TESSITURA	THICKENER	THYMIDINE
TAUTOLOGY	TELLURIDE	TESTAMENT	THICKHEAD	THYRATRON
TAUTONOMY	TELLURION	TESTATORS	THICKLEAF	THYRISTOR
TAXACEOUS	TELLURITE	TESTATRIX	THICKNESS	THYROXINE
TAX HAVENS	TELLURIUM	TEST CARDS	THIGHBONE	TICKETING
TAXIDERMY	TELLURIZE	TEST CASES	THINKABLE	TIDAL WAVE
TAXIMETER	TELLUROUS	TESTICLES	THINK TANK	TIDEMARKS
TAXI RANKS	TELOPHASE	TESTIFIED	THIO-ETHER	TIDEWATER
TAXONOMIC	TELPHERIC	TESTIFIER	THIOPHENE	TIED HOUSE
TAXPAYERS	TEMPERATE	TESTIMONY	THIRD-RATE	TIE-DYEING
TEA BREAKS	TEMPERING	TESTINESS	THIRSTIER	TIGHTENED
TEACHABLE	TEMPLATES	TESTINGLY	THIRSTILY	TIGHTENER
TEA CHESTS	TEMPORARY	TEST MATCH	THIRTIETH	TIGHTKNIT
TEA CLOTHS	TEMPORIZE	TEST PILOT	THITHERTO	TIGHTNESS
TEA COSIES	TEMPTABLE	TEST TUBES	THORNBACK	TIGHTROPE
TEAGARDEN	TEMPTRESS	TETCHIEST	THORNBILL	TIGRESSES
TEAHOUSES	TENACIOUS	TETE-A-TETE	THORNIEST	TIME BOMBS
TEAKETTLE	TENACULUM	TETHERING	THOUSANDS	TIME-LAPSE
TEALEAVES	TENANCIES	TETRAGRAM	THRALLDOM	TIMELIEST
TEAMSTERS	TENDEREST	TETRALOGY	THRASHING	TIME LIMIT
TEARAWAYS	TENDERING	TETRAPODY	THREADFIN	TIMEPIECE
TEARDROPS	TENDERIZE	TETRARCHY	THREADING	TIMESAVER
TEARFULLY	TENDINOUS	TETROXIDE	THREEFOLD	TIME SHEET
TEARINGLY	TENEBRISM	TEXTBOOKS	THREESOME	TIMETABLE
TEASINGLY	TENEBRIST	THALASSIC	THREE-STAR	TIME ZONES
TEASPOONS	TENEBROUS	THANKLESS	THREONITE	TIMISOARA
TEA TOWELS	TENEMENTS	THANK YOUS	THRESHERS	TIMOCRACY
TECHINESS	TENNESSEE	THATCHERS	THRESHING	TIMPANIST
TECHNICAL	TENSENESS	THATCHING	THRESHOLD	TINCTURES
TECHNIQUE	TENSILITY	THEACEOUS	THRIFTIER	TINDERBOX
TECTONICS	TENSIONAL	THEARCHIC	THRIFTILY	TINGALING
TEDDY BEAR	TENSORIAL	THEATRICS	THRILLERS	TINKERING

TINNINESS	TOP-SECRET	TRACTABLE	TRAVERSES	TRICYCLIC
TIN OPENER	TORCHWOOD	TRADE GAPS	TREACHERY	TRIDACTYL
TIPSINESS	TOREADORS	TRADEMARK	TREADMILL	TRIENNIAL
TIREDNESS	TOREUTICS	TRADE NAME	TREASURED	TRIENNIUM
TITCHIEST	TORMENTED	TRADE-OFFS	TREASURER	TRIFOLIUM
TIT FOR TAT	TORMENTIL	TRADESMAN	TREASURES	TRIFORIAL
TITILLATE	TORMENTOR	TRADESMAN	TREATABLE	TRIFORIUM
TITIVATED	TORNADOES	TRADEWIND	TREATISES	TRIGGERED
TITIVATOR	TORPEDOED	TRADITION	TREATMENT	TRIGONOUS
TITLE DEED	TORPEDOES	TRADUCERS	TREE FERNS	TRIHEDRAL
TITLE PAGE	TORPIDITY	TRADUCING	TREENWARE	TRIHEDRON
TITLE ROLE	TORRIDITY	TRAFALGAR	TREHALOSE	TRIHYDRIC
TITRATION	TORSIONAL	TRAGEDIAN	TREILLAGE	TRILINEAR
TITTERING	TORTILLAS	TRAGEDIES	TRELLISES	TRILLIONS
T-JUNCTION	TORTOISES	TRAINABLE	TREMATODE	TRILOBATE
TOADSTONE	TORTRICID	TRAININGS	TREMBLING	TRILOBITE
TOADSTOOL	TORTURERS	TRAIN SETS	TREMOLITE	TRILOGIES
TOBOGGANS	TORTURING	TRAIPSING	TREMOROUS	TRIMARANS
TOGLIATTI	TOTALIZER	TRAMLINERS	TREMULANT	TRIMEROUS
TOLERABLE	TOTALLING	TRAMMELER	TREMULOUS	TRIMESTER
TOLERABLY	TOTAQUINE	TRAMPLING	TRENCHANT	TRIMETRIC
TOLERANCE	TOTEM POLE	TRANSCEND	TRENCHERS	TRIMMINGS
TOLERATED	TOTTERING	TRANSEPTS	TRENDIEST	TRINITIES
TOLERATOR	TOUCHABLE	TRANSEUNT	TRENGGANU	TRINOMAL
TOLLBOOTH	TOUCH DOWN	TRANSFERS	TREPANNED	TRIOELEIN
TOLLGATES	TOUCHIEST	TRANSFORM	TREPHINED	TRIPLEXES
TOOLHOUSE	TOUCHLINE	TRANSFUER	TREPHINES	TRIPTYCHS
TOMAHAWKS	TOUCHMARK	TRANSFUSE	TRIAL RUNS	TRIPWIRES
TOMBOYISH	TOUCH-TYPE	TRANSIENT	TRIANGLES	TRISECTED
TOMBSTONE	TOUCHWOOD	TRANSLATE	TRIATOMIC	TRISECTOR
TOMMY GUNS	TOUGHENED	TRANSMUTE	TRIAZOLIC	TRISERIAL
TOMORROWS	TOUGHENER	TRANSONIC	TRIBADISM	TRITENESS
TONBRIDGE	TOUGH LUCK	TRANSPIRE	TRIBALISM	TRITURATE
TONE POEMS	TOUGHNESS	TRANSPORT	TRIBALIST	TRIUMPHAL
TONOMETER	TOURISTIC	TRANSPOSE	TRIBESMAN	TRIUMPHED
TONOMETRY	TOUT A FAIT	TRANSSHIP	TRIBESMEN	TRIUMPHER
TONSILLAR	TOWELLING	TRANSVAAL	TRIBOLOGY	TRIVALENT
TONSORIAL	TOWN CLERK	TRAPDOORS	TRIBUNALS	TRIVIALLY
TOOL-MAKER	TOWN CRIER	TRAPEZIAL	TRIBUNARY	TRIWEEKLY
TOOTHACHE	TOWN HALLS	TRAPEZIUM	TRIBUNATE	TROCHLEAR
TOOTHCOMB	TOWN HOUSE	TRAPEZIUS	TRIBUTARY	TROMBONES
TOOTHIEST	TOWNSCAPE	TRAPEZOID	TRICEPSES	TRONDHEIM
TOOTHLESS	TOWNSHIPS	TRAPPINGS	TRICHITIC	TROOPSHIP
TOOTHPICK	TOXAPHENE	TRAPPISTS	TRICHOMIC	TROOSTITE
TOOTHSOME	TOXICALLY	TRASHCANS	TRICHOSIS	TROPISTIC
TOOTHWORT	TOXICOSIS	TRASHIEST	TRICHROIC	TOPOLOGY
TOP DRAWER	TOXOPHILY	TRATTORIA	TRICKIEST	TROSSACHS
TOP-FLIGHT	TRABEATED	TRAUMATIC	TRICKLING	TROUBLING
TOPIARIAN	TRABECULA	TRAVAILED	TRICKSTER	TROUBLOUS
TOPIARIST	TRACEABLE	TRAVELING	TRICLINIC	TROUNCING
TOPICALLY	TRACHYTIC	TRAVELLED	TRICOLOUR	TROUSSEAU
TOPMINNOW	TRACKABLE	TRAVELLER	TRICOTINE	TROWELLER
TOPOLOGIC	TRACKLESS	TRAVERSAL	TRICUSPID	TROPORIFIC
TOPONYMIC	TRACKSUIT	TRAVERSED	TRICYCLES	TRUCK FARM

667

T
9 LETTERS to 10 LETTERS

TRUCKLING	TURNSTONE	TACHOMETRY	TAX SHELTER
TRUCKLOAD	TURNTABLE	TACITURNLY	TEA CADDIES
TRUCK STOP	TURPITUDE	TACTICALLY	TEA GARDENS
TRUCULENT	TURQUOISE	TACTICIANS	TEA PARTIES
TRUELOVES	TUSCARORA	TACTLESSLY	TEARJERKER
TRUE NORTH	TUTIORISM	TAENIACIDE	TEA SERVICE
TRUMP CARD	TUTIORIST	TAGLIATELE	TEA TROLLEY
TRUMPETED	TUTORIALS	TAILBOARDS	TECHNETIUM
TRUMPETER	TUT-TUTTED	TAILGATING	TECHNICIAN
TRUNCATED	TV DINNERS	TAILLIGHTS	TECHNIQUES
TRUNCHEON	TWAYTBLADE	TAILORBIRD	TECHNOCRAT
TRUNDLING	TWENTIETH	TAILPIECES	TECHNOLOGY
TRUNK CALL	TWICE-LAID	TAKINGNESS	TECTRICIAL
TRUNKFISH	TWICE-TOLD	TALEBEARER	TEDDY BEARS
TRUNK LOAD	TWIDDLING	TALISMANIC	TEENY WEENY
TRUSTABLE	TWINKLING	TALKING-TOS	TELECASTER
TRUST FUND	TWISTABLE	TAMABILITY	TELEGNOSIS
TRUSTIEST	TWISTEDLY	TAMAULIPAS	TELEGRAPHS
TSETSE FLY	TWISTIEST	TAMBOURINE	TELEGRAPHY
TUBBINESS	TWITCHING	TANANARIVE	TELEMETRIC
TUBULATOR	TWITTERING	TANGENTIAL	TELEPATHIC
TUCKERING	TWOPENCES	TANGERINES	TELEPHONED
TUG-OF-LOVE	TWO-SEATER	TANGLEMENT	TELEPHONER
TUG-OF-WAR	TWO-STROKE	TANTALIZED	TELEPHONES
TUILERIES	TWO-TIMERS	TANTALIZER	TELESCOPED
TUITIONAL	TWO-TIMING	TANTALUSES	TELESCOPES
TULIPWOOD	TYMPANIST	TAP DANCERS	TELESCOPIC
TUMBLE-DRY	TYMPANUMS	TAP DANCING	TELESCRIPT
TUMESCENT	TYPEFACES	TAPERINGLY	TELEVISING
TUMULUSES	TYPEWRITE	TAPESTRIED	TELEVISION
TUNEFULLY	TYPHLITIC	TAPASTRIES	TELEWRITER
TUNGSTITE	TYPHLITIS	TARANTELLA	TELIOSPORE
TUNGUSIAN	TYPHOIDAL	TARANTULAS	TELLING-OFF
TUNING PEG	TYPHOIDIN	TARDIGRADE	TELOPHASIC
TUNNELERS	TYPICALLY	TARMACKING	TELPHERAGE
TUNNELING	TYPIFYING	TARNISHING	TEMPERABLE
TUNNELLED	TYRANNIES	TARPAULINS	TEMPERANCE
TUNNELLER	TYRANNIZE	TASIMETRIC	TEMPORIZED
TUPPENCES	TYRANNOUS	TASK FORCES	TEMPORIZER
TURBIDITY	TZETZE FLY	TASKMASTER	TEMPTATION
TURBINATE		TASTEFULLY	TEMPTINGLY
TURBOJETS		TATTERSALL	TENABILITY
TURBOPROP	**10 LETTERS**	TATTLINGLY	TENDENCIES
TURBULENT	TABERNACLE	TATTOOISTS	TENDERABLE
TURFINESS	TABESCENCE	TAUNTINGLY	TENDERFEET
TURGIDITY	TABLECLOTH	TAUROMACHY	TENDERFOOT
TURKESTAN	TABLELANDS	TAUTOMERIC	TENDERIZED
TURNABOUT	TABLE LINEN	TAUTONYMIC	TENDERIZER
TURNCOATS	TABLESPOON	TAWDRINESS	TENDERLOIN
TURNCOCKS	TABULARIZE	TAXABILITY	TENDERNESS
TURNOVERS	TABULATING	TAXATIONAL	TENDRILLAR
TURNPIKES	TABULATION	TAXIDERMAL	TENEMENTAL
TURNROUND	TACHOGRAPH	TAXIMETERS	TENNESSEAN
TURNSTILE	TACHOMETER	TAXONOMIST	TENOTOMIST

668

TENSIMETER	THEOPHOBIA	THUMBNAILS	TITUBATION
TENTACULAR	THEORETICS	THUMBSCREW	T-JUNCTIONS
TENTERHOOK	THEORIZING	THUMBSTALL	TOADSTOOLS
TERATOLOGY	THEOSOPHIC	THUMBTACKS	TOBOGGANED
TERMAGANCY	THERAPISTS	THUMPINGLY	TOBOGGANER
TERMAGANTS	THEREAFTER	THUNDERERS	TOCOPHEROL
TERMINABLE	THEREUNDER	THUNDERING	TOILETRIES
TERMINALLY	THERMALIZE	THUNDEROUS	TOILET ROLL
TERMINATED	THERMIONIC	THURINGIAN	TOLERANTLY
TERMINATOR	THERISTOR	THWARTEDLY	TOLERATING
TERMINUSES	THERMOGRAM	TICKERTAPE	TOLERATION
TERRACOTTA	THERMOPILE	TICKING OFF	TOLERATIVE
TERRA FIRMA	THERMOSTAT	TICKLISHLY	TOLLBOOTHS
TERRAMYCIN	THEROPODAN	TIDAL WAVES	TOLLUIDINE
TERRE PLEIN	THESSALIAN	TIEBREAKER	TOLUIC ACID
TERRE VERTE	THETICALLY	TIED HOUSES	TOMBSTONES
TERRIFYING	THICKENERS	TIEMANNITE	TOMFOOLERY
TERRORISTS	THICKENING	TIGHTENING	TOMOGRAPHY
TERRORIZED	THIEVINGLY	TIGHTROPES	TONALITIES
TERRORIZER	THIEVISHLY	TILIACEOUS	TONELESSLY
TERRYCLOTH	THIMBLEFUL	TILLANDSIA	TONGUE-TIED
TESSELLATE	THINK TANKS	TIMBERHEAD	TONIC SOL-FA
TESTACEOUS	THIOURACIL	TIMBERLINE	TONIC WATER
TESTAMENTS	THIRD PARTY	TIMBERWORK	TONO METRIC
TESTICULAR	THIRD WORLD	TIMBERYARD	TOOL-MAKING
TESTIFYING	THIRSTIEST	TIMEKEEPER	TOOTHACHES
TEST PILOTS	THIRTEENTH	TIMELESSLY	TOOTHBRUSH
TESTUDINAL	THIRTIETHS	TIMELIMITS	TOOTHCOMBS
TETCHINESS	THIXOTROPY	TMELINESS	TOOTHINESS
TETE-A-TETES	THORIANITE	TIMEPIECES	TOOTHPASTE
TETRABASIC	THORNINESS	TIMESAVING	TOOTHPICKS
TETRABRACH	THOROUGHLY	TIMESERVER	TOPAZOLITE
TETRACHORD	THOUGHTFUL	TIME SHEETS	TOPGALLANT
TETRAGONAL	THOUGHT-OUT	TIME SIGNAL	TOP-HEAVILY
TETRAPLOID	THOUSANDTH	TIME SWITCH	TOPICALITY
TETRAPODIC	THREADBARE	TIMETABLED	TOPOGRAPHY
TETRARCHIC	THREADWORM	TIMETABLES	TOPOLOGIST
TETRASPORE	THREATENED	TIMEWORKER	TOPSY-TURVY
TETRASTICH	THREATENER	TIMOROUSLY	TORBERNITE
TETRATOMIC	THREEPIECE	TIMPANISTS	TORCHLIGHT
TEXTUALISM	THREE-SOMES	TINCTORIAL	TORMENTING
TEXTUALIST	THRENODIES	TINGALINGS	TORMENTORS
TEXTURALLY	THRESHOLDS	TINGLINGLY	TORPEDOING
THANKFULLY	THRIFTIEST	TIN OPENERS	TORRENTIAL
THEATRICAL	THROATLASH	TIRELESSLY	TORTUOSITY
THEME PARKS	THROMBOGEN	TIRESOMELY	TORTUOUSLY
THEME SONGS	THROMBOSES	TITANESQUE	TORTUREDLY
THEMSELVES	THROMBOSIS	TITILLATED	TOTEMISTIC
THENARDITE	THROMBOTIC	TITIVATING	TOTEM POLES
THEOCRATIC	THROTTLING	TITIVATION	TOTIPOTENT
THEODOLITE	THROUGHOUT	TITLE DEEDS	TOUCH-AND-GO
THEOLOGIAN	THROUGHPUT	TITLE PAGES	TOUCHDOWNS
THEOLOGIES	THROUGHWAY	TITLE ROLES	TOUCHINESS
THEOLOGIZE	THROWBACKS	TITRATABLE	TOUCHINGLY

TOUCHLINES	TRANSDUCER	TREPPANNER	TRISKELION
TOUCH PAPER	TRANSEPTAL	TRESPASSED	TRISTICHIC
TOUCHSTONE	TRANSFEREE	TRESPASSER	TRITANOPIA
TOUCH-TYPED	TRANSFEROR	TRESPASSES	TRITANOPIC
TOUGHENING	TRANSFIXED	TRIANGULAR	TRITURABLE
TOURMALINE	TRANSGRESS	TRIBRACHIC	TRITURATOR
TOURNAMENT	TRANSIENCE	TRICHIASIS	TRIUMPHANT
TOURNIQUES	TRANSIENCY	TRICHINIZE	TRIUMPHING
TOWER BLOCK	TRANSISTOR	TRICHINOUS	TRIVALENCY
TOWN CLERKS	TRANSITION	TRICHOCYST	TRIVANDRUM
TOWN CRIERS	TRANSITIVE	TRICHOGYNE	TRIVIALITY
TOWN HOUSES	TRANSITORY	TRICHOLOGY	TRIVIALIZE
TOWNSCAPES	TRANSKEIAN	TRICHOTOMY	TROCHANTER
TOWNSWOMAN	TRANSLATED	TRICHROISM	TROGLODYTE
TOXALBULMIN	TRANSLATOR	TRICHROMAT	TROLLEYBUS
TOXICOLOGY	TRANSLUNAR	TRICKINESS	TROMBONIST
TRABEATION	TRANSMUTED	TRICKINGLY	TROOPSHIPS
TRABECULAR	TRANSMUTER	TRICKSTERS	TROPAEOLIN
TRACHEIDAL	TRANSPIRED	TRICOLOURS	TROPAEOLUM
TRACHEITIS	TRANSPLANT	TRICOSTATE	TROPICALLY
TRACHYOID	TRANSPOLAR	TRICROTISM	TROPICBIRD
TRACK EVENT	TRANSPORTS	TRIDENTATE	TRIPOLOGIC
TRACKLAYER	TRANSPOSED	TRIDENTINE	TRIPOPAUSE
TRACKSUITS	TRANSPOSER	TRIFLINGLY	TROPOPHYTE
TRACTILITY	TRANSPUTER	TRIFOLIATE	TROTSKYISM
TRACTIONAL	TRANSUDATE	TRIFURCATE	TROTSKYITE
TRADEMARKS	TRANSVALUE	TRIGEMINAL	TROUBADOUR
TRADE NAMES	TRANSVERSE	TRIGGERING	TROUBLEDLY
TRADE PRICE	TRAPEZIUMS	TRIGLYPHIC	TROUSSEAUS
TRADE ROUTE	TRAPEZOIDS	TRIHYDRATE	TROUSSEAUX
TRADE UNION	TRASHINESS	TRILATERAL	TROY WEIGHT
TRADE WINDS	TRAUMATISM	TRILINGUAL	TRUCK FARMS
TRADITIONS	TRAUMATIZE	TRILLIONTH	TRUCKLOADS
TRADUCIBLE	TRAVAILLING	TRILOBITES	TRUCKSTOPS
TRAFFIC JAM	TRAVELLERS	TRILOCULAR	TRUCULENCE
TRAFFICKED	TRAVELLING	TRIMESTERS	TRUMP CARDS
TRAFFICKER	TRAVELOGUE	TRIMESTRAL	TRUMPETERS
TRAGACANTH	TRAVELSICK	TRIMONTHLY	TRUMPETING
TRAGEDIANS	TRAVERSING	TRIMORPHIC	TRUNCATING
TRAGICALLY	TRAVERTINE	TRINOCULAR	TRUNCATION
TRAGICOMIC	TRAVESTIES	TRIOECIOUS	TRUNCHEONS
TRAILINGLY	TREADMILLS	TRIPARTITE	TRUNK CALLS
TRAITOROUS	TREASURERS	TRIPHAMMER	TRUNK ROADS
TRAJECTILE	TREASURIES	TRIPHTHONG	TRUNK ROUTE
TRAJECTION	TREASURING	TRIPHYLITE	TRUSTFULLY
TRAJECTORY	TREATMENTS	TRIPINNATE	TRUTH-VALUE
TRAMONTANE	TREBLE CLEF	TRIPLE JUMP	TRYINGNESS
TRAMPOLINE	TREEHOPPER	TRIPLETAIL	TRYPTOPHAN
TRANCELIKE	TREMENDOUS	TRIPLICATE	TUBERCULAR
TRANQUILLY	TRENCHANCY	TRIPLICITY	TUBERCULIN
TRANSACTED	TRENCH COAT	TRIPPINGLY	TUBEROSITY
TRANSACTOR	TRENDINESS	TRIPTEROUS	TUB-THUMPER
TRANSCRIBE	TREPANNING	TRIRADIATE	TUBULARITY
TRANSCRIPT	TREPHINING	TRISECTING	TUBULATION

TUFFACEOUS	**11 LETTERS**	TELEKINETIC	TESTEMONIES
TUGS-OF-LOVE	TABERNACLES	TELEOLOGISM	TEST MATCHES
TULARAEMIA	TABLECLOTHS	TELEOLOGIST	TETANICALLY
TULARAEMIC	TABLESPOONS	TELEPATHIST	TETRADYMITE
TUMBLEDOWN	TABLE TENNIS	TELEPHONING	TETRAHEDRAL
TUMBLEWEED	TABULATIONS	TELEPHONIST	TETRAHEDRON
TUMESCENCE	TACHEOMETER	TELEPRINTER	TETRAMERISM
TUMULOSITY	TACHOGRAPHS	TELESCOPING	TETRAMEROUS
TUMULTUOUS	TACHOMETERS	TELESELLING	TETRAPLEGIA
TUNELESSLY	TACHOMETRIC	TELEVISIONS	TETRARCHATE
TUNING FORK	TACITURNITY	TELLINGS-OFF	TETRASPORIC
TUNING PEGS	TACTFULNESS	TEMERARIOUS	TETRAVALENT
TUNNELLING	TAGLIATELLE	TEMPERAMENT	THALIDOMIDE
TURBOPROPS	TAKE-HOME PAY	TEMPERATURE	THALLOPHYTE
TURBULENCE	TALE BEARERS	TEMPESTUOUS	THANKLESSLY
TURGESCENT	TALENT SCOUT	TEMPORALITY	THAUMATROPE
TURNABOUTS	TALKABILITY	TEMPORARILY	THEATREGOER
TURNAROUND	TALL STORIES	TEMPORIZING	THEATRICALS
TURNBUCKLE	TAMBLENESS	TEMPTATIONS	THENCEFORTH
TURNROUNDS	TAMBOURINES	TEMPTRESSES	THEOBROMINE
TURNSTILES	TANGIBILITY	TENACIOUSLY	THEOCENTRIC
TURNTABLES	TANTALIZING	TENDENTIOUS	THEODOLITES
TURPENTINE	TAPE MEASURE	TENDERFOOTS	THEODOLITIC
TURQUOISES	TARANTELLAS	TENDERIZING	THEOLOGIANS
TURTLEBACK	TARNISHABLE	TENEBROSITY	THEOLOGICAL
TURTLEDOVE	TARRADIDDLE	TENNIS ELBOW	THEOLOGIZER
TURTLENECK	TARTAR SAUCE	TENORRHAPHY	THEOPHOBAIC
TUT-TUTTING	TASK MASTERS	TENSIBILITY	THEOREMATIC
TWELVE-TONE	TASTELESSLY	TENISOMETER	THEORETICAL
TWENTIETHS	TAUTOLOGIES	TENTATIVELY	THEOSOPHISM
TWIN-BEDDED	TAUTOLOGIZE	TENTERHOOKS	THEOSOPHIST
TWINFLOWER	TAUTOMERIZE	TENUOUSNESS	THERAPEUTIC
TWINKLINGS	TAUTOMERISM	TEPEFACTION	THEREABOUTS
TWISTINGLY	TAXIDERMIST	TERATOGENIC	THEREMINIST
TWITTERING	TAX SHELTER	TERATOLOGIC	THERETOFORE
TYMPANITES	TEARFULNESS	TEREBIC ACID	THERIOMORPH
TYMPANITIC	TEAR JERKERS	TERMINATING	THERMIONICS
TYMPANITIS	TEA SERVICES	TERMINATION	THEREMOCLINE
TYPECASTER	TEA TROLLEYS	TERMINATIVE	THERMOGRAPH
TYPESCRIPT	TECHNICALLY	TERMINATORY	THERMOLYSIS
TYPESETTER	TECHNICIANS	TERMINOLOGY	THERMOLYTIC
TYPEWRITER	TECHNICOLOR	TERRESTRIAL	THERMOMETER
TYPHLOLOGY	TECHNOCRACY	TERRICOLOUS	THERMOMETRY
TYPHOGENIC	TECHNOCRATS	TERRIGENOUS	THERMOSCOPE
TYPING-POOL	TEDIOUSNESS	TERRIITORIAL	THERMOSTATS
TYPOGRAPHY	TEENYBOPPER	TERRITORIES	THERMOTAXIC
TYPOLOGIST	TEETOTALISM	TERRORISTIC	THERMOTAXIS
TYRANNICAL	TEETOTALLER	TERRORIZING	THESAURUSES
TYRANNIZED	TEGUCIGALPA	TERTIUM QUID	THICKHEADED
TYRANNIZER	TELEGNOSTIC	TESSELLATED	THICKNESSES
TYROCIDINE	TELEGRAPHED	TESTABILITY	THICK-WITTED
TYROSINASE	TELEGRAPHER	TESTAMENTAL	THIMBLEFULS
	TELEGRAPHIC	TESTICULATE	THIMBLEWEED
	TELEKINESIS	TESTIMONIAL	THINGAMAJIG

THIN-SKINNED	TOFFEE-NOSED	TRAFFICKERS	TRANSURANIC
THIOCYANATE	TOILET PAPER	TRAFFICKING	TRANSVAALER
THIRD-DEGREE	TOILET ROLLS	TRAGIDIENNE	TRANSVALUER
THIRD PERSON	TOILET WATER	TRAGICOMEDY	TRANSVERSAL
THIRSTINESS	TOLBUTAMIDE	TRAILBLAZER	TRAPSHOOTER
THIRTEENTHS	TOMBOYISHLY	TRAINBEARER	TRAUMATIZED
THISTLEDOWN	TONSILLITIS	TRAMPOILNER	TRAVEL AGENT
THIXOTROPIC	TOOTH POWDER	TRAMPOLINES	TRAVELOUGES
THORACOTOMY	TOPDRESSING	TRANQUILITY	TRAVERSABLE
THOROUGHPIN	TOPOGRAPHER	TRANSACTING	TRECHEROUS
THOUGHTLESS	TOPOGRAPHIC	TRANSACTION	TREACLINESS
THOUSANDTHS	TORCHBEARER	TRANSALPINE	TREASONABLE
THREADINESS	TORMENTEDLY	TRANSCEIVER	TREASONABLY
THREATENING	TORONTONIAN	TRANSCENDED	TREASURABLE
THREEPENCES	TORSIBILITY	TRANSCRIBED	TREBLE CLEFS
THRIFTINESS	TORTICOLLAR	TRANSCRIBER	TRELLISWORK
THRILLINGLY	TORTICOLLIS	TRANSCRIPTS	TREMBLINGLY
THROATINESS	TORTURESOME	TRANSECTION	TREMULOUSLY
THROBINGLY	TORTURINGLY	TRANSFERASE	TRENCHANTLY
THROMBOCYTE	TORTUROUSLY	TRANSFERRED	TRENCH COATS
THROUGHPUTS	TOTALIZATOR	TRANSFERRIN	TRENCHERMAN
THROUGHWAYS	TOTEMICALLY	TRANSFIGURE	TRENCHERMEN
THUMBSCREWS	TOTIPALMATE	TRANSFINITE	TRENDSETTER
THUNDERBIRD	TOTIPOTENCY	TRANSFIXING	TREPIDATION
THUNDERBOLT	TOUCHPAPERS	TRANSFIXION	TRESPASSING
THUNDERCLAP	TOUCHSTONES	TRANSFORMED	TRESTLETREE
THYROIDITIS	TOUCH-TYPING	TRANSFORMER	TRESTLEWORK
THYROTROPIN	TOUCH-TYPIST	TRANSFUSION	TRIABLENESS
TICKINGS OFF	TOUR DE FORCE	TRANSFUSIVE	TRIANGULATE
TICK-TACK-TOE	TOURMALINIC	TRANSHUMANT	TRIBULATION
TIDDLYWINKS	TOURNAMENTS	TRNSISTORS	TRIBUTARIES
TIEBREAKERS	TORNIQUENTS	TRANSITABLE	TRIBUTARILY
TIED COTTAGE	TOUT LE MONDE	TRANSITIONS	TRICERATOPS
TIGHTFISTED	TOWER BLOCKS	TRANSITIVES	TRICHINOSIS
TIGHT-LIPPED	TOWN PLANNER	TRANS-JORDAN	TRICHLORIDE
TIME CAPSULE	TOWNSPEOPLE	TRANSLATING	TRICHOMONAD
TIMEKEEPERS	TOXICOGENIC	TRANSLATION	TRICHOTOMIC
TIMESERVERS	TOXOPHILITE	TRANSLATORS	TRICKLINGLY
TIMESERVING	TOXOPLASMIC	TRANSLOCATE	TRICKSINESS
TIME-SHARING	TRACHEOTOMY	TRANSLUCENT	TRICUSPIALS
TIME SIGNALS	TRACK EVENTS	TRANSMITTAL	TRIGGERFISH
TIMETABLING	TRACKLAYERS	TRANSMITTED	TRILLIONTHS
TINDERBOXES	TRACK RECORD	TRANSMITTER	TRIMETROGON
TIN PAN ALLEY	TRACKSUITED	TRANSMUTING	TRIMORPHISM
TITANICALLY	TRADE PRICES	TRANSPADANE	TRINIDADIAN
TITILLATING	TRADE ROUTES	TRANSPARENT	TRIPALMITIN
TITILLATION	TRADES WOMAN	TRANSPIERCE	TRIPLICATES
TITILLATIVE	TRADE UNIONS	TRANSPIRING	TRIQUETROUS
TITLEHOLDER	TRADING POST	TRANSPLANTS	TRISTICHOUS
TITTERINGLY	TRADITIONAL	TRANSPONDER	TRISULPHIDE
TOASTMASTER	TRADUCEMENT	TRANSPORTED	TRITURATION
TOBACCONIST	TRADUCINGLY	TRANSPORTER	TRIUMVIRATE
TOBOGGANING	TRAFFICATOR	TRANSPOSING	TRIVIALIZED
TOFFEE APPLE	TRAFFIC JAMS	TRANSPUTERS	TROCHOPHORE

TROCORNERED
TROGLODYTES
TROGLODYTIC
TROJAN HORSE
TROMBONISTS
TROMPE L'OEIL
TROPHICALLY
TROPHOBLAST
TROPHOZOITE
TROPICALITY
TROPICALIZE
TROPISMATIC
TROPOPHYTIC
TROPOSPERE
TROTSKYISTS
TROUBADOURS
TROUBLESOME
TROUBLE SPOT
TROUBLINGLY
TRUCULENTLY
TRUEHEARTED
TRUMPETWEED
TRUNK ROUTES
TRUSTEESHIP
TRUSTWORTHY
TRYPANOSOME
TRYPSINOOGN
TSELINOGRAD
TSETSE FLIES
TUBERCULATE
TUBERCULOUS
TUB-THUMPERS
TUB-THUMPING
TUMBLE-DRIED
TUMBLE-DRYER
TUMEFACIENT
TUMEFACTION
TUNEFULNESS
TUNING FORKS
TURBINATION
TURBOCHARGE
TURBULAENTLY
TURGESCENCE
TURKISH BATH
TURNAROUNDS
TURRICULATE
TURTLEDOVES
TURTLENECKS
TUTTI FRUTTI
TWELVE MONTH
TWITCHINGLY
TYPECASTING
TYPESCRIPTS
TYPESETTERS

TYPEWRITERS
TYPEWRITINGG
TYPEWRITTEN
TYPICALNESS
TYPING POOLS
TYPOGRAPHER
TYPOGRAPHIC
TYPOLOGICAL
TYRANNICIDE
TYRANNIZING
TYROTHRICIN
TZETZE FLIES

12 LETTERS
TABERNACULAR
TABLE MANNERS
TABLE-TURNING
TACHEOMETRIC
TACHYCARDIAC
TACTLESSNESS
TALCUM POWDER
TALENT SCOUTS
TALKING POINT
TAMBOURINIST
TANGENTIALLY
TAPE MEASURES
TAPE RECORDER
TARAMASALATA
TARDENOISIAN
TARTARIC ACID
TASTEFULNESS
TAUROMACHIAN
TAUTOLOGICAL
TAXIDERMISTS
TECHNICALITY
TECHNOGRAPHY
TECHNOLOGIES
TECHNOLOGIST
TECTONICALLY
TEENYBOPPERS
TEETER-TOTTER
TEETOTALLERS
TELAESTHESIA
TELAESTHETIC
TELAUTOGRAPH
TELEGRAPHERS
TELEGRAPHESE
TELEGRAPHING
TELEOLOGICAL
TELEOLOGISTS
TELEPHONE BOX
TELEPHONISTS
TELEPRINTERS

TELEPROMPTER
TELEUTOSPORE
TELEVISIONAL
TELGENICALLY
TELLUROMETER
TEMPERAMNETS
TEMPERATURES
TEN-GALLON HAT
TERATOLOGIST
TERCENTENARY
TEREBINTHENE
TERGIVERSATE
TERMINATIONS
TERRIBLENESS
TERRIFICALLY
TERRIFYINGLY
TERRITORIALS
TESSELLATION
TESTAMENTARY
TESTIMENIALS
TESTOSTERONE
TEST-TUBE BABY
TETANIZATION
TETRACHORDAL
TETRACYCLINE
TETRAEDRITE
TETRAPTEROUS
TETRASTICHIC
TETRAVALENCY
TEUTONICALLY
THALAMICALLY
THALLOPHYTIC
THANKFULNESS
THANKSGIVING
THAUMATOLOGY
THEANTHROPIC
THEATREGOERS
THEATRICALLY
THEISTICALLY
THEMATICALLY
THEOCENTRISM
THEOPHYLLINE
THEORETICIAN
THEORIZATION
THERAPEUTICS
THEREINAFTER
THERMOCOUPLE
THERMOGENOUS
THERMOGRAPHY
THERMOLABILE
THERMOMETERS
THERMOMETRIC
THERMOSCOPIC
THERMOS FLASK

THERMOSIPHON
THERMOSPHERE
THERMOSTABLE
THERMOSTATIC
THERMOTROPIC
THEURGICALLY
THICK-SKINNED
THIEVISHNESS
THIGMOTACTIC
THIGMOROPIC
THINGAMAJIGS
THIOSINAMINE
THIOSULPHATE
THIRD PARTIES
THOROUGHBRED
THOROUGHFARE
THOROUGHNESS
THOUGHTFULLY
THREE-QUARTER
THREE-WHEELER
THROMBOCYTIC
THUNDERBOLTS
THNDERCLAPS
THUNDERCLOUD
THUNDERINGLY
THUNDEROUSLY
THUNDERSTONE
THUNDERSTORM
TICKLISHNESS
TIED COTTAGES
TIME CAPSULES
TIME EXPOSURE
TIME-HONOURED
TIMELESSNESS
TIME SWITCHES
TIMOROUSNESS
TIRELESSNESS
TITANIFEROUS
TITLEHOLDERS
TITTLE-TATTLE
TOASTING FORK
TOASTMASTERS
TABACCONISTS
TOFFEE APPLES
TOGETHERNESS
TOMFOOLERIES
TONE LANGUAGE
TONELESSNESS
TONSILLOTOMY
TOOTHBRUSHES
TOPDRESSINGS
TOP--HEAVINESS
TOPOGRAPHERS
TORMENTINGLY

TORREFACTION	TRANSFUSIBLE	TRICHOGYNIAL	TWO-WAY MIRROR
TORTUOUSNESS	TRANSFUSIONS	TRICHOLOGIST	TYPIFICATION
TOTALITARIAN	TRANSGRESSED	TRICHOPTERAN	TYPOGRAPHERS
TOTALIZATORS	TRANSGRESSOR	TRICHROMATIC	TYRANNICALLY
TOURIST CLASS	TRANSHUMANCE	TRICK OR TREAT	TYRANNICIDAL
TOUT ENSEMBLE	TRANSITIONAL	TRIFURCATION	
TOWN PLANNERS	TRANSITORILY	TRIGGER-HAPPY	
TOWN PLANNING	TRANSLATABLE	TRIGLYCERIDE	**13 LETTERS**
TOXICOLOGIST	TRANSLATIONS	TRIGONOMETRY	TALKATIVENESS
TOXOPHILITIC	TRANSLUCENCE	TRILINGUALLY	TALKING POINTS
TRACEABILITY	TRANSLUCENCY	TRIMOLECULAR	TANGENTIALITY
TRACE ELEMENT	TRANSMIGRANT	TRIPARTITION	TANTALIZATION
TRACHEOPHYTE	TRANSMIGRATE	TRIPHTHONGAL	TANTALIZINGLY
TRACHEOSTOMY	TRANSMISSION	TRIPLE-TONGUE	TAPE RECORDERS
TRACHOMATOUS	TRANSMISSIVE	TRIPLICATION	TASTELESSNESS
TRACING PAPER	TRANSMITTERS	TRIPOLITANIA	TAX-DEDUCTIBLE
TRACK RECORDS	TRANSMITTING	TRIUMPHANTLY	TAXONOMICALLY
TRACUCIANIST	TRANSMOGRIFY	TRIUMVIRATES	TECHNOLOGICAL
TRADESCANTIA	TRANSMUNDANE	TRIVIALITIES	TECHNOLOGISTS
TRADESPEOPLE	TRANSMUTABLE	TRIVIALIZING	TELEGRAPH POLE
TRADING POSTS	TRANSOCEANIC	TROCHOIDALLY	TELEMARKETING
TRADING STAMP	TRANSPARENCY	TROJAN HORSES	TELEPHOTO LENS
TRADITIONALIST	TRANSPIRABLE	TROLLEY BUSES	TELEPROMPTERS
TRADUCIANISM	TRANSPLANTED	TROMBIDIASIS	TELEVISIONARY
TRAFFICATORS	TRANSPLANTER	TROOP CARRIER	TEMPERABILITY
TRAFFIC LIGHT	TRANSPONDERS	TROPPOPHILOUS	TEMPERAMENTAL
TRAGEDIENNES	TRANSPORTER	TROUBLE MAKER	TEMPERATENESS
TRAILBLAZIING	TRANSPORTING	TROUBLE SPOTS	TEMPESTUOUSLY
TRAILER HOUSE	TRANSPORTIVE	TROUSER PRESS	TEMPORARINESS
TRAINBEARERS	TRANSPOSABLE	TRUSTABILITY	TEMPORIZATION
TRAITOROUSLY	TRANSUDATORY	TRUSTEESHIPS	TEMPORIZINGLY
TRAJECTORIES	TRANSVAALIAN	TRUSTFULNESS	TENACIOUSNESS
TRAMPISHNESS	TRANSVERSELY	TRUTHFULNESS	TENDENTIOUSLY
TRANQUILLITY	TRANSVESTISM	TRYPANOSOMAL	TENDERHEARTED
TRANQUILLIZE	TRANSVESTITE	TRYPARSAMIDE	TENDERIZATION
TRANSACTIONS	TRANSYLVANIA	TUBERCULOSIS	TEN-GALLON HATS
TRANSCENDENT	TRAPSHOOTING	TUMBLE-DRYERS	TENPIN BOWLING
TRANSCENDING	TRAUMATIZING	TUMBLE-DRYING	TENTATIVENESS
TRANSCRIBING	TRAVEL AGENCY	TUMULTUOUSLY	TERMINABILITY
TRANSCURRENT	TRAVEL AGENTS	TUNELESSNESS	TERMINATIONAL
TRANSDUCTION	TRBLE CHANCE	TUNNELVISION	TERMINOLOGIES
TRANSFERRABLE	TREELESSNESS	TURBELLARIAN	TERMINOLOGIST
TRANSFERENCE	TREMENDOUSLY	TURBIDIMETER	TERRESTRIALLY
TRANSFERRING	TRENDSETTERS	TURBOCHARGED	TERRORIZATION
TRANSFIGURED	TRENDSETTING	TURBOCHARGER	TETRACHLORIDE
TRANSFORMERS	TREPHINATION	TURKISH BATHS	TETRASYLLABIC
TRANSFORMING	TRIBULATIONS	TURNING POINT	TETRASYLLABLE
TRANSFORMISM	TRICHINIASIS	TWISTABILITY	THANKLESSNESS
TRANSFORMIST	TRICHOCYSTIC	TWO-FACEDNESS	THANKSGIVINGS

THEATRICALITY	TONGUE TWISTER	TRANSMUTATION
THEOLOGICALLY	TONSILLECTOMY	TRANSPARENTLY
THEORETICALLY	TOOTHSOMENESS	TRANSPLANTING
THERMODYNAMIC	TOPOGRAPHICAL	TRANSPORTABLE
THERMOGRAPHER	TOPOLOGICALLY	TRANSPORT CAFE
THERMOGRAPHIC	TORTOISESHELL	TRANSPORTEDLY
THERMONUCLEAR	TOXICOLOGICAL	TRANSPOSITION
THERMOPLASTIC	TOXICOLOGISTS	TRANSSHIPMENT
THERMOSETTING	TOXOPLASMOSIS	TRANSVESTITES
THERMOS FLASKS	TRADE UNIONISM	TRANSYLVANIAN
THERMOSTATICS	TRADE UNIONIST	TRAUMATICALLY
THERMOTHEAPY	TRADING ESTATE	TREACHEROUSLY
THERMOTROPISM	TRADING STAMPS	TREASURESHIP
THOROUGHBREDS	TRADITIONALLY	TREASURE TROVE
THOROUGHFARES	TRAFFIC CIRCLE	TREMULOUSNESS
THOROUGHGOING	TRAFFIC ISLAND	TRIANGULARITY
THOROUGHPACED	TRAFFIC LIGHTS	TRIANGULATION
THOUGHTLESSLY	TRAFFIC WARDEN	TRICENTENNIAL
THREATENINGLY	TRANQUILLIZED	TRICHOLOGISTS
THREE-CORNERED	TRANQUILLIZER	TRICHOMONDAL
THREE-DAY EVENT	TRANSATLANTIC	TRICHROMATISM
THREE-LINE WHIP	TRANSCENDENCE	TRIGONOMETRIC
THUNDERCLOUDS	TRANSCENDENCY	TRILATERATION
THUNDERSHOWER	TRANSCRIBABLE	TRILINGUALISM
THUNDERSTORMS	TRANSCRIPTION	TROOP CARRIERS
THUNDERSTRUCK	TRANSFIGURING	TROPHOBLASTIC
THYROIDECTOMY	TRANSFORMABLE	TROUBLEMAKERS
TIME-AND-MOTION	TRANSGRESSING	TRUSTWORTHILY
TIME-CONSUMING	TRANSGRESSION	TUBERCULATION
TIME EXPOSURES	TRANSGRESSIVE	TURBOCHARGERS
TIME SIGNATURE	TRANSGRESSORS	TURBOCHARGING
TINTINNABULAR	TRANSISTORIZE	TURBO-ELECTRIC
TINTINNABULUM	TRANSLATIONAL	TURING MACHINE
TITILLATINGLY	TRANSLATORIAL	TURNING CIRCLE
TITTLE-TATTLED	TRANSLITERATE	TURNING POINTS
TITTLE-TATTLER	TRANSLOCATION	TWO-WAY MIRRORS
TOAD-IN-THE-HOLE	TRANSMISSIBLE	TYPOGRAPHICAL
TOASTING FORKS	TRANSMISSIONS	TYRANNIZINGLY
TOILET-TRAINED	TRANSMITTANCE	TYRANNOSAURUS
TOLERABLENESS	TRANSMITTANCY	

U
3 LETTERS to 7 LETTERS

3 LETTERS	4 LETTERS				
UFO	UNFIX	UGRIAN	UNLASH	UPLAND	UDAIPUR
UGH	UNIAT	UJJAIN	UNLEAD	UPLIFT	UGANDAN
UHF	UNIFY	ULCERS	UNLESS	UPPERS	UGLIEST
UNI-	UNION	ULLAGE	UNLIKE	UPPISH	UKRAINE
URN	UNITE	ULSTER	UNLIVE	UPPITY	UKULELE
USE	UNITS	ULTIMA	UNLOAD	UPREAR	ULAN-UDE
	UNITY	UMBRAL	UNLOCK	UPRISE	ULLAGED
	UNLAY	UMBRIA	UNMADE	UPROAR	ULULANT
	UNMAN	UMLAUT	UNMAKE	UPROOT	ULULATE
4 LETTERS	UNPEG	UMPIRE	UNMASK	UPSETS	UMBRAGE
UCCA	UNPIN	UNABLE	UNMOOR	UPSHOT	UMBRIAN
UCAS	UNRIG	UNBELT	UNPACK	UPSIDE	UMBRIEL
UFOS	UNRIP	UNBEND	UNPAID	UPTAKE	UMLAUTS
UGLY	UNSAY	UNBIND	UNPICK	UPTILT	UMPIRED
ULNA	UNSET	UNBOLT	UNPLUG	UPTOWN	UMPIRES
UNDO	UNSEX	UNBORN	UNREAD	UPTURN	UMPTEEN
UNIT	UNTIE	UNCIAL	UNREAL	UPWARD	UNAIDED
UNTO	UNTIL	UNCLAD	UNREST	UPWIND	UNARMED
UPON	UNZIP	UNCLES	UNRIPE	URACIL	UNAWARE
URDO	UP-BOW	UNCLOG	UNROLL	URALIC	UNBONED
URGE	UPEND	UNCOIL	UNRULY	URANIC	UNBOSOM
URIC	UPPER	UNCORK	UNSAFE	URANUS	UNBOUND
URNS	UPSET	UNCURL	UNSAID	URANYL	UNBOWED
USED	URALS	UNDIES	UNSEAL	URRATIC	UNBRACE
USER	URATE	UNDOER	UNSEAM	URBANE	UNCAGED
USES	URBAN	UNDONE	UNSEAT	URCHIN	UNCANNY
UTAH	UREAL	UNDULY	UNSEEN	UREASE	UNCHAIN
UVEA	UREDO	UNEASE	UNSHIP	UREIDE	UNCINUS
	URGED	UNEASY	UNSNAP	URETER	UNCIVIL
5 LETTERS	URGER	UNESCO	UNSTEP	URETIC	UNCLASP
U-BOAT	URGES	UNEVEN	UNSTOP	URGENT	UNCLEAN
UDDER	URINE	UNFAIR	UNSUNG	URGING	UNCLEAR
UDINE	USAGE	UNFOLD	UNSURE	URINAL	UNCLOAK
UGRIC	USERS	UNFURL	UNTIDY	UROPOD	UNCLOSE
UIGUR	USHER	UNGUAL	UNTIED	URSINE	UNCOUTH
ULCER	USING	UNGUIS	UNTOLD	URTEXT	UNCOVER
ULNAR	USUAL	UNGULA	UNTRUE	USABLE	UNCROSS
ULNAS	USURP	UNHAIR	UNTUCK	USAGES	UNCTION
ULTRA-	USURY	UNHAND	UNUSED	USANCE	UNDERGO
UMBEL	UTERI	UNHOLY	UNVEIL	USEFUL	UNDOING
UMBER	UTTER	UNHOOK	UNWARY	USHERS	UNDRESS
UMBRA	U-TURN	UNICEF	UNWELL	USURER	UNDYING
UMIAK	UNVEAL	UNIONS	UNWEPT	UTAHAN	UNEARTH
UNAPT	UVULA	UNIPOD	UNWIND	UTERUS	UNEQUAL
UNARY	UZBEK	UNIQUE	UNWISE	UTMOST	UNFROCK
UNBAR		UNISEX	UNWRAP	UTOPIA	UNGODLY
UNCAP		UNISON	UNYOKE	U-TURNS	UNGULAR
UNCLE	6 LETTERS	UNITED	UPBEAT	UVULAE	UNHAPPY
UNCUS	U-BOATS	UNITER	UPCAST	UVULAR	UNHEARD
UNCUT	UDDERS	UNJUST	UPDATE	UVULAS	UNHINGE
UNDER	UDMURT	UNKIND	UPHELD		UNHORSE
UNDID	UGANDA	UNKNIT	UPHILL		UNICORN
UNDUE	UGLIER	UNLACE	UPHOLD		UNIFIED
UNFIT	UGLIFY	UNLAID	UPKEEP	7 LETTERS	UNIFIER

676

UNIFORM	UPPSALA	UTRICLE	UNCORKED	UNIPOLAR
UNITARY	UPRAISE	UT SUPRA	UNCOUPLE	UNIQUELY
UNITIES	UPRIGHT	UTTERED	UNCTUOUS	UNITEDLY
UNITING	UPRISER	UTTERER	UNDAMPED	UNIVALVE
UNITIVE	UPRIVER	UTTERLY	UNDERACT	UNIVERSE
UNKEMPT	UPSILON	UVEITIC	UNDERAGE	UNIVOCAL
UNKNOWN	UPSTAGE	UVEITIS	UNDERARM	UNKENNEL
UNLATCH	UPSTART	UVULARS	UNDERBUD	UNKINDER
UNLEARN	UPSURGE	UXORIAL	UNDERBUY	UNKINDLY
UNLEASH	UPSWEEP		UNDERCUT	UNKNOWNS
UNLOOSE	UPSWING		UNDERDOG	UNLAWFUL
UNLUCKY	UPTAKES	**8 LETTERS**	UNDERFUR	UNLIKELY
UNMAKER	UPTHROW	UBIQUITY	UNDERLAY	UNLIMBER
UNMANLY	UPTIGHT	UBI SUPRA	UNDERLTE	UNLISTED
UNMEANT	UPTURNS	UGLIFIER	UNDERLIE	UNLOADED
UNMORAL	UPWARDS	UGLINESS	UNDERPAY	UNLOADER
UNMOVED	URAEMIC	UIGURIAN	UNDERPIN	UNLOCKED
UNNAMED	URALITE	UKULELES	UNDERSEA	UNLOOSED
UNNERVE	URANIAN	ULCERATE	UNDERSET	UNLOOSEN
UNPAGED	URANIDE	ULCEROUS	UNDERTOW	UNLOVELY
UNQUIET	URANITE	ULTERIOR	UNDULANT	UNMANNED
UNQUOTE	URANIUM	ULTIMATA	UNDULATE	UNMARKED
UNRAVEL	URANOUS	ULTIMATE	UNEARNED	UNMASKER
UNREADY	URCHINS	ULTRAISM	UNEASIER	UNMUZZLE
UNREEVE	UREDIAL	ULTRAIST	UNEASILY	UNNERVED
UNSCREW	UREDIUM	UMBONATE	UNENDING	UNOPENED
UNSLING	URETHRA	UMBRGAES	UNERRING	UNPACKED
UNSNARL	URGENCY	UMBRELLA	UNEVENLY	UNPEOPLE
UNSOUND	URIDINE	UMPIRING	UNFAIRER	UNPICKED
UNSTICK	URINALS	UNABATED	UNFAIRLY	UNPLACED
UNSTRAP	URINANT	UNAWARES	UNFASTEN	UNPOLLED
UNSTUCK	URINARY	UNBACKED	UNFETTER	UNPRICED
UNSWEAR	URINATE	UNBARRED	UNFILIAL	UNPROVEN
UNTHINK	URINOUS	UNBEATEN	UNFOLDED	UNREASON
UNTRIED	URNLIKE	UNBELIEF	UNFOLDER	UNRIDDLE
UNTRUSS	UODELE	UNBIASED	UNFORCED	UNRIFLED
UNTRUTH	UROLITH	UNBIDDEN	UNFORMED	UNROLLED
UNTYING	UROLOGY	UNBODIED	UNFREEZE	UNSADDLE
UNUSUAL	URUAPAN	UNBOLTED	UNFURLED	UNSEATED
UNVOICE	URUGUAY	UNBRIDLE	UNGAINLY	UNSEEDED
UNWAGED	URUMCHI	UNBROKEN	UNGUENTS	UNSEEING
UNWOUND	USELESS	UNBUCKLE	UNGULATE	UNSEEMLY
UP-AND-UP	USHERED	UNBURDEN	UNHANDED	UNSETTLE
UPBRAID	USUALLY	UNBUTTON	UNHINGED	UNSHAPEN
UPBUILD	USURERS	UNCHASTE	UNHORSED	UNSHAVEN
UPDATED	USURPED	UNCHURCH	UNIATISM	UNSOCIAL
UPDATER	USURPER	UNCIFORM	UNIAXIAL	UNSOAKEN
UPDATES	UTENSIL	UNCINATE	UNICORNS	UNSTABLE
UPDRAFT	UTERINE	UNCLENCH	UNICYCLE	UNSTEADY
UPENDED	UTILITY	UNCLE SAM	UNIFORMS	UNSTRING
UPFRONT	UTILIZE	UNCLE TOM	UNIFYING	UNSUITED
UPGRADE	UTOPIAN	UNCLOTHE	UNIONISM	UNSWATHE
UPHEAVE	UTOPIAS	UNCOINED	UNIONIST	UNTANGLE
UPLANDS	UTRECHT	UNCOMMON	UNIONIZE	UNTAPPED

UNTAUGHT	URETHERAL	UNBENDING	UNDERSELL	UNIPAROUS
UNTHREAD	URETHRAS	UNBINDING	UNDERSHOT	UNIPLANAR
UNTIDILY	URGENTLY	UNBLESSED	UNDERSIDE	UNIRAMOUS
UNTIMELY	URGINGLY	UNBOSOMED	UNDERSOIL	UNISEXUAL
UNTIRING	URINATED	UNBOUNDED	UNDERSOLD	UNISONOUS
UNTITLED	URNFIELD	UNBRIDLED	UNDERTAKE	UNITARIAN
UNTOWARD	UROCHORD	UNBUCKLED	UNDERTINT	UNIT TRUST
UNTRUTHS	UROLOGIC	UNCANNIER	UNDERTONE	UNIVALENT
UNUSABLE	UROPODAL	UNCANNILY	UNDERTOOK	UNIVERSAL
UNVALUED	UROSCOPY	UNCEASING	UNDERWEAR	UNIVERSES
UNVEILED	UROSTYLE	UNCERTAIN	UNDERWENT	UNKINDEST
UNVERSED	URSULINE	UNCHARGED	UNDERWING	UNKNOWING
UNVOICED	URTICATE	UNCHARTED	UNDESIRED	UNLEARNED
UNWASHED	URUSHIOL	UNCHEKED	UNDEVIDED	UNLEASHED
UNWIELDY	USEFULLY	UNCONCERN	UNDOUBTED	UNLIMITED
UNWINDER	USHERING	UNCORKING	UNDRESSED	UNLOADERS
UNWISHED	USUFRUCT	UNCOUNTED	UNDULANCE	UNLOADING
UNWONTED	USURIOUS	UNCOUPLED	UNDULATED	UNLOCKING
UNWORTHY	USURPERS	UNCOUTHLY	UNDULATOR	UNLOOSING
UNZIPPED	USURPIING	UNCOVERED	UNEARTHED	UNLUCKILY
UP-ANCHOR	UTENSILS	UNCREATED	UNEARTHLY	UNMARRIED
UPCOMING	UTERUSES	UNCROWNED	UNEASIEST	UNMASKING
UPDATING	UTILIZED	UNDAUNTED	UNEATABLE	UNMATCHED
UPENDING	UTILIZER	UNDECAGON	UNEQUALLY	UNMEANING
UPGRADED	UTTERING	UNDECIEVE	UNETHICAL	UNMINDFUL
UPGRADED	UVULITIS	UNDECIDED	UNFAILING	UNMUSICAL
UPGROWTH	UXORIOUS	UNDERBODY	UNFAIREST	UNNATURAL
UPHEAVAL		UNDERBRED	UNFEELING	UNNERVING
UPHOLDER		UNDERCLAY	UNFEIGNED	UNNOTICED
UPLIFTED	**9 LETTERS**	UNDERCOAT	UNFITNESS	UNOPPOSED
UPLIFTER	UITLANDER	UNDERDOGS	UNFLEDGED	UNPACKING
UP-MARKET	UKRAINIAN	UNDERDONE	UNFOLDING	UNPICKING
UPPERCUT	ULCERATED	UNDERFEED	UNFOUNDED	UNPLUMBED
UPRAISER	ULMACEOUS	UNDERFELT	UNFROCKED	UNPOLITIC
UPRISING	ULOTRICHY	UNDERFOOT	UNFURLING	UNPOPULAR
UPROOTED	ULTIMATUM	UNDERGIRD	UNGUARDED	UNRAVELED
UPROOTER	ULULATION	UNDERGOER	UNGUINOUS	UNREALITY
UPSETTER	UMBELLATE	UNDERGONE	UNHANDLING	UNREFINED
UPSTAGED	UMBELLULE	UNDERHAND	UNHAPPILY	UNRELATED
UPSTAIRS	UMBILICAL	UNDERHUNG	UNHARNESS	UNRESERVE
UPSTARTS	UMBRELLAS	UNDERLAIN	UNHEALTHY	UNRIDDLER
UPSTREAM	UMPTEENTH	UNDERLAYS	UNHEARD-OF	UNROLLING
UPSTROKE	UNABASHED	UNDERLIER	UNHINGED	UNROUNDED
UPSURGES	UNADOPTED	UNDERLINE	UNHORSING	UNRUFFLED
UPSWINGS	UNADVISED	UNDERLING	UNHURRIED	UNSADDLED
UPTHRUST	UNALLOYED	UNDERMINE	UNICOLOUR	UNSAVOURY
UP-TO-DATE	UNANIMITY	UNDERMOST	UNIFIABLE	UNSCATHED
UPTURNED	UNANIMOUS	UNDERPAID	UNIFORMED	UNSCREWED
URALITIC	UNAPTNESS	UNDERPASS	UNIFORMLY	UNSEATING
URANITIC	UNASHAMED	UNDERPLAY	UNIJUGATE	UNSECURED
URANYLIC	UNASSUMED	UNDERPLOT	UNINSURED	UNSELFISH
URBANELY	UNBALANCED	UNDERPROP	UNIONISTS	UNSETTLED
URBANITY	UNBARRING	UNDERRATE	UNIONIZED	UNSHACKLE
URBANIZE	UNBEKNOWN	UNDERSEAL	UNION JACK	UNSHEATHE

UNSIGHTED
UNSIGHTLY
UNSKILFUL
UNSKILLED
UNSPARING
UNSPOTTED
UNSTOPPED
UNSTRIPED
UNSTUDIED
UNTANGLED
UNTENABLE
UNTOUCHED
UNTREATED
UNTUTORED
UNTYPICAL
UNUSUALLY
UNVEILING
UNWATCHED
UNWEARIED
UNWEIGHED
UNWELCOME
UNWILLING
UNWINDING
UNWITTING
UNWORLDLY
UNWRITTEN
UNZIPPING
UP-AND-DOWN
UPBRAIDED
UPBRAIDER
UP-COUNTRY
UPGRADING
UPHEAVALS
UPHOLDERS
UPHOLDING
UPHOLSTER
UPLIFTING
UPPER CASE
UPPERCUTS
UPPER HAND
UPPERMOST
UPRIGHTLY
UPRISINGS
UPROOTING
UPSETTING
UPSTAGING
URANINITE
URCEOLATE
URINATING
URINATION
URINATIVE
UROCHROME
UROGENOUS
UROLITHIC

UROLOGIST
UROPYGIAL
UROPYGIUM
UROSCOPIC
URSA MAJOR
URTICARIA
URUGUAYAN
USABILITY
USELESSLY
USHERETTE
USUALNESS
UTILITIES
UTILIZING
UTRICULAR
UTTERABLE
UTTERANCES
UVAROVITE
UXORICIDE

10 LETTERS
UBIQUITOUS
ULCERATING
ULCERATION
ULCERATIVE
ULTIMATELY
ULTIMATUMS
ULTRAFICHE
ULTRAISTIC
ULTRASHORT
ULTRASONIC
ULTRASOUND
ULTRAVIRUS
UMBILICATE
UMBILIFORM
UMBRAGEOUS
UMPIRESHIP
UMPTEENTHS
UNABRIDGED
UNAFFECTED
UN-AMERICAN
UNASSISTED
UNASSUMING
UNATTACHED
UNATTENDED
UNAVAILING
UNBALANCED
UNBEARABLE
UNBEARABLY
UNBEATABLE
UNBECOMING
UNBELIEVER
UNBENDABLE
UNBLINKING

UNBLUSHING
UNBOSOMING
UNBUCKLING
UNBURDENED
UNCANNIEST
UNCARED-FOR
UNCIVILITY
UNCOMMONLY
UNCONFINED
UNCOUPLING
UNCOVERING
UNCRITICAL
UNCTUOSITY
UNCTUOUSLY
UNDECEIVED
UNDECEIVER
UNDEFEATED
UNDEFENDED
UNDENIABLE
UNDENIABLY
UNDERACTED
UNDERBELLY
UNDERBRUSH
UNDERCOATS
UNDERCOVER
UNDERCROFT
UNDERDRAIN
UNDERFLOOR
UNDERGLAZE
UNDERGOING
UNDERGROWN
UNDERLINED
UNDERLINGS
UNDERLYING
UNDERMINED
UNDERMINER
UNDERNAMED
UNDERNEATH
UNDERPANTS
UNDERPRICE
UNDERPROOF
UNDERQUOTE
UNDERRATED
UNDERSCORE
UNDERSEXED
UNDERSHIRT
UNDERSHOOT
UNDERSIZED
UNDERSKIRT
UNDERSLUNG
UNDERSPEND
UNDERSTAND
UNDERSTATE
UNDERSTOCK

UNDERSTOOD
UNDERSTUDY
UNDERTAKEN
UNDERTAKER
UNDERTONE
UNDERTRICK
UNDERTRUMP
UNDERVALUE
UNDERWATER
UNDERWORLD
UNDERWRITE
UNDERWROTE
UNDETERRED
UNDIRECTED
UNDISPUTED
UNDRESSING
UNDULATING
UNDULATION
UNDULATORY
UNEARTHING
UNEASINESS
UNECONOMIC
UNEDIFYING
UNEDUCATED
UNEMPLOYED
UNEQUALLED
UNERRINGLY
UNEVENNESS
UNEVENTFUL
UNEXAMPLED
UNEXPECTED
UNFAIRNESS
UNFAITHFUL
UNFAMILIAR
UNFATHERED
UNFEMININE
UNFETTERED
UNFINISHED
UNFLAGGING
UNFORESEEN
UNFORGIVEN
UNFRIENDLY
UNFROCKING
UNFRUITFUL
UNGENEROUS
UNGRATEFUL
UNGRUDGING
UNGUENTARY
UNHALLOWED
UNHAMPERED
UNHANDSOME
UNHERALDED
UNHOLINESS
UNHOPED-FOR

UNHYGIENIC
UNICAMERAL
UNICOSTATE
UNICYCLIST
UNIFOLIATE
UNIFORMITY
UNILATERAL
UNILOCULAR
UNIMPOSING
UNIMPROVED
UNINFORMED
UNINSPIRED
UNINTENDED
UNIONISTIC
UNIONIZING
UNIQUENESS
UNISEPTATE
UNITARIANS
UNITEDNESS
UNIT TRUSTS
UNIVALENCY
UNIVERSITY
UNJUSTNESS
UNKINDNESS
UNKNOWABLE
UNLAWFULLY
UNLEARNING
UNLEASHING
UNLEAVENED
UNLETTERED
UNLICENSED
UNLOCKABLE
UNLOOSENED
UNMANNERED
UNMANNERLY
UNMEASURED
UNMERCIFUL
UNMORALITY
UNNUMBERED
UNOCCUPIED
UNOFFICIAL
UNORIGINAL
UNORTHODOX
UNPATENTED
UNPLAYABLE
UNPLEASANT
UNPREPARED
UNPROMPTED
UNPROVIDED
UNPROVOKED
UNPUNCTUAL
UNPUNISHED
UNRAVELING
UNRAVELLED

UNRAVELLER
UNREADABLE
UNREADABLY
UNRELIABLE
UNRELIEVED
UNREQUITED
UNRESERVED
UNRESOLVED
UNRIVALLED
UNRULINESS
UNSADDLING
UNSANITARY
UNSCHOOLED
UNSCRAMBLE
UNSCREENED
UNSCREWING
UNSCRIPTED
UNSEALABLE
UNSEASONED
UNSEEINGLY
UNSETTLING
UNSHAKABLE
UNSOCIABLE
UNSPECIFIC
UNSTEADILY
UNSTINTING
UNSTOPPING
UNSTRAINED
UNSTRESSED
UNSTRAITED
UNSUITABLE
UNSWERVING
UNTANGLING
UNTHANKFUL
UNTHINKING
UNTIDINESS
UNTIRINGLY
UNTOWARDLY
UNTRUTHFUL
UNWIELDILY
UNWINDABLE
UNWORKABLE
UNWORTHILY
UNWIELDING
UP-AND-UNDER
UPBRAIDING
UPBRINGING
UPHOLSTERY
UPLIFTMENT
UPPER CLASS
UPPER CRUST
UPPER HOUSE
UPPER VOLTA
UPPISHNESS

UPROARIOUS
UPSETTABLE
UPSIDE DOWN
UPWARDNESS
URAL-ALTAIC
URBANENESS
UREDOSORUS
UREDOSPORE
URETHRITIC
URETHRITIS
URINALYSIS
UROCORDAL
UROGENITAL
UROSCOPIST
URTICARIAL
URTICATION
USEFULNESS
USHERETTES
USTULATION
USURPATION
USURPATIVE
USURPINGLY
UTILIZABLE
UTO-AZTECAN
UTOPIANISM
UTTERANCES
UXORICIDAL
UZBEKISTAN

11 LETTERS
ULTRAFILTER
ULTRAMARINE
ULTRAMODERN
ULTRASONICS
ULTRAVIOLET
ULVERIZABLE
UMBELLULATE
UNACCOUNTED
UNADVISEDLY
UNALTERABLE
UNAMBIGUOUS
UNANIMOSITY
UNANNOUNCED
UNAVAILABLE
UNAVOIDABLE
UNAWARENESS
UNBALANCING
UNBALLASTED
UNBELIEVERS
UNBLEMISHED
UNBREAKABLE
UNBURDENING
UNCALLED-FOR

UNCERTAINLY
UNCERTAINTY
UNCHARTERED
UNCHRISTIAN
UNCIVILIZED
UNCLEANNESS
UNCOMMITTED
UNCONCERNED
UNCONCLUDED
UNCONNECTED
UNCONSCIOUS
UNCONTESTED
UNCONVERTED
UNCONVINCED
UNCOUNTABLE
UNCOUTHNESS
UNCRUSHABLE
UNDECEIVING
UNDECIDEDLY
UNDEMANDING
UNDERACTING
UNDERBIDDER
UNDERCHARGE
UNDEREXPOSE
UNDERGROUND
UNDERGROWTH
UNDERLETTER
UNDERLINING
UNDERMANNED
UNDERMINING
UNDERPASSES
UNDERPAYING
UNDERPINNED
UNDERPLAYED
UNDERRATING
UNDERSCORED
UNDERSELLER
UNDERSHIRTS
UNDERSIGNED
UNDERSTATED
UNDERTAKERS
UNDERTAKING
UNDERTHRUST
UNDERVALUED
UNDERVALUER
UNDERWEIGHT
UNDERWRITER
UNDESIGNING
UNDESIRABLE
UNDESIRABLE
UNDEVELOPED
UNDISCLOSED
UNDOUBTEDLY
UNDREAMED OF

UNDRINKABLE	UNREALISTIC	UMBILICATION	UNDERTAKINGS
UNDULATIONS	UNREASONING	UNACCEPTABLE	UNDERVALUING
UNEQUALNESS	UNREFLECTED	UNACCUSTOMED	UNDERWRITERS
UNEQUIVOCAL	UNREHEARSED	UNAQUAINTED	UNDERWRITING
UNESSENTIAL	UNRELENTING	UNAFFECTEDLY	UNDERWRITTEN
UNEXPLAINED	UNREMITTING	UNANSWERABLE	UNDESIRABLES
UNEXPRESSED	UNRIGHTEOUS	UNAPPEALABLE	UNDETERMINED
UNFAILINGLY	UNSATISFIED	UNASSAILABLE	UNDISCHARGED
UNFALTERING	UNSATURATED	UNASSUMINGLY	UNECONOMICAL
UNFLAPPABLE	UNSAVOURILY	UNATTAINABLE	UNEMPLOYABLE
UNFLAPPABLY	UNSCHEDULED	UNATTRACTIVE	UNEMPLOYMENT
UNFLINCHING	UNSCRAMBLED	UNBELIEVABLE	UNEVENTFULLY
UNFORTUNATE	UNSCRAMBLER	UNBELIEVABLY	UNEXPRESSIVE
UNFULFILLED	UNSCRATCHED	UNBIASEDNESS	UNEXPURGATED
UNGODLINESS	UNSHAKABLE	UNCHALLENGED	UNFAITHFULLY
UNGUICULATE	UNSPARINGLY	UNCHARITABLE	UNFATHOMABLE
UNGULIGRADE	UNSPEAKABLE	UNCHARITABLY	UNFATHOMABLY
UNHAPPINESS	UNSPEAKABLE	UNCHASTENESS	UNFAVOURABLE
UNHEALTHILY	UNSPECIFIED	UNCINARIASIS	UNFAVOURABLY
UNICELLULAR	UNSTOPPABLE	UNCLASSIFIED	UNFLAGGINGLY
UNIFICATION	UNSURPASSED	UNCOMMERCIAL	UNFLATTERING
UNIFORMNESS	UNSUSPECTED	UNCOMMONNESS	UNFORGIVABLE
UNINHABITED	UNTERWALDEN	UNCONFIRMITY	UNFORTUNATES
UNINHIBITED	UNTHINKABLE	UNCONSENTING	UNFREQUENTED
UNINITIATED	UNTOUCHABLE	UNCONSIDERED	UNGAINLINESS
UNINSPIRING	UNTRAVELLED	UNCONVINCING	UNGOVERNABLE
UNIPERSONAL	UNUTTERABLE	UNCOVENANTED	UNGRATEFULLY
UNIPOLARITY	UNUTTERABLY	UNCRITICALLY	UNHESITATING
UNIVERSALLY	UNVARNISHED	UNCTUOUSNESS	UNHYPHENATED
UNJUSTIFIED	UNWARRANTED	UNDECIEVABLE	UNIDENTIFIED
UNKEMPTNESS	UNWHOLESOME	UNDEMOCRATIC	UNIFOLIOLATE
UNKNOWINGLY	UNWILLINGLY	UNDERACHIEVE	UNILATERALLY
UNKNOWNNESS	UP-AND-COMING	UNDERBELLIES	UNIMAGINABLE
UNLOOKED-FOR	UPHOLSTERER	UNDERCHARGED	UNIMPRESSIVE
UNLOOSENING	UPRIGHTNESS	UNDERCLOTHES	UNINFLUENCED
UNLUCKINESS	UPS AND DOWNS	UNDERCURRENT	UNINTERESTED
UNMANLINESS	UPSTRETCHED	UNDERCUTTING	UNIONIZATION
UNMITIGATED	URANOGRAPHY	UNDERDEVELOP	UNISEXUALITY
UNNATURALLY	URINIFEROUS	UNDERDRESSED	UNITARIANISM
UNNECESSARY	UROCHORDATE	UNDEREXPOSED	UNIVERSALISM
UNOBTRUSIVE	URTICACEOUS	UNDERGARMENT	UNIVERSALIST
UNORGANIZED	USELESSNESS	UNDERGROUNDS	UNIVERSALITY
UNPALATABLE	UTILITARIAN	UNDERNOURISH	UNIVERSALIZE
UNPATRIOTIC	UTILITY ROOM	UNDERPAYMENT	UNIVERSITIES
UNPERTURBED	UTILIZATION	UNDERPINNING	UNKINDLINESS
UNPOLITICAL	UTRICULITIS	UNDERPLAYING	UNLAWFULNESS
UNPRACTISED		UNDERSCORING	UNLIKELIHOOD
UNPRINTABLE		UNDERSELLING	UNLIKELINESS
UNPROFESSED	**12 LETTERS**	UNDERSHERIFF	UNMANAGEABLE
UNPROMISING	UBIQUITOUSLY	UNDERSTAFFED	UNMEASURABLE
UNPUBLISHED	UGLIFICATION	UNDERSTATING	UNMISTAKABLE
UNQUALIFIED	UGLY DUCKLING	UNDERSTUDIED	UNMISTAKABLY
UNRAVELLING	ULTRAMONTANE	UNDERSTUDIES	UNOFFICIALLY
UNRAVELMENT	ULTRAMUNDANE	UNDERSURFACE	UNPARALELLED

UNPERFORATED
UNPLEASANTLY
UNPOPULARITY
UNPREJUDICED
UNPRINCIPLED
UNPRODUCTIVE
UNPROFITABLE
UNQUESTIONED
UNREASONABLE
UNREASONABLY
UNRECKONABLE
UNRECOGNIZED
UNREFLECTIVE
UNREGENERACY
UNREGENERATE
UNRESERVEDLY
UNRESPONSIVE
UNRESTRAINED
UNRESTRICTED
UNSANCTIONED
UNSATURATION
UNSCIENTIFIC
UNSCRAMBLING
UNSCRUPULOUS
UNSEARCHABLE
UNSEASONABLE
UNSEASONABLY
UNSEEMLINESS
UNSEGREGATED
UNSETTLEMENT
UNSTEADINESS
UNSTRATIFIED
UNSTRUCTURED
UNSUCCESSFUL
UNSUSPECTING
UNTENABILITY
UNTHINKINGLY
UNTIMELINESS
UNTOUCHABLES
UNTOWARDNESS
UNTRAMELLED
UNWIELDINESS
UNWORTHINESS
UNWRITTEN LAW
UPHOLSTERERS
UPHOLSTERING
UPRIGHT PIANO
UPROARIOUSLY
URBANIZATION
URETHROSCOPE
URETHROSCOPY
URINOGENITAL

USER FRIENDLY
UTILITY ROOMS
13 LETTERS
UGLY DUCKLINGS
UMBELLIFEROUS
UMBILICAL CORD
UNACCOMPANIED
UNACCOUNTABLE
UNACCOUNTABLY
UNADULTERATED
UNADVENTUROUS
UNASHAMEDNESS
UNBELIEVINGLY
UNBLESSEDNESS
UNCEREMONIOUS
UNCERTAINNESS
UNCLEANLINESS
UNCOMFORTABLE
UNCOMFORTABLY
UNCOMPENSATED
UNCOMPETITIVE
UNCOMPLAINING
UNCOMPLICATED
UNCONCERNEDLY
UNCONDITIONAL
UNCONDITIONED
UNCONFORMABLE
UNCONSCIOUSLY
UNCONSTRAINED
UNCONSUMMATED
UNCOORDINATED
UNDECIDEDNESS
UNDERACHIEVED
UNDERACHIEVER
UNDERBREEDING
UNDERCARRIAGE
UNDERCHARGING
UNDERCURRENTS
UNDERDRAINAGE
UNDEREMPLOYED
UNDERESTIMATE
UNDEREXPOSING
UNDEREXPOSURE
UNDERGARMENTS
UNDERGRADUATE
UNDERHANDEDLY
UNDERMININGLY
UNDERPAINTING
UNDERPINNINGS
UNDERSTANDING
UNDERSTUDYING
UNDISCIPLINED

UNENLIGHTENED
UNEQUIVOCALLY
UNEXCEPTIONAL
UNEXPERIENCED
UNFALTERINGLY
UNFAMILIARITY
UNFASHIONABLE
UNFEELINGNESS
UNFLINCHINGLY
UNFORESEEABLE
UNFORGETTABLE
UNFORGETTABLY
UNFORTUNATELY
UNFOUNDEDNESS
UNGUARDEDNESS
UNILATERALISM
UNILLUSTRATED
UNIMPEACHABLE
UNIMPEACHABLY
UNINHABITABLE
UNINHIBITEDLY
UNINTELLIGENT
UNINTENTIONAL
UNINTERRUPTED
UNITED NATIONS
UNIVERSALNESS
UNMENTIONABLE
UNNATURALNESS
UNNECESSARILY
UNOBTRUSIVELY
UNPRECEDENTED
UNPREDICTABLE
UNPRETENTIOUS
UNQUALIFIABLE
UNQUESTIONING
UNREADABILITY
UNRELENTINGLY
UNRELIABILITY
UNREMITTINGLY
UNREPRESENTED
UNRUFFLEDNESS
UNSAVOURINESS
UNSELFISHNESS
UNSERVICABLE
UNSIGHTLINESS
UNSOCIABILITY
UNSUBSTANTIAL
UNSUITABILITY
UNWILLINGNESS
UP-TO-THE-MINUTE

3 LETTERS	VISE	VIALS	VOWEL	VENDOR	VIDEOS
VAC	VOID	VIAND	V-SIGN	VENEER	VIENNA
VAN	VOLE	VIBES	VULVA	VENETO	VIENNE
VAT	VOTE	VICAR	VYING	VENIAL	VIEWED
VCR	VOWS	VICES		VENICE	VIEWER
VCS		VICHY		VENIRE	VIGILS
VDU		VIDEO	6 LETTERS	VENOSE	VIGOUR
VEG	5 LETTERS	VIEWS	VACANT	VENOUS	VIKING
VET	VADUZ	VIGIL	VACATE	VENTED	VILELY
VEX	VAGAL	VILER	VACUUM	VENTER	VILEST
VHF	VAGUE	VILLA	VADOSE	VENUES	VILIFY
VIA	VAGUS	VIMEN	VAGARY	VENULE	VILLAS
VIE	VALES	VINES	VAGINA	VERBAL	VILLUS
VIM	VALET	VINIC	VAINER	VERBID	VINERY
VIP	VALID	VINYL	VAINLY	VERDIN	VINOUS
VIZ	VALUE	VIOLA	VALAIS	VERGED	VINYLS
VOW	VALVE	VIOLS	VALETS	VERGER	VIOLAS
	VAMPS	VIPER	VALGUS	VERGES	VIOLET
	VANDA	VIRAL	VALINE	VERIFY	VIOLIN
4 LETTERS	VANES	VIREO	VALISE	VERILY	VIPERS
VACS	VAPID	VIRGA	VALIUM	VERSM	VIRAGO
VAIN	VARIA	VIRGO	VALLEY	VERIST	VIRGIN
VALE	VARIX	VIRTU	VALOUR	VERITY	VIRGOS
VAMP	VARNA	VIRUS	VALUED	VERMIN	VIRILE
VANE	VARUS	VISAS	VALUER	VERMIS	VIRTUE
VANS	VARVE	VISES	VALUES	VERNAL	VISAED
VARY	VASES	VISIT	VALVES	VERONA	VISAGE
VASE	VAULT	VISOR	VANDAL	VERSED	VISCID
VAST	VAUNT	VISTA	VANISH	VERSES	VISION
VATS	VEDDA	VITAL	VANITY	VERSOS	VISITS
VAUD	VEDIC	VITTA	VAPOUR	VERSUS	VISORS
VDUS	VEERY	VIVID	VARIED	VERTEX	VISTAS
VEAL	VEGAN	VIXEN	VARLET	VERVET	VISUAL
VEER	VEILS	V-NECK	VASSAL	VESICA	VITALS
VEIL	VEINS	VOCAB	VASTLY	VESPER	VITRIC
VEIN	VELAR	VOCAL	VAULTS	VESPID	VIVACE
VELD	VELUM	VODKA	VAUNTS	VESSEL	VIVIFY
VEND	VENAL	VOGUE	VECTOR	VESTAL	VIXENS
VENT	VENDA	VOGUL	VEERED	VESTED	VIZIAR
VERB	VENIN	VOICE	VEGANS	VESTRY	V-NECKS
VERY	VENOM	VOIDS	VEILED	VETOED	VOCABS
VEST	VENTS	VOILE	VEILER	VETOER	VOCALS
VETO	VENUE	VOLAR	VEINAL	VETOER	VOGUES
VETS	VENUS	VOLES	VEINED	VETTED	VOICED
VIAL	VERBS	VOLTA	VELARS	VEXING	VOICER
VICE	VERGE	VOLTS	VELATE	VIABLE	VOICES
VIED	VERSE	VOLVA	VELCRO	VIABLY	VOIDED
VIEW	VERSO	VOMER	VELLUM	VIANDS	VOIDER
VILE	VERVE	VOMIT	VELOCE	VIBIST	VOLANT
VINE	VESTA	VOTED	VELOUR	VIBRIO	VOLLEY
VINO	VESTS	VOTER	VELURE	VICARS	VOLUME
VIOL	VETCH	VOTES	VELVET	VICTIM	VOLUTE
VIPS	VEXED	VOUCH	VENDED	VICTOR	VOLVOX
VISA	VEXER	VOWED	VENDEE	VICUNA	VOODOO

VORTEX	VARIETY	VERISMO	VIOLATE	VOLTAGE
VOSGES	VARIOLA	VERMEIL	VIOLENT	VOLTAIC
VOSTOK	VARIOLE	VERMONT	VIOLETS	VOLUBLE
VOTARY	VARIOUS	VERNIER	VIOLINS	VOLUBLY
VOTERS	VARLETS	VERONAL	VIOLIST	VOLUMED
VOTING	VARMINT	VERRUCA	VIRAGOS	VOLUMES
VOTIVE	VARNISH	VERSANT	VIRELAY	VOLVATE
VOTYAK	VARSITY	VERSIFY	VIRGATE	VOMITED
VOWELS	VARYING	VERSION	VIRGINS	VOMITER
VOWING	VASSALS	VERTIGO	VIRGOAN	VOMITUS
VOX POP	VASTITY	VERVAIN	VIRGULE	VORLAGE
VOYAGE	VATICAN	VESICLE	VIRTUAL	VOTABLE
VOYEUR	VAUDOIS	VESPERS	VIRTUES	VOUCHED
V-SIGNS	VAULTED	VESPINE	VIRUSES	VOUCHER
VULGAR	VAULTER	VESSELS	VISAGES	VOX POPS
VULVAE	VAUNTED	VESTIGE	VISAING	VOYAGED
VULVAL	VAUNTER	VESTING	VIS-A-VIS	VOYAGER
VULVAS	VECTORS	VESTRAL	VISAYAN	VOYAGES
	VEDALIA	VESTURE	VISCERA	VOYEURS
	VEDDOID	VETCHES	VISCOID	VULGATE
7 LETTERS	VEDETTE	VETERAN	VISCOSE	VULTURE
VACANCY	VEERING	VETIVER	VISCOUS	
VACATED	VEGETAL	VETOING	VISIBLE	
VACCINE	VEHICLE	VETTING	VISIBLY	**8 LETTERS**
VACUITY	VEILING	VEXEDLY	VISIONS	VACANTLY
VACUOLE	VEINING	VIADUCT	VISITED	VACATING
VACUOUS	VEINLET	VIBRANT	VISITOR	VACATION
VACUUMS	VELAMEN	VIBRATE	VISTAED	VACCINAL
VAGRANT	VELIGER	VIBRATO	VISITOR	VACCINES
VAGUELY	VELLORE	VICENZA	VISTAED	VACCINIA
VAINEST	VELOURS	VICEROY	VISTULA	VACUOLAR
VALANCE	VELVETY	VICINAL	VITALLY	VACCUMED
VALENCE	VENALLY	VICIOUS	VITAMIN	VAGABOND
VALERIC	VENATIC	VICOMTE	VITEBSK	VAGARIES
VALIANT	VENDACE	VICTIMS	VITIATE	VAGANATE
VALIDLY	VENDING	VICTORS	VITORIA	VAGOTOMY
VALISES	VENDORS	VICTORY	VITRAIN	VAGRANCY
VALLEYS	VENEERS	VICTUAL	VITRIFY	VAGRANTS
VALONIA	VENISON	VICUNAS	VITRINE	VAINNESS
VALUERS	VENTAGE	VIDEOED	VITRIOL	VALANCED
VALUING	VENTING	VIDICON	VITTATE	VALANCES
VALVATE	VENTRAL	VIETNAM	VIVIDLY	VALENCIA
VALVULE	VENTURE	VIEWERS	VIYELLA	VALERIAN
VAMOOSE	VENULAR	VIEWING	VIZINERS	VALIANCE
VAMPIRE	VERANDA	VIKINGS	V-NECKED	VALIDATE
VANADIC	VERBENA	VILLAGE	VOCABLE	VALIDITY
VANDALS	VERBIFY	VILLAIN	VOCALIC	VALLETTA
VANILLA	VERBOSE	VILLEIN	VOCALLY	VALORIZE
VANTAGE	VERDANT	VILLOUS	VOICING	VALOROUS
VANWARD	VERDICT	VILNIUS	VOIDING	VALUABLE
VAPIDLY	VERDURE	VINASSE	VOLAPUK	VALUATOR
VAPOURS	VERGERS	VINEGAR	VOLCANO	VALVULAR
VARIANT	VERGING	VINTAGE	VOLLEYS	VAMBRACE
VARIATE	VERGLAS	VINTNER	VOLOGDA	VAMOOSED

VAMPIRES	VENOSITY	VIBRONIC	VISCOUNT	VORTEXES
VAMPIRIC	VENTURED	VIBURNUM	VISIONAL	VORTICAL
VANADATE	VENTURER	VICARAGE	VISITANT	VORTICES
VANADIUM	VENTURES	VICARIAL	VISITING	VOTARESS
VANADOUS	VENUSIAN	VICELIKE	VISITORS	VOTARIES
VANGUARD	VERACITY	VICENARY	VISUALLY	VOTARIST
VANILLIC	VERANDAS	VICEROYS	VITALISM	VOUCHERS
VANILLIN	VERBALLY	VICINITY	VITALIST	VOUCHING
VANISHED	VERBATIM	VICTORIA	VITALITY	VOUSSOIR
VANISHER	VERBIAGE	VICTUALS	VITALIZE	VOWELIZE
VANQUISH	VERBOTEN	VIDEOING	VITAMINS	VOYAGERS
VAPIDITY	VERDANCY	VIENNESE	VITELLIN	VOYAGING
VAPORIZE	VERDICTS	VIETCONG	VITIABLE	VULGARLY
VAPOROUS	VERIFIED	VIEWLESS	VITIATED	VULTURES
VAPOURER	VERIFIER	VIGILANT	VITIATOR	VULVITIS
VARACTOR	VERISTIC	VIGNETTE	VITILIGO	
VARANASI	VERITIES	VIGOROSO	VITREOUS	
VARIABLE	VERJUICE	VIGOROUS	VITULINE	**9 LETTERS**
VARIABLY	VERMOUTH	VILENESS	VIVACITY	VACANCIES
VARIANCE	VERONESE	VILIFIED	VIVARIUM	VACATABLE
VARIANTS	VERONICA	VILIFIER	VIVA VOCE	VACATIONS
VARICOSE	VERRUCAE	VILLAGER	VIVIFIER	VACCINATE
VARIETAL	VERRUCAS	VILLAGES	VIVISECT	VACCINIAL
VARIFORM	VERSICLE	VILLAINS	VIXENISH	VACILLANT
VARIOLAR	VERSIONS	VILLAINY	VLADIMIR	VACILLATE
VARIORUM	VERTEBRA	VILLANTIC	VOCALISE	VACUOLATE
VARISTOR	VERTEXES	VILLEINS	VOCALISM	VACUOUSLY
VARITYPE	VERTICAL	VINCULUM	VOCALIST	VACUUMING
VARMINTS	VERTICES	VINEGARY	VOCALITY	VAGABONDS
VASCULAR	VERTICIL	VINEYARD	VOCALIZE	VAGINITIS
VASCULUM	VESICANT	VINOSITY	VOCATION	VAGATONIA
VASELINE	VESICATE	VINTAGER	VOCATIVE	VAGUENESS
VASTERAS	VESICLES	VINTAGES	VOICE BOX	VAINGLORY
VASTNESS	VESPERAL	VINTNERS	VOICEFUL	VALENCIES
VAUCLUSE	VESPIARY	VIOLABLE	VOIDABLE	VALENTINE
VAULTERS	VESTIGES	VIOLATED	VOIDANCE	VALIANTLY
VAULTING	VESTMENT	VIOLATOR	VOLATILE	VALIDATED
VEGETATE	VESTRIES	VIOLENCE	VOLCANIC	VALIDNESS
VEHEMENT	VESTURAL	VIPERINE	VOLCANOS	VALLATION
VEHICLES	VESUVIAN	VIPEROUS	VOLIATION	VALLECULA
VEILEDLY	VESUVIUS	VIRAGOES	VOLIATIVE	VALUABLES
VELARIZE	VETERANS	VIRGINAL	VOLLEYED	VALUATION
VELOCITY	VEXATION	VIRGINIA	VOLLEYER	VALUELESS
VENILITY	VEXILLUM	VERIDIAN	VOLPLANE	VALVELESS
VENATION	VEXINGLY	VIRIDITY	VOLTAGES	VAMOOSING
VENDETTA	VIADUCTS	VIRILISM	VOLTAISM	VAMPIRISM
VENDIBLE	VIA MEDIA	VIRILITY	VOLUTION	VANASPATI
VENEERED	VIATICUM	VIROLOGY	VOLVULUS	VANCOUVER
VENEERER	VIBRANCY	VIRTUOSI	VOMERINE	VANDALISM
VENERATE	VIBRATED	VIRTUOSO	VOMITING	VANDALIZE
VENEREAL	VIBRATOR	VIRTUOUS	VOMITIVE	VANGUARDS
VENETIAN	VIBRATOS	VIRULENT	VOMITORY	VANISHING
VENGEFUL	VIBRIOID	VISCACHA	VORACITY	VAPIDNESS
VENOMOUS	VIBRISSA	VISCERAL	VORONEZH	VAPORETTO

VAPORIFIC	VERANDAED	VICARSHIP	VISUALIZE
VAPORIZED	VERATRINE	VICEGERAL	VITACEOUS
VAPORIZER	VERBALISM	VICENNIAL	VITALIZER
VAPOURISH	VERBALIST	VICEREGAL	VITAMINIC
VARANGIAN	VERBALIZE	VICEREINE	VITELLINE
VARIABLES	VERBOSELY	VICE VERSA	VITIATING
VARIANCES	VERBOSITY	VICIOUSLY	VITIATION
VARIATION	VERDIGRIS	VICTIMIZE	VITRIFIED
VARICELLA	VERDUROUS	VICTORIAN	VITRIFORM
VARICOSIS	VERIDICAL	VICTORIES	VITRIOLIC
VARIEGATE	VERIFYING	VICTULATED	VIVACEOUS
VARIETIES	VERITABLE	VIDELICET	VIVARIUMS
VARIOLATE	VERITABLY	VIDEODISC	VIVA VOCES
VARIOLITE	VERMICIDE	VIDEOTAPE	VIVERRINE
VARIOLOID	VERMIFORM	VEINTIANE	VIVIDNESS
VARIOUSLY	VERMIFUGE	VIEWPOINT	VOCALISTS
VARISCITE	VERMILLION	VIGESIMAL	VOCALIZER
VARITYPER	VERMINOUS	VIGILANCE	VOCATIONS
VARNISHED	VERMONTER	VIGILANTES	VOCATIVES
VARNISHER	VERNALIZE	VIGNETTES	VOICELESS
VARNISHES	VERNATION	VILIFYING	VOICE-OVER
VARSITIES	VERRUCOSE	VILLAGERS	VOL-AU-VENT
VARYINGLY	VERSATILE	VILLIFYING	VOLCANISM
VASECTOMY	VERSIFIER	VILLOSITY	VOLCANIZE
VASOMOTOR	VERSIONAL	VIMINEOUS	VOLCANOES
VASSALAGE	VERS LIBRE	VINACEOUS	VOLGOGRAD
VASSALIZE	VERTABRAE	VINDICATE	VOLLEYING
VECTORIAL	VERTEBRAL	VINEYARDS	VOLTE-FACE
VEERINGLY	VERY LIGHT	VIOLATING	VOLTMETER
VEGETABLE	VESICULAR	VIOLATION	VOLUMETRY
VEGETATED	VESTIBULE	VIOLATIVE	VOLUNTARY
VEHEMENCE	VESTIGIAL	VIOLATORS	VOLUNTEER
VEHICULAR	VESTMENTS	VIOLENTLY	VOODOOISM
VEINSTONE	VESTRYMEN	VIOLINIST	VOODOOIST
VELODROME	VETCHLING	VIRESCENT	VORACIOUS
VELVETEEN	VEXATIONS	VIRGINALS	VORTICISM
VENDETTAS	VEXATIOUS	VIRGINIAN	VORTICIST
VENDITION	VEXEDNESS	VIRGINITY	VOUCHSAFE
VENEERING	VEXILLARY	VIRGULATE	VOYEUISM
VENERABLE	VEXILLATE	VIRTUALLY	VULCANIAN
VENERATED	VIABILITY	VIRTUOSIC	VULCANIZE
VENERATOR	VIBRANTLY	VIRTUOSIS	VULGARIAN
VENEZUELA	VIBRANTILE	VIRULENCE	VULGARISM
VENGEANCE	VIBRATING	VIRULENCY	VULGARITY
VENIALITY	VIBRATION	VISCIDITY	VULGARIZE
VENTILATE	VIBRATIVE	VISCOSITY	VULNERARY
VENTRICLE	VIBRATORS	VISCOUNTS	VULTURINE
VENTURERS	VICARAGES	VISIONARY	VULTUROUS
VENTURING	VICARIATE	VISITABLE	VULVIFORM
VERACIOUS	VICARIOUS	VISUAL AID	

10 LETTERS

VACANTNESS
VACATIONED
VACATIONER
VACCINATED
VACILLATED
VACILLATOR
VACUUM PUMP
VAGINISMUS
VAGOTROPIC
VALENTINES
VALIDATING
VALIDATION
VALIDATORY
VALLADOLID
VALLECULAR
VALVULITIS
VAMPIRE BAT
VANADINITE
VANDALIZED
VANISHMENT
VANQUISHED
VANQUISHER
VAPOURIZING
VAPOURABLE
VARIATIONS
VARICELLAR
VARICOCELE
VARICOSOTY
VARIOCOTOMY
VARIEDNESS
VARIEGATED
VARIOLITIC
VARIOMETER
VARIOTYPIST
VANISHING
VASTNESSES
VAUDEVILLE
VAUNTINGLY
VEGETABLE
VEGETARIAN
VEGETATING
VEGETATION
VEGETATIVE
VEHEMENTLY
VELOCIPEDE
VELOCITIES
VELUTINOUS
VENATIONAL
VENDETTIST
VENERATING
VENERATION
VENEZUELAN
VENGEANCES

VENGEFULLY
VENOMOUSLY
VENOUSNESS
VENTILABLE
VENTILATED
VENTILATOR
VENTRICLES
VENTRICOSE
VERBALIZED
VERBALIZER
VERBAL NOUN
VERIFIABLE
VERMICELLI
VERMICIDAL
VERMICULAR
VERNISSAGE
VERSAILLES
VERTEBRATE
VERTICALLY
VESICATION
VESICULATE
VESPERTINE
VESTIBULAR
VESTIBULES
VESTMENTAL
VESTMENTED
VETERINARY
VIBRACULAR
VIBRACULUM
VIBRAPHONE
VIBRATIONS
VICEGERENT
VICEREINES
VICINITIES
VICOMTESSE
VITIMIZED
VICTIMIZER
VICTORIANS
VICTORIOUS
VICTUALING
VICTUALLED
VICTUALLER
VIDEODISCS
VIDEO NASTY
VIDEOPHONE
VIDEOTAPED
VIETNAMESE
VIEWFINDER
VIEWPOINTS
VIGILANTES
VIGILANTLY
VIGNETTING
VIGNETTIST
VIGOROUSLY

VIJAYAWADA
VILLAINOUS
VILLANELLA
VILLANELLE
VILLANOVAN
VINDICTABLE
VINDICATED
VINDICATOR
VINDICTIVE
VINIFEROUS
VINYLIDENE
VIOLACEOUS
VIOLATIONS
VIOLINISTS
VIRAGINOUS
VIRESCENCE
VIROLOGIST
VIRTUALITY
VIRTUOSITY
VIRTUOUSLY
VIRULENTLY
VISCOMETER
VISCOMETRY
VISCOUNTCY
VISIBILITY
VISITATION
VISITORIAL
VISUAL AIDS
VISUALIZED
VISUALIZER
VITALISTIC
VITAL SIGNS
VITRESCENT
VITRIFYING
VITRIOLIZE
VITUPERATE
VIVIPARITY
VIVIPAROUS
VIVISECTOR
VOCABULARY
VOCAL CORDS
VOCATIONAL
VOCIFERANT
VOCIFERATE
VOCIFEROUS
VOICE BOXES
VOICE-OVERS
VOICEPRINT
VOLATILITY
VOLATILIZE
VOL-AU-VENTS
VOLITIONAL
VOLLEYBALL
VOLT-AMPERE

VOLTE-FACES
VOLUBILITY
VOLUMETRIC
VOLUMINOUS
VOLUNTEERS
VOLUPTUARY
VOLUPTUOUS
VORALBERG
VORTICELLA
VOTIVENESS
VOUCHAFED
VOLCANIZED
VOLCANIZER
VULGARIZED
VULGARIZER
VULGARNESS
VULNERABLE
VULNERABLY
VULPECULAR

11 LETTERS

VACATIONERS
VACATIONING
VACCINATING
VACCINATION
VACILLATING
VACILLATION
VACUOUSNESS
VACUUM FLASK
VACUUM PUMPS
VAGABONDAGE
VAGABONDISM
VAGINECTOMY
VAGRANTNESS
VALEDICTION
VALEDICTORY
VALIDATIONS
VALUATIONAL
VAMPIRE BATS
VANDALISTIC
VANDALIZING
VANISHINLY
VANQUISHING
VAPORESCENT
VAPORIMETER
VAPORIZABLE
VAPOUR TRAIL
VARIABILITY
VARIABILITY
VARIATIONAL
VARICELLATE
VARIEGATION
VARIOLATION

V

11 LETTERS to 12 LETTERS

VARIOUSNESS
VASCULARITY
VASECTOMIES
VASODILATOR
VASOPRESSIN
VEGETARIANS
VELOCIPEDES
VENEREOLOGY
VENESECTION
VENTILLATING
VENTILATION
VENTILATIVE
VENTILATORS
VENTILATORY
VENTRICULAR
VENTRICULUS
VENTURESOME
VERACIOUSLY
VERATRIDINE
VERBALIZING
VERBAL NOUNS
VEREENIGING
VERISIMILAR
VERMICULATE
VERMICULITE
VERMINATION
VERMIVAROUS
VERNACULARS
VURRUCOSITY
VERSATILITY
VERSICOLOUR
VERTEBRATES
VERTICALITY
VERTIGINOUS
VESTIGIALLY
VETERANS DAY
VEXATIOUSLY
VEXILLOLOGY
VIBRACULOID
VIBRAPHONES
VIBRATILITY
VIBRATINGLY
VIBRATIONAL
VICARIOUSLY
VICEGERENCY
VICEROYALTY
VICEROYSHIP
VICHYSSOISE
VICIOUSNESS
VICISSITUDE

VICTIMIZING
VICTUALLING
VIDEOPHONIC
VIDEOTAPING
VIEWFINDERS
VINAIGRETTE
VINDICATING
VINDICATION
VINDICATORY
VINEDRESSER
VINEGARROON
VINEYARDIST
VINICULTURE
VINIFICATOR
VIOLABILITY
VIOLONCELLO
VIRGIN BIRTH
VIRIDESCENT
VIROLOGICAL
VISCOMETRIC
VISCOUNTESS
VISCOUSNESS
VISIBLENESS
VISIONARIES
VISITATIONS
VISUALIZING
VITICULTURE
VITRESCENCE
VITRIFIABLE
VITUPERATOR
VIVACIOUSLY
VIVISECTION
VLADIVSTOK
VOCIFERANCE
VOCIFERATED
VOCIFERATOR
VOLCANICITY
VOLCANOLOGY
VOLTAMMETER
VOLUNTARIES
VOLUNTARILY
VOLUNTARIST
VOLUNTEERED
VOODOOISTIC
VOORTREKKER
VORACIOUSLY
VORTIGINOUS
VOUCHSAFING
VOYEURISTIC
VULCANIZING

VULGARITIES
VULGARIZING
VULGAR LATIN

12 LETTERS

VACCINATIONS
VACILLATIONS
VACCUUM FLASKS
VACCUUM PACKED
VAINGLORIOUS
VALEDICTIONS
VALENCIENNES
VALORIZATION
VALUABLENESS
VANQUISHABLE
VANQUISHMENT
VANTAGE POINT
VAPORESCENCE
VAPORIZATION
VAPOROUSNESS
VAPOUR TRAILS
VARICOLOURED
VASODILATION
VAUDEVILLIAN
VAUDEVILLIST
VEGETATIONAL
VELARIZATION
VENERABILITY
VENERATIONAL
VANGEFULNESS
VENIPUNCTURE
VENTRICOSITY
VERBENACEOUS
VERIDICALITY
VERIFICATION
VERIFICATIVE
VERTEBRATION
VERTICILLATE
VESICULATION
VESTAL VIRGIN
VIBRAPHONIST
VICE-CHAIRMAN
VICISSITUDES
VICTORIANIISM
VICTORIA PLUM
VICTORIOUSLY
VIDEO NASTIES
VIGOROUSNESS
VILIFICATION

VILLEURBANE
VINDICTIVELY
VINICULTURAL
VIN ORDINAIRE
VIOLONCELLOS
VIRGIN'S BOWER
VIRIDESCENCE
VIRTUOUSNESS
VISCEROMOTOR
VISCOUNTCIES
VISITATIONAL
VISITATORIAL
VISITING CARD
VISTORS' BOOK
VITALIZATION
VITICULTURAL
VITICULTURER
VITREOUSNESS
VITUPERATION
VITUPERATIVE
VIVIFICATION
VIVISECTIONS
VIXENISHNESS
VOCABULARIES
VOCALIZATION
VOCIFERATING
VOCIFERATION
VOCIFEROUSLY
VOIDABLENESS
VOLCANICALLY
VOLTA REDONDA
VOLUMINOSITY
VOLUMINOUSLY
VOLUNTARYISM
VOLUNTARYIST
VOLUNTEERING
VOLUPTUARIES
VOLUPTUOUSLY
VOMITURATION
VOTE OF THANKS
VOWELIZATION
VULCANIZABLE

13 LETTERS

VACILLATINGLY
VACUUM CLEANER
VALUE-ADDED TAX
VALUE JUDGEMENT
VALUELESSNESS
VANTAGE POINTS
VAPOURABILITY
VAPOURISHNESS
VARICOSE VEINS
VARIOLIZATION
VASOINHIBITOR
VAULTING HORSE
VEGETARIANISM
VENEREOLOGIST
VENETIAN BLIND
VENTRILOQUIAL
VENTRILOQUISM
VENTRILOQUIST
VENTRILOQUIZE
VERACIOUSNESS
VERBALIZATION

VERBIFICATION
VERITABLENESS
VERMICULATION
VERMINOUSNESS
VERNACULARISM
VERNALIZATION
VERSIFICATION
VESTAL VIRGINS
VEXATIOUSNESS
VEXED QUESTION
VEXILLOLOGIST
VICARIOUSNESS
VICE PRESIDENT
VICIOUS CIRCLE
VICTIMIZATION
VICTORIA CROSS
VICTORIA PLUMS
VILIFICATIONS
VINDICABILITY
VINICULTURIST
VIOLONCELLIST
VISCOUNTESSES

VISIONARINESS
VISITING CARDS
VISITORS' BOOKS
VISUALIZATION
VITRIFICATION
VITRIOLICALLY
VIVACIOUSNESS
VIVISECTIONAL
VOCIFERATIONS
VOICELESSNESS
VOLATILIZABLE
VOLCANIZATION
VOLCANOLOGIST
VOLUNTARINESS
VOLUNTARISTIC
VOTE OF CENSURE
VOTES OF THANKS
VOUCHSAFEMENT
VULCANIZATION
VULGARIZATION
VULNERABILITY

3 LETTERS					
WAD	WATT	WIPE	WALLY	WHEAT	WIRES
WAG	WAUL	WIRE	WALTZ	WHELK	WISER
WAN	WAVE	WIRY	WANDS	WHELP	WISPS
WAR	WAVY	WISE	WANED	WHERE	WISPY
WAX	WAXY	WISH	WANES	WHICH	WITCH
WAY	WAYS	WISP	WANEY	WHIFF	WITHE
WEB	WEAK	WITH	WANLY	WHIGS	WITTY
WED	WEAL	WITS	WANTS	WHILE	WIVES
WEE	WEAN	WOAD	WARDS	WHIMS	WIZEN
WET	WEAR	WOES	WARES	WHINE	WOKEN
WHO	WEBS	WOKE	WARPS	WHINY	WOLDS
WHY	WEED	WOKS	WARTS	WHIPS	WOMAN
WIG	WEEK	WOLD	WARTY	WHIRL	WOMBS
WIN	WEEP	WOLF	WASPS	WHIRR	WOMEN
WIT	WEFT	WOMB	WASTE	WHIRS	WONKY
WOE	WEIR	WONT	WATCH	WHISK	WOODS
WOG	WELD	WOOD	WATER	WHIST	WOODY
WOK	WELL	WOOF	WATTS	WHITE	WOOED
WON	WELT	WOOL	WAVED	WHITS	WOOER
WOO	WEND	WOPS	WAVER	WHIZZ	WOOFS
WOP	WENT	WORD	WAVES	WHOE	WOOZY
WOT	WEPT	WORE	WAXED	WHOOP	WORDS
WOW	WEST	WORK	WAXEN	WHORE	WORDY
WPC	WETS	WORM	WAXER	WHORL	WORKS
WRY	WHAM	WORN	WEALD	WHOSE	WORLD
	WHAT	WOVE	WEALS	WICKS	WORMS
	WHEN	WPCS	WEARY	WIDEN	WORMY
	WHET	WRAP	WEAVE	WIDER	WORRY
	WHEW	WREN	WEBBY	WIDES	WORSE
4 LETTERS	WHEY	WRIT	WEBER	WIDOW	WORST
WADE	WHIG		WEDGE	WIDTH	WORTH
WADI	WHIM		WEDGY	WIELD	WOULD
WADS	WHIP	5 LETTERS	WEEDS	WIGHT	WOUND
WAFT	WHIR	WACKY	WEEDY	WILCO	WOVEN
WAGE	WHIT	WADED	WEEKS	WILDS	WOWED
WAGS	WHIZ	WADER	WEENY	WILES	WRACK
WAIF	WHOA	WADGE	WEEPY	WILLS	WRAPS
WAIL	WHOP	WADIS	WEIGH	WIMPS	WRATH
WAIT	WHYS	WAFER	WEIRD	WIMPY	WREAK
WAKE	WICK	WAGED	WEIRS	WINCE	WREAK
WALK	WIDE	WAGER	WELCH	WINCH	WRECK
WALL	WIFE	WAGES	WELDS	WINDS	WRENS
WAND	WIGS	WAGON	WELLS	WINDY	WREST
WANE	WILD	WAHOO	WELLY	WINED	WRING
WANK	WILL	WAIFS	WELSH	WINES	WRIST
WANT	WILT	WAIST	WELTS	WINGE	WRITE
WARD	WILY	WAIVE	WENCH	WINGS	WRITS
WARM	WIMP	WAKED	WETLY	WINKS	WRONG
WARN	WIND	WAKEN	WHACK	WINZE	WROTE
WARP	WINE	WAKER	WHALE	WIPED	WROTH
WARS	WING	WAKES	WHAMS	WIPER	WRUNG
WART	WINK	WALKS	WHANG	WIPES	WRYER
WARY	WINS	WALLS	WHARF	WIRED	WRYLY
WASY	WINY	WALLY	WHEAL	WIRER	
WASP					

6 LETTERS	WARILY	WEEVER	WIDELY	WISHED
WADDLE	WARMED	WEEVIL	WIDEST	WISHER
WADERS	WARMER	WEE-WEE	WIDGET	WISHES
WADGES	WARMLY	WEIGHT	WIDISH	WITHAL
WADING	WARMTH	WEIRDO	WIDOWS	WITHER
WAFERS	WARM-UP	WELDED	WIDTHS	WITHIN
WAFFLE	WARNED	WELDER	WIELDY	WIZARD
WAFTED	WARNER	WELKIN	WIFELY	WOBBLE
WAFTER	WARPED	WELKOM	WIGEON	WOBBLY
WAGERS	WARRED	WELLED	WIGGED	WOEFUL
WAGGED	WARREN	WELTER	WIGGLE	WOLFED
WAGGLE	WARSAW	WENDED	WIGHTS	WOLVER
WAGGLY	WARTED	WESTER	WIGWAG	WOLVES
WAGING	WASHED	WETHER	WIGWAM	WOMBAT
WAGONS	WASHER	WETTED	WILDER	WONDER
WAILED	WASHES	WHACKS	WILDLY	WONTED
WAILER	WASHIN	WHALER	WILFUL	WOODED
WAISTS	WASTED	WHALES	WILIER	WOODEN
WAITED	WASTER	WHARFS	WILLED	WOOERS
WAITER	WASTES	WHARVE	WILLER	WOOFER
WAIVED	WATERS	WHEELS	WILLET	WOOING
WAIVER	WATERY	WHEEZE	WILLOW	WOOLLY
WAKING	WATTLE	WHEEZY	WILTED	WORDED
WALKED	WATUSI	WHELKS	WIMBLE	WORKED
WALKER	WAVIER	WHELPS	WIMPLE	WORKER
WALK-IN	WAVILY	WHENCE	WINCED	WORLDS
WALK-ON	WAVING	WHERRY	WINCER	WORMED
WALK-UP	WAXIER	WHEYEY	WINCES	WORMER
WALLAH	WAXILY	WHIFFS	WINCEY	WORSEN
WALLED	WAXING	WHIFFY	WINDED	WORTHY
WALLET	WAYLAY	WHILED	WINDER	WOUNDS
WALLOP	WAY-OUT	WHILST	WINDOW	WOWING
WALLOW	WEAKEN	WHIMSY	WINGED	WRAITH
WALNUT	WEAKER	WHINED	WINGER	WRASSE
WALRUS	WEAKLY	WHINER	WINGES	WREATH
WAMPUM	WEALTH	WHINES	WINING	WRECKS
WANDER	WEANED	WHINGE	WINKED	WRENCH
WANGLE	WEAPON	WHINNY	WINKED	WRETCH
WANING	WEARER	WHIPPY	WINKER	WRIEST
WANNED	WEASEL	WHIRLS	WINKLE	WRIGHT
WANNER	WEAVER	WHISKS	WINNER	WRISTS
WANT AD	WEAVES	WHISKY	WINNOW	WRISTY
WANTED	WEBBED	WHITEN	WINTER	WRITER
WANTER	WEDDED	WHITER	WINTRY	WRITHE
WANTON	WEDELN	WHITES	WIPING	WRONGS
WAPITI	WEDGED	WHOLLY	WIRIER	WRYEST
WARBLE	WEDGES	WHOOPS	WIRILY	WRYING
WAR CRY	WEEDED	WHOOSH	WIRING	WYVERN
WARDED	WEEDER	WHORLS	WIRRAL	
WARDEN	WEEING	WICKED	WISDOM	
WARDER	WEEKLY	WICKER	WISELY	
WARIER	WEEPER	WICKEY	WISEST	

7 LETTERS	WANTING	WAVIEST	WELLING	WHINING
WADABLE	WAPITIS	WAXBILL	WELL-OFF	WHIPPED
WADDING	WARBLED	WAXIEST	WELL-SET	WHIPPER
WADDLED	WARBLER	WAXLIKE	WELSHED	WHIPPET
WADDLER	WARDENS	WAXWING	WELSHER	WHIPSAW
WADDLES	WARDERS	WAXWORK	WEMBLEY	WHIRLED
WAFFLED	WARDING	WAXBILL	WENCHED	WHIRLER
WAFFLES	WARFARE	WAYLAID	WENCHER	WHIRRED
WAFTAGE	WAR GAME	WAYLAIN	WENCHES	WHISKED
WAFTING	WARHEAD	WAYSIDE	WENDING	WHISKER
WAGERED	WARIEST	WAYWARD	WENDISH	WHISKEY
WAGERER	WARLIKE	WEAKEST	WEST END	WHISPER
WAGGING	WARLOCK	WEALTHY	WESTERN	WHISTLE
WAGGISH	WARLORD	WEANING	WESTING	WHITEST
WAGGLED	WARLORD	WEAPONS	WET-LOOK	WHITHER
WAGGLES	WARMEST	WEARIED	WETNESS	WHITING
WAGONER	WARMING	WEARIER	WETSUIT	WHITLOW
WAGTAIL	WARM-UPS	WEARILY	WETTEST	WHITSUN
WAILFUL	WARNING	WEARING	WETTING	WHITTLE
WAILING	WARPAGE	WEASELS	WETTISH	WHIZZED
WAISTED	WARPATH	WEATHER	WHACKED	WHIZZES
WAITERS	WARPING	WEAVERS	WHACKER	WHOEVER
WAITING	WARRANT	WEAVING	WHALERS	WHOOPED
WAIVERS	WARRENS	WEBBING	WHALING	WHOOPEE
WAIVING	WARRING	WEBFOOT	WHANGEE	WHOO[ER
WAKENED	WARRIOR	WEB-TOED	WHARVES	WHOPPERD
WAKENER	WARSHIP	WEDDING	WHAT FOR	WHOPPER
WALKERS	WARTHOG	WEDGING	WHATNOT	WHORISH
WALKIES	WARTIME	WEDLOCK	WHATSIT	WHORLED
WALKING	WARWICK	WEEDIER	WHEATEN	WICHITA
WALKMAN	WASHDAY	WEEDILY	WHEEDLE	WICKETS
WALK-ONS	WASHERS	WEEDING	WHEELED	WIDE BAY
WALKOUT	WASHERY	WEEKDAY	WHEELER	WIDENED
WALK-UPS	WASHING	WEEKEND	WHEELIE	WIDENER
WALLABY	WASHOUT	WEENIER	WHEEZED	WIDGEON
WALLAHS	WASHTUB	WEEPING	WHEEZER	WIDOWED
WALLETS	WASPILY	WEEVILS	WHEEZES	WIDOWER
WALLEYE	WASPISH	WEEVILY	WHEREAS	WIELDED
WALLIES	WASSAIL	WEIGELA	WHEREAT	WIELDER
WALLING	WASTAGE	WEIGHED	WHEREBY	WIGGING
WALLOON	WASTERS	WEIGHER	WHEREIN	WIGGLED
WALLOPS	WASTING	WEIGHTS	WHEREOF	WIGGLER
WALLOWS	WASTREL	WEIGHTY	WHEREON	WIGGLES
WALNUTS	WATCHED	WEIRDER	WHERETO	WIGWAMS
WALTZED	WATCHER	WEIRDIE	WHERRIT	WILDCAT
WALTZER	WATCHES	WEIRDLY	WHETHER	WILDEST
WALTZES	WATERED	WEIRDOS	WHETTED	WILDING
WANGLED	WATERER	WELCHED	WHETTER	WILIEST
WANGLER	WATTAGE	WELCOME	WHICKER	WILLIES
WANGLES	WATTLES	WELDERS	WHIFFLE	WILLING
WANNESS	WAVELET	WELDING	WHILING	WILLOWS
WANNEST	WAVEOFF	WELFARE	WHIMPER	WILLOWY
WANNING	WAVERED	WELL-FED	WHINERS	WILTING
WANT ADS	WAVERER	WELLIES	WHINGED	WIMPIES

WIMPISH	WOODCUT	WRESTER	WANGLING	WAVEFORM
WIMPLES	WOODIER	WRESTLE	WANTONLY	WAVELIKE
WINCHED	WOODMAN	WRIGGLE	WARANGAL	WAVERERS
WINCHER	WOODSIA	WRINGER	WARBLERS	WAVERING
WINCHED	WOOFERS	WRINKLE	WARBLING	WAVINESS
WINCHER	WOOLLEN	WRINKLY	WAR CRIMES	WAXBERRY
WINCHER	WOOMERA	WRITE-IN	WAR CRIME	WAXINESS
WINCHES	WOOZIER	WRITERS	WAR DANCE	WAXPLANT
WINCING	WOOZILY	WRITE-UP	WARDENRY	WAXWORKS
WINDAGE	WORDAGE	WRITHED	WARDRESS	WAYBILLS
WINDBAG	WORDIER	WRITHER	WARDROBE	WATFARER
WINDIER	WORDILY	WRITING	WARDROOM	WAYLEYER
WINDILY	WORDING	WRITTEN	WARDSHIP	WEAKENED
WINDING	WORKBAG	WROCLAW	WARFARIN	WEAKENER
WINDOWS	WORKBOX	WRONGED	WAR GAMES	WEAKFISH
WINDROW	WORKDAY	WRONGER	WARHEADS	WEAKLING
WINDSOR	WORKERS	WRONGLY	WARHORSE	WEAPONED
WINE BAR	WORKING	WROUGHT	WARINESS	WEAPONRY
WINGERS	WORKMAN	WRYBILL	WARLOCKS	WEARABLE
WINGING	WORKMEN	WRYNECK	WARLORDS	WEARIEST
WINGLET	WORKOUT	WRYNESS	WARMNESS	WEARYING
WING NUT	WORKSHY	WYCHELM	WARNINGS	WEASELED
WINKERS	WORKTOP	WYOMING	WAR PAINT	WEASELLY
WINKING	WORLDLY	WYVERNS	WARPATHS	WEDDINGS
WINKLED	WORMIER		WARPLANE	WEDGWOOD
WINKLES	WORMING		WARRANTS	WEEDIEST
WINNERS	WORN-OUT	**8 LETTERS**	WARRANTY	WEEKDAYS
WINNING	WORRIED	WADDLING	WARRIORS	WEEKENDS
WINSOME	WORRIER	WAFFLING	WARSHIPS	WEEKLIES
WINTERS	WORRIES	WAGERING	WARTHOGS	WEENIEST
WIRETAP	WORSHIP	WAGGLING	WASHABLE	WEIGHING
WIRIEST	WORSTED	WAGON-LIT	WASHBOWL	WEIGHTED
WISE GUY	WOTCHED	WAGTAILS	WASHDAYS	WEIGHTER
WISHFUL	WOTCHER	WAINSCOT	WASHED-UP	WEIRDEST
WITCHES	WOULD-BE	WAITRESS	WASHOUTS	WELCHING
WITHERS	WOULDN'T	WAKELESS	WASHROOM	WELCOMED
WITHOUT	WOUNDED	WAKENING	WASTABLE	WELCOMER
WITLESS	WOUNDER	WALKABLE	WASTEFUL	WELCOMES
WITNESS	WOUND-UP	WALKAWAY	WASTRELS	WELDABLE
WITTIER	WRAITHS	WALKMANS	WATCHDOG	WELL-BRED
WITTILY	WRANGLE	WALKOUTS	WATCHFUL	WELL-DONE
WIZARDS	WRAPPED	WALKOVER	WATCHING	WELLHEAD
WIZENED	WRAPPER	WALLAROO	WATCHMAN	WELL-HUNG
WOBBLED	WREAKED	WALLEYED	WATCHMEN	WELL-KNIT
WOBBLER	WREAKER	WALL-LIKE	WATERAGE	WELL-NIGH
WOBBLER	WREATHE	WALLOPED	WATERBED	WELL-READ
WOBBLES	WREATHS	WALLOPER	WATER ICE	WELL-TO-DO
WOLFING	WREAKED	WALLOWED	WATERING	WELL-WORN
WOLFISH	WREAKER	WALLOWER	WATERLOO	WELSHERS
WOLFRAM	WREATHE	WALRUSES	WATER RAT	WELSHING
WOMANLY	WREATHS	WALTZING	WATER-SKI	WENCHING
WOMBATS	WRECKED	WANDERED	WATERWAY	WEREWOLF
WONDERS	WRECKER	WANDERER	WATT-HOUR	WESLEYAN
WONKIER	WRESTED	WANDEROO	WAVE BAND	WESTERLY

W 8 LETTERS

WESTERNS	WHITE-EYE	WINDGALL	WOEFULLY	WORMWOOD
WESTWARD	WHITEFLY	WINDIEST	WOLFFISH	WORRIERS
WET NURSE	WHITE-HOT	WINDLASS	WOLFLIKE	WORRYING
WET SUITS	WHITE LIE	WINDMILL	WOMANISH	WORSENED
WETTABLE	WHITENED	WINDPIPE	WOMANIZE	WORSE-OFF
WETTINGS	WHITENER	WINDSAIL	WOMBLIKE	WORSHIPS
WHACKING	WHITEOUT	WINDSOCK	WONDERED	WORSTING
WHARFAGE	WHITE-TIE	WINDWARD	WONDERER	WORST-OFF
WHATEVER	WHITLINGS	WINE BARS	WONDROUS	WORTHIER
WHATNOTS	WHITLOWS	WINESHKIN	WONKIEST	WORTHIES
WHATSITS	WHITTLED	WINGLESS	WOODBINE	WORTHILY
WHEATEAR	WHITTLER	WINGLIKE	WOODCHAT	WOUNDING
WHEEDLED	WHIZ-BANG	WING NUTS	WOODCOCK	WRANGLED
WHEEDLER	WHIZZING	WINGOVER	WOODCUTS	WRANGLER
WHEELIES	WHIZZ KID	WINGSPAN	WOODENLY	WRANGLES
WHEELING	WHODUNIT	WINKLING	WOODIEST	WRAPOVER
WHEEZILY	WHOMEVER	WINNABLE	WOODLAND	WRAPPERS
WHEEZING	WHOOPEES	WINNINGS	WOODLARK	WRAPPING
WHENEVER	WHOOPING	WINNIPEG	WOODLICE	WRATHFUL
WHEREVER	WHOOSHES	WINNOWED	WOODNOTE	WREAKING
WHETTING	WHOPPERS	WINNOWER	WOODPILE	WREATHED
WHEYFACE	WHOPPING	WINTERED	WOOD PULP	WRECKAGE
WHICKERS	WICKEDLY	WINTERER	WOODRUFF	WRECKERS
WHIFFIER	WIDE BOYS	WINTRIER	WOODRUSH	WRECKING
WHIGGERY	WIDE-EYED	WINTRILY	WOODSHED	WRENCHED
WHIGGISH	WIDENESS	WIPED OUT	WOODSMAN	WRENCHES
WHIMBREL	WIDENING	WIREDRAW	WOODSMEN	WRESTING
WHIMPERS	WIDE-OPEN	WIRELESS	WOODWIND	WRESTLED
WHIMSIES	WIDGEONS	WIRETAPS	WOODWORK	WRESTLER
WHINCHAT	WIDOWERS	WIRE WOOL	WOODWORM	WRETCHED
WHINGING	WIELDERS	WIREWORK	WOOLLENS	WRETCHES
WHINNIED	WEILDING	WIREWORM	WOOLLIER	WRIGGLED
WHINNIES	WIGGINGS	WIRE-WOVE	WOOLLIES	WRIGGLER
WHIPCORD	WIGGLING	WIRINESS	WOOLLILY	WRIGGLES
WHIP HAND	WILD BOAR	WISEACRE	WOOLPACK	WRINGERS
WHIPLASH	WILDCATS	WISE GUYS	WOOLSACK	WRINGING
WHIPLIKE	WILD-EYED	WISENESS	WOOZIEST	WRINKLED
WHIPPETS	WILDFIRE	WISHBONE	WORDBOOK	WRINKLES
WHIPPING	WILDFOWL	WISPIEST	WORKDAYS	WRISTLET
WHIPWORM	WILDLIFE	WISTERIA	WORKED UP	WRITE-INS
WHIRLING	WILDNESS	WITCHERY	WORKINGS	WRITE-OFF
WHIRRING	WILD OATS	WITCHING	WORKLOAD	WRITE-UPS
WHISKERS	WILD WEST	WITHDRAW	WORKOUTS	WRITHING
WISKERY	WILFULLY	WITHDREW	WORKROOM	WRITINGS
WHISKIES	WILINESS	WITHERED	WORKSHOP	WRONGFUL
WHISKING	WILLABLE	WITHERER	WORKTOPS	WRONGING
WHISPERS	WILLIWAW	WITHHELD	WORM CAST	WURZBURG
WHISTLED	WINCHING	WITHHOLD	WORM GEAR	
WHISTLER	WINDABLE	WITTIEST	WORMHOLE	**9 LETTERS**
WHISTLES	WINDBAGS	WIZARDRY	WORMIEST	WACKINESS
WHITE ANT	WINDBURN	WOBBLIER	WORMLIKE	WAD MEDANI
WHITECAP	WINDFALL	WOBBLING	WORMSEED	WAFER-THIN

WAGE SLAVE	WATER ICES	WELCOMING	WHITE ANTS
WAGGISHLY	WATER JUMP	WELL-ACTED	WHITEBAIT
WAGONETTE	WATERLESS	WELL-AWARE	WHITECAPS
WAGONLOAD	WATERLILY	WELLBEING	WHITEDAMP
WAILINGLY	WATERLINE	WELL-FOUND	WHITEFISH
WAINSCOTS	WATER MAIN	WELL-KNOWN	WHITE FLAG
WAISTBAND	WATERMARK	WELL-LINED	WHITEHALL
WAISTCOAT	WATERMILL	WELL-MEANT	WHITE HEAT
WAISTLINE	WATER PIPE	WELL-OILED	WHITE HOPE
WAKEFULLY	WATER POLO	WELL-TIMED	WHITE LEAD
WAKE-ROBIN	WATER RATE	WELL-TRIED	WHITE LIES
WALKABOUT	WATER RATS	WERNERITE	WHITE MEAT
WALKWAYS	WATERSHED	WESLEYANS	WHITENESS
WALKOVERS	WATER-SICK	WESTBOUND	WHITENING
WALLABIES	WATERSIDE	WESTERING	WHITEWALL
WALLBOARD	WATER VOLE	WESTENER	WHITEWASH
WALLCHART	WATERWAYS	WESTWARDS	WHITEWOOD
WALLOPING	WATERWEED	WET DREAMS	WHITTLERS
WALLOWING	WATERWORN	WET-NURSED	WHITTLING
WALLPAPER	WATTMETER	WET NURSES	WHIZZ KIDS
WANDERER	WAVE BANDS	WHACKINGS	WHODUNITS
WANDERING	WAVEGUIDE	WHALEBOAT	WHOLEFOOD
WAR CLOUDS	WAVELLITE	WHALEBONE	WHOLEMEAL
WAR CRIMES	WAVEMETER	WHEAT GERM	WHOLENESS
WAR DANCES	WAXWORKS	WHEATWORM	WHOLE NOTE
WARDROBES	WAYFARERS	WHEEDLING	WHOLESALE
WARDROOMS	WAYFARING	WHEELBASE	WHOLESOME
WAREHOUSES	WAYLAYING	WHEELWORK	WHOSOEVER
WARHORSES	WEAKENING	WHEREFORE	WIDE-ANGLE
WARMONGER	WEAKER SEX	WHEREUPON	WIDE-AWAKE
WARRANTED	WEAK-KNEED	WHEREWITH	WIDOWHOOD
WARRANTEE	WEAKILINGS	WHERRYMAN	WIDTHWISE
WARRANTOR	WEALTHIER	WHETSTONE	WIELDABLE
WASHBASIN	WEALTHILY	WHICHEVER	WIGWAGGER
WASHBOARD	WEAPONEER	WHICKERED	WILD BOARS
WASHCLOTH	WEARINESS	WHIFFIEST	WILDFIRES
WASHED-OUT	WEARINGLY	WHIMPERED	WILLEMITE
WASHINESS	WEARISOME	WHIMPERER	WILLINGLY
WASHING-UP	WEARPROOF	WHIMSICAL	WILLPOWER
WASHROOMS	WEASELING	WHININGLY	WILTSHIRE
WASHSTAND	WEATHERED	WHINNYING	WINCINGLY
WASPINESS	WEATHERER	WHINSTONE	WINDBLOWN
WASPISHLY	WEB-FOOTED	WHIPPER-IN	WIND-BORNE
WASSAILER	WEB OFFSET	WHIPPINGS	WINDBOUND
WASTELAND	WEDNESDAY	WHIP-AROUND	WINDBREAK
WATCHDOGS	WEEDINESS	WHIPSTALL	WINSBURNT
WATCHWORD	WEEKENDED	WHIPSTOCK	WINDFALLS
WATER BIRD	WEEKENDER	WHIRLIGIG	WIND GAUGE
WATERBUCK	WEEKNIGHT	WHIRLPOOL	WINDINESS
WATER BUTT	WEEPINESS	WHIRLWIND	WINDINGLY
WATER-COOL	WEEPINGLY	WHISKERED	WINDMILLS
WATERFALL	WEIGHABLE	WHISPERED	WINDOW BOX
WATERFOWL	WEIGHTILY	WHISPERER	WINDPIPES
WATERHOLE	WEIRDNESS	WHISTLING	WINDROWER

WINDSOCKS	WOODSCREW	WYANDOTTE	WATER JUMPS
WINDSTORM	WOODSHEDS	WYCH-HAZEL	WATER LEVEL
WINDSWEPT	WOOLLIEST		WATER MAINS
WINEGLASS	WOOZINESS		WATERMARKS
WINEPRESS	WORCESTER	**10 LETTERS**	WATERMELON
WINGSPANS	WORDBREAK	WADDLINGLY	WATERMILLS
WINNEBAGO	WORDINESS	WADING POOL	WATER PIPES
WINNOWING	WORKBENCH	WAGE SLAVES	WATERPOWER
WINSOMELY	WORKBOOKS	WAGGA WAGGA	WATERPROOF
WINTERING	WORKFORCE	WAGGLINGLY	WATER RATES
WINTRIEST	WORKHORSE	WAGON-TRAIN	\WATERSCAPE
WIRE GAUGE	WORKHOUSE	WAINWRIGHT	WATERSHEDS
WIREWORKS	WORKLOADS	WAISTBANDS	WATERSKIER
WIREWORMS	WORKPIECE	WAISTCOATS	WATERSPOUT
WISCONSIN	WORKPLACE	WAISTLINES	WATER TABLE
WISECRACK	WORKROOMS	WAKEY WAKEY	WATERTIGHT
WISHBONES	WORKSHOP	WALKABOUTS	WATER VOLES
WISPINESS	WORK-STUDY	WALK OF LIFE	WATERWHEEL
WISTFULLY	WORKTABLE	WALL CHARTS	WATERWINGS
WITCH-HUNT	WORLD BANK	WALLFLOWER	WATERWORKS
WITCHLIKE	WORLDLIER	WALLPAPERS	WATTLEBIRD
WITHDRAWN	WORLDLING	WALL STREET	WAVELENGTH
WITHERING	WORLDWIDE	WALL-TO-WALL	WAVERINGLY
WITHERITE	WORM CASTS	WANDERING	WAXED PAPER
WITHSTAND	WORM-EATEN	WANDERLUST	WEAKLINESS
WITHSTOOD	WORM GEARS	WANTONNESS	WEAK WILLED
WITLESSLY	WORMHOLES	WAREHOUSES	WEALTHIEST
WITNESSED	WORRIEDLY	WARMING PAN	WEARYINGLY
WITNESSER	WORRISOME	WARMONGERS	WEATHERING
WITNESSES	WORRYWART	WARRANTIES	WEATHERMAN
WITTICISM	WORSENING	WARRANTING	WEATHERMEN
WITTINESS	WORSHIPED	WASHBASINS	WEAVERBIRD
WOBBLIEST	WORTHIEST	WASHCLOTHS	WEDNESDAYS
WOEBEGONE	WORTHLESS	WASHING DAY	WEEDKILLER
WOLFHOUND	WOUNDABLE	WASHINGTON	WEEKENDERS
WOLFSBANE	WOUNDWORT	WASHSTANDS	WEEKENDING
WOLVERINE	WRANGLERS	WASTEFULLY	WEEKNIGHTS
WOMANHOOD	WRANGLING	WASTELANDS	WEIGHTLESS
WOMANIZED	WRAPPINGS	WASTE PAPER	WELL-ARGUED
WOMANIZER	WREATHING	WATCHFULLY	WELL-CHOSEN
WOMANKIND	WRECKFISH	WATCHMAKER	WELL-EARNED
WOMAN-LIKE	WRENCHING	WATCHSTRAP	WELL-HEELED
WOMENFOLK	WRESTLERS	WATCHTOWER	WELLINGTON
WOMEN'S LIB	WRIGGLING	WATCHWORDS	WELL-JUDGED
WONDERFUL	WRINKLING	WATER BIRDS	WELL-SPOKEN
WONDERING	WRISTBAND	WATERBORNE	WELLSPRING
WOODBLOCK	WRISTLETS	WATER BUTTS	WELL-TURNED
WOODBORER	WRISTLOCK	WATERCRAFT	WELL-WISHER
WOODCHUCK	WRITE-OFFS	WATERCRESS	WELL-WORDED
WOODCOCKS	WRONGDOER	WATERFALLS	WENTLETRAP
WOODCRAFT	WRONGNESS	WATERFOWLS	WEREWOLVES
WOODINESS	WROUGHT-UP	WATERFRONT	WESTERLIES
WOODLOUSE	WULFERTINE	WATERHOLES	WESTERNERS
WOODPRINT	WUPPERTAIL	WATERINESS	WESTERNISM

696

WESTERNIZE	WILDFOWLER	WOODENNESS	WARM-BLOODED
WEST INDIAN	WILFULNESS	WOODLANDER	WARM-HEARTED
WESTPHALIA	WILLOWHERB	WOODPECKER	WARMING PLANS
WET BLANKET	WILLY-NILLY	WOODWORKER	WAR OF NERVES
WET-NURSING	WINCEYETTE	WOODGROWER	WARRANTABLE
WHARFINGER	WINCHESTER	WOOLLINESS	WASHABILITY
WHATSOEVER	WINDBREAKS	WORDLESSLY	WASHD RAWING
WHEEL BASES	WIND BROKEN	WORKAHOLIC	WASHERWOMAN
WHEELCHAIR	WINDEDNESS	WORKBASKET	WASHERWOMEN
WHEELHOUSE	WINDFLOWER	WORK-HARDEN	WASHING DAYS
WHEEZINESS	WINDGALLED	WORK HORSES	WASPISHNESS
WHEEZINGLY	WIND GAUGES	WORKING DAY	WATCHMAKERS
WHENSOEVER	WINDJAMMER	WORKINGMAN	WATCHMAKING
WHEREFORES	WINDLASSES	WORKPEOPLE	WATCHSTRAPS
WHETSTONES	WINDOWPANE	WORK PLACES	WATCHTOWERS
WHICKERING	WINDOW-SHOP	WORK-TO-RULE	WATER CANNON
WHIPLASHES	WINDOWSILL	WORLD CLASS	WATER CLOSET
WHIP-ROUNDS	WINDSCREEN	WORLDLIEST	WATER COLOUR
WHIPSTITCH	WINDSHIELD	WORLD POWER	WATER COURSE
WHIRLABOUT	WINDSTORMS	WORLD-WEARY	WATERED-DOWN
WHIRLIGIGS	WINDSUCKER	WORRYINGLY	WATERFRONTS
WHIRLINGLY	WIND-SURFER	WORRYWORTS	WATERING CAN
WHIRLPOOLS	WIND TUNNEL	WORSHIPFUL	WATER LEVELS
WHIRLWINDS	WINEBIBBER	WORSHIPING	WATER LILIES
WHIRLYBIRD	WINTERFEED	WORSHIPPED	WATERLOGGED
WHISPERERS	WINTERTIME	WORSHIPPER	WATER MEADOW
WHISPERING	WINTRINESS	WORTHINESS	WATERMELONS
WHIST DRIVE	WIREHARED	WORTHWHILE	WATERPROOFS
WHITE BOARD	WIRE-HAIRED	WOUNDINGLY	WATER SKIERS
WHITE DWARF	WIRELESSES	WRAITHLIKE	WATER SKIING
WHITE FLAGS	WIREWORKER	WRATHFULLY	WATERSPOUTS
WHITE HOPES	WISECRACKS	WRETCHEDLY	WATER SUPPLY
WHITE HORSE	WISHY-WASHY	WRISTBANDS	WATER TABLES
WHITE HOUSE	WAITCHCRAFT	WRISTWATCH	WATER VAPOUR
WHITE MAGIC	WITCH-HAZEL	WRITHINGLY	WATERWHEELS
WHITE METAL	WITCH-HUNTS	WRONGDOERS	WAVELENGTHS
WHITE PAPER	WITHDRAWAL	WRONGDOING	WAYWARDNESS
WHITE SAUCE	WITHDRAWER	WRONGFULLY	WEALTHINESS
WHITESMITH	WITHHOLDER	WUNDERKIND	WEARABILITY
WHITEWATER	WITNESS BOX		WEAR AND TEAR
WHITTLINGS	WITNESSING		WEATHERCOCK
WHOLEFOODS	WITTICISMS	**11 LETTERS**	WEATHER SHIP
WHOLE NOTES	WOBBLINESS	WADING POOLS	WEATHER VANE
WHOLESALER	WOEFULNESS	WAGGISHNESS	WEATHER-WISE
WHOREHOUSE	WOLFHOUNDS	WAINSCOTING	WEDDING RING
WICKEDNESS	WOLFRAMITE	WAINSCOTTED	WEIGHBRIDGE
WICKERWORK	WOMANIZERS	WAITING GAME	WEIGHTINESS
WICKET GATE	WOMANIZING	WAITING LIST	WELCOMENESS
WIDE SCREEN	WONDERLAND	WAITING ROOM	WELDABILITY
WIDESPREAD	WONDERMENT	WAKEFULNESS	WELL-ADAPTED
WIFELINESS	WONDERWORK	WALKS OF LIFE	WELL-ADVISED
WILDCATTED	WOODBLOCKS	WALLFLOWERS	WELL-BEHAVED
WILDEBEEST	WOODCARVER	WALLPAPERED	WELL-DEFINED
WILDERNESS	WOODCUTTER	WANDERINGLY	WELL-ENDOWED

WELL-FOUNDED
WELL-GROOMED
WELLINGTONS
WELL-MEANING
WELL-ROUNDED
WELLSPRINGS
WELL-WISHERS
WELL-WISHING
WELWITSCHIA
WENSLEYDALE
WESLEYANISM
WEST COUNTRY
WESTERNIZED
WESTERNMOST
WESTMINSTER
WESTPHALIAN
WET BLANKETS
WETTABILITY
WHEEDLINGLY
WHEELBARROW
WHEELCHAIRS
WHEELHOUSES
WHEELWRIGHT
WHEREABOUTS
WHERESOEVER
WHEREWITHAL
WHIFFLETREE
WHIMSICALLY
WHIPPING BOY
WHIRLYBIRDS
WHIST DRIVES
WHITEBOARDS
WHITE-COLLAR
WHITE DWARFS
WHITE HORSES
WHITE KNIGHT
WHITE METALS
WHITE PAPERS
WHITE PEPPER
WHITE-SLAVER
WHITE SPIRIT
WHITETHROAT
WHITEWASHED
WHITEWASHER
WHITEWASHES
WHITSUN TIDE
WHOLE NUMBER
WHOLESALERS
WHOREHOUSES
WICKET GATES
WILDEBEESTS
WILDFOWLING
WILLINGNESS
WINDCHEATER

WINDJAMMERS
WINDOW BOXES
WINDOWPANES
WINDOW SHADE
WINDOWSILLS
WIND SCREENS
WINDSHIELDS
WIND-SUCKING
WIND-SURFERS
WIND-SURFING
WIND TUNNELS
WIND TURBINE
WINDBIBBING
WINNINGNESS
WINNING POST
WINNIPEGGER
WINSOMENESS
WINTERGREEN
WIRE NETTING
WIRE-TAPPING
WISDOM TEETH
WISDOM TOOTH
WISECRACKED
WISECRACKER
WISHFULNESS
WITCHDOCTOR
WITCH-HUNTER
WITHDRAWALS
WITHDRAWING
WITHHOLDING
WITHSTANDER
WITLESSNESS
WITNESSABLE
WOLFISHNESS
WOLF WHISTLE
WOMANLINESS
WONDERFULLY
WONDERINGLY
WONDERLANDS
WOOD ALCOHOL
WOODCARVING
WOODCUTTERS
WOODCUTTING
WOODEN SPOON
WOODPECKERS
WOODWORKING
WOOLGROWING
WORD-PERFECT
WORKABILITY
WORKAHOLICS
WORKAHOLISM
WORKBASKETS
WORKBENCHES
WORKING DAYS

WORKING WEEK
WORKMANLIKE
WORKMANSHIP
WORKSTATION
WORLD BEATER
WORLDLINESS
WORLDLY-WISE
WORLD POWERS
WORLD SERIES
WORSHIPPABLE
WORSHIPPERS
WORSHIPPING
WORTHLESSLY
WRIGGLINGLY
WRITING DESK
WRONG DOINGS
WRONG HEADED
WROUGHT IRON

12 LETTERS
WAITING LISTS
WAITING ROOMS
WALKIE-TALKIE
WALKING STICK
WALL PAINTING
WALL PAPERING
WAREHOUSEMAN
WARMONGERING
WARS OF NERVES
WASH DRAWINGS
WASTEFULNESS
WASTE PRODUCT
WATCHFULNESS
WATER BISCUIT
WATER BUFFALO
WATER CANNONS
WATER CLOSETS
WATERCOLOURS
WATERCOURSES
WATERING CANS
WATERING HOLE
WATERMANSHIP
WATERPROOFED
WEATHERBOARD
WEATHER-BOUND
WEATHERCOCKS
WEATHERGLASS
WEATHERPROOF
WEATHER SHIPS
WEATHER VANES
WEDDING RINGS
WEIGH BRIDGES
WEIGHTLESSLY

WEIGHT LIFTER
WELFARE STATE
WELL-ADJUSTED
WELL-ASSORTED
WELL-ATTENDED
WELL-BALANCED
WELL-DESERVED
WELL-DISPOSED
WELL-EDUCATED
WELL-EQUIPPED
WELL-FAVOURED
WELL-INFORMED
WELL-MANNERED
WELL-PROVIDED
WELL-RECEIVED
WELL-SITUATED
WELL-TEMPERED
WELSH RAREBIT
WELTERWEIGHT
WESLEYDALES
WESTERLINESS
WESTERNIZING
WETTING AGENT
WHEELBARROWS
WHEELWRIGHTS
WHENCESOEVER
WHEREWITHALS
WHIGGISHNESS
WHIMPERINGLY
WHIMSICALITY
WHIPPING BOYS
WHIPPOORWILL
WHITE KNIGHTS
WHITE-LIVERED
WHITE SLAVERY
WHITEWASHING
WHITEWEDDING
WHOLE-HEARTED
WHORTLEBERRY
WICKET KEEPER
WIFE SWAPPING
WILDERNESSES
WILL-O'-THE-WISP
WINDCHEATERS
WINDING SHEET
WINDOW SHADES
WIND TURBINES
WINEGLASSFUL
WINGLESSNESS
WINTER SPORTS
WISCONSINITE
WISECRACKING
WITCHDOCTORS
WITCH-HUNTING

WITCHING HOUR
WITHDRAWABLE
WITHEREDNESS
WITHSTANDING
WITNESS BOXES
WOLF WHISTLES
WOLLASTONITE
WOMANISHNESS
WONDER-WORKER
WONDROUSNESS
WOODENHEADED
WOOL GATHERER
WOOLLY-HEADED
WORDLESSNESS
WORKER-PRIEST
WORKING CLASS
WORKING ORDER
WORKING PARTY
WORKING WEEKS
WORKING WOMAN
WORK STATIONS
WORLD-BEATERS
WORLD-BEATING
WORLDSHAKING
WRATHFULNESS
WRETCHEDNESS
WRISTWATCHES
WRITER'S CRAMP
WRITING DESKS
WRITING PAPER
WRONGFULNESS

13 LETTERS
WALKIE-TALKIES
WALKING PAPERS
WALKING STICKS
WALL PAINTINGS
WARM-HEARTEDLY
WASHINGTONIAN
WASTE PRODUCTS
WATER BISCUITS
WATER BUFFALOS
WATERING HOLES
WATERING PLACE
WATERPROOFING
WATER SOFTENER
WATER SUPPLIES
WATTLE AND DAUB
WEARISOMENESS
WEATHER-BEATEN
WEATHERBOARDS
WEIGHT LIFTERS
WEIGHT LIFTING
WELFARE STATES
WELL-APPOINTED
WELL-CONNECTED
WELL-DEVELOPED
WELL-PRESERVED
WELL-QUALIFIED
WELL-SUPPORTED
WELL-THOUGHT-OF
WELSH RAREBITS
WELTERWEIGHTS
WEST-NORTHWEST
WEST-SOUTHWEST

WHEELER-DEALER
WHIMSICALNESS
WHIPPOORWILLS
WHITE ELEPHANT
WHITE WEDDING
WHOLESOMENESS
WHOOPING COUGH
WICKET KEEPERS
WIDE-AWAKENESS
WILDCAT STRIKE
WILHELMSHAVEN
WILL-O'-THE WISPS
WILLOW PATTERN
WINDING SHEETS
WINDOW-DRESSER
WINDOW-SHOPPED
WINDOW-SHOPPER
WING COMMANDER
WITHDRAWNNESS
WITHERINGNESS
WITWATERSRAND
WOLVERHAMPTON
WOMEN'S STUDIES
WONDERFULNESS
WONDER-WORKING
WOODCRAFTSMAN
WOOLGATHERING
WORD BLINDNESS
WORD PROCESSOR
WORK-HARDENING
WORSHIPPINGLY
WORTHLESSNESS
WRONGHEADEDLY

X 4 LETTERS to 13 LETTERS

4 LETTERS
XMAS
X-RAY

5 LETTERS
X-AXIS
XENIA
XENON
XERIC
XEROX
XHOSA
X-RAYS
X-UNIT
XYLAN
XYLEM
XYLOL
XYLYL

6 LETTERS
XENIAL
XEROMA
YHOSAN
XMASES
X-RATED
X-RAYED
XYLENE
XYLOID
XYLOSE
XYSTER

7 LETTERS
XANTHIC
XANTHIN
XERARCH
XEROSIS
XEROTIC
XEROXED
XEROXES
XIPHOID
X-RATING
X-RAYING

8 LETTERS
XANTHATE
XANTHEAN
XANTHEIN
XANTHENE
XANTHINE
XANTHOMA
XANTHOUS
XENOGAMY
XENOLITH
XEROSERE
XEROXING
XYLIDINE
XYLOCARP
XYLOTOMY

9 LETTERS
XENOCRYST
XENOPHILE
XENOPHOBE
XERICALLY
XERODERMA
XEROPHILY
XEROPHYTE
XYLOGRAPH
XYLOPHONE

10 LETTERS
XENOGAMOUS
XENOLITHIC
XENOPHOBIA
XENOPHOBIA
XENOPHOBIC
XEROGRAPHY
XEROPHYTIC
X-RADIATION
XYLOGRAPHY
XYLOPHONES
XYLOPHONIC
XYLOTOMIST
XYOTOMOUS

11 LETTERS
XANTHOPHYLL
X CHROMOSOME
XENOGENESIS
XENOGENETIC
XENOGLOSSIA
XENOMORPHIC
XEROGRAPHER
XEROGRAPHIC
XEROMORPHIC
XEROPHILOUS
XEROPHYTISM
XYLOCARPOUS
XYLOGRAPHER
XYLOGRAPHIC
XYLOPHAGOUS
XYLOPHONIST

12 LETTERS
X CHROMOSOMES
XERODERMATIC
XIPHISTERNUM

13 LETTERS
XANTHOCHROISM
XEROPHTHALMIA
XEROPHTHALMIC

700

3 LETTERS	5 LETTERS	6 LETTERS	7 LETTERS	YEANLING
YAK	YACHT	YACHTS	YAKKING	YEARBOOK
YAM	YAHOO	YAKKED	YAKUTSK	YEARLING
YAP	YAKUT	YAMMER	YANGTZE	YEARBOOK
YAW	YALTA	YANKED	YANKEES	YEARLING
YEA	YANKS	YANKEE	YANKING	YEARLONG
YEN	YAPOK	YAPPED	YAOUNDE	YEARNING
YES	YARDS	YAPPER	YAPPING	YEASTILY
YET	YARNS	YARNED	YARDAGE	YELLOWED
YEW	YAWED	YARROW	YARDARM	YEOMANLLY
YIN	YAWLS	YAUPON	YARNING	YEOMANELY
YOB	YAWNS	YAUTIA	YASHMAK	YEILDING
YOU	Y-AXIS	YAWING	YAWNING	YODELING
	YEARN	YAWNED	YEAR DOT	YODELLED
	YEARS	YAWNER	YEARNED	YODELLER
4 LETTERS	YEAST	YEARLY	YEARNER	YOKELISH
YAKS	YELLS	YEASTY	YELLING	YOKOHAMA
YAMS	YELPS	YELLED	YELLOWS	YOUNGEST
YANG	YEMEN	YELLER	YELPING	YOUNGISH
YANK	YERBA	YELLOW	YEREVAN	YOURSELF
YAPS	YETIS	YELPED	Y-FRONTS	YOUTHFUL
YARD	YIELD	YELPER	YIDDISH	YTTERBIA
YARN	YODEL	YEMENI	YIELDED	YUCKIEST
YAWL	YOGIC	YENTAI	YIELDER	YUGOSLAV
YAWN	YOGIS	YEOMAN	YODELED	YULE LOGS
YAWS	YOKED	YEOMEN	YOGHURT	YULETIDE
YEAH	YOKEL	YES-MAN	YONKERS	YVELINES
YEAR	YOKES	YES-MEN	YORKIST	
YELL	YOKES	YIELDS	YUROBAN	
YELP	YOLKS	YIPPEE	YOUNGER	9 LETTERS
YENS	YOLKY	YODELS	YOWLING	YACHTINGS
YETI	YONNE	YOGISM	YTTRIUM	YACHTSMAN
YEWS	YOUNG	YOKELS	YUKATAN	YACHTSMAN
YIDS	YOURS	YOKING	YUCKIER	YAMMERING
YOBS	YOUTH	YONDER	YUKONER	YANKEEISM
YOGA	YOWLS	YORKER	YULE LOG	YARDSTICK
YOGI	YOYOS	YORUBA	YUPPIES	YAWNINGLY
YOKE	YUCCA	YOUTHS		YEARBOOKS
YOLK	YUCKY	YOWLED		YEARLINGS
YORE	YUKON	YOWLER	8 LETTERS	YEARNINGS
YOUR	YULAN	YTTRIA	YACHTING	YELLOWING
YOWL	YUMAN	YTTRIC	YAHOOISM	YELLOWISH
YOYO		YUCCAS	YAMMERED	YESTERDAY
YUAN		YUNNAN	YAMMERER	YIELDABLE
YUCK		YUPPIE	YARDARMS	YODELLING
YULE			YARN-DYED	YOUNGSTER
			YASHMAKS	

10 LETTERS
YARDSTICKS
YEASTINESS
YELLOWBIRD
YELLOWTAIL
YELLOWWEED
YESTERDAYS
YESTERYEAR
YIELDINGLY
YLANG-YLANG
YOUNGSTERS
YOURSELVES
YOUTHFULLY
YUGOSLAVIA

11 LETTERS
YACHTSWOMAN
YACHTSWOMEN
Y CHROMOSOME
YELLOW FEVER
YELLOW PAGES
YELLOWSTONE
YOUTH HOSTEL
YUGOSLAVIAN

12 LETTERS
Y CHROMOSOMES
YELLOWHAMMER
YIELDINGNESS
YOUTHFULNESS
YOUTH HOSTELS

13 LETTERS
YACHTSMANSHIP
YEOMAN SERVICE
YOUNG MARRIEDS

3 LETTERS
ZAP
ZED
ZEN
ZIP
ZIT
ZOO

4 LETTERS
ZANY
ZEAL
ZEBU
ZEDS
ZEIN
ZERO
ZEST
ZINC
ZION
ZIPS
ZITS
ZIZZ
ZOND
ZONE
ZOOM
ZOOS
ZULU

5 LETTERS
ZAIRE
ZAMIA
ZAPPY
ZARGA
Z-AXIS
ZABRA
ZEIAT
ZANIC
ZEROS
ZESTY
ZIBET
ZINGY
ZIPPY
ZLOTY
ZONAL
ZONED
ZONES
ZOOID

6 LETTERS
ZABRZE
ZAFFER
ZAGREB

ZAMBIA
ZANIER
ZANILY
ZAPPED
ZAREBA
ZEALOY
ZEBRAS
ZENIST
ZENITH
ZEPHYR
ZEROED
ZEROES
ZEUGMA
ZIGZAG
ZINCIC
ZINCKY
ZINNIA
ZIPPED
ZIPPER
ZIRCON
ZITHER
ZODIAC
ZOMBIE
ZONATE
ZONING
ZONKED
ZONULE
ZOOMED
ZOSTER
ZOYSIA
ZURICH
ZYGOMA
ZYGOSE
ZYGOTE
ZYMASE
ZYRIAN

7 LETTERS
ZAGAZIG
ZAIRESE
ZAMBIAN
ZANIEST
ZAPOTEC
ZAPPIER
ZAPPING
ZEALOTS
ZEALOUS
ZABRINE
ZEDOARY
ZEELAND
ZENITHS
ZEOLITE
ZEPHYRS

ZEROING
ZESTFUL
ZHDANOV
ZIGZAGS
ZILLION
ZINCATE
ZINCITE
ZIONISM
ZIONIST
ZIP CODE
ZIPPERS
ZIPPIER
ZIPPING
ZITHERS
ZODIACS
ZOISITE
ZOMBIES
ZONALLY
ZONULAR
ZOOLOGY
ZOOMING
ZOOTOMY
ZORILLA
ZWICKAU
ZYGOSIS
ZYGOTIC
ZYMOGEN
ZYMOSIS
ZYMOTIC
ZYMURGY

8 LETTERS
ZAIBATSU
ZANINESS
ZANZIBAR
ZAPPIEST
ZAROGOZA
ZARATITE
ZEALOTRY
ZACCHINO
ZENITHAL
ZEOLITIC
ZEPPELIN
ZERO HOUR
ZHITOMIR
ZIBELINE
ZILLIONS
ZIMBABWE
ZIONISTS
ZIP CODES
ZIPPIEST
ZIRCONIA
ZIRCONIC

ZLATOUST
ZODIACAL
ZOMBIISM
ZONATION
ZONETIME
ZOOCHORE
ZOOGLOEA
ZOOLATER
ZOOLATRY
ZOOMETRY
ZOOM LENS
ZOONOSIS
ZOOPHILE
ZOOPHYTE
ZOOSPERM
ZOOSPORE
ZOOTOMIC
ZOOTOXIC
ZOOTOXIN
ZOCCHINI
ZUGZWAG
ZULULAND
ZWIEBACK
ZYGOTENE
ZYMOLOGY

9 LETTERS
ZACATECAS
ZAMBEZIAN
ZANZIBARI
ZAPOTECAN
ZEALOUSLY
ZEBRA-LIKE
ZEBRAWOD
ZEEBRUGGE
ZEELANDER
ZEITGEIST
ZEPPELINS
ZESTFULLY
ZEUGMATIC
ZIGZAGGED
ZIGZAGGER
ZINKENITE
ZIONISTIC
ZIRCALLOY
ZIRCONIUM
ZITHERIST
ZOOGLEOAL
ZOOGRAPHY
ZOOMETRIC
ZOOPHILIA
ZOOPHILIC
ZOOPHOBIA

ZOOPHYTIC
ZOOPLASTY
ZOOSPORIC
ZOOSTEROL
ZOOTOMIST
ZUCCHINIS
ZUIDER ZEE
ZYGOMATIC
ZYGOPHYTE
ZYGOSPORE
ZYGMOGENIC
ZYMOLOGIC
ZYMOLYSIS
ZYMOLYTIC
ZYNOMETER

10 LETTERS
ZAPOROZHYE
ZIGZAGGING
ZINCOGRAPH
ZOOGRAPHER
ZOOGRAPHIC
ZOOLATROUS

ZOOLOGICAL
ZOOLOGISTS
ZOOM LENSES
ZOOMORPHIC
ZOOPHAGOUS
ZOOPHILISM
ZOOPHILOUS
ZOOPHOBOUS
ZOOPLASTIC
ZWITTERION
ZYGODACTYL
ZYGOSPHORIC
ZYMOLOGIST

11 LETTERS
ZANTHOXYLUM
ZEALOUNESS
ZESTFULNESS
ZINCOGRAPHY
ZOOCHEMICAL
ZOOMORPHISM
ZOOPLANKTON
ZOOTECHNICS

12 LETTERS
ZINCOGRAPHER
ZINCOGRAPHIC
ZOOCHEMISTRY
ZOOGEOGRAPHY
ZOOSPERMATIC
ZOOTOMICALLY
ZYGAPOPHYSIS
ZYGOMORPHISM

13 LETTERS
ZEBRA CROSSING
ZEUGMATICALLY
ZIGZAGGEDNESS
ZINJANTHROPUS
ZOOGEOGRAPHER
ZOOGEOGRAPHIC
ZOOSPORANGIAL
ZOOSPORANGIUM
ZYGAPOPHYSEAL
ZYGODACTYLISM
ZYGODACTYLOUS

APPENDICES

ABBREVIATIONS

AA (Alcoholics Anonymous; Automobile Association)
AAA (Amateur Athletics Association)
AB (able-bodied seaman)
ABA (Amateur Boxing Association)
ABP (archbishop)
ABTA (Association of British Travel Agents)
AC (alternating current)
a/c (account)
ACA (Associate of the Institute of Chartered Accountants)
ACAS (Advisory Conciliation and Arbitration Service)
ACIS (Associate of the Chartered Institute of Secretaries)
AD (Anno Domini)
ADC (aide-de-camp; amateur dramatic club)
ADJ (adjective)
ADM (admiral)
ADV (adverb)
AD VAL (ad valorem)
AF (Admiral of the Fleet)
AFA (Amateur Football Association0
AFC (Air Force Cross)
AFM (Air Force Medal)
AG (Adjutant-General)
AGM (annual eneral meeting)
AI (artificial insemination; artificial intelligence)
AIB (Associate of the Institute of Bankers)
AIDS (Acquired Immune Deficiency Syndrome)
AK (Alaska)
AL (Alabama)
ALA (American Library Association)
AM (ante meridiem)
AMU (atomic mass unit)
ANON (anonymous)
AOB (any other business)
AOC (Air Officer Commanding)
AP (Associated Press)
APEX (Association of Professional, Executive, Clerical and Computer Staff)
APOCR (Apocrypha)
APPROX (approximate)
APT (Advanced Passenger Train)
AR (Arkansas)
ARA (Associate of the Royal Academy)
ARAM (Associate of the Royal Academy of Music)
ARCS (Associate of the Royal College of Science)

ARIBA (Associate of the Royal Institute of British Architects)
ASA (Advertising Standards Agency)
ASAP (as soon as possible)
ASH (Action on Smoking and Health)
ASLEF (Associated Society of Locomotive Engineers and Firemen)
AT (atomic)
ATC (air traffic control; Air Training Corps)
ATS (Auxiliary Territorial Service)
ATTN (for the attention of)
ATTRIB (attributive)
AT WT (atomic weight)
AU (Angström unit; astronomical unit)
AUEW (Amalgamated Union of Engineering Workers)
AUG (August)
AV (ad valorem; Authorized Version, average)
AVDP (avoirdupois)
AVE (avenue)
AWOL (absent without leave)
AZ (Arizona)

BA (Bachelor of Arts; British Academy; British Airways; British Association)
BAA (British Airports Association)
BAFTA (British Academy of Film and Television Arts)
B ARCH (Bachelor of Architecture)
BART (baronet)
BB (Boys' Brigade)
BBC (British Broadcasting Corporation)
BC (Before Christ; British Columbia)
BCH (Bachelor of Surgery)
BCL (Bachelor of Civil Law)
BCOM (Bachelor of Commerce)
BD (Bachelor of Divinity)
BDA (British Dental Association)
BDS (Bachelor of Dental Surgery)
BE (bill of exchange)
B Ed (Bachelor of Education)
B ENG (Bachelor of Engineering)
BHP (brake horsepower)
BIM (British Institute of Management)
BL (bill of lading)
B LITT (Bachelor of Letters)
BM (British Museum)
BMA (British Medical Association)
BMC (British Medical Council)
BMJ (British Medical Journal)

ABBREVIATIONS

BMUS (Bachelor of Music)
BN (billion)
BOC (British Oxygen Company)
BP (bishop, boiling point; British Petroleum; British Pharmacopoeia)
BPAS (British Pregnancy Advisory Centre)
BPHARM (Bachelor of Pharmacy)
BPHIL (Bachelor of Philosophy)
BR (British Rail)
BRCS (British Red Cross Society)
BROS (brothers)
BSC (Bachelor of Science)
BSI (British Standards Institution)
BST (British Standard Time; British Summer Time)
BT (Baronet; British Telecom)
BTA (British Tourist Authority)
BVA (British Veterinary Association)

C (centigrade, circa)
CA (chartered accountant; California)
CAA (Civil Aviation Athority)
CAD (computer-aided design)
CADCAM (computer-aided design and manufacture)
CAL (calorie)
CAM (computer-aided manufacture)
CAMRA (Campaign for Real Ale)
C and G (City and Guilds)
C and W (country and western)
CANT (canticles)
CANTAB (of Cambridge - used with academic awards)
CAP (capital)
CAPT (captain)
CARD (carinal)
CB (Citizens' Band; Companion of the Order of Bath; confined to barracks)
CBE (Commander of the British Empire)
CBI (Confederationof British Industry)
CC (County Council; City Council; Cricket Club; cubic centimetre; carbon copy)
CD (compact disc; civil defence; corps diplomatique)
CDR (Commander)
CDRE (Commodore)
CE (Church of England; civil engineer)
CEGB (Central Electricity Generating Board)
C ENG (Chartered Engineer)
CENTO (Central Treaty Organization)
CERT (certificate, certified, certify)
CET (Central European Time)
CF (compare; Chaplain to the Forces)
CFE (College of Further Education)

CFI (cost, freight, and insurance)
CGM (Conspicuous Gallantry Medal)
CH (chapter; church; Companion of Honour)
CHAS (Charles)
CI (Channel Islands; Lady of Imperial Order of the Crown of India)
CIA (Central Intelligence Agency)
CID (Criminal Investigation Depatment)
CIE (Companion of the Indian Empire)
CIF (cost, insurance, and freight)
CII (Chartered Insurance Institute)
C in C (Commander in Chief)
CIS (Chartered Institute of Secretaries)
CJ (Chief Justice)
CL (centilitre; clause; class; Companion of Literature)
CLLR (councillor)
cm (centimetre)
CMG (Companion of Saint Michael and Saint George)
CNAA (Council for National Academic Awards)
CND (Campaign for Nuclear Disarmament)
CO (commanding officer; company; county; Colorado; concientious objector)
c/o (care of)
COD (cash on delivery)
C of E (Church of England)
C of S (Church of Scotland)
COHSE (Confederation of Health Service Employees)
COL (colonel; Colossians)
CONT (continued)
COR (Corinthians)
COS (cosine)
CP (Communist Party)
CR (credit)
CRO (cathode ray oscilloscope; Criminal Records Office)
CSE (Certificate of Secondary Education)
CSI (Companion of the Star of India)
CSM (Company Segeant Major)
CT (Connecticut; Civic Trust)
CU (cubic; Cambridge University)
CV (curriculum vitae)
CVO (Commander of the Victorian Order)
CWT (hundredweight)

D (daughter; died; penny)
DA (District Attorney)
dB (decibel)
DAN (Daniel)
DBE (Dame Commander of the British Empire)

DC (Detective Constable; direct current; from the beginning; District of Columbia)
DCB (Dame Commander of the Bath)
DCL (Doctor of Civil Law)
DCM (Distinguished Conduct Medal)
DCMG (Dame Commander of Saint Michael and Saint George)
DCVO (Dame Commander of the Victorian Order)
DD (direct debit; Doctor of Divinity)
DDS (Doctor of Dental Surgery)
DE (Delaware)
Dept (department)
DES (Department of Education and Science)
Deut (Deuteronomy)
DF (Defender of the Faith)
DFC (Distinguished Flying Cross)
DFM (Distinguished Flying Medal)
DG (Dei gratia - by the Grace of God; Deo gratias – thanks be to God)
DHSS (Department of Health and Socal Security)
DI (Detective Inspector)
DIAL (dialect)
DIP (Diploma)
DIP ED (Diploma in Education)
DIY (do it yourself)
DK (Dakota)
DL (Deputy Lieutenant)
D LITT (Doctor of Literature)
DM (Deutschmark; Doctor of Medicine)
D MUS (Doctor of Music)
DNB (Dictionary of National Biography)
DO (ditto)
DOA (dead on arrival)
DOB (date of birth)
DOD (date of death)
DOE (Department of the Enviroment)
DOM (to God, the best and the greatest)
DOZ (dozen)
DPHIL (Doctor of Philosophy)
DPP (Director of Public Prosecutions)
DHSS (Department of Health and Socal Security)
DI (Detective Inspector)
DIAL (dialect)
DIP (Diploma)
DIP ED (Diploma in Education)
DIY (do it yourself)
D LITT (Doctor of Literature)
DM (Doctor of Medicine)
D MUS (Doctor of Music)
DNB (Dictionary of National Biography)
DO (ditto)

DOA (dead on arrival)
DOB (date of birth)
DOE (Department of the Enviroment)
DOM (to God, the best and the greatest)
DOZ (dozen)
DPHIL (Doctor of Philosophy)
DPP (Director of Public Prosecutions)
DR (debter; doctor; drive; Drachma)
DSC (Distinguished Service Cross; Doctor of Science)
DSM (Distinguished Service Medal)
DSO (Distinguished Service Order)
DT (delirium tremens)
DV (Deo volente – God willing)
DVLC (Driver and Vehicle Licencing Centre)

E (East; Easterly, Eastern)
EA (each)
EC (East Central London postal district; European Community; electricity council)
ECCLES (Ecclesiastes)
ECCLUS (Ecclesiasticus)
ECG (electrocardiogram)
ECS (European Communicating Satellite)
Ed (editor)
EE (Early English; Electrical engineer; errors accepted)
EEC (European Economic Community)
EEG (electroencephalogram)
EFTA (European Free Trade Association)
EG (exempli gratia – for example)
EMA (Europen Monetry Agreement)
EMF (electromotive force)
ENC (enclosed; enclosure)
ENE (east-northeast)
ENSA (Entertainments National Service Association)
ENT (ear, nose and throat)
EOC (Equal Opportunities Commission)
EOF (end of file)
EP (electroplatde; epistle' extended play)
EPH (Ephesians)
EPNS (electropated nickel silver)
EPROM (erasable programmable read only memory)
eq (equal)
ER (Edward Rex; Elizabeth Regina)
ERNIE (Electronic Random Number Indicator Equipment)
ESE (east-southeast)
ESN (educationally subnormal)
ESQ (esquire)
ETA (estimated time of arrival)
ETC (etcetera)

ABBREVIATIONS

ETD (estimated time of departure)
ET SEQ (and the following one)
EU (European Union)
EX DIV (without dividend)
EX LIB (from the books)
EXOD (Exodus)
EZEK (Ezekiel)

F (Fahrenheit; franc)
FA (Football Association)
FAS (free alongside ship)
FBA (Fellow of the British Academy)
FBI (Federal Bureau of Investigation)
FC (Football Club)
FCA (Fellow of the Institute of Chartered Accountants)
FCII (Fellow of the Chartered Insurance Institute)
FCIS (Fellow of the Chartered Institute of Secretaries)
FCO (Foreign Commonwealth Office)
ff (fortissimo)
FH (fire hydrant)
FIFA (International Football Federation)
FL (flourished; Florida)
FM (Field Marshall; frequency modulation)
FO (Field Officer; Flying Officer; Foreign Office; folio)
FOB (free on board)
FOC (Father of the Chapel; free of charge)
fp (freezing point)
FPA (Family Planning Association)
Fr (French)
FRAM (Fellow of the Royal Academy of Music)
FRAS (Fellow of the Royal Astronomical Society)
FRCM (Fellow of the Royal College of Music)
FRCO (Fellow of the Royal College of Organists)
FRCOG (Fellow of the Royal College of Obstetricians and Gynaecologists)
FRCP (Fellow of the Royal College of Physicians)
FRCS (Fellow of the Royal College of Surgeons)
FRCVS (Fellow of the Royal College of Veterinary Surgeons)
FRGS (Fellow of the Royal Geographical Society)
FRIBA (Fellow of the Royal Institute of British Architects)
FRIC (Fellow of the Royal Institute of Chemistry)
FRICS (Fellow of the Royal Institute of Chartered Surveyers)

FRPS (Fellow of the Royal Photographic Society)
FRS (Fellow of the Royal Society)
FRSA (Fellow of the Royal Society of Arts)
FSA (Fellow of the Society of Antiquaries)
ft (feet; foot)
FZS (Fellow of the Zoological Society)

G (gram)
GA (Georgia)
GAL (Galatians)
GATT (General Agreement on Tarrifs and Trade)
GB (Great Britain)
GBE (Knight/Dame Grand Cross of the British Empire)
GBH (grievous bodily harm)
GC (George Cross)
GCB (Knight/Dame Grand Cross of the Bath)
GCE (General Certificate of Education)
GCHQ (Government Communication Head Quarters)
GCIE (Grand Commander of the Indian Empire)
GCMG (Knight/Dame Grand Cross of Saint Michael and Saint George)
GCSE (Ge neral Certificate of Secondary Education)
GCVO (Knight/Dame Grand Cross of the Victorian Order)
GDNS (gardens)
GDP (gross domestic product)
GDR (German Democratic Republic)
GEO (George)
GER (German)
GHQ (General Head Quarters)
GI (governement issue; US soldier)
GIB (Gibralter)
GLC (Greater London Council)
gm (gram)
GM (George Medal; Grand Master)
GMT (Greenwich Mean Time)
GNP (gross national product)
GOM (grand old man)
GP (general practitioner)
GPO (general post office)

H (hour)
HCF (highest common factor)
HEB (Hebrews)
HF (high frequency)
HGV (heavy goods vehicle)

HI (Hawaii)
HIH (His/Her Imperial Highness)
HIM (His/Her Imperial Majesty)
HM (headmaster/headmistress; His Her Majesty)
HMI (His/Her Majesty's Inspector)
HMS (His/Her Majesty's Ship)
HMSO (His/Her Majesty's Stationary Office)
HND (Higher National Diploma)
HO (Home Office; house)
HON (honorary; honour; honourable)
HONS (honours)
HON SEC (Honorary Secretary)
HOS (Hosea)
HP (hire purchase; horsepower)
HQ (headquarters)
HR (holiday route; hour)
HRH (His/Her Royal Highness)
HSH (His/Her Serene Highness)
HT (height)
HV (high velocity; high voltage)

IA (Institute of Actuaries; Iowa)
IAAF (International Amateur Athletic Federation)
IABA (International Amateur Boxing Association)
IATA (International Air Transport Association)
IB (ibidem; Institute of Bankers)
IBA (Independent Broadcasting Authority)
IBID (ibidem)
IC (in charge; intergrated circuit)
ICE (Institution of Civil Engineers)
ICHEME (Institute of Chemical Engineers)
ID (idem; identification; Idaho)
IE (that is)
IEE (Institute of Electrical Engineers)
IHS (Jesus)
IL (Illinois)
I MECH E (Institution of Mechanical Engineers)
IMF (International Monetary Fund)
IN (Indiana)
INC (incorporated)
INCL (included; including; inclusive)
INST (instant)
IOM (Isle of Man)
IOW (Isle of Wight)
IPA (International Phonetic Alphabet)
IQ (intelligence quotient)
IR (Inland Revenue)
IRA (Irish Republican Army)
IS (Isaiah)
ISO (Imperial Service Order)

ITA (initial teaching alphabet)
ITAL (italic; italicized)
ITV (Independent Television)

JAM (James)
JC (Jesus Christ; Julius Caesar)
JER (Jeremiah)
JNR (junior)
JP (Justice of the Peace)
JR (junior)

KB (King's Beach)
KBE (Knight Commander of the British Empire)
KC (King's Council)
KCB (Knight Commander of the Bath)
KCIE (Knight Commander of the Indian Empire)
KCMG (Knight Commander of Saint Michael and Saint George)
KCSI (Knight Commander of the Star of India)
KCVO (Knight Commander of the Victorian Order)
KG (kilogram; Knight of the Garter)
KGB (Soviet State Security Commitee)
KKK (Ku Klux Klan)
KM (kilometre)
KO (knock out)
KP (Knight of Saint Patrick)
KS (Kansas)
KSTJ (Knight of Saint John)
KT (Knight of the Thistle)
KY (Kentucky)

L (Latin; learner; pound)
LA (Louisiana; Los Angeles)
LAT (latitude)
LB (pound)
LBW (leg before wicket)
lc (lower case)
LCD (liquid crystal display; lowest common denominator)
LCJ (Lord Chief Justice)
LEA (Local Education Authority)
LEV (leviticus)
LF (low frequency)
LIEUT (Lieutenant)
LITT D (Doctor of Letters; Doctor of Literature)
LJ (Lord Justice)
LLB (Bachelor of Laws)
LLD (Doctor of Laws)
LLM (Master of Laws)

ABBREVIATIONS

LOC CIT (in the place cited)
LOQ (he/she speaks)
LP (long playing)
LPG (liquefied petroleum gas)
LPO (London Philharmonic Orchestra)
LPS (London Privy Seal)
LRAM (Licentiate of the Royal Academy of Music)
LRCM (Licentiate of the Royal College of Music)
LRCP (Licentiate of the Royal College of Physicians)
LRCS (Licentiate of the Royal College of Surgeons)
LS (locus sigilli)
LSD (pounds, shillings, pence)
LSE (London School of Economics)
LSO (London Symphony Orchestra)
LTD (limited)
LW (long wave)

M (male; married; motorway; thousand)
MA (Master of Arts; Massachusetts)
MAJ (Major)
MAL (Malachi)
MASH (moblie army surgical hospital)
MATT (Matthew)
MB (Bachelor of Medicine)
MBE (Member of the British Empire)
MC (Master of Ceremonies)
MCC (Marylebone Cricket Club)
MCP (male chauvinist pig)
MD (Doctor of Medicine; Managing Director, Maryland)
ME (Maine)
MEP (Member of the European Parliament)
MET (meteorological; meteorology; metropolitan)
MF (medium frequency)
mg (milligram)
MI (Michigan)
MICE (Member of the Institution of Civil Engineers)
MIEE (Member of the Institution of Mechanical Engineers)
ML (millilitre)
M LITT (Master of Letters)
MLR (minimum lending rate)
mm (millimetre)
MN (Minnesota)
MO (Medical Officer; Missouri)
MOC (Mother of the Capel)
MOD (Ministry of Defence)
MOH (Medical Officer of Health)

MP (Member of Parliament; Metropolitan Police; Military Police)
MPG (miles per gallon)
MPH (miles per hour)
MPHIL (Master of Philosophy)
MR (Master of the Rolls)
MRCOG (Member of the Royal College of Obstetricians and Gynacologists)
MRCP (Member of the Royal College of Physicians)
MRCS (Member of the Royal College of Surgeons)
MRCVS (Member of the Royal College of Veterinary Surgeons)
MS (manuscript; multiple sclerosis; Mississippi)
MSC (Master of Scienec)
MSM (Meritorious Service Medal)
MSS (manuscripts)
MT (Mount; Montana)
MVO (Memeber of the Victorian Order)

N (north)
NA (North America; not applicable)
NAAFI (Navy, Army, and Air Force Institutes)
NALGO (National and Local Government Officers Association)
NATO (North Atlantic Treaty Organisation)
NATSOPA (National Society of Operative Printers, Graphical, and Media Personnel)
NB (note well)
NC (North Carolina)
NCB (National Coal Board)
NCO (non-commissioned officer)
NCP (National Car Parks)
NCT (National Childbirth Trust)
NCV (no commercial value)
ND (North Dakota)
NE (northeast; Nebraska)
NEC (National Executive Commitee)
NF (National Front)
NFU (National Farmers' Union)
NGA (National Geographical Association)
NH (New Hampshire)
NHS (National Health Service)
NI (National Insurance; Northern Ireland)
NJ (New Jersey)
NM (New Mexico)
NNE (north-northeast)
NNW (north-northwest)
NO (not out; number)
NORM (normal)
NOS (numbers)
NP (new paragraph)
NR (near; Northern Region)

NRA (National Rifle Association)
NSB (National Savings Bank)
NSPCC (National Society fot the Provention of Cruelty to Children)
NSW (New South Wales)
NT (National Trust; New Testament)
NUBE (National Union of Bank Employees)
NUGMW (National Union of General and Municipal Workers)
NUJ (National Union of Journaists)
NUM (National Union of Mineworkers)
NUPE (National Union of Public Employees)
NUR (National Union of Railwaymen)
NUS (National Union of Seamen; National Union of Students)
NUT (National Union of Teachers)
NV (Nevada)
NW (northwest)
NY (New York)
NZ (New Zealand)

OAP (old-age pensioner)
OB (outside broadcast)
OBE (Officer of the British Empire)
OCTU (Officer Cadets Training Unit)
OECD (Organization for Economic Co-operation and Development)
OFM (Order of Friars Minor)
OH (Ohio)
OHMS (On His/Her Majesty's Service)
OK (okay; Oklahoma)
OM (Order of Merit)
ONC (Ordinary National Certificate)
OND (Ordinary National Diploma)
ONO (or near offer)
OP (opus)
OP CIT (in the work cited)
OPEC (Organisation of Petroleum Exporting Countries)
OPS (operations)
OR (Oregon)
OS (ordinary seamen; Ordanace Survey)
OSA (Order of Saint Augustine)
OSB (Order of Saint Benedict)
OSF (Order of Saint Francis)
OT (occupational therapy; Old Testament)
OTC (Officers' Training Corps)
OU (Open University)
OUDS (Oxford University Dramatic Society)
OXFAM (Oxford Commitee for Famine Relief)
OZ (ounce)

P (page; penny; purl)
PA (Pennsylvania; per annum; personal assistant; public address system)
PAYE (pay as you earn)
PC (per cent; personal computer; police constable; politically correct)
PD (paid)
PDSA (Peaple's Dispensary for Sick Animals)
PE (physical education)
PEI (Prince Edward Island)
PER PRO (by the agency of)
PG (paying guest; post graduate)
PHD (Doctor of Philosophy)
PL (place; plural)
PLC (public limited company)
PLO (Palestine Liberation Organisation)
PM (post meridiem; Prime Minister)
PO (Petty Office; Pilot Officer; postal order; Post Office)
POW (prisoner of war)
PP (pages; per pro)
PPS (further postscript; Parliamentary Private Secretary)
PR (public relations)
PRAM (programmable random access memory)
PRO (Public Records Office; public relations officer)
PROM (programmable read-only memory)
PROV (Proverbs)
PS (postscript; private secretary)
PT (physical training)
PTA (Parent-Teacher Association)
PTO (please turn over)
PVA (polyvinyl acetate)
PVC (polyvinyl chloride)

QB (Queen's Bench)
QC (Queen's Council)
QUD (which was to be demonstrated)
QM (quartermaster)
QR (quarter; quire)
QT (quart)
QV (which see)

R (king; queen; right; river)
RA (Royal Academy; Royal Artillery)
RAC (Royal Automoile Club)
RADA (Royal Academy of Dramatic Art)
RAF (Royal Air Force)
RAM (random access memory; Royal Academy of Music)
RAMC (Royal Army Medical Corps)
RAOC (Royal Army Ordnance Corps)

ABBREVIATIONS

R and D (research and development)
RBA (Royal Society of British Arts)
RBS (Royal Society of British Sculpters)
RC (Roman Catholic)
RCA (Royal College of Art)
RCM (Royal College of Music)
RCN (Royal College of Nursing)
RCP (Royal College of Physicians)
RCS (Royal College of Surgeons)
RCVS (Royal College of Veterinary Surgeons)
RD (road)
RE (religious education; Royal Engineers)
REME (Royal Electrical and Mechanical Engineers)
REV (Reverend)
RFC (Royal Flying Corps)
RH (Royal Highness; right hand)
RHA (Royal Horse Artillery)
RI (religious instruction; Rhode Island)
RIBA (Royal Institute of British Architects)
RIC (Royal Institute of Chemistry)
RICS (Royal Institution of Chartered Surveyors)
RIP (may he rest in peace)
RK (religious knowledge)
RM (Resident Magistrate; Royal Mail; Royal Marines)
RMA (Royal Military Academy)
RN (Royal Navy)
RNIB (Royal National Institute for the Blind)
RNLI (Royal National Lifeboat Association)
ROM (read only memory)
ROSPA (Royal Society for the Prevention of Accidents)
RPM (revolutions per minute)
RSA (Royal Society of Arts)
RSC (Royal Shakespeare Company)
RSM (Regimental Sereant Major; Royal Society of Medicine)
RSPB (Royal Society for the Protection of Birds)
RSPCA (Royal Society for the Prevention of Cruelty to Animals)
RSVP (please answer)
RT HON (Right Honorable)
RT REV (Right Reverend)
RU (Rugby Union)
RUC (Royal Ulster Constabulary)

S (second; shilling; South)
SA (Salvation Army; Sex Appeal; South Africa)
SAE (stamped addressed envelope)
SALT (Strategic Arms Limitation Talks)

SAS (Special Air Service)
SATB (soprano, alto, tenor, bass)
SAYE (save as you earn)
SC (South Carolina)
SCD (Doctor of Science)
SD (South Dakota)
SE (southeast)
SEATO (South-East Asia Treaty Organization)
SEC (second; secretary)
SEN (senior; State Enrolled Nurse)
SEQ (the following)
SF (science fiction)
SGT (Sergeant)
SHAPE (Supreme Headquarters Allied Powers in Europe)
SI (Internatiuonal System of Units)
SINE (sine)
SLADE (Society of Lithographic Artists, Designers, and Etchers)
SLR (single lens reflex)
SNCF (French National Railways)
SNP (Scottish National Party)
SNR (senior)
SOGAT (Society of Graphical and Allied Trades)
SOP (soprano)
SQ (square)
SRN (State Registered Nurse)
SSE (south-southeast)
SSW (south-southwest)
ST (saint; street)
STD (sexually transmitted disease; subscriber trunk dialling)
SW (southwest)

TA (Territorial Army)
TAN (tangent)
TB (tubercle bacillus)
TCCB (Test and County Cricket Board)
TEFL (teaching English as a foreign language)
TGWU (Transport and General Workers' Union)
THOS (Thomas)
TM (tademark; transcendental meditation)
TN (Tennesee)
TOPS (Training Opportunities Scheme)
TSB (Trustee Savings Bank)
TT (teetotal; teetotaller; time trials)
TU (trade union)
TUC (Trades Union Congress)
TV (television)
TX (Texas)

UC (upper case)
UCAS (University and Colleges Admissions Service)
UCATT (Union of Construction, AlliedTrades, and Technicians)
UCCA (Universities Central Council on Admissions)
UCL (University College, London)
UDI (unilateral declaration of independence)
UEFA (Union of European Football Assosiations)
UHF (ultrahigh frequency)
UHT (ultrahigh temperature)
UK (United Kingdom)
ULT (ultimo)
UN (United Nations)
UNCTAD (United Nations Commission for Trade and Development)
UNESCO (United Nations Educational, Scientific, and Cultural Organisation)
UNICEF (United Nations International Children's Emergency Fund)
UNO (United Nations Organisation)
UPOW (Union of Post Office Workers)
US (United States)
USA (United States of America)
UT (Utah)

V (verse; versus; volt)
VA (Order of Victoria and Albert; Virginia)
VAT (value-added tax)
VB (verb)
VC (Vice Chancellor; Victoria Cross)
VD (venereal disease)
VDU (visual display unit)
VE (Victory in Europe)
VG (very good)
VHF (very high frequency)
VIP (very important person)

VIZ (namely)
VLF (very low frequency)
VR (Victoria Regina; Volunteer Reserve)
VS (veterinary surgeon; vital statistics)
VSO (Voluntary Service Overseas)
VT (Vermont)

W (west)
WA (Washington)
WAAC (Woman's Army Auxiliary Corps)
WAAF (Woman's Auxiliary Air Force)
WC (water closet; West Central)
WI (West Indies; Wisconsin; Woman's Institute)
WK (week)
WM (William)
WNW (west-northwest)
WO (Warrent Officer)
WP (word processor)
WPC (Woman Police Constable)
WPM (words per minute)
WRAC (Woman's Royal Army Corps)
WRAF (Woman's Royal Air Force)
WRNS (Woman's Royal Naval Service)
WRVS (Woman's Royal Voluntary Service)
WSW (west-southwest)
WT (weight)
WV (West Virginia)
WW (World War)
WWF (World Wildlife Fund)
WY(Wyoming)

XL (extra large)

YHA (Youth Hostels Association)
YMCA (Young Men's Christian Association)
YR (year)
YWCA (Young Woman's Christian Association)

PALINDROMES

3	GAG	PIP	4	5	SOLOS
AHA	GIG	POP	BOOB	CIVIC	TENET
BIB	HAH	PUP	DEED	KAYAK	**6**
BOB	HUH	SIS	KOOK	LEVEL	DENNED
DAD	MAM	SOS	MA'AM	MADAM	HALLAH
DID	MOM	TAT	NOON	MINIM	HANNAH
DUD	MUM	TIT	PEEP	RADAR	REDDER
ERE	NUN	TNT	POOP	REFER	TERRET
EVE	OHO	TOT	SEES	ROTOR	TUT-TUT
EWE	PAP	TUT	TOOT	SAGAS	
EYE	PEP	WOW		SEXES	

BACK WORDS

2
AH - HA
AM - MA
AT - TA
EH - HE
HA - AH
HE - EH
HO - OH
IT - TI
MA - AM
MP - PM
NO - ON
OH - HO
ON - NO
PM - MP
TA - AT
TI - IT
3
AND -DNA
BAD - DAB
BAG - GAB
BAN - NAB
BAT - TAB
BIN - NIB
BOG - GOB
BOY - YOB
BUD - DUB
BUN - NUB
BUS - SUB
BUT - TUB
DAB BAD
DAM - MAD
DEW - WED
DIM - MID
DNA - AND
DOG - GOD
DOH - HOD
DON - NOD
DOT - TOD
DUB - BUD
EEL - LEE
GAB - BAG
GAL - LAG
GAS - SAG
GEL - LEG
GOB - BOG
GOT - TOG
GOD - DOG

GUM - MUG
GUT - TUG
HOD - DOH
JAR - RAG
LAG - GAL
LAP - PAL
LEE - EEL
LEG - GEL
MAD - DAM
MAR - RAM
MAY - YAM
MID - DIM
MUG - GUM
NAB - BAN
NAP - PAN
NET - TEN
NIB - BIN
NIP - PIN
NIT - TIN
NOD - DON
NOT - TOD
NOW - WON
NUB - BUN
PAL - LAP
PAN - NAP
PAR - RAP
PAT - TAP
PAY - YAP
PER - REP
PIN - NIP
PIT - TIP
POT - TOP
PUS - SUP
RAJ - JAR
RAM - MAR
RAT - TAR
RAW - WAR
REP - PER
ROT - TOR
SAG - GAS
SUB - BUS
SUP - PUS
TAB - BAT
TAP - PAT
RAT - TAR
TEN - NET
TIN - NIT
TIP - PIT

TOD - DOT
GOT - TOG
TON - NOT
TOP - POT
TOR - ROT
TUB - BUT
TUG - GUT
WAR RAW
WAY - YAW
WED - DEW
WON - NOW
YAM - MAY
YAP - PAY
YAW - WAY
YOB - BOY
4
ABLE - ELBA
ABUT - TUBA
BARD - DRAB
BATS - STAB
BRAG - GARB
BUNS - SNUB
BUTS - STUB
DEER - REED
DIAL - LAID
DOOM - MOOD
DOOR - ROOD
DRAB - BARD
DRAW - WARD
DRAY - YARD
DUAL - LAUD
EDAM - MADE
EDIT - TIDE
ELBA - ABLE
EMIR -RIME
EMIT -TIME
ERGO - ORGE
ET AL - LATE
EVIL - LIVE
FLOG - GOLF
FLOW - WOLF
GALS - SLAG
GARB - BRAG
GNAT - TANG
GOLF - FLOG
GULP - PLUG
GUMS - SMUG
HOOP POOH

KEEL - LEEK
KEEP - PEEK
LAID - DAIL
LAIR - RIAL
LATE -ET AL
LAUD -DUAL
LEEK - KEEL
LEER - REEL
LIAR - RAIL
LIVE - EVIL
LOOP - POOL
LOOT - TOOL
MACS - SCAM
MADE - EDAM
MAPS - SPAM
MAWS - SWAM
MEET - TEEM
MOOD - DOOM -
NAPS - SPAN
NIPS - SPIN
NUTS - STUN
OGRE - ERGO
PALS - SLAP
PANS - SNAP
PART - TRAP
PAWS - SWAP
PEEK - KEEP
PETS - STEP
PINS - SNIP
PLUG - GULP
POOH - HOOP
POOL - LOOP
POTS - STOP
RAIL - LIAR
RAPS - SPAR
RATS - STAR
REED - DEER
REEL - LEED
RIAL - LAIR
RIME - EMIR
ROOD - DOOR
SCAM - MACS
SLAG - GALS
SLAP - PALS
SMUG - GUNS
SPAM - MAPS
SPAN - NAPS
SPAR - RAPS

4 continued

SPAY -YAPS
SPIN -TIPS
SPOT - TOPS
STAB - BATS
STAR - RATS
STEP - PETS
STEW - WETS
STOP - POTS
STUB - BUTS
STUN - NUTS
SWAM - MAWS
SWAP - PAWSS-
WAY -YAWS
SWOT - TOWS
TANG - GNAT
TAPS - SPAT
TEEM - MEET
TIDE - EDIT
TIME - EMIT
TIPS - SPIT
TONS - SNOT
TOOL - LOOT
TOPS - SPOT
TORT - TROT
TOWS - SWOT
TRAP - PART
TROT - TROT

TUBA - ABUT
WARD - DRAW
WETS - STEW
WOLF - FLOW
YAPS - SPAY
YARD - DRAY
YAWS - SWAY

5

ANNAM - MANNA
ATLAS - SALTA
CARES - SERAC
DARAF - FARED
DECAL - LACED
DENIM - MINED
DEVIL - LIVED
FARAD - DARAF
FIRES - SERIF
KEELS - SLEEK
LACED - DECAL
LAGER - REGAL
LEPER - REPEL
LEVER - REVEL
LIVED - DEVIL
LOOPS - SPOOL
MANNA - ANNAM
MINED - DENIM
PACER - RECAP
PARTS --STRAP

POOLS - SLOOP
PORTS - STROP
REBUT - TUBER
RECAP - PACER
REGAL - LAGER
REMIT - TIMER
REPEL - LEPER
REVEL - LEVER
SALTA - ATLAS
SERAC - CARES
SERIF - FIRES
SLEEK - KEELS
SLOOP - POOLS
SMART - TRAMS
SNIPS - SPINS
SPINS - SNIPS
SPOOL - LOOPS
SPOTS - STOPS
STRAP - PARTS
STRAW - WARTS
STROP - PORTS
TIMER - REMIT
TRAMS - SMART
TUBER - REBUT
WARTS - STRAW

6

ANIMAL - LAMINA
DELIAN - NAILED

DENIER - RENIED
DIAPER - REPAID
DRAWER - REWARD
HARRIS - SIRRAH
LAMINA - ANIMAL
LOOTER - RETOOL
NAILED - DELIAN
PUPILS - SLIP-UP
RECAPS - SPACER
REINED - DENIER
RENNET - TENNER
REPAID - DAIPER
RETOOL - LOOTER
REWARD - DRAWER
SERVES - SEVRES
SEVRES - SERVES
SIRRAH - HARRIS
SLIP-UP - PUPILS
SNOOPS - SPOONS
SPACER - RECAPS
SPOONS - SNOOPS
TENNER - RENNET

8

DESSERTS -
    STRESSED
STRESSED -
    DESSERTS

HOMOPHONES

SPAT - TAPS
ACCESSARY - ACCESSO-
RY
ACCESSORY - ACCES-
SARY
AERIAL - ARIEL
AERIE - AIRY
AIL - ALE
AIR - AIRE, E'ER, ERE,
EYRE,HEIR
AIRE - AIR,E'ER, ERE,
EYRE, HEIR
AIRSHIP - HEIRSHIP
AIRY - AERIE
AISLE - I'LL, ISLE
AIT - EIGHT, ATE
ALE - AIL
ALL - AWL, ORLE
ALMS - ARMS
ALTAR - ALTER

ALTER - ALTAR
AMAH - ARMOUR
ANTE - ANTI
ANTI - ANTE
ARC - ARK
ARMOUR - AMAH
ARMS - ALMS
ASCENT - ASSENT
ASSENT - ASCENT
ATE - AIT, EIGHT
AUK - ORC
AUNT - AREN'T
AURAL - ORAL
AUSTERE - OSTIA
AWAY - AWEUGH
AWE - OAR, O'ER, ORE
AWEIGH - AWAY
AWL - ALL, ORLE
AXEL - AXLE
AXLE - AXEL

AY - AYE, EYE, I
AYAH - IRE
AYE - AY, EYE, I
AYES - EYES
BAA - BAH, BAR
BAAL - BASLE
BAH - BAA, BAR
BAIL - BALE
BALL - BAWL
BALM - BARM
BAR - BAA, BAH
BARE - BEAR
BARM - BALM
BARMY - BALMY
BARON - BARREN
BARREN - BARON
BASE - BASS
BASLE - BAAL
BASS - BASE
BAUD - BAWD, BOARD

717

HOMOPHONES

BAWD - BAUD, BOARD
BAWL - BALL
BAY - BEY
BEACH - BEECH
BEAN - BEEN
BEAR - BARE
BEAT - BEET
BEATER - BETA
BEAU - BOH, BOW
BEECH - BEACH
BEEN - BEAN
BEER - BIER
BEET - BEAT
BEL - BELL,BELLE
BELL - BEL, BELLE
BELLE - BEL, BELL
BERRY -BURY
BERTH - BIRTH
BETA - BEATER
BEY - BAY
BHAI - BI, BUY, BY, BYE
BI - BHAI, BUY, BY, BYE
BIER - BEER
BIGHT -
BITE, BYTE
BIRTH - BERTH
BITE - BYTE, BIGHT
BLEW - BLUE
BLUE - BLEW
BOAR - BOER, BOOR, BORE
BOARD - BAUD, BAWD
BOARDER - BORDER
BOART - BOUGHT
BOER - BOAR, BOOR, BORE
BOOTIE - BOOTY
BOOTY - BOOTIE
BORDER - BOARDER
BORE - BOAR, BOER, BOOR
BORN - BORNE
BORNE - BORN
BOUGH -BOW
BOUGHT - BOART
BOULT - BOLT
BOW - BEAU,BOH
BOW - BOUGH
BOWL - BOLE
BOY - BOUY
BRAKE - BREAK
BREAD - BRED
BREAK - BRAKE
BRED - BREAD

BREDE - BREED, BREID
BREED - BREDE, BREID
BREID - BREDE, BREED
BRIDAL - BRIDLE
ACCESSARY - ACCESSORY
ACCESSORY - ACCESSARY
AERIAL - ARIEL
AERIE - AIRY
AIL - ALE
AIR - AIRE, E'ER, ERE, EYRE,HEIR
AIRE - AIR,E'ER, ERE, EYRE, HEIR
AIRSHIP - HEIRSHIP
AIRY - AERIE
AISLE - I'LL, ISLE
AIT - EIGHT, ATE
ALE - AIL
ALL - AWL, ORLE
ALMS - ARMS
ALTAR - ALTER
ALTER - ALTAR
AMAH - ARMOUR
ANTE - ANTI
ANTI - ANTE
ARC - ARK
ARMOUR - AMAH
ARMS - ALMS
ASCENT - ASSENT
ASSENT - ASCENT
ATE - AIT, EIGHT
AUK - ORC
AUNT - AREN'T
AURAL - ORAL
AUSTERE - OSTIA
AWAY - AWEUGH
AWE - OAR, O'ER, ORE
AWEIGH - AWAY
AWL - ALL, ORLE
AXEL - AXLE
AXLE - AXEL
AY - AYE, EYE, I
AYAH - IRE
AYE - AY, EYE, I
AYES - EYES
BAA - BAH, BAR
BAAL - BASLE
BAH - BAA, BAR
BAIL - BALE
BALL - BAWL
BALM - BARM
BAR - BAA, BAH
BARE - BEAR

BARM - BALM
BARMY - BALMY
BARON - BARREN
BARREN - BARON
BASE - BASS
BASLE - BAAL
BASS - BASE
BAUD - BAWD, BOARD
BAWD - BAUD, BOARD
BAWL - BALL
BAY - BEY
BEACH - BEECH
BEAN - BEEN
BEAR - BARE
BEAT - BEET
BEATER - BETA
BEAU - BOH, BOW
BEECH - BEACH
BEEN - BEAN
BEER - BIER
BEET - BEAT
BEL - BELL,BELLE
BELL - BEL, BELLE
BELLE - BEL, BELL
BERRY -BURY
BERTH - BIRTH
BETA - BEATER
BEY - BAY
BHAI - BI, BUY, BY, BYE
BI - BHAI, BUY, BY, BYE
BIER - BEER
BIGHT -
BITE, BYTE
BIRTH - BERTH
BITE - BYTE, BIGHT
BLEW - BLUE
BLUE - BLEW
BOAR - BOER, BOOR, BORE
BOARD - BAUD, BAWD
BOARDER - BORDER
BOART - BOUGHT
BOER - BOAR, BOOR, BORE
BOOTIE - BOOTY
BOOTY - BOOTIE
BORDER - BOARDER
BORE - BOAR, BOER, BOOR
BORN - BORNE
BORNE - BORN
BOUGH -BOW
BOUGHT - BOART
BOULT - BOLT

BOW - BEAU,BOH
BOW - BOUGH
BOWL - BOLE
BOY - BOUY
BRAKE - BREAK
BREAD - BRED
BREAK - BRAKE
BRED - BREAD
BREDE - BREED, BREID
BREED - BREDE, BREID
BREID - BREDE, BREED
BRIDAL - BRIDLE
FORTY - FORTE
FOUGHT - FORT
FOUL - FOWL
FOUR - FAUGH, FOR, FORE
FOURTH - FORTH
FOWL - FOUL
FRIAR - FRIER
FRIER - FRIAR
FUR - FIR
GAIL - GALE
GAIT - GATE
GALE - GAIL
GALLOP - GALLUP
GALLUP - GALLOP
GAMBLE - GAMBOL
GAMBOL - GAMBLE
GATE - GAIT
GAWKY - GORKY
GENE - JAEN
GIN - JINN
GLADDEN - GLADDON
GLADDON - GLADDEN
GNASH - NASH
GNAT - NAT
GNAW - NOR
GORKY - GAWKY
GRATER - GREATER
GREATER - GRATER
GROAN - GROWN
GROWN - GROAN
HAE - HAY, HEH, HEY
HAIL - HALE
HAIR - HARE
HALE - HAIL
HALL - HAUL
HANDEL - HANDLE
HANDLE - HANDEL
HANGAR - HANGER
HANGER - HANGAR

719

HARE - HAIR
HART - HEART
HAUD - HOARD, HORDE
HAUL - HALL
HAW - HOARE, WHORE
HAY - HAE, HEH, HEY
HEIR - AIR, AIRE, E'ER, ERE, EYRE
HEIRSHIP - AIRSHIP
HERE - HEAR
HEROIN - HEROINE
HEROINE - HEROIN
HEW - HUE
HEY - HAE, HAY, HEH
HIE - HIGH
HIGH - HIE
HIGHER - HIRE
HIM - HYMN
HIRE - HIGHER
HO - HOE
HOAR - HAW, WHORE
HOARD - HAUD, HORDE
HOARSE - HORSE
HOE - HO
HOLE - WHOLE
HOO - WHO
HORDE - HAUD, HOARD
HORSE - HOARSE
HOUR - OUR
HOURS - OURS
HUE - HEW
HYMN - HIM
I - AY, AYE, EYE
I'D - EYED, IDE
IDA - EIDER
IDE - EYED, I'D
IDLE - IDOL
IDOL - IDLE
I'LL - AISLE, ISLE
ILLAATION - ELATION
ILLICIT - ELICIT
ILLUDE - ELUDE
ILLUSIONARY - ELUSORY
IMMERGE - EMERGE
IMMERSED - EMERSED
IMMERSION - EMERSION
IN - INN
INCITE - INSIGHT
INDICT - INDITE
INDITE - INDICT
INN - IN
INSIGHT - INCITE

INSOLE - INSOUL
INSOUL - INSOLE
ION - IRON
IRE - AYAH
IRK - ERK
IRON - ION
ISLE - AISLE, I'LL
ISLET - EYELET
JAM - JAMB, JAMBE
JAMB - JAM, JAMBE
JAMBE - JAM, JAMB
JEAN - GENE
JINKS - JINX
JINN - GIN
JINX - JINKS
KAIN - CAIN, CANE
KARAT - CARAT, CARROT
KARST - CAST, CASTE
KART - CART, CARTE
KASHMIR - CASHMERE
KERB - CURB
KERNEL - COLONEL
KEW - KYU, QUEUE
KEY - QUAY
KNAVE - NAVE
KNEAD - NEED
KNEW - NEW, NU
KNOGHT - NIGHT
KNIGHTLY - NIGHTLY
KNIT - NIT
KNOW - NOH, NO
KNOWS - NOES, NOSE
KOHL - COAL, COLE
KYU - KEW, QUEUE
LACKER - LACQUER
LACQUER - LACKER
LAIN - LANE
LANCE - LAUNCE
LANE - LAIN
LAUD - LORD
LAUNCE - LANCE
LAW - LORE
LAY - LEI,LEY
LAYS - LAZE
LAZE - LAYS
LEAD - LED
LEAF - LIEF
LEAH - LEAR, LEER, LEHR
LEAK - LEEK
LEANT - LENT
LEAR - LEAH, LEER, LEHR

LED - LEAD
LEEK - LEAK
LEER - LEAH, LEAR, LEHR
LEHR - LEAH, LEAR, LEER
LEI - LAY, LEY
LEMAN
LEMON
LEMON - LEMAN
LENT - LEANT
LESSEN - LESSON
LESSON - LESSEN
LEY - LAY, LEI
LIAR - LYRE
LIEF - LEAF
LINCS - LINKS, LYNX
LINKS - LINCS, LYNX
LOAD - LODE
LOAN - LONE
LODE - LOAD
LONE - LOAN
LORD - LAUD
LORE - LAW
LUMBAR - LUMBER
LUMBER - LUMBAR
LYMX - LINCS, LINKS
LYRE - LIAR
MA - MAAR, MAR
MADE - MAID
MAID - MADE
MAIL - MALE
MAIN - MAINE , MANE
MAINE - MAIN, MANE
MAIZE - MAZE
MALE - MAIL
MALL - MAUL
MANE - MAIN, MAINE
MANNA - MANNER, MANOR
MANNER - MANNA, MANOR
MANOR - MANNA, MANNER
MAQUIS - MARQUEE
MAR - MA, MAAR
MARC - MARK, MARQUE
MARQUE - MARC, MARK
MARQUEE - MARQUIS
MAUL - MALL
MAW - MOR, MORE, MOOR
MAYOR - MARE
MAZE - MAIZE
MEAN - MESNE, MIEN
MEAT - MEET, METE
MEDAL - MEDDLE

MEDDLE - MEDAL
MEET - MEAT, METE
MESNE - MIEN, MEAN
METAL - METTLE
METE - MEAT, MEET
METTLE - METAL
MEWS - MUSE
MIEN - MESNE, MEAN
MIGHT - MITE
MINER - MINOR
MINOR - MINER
MITE - MIGHT
MOAN - MOWN
MOAT - MOTE
MOCHA - MOCKER
MOCKER - MOCHA
MOOR - MAW, MOR, MORE
MOOSE - MOUSSE
MOR - MAW, MORE, MOOR
MORE - MAW, MORE, MOOR
MORN - MOURN
MORNING - MOURNING
MOTE - MOAT
MOURN - MORN
MOURNING - MORNING
MOUSSE - MOOSE
MOWN - MOAN
MUSCLE - MUSSEL
MUSE - MEWS
MUSSEL - MUSCLE
NAE - NAY, NEAGH, NEIGH, NEY
NEAGH - NAE, NAY, NEIGH, NEY
NEED - KNEAD
NEIGH - NAE, NAY, NEAGH
NEY
NEUK - NUKE
NEW - KNEW, NU
NEY - NAE, NAY, NEAGH, NEIGH
NIGH - NYE
NIGHT - KNIGHT
NIGHTLY - KNIGHTLY
NIT - KNIT
NO - KNOW, NOH
NOES - KNOWS, NOSE
NOH - KNOW, NO
NONE - NUN
NOR - GNAW
NOSE - KNOWS, NOES
NOUGHT - NAUGHT
NU - KNEW, NEW
NUKE - NEUK

HOMOPHONES

NUN - NONE
NYE - NIGH
OAR - AWE, O'ER, ORE
O'ER - AWE, OAR, ORE
OFFA - OFFER
OFFER - OFFA
OH - OWE
ORAL - AURAL
ORC - AUK
ORE - AWE, OAR, O'RE
ORLE - ALL, AWL
OSTIA - AUSTERE
OUR - HOUR
OURS - HOURS
OUT - OWT
OVA - OVER
OWE - OH
OWT - OUT
PA - PAH, PAR, PARR, PAS
PACKED - PACT
PAH - PA, PAR, PARR, PAS
PAIL - PALE
PAIR - PARE, PEAR
PALATE - PALETTE, PALLET
PANDA - PANDER
PANDER - PANDA
PAR - PA, PAH, PARR, PAS
PARE - PEAR, PAIR
PARR - PA, PAH, PAR, PAS
PAS - PA, PAH, PAR, PARR
PAW - POOR, PORE, POUR
PAWKY - PORKY
PAWN - PORN
PEA - PEE
PEACE - PIECE
PEAK - PIQUE
PEAKE - PEEK, PEKE
PEAL - PEEL
PEAR - PARE, PAIR
PEARL - PURL
PEARLER - PURLER
PEDAL - PEDDLE
PEDDLE - PEDAL
PEE - PEA
PEEK - PEAKE, PEKE
PEEL - PEAL
PEKE - PEAKE, PEEK
PER - PURR
PETREL - PETROL
PETROL - PETREL
PHARAOH - FARO

PHASE - FAZE
PHEW - FEU, FEW
PHIZ - FIZZ
PI - PIE, PYE
PIE - PI, PYE
PIECE - PEACE
PILATE - PILOT
PILOT - PILATE
PIQUE - PEAK
PLACE - PLAICE
PLAICE - PLACE
PLAIN - PLANE
PLANE - PLAIN
POLE - POLL
POLL - POLE
POMACE - PUMICE
POMMEL - PUMMEL
POOR - PAW, PORE, POUR
PORKY - PAWKY
PORN - PAWN
POUR - PAW, POOR, PORE
PRAY - PREY
PREY - PRAY
PRINCIPAL - PRINCIPLE
PRINCIPLE - PRINCIPAL
PROFIT - PROPHET
PROPHET - PROFIT
PSALTER - SALTER
PUCKA - PUCKER
PUCKER - PUCKA
PUMICE - POMACE
PUMMEL - POMMEL
PURL - PEARL
PURLER - PEARLER
PURR - PER
PYE - PI, PIE
QUAY - KEY
QUEUE - KEW, KYU
QUIRE - CHOIR
RACK - WRACK
RACKET - RACQUET
RACQUET - RACKET
RAIN - REIGN, REIN
RAINS - REINS
RAISE - RASE
RAW - ROAR
READ - REDE, REED
REED - READ, READ
REEK - WREAK
REIGN - RAIN, REIN
REIN - RAIN, REIGN

722

REINS - RAINS
RENNES - WREN
RETCH - WRETCH
REVERE - REVERS
REVERS - REVERE
RHEUM - ROOM
RHEUMY - ROOMY
RHO - ROW, ROE
RHÔNE - ROAN, RONE
RIGHT - RITE, WRIGHT, WRITE
RING - WRING
RINGER - WRINGER
RITE - RIGHT, WRIGHT, WRITE
ROAM - ROME
ROAN - RHÔNE, RONE
ROAR - RAW
ROE - RHO, ROW
ROLE - ROLL
ROLL - ROLE
ROME - ROAM
RONE - RHÔNE, ROAN
ROOD - RUDE
ROOM - RHEUM
ROOMY - RHEUMY
ROOSE - RUSE
ROOT - ROUTE
RORT - WROUGHT
ROTE - WROTE
ROUGH - RUFF
ROUTE - ROOT
ROW - RHO, ROE
RUDE - ROOD
RUFF - ROUGH
RUNG - WRUNG
RUSE - ROOSE
RYE - WRY
SAIL - SALE
SAIN - SANE, SEINE
SALE - SAIL
SALTER - PSALTER
SANE - SAIN, SEINE
SAUCE - SOURCE
SAUT - SORT, SOUGHT
SAW - SOAR, SORE
SAWN - SORN
SCENE - SEEN
SCENT - CENT, SENT
SCULL - SKULL
SEEL - SEIL, SEAL
SEEM - SEAM
SEEN - SCENE

SEER - CERE, SEER
SEED - CEDE
SEDER - CEDAR
SEIK - SEEK, SIKH
SEINE - SAIN, SANE
SELL - CELL, SZELL
SELLER - CELLAR
SENSOR - CENSER, CENSOR
SENT - CENT, SCENT
SERF - SURF
SERGE - SURGE
SERIAL - CEREAL
SESSION - CESSION
SSEW - SO, SOH, SOW
SEWN - SONE, SOWN
SHAKE - SHEIK
SHEIK - SHAKE
SHIER - SHYER, SHIRE
SHIRE - SHIER, SHYER
SHOE - CHOU, SHOO
SHOO - CHOU, SHOE
SHOOT - SHUTE, CHUTE
SHOT - SHOTT, CHOTT
SHOTT - SHOT, CHOTT
SHUTE - SHOOT, CHUTE
SHYER - SHIER, SHIRE
SIGHT - CITE, SITE
SIGN - SYN
SIGNET - CYGNET
SIKH - SEEK, SEIK
SIOUX - SOU
SITE - CITE, SIGHT
SKULL - SCULL
SKY - SKYE
SKYE - SKY
SLAY - SLEIGH
SLEAVE - SLEEVE
SLEEVE - SLEAVE
SLEIGH - SLAY
SLOE - SLOW
SLOW - SLOE
SO - SEW, SOH, SOW
SOAR - SAW, SORE
SOH - SEW, SO, SOW
SOLE - SOUL
SOME - SUM
SON - SUN, SUNN
SONE - SEWN, SOWN
SONNY - SUNNI, SUNNY
SORE - SAW, SOAR
SORN - SAWN

SORT - SAUT, SOUGHT
SOU - SIOUX
SOUGHT - SAUT, SORT
SOUL - SOLE
SOURCE - SAUCE
SOW - SEW, SO, SOH
SOWN - SEWN, SONE
STAIR - STARE
STAKE - STEAK
STALK - STORK
STARE - STAIR
STEAK - STAKE
STEAL - STEEL
STEEL - STEAL
STOREY - STORY
STORK - STALK
STORY - STOREY
SUITE - SWEET
SUM - SOME
SUN - SON, SUNN
SUNDAE - SUNDAY
SUNDAY - SUNDAE
SUNN - SON, SUN
SUNNI - SONNY, SUNNY
SUNNY - SONNY, SUNNI
SURF - SERF
SURGE - SERGE
SWAT - SWOT
SWEET - SUITE
SWOT - SWAT
SYMBOL - CYMBAL
SYN - SIGN
SZELL - CELL, SELL
TACIT - TASSET
TAI - TAILLE, THAI, TIE
TAIL - TALE
TAILLE - TAI, THAI, TIE
TALE - TAIL
TALK - TORC, TORQUE
TARE - TEAR
TASSET - TACIT
TAUGHT - TAUT, TORT, TORTE
TAUT - TAUGHT, TORT, TORTE
TEA - TEE, TI
TEAM - TEEM
TEAR - TARE
TEE - TEA, TI
TEEM - TEAM
TENNER - TENOR
TENOR - TENNER
TERNE - TURN

THAI - TAI, TAILLE, TIE
THAW - THOR
THEIR - THERE, THEY'RE
THERE - THEIR, THEY'RE
THEY'RE - THEIR, THERE
THOR - THAW
THREW - THOUGH, THRU
THROE - THROW
THRONE - THROWN
THROUGH - THREW, THRU
THROW - THROE
THROWN - THRONE
THRU - THREW, THROUGH
THYME - TIME
TI - TEA, TEE
TIC - TICK
TICK - TIC
TIDE - TIED
TIE - TAI, TAILLE, THAI
TIED - TIDE
TIER - TIRE, TYRE
TIGHTEN - TITAN
TMBER - TIMBRE
TIMBRE - TIMBER
TIME - THYME
TIRE - TIER, TYRE
TITAN - TIGHTEN
TO - TOO, TWO
TOAD - TOED, TOWED
TOO - TO, TWO
TOR - TORE
TORC - TALK,TORQUE
TORE - TOR
TORQUE - TALK, TORC
TORT - TAUGHT, TAUT, TORTE
TORTE - TAUGHT, TAUT, TORT
TOW - TOE
TOWED - TOAD, TOED
TROOP - TOUPE
TROUPE - TROOP
TUNA - TUNER
TUNER - TUNA
TURN - TERNE
TWO - TO, TOO
TYRE - TIER, TIRE
UR - ERR
URN - EARN
VAIL - VALE, VEIL
VAIN - VANE, VEIN
VALE - VAIL, VEIL
VANE - VAIN, VEIN

VELD - FELT, VELDT
VELDT - FELT, VELD
WAE - WAY, WHEY
WAIL - WHALE
WAIN - WANE, WAYNE
WAR - WAUGH, WAW, WORE
WARE - WEAR, WHERE
WARN - WORN
WASTE - WAIST
WATT - WHAT, WOT
WAUGH - WAR, WAW, WORE
WAVE - WAIVE
WAW - WAR, WAUGH, WORE
WAY - WAE, WHEY
WAYNE - WAIN, WANE
WEAK - WEEK
WEAKLY - WEEKLY
WEAR - WARE, WHERE
WEAVE - WE'VE
WHALE - WAIL
WHAT - WATT, WOT
WHEAL - WEEL, WE'LL, WHEEL
WHEEL - WEEL, WE'LL, WHEAL
WHEN - WEN
WHERE - WARE, WEAR
WHEY - WAE, WAY
WHICH - WITCH
WHINE - WINE
WHIRR - WERE
WHITE - WIGHT, WITE
WHITHER - WITHER
WHO - HOO
WHOA - WO, WOE
WHOLE - HOLE
WHORE - HAW, HOAR

WIGHT - WHITE, WITE
WINE - WHINE
WITCH - WHICH
WITE - WHITE, WIGHT
WITHER - WHITHER
WO - WHOA, WOE
WOE - WHOA, WO
WORE - WAR, WAUGH, WAW
WORN - WARN
WOT - WATT, WHAT
WRACK - RACK
WRAP - RAP
WRAPPED - RAPT
WREAK - REEK
WRECK - RECK
WREN - RENNES
WRETCH - RETCH
WRIGHT - RIGHT, RITE, WRITE
WRING - RING
WRINGER - RINGER
WRITE - RIGHT, RITE, WRIGHT
WROTE - ROTE
WROUGHT - RORT
WRUNG - RUNG
WRY - RYE
YAW - YORE, YOUR
YAWS - YOURS
YEW - EWE, YOU
YOKE - YOLK
YORE - YAW, YOUR
YOU - EWE, YEW
YOU'LL - YULE
YOUR - YAW, YORE
YOURS - YAWS
YULE - YOU'LL